Employment Law for Business

Seventh Edition

Dawn D. Bennett-Alexander
University of Georgia

Laura P. Hartman
DePaul University

McGraw-Hill Irwin

EMPLOYMENT LAW FOR BUSINESS, SEVENTH EDITION

Published by McGraw-Hill, a business unit of The McGraw-Hill Companies, Inc., 1221 Avenue of the Americas, New York, NY 10020. Copyright © 2012 by The McGraw-Hill Companies, Inc. All rights reserved. Previous editions © 2009, 2007, and 2004. Printed in the United States of America. No part of this publication may be reproduced or distributed in any form or by any means, or stored in a database or retrieval system, without the prior written consent of The McGraw-Hill Companies, Inc., including, but not limited to, in any network or other electronic storage or transmission, or broadcast for distance learning.

Some ancillaries, including electronic and print components, may not be available to customers outside the United States.

♻This book is printed on recycled, acid-free paper containing 10% postconsumer waste.

1 2 3 4 5 6 7 8 9 0 DOC/DOC 1 0 9 8 7 6 5 4 3 2 1

ISBN 978-0-07-352496-2
MHID 0-07-352496-4

Vice President & Editor-in-Chief: *Michael Ryan*
Vice President & Director of Specialized Publishing: *Janice M. Roerig-Blong*
Publisher: *Paul Ducham*
Sponsoring Editor: *Daryl Bruflodt*
Marketing Coordinator: *Colleen Havens*
Project Manager: *Erin Melloy*
Design Coordinator: *Brenda A.Rolwes*
Cover Designer: *Studio Montage, St. Louis, Missouri*
Cover Image: © *Anne Alexis Bennett-Alexander*
Buyer: *Susan K. Culbertson*
Media Project Manager: *Balaji Sundaraman*
Compositor: *Aptara®, Inc.*
Typeface: *10/12 Times New Roman*
Printer: *RR Donnelley, Crawfordsville*

All credits appearing on page or at the end of the book are considered to be an extension of the copyright page.

Library of Congress Cataloging-in-Publication Data

Bennett-Alexander, Dawn.
    Employment law for business / Dawn D. Bennett-Alexander, Laura P. Hartman. — 7th ed.
        p. cm.
    Includes index.
    ISBN-13: 978-0-07-352496-2 (alk. paper)
    ISBN-10: 0-07-352496-4 (alk. paper)
        1. Labor laws and legislation—United States. 2. Discrimination in employment—Law and legislation—United States.   I. Hartman, Laura Pincus.
    II. Title.
    KF3455.B46 2012
    344.7301—dc23   2011033378

Dedication

For my very first grandson, Edward Christian Jones, b. 1/8/2011, whose double dimples, giggles, babblings and smiles light up my life. And to my Ancestors. Thank you.

D D B-A

For those who have accomplished so much with so little, and so many challenges in their way, I honor your strength of determination. **Mwen respekte nou tout anpil, zanmi ayisyen mwen.**

L P H

About the Cover

Acrylic on canvas, the art on this text was created by Anne Alexis Bennett-Alexander, daughter of author Dawn D. Bennett-Alexander. Anne Alexis, a 2011 Masters in Mental Health Counseling graduate, sold her art to finance her first solo trip to Europe after graduating from the University of Georgia with degrees in psychology and criminal justice before going on to receive her grande diplome at Le Cordon Bleu Cooking School in Paris and London. She has sold many pieces since. Fascinated by shapes, colors, and tactile mediums and surfaces for her work, Anne Alexis's art is unpredictable, surprising and allegorical, containing elements of realism, fantasy, fascinating shapes, and surprising three-dimensional elements such as actual shells, butterflies, and bees and odd surfaces such as ceiling tiles and wooden two-by-fours. Her first book cover art was for McGraw-Hill's *Legal, Ethical, and Regulatory Environment of Business in a Diverse Society* by Bennett-Alexander and Harrison, released in January 2011. Anne Alexis believes art is a personal experience for the viewer and prefers viewers to bring themselves to her art and interpret it for what it means for them, rather than shape meaning for them by naming or explaining her pieces. Anne Alexis can be reached at annealexisba@gmail.com.

About the Authors

Dawn D. Bennett-Alexander *University of Georgia*

Dawn D. Bennett-Alexander, Esq., is a multi-award-winning tenured associate professor of employment law and legal studies at the University of Georgia's Terry College of Business and an attorney admitted to practice in the District of Columbia and six federal jurisdictions. She is a *cum laude* graduate of the Howard University School of Law and a *magna cum laude* graduate of the Federal City College, now the University of the District of Columbia. She authors, with linda f. harrison, McGraw-Hill's groundbreaking text *The Legal, Ethical, and Regulatory Environment of Business in a Diverse Society*, published in 2011. She was cofounder and cochair, with her coauthor, of the Employment and Labor Law Section of the Academy of Legal Studies in Business and coeditor of the section's *Employment and Labor Law Quarterly;* past coeditor of the section's newsletter; and past president of the Southeastern Academy of Legal Studies in Business. Bennett-Alexander taught employment law in the University of North Florida's MBA program from 1982 to 1987 and has been conducting employment law seminars for managers and supervisors since 1985. Prior to teaching, Bennett-Alexander worked at the Federal Labor Relations Authority, the White House Domestic Council, the U.S. Federal Trade Commission, Antioch School of Law, and the U.S. Department of Justice, and as law clerk to the Honorable Julia Cooper Mack at the highest court in the District of Columbia, the D.C. Court of Appeals. Bennett-Alexander publishes widely in the employment law area; is a noted expert on employment law and diversity issues; was asked to write the first-ever sexual harassment entry for *Grolier Encyclopedia;* edited the National Employee Rights Institute's definitive book on federal employment; has chapters in several other books including five employment law entries in Sage Publications' *Encyclopedia of Business Ethics and Society;* has been widely quoted on TV and radio, and in the print press, including *USA Today, The Wall Street Journal,* and *Fortune* magazine; and was founder of Practical Diversity, consultants on diversity and employment law issues. Bennett-Alexander was a 2000–2001 recipient of the Fulbright Senior Scholar Fellowship under which she taught at the Ghana School of Law in Ghana, West Africa, and conducted research on race and gender in employment. She has also taught in Budapest, Krakow, Austria, Prague, Australia, New Zealand, and Costa Rica. She is the recipient of the 2011 University of Georgia President's Martin Luther King, Jr., Fulfilling the Dream Award for her outstanding work in building bridges to understanding and unity, the 2010 recipient of the University of Georgia's Terry College of Business inaugural Diversity Award, and the 2009 recipient of the Ernst & Young Inclusive Excellence Award for Accounting and Business School faculty. She dedicates all her research and writing to her ancestors, three daughters, and two grandchildren.

Laura P. Hartman *DePaul University*

Laura Hartman is Vincent de Paul Professor of Business Ethics and Legal Studies in DePaul University's College of Commerce, and special assistant to the president for DePaul's Haiti Initiatives. She also serves as research director of DePaul's Institute for Business and Professional Ethics. In her work in the private sector, she is director of external partnerships for Zynga.org, the philanthropic arm of Zynga Game Network. She has received the university's Excellence in Teaching Award, the Spirit of DePaul Award, and the Woman of Spirit and Action Award in honor of St. Louise de Marillac, the college's Outstanding Service Award and numerous university and college competitive research grants.

From 2009 to 2010, she represented DePaul University on the Worldwide Vincentian Family's Vincentian Board for Haiti, a committee responsible for hands-on design and implementation of a micro-development, finance and education system for the poor of Haiti (including its online project, www.zafen.org) and is currently involved in the development of a K-12 school in Mirebalais, Haiti. She was named to that effort after returning to the faculty, having served for a number of years as associate vice president for academic affairs for the university. In that capacity, she was responsible for, among other programs, the administration and adjudication of the Academic Integrity Policy across the entire university (24,000+ students). Hartman also chaired DePaul's Task Force on Speech and Expression Principles at the request of its president, among numerous other service contributions.

Hartman's academic scholarship focuses on the alleviation of global poverty through profitable corporate partnerships as well as the ethics of the employment relationship with a primary emphasis on global labor conditions and standards, corporate governance and corporate culture, and the impact of technology on the employment relationship. Hartman has published over 80 books and cases and articles in, among other journals, *Business Ethics Quarterly, Business & Society Review, Business Ethics: A European Review,* and the *Journal of Business Ethics.* Her research and consulting efforts have also garnered national media attention by publications such as *Fortune Small Business,* where she was named one of the "Top 10 Minds for Small Business," as well as *The Wall Street Journal, Business-Week,* and *The New York Times.* She also has written or co-written a number of texts, including *Alleviating Poverty through Profitable Partnerships: Globalization, Markets & Economic Well-Being; Effective & Ethical Practices in Global Corporations; Rising above Sweatshops: Innovative Management Approaches to Global Labor Challenges; Employment Law for Business; Perspectives in Business Ethics;* and *Business Ethics.*

Previously, Hartman has served as an invited professor at INSEAD (France), HEC (France), the Gourlay Professor at the Melbourne Business School/Trinity College at the University of Melbourne (2007–2008), the Université Paul Cezanne Aix Marseille III, and the Grenoble Graduate School of Business, among other universities. She has also held DePaul's Wicklander Chair in Professional Ethics and subsequently was named the Grainger Chair of Business Ethics at the University of Wisconsin–Madison School of Business, where she was identified as one of the top five professors of the year. She was also an adjunct professor of business law and ethics at Northwestern University's Kellogg Graduate School of Management, where she was placed on the Honor Roll for Excellence in Teaching.

Hartman graduated *magna cum laude* from Tufts University and received her law degree from the University of Chicago Law School. She lives in Chicago with her two daughters, Emma and Rachel.

Preface

- Must an employer provide breaks for a nursing mother to express milk, and a private place in which to do it?
- Must an employee allow time off to care for a sick child if the employee is gay and is raising a child not his own, with his partner of several years?
- If a disabled employee could perform the job requirements when hired, but the job has progressed and the employee is no longer able to perform, must the employer keep her on?
- Is an employer liable when a supervisor sexually harasses an employee, but the employer knew nothing of it?
- Is an employer liable for racial discrimination because she terminates a black male who refuses to abide by the "no-beard" rule?
- Can an employer be successfully sued for "reverse discrimination" by an employee who feels harmed by the employer's affirmative action plan?
- Can an employer institute a policy prohibiting Muslim women from wearing their hijab (head scarf)?
- If an employer has two equally qualified applicants from which to choose and prefers the white one to the black one, is it illegal discrimination for the employer to hire the white applicant, or must the employer hire the black one?
- Must an employer send to training the employee who is in line to attend, if that employee will retire shortly?
- Can an employer terminate a female employee because male employees find her pleasing shape too distracting?
- Is it a violation of wage and hour laws for an employer to hire his 13-year-old daughter to pick strawberries during the summer?
- Is an ex-employer liable for defamation if he gives a negative recommendation about an ex-employee to a potential employer who inquires?
- Must an employer disclose to employees that chemicals with which they work are potentially harmful?
- Can an employer stop employees from forming a union?

These types of questions, which are routinely decided in workplaces every day, can have devastating financial and productivity consequences if mishandled by the employer. Yet few employers or their managers and supervisors are equipped to handle them well. That is why this textbook was created.

Between fiscal years 1970, when newly enacted job discrimination legislation cases started to rise, and 2010, the number of federal discrimination suits grew from fewer than 350 per year to just shy of 100,000. A major factor in this statistic is that the groups protected by Title VII of the Civil Rights Act of 1964 and similar legislation, including minorities, women, and white males over 40, now constitute over 70 percent of the total workforce. Add to that number those protected by laws addressing disability, genetic and family medical history, wages and hours, and unions; workplace environmental right-to-know laws; tort laws; and occupational safety and health laws, and the percentage increases even more. The U.S. Department of Labor alone administers more than 180 federal laws covering about 10 million employers and 125 million workers (http://www. dol.gov/opa/aboutdol/lawsprog.htm).

It is good that employers and employees alike are now getting the benefits derived from having a safer, fairer workplace and one more reflective of the population. However, this is not without its attendant challenges. One of those challenges is reflected in the statistics given above. With the advent of workplace regulation by the government, particularly the Civil Rights Act of 1964, there is more of an expectation by employees of certain basic rights in the workplace. When these expectations are not met, and the affected population constitutes more than 70 percent of the workforce, problems and their attendant litigation will be numerous.

Plaintiffs generally win nearly 50 percent of lawsuits brought for workplace discrimination. The median monetary damage award is $155,000 ("Civil Rights Complaints in U.S. District Courts, 2000," 7/1/2002, U.S. Department of Justice, Office of Justice Programs, Bureau of Justice Statistics, http://www.bjs. ojp.usdoj.gov/content/pub/pdf/cicus00.pdf). As you will soon see, the good news is that the vast majority of the litigation and liability arising in the area covered by these statistics is completely avoidable. Many times the only difference between an employer being sued or not is a manager or supervisor who recognizes that the decision being made may lead to unnecessary litigation and thus avoids it.

When we first began this venture more than 15 years ago, we did not know if we would be able to sell enough copies of the textbook to justify even having a second edition. Luckily, we had a publisher who understood the situation and made a commitment to hang in there with us. The problem was that there was no established market for the text. There were so few classes in this area that they did not even show up as a blip on the radar screen. Actually, we only knew of two. But having worked in this area for years, we knew the need was there, even if the students, faculty, and even employers were not yet aware of it.

We convinced the publishers that "if you publish it, they will come."

And come they did. From the minute the book was first released, it was embraced. And just as we thought, classes were developed, students flooded in, and by the time the smoke cleared, the first edition had exceeded all the publisher's forecasts and expectations. The need that we knew was there really was there, and an entire discipline was created. The textbook spawned other such texts, but remains the leading textbook of its kind in the country.

We cannot thank the publishers enough for being so committed to this textbook. Without their commitment, none of this would have happened. And we cannot thank professors and students enough for being there for us, supporting us, believing in the textbook and our voices, and trusting that we will honor the law and our commitment to bring the best to faculty and students.

We have seen what types of employment law problems are most prevalent in the workplace from our extensive experience in the classroom and in our research and writing, as well as in conducting over the years many employment seminars for managers, supervisors, business owners, equal employment opportunity officers, human resources personnel, general counsels, and others. We have seen how management most often strays from appropriate considerations and gets into avoidable legal trouble, exposing it to potential increased liability. We came to realize that many of the mistakes were based on ignorance rather than malice. Often employers simply did not know that a situation was being handled incorrectly.

Becoming more aware of potential liability does not mean the employer is not free to make legitimate workplace decisions it deems best. It simply means that those decisions are handled appropriately in ways that lessen or avoid liability. The problem does not lie in not being able to terminate the female who is chronically late for work because the employer thinks she will sue for gender discrimination. Rather, the challenge lies in doing it in a way that precludes her from being able to file a successful gender discrimination claim. It does not mean the employer must retain her, despite her failure to adequately meet workplace requirements. Rather, it means that the employer must make certain the termination is beyond reproach. If the employee has performed in a way that results in termination, this should be documentable and, therefore, defensible. Termination of the employee under such circumstances should present no problem, assuming similarly situated employees consistently have been treated the same way. The employer is free to make the management decisions necessary to run the business, but it simply does so correctly.

Knowing how to do so correctly does not just happen. It must be learned. We set out to create a textbook aimed at anyone who would, or presently does, manage people. Knowing what is in this book is a necessity. For those already in the workplace, your day is filled with one awkward situation after another—for which you wish you had the answers. For those in school, you will soon be in the workplace, and in the not-too-distant future you will likely be in a position managing others. We cannot promise answers to every one of your questions, but we can promise that we will provide the information and basic considerations in most areas that will help you arrive at an informed, reasonable, and defensible decision about which you can feel more comfortable. You will not walk away feeling as if you rolled the dice when you made a workplace decision, and then wait with anxiety to see if the decision will backfire in some way.

In an effort to best inform employers of the reasoning behind legal requirements and to provide a basis for making decisions in "gray areas," we often provide background in relevant social or political movements, or both, as well as in legislative history and other relevant considerations. Law is not created in a vacuum, and this information gives the law context so the purpose is more easily understood. Often understanding why a law exists can help a manager make the correct choices in interpreting the law when making workplace decisions with no clear-cut answers. We have found over the years that so few people really understand what any of this is really about. They know they are not supposed to discriminate on the basis of, say, gender, but they don't always realize (1) when they are doing it, and (2) why the law prohibits it. Understanding the background behind the law can give extremely important insight into areas that help with both of these issues and allow the manager to make better decisions, particularly where no clear-cut answer may be apparent.

Legal cases are used to illustrate important concepts; however, we realize that it is the managerial aspects of the concepts with which you must deal. Therefore, we took great pains to try to rid the cases of unnecessary "legalese" and procedural matters that would be more relevant to a lawyer or law student. We also follow each case with questions designed to aid in thinking critically about the issues involved from an employer's standpoint, rather than from a purely legal standpoint. We understand that *how* employers make their decisions has a great impact on the decisions made. Therefore, our case-end questions are designed as critical-thinking questions to get the student to go beyond the legal concepts and think critically about management issues. This process of learning to analyze and think critically about issues from different points of view will greatly enhance students decision-making abilities as future managers or business owners. Addressing the issues in the way they are likely to arise in life greatly enhances that ability. You may wonder why we ask questions such as whether you agree with the court's decision or what you would do in the situation. This is important in getting you to think about facts from your perspective as a potential manager or supervisor. Your thoughts matter just as much as anyone else's and you should begin to think like a manager if you are going to be one. Nothing magic happens once you step into the workplace. You bring an awful lot of your own thoughts, preconceived notions, and prejudgments with you. Sometimes these are at odds with the law, which can lead to liability for the employer. The questions are a way to ferret out your own thoughts, to explore what is in your own head that can serve as the basis of decisions you make in the workplace. You can then make any needed adjustments to avoid liability.

It is one thing to know that the law prohibits gender discrimination in employment. It is quite another to recognize such discrimination when it occurs and govern oneself accordingly. For instance, a female employee says she cannot use a "filthy" toilet, which is the only one at the work site. The employer can dismiss the complaint and tell the employee she must use the toilet, and perhaps later be held liable for gender discrimination. Or the employer can think of what implications this may have, given that this is a female employee essentially being denied a right that male employees have in access to a usable toilet. The employer then realizes there may be a problem and is more likely to make the better decision.

This seemingly unlikely scenario is based on an actual case, which you will later read. It is a great example of how simple but unexpected decisions can create liability in surprising ways. Knowing the background and intent of a law often can help in situations where the answer to the problem may not be readily apparent. Including the law in your thinking can help the thought process for making well-founded decisions.

You may notice that, while many of our cases are extremely timely and have a "ripped from the headlines" feel to them, others are somewhat older. There are two reasons why we include those older cases. First, some of them are called "seminal" cases that created the foundation for all of the legal decisions that came afterwards, so you need to be aware of them. The other reason is much more practical. Because our goal is to teach you to avoid liability in the workplace, part of our means of reaching the goal is to use fact patterns that we think do the best job of illustrating certain points. Most law texts try to bring you *only* the latest cases. Of course, we also do that; but our primary goal is to use those cases that we think best illustrate our point. The clearest, most illustrative fact pattern might be an older case rather than a newer one. We will not include newer cases just because they are new. We provide cases that best illustrate our points for you and, if they happen to be older cases that are still good law, we will use them. We are interested in facts that will help you learn what you need to know, rather than case dates. We look at the cases that have come out between editions and, if none do the job of illustrating our point better, we go with what is best geared to show you how to think through an issue.

In this edition, we have, for the first time, made the decision to limit the number of cases in each chapter to between three and five. Most chapters have three or four. Even though the subject matter from chapter to chapter may lend itself to different numbers of cases, we decided to try for consistency in this edition. Hopefully, the carefully chosen cases will still accomplish our purpose.

We also have included endnotes and boxed items from easily accessible media sources that you come across every day, such as *People* magazine, *The New York Times, The Wall Street Journal,* and *USA Today.* The intent is to demonstrate how the matters discussed are interesting and integrated into everyday life, yet they can have serious repercussions for employers. In earlier editions, we opted for reading continuity and thus did not include a lot of our research material as endnotes. In this edition, we have decided to include more sources as endnotes. Hopefully, what is lost in seeing the endnote callout as you read will be balanced out with the fact that you now have the resources to do further investigation on your own since you now have the resources to do so.

Much of today's litigation results from workplace decisions arising from unfortunate ideas about various groups and from lack of awareness about what may result in litigation. We do not want to take away anyone's right to think whatever he or she wants about whomever he or she wants, but we do want to teach that those thoughts may result in legal trouble when they are acted on.

Something new and innovative must be done if we are to break the cycle of insensitivity and myopia that results in spiraling numbers of unnecessary workplace lawsuits. Part of breaking this cycle is using language and terminology that more accurately reflects those considerations. We therefore, in writing the text, made a rather unorthodox move and took the offensive, creating a path, rather than following one.

For instance, the term *sex* is generally used in this text to mean sex only in a purely sexual sense—which means we do not use it very much. The term *gender* is used to distinguish males from females. With the increasing use of sexual harassment as a cause of action, it became confusing to continue to speak of sex as meaning gender, particularly when it adds to the confusion to understand that sex need *not* be present in a sexual harassment claim but gender differences *are* required. For instance, to say that a claim must be based on "a difference in treatment based on sex" leaves it unclear as to whether it means gender or sexual activity. Since it actually means gender, we have made such clarifications. Also, use of the term *sex* in connection with gender discrimination cases, the majority of which are brought by women, continues to inject sexuality into the equation of women and work. This, in turn, contributes to keeping women and sexuality connected in an inappropriate setting (employment). Further, it does so at a time when there is an attempt to decrease such connections and, instead, concentrate on the applicant's qualifications for the job. The term is also confusing when a growing number of workplace discrimination claims have been brought by transgenders, for whom gender, sex, and sexuality intersect, and can cause confusion if language is not intentional, accurate, conscious, and thoughtful.

So, too, with the term *homosexuality*. In this text, the term *affinity orientation* is used instead. The traditional term emphasizes, for one group and not others, the highly personal yet generally irrelevant issue of the employee's sexuality. The use of the term sets up those within that group for consideration as different (usually interpreted to be "less than"), when they may well be qualified for the job and otherwise acceptable. With sexuality being highlighted in referring to them, it becomes difficult to think of them in any other light. The term also continues to pander to the historically more sensational or titillating aspects of the applicant's personal life and uses it to color her or his entire life when all that should be of interest is ability to do the job. Using more appropriate terminology will hopefully keep the focus on that ability.

The term *disabled* is used rather than *handicapped* to conform to the more enlightened view taken by the Americans with Disabilities Act of 1990. It gets away from the old notion noted by some that those who were differently abled went "cap in hand" looking for handouts. Rather, it recognizes the importance of including in employment these 43 million Americans who can contribute to the workplace despite their physical or mental condition.

There is also a diligent effort to use gender-inclusive or neutral terminology—for example, police officers, rather than policemen; firefighters, rather than firemen; servers, rather than waiters or waitresses; and flight attendants, rather than stewards or stewardesses. We urge you to add to the list and use such language in your conversations. To use different terminology for males and females performing the same job reflects a gender difference when there is no need to do so. If, as the law requires, it is irrelevant because it is the job itself on which we wish to focus, then our language should reflect this.

It is not simply a matter of terminology. Terminology is powerful. It conveys ideas to us about the matter spoken of. To the extent we change our language to be more neutral when referring to employees, it will be easier to change our ingrained notions of the "appropriateness" of traditional employment roles based on gender, sexuality, or other largely irrelevant criteria and make employment discrimination laws more effective.

This conscious choice of language also is not a reflection of temporal "political correctness" considerations. It goes far beyond what terming something *politically correct* tends to do. These changes in terminology are substantive and nontrivial ones that attempt to have language reflect reality, rather than have our reality shaped and limited by the language we use. Being sensitive to the matter of language can help make us more sensitive to what stands behind the words. That is an important aid in avoiding liability and obeying the law.

The best way to determine what an employer must do to avoid liability for employment decisions is to look at cases to see what courts have used to determine previous liability. This is why we have provided many and varied cases for you to consider. Much care has been taken to make the cases not only relevant, informative, and illustrative but also interesting, up to date, and easy to read. There is a good mix of new cases, along with the old standards that still define an area. We have assiduously tried to avoid legalese and intricate legal consideration. Instead, we emphasize the legal managerial aspects of cases—that is, what does the case mean that management should or should not do to be best protected from violating the law?

We wanted the textbook to be informative and readable—a resource to encourage critical and creative thinking about workplace issues and to sensitize you to the need for effective workplace management of these issues. We think we have accomplished our goal. We hope the text is as interesting and informative for you to read and use as it was exciting and challenging for us to write.

As we have done with other editions, in this seventh edition we have continued to make updates and improvements that we think will help students understand the material better. We have learning objectives for each chapter, new cases where appropriate, updated background and context information, new boxed information, up-to-the-minute legal issues, more insights, and a modified structure. We have kept the things you tell us you love, and added to them. For instance, a reader suggested that we address the issue of the redundancy of examining certain issues in each chapter where they are raised. Based on this excellent suggestion, which we had considered ourselves over the years, in this edition we now have a "Toolkit" that does this. In the Toolkit chapter, Chapter 2, "The Employment Law Toolkit: Resources for Understanding the Law and Recurring Legal Concepts," we introduce you to concepts that you will see throughout the text but, rather than repeat them in each chapter, we have added Toolkit icons instead. These icons will be an indication to you that the issue referred to was included in the Toolkit chapter, and you can go back to that chapter and review the issue again if you would like a refresher.

As always, we *truly* welcome your feedback. We are the only textbook we know of that actually gets fan letters! Keep them coming! ☺ We urge you to e-mail us about any thoughts you have about the text, good or bad, as well as suggestions, unclear items you don't understand, errata, or anything else you think would be helpful. Our contact information is

Dawn D. Bennett-Alexander
University of Georgia
Terry College of Business
202 Brooks Hall
Athens, GA 30602-6255
(706) 542-4290
E-mail: dawndba@uga.edu

Laura P. Hartman
DePaul University
Department of Management
1 E. Jackson Blvd., Ste. 7000
Chicago, IL 60604-2787
(312) 362-6569
E-mail: lhartman@depaul.edu

And again as always, we hope you have as much fun reading the book as we did writing it. It really is a pleasure. Enjoy!

Dawn D. Bennett-Alexander, Esq.

Athens, GA

August 28, 2011

Acknowledgments

The authors would like to honor and thank the following individuals, without whose assistance and support this text would never have been written: McGraw-Hill Higher Education editorial support, including Craig Beytien, for having the insight and courage to sign the first employment law text of its kind before many others were able to see the vast but undeniable merit of doing so; McGraw-Hill editors Daryl Bruflodt and Laura Hurst Spell, and former McGraw-Hill editor Dana Woo; and editor Robin Bonner, of Aptara, Inc. Finally, for their contributions to our seventh edition revisions, we would like to thank the scholars who have class tested and reviewed this manuscript, including the following:

Glenda Barrett

University of Maryland–University College

Walter Bogumil

University of Central Florida

Gerald Calvasina

Salisbury University

William Carnes

University of South Florida–St. Petersburg

Carol M. Carnevale

SUNY Empire State College

Mitchell Crocker

Austin State University–Texas

Richard Dibble

New York Institute of Technology

Anthony DiPrimio

Holy Family University

Dennis R. Favaro

William Rainey Harper College

Dean Gualco

Warren National University

Shumon Johnson

Columbia Southern University

Rhonda Jones

University of Maryland

Doug Kennedy

University of Wisconsin–Stout

Dale F. Krieg

Oakland City University

Clif Koen

University of New Orleans

Jonathan Kulaga

Spring Arbor University

Cheryl Macon

Butler County Community College

Stan Malos

San Jose State University

Michael McKinney

East Tennessee State University

Richard O. Parry

California State University–Fullerton

John Poirier

Bryant University

Douglas Reed

Milwaukee School of Engineering

Mike Rhymes

Louisiana Tech

Stacey Scroggins

Troy University

Stephanie Sipe

Georgia Southern University

Laura Smagala
Carlow University

Joanie Sompayrac
University of Tennessee

Vicki Spivey
Southeastern Technical College

Lamont Stallworth
Loyola University–Chicago

Dave Stokes
MATC–Madison

Maris Stella Swift
Grand Valley State University

Cheryl Thomas
Fayetteville Tech

Jan Tucker
Warren National University

Thomas Tudor
*University of Arkansas–
Little Rock*

Clark Wheeler
Santa Fe Community College

Glynda White
*College of Southern Nevada–West
Charles*

Bennett-Alexander: I would like to thank (1) my co-author, Laura Pincus Hartman, for her intellect, energy, support, and hard work; (2) our publishers, editors, and other support staff who love this project as much as we do; (3) my daughters Jennifer Dawn Bennett-Alexander Jones, Anne Alexis Bennett-Alexander, and Tess Alexandra Bennett-Harrison for being my special gifts from above and for knowing that my very favorite thing in the whole world is being their Mama— even though they drive me crazy ☺; (4) my grandchildren, Makayla Anne Jones and Edward Christian Jones, who are the delight of my existence. Thank you for loving Nana so; (5) my sisters, Brenda Bennett Watkins and Dr. Gale C. Bennett-Harris, and brother, Rev. Dr. William H. Bennett II, for their unwavering confidence, love, support, and laughs; (6) Edward Demont Jones (Ed), for loving my Jen, Makayla, and Christian so, and being there to always make me laugh; (7) my BFF, linda f. harrison, who can always be counted on for whatever, including smoothing ruffled feathers and a great belly laugh. I don't know how it works, but it's been doing it for 31 years; (8) my ancestors, who made it all possible. I am eternally grateful for your strength, perseverance, sacrifices, and unwavering hope; (9) Leonard Peragine and Jeffrey Baracco, my contractor and his helper who created such an incredible place of peace, contentment, renewal, and solitude for me to work. That is so important to my task and you did an incredible job; (10) my department chair, Dr. Rob Hoyt, who is supportive in so many ways; (11) the thousands of managers, supervisors, employers, and employees who have shared their experiences and insights over the years; (12) my colleagues from across the country who have been so very supportive of this text; and, last but *certainly* not least, (13) my favorites, my students, who are a never-ending source of utter wonder, insight, and fun for me. Do we have a good time, *or what?*

   This text is *immeasurably* richer for having the contributions of *each* of you.

DDB-A

Hartman: This book would not exist without the passionate dedication of my co-author, Dawn D. Bennett-Alexander. She has been by my (metaphorical) side during many of the most gratifying times in my life. But it has been her stalwart commitment to our friendship during some of the more challenging times that evidences the depth of her generosity of character. She represents—truly—the values that both of us hope to engender in our teaching and in our scholarship, and perhaps the original reason that we began the adventure of this text several decades ago. Who would have thought, right, D?

A text is often the work not only of its original authors but also other contributors, and those who have supported us during the lengthy process that has brought the text into existence. This edition could not have been completed without the extraordinary support and assistance of all of the brains and stamina from those who contributed to it. Heartfelt gratitude goes to Bob Bennett for his fabulous updates and to Crina Archer for her eagle eye help with the instructors' manual. All errors—and, *yes, we know* they are there, dear readers, so send them in—are completely my own. There are others, finally, who did not necessarily write a word for this text, but who simply exist on the earth and thereby make me happier that I do, as well. I thank you, each, my sister, brother, steps and their partners, Ma, Shelly, Pop (thank goodness), Sherri, Kathy & A, Kim & David, Carol, Née & Jenn, Leah, Pat, Suzy, Malcolm & Scott, and, of course, Em and Ray.

LPH

Text Organization

Part 1 gives the foundations for employment law, covering introductory topics and cases to set the stage for later coverage. This initial section now includes more material to give students a more thorough grounding.

Chapter 1 provides an introduction to the employment environment, explains the freedom to contract and the current regulatory environment for employment. It now includes an expanded discussion of employment-at-will and showcases a recent case, *Estrada v. FedEx.*

Chapter 2 is the Toolkit chapter that provides information on several topics that run throughout the text. Chapters thereafter that mention these issues will use a toolkit icon to notify the reader to go back to the Toolkit chapter if a refresher is needed.

Chapter 3 covers Title VII of the Civil Rights Act in order to illustrate the foundational nature this groundbreaking legislation has for employment law.

Chapter 4 introduces the reader to the regulation of the employment process, such as recruitment, selection, and hiring. In examining the variety of methods of information gathering through testing and other media, it also explores the issue of employers' access to extraordinary amounts of information via evolving technology. The chapter has been extensively updated with illustrative and supporting empirical data integrated throughout the chapter, including information relating to corporate use of employee referral programs, workplace violence., employer use of online sources for background investigation, corporate use of personality and integrity tests in the hiring process and recent legislation regulating genetic testing in employment.

Part 2 covers various types of discrimination in employment, with each chapter revised to reflect recent changes.

Chapter 5 includes a discussion on recent revisions to affirmative action regulations and misuse of affirmative action, including the famous U.S. Supreme Court decision on the firefighters in New Haven, Connecticut.

Chapter 6 presents a historical overview of racism in the United States, giving students a deeper understanding of how prevalent racial discrimination still is, so managers can better recognize potential liability as it arises. In addition, contemporary race issues and racial harassment are addressed.

Chapter 7 directly follows Chapter 6 in order to link and distinguish the concepts of race and national origin in U.S. laws and culture.

Chapter 8 features coverage of how gender impacts the workplace, including gender discrimination, pregnancy discrimination, gender stereotyping, workplace grooming codes, fetal protection policies, lactation break requirements, and comparable worth.

Employment Law for Business, 7e has been revised and updated to maintain its currency amid a rapidly changing landscape in the area of employment law. Some of its content has also been streamlined to provide a more realistic opportunity for instructors to cover key concepts in one semester. Learning objectives at the start of each chapter alert instructor and students to key concepts within. Cases are found at the end of the chapter to facilitate a smoother read, with case icons inserted into the text where references are appropriate.

Chapter 9 explores the law relating to sexual harassment, clearly explaining the difference between quid pro quo and hostile environment sexual harassment as well as how to avoid employer liability in this important area.

Chapter 10 discusses developments in affinity orientation discrimination and gender identity issues and offers management tips on how to handle this quickly evolving topic.

Chapter 11 gives students up-to-date considerations on the many aspects of religious discrimination, including explanations of the legal definition of religion, points on the employer's duty to reasonably accommodate employees, and information on the correct usage of religion as a BFOQ. Issues of increasing frequency such as Muslim employee workplace conflicts are discussed and methods provided for how to handle these matters.

Chapter 12 provides a comprehensive review of age discrimination laws in the workplace and has been updated with current statistical information with regard to age discrimination and also includes comparisons of perceptions of age in the United States and other countries. Additional updates include state age discrimination laws and the legal standard prohibiting an employer from engaging in retaliatory behavior in response to an age discrimination filing.

Chapter 13 offers a complete analysis of the legal environment with regard to workers with disabilities with an expanded discussion of the legal history of protection against discrimination on the basis of disability. The chapter is comprehensive in its coverage of both the recent Genetic Information Non-Discrimination Act and the Americans with Disabilities Amendments Act (ADAAA) and offers examples to managers of ways to create more inclusive working environments.

Part 3 lays out additional regulatory processes and dilemmas in employment. Several chapters on various regulatory issues have been merged to form the final chapter.

Chapter 14 examines the roles of both the employer and the employee in connection with privacy in the workplace and has been thoroughly updated to keep step with the practically daily changes in technology and how they affect employee privacy. These developments include reference to blogging, social media, RFIDs, GPS, and expanded legal frameworks, both domestic and global; the chapter also includes discussion of new cases such as *U.S. v. Ziegler.*

Chapter 15 addresses collective bargaining and unions in a chapter on labor law.

Chapter 16 combines the Fair Labor Standards Act (FLSA), the Family Medical Leave Act (FMLA), including the newly enacted amendments for military families preparing for active duty or injured in active duty, the Occupational Safety and Health Act (OSHA), and the Employee Retirement Income Security Act (ERISA) into a chapter on selected additional employment laws and regulations.

Key Features for the Seventh Edition

Learning Objectives

Each chapter has active learning objectives, posted before addressing the subject matter, that give a clear picture of specifically what readers should know when they finish studying the chapter. In addition, the learning objectives are noted at the place in the chapter in which the information appears.

Learning Objectives

After completing this chapter, you should be able to:

LO1 Explain why employers might be concerned about ensuring protections for equal opportunity during recruitment, in particular.

LO2 Describe how the recruitment environment is regulated, by both statutes and common law.

LO3 Describe the employer's opportunities during the information-gathering process to learn as much as possible about hiring the most effective worker.

LO4 Explain how the employer might be liable under the theory of negligent hiring.

LO5 Identify the circumstances under which an employer may be responsible for an employee's compelled self-publication, thus liable for defamation.

LO6 Explain the difference between testing for eligibility and testing for ineligibility, and provide examples of each.

Opening Scenarios

Based on real cases and situations, chapter-opening scenarios introduce topics and material that illustrate the need for chapter concepts. Scenarios are then revisited throughout the chapter text as material pertinent to the opening scenario is discussed. When you encounter the scenario icon in the chapter body, return to the corresponding opening scenario to see if you can now articulate the correct way to solve the problem.

Opening Scenarios

SCENARIO 1
A union has not permitted African-Americans to become a part of its ranks because of opposition from white union members. Black employees win when they sue to join. The court orders appropriate remedies. The union still resists African-Americans as members. Eventually the court orders that the union admit a certain number of African-Americans by a certain time or be held in contempt of court. Is this a permissible remedy under Title VII?

SCENARIO 2
An employer is concerned that her workplace has only a few African-Americans, Hispanics, and women, under the

women and minorities. Employer decides to institute a program that will increase the numbers of minorities and women in management and skilled-labor positions. Is this permissible? Do you have all relevant facts needed to decide? Explain.

SCENARIO 3
An employer is found by a court to have discriminated. As part of an appropriate remedy, employer is ordered to promote one female for every male that is promoted, until the desired goal is met. Male employees who would have been next in line for promotions under the old system sue the employer, alleging reverse discrimination in that the new promotees are being chosen on the basis of gender, rather than ability. Is the employer

Toolkit Icons

Key concepts used in several different chapters have been combined into one chapter to prevent redundancy. That chapter is Chapter 2, "The Employment Law Toolkit: Resources for Understanding the Law and Recurring Legal Concepts." Where a toolkit chapter concept arises in a subsequent chapter a notation is made that it can be found in the Toolkit chapter, with an icon placed in the margin.

respondent or responding party
Person alleged to have violated Title VII, usually the employer.

Within 10 days of the employee filing a claim with the EEOC, the EEOC serves notice of the charge to the employer (called **respondent** or **responding party**). As discussed in the toolkit chapter, Title VII also includes antiretaliation provisions. It is a separate offense for an employer to retaliate against an employee for pursuing rights under Title VII. Noting that retaliation claims had doubled since 1991, in 1998 the EEOC issued retaliation guidelines to make clear its view on what constitutes retaliation for pursuing Title VII rights and how seriously it views such claims by employees.²⁷ In fiscal year 2010, at 36.3 percent retaliation claims for the first time were the largest percentage of claims filed under the protective legislation with race at 35.9 percent and gender at 29.1 percent.²⁸

LO7 **Mediation**
The EEOC's approach to mediation has been very aggressive in the past decade or so. In response to complaints of a tremendous backlog of cases and claims that went on for years, in recent years the EEOC has adopted several important steps to

Cases

Excerpted cases are placed at the end of the chapter rather than throughout so that reading can be accomplished without interruption. There are reference icons in the chapter when a case is discussed. There is a minimum of legalese and only facts relevant to the employment law issues are included. Each digested case has a short introductory paragraph to explain the facts and issues in the case and is followed by three critical thinking questions created to build and strengthen managerial liability-avoidance skills.

Management Tips

These boxes, included near the conclusion of each chapter, encapsulate how key concepts relate to managerial concerns. The authors offer concise tips on how to put chapter material into practice in the real world.

Key Terms

Key terms are printed larger, in boldface with alternate color, and defined in the margin during early usage. The terms are also listed in the Glossary at the end of the book for quick reference.

 Case 3 Ali v. Mount Sinai Hospital *68 Empl. Prac. Dec. (CCH) 44,188, 1996 U.S. Dist. LEXIS 8079 (S.D.N.Y. 1996)*

An employee sued the employer for racial discrimination in violation of Title VII, for discriminatory enforcement of the employer's dress code. She alleged she was disciplined for violating the code but whites were not. The court found that the employee had offered no evidence of discriminatory enforcement, so the court had no choice but to find in favor of the employer.

Gershon, J.

***

It is undisputed that, at all relevant times, the Hospital had a detailed three page dress code for all of its nursing department staff, including unit clerks. It expressly provided that "the style chosen be conservative and in keeping with the professional image in nursing" and that the . . .

look like I [am] . . . going to a disco or belong in a disco or something to that effect." Dr. Shields testified: "I told her about the whole outfit. She had red boots, red dress, in the unit. This is the post open heart unit. People come out of here after . . . having cracked their chest. We were . . .

Management Tips

LO9 Since potentially all employees can bind employers by their discriminatory actions, it is important for all employees to understand the law. This not only will greatly aid them in avoiding acts that may cause the employer liability, but it will also go far in creating a work environment in which discrimination is less likely to occur. Through training, make sure that all employees understand:

- What Title VII is.
- What Title VII requires.
- Who Title VII applies to.
- How the employees' actions can bring about liability for the employer.

The three post–Civil War statutes are now codified as 42 U.S.C. sections 1981, 1983, and 1985. They prohibit discrimination on the basis of race in making and enforcing contracts; prohibit the denial of civil rights on the basis of race by someone behaving as if they are acting on behalf of the government (called **under color of state law**); and prohibit concerted activity to deny someone their rights based on race.

under color of state law Government employee is illegally discriminating against another during performance of his or her official duties.

Sections 1981 and 1983 are the laws most frequently used in the employment setting if a claim is not brought using Title VII. Since Title VII is part of a comprehensive statutory scheme to prohibit race and other discrimination, it is the preferred method of enforcing employment discrimination claims. As we have seen, a complete and comprehensive administrative structure has been set up to deal with such claims. The post–Civil War statutes do not offer such a structure. Employees bringing claims under Title VII go to the EEOC to file their claim and do not have to pay. Employees bringing claims under the post–Civil War statutes are on their own and must go to an attorney and must pay. On the other hand, the statute of limitations for the post–Civil War statutes is longer than . . .

Exhibits

Numerous exhibits are included throughout the text to reinforce concepts visually and to provide students with essential background information.

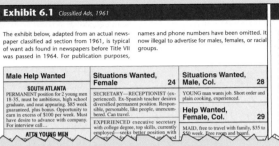

Exhibit 6.1 *Classified Ads, 1961*

The exhibit below, adapted from an actual newspaper classified ad section from 1961, is typical of want ads found in newspapers before Title VII was passed in 1964. For publication purposes, names and phone numbers have been omitted. It now illegal to advertise for males, females, or racial groups.

Male Help Wanted	Situations Wanted, Female	24	Situations Wanted, Male, Col.	28
SOUTH ATLANTA PERMANENT position for 2 young men 18-35, must be ambitious, high school graduate, and neat appearing. $85 week guaranteed, plus bonus. Opportunity to earn in excess of $100 per week. Must have desire to advance with company. For interview call... **ATTN YOUNG MEN**	SECRETARY—RECEPTIONIST (experienced). Ex-Spanish teacher desires diversified permanent position. Responsible, personable, like people, unencumbered. Can travel. EXPERIENCED executive secretary with college degree, top skills, currently employed—seeks better position with		YOUNG man wants job. Short order and plain cooking, experienced. **Help Wanted, Female, Col.** 29	
			MAID, free to travel with family, $35 to $50 week. Free room and board.	

Exhibit 6.4 *Hispanic: Race or National Origin—and Who Is Included?*

Ever wonder where racial categories come from? In this interesting exhibit, you get to see (1) how a court addresses certain groups being left out of a definition of Hispanic (note especially footnote 1) and (2) how the government comes up with racial classifications and how they find their way into the mainstream. The first is an excerpt from a discrimination case; the second is a document from the U.S. Census Bureau about how Asians will be added to the minimum categories and how Hispanics will be classified in the census. While reading the document and noting all the effort and energy given to this issue, ponder the necessity of having such classifications at all.

"The purpose of strict scrutiny is to 'smoke out' illegitimate uses of race by assuring that the legislative body is pursuing a goal important enough to warrant use of a highly suspect tool."

But once the government has shown that its decision to resort to explicit racial classifications survives strict scrutiny by being narrowly tailored to achieve a compelling interest, its program is no longer presumptively suspect. We do not think that it is appropriate to apply automatically strict scrutiny a second time in determining whether an otherwise valid affirmative action program is underinclusive for having excluded a particular plaintiff. In order to trigger strict scrutiny, such a

Chapter Summaries

Each chapter closes with a summary section, giving students and instructors a tool for checking comprehension. Use this bulleted list as an aide in retaining key chapter points.

Chapter Summary

- Title VII prohibits employers, unions, joint labor–management committees, and employment agencies from discriminating in any aspect of employment on the basis of race, color, religion, gender, or national origin.
- Title VII addresses subtle as well as overt discrimination and discrimination that is intentional as well as unintentional.
- The law allows for compensatory and punitive damages, where appropriate, as well as jury trials.
- The post–Civil War statutes add another area of potential liability for the employer and have a much longer statute of limitations and unlimited compensatory and punitive damages.
- The employer's best defense is a good offense. A strong, top-down policy of non-discrimination can be effective in setting the right tone and getting the

125

Guide to Reading Cases

This guide gives succinct direction on how to get the most out of text cases. Terminology definitions, case citation explanations, and a walkthrough of the trial process are all included to help facilitate student comprehension.

Guide to Reading Cases

Thank you very much to the several students who have contacted us and asked that we improve your understanding by including a guide to reading and understanding the cases. We consider the cases an important and integral part of the chapters. By viewing the court decisions included in the text, you get to see for yourself what the court considers important when deciding a given issue. This in turn gives you as a decision maker insight into what you need to keep in mind when making decisions on similar issues in the workplace. The more you know about how a court thinks about issues that may end up in litigation, the better you can avoid it.

We provide the following in order to help you better understand the cases so that you can use them to their fullest. In order to tell you about how to view the cases, we have to give you a little background on the legal system. Hopefully, it will only be a refresher of your previous law or civics courses.

End of Chapter Material

Included at the end of each chapter is a complete set of questions incorporating chapter concepts. Use these as tools to assess your understanding of chapter material.

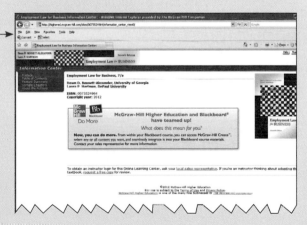

You Be the Judge Online

You Be the Judge Online video segments include 18 hypothetical business law cases that are based on actual cases. Each case allows you to watch interviews of the plaintiff and defendant before the courtroom argument, see the courtroom proceedings, view relevant evidence, read other actual cases relating to the issues in the case, and then create your own ruling. After your verdict is generated, view what an actual judge ruled (unscripted) in the case and then get the chance to defend or change your ruling. Students can buy access via e-commerce through the book's Web site for $10. Professors: Ask your McGraw-Hill sales representative how to obtain premium content to accompany *Employment Law for Business* for your course.

Online Learning Center

The Online Learning Center for this text gives a complete overview of its organization, features, and supplements. Students can study chapter objectives, view the Guide to Reading Cases, access the book's Glossary, and assess their learning with quizzes pertaining to every chapter. Instructors using the OLC can view all student materials as well as gain access to exclusive instructor resources, including teaching notes, class discussion starters, PowerPoint presentations, solutions to chapter-end questions, and a comprehensive Test Bank in document and computerized formats. Jump start your learning now by visiting www.mhhe.com/emplaw7e.

Brief Contents

Contents

Chapter 10

Affinity Orientation Discrimination   432

Chapter 11

Religious Discrimination   476

Chapter 12

Age Discrimination   516

Guide to Reading Cases

Thank you very much to the several students who have contacted us and asked that we improve your understanding by including a guide to reading and understanding the cases. We consider the cases an important and integral part of the chapters. By viewing the court decisions included in the text, you get to see for yourself what the court considers important when deciding a given issue. This in turn gives you as a decision maker insight into what you need to keep in mind when making decisions on similar issues in the workplace. The more you know about how a court thinks about issues that may end up in litigation, the better you can avoid it.

We provide the following in order to help you better understand the cases so that you can use them to their fullest. In order to tell you about how to view the cases, we have to give you a little background on the legal system. Hopefully, it will only be a refresher of your previous law or civics courses.

Stare Decisis and Precedent

The American legal system is based on *stare decisis,* a system of using legal precedent. Once a judge renders a decision in a case, the decision is generally written and placed in a *law reporter* and must be followed in that jurisdiction when other similar cases arise. The case thus becomes precedent for future cases.

Most of the decisions in the chapters are from federal courts since most of the topics we discuss are based on federal law. Federal courts consist of trial courts (called the "U.S. District Court" for a particular district), courts of appeal (called the "U.S. Circuit Court" for a particular circuit), and the U.S. Supreme Court. U.S. Supreme Court decisions apply to all jurisdictions, and once there is a U.S. Supreme Court decision, all courts must follow the precedent. Circuit court decisions are mandatory precedent only for the circuit in which the decision is issued. All courts in that circuit must follow the U.S. Circuit Court precedents. District court decisions (precedent) are applicable only to the district in which they were made. When courts that are not in the jurisdiction are faced with a novel issue they have not decided before, they can look to other jurisdictions to see how they handled the issue. If such a court likes the other jurisdiction's decision, it can use the approach taken by that jurisdiction's court. However, it is not bound to follow the other court's decision if that court is not in its jurisdiction.

Understanding the Case Information

With this in mind, let's take a look at a typical case included in this book. Each of the cases is an actual decision written by a judge. The first thing you will see is the *case name.* This is derived from the parties involved—the one suing (called *plaintiff* at the district court level) and the one being sued (called *defendant* at the district court level). At the court of appeals or Supreme Court level, the first name generally reflects who appealed the case to that court. It may or may not be the party who initially brought the case at the district court level. At the court of appeals level, the person who appealed the case to the court of appeals is known as the *appellant* and the other party is known as the *appellee*. At the Supreme Court level they are known as the *petitioner* and the *respondent*.

Under the case name, the next line will have several numbers and a few letters. This is called a *case citation*. A case citation is the means by which the full case can be located in a law reporter if you want to find the case for yourself in a law library or a legal database such as LEXIS/NEXIS or Westlaw. Reporters are books in which judges' case decisions are kept for later retrieval by lawyers, law students, judges, and others. Law reporters can be found in any law library, and many cases can be found on the Internet for free on Web sites such us Public Library of Law (plol.org) or FindLaw.com.

Take a minute and turn to one of the cases in the text. Any case will do. A typical citation would be "72 U.S. 544 (2002)." This means that you can find the decision in volume 72 of the *U.S. Supreme Court Reporter* at page 544 and that it is a 2002 decision. The U.S. reporters contain U.S. Supreme Court decisions. Reporters have different names based on the court decisions contained in them; thus, their citations are different.

The citation "43 F.3d 762 (9th Cir. 2002)" means that you can find the case decision in volume 43 of the *Federal Reporter* third series, at page 762 and that the decision came out of the U.S. Circuit Court of Appeals for the Ninth Circuit in the year 2002. The federal reporters contain the cases of the U.S. Circuit Courts of Appeal from across the country.

Similarly, the citation "750 F. Supp. 234 (S.D. N.Y. 2002)" means that you can find the case decision in volume 750 of the *Federal Supplement Reporters,* which contain U.S. district court cases, at page 234. The case was decided in the year 2002 by the U.S. District Court in the Southern District of New York.

In looking at the chapter cases, after the citation we include a short blurb on the case to let you know before you read it what the case is about, what the main issues are, and what the court decided. This is designed to give you a "heads up," rather than just dumping you into the case cold, with no background on what you are about to read.

The next line you see will have a last name and then a comma followed by "J." This is the name of the judge who wrote the decision you are reading. The "J" stands for "judge" or "justice." Judges oversee lower courts, while the term for them used in higher courts is "justices." "C. J." stands for "chief justice."

The next thing you see in looking at the chapter case is the body of the decision. Judges write for lawyers and judges, not for the public at large. As such, they use a lot of legal terms (which we call "legalese") that can make the decisions difficult for a nonlawyer to read. There are also many procedural issues included in cases, which have little or nothing to do with the issues we are providing the case to illustrate. There also may be many other issues in the case that are not relevant for our purposes. Therefore, rather than give you the entire decision of the court, we instead usually give you a shortened, excerpted version of the case containing only the information relevant for the issue being discussed. If you want to see the entire case for yourself, you can find it by using the citation provided just below the name of the case, as explained above. By not bogging you down in legalese, procedural matters, and other issues irrelevant to our point, we make the cases more accessible and understandable and much less confusing, while still giving you all you need to illustrate our point.

The last thing you will see in the chapter cases is the final decision of the court itself. If the case is a trial court decision by the district court, it will provide relief either for the plaintiff bringing the case or for the defendant against whom the case is brought.

If a defendant makes a *motion to dismiss,* the court will decide that issue and say either that the motion to dismiss is *granted* or that it is *denied.* A defendant will make a motion to dismiss when he or she thinks there is not enough evidence to constitute a violation of law. If the motion to dismiss is granted, the decision favors the defendant in that the court throws the case out. If the motion to dismiss is denied, it means the plaintiff's case can proceed to trial.

The parties also may ask the court to grant a *motion for summary judgment.* This essentially requests that the court take a look at the documentary information submitted by the parties and make a judgment based on that, as there is allegedly no issue that needs to be determined by a jury. Again, the court will either grant the motion for summary judgment or deny it. If the court grants a motion for summary judgment, it also will determine the issues and grant a judgment in favor of one of the parties. If the court dismisses a motion for summary judgment, the case proceeds to trial.

If the case is in the appellate court, it means that one of the parties did not like the trial court's decision. This party appeals the case to the appellate court, seeking to overturn the decision based on what it alleges are errors of law committed by the court below. Cases cannot be appealed simply because one of the parties did not like the facts found by the lower court. After the appellate court reviews the lower court's decision, the court of appeals will either *affirm* the lower court's decision, which means the decision is allowed to stand, or it will *reverse* the lower court's decision, which means the lower court's decision is overturned. If there is work still to be done on the case, the appellate court also will order *remand.* Remand is an order by the court of appeals to the lower court telling it to take the case back and do what needs to be done based on the court's decision.

It is also possible that the appellate court will issue a *per curiam* decision. This is merely a brief decision by the court, rather than a long one.

Following the court's decision is a set of questions that are intended to translate what you have read in the case into issues that you would likely have to think about as a business owner, manager, or supervisor. The questions generally are included to make you think about what you read in the case and how it would impact your decisions as a manager. They are provided as a way to make you think critically and learn how to ask yourself the important questions that you will need to deal with each time you make an employment decision.

The opening scenarios, chapter cases, and case-end questions are important tools for you to use to learn to think like a manager or supervisor. Reading the courts' language and thinking about the issues in the opening scenarios and case-end questions will greatly assist you in making solid, defensible workplace decisions as a manager or supervisor.

Part 1

The Regulation of the Employment Relationship

Chapter 1

The Regulation of Employment

Learning Objectives

When you complete this chapter, you should be able to:

LO1 Describe the balance between the freedom to contract and the current regulatory environment for employment.

LO2 Identify who is subject to which employment laws and understand the implication of each of these laws for both the employer and employee.

LO3 Delineate the risks to the employer of employee misclassification.

LO4 Explain the difference between an employee and an independent contractor and the tests that help us in that determination.

LO5 Articulate the various ways in which the concept "employer" is defined by the various employment-related regulations.

LO6 Describe the permissible parameters of non-compete agreements.

Opening Scenarios

SCENARIO 1

1) Scenario

Nan works for an industrial products firm as an outside sales representative. Of the firm's 1,200 clients across several states in the northeast United States, Nan is responsible for 60, spread throughout the firm's region. She visits these customers on a regular basis and maintains very close relationships with them. She is the only connection that most of these customers have with the firm, and they might not even have an idea of how else to reach the firm except through Nan. When she joined the firm, she signed a non-compete agreement that stipulated that, if she were to cease her relationship with the firm, she would not engage in any business of any kind with any customer of the firm for a period of one year. Because of her success in building client relationships, Nan is courted by a competing firm that does business in the same region and she accepts an offer. She begins to call on both her original customers as well as other customers of her previous employer. When her previous employer files a cause of action for breach of the non-compete, Nan defends. What are her strongest arguments?

SCENARIO 2

2) Scenario

Serafine worked as a secretary for Creole Construction Corp. (CCC). Gustave was her supervisor. Gustave subjected her to sexual harassment whenever both were at their job site. The harassment consisted of unwanted physical contact, including touching Serafine's body parts and kissing her, as well as other sexual advances and comments. Gustave also made an uninvited visit to Serafine's home. When Serafine rejected Gustave's advances, he retaliated by criticizing her work performance. Serafine complained to CCC's Human Resources department, initially asking the department to keep her complaint confidential. However, she later informed the department that she could no longer work with Gustave. CCC investigated her complaint and subsequently suspended Gustave. Serafine appreciates CCC's action but remains frustrated that Gustave is simply suspended and finds that she really has no remedy against Gustave through CCC; so she files a complaint against him with the Equal Employment Opportunity Commission. Will the EEOC case be successful?

SCENARIO 3

3) Scenario

Ariana worked on a contract basis as a tax accountant for the clients of a small accounting firm. Whenever there was too much work for the employees of the firm, Ariana would receive a call and be assigned by the firm to a particular client for a specific job. When the job was completed, she was paid a commission for her work based on the amount paid by that client to the accounting firm. This commission was established in the contract Ariana was offered when she accepted the position. During the time she was working, she was paid weekly, was free to use office space within the accounting firm's office, and also could use whatever equipment and supplies were necessary to complete the job. In order to ensure a consistent quality among all of its workers, as well as to be sure that it complied with all regulations that might govern the job, the firm asked Ariana to submit her work through a supervisor, who then sent it on to the client. This process also ensured that clients saw all of the firm's workers as equivalent quality. Ariana is laid off in the middle of a job and she files for unemployment compensation. The firm defends the claim, arguing that she was not an employee. Was Ariana an employee or an independent contractor?

Introduction to the Regulatory Environment

How is the employer regulated? To what extent can Congress or the courts tell an employer how to run its business, whom it should hire or fire, or how it should treat its employees?

3

Exhibit 1.1   *Realities about the Regulation of Employment*

1. Generally, you do not have a right to your job.
2. This means that, once you are hired, your employer may choose to fire you, even for reasons that seem unjustified, as long as the termination is not in violation of a contract or for one of the few bases discussed in this textbook. But, basically, there are far more reasons a boss can fire you than not.

3. As an employer, you may fire someone for a good reason, for a bad reason, or even for no reason, just not for an illegal reason.
4. You may terminate someone simply because you do not get along with them. However, you must ensure that bias or perception, which might serve as the basis of a discrimination claim, is not interfering with judgment.

If an employer wants to hire someone to work every other hour every other week, it should be allowed to do that, as long as it can locate an employee who wants that type of job. Or, if an employer requires that all employees wear a purple chicken costume throughout the workday, there is no reason why that requirement could not be enforced, as long as the employer can find employees to accept that agreement.

The freedom to contract is crucial to freedom of the market; an employee may choose to work or not to work for a given employer, and an employer may choose to hire or not to hire a given applicant.

LO1   As a result, though the employment relationship is regulated in some important ways, Congress tries to avoid telling employers how to manage their employees or whom the employer should or should not hire. It is unlikely that Congress would enact legislation that would require employers to hire certain individuals or groups of individuals (like a pure quota system) or that would prevent employers and employees from freely negotiating the responsibilities of a given job. (See Exhibit 1.1, "Realities about the Regulation of Employment.")

Employers historically have had the right to discharge an employee whenever they wished to do so. In one clear example, after the Chicago Bears football team lost to the Green Bay Packers in January 2010 and thereby failed to clinch a spot in that year's Super Bowl, John Stone wore a Packers tie to his job at a Chicago car dealership to honor his grandmother, a Packers fan who had recently died. When he was asked by the general manager to remove the tie, he thought the guy was joking and returned to work. He was later fired. While the lesson learned is that Title VII (or any other statute, for that matter) does not protect on the basis of team allegiances, Mr. Stone was offered a job at a competing dealership that very day.[1]

However, Congress has passed employment-related laws when it believes that there is some imbalance of power between the employee and the employer. For example, Congress has passed laws that require employers to pay minimum wages and avoid using certain criteria such as race or gender in reaching specific employment decisions. These laws reflect the reality that employers stand in a position of power in the employment relationship. Legal protections granted to employees seek to make the "power relationship" between employer and employee one that is fair and equitable.

Is Regulation Necessary?

There are scholars who do not believe that regulation of discrimination and other areas of the employment relationship is necessary. Proponents of this view believe that the market will work to encourage employers' rational, non-biased behavior. For example, one of the main subjects of this textbook—Title VII of the Civil Rights Act of 1964 (Title VII)—prohibits discrimination based on race and gender, among other characteristics. (For detailed discussion of Title VII, see Chapter 3.) Some economists have argued that rational individuals interested in profit maximization will never hesitate to hire the most qualified applicants, regardless of their race. Decisions that are dependent on race or gender would be inefficient, they argue, since they are based on the (generally) incorrect belief that members of one class are less worthy of a job than those of another. The employers who are blind to gender or race, for instance, know that, if they were to allow their prejudices to govern or to influence their employment decisions, they may overlook the most qualified applicant because that applicant was African-American or a woman. Therefore, they will not let prejudices cause them to hire less qualified individuals and employ a less efficient workforce.

However, opponents of this position contend that discrimination continues because often employers are faced with the choice of two *equally* qualified applicants for a position. In that case, the prejudiced employer suffers no decrease in efficiency of her or his firm as a result of choosing the white or male applicant over the minority or female applicant. In addition, human beings do not always act rationally or in ways that society might deem to be in the best interests of society, as a whole. As Judge Richard Posner of the Seventh Circuit explained, "[t]he pluralism of our society is mirrored in the workplace, creating endless occasions for offense. Civilized people refrain from words and conduct that offend the people around them, but not all workers are civilized all the time."[2] Finally, given the composition of the work force, if a biased firm chooses only from the stock of white males, it still might have a pretty qualified stock from which to choose; so it can remain awfully competitive. Therefore, economic forces do not afford absolute protection against employment discrimination where the discrimination is based on race, gender, national origin, or other protected categories.

Who Is Subject to Regulation?

LO2

The issue of whether someone is an employer or employee is a critical one when it comes to regulation, but like many areas of the law, it is not one with an easy

---

Exhibit 1.2 *Realities about Who Is an Employee and Who Is Not*

1. You are not an employee simply because you are paid to work.
2. Choosing how to perform your job is not a clear indicator of independent contractor status.
3. Just because you hire a worker does not mean that you are necessarily liable for anything that the employee does in the course of his or her employment.
4. If you are an employee under one statute, you are not always considered an employee under all employment-related statutes.
5. If you are considered an employer for purposes of one statute, you are not always considered an employer for all statutes.
6. It is not always better to hire someone as an independent contractor rather than as an employee.
7. A mistake in the categorization of a business's workers can be catastrophic to that business from a financial and other perspectives.

---

answer. (See Exhibit 1.2, "Realities about Who Is an Employee and Who Is Not.") Business decisions made in one context, for instance, may give rise to liability when there may be no liability in another (depending on factors such as the size of the business organization). In addition, defining an individual as an employee allows that person to pursue a claim that an independent contractor might not have.

In this section, we will examine who is considered to be an employer and an employee and how it is decided. These definitions are not just the concern of the employer's lawyer and accountant. Instead, concepts such as temporary help, leased workers, independent contractors, vendors, outsourcing, and staffing firms have become common elements of the employment landscape. While employers might not consider some of these workers to be employees, mere labels will not stop a court or agency from determining that the worker has been misclassified and that an employment relationship exists.[3]

Origins in Agency Law

The law relating to the employment relationship is based on the traditional law called *master and servant,* which evolved into the law of agency. It may be helpful to briefly review the fundamentals of the law of agency in order to gain a better perspective on the legal regulation of the employment relationship that follows.

In an agency relationship, one person acts on behalf of another. The actor is called the *agent,* and the party for whom the agent acts and from whom that agent derives authority to act is called the *principal.* The agent is basically a substitute appointed by the principal with power to do certain things. In the employment context, an employee is the agent of the employer, the principal. For example, if Alex hires Emma as an employee to work in his store selling paintings on his behalf, Alex would be the principal and employer, and Emma would be his agent and employee.

In an employment–agency relationship, the employee–agent is under a specific duty to the principal to act only as *authorized*. As a rule, if an agent goes beyond her authority or places the property of the principal at risk without authority, the principal is now responsible to the third party for all loss or damage naturally resulting from the agent's unauthorized acts (while the agent remains liable to the principal for the same amount). In other words, if Alex told Emma that one of the paintings in the store should be priced at $100, and she sells it instead for $80, she would be acting without authority. Emma would be liable to Alex for his losses up to the amount authorized, $20, but Alex would still be required to sell the painting for the lower price because a customer in the store would reasonably believe the prices as marked. In addition, an agent has a duty to properly conduct herself when representing the principal and is liable for injuries resulting to the principal from her unwarranted misconduct. So, if Emma misses an appointment at which someone intended to purchase the painting because she overslept, again she would be liable.

Throughout the entire relationship, the principal/employer has the obligation toward the agent to exercise good faith in their relationship, and the principal has to use care to prevent the agent from coming to any harm during the agency relationship. This requirement translates into the employer's responsibility to provide a safe and healthy working environment for the workers.

In addition to creating these implied duties for the employment relationship, the principal–agent characterization is important to the working relationship for other reasons, explained in the next section.

Why Is It Important to Determine Whether a Worker Is an Employee?

independent contractor
Generally, a person who contracts with a principal to perform a task according to her or his own methods, and who is not under the principal's control regarding the physical details of the work.

You just received a job offer. How do you know if you are being hired as an employee or as an **independent contractor**? While some workers may have no doubt about their classification, the actual answer may vary, depending on the statute, case law, or other analysis to be applied. The courts, employers, and the government are unable to agree on one definition of "employee" and "employer," so it varies, depending on the situation and the law being used. In addition, some statutes do not give effective guidance. For instance, the Employee Retirement Income Security Act (ERISA, discussed in detail in Chapter 12) defines employee as "any individual employed by an employer." But, as one court chastised the legislators who wrote it, this nominal definition is "completely circular and explains nothing." The distinction, however, is significant for tax law compliance and categorization, for benefit plans, for cost reduction plans, and for discrimination claims. For instance, Title VII applies to employers and prohibits them from discriminating against employees. It does not, however, cover discrimination against independent contractors. In addition, employers will not be liable for most torts committed by an independent contractor within the scope of the working relationship.

The definition of employee is all the more important as companies hire supplemental or contingent workers on an independent-contractor basis to cut costs.

Generally, an employer's responsibilities increase when someone is an employee. This section of the chapter will discuss the varied implications of this characterization and why it is important to determine whether a worker is an employee. A later section in this chapter—"The Definition of Employee"—will present the different ways to figure it out.

Employer Payroll Deductions

An employer paying an employee is subject to requirements different from those for paying an independent contractor. An employer who maintains employees has the responsibility to pay Social Security (FICA), the FICA excise tax, Railroad Retirement Tax Act (RRTA) withholding amounts, federal unemployment compensation (FUTA), IRS federal income tax withholdings, Medicare, and state taxes. In addition, it is the employer's responsibility to withhold a certain percentage of the employee's wages for federal income tax purposes.

On the other hand, an independent contractor has to pay all of these taxes on his or her own. This is usually considered to be a benefit for the employer because it is able to avoid the tax expenses and bookkeeping costs associated with such withholdings.

Benefits

When you have taken jobs in the past, were you offered a certain number of paid vacation or sick days, a retirement plan, a parking spot, a medical or dental plan? These are known as *benefits,* and they cost the employer money outside of the wages the employer must pay the employee. In an effort to attract and retain superior personnel, employers offer employees a range of benefits that generally are not required to be offered such as dental, medical, pension, and profit-sharing plans. Independent contractors have no access to these benefits.

We will discuss the Fair Labor Standards Act of 1938 (FLSA) in detail in Chapter 16 but introduce it here merely to identify it as another vital reason to ensure correct classification of workers. The FLSA was enacted to establish standards for minimum wages, overtime pay, employer record keeping, and child labor. Where a worker is considered an employee, the FLSA regulates the amount of money an employee must be paid per hour and overtime compensation. Employers may intentionally misclassify employees in order to avoid these and other costs and liabilities. A willful misclassification under FLSA may result in imprisonment and up to a $10,000 fine, imposed by the Department of Labor.

Discrimination and Affirmative Action

As you will learn in Chapter 3, Title VII and other related anti-discrimination statutes only protect *employees* from discrimination by employers; therefore, an independent contractor cannot hold an employer liable for discrimination on this basis and employers are protected from some forms of discrimination and wrongful discharge claims where the worker is an independent contractor. (Coverage of employers by various statutes is discussed later in the chapter.)

However, as will be explored throughout this chapter, merely labeling a worker as an "independent contractor" does not protect against liability under federal anti-discrimination statutes such as Title VII. Courts and the EEOC will examine a variety of factors to determine the true meaning of the relationship between the worker and the organization. If the worker is more appropriately classified as an employee, then the label will be peeled off, allowing for anti-discrimination statutes to apply.

Additionally, the National Labor Relations Act protects only employees and not independent contractors from unfair labor practices. Note, however, that independent contractors may be considered to be *employers;* so they may be subject to these regulations from the other side of the fence.

Cost Reductions

It would seem to be a safe statement that an objective of some, if not most, employers is to reduce cost and to increase profit. The regulations previously discussed require greater expenditures on behalf of employees, as does the necessity of hiring others to maintain records of the employees. In addition to avoiding those costs, hiring independent contractors also avoids the cost of overtime (the federal wage and hour laws do not apply to independent contractors) and the employer is able to avoid any work-related expenses such as tools, training, or traveling. The employer is also guaranteed satisfactory performance of the job for which the contractor was hired because it is the contractor's contractual obligation to adequately perform the contract with the employer, while the employee is generally able to quit without incurring liability (the at-will doctrine). If there is a breach of the agreement between the employer and the independent contractor, the independent contractor not only stands to lose the job but also may be liable for resulting damages. An employee is usually compensated for work completed with less liability for failure to perfectly perform. Some managers also contend that independent contractors are more motivated and, as a result, have a higher level of performance as a consequence of their freedom to control their own work and futures.

vicarious liability
The imposition of liability on one party for the wrongs of another. Liability may extend from an employee to the employer on this basis if the employee is acting within the scope of her or his employment at the time the liability arose.

In addition, the employee may actually cause the employer to have greater liability exposure. An employer is **vicariously liable** if the employee causes harm to a third party while the employee is in the course of employment. For instance, if an employee is driving a company car from one company plant to another and, in the course of that trip, sideswipes another vehicle, the employer may be liable to the owner of the other vehicle. While the employee may be required to reimburse the employer if the employer has to pay for the damages, generally the third party goes after the employer because the employee does not have the funds to pay the liability. The employer could of course seek repayment from the employee but, more likely, will write it off as an expense of doing business.

Questions might arise in connection with whether the worker is actually an employee of the employer and, therefore, whether the employer is liable at all, a question examined later in this chapter. For instance, if a hospital is sued for the malpractice of one of its doctors, the question of the hospital's vicarious liability will be determined based on whether the doctor is an employee or an independent contractor of the hospital.

In some situations, notwithstanding the decrease in the amount of benefits that the employer must provide, independent contractors may still be more expensive to employ. This situation may exist where the employer finds that it is cheaper to have its employees perform certain types of work that are characteristically expensive to contract. Often a large firm will find it more profitable to employ a legal staff, and pay their benefits and salaries, than to employ a law firm every time a legal question arises. Or a school may find it less expensive to maintain a full janitorial staff than to employ a professional cleaning crew whenever something needs to be taken care of at the school.

LO3   *The Cost of Mistakes*

Workers and employers alike make mistakes about whether a worker is an independent contractor or an employee. If a worker is classified as an independent contractor but later is found to constitute an employee, the punishment by the IRS is harsh. The employer is not only liable for its share of FICA and FUTA taxes but is also subject to an additional penalty equal to 20 percent of the FICA taxes that should have been withheld. In addition, the employer is liable for 1.5 percent of the wages received by the employee. These penalty charges apply if 1099 forms (records of payments to independent contractors) have been compiled for the worker. If, on the other hand, the forms have not been completed, the penalties increase to 40 percent of the FICA taxes and 3 percent of wages. Where the IRS determines that the worker was *deliberately* classified as an independent contractor to avoid paying taxes, the fines and penalties can easily run into six figures for even the smallest business.

In one case, the court ordered a cleaning services company to pay $4.5 million in back pay and damages for its failure to pay minimum wages and overtime pay to almost 400 house cleaners when it violated the Fair Labor Standards Act by misclassifying its workers as independent contractors.[4] Because the employer did not respond to the Department of Labor's request for an admission that the workers were employees, the court held that the employer basically admitted that it was continually aware of its FLSA violations.

In late 2009, the Illinois Department of Labor levied a $328,500 penalty against one Chicago-area housing contractor for failing records and the misclassification of 18 workers. Meanwhile other states such as Iowa, Michigan, New York, and Wisconsin are searching for misclassifications through special task forces and asking for new legislation. The New York task force reported in 2009 that it discovered 12,300 cases of misclassification leading to approximately $6 million in penalties, employment taxes, and workers compensation fines.

In addition to potential IRS violations, the employer may be liable for violations of the National Labor Relations Act of 1935 (NLRA), FLSA, as mentioned above, the Social Security Act of 1935, and state workers' compensation and un-employment compensation laws. The fines for each violation are substantial. For example, any person who willfully violates the FLSA is subject to a fine of $10,000 and six months' imprisonment.

Why is the IRS so intent on ensuring that improper classification does not occur? The IRS estimates that it loses over $3.3 billion a year in uncollected taxes that should have been paid by employers or the independent contractors whom they have hired. The IRS last estimated a misclassification of 3.4 million workers as independent contractors; in some fields, misclassification rates run as high as 92 percent. As one scholar has written, IRS agents are told, "Go forth and find employees!" The IRS will generally attempt to "match" workers who claim to be independent contractors with their companies. If an independent contractor earned more than $10,000 from one source during a one-year period, the independent status of that individual is suspect.

While we will discuss below the process for correct worker classification, the IRS provides a small "safe harbor" through the 1978 Revenue Act for employers who have always and consistently defined a class of workers as independent contractors. Section 530 cites four criteria required to claim a worker as an independent contractor. Where these conditions have been satisfied, the employer is not liable for misclassification.

1. First, the business must have never treated the worker as an employee for the purposes of employment taxes for any period (e.g., the company has never withheld income or FICA tax from its payments).
2. Second, all federal tax returns with respect to this worker were filed consistently with the worker being an independent contractor.
3. Third, the company has treated all those in positions substantially similar to that of this worker as independent contractors.
4. Fourth, the company has a reasonable basis for treating the worker as an independent contractor. Such a reasonable basis may include a judicial precedent or published IRS ruling, a past IRS audit of the company, or long-standing industry practices, as will be discussed in greater detail later in this chapter.

The Definition of "Employee"

Courts have offered various ways to determine whether a worker is an employee. Generally, the interpretation used depends on the factual circumstances presented by each case, as well as which law is at issue.

An older but consistently cited case that illustrates the effect of the difference between classification as an independent contractor and as an employee is *Lemmerman v. A.T. Williams Oil Co.,*[5] where an eight-year-old boy frequently performed odd jobs for his mother's employer, the Wilco Service Station. He was paid $1 a day to stock shelves and to sweep up. One day the boy fell and cut his hand. The boy sought damages in the form of lost wages, pain and suffering. The main issue in this case was whether he was an employee. If he was an employee, then his sole remedy was in the form of workers' compensation; however, if instead he was an independent contractor, Wilco would lose the protection of the workers' compensation limits and would be liable in tort for much higher amounts. Over a strong dissenting opinion, the court in *Lemmerman* determined that the boy was actually an employee of the defendant and, therefore, could not recover beyond a standard workers' compensation claim.

Several tests have been developed and are commonly used by courts to classify employees and independent contractors. These tests include the common-law test of agency, which considers several factors but focuses on who has the right to control the work; the Internal Revenue Service (IRS) 20-factor analysis; and the economic realities analysis. Several courts also use a hybrid approach, using one test that combines factors from other tests. While some courts continue to refer to all three tests as available for consideration, and therefore we will include a discussion of them here, there is a trend toward recognizing a convergence. In other words, as the court explains in *Murray v. Principal Financial Group, Inc., et al.,*[6] included at the end of the chapter, the three tests are "functionally equivalent," with the common-law test controlling.

LO4

common-law agency test
A test used to determine employee status; though it considers several factors, the most critical is whether the employer has the right or ability to control the work.

Under what is now considered to be the leading test to determine status, the **common-law agency test**, a persuasive indicator of independent-contractor status, is the ability to control how the work is performed. This test originated in the master and servant law discussed at the beginning of the chapter. Using the language of those origins, since the master (employer) had control over the servant (worker), the servant was considered similar to common-law property of the master and, therefore, originally governed by property law rather than contract law. Though today we have adopted contract or agency principles to negotiate this relationship, the element of control has persisted in our interpretation of the distinction between an employee and an independent contractor. *The right to control remains the predominant factor.*

Under the common-law agency approach applied by the courts, the employer need not actually control the work, but must merely *have the right or ability* to control the work for a worker to be classified an employee. Although this is a strong indication that the worker is an employee, other factors usually are considered. For example, sometimes the courts will review whether the worker is paid in standard wages or through an expectation of profit based on the price the worker "charges" for the job. The common-law test is specifically and consistently used to determine employee status in connection with employment taxes (e.g., FUTA and FICA), as well as in federal income tax withholding.

In *Estrada v. FedEx Ground Package System, Inc.,* the California Court of Appeals evaluated whether Federal Express ground package drivers were employees entitled to reimbursement for work-related expenses. The court applied the common-law test and found that they were, in fact, employees. "FedEx's control over every exquisite detail of the drivers' performance, including the color of their socks and the style of their hair, supports the trial court's conclusion that the drivers are employees, not independent contractors." In agreeing with the lower court's opinion, the Court of Appeals explained at one point that "the essence of the trial court's statement of decision is that if it looks like a duck, walks like a duck, swims like a duck, and quacks like a duck, it is a duck." One might begin to understand the magnitude of a decision such as this one when one learns that the fallout was an order by the Internal Revenue Service that Federal Express pay $319 million in back taxes based on the misclassification—and the *Estrada* case only applied to workers over the course of *one single year*. Not all courts or circuits agree with California on this issue, however. In cases since, courts have also found in favor of FedEx, holding that the workers' ability to hire their own employees, manage multiple routes, and to sell those routes without FedEx's permission, "as well as the parties' intent expressed in the contract, argues strongly in favor of independent contractor status."[7] Clearly, it is not a clear-cut answer.

IRS 20-factor analysis
A list of 20 factors to which the IRS looks to determine whether someone is an employee or an independent contractor. The IRS compiled this list from the results of judgments of the courts relating to this issue.

The IRS does have a secondary analysis, called the **IRS 20-factor analysis**; however, even the IRS itself explains that "this Twenty Factor Test is an analytical tool and *not* the legal test used for determining worker status. The legal test is whether there is a right to direct and control the means and details of the work" (emphasis in original).[8]

Notwithstanding its own disclaimer, the following 20 factors have been continually articulated by courts, regulatory agencies, commentators, and scholars as critical to the determination of the status of an individual worker. Suffice it to say that, when these factors are satisfied, courts are more likely to find "employee" status. In addition, the IRS stated that these 20 factors are not inclusive but that "every piece of information that helps determine the extent to which the business retains the right to control the worker is important." (See Exhibits 1.3, "Employee

---

Exhibit 1.3   *Employee or Independent Contractor?*

The IRS, in its training materials, offers this case study on the question of whether someone is an employee or an independent contractor:

A computer programmer is laid off when company X downsizes. Company X agrees to pay the programmer $10,000 to complete a one-time project to create a certain product. It is not clear how long it will take to complete the project, and the programmer is not guaranteed any minimum payment for the hours spent on the project. The programmer does the work on a new high-end computer, which was purchased by the company.

The programmer works at home, but may attend meetings of the software development group at the firm. Company X provides the programmer with no instructions beyond the specifications for the product itself. The programmer and company X have a written contract, which provides that the programmer is considered to be an independent contractor, is required to pay her own taxes, and receives no benefits from company X.

Is she an employee?

Source: Internal Revenue Service; case modified slightly by the author.

or Independent Contractor?" and 1.4, "Internal Revenue Service 'Independent Contractor or Employee?' Publication 1779.")

1. *Instructions.* A worker who is required to comply with other persons' instructions about when, where, and how to perform the work is ordinarily considered to be an employee.
2. *Training.* Training a worker indicates that the employer exercises control over the means by which the result is accomplished.
3. *Integration.* When the success or continuation of a business depends on the performance of certain services, the worker performing those services is subject to a certain amount of control by the owner of the business.
4. *Personal rendering of services.* If the services must be rendered personally, the employer controls both the means and the results of the work.
5. *Hiring, supervising, and paying of assistants.* Control is exercised if the employer hires, supervises, and pays assistants.
6. *Continuing relationships.* The existence of a continuing relationship between the worker and the employer indicates an employer–employee relationship.
7. *Set hours of work.* The establishment of hours of work by the employer indicates control.
8. *Full-time requirement.* If the worker must devote full time to the employer's business, the employer has control over the worker's time. An independent contractor is free to work when and for whom she or he chooses.
9. *Work performed on the employer's premises.* Control is indicated if the work is performed on the employer's premises.
10. *Order or sequence set.* Control is indicated if a worker is not free to choose his or her own pattern of work but must perform services in the sequence set by the employer.
11. *Oral or written reports.* Control is indicated if the worker must submit regular oral or written reports to the employer.
12. *Furnishing of tools and materials.* If the employer furnishes significant tools, materials, and other equipment, an employer–employee relationship usually exists.
13. *Payment by hour, week, or month.* Payment by the hour, week, or month points to an employer–employee relationship, provided that this method of payment is not just a convenient way of paying a lump sum agreed on as a cost of a job. However, hourly pay may not be evidence that a worker is an employee if it is customary to pay an independent contractor by the hour (an attorney, for example). An independent contractor usually is paid by the job or on a straight commission.
14. *Payment of business or traveling expenses.* Payment of the worker's business or traveling expenses, or both, is indicative of an employer–employee relationship. However, this factor is less important because companies do reimburse independent contractors.

INDEPENDENT CONTRACTOR OR EMPLOYEE

Which are you?

For federal tax purposes, this is an important distinction. Worker classification affects how you pay your federal income tax, social security and Medicare taxes, and how you file your tax return. Classification affects your eligibility for employer and social security and Medicare benefits and your tax responsibilities. If you aren't sure of your work status, you should find out now. This brochure can help you.

The courts have considered many facts in deciding whether a worker is an **independent contractor** or an **employee**. These relevant facts fall into three main categories: *behavioral control, financial control,* and *relationship of the parties.* In each case, it is very important to consider all the facts – no single fact provides the answer. Carefully review the following definitions.

BEHAVIORAL CONTROL

These facts show whether there is a right to direct or control how the worker does the work. A worker is an employee when the business has the right to direct and control the worker. The business does not have to actually direct or control the way the work is done – as long as the employer has the right to direct and control the work. For example:

- **Instructions** – if you receive extensive instructions on how work is to be done, this suggests that you are an **employee**. Instructions can cover a wide range of topics, for example:
  - how, when, or where to do the work
  - what tools or equipment to use

- what assistants to hire to help with the work
- where to purchase supplies and services

If you receive less extensive instructions about what should be done, but not how it should be done, you may be an **independent contractor**. For instance, instructions about time and place may be less important than directions on how the work is performed.

- **Training** – if the business provides you with training about required procedures and methods, this indicates that the business wants the work done in a certain way, and this suggests that you may be an **employee**.

FINANCIAL CONTROL

These facts show whether there is a right to direct or control the business part of the work. For example:

- **Significant Investment** – if you have a significant investment in your work, you may be an **independent contractor**. While there is no precise dollar test, the investment must have substance. However, a significant investment is not necessary to be an **independent contractor**.

- **Expenses** – if you are not reimbursed for some or all business expenses, then you may be an **independent contractor**, especially if your unreimbursed business expenses are high.

- **Opportunity for Profit or Loss** – if you can realize a profit or incur a loss, this suggests that you are in business for yourself and that you may be an **independent contractor**.

RELATIONSHIP OF THE PARTIES

These are facts that illustrate how the business and the worker perceive their relationship. For example:

- **Employee Benefits** – if you receive benefits, such as insurance, pension, or paid

leave, this is an indication that you may be an **employee**. If you do not receive benefits, however, you could be either an **employee** or an **independent contractor**.

- **Written Contracts** – a written contract may show what both you and the business intend. This may be very significant if it is difficult, if not impossible, to determine status based on other facts

When You Are an Employee

- Your employer must withhold income tax and your portion of social security and Medicare taxes. Also, your employer is responsible for paying social security, Medicare, and unemployment (FUTA) taxes on your wages. Your employer must give you a Form W-2, *Wage and Tax Statement,* showing the amount of taxes withheld from your pay.

- You may deduct unreimbursed employee business expenses on Schedule A of your income tax return, but only if you itemize deductions and they total more than two percent of your adjusted gross income.

When You Are an Independent Contractor

- The business may be required to give you Form 1099-MISC, *Miscellaneous Income,* to report what it has paid to you.

- You are responsible for paying your own income tax and self-employment tax (Self-Employment Contributions Act – SECA). The business does not withhold taxes from your pay. You may need to make estimated tax payments during the year to cover your tax liabilities.

- You may deduct business expenses on Schedule C of your income tax return.

Source: Internal Revenue Service Publication 1779 (Rev. 1-2007). Catalog No. 16134L. (http://www.irs.gov/pub/irs-pdf/p1779.pdf).

15. *Significant investment.* A worker is an independent contractor if she or he invests in facilities that are not typically maintained by employees such as the maintenance of an office rented at fair value from an unrelated party. An employee depends on the employer for such facilities.

16. *Realization of profit or loss.* A worker who can realize a profit or loss (in addition to the profit or loss ordinarily realized by employees) through management of resources is an independent contractor. The worker who cannot is generally an employee.

17. *Work performed for more than one firm at a time.* If a worker performs more than *de minimis* services for a number of unrelated persons at the same time, she or he is usually considered an independent contractor.

18. *Service made available to the general public.* A worker is usually an independent contractor if the services are made available to the general public on a regular or consistent basis.

19. *Right to discharge.* The right of the employer to discharge a worker indicates that he or she is an employee.

20. *Right to terminate.* A worker is an employee if the right to end the relationship with the principal is available at any time he or she wishes without incurring liability.

In addition to the basic analysis under the IRS test, writer Christina Morfeld provides a helpful analysis to consider when determining whether an individual is more appropriately classified as an employee or independent contractor (IC) (see Exhibit 1.5, "Employee or Independent Contractor? Twenty Questions").

Finally, under the **economic realities test**, courts consider whether the worker is economically dependent on the business or, as a matter of economic fact, is in business for himself or herself. In applying the economic realities test, courts look to the degree of control exerted by the alleged employer over the worker, the worker's opportunity for profit or loss, the worker's investment in the business, the permanence of the working relationship, the degree of skill required by the worker, and the extent the work is an integral part of the alleged employer's business. Typically, all of these factors are considered as a whole with none of the factors being determinative.

In *NLRB v. Friendly Cab Co.,* included at the end of this chapter, the taxi company identified its workers as independent contractors in its auto leases with its drivers. In fact, the agreements specifically explained that no employee–employer relationship existed and, as a result, the cab company was not responsible for standard employer responsibilities such as withholding payroll taxes or providing workers' compensation insurance. The circuit court, however, held that, notwithstanding the insistence of the employer that the drivers were independent contractors, the economic realities of the relationship actually would determine its ultimate legal definition. In short, calling something an apple does not always make it an apple; it must actually grow on an apple tree.

economic realities test
A test to determine whether a worker qualifies as an employee. Courts use this test to determine whether a worker is economically dependent on the business or is in business for himself or herself. To apply the test, courts look to the degree of control exerted by the alleged employer over the worker, the worker's opportunity for profit or loss, the worker's investment in the business, the permanence of the working relationship, the degree of skill required by the worker, and the extent the work is an integral part of the alleged employer's business.

Exhibit 1.5 *Employee or Independent Contractor? Twenty Questions*

Query	Yes	No
1. Is the individual's work vital to the company's core business?	Employee activities are integrated with the organization's business operations.	IC services are typically limited to nonessential business activities.
2. Did you train the individual to perform tasks in a specific way?	Employees are usually taught the specific work procedures that they are expected to follow and must comply with any other employer requirements with regard to these activities.	ICs are generally considered "experts" in their field and, as such, can determine which work methods are most appropriate. Additionally, they are typically held accountable only for outcomes, not the means with which they are achieved.
3. Do you (or can you) instruct the individual as to when, where, and how the work is performed?		
4. Do you (or can you) control the sequence or order the work is performed?		
5. Do you (or can you) set the hours of work for the individual?	Employees generally work on a schedule determined by their employer.	ICs can work whatever hours they choose, provided that agreed-upon deadlines are met.
6. Do you (or can you) require the individual to perform the work personally?		ICs are free to delegate to their own staff or subcontract the work to others.
7. Do you (or can you) prohibit the individual from hiring, supervising, and paying assistants?	Employees must do the tasks for which they were hired themselves.	
8. Does the individual perform regular and continuous services for you?	Employees typically have an open-ended relationship with a company, even if the work is performed at irregular intervals.	ICs work on a project-by-project basis, each time with a new contract.
9. Does the individual provide services on a substantially full-time basis to your company?	Employees are usually expected to devote all working hours to their employer.	ICs do not spend so much time with any one company that they are restricted from doing projects for others and, in fact, generally work for multiple clients concurrently.

continued

Exhibit 1.5 *continued*

10. Is your company the sole or major source of income for the individual?		
11. Is the work performed on your premises?	Employees are ordinarily required to work on-site.	ICs are free to work off-site, such as in a home office.
12. Do you (or can you) require the individual to submit regular reports, either written or oral?	Employees may be asked to provide status or activity reports on a regular basis.	ICs are responsible for producing a final deliverable and are not, therefore, required to provide interim reports.
13. Do you pay the individual by the hour, week, or month?	Employees are usually paid at fixed intervals.	ICs are generally paid for their results, not the amount of time worked.
14. Do you pay the individual's travel and business expenses?	Employees who incur work-related expenses are typically reimbursed by their employer.	ICs are usually expected to incorporate out-of-pocket expenses into their project fee rather than be directly reimbursed for them.
15. Do you furnish tools or equipment for the individual?	Employees generally use company-provided supplies.	ICs are expected to own and use their own supplies.
16. Does the individual have a significant investment in facilities, tools, or equipment?	Employees typically use their company's facilities, tools, and equipment.	ICs incur expenses related to work space, equipment, etc., like any other business owner.
17. Can the individual realize a profit or loss from his or her services to your company?	Employees can usually expect steady paychecks.	ICs run the risk of nonpayment if a project is not completed according to the specifications detailed in the contract.
18. Does the individual make his or her services available to the general public?	Employees do not typically position and market themselves as service providers.	ICs publicize their services to a wide range of potential clients via direct mail, advertising, etc.
19. Can the individual terminate the relationship without liability?	Employees can quit at any time and can typically be released "at-will" by their employers.	ICs are legally obligated to complete projects according to contract provisions and can only be dismissed if they fail to do so.
20. Do you have the right to discharge the individual at any time?		

Source: Reprinted from Christina Morfeld, "Employee vs. Independent Contractor: A Game of 20 Questions," http://affinitybizcomm.com/EEvsIC.htm, with permission of the author, Christina Morfeld.

Scenario

Applying the tests to Scenario 3, we find that control plays an even more significant role in the final determination. In Ariana's case, though, she likely held herself out as a tax consultant or independent contractor; indeed, she had very little control over any details of her work. She was at no point in a position to impact the financial bottom line of her own enterprise. She did not have the ability to name her own contract fee; she did not hire or fire her own staff, or choose her own clients. Though she could direct how her work was done, in the end, she had no control over nor even responsibility for how her work was completed and delivered to the client. Ariana would therefore be considered an employee.

Contingent or Temporary Workers

A *contingent worker* is one whose job with an employer is temporary, is sporadic, or differs in any way from the norm of full-time employment. As used by the EEOC, the term *contingent worker* includes those who are hired by an employer through a staffing firm, as well as temporary, seasonal, and part-time workers, and those considered to be independent contractors rather than employees.[9]

When using contingent and temporary workers, an employer must be aware of the advantages and disadvantages. Although contingent or temporary workers provide a cost savings as a short-term benefit, depending on their classification they could be entitled to protection under the employment laws. It is important to be sure the classification given is the true classification.

Joint Employers and Staffing Firms

Title VII prohibits staffing firms from illegally discriminating against workers in assignments and opportunities for employment. Staffing firms can be considered to be employers, as well, such as when they pay the worker and provide training and workers' compensation coverage.

If a client of a staffing firm supervises, trains, and otherwise directs the worker with whom it has a continuing relationship, then perhaps the client will become an employer of the worker. In this way, *both* the staffing firm *and* the client may share liability as employers of the worker. This is called *joint* and *several* liability, and the worker may collect compensatory damages from either one or both of the entities combined if a wrong is proven.

Whether a contingent worker who is placed by a staffing firm with the firm's clients qualifies as an employee depends on a number of factors, including whether the staffing firm or the client retains the right to control when, where, and how the worker performs the job and whether there is a continuing relationship with the worker, among other factors. What is unique about the worker placed by a staffing firm is the potential for joint liability between the staffing firm and the client.

In a case that sought to determine liability for wage and hour violations, the Second Circuit Court of Appeals considered whether the right to control is necessary to create liability based on joint employment. In *Zheng v. Liberty Apparel*

Co.,[10] Liberty was a clothing manufacturer that subcontracted with a garment factory to produce its clothing. In finding liability based on the joint employer concept, the court held not all outsourcing relationships would be classified as joint employers and that that all relevant factors should be considered, including (but not limited to)

1. Whether the work was done on the employer's premises.
2. Whether the subcontractor brought his business from one employer to another.
3. Whether the subcontractor performed a specific role that was integral to the employer's work process of production.
4. Whether the responsibility under the contract could pass from one subcontractor to another without a lot of change.
5. The degree to which the employer supervised the subcontractor's work.
6. Whether the subcontractors worked exclusively or predominantly for the employer.[11]

Further, employers may be held liable as "third-party interferers" under Title VII. For example, if an employer decides to ask its staffing firm to replace the temporary receptionist with one of another race, the receptionist could proceed with a Title VII claim against the employer because it improperly interfered with her employment opportunities with the staffing firm. Therefore, an employer using a staffing firm cannot avoid liability for discriminating against a temporary worker merely because it did not "employ" the worker.

Defining "Applicant"

Since federal regulations often require employers to track applicants on the basis of race, gender, and ethnicity, it is important to have a clear and consistent definition of who is an *applicant*. Moreover, in this electronic age, technology has changed the way that people apply for jobs. As a result, the Uniform Guidelines on Employee Selection Procedures were modified to include the following expanded definition of applicant in the context of the Internet and related electronic data processing technologies: An applicant exists when three conditions have been met:

1. The employer has acted to fill a particular position.
2. The individual has followed the employer's standard procedures for submitting applications.
3. The individual has indicated an interest in the particular position.

Where the applicant is instead a traditional job seeker, the original definition still applies—an applicant is someone who has "indicated an interest in being considered" for employment. The impact of this change is that an e-mail inquiry about a job does not qualify the sender as an applicant, nor does the posting of a résumé on a third-party job board.

Management Tips *Employee Status*

- For reasons cited earlier in this chapter, an employer may hire someone with the intent of establishing an employment relationship or an independent-contractor relationship. A variety of protections available to the employer allow the employer some measure of control over this seemingly arbitrary categorization process. However, none will guarantee a court determination of employee or independent-contractor status.

- As in most relationships, a written document will help to identify the nature of the association between the parties and their rights and obligations, provided that the role of the worker is consistent with the duties of an employee or independent contractor. While the classification made in this document is not binding in any way on the courts or the IRS, it may serve as persuasive evidence about the parties' intentions.

- If the person is hired as an employee, and it is so stipulated in the document, the written agreement may be considered an employment agreement. The employer should be careful to discuss whether the employment duration will remain at-will or for a specified time period.

- If the employer intends to hire the worker as an independent contractor, the agreement should articulate the extent of the worker's control over her or his performance and the outcome to be produced pursuant to the contract. Further, where the agreement specifies particular hours to be worked, rather than a deadline for completion, it is more likely that the worker will be considered an employee.

- Included in the written agreement should be a discussion of who is responsible for the payment of income taxes and benefits and for the division of responsibility for office expenses and overhead such as tools, supplies, and office rent.

- The independent contractor should be paid on the basis of the nature of the job completed, rather than the hours worked to complete it.

- No training should be offered to an independent contractor; courts hypothesize that the reason an employer would hire outside help is to reduce these costs. On the other hand, where an employer provides extensive training and support, it is likely that the employer seeks to reap a benefit from this investment in the long run through continued service of its employee.

- Where additional assistance is required, an independent contractor will be made to supply that extra assistance, while an employer would be the party to provide the aid if the worker is an employee. The employer may offer to guarantee a loan to the contractor to allow her or him to obtain the assistance, or new tools, or other equipment if necessary without threatening the independent-contractor status.

- Finally, where the risk of misclassification is great—for instance, where the failure to correctly categorize the worker may result in large financial penalties—the employer may choose to obtain an advance ruling from the IRS regarding the nature of the relationship. This is accomplished through the filing of IRS Form SS-8 (see Exhibit 1.6, "IRS Form SS-8").

Exhibit 1.6 *IRS Form SS-8*

Form **SS-8**
(Rev. June 2003)
Department of the Treasury
Internal Revenue Service

Determination of Worker Status
for Purposes of Federal Employment Taxes
and Income Tax Withholding

OMB No. 1545-0004

Name of firm (or person) for whom the worker performed services

Worker's name

Firm's address (include street address, apt. or suite no., city, state, and ZIP code)

Worker's address (include street address, apt. or suite no., city, state, and ZIP code)

Trade name

Telephone number (include area code)
( )

Worker's social security number

Telephone number (include area code)
( )

Firm's employer identification number

Worker's employer identification number (if any)

If the worker is paid by a firm other than the one listed on this form for these services, enter the name, address, and employer identification number of the payer.

Important Information Needed To Process Your Request

We must have your permission to disclose your name and the information on this form and any attachments to other parties involved with this request. **Do we have your permission to disclose this information?** . . . . □ **Yes** □ **No**
If you answered "No" or did not mark a box, we will not process your request and will not issue a determination.

You must answer ALL items OR mark them "Unknown" or "Does not apply." If you need more space, attach another sheet.

A This form is being completed by: □ Firm □ Worker; for services performed _____ to _____ .
(beginning date)   (ending date)

B Explain your reason(s) for filing this form (e.g., you received a bill from the IRS, you believe you received a Form 1099 or Form W-2 erroneously, you are unable to get worker's compensation benefits, you were audited or are being audited by the IRS). ----------------------------
----

C Total number of workers who performed or are performing the same or similar services _____ .

D How did the worker obtain the job? □ Application   □ Bid   □ Employment Agency   □ Other (specify) _____ .

E Attach copies of all supporting documentation (contracts, invoices, memos, Forms W-2, Forms 1099, IRS closing agreements, IRS rulings, etc.). In addition, please inform us of any current or past litigation concerning the worker's status. If no income reporting forms (Form 1099-MISC or W-2) were furnished to the worker, enter the amount of income earned for the year(s) at issue $ _____ .

F Describe the firm's business. ---

G Describe the work done by the worker and provide the worker's job title. ------------------------------
----

H Explain why you believe the worker is an employee or an independent contractor. ---------------------
----

I Did the worker perform services for the firm before getting this position? . . . . □ Yes □ No □ N/A
If "Yes," what were the dates of the prior service? --
If "Yes," explain the differences, if any, between the current and prior service. ------------------------------
----

J If the work is done under a written agreement between the firm and the worker, attach a copy (preferably signed by both parties). Describe the terms and conditions of the work arrangement. --
----

For Privacy Act and Paperwork Reduction Act Notice, see page 5.   Cat. No. 16106T   Form **SS-8** (Rev. 6-2003)

continued

Part I   Behavioral Control

1   What specific training and/or instruction is the worker given by the firm? ....

2   How does the worker receive work assignments? ....

3   Who determines the methods by which the assignments are performed? ....

4   Who is the worker required to contact if problems or complaints arise and who is responsible for their resolution? ....

5   What types of reports are required from the worker? Attach examples. ....

6   Describe the worker's daily routine (i.e., schedule, hours, etc.). ....

7   At what location(s) does the worker perform services (e.g., firm's premises, own shop or office, home, customer's location, etc.)? ....

8   Describe any meetings the worker is required to attend and any penalties for not attending (e.g., sales meetings, monthly meetings, staff meetings, etc.). ....

9   Is the worker required to provide the services personally? . . . . ☐ Yes   ☐ No

10   If substitutes or helpers are needed, who hires them? ....

11   If the worker hires the substitutes or helpers, is approval required? . . . . ☐ Yes   ☐ No
     If "Yes," by whom? ....

12   Who pays the substitutes or helpers? ....

13   Is the worker reimbursed if the worker pays the substitutes or helpers? . . . . ☐ Yes   ☐ No
     If "Yes," by whom? ....

Part II   Financial Control

1   List the supplies, equipment, materials, and property provided by each party:
     The firm ....
     The worker ....
     Other party ....

2   Does the worker lease equipment? . . . . ☐ Yes   ☐ No
     If "Yes," what are the terms of the lease? (Attach a copy or explanatory statement.) ....

3   What expenses are incurred by the worker in the performance of services for the firm? ....

4   Specify which, if any, expenses are reimbursed by:
     The firm ....
     Other party ....

5   Type of pay the worker receives: ☐ Salary   ☐ Commission   ☐ Hourly Wage   ☐ Piece Work
     ☐ Lump Sum   ☐ Other (specify) ....
     If type of pay is commission, and the firm guarantees a minimum amount of pay, specify amount $ _____ .

6   Is the worker allowed a drawing account for advances? . . . . ☐ Yes   ☐ No
     If "Yes," how often? ....
     Specify any restrictions. ....

7   Whom does the customer pay? . . . . ☐ Firm   ☐ Worker
     If worker, does the worker pay the total amount to the firm? ☐ Yes   ☐ No   If "No," explain. ....

8   Does the firm carry worker's compensation insurance on the worker? . . . . ☐ Yes   ☐ No

9   What economic loss or financial risk, if any, can the worker incur beyond the normal loss of salary (e.g., loss or damage of equipment, material, etc.)? ....

Form **SS-8** (Rev. 6-2003)

continued

23

Exhibit 1.6 *continued*

Part III　　**Relationship of the Worker and Firm**

1　List the benefits available to the worker (e.g., paid vacations, sick pay, pensions, bonuses). ----------------------------
----

2　Can the relationship be terminated by either party without incurring liability or penalty? . . . . ☐ **Yes**　☐ **No**
　　If "No," explain your answer. --

3　Does the worker perform similar services for others? . . . . ☐ **Yes**　☐ **No**
　　If "Yes," is the worker required to get approval from the firm? . . . . ☐ **Yes**　☐ **No**

4　Describe any agreements prohibiting competition between the worker and the firm while the worker is performing services or during any later
　　period. Attach any available documentation. --

5　Is the worker a member of a union? . . . . ☐ **Yes**　☐ **No**

6　What type of advertising, if any, does the worker do (e.g., a business listing in a directory, business cards, etc.)? Provide copies, if applicable.

7　If the worker assembles or processes a product at home, who provides the materials and instructions or pattern? --------------
----

8　What does the worker do with the finished product (e.g., return it to the firm, provide it to another party, or sell it)? --------------
----

9　How does the firm represent the worker to its customers (e.g., employee, partner, representative, or contractor)? --------------
----

10　If the worker no longer performs services for the firm, how did the relationship end? --------------------------------------
----

Part IV　　**For Service Providers or Salespersons**—Complete this part if the worker provided a service directly to
　　　　　　　customers or is a salesperson.

1　What are the worker's responsibilities in soliciting new customers? --
----

2　Who provides the worker with leads to prospective customers? --

3　Describe any reporting requirements pertaining to the leads. --
----

4　What terms and conditions of sale, if any, are required by the firm? --

5　Are orders submitted to and subject to approval by the firm? . . . . ☐ **Yes**　☐ **No**

6　Who determines the worker's territory? --

7　Did the worker pay for the privilege of serving customers on the route or in the territory? . . . . ☐ **Yes**　☐ **No**
　　If "Yes," whom did the worker pay? --
　　If "Yes," how much did the worker pay? . . . . $ _____ .

8　Where does the worker sell the product (e.g., in a home, retail establishment, etc.)? ---
----

9　List the product and/or services distributed by the worker (e.g., meat, vegetables, fruit, bakery products, beverages, or laundry or dry cleaning
　　services). If more than one type of product and/or service is distributed, specify the principal one. -----------------------------
----

10　Does the worker sell life insurance full time? . . . . ☐ **Yes**　☐ **No**

11　Does the worker sell other types of insurance for the firm? . . . . ☐ **Yes**　☐ **No**
　　If "Yes," enter the percentage of the worker's total working time spent in selling other types of insurance. . . . _____%

12　If the worker solicits orders from wholesalers, retailers, contractors, or operators of hotels, restaurants, or other similar
　　establishments, enter the percentage of the worker's time spent in the solicitation. . . . . _____%

13　Is the merchandise purchased by the customers for resale or use in their business operations? . . . . ☐ **Yes**　☐ **No**
　　Describe the merchandise and state whether it is equipment installed on the customers' premises. ---------------------------
----

Part V　　**Signature** (see page 4)

Under penalties of perjury, I declare that I have examined this request, including accompanying documents, and to the best of my knowledge and belief, the facts
presented are true, correct, and complete.

Signature ▶ _____ Title ▶ _____ Date ▶ _____
　　　　　　　(Type or print name below)

Source: www.irs.gov/pub/irs-pdf/fss8.pdf.

The Definition of "Employer"

LO5

While *employees* are hard to define, courts and regulatory agencies have not experienced great difficulty in defining the term *employer*. Depending on the applicable statute or provision, an *employer* is simply one who employs or uses others to do his or her work, or to work on his or her behalf. Most statutes specifically include in this definition employment agencies, labor organizations, and joint labor–management committees.

Issues may arise where an entity claims to be a private membership club (exempt from Title VII prohibitions) or a multinational company that may or may not be subject to application of various U.S. laws. A determination also must be made whether the employer receives federal funds or maintains federal contracts for coverage under the Rehabilitation Act of 1973, among others.

Another question is whether an individual, such as a supervisor, is also considered an employer under employment-related statutes and, therefore, can be held personally liable for her or his actions. Though most statutes are silent on the issue, the majority of courts have concluded that federal anti-discrimination statutes do *not* permit the imposition of this liability.

2
Scenario

Therefore, in this chapter's Scenario 2, Serafine would not be able to sustain her case through the EEOC against Gustave. The court would instead find that her only cause of action would be against her employer, CCC. Since, in this scenario, CCC has a system, investigated Serafine's complaint promptly, and then took swift and decisive action against Gustave, employer CCC is not liable for his harassment of Serafine. Basically, an employee is entitled to an appropriate response by the employer to solve the problem, what the courts call "considerable recompense, albeit not in monetary form." In the case on which this scenario is based, the court helpfully explained the rationale for this limitation:

> She has an employer who was sensitive and responsive to her complaint. She can take comfort in the knowledge that she continues to work for this company, while her harasser does not—and that the company's prompt action is likely to discourage other would-be harassers. This is precisely the result Title VII was meant to achieve.[12]

The most exacting issue is usually how many employees an employer must have in order to be subject to a given statute. It is crucial for employers to be familiar with the statutes to which they are subject and those from which they are immune. (See Exhibit 1.7 for an overview of the various statutory definitions of employer.)

The "Freedom" to Contract in the Regulatory Employment Environment

In the age of increasingly complex regulations governing the workplace, the relationship between employer and employee essentially is still based on an

Exhibit 1.7 *Statutory Definitions of Employer*

The Civil Rights Act of 1866

- *Purpose:* Regulates the actions of all individuals or entities when entering into a contract to employ someone else.
- *Definition of Employer:* No requirement for a minimum number of employees in order to qualify as an employer under the CRA of 1866.
- *Other:* The Civil Rights Act of 1991 added a section to the CRA of 1866 to cover actions by the employer after the contract has been formed, including discrimination during employment or termination.

Title VII of the Civil Rights Act of 1964

- *Purpose:* Prohibits discrimination in employment based on specified protected classes.
- *Definition of Employer:* Applies to all firms or their agents engaged in an industry affecting commerce that employ 15 or more employees for each working day in each of 20 or more weeks in the current or preceding calendar year.[1]
- *Exemptions:* Government-owned corporations, Indian tribes, and bona fide private membership clubs.

Title VI of the Civil Rights Act of 1964

- *Purpose:* Applies the race, color, and national origin proscriptions of Title VII to any program or activity that receives federal financial assistance. Unless it falls within one of several exemptions, a government contractor is also prohibited from discriminating on the bases of race, color, religion, gender, or national origin by Executive Order 11246.[2]
- *Definition of Employer:* Any government agency that receives federal funding.

Age Discrimination in Employment Act of 1967

- *Purpose:* Prohibits discrimination in employment against anyone over the age of 40.
- *Definition of Employer:* Applies to all entities or their agents that employ 20 or more employees on each working day for 20 or more weeks during the current or preceding calendar year.
- *Exemptions:* American employers who control foreign firms where compliance with the ADEA in connection with an American employee would cause the foreign firm to violate the laws of the country in which it is located. The ADEA, unlike Title VII, does *not* exempt Indian tribes or private membership clubs.

Title I of the Americans with Disabilities Act

- *Purpose:* Prohibits discrimination in employment against otherwise qualified individuals with disabilities who cannot perform the essential functions of their jobs, with or without reasonable accommodations.
- *Definition of Employer:* The Americans with Disabilities Act (ADA) applies to all employers

[1] "Working day" is generally computed by counting the number of employees maintained on the payroll in a given week, as opposed to the number of employees who work on any one day. This calculation provides for a more expansive definition of "employer" since it includes hourly and part-time workers. *Walters v. Metropolitan Educational Enterprises, Inc.,* 72 FEP Cases (BNA) 1211 (1997). Note, however, that this form of calculation is merely the majority approach; other courts have found that part-time employees who work for any part of each day of the workweek should be counted, while part-time employees who work full days for only a portion of the workweek should not be counted.

[2] The order exempts (1) employers with contracts of less than $10,000 from the requirement to include an equal employment opportunity clause in each of their contracts; (2) contracts for work performed outside the United States by employees not recruited within the United States; (3) contracts with state and local governments by providing that the EEO requirements do not apply to any agency of that government that is not participating in the work of the contract; (4) religious educational institutions that hire only people of that religion; (5) preferences offered to Native Americans living on or near a reservation in connection with employment on or near the reservation; and (6) certain contracts on the basis of national interest or security reasons.

continued

engaged in interstate commerce with 15 or more workers, including state and local government employers, employment agencies, labor unions, and joint labor–management committees.

- *Exemptions:* Executive agencies of the U.S. government are exempt from the ADA, but these agencies are covered instead by similar non-discrimination requirements and additional affirmative employment requirements under section 501 of the Rehabilitation Act of 1973 (see below). Also exempted from the ADA, similar to Title VII, are corporations fully owned by the U.S. government, Indian tribes, and bona fide private membership clubs that are not labor organizations and that are exempt from taxation under the Internal Revenue Code. Religious organizations are covered by the ADA, but they may give employment preference to people of their own religion or religious organization.

The Fair Labor Standards Act

- *Purpose:* Mandates wages, hours, and ages for employment in the United States, among other labor standards.
- *Definition of Employer:* Offers coverage to workers not necessarily based on a particular definition of "employer" but on two distinct forms of coverage: "enterprise coverage" and "individual coverage." *Enterprise coverage* refers to the protections offered to employees who work for certain businesses or organizations (i.e., "enterprises") that have at least two employees and do at least $500,000 a year in business, or that are involved in certain specified industries such as hospitals, businesses providing medical or nursing care for residents, schools and preschools, and government agencies. *Individual coverage* refers to the protections offered to employees if their work regularly involves them in commerce between states ("interstate commerce"). The FLSA provides coverage, even when there is no enterprise coverage, to workers who are "engaged in commerce or in the production of goods for commerce." This coverage may include workers who produce goods that will be sent out of state, who regularly make telephone calls as part of their job to persons located in other states, or who travel to other states for their jobs. Also, domestic service workers (such as housekeepers, full-time babysitters, and cooks) are normally covered by the law.

The Rehabilitation Act of 1973

- *Purpose:* Prohibits covered agencies from discriminating against otherwise qualified disabled individuals, similar to the ADA.
- *Definition of Employer:* Applies not only to all entities, programs, and activities that receive federal funds and to government contractors, but also to all programs and activities of any executive agency as well as the U.S. Postal Service. A covered federal contractor is one who maintains a contract with the federal government in excess of $10,000 annually for the provision of personal property or nonpersonal services.

agreement. As you will see throughout this text, terms and conditions of employment may be subject to regulation or open to contractual negotiation, and either expressed or implied. Though an employer is generally free to design contract terms of any kind, the terms and conditions set by an employer cannot violate the letter or the spirit of the applicable laws we have discussed or will discuss in chapters to come.

In addition, you will learn that courts and legislatures sometimes determine that certain types of agreements between employer and employee are *unenforceable*. The focus of our discussion, therefore, is how the employment relationship is regulated, in general.

Covenants Not to Compete (Non-compete Agreements)

LO6

non-compete agreement (or covenant not to compete)
An agreement by the employee not to disclose the employer's confidential information or enter into competition with the employer for a specified period of time and/or within a specified region.

One employment constraint that has received varying degrees of acceptance by different states is the **covenant not to compete** or **non-compete agreement**. While individuals in positions of trust and confidence already owe a duty of loyalty to their employers during employment, even without a non-compete agreement, a non-compete agreement usually includes prohibitions against disclosure of trade secrets, soliciting the employer's employees or customers, or entering into competition with the employer if the employee is terminated. All states allow employers *some* control over what information a former worker can use or disclose in a competing business and whether a former worker can encourage clients, customers, and former co-workers to leave the employer.

However, not all states allow employers to prevent former workers from competing with them. States vary widely, from explicitly permitting non-compete agreements, to permitting agreements under certain circumstances, to strictly prohibiting agreements that limit for whom a former employee can work and where he or she can work. Notably, while California and North Dakota severely *restrict* the use of non-competes, in 2010 Georgia voters enacted a state constitutional amendment specifically expanding the enforcement of reasonable non-competes in order to make that state more economically attractive to business.[13]

In some states, certain professions are exempted from these prohibitions. For example, in certain states, prior employers can enforce non-competes against "management personnel" while they may not enforce the agreements against other types of workers; some regions instead specifically exempt security guards and broadcast employees. In many states, an employer may restrict a past employee based on location, length of time, and the type of work she or he may conduct, as long as the restrictions are reasonable and necessary to protect a business interest.[14] Because of these state-by-state differences, it is critical to have **forum selection clauses** in contracts that stipulate the state law that will apply to the contract in question.

forum selection clause
A clause in a contract that identifies the state law that will apply to any disputes that arise under the contract.[15]

But how do you know what will be considered *reasonable* restrictions on an employee's ability to compete after the employment relationship has ended? The common law generally *prohibits* the restriction if it is more broad than necessary to protect the employer's legitimate interests or if the employer's need is outweighed by the hardship to the employee and likely injury to the public.[16]

To determine reasonableness, courts look to the location and time limitations placed on the employee's ability to compete. The definition of competition under the non-compete agreement is also relevant: Is the employee prohibited from working in any capacity with a competitor or merely restricted from entering into direct competition with the employer? Restrictions that are for an indefinite period of time, or that prohibit the employee from working "anywhere in the United States," would likely be considered unreasonable. However, as an example, restricting an employee from engaging in direct competition with the employer for one year from the end of their employment relationship within the same county may be considered reasonable. Generally, in order to be considered reasonable, the restrictive covenant should not prevent the employee from earning a living of any sort under its terms.

1
Scenario

It is generally accepted that a valid restrictive covenant will meet the following qualifications:

1. It protects a legitimate business interest.
2. It is ancillary to a legitimate business relationship.
3. It provides a benefit to both the employee and employer.
4. It is reasonable in scope and duration.
5. It is not contrary to the public interest.[17]

Consider the example of *DoubleClick, Inc. v. Henderson,*[18] where the court was asked to impose a non-compete injunction that would have prohibited executives from one of the most successful Internet advertising businesses from engaging in a competing start-up business for one year. Recognizing the concept that time is relative, the judge considered one year in Internet time to be too burdensome. In arriving at this conclusion, the judge assessed the characteristics of the Internet advertising industry, which is dynamic, constantly evolving, and lacking geographical borders.

A lesson learned from *DoubleClick* applies to all employers considering the use of non-compete agreements: Reasonableness is measured by the realities of the industry and the nature of the employee's occupation.

As mentioned above, covenants not to compete sometimes also include provisions with regard to trade secrets or confidentiality with regard to other elements of employer intellectual property. This property might also include, for instance, customer relations and goodwill, specialized training, or particular skills unique to the workplace. The agreement often depends on what an employer considers to be trade secrets versus information in the public domain or commonly known in an industry. Confidential customer lists or customer preferences are often the source of trouble since they are usually maintained by individual workers based on professional relationships; however, most courts deem them property of the employer. Pricing, revenue, and other projections and marketing strategies are also commonly considered to be trade secrets. On the other hand, processes that are known by many in a particular industry or other information that is otherwise available through external sources are not considered to be company property. Note that customer lists, if accessible through public means, would therefore no longer fall under the rubric of trade secrets.

inevitable disclosure
The theory under which a court may prohibit a former employee from working for an employer's competitor if the employer can show that it is inevitable that the former employee will disclose a trade secret by virtue of her or his position.

Under the theory of **inevitable disclosure**, employers are protected against disclosure of trade secrets even if no non-compete applies. A court may prohibit a former employee from working for an employer's competitor if the employer can show that there is imminent threat that a trade secret will be shared. The courts look to (1) whether the employee's knowledge is exceptionally specialized and technical, (2) which would give either business (former or new) a significant advantage in the market, and (3) the employee could perform her or his work without it. It might be highly unlikely, if not impossible, in some instances for some of these workers to conduct their work without disclosing the trade secret.

Management Tips

In one of the landmark cases in the area, for instance, Continental Aviation tried to purchase a very particular type of fuel injector pump from Allis-Chalmers, one of only three companies that marketed the pump in the world. When they were unable to reach terms, Continental instead simply hired the original designer of the pump from Allis-Chalmers to design the pump for Continental. In finding inevitable disclosure and imposing an injunction that prohibited the engineer from working at Continental, the court pointed out the "virtual impossibility of Mr. Wolff [the engineer] performing all of his prospective duties for Continental to the best of his ability, without in effect giving it the benefit of Allis-Chalmers' confidential information."[19]

The Uniform Trade Secrets Act is a model act that strives to provide guidance to states developing statutes in this and other related areas; 44 states and the District of Columbia have adopted its structure. The UTSA provides relief in the form of monetary damages, attorney's fees, and injunctive relief for misappropriation of trade secrets and does include a provision for inevitable disclosure.

Once a non-compete agreement has been found to be valid, in order to be enforceable, it must also be supported by consideration offered in a bargained-for exchange. In other words, the agreement by the employee not to compete with the employer is *only* enforceable if the employee also receives something in exchange for this agreement. Often, non-competes are signed at the time an employee is first hired; so the offer of employment on its own is considered sufficient consideration. However, if an employee is asked to sign a non-compete agreement after being hired and is not offered any additional consideration, some states do not treat continued at-will employment as sufficient.[20] It depends on the state in which the agreement is signed.[21]

Chapter Summary

- No matter the size of your organization, as long as you have hired one individual to work for you, you are considered an employer and potentially subject to numerous federal and other regulations, as well as to wrongful termination liability.

- Why is the definition of "employee" important? The distinction between employees and independent contractors is crucial from a financial perspective. Because many regulations require different responsibilities from employers of employees and independent contractors, it is imperative that an employer be confident of the classification of its employees.

- How does an employer make the distinction between employees and independent contractors? The classification of employees may vary depending on the statute that is to be applied or on the court in which a given case is scheduled to be heard. However, the common thread is generally the right of the employer to control the actions of the worker. Where this is present, the worker is likely to be considered an employee. Other factors to be considered include those that are part of the economic realities test, which evaluates the economics of the employment situation. Finally, some workers may be classified statutorily as employees, making the distinction all the easier.

- Who is an "employer"? The definition of employer is generally agreed on. An employer is usually thought to be one who employs or uses others (either employees or independent contractors, or both) to do its work, or to work on its behalf.

Chapter-End Questions

1. Campion is a firm that provides psychological services to police departments. The City of Minneapolis terminated its contract with Campion and entered into a new contract with Detrick. Campion contends that it is because it is affiliated with the Illinois Family Institute, an organization that happens to have conservative perspectives on issues such as marriage, abortion, homosexuality, and stem cell research. Campion filed a claim against the City of Minneapolis (a public entity) claiming that the termination violated its First Amendment freedom of association. Is the firm's contract protected under the First Amendment? What would the firm have to demonstrate in order to prove a *prima facie* case here? [*Campion, Barrow & Assocs. of Illinois, Inc. v. City of Minneapolis*, 652 F. Supp. 2d 986, 2009 U.S. Dist. LEXIS 70993 (D. Minn. 2009).]

2. A staffing firm provides landscaping services for clients on an ongoing basis. The staffing firm selects and pays the workers, provides health insurance, and withholds taxes. The firm provides the equipment and supplies necessary to do the work. It also supervises the workers on the clients' premises. Client A reserves the right to direct the staffing-firm workers to perform particular tasks at particular times or in a specified manner, although it does not generally exercise that authority. Client A evaluates the quality of the workers' performance and regularly reports its findings to the firm. It can require the firm to remove a worker from the job assignment if it is dissatisfied. Who is the employer of the workers?

3. Alberto Camargo was killed when his tractor rolled over as he was driving over a large mound of manure in a corral belonging to Tjaarda Dairy. Camargo was an employee of Golden Cal Trucking, and Golden Cal Trucking was an independent contractor that Tjaarda Dairy had hired to scrape the manure out of its corrals and to haul it away in exchange for the right to purchase the manure at a discount. Plaintiffs, Camargo's wife and five children, sued defendants Tjaarda Dairy and Perry Tjaarda on the theory, among others, that they were *negligent in hiring* Golden Cal Trucking because they failed to determine whether Camargo was qualified to operate the tractor safely. Is Tjaarda Dairy liable for Camargo's death? [*Camargo v. Tjaarda Dairy,* 25 Cal. 4th 1235 (2001).]

4. Farlow graduated from law school in 1988 and was employed by Wachovia Bank of North Carolina to represent it. In 1993, Wachovia discussed the possibility of Farlow's working as in-house counsel for Wachovia to handle recovery and bankruptcy cases. On her employment application, Farlow disclosed that she had been convicted of two counts of misdemeanor larceny in 1982. Those convictions made it unlawful for her to become an employee of Wachovia without FDIC approval. Wachovia proceeded with its working relationship with Farlow, who closed her private practice and moved on site with Wachovia. The parties executed a written contract under which Farlow would provide legal services as an independent contractor. Both parties intended that Farlow would not be considered an employee unless the FDIC waiver was obtained. Such a waiver was never sought for Farlow.

    Farlow was considered an independent contractor for tax purposes and was never paid a salary by Wachovia but, instead, was paid for the bills she submitted. She received no benefits or compensation for business travel. She used letterhead that designated her simply as an attorney-at-law and did not receive business cards. However, she was provided with on-site office space, support, staff, equipment, and the use of company vehicles. She was paid for continuing education. Wachovia exercised control over the hours in which she had access to her office.

    After complaining about a sexually and racially hostile work environment, Farlow was terminated. She filed several claims under Title VII. Was Wachovia Farlow's employer? [*Farlow v. Wachovia Bank of North Carolina,* 259 F.R.D. 309 (4th Cir. 2001).]

5. Wojewski was a heart surgeon with staff privileges at Rapid City Regional Hospital. He took a leave of absence based on his bipolar disorder and, upon his return, was subject to various restrictions in his work in order to ensure that he did not place patients at risk. These restrictions included meeting regularly with another physician to monitor his work, participating in therapy sessions, taking only prescribed medication, submitting to competency exams, submitting to random drug testing, taking mandatory vacations, and submitting to a review of all of his cases for the past six months. After he had an "acute episode" of his disorder during surgery, the hospital terminated his privileges and he sued based on disability discrimination under the Americans with Disabilities Act. The hospital claimed that he did not have a claim as he was not an employee. Is the hospital correct? What additional information might you wish to know to answer this question? [*Wojewski v. Rapid City Regional Hospital Inc. et al.,* 450 F.3d 338 (8th Cir. 2006).]

6. A group of individuals began work for Microsoft as freelancers between 1987 and 1990 and were asked to sign agreements stating that they were independent contractors and were responsible for all their own benefits. Many of them had served continuously for more than two years, working at the Microsoft facility, engaging in the same

functions as Microsoft employees, sharing supervisors, and working the same basic shifts. However, aside from those agreements, the only other difference was that these workers received their pay through accounts payable rather than through the payroll department and they were not be eligible for benefits.

Notwithstanding the agreements, in 1989 and 1990, the IRS reclassified the workers as employees. Microsoft then offered the workers new positions as either regular employees or as employees of a new Microsoft-owned employment agency, but continued to pay the workers in the same manner. The workers then sought to claim benefits, but were denied. Microsoft claimed it only offered benefits to an employee "who is on the United States payroll of the employer." Since the workers were paid through the accounts payable department and not through the payroll department, it claimed that the workers were not "on the payroll of the employer." Does Microsoft win? [*Vizcaino v. Microsoft Corporation,* 97 F.3d 1187 (9th Cir. 1996).]

7. Consultants for Long View Systems signed agreements stating they were independent contractors, which also contained non-compete provisions. However, after one exclusive, three-month engagement for computer consulting, during which Long View paid Lucero personally, by the hour, Gino Lucero filed for unemployment benefits claiming that he was an employee.

   Though Lucero had signed the agreement and was paid directly by Long View, he provided the services to a third party who oversaw his work, provided the tools he used, and established (with Lucero's agreement) the schedule for the work. The Colorado statute that governed this relationship requires that, for Long View to show that Lucero was an independent contract, Long View had to show that he was (1) free from control and direction in the performance of the service, *and* (2) customarily engaged in an independent trade, occupation, profession, or business related to the service performed for Long View. Should Lucero be considered Long View's employee? [*Long View Systems Corp v. Lucero,* No. 07CA2284 (2008).]

8. Arman was hired to drive an airport shuttle for a rental car company back and forth from the airport to the rental car company's off-site parking lot. When Arman was hired, he signed a written contract that stated specifically that he was an independent contractor. He was paid every two weeks, based on a rate per mile plus an hourly rate for waiting time. He drove the shuttle at times and to locations directed by the rental car company and was on call twenty-four hours a day. Is Arman an employee or an independent contractor?

9. Eugene McCarthy began working for Nike in 1993 and was promoted to a footwear sales manager position in 1997. Following his promotion, McCarthy signed a covenant not to compete that stated, "during Employee's employment by Nike . . . and for one (1) year thereafter, Employee will not directly or indirectly . . . be employed by, consult for, or be connected in any manner with, any business engaged anywhere in the world in the athletic footwear, athletic apparel or sports equipment and accessories business, or any other business which directly competes with Nike or any of its subsidiaries or affiliated corporations." In 1999, McCarthy was promoted again, to director of sales for the Brand Jordan division, but he was not required to sign a new non-compete agreement. In the spring of 2003, McCarthy accepted a job at Reebok as vice president of U.S. footwear sales and merchandising, and he resigned from Nike. Once McCarthy began working at Reebok, Nike filed a suit against him, claiming breach of contract and that McCarthy's employment

with Reebok violated the covenant not to compete. Is Nike's non-compete agreement "reasonable"? Why or why not? [*Nike v. McCarthy,* 379 F.3d 576 (9th Cir. 2004).]

10. Quaker Oats makes Gatorade, and PepsiCo competes with its All Sport brand sports drink. Quaker Oats also makes Snapple fruit drinks, while in the 1990s PepsiCo worked to compete in that market through joint ventures with Ocean Spray Cranberries and the Lipton Company. Redmond held a position as a highly placed executive with PepsiCo when he accepted a position at Quaker Oats. PepsiCo sought an injunction based on inevitable disclosure since Redmond had helped to develop PepsiCo's marketing plans and strategies for the upcoming year, including a great deal of confidential pricing and competitive information regarding how they would take over market share from competitors such as Redmond's new employer. Should the court issue the injunction? If so, how long would be reasonable? [*PepsiCo v. Redmond,* 54 F.3d 1262 (7th Cir. 1995).]

End Notes

1. Rhodes, D. and R. Haggerty, "Packers Necktie Gets Car Salesman Fired," *WGN-TV News* (Jan. 25, 2011), http://www.chicagobreakingnews.com/news/local/chibrknews-packers-necktie-gets-car-sales-01242011,0,839232.story.

2. *Yuknis v. First Student, Inc.,* 481 F.3d 552 (7th Cir. 2007).

3. Kenneth J. Turnbull, "Using Contingent Workers Can Create Complications," *New York Law Journal,* January 12, 2001.

4. *Chao v. Southern California Maid Services & Carpet Cleaning, Inc.,* No. CV-06-3903 (C.D. Cal. 2007).

5. 318 N.C. 577, 350 S.E.2d 83, reh'g denied, 318 N.C. 704, 351 S.E.2d 736 (1986).

6. *Murray v. Principal Financial Group et al.,* No. 09-16664 (9th Cir. July 27, 2010).

7. *FedEx Home Delivery v. NLRB,* 563 F.3d 492 (D.C. Cir. 2009).

8. Department of Treasury, Internal Revenue Service, "Employee or Independent Contractor?" Training 3320-102 (July 1996).

9. See "EEOC Enforcement Guidance on Application of EEO Laws to Contingent Workers Placed by Temporary Employment Agencies and Other Staffing Firms," *EEOC Enforcement Guidance,* December 1997.

10. 355 F.3d 61 (2d Cir. 2003).

11. Ibid. at 72.

12. *Williams v. Banning,* 72 F.3d 552 (7th Cir. 1995).

13. Georgia Employment Contract Enforcement, Amendment 1 (Nov. 2, 2010), http://www.ballotpedia.org/wiki/index.php/Georgia_Employment_Contract_Enforcement,_Amendment_1_%282010%29.

14. Shannon Miehe, *How to Create a Noncompete Agreement* (Berkeley, CA: Nolo Press, 2001), pp. 1/3, 1/4.

15. For an example of application, see *In re AutoNation, Inc.,* 2007 Tex. LEXIS 604, 50 Tex. Sup. J. 960 (Tex. June 29, 2007).

16. Restatement (Second) of Contracts.

17. W. Martucci and J. Place, "Covenants Not to Compete," *Employment Relations Today* 21 (1998), pp. 77–83.

18. No. 116914/97, 1997 WL 731413 (N.Y. Sup. Ct. Nov. 7, 1997).

19. 255 F. Supp. 645, 654 (E.D. Mich. 1966).

20. *Labriola v. Pollard Group, Inc.*, 100 P.3d 791 (Wash. 2004).

21. Compare *Camco Inc. v. Baker*, 936 P.2d 829 (Nev. 1997) (an at-will employee's continued employment constitutes adequate consideration).

Cases

Case 1

MURRAY v. PRINCIPAL FINANCIAL GROUP, INC.
No. 09-16664 (9th Cir. July 27, 2010)

Plaintiff Patricia Murray is a "career agent," selling defendant Principal Financial Group's products, including a wide range of financial products and services, including annuities, disability income, 401(k) plans, and insurance. Murray sued Principal for sex discrimination in violation of Title VII and the court had to determine whether Murray was an employee or an independent contractor within the meaning of that statute since she would be entitled to the protections of Title VII only if she is an employee. The circuit court determines that she is not an employee but the case is important for its analysis of the type of test to be applied.

Schroeder, C.J.

***

[2] We write principally to clarify the source of the appropriate test to apply in this federal statutory context. The able district judge viewed our decisions as reflecting three different formulations of the test to determine whether an individual is an independent contractor or an employee for purposes of Title VII: a "common law agency" test, an "economic realities" test, and a "common law hybrid" test. The district court characterized the common law agency test as "focus[ing] on `the hiring party's right to control the manner and means by which the product is accomplished,'" and quoted the factors identified by the Supreme Court in *Nationwide Mutual Insurance Co. v. Darden*, 503 U.S. 318 (1992). The district court perceived the second test to have been set forth by our court in *Adcock*, where we said that "[d]etermining whether a relationship is one of employment or independent contractual affiliation requires a fact-specific inquiry which depends on the economic realities of the situation." 166 F.3d at 1292 (internal quotation marks omitted). The district court

stated, however, that the "primary factor" of that test is "the extent of the employer's right to control the means and manner of the worker's performance." The district court saw still a third test in *Lutcher v. Musicians Union Local 47,* where we enumerated more factors. The district court characterized this as combining the common law and economic realities tests to form a "common law hybrid test."

[3] We take this opportunity to clarify what the district court ultimately recognized: there is no functional difference between the three formulations. Even if the differences in formulation might suggest a difference in practical application, however, *Darden*'s common law test as pronounced by the Supreme Court would have to control. We have previously said that the Supreme Court intended the *Darden* analysis to control whenever an employment statute defines the term "employee" in the way ERISA does, and the statute in question does not otherwise suggest that the common law test would be inappropriate. Both ERISA and Title

VII define "employee" in a circular manner as "an individual employed by an employer." There is no reason why the *Darden* test would be inappropriate in the Title VII context.

[4] Thus, when determining whether an individual is an independent contractor or an employee for purposes of Title VII, a court should evaluate "the hiring party's right to control the manner and means by which the product is accomplished." The factors relevant to this inquiry, as identified by the Supreme Court, are:

[1] the skill required; [2] the source of the instrumentalities and tools; [3] the location of the work; [4] the duration of the relationship between the parties; [5] whether the hiring party has the right to assign additional projects to the hired party; [6] the extent of the hired party's discretion over when and how long to work; [7] the method of payment; [8] the hired party's role in hiring and paying assistants; [9] whether the work is part of the regular business of the hiring party; [10] whether the hiring party is in business; [11] the provision of employee benefits; and [12] the tax treatment of the hired party.

Applying these factors to Murray's case, we find Murray's situation to be virtually indistinguishable from that which we considered in *Barnhart,* when we decided that an insurance agent was an independent contractor under the *Darden* test for purposes of discrimination under the ADEA and ERISA. We concluded that the district court had correctly granted summary judgment to the defendant because the plaintiff was an independent contractor. We reach the same result here.

[5] Here, as in *Barnhart,* several factors strongly favor classifying Murray as an independent contractor. Like Barnhart, Murray is "free to operate [her] business as [she] s[ees] fit without day-to-day intrusions." Murray decides when and where to work, and in fact maintains her own office, where she pays rent. She schedules her own time off, and is not entitled to vacation or sick days.

Also like Barnhart, Murray is paid on commission only, reports herself as self-employed to the IRS, and sells products other than those offered by Principal in limited circumstances.

[6] There are a few factors present in Murray's case, as there were in *Barnhart,* that support the argument that Murray is an employee. Murray receives some benefits, has a long-term relationship with Principal, possesses an at-will contract, and is subject to some minimum standards imposed by the hiring party. These, however, on balance, are insufficient to overcome the strong indications that Murray is an independent contractor.

[7] The parties dispute the minutiae of some aspects of Murray's relationship with Principal, relating to who bears responsibility for providing some of the instrumentalities and tools required for Murray to perform her job, the degree of autonomy that Murray has to select and retain her assistant, and the degree to which Principal requires Murray to document and report her work. Even when all of these issues are resolved in Murray's favor, however, the overall picture presented by Murray's relationship with Principal is still one of an independent contractor rather than an employee. The defendants do not control the manner and means by which Murray sells their financial products.

AFFIRMED.

Case Questions

1. Do you agree with the court that there is no "functional difference" between the three tests—the "common law agency" test, the "economic realities" test, and the "common law hybrid"—test for whether someone is an employee or an independent contractor?

2. Even if it might not be vital in this situation, could you imagine a circumstance where the distinction could be great and a different decision would result under one or several of these tests?

3. What is the value in the court's decision in reaching convergence among the three tests in *Murray*?

Case 2

NLRB v. Friendly Cab Co. *512 F.3d 1090* (*9th Cir. 2008*)

Friendly is a taxi company in Oakland, California, run by Surinder Singh, the chief administrator, and her husband, Baljit Singh, the president of the company. After tension arose between Friendly and its drivers, the drivers' union filed a petition with the National Labor Relations Board seeking a declaration that Friendly's taxicab drivers were indeed employees rather than independent contractors, and therefore entitled to representation for collective bargaining purposes. The court explores the myriad facts that might support either conclusion to determine the drivers' classification.

Callahan, C. J.

***

I. Background

Friendly, along with six other taxicab entities, operates out of a facility in Oakland, California, and is under the control of Surinder Singh, the chief administrator, and her husband, Baljit Singh, the president of the company. Friendly owns approximately eighty taxicabs (fifty of which are designated as airport cabs) and leases these cabs to its drivers . . . These leases typically state that the taxicabs are rented for seven days, renew automatically, and provide the drivers with six days of service and one day of mandatory maintenance per week. Each of Friendly's drivers is required to pay a fee or "gate," which ranges from $450 to $600 per week based on Friendly's discretion. In determining this fee, Friendly takes into account the cab model, as well as the driver's driving record, driving ability, and prior accidents. Friendly has a limited number of permits to operate at the Oakland Airport, which are in high demand and are typically held by drivers with more experience. Although drivers designate which entity they want to work for, Friendly retains the discretion to assign drivers to different taxicab entities, taxicab models, and the type of cab (airport or street cabs). These leases also specify that there is no employer–employee relationship between Friendly and its taxicab drivers, and that Friendly is not responsible for withholding any federal or state taxes or providing workers' compensation insurance.

As part of the lease, Friendly's drivers agree to comply with Friendly's Taxicab Company Policy Manual ("Manual") and its Standard Operating Procedures ("SOP"). Although Friendly's Manual and SOP cover a broad range of topics that are common to the operation of a taxi service (*e.g.*, safety concerns, non-discrimination

policy, etc.), there are a number of regulations that concern Friendly's control over its drivers. For example, the Manual instructs drivers that: "[a]cceleration should be smooth," they should "[a]void abrupt stops," they should "not stop next to puddles or in front of obstacles such as signs, trees or hydrants," and that "[w]hen stopping at curbs, stop either right next to curb or out away from the curb." Friendly's Manual also imposes a dress code, which requires that all taxicab drivers "maintain good personal hygiene and dress appropriately and professionally: collared shirts with sleeves, slacks or knee-high skirts, closed shoes with socks or hose."

Friendly's SOP contains a number of relevant regulations as well. Of particular significance to this case, the SOP restricts outside business opportunities for Friendly's drivers by stating that: "[a]ll calls for service must be conducted over company provided communications system and telephone number. No private or individual business cards or phone numbers are allowed for distribution to customers as these constitute an interference in company business and a form of competition not permitted while working under the lease." The SOP also provides that "[d]rivers must service all reasonable customer calls from dispatchers." Several drivers testified that the dispatcher will ignore or bypass them if they refuse or are late to a dispatch. One driver testified that if drivers do not respond in a certain amount of time, the dispatcher reminds drivers over the radio that "we run the show, you guys are just the driver. Just drive. That's it."

***

In addition to the requirements contained in the Manual and the SOP, Friendly imposes a number of additional restrictions on its drivers. For example, Friendly's general manager testified that taxicab drivers are not able to sublease their vehicles to other drivers. Friendly also requires that its taxicabs carry advertisements for outside vendors on the roofs of the taxicabs. Drivers must return to the station to replace these advertisements at Friendly's discretion. Furthermore, Friendly requires that its drivers attend, at their expense, annual classes on company policies and laws dealing with discrimination. Finally, if the drivers do not comply with Friendly's policies, Friendly can terminate their leases. Friendly employs a "road manager" who monitors the drivers' appearance and compliance with Friendly's policies.

As a result of tension between Friendly and its drivers, the Union was appointed as the representative of a number of Friendly's drivers. The Union filed a petition under Section 9(c) of the Act with the NLRB for a declaration that Friendly's taxicab drivers were employees and thus entitled to representation for collective bargaining purposes. [After a number of administrative actions, the court in the current case evaluates whether the drivers are employees or independent contractors for purposes of representation under the NLRA.]

***

III. Analysis

In order to distinguish an "employee" from an "independent contractor," we must undertake a fact-based inquiry applying common law principles of agency. Although courts must look to the totality of the circumstances, "[t]he essential ingredient of the agency test is the extent of control exercised by the 'employer.' It rests primarily upon the amount of supervision that the putative employer has a right to exercise over the individual, particularly regarding the details of the work." Additional factors that are relevant to this determination include "entrepreneurial aspects of the individual's business; risk of loss and opportunity for profit; and the individual's proprietary interest in his business." We must assess and weigh all of the incidents of the relationship with the understanding that no one factor is decisive, and that "[i]t is the rare case where the various factors will point with unanimity in one direction or the other."

We cannot displace the NLRB's conclusion that Friendly's drivers are "employees" within the meaning of the Act because there is substantial evidence in the record that Friendly exercises significant control over the means and manner of its drivers' performance. In finding that the incidents of the relationship between Friendly and its drivers militate in favor of "employee" status, we place particular significance on Friendly's requirement that its drivers may not engage in any entrepreneurial opportunities.

A. Evidence of Independent Contractor Status

The payment by taxicab drivers of a fixed rental rate to an employer where drivers retain all fares collected without accounting to that employer typically creates a "strong inference" that the employer does not exert control over the means and manner of the drivers' performance. The rationale behind this "strong inference" is that the employer does not have an incentive to control the means and manner of the drivers' performance when the employer makes the same amount of money irrespective of the fares received by the drivers.

Here, the NLRB accepted that this "strong inference" exists because Friendly's drivers pay a flat fee and are not required to account for the amount of fares or tips they collect. Although Friendly received the benefit of this inference, the NLRB was generous to give it. There is nothing flat about this fee since it varies among the drivers between $450 and $600, depending on their cab model, driving record, driving ability and prior accidents. Those drivers that do not incur additional expenses for Friendly—for example, in the form of higher automobile insurance rates for poor driving records or increased costs for repairs of taxicabs damaged in accidents—are presumably rewarded with lower rental rates. Friendly's rental fees thus do in fact reflect some control over the drivers' performance. In addition to Friendly's rental fees, the NLRB found additional indicia of independent contractor status. These include the facts that Friendly's drivers do not work set hours or a minimum number of hours, the taxicab lease agreements provide that the drivers are independent contractors, Friendly does not provide any benefits to drivers, and Friendly does not withhold social security or other taxes on behalf of the drivers. However, the NLRB properly concluded that such factors are substantially outweighed by the evidence in the record of significant control by Friendly over the means and manner of its drivers' performance.

B. Evidence of Employee Status

The ability to operate an independent business and develop entrepreneurial opportunities is significant in any analysis of whether an individual is an "employee" or an "independent contractor" under the common law agency test. Friendly's restrictions against its drivers' operating independent businesses or developing entrepreneurial opportunities strongly support the NLRB's determination that Friendly's drivers are employees . . .

In the Underlying Representation Proceeding, the NLRB stated that "[t]he most significant evidence of Employer control in this case is that the drivers are not permitted to operate independent businesses." A review of the record supports this conclusion. Friendly's own general manager testified that drivers can use the taxicabs only to respond to dispatches from Friendly and not for outside business. The SOP prohibits drivers from soliciting customers, stating that "all calls for service must be conducted over company provided communications system and telephone number." It also requires that drivers maintain company business cards at all times in the taxicab and prohibits drivers from distributing any private business cards or telephone numbers to customers because this would "constitute an interference in company business and a form of competition not permitted while working under the lease." Drivers cannot accept calls for service on personal cellular telephones and, in fact, cannot even use cellular telephones while driving.

These limitations do not allow Friendly's drivers the entrepreneurial freedom to develop their own business interests like true independent contractors . . . Here, it is telling that Friendly's SOP mandates that its drivers must operate the taxis "in such a manner as to protect the goodwill that exists between the company and its customers."

Additional entrepreneurial characteristics—such as substantial investment in property and the ability to employ others—are also absent. Friendly's taxicab drivers do not own the taxicabs, but must lease them from Friendly. Friendly also prohibits its drivers from employing others by preventing the subleasing of its taxicabs. One former driver testified that while he was hospitalized, he was instructed by Mrs. Singh that drivers were prohibited from subleasing the vehicles, even to other Friendly drivers.

Friendly maintains direct control over the performance of its drivers' duties by exercising "discretion to determine which entity a driver is assigned to, the model of the vehicle assigned to a driver, . . . and whether a driver may drive an airport cab." Friendly's Manual further instructs drivers in the manner they should accelerate and stop their vehicles, as well as factors they should consider in choosing where to stop their taxicabs. Thus, Friendly's interest in controlling the means and manner

of its drivers' performance extends to the actual details of the operation of the taxicabs.

***

The type of control Friendly exercises over its drivers exceeds that found in the typical case in which a company requires its workers [to] place advertisements on work vehicles . . . In this case, Friendly's requirement constitutes significantly greater control. Friendly's advertising requirement represents a form of control that inures to the benefit of Friendly at the financial expense of the drivers.

***

In *City Cab of Orlando II*, the court cited the extensive dress code the taxicab company required of its drivers as one of the factors that led the court to conclude the taxicab drivers were employees. There, the drivers were required to wear a shirt with a collar, not to wear jeans or short pants, to be clean-shaven, not to wear tennis shoes, and, if the driver chose to wear a hat, it had to be a designated "cab drivers hat." Friendly's dress code is very similar to the one in *City Cab of Orlando II*. Although this court and others have not given a dress code requirement much weight, Friendly's extensive dress code is an additional factor supporting the NLRB's determination.

Friendly's training policy outlined in its Manual, which incorporates both local government regulations and company specific regulations, also constitutes another minimal indicium of control over the drivers. While the incorporation of government regulations into a company's manual is not evidence of an employer–employee relationship, the NLRB reasonably found that Friendly's training requirements exceed those required by the City of Oakland's ordinance and constitute some degree of control over the drivers. Friendly describes its mandatory two-day training class as being "in addition to the class conducted by the City of Oakland Police Taxi Detail." It covers sensitivity training, operating procedures, hands-on practical training, record keeping, and local geography training. Like the dress code requirement, we find the training requirement supports the NLRB's determination that Friendly's drivers are employees.

***

V. Conclusion

In sum, we conclude there is substantial evidence in the record to support the NLRB's determination that Friendly's taxicab drivers are "employees" within the meaning of the Act. The NLRB relied on a number of factors that in their totality compel a finding of employee status, the most significant of these being Friendly's prohibition on its drivers' operating an independent business and developing entrepreneurial opportunities with customers. Additional salient indicia of control by Friendly over the means and manner of its drivers' performance include: (1) regulating the details of how drivers must operate their taxicabs, (2) imposing discipline for refusing or delays in responding to dispatches, (3) requiring drivers to carry advertisements without receiving revenue, (4) requiring drivers to accept vouchers subject to graduated "processing fees," (5) prohibiting subleases, (6) imposing a strict dress code, and (7) requiring training in excess of government regulations. Although some of these factors individually may not constitute substantial control, the NLRB reasonably concluded that these factors taken together overcame any evidence of independent contractor status. We therefore affirm the NLRB's decision.

AFFIRMED.

Case Questions

1. Though the court was quite clear that simply identifying workers as employees is insufficient to qualify them as employees, does the name by which an employer calls its workers matter at all? In other words, does it matter at all whether the employer calls its workers independent contractors or employees, or is it completely irrelevant?

2. Of the factors considered critical by the court in reaching its conclusion, which seem more critical to a determination of employment status? If you were advising Friendly Cab Co. to modify its employment relationship in order to ensure a determination of independent contractor status rather than employee status, which elements would you advise changing?

3. What are the public policy reasons why Friendly *should* be required to consider these workers as employees rather than as independent contractors?

Chapter 2

The Employment Law Toolkit: Resources for Understanding the Law and Recurring Legal Concepts

Learning Objectives

After studying the chapter, you should be able to:

LO1   Understand how to read and digest legal cases and citations.

LO2   Explain and distinguish the concepts of *stare decisis* and precedent.

LO3   Evaluate whether an employee is an at-will employee.

LO4   Determine if an at-will employee has sufficient basis for wrongful discharge.

LO5   Recite and explain at least three exceptions to employment-at-will.

LO6   Distinguish between disparate impact and disparate treatment discrimination claims.

LO7   Provide several bases for employer defenses to employment discrimination claims.

LO8   Determine if there is sufficient basis for a retaliation claim by an employee.

LO9   Identify sources for further legal information and resources.

41

Opening Scenarios

SCENARIO 1

1 Mark Richter is about to retire as a candy salesperson when he closes on a deal the candy company has been trying to land for a long time. Just before Mark is to collect his substantial commission, he is terminated. Does Mark have a basis on which to sue for unlawful termination?

SCENARIO 2

2 Jenna Zitron informs her employer that she has been summoned to serve jury duty for a week. Though rescheduling her duties is not a problem, Jenna is told by her employer that, if she serves jury duty rather than trying to be relieved of it, she will be terminated. Jenna refuses to lie to be relieved of jury duty. Does Jenna have a basis on which to sue for unlawful termination?

SCENARIO 3

3 Demetria, 5' 2", 120 pounds, applies for a position with her local police department. When the department sees that she is applying for a position as a police officer, it refuses to take her application, saying that she doesn't meet the department's requirement of being at least 5 feet 4 inches tall and at least 130 pounds. Is the department's policy legal?

SCENARIO 4

4 Jill, an interviewer for a large business firm, receives a letter from a consulting firm inviting her to attend a seminar on Title VII issues. Jill feels she doesn't need to go since all she does is interview applicants, who are then hired by someone else in the firm. Is Jill correct?

Introduction

We understand that this is not a textbook intended to create or enlighten lawyers. In fact, some of you may never have taken a law course before. Thus, we thought it might be useful to take some time up front to introduce you to helpful information that will make your legal journey easier. We have taken out much of the legalese that tends to stump our readers and have tried to make the legal concepts as accessible as we can for the non-legal audience.

In this chapter, we offer several tools to help you navigate the text. As a procedural matter, we offer a guide to reading cases and understanding what it takes to have a legally recognized cause of action. In addition, several of the substantive issues you will face in the chapters ahead will use information that is based on the same legal concepts. Rather than repeat the information in each chapter's discussion, we explain the concept once in this "toolkit" chapter.

There is a corresponding icon used throughout the text. When you see the toolkit icon, know that the text is referring to information that has been covered in this toolkit chapter and, if you need to, refer to this chapter to refresh your recollection. Part one explains how to read the cases and a couple of important concepts to keep in mind for all legal cases. Part two provides information on the concept of employment-at-will, part three discusses the theoretical bases for all employment discrimination actions, and part four describes legal resources for searching for further legal information.

Guide to Reading Cases

Thank you very much to the several students who have contacted us and asked that we improve your understanding by including a guide to reading and understanding the cases. We consider the cases an important and integral part of the chapters. By viewing the court decisions included in the text, you get to see for yourself what the court considers important when deciding a given issue. This in turn gives you as a decision maker insight into what you need to keep in mind when making decisions on similar issues in the workplace. The more you know about how a court thinks about issues that may end up in litigation, the better you can avoid it.

In order to tell you about how to view the cases for better understanding, we have to give you a little background on the legal system. Hopefully, it will only be a refresher of your previous law or civics courses.

LO2 *Stare Decisis* **and Precedent**

The American legal system is based on *stare decisis,* a system of using legal precedent. Once a judge renders a decision in a case, the decision is generally written and placed in a law reporter and must be followed in that jurisdiction when other similar cases arise. The case thus becomes precedent for future cases involving that issue.

Most of the cases in our chapters are from federal courts since most of the topics we discuss are based on federal law. Federal courts consist of trial courts (called the U.S. District Court for a particular district), courts of appeal (called the U.S. Circuit Court for a particular circuit), and the U.S. Supreme Court. U.S. Supreme Court decisions apply to all jurisdictions, and once there is a U.S. Supreme Court decision, all courts must follow the precedent. Circuit court decisions are mandatory precedent only for the circuit in which the decision is issued. All courts in that circuit must follow that circuit's precedents. District court precedents are applicable only to the district in which they were made. When courts that are not in the jurisdiction are faced with a novel issue they have not decided before, they can look to other jurisdictions to see how the issue was handled. If such a court likes the other jurisdiction's decision, it can use the approach taken by that jurisdiction's court. However, it is not bound to follow the other court's decision since that court is not in its jurisdiction.

States have court systems parallel to the federal court system. They vary from state to state, but generally there is also a trial court, an intermediate court of appeals, and a state supreme court. For our purposes, the state court system works very much like the federal system in terms of appeals moving up through the appellate system, though some states have more levels. Once the case is decided by the state supreme court, it can be heard by the U.S. Supreme Court if there is a basis for appealing it to that court.

On the federal side, once a case is heard by the U.S. Supreme Court, there is no other court to which it can be appealed. Under our country's constitutionally based system of checks and balances, if Congress, who passed the law the Court interpreted, believes the Court's interpretation is not in keeping with the law's intended purpose, Congress can pass a law that reflects that determination. This has been done many times. Perhaps the most recent is the Lilly Ledbetter Fair Pay Act of 2009 discussed in the gender chapter. The Supreme Court interpreted Title VII of the 1964 Civil Rights Act barring workplace discrimination on the basis of gender such that even though it was clear that gender-based pay discrimination had occurred, there was no basis for a remedy. Ledbetter did not find out about the pay discrimination for 19 years. By that time, the 180-day statute of limitations had long expired. Congress responded to this Supreme Court decision with the Lilly Ledbetter Fair Pay Act, which allows the statute of limitations to begin to run anew each time an employee receives a paycheck based on discrimination.

LO1

Understanding the Case Information

plaintiff
One who brings a civil action in court.

defendant
One against whom a case is brought.

appellant
One who brings an appeal.

appellee
One against whom an appeal is brought.

petitioner
One who appeals a case to the Supreme Court.

respondent
One against whom a case is appealed at the Supreme Court.

With this in mind, let's take a look at a typical case included in this book. Each of the cases is an actual law case written by a judge. Choose a case, any case, to go through this exercise. The first thing you will see is the *case name*. This is derived from the parties involved—the one suing (called **plaintiff** at the district court level) and the one being sued (called **defendant** at the district court level). At the court of appeals or Supreme Court level, the first name reflects who appealed the case to that court. It may or may not be the party who initially brought the case at the district court level. At the court of appeals level, the person who appealed the case to the court of appeals is known as the **appellant** and the other party is known as the **appellee**. At the Supreme Court level they are known as the **petitioner** and the **respondent**.

Under the case name, the next line will have several numbers and a few letters. This is called a *case citation*. A case citation is the means by which the full case can be located in a law reporter if you want to find the case for yourself in a law library or a legal database such as LEXIS/NEXIS or Westlaw. Reporters are books in which judges' case decisions are kept for later retrieval by lawyers, law students, judges, and others. Law reporters can be found in any law library, and many cases can be found on the Internet for free on Web sites such us Public Library of Law (plol.org) or FindLaw.com.

Take a minute and turn to one of the cases in the text. Any case will do. A typical citation would be "72 U.S. 544 (2002)." This means that you can find the decision in volume 72 of the *U.S. Supreme Court Reporter* at page 544 and that it is a 2002 decision. The U.S. reporters contain U.S. Supreme Court decisions. Reporters have different names based on the court decisions contained in them; thus, their citations are different.

The citation "43 F.3d 762 (9th Cir. 2002)" means that you can find the case decision in volume 43 of the *Federal Reporter* third series, at page 762, and that the decision came out of the U.S. Circuit Court of Appeals for the Ninth Circuit in the year 2002. The *Federal Reporters* contain the cases of the U.S. Circuit Courts of Appeal from across the country.

Similarly, the citation "750 F. Supp. 234 (S.D.N.Y. 2002)" means that you can find the case decision in volume 750 of the *Federal Supplement Reporters,* which contain U.S. district court cases, at page 234. The case was decided in the year 2002 by the U.S. District Court in the Southern District of New York.

In looking at the chapter cases, after the citation we include a short paragraph to tell you what the case is about, what the main issues are, and what the court decided. This is designed to give you a heads-up to make reading the case easier.

The next line you see will have a last name and then a comma followed by "J." This is the name of the judge who wrote the decision you are reading. The J stands for *judge* or *justice*. Judges oversee lower courts, while the term for them used in higher courts is *justices*. C. J. stands for *chief justice*.

The next thing you see in looking at the chapter case is the body of the decision. Judges write for lawyers and judges, not for the public at large. As such, they use a lot of legal terms (which we call *legalese*) that can make the decisions difficult for a nonlawyer to read. There are also many procedural issues included in cases, which have little or nothing to do with the issues we are illustrating. There also may be many other issues in the case that are not relevant for our purposes. Therefore, we usually give you a shortened, excerpted version of the case containing only relevant information.

If you want to see the entire case for yourself, you can find it by using the citation provided just below the name of the case, as explained above, using the legal resources provided at the end of the chapter. By not bogging you down in legalese, procedural matters, and other issues irrelevant to our point, we make the cases more accessible and understandable and much less confusing, while still giving you all you need to illustrate the matter at hand.

The last thing you will see in the chapter cases is the final decision of the court itself. If the case is a trial court decision by the district court based on the merits of the claim, the court will provide relief either for the plaintiff or for the defendant.

Sometimes, the court does not reach the actual merits of the case, however. If a defendant makes a **motion to dismiss**, the court will decide that issue and say either that the motion to dismiss is *granted* or that it is *denied*. A defendant will make a motion to dismiss when he or she thinks there is not enough evidence to constitute a violation of law. If the motion to dismiss is granted, the decision favors the defendant in that the court dismisses the case. If the motion to dismiss is denied, it means the plaintiff's case can proceed to trial. Notice that this does not mean that the ultimate issues have been determined, but only that the case can or cannot, as the case may be, proceed further. This decision can be appealed to the next court.

The parties also may ask the court to grant a **motion for summary judgment**. This essentially requests that the court take a look at the documentary information submitted by the parties and make a judgment based on that, as there is allegedly no issue that needs to be determined by a jury. Again, the court will either grant the motion for summary judgment or deny it. If the court grants a motion for summary judgment, it also will determine the issues and grant a judgment in favor of one of the parties. If the court dismisses a motion for summary judgment, the court has determined that there is a need for the case to proceed to trial. This, too, can be appealed.

motion to dismiss
Request by a defendant for the court to dismiss the plaintiff's case.

motion for summary judgment
Defendant's request for the court to rule on the plaintiff's case based on the documents submitted, alleging there are no triable issues of fact to be decided.

If the case is in the appellate court, it means that one of the parties did not agree with the trial court's decision. This party, known as the *appellant,* appeals the case to the appellate court, seeking to overturn the decision based on what the appellant alleges are errors of law committed by the court below. The *appellee* is the party against whom an appeal is brought. Cases cannot be appealed simply because one of the parties did not like the facts found in the lower court. The appeal must be based on errors of law.

After the appellate court reviews the lower court's decision, the court of appeals will either *affirm* the lower court's decision and the decision is allowed to stand, or it will *reverse* the lower court's decision, which means the lower court's decision is overturned. If there is work still to be done on the case, the appellate court also will order *remand.* Remand is an order by the court of appeals to the lower court telling it to take the case back and do what needs to be done based on the court's decision.

It is also possible that the appellate court will issue a *per curiam* decision. This is merely a brief decision by the court, rather than a long one, and is not issued by a particular judge. Rather than seeing a judge's name, you will simply see the words *Per Curiam.*

Following the court's decision is a set of questions we developed that is intended to translate what you have read in the case into issues that you would be likely to have to think about as a business owner, manager, or supervisor. The questions generally are included to make you think about what you read in the case and how it would impact your decisions as a manager. They are provided as a way to make you think critically and learn how to ask yourself the important questions that you will need to deal with each time you make an employment decision.

The opening scenarios, chapter cases, and the case-end questions are important tools for you to use to learn to think like a manager or supervisor who avoids unnecessary and costly liability. Reading the courts' language and analyzing and thinking critically about the issues in the opening scenarios and case-end questions will greatly assist you in making solid, defensible workplace decisions as a business owner, manager, or supervisor.

Prima Facie Case

cause of action
Right provided by law for a party to sue for remedies when certain legal rights is violated.

prima facie case
The evidence that fits each requirement of a cause of action.

When a legal case is brought, it must be based on legal rights provided by statutes or common law. When an individual's legal rights have been violated, the ability to file a case on that basis is known as having a **cause of action**. Each cause of action has certain requirements that the law has determined constitute the cause of action. In court if it can be shown that those requirements are met, then the party bringing the cause of action is said to have established a ***prima facie case*** for that cause of action. Generally, if the claimant is not able to present evidence to establish a *prima facie* case for his or her claim, the claim will be dismissed by the court, generally based on a motion to dismiss discussed above, asserting that the claimant has not established all the elements of the claim and, therefore, there is no basis for the court to proceed. Sometimes the court allows the claimant leave to re-file the claim, depending on what was lacking. If the claimant establishes a *prima facie* case, then the claim may advance to the next step in the proceedings.

Employment-at-Will Concepts

LO3

LO4

Wrongful Discharge and the Employment-at-Will Doctrine

In this part of the chapter, we will examine the common law and statutes that govern the employment relationship between the employer and employee, how they come together to form the relationship, and in some cases, how they come apart. Though it might appear strange or awkward to discuss *ending* the employment relationship so early in the book, when many of the discussions that follow involve what occurs *within* the employment environment, it is vital that we raise these issues at this point. In many of the succeeding chapters, you will read about protections offered to individuals based on their inclusion in particular classes. If we omit to mention what they might be protected *from,* the book's conversation loses a bit of its urgency. In addition, in almost all of the cases that you will read throughout this text, you will need to understand the laws that govern the employment relationship, at-will employment, and discharge, in order to understand the court's judgment of the case.

The American employer–employee relationship was originally based on the English feudal system. When employers were the wealthy landowners who owned the land on which serfs (workers) toiled, employers met virtually all of the workers' needs, took care of disputes that arose, and allowed the workers to live their entire lives on the land, even after they could no longer be the productive serfs they once were. The employer took care of the employees just as parents would take care of their children.

When we moved from an agrarian to an industrialized society, the employee–employer relationship became further removed than before: The employee could work for the employer as long as the employee wished and leave when the employee no longer wished to work for the employer (therefore, the employees worked at their own will). The reverse was also true: The employer employed the employee for as long as the employer wished, and when the employer no longer wished to have the employee in his or her employ, the employee had to leave. This relationship was called **at-will employment**.

at-will employment
An employment relationship where there is no contractual obligation to remain in the relationship; either party may terminate the relationship at any time, for any reason, as long as the reason is not prohibited by law, such as for discriminatory purposes.

Both parties were free to leave at virtually any time for any reason. If, instead, there is a contract between the parties, either as a collective bargaining agreement or an individual contract, the relationship is not governed by the will of the parties, but rather by the contract. Further, government employees generally are not considered at-will employees. Limitations are imposed on the government employer through rules governing the terms and termination of the federal employment relationship. Thus, excluded from at-will employment are government employees, employees under a collective bargaining agreement, or employees who have an individual contract with their employer.

As you might imagine, the employment-at-will relationship has not always been considered the most balanced. Employers have had a bit of an upper hand in terms of the power, and the connection looks less and less like that familial affiliation where employment might have begun and more like the hierarchical structure present in some workplaces today. The at-will environment has spread throughout the United States as each state has sought to attract more employers by offering greater freedoms within the employment context.[1]

When equal employment opportunity legislation entered the equation, the employer's rights to hire and fire were circumscribed to a great extent. While an employer was free to terminate an employee for no particular reason, it could not terminate a worker based on race, gender, religion, national origin, age, or disability. Providing protection for members of historically discriminated-against groups through such laws as Title VII of the Civil Rights Act of 1964, the Age Discrimination in Employment Act, and the Americans with Disabilities Act also had the predictable effect of making all employees feel more empowered in their employment relationships. While virtually no employees sued employers before such legislation, after the legislation was passed employees were willing to challenge employers' decisions in legal actions.

With women, minorities, older employees, disabled employees, and veterans given protection under the laws, it was not long before those who were not afforded specific protection began to sue employers based on their perception that it "just wasn't right" for an employer to be able to terminate them for any reason even though their termination did not violate anti-discrimination statutes! To them it was beside the point that they did not fit neatly into a protected category. They had been "wronged" and they wanted their just due.

However, since our system is one of at-will employment, an employer is only prohibited from terminating employees based on what the law dictates. It does not protect the employee fired because the employer did not like the employee's green socks, or the way the employee wore her hair, or the fact that the employee blew his attempt to get his first account after being hired. There is no recourse for these workers because, since the relationship is at-will, the employer can fire the employee for whatever reason the employer wishes, as long as it is not a violation of the law. Any terminated at-will employee may bring suit against the employer, seeking reinstatement or compensatory and punitive damages for the losses suffered on the basis of *unjust dismissal* or *wrongful termination*. However, if there is a legally prohibited reason for the termination, such as race or gender, the law provides its own means of pursuing those cases, discussed in the Title VII chapter.

Probably because the law also began to recognize certain basic rights in its concept of the employment relationship, and because of the basic unfairness involved in some of the cases that the courts were asked to decide, courts all over the country began making *exceptions* to the at-will doctrine. Since each state is free to make its own laws governing at-will employment, the at-will doctrine developed on a state-by-state basis and varies from state to state. (See Exhibit 2.1, "Exceptions to the Doctrine of Employment-at-Will.") Congress has entertained proposals to deal with the doctrine on the federal level, but as of yet, none has been successful. To bring uniformity, predictability, and consistency to the area, in 1991,

---

Exhibit 2.1 *Exceptions to the Doctrine of Employment-at-Will*

States vary broadly in terms of their recognition of the exceptions to the doctrine of employment-at-will. Some states recognize one or more exceptions, while others might recognize none at all. In addition, the definition of these exceptions also may vary from state to state.

- Bad faith, malicious, or retaliatory termination may serve as a violation of **public policy**.
- Termination in breach of the **implied covenant of good faith and fair dealing**.

- Termination in breach of some other implied **contract term**, such as those that might be created by employee handbook provisions (in certain jurisdictions).
- Termination in violation of the doctrine of **promissory estoppel** (where the employee reasonably relied on an employer's promise, to the employee's detriment).
- Other exceptions as determined by **statutes** (such as WARN, discussed later).

---

the Commission on Uniform State Laws issued a model termination act that states may use. This model act, and its status, will be discussed later in the chapter.

The state-by-state approach to addressing the exceptions to the at-will doctrine has created a crazy quilt of laws across the country. (See Exhibit 2.2, "State Rulings Chart.") In some states, the at-will doctrine has virtually no exceptions and, therefore, remains virtually intact. In other states, the courts have created judicial exceptions to the at-will doctrine that apply in certain limited circumstances. In still other states, the state legislature has passed laws providing legislative exceptions to the at-will doctrine. At this time, the at-will doctrine still survives as the default rule in 49 of the 50 states, with Montana remaining as the single state holdout.[2]

LO5 Exceptions to the At-Will Doctrine

Even though an employer can terminate an employee for any legal reason, if the reason is one that falls within an exception to the at-will doctrine, the employee can claim wrongful termination and receive either damages or reinstatement.

Though they are difficult cases for employees to prove, state courts and state legislation have been fairly consistent in holding that exceptions will be permitted where the discharge is in violation of some recognized public policy, where the employer breaches an implied covenant of good faith and fair dealing, or where an implied contract or implied promise to the employee was breached (the latter involves the legal concept of *promissory estoppel*). We will discuss each of these in more detail, below.

Keep in mind that, if the employee and employer have an individual contract or a collective bargaining agreement, then the employment relationship is governed by that agreement. However, the contract, of course, can be one that states simply that the relationship is at-will; that the employer's right to discharge or take any other action is at its discretion; that the relationship may be terminated at any time by either side, with or without cause; and that the employee understands the nature of this arrangement.[3] In addition, if the employer is the government, then the employment relationship regarding dismissals is governed by relevant government regulations. It is the other 65 percent of the workforce that is covered by the employment-at-will doctrine.

Exhibit 2.2 *State Rulings Chart*

Availability of common-law exceptions to the employment-at-will doctrine on state-by-state basis. (Implied contract includes implications through employer policies, handbooks, promises, or other representations.)

	Implied Contract	Public Policy	Good Faith		Implied Contract	Public Policy	Good Faith
Alabama	Yes	No	No	Missouri	No	Yes	No
Alaska	Yes	Yes	Yes	Montana	Yes	Yes	Yes
Arizona	Yes	Yes	Yes	Nebraska	Yes	Yes	No
Arkansas	No	Yes	Yes	Nevada	Yes	Yes	No
California	Yes	Yes	Yes	New Hampshire	Yes	Yes	Yes
Colorado	Yes	Yes	No	New Jersey	Yes	Yes	Yes
Connecticut	Yes	Yes	Yes	New Mexico	Yes	Yes	No
Delaware	Yes	Yes	Yes	New York	Yes	No	No
District of Columbia	Yes	Yes	No	North Carolina	Yes	Yes	No
				North Dakota	Yes	Yes	No
Florida	No	No	No	Ohio	Yes	Yes	No
Georgia	Yes	No	No	Oklahoma	Yes	Yes	No
Hawaii	Yes	Yes	No	Oregon	Yes	Yes	No
Idaho	Yes	Yes	Yes	Pennsylvania	Yes	Yes	No
Illinois	Yes	Yes	No	Rhode Island	NC	No	No
Indiana	Yes	Yes	No	South Carolina	Yes	Yes	No
Iowa	Yes	Yes	No	South Dakota	Yes	Yes	No
Kansas	Yes	Yes	No	Tennessee	Yes	Yes	No
Kentucky	Yes	Yes	No	Texas	Yes	Yes	No
Louisiana	No	No	No	Utah	Yes	Yes	Yes
Maine	Yes	No	No	Vermont	Yes	Yes	No
Maryland	Yes	Yes	No	Virginia	Yes	Yes	No
Massachusetts	Yes	Yes	Yes	Washington	Yes	Yes	No
Michigan	Yes	Yes	No	West Virginia	Yes	Yes	No
Minnesota	Yes	Yes	No	Wisconsin	Yes	Yes	No
Mississippi	Yes	Yes	No	Wyoming	Yes	Yes	Yes

public policy
A legal concept intended to ensure that no individual lawfully do that which has a tendency to be injurious to the public or against the public good. Public policy is undermined by anything that harms a sense of individual rights.

Scenario

Violation of Public Policy

One of the most visible exceptions to employment at-will that states are fairly consistent in recognizing, either through legislation or court cases, has been a violation of **public policy**; at least 44 states allow this exception. Violations of public policy usually arise when the employee is terminated for acts such as refusing to violate a criminal statute on behalf of the employer, exercising a statutory right, fulfilling a statutory duty, or reporting violations of statutes by an employer. States vary in terminology for the basis of a cause of action against her or his employer on this basis, and some require that the ex-employee show that the employer's actions were motivated by bad faith, malice, or retaliation.

For instance, a state may have a law that says that qualified citizens must serve jury duty, unless they come within one of the statutory exceptions. The employer does not want the employee to miss work just because of jury duty. The employee serves jury duty and the employer fires the worker. The employee sues the employer for unjust dismissal. The employer counters with the at-will doctrine, which states that the employer can terminate the employee for any reason. The Jury System Improvements Act prohibits employers from discriminating based on jury service in federal courts. States vary in terms of their protection for state and local jury service. Even in states where the protection is less clear, many courts have then held that the employer's termination of the employee under these circumstances would be a violation of public policy. Terminating the employee for fulfilling that statutory duty would therefore be a violation of public policy by the employer.

In a Washington State Supreme Court case, *Gardner v. Loomis Armored, Inc.,*[4] the court ruled that an employer violated public policy when it fired an armored-truck driver after the driver left the vehicle in order to rescue a robbery hostage. In that case, the driver was making a routine stop at a bank. When he saw the bank's manager running from the bank followed by a man wielding a knife, he locked the truck's door and ran to her rescue. While the woman was saved, the driver was fired for violating his employer's policy prohibiting him from leaving his vehicle. The court held that his termination violated the public policy encouraging such "heroic conduct." Understanding the confusion sometimes left in the wake of decisions surrounding public policy (since it did not wish to create a responsibility for people to be Good Samaritans), the court explained that

> [t]his holding does not create an affirmative legal duty requiring citizens to intervene in dangerous life threatening situations. We simply observe that society values and encourages voluntary rescuers when a life is in danger. Additionally, our adherence to this public policy does nothing to invalidate [the firm's] work rule regarding drivers' leaving the trucks. The rule's importance cannot be understated, and drivers do subject themselves to a great risk of harm by leaving the driver's compartment. Our holding merely forbids [the firm] from firing [the driver] when he broke the rule because he saw a woman who faced imminent life-threatening harm, and he reasonably believed his intervention was necessary to save her life. Finally, by focusing on the narrow public policy encouraging citizens to save human lives from life threatening situations, we continue to protect employers from frivolous lawsuits.[5]

On the other hand, while courts often try to be sensitive to family obligations, being there for one's family is not a sufficient public policy interest; and a refusal to work overtime in consideration of those obligations was deemed a legal basis for termination. The termination of an at-will employee for meeting family obligations did not violate a public policy or any legally recognized right or duty of the employee.[6] While the courts that have adopted the public policy exception agree that the competing interests of employers and society require that the exception be recognized, there is considerable disagreement in connection with *what is the public policy* and *what constitutes a violation of the policy.*

Whistle-Blowing   Some states have included terminations based on whistle-blowing under the public policy exception. Whistle-blowing occurs when an employee reports an employer's wrongdoing. One of the most infamous cases of whistle-blowing occurred when Sherron Watkins chose to speak up in connection with Enron's wrongdoings with regards to its accounting procedures.

In 1982, Congress enacted the Federal Whistleblower Statute, which prohibits retaliatory action specifically against defense contractor employees who disclose information pertaining to a violation of the law governing defense contracts. The statute is administered by the Department of Defense and is enforced solely by that department; that is, an individual who suffers retaliatory action under this statute may not bring a private, common-law suit. The statute states specifically:

> An employee of a defense contractor may not be discharged, demoted, or otherwise discriminated against as a reprisal for disclosing to a Member of Congress or an authorized official of the Department of Defense or of Justice information relating to a substantial violation of law related to a defense contract (including the competition for or negotiation of a defense contract).

Additionally, in 1989 Congress amended the Civil Service Reform Act of 1978 to include the Whistleblowers Protection Act, which expands the protection afforded to federal employees who report government fraud, waste, and abuse. The act applies to all employees appointed in the civil service who are engaged in the performance of a federal function and are supervised by a federal official. Employees of federal contractors, therefore, are not covered by the act since they are hired by the contractor and not the government itself. Of course, none of these statutes apply to other private sector workers.

Certain statutes on other subjects or specific professions include whistle-blowing protections. For example, the Health Care Worker Whistleblower Protection Act protects nurses and other health care workers from harassment, demotion, and discharge for filing complaints about workplace conditions. These complaints often report on improper patient care or business methods and can affect the patient care and staff in a positive way. The act also protects employers from disgruntled ex-employees by allowing the employer an opportunity to correct allegations and by having a compliance plan to maintain an internal file for complaints of violations. Twenty-one states have implemented their own form of this act.[7]

At least 43 states, including California, Florida, New York, and Texas, also provide some additional and general form of legislative protection for whistle-blowers. Almost half of these state whistle-blower protection statutes protect both public and private sector employees who report wrongdoings of their employer. Some states limit protection to the reporting of violation of federal, state, or local laws. However, an increasing number of states, including California, Colorado, and Illinois, protect the reporting of mismanagement or gross waste of public funds or of a substantial and specific danger to public health and safety. A few states, such as Alaska, Louisiana, Maine, and Pennsylvania, require that whistle-blowing reports be made in "good faith." (See Exhibit 2.3, "States with Whistle-Blower Protection Statutes.")

Exhibit 2.3 *States with Whistle-Blower Protection Statutes*

STATES WITH WHISTLE-BLOWER PROTECTION STATUTES FOR BOTH PRIVATE AND PUBLIC EMPLOYEES

Alabama, Alaska, Arkansas, California, Connecticut,[1] Delaware, Florida, Hawaii, Kentucky, Louisiana, Maine, Michigan, Minnesota,[2] Montana, New Hampshire,[3] Nevada, New Jersey, New York, North Carolina, Ohio, Oregon, Pennsylvania[11] Rhode Island, South Carolina, Tennessee,[4] Vermont, Washington.

STATES THAT OFFER SPECIAL WHISTLE-BLOWER PROTECTIONS ONLY FOR THEIR OWN STATE OR LOCAL GOVERNMENT EMPLOYEES

Alaska,[9] Arizona, California, Colorado, Connecticut, Georgia,[5] Hawaii, Illinois, Indiana, Iowa, Kansas, Kentucky, Louisiana, Maryland,[6] Massachusetts, Missouri, Nebraska,[10] New Mexico, Nevada, Oklahoma, Pennsylvania,[7] South Carolina, South Dakota, Texas, Utah, Washington, West Virginia, Wisconsin.[8]

Separate laws in Nevada cover state employees and peace officers.

Montana also protects public and private sector whistle-blowers through its Wrongful Discharge from Employment Act.

Source: R. A. Guttman et al., *The Law: An Overview* (undated), http://whistleblowerlaws.com/protection.htm (accessed December 7, 2007); Bureau of National Affairs, Inc., *Individual Employment Rights Manual*, No. 133, 505:28–29 (July 2001). http://www.taterenner.com/stchart.htm, http://law.jrank.org/pages/11824/Whistleblower-Statutes.html, http://www.ncsl.org/IssuesResearch/EmploymentWorking-Families/StateWhistleblowerLaws/tabid/13390/Default.aspx.

[1] Connecticut has separate laws extending whistle-blower protection to public service, nuclear-power, and state and local employees who report hazardous conditions.

[2] The laws in Minnesota and New Hampshire specifically exclude independent contractors.

[3] See note 2.

[4] Tennessee has two whistle-blower laws, one that covers only local school-system employees and the other covering any employee who reports, or refuses to participate in, illegal activities.

[5] Georgia and Wisconsin exclude employees of the office of the governor, the legislature, and the courts.

[6] Maryland restricts coverage to employees and classified-service applicants within the executive branch of state government.

[7] Pennsylvania's law excludes teachers, although school administrators are covered. Pennsylvania also has a separate law governing public utility employees.

[8] See note 5.

[9] Arizona SOL 10 days for state employees

[10] Nebraska state employees are covered by the State Government Effectiveness Act- R.R.S. Neb. § 81-2701. SOL 4 years.

[11] Pennsylvania public policy tort recognized where employees have a duty to report or prove actual violation.

If there is a statute permitting an employee to take certain action or to pursue certain rights, the employer is prohibited from terminating employees for engaging in such activity. Examples of this type of legislation include state statutes permitting the employee to file a workers' compensation claim for on-the-job injuries sustained by the employee. Another example is the Sarbanes-Oxley Act, which primarily addresses issues relating to accountability and transparency in corporate governance (such as the issues that arose during the infamous Enron debacle). The act provides protection to employees of publicly traded companies who disclose corporate misbehavior, even if the disclosure was made only internally to management or to the board of directors and not necessarily to relevant government authorities. The *Palmateer* case at the end of the chapter is a seminal one in this area, exploring whether employees who assist law enforcement agencies should be protected as a matter of public policy.

Case 1

In *Green v. Ralee Engineering Co.*,[8] decided after *Palmateer,* an employee was terminated after calling attention to the fact that parts that had failed inspection were still being shipped to purchasers. He sued for wrongful discharge, asserting a public policy exception to the at-will employment rule. The court explored whether public safety regulations governing commercial airline safety could provide a basis for declaring a public policy in the context of a retaliatory discharge action. The court found that the regulations furthered important safety policies affecting the public at large and did not merely serve either the employee's or the employer's personal or proprietary interest; "[t]here is no public policy more important or more fundamental than the one favoring the effective protection of the lives and property of citizens." The court agreed that the termination violated public policy.

LO8

Retaliatory Discharge   Retaliatory discharge is a broad term that encompasses terminations in response to an employee exercising rights provided by law. We will discuss this basis for discharge later as it relates to the areas of discrimination and regulatory protections. However, the basis for the claim remains the same, which is why it is included in this toolkit. Courts are sensitive to claims of retaliation in order to protect an employee's right to protest adverse employment actions. If workers are not protected against retaliation, there would be a strong deterrent to asserting one's rights. On the other hand, if the employer's actions are legitimately based in law, the employer's actions are protected.

In order to prove a retaliatory discharge claim, an employee must show that he or she was participating in a protected activity, there was an adverse employment action toward the employee by the employer, and there is causal connection between the employee's protected activity and the adverse action taken by the employer. (See Exhibit 2.4, "Retaliatory Discharge: *Prima Facie* Case.") For instance, if an employee is given a right to serve jury duty but is terminated by the employer for doing so, with no other apparent reason for the termination, that employee has a basis for a retaliation claim.

In determining whether the adverse action is sufficient to support a claim, courts will look to an objective standard and measure whether a "reasonable employee" would view the retaliatory harm as *significant*. In *Burlington Northern*

Exhibit 2.4   *Retaliatory Discharge:* Prima Facie *Case*

Participation in a **protected activity** → An **adverse employment action** → **Causal connection** between the protected activity and the adverse action

Source: EEOC, "Guidance and Instructions for Investigating and Analyzing Claims of Retaliation," *EEOC Compliance Manual,* www.eeoc.gov/policy/docs/retal.html (May 20, 1998).

& Santa Fe Railway Co. v. White,[9] the U.S. Supreme Court reviewed the context of the retaliatory action and determined that, even though the employee received back pay for a 37-day suspension, that suspension, along with a reassignment to a job that was more physically demanding, would have "dissuaded a reasonable worker from making or supporting a charge of discrimination."[10] The case is viewed as important since it expands retaliatory discharge to include not only "ultimate" employment actions such as refusal to hire, discharge, or demotion, but also any action that satisfies this new standard of "dissuasion." The impact may be that, even in cases where no violation occurred in the original decision, the court might find retaliation against the employee who complained about the alleged violation. You may wish to review the *Herawi* case at the end of the chapter, which demonstrates a fact pattern where motives for the adverse action involved are a bit more complicated since they involve several proposed justifications.

Finally, the third element of retaliatory discharge requires a causal connection between the first two elements. Courts often require more than a simple showing of close timing; however, when the adverse employment action happens immediately after the protected activity, courts recognize that there may be no time for any other evidence to amass.[11]

It is important to understand that, if an employee originally claims wrongful behavior on the part of the employer and suffers retaliation, it does not matter whether the employer proves that the original wrongful behavior actually occurred. The question is only whether there was retaliation for engaging in protected activity.

Constitutional Protections   Though perhaps it goes without saying, an employer is prohibited from terminating a worker or taking other adverse employment action against a worker on the basis of the worker's engaging in constitutionally protected activities. However—and this is a significant limitation—this prohibition applies only where the employer is a public entity, since the Constitution protects against government action rather than action by private employers.

For instance, a public employer may not terminate a worker for the exercise of free speech (including whistle-blowing, under most circumstances) or based on a particular political affiliation. So, an employee who refused to participate in an employer's public lobbying campaign is protected. There are exceptions in the private sector when an adverse employment action would violate some recognized expression of public policy, even without state action; but, as mentioned above, these protections vary from state to state.

Breach of Implied Covenant of Good Faith and Fair Dealing

covenant of good faith and fair dealing
Implied contractual obligation to act in good faith in the fulfillment of each party's contractual duties.

Another exception to the presumption of an at-will employment relationship is the implied **covenant of good faith and fair dealing** in the performance and enforcement of the employee's work agreement. This requirement should not be confused with a requirement in some contracts of "good cause" prior to termination. A New York court defined this particular duty as follows:

> In every contract there is an implied covenant that neither party shall do anything which will have the effect of destroying or injuring the right of the other party to receive the fruits of the contract, which means that in every contract there exists an implied covenant of good faith and fair dealing. While the public policy exception to the at-will doctrine looks to the law to judge the employer's actions and deems them violations of public policy or not, the breach of implied covenant of good faith looks instead to the actions between the parties to do so.

The implied covenant of good faith and fair dealing means that any agreement between the employer and the employee includes a promise that the parties will deal with each other fairly and in good faith. Imagine a situation where an employer and employee have entered into an employment contract but fail to specify why and when the employee could be terminated. Assume the employee is then terminated and the employee claims that the reason is unwarranted. The court will first look to the contract and will find that the matter is not discussed. If the situation occurs in a state that recognizes the implied covenant, the court will then look to the facts to see whether the termination is in breach of the implied covenant of good faith and fair dealing.

Only 13 states recognize this covenant as an exception to at-will employment. Some states allow the cause of action but limit the damages awarded to those that would be awarded under a breach of contract claim, while other states allow the terminated employee to recover higher tort damages.

Scenario

In connection with Scenario 1, Mark Richter may have a claim against his employer for breach of the covenant of good faith and fair dealing. Mark's employer is, in effect, denying Mark the fruits of his labor.

Critics of this implied agreement argue that, where an agreement is specifically nondurational, there should be no expectation of guaranteed employment of any length. As long as both parties are aware that the relationship may be terminated at any time (which arguably would be the case if they both signed the contract), it would be extremely difficult to prove that either party acted in bad faith in terminating the relationship. Courts have supported this contention in holding that an implied contract or covenant seems to upset the balance between the employee's interest in maintaining her or his employment and the employer's interest in running its business as it sees fit. "The absence of good cause to discharge an employee does not alone give rise to an enforceable claim for breach of a condition of good faith and fair dealing." To the contrary, as mentioned, in most states, employers may terminate an individual for any reason, as long as the true reason is not contradictory to public policy, against the law, or in contravention of another agreement. The *Guz* case at the end of the chapter seeks to clarify this distinction.

Breach of Implied Contract

implied contract
A contract that is not expressed but, instead, is created by other words or conduct of the parties involved.

What happens when the employer is not violating an express contractual agreement, nor the implied covenant of good faith and fair dealing, yet it seems to the employee that an injustice was done? Courts might identify instead an **implied contract** from several different sources. Though primarily an implied contract arises from the acts of the parties, the acts leading to the creation of an implied contract vary from situation to situation.

Courts have found contracts implied from off-hand statements made by employers during preemployment interviews, such as a statement that a candidate will become a "permanent" employee after a trial period, or quotes of yearly or other periodic salaries, or statements in employee handbooks. In such cases, when the employee has been terminated in less than the time quoted as the salary (e.g., $50,000 per year), the employee may be able to maintain an action for the remainder of the salary on the theory of this establishing an implied contract for a year's duration. However, these statements must be sufficiently specific to be enforceable. In *Melott v. ACC Operations, Inc.,*[12] the promise of the employee's manager to help her in "any way" he could did not create an implied contract that changed her at-will employment status.

Court rulings finding implied contracts based on statements of employers have caused some employers to restructure terms of agreements, employee handbooks, or hiring practices to ensure that no possible implied contract can arise. Some commentators believe that this may not result in the fairest consequence to employees.[13] The *Guz* case at the end of the chapter highlights the fact that the employer's failure to abide by those policies or documents mentioned above may be the cause of subsequent litigation and liability if an employee is harmed by the employer's failure to do so.

Some employers have tried to avoid the characterization of their employment policies or handbooks as potential contract terms by including in those documents a disclaimer such as the following:

> Our employment relationship is to be considered "at-will" as that term is defined in this state. Nothing in this policy [or handbook] shall be construed as a modification to that characterization and, where there is an apparent conflict between the statements in this policy [or handbook], the policy [or handbook] shall be construed to support a determination of an at-will relationship or shall become null.

Employers should be careful when creating an employment policy manual that includes a statement that employees will only be terminated for good cause,

---

Exhibit 2.5 *Promissory Estoppel:* Prima Facie *Case*

The employer made a ***promise*** → On which the worker ***reasonably relied*** → To the employee's ***detriment***

---

or that employees become "permanent" employees once they successfully complete their probationary period. This type of language has been held to create binding agreements between the employer and the employee; and the employer's later termination of the employee, if inconsistent with those statements, has resulted in liability.[14]

Exception Based on Promissory Estoppel Promissory estoppel is another exception to the at-will rule. Promissory estoppel is similar to the implied contract claim except that the promise, implied or expressed, does not rise to the level of a contract. It may be missing an element; perhaps there is no mutual consideration or some other flaw; however, promissory estoppel is still a possible exception to an employer's contention of an at-will environment. For a claim of estoppel to be successful, the plaintiff must show that the employer or prospective employer made a *promise* upon which the worker *reasonably relied* to her or his *detriment*. (See Exhibit 2.5, "Promissory Estoppel: *Prima Facie* Case.") Often the case turns on whether it was reasonable for the worker to rely on the employer's promise without an underlying contract. In addition, it is critical to have a clear and unambiguous promise.

Statutory Exceptions to Employment at-Will In addition to the exceptions that have been discussed in this section, and any contractual constraints on discharge to which the parties might have previously agreed, a number of statutory exceptions also exist that limit the nature of employment-at-will. For instance, by legislation, an employer may not terminate an employee for exercising her or his rights to a safe working environment (Occupational Safety and Health Act), fair pay (Fair Labor Standards Act), or being pregnant (Pregnancy Discrimination Act, which amended Title VII). As you will see throughout this text, several statutes exist that serve to guide the employer away from decisions on bases that perpetuate wrongful discrimination such as decisions based on race, sex, national origin, or disability status.[15]

However, though some employers have argued that the list of exceptions makes mockery of the at-will rule, the list itself is actually finite rather than limitless. Employers are, in fact, free to make business decisions based on managerial discretion outside of certain judicially limited and legislatively imposed parameters.

As discussed above, if there is no express agreement or contract to the contrary, employment is considered to be at-will; that is, either the employer or the employee may terminate the relationship at her or his discretion. Nevertheless, even where a discharge involves no statutory discrimination, breach of contract, or traditional exception to the at-will doctrine discussed above, the termination may still be considered wrongful and the employer may be liable for "wrongful discharge," "wrongful termination," or "unjust dismissal." Therefore, in addition to ensuring that workplace policies do not wrongfully discriminate against employees and do not fall under other exceptions, the employer also must beware of situations in which the employer's policy or action in a termination can form the basis for unjust dismissal. Since such bases can be so diverse, the employer must be vigilant in its attention to this area, and employees should be fully aware of their rights, even though the relationship may be considered at-will.

Constructive Discharge

constructive discharge
Occurs when the employee is given no reasonable alternative but to end the employment relationship; considered an involuntary act on the part of the employee.

The "discharge" addressed throughout this chapter and the remainder of this text may refer either to traditional termination or to an employee's decision to leave under certain intolerable circumstances. **Constructive discharge** exists where the employee sees no alternative but to quit her or his position; that is, the act of leaving was not truly voluntary. Therefore, while the employer did not actually fire the employee, the actions of the employer caused the employee to leave. Constructive discharge usually evolves from circumstances where an employer knows that it would be wrongful to terminate an employee for one reason or another. So, to avoid being sued for wrongful termination, the employer creates an environment where the employee has no choice but to leave. If courts were to allow this type of treatment, those laws that restrict employers' actions from wrongful termination, such as Title VII, would have no effect.

The test for constructive discharge is whether the employer made the working conditions so intolerable that no reasonable employee should be expected to endure. The courts have softened this language somewhat so that an employee need not demonstrate that the environment is literally unbearable but simply that she or he "has no recourse within the employer's organization or reasonably believes there is no chance for fair treatment," then or in the future.[16] The circumstances might present one horrendous event or a number of minor instances of hostile behavior, similar to the standard you will learn for sexual harassment later in the text.

A police officer in *Paloni v. City of Albuquerque Police Department*[17] sued her police department claiming constructive discharge after she had been found in violation of the department's use of force policy and asked to go through a retraining on the practice. Because she could not provide evidence that other officers had lost confidence in her or that the situation was made intolerable because of the retraining, the Tenth Circuit found that there was no constructive discharge. Similarly, when Allstate imposed a new job requirement that agents be present in the office during all operating hours, the agents could not show that this made the position so intolerable that they could not be expected to continue.

On the other hand, in *Nassar v. Univ. of Texas Southwestern Medical Center at Dallas,*[18] Dr. Nassar was subjected to such extreme harassment on the basis of race and national origin that no reasonable employee should have to tolerate within his or her working environment. Nassar, a U.S. citizen of Egyptian origin, was subject to challenges to his work that were unsupported by facts, derogatory statements from his supervisor such as "middle easterners were lazy," and alleged retaliation for his complaints when he tried to get an alternate position. Nassar was awarded more than $3.6 million in both compensatory damages and back pay and has a pending claim of up to $4 million for front pay.

Conditions that one might consider to be traditionally intolerable, such as harassment, are not required to find constructive discharge. Courts have found that a failure to accommodate a disability,[19] or even an employer's offer of a severance package without a release of claims[20] (but be wary of the Older Workers Benefit Protection Act, discussed in a later chapter), is grounds for constructive discharge.

The Worker Adjustment and Retraining Notification Act

In addition to the exceptions to employment-at-will mentioned above, the Worker Adjustment and Retraining Notification (WARN) Act is included in this section because it also places restrictions on an employer's management of its workforce in terms of discharging workers. Before termination, WARN requires that employers with over 100 employees must give 60 days' advance notice of a plant closing or mass layoff to affected employees. A plant closing triggers this notice requirement if it would result in employment loss for 50 or more workers during a 30-day period.

Mass layoff is defined as employment losses at one location during any 30-day period of 500 or more workers, or of 50–499 workers if they constitute at least one-third of the active workforce. Employees who have worked less than 6 months of the prior 12 or who work less than 20 hours a week are excluded from both computations. If an employer does not comply with the requirements of the WARN Act notices, employees can recover pay and benefits for the period for which notice was not given, up to a maximum of 60 days. All but small employers and public employers are required to provide written notice of a plant closing or mass layoff no less than 60 days in advance.

The number of employees is a key factor in determining whether the WARN Act is applicable. Only an employer who has 100 or more full-time employees or has 100 or more employees who, in the aggregate, work at least 4,000 hours per week are covered by the WARN Act. In counting the number of employees, U.S. citizens working at foreign sites, temporary employees, and employees working for a subsidiary as part of the parent company must be considered in the calculation.

There are three exceptions to the 60-day notice requirements. The first, referred to as the *faltering company* exception, involves an employer who is actively seeking capital and who in good faith believes that giving notice to the employees will preclude the employer from obtaining the needed capital. The second exception occurs when the required notice is not given due to a "sudden, dramatic, and unexpected" business circumstance not reasonably foreseen and outside the employer's control. The last exception is for actions arising out of a "natural disaster" such as a flood, earthquake, or drought.

Wrongful Discharge Based on Other Tort Liability

A *tort* is a violation of a duty, other than one owed when the parties have a contract. Where a termination happens because of intentional and outrageous conduct on the part of the employer and causes emotional distress to the employee, the employee may have a tort claim for a wrongful discharge in approximately half of the states in the United States. For example, in one case, an employee was terminated because she was having a relationship with a competitor's employee. The court determined that forcing the employee to choose between her position at the company and her relationship with a male companion constituted the tort of outrageous conduct.

One problem exists in connection with a claim for physical or emotional damages under tort theories: In many states, an employee's damages are limited by workers' compensation laws. Where an injury is work-related, such as emotional distress as a result of discharge, these statutes provide that the workers' compensation process is a worker's *exclusive* remedy. An exception exists where a claim of injury is based solely on emotional distress; in that situation, many times workers' compensation will be denied. Therefore, in those cases, the employee may proceed against the employer under a tort claim. If an employer seeks to protect against liability for this tort, it should ensure that the process by which an employee is terminated is respectful of the employee, as well as mindful of the interests of the employer.

One tort that might result from a discharge could be a tort action for defamation, under certain circumstances. To sustain a claim for defamation, the employee must be able to show that (1) the employer made a *false and defamatory statement* about the employee, (2) the statement was *communicated* to a third party *without the employee's consent,* and (3) the communication *caused harm* to the employee. Claims of defamation usually arise where an employer makes statements about the employee to other employees or her or his prospective employers. This issue is covered in more detail in Chapter 13 relating to the employee's privacy rights and employer references.

Finally, where the termination results from a wrongful invasion of privacy, an employee may have a claim for damages. For instance, where the employer wrongfully invades the employee's privacy, searches her purse, and consequently terminates her, the termination may be wrongful.

As you can see, employment-at-will is a broad power for both the employer and the employee. However, the most likely challenge in employment-at-will is the employee being terminated rather than the employee quitting the job. There are, however, many bases upon which the employee can challenge what is perceived to be the employer's wrongful termination. If the facts of the termination fall within one of the several exceptions to employment-at-will, then the wrongful termination action can be successful for the employee. It therefore behooves the employer to make sure that there are appropriate safeguards in place that allow terminations that will not bounce back to the employer like a rubber ball.

Employment Discrimination Concepts

In part two of the chapter, we move from the concept of employment-at-will to concepts that will be visited many times in later chapters, that is, employment discrimination under Title VII of the Civil Rights Act of 1964. The chapters on Title VII constitute a good portion of this text and it will be helpful for you to have a single chapter to which you can refer for repeating concepts throughout the chapters. You may find it a bit awkward to be exposed to these concepts before you actually get to the chapters that explain the law itself, but we have worked to make the situation as clear as possible. For now, in reviewing the information in this section, just keep in mind something you already know: Federal law prohibits employment discrimination on the basis of race, color, gender, religion, national origin, age, and disability.

In the chapters on Title VII, the Americans with Disabilities Act, and the Age Discrimination in Employment Act, you will find out more of the details of the law, such as to whom it applies, how cases are brought, and so on. You will discover the particulars of what is involved in avoiding costly workplace liability for each of the prohibited categories. However, for our present purposes, we will be concentrating only on the theories used to prove employment discrimination claims under the protective legislation. Since Title VII was the first comprehensive protective legislation for workplace discrimination, most of the law was developed under it, and for that reason we often refer to Title VII. However, as the age discrimination and pregnancy discrimination and disability discrimination law was later passed, the legal considerations were applied to those categories as appropriate. So, in this part of the chapter discussing these concepts, know that the basis of the claim may vary depending on the category, but the underlying legal concepts remain applicable.

In alleging discrimination, an employee plaintiff must use one of two theories to bring suit under Title VII and protective legislation: disparate treatment or disparate impact. The suit must fit into one theory or the other to be recognized under the protective legislation. A thorough understanding of each will help employers make sounder policies that avoid litigation in the first place and enhance the workplace in the process.

LO6

Disparate Treatment

disparate treatment
Treating similarly situated employees differently because of prohibited Title VII factors.

Disparate treatment is the theory of discrimination used in cases of individual and overt discrimination and is the one you probably think of when you think of discrimination. The plaintiff employee (or applicant) bringing suit alleges that the employer treated the employee in a way different from other similarly situated employees based on one or more of the prohibited categories. Disparate treatment is considered intentional discrimination, but the plaintiff need not actually know that unlawful discrimination is the reason for the difference. That is, the employee need not prove that the employer actually said that race, gender, and so on was the reason for the decision. In disparate treatment cases, the employer's policy is discriminatory on its face, such as a

Exhibit 2.6 *Disparate Treatment Discrimination:* Prima Facie *Case*

* Employee belongs to a class protected under Title VII

* Employee applied for and was qualified for a job for which the employer was seeking applicants

* Employee was rejected and, after the rejection, the position remained open

* Employer continued to seek applicants with the rejected applicant's qualifications

policy of not hiring women to load boxes. Keep in mind that it is not the employer's subjective intent that is important. There need not be evil intent to discriminate. It must simply be able to be shown that the difference in treatment occurred and had no sustainable justification, leaving a prohibited category as the only remaining conclusion.

As you will see in *McDonnell Douglas Corp. v. Green,* included at the end of the chapter, the U.S. Supreme Court has developed a set of indicators that leaves discrimination as the only plausible explanation when all other possibilities are eliminated. (See Exhibit 2.6, "Disparate Treatment Discrimination.") Under the *McDonnell Douglas* case, in order to make out a *prima facie* case of disparate treatment discrimination, please see Exhibit 2.6.

The effect of the *McDonnell Douglas* inquiries is to set up a legal test of all relevant factors that are generally taken into consideration in making employment decisions. Once those considerations have been ruled out as the reason for failure to hire the applicant, the only factor left to consider is the applicant's membership in one of the prohibited categories (e.g., race, color, gender, religion, national origin or other protected category).

The *McDonnell Douglas* Court recognized that there would be scenarios under the law other than failure to rehire involved in that case (i.e., failure to promote or train, discriminatory discipline, and so on) and its test would not be directly transferrable to them, but it could be modified accordingly. For instance, the issue may not be a refusal to rehire; it may, instead, be a dismissal. In such a case, the employee would show the factors as they relate to dismissal.

If an employer makes decisions in accordance with these requirements, it is less likely that the decisions will later be successfully challenged by the employee in court. Disparate treatment cases involve an employer's variance from the normal scheme of things, to which the employee can point to show he or she was treated differently. Employers should therefore consistently treat similarly situated employees similarly. If there are differences, ensure that they are justifiable.

Think carefully before deciding to single out an employee for a workplace action. Is the reason for the action clear? Can it be articulated? Based on the information the employer used to make the decision, is it reasonable? Rational? Is the information serving as the basis for the decision reliable? Balanced? Is the justification job related? If the employer is satisfied with the answers to these questions, the decision is probably defensible. If not, reexamine the considerations for the decision, find its weakness, and determine what can be done to address the weakness. The employer will then be in a much better position to defend the decision and show it is supported by legitimate, non-discriminatory reasons.

Keep in mind that these requirements are modified to conform to the situation forming the basis of the suit, as appropriate. For instance, if it was termination rather than failure to hire, or discipline rather than termination, the requirements would be adjusted accordingly.

> *Employer's Defense:* The employer can defend by showing that the action was taken for a legitimate, non-discriminatory reason.

> *Employee's Counter:* After the employer's defense, the employee can counter with evidence that the employer's legitimate, non-discriminatory reason was actually a mere pretext for the employer to discriminate.

Legitimate, Non-discriminatory Reason Defense

LO7

Even if the employee establishes all the elements of the *prima facie* case of disparate treatment, it is only a rebuttable presumption. That is, establishing the *prima facie* case alone does not establish that the employer discriminated against the employee. There may be some other explanation for what the employer did. As the Court stated in *McDonnell Douglas,* the employer may defend against the *prima facie* case of disparate treatment by showing that there was a legitimate, non-discriminatory reason for the decision. That reason may be virtually anything that makes sense and is not related to prohibited criteria. It is only discrimination on the basis of prohibited categories that is protected by the law. For instance, the law does not protect the category of jerks. If it can legitimately be shown that the action was taken because the employee was acting like a jerk, then the employee has no viable claim for employment discrimination. However, if it turns out that the only jerks terminated are those of a particular race, gender, ethnicity, and the like, then the employer is in violation Title VII.

Even if the employer can show a legitimate, non-discriminatory reason for the action toward the employee, the analysis does not end there. The employee can then counter the employer's defense by showing that the legitimate, non-discriminatory reason being shown by the employer is a mere pretext for discrimination. That is, that while on its face the employer's reason may appear legitimate, there is actually something discriminatory going on. For instance, in *McDonnell Douglas,* the employer said it would not rehire Green because he engaged in unlawful activity. This

---

Exhibit 2.7 *BFOQ Test*

If an employer can answer yes to both of these questions, there may be a legitimate basis for the employer to limit employees to one gender and use the BFOQ defense if sued for discrimination.

1. **Does the job require that the employee be of one gender only?** This requirement is designed to test whether gender is so essential to job performance that a member of the opposite gender simply could not do the same job. In our bunny case, being a Playboy bunny requires being female and a male could not be the bunny envisioned by *Playboy* magazine (though we understand that there are males who do a very good job of looking female).

2. **If the answer to question 1 is yes, is that requirement reasonably necessary to the "essence" of the employer's particular business?** This requirement is designed to ensure that the qualification being scrutinized is so important to the operation of the business that the business would be undermined if employees of the "wrong" gender were hired. Keep in mind that the BFOQ must be necessary, not just convenient. Here, having bunnies that look like the *Playboy* magazine bunnies is the essence of the employer's business.

Contrast Southwest with Hooters restaurants, where Hooters asserted that its business is serving spicy chicken wings. Since males can serve chicken wings just as well as females, being female is not a BFOQ for being a Hooters server. However, if Hooters had said the purpose of its business is to provide males with scantily clad female servers for entertainment purposes, as it was with the Playboy clubs, then being female would be a BFOQ.

---

is a perfectly reasonable, legitimate, non-discriminatory reason. However, if Green could show that the employer had rehired white employees who had engaged in similar unlawful activities, then McDonnell Douglas's legitimate, non-discriminatory reason for Green's treatment would appear to be a mere pretext for discrimination since white employees who engaged in similar activities had been rehired despite their activity, but Green, who was black, had not.

The Bona Fide Occupational Qualification Defense

LO7

bona fide occupational qualification (BFOQ)
Permissible discrimination if legally necessary for an employer's particular business.

Employers also may defend against disparate treatment cases by showing that the basis for the employer's intentional discrimination is a **bona fide occupational qualification (BFOQ)** reasonably necessary for the employer's particular business. This is available only for disparate treatment cases involving gender, religion, and national origin and is not available for race or color. BFOQ is legalized discrimination and, therefore, very narrowly construed by the courts.

To have a successful BFOQ defense, the employer must be able to show that the basis for preferring one group over another goes to the essence of what the employer is in business to do and that predominant attributes of the group discriminated against are at odds with that business. (See Exhibit 2.7, "BFOQ Test.") The evidence supporting the qualification must be credible, and not just the employer's opinion. The employer also must be able to show it would be impractical to determine if each individual member of the group who is discriminated against could qualify for the position.

For instance, it has been held, based on expert evidence, that, because bus companies and airlines are in the business of safely transporting passengers from one place to another, and driving and piloting skills begin to deteriorate at a certain age, a maximum age requirement for hiring is an appropriate BFOQ for bus drivers and pilots.

As you can see from *Wilson v. Southwest Airlines Company,* included at the end of the chapter, not every attempt to show a BFOQ is successful. Southwest argued that allowing only females to be flight attendants was a BFOQ. However, the court held that the essence of the job of flight attendants is to be able to assist passengers if there is an emergency, and being female was not necessary for this role. Weigh the business considerations in the case against the dictates of Title VII and think about how you would decide the issue.

Make sure that you understand the distinction the court made in *Southwest Airlines* between the essence of *what* an employer is in business to do and *how* the employer chooses to do it. People often neglect this distinction and cannot understand why business owners cannot simply hire whomever they want (or not, as the case may be) if they have a marketing scheme they want to pursue. Marketing schemes go to the "how" of the employer's business, as in how an employer chooses to conduct his or her business or attract people to it, rather than the "what" of the business, which is what the actual business itself is set up to do. Getting passengers safely from one point to another is the "what" in *Southwest.* How the airline chose to market that business to customers is another matter and has little to do with the actual conduct of the business itself. Marketing schemes are not protected by law as BFOQs are. Perhaps the Playboy Club bunnies will make it clearer.

After the success of *Playboy* magazine, Playboy opened several Playboy clubs in which the servers were dressed as Playboy bunnies. The purpose of the clubs was not to serve drinks as much as it was to extend *Playboy* magazine and its theme of beautiful women dressed in bunny costumes into another form for public consumption. *Playboy* magazine and its concept were purely for the purpose of adult male entertainment. The bunnies serving drinks were not so much drink servers as they were Playboy bunnies in the flesh rather than on a magazine page. That is what the business of the clubs was all about. Though it later chose to open up its policies to include male bunnies, being female was a defensible BFOQ for being a bunny server in a Playboy club because having female bunnies was what the club was in business to do. Having sexy female flight attendants was not what Southwest Airlines was in the business to do.

As you saw in *Southwest,* in order for an employer to establish a successful bona fide occupational qualification reasonably necessary for the employer's particular business that will protect the employer from liability for discrimination, the courts use a *two-part test.* The employer has the burden of proving that it had reasonable factual cause to believe that all or substantially all members of a particular group would be unable to perform safely and efficiently the duties of the job involved. This is most effective if the employer has consulted with an expert in the area who provides a scientific basis for the belief—for example, using a doctor who can attest to factors that applicants over 35 years of age for professional driving positions need at least 15 years to become a really competent driver, but after age 50 would begin to lose physical attributes needed for safe driving. The attributes must occur so frequently within the group being screened out that it would be safe to say the group as a whole could be kept out. The two-part test must answer the following questions affirmatively: (1) Does the job require that the employee be of one gender, and (2) if yes, is that reasonably necessary to the "essence" of the employer's particular business? Keep in mind that since a BFOQ is legalized discrimination, the bar to obtaining it is set very high. (See Exhibit 2.7, "BFOQ Test.")

Disparate Impact

LO6

disparate/adverse impact
Deleterious effect of a facially neutral policy on a Title VII group.

facially neutral policy
Workplace policy that applies equally to all appropriate employees.

Scenario

While disparate treatment is based on an employee's allegations that she or he is treated differently as an individual based on a policy that is discriminatory on its face, **disparate impact** cases are generally statistically based group cases alleging that the employer's policy, while neutral on its face (**facially neutral**), has a disparate or adverse impact on a protected group. If such a policy impacts protected groups more harshly than others, illegal discrimination may be found if the employer cannot show that the requirement is a legitimate business necessity. This is why the police department's policy fails in the opening scenario. The 5-foot-4, 130-pound policy would screen out many more females than males and would therefore have to be shown to be job-related in order to stand. Statistically speaking, females, as a group, are slighter and shorter than males, so the policy has a disparate impact on females and could be gender discrimination in violation of Title VII. Actually, this has also been determined by courts to be true of males in certain ethnic groups, such as some Hispanics and Asians, who statistically tend to be lighter and shorter than the requirement.

The disparate impact theory was set forth by the U.S. Supreme Court in 1971 in *Griggs v. Duke Power Co.,* included at the end of the chapter. *Griggs* is generally recognized as the first important case under Title VII, setting forth how Title VII was to be interpreted by courts. Even though Title VII was passed in 1964 and became effective in 1965, it was not until *Griggs* in 1971 that it was taken seriously by most employers. *Griggs* has since been codified into law by the Civil Rights Act of 1991. In *Griggs,* the employer had kept a segregated workforce before Title VII as enacted, with African-American employees being consigned to the coal-handling department, where the highest-paid coal handler made less than the lowest-paid white employee in any other department. The day after Title VII became effective, the company imposed a high school diploma requirement and passing scores on two general intelligence tests in order for employees to be able to move from coal handling to any other department. Employees working in all other departments of the company, all of whom were white, were grandfathered in and did not have to meet these requirements.

While the policy looked neutral on its face, the impact was to effectively keep the status quo and continue to keep blacks in coal handling and whites in the other, higher-paying, departments. The Supreme Court struck down Duke Power Company's new requirements as a violation of Title VII due to its disparate impact on African Americans. Notice the difference between the theories in the

---

Exhibit 2.8   *Disparate Impact Screening Devices*

Court cases have determined that the following screening devices have a disparate impact:

- Credit status—gender, race.
- Arrest record—race.
- Unwed pregnancy—gender, race.
- Height and weight requirements—gender, national origin.
- Educational requirements—race.

- Marital status—gender.
- Conviction of crime unrelated to job performance—race.

Keep in mind that finding that a screening device has a disparate impact does not mean that it will automatically be struck down as discriminatory. The employer can always show that the screening device is based on a legitimate business necessity, as discussed shortly.

Griggs case involving disparate impact and the *McDonnell Douglas* case involving disparate treatment.

 Griggs stood as good law until 1989 when the U.S. Supreme Court decided *Wards Cove Packing Co. v. Atonio.*[21] In that case, the Court held that the burden was on the employee to show that the employer's policy was *not* job related. In *Griggs* the burden was on the *employer* to show that the policy *was* job related. This increase in the employee's burden was taken as a setback in what had been considered settled civil rights law. It moved Congress to immediately call for *Griggs* and its 18-year progeny to be enacted into law so it would no longer be subject to the vagaries of whoever was sitting on the U.S. Supreme Court. The Civil Rights Act of 1991 did this.

screening device
Factor used to weed out applicants from the pool of candidates.

 Disparate impact cases can be an employer's nightmare. No matter how careful an employer tries to be, a policy, procedure, or **screening device** may serve as the basis of a disparate impact claim if the employer is not vigilant in watching for its indefensible disparate impact. Even the most seemingly innocuous policies can turn up unexpected cases of disparate impact. (See Exhibit 2.8, "Disparate Impact Screening Devices.") Employers must guard against analyzing policies or actions for signs of intentional discrimination, yet missing those with a disparate impact. Ensure that any screening device is explainable and justifiable as a legitimate business necessity if it has a disparate impact on protected groups. This is even more important now that the EEOC has adopted its new E-RACE initiative. The purpose of the initiative is to put a renewed emphasis on employers' hiring and promotion practices in order to eliminate even the more subtle ways in which employers can discriminate. For instance, screening applicants on the basis of names, arrest or conviction records, credit scores, or employment and personality tests may have a disparate impact on people of color.

What Constitutes a Disparate Impact?

We have talked about disparate impact in general, but we have not yet discussed what actually constitutes a disparate impact. Any time an employer uses a factor as a screening device to decide who receives the benefit of any type of employment decision—from hiring to termination, from promotion to training, from raises to employee benefit packages—it can be the basis for disparate impact analysis.

Title VII does not mention disparate impact. On August 25, 1978, several federal agencies, including the EEOC and the Departments of Justice and Labor, adopted a set of uniform guidelines to provide standards for ruling on the legality of employee selection procedures. The Uniform Guidelines on Employee Selection Procedures takes the position that there is a 20 percent margin permissible between the outcome of the majority and the minority under a given screening device. This is known as the **four-fifths rule**. Disparate impact is statistically demonstrated when the selection rate for groups protected by the law is less than 80 percent, or four-fifths, that of the higher-scoring majority group.

For example, 100 women and 100 men take a promotion examination. One hundred percent of the women and 50 percent of the men pass the exam. The men have only performed 50 percent as well as the women. Since the men did not pass at a rate of at least 80 percent of the women's passage rate, the exam has a disparate impact on the men. The employer would now be required to show that the exam is a legitimate business necessity. If this can be shown to the satisfaction of the court, then the job requirement will be permitted even though it has a disparate impact. Even then the policy may still be struck down if the men can show there is a way to accomplish the employer's legitimate goal in using the exam without it having such a harsh impact on them.

For example, suppose a store like Sears has a 75-pound lifting requirement for applicants who apply to work as mechanics in their car repair facilities. A woman who is not hired sues on the basis of gender discrimination, saying the lifting requirement has a disparate impact on women because they generally cannot lift that much weight. The store is able to show that employees who work in the car repair facilities move heavy tools from place to place in the garage. The lifting requirement is therefore a legitimate business necessity. Though the lifting policy screens out women applying for jobs as mechanics at a higher rate than it does men, and, for argument's sake, let's say women only do 20 percent as well as men on the lifting requirement, thus not meeting the four-fifths rule, the employer has provided a legitimate, non-discriminatory reason for the lifting policy.

But suppose the applicant can counter that if the employer used a rolling tool cart (which is actually sold by Sears), then the policy would not have such a harmful impact on women and would still allow Sears what it needs. Even though Sears has given a legitimate, non-discriminatory reason for its policy, it has been demonstrated that the policy can be made less harsh by allowing use of the carts.

The four-fifths rule guideline is only a rule of thumb. The U.S. Supreme Court stated in *Watson v. Fort Worth Bank and Trust* [22] that it has never used mathematical precision to determine disparate impact. What is clear is that the employee is required to show that the statistical disparity is significant and has the effect of selecting applicants for hiring and promotion in ways adversely affecting groups protected by the law.

The terminology regarding scoring is intentionally imprecise because the "outcome" depends on the nature of the screening device. The screening device can be

four-fifths rule
The minority must do at least 80 percent, or four-fifths, as well as the majority on a screening device or a presumption of disparate impact arises, and the device must then be shown to be a legitimate business necessity.

anything that distinguishes one employee from another for workplace decision purposes, such as a policy of hiring only ex-football players as barroom bouncers (most females would be precluded from consideration since most of them have not played football); a minimum passing score on a written or other examination; physical attributes such as height and weight requirements; or another type of differentiating factor. Disparate impact's coverage is very broad and virtually any policy may be challenged.

If the device is a written examination, then the outcomes compared will be test scores of one group (usually whites) versus another (usually African Americans or, more recently, Hispanics). If the screening device is a no-beard policy, then the outcome will be the percentage of black males affected by the medical condition pseudofolliculitis barbae that is exacerbated if they shave, versus the percentage of white males so affected. If it is a height and weight requirement, it will be the percentage of females or members of traditionally shorter and slighter ethnic groups who can meet that requirement versus the percentage of males or majority members who can do so. The hallmark of these screening devices is that they appear neutral on their face. That is, they appear on the surface to apply equally to everyone, yet upon closer examination, they have a harsher impact on a group protected by the law.

Disparate Impact and Subjective Criteria

When addressing the issue of the disparate impact of screening devices, subjective and objective criteria are a concern. *Objective criteria* are factors that are able to be quantified by anyone, such as scores on a written exam. *Subjective criteria* are, instead, factors based on the evaluator's personal thoughts or ideas (e.g., a supervisor's opinion as to whether the employee being considered for promotion is "compatible" with the workplace).

Initially it was suspected that subjective criteria could not be the basis for disparate impact claims since the Supreme Court cases had involved only objective factors such as height and weight, educational requirements, test scores, and the like. In *Watson v. Fort Worth Bank,* mentioned above, the Supreme Court, for the first time, determined that subjective criteria also could be the basis for a disparate impact claim.

In *Watson,* a black employee had worked for the bank for years and was constantly passed over for promotion in favor of white employees. She eventually brought suit, alleging racial discrimination in that the bank's subjective promotion policy had a disparate impact upon black employees. The bank's policy was to promote employees based on the recommendation of the supervisor (all of whom were white). The Supreme Court held that the disparate impact analysis could indeed be used in determining illegal discrimination in subjective criteria cases.

Disparate Impact of Preemployment Interviews and Employment Applications

Quite often questions asked during idle conversational chat in preemployment interviews or included on job applications may unwittingly be the basis for discrimination claims. Such questions or discussions should therefore be scrutinized for their potential impact, and interviewers should be trained in potential trouble areas to be avoided. If the premise is that the purpose of questions is to elicit information to be used in the evaluation process, then it makes sense to the applicant that if the question is asked, the employer will use the information. It may seem like innocent conversation to the interviewer, but if the applicant is rejected, then whether or not the information was gathered for discriminatory purposes, the applicant has the foundation for alleging that it illegally impacted the decision-making process. (See Exhibit 2.8.) Only questions relevant to legal considerations for evaluating the applicant should be asked. There is virtually always a way to elicit legal, necessary information without violating the law or exposing the employer to potential liability. A chatty, untrained interviewer can innocently do an employer a world of harm.

For example, idle, friendly conversation has included questions by interviewers such as "What a beautiful head of gray hair! Is it real?" (age); "What an interesting last name. What sort of name is it?" (national origin); "Oh, just the one child? Are you planning to have more?" (gender); "Oh, I see by your engagement ring that you're getting married! Congratulations! What does your fiancée do?" (gender). These questions may seem, or even be, innocent, but they can come back to haunt an employer later. Training employees who interview is an important way to avoid liability for unnecessary discrimination claims.

Conversation is not the only culprit. Sometimes it is job applications. Applications often ask the marital status of the applicant. Since there is often discrimination against married women holding certain jobs, this question has a potential disparate impact on married female applicants (but not married male applicants for whom this is generally not considered an issue). If the married female applicant is not hired, she can allege that it was because she was a married female. This may have nothing whatsoever to do with the actual reason for her rejection, but since the employer asked the question, the argument can be made that it did. In truth, employers often ask this question because they want to know whom to contact in case of an emergency should the applicant be hired and suffer an on-the-job emergency. Simply asking who should be contacted in case of emergency, or not soliciting such information until after the applicant is hired, gives the employer exactly what the employer needs without risking potential liability by asking questions about protected categories that pose a risk. That is why in opening Scenario 4, Jill, as one who interviews applicants, is in need of training, just like those who actually hire applicants.

Scenario

The Business Necessity Defense

LO7

business necessity
Defense to a disparate impact case based on the employer's need for the policy as a legitimate requirement for the job.

In a disparate impact claim, the employer can use the defense that the challenged policy, neutral on its face, that has a disparate impact on a group protected by law is actually job related and consistent with **business necessity**. For instance, an employee challenges the employer's policy of requesting credit information and demonstrates that, because of shorter credit histories, fewer women are hired than men. The employer can show that it needs the policy because it is in the business of handling large sums of money and that hiring only those people with good and stable credit histories is a business necessity. Business necessity may not be used as a defense to a disparate treatment claim.

In a disparate impact case, once the employer provides evidence rebutting the employee's *prima facie* case by showing business necessity or other means of rebuttal, the employee can show that there is a means of addressing the issue that has less of an adverse impact than the challenged policy. If this is shown to the court's satisfaction, then the employee will prevail and the policy will be struck down.

Knowing these requirements provides the employer with valuable insight into what is necessary to protect itself from liability. Even though disparate impact claims can be difficult to detect beforehand, once they are brought to the employer's attention by the employee, they can be used as an opportunity to revisit the policy. With flexible, creative, and innovative approaches, the employer is able to avoid many problems in this area.

Other Defenses to Employment Discrimination Claims

Once an employee provides *prima facie* evidence that the employer has discriminated, in addition to the BFOQ, legitimate non-discriminatory reason, and business necessity defenses discussed, the employer may perhaps present evidence of other defenses:

- That the employee's evidence is not true—that is, this is not the employer's policy as alleged or it was not applied as the employee alleges, the employee's statistics regarding the policy's disparate impact are incorrect and there is no disparate impact, or the treatment the employee says she or he received did not occur.

- That the employer's "bottom line" comes out correctly. We initially said that disparate impact is a statistical theory. Employers have tried to avoid litigation under this theory by taking measures to ensure that the relevant statistics will not exhibit a disparate impact. In an area in which they feel they may be vulnerable, such as in minorities' passing scores on a written examination, they may make decisions to use criteria that make it appear as if minorities do at least 80 percent as well as the majority, so the *prima facie* elements for a disparate impact case are not met. This attempt at an end run around Title VII was soundly rejected by the U.S. Supreme Court in *Connecticut v. Teal*.[23] In that case, an employer's written test exhibited a disparate impact on black employees who had already held their supervisory positions on a provisional basis for two years. Without a passing score on the written test, none of their other qualifications mattered and they could not move forward in the promotion process. To avoid liability, Connecticut used an unknown method to render the test scores as not having a disparate impact. The Supreme Court said this was not permissible, as it was equal employment opportunity required by law, not equal employment. Doing something to the test scores so that they no longer exhibited a disparate impact still left the black employees without an equal opportunity for the promotions. Note that this is also very often the reason you hear someone say there are "quotas" in a workplace. They are there *not* because the law requires them—it doesn't—but rather because the employer has self-imposed them to try to avoid liability. *Not* a good idea. The best policy is to have an open, fair employment process. Manipulating statistics to reach a "suitable" bottom-line outcome is *not* permitted.

Teal demonstrates that protective legislation requires equal employment *opportunity,* not simply equal *employment.* This is *extremely* important to keep in mind. It is *not* purely a "numbers game" as many employers, including the state of Connecticut, interpret the law. Under the Civil Rights Act of 1991, it is an unfair employment practice for an employer to adjust the scores of, or to use different cutoff scores for, or to otherwise alter the results of, an employment-related test on the basis of a prohibited category as was done in *Teal.*

Employers' policies should ensure that everyone has an equal chance at the job, based on qualifications. The *Teal* employees had been in their positions on a provisional basis for nearly two years before taking the examination. The employer therefore had nearly two years of actual job performance that it could consider to determine the applicant's promotability. Instead, an exam was administered, requiring a certain score, which exam the employer could not show to be related to the job. Of course, the logical question is, "Then why give it?" Make sure you ask yourself that question before using screening devices that may operate to exclude certain groups on a disproportional basis. If you cannot justify the device, you take an unnecessary risk by using it.

Accommodation

The next legal concept we will discuss is that of the accommodation requirement. Religious discrimination under Title VII, as well as disability discrimination under the Americans with Disabilities Act (ADA), both require that employers attempt to accommodate workplace conflicts based on these categories. Discrimination is simply prohibited on the basis of race, color, gender, national origin, or age. However, discrimination on the basis of religion or disability is prohibited only as long as trying to accommodate the conflict between the status and the workplace policy does not create an undue hardship for the employer. We only introduce you to the generalities of the concept here, but understand that the considerations are quite different for religious accommodation and accommodation of those with disabilities and they will be discussed in their own chapters. Suffice it to say that in both cases, rather than an out-and-out prohibition against discrimination, the employer must try to accommodate conflicts, but only up to the point that it creates an undue hardship on the employer. What constitutes an undue hardship varies and will be discussed in more detail in the chapters, but the concept of trying to accommodate conflicts is present for both religion and disability discrimination.

Exhaustion of Administrative Remedies

The statutory schemes set out for employment discrimination claims require that claimants first pursue their grievances within the agency created to handle such claims, the Equal Employment Opportunity Commission (EEOC). The EEOC

exhaustion of administrative remedies
Going through the EEOC administrative procedure before being permitted to seek judicial review of an agency decision.

back pay
Money awarded for time an employee was not working (usually due to termination) because of illegal discrimination.

front pay
Equitable remedy of money awarded to a claimant when reinstatement is not possible or feasible.

retroactive seniority
Seniority that dates back to the time the claimant was treated illegally.

make-whole relief
Attempt to put the claimant in position he or she would have been in had there been no discrimination.

compensatory damages
Money awarded to compensate the injured party for direct losses.

punitive damages
Money over and above compensatory damages, imposed by the court to punish the defendant for willful acts and to act as a deterrent.

will be discussed in detail in the Title VII chapter. All of the protective statutes provide for courts to hear employment discrimination claims only after the claimant has done all that can be done at the agency level. This is called **exhaustion of administrative remedies.**

Employment Discrimination Remedies

Title VII and other protective legislation have specific remedies available to employee claimants. Keep in mind that the tort remedies discussed in the employment-at-will part of the chapter are separate from the administrative remedies available to discrimination claimants. Also, these remedies are the basic ones available for winning employees, but some of the statutes may contain variations that you will learn as you read the chapters for those specific categories.

If the employee in an EEOC case is successful, the employer may be liable for **back pay** of up to two years before the filing of the charge with the EEOC; for **front pay** for situations when reinstatement is not possible or feasible for claimant; for reinstatement of the employee to his or her position; for **retroactive seniority**; for injunctive relief, if applicable; and for attorney fees. Until passage of the Civil Rights Act of 1991, remedies for discrimination under Title VII were limited to **make-whole relief** and injunctive relief.

The Civil Rights Act of 1991 added **compensatory damages** and **punitive damages** as available remedies. Punitive damages are permitted when it is shown that the employer's action was malicious or was done with reckless indifference to federally protected rights of the employee. They are not allowed under the disparate/adverse impact or unintentional theory of discrimination (to be discussed shortly) and may not be recovered from governmental employers. Compensatory damages may include future pecuniary loss, emotional pain, suffering, inconvenience, mental anguish, loss of enjoyment of life, and other nonpecuniary losses. (See Exhibit 2.9, "Employment Discrimination Remedies.")

There are certain limitations on the damages under the law. Gender discrimination (including sexual harassment) and religious discrimination have a $300,000 cap total on nonpecuniary (pain and suffering) compensatory and punitive damages. There is no limitation on medical compensatory damages. The cap depends on the number of employees the employer has. (See Exhibit 2.10, "Compensatory and Punitive Damages Caps.") Juries may not be told of the caps on liability. Since race and national origin discrimination cases also can be brought under 42 U.S.C. § 1981, which permits unlimited compensatory damages, the caps do not apply to these categories. In 2001, the U.S. Supreme Court ruled that, though compensatory damages are capped by the law, the limitations do not apply to front pay.[24] Also, as previously discussed, the U.S. Supreme Court's *Hoffman* decision[25] foreclosed the ability of undocumented workers to receive post-discharge back pay, and the EEOC rescinded its policy guidance suggesting otherwise.

With the addition of compensatory and punitive damages possible in Title VII cases, litigation increased dramatically. It is now more worthwhile for employees

---

Exhibit 2.9   *Employment Discrimination Remedies*

These are the basic remedies available, but as mentioned, some of the protective statutes provide additional remedies that will be discussed in those chapters.

Basic remedies

- Back pay
- Front pay
- Reinstatement
- Seniority
- Retroactive seniority
- Injunctive relief
- Compensatory damages
- Punitive damages
- Attorney fees
- Medical costs

Exhibit 2.10   *Compensatory and Punitive Damages Caps*

For employers with:

15 to 100 employees	Cap = $50,000
101 to 200 employees	Cap = $100,000
201 to 500 employees	Cap = $200,000
> 500 employees	Cap = $300,000

to sue and for lawyers to take the cases. The possibility of monetary damages also makes it more likely that employers will settle more suits rather than risk large damage awards. Again, the best defense against costly litigation and liability is solid, consistently applied workplace policies.

Additional Legal Resources

LO9 One of the things students often tell us is that they found this text so helpful that they decided to keep it rather than sell it after the course was over. They later find it quite helpful once they enter the workplace. With this in mind, and because we also understand that the text may not cover every single issue that may be of interest to you, we are including a section on how to find additional legal resources once you have been exposed to the law. Our section is not exhaustive but will give you quite enough to be able to search for additional information when the need arises. With the resources now available to everyone, there is no excuse not to be informed.

Law Libraries

Law libraries can be found everywhere from private firms to public courthouses and can contain only a few necessary legal resources or vast ones. While many of these are closed to the general public, check with your local sources to be certain. If you are lucky enough to live in or near a town that has a law school, there will inevitably be a law library and the legal world is within your reach. In addition to reporters containing law cases, there will also be law journals from around the world, legal treatises on any area of law you can imagine, books on legal issues, legal research updating sources, and local, state, federal and international legal resources. You do not need to be a lawyer or law student to be able to access most libraries and find what you are looking for. Most institutions open their doors to everyone, and that is certainly the case at public institutions. Depending on the nature of your inquiry, you may be able to simply place a call to the law librarian and ask for help with what you need. Law librarians are incredible founts of knowledge about legal resources available, how best to access them, and where to find what you need.

The Internet

One of the most exciting things that has happened since we first began writing this text is the advent of the Internet and its now virtually omnipresent use. We have rejoiced as it has expanded from a time when information was available only if you knew a Web site to which you could go directly, to the present time when search engines can find whatever you want in seconds. This evolution has been very exciting for us to watch as the Internet includes more and more legal databases for public consumption, taking the law out of the hands of the lucky few who could access it as lawyers and law students and giving it to the public at large who could now be much more informed. Such access is imperative for an informed democratic society. If you had not thought so before, surely you did as you watched the recent political situations unfold in Tunisia, Egypt, Libya, and elsewhere in North Africa and the Middle East. Knowledge is powerful, and the Internet brings unbelievable legal resources to your computer. A few well-chosen search terms can quickly bring you exactly what you are looking for.

We will list a few Web sites on which you can find legal resources for free, but there are also other legal databases that cost to access. Check with your institution or employer to see if they have available for you the legal databases of Westlaw or Lexis/Nexis. Both of these are vast full-service legal databases, but as you will see below, Lexis has limited free public access for at least the cases. In addition, many law firms maintain as part of their Web sites free recent information on issues they deal with. If you enter into a search engine the particular issue you wish to research, you will likely find many resources in addition to the ones listed here. At the end of the listings below, you will find two compilation resources that allow you to stay up to date by subject matter based on many of these resources created by law firms. Of course, we would welcome suggestions by students and faculty alike for general resources to add to this list.

- FindLaw is a great legal research Web site that is easy to navigate and has extensive legal resources. http://www.public.findlaw.com
- The U.S. Supreme Court maintains a Web site that includes access to its decisions. http://www.supremecourt.gov/
- The Oyez Project Web site has easily searchable major U.S. Supreme Court decisions that include media such as the Court's oral arguments. http://www.oyez.org/
- The Government Printing Office maintains a searchable Web site for federal agency regulations in the Code of Federal Regulations. http://www.gpoaccess.gov/cfr/index.html
- Municode.com provides links to municipal codes all over the country in an easily searched format. http://www.municode.com/Library/Library.aspx
- LexisOne is the public Web site adjunct of the Lexis/Nexis legal database and provides a searchable database of free cases. http://law.lexisnexis.com/webcenters/lexisone/
- Government Information Resources maintained by the University of Virginia provides links to administrative agency decisions and actions. http://www2.lib.virginia.edu/govtinfo/fed_decisions_agency.html
- Washlaw is a pretty comprehensive Web site maintained by the Washburn School of Law with free access to the public. http://www.washlaw.edu/uslaw/index.html
- The Social Science Research Network has an extensive library of journal articles and working papers on many topics, including law. http://papers.ssrn.com/sol3/DisplayAbstractSearch.cfm
- The Directory of Open Access Journals provides links to thousands of journals, including legal journals, that do not charge for access. http://www.doaj.org/
- Usa.gov is the opening portal to all types of government resources, including legal. http://www.usa.gov

- You are always allowed to hire the best person for a job; the law merely states that you may not make this decision based on prejudice or stereotypes. In order to avoid a wrongful discharge suit and, more importantly, to ensure the ethical quality of your decisions, do not fire someone for some reason that violates basic principles of dignity, respect, or social justice.

- Make sure that your policies and procedures create a space for employees to voice any concerns and complaints. It is most effective for employees to be able to share these issues with you long before they reach a breaking point. Then, make sure that everyone knows about them through appropriate training.

- You have the right to fire an employee for *any* reason as long as it is not for one of the specific reasons prohibited by law. On the other hand, if you do not have sufficient documentation or other evidence of the appropriate reason for your decision, a court might infer that your basis is wrongful.

- While it is unfortunate, to say the least, when an employee reports wrongdoing occurring at your firm, you may not retaliate against that person. Be sure to avoid even the *appearance* of retaliation, as the actual motivation for employment decisions is often difficult to prove.

- Have termination decisions be subject to internal review. Unilateral decisions to fire an employee may lead to emotion—or the *appearance of emotion*—rather than reason being used to determine terminations. Additional review can protect against this consequence.

- In the event of a layoff:
  - Clearly explain to employees the reasons for the actions taken: Document all efforts to communicate with employees.
  - Prepare the managers who will deliver the message.
  - Speak plainly and do not make promises.
  - Avoid euphemisms such as "We are all family and we will be together again someday."
  - Emphasize that it is not personal.
  - Know how layoffs will affect the demographic breakdown of the staff.

- Make sure employees are aware of their rights under the law regarding any protected category to which they may belong.

- Do not retaliate for employees pursuing legally protected rights!

- Do not forget that certain protected categories must be accommodated to the extent that such accommodation does not present an undue burden on the employer.

Source: Partially adapted from Matthew Boyle, "The Not-So-Fine Art of the Layoff," *Fortune,* March 19, 2001, pp. 209–210.

- The U.S. Senate's Web site can access information on U.S. laws, pending bills and other Senate business. Its Virtual Reference Desk is particularly helpful in accessing information organized around a particular topic. http://www.senate.gov/
- The Web site for the U.S. House of Representatives provides information on all aspects of pending and passed legislation for that body. http://www.house.gov/
- THOMAS is the Library of Congress's Web site that provides a wealth of information on legislation, including laws, treaties, and other legislative matters. http://thomas.loc.gov/
- The Legal Information Institute (LII) at Cornell University is one of the earliest public access legal databases formed with the intention to make the law accessible to all in an understandable way. It contains links to federal, state, and other legal resources. http://www.law.cornell.edu/
- The Congressional Research Service, which prepares reports on virtually any topic for members of Congress, maintains an open Web site to provide these reports to the public. http://opencrs.com/
- The Government Printing Office has a searchable database of all federal agency actions in the Federal Register. http://www.gpoaccess.gov/fr/index.html
- Mondaq provides legal, regulatory, and financial commentaries on recent rulings and other statutory events, organized by subject matter. You can subscribe to e-mail alerts organized by subject matter in order to stay current on those areas of the law that interest you (and related to over 70 countries). http://www.mondaq.com/
- In association with the Association of Corporate Counsel, http://www.lexology.com/ provides a service similar to Mondaq, with a greater focus on legal cases and their implications.

Chapter Summary

- With the concepts and information provided in this chapter, not only will you be able to navigate more easily and efficiently through the subsequent chapters, but you also have resources to use if you wish to know more or even to explore your own legal issues.
- Given the possibility of unlimited compensatory and punitive damage awards in wrongful discharge actions, employers are cautioned regarding their interpretation and implementation of the at-will employment arrangement. Employees' protections from unjust dismissal are not limited to statutes prohibiting employment discrimination based on certain factors. Increasingly, employees are able to rely on promises made by the employer through, for example, the employment policy manual.
- Further, public policy considerations beyond anti-discrimination protections also place limits on the manner in which an employer may terminate an employment relationship. An employer is prohibited from acting in a manner that undermines public policy, however defined.

- In employment discrimination cases, employee's facts must fit within one of two bases in order to be recognized under protective employment legislation. Disparate treatment and disparate impact each have their own unique requirements.
- It is not enough for an employee to simply feel there has been discrimination; the facts must fit within the law.
- Retaliation against an employee for pursuing rights provided by the law is a separate cause of action from the underlying employer action itself and can be found even when the underlying basis is not.
- Given the rise in retaliation claims in the courts and EEOC, it is imperative that employers not take adverse action against their employees for pursuing legitimate legal claims.

Chapter-End Questions

1. Ron and Megan Dible needed some extra money so they decided to charge money for viewing some sexually explicit photographs and videos of themselves that they had posted on the Internet. While this was an otherwise legal act, Ron Dible was a police officer, and after the Chandler Police Department, his employer, learned of his actions, he was terminated. Is his termination in violation of his right to freedom of expression under the First Amendment? [*Dible v. City of Chandler,* 502 F.3d 1040 (9th Cir. 2007).]

2. Think about the following questions from the point of view of violation of public policy or breach of a covenant of good faith and fair dealing, and see what the outcome would be.

   a. A female child care worker alleges that she was unlawfully terminated from her position as the director of a child care facility after continually refusing to make staff cuts. The staff cuts she was asked to make resulted in violation of state regulations governing the minimum ratios between staff and child. After the employee was terminated, the employer's child care center was in violation of the staff-to-child ratio. [*Jasper v. H. Nizam, Inc.,* 764 N.W.2d 751, 2009 Iowa Sup.]

   b. A machine operator employee with a major depressive disorder intermittently takes leaves under the Family and Medical Leave Act, resulting in alleged harassment by her employer surrounding her FMLA usage as well as a transfer to various difficult machines after her return from leave. Two months after her last FMLA leave, she is terminated for "improper phone usage." [*Hite v. Vermeer Mfg. Co.,* 361 F. Supp. 2d 935 (S.D. Iowa, 2005).]

   c. A nurse is asked by her employer to sign a backdated Medicare form. She refuses and is terminated that day. As a health care provider, she is required to complete that particular form. [*Callantine v. Staff Builders, Inc.,* 271 F.3d 1124 (8th Cir. 2001).]

   d. A legal secretary to a county commissioner is terminated because of her political beliefs. [*Armour v. County of Beaver,* 271 F.3d 417 (3d Cir. 2001).]

   e. A teacher under contract is terminated after insisting that his superiors report a situation where a student was being physically abused. The teacher refused to commit an illegal act of not reporting the suspected abuse to family services. [*Keveney v. Missouri Military Academy,* 304 S.W.3d 98 (MO 2010).]

f. A recent college graduate found a job with an office supply company as a reverse logistics analyst. Soon after being hired, he found that some practices within the department could be deemed unlawful and unethical. Three specific types of practices were written up in a formal complaint to his supervisor: (1) the issuing of monetary credits to customers without proper documentation, thus overpaying customers without returned goods; (2) the department's knowingly withholding from contract customers by underissuing credits over $25; and (3) the canceling and reissuing of pickup orders that could allow couriers to overbill the company. After his formal complaint and multiple meetings on the procedures of the department, the employee was terminated based on his insubordination and inflexibility. [*Day v. Staples Inc.*, 28 IER Cases 1121 (1st Cir. 2009).]

g. An employee engaged in protected whistle blowing activity after filing a complaint against his employer for his termination. The employee, a licensed optician, claimed his employer was violating state statute by allowing unlicensed employees to sell optical products without a licensed optician present. There was also a complaint filed to his supervisor about the promoting and hiring of unlicensed employees. [*Dishmon v. Wal-Mart Stores Inc.*, 28 IER Cases 1393 (M.D. Tenn. 2009).]

h. A legal secretary was hired by a law firm. The Letter of Employment stated, "In the event of any dispute or claim between you and the firm . . . including, but not limited to claims arising from or related to your employment or the termination of your employment, we jointly agree to submit all such disputes or claims to confidential binding arbitration, under the Federal Arbitration Act." On his third day of work, the employee informed his superiors that he would not agree to arbitrate disputes. He was told that the arbitration provision was "not negotiable" and that his continued employment was contingent upon signing the agreement. The employee declined to sign the agreement and was discharged [*Lagatree v. Luce, Forward, Hamilton & Scripps*, 74 Cal. App. 4th 1005 (Cal. App. 2d Div. 1 1999).]

i. An employee is licensed to perform certain medical procedures, but he is terminated for refusing to perform a procedure he is not licensed to perform. [*O'Sullivan v. Mallon*, 390 A.2d 149 (N.J. Super. Ct. Law Div. 1978).]

j. An employee was fired from his job as security manager for a medical center because he was suspected of making an obscene phone call to another employee and refused to submit to voice print analysis to confirm or refute the accusation. He sued the employer for wrongful discharge, claiming that the employer's request violated public policy. A state statute prohibits an employer from requiring an employee to submit to a polygraph examination as a condition or precondition of employment. [*Theisen v. Covenant Medical Center*, 636 N.W.2d 74 (Iowa 2001).]

3. Mariani was a licensed CPA who worked for Colorado Blue Cross and Blue Shield as manager of general accounting for human resources. She complained to her supervisors about questionable accounting practices on a number of occasions and was fired. She claims that her termination was in violation of public policy in favor of accurate reporting, as found in the Board of Accountancy Rules of Professional Conduct. BCBS claims that the rules are not an arbiter of public policy as ethics codes are too variable. Who is correct? [*Rocky Mountain Hospital v. Mariani*, 916 P.2d 519 (Colo. 1996).]

4. Patricia Meleen, a chemical dependency counselor, brought charges alleging wrongful discharge, defamation, and emotional distress against the Hazelden Foundation, a

chemical dependency clinic, in regard to her discharge due to her alleged sexual relations with a former patient. Hazelden's written employment policies prohibited unprofessional and unethical conduct, including sexual contact between patients and
counselors. A former patient alleged that Meleen had initiated a social and sexual .
relationship with him within one year of his discharge. A committee appointed by
Hazelden told Meleen of the allegation against her and suspended her with pay in spite
of Meleen's denial that she was involved in any improper relations or sexual contact
with the former patient. Hazelden offered Meleen a nonclinical position, and when she
refused, she was dismissed. Is the dismissal wrongful? [*Meleen v. Hazelden Foundation,* 928 F.2d 795 (8th Cir. 1991).]

5. Max Huber was the agency manager at Standard Insurance's Los Angeles office. He
   was employed as an at-will employee, and his contract did not specify any fixed duration of guaranteed employment. Huber was discharged by the company after eight
   years because of his alleged negative attitude, the company's increasing expense ratio,
   and the agency's decreasing recruiting. Huber provided evidence that he had never received negative criticism in any of his evaluations, and that his recruiting had been
   successful. Huber demonstrated that, even though the company had a decrease in recruitment during his employment, he himself had a net increase of contracted agents of
   1,100 percent. Huber claims that he was discharged because he was asked to write a
   letter of recommendation about his supervisor, Canfield, whose termination was being
   considered. Johnson, Canfield's supervisor, was disappointed with the positive recommendation that Huber wrote because it made Canfield's termination difficult to execute.
   Johnson is alleged to have transferred Huber to expedite Canfield's termination, and he
   eventually discharged Huber in retaliation for the positive letter of recommendation. If
   Huber files suit, what will the result be? [*Huber v. Standard Insurance Co.,* 841 F.2d
   980 (9th Cir. 1988).]

6. A new employer policy at a dental office stated that the employees were unable to leave
   the office except to use the restroom, even with a patient cancellation. A husband of an
   employee e-mailed the employer that he had discussed the new rules with an attorney
   who noted they were in violation of state law. The employer let the employee go soon
   after the complaint. Does the employee have a claim? [*Bonidy v. Vail Valley Ctr. for
   Aesthetic Dentistry, P.C.,* 186 P.3d 80, 2008 Colo.]

7. Althea, black, has been a deejay for a local Christian music station for several years.
   The station got a new general manager and within a month he terminated Althea. The
   reason he gave was that it was inappropriate for a black deejay to play music on a white
   Christian music station. Althea sues the station. What is her best theory for
   proceeding?

8. An employee files a race discrimination claim against the employer under Title VII.
   The employee alleges that after filing a claim with the EEOC, her rating went from
   outstanding to satisfactory and she was excluded from meetings and important
   workplace communications, which made it impossible for her to satisfactorily
   perform her job. The court denied the race discrimination claim. Must it also deny
   the retaliation claim? [*Lafate v. Chase Manhattan Bank,* 123 F. Supp. 2d 773
   (D. Del. 2000).]

9. Day Care Center has a policy stating that no employee can be over 5 feet 4 inches because the employer thinks children feel more comfortable with people who are closer to
   them in size. Does Tiffany, who is 5 feet 7 inches, have a claim? If so, under what theory could she proceed?

End Notes

1. For an expanded discussion of the evolution of the at-will environment, see Richard Bales, "Explaining the Spread of At-Will Employment as an Inter-Jurisdictional Race-to-the-Bottom of Employment Standards," *Tennessee Law Review* 75, no. 3 (2007), p. 1, http://ssrn.com/abstract=989013; Deborah A. Ballam, "Exploding the Original Myth Regarding Employment-at-Will: The True Origins of the Doctrine," *Berkeley Journal of Employment & Labor Law* 17 (1996), p. 91.

2. Bales, op. cit 128 Wash. 2d 931, 913 P.2d 377 (1996).

3. If the employer uses a contract to create the at-will relationship, the contract should state that the written document is their entire agreement and that only modifications in writing and signed by the employer will be valid.

4. 128 Wash. 2d 931, 913 P.2d 377 (1996).

5. Ibid. at 950 (emphasis added).

6. *Upton v. JWP Businessland*, 682 N.E.2d 1357 (Mass. 1997).

7. These states include Arizona, California, Colorado, Florida, Georgia, Hawaii, Illinois, Indiana, Maine, Maryland, Minnesota, Nevada, New Jersey, New York, Ohio, Oregon, Texas, Utah, Vermont, Virginia and West Virginia.

8. 78 Cal. Rptr. 2d 16 (Cal. 1998).

9. 126 S. Ct. 2405 (2006).

10. Ibid. at 2415.

11. *Mickey v. Zeidler Tool & Die Co., et al.,* 516 F.3d 516, 525 (6th Cir. 2008).

12. No. 2:05-CV-063, 2006 U.S. Dist. LEXIS 46328 (S.D. Ohio, 2006).

13. For a more detailed discussion of the implications of these holdings, see, e.g., J. W. Fincman, "The Inevitable Demise of the Implied Employment Contract," University of Colorado Law Legal Studies Research Paper No. 07-25 (September 17, 2007), http://ssrn.com/abstract=1015136.

14. See also *Buttrick v. Intercity Alarms, LLC,* No. 08-ADMS-40004, Massachusetts District Court, Appellate Division (June 17, 2009) (held not unreasonable for the employee to regard the employee manual as a binding commitment, thus implied contract).

15. For a comprehensive list, see Littler Mendelson, *The National Employer 2007–2008* (2007), www.littler.com.

16. *Anderson v. First Century Fed. Credit Union,* 738 N.W.2d 40, 46 (S.D. 2007); *Van Meter Industries v. Mason City Human Rights Commission,* 675 N.W.2d 503 (Iowa 2004). A minority of courts hold additional requirements such as that the former employee must also show that the employer created the intolerable working conditions with the specific intent of forcing the employee to quit. However, this intent can be inferred where the employee's departure is a reasonably foreseeable consequence of the employer's actions. *Martin v. Cavalier Hotel Corp.,* 67 FEP Cases 300 (4th Cir. 1995).

17. 2006 U.S. App. LEXIS 31895 (10th Cir. May 22, 2006).

18. Tex., No. 08-1337, jury verdict, May 26, 2010.

19. *Talley v. Family Dollar Stores of Ohio,* 542 F.3d 1099 (6th Cir. 2008).

20. *Coryell v. Bank One Trust,* 2008 Ohio 2698 (C.A. 2008).

21. 490 U.S. 642 (1989).

22. 487 U.S. 997 (1988).

23. 457 U.S. 440 (1982).

24. *Pollard v. E.I. du Pont de Nemours & Co.,* 532 U.S. 843 (2001).

25. *Hoffman Plastic Compounds, Inc. v. NLRB,* 535 U.S. 137 (2002).

26. We do not suggest the covenant of good faith and fair dealing has no function whatever in the interpretation and enforcement of employment contracts. As indicated above, the covenant prevents a party from acting in bad faith to frustrate the contract's *actual* benefits. Thus, for example, the covenant might be violated if termination of an at-will employee was a mere pretext to cheat the worker out of another contract benefit to which the employee was clearly entitled, such as compensation already earned. We confront no such claim here.

Palmateer v. International Harvester Company
85 Ill. 2d 124, 421 N.E.2d 876 (1981)

Case 1

Ray Palmateer had worked for International Harvester (IH) for 16 years at the time of his discharge. Palmateer sued IH for retaliatory discharge, claiming that he was terminated because he supplied information to local law enforcement authorities regarding a co-worker's criminal activities and for offering to assist in the investigation and trial of the co-worker if necessary. The court agreed and found in favor of Palmateer.

Simon, J.

***

[The court discusses the history of the tort of retaliatory discharge in Illinois and explains that the law will not support the termination of an at-will employment relationship where the termination would contravene public policy.] But the Achilles heel of the principle lies in the definition of public policy. When a discharge contravenes public policy in any way, the employer has committed a legal wrong. However, the employer retains the right to fire workers at-will in cases "where no clear mandate of public policy is involved."

There is no precise definition of the term. In general, it can be said that public policy concerns what is right and just and what affects the citizens of the State collectively. It is to be found in the State's constitution and statutes and, when they are silent, in its judicial decisions. Although there is no precise line of demarcation dividing matters that are the subject of public policies from matters purely personal, a survey of cases in other States involving retaliatory discharge shows that a matter must strike at the heart of a citizen's social rights, duties, and responsibilities before the tort will be allowed.

It is clear that Palmateer has here alleged that he was fired in violation of an established public policy. There is no public policy more basic, nothing more implicit in the concept of ordered liberty than the enforcement of a State's criminal code. There is no public policy more important or more fundamental than the one favoring the effective protection of the lives and property of citizens.

No specific constitutional or statutory provision requires a citizen to take an active part in the ferreting out and the prosecution of crime, but public policy nevertheless favors citizen crime-fighters. Public policy favors Palmateer's conduct in volunteering information to the law enforcement agency. Palmateer was under a statutory duty to further assist officials when requested to do so.

The foundation of the tort of retaliatory discharge lies in the protection of public policy, and there is a clear public policy favoring investigation and prosecution of criminal offenses. Palmateer has stated a cause of action for retaliatory discharge.

Case Questions

1. Is there a difference between the court's protection of an employee who reports a rape by a co-worker or the theft of a car, and an employee who is constantly reporting the theft of the company's paper clips and pens?

2. Should the latter employee in the above question be protected? Consider that the court in Palmateer remarked that "the magnitude of the crime is not the issue here. It was the General Assembly who decided that the theft of a $2 screwdriver was a problem that should be resolved by resort to the criminal justice system."

3. What are other areas of public policy that might offer protection to terminated workers?

Herawi v. State of Alabama, Department of Forensic Sciences *311 F. Supp. 2d 1335 (M.D. Ala. 2004)*

Herawi is an Iranian doctor whose employment was terminated. She filed a complaint against the defendant, the state Department of Forensic Sciences, alleging national origin discrimination and retaliation. The state responded that it had legitimate non-discriminatory reasons for terminating her (insubordination and poor job performance). The district court found that Herawi's national origin discrimination claim would not be dismissed on summary judgment because her supervisor's threat that she would report the doctor's national origin to law enforcement made clear that her supervisor was antagonistic towards her because of her Iranian heritage, and that the timing of the doctor's termination (three weeks after complaining about the supervisor's behavior) suggested that the supervisor's apparent dislike for her national origin may have infected the process of evaluating the doctor. Herawi also prevailed against summary judgment on the retaliatory discharge claim. (Herawi also claimed hostile environment but did not succeed and the discussion of that claim is not included below.)

OPINION BY: Myron H. Thompson, J.

***

II. Factual Background

During the relevant time period, Herawi's supervisor in the Montgomery office [of the Alabama Department of Forensic Sciences] was Dr. Emily Ward. Herawi, like all state employees, was a probationary employee for her first six months on the job.

Ward was highly critical of Herawi almost immediately upon her arrival in the Montgomery office. On her first day at work, Ward accused Herawi of being inconsiderate for not offering to help her. Ward looked at Herawi with a "hatred filled stare" and mocked her by repeating her in a high-pitched voice. On or about October 22, 2001, Ward became enraged at Herawi, shouted at her, accused her of wrongdoing, and said she had had enough of Herawi and that Herawi was the rudest person she had ever met. When Herawi tried to explain her actions, Ward yelled louder and said that she did not like Herawi and that no one else liked her either.

On October 24, Herawi expressed to Craig Bailey, the office director, her concerns about the way Ward was treating her. Bailey later told Herawi that, after his conversation with her, he spoke to Ward to find out if she had a problem with people of Middle Eastern descent. Bailey told Herawi that people from the Middle East were perceived as rude and aggressive.

On November 7, Ward "implied" to Herawi that she was getting calls from people asking about Herawi's background and her accent, and she threatened to expose Herawi's nationality to law enforcement agencies. Ward also said that she was getting calls from people asking who Herawi was, asking why she was there, and stating that she did not belong there.

Herawi had two more run-ins with Ward in December 2001, after Herawi had taken time off in November to visit her mother in California after the death of her father. On December 6, Ward called Herawi into her office, where Bailey yelled at Herawi, accusing her of neglecting the office after her father died and not performing enough autopsies. Bailey also questioned Herawi about whether she was looking for a job in California. On or about December 25, Herawi confronted Ward about whether Ward had spread a rumor that Herawi was looking for a job in California. [The court outlines additional, subsequent circumstances, which it discusses later in this opinion.]

On January 2, 2002, Herawi received an "employee probationary performance appraisal" and an attached narrative performance appraisal, dated November 15, 2001. The narrative performance appraisal states that Herawi "appears to be a very intelligent and dedicated Forensic Pathologist" and that she "seems to have been well trained." The narrative appraisal, however, goes on to state that "her performance has been problematic in four inter-related areas: expectations of co-workers, recognition of and subordination to authority, incessant inquisitiveness, and lack of organization." It also states that Herawi "comes across as very self-centered and projects an 'entitlement complex'"; that she "has also refused to comply with departmental regulations and/or rules if she doesn't agree with them"; and that her "work habits leave room for improvement." The narrative was signed by Ward and Downs, [J.C. Upshaw Downs, the Director of

the Alabama Department of Forensic Sciences and the Chief Medical Examiner for Alabama, and others.]

Herawi brought her concerns about Ward to Downs on January 4, 2002. Herawi told Downs that Ward had threatened to expose her nationality; Herawi also told Downs that she felt confused and intimidated. Downs told Herawi that Middle Eastern people were generally facing troubles in the wake of the terrorist attacks on September 11, 2001, and that Herawi should turn the other cheek. However, Downs said he would speak to Ward.

On January 9, 2002, Downs wrote a letter to Thomas Flowers, the state personnel director, requesting that Herawi's probationary period be extended by three months. Downs wrote that Herawi "requires additional training in autopsy procedures to take a more organized approach to the process" and that she "must also learn to use the chain of command."

***

Ward alluded to Herawi's nationality again on March 7, 2002. Ward told Herawi that nobody liked her, that everybody complained about her, that she did not belong there, that should leave, and that her English was bad. After this incident, Herawi complained to Downs again on March 21, about Ward's hostility. At this meeting, Downs told Herawi that he would start an investigation, and Herawi told Downs that she had contacted a lawyer. Herawi also complained to Samuel Mitchell, the department chief of staff, on March 25.

Events came to a head on March 28, at a meeting attended by Herawi, Ward, Bailey and Steve Christian, the department's personnel Manager. Herawi claims that she was terminated during the meeting and that when she met with Christian shortly after the meeting, he told her it was unofficial policy that terminated employees could submit a letter of resignation. Memoranda written by Ward, Bailey and Christian present slightly different accounts. According to Ward, she informed Herawi that the situation was not working out and that the department had not seen any improvement in the areas identified in Herawi's performance appraisal. According to Ward, before she could finish, Herawi interrupted her to say she would quit. According to Bailey, Ward requested Herawi's resignation, and Herawi agreed. According to Christian, Ward told Herawi that an offer of permanent employment would not be forthcoming and then told Herawi to speak with him later that day. When they met, according to Christian, he told her it was the department's unofficial policy to allow employees to resign to make it easier to look for work in the future.

Herawi submitted a letter of resignation on April 1, 2002. A letter from Downs, dated April 18, confirmed Herawi's "separation from employment" at the department effective April 19. Downs's letter states that the reason for Herawi's separation is that she continued "to require additional training in autopsy procedures and failure to properly use the chain of command."

III. Analysis

Herawi claims that (1) she was terminated because of her Iranian origin; (2) she was fired in retaliation for her complaints about Ward; and (3) she was harassed because of her national origin [not addressed in this excerpt]. The Forensic Department has moved for summary judgment on the ground that its decision not to offer her a permanent position was based on legitimate, non-discriminatory reasons. The court will consider Herawi's claims in order.

A. Termination

***

iv.

Applying *McDonnell Douglas*, this court concludes that Herawi has met her *prima-facie* burden of producing "evidence adequate to create an inference that [the Forensic Department's] employment decision was based on an [illegal] discriminatory criterion." To establish a *prima-facie* case of discriminatory discharge, she must show the following: (1) she is a member of a protected class; (2) she was qualified for the position at issue; (3) she was discharged despite her qualification; and (4) some additional evidence that would allow an inference of discrimination. [The court evaluates Herawi's evidence of these elements and finds that Herawi satisfies the first three elements; it then continues in its analysis of the fourth requirement, below.]

In this case, Ward made remarks related to Herawi's national origin on three occasions. On November 7, 2001, Ward threatened to report Herawi's national origin to law enforcement agencies. On January 2, 2002, Ward told Herawi that she was getting calls asking who Herawi was and why she was working there; Ward suggested that she was getting these calls because of Herawi's accent. Finally, on March 7, 2002, Ward told Herawi that no one liked her, that she did not belong at the department, that she should leave, and that her English was bad. It is undisputed that Ward was Herawi's direct supervisor when she made these remarks and that Ward had substantial input into the ultimate decision to terminate Herawi. In fact, Ward conducted Herawi's January 2002 performance appraisal, and she wrote the four memoranda in February and March of 2002 documenting incidents involving Herawi. Given this evidence, the court is satisfied that Herawi has raised the inference that her national origin was a motivating factor in the department's decision to terminate her.

The burden thus shifts to the Forensic Department to articulate a legitimate non-discriminatory reason for its decision to fire Herawi. The department has met this "exceedingly light" burden. It asserts that Herawi was not retained because she "had problems with autopsy procedures and with the chain of command." Plainly, job performance, failure to follow instructions, and insubordination are all legitimate, non-discriminatory considerations.

Because the department has met its burden, Herawi must show that its asserted reasons are pretextual. The court finds, again, that the evidence of Ward's comments about Herawi's national origin is sufficient for Herawi to meet her burden. Comments or remarks that suggest discriminatory animus can be sufficient circumstantial evidence to establish pretext. "Whether comments standing alone show pretext depends on whether their substance, context, and timing could permit a finding that the comments are causally related to the adverse employment action at issue."

In this case, Ward's comments "might lead a reasonable jury to disbelieve [the department's] proffered reason for firing" Herawi. Ward's threat that she would report Herawi's nationality to law enforcement makes it clear that she was antagonistic towards Herawi because of Herawi's Iranian origin. Ward's later comment that Herawi did not belong in the department, made at the same time she commented on Herawi's accent, further evinced discriminatory animus. Standing alone, this might not be enough evidence to establish a genuine question of pretext, but Ward was Herawi's supervisor, conducted her performance appraisal, and wrote four memoranda containing negative evaluations of her. In this context, the evidence suggests that Ward's evident dislike for Herawi's national origin may have infected the process of evaluating Herawi. The timing of Ward's remarks reinforces this conclusion. The first incident in which Ward referred to Herawi's nationality occurred one week before the narrative performance appraisal of Herawi was written, the second incident occurred on the same day—January 2, 2002—that Ward completed the performance appraisal form, and her final remarks were made three weeks before Herawi was fired. Because of this close temporal proximity, a jury could reasonably conclude that discriminatory attitude evidence in Ward's remarks motivated the decision to fire Herawi. Accordingly, the court finds that Herawi has met her burden and that summary judgment on her termination claim is not appropriate.

B. Retaliation

Herawi contends that the Forensic Department retaliated against her for complaining to Downs and to Mitchell about Ward's conduct. The department has moved for summary judgment, again, on the basis that its employment decision was motivated by legitimate, non-discriminatory reasons.

Under Title VII, it is an unlawful employment practice for an employer to discriminate against an employee "because [s]he has opposed any practice made an unlawful employment practice by this subchapter, or because [s]he has made a charge, testified, assisted, or participated in any manner in an investigation, proceeding, or hearing under this subchapter." The same *McDonnell Douglas* burden-shifting framework that applies to claims of discriminatory discharge applies to claims for retaliation.

The Eleventh Circuit has established broad standards for a *prima-facie* case of retaliation. An individual alleging retaliation under Title VII must establish her *prima-facie* case by demonstrating "(1) that she engaged in statutorily protected activity, (2) that an adverse employment action occurred, and (3) that the adverse action was causally related to [her] protected activities." "The causal link element is construed broadly so that a plaintiff merely has to prove that the protected activity and the negative employment action are not completely unrelated."

Herawi has established the elements of a *prima-facie* case of retaliation. First, she was engaged in protected activity on the two occasions that she spoke with Downs and on the one occasion she spoke to Mitchell. Second, Herawi was terminated. Third, Herawi satisfies the causality requirement because she was terminated only a week after her meeting with Downs and three days after her meeting with Mitchell.

Because Herawi has produced evidence sufficient to meet her *prima-facie* burden, the burden of production shifts to the Forensic Department to produce a legitimate, non-retaliatory reason for its decision. As discussed above, the department has offered legitimate reasons for its decision. The department contends that it fired Herawi because of her problems with autopsy procedure and her problems following the chain of command. The burden thus shifts to Herawi to come forward with evidence sufficient for a reasonable fact finder to conclude that the department's asserted reasons were pretext for retaliation.

Herawi has met this burden. As discussed above, Herawi has presented substantial evidence of Ward's animus towards her and thus raised a very real question about the extent to which the department's assessment of her might have been influenced by Ward's attitude. There is also evidence from which a reasonable fact finder could conclude that Ward's assessment of Herawi was infected by a retaliatory motive. In October 2001, Bailey reported to Ward that Herawi had complained to him about her, and, in January 2002, Downs spoke to Ward about Herawi's complaints. Thus, at the same time that Ward was evaluating and assessing Herawi's job performance in the fall of 2001, and the winter of 2002, she was aware that Herawi had gone to various supervisors to complain about her. The court also considers it relevant to determining pretext that Herawi was dismissed so soon after she complained to Downs and Mitchell. While temporal proximity, standing alone, may not be enough to create a genuine issue of pretext, it is a relevant factor. Thus, taking into consideration the evidence of Ward's discriminatory animus, her possible retaliatory motive, and the extreme closeness in time between Herawi's complaints and her dismissal, the court concludes that Herawi has evidence sufficient for a reasonable fact finder to conclude that the department's asserted reasons for her dismissal were pretextual.

***

IV. Conclusion

For the reasons given above, it is ORDERED as follows:

(1) The motion for summary judgment, filed by defendant Alabama Department of Forensic Sciences on November 12, 2003 (doc. no. 20), is granted with respect to plaintiff Mehsati Herawi's hostile-environment claim.

Case Questions

1. Are you persuaded by the state's evidence that it had an individual of a different national origin who was

treated similarly to Herawi? If Ward (or other managers) treated everyone equally poorly, perhaps there is no national origin claim. What if Ward's defense is simply that her poor treatment of Herawi had nothing to do with national origin, but that she just really did not like Hewari, specifically? Would that be an acceptable defense and could it have saved the state's case?

2. The court explains that pretext may be based on comments depending on "whether their substance, context, and timing could permit a finding that the comments are causally related to the adverse employment action at issue." What elements would you look to in order to find pretext, if you were on a jury?

3. The court explains that timing, alone, would not be enough to satisfy the causality requirement of retaliatory discharge. Given the facts of this case, if you were in charge of the department, and if Hewari truly were not performing at an acceptable level and you wished to terminate her after all of these circumstances, how might you have better protected the department from a retaliatory discharge claim?

Case 3 — Guz v. Bechtel National Inc. *100 Cal. Rptr. 2d 352 (Cal. 2000)*

Plaintiff John Guz, a longtime employee of Bechtel National, Inc. (BNI), was terminated at age 49 when his work unit was eliminated as a way to reduce costs. At the time he was hired and at his termination, Bechtel had a Personnel Policy (no. 1101) on the subject of termination of employment which explained that "Bechtel employees have no employment agreements guaranteeing continuous service and may resign at their option or be terminated at the option of Bechtel." Guz sued BNI and its parent, Bechtel Corporation, alleging age discrimination, breach of an implied contract to be terminated only for good cause, and breach of the implied covenant of good faith and fair dealing. The trial court found in favor of Bechtel and dismissed the action. The Court of Appeals reversed and determined that the trial should instead be permitted to proceed. Bechtel appealed to the Supreme Court of California, which in this opinion reverses the judgment of the Court of Appeals based on a finding that no *implied* contract exists and remands only for a determination of whether there are any enforceable *express* contract terms.

Baxter, J.

***

III. Implied Covenant Claim

Bechtel urges that the trial court properly dismissed Guz's separate claim for breach of the implied covenant of good faith and fair dealing because, on the facts and arguments presented, this theory of recovery is either inapplicable or superfluous. We agree.

The sole asserted basis for Guz's implied covenant claim is that Bechtel violated its established personnel policies when it terminated him without a prior opportunity to improve his "unsatisfactory" performance, used no force ranking or other objective criteria when selecting him for layoff, and omitted to consider him for other positions for which he was qualified. Guz urges that *even if his contract was for employment at-will,* the implied covenant of good faith and fair dealing precluded Bechtel from "unfairly" denying him the contract's benefits by failing to follow its own termination policies.

Thus, Guz argues, in effect, that the implied covenant can impose substantive terms and conditions beyond those to which the contract parties actually agreed. However, as indicated above, such a theory directly contradicts our conclusions in *Foley v. Interactive Data Corp.* (1988). The covenant of good faith and fair dealing, implied by law in every contract, exists merely to prevent one contracting party from unfairly frustrating the other party's right to receive the *benefits of the agreement actually made.* The covenant thus cannot "be endowed with an existence independent of its contractual underpinnings." It cannot impose substantive duties or limits on the contracting parties beyond those incorporated in the specific terms of their agreement.

. . . The mere existence of an employment relationship affords no expectation, protectable by law, that employment will continue, or will end only on certain conditions, unless the parties have actually adopted such terms. Thus if the employer's termination decisions, however arbitrary, do not breach such a substantive contract provision, they are not precluded by the covenant.

This logic led us to emphasize in *Foley* that "breach of the implied covenant cannot logically be based on a claim that [the] discharge [of an at-will employee] was made without good cause." As we noted, "[b]ecause the implied covenant protects only the parties' right to receive the benefit of their agreement, and, in an at-will relationship there is no agreement to terminate only for good cause, the implied covenant standing alone cannot be read to impose such a duty."

The same reasoning applies to any case where an employee argues that even if his employment was at-will, his arbitrary dismissal frustrated his contract benefits and thus violated the implied covenant of good faith and fair dealing. Precisely because employment at-will *allows* the employer freedom to terminate the relationship as it chooses, the employer does not frustrate the employee's contractual rights merely by doing so. In such a case, "the employee cannot complain about a deprivation of the benefits of continued employment, for the agreement never provided for a continuation of its benefits in the first instance."

At odds with *Foley* are suggestions that independent recovery for breach of the implied covenant may be available if the employer terminated the employee in "bad faith" or "without probable cause," i.e., without determining "honestly and in good faith that good cause for discharge existed." Where the employment contract itself allows the employer to terminate at-will, its motive and lack of care in doing so are, in most cases at least, irrelevant.

A number of Court of Appeal decisions since *Foley* have recognized that the implied covenant of good faith and fair dealing imposes no independent limits on an employer's prerogative to dismiss employees . . . We affirm that this is the law.

Of course, as we have indicated above, the employer's personnel policies and practices may become *implied-in-fact terms* of the contract between employer and employee. If that has occurred, the employer's failure to follow such policies when terminating an employee is a breach of the contract itself.

A breach of the contract may also constitute a breach of the implied covenant of good faith and fair dealing. But insofar as the employer's acts are directly actionable as a breach of an implied-in-fact contract term, a claim that merely realleges that breach as a violation of the covenant is superfluous. This is because, as we explained at length in *Foley,* the remedy for breach of an employment agreement, including the covenant of good faith and fair dealing implied by law therein, is *solely contractual.* In the employment context, an implied covenant theory affords no separate *measure of recovery,* such as tort damages. Allegations that the breach was wrongful, in bad faith, arbitrary, and unfair are unavailing; there is no tort of "bad faith breach" of an employment contract.

We adhere to these principles here. To the extent Guz's implied covenant cause of action seeks to impose limits on Bechtel's termination rights *beyond* those to which the parties actually agreed, the claim is invalid. To the extent the implied covenant claim seeks simply to invoke terms to which the parties *did* agree, it is superfluous. Guz's remedy, if any, for Bechtel's alleged violation of its personnel policies depends on proof that they were contract terms to which the parties actually agreed. The trial court thus properly dismissed the implied covenant cause of action.[26]

Case Questions

1. Based on *Guz,* can the implied covenant of good faith and fair dealing apply to any conditions not actually stated in a contract? In other words, can the covenant apply to anything beyond that which is actually stated in an employment contract? If not, is there no implied covenant as long as someone is at-will without a contract?

2. Explain the distinction between the court's discussion of the covenant of good faith and fair dealing and the possibility of an implied contract term.

3. How might an employer create an "implied-in-fact term" and how could a failure to follow such policies when terminating an employee create a breach of the contract?

McDonnell Douglas Corp. v. Green *411 U.S. 792 (1973)*

Green, an employee of McDonnell Douglas and a black civil rights activist, engaged with others in "disruptive and illegal activity" against his employer in the form of a traffic stall-in. The activity was done as part of Green's protest that his discharge from McDonnell Douglas was racially motivated, as were the firm's general hiring practices. McDonnell Douglas later rejected Green's reemployment application on the ground of the illegal conduct. Green sued, alleging race discrimination. The case is important because it is the first time the U.S. Supreme Court set forth how to prove a disparate treatment case under Title VII. In such cases the employee can use an inference of discrimination drawn from a set of inquiries the Court set forth.

Powell, J.

***

The critical issue before us concerns the order and allocation of proof in a private, nonclass action challenging employment discrimination. The language of Title VII makes plain the purpose of Congress to assure equality of employment opportunities and to eliminate those discriminatory practices and devices which have fostered racially stratified job environments to the disadvantage of minority citizens.

The complainant in a Title VII trial must carry the initial burden under the statute of establishing a *prima facie* case of racial discrimination. This may be done by showing (i) that he belongs to a racial minority; (ii) that he applied and was qualified for a job for which the employer was seeking applicants; (iii) that, despite his qualifications, he was rejected; and (iv) that, after his rejection, the position remained open and the employer continued to seek applicants from persons of complainant's qualifications. The facts necessarily will vary in Title VII cases, and the specification of the *prima facie* proof required from Green is not necessarily applicable in every respect to differing factual situations.

In the instant case, Green proved a *prima facie* case. McDonnell Douglas sought mechanics, Green's trade, and continued to do so after Green's rejection. McDonnell Douglas, moreover, does not dispute Green's qualifications and acknowledges that his past work performance in McDonnell Douglas' employ was "satisfactory."

The burden then must shift to the employer to articulate some legitimate, non-discriminatory reason for the employee's rejection. We need not attempt to detail every matter which fairly could be recognized as a reasonable basis for a refusal to hire. Here McDonnell Douglas has assigned Green's participation in unlawful conduct against it as the cause for his rejection. We think that this suffices to discharge McDonnell Douglas' burden of proof at this stage and to meet Green's *prima facie* case of discrimination.

But the inquiry must not end here. While Title VII does not, without more, compel the rehiring of Green, neither does it permit McDonnell Douglas to use Green's conduct as a pretext for the sort of discrimination prohibited by Title VII. On remand, Green must be afforded a fair opportunity to show that McDonnell Douglas' stated reason for Green's rejection was in fact pretext. Especially relevant to such a showing would be evidence that white employees involved in acts against McDonnell Douglas of comparable seriousness to the "stall-in" were nevertheless retained or rehired.

McDonnell Douglas may justifiably refuse to rehire one who was engaged in unlawful, disruptive acts against it, but only if this criterion is applied alike to members of all races. Other evidence that may be relevant to any showing of pretext includes facts as to McDonnell Douglas' treatment of Green during his prior term of employment; McDonnell Douglas' reaction, if any, to Green's legitimate civil rights activities; and McDonnell Douglas' general policy and practice with respect to minority employment.

On the latter point, statistics as to McDonnell Douglas' employment policy and practice may be helpful to a determination of whether McDonnell Douglas' refusal to rehire Green in this case conformed to a general pattern of discrimination against blacks. The District Court may, for example, determine after reasonable discovery that "the [racial] composition of defendant's labor force is itself reflective of restrictive or exclusionary practices." We caution that such general determinations, while helpful, may not be in and of themselves controlling as to an individualized hiring decision, particularly in the presence of an otherwise justifiable reason for refusing to rehire. In short, on the retrial Green must be given a full and fair opportunity to demonstrate by competent evidence that the presumptively valid reasons for his rejection were in fact a cover up for a racially discriminatory decision. VACATED and REMANDED.

Case Questions

1. Do you think the Court should require actual evidence of discrimination in disparate treatment cases rather than permitting an inference? What are the advantages? Disadvantages?

2. Practically speaking, is an employer's burden really met after the employer "articulates" a legitimate nondiscriminatory reason for rejecting the employee? Explain.

3. Does the Court say that Green must be kept on in spite of his illegal activities? Discuss.

Case 5

Wilson v. Southwest Airlines Company
517 F. Supp. 292 (N.D. Tex. Dallas Div. 1981)

A male sued Southwest Airlines after he was not hired as a flight attendant because he was male. The airline argued that being female was a BFOQ for being a flight attendant. The court disagreed.

Higginbotham, J.

***

Memorandum Opinion

Southwest conceded that its refusal to hire males was intentional. The airline also conceded that its height–weight restrictions would have an adverse impact on male applicants, if actually applied. Southwest contends, however, that the BFOQ exception to Title VII's ban on gender discrimination justifies its hiring only females for the public contact positions of flight attendant and ticket agent. The BFOQ window through which Southwest attempts to fly permits gender discrimination in situations where the employer can prove that gender is a "bona fide occupational qualification reasonably necessary to the normal operation of that particular business or enterprise." Southwest reasons it may discriminate against males because its attractive female flight attendants and ticket agents personify the airline's sexy image and fulfill its public promise to take passengers skyward with "love." The airline claims maintenance of its females-only hiring policy is crucial to its continued financial success.

Since it has been admitted that Southwest discriminates on the basis of gender, the only issue to decide is whether Southwest has proved that being female is a BFOQ reasonably necessary to the normal operation of its particular business.

As an integral part of its youthful, feminine image, Southwest has employed only females in the high customer contact positions of ticket agent and flight attendant. From the start, Southwest's attractive personnel, dressed in high boots and hot-pants, generated public interest and "free ink." Their sex appeal has been used to attract male customers to the airline. Southwest's flight attendants, and to a lesser degree its ticket agents, have been featured in newspaper, magazine, billboard, and television advertisements during the past 10 years. According to Southwest, its female flight attendants have come to "personify" Southwest's public image.

Southwest has enjoyed enormous success in recent years. From 1979 to 1980, the company's earnings rose from $17 million to $28 million when most other airlines suffered heavy losses.

The broad scope of Title VII's coverage is qualified by Section 703(e), the BFOQ exception. Section 703(e) states:

(e) Notwithstanding any other provision of this subchapter,

(1) It shall not be an unlawful employment practice for an employer to hire . . . on the basis of his religion, gender, or national origin in those certain instances

where religion, gender, or national origin is a bona fide occupational qualification reasonably necessary to the normal operation of that particular business or enterprise.

The BFOQ defense is not to be confused with the doctrine of "business necessity" which operates only in cases involving unintentional discrimination, when job criteria which are "fair in form, but discriminatory in operation" are shown to be "related to" job performance.

This Circuit's decisions have given rise to a two step BFOQ test: (1) does the particular job under consideration require that the worker be of one gender only; and if so, (2) is that requirement reasonably necessary to the "essence" of the employer's business. The first level of inquiry is designed to test whether gender is so essential to job performance that a member of the opposite gender simply could not do the same job.

To rely on the bona fide occupational qualification exception, an employer has the burden of proving that he had reasonable cause to believe, that is, a factual basis for believing, that all or substantially all women would be unable to perform safely and efficiently the duties of the job involved. The second level is designed to assure that the qualification being scrutinized is one so important to the operation of the business that the business would be undermined if employees of the "wrong" gender were hired. . . . The use of the word "necessary" in section 703(c) requires that we apply a business necessity test, not a business convenience test. That is to say, discrimination based on gender is valid only when the essence of the business operation would be undermined by not hiring members of one gender exclusively.

Applying the first level test for a BFOQ to Southwest's particular operations results in the conclusion that being female is not a qualification required to perform successfully the jobs of flight attendant and ticket agent with Southwest. Like any other airline, Southwest's primary function is to transport passengers safely and quickly from one point to another. To do this, Southwest employs ticket agents whose primary job duties are to ticket passengers and check baggage, and flight attendants, whose primary duties are to assist passengers during boarding and deboarding, to instruct passengers in the location and use of aircraft safety equipment, and to

serve passengers cocktails and snacks during the airline's short commuter flights. Mechanical, nongender-linked duties dominate both these occupations. Indeed, on Southwest's short-haul commuter flights there is time for little else. That Southwest's female personnel may perform their mechanical duties "with love" does not change the result. "Love" is the manner of job performance, not the job performed.

Southwest's argument that its primary function is "to make a profit," not to transport passengers, must be rejected. Without doubt the goal of every business is to make a profit. For purposes of BFOQ analysis, however, the business "essence" inquiry focuses on the particular service provided and the job tasks and functions involved, not the business goal. If an employer could justify employment discrimination merely on the grounds that it is necessary to make a profit, Title VII would be nullified in short order.

In order not to undermine Congress' purpose to prevent employers from "refusing to hire an individual based on stereotyped characterizations of the genders," a BFOQ for gender must be denied where gender is merely useful for attracting customers of the opposite gender, but where hiring both genders will not alter or undermine the essential function of the employer's business. Rejecting a wider BFOQ for gender does not eliminate the commercial exploitation of sex appeal. It only requires, consistent with the purposes of Title VII, that employers exploit the attractiveness and allure of a gender-integrated workforce. Neither Southwest, nor the traveling public, will suffer from such a rule. More to the point, it is my judgment that this is what Congress intended.

Case Questions

1. What should be done if, as here, the public likes the employer's marketing scheme?

2. Do you think the standards for BFOQs are too strict? Explain.

3. Should a commercial success argument be given more weight by the courts? How should that be balanced with concern for Congress's position on discrimination?

Griggs v. Duke Power Co. *401 U.S. 424 (1971)*

Case 6

Until the day Title VII became effective, it was the policy of Duke Power Co. that blacks be employed in only one of its five departments: the Labor Department. The highest-paid black employee in the Labor Department made less than the lowest-paid white employee in any other department. Blacks could not transfer out of the Labor Department into any other department. The day Title VII became effective, Duke instituted a policy requiring new hires to have a high school diploma and passing scores on two general intelligence tests in order to be placed in any department other than Labor and a high school diploma to transfer to other departments from Labor. Two months later, Duke required that transferees from the Labor or Coal Handling Departments who had no high school diploma pass two general intelligence tests. White employees already in other departments were grandfathered in under the new policy and the high school diploma and intelligence test requirements did not apply to them. Black employees brought this action under Title VII of the Civil Rights Act of 1964, challenging the employer's requirement of a high school diploma and the passing of intelligence tests as a condition of employment in or transfer to jobs at the power plant. They alleged the requirements are not job related and have the effect of disqualifying blacks from employment or transfer at a higher rate than whites. The U.S. Supreme Court held that the act dictated that job requirements which have a disproportionate impact on groups protected by Title VII be shown to be job related.

Burger, J.

***

We granted the writ in this case to resolve the question of whether an employer is prohibited by Title VII of the Civil Rights Act of 1964 from requiring a high school education or passing of a standardized general intelligence test as a condition of employment in or transfer to jobs when *(a)* neither standard is shown to be significantly related to successful job performance, *(b)* both requirements operate to disqualify Negroes at a substantially higher rate than white applicants, and *(c)* the jobs in question formerly had been filled only by white employees as part of a longstanding practice of giving preference to whites.

What is required by Congress [under Title VII] is the removal of artificial, arbitrary, and unnecessary barriers to employment when the barriers operate invidiously to discriminate on the basis of racial or other impermissible classifications.

The act proscribes not only overt discrimination but also practices that are fair in form, but discriminatory in operation. The touchstone is business necessity. If an employment practice which operates to exclude Negroes cannot be shown to be related to job performance, the practice is prohibited.

On the record before us, neither the high school completion requirement nor the general intelligence test is shown to bear a demonstrable relationship to successful performance of the jobs for which it was used. Both were adopted without meaningful study of their relationship to job performance ability.

The evidence shows that employees who have not completed high school or taken the tests have continued to perform satisfactorily and make progress in departments for which the high school and test criteria are now used.

Good intent or absence of discriminatory intent does not redeem employment procedures or testing mechanisms that operate as "built-in head winds" for minority groups and are unrelated to measuring job capability.

The facts of this case demonstrate the inadequacy of broad and general testing devices as well as the infirmity of using diplomas or degrees as general measures of capability. History is filled with examples of men and women who rendered highly effective performance without the conventional badges of accomplishment in terms of certificates, diplomas, or degrees. Diplomas and tests are useful servants, but Congress has mandated the commonsense proposition that they are not to become masters of reality.

Nothing in the act precludes the use of testing or measuring procedures; obviously they are useful. What

Congress has forbidden is giving these devices and mechanisms controlling force unless they are demonstrably a reasonable measure of job performance. Congress has not commanded that the less qualified be measured or preferred over the better qualified simply because of minority origins. Far from disparaging job qualifications as such, Congress has made such qualifications the controlling factor, so that race, religion, nationality, and sex become irrelevant. What Congress has commanded is that any tests used must measure the person for the job and not the person in the abstract. REVERSED.

Case Questions

1. Does this case make sense to you? Why? Why not?

2. The Court said the employer's intent does not matter here. Should it? Explain.

3. What would be your biggest concern as an employer who read this decision?

Chapter 3

Title VII of the Civil Rights Act of 1964

Learning Objectives

When you finish this chapter you should be able to:

LO1 Explain the history leading up to passage of the Civil Rights Act of 1964.

LO2 Give examples of the ways that certain groups of people were treated differently before passage of the Civil Rights Act.

LO3 Discuss what is prohibited by Title VII.

LO4 Recognize who is covered by Title VII and who is not.

LO5 State how a Title VII claim is filed and proceeds through the administrative process.

LO6 Determine if a Title VII claimant is able to proceed after receiving a no–reasonable-cause finding.

LO7 Distinguish between the various types of alternative dispute resolution used by EEOC.

LO8 Explain the Post-Civil War Statutes, including what each is and what it does.

LO9 Discuss what management can do to comply with Title VII.

Opening Scenarios

SCENARIO 1

1 Scenario Jack feels he has been discriminated against by his employer, based on national origin. After a particularly tense incident one day, Jack leaves work and goes to his attorney and asks the attorney to file suit against the employer for violation of Title VII of the Civil Rights Act of 1964. Will the attorney do so?

SCENARIO 2

2 Scenario Shelly receives an anonymous tip that she is making less money than all the other managers on her level, all of whom are male. Shelly believes it began when she did not receive a raise because she rejected advances by her supervisor six years before, and the wage gap has now grown far more than she realized. Shelly files a claim with the EEOC. Will she prevail?

SCENARIO 3

3 Scenario When Rinson did not receive the promotion he believed was his, he became upset. Rinson believes he did not receive the raise because his boss hates him and always judges Rinson's work harshly. If Rinson can prove this is true, does he have a valid claim for damages under Title VII?

Statutory Basis

Title VII of the Civil Rights Act of 1964

(a) It shall be an unlawful employment practice for an employer—

(1) to fail or refuse to hire or to discharge any individual, or otherwise to discriminate against any individual with respect to his compensation, terms, conditions, or privileges of employment, because of such individual's race, color, religion, sex, or national origin; or

(2) to limit, segregate, or classify his employees or applicants for employment in any way which would deprive or tend to deprive any individual of employment opportunities or otherwise adversely affect his status as an employee, because of such individual's race, color, religion, sex, or national origin. Title VII of the Civil Rights Act of 1964, as amended, 42 U.S.C.A. sec. 2000e et seq., sec. 703 (a).

A Historic Rights Act

LO1 "A strong and prosperous nation secured through a fair and inclusive workplace."[1]

LO2 Such a simple statement. Who could disagree with such a vision? It is the vision of the Equal Employment Opportunity Commission (EEOC), the federal agency charged with enforcing laws that were created to make that statement a reality. However, not everyone agrees with that vision, or realizes when they may not be acting consistent with it, so though we have come a long way in the 40+ years since the law was passed creating the agency, unfortunately, there is still much work to be done.

Title VII of the Civil Rights Act of 1964 is the single most important piece of legislation that has helped to shape and define employment law rights in this country. It was an ambitious piece of social legislation, the likes of which had never been attempted here, so passage of the law was not an easy task.

The Civil Rights Act of 1964 prohibits discrimination in education, employment, public accommodations, and the receipt of federal funds on the basis of race, color, gender, national origin, and religion. Although several categories of discrimination are included in the law, it was racial discrimination that was truly the moving force for its enactment. Since the world you live in today is so different from the one that existed when Title VII was passed, it is important for you to understand the world as it was then or the law will not seem to make much sense. We will take a few minutes to paint a picture for you. Some of the picture you may be vaguely aware of, but may not truly understand the import of.

Historical Context Leading to the Need for the Civil Rights Act of 1964

We know most students' eyes glaze over when the word *history* is mentioned, but not only is this history interesting, it is imperative for you to know in order to understand the law with which we will be dealing. Just bear with us for a few minutes, and we promise it will be worth your while.

Africans had been brought to America from Africa to be slaves, period. No other role was envisioned for them. It was thus not surprising that when slavery ended 246 years later, the country struggled mightily with the idea of forging a new relationship with African Americans with whom they had no legal or social relationship other than ownership or African Americans serving their needs in the most menial ways. After the Civil War ended slavery, the next 99 years saw many in the country resisting that change, learning how they could live with that change but, in many ways, still retain the familiar world they had known.

The overall response was Jim Crow laws. This was a system of racial segregation practiced virtually everywhere in the United States. The system was enforced through law, ironclad social custom, and, many times, violence.

The separation between the races was complete. There were laws regulating the separation of blacks and whites in every facet of life from birth to death.[2] Laws prohibited blacks and whites from marrying, going to school together, and working together. Every facility imaginable was segregated, including movie theaters, restaurants, hospitals, cemeteries, libraries, funeral homes, doctors' waiting rooms, swimming pools, taxicabs, churches, housing developments, parks, water fountains, colleges, public transportation, recreational facilities, toilets, social organizations, and stores. Blacks could not vote, sue whites, testify against them, raise their voice to them, or even look them in the eye or stay on the sidewalk if they passed by. If an African American wanted to buy shoes, he or she had to bring a paper cutout of the foot, rather than try the shoe on in the store. If he needed pants, he brought to the store a length of string the size of his waist. Of course it was unthinkable to allow an item purchased by an African American customer to be returned, even if it did not fit. If blacks wanted food from a restaurant, they had to go to the back door and order it to be taken away. For young black boys, the first few days of school were spent in book repositories taping up old, outdated books no longer used by white schools, which could now be used by blacks who never received new ones. However, even this was for only the lucky black students who did not have to forgo school to pick the cotton crop when it was ready for harvest.

The South attempted to maintain its cheap labor force of blacks in several ways. These included instituting peonage laws that allowed blacks without the means of making bail to be arrested for virtually anything, then "loaned out" by the sheriff to white farmers or others needing cheap labor, ostensibly under the guise of working off their bond. Sharecropping was common, with the white owner of the property hiring blacks to work it in return for a share of the proceeds from the crop. Land-owners routinely cheated blacks out of their share of the earnings, so that the destitute sharecropper, often in debt to the landowner, would have to continue to work for the landowner.[3] For those blacks who stepped out of line, the consequences were dire. Termination, being thrown off the farms and plantations (yes, there were still plantations in the early 1960s) they worked on if they challenged any decision of the owner, burning of homes, beatings, and lynchings were all common.[4]

Separation of the races was complete under Jim Crow, and Jim Crow was only outlawed in 1964, the year the Beatles descended upon America from Britain and rocked the music world. (See Exhibit 3.1, "June 1961

Exhibit 3.1 *June 1961 (Pre–Title VII) Newspaper Want Ad*

This exhibit, taken from an actual newspaper, is typical of the index to want ads from the classified section found in newspapers in the United States before Title VII was passed in 1964. Note the separate categories based on race and gender. This is no longer legal under Title VII.

INDEX TO WANT ADS	Colored Employment
Announcements	26—Help Wanted Male, Colored
1—Funeral Notices	27—Employment Agency Male, Colored
2—Funeral Notices, Colored	28—Situations Wanted Male, Colored
	29—Help Wanted Female, Colored
Male Employment	30—Employment Agency Female, Colored
	31—Situations Wanted Female, Colored
14—Male Help Wanted	
15—Male Employment Agencies	
16—Situations Wanted, Male	
17—Male, Female Help Wanted	
Female Employment	
22—Female Help Wanted	
23—Female Employment Agencies	
24—Situations Wanted, Female	

Newspaper Want Ad.") This may not be pleasant to read but imagine living it. It simply was the way things were and had been in the 99 years since slavery ended.[5] It is not happenstance that the blues, a uniquely American genre of music known and loved around the world, was borne of these circumstances.

The doctrine of separate but equal educational facilities had fallen 10 years before passage of the Civil Rights Act, with the U.S. Supreme Court's 1954 decision in *Brown v. Topeka Board of Education.*[6] However, states were still fighting the change in any number of ways, from closing down public schools completely, to using public revenue to fund all-white private schools established after the Supreme Court's decision.[7]

But blacks began pushing back. Citizens were challenging infringements upon the right of blacks to vote. There were boycotts, "freedom rides," and sit-in demonstrations for the right to nonsegregated public accommodations, transportation, municipal parks, swimming pools, libraries, and lunch counters. There was racial unrest, strife, marches, and civil disobedience on as close to a mass scale as this country has ever experienced.[8] Something had to give.

In an impressive show of how important societal considerations can be in shaping law, the 1964 Civil Rights Act was passed the year after the historic August 28, 1963, March on Washington. It was at this march that the late Rev. Dr. Martin Luther King Jr. gave his famous "I Have a Dream" speech (see Exhibit 3.2, "Dr. Martin Luther King Jr.'s 'I Have a Dream Speech'") on the steps of the Lincoln Memorial. In the largest march of its kind ever held in this country until then, hundreds of thousands of people of all races, creeds, colors, and walks of life traveled from around the world to show legislators that legalized racism was no longer tolerable in a society that considered itself to be civilized. Just two weeks later, 4 little black girls were killed and 20 others injured by a bomb tossed into the Sixteenth Street Baptist Church by whites in Birmingham, as the girls donned their robes and prepared to sing in the choir at Sunday's church service. Two months later, President Kennedy, who had proposed the bill, was assassinated. These and other factors demonstrated in stark terms that it was time to change the status quo and move from the racially segregated Jim Crow system the country had employed in the 99 years since the end of the Civil War, to something more akin to the equality the Constitution promised to all.

The 54-day Senate filibuster against the bill was led by Sen. Richard Russell (D-GA), who had the reputation of being the leader of white supremacists in the Senate and the head of the very powerful southern voting bloc. In opposing the bill, Russell famously said, "We will resist to the bitter end any measure or any movement which would have a tendency to bring about social equality and intermingling and amalgamation of the races in our southern states."[9]

The legislation eventually passed and President Johnson used 72 commemorative ink pens to sign it into law.

Title VII: The Legislation

Title VII of the Civil Rights Act of 1964 is the employment section of the act, but it is only one title of a much larger piece of legislation. The Civil Rights Act of 1964 also created the legal basis for non-discrimination in education, public accommodations, and federally assisted programs. Since employment in large measure defines the availability of the other matters, the case law in Title VII of the Civil Rights Act quickly became the most important arbiter of rights under the new law. In President John F. Kennedy's original message to Congress upon introducing the bill in 1963, he stated: "There is little value in a Negro's obtaining the right to be admitted to hotels and restaurants if he has no cash in his pocket and no job."

The face of the workplace has changed dramatically since the passage of the act. Because of the law, more women and minorities than ever before are engaged in meaningful employment. While Title VII applies equally to everyone, because of the particular history behind the law it gave new rights to women and minorities, who had only limited access to the workplace and limited legal recourse for job discrimination before the act. As discussed in the toolkit chapter, with the passage of Title VII, the door was opened to prohibiting job discrimination and creating expectations of fairness in employment overall. It was not long before additional federal legislation followed providing similar protection from discrimination in the workplace based on age, Vietnam veteran status, disabilities, and, later, genetic information. Like a ripple effect, not only did the law usher in the expectations that you now have that you will be treated equally because you live in the United States and we have such laws, but anti-discrimination laws were enacted all over the world in the wake of the Civil Rights Act of 1964. The courage exhibited by African Americans and their supporters in standing up to the government and challenging long-held beliefs relegating them to second-class citizenship emboldened other groups here and around the world to challenge their treatment as well.

State and local governments passed laws paralleling Title VII and the other protective legislation. Some laws added categories such as marital status, political affiliation, affinity orientation, or receipt of public benefits, as prohibited categories of discrimination. For instance, California prohibits discrimination on the basis of being a victim of domestic violence and imposed personal liability on co-workers regardless of whether the employer knew or should have known of the conduct and failed to take immediate corrective action. Washington, D.C., added personal appearance to its list of prohibited categories. Michigan is the only state that includes protection on the basis of obesity.

The new expectations did not stop there. As we saw in the toolkit chapter, others not included in the coverage of the statutes came to have heightened expectations about the workplace and their role within it and were willing to pressure legislators and sue employers in pursuit of these expected rights. The exceptions created in the employment-at-will doctrine largely owe their existence to the expectations caused by Title VII. Once Title VII protected employees from unjust

Exhibit 3.2   *Dr. Martin Luther King Jr.'s "I Have A Dream" Speech*

Now that you have some of the historical background behind the need for a civil rights law, you are also better able to see that Dr. King did an excellent job of capturing the state of race in America in the year before the Civil Rights Act of 1964 was enacted. While many, many factors resulted in the eventual passage of the law, the year after this speech, the Civil Rights Act of 1964 was passed by Congress and Dr. King won the Nobel Peace Prize. Dr. King was the face of "speaking truth to power," but there were thousands of nameless, "foot soldiers for justice" behind him that took their physical and economic lives and those of their families into their hands when they made the decision to stand up to oppression.[10] The speech became a rallying cry for people all over the world who suffered oppression at the hands of their governments and/or societies. You have no doubt heard excerpts of the speech at some point, but it may well prove helpful to actually read in its entirety the words that were so powerful that they helped change the laws of a nation, release millions of its citizens from a racial prison of long standing, and dismantle the system that kept them there for so long.

I am happy to join with you today in what will go down in history as the greatest demonstration for freedom in the history of our nation.

Five score years ago, a great American, in whose symbolic shadow we stand today, signed the Emancipation Proclamation. This momentous decree came as a great beacon light of hope to millions of Negro slaves who had been seared in the flames of withering injustice. It came as a joyous daybreak to end the long night of their captivity.

But one hundred years later, the Negro still is not free. One hundred years later, the life of the Negro is still sadly crippled by the manacles of segregation and the chains of discrimination. One hundred years later, the Negro lives on a lonely island of poverty in the midst of a vast ocean of material prosperity. One hundred years later, the Negro is still languishing in the corners of American society and finds himself an exile in his own land. So we have come here today to dramatize a shameful condition.

In a sense we have come to our nation's capital to cash a check. When the architects of our republic wrote the magnificent words of the Constitution and the Declaration of Independence, they were signing a promissory note to which every American was to fall heir. This note was a promise that all men, yes, black men as well as white men, would be guaranteed the unalienable rights of life, liberty, and the pursuit of happiness.

It is obvious today that America has defaulted on this promissory note insofar as her citizens of color are concerned. Instead of honoring this sacred obligation, America has given the Negro people a bad check, a check which has come back marked "insufficient funds." But we refuse to believe that the bank of justice is bankrupt. We refuse to believe that there are insufficient funds in the great vaults of opportunity of this nation. So we have come to cash this check—a check that will give us upon demand the riches of freedom and the security of justice. We have also come to this hallowed spot to remind America of the fierce urgency of now. This is no time to engage in the luxury of cooling off or to take the tranquilizing drug of gradualism. Now is the time to make real the promises of democracy. Now is the time to rise from the dark and desolate valley of segregation to the sunlit path of racial justice. Now is the time to lift our nation from the quick sands of racial injustice to the solid rock of brotherhood. Now is the time to make justice a reality for all of God's children.

It would be fatal for the nation to overlook the urgency of the moment. This sweltering summer of the Negro's legitimate discontent will not pass until there is an invigorating autumn of freedom and equality. Nineteen sixty-three is not an end, but a beginning. Those who hope that the Negro needed to blow off steam and will now be content will have a rude awakening if the nation returns to business as usual. There will be neither rest nor tranquility in America until the Negro is granted his citizenship rights. The whirlwinds of revolt will continue to shake the foundations of our nation until the bright day of justice emerges.

But there is something that I must say to my people who stand on the warm threshold which leads into the palace of justice. In the process of gaining our rightful place we must not be guilty of wrongful deeds. Let us not seek to satisfy our thirst for freedom by drinking from the cup of bitterness and hatred.

We must forever conduct our struggle on the high plane of dignity and discipline. We must not allow our creative protest to degenerate into physical violence. Again and again we must rise to the majestic heights of meeting physical force with soul force. The marvelous new militancy which has engulfed the

continued

Negro community must not lead us to distrust of all white people, for many of our white brothers, as evidenced by their presence here today, have come to realize that their destiny is tied up with our destiny and their freedom is inextricably bound to our freedom. We cannot walk alone.

As we walk, we must make the pledge that we shall march ahead. We cannot turn back. There are those who are asking the devotees of civil rights, "When will you be satisfied?" We can never be satisfied as long as the Negro is the victim of the unspeakable horrors of police brutality. We can never be satisfied, as long as our bodies, heavy with the fatigue of travel, cannot gain lodging in the motels of the highways and the hotels of the cities. We can never be satisfied as long as a Negro in Mississippi cannot vote and a Negro in New York believes he has nothing for which to vote. No, no, we are not satisfied, and we will not be satisfied until justice rolls down like waters and righteousness like a mighty stream.

I am not unmindful that some of you have come here out of great trials and tribulations. Some of you have come fresh from narrow jail cells. Some of you have come from areas where your quest for freedom left you battered by the storms of persecution and staggered by the winds of police brutality. You have been the veterans of creative suffering. Continue to work with the faith that unearned suffering is redemptive.

Go back to Mississippi, go back to Alabama, go back to South Carolina, go back to Georgia, go back to Louisiana, go back to the slums and ghettos of our northern cities, knowing that somehow this situation can and will be changed. Let us not wallow in the valley of despair.

I say to you today, my friends, so even though we face the difficulties of today and tomorrow, I still have a dream. It is a dream deeply rooted in the American dream.

I have a dream that one day this nation will rise up and live out the true meaning of its creed: "We hold these truths to be self-evident: that all men are created equal."

I have a dream that one day on the red hills of Georgia the sons of former slaves and the sons of former slave owners will be able to sit down together at the table of brotherhood.

I have a dream that one day even the state of Mississippi, a state sweltering with the heat of injustice, sweltering with the heat of oppression, will be transformed into an oasis of freedom and justice.

I have a dream that my four little children will one day live in a nation where they will not be judged by the color of their skin but by the content of their character.

I have a dream today.

I have a dream that one day, down in Alabama, with its vicious racists, with its governor having his lips dripping with the words of interposition and nullification; one day right there in Alabama, little black boys and black girls will be able to join hands with little white boys and white girls as sisters and brothers.

I have a dream today.

I have a dream that one day every valley shall be exalted, every hill and mountain shall be made low, the rough places will be made plain, and the crooked places will be made straight, and the glory of the Lord shall be revealed, and all flesh shall see it together.

This is our hope. This is the faith that I go back to the South with. With this faith we will be able to hew out of the mountain of despair a stone of hope. With this faith we will be able to transform the jangling discords of our nation into a beautiful symphony of brotherhood. With this faith we will be able to work together, to pray together, to struggle together, to go to jail together, to stand up for freedom together, knowing that we will be free one day.

This will be the day when all of God's children will be able to sing with a new meaning, "My country, 'tis of thee, sweet land of liberty, of thee I sing. Land where my fathers died, land of the pilgrim's pride, from every mountainside, let freedom ring."

And if America is to be a great nation this must become true. So let freedom ring from the prodigious hilltops of New Hampshire. Let freedom ring from the mighty mountains of New York. Let freedom ring from the heightening Alleghenies of Pennsylvania!

Let freedom ring from the snowcapped Rockies of Colorado!

Let freedom ring from the curvaceous slopes of California!

But not only that; let freedom ring from Stone Mountain of Georgia!

Let freedom ring from Lookout Mountain of Tennessee!

Let freedom ring from every hill and molehill of Mississippi. From every mountainside, let freedom ring.

And when this happens, when we allow freedom to ring, when we let it ring from every village and every hamlet, from every state and every city, we will be able to speed up that day when all of God's children, black men and white men, Jews and Gentiles, Protestants and Catholics, will be able to join hands and sing in the words of the old Negro spiritual, "Free at last! free at last! thank God Almighty, we are free at last!"

Source: www.usconstitution.net/dream.html, accessed July 27, 2007.

dismissal on the basis of discrimination, it made it easier for judges and legislators to take the step of extending it to other terminations that came to be considered as not in keeping with this evolving view of the employment relationship.

For employers, Title VII meant that the workplace was no longer a place in which decisions regarding hiring, promotion, and the like could go unchallenged. Now there were prohibitions on some of the factors that had previously been a part of many employers' considerations such as race and gender (again, see, e.g., Exhibit 3.1 showing the text of an actual newspaper classified ad categorized by race and gender). Employers had been feeling the effects of federal regulation in the workplace for some time. Among other regulations, wage and hour and child labor laws governed minimum ages, wages, and permissible work hours that employers could impose, and labor laws protected collective bargaining. Now came Title VII, prohibiting certain bases an employer could use to hire or promote employees. The idea of evolving from employment-at-will to these "intrusions" into the employer's heretofore sole domain of making workplace decisions took some getting used to.

After enactment, Title VII was amended several times to further strengthen it. There were amendments in 1972 and 1978, with the passage of the Equal Employment Opportunity Act of 1972 and the Pregnancy Discrimination Act of 1978. The 1972 amendment expanded Title VII's coverage to include government employees and to strengthen the enforcement powers of the enforcing agency created by the law, the Equal Employment Opportunity Commission (EEOC). The 1978 amendment added discrimination on the basis of pregnancy as a type of gender discrimination. In addition, Title VII and other workplace protections were extended to congressional employees in the Congressional Accountability Act of 1995.

In the most far-reaching overhaul since its passage, the act was also amended by the Civil Rights Act of 1991. This amendment added jury trials, compensatory and punitive damages where appropriate, and several other provisions, further strengthening the law. (See Exhibit 3.3, "The Civil Rights Act of 1991.")

The EEOC is now the lead agency for handling issues of job discrimination and deals with most matters of employment discrimination arising under federal laws, including age, disability, and genetic information and family medical history. The U.S. Department of Justice handles cases involving most government agencies such as police and fire departments. The Office of Federal Contract Compliance Programs (OFCCP) enforces Executive Order 11246 prohibiting employment discrimination by those receiving government contracts and imposing affirmative action under certain circumstances. The EEOC has implemented regulations that govern agency procedures and requirements under the law, and it provides guidelines to employers for dealing with employment discrimination laws.[11]

Most employers have come to accept the reality of Title VII. Some have gone beyond acceptance and grown to appreciate the diversity and breadth of the workplace that the law engenders. Most of the work at this point is in fine-tuning what it means to not discriminate in employment and keeping a reign on employers who engage in such activity. For instance, there have been growing complaints of

Exhibit 3.3 *The Civil Rights Act of 1991*

When the Civil Rights Act of 1991 was signed into law by President George Bush on November 21, 1991, it was the end of a fierce battle that had raged for several years over the increasingly conservative decisions of the U.S. Supreme Court in civil rights cases. The new law was a major overhaul for Title VII. The law's nearly 30-year history was closely scrutinized. It is significant for employers that, when presented the opportunity, Congress chose to strengthen the law in many ways, rather than lessen its effectiveness. Among other things, the new law for the first time in Title VII cases:

- Permitted:
  —Jury trials where compensatory or punitive damages are sought.
  —Compensatory damages in religious, gender, and disability cases (such damages were already allowed for race and national origin under related legislation).
  —Punitive damages for the same (except against governmental agencies).
  —Unlimited medical expenses.
- Limited the extent to which "reverse discrimination" suits could be brought.

- Authorized expert witness fees to successful plaintiffs.
- Codified the disparate impact theory.
- Broadened protections against private race discrimination in 42 U.S.C. § 1981 cases.
- Expanded the right to bring actions challenging discriminatory seniority systems.
- Extended extraterritorial coverage of Title VII to U.S. citizens working for U.S. companies outside the United States, except where it would violate the laws of the country.
- Extended coverage and established procedures for Senate employees.
- Established the Glass Ceiling Commission.
- Established the National Award for Diversity and Excellence in American Executive Management (known as the Frances Perkins–Elizabeth Hanford Dole National Award for Diversity and Excellence in American Executive Management) for businesses who "have made substantial efforts to promote the opportunities and development experiences of women and minorities and foster advancement to management and decision-making positions within the business."

nooses found in black employees' work areas, a growing number of class action suits regarding unequal pay and promotions for women, and a surge in discrimination against Muslims in the workplace, ranging from harassment to failure to accommodate their prayer schedules.

The EEOC has moved into the "new frontier" of combatting human trafficking as it relates to race, national origin, and sexual harassment.[12] In light of the enormous impact of unemployment and housing foreclosures, the EEOC is also exploring the impact of those events, as well as of the use of credit histories on women, minorities and the disabled as an unlawful employment screening device.[13] As interracial marriages increased, with the accompanying increase in multiracial employees, the agency introduced its E-RACE (Eradicating Racism and Colorism in Employment) Initiative to address the more subtle manifestations of color discrimination. The agency also testified on the Paycheck Fairness Act before the Senate hearing "A Fair Share for All: Pay Equity in the New American Workplace" about the continuing pay gap between men and women in the workplace.[14] The impact on gender of what was happening to adversely impact caregivers in the graying of America was also the subject of EEOC guidance.[15] As society gains more knowledge of the ways in which unlawful discrimination is manifested by workplace policies, the agency tries to address them accordingly.

As then-EEOC Chair Naomi C. Earp said in presenting the EEOC's Performance and Accountability Report for FY 2006,

> Employment discrimination has changed fairly dramatically over the past 40 years. In the years before and immediately after Title VII was passed, discrimination was blatant and pervasive. Newspapers published sex-segregated job ads, and employers implemented or continued policies of segregating employment facilities by race, paying female employees less than male employees, restricting employment and promotion opportunities for women and minorities, and enforcing mandatory retirement policies to force older workers out. Today, discrimination has become more subtle and thus more difficult to prove . . . [C]urrent demographic changes, such as the graying of the workforce and the increased gender and ethnic diversity of the workforce, also present new challenges and opportunities for employees, employers, and the Commission.[16]

The EEOC has changed also. Forty-plus years after the effective date of the 1964 Civil Rights Act, it is clear that the agency has maintained its mission to eradicate workplace discrimination but changed some of its tactics as it has gained experience.

While its mission has always been conciliation based, it did not always seem that way. In carving out its new, untrod territory, it aggressively went after employers in order to establish its presence and place in the law (which, along with being "the feds," caused more than a little employer resentment). Once that place was firmly established, the EEOC began living up to its conciliation mission.

The EEOC now prefers to be proactive and have employers avoid litigation by thoroughly understanding the law and its requirements. The EEOC has sponsored thousands of outreach programs to teach employers and employees, alike, about the law; has initiated extensive mediation programs to try to handle discrimination claims quickly, efficiently, and without litigation; and maintains an informative Web site that makes help readily accessible for employers and employees alike. (See Exhibit 3.4, "EEOC on Call.")

Exhibit 3.4　*EEOC on Call*

The EEOC's National Contact Center may be reached 24 hours a day at 1-800-669-4000 or 1-800-669-6820 TTY, or via e-mail at info@ask.eeoc.gov. Constituents can now communicate with the agency in more than 150 languages by telephone, e-mail, and Web inquiries to obtain quick, accurate information. Additionally, through Frequently Asked Questions posted on the EEOC's Web page and an Interactive Voice Response telephone system available 24 hours a day, customers are getting their questions answered through the use of the agency's technology.

Source: http://eeoc.gov/abouteeoc/plan/par/2006/management_discussion.html#highlights.

As the demographics and the workplace change, the EEOC has incorporated these changes into its mission,. For instance, EEOC has developed several programs targeted to the needs of specific groups such as:

- TIGAAR (The Information Group for Asian-American Rights) initiative to promote voluntary compliance with employment laws by Asian-American employers and to educate Asian-American employees about their workplace rights.
- Programs with Sikh and Muslim communities in response to post-9/11 religious and national origin discrimination.
- The Council of Tribal Employment Rights (CTER) to work with Native Americans to eliminate workplace discrimination on or near Native American reservations, secure Native American preference agreements with employers operating on or near reservations, and process employment discrimination complaints.
- The new E-RACE initiative to reinvigorate its efforts in the area of race and color discrimination, discussed in a later chapter.
- Youth@Work initative to put renewed emphasis on discriminatory recruitment and hiring practices and discrimination against youth.

Much work, however, remains. The EEOC still receives a large number of discrimination charges. In fact, in fiscal year 2010, EEOC received more charges than any other year in its history (99,922).[17] (See Exhibit 3.5, "EEOC Charge Statistics.) Charges of race discrimination have increased every decade since the inception of Title VII. Retaliation charges and "egregious discrimination" charges are increasing.[18] While it prefers conciliation, the EEOC will still aggressively pursue employers when conciliation does not work to its satisfaction. There are other changes as well. The best way to avoid violations of employment discrimination laws is to know and understand their requirements. That is what the following sections and chapters will help you do.

Keep Exhibit 3.6, "Cages," in mind as you go through this section of the text. Most of us look at things microscopically. That is, we tend to see only the situation in front of us and don't give much thought to the larger picture into which it fits. But it is this larger picture within which we actually operate. It is the one the law considers when enacting legislation, the courts consider in interpreting the law and deciding cases, and thus the one an employer should consider when developing workplace policies or responding to workplace situations. Often, a situation, in and of itself, may seem to us to have little or no significance. "Why are they whining about this?" we say; "Why can't they just go along? Why are they being so sensitive?" But we are often missing the larger picture and how this situation may fit into it. Like the birdcage in Exhibit 3.6, each thing, in and of itself, may not be a big deal, but put each of these things together, and a picture is revealed of a very different reality for those who must deal with the "wires."

Many of the situations you see in the following chapters are "wires" that Title VII and other protective legislation try to eradicate in an effort to break down the seemingly impenetrable invisible barriers we have erected around issues of race, gender, disabilities, ethnicity, religion, age, family medical history, and genetic

Exhibit 3.5 *EEOC Charge Statistics FY 1997 through FY 2010*

In this chart you can see for yourself the numbers of charges filed with the EEOC over the years, including the percentages by type.

	FY 1997	FY 1998	FY 1999	FY 2000	FY 2001	FY 2002	FY 2003	FY 2004	FY 2005	FY 2006	FY 2007	FY 2008	FY 2009	FY 2010
Total Charges*	80,680	79,591	77,444	79,896	80,840	84,442	81,293	79,432	75,428	75,768	82,792	95,402	93,277	99,922
Race	29,199	28,820	28,819	28,945	28,912	29,910	28,526	27,696	26,740	27,238	30,510	33,937	33,579	35,890
	36.2%	36.2%	37.3%	36.2%	35.8%	35.4%	35.1%	34.9%	35.5%	35.9%	37.0%	35.6%	36.0%	35.9%
Sex	24,728	24,454	23,907	25,194	25,140	25,536	24,362	24,249	23,094	23,247	24,826	28,372	28,028	29,029
	30.7%	30.7%	30.9%	31.5%	31.1%	30.2%	30.0%	30.5%	30.6%	30.7%	30.1%	29.7%	30.0%	29.1%
National Origin	6,712	6,778	7,108	7,792	8,025	9,046	8,450	8,361	8,035	8,327	9,396	10,601	11,134	11,304
	8.3%	8.5%	9.2%	9.8%	9.9%	10.7%	10.4%	10.5%	10.7%	11.0%	11.4%	11.1%	11.9%	11.3%
Religion	1,709	1,786	1,811	1,939	2,127	2,572	2,532	2,466	2,340	2,541	2,880	3,273	3,386	3,790
	2.1%	2.2%	2.3%	2.4%	2.6%	3.0%	3.1%	3.1%	3.1%	3.4%	3.5%	3.4%	3.6%	3.8%
Retaliation—all statutes	18,198	19,114	19,694	21,613	22,257	22,768	22,690	22,740	22,278	22,555	26,663	32,690	33,613	36,258
	22.6%	24.0%	25.4%	27.1%	27.5%	27.0%	27.9%	28.6%	29.5%	29.8%	32.3%	34.3%	36.0%	36.3%
Retaliation—Title VII only	16,394	17,246	17,883	19,753	20,407	20,814	20,615	20,240	19,429	19,560	23,371	28,698	28,948	30,948
	20.3%	21.7%	23.1%	24.7%	25.2%	24.6%	25.4%	25.5%	25.8%	25.8%	28.3%	30.1%	31.0%	31.0%
Age	15,785	15,191	14,141	16,008	17,405	19,921	19,124	17,837	16,585	16,548	19,103	24,582	22,778	23,264
	19.6%	19.1%	18.3%	20.0%	21.5%	23.6%	23.5%	22.5%	22.0%	21.8%	23.2%	25.8%	24.4%	23.3%
Disability	18,108	17,806	17,007	15,864	16,470	15,964	15,377	15,376	14,893	15,575	17,734	19,453	21,451	25,165
	22.4%	22.4%	22.0%	19.9%	20.4%	18.9%	18.9%	19.4%	19.7%	20.6%	21.4%	20.4%	23.0%	25.2%
Equal Pay Act	1,134	1,071	1,044	1,270	1,251	1,256	1,167	1,011	970	861	818	954	942	1,044
	1.4%	1.3%	1.3%	1.6%	1.5%	1.5%	1.4%	1.3%	1.3%	1.1%	1.0%	1.0%	1.0%	1.0%
GINA (Genetic Information Nondiscrimination Act)														201
														0.2%

*The number for total charges reflects the number of individual charge filings. Because individuals often file charges claiming multiple types of discrimination, the number of total charges for any given fiscal year will be less than the total of the eight types of discrimination listed.

Source: Data are compiled by the Office of Research, Information and Planning from data reported via the quarterly reconciled Data Summary Reports and compiled from EEOC's Charge Data System and, from FY 2004 forward, EEOC's Integrated Mission System, http://www.eeoc.gov/eeoc/statistics/enforcement/charges.cfm.

Exhibit 3.6 *Cages*

Cages. Consider a birdcage. If you look very closely at just one wire in the cage, you cannot see the other wires. If your conception of what is before you is determined by this myopic focus, you could look at that one wire, up and down the length of it, and be unable to see why a bird would not just fly around the wire any time it wanted to go somewhere. Furthermore, even if, one day at a time, you myopically inspected each wire, you still could not see why a bird would have trouble going past the wires to get anywhere. There is no physical property of any one wire, nothing that the closest scrutiny could discover, that will reveal how a bird could be inhibited or harmed by it except in the most accidental way. It is only when you step back, stop looking at the wires one by one, microscopically, and take a macroscopic view of the whole cage, that you can see why the bird does not go anywhere; and then you will see it in a moment. It will require no great subtlety of mental powers. It is perfectly obvious that the bird is surrounded by a network of systematically related barriers, no one of which would be the least hindrance to its flight, but which, by their relations to each other, are as confining as the solid walls of a dungeon.

Source: From "Oppression," by Marilyn Frye, The Politics of Reality, reprinted in *Race, Class and Gender: An Anthology*, Margaret L. Anderson and Patricia Hill Collins, 1992, Wadsworth Press. Used by permission.

information for generations. As you go through the cases and information, think not only about the micro picture of what is going on in front of you but also about the larger macro picture that it fits into. Sometimes what makes little sense in one setting, makes perfect sense in the other.

Another way to look at it is as if it is one of those repeating-pattern "Magic Eye" pictures so popular a few years ago. If you stare at one the correct way, you get to see the detailed 3-D picture you'd never see by just glancing at the surface picture. The picture hasn't changed, but you've looked at it in a way that now lets you see another, richly detailed picture you didn't even know was there. Learning about employment discrimination will not change the reality you already know (the repeating-pattern picture you see at a glance), but will instead help you to see another, richer, more detailed picture inside this one—one that will greatly assist you in being an effective manager who is less likely to be responsible for workplace discrimination claims and liability.

What does this all mean? Let's look at an example. A female who works in a garage comes in one day and there are photos of nude females all around the shop. She complains to the supervisor and he tells her that the men like the photos and if she doesn't like it, just don't look at them. The guys she works with begin to rib her about complaining. They tell her she's a "wuss," "can't cut the mustard," and "can't hang with the big boys." "What's the big deal?" you say. "Why didn't she just shut up and ignore the photos?"

Well, in and of itself the photos may not seem like much. But when you look at the issue in its larger context, it looks quite different. Research shows that in workplaces in which nude photos, adult language, sexual teasing, jokes, and so on are present, women tend to be paid less and receive fewer and less-significant raises, promotions, and training. It is not unlikely that the environment that supports such photos doesn't clearly draw lines between the people in the photos and females at work. Case after case bears it out. So the photos themselves aren't really the whole issue. It's the micro picture, the repeating-pattern picture you see at a glance. But the macro picture, the 3-D picture, is the objectification of women and what contributes to women being viewed as less than men and not as capable in a workplace in which they may well be just as capable as anyone else. What might have seemed like harmless joking or photos in the micro view takes on much more significance in the macro view and has much more of a potential negative impact on the work experience of the female employee who is less likely to be trained, promoted, or given a raise for which she is qualified.

Again, as you go through the following chapters, try to look at the micro as well as the macro picture—the repeating-pattern surface picture as well as the 3-D picture inside. You will also benefit from the case questions, which help you view what you have read in a larger context. Again, it is this context that will be under scrutiny when the policies of a workplace form the basis of a lawsuit. Thinking about that context beforehand and making policies consistent with it will give the employer a much greater chance of avoiding embarrassing and costly litigation.

The Structure of Title VII

What Is Prohibited under Title VII?

Title VII prohibits discrimination in hiring, firing, training, promotion, discipline, or other workplace decisions on the basis of an employee or applicant's race, color, gender, national origin, or religion. Included in the prohibitions are discrimination in pay, terms and conditions of employment, training, layoffs, and benefits. Virtually any workplace decision can be challenged by an applicant or employee who falls within the Title VII categories. (See Exhibit 3.7 "Title VII Provisions.")

Exhibit 3.7 *Title VII Provisions*

An employer cannot discriminate on the basis of:

- Race
- Color
- Gender
- Religion
- National origin

in making decisions regarding:

- Hiring
- Firing
- Training
- Discipline
- Compensation
- Benefits
- Classification
- Or other terms or conditions of employment

Exhibit 3.8 *Who Must Comply*

- Employers engaged in interstate commerce if they have:
  - Fifteen or more employees for each working day in each of 20 or more calendar weeks in the current or preceding calendar year.
- Labor organizations of any kind that exist to deal with employers concerning labor issues, engaged in an industry affecting commerce.

- Employment agencies that, with or without compensation, procure employees for employers or opportunities to work for employees.

Who Must Comply?

Title VII applies to employers, unions, and joint labor and management committees making admission, referral, training, and other decisions, and to employment agencies and other similar hiring entities making referrals for employment. It applies to all private employers employing 15 or more employees, and to federal, state, and local governments. (See Exhibit 3.8, "Who Must Comply.")

Who Is Covered?

Title VII applies to public (governmental) and private (nongovernmental) employees alike. Unlike labor laws that do not apply to managerial employees or wage and hour laws that exempt certain types of employees, Title VII covers all levels and types of employees. The Civil Rights Act of 1991 further extended Title VII's coverage to U.S. citizens employed by American employers outside the United States. Non-U.S. citizens are protected in the United States but not outside the United States.

Undocumented workers also are covered by the law, but after the U.S. Supreme Court's 2002 ruling in *Hoffman Plastic Compounds, Inc. v. NLRB*,[19] the EEOC reexamined its position on remedies for undocumented workers. In *Hoffman*, the Court said that U.S. immigration laws outweighed the employer's labor violations; therefore, the employee could not recover back pay for violations of the labor law. The EEOC had been treating undocumented worker claims of employment discrimination under Title VII like violations against any other worker. After *Hoffman*, the EEOC said that employment discrimination against undocumented workers is still illegal, and they will not ask their status in handling their discrimination claims, but *Hoffman* affected the availability of some forms of relief, such as reinstatement and back pay for periods after discharge or failure to hire.[20]

Who Is Not Covered?

Exemptions under Title VII are limited. Title VII permits businesses operated on or around Native American reservations to give preferential treatment to

---

Exhibit 3.9 *Employees Who Are Not Covered by Title VII*

- Employees of employers having less than 15 employees.
- Employees whose employers are not engaged in interstate commerce.
- Non-U.S. citizens employed outside the United States.
- Employees of religious institutions, associations, or corporations hired to perform work connected with carrying on religious activities.

- Members of Communist organizations.
- Employers employing Native Americans living in or around Native American reservations.
- Employers who are engaged in interstate commerce but do not employ 15 or more employees for each of 20 or more calendar weeks in the current or preceding calendar year.

Native Americans. The act specifically states that it does not apply to actions taken with respect to someone who is a member of the Communist Party or other organization required to register as a Communist-action or Communist-front organization (keep in mind that Title VII was passed while the country was still reeling from the McCarthy hearings investigating suspicion of Communist infiltration of the government). The law permits religious institutions and associations to discriminate when performing their activities. For instance, a Catholic priest could not successfully sue under Title VII alleging religious discrimination for not being hired to lead a Jewish synagogue. (See Exhibit 3.9 "Employees Who Are Not Covered by Title VII.") In the case of *Petruska v. Gannon University,* included at the end of the chapter, the employee was not able to effectively bring her claim for gender discrimination because of this limitation on religious claims.

Keep in mind that the law covers what it covers and no more. In order to have a valid claim under Title VII, the employee or applicant must be able to show that he or she has been discriminated against on one of the bases in the law. If the employee cannot show this, then there is no basis for a Title VII claim. That is why in Opening Scenario 3, Rinson has no cause of action. There is no indication that the reason for the supervisor treating Rinson poorly has anything to do with any of Title VII's prohibited classes of race, color, gender, religion, or national origin.

Filing Claims under Title VII

claimant or charging party
The person who brings an action alleging violation of Title VII.

Nonfederal employees who believe they have experienced employment discrimination may file a charge or claim with the EEOC. An employee filing such a claim is called a **claimant** or a **charging party**. Employers should be aware that it costs an employee only time and energy to go to the nearest EEOC office and file a claim. By law, the EEOC must in some way handle every claim it receives. To discourage claims and ensure the best defense when they arise, employers should ensure that their policies and procedures are legal, fair, and consistently applied.

However, just because filing with the EEOC is free does not mean that every employee who thinks he or she has a claim is making a beeline to the EEOC office. Filing a claim against an employer is a serious matter. Most employees work because they must in order to finance their lives. Doing anything to interfere with that is a shaky business. There are far more people who have legitimate claims who choose not to pursue them than those who do so, or who do so for questionable reasons. You, yourself, may have had a basis for a claim and just let it go, perhaps thinking it wasn't worth the hassle and you had other pressing matters to deal with such as school. There are many reasons employees may choose not to pursue a claim:

- They may not know their rights under the law.
- They may be afraid.
- They may fear retaliation.
- They may feel it is easier to just go along or to find another job.
- They may have valued friendships they wish to maintain.
- They may feel the process takes too long and feels too uncertain.
- They may fear the emotional cost of the proceedings.
- They may not wish to risk the ire of their fellow employees.
- They may find it too uncomfortable to work in the workplace where they have filed claims against the employer.
- They may think things will get better on their own.
- The job market may make their present situation seem like the best choice under the circumstances.
- They may not want to put their families at risk.

Keep in mind that even with the best case in the world, there are no guarantees. A claim can drag on for years, and during that time the claimant, who may have been terminated in violation of Title VII, must still eat. He or she must obtain other employment and, by the time the case is finished, may have moved on with his or her life. As we write this, the U.S. Supreme Court this week heard oral arguments in a case against Wal-Mart[21] that has already been going on for 10 years. The decision for the Court is not even about the substantive issue of whether Wal-Mart engaged in gender discrimination against its female employees, but rather whether it was correct for the trial court and court of appeals to allow the employees to be certified as a class for bringing the lawsuit. Ten years and the case has not even been heard on the merits yet. So, while it is easy for employers to sue, the bigger concern is the ones who have legitimate cases that were easily avoided by good workplace practices.

Regarding the ease of bringing EEO claims, there is good news and bad news for employers. The good news is that the vast majority of charges are sifted out of the system for one reason or another. For instance, in fiscal year 2010, of the 99,922 charges filed with the EEOC, 9.3 percent were settled, 16.5 percent had administrative closures (failure of the claimant to pursue the claim, loss of contact with the claimant, etc.), 64.3 percent resulted in findings of no reasonable cause, and reasonable cause was found in only 4.7 percent of the charges. Conciliation was successful in only 1.3 percent of the cases, and unsuccessful in 13 percent.[22]

The bad news is that the EEOC's success rate in litigation has been at least 90 percent for years. In fiscal year 2010, the EEOC obtained $319.4 million in monetary benefits even though only 14 percent of the charges settled or had a reasonable cause finding. This is the highest level of monetary relief through administrative enforcement in EEOC history.[23] There is no doubt that shareholders of companies that had to pay out this money in settlements and judgments believe that the avoidable $319.4 million could have been put to more productive use.

Understanding and implementing effective workplace policies can do that. These are not good numbers for employers facing the EEOC. The best defense is a good offense. Avoiding trouble in the first place lessens the chances of having to deal with the EEOC and therefore the chances of being unsuccessful.

Nonfederal government employee claims must be filed within 180 days of the discriminatory event, except as noted in the next section involving 706 agencies. For federal employees, claims must be filed with their employing agency within 45 days of the event. In a significant U.S. Supreme Court case, *National Railroad Passenger Corp. (Amtrak) v. Morgan,*[24] these deadlines were made a bit more flexible by the Court for harassment cases. In the *Morgan* case, the Supreme Court said that since on-the-job harassment is part of a pattern of behavior, if a charge is filed with the EEOC within the statutory period, a jury can consider actions that occurred outside the statutory period. The violation is considered to be a continuing one, so the claimant is not limited to only evidence relating to the specific event resulting in the lawsuit. Note, however, as briefly discussed in the toolkit chapter, that in 2007, the U.S. Supreme Court held that it was not a continuing violation each time an employer issued a paycheck based on gender-based wage discrimination. In *Ledbetter v. Goodyear Tire and Rubber Co., Inc.,*[25] discussed in more detail in the gender chapter (Chapter 9), the Court rejected the paycheck accrual rule that would have allowed the employee to restart the statute of limitations each time she was paid. The Court distinguished *Morgan* by saying the act of wage discrimination was a discrete act rather than a pattern and, thus, did not merit the same treatment as the harassment in the *Morgan* case. Congress, however, responded by passing the Lilly Ledbetter Fair Pay Act of 2009 that adopted the paycheck accrual rule. Under that law, the 180-day statute of limitations begins to run all over again each time a paycheck is issued based on pay discrimination. That is why in Opening Scenario 2, Shelly is still able to bring her claim even though it has been more than 180 days since the event.

Scenario

The reason for the fairly short statute of limitations in Title VII is an attempt to ensure that the necessary parties and witnesses are still available and that events are not too remote to recollect accurately. Violations of Title VII may also be brought to the EEOC's attention because of its own investigation or by information

record keeping and reporting requirements
Requirement under Title VII that certain documents must be maintained and periodically reported to the EEOC.

provided by employers meeting their **record keeping and reporting requirements** under the law.

The filing process is somewhat different for federal employees, although the EEOC is seeking to make it conform more closely to the nonfederal employee regulations.[26] Federal employees are protected by Title VII, but the procedures for handling their claims simply follow a different path.

State Law Interface in the Filing Process

Since most states have their own fair employment practice laws that track Title VII, they also have their own state and local enforcement agencies for employment discrimination claims. Most of these agencies contract with the EEOC to act as a **706 agency** (named for the section of the law that permits them). On the basis of a work-sharing agreement with the EEOC, these agencies receive and process claims of discrimination for the EEOC in addition to carrying on their own state business.

706 agency
State agency that handles EEOC claims under a work-sharing agreement with the EEOC.

conciliation
Attempting to reach agreement on a claim through discussion, without resort to litigation.

Title VII's intent is that claims be **conciliated** if possible. Local agencies serve as a type of screening process for the more serious cases. If the complaint is not satisfactorily disposed at this level, it may eventually be taken by the EEOC and, if necessary, litigated. State and local agencies have their own procedures, which are similar to those of the EEOC.

If there is a 706 agency in the employee's jurisdiction, the employee has 300 days rather than 180 days within which to file. If an employee files his or her claim with the EEOC when there is a 706 agency in the jurisdiction, the EEOC defers the complaint to the 706 agency for 60 days before investigating. The employee can file the complaint with the EEOC, but the EEOC sends it to the 706 agency, and the EEOC will not move on the claim for 60 days.

In further explaining the process, reference will only be made to the EEOC as the enforcing agency involved.

Proceeding through the EEOC

respondent or responding party
Person alleged to have violated Title VII, usually the employer.

Within 10 days of the employee filing a claim with the EEOC, the EEOC serves notice of the charge to the employer (called **respondent** or **responding party**). As discussed in the toolkit chapter, Title VII also includes antiretaliation provisions. It is a separate offense for an employer to retaliate against an employee for pursuing rights under Title VII. Noting that retaliation claims had doubled since 1991, in 1998 the EEOC issued retaliation guidelines to make clear its view on what constitutes retaliation for pursuing Title VII rights and how seriously it views such claims by employees.[27] In fiscal year 2010, at 36.3 percent retaliation claims for the first time were the largest percentage of claims filed under the protective legislation with race at 35.9 percent and gender at 29.1 percent.[28]

LO7

Mediation

The EEOC's approach to mediation has been very aggressive in the past decade or so. In response to complaints of a tremendous backlog of cases and claims that went on for years, in recent years the EEOC has adopted several important steps to try to streamline its case-handling process and make it more efficient and effective, and less time-consuming for claimants. Primary among the steps is its adoption of mediation as an alternative to a full-blown EEOC investigation. In furtherance of this, the EEOC has begun several different programs involving mediation. In 1999 it launched the expanded mediation program discussed in the next paragraph. In 2003, in recognition that many private sector employers already have extensive mediation programs set up to handle workplace issues, the EEOC began a "referral-back" program. Private sector employment discrimination claims are referred back to participating employers for mediation by the employer's own mediation program to see if they can be resolved without going any further. The same year, the EEOC ushered in a pilot program to have local fair employment practice offices mediate claims on the EEOC's behalf. In response to the EEOC's finding that there were more employees willing to mediate than there were employers willing to do so, the EEOC instituted "universal mediation agreements," under which employers agree to have their claims mediated by the EEOC when discrimination charges are filed.

As of the end of fiscal year 2010, the EEOC had signed universal agreements to mediate with 214 national corporations and more than 1,570 regional and local employers.[29] National universal mediation agreements have been signed with such employers as Ford Motor Company; Huddle House, Inc.; Ryan's Restaurant Group, Inc.; and Southern Company. While overall, mediation has accounted for only a very small percentage of claim decisions, in fiscal year 2010, there was a 10 percent increase in the number of resolutions over the previous year, making it the highest number of resolutions in the history of the program. Mediation resolutions accounted for over $142 million in monetary benefits to employees.[30]

Generally, the way mediation works is that, after a discrimination charge is filed by the employee and notice of the charge is given to the employer, the EEOC screens the charge to see if it is one that is appropriate for mediation. If it is appropriate for mediation, the EEOC will offer that option to the parties. Complex and weak cases are not offered mediation. The agency estimates that it offers mediation to 60 to 70 percent of its incoming workload of nearly 100,000 cases per year. Of those, about 15 percent are actually mediated. Both parties are sent letters offering mediation, and the decision to participate is voluntary for both parties. Each side has 10 days to respond to the offer to mediate. If both parties elect mediation, the charge must be mediated within 60 days for in-house mediation or 45 days for external mediation. The EEOC has expanded its mediation program to allow a request for mediation at any stage of the administrative process, even after a finding of discrimination has been issued.

If the parties choose to mediate, during mediation they will have the opportunity to present their positions, express their opinions, provide information, and express their request for relief. Any information disclosed during this process is not to be revealed to anyone, including EEOC employees. If the parties reach agreement, that agreement is as binding as any other settlement agreement. From 1999, when its mediation program was fully implemented, to 2010, the EEOC conducted over 100,000 mediations, with a satisfaction rate of well over 90 percent.[31]

reasonable cause
EEOC finding that Title VII was violated.

no reasonable cause
EEOC finding that evidence indicates no reasonable basis to believe Title VII was violated.

right-to-sue letter
Letter given by the EEOC to claimants, notifying them of the EEOC's no-cause finding and informing them of their right to pursue their claim in court.

EEOC Investigation

If the parties choose not to mediate the charge or if the mediation is not successful, the charge is referred back to the EEOC for handling. The EEOC investigates the complaint by talking with the employer and employee and any other necessary witnesses, as well as viewing any documents or even visiting the workplace. The average time for an investigation is about 182 days.[32]

EEOC's Determination

After appropriate investigation, the EEOC makes a determination as to whether there is **reasonable cause** or no reasonable cause for the employee to charge the employer with violating Title VII. Once there has been an investigation and a cause or no-cause finding, either party can ask for reconsideration of the EEOC's decision.

No-Reasonable-Cause Finding

After investigation, if the EEOC finds there is **no reasonable cause** for the employee's discrimination complaint, the employee is given a dismissal and notice of rights, often known as a **right-to-sue letter**. If the employee wants to pursue the matter further despite the EEOC's conclusion that Title VII has not been violated, the employee is now free to do so, having exhausted the administrative remedies of the EEOC. The employee can then bring suit against the employer in federal court within 90 days of receiving the notice. (See Exhibit 3.10, "The Procedure for Bringing a Claim within the EEOC.")

Exhibit 3.10 *The Procedure for Bringing a Claim within the EEOC*

- Employee goes to the EEOC office and files the complaint.
- Agency sends a notice to the employer accused of discrimination.
- Parties receive referral to mediation (if appropriate).
- If both parties elect mediation, the charge is mediated.
- If the parties agree in mediation, the negotiated settlement is binding. Complaint is resolved and closed.
- If mediation is not successful or parties choose not to mediate, the EEOC investigates the claim.
- If the EEOC's investigation shows reasonable cause to believe discrimination has occurred, the parties meet and try to conciliate.

- If agreement is reached during conciliation, the claim is resolved and closed.
- If no agreement is reached during conciliation, the EEOC makes a determination of reasonable cause or no reasonable cause to believe discrimination occurred.
- If reasonable cause is found, the EEOC notifies the employer of the proposed remedy.
- If no reasonable cause is found, parties are notified and the charging party is issued a dismissal and the notice of rights letter.
- If the employer disagrees, he or she appeals the decision to the next agency level.

Reasonable-Cause Finding

If the EEOC finds there is reasonable cause for the employee to charge the employer with discrimination, it will attempt to have the parties meet together and conciliate the matter. That is, the EEOC will bring the parties together in a fairly informal setting with an **EEO investigator**.

The EEO investigator sets forth what has been found during the investigation and discusses with the parties the ways the matter can be resolved. Often the employee is satisfied if the employer simply agrees to provide a favorable letter of recommendation. The majority of claims filed with the EEOC are adequately disposed of at this stage of the proceedings. If the claim is not adequately disposed of, the EEOC can take the matter further and eventually file suit against the employer in federal district court if it is deemed justified by the EEOC.

Judicial Review

If no conciliation is reached, the EEOC may eventually file a civil action in federal district court. As we have seen, if the EEOC originally found no cause and issued the complaining party a right-to-sue letter, the employee can take the case to court, seeking **judicial review**. Title VII requires that courts accord EEOC decisions *de novo* **review**. A court can only take a Title VII discrimination case for judicial review after the EEOC has first disposed of the claim. Thus, in Opening Scenario 1, Jack cannot immediately file a discrimination lawsuit against his employer because he has not yet gone through the EEOC's administrative process and exhausted his administrative remedies.

Under de novo review, upon going to court, the case is handled entirely as if it were new, as if there had not already been a finding by the EEOC. Employees proceeding with a no-reasonable-cause letter are also free to develop the case however they wish without being bound by the EEOC's prior determination. If a party is not satisfied with the court's decision and has a basis upon which to appeal, the case can be appealed up to, and including, the U.S. Supreme Court, if it agrees to hear the case.

Before we leave the topic of judicial review, we need to discuss a matter that has become important in the area of employees' pursuing their rights under Title VII and having the right to judicial review of the EEOC's decisions. In recent years, **mandatory arbitration agreements** have gained tremendously in popularity. Previously confined almost exclusively to unions and the securities industry, these agreements are entered into by employees with their employers when they are hired and stipulate that any workplace disputes will be disposed of by submitting them to arbitration rather than to the EEOC or the courts.

The appeal of mandatory arbitration clauses is that they greatly decrease the time and resources parties would spend by fighting workplace legal battles in court. There are at least two major drawbacks for employees: (1) When they are trying to obtain employment, potential employees generally feel they have little choice about signing away their rights to go to court and (2) once a case goes to arbitration, the arbitrator's decision is not subject to judicial review by the courts

EEO investigator
Employee of the EEOC who reviews Title VII complaints for merit.

Scenario

judicial review
Court review of an agency's decision.

***de novo* review**
Complete new look at an administrative case by the reviewing court.

mandatory arbitration agreement
Agreement an employee signs as a condition of employment, requiring that workplace disputes be arbitrated rather than litigated.

unless the decision can be shown to be the result of fraud or collusion, is unconstitutional, or suffers some similar malady. This means that the vast majority of arbitration awards, many rendered by arbitrators with no legal background or grounding in Title VII issues, remain intact, free from review by the courts. It also means that while employers gain the advantage of having fewer cases in court, employees have the disadvantage of essentially having the courts closed to them in Title VII cases, even though Title VII provides for both an administrative process and judicial review.

With few downsides for employers, mandatory arbitration agreements have become so popular with employers that they are now fairly routine. Employees who come to the EEOC intending to file claims of employment discrimination are told that they cannot do so because they have entered into a mandatory arbitration agreement with their employer, which requires them to seek redress through arbitration, *not* the EEOC or the courts. This happened recently in New York City to a female Citibank investment banker who was terminated because her supervisor said that her figure was too distracting to the male employees.[33]

Two recent U.S. Supreme Court cases have decided important issues in this area. In *Circuit City v. Adams,*[34] the Supreme Court held that mandatory arbitration clauses requiring arbitration of workplace claims, including those under Title VII, are enforceable under the Federal Arbitration Act. In *EEOC v. Waffle House, Inc.,*[35] the Court held that even though an employee is subject to a mandatory arbitration agreement, since the EEOC is not a party to the agreement, the agreement does not prevent the EEOC from pursuing victim-specific relief such as back pay, reinstatement, and damages as part of an enforcement action.

So, the EEOC claims can be the subject of mandatory arbitration, but this does not prevent the EEOC from bringing its own enforcement action against the employer and even asking for victim-specific relief for the employee. An employer can avoid a Title VII court case by requiring mandatory arbitration of workplace claims, but still may have to contend with the EEOC bringing suit on its own.

Legislation to overturn *Circuit City* and only permit voluntary arbitration agreements was introduced in both the House and Senate shortly after the decision, but did not pass. Perhaps this was, at least in part, because the Supreme Court gave further indication of how it will view mandatory arbitration agreements in a later *Circuit City* case. In its initial decision, the Supreme Court required the *Circuit City* case to be remanded to the lower court for actions not inconsistent with its ruling. On remand, the court of appeals applied the Federal Arbitration Act and ruled that the employer's mandatory arbitration agreement was unconscionable and unenforceable because it was offered on a take-it-or-leave-it basis, did not require the company to arbitrate claims, limited the relief available to employees, and required employees to pay half of the arbitration costs. When the court of appeals' decision came back to the Supreme Court for review, the Court declined to hear it, leaving the court of appeals' refusal to enforce the mandatory arbitration agreement intact.[36]

Perhaps also, at least in part in response to mandatory arbitration agreements, the EEOC stepped up its mediation programs in order to provide employers with an alternative between litigation and mandatory arbitration. Since 1991 the EEOC had been moving in the direction of mediation, but the issue heated up after the Supreme Court decisions on mandatory arbitration. The EEOC's subsequent litigation alternatives heavily favoring mediation included plans aimed squarely at employers, with its adoption of the national uniform mediation agreements (NUMAs) and referral-back programs. As discussed earlier, the NUMAs specifically commit employers to mediation of Title VII claims, while the referral-back programs allow employers to use their own in-house ADR programs to attempt to settle such claims.

Remedies

For remedies available under Title VII, see Chapter 2: "The Employment Law Toolkit."

Jury Trials

The Civil Rights Act of 1991 also added jury trials to Title VII. From the creation of Title VII in 1964 until passage of the 1991 Civil Rights Act 27 years later, jury trials were not permitted under Title VII. Jury trials are now permitted under Title VII at the request of either party when compensatory and punitive damages are sought.

There is always less predictability about case outcomes when juries are involved. Arguing one's cause to a judge who is a trained member of the legal profession is quite different from arguing to a jury of 6 to 12 jurors, all of whom come with their own backgrounds, prejudices, predilections, and little knowledge of the law. Employers now have even more incentive to ensure that their policies and actions are well reasoned, business-related, and justifiable—especially since employees have even more incentive to sue.

The Reconstruction Civil Rights Acts

LO8   In this chapter we have been discussing race discrimination under Title VII of the Civil Rights Act of 1964. However, the Civil Rights Act of 1964 was not the first piece of legislation aimed at prohibiting racial discrimination. Since these other laws are still used today, a chapter on race discrimination in employment would not be complete without including some mention of them. It is important to know the full range of potential employer liability for discrimination lawsuits by employees.

There are three main pre–Title VII laws. (See Exhibit 3.11, "The Reconstruction Civil Rights Acts.") Collectively, they are known as the post–Civil War statutes, or the Reconstruction Civil Rights Acts. They were passed by Congress after the Civil War ended in 1865 in an effort to provide a means of enforcing

Exhibit 3.11 *The Reconstruction Civil Rights Acts*

42 U.S.C. Section 1981. Equal Rights under the Law

All persons within the jurisdiction of the United States shall have the same right in every State and Territory to make and enforce contracts. . . as is enjoyed by white citizens.

42 U.S.C. Section 1983. Civil Action for Deprivation of Rights

Every person who, under color of any statute, ordinance, regulation, custom, or usage, of any State or Territory, subjects, or causes to be subjected, any citizen of the United States or other person within the jurisdiction thereof to the deprivation of any rights, privileges, or immunities secured by the Constitution and laws, shall be liable to the party injured in an action at law, suit in equity, or other proper proceeding for redress.

42 U.S.C. Section 1985. Conspiracy to Interfere with Civil Rights—Preventing Officer from Performing Duties ("Ku Klux Klan Act")

Depriving persons of rights or privileges . . .

(3) If two or more persons in any State or Territory conspire or go in disguise on the highway or on the premises of another, for the purpose of depriving, either directly or indirectly, any person or class of persons of the equal protection of the laws, or of equal privileges and immunities under the laws; in any case of conspiracy set forth in this section, if one or more persons engaged therein do, or cause to be done, any act in furtherance of the object of such conspiracy, whereby another is injured in his person or property, or deprived of having and exercising any rights or privileges of a citizen of the United States, the party so injured or deprived may have an action for the recovery of damages, occasioned by such injury or deprivation, against any one or more of the conspirators.

the new status of the ex-slaves as free citizens. In 1865, passage of the Thirteenth Amendment to the Constitution abolishing slavery had merely set African Americans free. Nothing on the books at that point said what that picture had to look like. In fact, largely in response to the Thirteenth Amendment, states enacted "Black Codes"—mostly revisions of their pre–Civil War "Slave Codes"—that codified discrimination on the basis of race and limited the rights of the newly free slaves.[37]

Beginning in 1866, Congress began enacting the post–Civil War statutes, understanding that without legislation providing rights for the new status of African Americans, things would almost certainly revert to pre–Civil War status. It passed section 1981, making all African Americans born in the United States citizens and ensuring them the right to make and enforce contracts the same "as enjoyed by white citizens." In 1868, Congress passed the Fourteenth Amendment to make its laws applicable to the states, dictating that no state "shall make or enforce any law which shall abridge the privileges or immunities of the citizens of the United States . . . [or] deprive any person of life, liberty, or property, without due process of law, [or] deny to any person within its jurisdiction the equal protection of the laws."

The three post–Civil War statutes are now codified as 42 U.S.C. sections 1981, 1983, and 1985. They prohibit discrimination on the basis of race in making and enforcing contracts; prohibit the denial of civil rights on the basis of race by someone behaving as if they are acting on behalf of the government (called **under color of state law**); and prohibit concerted activity to deny someone their rights based on race.

under color of state law
Government employee is illegally discriminating against another during performance of his or her official duties.

Sections 1981 and 1983 are the laws most frequently used in the employment setting if a claim is not brought using Title VII. Since Title VII is part of a comprehensive statutory scheme to prohibit race and other discrimination, it is the preferred method of enforcing employment discrimination claims. As we have seen, a complete and comprehensive administrative structure has been set up to deal with such claims. The post–Civil War statutes do not offer such a structure. Employees bringing claims under Title VII go to the EEOC to file their claim and do not have to pay. Employees bringing claims under the post–Civil War statutes are on their own and must go to an attorney and must pay. On the other hand, the statute of limitations for the post–Civil War statutes is longer than under Title VII. While Title VII's basic statute of limitations is 180 days from the precipitating event, the U.S. Supreme Court has ruled that the statute of limitations on race cases under section 1981 is four years.[38] In addition, the damages under section 1981 are unlimited, unlike those under Title VII that have caps.

When you put the post–Civil War statutes' limitations together with the historical context in which African Americans operated after the Civil War until passage of the Civil Rights Act in 1964, 99 years later, it makes sense that these laws were not used as much as Title VII. From the end of the Civil War until passage of the Civil Rights Act of 1964, Jim Crow laws and iron-clad social customs segregated African Americans and denied them basic rights. This was often enforced through violence. Few African Americans had the money to sue. Between not having the legal right to have a job based on their race, not being able to afford to bring lawsuits, and taking their lives into their hands if they tried to enforce any rights they did have under these law, the post–Civil War statutes provided little relief to African Americans facing employment discrimination.

Still, they remain a viable source of employer liability and, as such, you should have some exposure to them. Note also that the laws were created to address the issue of the newly freed slaves, but the language applies to anyone, so national origin cases are also brought under the statutes. By and large, most of the cases are brought under these statutes as opposed to Title VII either because the claimant was outside the Title VII statute of limitations deadline or because the claim involves a government employer.

42 U.S.C. Section 1981

Section 1981. Equal Rights under the Law

All persons within the jurisdiction of the United States shall have the same right in every State and Territory to make and enforce contracts . . . as is enjoyed by white citizens.

This provision of the post–Civil War statutes has been used to a limited extent in the past as a basis for employees suing employers for racial discrimination in employment. In a case of first impression, the Second Circuit Court of Appeals recently held that section 1981 did not cover a race discrimination claim filed by an African American employee for actions occurring while he was on temporary work assignment in South Africa because, by its terms, the law only covers those within the jurisdiction of the United States.[39]

In 1975, the U.S. Supreme Court held that section 1981 prohibits purely private discrimination in contracts, including employment contracts. In *Patterson v. McLean Credit Union,* given for your review, the limitations of section 1981 become evident. *Patterson* was nullified by the Civil Rights Act of 1991. The act overturned *Patterson*'s holding that section 1981 does not permit actions for racial discrimination during the performance of the contract, but only in making or enforcing the contract. Note that the limitation on damages the Court spoke of as part of Title VII's administrative scheme no longer applies. The Civil Rights Act of 1991 now permits recovery of compensatory and punitive damages. How do you think this squares with the Court's statement "Neither party would be likely to conciliate if there is the possibility of the employee recovering the greater damages permitted by section 1981"?

As you read the case for historical and analytical purposes, see if you can determine why Congress would want to overrule the Supreme Court's decision by enacting the 1991 legislation. *Patterson* was specifically chosen for inclusion here to demonstrate how seemingly small, insignificant matters can accumulate and provide a solid picture of discriminatory treatment leading to employer liability. Again, vigilance pays off. Managers should curtail discriminatory activity as soon as they see it, so that it does not progress and result in liability.

42 U.S.C. Section 1983

Section 1983. Civil Action for Deprivation of Rights

Every person who, under color of any statute, ordinance, regulation, custom, or usage, of any State or Territory, subjects, or causes to be subjected, any citizen of the United States or other person within the jurisdiction thereof to the deprivation of any rights, privileges, or immunities secured by the Constitution and laws, shall be liable to the party injured in an action at law, suit in equity, or other proper proceeding for redress.

The Civil Rights Act of 1871, codified as 42 U.S.C. section 1983, protects citizens from deprivation of their legal and constitutional rights, privileges, and immunities, under color of state law. That is, someone acting on behalf of the state cannot deprive people of their rights. Examples would be (1) the New Jersey state troopers who were convicted in 2002 when racial profiling admittedly caused them to shoot 11 bullets into a car with four unarmed black and Latino students, wounding three, and (2) the police officers who were videotaped beating

Rodney King during his arrest in Los Angeles in 1991. While performing their duties as government employees, they were alleged to have deprived King of his rights by using excessive force and thus depriving him of his rights as if it were a legitimate part of their duties.

In the employment area, section 1983 cases arise when, for instance, a city fire department or municipal police department discriminates against an employee on the basis of race, gender, or one of the other bases protected under federal or state law.

Neither the Fourteenth Amendment nor section 1983 may be used for discrimination by private employers. They both redress actions by government personnel. The government may not be sued without its permission because of the Eleventh Amendment to the Constitution, so the action is brought against the government official in his or her individual and official capacity.

An Important Note

One of the prevalent misconceptions about Title VII is that all an employee must do is file a claim and the employer is automatically deemed to be liable for discrimination. This is not true. Discrimination claims under Title VII and other employment discrimination legislation must be proved just as any other lawsuits. It is not enough for an employee to allege he or she is being discriminated against. The employee must offer evidence to support the claim. As shown, at the conclusion of the chapter, in *Ali v. Mount Sinai Hospital,* not doing so has predictable results.

Many times managers do not discipline or even terminate employees with Title VII protection for fear of being sued. This should not be the approach. Rather, simply treat them and their actions as you would those of any other similarly situated employee and be consistent. There is no need to walk on eggshells. If an employee is not performing as he or she should, Title VII affords them no protection whatsoever just because they are in a protected class based on race, gender, national origin, and so forth. Title VII is not a job guarantee for women and minorities. Instead, it requires employers to provide them with equal employment opportunity, including termination if it is called for. No one can stop the employee from suing. The best an employer can do is engage in consistency and evenhandedness that makes for a less desirable target, and to have justifiable decisions to defend once sued.

In *Ali v. Mt. Sinai Hospital,* an African-American employee sued her employer for race discrimination after being disciplined for violating the hospital's detailed three-page dress code requiring that dress be "conservative and in keeping with the professional image of nursing," in deference to working in the post–open heart surgery unit. Ali said enforcement of the dress code against her was discriminatory but did not show proof of this, and her case was therefore dismissed. As you read *Ali,* take note of the inadvisability of the questionable parts of the encounter between the employer and the employee.

Management Tips

LO9   Since potentially all employees can bind employers by their discriminatory actions, it is important for all employees to understand the law. This not only will greatly aid them in avoiding acts that may cause the employer liability, but it will also go far in creating a work environment in which discrimination is less likely to occur. Through training, make sure that all employees understand:

- What Title VII is.
- What Title VII requires.
- Who Title VII applies to.
- How the employees' actions can bring about liability for the employer.
- What kinds of actions will be looked at in a Title VII proceeding.
- That the employer will not allow Title VII to be violated.
- That all employees have a right to a workplace free of illegal discrimination.
- That the workplace will try hard to be inclusive, understanding that failure to include traditionally excluded groups leads to discrimination claims.
- That the workplace will use all its available resources among its personnel to attempt to determine where support is needed in order to head off problems before they become legal liabilities.
- The need for the employer to be proactive rather than reactive in the workplace to better protect the workplace from unnecessary claims of employment discrimination.
- The need for not only specific and obvious compliance with the law, but also the historical reasons why certain actions can be interpreted differently by different groups and unwittingly create employer liability. Inclusion in the workplace of those historically excluded becomes important when it is clear that exclusion can serve as the basis for Title VII and other protective legislation claims.

Chapter Summary

- Title VII prohibits employers, unions, joint labor–management committees, and employment agencies from discriminating in any aspect of employment on the basis of race, color, religion, gender, or national origin.
- Title VII addresses subtle as well as overt discrimination and discrimination that is intentional as well as unintentional.
- The law allows for compensatory and punitive damages, where appropriate, as well as jury trials.
- The post–Civil War statutes add another area of potential liability for the employer and have a much longer statute of limitations and unlimited compensatory and punitive damages.
- The employer's best defense is a good offense. A strong, top-down policy of non-discrimination can be effective in setting the right tone and getting the

message to managers and employees alike that discrimination in employment will not be tolerated.

- Strong policies, consistently and appropriately enforced, as well as periodic training and updating as issues emerge, and even as a means of review, are most helpful.

- To the extent that an employer complies with Title VII, it can safely be said that workplace productivity will benefit, as will the employer's coffers, because unlawful employment discrimination can be costly to the employer in more ways than one.

Chapter-End Questions

1. While reviewing preemployment reports as part of her job, the claimant read a report in which an applicant admitted commenting to an employee at a prior job that "making love to you is like making love to the Grand Canyon." Later, at a meeting convened by her supervisor, the supervisor read the quote and said he didn't understand it. A male subordinate said he would explain it to him later, and both chuckled. The claimant interpreted the exchange as sexual harassment and reported it internally. The claimant alleges that nearly every action after the incident constituted retaliation for her complaint, including a lateral transfer. Will the court agree? [*Clark County School District v. Breeden,* 121 S. Ct. 1508 (2001).]

2. How long does a private employee have to file a claim with the EEOC or be barred from doing so?

3. Lin Teung files a complaint with the EEOC for national origin discrimination. His jurisdiction has a 706 agency. When Teung calls up the EEOC after 45 days to see how his case is progressing, he learns that the EEOC has not yet moved on it. Teung feels the EEOC is violating its own rules. Is it?

4. Melinda wants to file a sexual harassment claim against her employer but feels she cannot do so because he would retaliate against her by firing her. She also has no money to sue him. Any advice for Melinda?

5. Saeid, a Muslim, alleges that his supervisor made numerous remarks belittling his Muslim religion, Arabs generally, and him specifically. The comments were not made in the context of a specific employment decision affecting Saeid. Is this sufficient for the court to find discriminatory ill will? [*Maarouf v. Walker Manufacturing Co.,* 210 F.3d 750 (7th Cir. 2000).]

6. A construction company was sued for harassment when it failed to take seriously the complaints about offensive graffiti scrawled on rented portable toilets. The employer defended by saying (1) employees should be used to such rude and crude behavior; (2) the employer did not own or maintain the equipment, which came with graffiti already on it; (3) it took action after a formal employee complaint; and (4) the graffiti insulted everyone. Will the defenses be successful? [*Malone v. Foster-Wheeler Constructors,* 21 Fed. Appx. 470 (Westlaw) (7th Cir. 2001) (unpub. opinion).]

7. During the interview Gale had with Leslie Accounting Firm, Gale was asked whether she had any children, whether she planned to have any more children, to what church she belonged, and what her husband did for a living. Are these questions illegal? Explain.

8. Any claimant who has a cause of action for employment discrimination can bring his or her claim under the post–Civil War statutes, True or False? Explain.

9. Laurie, a lesbian and French national, was hired as a flight attendant to work in United Airlines' hub in Paris. Laurie was terminated at age 40. She sues United Airlines alleging employment discrimination on the basis of age, gender, and affinity orientation (the latter based on the Illinois Human Rights Act). The airline asks the court to dismiss Laurie's action on the basis that she does not live in the U.S., so the employment protection laws do not apply to her. Will the court do so? Explain. [*Rabé v. United Airlines, Inc.* 2011 WL677946 (7th Cir. 2011).]

10. Ted, the white coach of a local high school, has been at the school as a teacher, athletic director, and coach for 25 years. Over the years the neighborhood has changed from predominantly white to predominantly black. When a new principal is appointed, he and Ted do not get along well at all. Ted alleges that the principal took away a good deal of his authority and publicly castigated him for the football team's performance. Ted waits too long to sue under Title VII for race discrimination but hears about section 1981. He wants to sues for race discrimination under section 1981 but thinks he cannot do so because he is white. Is Ted correct? Explain. [*Jett v. Dallas Independent School District,* 491 U.S. 701 (1989).]

End Notes

1. http://eeoc.gov/abouteeoc/plan/par/2006/index.html.

2. See, e.g., Stetson Kennedy, *The Jim Crow Guide to the U.S.,* London: Lawrence & Wishart, 1959; Jerrold M. Packard, *American Nightmare: The History of Jim Crow,* New York: St. Martin's Press, 2002; Thomas Adams Upchurch, *Legislating Racism: The Billion Dollar Congress and the Birth of Jim Crow,* The University Press of Kentucky, 2004; and David K. Fremon, *Jim Crow Laws and Racism in American History,* New Jersey: Enslow Publishers, 2000.

3. See, e.g., Douglas A. Blackmon, *Slavery by Another Name: The Re-Enslavement of Black Americans from the Civil War to World War II,* New York: Anchor Books, 2008; David M. Oshinsky, *Worse Than Slavery: Parchman Farm and the Ordeal of Jim Crow Justice,* New York: Free Press Paperbacks, 1996.

4. Donald L. Grant, *The Way It Was in the South: The Black Experience in Georgia,* Athens, GA: University of Georgia Press, 1993; Philip Dray, *At the Hands of Persons Unknown: The Lynching of Black America,* New York: Random House, 2002; James Allen et al., *Without Sanctuary: Lynching Photography in America,* New Mexico: Twin Palms, 2005; James W. Loewen, *Sundown Towns: A Hidden Dimension of American Racism,* New York: Touchstone, 2005; Alex A. Alston, Jr., and James L. Dickerson, *Devil's Sanctuary: An Eyewitness History of Mississippi Hate Crimes,* Chicago, IL: Lawrence Hill Books, 2009.

5. For fascinating glimpses of life at the time, see, e.g., Melton A. McLaurin, *Separate Pasts: Growing Up White in the Segregated South,* Athens, GA: University of Georgia Press, 1987; Virginia Foster Durr, *Outside the Magic Circle: The Autobiography of Virginia Foster Durr,* New York: University of Alabama Press, 1985; Lillian Smith, *Killers of the Dream,* New York: W.W. Norton, 1949; and Leon F. Litwack, *Trouble in Mind: Black Southerners in the Age of Jim Crow,* New York: Vintage Books, 1998.

6. 347 U.S. 483 (1954).

7. See, e.g., Charles J. Ogletree, Jr., *All Deliberate Speed: Reflections on the First Half Century of Brown v. Board of Education,* New York: W.W. Norton, 2004; Elizabeth Jacoway, *Turn Away Thy Son: Little Rock, the Crisis That Shocked the Nation,* New York: Free Press, 2007; Derrick A. Bell, Jr., *Race, Racism and American Law,* Boston: Little, Brown, 1980.

8. Adam Fairclough, *To Redeem the Soul of America: The Southern Christian Leadership Conference and Martin Luther King, Jr.,* Athens, GA: University of Georgia Press, 1987; Juan Williams, *Eyes on the Prize: America's Civil Rights Years, 1954-1965,* New York: Viking Press, 1987; Clive Webb, *Massive Resistance: Opposition to the Second Reconstruction,* New York: Oxford University Press, 2005; Maurice C. Daniels, *Horace T. Ward: Desegregation of the University of Georgia, Civil Rights Advocacy, and Jurisprudence,* Athens, GA: Clark Atlanta University Press, 2001; Mark V. Tushnet, Ed., *Thurgood Marshall: His Speeches, Writings, Arguments, Opinions and Reminiscences,* Chicago, IL: Lawrence Hill Books, 2001.

9. See David C. Cozak and Kenneth N. Ciboski, Eds., *The American Presidency,* Nelson Hall, 1985, http://faculty1.coloradocollege.edu/%7Ebloevy/CivilRightsActOf1964/; Charles Whalen and Barbara Whalen, *The Longest Debate: A Legislative History of the 1964 Civil Rights Act,* Santa Ana, CA: Seven Locks Press, 1985.

10. See., e.g., The Foot Soldiers for Equal Justice Project at the University of Georgia at footsoldier.uga.edu.

11. The EEOC's regulations can be found in the Code of Federal Regulations (e.g., 29 C.F.R. § 1604.1–9, Guidelines on Discrimination Because of Sex; 29 C.F.R. § 1604.10, Guidelines on Discrimination Because of Sex, Pregnancy and Childbirth; 29 C.F.R. part 1606, Guidelines on Discrimination Because of National Origin; 29 C.F.R. part 1607, Employee Selection Procedures; 29 C.F.R. § 1613.701–707, Guidelines on Discrimination Because of Disability; 45 C.F.R. part 90, Guidelines on Discrimination Because of Age; 29 C.F.R. 1635 Regulations Under the Generic Information Nondiscrimination Act of 2008 Final Rule).

12. "Employment Discrimination Laws 'New Frontier' in War Against Human Labor Trafficking," 1/19/11 http://www.eeoc.gov/eeoc/newsroom/release/1-19-11.cfm.

13. "EEOC Public Meeting Explores The Use of Credit Histories as Employment Selection Criteria," 10/20/10 http://www.eeoc.gov/eeoc/newsroom/release/10-20-10b.cfm.

14. "Statement of Stuart J. Ishimaru, Acting Chairman U.S. Equal Employment Opportunity Commission Before the Committee on Health, Education, Labor and Pensions, U.S. Senate," 3/11/10 http://www.eeoc.gov/eeoc/events/ishimaru_paycheck_fairness.cfm.

15. "Enforcement Guidance: Unlawful Disparate Treatment of Workers with Caregiving Responsibilities," 5/23/07 http://www.eeoc.gov/policy/docs/caregiving.html.

16. http://eeoc.gov/abouteeoc/plan/par/2006/chair_message.html.

17. http://eeoc.gov/eeoc/statistics/enforcement/charges.cfm

18. Ibid.

19. 535 U.S. 137 (2002).

20. 6/27/02, EEOC, Rescission of Enforcement Guidance on Remedies Available to Undocumented Workers under Federal Employment Discrimination Laws, http://www.eeoc.gov/policy/docs/undoc-rescind.html; 10/26/99, EEOC Issues Guidance on Remedies for Undocumented Workers under Federal Laws Prohibiting Employment Discrimination, http://www.eeoc.gov/eeoc/newsroom/release/10-26-99.cfm.

21. *Dukes v. Wal-Mart,* Docket No. 10-277. For a look at the parties' briefs, oral argument points and other information on the case, see the Supreme Court of the United States blog: http://www.scotusblog.com/case-files/cases/wal-mart-v-dukes/.

22. http://www.ccoc.gov/eeoc/statistics/enforcement/all.cfm.

23. "Fiscal Year 2012 Congressional Budget Justification," http://www.eeoc.gov/eeoc/plan/2012budget.cfm.

24. 536 U.S. 101 (2002).

25. 550 U.S.__, 127 S. Ct. 2162, 167 L. Ed. 2d 982, 2007 U.S. LEXIS 6295 (2007).

26. EEOC Solicits Comments on Proposed Improvements to Federal Employee Discrimination Complaint Process, 12/22/09 http://www.eeoc.gov/eeoc/newsroom/release/12-21-09.cfm.

27. EEOC Compliance Manual, Section 8—Retaliation, http://www.eeoc.gov/policy/docs/retal.html; "Facts About Retaliation," http://www.eeoc.gov/laws/types/facts-retal.cfm.

28. http://www.eeoc.gov/eeoc/statistics/enforcement/charges.cfm.

29. "Fiscal Year 2012 Congressional Budget Justification," http://www.eeoc.gov/eeoc/plan/2012budget.cfm.

30. "Fiscal Year 2010 Performance and Accountability Report Highlights," http://www.eeoc.gov/eeoc/plan/2010parhigh_discussion.cfm.

31. Ibid.

32. http://eeoc.gov/employers/investigations.html.

33. "Is This Woman Too Hot To Be a Banker?," Elizabeth Dwoskin, *The Village Voice News,* 6/21/10 http://www.villagevoice.com/2010-06-01/news/is-this-woman-too-hot-to-work-in-a-bank/.

34. 532 U.S. 105 (2001).

35. 534 U.S. 279 (2002).

36. *Circuit City Stores, Inc. v. Adams,* 535 U.S. 1112 (2002).

37. Jerrold M. Packard, *American Nightmare: The History of Jim Crow,* St. Martin's Press, 2002; Thomas Adams Upchurch, *Legislating Racism: The Billion Dollar Congress and the Birth of Jim Crow,* The University Press of Kentucky, 2004; and David K. Fremon, *Jim Crow Laws and Racism in American History,* Enslow Publishers, 2000.

38. *Jones v. R.R. Donnelley & Sons Co.,* 541 U.S.369 (2004).

39. *Ofori-Tenkorang v. AIG,* 460 F.3d 296 (2d Cir. 2006).

Cases

Petruska v. Gannon University 462 F. 3d 294 (3d Cir. 2006)

Case 1

Employee, the chaplain of a Catholic university, sued for gender-based employment discrimination in violation of, among other things, Title VII. The court dismissed the action, saying that the university, as a religious institution, was not subject to Title VII.

Smith, J.

***

Gannon University is a private, Catholic, diocesan college established under the laws of the Commonwealth of Pennsylvania. Plaintiff employee was initially hired by Gannon as Director for the University's Center for Social Concerns and in considering and accepting this position, relied upon Gannon's self-representation as an equal opportunity employer that does not discriminate on the basis of, among other things, gender.

Following [Gannon's President] Rubino's resignation [after allegations of a sexual affair with a subordinate], Gannon engaged in a campaign to cover up Rubino's sexual misconduct. Employee was vocal in opposing this and other of the Administration's policies and procedures, which she viewed as discriminatory toward females. One such policy was [Bishop of the Roman Catholic Diocese of Erie] Trautman's willingness to allow allegedly abusive clergy to remain on campus, including at least one former Gannon priest who had been removed because of sexual misconduct directed at students.

Employee also strongly opposed the University's efforts, during the time that Rubino was coming under investigation for alleged sexual harassment of females, to limit the time frame within which victims of sexual harassment could file grievances. As Chair of the University's Institutional Integrity Committee, employee was instrumental in submitting a Middle States accreditation report which raised issues of gender-based inequality in the pay of Gannon's female employees and which was critical of the University's policies and procedures for addressing complaints of sexual harassment and other forms of discrimination. Despite pressure from the University's administration, employee refused to change those portions of the report which were critical of the University.

Employee contends that, in retaliation for the foregoing conduct and because of her gender, she was discriminated against in the terms and conditions of her employment. Believing that she was about to be fired,

employee served Gannon with two weeks notice of her resignation. Employee was advised the following day that her resignation was accepted effective immediately and that she was to pack her belongings and leave the campus. Her access to the campus and to students was strictly limited thereafter. Following employee's departure, her supervisor stated on several occasions to both students and staff that a female would not be considered to replace employee as Chaplain.

The University has moved to dismiss all claims on the ground that they are barred by the so-called "ministerial exception," which is frequently applied in employment discrimination cases involving religious institutions. The ministerial exception is rooted in the First Amendment which provides that "Congress shall make no law respecting an establishment of religion, or prohibiting the free exercise thereof." Among the prerogatives protected by the Free Exercise Clause is the right of religious institutions to manage their internal affairs.

The Establishment Clause prohibits laws "respecting an establishment of religion." The Supreme Court held that a statute comports with the Establishment Clause if it has a secular legislative purpose, if its principal or primary effect neither advances nor inhibits religion, and if it does not foster an "excessive government entanglement with religion." Unconstitutional entanglement with religion may arise in situations "where a 'protracted legal process pit(s) church and state as adversaries,' and where the Government is placed in a position of choosing among 'competing religious visions.' "

The questions presented in this case are whether applying Title VII to Gannon's decision to restructure would infringe upon its free exercise rights and whether adjudication of Petruska's Title VII claims would result in unconstitutional entanglement under the Establishment Clause. Every one of our sister circuits to consider the issue has concluded that application of Title VII to a minister-church relationship would violate—or would risk violating—the First Amendment and, accordingly,

Petruska alleges that Gannon demoted and constructively discharged her from her position as University Chaplain based on her gender and retaliated against her on the basis of her opposition to sexual harassment at the University. Her discrimination and retaliation claims are premised upon Gannon's decision to restructure, a decision which Petruska argues was merely pretext for gender discrimination. It is clear from the face of Petruska's complaint, however, that Gannon's choice to restructure constituted a decision about who would perform spiritual functions and about how those function would be divided. Accordingly, application of Title VII's discrimination and retaliation provisions to Gannon's decision to restructure would violate the Free Exercise Clause. For that reason, Petruska's Title VII claims should be dismissed.

The First Amendment protects a church's right to decide matters of faith and to declare its doctrine free from state interference. A church's ability to select who will perform particular spiritual functions is a necessary corollary to this right. The function of Petruska's position as University Chaplain was ministerial in nature, and therefore, her Title VII, civil claim must be dismissed. Based upon the foregoing reasons, the trial court's decision is AFFIRMED and REMANDED. [Petruska petitioned the U.S. Supreme Court to hear an appeal from this case and the Court denied the petition.]

Case Questions

1. Do you agree with the court's decision? Explain.
2. As a manager in this situation, how do you think you would have handled the chaplain's complaints?
3. Given the power that religious organizations have under Title VII, how do you think employment discrimination concerns can be addressed in the religious workplace?

Case 2

Patterson v. McLean Credit Union
491 U.S. 164 (1989)

A black female alleged racial discrimination in violation of section 1981 in that she was treated differently from white employees and not promoted, on the basis of race. The Court held that section 1981 was not available to address this problem since the case did not involve the making of a contract, but rather its performance.

Kennedy, J.

***

Patterson, a black female, worked for the McLean Credit Union (MCU) as a teller and file coordinator for 10 years. She alleges that when she first interviewed for her job, the supervisor, who later became the president of MCU, told her that she would be working with all white women and that they probably would not like working with her because she was black. According to Patterson, in the subsequent years, it was her supervisor who proved to have the problem with her working at the credit union.

Patterson alleges that she was subjected to a pattern of discrimination at MCU which included her supervisor repeatedly staring at her for minutes at a time while she performed her work and not doing so to white employees; not promoting her or giving her the usually perfunctory raises which other employees routinely received; not arranging to have her work reassigned to others when she went on vacation, as was routinely done with other employees, but rather, allowing Patterson's work to accumulate during her absence; assigning her menial, non-clerical tasks such as sweeping and dusting, while such tasks were not assigned to other similarly situated employees; being openly critical of Patterson's work in staff meetings, and that of one other black employee, while white employees were told of their shortcomings privately; telling Patterson that it was known that "blacks are known to work slower than whites, by nature" or, saying in one instance, "some animals [are] faster than other animals"; repeatedly suggesting that a white would be able to perform Patterson's job better than she could; unequal work assignments between Patterson and other similarly situated white employees, with Patterson receiving more work than others; having her work scrutinized more closely and criticized more severely than white employees; despite her desire to "move up and advance," being offered no training for higher jobs during her 10 years at the credit union, while white employees were offered training, including those at the same level, but with less seniority (such employees were later promoted); not being informed of job openings, nor interviewed for them, while less senior whites were informed of the positions and hired; and when another manager recommended to Patterson's supervisor a different black to fill a position as a data processor, the supervisor said that he did not "need any more problems around here," and would "search for additional people who are not black."

When Patterson complained about her workload, she was given no help, and in fact was given more work and told she always had the option of quitting. Patterson was laid off after 10 years with MCU. She brought suit under 42 U.S.C. section 1981, alleging harassment, failure to promote and discharge because of her race.

None of the racially harassing conduct which McLean engaged in involved the section 1981 prohibition against refusing to make a contract with Patterson or impairing Patterson's ability to enforce her existing contract rights with McLean. It is clear that Patterson is attacking conditions of employment which came into existence after she formed the contract to work for McLean. Since section 1981 only prohibits the interference with the making or enforcement of contracts because of race, performance of the contract is not actionable under section 1981.

Section 1981's language is specifically limited to making and enforcing contracts. To permit race discrimination cases involving post-formation actions would also undermine the detailed and well-crafted procedures for conciliation and resolution of Title VII claims. While section 1981 has no administrative procedure for review or conciliation of claims, Title VII has an elaborate system which is designed to investigate claims and work toward resolution of them by conciliation rather than litigation. This includes Title VII's limiting recovery to back pay, while section 1981 permits plenary compensatory and punitive damages in appropriate cases. Neither party would be likely to conciliate if there is the possibility of the employee recovering the greater damages permitted by section 1981. There is some overlap between Title VII and section 1981, and when conduct is covered by both, the detailed procedures of Title VII are rendered a dead letter, as the plaintiff is free to pursue a claim by bringing suit under section 1981 without resort to those statutory prerequisites.

Regarding Patterson's failure to promote claim, this is somewhat different. Whether a racially discriminatory failure to promote claim is cognizable under section 1981 depends upon whether the nature of the change in positions is such that it involved the opportunity to enter into a new contract with the employer. If so, then the employer's refusal to enter the new contract is actionable under section 1981. AFFIRMED in part, VACATED in part, and REMANDED.

Case Questions

1. Do you think justice was served in this case? Explain. Why do you think Patterson waited so long to sue?

2. If you had been the manager when Patterson was initially interviewed, would you have made the statement about whites not accepting her? Why or why not?

3. When looking at the list of actions Patterson alleged McLean engaged in, do any seem appropriate? Why do you think it was done or permitted?

Ali v. Mount Sinai Hospital *68 Empl. Prac. Dec. (CCH) 44,188, 1996 U.S. Dist. LEXIS 8079 (S.D.N.Y. 1996)*

An employee sued the employer for racial discrimination in violation of Title VII, for discriminatory enforcement of the employer's dress code. She alleged she was disciplined for violating the code but whites were not. The court found that the employee had offered no evidence of discriminatory enforcement, so the court had no choice but to find in favor of the employer.

Gershon, J.

***

It is undisputed that, at all relevant times, the Hospital had a detailed three-page dress code for all of its nursing department staff, including unit clerks. It expressly provided that "the style chosen be conservative and in keeping with the professional image in nursing" and that the "Unit clerks wear the blue smock provided by the Hospital with conservative street clothes." The wearing of boots, among other items of dress, was expressly prohibited. With regard to hair, the dress code provided that "it should be clean and neatly groomed to prevent interference with patient care" and only "plain" hair barrettes and hairpins should be worn. As plaintiff acknowledges, "The hallmark of said code was that the staff had to dress and groom themselves in a conservative manner."

It is also undisputed that Ms. Ali violated the dress code. Ms. Ali reported to work at the CSICU wearing a red, three-quarter length, cowl-necked dress and red boots made of lycra fabric which went over her knees. Over her dress, Ms. Ali wore the regulation smock provided by the Hospital. She wore her hair in what she says she then called a "punk" style. She now calls it a "fade" style, which she describes as an "Afro hairstyle." It was shorter on the sides than on the top and was in its natural color, black. According to Dr. Shields, Ms. Ali's hair was not conservative because it "was so high" and "you noticed it right away because it was high and back behind the ears and down. It certainly caused you to look at her. It caused attention." Deposition of Dr. Elizabeth Shields: Her hair "had to be at least three to five inches high down behind her ears." This description by Dr. Shields has not been disputed.

According to the employee, Dr. Shields approached her and asked her to look in the mirror and see what looks back at her. Ali responded that she looked beautiful. Ms. Ali testified that Dr. Shields told her that "I belong in a zoo, and then the last thing she said was I look like I [am] . . . going to a disco or belong in a disco or something to that effect." Dr. Shields testified: "I told her about the whole outfit. She had red boots, red dress, in the unit. This is the post open heart unit. People come out of here after just having cracked their chest. We were expected to be conservative."

Title VII makes it an unlawful employment practice for an employer "to fail or refuse to hire or to discharge any individual, or otherwise to discriminate against any individual with respect to his compensation, terms, conditions, or privileges of employment, because of such individual's race, color, religion, sex, or national origin. . . ." Defendants seek summary judgment dismissing the complaint on the ground that plaintiff cannot make a *prima facie* showing that they engaged in discriminatory conduct.

To establish a *prima facie* case of individualized disparate treatment from an alleged discriminatory enforcement of the dress code, plaintiff must show that she is a member of a protected class and that, at the time of the alleged discriminatory treatment, she was satisfactorily performing the duties of her position. This she has done. However, her *prima facie* showing must also include a showing that Mount Sinai Hospital had a dress code and that it was applied to her under circumstances giving rise to an inference of discrimination.

Reviewing all of the evidence submitted on the motion, employee does not raise an issue of fact as to whether the enforcement of the code against her was discriminatory. There is no dispute that employee was in violation of the dress code. Her claim is that the dress code was enforced against her but not against others, who also violated its requirements, but were not black. The problem is the utter lack of evidence supporting this position.

Employee offers no evidence that the dress code was not enforced against other Hospital employees as it was against her. Dr. Shields' testimony that the dress code had been enforced against other nurses was not disputed. Although Ms. Ali identified certain Caucasian women whom she believed were in violation of the code, she failed to set forth any evidence to show a lack of enforcement.

All that employee's testimony establishes is that she was unaware of the enforcement of the dress code against others. Following a full opportunity for discovery, employee has not proffered any additional evidence to support her claim of disparate treatment. On this record, there is no reason to believe that she will be able to offer at trial evidence from which a jury could reasonably conclude that there was racially discriminatory enforcement of the dress code.

It is not enough that Ms. Ali sincerely believes that she was the subject of discrimination; "[a] plaintiff is not entitled to a trial based on pure speculation, no matter how earnestly held." Summary judgment is appropriate here because employee has failed to raise an issue of fact as to whether the dress code was enforced against her under circumstances giving rise to an inference of discrimination. Motion to dismiss GRANTED.

Case Questions

1. What do you think of the way in which Ali was approached by Dr. Shields about her violation of the dress code? Does this seem advisable to you?

2. How much of a role do you think different cultural values played in this situation? Explain.

3. What can the employer do to avoid even the appearance of unfair enforcement of its dress policy in the future?

Chapter 4

Legal Construction of the Employment Environment

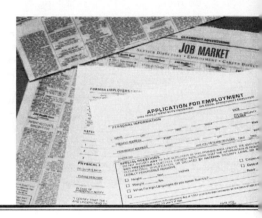

Learning Objectives

After completing this chapter, you should be able to:

LO1 Explain why employers might be concerned about ensuring protections for equal opportunity during recruitment, in particular.

LO2 Describe how the recruitment environment is regulated, by both statutes and common law.

LO3 Describe the employer's opportunities during the information-gathering process to learn as much as possible about hiring the most effective worker.

LO4 Explain how the employer might be liable under the theory of negligent hiring.

LO5 Identify the circumstances under which an employer may be responsible for an employee's compelled self-publication, thus liable for defamation.

LO6 Explain the difference between testing for eligibility and testing for ineligibility, and provide examples of each.

LO7 Identify the key benefits of performance appraisal structures, as well as their areas of potential pitfalls.

Opening Scenarios

SCENARIO 1

1
Scenario

Wendy Swan is asked to fill two new positions at her company. The first requires complicated engineering knowledge; the second has no prerequisites and no opportunity for advancement without a college degree. Wendy wants to hire younger workers so they will be more likely to have a long tenure at the firm. The advertisement for the positions placed in a newspaper of general circulation requests résumés from "recent college graduates," engineering degrees preferred. Is Wendy's firm subject to any liability based on this advertisement?

SCENARIO 2

2
Scenario

Shefali Trivedi is the manager at a large food store and has hired many young employees to work for her on a part-time basis. During the past few weeks, she has noticed that she is missing a sizable amount of her stock in many different areas. She has no idea where to begin a search for suspects but is convinced that it is an "inside" job because her security during nonworking hours is excellent. Can she simply notify each of her employees that they will all be required to submit to a polygraph test to determine who is involved, or should she perform additional investigation and use the polygraph test only as a means of confirmation of suspicion?

In addition, Shefali has not yet purchased computerized checkout scanners, and therefore all of the product prices must be input by hand to the store registers. Shefali has found in the past that certain employees are able to perform this task at a much more rapid pace than others. To maintain store efficiency, she decides to test all applicants relating to their ability to input prices into the register. After administering an on-site timed test, she finds that 12 white applicants, 2 black applicants, and 1 Hispanic applicant are represented among the top 15 performers, in that order of performance. Shefali has five positions available. Will she be subject to liability for disparate impact discrimination if she proceeds to hire the five top performers, all of whom are white?

SCENARIO 3

3
Scenario

Mark-Jonathan is the supervisor of 12 employees, most of whom generally perform adequate work in conformance with company job descriptions and standards. However, he has had problems in completing the performance appraisals of two employees.

The first employee is Gordie, a young man who went through a divorce during the past year. He was awarded custody of his children and has had a difficult time throughout this past year balancing his increased familial responsibilities with his job requirements. He has missed several important meetings as a result. Gordie has received two written warnings about his inadequate performance, and a poor year-end performance appraisal would mean an automatic dismissal. However, Mark-Jonathan is confident that Gordie will be able to successfully manage these two priorities in the coming year, if only given the chance. Does Mark-Jonathan draft an honest appraisal of his past performance with the knowledge that it would mean Gordie would lose his job according to company policy, or does he decide to use his discretion and offer a less-than-truthful assessment, knowing that it is in the company's best interest to retain this employee?

Mark-Jonathan's dilemma is accentuated by the fact that he is to review Julio, an Argentinean worker who holds a position similar to Gordie's. Julio is consistently late for work and also has received two written warnings about his inadequate performance. Mark-Jonathan has no idea why Julio arrives late, and, when asked, Julio offers no sufficient justification. If Mark-Jonathan writes a performance evaluation that highlights this poor behavior, similar to Gordie's, and terminates Julio but not Gordie (a white male), he is concerned about the potential for discrimination implications.

Evolution of the Employment Relationship

The people who work at a firm—its human resources—are among its most valuable assets; consequently, the utmost care must be used in their selection process. The law therefore permits employers much leeway in choosing and managing employees (and in their terminations, as you saw in Chapter 2). Basically, the only restrictions on the employment relationship are the laws that protect certain groups from employment discrimination (as will be discussed) since history has demonstrated a need for such protection. As we will see, discrimination in employment, whether intentional or unintentional, actually is allowed unless it is based on or has a different impact on people based on their membership in a particular category, such as gender, race, religion, disability, and so on. Employers looking for a salesperson may discriminate against applicants who cannot get along well with others; employers hiring computer technicians may discriminate on the basis of computer training; and other individuals may be discriminated against for equally permissible reasons. (See Exhibit 4.1, "Realities about Hiring Employees or Finding a Job.")

The focus of this chapter will be on the evolution of the employment relationship, from recruitment of appropriate candidates through hiring, testing, and performance appraisals. Though the chapter will not reiterate completely the nature of Title VII regulation discussed in Chapter 3, it is difficult to discuss the regulation of this evolution without heavily drawing on those concepts. Accordingly, we will briefly mention appropriate and applicable laws as they arise, though fuller coverage will be given to these issues in the chapters that follow.

The employment relationship usually begins with recruitment. Employers use a variety of techniques to locate suitable applicants. Once the employer has a group from which to choose, information gathering begins. This stage

---

Exhibit 4.1 *Realities about Hiring Employees or Finding a Job*

1. The best way to promote workplace unity may *not* be to seek guidance only from those who already work there.

2. If an employer places an advertisement only at limited locations within the city where hiring is to be done, it might risk being accused of selective recruiting.

3. The purpose of this interview is not only for the employer to find out information about the employee. It is also for the employer to share information about itself so that the potential employee may learn whether it is the best fit for her or him.

4. While promoting from within may raise employee morale and encourage loyalty, the strategy has the potential to lead to either a real or perceived lack of balance or discriminatory impact.

5. Though nepotism (favoring family members in hiring decisions) occurs with frequency, it has the potential to create challenges in the workplace.

consists of soliciting information from the applicant through forms, interviews, references, and testing. Targeting recruitment and selection has been found to be the most effective way to reduce employment discrimination charges.

Recruitment

LO1

Recruitment practices are particularly susceptible to claims of discrimination as barriers to equal opportunity. If applicants are denied access to employment opportunities on the basis of membership in a protected class, they may have a claim against the potential employer for discriminatory practice.

Statutes such as Title VII of the Civil Rights Act of 1964 and others require, in part, that an employer not only recruit from a diverse audience but also design employment announcements that will encourage a diverse group of people to apply. How does the employer create an applicant pool? Does it place an advertisement in a local newspaper, advertise on the radio in a given neighborhood, ask certain people to submit résumés, or ask current employees for suggestions? Does the advertisement contain gender-specific language that would discourage certain groups from applying for the position? Each of these possibilities has potential hazards. Each of these recruitment practices could easily result in an adverse impact on a protected group even if the employer had no intent to discriminate.

Federal Statutory Regulation of Recruitment

LO2

Though a number of statutes apply to recruitment (see Exhibit 4.2), the EEOC has offered important guidance on disability-related inquiries of applicants as well as employees under the Americans with Disabilities Act, which is covered in greater detail in Chapter 13. For example, prior to an offer of employment, an employer may not ask disability-related questions or require any medical examinations, even if they seem to be related to the job. However, the EEOC's Enforcement Guidelines explain that an employer may ask whether an applicant will need a "reasonable accommodation" during the hiring process (e.g., interview, written test, job demonstration). The employer also may inquire whether the applicant will need a reasonable accommodation for the job if the employer knows that an applicant has a disability (i.e., if the disability is obvious or the applicant has voluntarily disclosed the information, and the employer reasonably believes that the applicant will need a reasonable accommodation).

The employer must provide a reasonable accommodation to a qualified applicant with a disability even if it believes that it would be unable to provide this individual with a reasonable accommodation on the job if the person were eventually hired. According to the EEOC, in many instances, employers will be unable to determine whether an individual needs reasonable accommodation to perform the job based solely on a request for accommodation during the application process, or whether the same type or degree of accommodation will be needed on the job as was required for the application process.

Exhibit 4.2 *Federal Laws Regulating Recruitment*

TITLE VII OF THE CIVIL RIGHTS ACT OF 1964

Section 703(a)(1)   It shall be an unlawful employment practice for an employer to fail or refuse to hire . . . any individual or otherwise to discriminate against any individual with respect to his [sic] compensation, terms, conditions, or privileges of employment, because of such individual's race, color, religion, sex, or national origin.

   Section 704(b)   It shall be an unlawful employment practice for an employer, . . . to print or cause to be printed or published any notice or advertisement relating to employment by such an employer indicating any preference, limitation, specification, or discrimination based on race, color, religion, sex, or national origin, except that such a notice or advertisement may indicate a preference, limitation, specification, or discrimination based on religion, sex, or national origin when religion, sex, or national origin is a bona fide occupational qualification for employment.

VOCATIONAL REHABILITATION ACT OF 1973 AND THE AMERICANS WITH DISABILITIES ACT OF 1990

The Rehabilitation Act and the Americans with Disabilities Act, which will be covered in depth in Chapter 13, protect otherwise qualified individuals with disabilities. The former regulates the employment practices of federal contractors, agencies, and employers, while the latter act applies similar standards to private-sector employers of 25 (15, effective July 1993) employees or more.

   The Rehabilitation Act specifically provides that, in connection with recruitment, contractors and their subcontractors who have contracts with the government in excess of $10,000 must design and commit to an affirmative action program with the purpose of providing employment opportunities to disabled applicants. Affirmative action recruitment programs may include specific recruitment plans for universities for the disabled, designing positions that will easily accommodate a disabled employee, and adjusting work schedules to conform to the needs of certain applicants.

AGE DISCRIMINATION IN EMPLOYMENT ACT OF 1967

All employers of 20 or more employees are subject to the act, which prohibits discrimination against an individual 40 years of age or older, unless age is a bona fide occupational qualification. In addition, the act states:

> *Section 4(e)*   It shall be unlawful for an employer . . . to print or publish, or cause to be printed or published, any notice or advertisement relating to employment . . . indicating any preference, limitation, specification or discrimination based on age.

IMMIGRATION REFORM AND CONTROL ACT OF 1986

IRCA is slightly different in its regulation of recruitment. IRCA applies to all employers. IRCA's purpose is to eliminate work opportunities that attract illegal aliens to the United States. With regard to discrimination based on national origin, the act provides that all employers must determine the eligibility of each individual they intend to hire, prior to the commencement of employment. In this way, IRCA condones discrimination against illegal aliens in recruitment. Note that while IRCA applies to all employers, its discrimination provisions apply only to those with four employees or more.

State Employment Law Regulation

Many states have enacted legislation specifically aimed at expansion of the federal statutes above. For instance, many states have human rights acts that include in their protections the prohibitions against discrimination based on marital status or affinity orientation. The statutes generally establish a state human rights commission, which hears claims brought under the state act. Several other states have enacted legislation that closely mirrors Title VII but covers a larger number of employers.

Common Law: Misrepresentations and Fraud

In addition to statutes, recruitment is also governed by the common law; and one area where employers sometimes get into hot water in this regard involves statements and promises made during the recruitment process. A company representative who makes an intentional or negligent misrepresentation that encourages an applicant to take a job may be liable to that applicant for any harm that results. Misrepresentations may include claims regarding the terms of the job offer, including the type of position available, the salary to be paid, the job requirements, and other matters directly relating to the representation of the offer. (See Exhibit 4.3, "Common-Law Recruitment Violations," for elements of the *prima facie* cases.)

For example, assume an applicant is told by an employer at the time when she is hired that she will automatically receive a raise at her six-month review. Based

---

Exhibit 4.3 *Common-Law Recruitment Violations*

Fraud
- Misrepresentation
- ... of a material fact
- ... with intent to deceive, or recklessness about its truth or falsity
- ... on which the applicant reasonably relies
- ... to her or his detriment.

Misrepresentation
- False statement.
- True statement creating a false impression.
- Silence where:
  - It is necessary to correct applicant's mistaken belief about material facts.
  - There is active concealment of material facts.
  - It is necessary to correct an employer's statement that was true at the time made, but which subsequently became false.

Material facts
- Statement of fact
- ... which will influence
- ... a reasonable person
- ... regarding whether to enter into a contract.
- *Note that an opinion is not a material fact because it would be generally unreasonable to rely only on the opinion of another in arriving at a decision.*

on this representation, the applicant accepts an offer. Six months pass and she does not receive the promised raise. She may be able to sue her employer for the misrepresentation that induced her to take the job, even if she is an at-will employee working without a contract.

Additionally, the misrepresentation need not actually be a false statement: Where a statement creates a false impression, the employer also may be liable for fraud if the employee's impression was reasonable. Or, where the employer is aware that the applicant is under a mistaken belief about the position or the company, the employer's silence may constitute misrepresentation.

Where the employer hides certain bits of information, the employer's silence may again be considered misrepresentation. For instance, suppose an employer needs someone to serve as an assistant to the president of the company. The president has a reputation for being unpleasant to his assistants and for constantly firing them. The employer, therefore, solicits applications for a general administrative position, "with specific duties to be assigned later," knowing the hiree will spend the majority of the time working for the president.

Someone applies for the job and states during his interview that he would like the position and says he is glad that it is not the assistant-to-the-president position for which they were interviewing last month. He is offered the job, and even though he has an excellent offer from another company for more money, decides to take the job because he likes the work environment. Later, he is told that he will be spending a large part of his workday with the president. The employee could sue the employer for misrepresentation, even though the employer did not respond to his statement about the president during the interview.

Employers also may be liable for fraud in recruitment when misstatements are used to discourage potential applicants from pursuing positions. For instance, an employer who wishes to maintain a male-dominated workforce may intentionally present an excessively negative image of the position or the company in an effort to persuade females not to apply. If all candidates are offered the same information, there may be no basis for a discrimination claim. However, if only the female applicants receive this discouraging outlook, the practice presents to the female applicants a "chilling" effect and the employer may be subject to claims of gender discrimination.

Application of Regulation to Recruitment Practices
Advertisements

Statutes and the common-law claim of fraud protect applicants from discriminatory recruitment practices, ranging from a refusal to interview Latinos to a job notice that is posted only in the executive suite where it will be seen primarily by white males. Assume, for instance, that an employer advertises in a newspaper that is circulated in a neighborhood that has an extremely high Asian population with very few other minorities represented. You might also assume that the employer can expect to see almost all of its applications from Asians and few, if any, applications from other groups. While there may be no intent to discriminate, the effect of the practice is an unbalanced workforce with a disparate impact on non-Asians.

Scenario

In connection with Scenario 1, recall that Wendy is concerned about placing an advertisement requesting résumés from "recent college grads." Older workers may claim that they are discouraged from applying due to the language—they are less likely to be "recent" college grads. On the other hand, language such as this does not constitute a per se violation. Instead, the applicant would have to establish a *prima facie* case of age discrimination. Though terminology such as this seems to be a minor concern to some, courts have found that it may lead to a belief that stereotyping or pigeonholing of one gender or a certain age group in certain positions is condoned by the law. Consider Dominick's supermarket's experience when it named the second-in-command of its deli section the "Second Deli Man," notwithstanding whether the person was male or female. Maybe someone at Dominick's noticed the inconsistency this might create, but probably no one expected a class action suit by 1,500 women alleging gender discrimination! While this was only one of numerous pieces of evidence, it may have made a difference in encouraging a settlement.

Word-of-Mouth Recruiting

The same discriminatory effect may occur where an employer obtains its new employees from referrals from within its own workforce, or "word-of-mouth" recruiting. Generally most people know and recommend others similar to themselves. Word-of-mouth recruiting generally results in a homogeneous workplace.

This type of recruiting is not necessarily harmful where precautions are taken to ensure a balanced applicant pool or where it is necessary to ensure the hiring of the safest and most competent workers. Benefits of this type of recruitment include the preliminary screening accomplished by the current employees before they even recommend the applicant for the position, and the propensity for long-term service and loyalty among the new hires. Since they already have bonds to the company, a family attitude toward the firm, resulting in increased productivity, is more easily developed. In fact, a 2010 study found that 25.7 percent of hires in 2009 were part of an employee referral program.[1] The vast majority of respondents reported that referrals were the number one source of above-average applicants. The study found a turnover rate among referred hires 32 percent lower than for other hires, the highest satisfaction among all hires, and an 82 percent ROI measured across all indices.[2] But consider how this might lead to liability under Title VII.

There is a significant difference between *disparate impact* and *disparate treatment* in the context of word-of-mouth recruiting. The Seventh Circuit decided two important cases in this area, one that explained the difference and one that subsequently applied it. In *EEOC v. Chicago Miniature Lamp Works,*[3] the EEOC claimed that Chicago Miniature Lamp Works discriminated against blacks in its recruitment and hiring of its entry-level workers because it recruited primarily through an informal word-of-mouth process. Current employees would simply tell their relatives and friends about a job; if interested, these people then would come to Miniature's office and complete an application form. Miniature did not tell or encourage its employees to recruit this way.

Between 1978 and 1981, Miniature hired 146 entry-level workers. Nine of these workers (6 percent) were black. The trial court concluded that "the statistical probability of Chicago Miniature's hiring so few blacks in the 1978–81 period, in the absence of racial bias against blacks in recruitment and hiring, is virtually zero."

The Seventh Circuit evaluated the EEOC's arguments for both discriminatory treatment and impact. It dismissed the treatment claim, which requires intent, explaining that "[i]ntent means a subjective desire or wish for these discriminatory results to occur." Since there was no evidence whatsoever of any desire for the results, with regard to impact, the Seventh Circuit also dismissed the claims. "[A] Title VII plaintiff does not make out a case of disparate impact simply by showing that, 'at the bottom line,' there is a racial imbalance in the work force." Instead, the plaintiff must identify a *particular practice* that caused the disparate impact. In a seminal ruling that has been cited significantly since, the court held:

> The EEOC does not allege that Miniature affirmatively engaged in word-of-mouth recruitment of the kind where it told or encouraged its employees to refer applicants for entry-level jobs. Instead, it is uncontested that Miniature passively waited for applicants who typically learned of opportunities from current Miniature employees. The court erred in considering passive reliance on employee word-of-mouth recruiting as a particular employment practice for the purposes of disparate impact. The practices here are undertaken solely by employees.

The vital lesson from *Miniature* is the distinction in liability between acts of the general workforce and acts of the employer, itself. Where workers learn of opportunities on their own and share these opportunities with those in their social networks (posting an open position notice through Facebook, for instance), *Miniature* tells us that this would not be considered a practice of the employer unless the employee were asked to do so by the employer.

The same court followed *Miniature* with its decision in *EEOC v. Consolidated Service System* (included at the end of this chapter), an extraordinary statement by the court, authored by Judge Posner, a noted economist, that contains some quite interesting conclusions. In that case, a janitorial firm owned by a Korean immigrant and staffed mostly by Koreans used word-of-mouth recruiting for its hires. Between 1983 and 1987, the firm hired 81 percent Korean workers, while less than 1 percent of the workforce in its surrounding community is Korean.

In this disparate treatment case, the court basically said that, just because the end result is completely askew, we cannot draw a conclusion that discrimination was involved. "If the most efficient method of hiring adopted *because* it is the most efficient . . . just happens to produce a workforce whose racial or religious or ethnic or national-origin or gender composition pleases the employer, this is not intentional discrimination." The court does suggest that, if the case were instead based on disparate impact, which it is not, "then the advantages of word-of-mouth recruitment would have to be balanced against its possibly discriminatory effect when the employer's current workforce is already skewed along racial or other disfavored lines."

As you will see by the conclusion in that case, the Seventh Circuit apparently grew frustrated with the EEOC's conception of "disparate impact," even suggesting that the defendant consider suing to recoup its fees based on *groundless* prosecution!

Promoting from Within

While promoting from within the company is not in and of itself illegal, it also has the potential for discriminatory results, depending on the process used and the makeup of the workforce. Some employers use a secretive process, quietly soliciting interest in a position from a few upper-level employees who have been selected based on recommendations by their supervisors. The employer then conducts interviews with the candidates and extends an offer. After the employee accepts the offer, a notice is posted announcing the promotion. If women and minorities are not well represented in a firm, such a process may result in a disparate impact against them, even where the purpose of the employer is merely to locate and promote the most qualified candidate.

A process that could avoid a finding of disparate impact would be to post a notice of position availability in which all employees are offered the opportunity to compete for open positions. The employer is less vulnerable to attack for discriminatory policies as long as the workforce is relatively balanced so there is equal employment opportunity.

Venue Recruiting

Employers may decide to conduct recruiting at a university or high school. Similar precautions must be taken to attract diverse applicants in a locale that may be either purposefully or unintentionally uniform. The same effect may result when an employer recruits with a preference for experienced applicants for entry-level jobs—for instance, recruiting firefighters and specifying a preference for applicants with experience in volunteer fire departments. The court held in one case that this recruitment practice was wrongful because volunteer fire departments tended in the past to be hostile to minorities and to women as firefighters. Preference for firefighters with this experience, therefore, would lead to few, if any, women and minorities being hired. Employers should be aware of the effects of the composition of their workforce on protected groups and the effects of the sources of their recruitment.

Walk-In Applicants

Recruiting may not be necessary where the company is constantly receiving unsolicited applications. Depending on the profession, potential employees may send their résumés to prospective employers in hopes of locating an open position, or of persuading them to create one. While this strategy may be effective in locating employees and reducing costs of actual formal recruiting, the company may find that its reputation attracts only one type of employee, while others are intimidated by, unaware of, or uninterested in the firm. Equal employment opportunity is again lost.

Neutral Solicitation

While selecting an appropriate source from which to choose applicants is crucial, fashioning the process to encourage diverse applicants is also important. For instance, an advertisement that requests "recent college grads" may discourage older workers from applying and result in an adverse impact on them. Or a job announcement that states the employer is looking for "busboys" or "servicemen" may deter females from applying. Other terms that at first appear innocuous are discouraging to one group or another as well, including "draftsman," "saleswoman," "repairman," "waiter," "host," and "maid." The announcement or solicitation should invite applications from all groups and should not suggest a preference for any one class of individual.

Information Gathering and Selection

Once the employer has recruited a group of applicants, how does the employer reach a final conclusion about whether to hire a particular applicant? The next step is for the employer to balance some additional information about the applicant—her or his experience, education, fit with the company, and other information gained through interviews, reference checks, testing, and application forms—with the needs of the company along with any negative information on the candidate discovered during the course of the information gathering. Amassing this information is a time-consuming, yet important, process that is subject to suspicion by applicants and others because of its potential for the invasion of privacy and discriminatory treatment. While we will discuss the extent to which an employer is prohibited from delving into private information about an employee on the basis of invasion of privacy in Chapter 14, this section will examine the information that the employer may or may not obtain during this particular stage of the employment process.

The Application Phase

The hiring process usually begins with an application for employment. Most of us at some point have filled out an employment application. Did you ever stop to think about whether the employer actually had a right to ask these questions? Under most circumstances, the application requests information that will serve as the basis for screening out applicants because of education or experience requirements. Questions that are business related and used for a non-discriminatory purpose are appropriate. The form will generally ask for name, address, educational background, work experience, and other qualifications for the position; but it may additionally request your date of birth, nationality, religion, marital status, number of children, or ethnicity.

LO3   There are only a few questions that are strictly prohibited by federal law from being asked on an application and during the interview process. Any questions concerning disability, specific health inquiries, and workers' compensation history are prohibited by the Americans with Disabilities Act of 1990. Other questions regarding age, sex, religion, marital status, nationality, and ethnicity are not prohibited by federal statute, but they raise some dangerous issues and employers are strenuously advised to avoid them. Questions about these topics must be related to the position for which the applicant applies in order for an employer to be able to ask them. If they are not related and, even if the employer does not base its employment decision on the responses to these inquiries, the selection process results in a disparate impact against a protected group, the employer could be liable.

Nevertheless, research has shown that companies frequently violate EEOC guidelines regarding appropriate application and interview questions. You may even be thinking right now that you have answered these questions on some form in the past. The areas of inquiry that are most often violated include education (where not business justified and where questions relate to religious affiliation of the school, and so on), arrest records, physical disabilities, and age. Even the most innocuous remark may be inappropriate. For instance, an employer is advised not to ask questions during an interview regarding the name of the applicant, other than what it is (it may be perceived as national origin discrimination). For example, questions relating to other names by which the applicant may be known are proper, while questions regarding the origins of an interesting surname or whether it is a maiden name are improper (it may be perceived as marital status discrimination, prohibited in some states).

Moreover, while most applicants are used to filling in the response to a question regarding gender on an application, an employer actually has no right to that knowledge unless gender is a bona fide occupational qualification. As hair and eye color may lead to an inference regarding the applicant's race or color, these questions, too, may be inappropriate, but not per se illegal if it is a bona fide qualification.

The Interview

The second step in the process is usually an interview conducted by a representative of the employer. Discrimination may occur during the interview in the same manner in which it is present on application forms. An improper question on the application is just as improper in an interview.

Questions are not the only source of discrimination during an interview. In a recent study conducted by the Urban Institute, researchers found that black applicants were treated more harshly during interviews than white applicants with identical qualifications. Researchers submitted pairs of applications of black and white applicants for available positions. The researchers found that blacks were treated more favorably than whites in 27 percent of the interview situations, while they were treated less favorably than whites in half of the interviews. Black applicants suffered greater abuses, including longer waiting times, shorter interviews, and being interviewed by a greater number of individuals. White applicants were found to be more likely to receive a job offer. All of this occurred under controlled circumstances where the applications of the pairs were kept equal in terms of qualifications and experience. An interview, therefore, must be nondiscriminatory not only in terms of the information solicited but also in terms of the process by which it is conducted.

There are four areas of potential problems in connection with the interview. First, the employer must ensure that the interview procedures do not discourage women, minorities, or other protected groups from continuing the process. Second, employers should be aware that all-white or all-male interviewers, or interviewers who are not well trained, may subject the employer to liability. Third, the training of the interviewers is crucial to avoid biased questions, gender-based remarks, and unbalanced interviews. Fourth, the evaluation of the applicant subsequent to the interview should follow a consistent and evaluative process rather than reflect arbitrary and subjective opinions.

Exhibit 4.4, "Preemployment Inquiry Guidelines," offers guidance on developing acceptable questions for an interview. Questions should be uniformly applied to all applicants.

Exhibit 4.4 *Preemployment Inquiry Guidelines*

Subject	Acceptable	Unacceptable
Name	"Have you ever used another name?"	"What is your maiden name?"
Citizenship	"After an offer of employment, can you submit verification of your legal authorization to work in the United States?" or statement that such proof may be required after a decision is made to hire the candidate.	"Are you a U.S. citizen?"; citizenship of spouse, parents, or other relative; birthplace of applicant, applicant's parents, spouse, or other relative; requirements that applicant produce naturalization papers, alien card, etc., prior to decision to hire applicant.
National origin	Questions as to languages applicant reads, speaks, or writes, if use of a language other than English is relevant to the job for which applicant is applying.	Questions as to nationality, lineage, ancestry, national origin, descent, or parentage of applicant, applicant's parents, or spouse; "What is your native language?"; "What language do you use most?"; "How did you acquire the ability to speak [language other than English]?"
Sex, family	Statement of company policy regarding work assignment of employees who are related; name and address of parent or guardian if applicant is a minor; ability to work overtime or to travel; experience working with a certain age group.	Questions to indicate applicant's sex, marital status, number and/or ages of children or dependents; provisions for child care; "Are you pregnant?"; "Are you using birth control?"; spouse's name or contact information.
Physical or mental disability	"Can you perform [specific job-related tasks]?"; statement that employment offer may be made contingent upon passing a job-related mental or physical examination; questions about illegal drug use, missed days of work during previous year.	"Are you in good health?"; "Have you ever received workers' compensation?"; "Do you have any disabilities?"; any inquiry into the applicant's general health, medical condition, or mental/physical disability, requiring a psychological or medical examination of any applicant.
Religion	Statement by employer of regular days, hours, or shifts to be worked.	Religion or religious days observed; "Does your religion prohibit you from working weekends or holidays?"

Source: Adapted from State of California Department of Fair Employment and Housing, DFEH-161 (rev. 8/01), http://www.dfeh.*ca.gov/DFEH/Publications/PublicationDocs/DFEH-161.pdf.*

Background or Reference Check, Negligent Hiring, and Googling Employees

Once the applicant has successfully completed the interview process, the next step for the employer is to check the applicant's background and references. This is how the employer discovers whether the information in the application and the interview is true, and whether there is any additional information that might be relevant to the person's employment. The *Small Business Report* found that 80 percent of job applications contain false information regarding prior work history, while 30 percent of the information related to educational background is false. On the other hand, as the level of job responsibility decreases, the employer is less likely to verify all of the information provided by the applicant. A check, therefore, is crucial to verify the information given on the application and in the interview. (See Exhibit 4.5, "Tips for Tracing Lies.")

LO4

It is important, as well, to ensure that there is no information that, if discovered, would disqualify the applicant from employment or could subject other employees, clients, or customers to a dangerous situation. That type of information also could subject the employer to a claim of **negligent hiring**, recognized as a cause of action in at least 47 states.[4] For these reasons, employers may verify not only education and experience, but also driving records, credit standing, refusals of bonds, or exclusion from government programs. An employer is liable for negligent hiring where an employee causes harm that could have been prevented if the employer had conducted a reasonable and responsible background check on the employee; in other words, when the employer knew or should have known that the worker was not fit for the job. The person injured may claim that the **negligence** of the employer placed the employee in a position where harm could result, and, therefore, the employer contributed to that harm (see Exhibit 4.6, "Grounds for Negligent Hiring Claim"). More than 500 workers are murdered at work each year in America, while more than 800 suffer same type of assault.[5] Since 20 percent of workplace attacks are committed by co-workers or former co-workers, this is a critical area of caution.[6]

negligent hiring
Employment of a person who causes harm that could have been prevented if the employer had conducted a reasonable and responsible background check on the employee. The standard against which the decision is measured is when the employer knew or should have known that the worker was not fit for the job.

negligence
Failing to do something in such a way or manner as a reasonable person would have done; doing something that a reasonable person would not do; or failing to raise one's standard of care to the level of care that a reasonable person would use in a given situation.

For instance, VIP Companion Care reached a settlement with the New York attorney general after it was found to have hired workers with criminal histories to provide companion care in the homes of aged and infirm clients. One of these workers later stole the credit card of an elderly woman for whom she was caring. As part of its settlement, VIP was required to conduct criminal background checks of all of its employees, as well as pay restitution, fines, and penalties.

An additional wrinkle is added in the case of temporary or contingent workers. Employers often hire their workforce from temporary employment agencies, which have engaged in background screening of the worker on their own. It is arguable that, as long as the employer ensures the reasonableness and diligence of these third-party checks, it is sufficiently protected from liability for negligently hiring these workers (the EEOC Guidelines suggest this framework).[7] However, the court decisions are not uniform and research suggests that screening of temporary workers by agencies is inconsistent and not reliable.[8]

Exhibit 4.5 *Tips for Tracing Lies*

20 TIPS FOR CATCHING RÉSUMÉ FRAUD

1. Carefully note the order of the material given on the résumé. What is given up front is generally what the applicant wishes to emphasize. But what is hidden below may well be more revealing.

2. Concentrate on the most important points in the applicant's résumé. Diverting attention to too many insignificant details draws focus away from key areas.

3. See if the applicant's history follows a logical sequence. For example, has there been a consistent upward progression during the career? Or has there been a downward trend? People do not tend to leave better jobs for poorer ones.

4. Look for conflicting details or overlapping dates.

5. Look for gaps in dates. It is common for applicants who wish to cover something up to try to omit it.

6. Look for omissions of any kind.

7. Pay attention to what the applicant does not say as much as to what he or she does say. You will probably find the most valuable information in those areas your applicant does not want to discuss.

8. Get particulars about various subjects. For example, if the applicant says he or she studied business at Harvard, find out what courses he or she took. Casually ask some questions about the campus or physical environment—just to determine if he or she really was there. People who are dishonest will probably stumble on questions like those.

9. Be sure to discuss all key points.

10. Question the applicant about details as you review the résumé. It will be much harder for him or her to remember false information.

11. Probe the applicant's reasons for leaving past jobs, or for jumping from school to school.

12. Notice how quick and sharp the applicant's answers are. Do they sound rehearsed? An honest person has no need to hesitate or rehearse.

13. Notice body language. Does the applicant look you in the eye?

14. Ask the applicant if he or she minds if you verify information. Then assure him or her that you will need to verify every detail. Imposters likely will drop out at that point.

15. Ask colleagues to sit in on your interview. Your associates may catch vital signs or details that you might miss. They also might think of revealing questions to ask.

16. When confirming information by phone, begin by asking for the company operator. That will help you be sure that the place you are calling is a genuine company. Then move on to the personnel department, and then to the particular manager indicated.

17. Send something in the mail. That will enable you to determine if the address given is genuine.

18. Ask references that you are given for other references. The applicant is bound to provide only favorable references. But those sources may be aware of others.

19. If the applicant sought the help of a résumé service or other career placement service, ask him or her why. The reasons may be legitimate. But they also may be revealing.

20. If the résumé is not very clear, or if it has been produced by a professional service, consider asking the applicant to redo it in his or her own way.

Source: *Workforce Online,* reprinted from Christopher J. Bachler, *Personnel Journal* 74, no. 6 (June 1995), p. 55.

Exhibit 4.6   *Grounds for Negligent Hiring Claim*

Negligent hiring

To state a claim for **negligent hiring**, the plaintiff must show:

- The existence of an employer–employee relationship.
- The employee's incompetence or inappropriateness for the position assumed.
- The employer's actual or constructive knowledge of such incompetence or inappropriateness, or the employer's ability.
- That the employee's act or omission caused the plaintiff's injuries.
- That the employer's negligence in hiring or retaining the employee was the proximate cause of the plaintiff's injuries
  - (*i.e., on investigation, the employer could have discovered the relevant information and prevented the incident from occurring*).

To carefully and adequately check on an applicant's references in order to insulate oneself from negligent hiring liability, the employer might try several strategies. First, the employer might contact the reference in person, by telephone, or by letter and request a general statement about whether the information stated in the application and interview is correct. Second, the contact might be much more specific, posing questions about the applicant's abilities and qualifications for the available position. Third, the employer may undertake an independent check of credit standing through a credit reporting agency, military service and discharge status, driving record, criminal record, or other public information to obtain the most complete information on the applicant.

There are problems inherent in each form of query:

- Most employers are willing to verify the employment of past employees, but obtaining this limited information may not necessarily satisfy the standard of care required to avoid a claim of negligent hiring.
- Certain information is not available to employers and is protected by state law. For instance, if an employer asks about the applicant's prior criminal arrest record, or even certain convictions, in one of several states that statutorily protect disclosure of this type of information, the employer may be subject to a claim of invasion of privacy or other statutory violations.
- There also may be the basis for a claim of disparate impact where it can be shown that those of one protected class are arrested more often than others. In that case, asking about an arrest record where the offense is not necessarily related to job performance may result in adverse impact. Note that arrests and convictions are not the same. Employers are more limited in inquiring about arrest records than about convictions relevant to the job.
- The Fair Credit Reporting Act requires that an employer notify the applicant in writing of its intention to conduct an investigative consumer report and inform the applicant of the information it seeks. It further requires the employer to

obtain written authorization to obtain the report. In addition, if the employer plans to take an adverse employment action based on the report, it must notify the employee of the reporting agency and give notice that he or she can get a free copy of the report and that he or she can dispute its contents.

- The reference and background information-gathering process is a lengthy one and may be unmanageable, given the employer's position requirements.
- Employers may not be willing to offer any further information than that the applicant worked at that company for a time. Employers have cause for concern, given the large number of defamation actions filed against employers based on references. (See Exhibit 4.7, "Checklist for Safe Hiring"; see also Chapter 14.)

Exhibit 4.7 *Checklist for Safe Hiring*

Lester S. Rosen of Employment Screening Resources suggests that the following could be placed in every applicant's file prior to the applicant coming onto the premises:

Task	Yes/No	Date/Initial	Notes
Application Process			
Did applicant sign consent for background investigation?			
Is application complete?			
Did applicant sign and date application?			
Did applicant leave criminal questions blank?			
Did applicant indicate a criminal record?			
Did applicant explain why he or she had left past jobs?			
Did applicant explain gaps in job history?			
Did applicant clearly identify previous employers?			
Did applicant provide supervisor names?			
Were there excessive changes?			
Interview			
Did applicant explain excessive changes?			
Leaving past jobs: Did applicant explain satisfactorily?			
Leaving past jobs: Was reason consistent with application?			

continued

Task	Yes/No	Date/Initial	Notes
Employment gaps: Did applicant explain satisfactorily?			
Employment gaps: Explanations consistent with application?			
"Our firm has a standard policy of background checks and drug tests on all applicants. Do you have any concerns you would like to share with me about our procedure?"			Response:
"When we contact past employers, pursuant to the release you have signed, would any of them tell us you were terminated, disciplined, or not eligible for rehire?"			Response:
"When we contact past employers, pursuant to the release you have signed, what do you think they would tell us about you?"			Response:
"When we contact the courthouse or police department, would we locate any criminal convictions or pending cases?"			Response:
Reference Checks (by employer or third party)			
Have references been checked for at least the last five years, regardless of whether past employers will give details?			
Have efforts been documented and placed in the file?			
Discrepancies between information located and what applicant reported on application:			
a. Dates/salary/job title/duties b. Reason for leaving			
Background Check			
Submitted for background check?			
Check completed?			By:
Background check reviewed for discrepancies/issues			
NOT CLEAR or SATISFACTORY, action taken per policy and procedures.			Describe:

Source: © 2007 Lester S. Rosen, Employment Screening Resources, www.ESRcheck.com, reprinted with permission.

The most effective means by which to avoid these potential stumbling blocks is to request that the applicant sign a statement on the application form, which states that former employers are released from liability for offering references on her or his behalf. In the course of making a request for a reference from those former employers, the release should be sent to the former employer along with a copy of the applicant's entire application.

In addition, in this environment of enhanced access to information, perhaps the standard of what a reasonable employer should do is also heightened. For instance, if people Google their blind dates as standard practice, is it really asking too much for an employer to simply Google a prospective employee to see what can be uncovered through a basic Internet search? If a number of employers begin to use the Internet as a method of information gathering, does that practice become the norm, thus raising the bar for other employers? The bar does seem to be rising—while a 2006 survey reported that at least one in four employers used the Web to obtain personal information on candidates, and 10 percent had used "social networking sites" (including Facebook.com or MySpace.com) for the same purpose,[9] a survey just one year later[10] in 2007 found 44 percent of another group of respondents to have engaged in the practice (one cannot compare the numbers exactly since they represented different survey populations; but it demonstrates a trend). A 2009 survey found numbers comparable to 2007 (see Exhibit 4.8).[11] The earlier survey found that an overwhelming majority of employers did not hire the employee after conducting the search, having found job candidates who bad-mouthed prior employers over the Internet or simply handled themselves online in such an unprofessional manner as to warrant the rejection letter. Provocative photos were cited in the 2009 survey as reasons not to hire, as well as references to drinking and drugs (see Exhibit 4.9).

Exhibit 4.8 *Where Do Employers Get Their Info?*

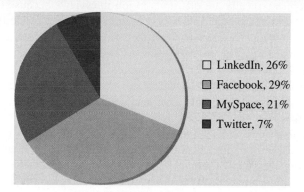

- ☐ LinkedIn, 26%
- ☐ Facebook, 29%
- ■ MySpace, 21%
- ■ Twitter, 7%

Source: Adapted from J. Grasz, "45% Employers Use Facebook-Twitter to Screen Job Candidates," *Oregon Business Report* (Aug. 24, 2009), http://oregonbusinessreport.com/2.009/08/45-employers-use-facebook-twitter-to-screen-job-candidates.

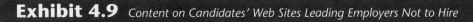

Exhibit 4.9 *Content on Candidates' Web Sites Leading Employers Not to Hire*

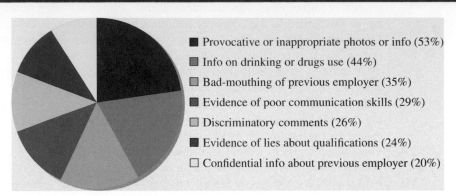

- ■ Provocative or inappropriate photos or info (53%)
- ■ Info on drinking or drugs use (44%)
- ☐ Bad-mouthing of previous employer (35%)
- ■ Evidence of poor communication skills (29%)
- ☐ Discriminatory comments (26%)
- ■ Evidence of lies about qualifications (24%)
- ☐ Confidential info about previous employer (20%)

Source: Adapted from J. Grasz, "45% Employers Use Facebook-Twitter to Screen Job Candidates," *Oregon Business Report* (Aug. 24, 2009), http://oregonbusinessreport.com/2009/08/45-employers-use-facebook-twitter-to-screen-job-candidates.

However, employers should exercise caution when using online sources for background checks. While they may find valuable information about prospective employees, if they use (or appear to use) certain information, such as age, race, marital status, or other defining features of potentially protected classes, to screen job candidates, it could serve as grounds for a discrimination suit. Researcher Ed Frauenheim suggests that "using social networking sites for background checking has emerged as a new tool for recruiters and employers, but it may be a risky one. Web sites such as MySpace.com and Facebook.com can contain details about candidates that make employers think twice about hiring them . . . By looking at the highly personal sites, employers can inadvertently learn about matters such as candidates' age, marital status, medical problems, and plans to start a family. These topics typically are off limits in job interviews because they can be grounds for discrimination lawsuits if people aren't hired."[12] In addition, some of these sites have terms of use that ban recruiters from copying or sharing any of the information found on the site. MySpace states, "The MySpace Services are for the personal use of Members only and may not be used in connection with any commercial endeavors except those that are specifically endorsed or approved by MySpace.com."[13]

In considering a claim of negligent hiring, you might notice the inherent conflicts between the potential liability involved in hiring someone without sufficient information and the alternate liability involved in intrusion into a candidate's personal information. As we have noted and will discuss, certain subjects are not acceptable areas of inquiry for employers except under specific circumstances. In addition, while the Occupational Safety and Health Act (OSHA) mandates that employers protect the workplace from "recognized" workplace safety and health hazards that are likely to cause serious injury or death, until those threats are manifested, it may be difficult to identify some of them before they enter the workplace.

Therefore, the amount of background and reference checking for an employer to shield itself from a claim of negligent hiring should both be based on a written workplace policy that applies a standard procedure across the board and maintains a zero tolerance bar for any threats of violence whatsoever, but also should be sufficiently flexible to vary from situation to situation, as needed. A position that provides for absolutely no contact with clients, customers, or other employees may necessitate a quick check of the information contained on the application, while a position that requires a great deal of personal contact, such as an intensive care nurse, would require an investigation into the applicant's prior experiences and background. An employer must exercise reasonable care in hiring applicants who may pose a risk to others as a result of their employment and the employer's negligent failure to obtain more complete information. The standard of care to be met is what would be exercised by a reasonable employer in similar circumstances. If an employer had no means by which to learn of a dangerous propensity, or if discovery of this information would place a great burden on the employer, a court is more likely to deny a claim for negligent hiring.

Reference Checks: Potential Liability for *Providing* References?

Due to an increasing risk of lawsuits as a result of reference checks, many employers have adopted an official policy of providing only name, position held, and salary, or simply saying, "No comment." However, employers should be aware that, should an employer choose not to provide reference information on prior employees, it could face liability for injuries to the prospective employer who sought the reference, or even third parties. In one case, a former employer settled for an undisclosed amount after allegedly sending an incomplete referral letter that neglected to mention that the former employee had been fired for bringing a gun to work. The employee was subsequently hired by an insurance company and went on a rampage, killing three and wounding two of his co-workers, before killing himself.[14]

While employers may not have an affirmative duty to respond to a reference inquiry, those who choose to respond may be held liable for negligent misrepresentation based on misleading statements made in employment references. Therefore, while there is no affirmative duty to respond, once an employer chooses to do so, some courts have held that it creates a duty to respond fully and honestly, to avoid foreseeable harm.[15]

One possible safeguard an employer can utilize is requiring a written release from former employees before any information is released. However, the written release should be voluntary, should allow the former employee to discuss the waiver with an attorney, and should include the employee's agreement not to contest his or her termination or the contents of the personnel file. For additional guidance, see Exhibit 4.10, "Employer Strategies for Avoiding Negligent Hiring, References, and Supervision" and Exhibit 4.11, "Tips for Employer Protection."

Employers also can be liable for reference checks in an unexpected manner—from an ex-employee's own mouth through **compelled self-publication**. Compelled self-publication occurs when an ex-employee is forced to repeat the reason for her or his termination and thereby has the basis for a claim for

LO5

compelled self-publication
Occurs when an ex-employee is forced to repeat the reason for her or his termination and thereby has the basis for a claim for defamation.

Exhibit 4.10 *Employer Strategies for Avoiding Negligent Hiring, References, and Supervision*

Former Employees	
Strategy	**Considerations**
Examine state law to determine whether statutory protection is available for employers giving references. • If yes, conform reference policy for former employees to state law. • If no, develop a policy that balances the potential legal costs with the future employers' need for information regarding the former employee.	• Possible protection under General Liability Policy. • Require form signed by former employee authorizing release of information.

Current and Future Employees	
Strategy	**Considerations**
Preemployment:	
For each new hire or position change, review position to determine risk factors. Based on assessment, determine scope of necessary applicant investigation.	Risk factors include: • Contact with the public/children/infirm. • Access to employer property. • Operation of motor vehicles/dangerous equipment.
Employment application should include:	
• Statement that any misrepresentation is grounds for dismissal, no matter when discovered. • Inquiry as to any criminal convictions. • Signed permission for all former employers to release reference information, including reason for separation and eligibility for rehire. • Data on all education, certifications, and experience relevant to position. If applicant is deemed to be qualified via personal interviews, skills, or other preemployment tests, begin background check commensurate with prior review of position and risk factors.	If applicant discloses a criminal conviction, determine the nature of the crime and whether it is within the scope of job requirements or job related.
In particular, the employer should:	
• Verify all claimed credentials and certifications. • Instigate any necessary criminal background checks. • Send signed consent form to past employers requesting appropriate information.	Where former employer does not respond, employer will need to follow up and document due diligence. Where former employer has a "no comment" reference policy, depending on position's risk factors, remind former employer of potential negli-

continued

- Request any other pertinent information, given job duties/responsibilities.

gent reference issues and allow former employer opportunity to reconsider. Document due diligence.

Where negative information is received, consider risk factors, consider investigating further, or seek applicant's rebuttal to information received, and make best decision possible for all concerned.

During Employment:

If an employee exhibits any display of greater than ordinary temper or violent behavior:

- Remove employee from potentially hazardous duties (i.e., working closely with public, children, or the infirm).
- Require anger management or similar counseling before reinstatement to prior duties.

Postemployment:

When employee is terminating employment, present Reference Permission Form for employee to sign during exit interview and inform employee that factual information will be provided to future employers.

If contacted for reference of past employee:

- Provide data as prescribed by Reference Permission Form.
- Consider potential position risk factors, including risk to third parties, when deciding whether to release additional relevant factual information.

Source: S. Arsenault, D. Jessup, M. Hass, and J. Philbrick, "The Legal Implications of Workplace Violence: Negligent References, Negligent Hiring, and Negligent Supervision and Retention," *Journal of Legal Studies in Business* 9 (2002), pp. 31–63. Reprinted by permission of the authors and *Journal of Legal Studies in Business*.

defamation. When the reason for the termination is allegedly defamatory (for instance, termination based on false accusations of insubordination or theft), then courts have held that self-publication can satisfy the *prima facie* requirements of defamation since the employee was compelled to publish the defamatory statement to a third person (the potential new employer), and since it was foreseeable to the employer that the employee would have to repeat the basis for termination. The tort of compelled self-publication, however, is recognized in a minority of states.[16]

The discussion above about negligent hiring standards also applies to situations involved in negligent training, supervision, and retention. Some courts recognize a responsibility of employers in certain industries to appropriately train their employees when third parties will rely on that training, such as in the medical environment.

Exhibit 4.11   *Tips for Employer Protection*

	So how does the employer protect itself? **Precaution.**
During the interview process	• Obtain releases from all applicants allowing the employer to check on previous employment. • Request that all applicants obtain copies of their personnel files from previous employers.
Before a position is offered to the candidate	• Investigate the employment record, including all gaps, missing data, and positions held. • Review educational records carefully. Contact the institutions listed to verify their existence, the years attended, the course of study, and, most important, actual graduation with degree. • Check references, especially when several are reluctant to speak. This may be viewed as a warning beacon that they do not have much good to say or have no desire to support the candidate. (On the other hand, ensure that this unwillingness is not the result of a bad relationship with the person. Allow the candidate the opportunity to explain.)
After the candidate is hired	• Maintain clear, consistent policies relating to employment decisions. • Follow up on the implementation and enforcement of these policies.

Negligent supervision exists where an employer fails to adequately oversee the activities of an employee who threatens violent conduct. Negligent retention occurs when the employee's conduct gives rise to employer action such as suspension or dismissal, but the employer fails to take such action and a third party suffers damages.

"After-Acquired Evidence" Defense in Wrongful Termination Suits

While the previous discussion has focused on potential for employer mistakes, omissions, or wrongdoing, what happens when the applicant is the wrongdoer, such as when she or he includes misstatements on her or his application? According to a 1995 Supreme Court decision,[17] an employer may fire someone for that reason. Often, this situation will come up after someone has been fired for another, allegedly wrongful reason. The "after-acquired evidence" of the misstatements is admissible to

Exhibit 4.12   *Reasons for Not Hiring*

Possible Lawful Reasons for Choosing to Reject a Candidate

- No positions available.
- Not interested in positions available.
- Not qualified for positions available.
- Not qualified for position being sought.
- Better qualified persons were hired instead.
- Cannot work hours offered.
- Rejected our job offer.

- Unable to communicate effectively in the English language (if required for position).
- Obviously under the influence of drugs or alcohol during the employment interview.
- Did not return for follow-up interview or otherwise failed to complete the preemployment process.
- Employment interview revealed no interest in type of work.

show the court that, whether or not the employer had unlawful reasons for the action, it also had this legal justification for the action. In *McKennon,* the court held that a discharge in violation of the ADEA was acceptable where the employer would have terminated the employment anyway because of a breach of confidentiality.

Documentation of Failure to Hire

No federal statute or guideline requires that employers document the reasons for failing to hire any specific applicant. However, it may be in the best interests of the employer to articulate the reasons in order to avoid the presumption of inappropriate reasons. (See Exhibit 4.12, "Reasons for Not Hiring.") In addition, since a claim under Title VII or other statutes may come long after the decision was made, documentation will help an employer recall the particular reasons why a certain applicant was rejected so that she or he is not left, perhaps on the witness stand, to say, "I don't remember!" Moreover, the individuals who originally made the decision about this candidate may no longer be with the firm. Finally, a firm may choose to document in order to supplement statistical data proving a lack of discrimination. This paper trail may serve to prove that others who were similarly situated were treated the same way, not differently. For instance, in a gender discrimination action, the documentation may demonstrate that no one with a certain low level of experience was hired, male or female.

On the other hand, some might argue that documentation also may serve to demonstrate facts to which the employer does not want to be bound. Once the reason for failing to hire is on paper, the employer is now bound to use that, alone, as the reason for the decision. Further, while any one decision may seem appropriate, systematic documentation of these decisions may demonstrate a pattern of adverse impact that one might not notice if nothing is ever recorded. But, just because the employer can document this information more easily, this does not mean that it is not able to be recorded at all by others. So, in the long run, it is in the employer's best interests to document, document, document so that it is in the

- If you are looking for the most qualified candidate, make sure that you are advertising in *all* of the places where that candidate might look for employment—not just the obvious places where you are sure to find the same type of workers as those that already work for you.
- Be wary of representations about the firm that are made during recruitment interviews. While, of course, you want to encourage the best candidates to work for your firm, sometimes glowing accounts of life at the firm might cross the line to misrepresentations. Also, be cautious about promises made to prospective employees as these might be construed as part of the individual's contract with the firm.
- While word-of-mouth recruiting, nepotism, and promoting from within may appear on the surface to be an easy method for locating a new employee, these methods are likely to produce new employees quite similar to your present employees. Make sure that you employ additional methods to prevent discrimination in developing your applicant pool.
- Take a look at your written applicant form. Does it ask for any information that is not relevant to the candidate's potential ability to do the job? Is there any information upon which you are prohibited from basing an employment decision, such as age?
- Background checks are relevant to most positions. If you fail to conduct a check, you might be liable for any actions that you would have learned about in the check, such as previous workplace violence. From a cost–benefit perspective, conducting the check usually wins.

best position to know its own vulnerabilities and make changes, where necessary, before it is too late—and much more expensive—to do so on its own.

Employers may then discover problem areas and respond appropriately and lawfully to them once observed. As long as an employer's policies about hiring are consistently applied and are reasonable, there should be no problems—whether recorded in writing or not.

Testing in the Employment Environment

The third step beyond recruitment and information gathering is to hone in on the particular information that would tell the employer if this is the right worker to satisfy the job's essential requirements. Testing may allow the employer to do so. However, while preemployment testing can help locate ideal employees, it also may land the employer in court. Managing the risk created by use of preemployment tests requires an understanding of the types of preemployment tests used, the benefits they offer, and their possible costs, beyond the monetary expenditures involved in testing. This balance is critical, given the high rate of résumé fraud (a recent survey by Colorado-based Avert, Inc., of 2.6 million job applications revealed that 44 percent of the résumés contained lies).[18]

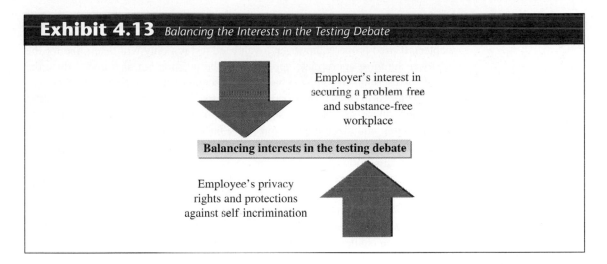

Exhibit 4.13   *Balancing the Interests in the Testing Debate*

Employer's interest in securing a problem free and substance-free workplace

Balancing interests in the testing debate

Employee's privacy rights and protections against self incrimination

preemployment testing
Testing that takes place before hiring, or sometimes after hiring but before employment, in connection with such qualities as integrity, honesty, drug and alcohol use, HIV, or other characteristics.

Preemployment testing began in the 1950s as a response to the inefficiencies that were purportedly present in American business. Since that time, preemployment testing has been considered a necessity to the selection process. The majority of selection tests originally given were conducted as a means of bettering the company's position in a competitive market. Testing was seen as the answer to workplace personnel problems, ineffective hiring programs, and the inappropriate job placement of hirees. Employers believed they would be more competitive if they could test applicants to "weed out" those who failed the tests. These tests became the wave of the future. However, many managers administered tests that had never been validated as indicators of performance or were not specifically job-related in any way. (See Exhibit 4.13, "Balancing the Interests in the Testing Debate.")

In 1990, former U.S. Surgeon General C. Everett Koop estimated that between 14 and 25 percent of employees between the ages of 18 and 40 would test positive for illegal substances on any given day. The U.S. Department of Health and Human Services estimates that the cost of substance abuse in the workplace in the form of lost productivity amounts to approximately $81 billion per year, and alcoholism is specifically responsible for at least 500 million lost workdays each year.[19] In 2004, it was estimated that approximately three-fourths of all illegal drug users over 18 were employed[20] and the National Institute on Drug Abuse reports that those employees are about twice as costly to their employers in medical and workers' compensation claims as their drug-free co-workers.[21] The enormity of these figures is one of the reasons why approximately 22 million employees were tested in 1992 alone.

LO6

Testing in the workplace has taken two forms: tests for the purpose of finding the best individual for a position and tests to ensure that the individual is free of problems that would prevent her or him from performing the position's functions. Examples of the former include achievement tests and personality indicators. The problem with this type of eligibility test is that, while appearing facially neutral, it may have a disparate impact on a protected class. Pursuant to Title VII of the

Civil Rights Act of 1964, where adverse impact has been shown, the test may still be used if it has been professionally developed and validated (discussed later in this chapter). If used properly, however, a validated test not only will determine for the employer the most appropriate applicant for the position but also may reduce the chance for discriminatory choices based on conscious or subconscious employer bias.

The latter form of examination refers to tests for ineligibility, such as for drug and alcohol abuse, and other impairments that may limit an applicant's ability to perform. Drug and alcohol addictions have become pervasive issues in our society. Highly publicized mishaps, such as the alcohol-related Exxon *Valdez* disaster and drug-related railway incidents, have added to our consternation. Other addictions have evolved, resulting from the impact of technology on our society. Though some may be the subject of jokes, like the "crackberry" addict—the individual who cannot leave his or her personal mobile communicators at home—others can be far more serious.

Clearly, the challenges of addiction have permeated almost every facet of our lives, including the workplace. Employers have institutionalized prevention programs, not only for the safety of their workers but also in an effort to ensure high productivity and quality output. As technology has improved, impairment tests have become more efficient, less expensive, and therefore more prevalent.

In an effort to protect individual employee rights, courts do a balancing test to determine the legality of ineligibility testing. "At some point, an individual's privacy interests trump an employer's efficiency concerns. That point is when the invasion of privacy is 'substantially and highly offensive to the reasonable person,'" one judge stated. The courts accordingly weigh the conflicting interest of the employer in securing a problem-free or substance-free workplace against the privacy rights of the employee and protections against self-incrimination.

As many of the protections offered to the employee come from the Constitution (Fourth Amendment protection against unreasonable searches and seizures, Fifth Amendment right against self-incrimination, and Fifth and Fourteenth Amendments' protections of due process), government employees and contractors generally receive greater protection in these areas than do employees in the private sector. However, state constitutions can be a source of protection in the private sector as well. The issue of privacy rights is more completely discussed in Chapter 14. This discussion, instead, will be concerned with the potential for discrimination in the course of testing procedures and requirements, and the various statutes that protect against related discrimination.

Legality of Eligibility Testing

eligibility testing
Tests an employer administers to ensure that the potential employee is capable and qualified to perform the requirements of the position.

Eligibility testing refers to tests that an employer administers to ensure that the potential employee is capable and qualified to perform the requirements of the position. Some tests also are used to determine who is most capable among applicants. These tests may include intelligence tests, tests of physical stamina, eye exams, tests for levels of achievement or aptitude, or tests for the presence of certain personality traits. Tests for ineligibility, on the other hand, test for disqualifying factors, for example, drug and alcohol tests, polygraphs, and HIV testing.

Of course, a test may cross the line between the two. For instance, an employer may administer a preemployment, post-offer medical exam to determine whether the applicant is sufficiently healthy to perform the job requirements. If the individual fails the medical examination, the test has determined that she or he is not qualified for the position and, therefore, is ineligible.

Employers may conduct eligibility tests for a variety of reasons. For example, the position may require a unique skill for which the employer wishes to test the applicants. Those applicants who possess that skill will continue in the application process. Or perhaps the employer may need to ensure that the applicants meet minimum standards to satisfy requirements of the position. For instance, an eye exam may be required for all potential bus drivers, or an English language competency examination for all applicants for customer relations positions. These tests, however, in their implementation may have a disparate impact on members of a protected class. To illustrate, the employer's test for English language competency would have an adverse impact on individuals of non-English-speaking origin. Where discrimination on the basis of national origin has been shown, the employer may continue to use the test only where it can establish that the requirement is a bona fide occupational qualification.

Eligibility tests that have been professionally developed are specifically exempt from claims of disparate impact, as long as the test is not designed, intended, or used to discriminate on the basis of membership in a protected class. For an eligibility test to be legally validated as an effective gauge of performance other than through this exemption, an employer must show that the test is job-related and consistent with **business necessity**.

For example, most people would agree a test of general math is probably related to successful performance as a cashier. Thus, even if this type of test had disparate impact against a particular group, it would be allowable if the employer provided **job analysis** data supporting its claim that math skills were required to perform the job. In general, the more abstract the trait the instrument purports to test (such as "creativity"), the more difficult it becomes to establish evidence of validity. Note that a test may be challenged if there exists a less discriminatory alternative.

The Seventh Circuit held in *Melendez v. Illinois Bell Telephone Co.*[22] that an employer's aptitude test had a disparate impact on Hispanic job applicants because there was no significant correlation between an applicant's test score and his or her ability to perform the duties of an entry-level manager. The plaintiff's expert testified that the aptitude tests could "predict a person's job performance only 3 percent better than chance alone."

Test Validity

Scenario

In 1975, the Supreme Court decided *Albemarle Paper Co. v. Moody*,[23] a seminal case with regard to test validation. In that case, Albemarle Paper imposed a requirement that those in skilled labor positions have a high school diploma and pass two tests. The court found it a critical error that Albemarle Paper made no attempt to validate that the tests were related to the job; instead, the employer simply adopted a national norm score as a cutoff point for its new applicants. The Court held that "discriminatory tests are impermissible unless shown, by professionally

---

business necessity
Defense to a disparate impact case based on the employer's need for the policy as a legitimate requirement for the job.

job analysis
Information regarding the nature of the work associated with a job and the knowledge, skills, and abilities required to perform that work.

acceptable methods, to be predictive of or significantly correlated with important elements of work behavior that constitute or are relevant to the job or jobs for which employees are being evaluated." Because of defects in the validation process, the court found that Albemarle was liable for discrimination for failure to evidence job relatedness of a discriminatory test process.

In 1978, the EEOC, with the assistance of several other government agencies, developed the *Uniform Guidelines on Employee Selection Procedures* as a framework for employers in connection with the determination of the proper use of tests and other selection procedures. Where a selection test has been shown to have an adverse impact on a protected class, the guidelines identify three approaches to gathering evidence of validity; the choice of **validation** strategy depends on the type of inference the user wishes to draw from the test scores. The guidelines define an adverse impact on a protected class as any procedure that has a selection rate for any group of less than 80 percent of the selection rate of the group with the highest rate.

validation

Evidence that shows that a test evaluates precisely what it claims to evaluate.

The most traditional type of test validation is criterion-related validity. To validate using criteria, one collects data relating to job performance from a simulated exercise or on-the-job measures of performance. The test is developed using these measurements of critical work behaviors once a systematic relationship between the criteria and the test scores has been demonstrated.

The second form of validity that is identified by the Guidelines is content validation. Content validation is based on a careful job analysis and definition that identifies important tasks, behaviors and knowledge that the job requires. The test is then developed involving a representative sample of these tasks, behaviors, and knowledge. Employers should be particularly concerned with this type of validity during test construction, as there is a vulnerability toward lack of representativeness at this stage.

The third strategy to validate tests under the Guidelines is construct validity, an approach that is generally most useful when the employer is seeking to measure a psychological characteristic such as reasoning ability, introversion (a personality characteristic), leadership behaviors, and others. Construct validation is a relatively technical area, dependent on intercorrelation of test items, but relevant for employers are the following considerations. First, the characteristic sought needs to be important for job performance. As with content validity, this is done through the use of careful job analysis. In addition, the characteristic should be well defined.

Integrity and Personality Tests

Because employers have been restricted in their use of polygraph tests (to be discussed in the next section), many have resorted to subjective tests that purport to measure personality, honesty or integrity through analysis of written or oral answers to numerous questions, with as many as 40 percent of Fortune 100 companies using personality or integrity tests each year.[24]

There are a number of traits for which employers test but only general agreement that attention to detail (conscientiousness) has a strong correlation to on-the-job behavior.[25] Because of research that demonstrates that intentional faking can be successful,[26] their results have been deemed suspect by courts. However, perhaps because the tests have not been shown to have a consistently adverse impact on any one protected group, employers continue to use them to measure a wide variety of constructs, such as honesty, integrity, propensity to steal, attitude, and counterproductivity.

Personality or psychological tests for preemployment selection screening, however, must be used with caution. Their use pre-offer is inconsistent with the Americans with Disabilities Act. The Seventh Circuit upheld a claim against an employer on the basis of disability discrimination because of its use one of the most popular personality test, the Minnesota Multiphasic Personality Indicator.[27] In a class action lawsuit against the furniture rental company Rent-a-Center, the court found that the use of the screening test would likely exclude employees with mental impairments from promotions. In this case, the court noted that the ADA limits medical exams as a condition of employment; they may only be required after the offer is made and, even then, only when all entering employees are required to take the test, any medical results are maintained in a confidential manner, and the "examination or inquiry is shown to be job-related and consistent with business necessity."[28] Simply because a test is an accepted psychological measure does not make that test relevant to a particular job, nor does it validate its use in any situation.

Personality tests should not be confused with intelligence tests, which have suffered a great deal of criticism in connection with their potential for disparate impact discrimination against various minority groups. Notwithstanding these concerns, basic intelligence testing does remain one of the single best predictors of job performance across all jobs.[29]

Physical Ability Tests

Physical ability tests are administered to applicants seeking particularly physically demanding jobs in order to increase the likelihood that candidates will be able to perform the essential physical functions of the job in question. General tests of fitness may no longer be an appropriate means of testing for physical fitness for a particular position since these tests might exclude individuals who could still perform the essential functions of that position. For instance, physical ability tests in the past might have required applicants to perform sit-ups, lift weights, and run certain distances—not all of which might be required by every job. The logic of this test approach is that those who do better on these events are more physically fit and thus better able to perform the physical tasks of any job.

Under current laws, physical ability testing usually results in some type of job simulation. For example, a physical ability exam for entry-level firefighters might require applicants to drag hoses, open fire hydrants, or climb ladders. Job simulations imply a content approach to test validation because the test components are direct samples of the job domain. This approach to physical ability testing is used extensively in the public sector.

Medical Tests

Many employers require preemployment, post-offer medical tests to ensure that the applicant is physically capable of performing the requirements of the position.

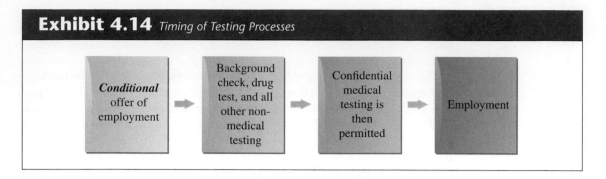

Exhibit 4.14 *Timing of Testing Processes*

Conditional offer of employment ➡ Background check, drug test, and all other non-medical testing ➡ Confidential medical testing is then permitted ➡ Employment

Medical examinations are prohibited only prior to the offer to protect against wrongful discrimination based on a discovered disability.

Medical examinations subsequent to the offer of employment, but prior to the actual employment, are allowed under the acts for the purpose of determining whether an employee is able to perform the job for which she or he has been hired. The order is not a minor issue. In one case, an offer was made, conditional on a drug test, medical examination, and background check. The employee happened to do the medical examination first. The blood test uncovered the employee's HIV-positive status and the employer rescinded the offer, but the employee prevailed in court. The court found that no medical examinations were permitted until after all of the nonmedical aspects of the application process, including the background check. (See Exhibit 4.14, "Timing of Testing Processes.")

The acts also require that all employees within the same job category are subject to the medical examination requirement; individual applicants may not be singled out. In addition, all information generated through the examination process must be maintained in confidential files, separate from other general personnel-related information.

Subsequent to the applicant's employment, no medical examination may be required unless the test is job-related and justified by business necessity.

Legality of Ineligibility Testing

A variety of factors encourage workplace testing for ineligibility. First, the employer may wish to reduce workplace injury or to provide a safer working environment. For instance, drug testing has been shown to drastically reduce the number of workplace injuries and personal injury claims. Second, an employer may use drug tests to predict employee performance or to deter poor performance; in addition to a reduction in accident rates, "absenteeism, tardiness, employee theft and behavioral problems typically decrease with the implementation and maintenance of drug testing. Productivity and employee morale rise with improved attendance, attention to work and improved performance."[30] Third, testing can reduce the employer's financial responsibility to the state workers' compensation system. The use of an illegal substance, which contributes to the claimant's injury, may serve as a defense to the employer's liability.

Despite the fact that the Constitution only protects employees from invasive or wrongful action by the state, an employee may make a number of possible claims against testing. Portions of the constitutions or state statutes of certain states establish private-sector requirements for workplace testing. For example, San Francisco has enacted an ordinance that requires reasonable suspicion based on evidence of job impairment or danger to others before testing is deemed appropriate. Mandatory or random testing would not be allowed in this jurisdiction.

There is also some support for a claim of common-law invasion of privacy in connection to private-sector testing, under certain circumstances.[31] We will examine the balance of rights surrounding drug testing in much greater detail when we discuss privacy issues in Chapter 14.

Generally, congruent with fundamental theories of employment law, a discharge resulting from an employee's failure to take a test for ineligibility is protected under the employment-at-will doctrine. The employment relationship is based on the consent of both parties; if the employee does not wish to be subject to various requirements or conditions of employment, the employee may refuse and leave. If the employee, for instance, is uncomfortable with the idea of random drug testing, that employee may quit and work in an environment in which she or he is more comfortable.

Polygraphs

polygraph
A lie-detecting device that measures biological reactions in individuals when questioned.

Scenario

A relatively newsworthy area of testing is the **polygraph** or lie detector. In each year during the past decade, more than 2 million private-sector employees were asked to take a lie detector test. While the actual number of polygraph tests administered is unknown, it is instructive that there are between 2,000 and 3,500 polygraphers practicing in the United States. There are at least nine schools of polygraph analysis that graduate hundreds more each year.

A polygraph test measures three physiological indicators of arousal: rate and depth of respiration, cardiovascular activity, and perspiration. The examiner asks a structured set of questions, and the subject is evaluated as honest or deceitful based on the pattern of arousal responses. The test has been criticized, however, because catalysts other than dishonesty may produce similar effects in an individual subject. For instance, if an individual is aware that the basis for the test is a concern regarding theft, she or he may become innocently aroused when asked questions relating to the theft. On the other hand, the individual who has actually committed the theft may not be concerned at all; if the person was capable of theft, she or he may be just as comfortable with deceit.

The desire of employers to use polygraphs is perplexing when one considers the reliability of these tests (or lack thereof). In 1983, the Congressional Office of Technology Assessment conducted a study of polygraph reliability. The office found there is a dearth of research or scientific evidence to prove the polygraph is valid for screening purposes. In fact, it has been found that accuracy rates range from 90 to 50 percent.

Because of the large number of false positives and inaccuracies of the polygraph test, a loud outcry from those wrongly accused of improper behavior resulted in the enactment of the federal Employee Polygraph Protection Act (EPPA) of 1988. To a great extent, this act put an end to polygraph use in selection and greatly restricts its use in many other employment situations. The act provides that an employer may not

1. Directly or indirectly require, request, suggest, or cause any employee to take or submit to any lie detector test (e.g., a polygraph, deceptograph, voice-stress analyzer, psychological-stress evaluator, and any similar mechanical or electrical device used to render a diagnostic opinion about the honesty of an individual).
2. Use, accept, refer to, or inquire about the results of any lie detector test of any job applicant or current employee.
3. Discharge, discipline, discriminate against, or deny employment or promotion to (or threaten to take such adverse action against) any prospective or current employee who refuses, declines, or fails to take or submit to a lie detector test or who fails such a test.

However, see Exhibits 4.15 and 4.16 for EPPA employer exemptions, as well as certain conditions under which private employers are permitted to administer a polygraph test.

The Employee Polygraph Protection Act also provides that, except in limited settlement-related circumstances, employees may not waive their rights under the act, nor is an employer allowed to offer financial incentives to employees to take the test or to waive their rights.

Violations of the act are subject to fines as high as $10,000 per violation, as well as reinstatement, employment, or promotion, and the payment of back wages and benefits to the adversely affected individual. The Wage and Hour Division of the Employment Standards Administration of the Department of Labor has the authority to administer the Employee Polygraph Protection Act.

Exhibit 4.15   *Employers Exempted from EPPA*

Employers exempted from EPPA:

Private employers whose primary business purpose is to provide security services.	Employers involved in the manufacture, distribution, or dispensing of controlled substances.	Federal, state, and local government employers.
Such as: the protection of nuclear power facilities; shipments or storage of radioactive or other toxic waste materials; public transport of currency, negotiable securities, precious commodities, or proprietary information.	Such as: the direct access to the manufacture, storage, distribution, or sale of a controlled substance.	Federal government may also test private consultants or experts under contract to the Defense Department, the National Security Agency, the Defense Intelligence Agency, the CIA, and the FBI.

Exhibit 4.16   *Conditions under Which Private Employers Are Permitted to Administer a Polygraph Test*

**Private employers may test current employees
if the following four conditions exist:**
(*Note*: Notwithstanding this safe harbor, an employer **cannot** discharge, discipline, or otherwise discriminate against the employee in any manner on the basis of the polygraph results or even the refusal to take the polygraph test, without **additional supporting evidence**. This is called the **investigation exemption**.)

1. The test must be administered in connection with a workplace theft or incident investigation.	2. The employee must have had reasonable access to the missing property or loss incurred.	3. The employer must have reasonable suspicion that this particular employee was involved.	4. The employee must have been given written information regarding the basis for the investigation and for the suspicion that she or he is involved.

In addition to the regulations enacted by Congress, 33 states have statutes that either prohibit or restrict the use of polygraph examinations for use in employment decisions. Where a state law is more restrictive than the federal act, the statute governs.

Drug and Alcohol Tests

In response to the growing problem of drugs in the workplace and injuries and accidents related to their use, former President George H. W. Bush enacted the Drug-Free Workplace Act in 1988, which authorized the drug testing (also called *biochemical surveillance,* in more legalistic terms) of federal employees under certain circumstances. It also required government service contractors with contracts of $100,000 or more to be performed within the United States to publish a statement about the act, to establish a drug-free awareness program, and to give each employee a copy of the workplace policy. The cost to businesses of drug use in the workplace, based on the figures discussed earlier in the chapter, include a 66 percent higher absenteeism rate among drug users, 300 percent higher rate of health benefit utilization, and 90 percent higher rate of disciplinary actions, as well as findings that 47 percent of workplace accidents are drug-related and that employee turnover is significantly higher. (See Exhibits 4.17, "Executive Order 12564, September 15, 1986: Drug-Free Federal Workplace Act," and 4.18, "Benefits and Drawbacks of a Drug-Free Workplace Policy (DFWP).") However, testing is not without costs. In 2004, approximately 35 million workplace drug tests were performed at a cost of more than $1 billion.[32]

Exhibit 4.17   *Executive Order 12564, September 15, 1986: Drug-Free Federal Workplace Act*

I, Ronald Reagan, President of the United States of America, find that:

Drug use is having serious adverse effects upon a significant proportion of the national work force and results in billions of dollars of lost productivity each year;

The Federal government, as an employer, is concerned with the well-being of its employees, the successful accomplishment of agency missions, and the need to maintain employee productivity;

The Federal government, as the largest employer in the nation, can and should show the way towards achieving drug-free workplaces through a program designed to offer drug users a helping hand and, at the same time, demonstrating to drug users and potential drug users that drugs will not be tolerated in the Federal workplace.

Preemployment screening of job applicants and testing as a part of a rehabilitation program are allowed by the act. In addition, the act requires that federal contractors and grant recipients satisfy certain requirements designed to eliminate the effects of illicit drugs from the workplace. In response to the act, all federal agencies established individual drug-use testing programs designed to ensure the safety and security of the government and the public. For example, the Department of Defense has an employee assistance program that focuses on counseling and rehabilitation, in addition to self and supervisory referrals to substance abuse treatment clinics.

The act also provides that, for a drug-use testing program to be legal, the covered employers must post and distribute a policy statement explaining that the unlawful manufacture, distribution, dispensation, possession, or use of controlled substances is prohibited. Discipline or sanctions against the offending employee are left to the employer's discretion. However, if a criminal conviction arises from a workplace substance abuse offense, the employer is required to administer an employment sanction or to advise and direct the employee to an approved substance abuse treatment program. To protect the employee's right to due process, the employer must educate the workforce of any drug/alcohol policy and testing procedures. In addition, laboratory and screening procedures must meet certain standards. In one case, *Fraternal Order of Police, Lodge No. 5 v. Tucker,*[33] the court concluded that the employees were denied due process because they were not informed of the basis of the employer's suspicion and because they were not offered the opportunity to rebut the employer's claims.

Substance abuse testing is also governed by state laws. Therefore, employers are cautioned to evaluate programs according to the laws of the state or states in which their operations are located. For instance, the laws of California include the privacy provisions of its state constitution, which, unlike most state constitutional provisions, extend to private employers. Random testing is permitted in California for those in safety-sensitive work (though that definition remains open to interpretation) and an employer is under no obligation to hire or retain individuals who fail a drug test. *National Treasury Employees Union v. Von Raab* is a critical

Case 2

Exhibit 4.18 *Benefits and Drawbacks of a Drug Free Workplace Policy (DFWP)*

THE BENEFITS

- Ridding the workplace of substance abuse can improve morale, increase productivity and create a competitive advantage.
- A comprehensive program may qualify an employer for discounts on workers' compensation and other insurance premiums.
- The prevention of a single accident or injury may pay for the entire program costs for several years.
- Some contractors may need to have a DFWP to be eligible for business.
- Many employers have successfully formulated policies which deal with ethical and privacy issues, and have successfully controlled their responsibility for, and the costs associated with, treatment and rehabilitation benefits.
- Unions have initiated DFWPs with employers to promote good public relations and recapture work for their members.
- Having a DFWP sends a very clear message to employees, their families and the community as to the company's position on illegal drug use.

THE DRAWBACKS

- A DFWP can increase distrust between management and workers, and degrade morale and productivity in some workplaces.
- A comprehensive DFWP could add significantly to the cost of doing business.
- False accusations, misidentification of employees as drug users, unjustified dismissals and violation of confidentiality obligations could prompt burdensome litigation.
- Identifying substance users may entail an obligation to provide costly counseling and treatment for a relapsing condition. It is not always easy to contain the financial drain, and health insurance premiums could rise.
- A DFWP, particularly one that features drug testing, can raise serious ethical and privacy issues.

- Where the workplace is organized, the employer faces additional negotiations with the union.

DRUG-FREE WORKPLACE POLICY CHECKLIST

1. What is our current company policy regarding the use of alcohol and other drugs?
2. How much of a drug or alcohol problem does our company have at the present time?
3. What is the nature of the problem (absenteeism, quality, productivity, safety, etc.)?
4. How much does this problem cost the company?
5. What type of DFWP would be most likely to improve the situation?
   a. urine testing
   b. impairment testing
   c. under the influence testing
   d. better supervision and quality control
   e. Employee Assistance Plan
   f. a combination of the above
6. If testing is involved, who will be tested?
   a. applicants
   b. employees in safety sensitive positions
   c. all employees
7. Under what circumstances will testing be done?
   a. pre-employment
   b. for cause
   c. random
   d. combination
8. What will be done with those who fail the test?
9. What action will be taken regarding those who refuse to be tested?
10. What would be the costs of such a program?
11. What would be the benefits? How much would the problems described in 3 and 4 above be reduced by the program? How great is the financial benefit of the reduction?
12. Do the projected benefits justify the costs?

continued

Exhibit 4.18 *continued*

13. Which proposed components of the DFWP are cost effective?

14. How do the company's employees feel about the proposed DFWP? Would they be more supportive of another option? Have we sought their input?

15. (If the company is organized) Has the proposed DFWP been negotiated with the union?

16. Is the proposed DFWP consistent with company values?

17. Is the proposed DFWP legal in the jurisdictions where it will be implemented?

CHOOSING A POLICY

The first step in developing a policy is to decide whether to have a DFWP. Some employers may choose instead to judge employees simply on the basis of performance. Once a company has made a basic policy choice, it can consider in more detail the objectives it intends to achieve. There are a variety of possible motivations for pursuing such a program:

1. *Complying with legal requirements.* Under federal law, some employers are required to establish DFWPs, including engaging in drug (and possibly alcohol) testing.

2. *Reducing liability risks.* Having a DFWP may be viewed as assisting in the defense against certain legal actions, although DFWPs may also generate other kinds of claims.

3. *Reducing business costs due to accidents, absenteeism. and ill health.* Eliminating drug use is seen as a way to promote safety and efficiency, improve the health of the workforce and curtail use of sick leave, medical benefits, and workers' compensation.

4. *Ensuring the integrity of employees.* A potential cause of theft, pilferage, and blackmail is removed, and workers' confidence in each other is enhanced.

5. *Determining fitness for duty and corroborating evidence of misconduct.* A DFWP may help establish uniformity in standards of behavior and in discipline imposed. To establish the DFWP the employer must determine the proper balance between punitive and rehabilitative elements of the program. Being identified as a substance abuser may lead to discharge, but there may also be an attempt at rehabilitating employees and returning them to duty.

6. *Assuring public confidence in the business.* The employer prevents embarrassment by taking genuine steps to deal with employees who are affected by substance abuse.

7. Promoting *a "drug-free" society.* Many employers, seeing themselves as responsible members of society, sense a moral obligation to support law enforcement efforts against illicit drugs. NIDA has stated its "belief that the fight against illegal drugs in the workplace is critical to the nation's war against drug use." It has encouraged private employers to adopt DFWPs.

Source: ABA Section of Labor and Employment Law, *Attorney's Guide to Drugs in the Workplace* (1996). Reprinted with permission.

statement by the Supreme Court on the subject of drug-screening program standards for safety-sensitive positions and can be found at the end of this chapter.

As discussed in other contexts in this chapter, the legality of drug testing relies, in part, on the reliability and effectiveness of the testing procedure itself. Some employers opt for the most common form of employee drug-use screening, an *immunoassay test,* otherwise known as a urine test.

The immunoassay test has several limitations. First, the test is subject to cross-reactivity, where the test detects small amounts of similarly structured drugs, some of which are not illegal. Second, the test does not evidence the time or quantity of ingestion, or the effects of the impairment on job performance. In addition, the test only investigates the presence of one drug at a time.

A second form of drug testing, testing hair follicles (*radioimmunoassay of hair*), has therefore become more popular among employers. This test works on the theory that substances are absorbed into the bloodstream and incorporated into the hair as it grows. A hair follicle test can purportedly determine the chronology and degree of the subject's drug use by reporting what was in the body at the time the hair was formed in the follicle. Any positive response is confirmed by a more sensitive gas chromatography/mass spectrometry test. The procedure involves cutting a small amount of hair from the subject, approximately 1½ inches in length from the back of the head so as to remain physically unnoticed. The sample is placed in a collection envelope, which is immediately sealed and transported to a testing facility.

Because of the sampling technique, hair follicle testing is slightly less intrusive than are urinalyses. Many urinalysis examinations are monitored to prevent tampering or contamination; this type of intrusion into personal activities would not be required in a follicle exam. In addition, the window of detection opened by a follicle test is much greater than that of a urinalysis. The follicle test is reliable up to a period of approximately three months, compared with the one- to three-day window of reliability for urinalysis.

On the other hand, many of the arguments that arise in connection with urinalysis drug testing can be repeated here. Hair follicle testing provides much quantifiable information regarding the amount of drugs ingested and the time over which the drugs were taken. Given its ability to reveal extensive information, follicle testing has been attacked as an unreasonable intrusion into the subject's private life in connection with unregulated and unrelated off work activities.

In a study performed by Steelcase Corporation, the firm found that the overall positive response rate jumped from 2.7 percent, when urinalyses were used to detect marijuana and cocaine usage, to 18.0 percent, when hair follicle testing was used. In follow-up interviews, individuals who tested negative for substance usage according to the urinalysis but positive according to the follicle test reported that they did actually use illegal substances some time within the three months prior to the examination.

One additional issue raised by drug and alcohol testing involves the Americans with Disabilities Act. The act, which applies to private-sector employers and is discussed in much greater detail in Chapter 13, provides that individuals who currently use illegal drugs are not considered individuals with disabilities. However, if an employee or applicant is pursuing or has successfully completed a rehabilitation program and demonstrates that she or he has a disability based on prior use, she or he is covered by the act and therefore entitled to reasonable accommodation.

The Drug-Free Workplace Act does not apply to private-sector employers. An increasing number of private employers have implemented drug programs for their employees. Ninety-eighty percent of Fortune 200 companies have drug-free workplace programs in place. Private employers have generally followed the guidelines set forth in the act of 1989 in the institution of their own programs, and such programs have generally been upheld where reasonable procedures are followed. There do exist several occupation-specific regulations that restrict or require drug testing of employees. Where the government requires or actively encourages testing by the private sector, the testing may be subject to constitutional scrutiny. For instance, the Department of Transportation (DOT) requires private-sector transportation employers to randomly drug test employees in safety or security-related positions. In addition, under certain circumstances, DOT requires preemployment and periodic testing, testing where reasonable cause exists, and testing subsequent to any accidents. An employee who tests positive is removed from her or his position and can only return after successful completion of a rehabilitation program. These requirements must meet constitutional requirements of privacy and due process, even though the testing is actually carried out by private employers.

On June 23, 1998, the House of Representatives passed the Drug-Free Workplace Act of 1998, aimed at providing small businesses—which often lack the resources and infrastructure to conduct employee drug tests—with financial resources and technical assistance for implementing drug-testing programs. The three purposes of the act are to (1) educate small business concerns about the advantages of a drug-free workplace, (2) provide financial incentives and technical assistance to enable small business concerns to create a drug-free workplace, and (3) assist working parents in keeping their children drug free. The Drug-Free Workplace Act of 1998 provides a $10 million grant program for nonprofit organizations that have the ability to provide technical assistance to small businesses in establishing drug-free policies.

Additionally, 23 states have enacted legislation designed to protect the privacy of private-sector employees. These state laws vary in their approach; some states offer a great deal of protection for employees and may be classified as pro-employee (such as Connecticut, California, and Minnesota), while other states allow testing after satisfaction of only modest burdens and are classified as pro-employer (such as Utah).

It should be noted that some legal scholars do not believe there is a connection between the recreational use of drugs and low productivity. Some researchers have been shocked by low levels of drug-related absenteeism and terminations in their studies. Others have found no effect from drug use on worksite performance and have criticized misleading characteristics of pro-drug-testing data. Instead, they contend that, even if the data were supportive of testing, drug testing ignores the presumption of innocence guaranteed to each individual. In many situations, a refusal to submit to a drug test is treated as an admission of drug usage.

genetic testing
Investigation and evaluation of an individual's biological predispositions based on the presence of a specific disease-associated gene on the individual's chromosomes.

Genetic Tests

Genetic testing is a scientific development that involves the use of laser and computer technology. Scientists make diagnostic predictions by locating a specific disease-associated gene on an individual's chromosomes. This type of testing evolved in the 1960s in connection with research regarding individuals who were "hypersusceptible" to certain chemicals used in certain workplaces.

By testing an applicant's genes, the researchers were able to ascertain which applicants would be expected to experience negative reactions to various chemicals.

Today, with the tremendous advances in medicine and technology, employers who choose to use genetic testing will have tremendous amounts of information at their fingertips. The map of the entire human genome will allow us to prevent and to treat countless health problems. Only recently, with the passage of the Genetic Information Non-Discrimination Act, does federal legislation begin to restrict the use of this personal, private, and potentially volatile information. (See Chapter 13 for additional discussion of how this issue relates to disability discrimination.) One area of concern is that an employer might discover something about an individual's genetic makeup that points to the *potential* for a debilitating disease and therefore may choose not to hire the individual based on that potential, even though the person may never develop that disease. In addition, the individual might have no previous knowledge of her or his disposition toward the disease and, in fact, might not want to know. Should the employer let that person know the reasons for her or his failure to get the job? Taken to an extreme, genetic testing might allow society to separate individuals on the basis of their potential for disease—a prospect that should not be taken lightly. Simply because we have the ability to test for something, does that mean that we should?

Moreover, genetic testing is far from perfect. Researchers have discovered that some of the genetic differences found in the test might be due to damage to the genes from the test itself. Similarly, the tests (in their present technological state) evidence only the response of the sample to the presence of a certain toxic agent. The results show merely that the subject is more susceptible to that toxic agent than someone else. Only infrequently can the test show more than this mere susceptibility or potentiality.

One additional issue raised by genetic testing is based on the fact that the genetic irregularities that may substantially impair a major life activity may be considered protected disabilities under the Americans with Disabilities Act and the Vocational Rehabilitation Act. A genetic test may encourage discrimination based on myths, fears, and stereotypes about genetic differences.

In addition, at least 26 states prohibit or limit genetic testing as a matter of law. Except to determine an employee's susceptibility or level of exposure to potentially toxic chemicals in the workplace, employers in several states, including Illinois, New Hampshire, North Carolina, Rhode Island, Vermont, and Wisconsin, are prohibited from using genetic testing as a condition of employment. Many states also prohibit discrimination and employment decisions made on the basis of genetic information.

Unique Considerations of HIV/AIDS Testing

Employers unreasonably fearful about the onslaught of **AIDS/HIV** in the workplace and the effect it will have on their workforces are anxious to test their employees or applicants for the presence of HIV. However, the HIV test in the workplace is inappropriate for two reasons. First, for the test to be justified, it must serve a legitimate business purpose. Because HIV is not transmitted by casual contact of the sort that takes place in a work environment, an HIV test is improper for most

AIDS
Acquired immune deficiency syndrome, a syndrome in which the individual's immune system ceases to function properly and during which the individual is susceptible, in most cases fatally, to opportunistic diseases. AIDS is not transmitted through casual contact; to transmit the disease, there must be an exchange of fluids. The disease may be transmitted through sexual contact, during which there is an exchange of bodily fluids; needle sharing; or an exchange of blood.

HIV
Human immunodeficiency virus, the virus that causes AIDS.

positions. Second, the test reports only the subject's past status; the test does not determine the HIV status of the individual as of the day of the examination. Therefore, unless the employer monitors and restricts the employee's off-work activities prior to the test and between testing, the inquiry is inefficient and ineffective.

In addition, an employer may not take an adverse employment action against an employee merely based on the knowledge that the individual is HIV-positive. That employee or applicant may be protected by both the federal Vocational Rehabilitation Act and the Americans with Disabilities Act. These acts provide that an employer may not make an employment decision based on the individual's HIV status, where the person is otherwise qualified to perform the essential requirements of the position.

Management Considerations: Testing

A workplace substance abuse program should incorporate (1) a written abuse policy that has been drafted after input from employees, (2) a supervisory training program, (3) an employee education and awareness program, (4) access to an employee assistance program, and (5) a drug-testing program, where appropriate.

There are three possible corporate approaches for testing employees for ineligibility. First, the employer may establish mandatory testing, which requires that all employees be tested for drug or alcohol use or some other form of ineligibility when they enter a specific program or at the time of their annual physical. Second, an employer may implement "probable cause" testing, where an employer tests employees only if there is suspicion of ineligibility, and testing is implemented for the purpose of discovering a safety, conduct, or performance problem. Third, employers may implement random testing.

The decision about what method to use for testing will depend on the goals of the employer. Does it want to test its entire workforce? Or merely potential problem employees? In any case, an employer should, first, look carefully at state and local laws in connection with specific test-related legislation, as well as at statutes regarding privacy and so on. Second, the employer should clearly articulate its policy regarding substance use, lie detectors, and other tests, as well as its purpose, the procedure by which this policy is enforced, and the appeals process. Third, the policy must be consistently implemented and diligently documented. Possible human and laboratory errors must be minimized. Fourth, all positive results should be confirmed with additional tests.

Performance Appraisals, Evaluation, and Discipline Schemes

Once a worker is chosen and hired, the next step in the employment relationship involves its management, which might include the employee's professional development. Generally, employees want to enter organizations and rise as high as they can go. Generally, employers want qualified employees who can handle what

Management Tips *Testing*

- Private-sector employers are *not* generally restricted by the Fourth Amendment protection against unreasonable searches. Therefore, as a private employer, you are allowed to conduct searches under a lower standard. On the other hand, common-law protections against invasions of privacy do apply in the private sector.
- You have an absolute right to determine whether someone is sufficiently healthy to do a job. The problem arises where your tests don't quite tell you that information or where you are testing for eligibility beyond the job's requirements. Make sure that your test will yield results that are relevant to the job in question.
- Health or eligibility testing should be conducted post-offer, preemployment.
- All tests should be validated; that is, they should be shown to test what they intend to test. Using an invalid test might subject you to liability.
- Restrict access to the information gained during testing. If you disclose the information to individuals who don't have a need to know it, you may be liable for an invasion of privacy or for defamation should the information turn out to be false.
- If you choose to try a polygraph test on workers, be wary of the restrictions imposed by the Employee Polygraph Protection Act.
- Since being HIV-free or AIDS-free is seldom (if ever) a BFOQ, testing for HIV is most likely to be unwarranted and a wrongful invasion of privacy.

performance appraisal
A periodic assessment of an employee's performance, usually completed by her or his immediate supervisor and reviewed, at times, by others in the company.

LO7

must be done to accomplish the job. Employees who want to succeed in their work do so by meeting their employers' expectations in an exemplary way. Success is usually documented by both sides through **performance appraisals (PAs)**. Employers wishing to have employees best suited for the job need to identify these employees for promotion, retention, transfers, training, bonuses, and raises; and they gather this necessary information through the periodic evaluation of employees. Disputes may arise when an employer's expectations of an employee are not aligned with the employee's understanding of the performance expected or offered; and they are most often brought to light through the evaluation system.

Above all, the purpose of the performance appraisal should be to identify those characteristics the employer hopes the employee will accentuate and to dissuade the employee from exhibiting characteristics not in keeping with the organization's objectives. Performance appraisals have the potential for discriminatory effect because discrimination may exist in the way the employer utilizes the evaluations, as well as in the manner the appraisal is conducted.

Employers are not required to maintain poor performers. Termination as a result of inadequate work performance is justified by business considerations. It is the measure of adequacy that often results in an adverse impact or is the consequence of adverse treatment, which must be avoided by employers. (See Exhibit 4.19, "Realities about Performance Evaluations.")

Exhibit 4.19 *Realities about Performance Evaluations*

1. An employer might be liable for giving a negative reference even when it is based on a valid performance evaluation.

2. An employer need not lower its standards or qualifications in order to accommodate an individual employee's or applicant's needs (such as a disability).

3. Performance appraisal systems, though inherently dependent on the evaluation of workers by other workers, can still rely on objective measures.

4. Performance incentive systems *can* be effective. They do not involve rewarding workers for doing the basics of their jobs, but instead recognize *outstanding* performance and leadership.

5. The greater legal challenges in evaluation structures are not always found in the objectives, motivation or incentives, but often in areas of implementation, monitoring and accountability.

Of the many ways in which an employer may assess employees' performance levels, the most efficient and effective methods are those that utilize a variety of schemes to obtain the most complete job-related information.

Legal Implications of Performance Appraisal Systems

Given their potential for subjectivity, as well as biased or skewed results, performance appraisal schemes are susceptible to abuse and criticism. It is undeniable that it is integral to the proper management of any workplace to have the ability to evaluate the performance of its employees, but concerns remain regarding the efficacy and propriety of the evaluation systems available.

Moreover, courts differ greatly in their decisions regarding similar performance appraisal methods; therefore, a rational and predictable conclusion is almost impossible about the propriety of any single method. What one is left with is merely direction.

Disparate Impact

The legal implications of performance appraisals become relevant when their information is used as the basis for any employment-related decision. The Uniform Guidelines on Employee Selection Procedures apply to "tests and other selection procedures which are used as the basis for any employment decision;" therefore, the guidelines regulate the design and use of performance appraisals. Improper performance appraisal systems are those that do not fairly or adequately evaluate performance but, instead, perpetuate stereotypes that have an adverse impact on protected classes.

four-fifths rule
Presumption of discrimination where the selection rate (for any employment decision) of the protected group is less than 80 percent of the selection rate of the nonminority group.

Disparate impact may be determined by a number of methods, the most common of which is described in the Guidelines as the **four-fifths rule**. The four-fifths rule holds that there is a presumption of discrimination where the selection rate (for any employment decision) of the protected group is less than 80 percent of the selection rate of the nonminority group. For example, if the number of males and females at a firm is equal, but the performance evaluation system results in promotions of 85 percent of the males and only 3 percent of the females, a court will presume discrimination. The employer could always attempt to rebut this presumption, but the default is to presume discriminatory reasons for this result.

As with other areas in which disparate impact is shown, the employer may still defend the system used, as long as the performance appraisal was sufficiently job related. There must be some reasonable need for it, and some means by which to ensure the system's objectivity and fairness. If, for example, a checklist system for appraisal is instituted, the employer must show that the person doing the checking is reasonably free of bias, and that the list itself is a fair representation of what is to be expected of the reasonable or "common" employee. This is called *validation* and is strictly regulated by the Guidelines.

The U.S Supreme Court provided some guidance to employers with regard to performance appraisal systems in *Ricci v. DeStefano,* a decision that demonstrated how prevention of unintentional discrimination against some employees can lead to perceived intentional discrimination against others. *Ricci* involved a test by the city of New Haven, Connecticut, for promotion of firefighters. The city subsequently learned that the test resulted in a statistically significant lower pass rate for African Americans than for other employees. Out of concern for potential liability, the city opted not to use the test for promotions. However, New Haven was then sued for discrimination by 18 firefighters (17 white and one Hispanic) who had already passed the test, claiming that they were denied their due promotions.

The court found that tossing out the test results amounted to intentional discrimination against those who did well unless the employer could demonstrate a "strong basis in evidence" that the test would lead to liability. To the contrary, as long as the test was "job related and consistent with business necessity" and the employer did not refuse to use other methods with less discriminatory impact, the employer needed to maintain the original test.

The holding in *Ricci* provides a strong incentive for employers to examine thoroughly any test before integrating it into an evaluation system. One effective strategy is to evaluate the passing rate of current successful employees in order to establish a benchmark for promotions overall.

Disparate Treatment

A performance appraisal also may result in disparate *treatment,* such as where a female employee is rated subject to different criteria than are the male employees. An example of this type of sexual stereotyping was at issue in the *Hopkins v. Price Waterhouse* case.[34] In that case, a female accounting executive was refused a promotion to partner based on her performance evaluation. During the evaluation, the plaintiff had been told that she needed to "take a charm school course"; maintain more social grace; "walk, talk, and dress more like a woman"; use less profanity; and act less "macho."

The Supreme Court ruled in favor of the employee, even though the employer offered evidence of various non-discriminatory bases for the denial of the partnership. The Court found that, as long as the sexual stereotype and discriminatory appraisal were "motivating factors" in the employer's denial, the motive was

- Documentation such as written performance appraisals can be your protection against wrongful lawsuits charging discrimination. As mentioned before, you are allowed to terminate someone for any reason *except* for certain prohibited reasons. As long as you document poor or deteriorating performance, you may generally terminate an individual on that basis and have protection against claims of discrimination.

- On the other hand, if you do conduct written performance appraisals but treat workers with similar appraisals differently, you may be subject to charges of discrimination.

- Where performance appraisals are conducted by a manager on the basis of stereotypes or prejudice, you are subject to claims of either disparate treatment or disparate impact. Therefore, make sure that all supervisors undergo training in connection with nonbiased reporting and evaluations that are free from prejudgments.

- Make sure that there are precautions against inappropriate disclosures. An employer may be subject to claims of privacy invasions or defamation under certain circumstances.

- If your employee manual or other materials state that you will conduct appraisals, failure to conduct them may be a problem. Make sure that you are willing to live with the claims you make regarding the regularity of appraisals and other promises.

An employee who is subject to discipline has a right to request that a co-worker be present as a witness during an investigatory interview. This right is not limited to the union employee: Nonunion employees have a right to representation under *Epilepsy Foundation of Northeast Ohio v. NLRB*.[44]

Documentation of discipline, as well as of appraisals, warnings, and commendations, should be retained in each employee's file and should be given to the employee to provide her or him with the opportunity to appeal the action.

Chapter Summary

- Employers believe that freedom of contract should permit them to hire whom they please. However, such statutes as Title VII and IRCA require the employer to ensure that all qualified employees are provided with equal employment opportunity and that decisions to hire are based solely on appropriate concerns and not on prejudice or bias that is neither supported nor relevant to business necessities.

- An ethic of non-discrimination must permeate the hiring process, from advertising the position to drafting the application form to making the decision to hire.

- One of the most effective means by which an employer can protect itself from claims of discrimination in the recruitment/application process is to have a clear view of the job to be filled and the best person to fill that job (i.e., an adequate, specific job description for each position within the company).

- After the employer has conducted the analysis, it should implement those results by reviewing the written job descriptions to ensure that they are clear and specific in line with the analysis; all nonessential job requirements should be deleted or defined as nonessential, and minimum requirements should be listed.

- Employers are cautioned, however, that the court or enforcement agency will look first to the actual job performance, then to the description only to the extent that it accurately reflects what the employee really does in that position. If the employer fails to include a function in the description, that may be used as an admission that the function is nonessential. If the function is nonessential, it is likely that an employment decision made on that basis will be suspect.

- Employers should ensure that recruitment procedures not only seek to obtain the most diversified applicant pool by reaching diverse communities but also encourage diverse applicants through the language used and the presentation of the firm.

- Employers should establish efficient, effective procedures to guarantee that they know whom they are hiring. If an employer wants a certain type of person to fill a position, ensure that the one hired is such a person. Failure to do so may result in liability under a theory of negligent hiring.

- Employers should review their applications to ensure they are asking only for information that is defensibly job-related or necessary to make a decision about whether to hire the candidate.

- Since employers are liable for negligent hiring based on what they knew or should have known, it is critical to do a thorough background check on each new hire. This may include new hires through employment agencies, as well, since those agencies do not always conduct background checks sufficient to insulate the ultimate employer.

- Though prior employers are not obligated to provide references beyond the individual's position, salary, and dates of work, if the employer chooses to do so beyond that basic level, the reference must be complete and honest to prevent foreseeable harm.

- Testing for eligibility and ineligibility is a necessary component of the selection procedure. No employer would hire an unqualified employee if it knew the qualifications of the employee in advance of the hiring determination.

- Designing the appropriate preemployment tests in order to ensure applicants can perform the functions of the job is critical, not only to effective selection procedures but also to the prevention of liability for disparate results of your procedure.

- To keep an employer's evaluation techniques within parameters that are relatively safe from criticism, the employer should first describe precisely what is required of each position to be evaluated. An adequate description will include the following:

1. Position title.
2. Department or division in which the position is located.

3. Title of supervisor (not name, as the individual may change while the supervisory position would not).

4. Function or purpose of position.

5. Scope of responsibility for accomplishing that purpose.

6. Specific duties and responsibilities.

7. Knowledge, experience, or qualifications necessary for performance of the above duties and responsibilities (the connection should be apparent or explained).

8. Organizational relationship, persons to whom the employee should report, those employees who report to this supervisor, and those employees over whom the supervisor has direct supervisory responsibilities.

- No unwritten qualifications should exist. These may have a disparate impact on those employees outside the loop of information, pursuant to which employees learn of the "real" way of obtaining promotions and other workplace benefits.

- The employer should communicate to its employees the nature, content, timing, and weight of the performance appraisal and ensure that the employees understand each of the standards pursuant to which they will be evaluated.

- The bases for the evaluation should be specific and job- or task-defined, rather than subjective, global measures of job performance. For example, a performance measure such as "ability to finish tasks within specified time period" is preferable to "timeliness." "Suggests new approaches" would be preferable to "industrious." This is because the supervisor evaluating the individual is using baselines and vantage points such as the schedules that she or he has given the employee, rather than being forced to reach a conclusion about the employee's timeliness in general.

- The employer should request justifications of ratings wherever possible. Some researchers have suggested that documentation should be required only where a rating is extreme; however, this may be construed by the court as bending over backward only in those circumstances where the rating may be questioned. To the contrary, where an employer maintains a policy that each evaluation should be documented, the consistency of treatment is a defense in itself.

- In addition to affording the employee the opportunity to be heard during the process, the employer should establish a formal appeals process, which the employee may follow subsequent to receipt of the final appraisal. This process may be implemented by the employer through its supervisors, a committee composed of representatives from all levels of the company, or a committee composed of the employee's peers. Under most circumstances, appeals processes act as a means to air differences and to explain misunderstandings, deterring later litigation.

Chapter-End Questions

1. In the process of its recruitment of Peters, Security Pacific informed Peters that the company was doing "just fine" and Peters would have "a long tenure" at Security Pacific should he accept the position offered. In doing so, Security Pacific concealed its financial losses and the substantial, known risk that the project on which Peters was hired to work might soon be abandoned and Peters laid off. Peters accepted the position and moved from New Orleans to Denver to begin his new job. Two months later, Peters was laid off as a result of Security Pacific's poor financial condition. Does Peters have a cause of action?

2. A school district performs standard teacher evaluations including unannounced visits to classrooms, and messages are often delivered to the classroom throughout the day. It is discovered that a teacher engaged in intimate sexual contact with a student during the school day. Is the school district liable for negligent hiring? Should the employer have known that this could happen? [*P. L. v. Aubert,* 545 N.W.2d 666 (Minn. 1996).]

3. Can an employer automatically exclude all applicants with criminal conviction records? What if the policy was limited to felony convictions?

4. In 1997, Bobby Randall was hired at Walmart. At the time, Randall was not a convicted felon but had been previously convicted three times on misdemeanor charges for indecent exposure. At the time of his hiring, Walmart did not have a policy in place that required criminal background checks for employees. In September 2000, Randall fondled a 10-year-old girl while on the job in the Walmart store in which he worked. The girl's mother sued Walmart for negligent hiring, claiming that they should have known of his status as a sex offender through a background check. Was Walmart liable?

5. Phillips, an African-American woman, applied for a position as secretary at the Mississippi legislature as a "walk-in" applicant. Phillips worked in the same building, which was made up of approximately 80 percent African-American employees. She stopped by the office one day to ask if the office was hiring clerical help. She was told that the office was and she was given an application to fill out. After not hearing a response from the office regarding the position, she called and learned that a white woman with similar qualifications had filled the position, even though Phillips applied before this woman. The office defended itself, claiming only that it has a practice of not contacting walk-in applicants for positions. Phillips claims that this policy disfavors African-American applicants who work in the building and is, therefore, illegal based on disparate impact. What result?

6. In December 2001, Mervyn Losing, a manager at a Food Lion grocery store, was selected to take a random drug test. The test result came back as "substituted," meaning the sample submitted did not appear to be human urine. The laboratory performed a confirmation test that also came back "substituted." Under Food Lion's substance abuse policy, "substituted" results are considered positive screens for drug use. Food Lion had a zero-tolerance policy, so Losing was fired. He insisted on a retest, which came back negative. Food Lion accepted that the first test could have been a false positive and reinstated him in the same position. In March 2002, Losing was suspended for a week for failing to follow a Food Lion policy. Upon his return, he claimed he was continually harassed by co-workers and said that his supervisor had talked about his failed drug test to other employees, suggesting that he had substituted nonhuman urine in his first drug test. He admitted that he did not ever hear the supervisor make statements to his co-workers, but says he never told anyone, so the only way they could have known was

through the supervisor. In 2005, Losing sued Food Lion, claiming defamation based on slander. Can he state a claim?

7. Sabrina Polkey was a supervisor and one of six Transtecs Corp. employees working in a mailroom at Pensacola Naval Air Station (NAS), through a Department of Defense (DoD) contract. One day, Polkey returned to the mailroom after working hours and discovered 14 opened and undelivered Christmas cards in the wastebasket at the front desk. Each of the six mailroom employees was questioned and each denied opening the mail. Transtecs arranged for polygraph exams for all six employees to absolve the company of any wrongdoing in the event that charges were pursued against the perpetrator. Employees were informed that the polygraph was voluntary and they each signed a general release form for the polygraph. Only one employee agreed to and took the polygraph test; Polkey did not. Less than a week later, Polkey was fired for a separate incident that supervisors claimed was a violation of NAS security procedures. Polkey believed that her refusal to take the polygraph was the true reason for her termination and claimed that the request to take a polygraph was a violation of the Employee Polygraph Protection Act (EPPA). Transtecs claimed that their request fell within EPPA's exemptions for an ongoing investigation and national security (based on the contract with the DoD). Who is correct? [*Polkey v. Transtecs Corp.,* 404 F.3d 1264 (11th Cir. 2005).]

8. Please respond to the following in connection with recruitment, selection, or employment procedures:

   a. When, if ever, may an employer ask a candidate or employee for a photograph as part of recruitment, selection or employment procedures?

   b. May an employer ask a candidate or current employee to which organizations the individual belongs?

   c. If a contract is intended to be at-will, must it include a statement to that effect?

9. An individual contacts you in connection with a reference for one of your worst employees, who was just recently terminated for poor performance. This individual asks whether you believe the former employee will perform well in a similar position at a new company. How do you respond? Is your response different if the former employee was terminated for stealing, and the individual asks whether this employee can be trusted?

10. Which of the following statements would be acceptable in a performance evaluation?

    • "Even though Jacquie was out on a few religious retreats, she exceeded June sales goals by 10 percent."

    • "Although a new, young college graduate, Spiro was very capable in leading the sales meeting."

    • "Despite time off for medical leaves, Renee was able to surpass productivity of many of her colleagues."

    • "Though a bit tough to understand, Margeaux has received excellent reviews for her customer service."

11. The city of Bozeman, Montana, requires job candidates to list their social networking sites, usernames, and passwords on the city employee application. City Attorney Greg Sullivan explained that the city has "positions ranging from fire and police, which require people of high integrity for those positions, all the way down to the lifeguards and the folks that work in city hall here. So we do those types of investigations to make sure the people that we hire have the highest moral character and are a good fit

for the City." No prospective employee has yet to remove his/her name because of the requirement. Yet, with such high access to a prospect's profile, it could become difficult for human resources to not be aware of a candidate's ethnicity or even religious affiliation. Has the city justified its decision to ask for this information? Would you be comfortable if a prospective employer asked you for this information? Why or why not?

End Notes

1. Crispin, G., and Mehler, M., *CareerXroads 9th Annual Source of Hire Study* (2010).

2. Sullivan, John, http://www.slideshare.net/beeshields/making-your-employee-referral-program-work-smarter (June 16, 2010).

3. *Equal Employment Opportunity Commission v. Chicago Miniature Lamp Works,* 947 F.2d 292 (7th Cir. 1991).

4. Littler Mendelson, "Hiring Strategies for the Changing American Workforce" (2007).

5. Kerry Parker, "Workplace Violence Considerations for Employers," *New Jersey Lawyer,* April 1999, p. 18.

6. Dawn Anfuso, "Deflecting Workplace Violence," *Personnel Journal* 73, no. 10 (October 1994), pp. 66–67.

7. EEOC Enforcement Guidance on Application of EEO Laws to Contingent Workers (December 3, 1997).

8. Charles White and Joanie Sompayrac, "Employee Screening Practices and the Temporary Help Industry," unpublished manuscript.

9. Eileen Duffy, "Employers Use Facebook in Hiring Process," *The Observer* (online), November 1, 2006, http://media.www.ndsmcobserver.com/media/storage/paper660/news/2006/11/01/News/Employers.Use.Facebook.In.Hiring.Process-2414357.shtml. See also A. L. Rupe, "Facebook Faux Pas," *Workforce Management,* March 2007.

10. G. Maatman, "Lawyers Warn Facebook a Risky Tool for Background Checks," *Workforce Management* (undated), http://www.workforce.com/section/06/feature/25/45/83/254585.html.

11. Wortham, Jenna, "More Employers Use Social Networks to Check Out Applicants," *The New York Times* (Aug. 20, 2009), http://bits.blogs.nytimes.com/2009/08/20/more-employers-use-social-networks-to-check-out-applicants/.

12. E. Frauenheim, "Caution Advised When Using Social Networking Web Sites for Recruiting, Background Checking," *Workforce Management,* March 2007.

13. Ibid.

14. *Allstate Insurance Co. v. Jerner,* Case No. 93-09472 (Fla. Cir. Ct. 1993), cert. denied, 650 So. 2d 997 (Fla. Ct. App. 1995).

15. *Randi W. v. Muroc Joint Unified School Dist.,* 14 Cal. 4th 1066 (1997).

16. See review of caselaw in *Cweklinsky v. Mobil Chemical Co.,* 837 A.2d 759, 765 (Conn. 2004). States include Colorado, Iowa, Minnesota, Connecticut, and California.

17. 115 S. Ct. 879 (1995).

18. See Jeffrey Kluger, "Pumping Up Your Past," *Time,* June 10, 2002, p. 41.

19. U.S. Department of Health and Human Services, Substance Abuse and Mental Health Services Administration, "Drugs in the Workplace," April 19, 2006, http://workplace.samhsa.gov/DrugTesting/Files_Drug_Testing/FactSheet/SAMSA_Drugs_workplace508.pdf.

20   U.S. Department of Health and Human Services, Substance Abuse and Mental Health Services Administration, Office of Applied Studies, Results from the *2004 National Survey on Drug Use and Health: National Findings* (Rockville, MD: DHHS, 2005).

21. National Institutes of Health, National Institute on Drug Abuse, "NIDA InfoFacts: Workplace Trends," November 2, 2006, http://www.drugabuse.gov/Infofacts/workplace.html.

22. 79 F.3d 661, 665–69 (7th Cir. 1996).

23. 422 U.S. 405 (1975).

24. "Personality Testing as Part of the Hiring Process," RD411.com (Nov. 2009, accessed July 19, 2010), http://www.rd411.com/index.php?option=com_content&view=article&id=1155:personality-testing-as-part-of-the-hiring-process&catid=70:clinical-management&Itemid=349.

25. Barrick, M. R., and Mount, M. K., "The Big Five Personality Dimensions and Job Performance: A Meta-analysis," *Personnel Psychology,* 44 (1991), pp. 1–26.

26. Martin, B. A., Bowen, C. C., and Hunt, S. T., "How Effective Are People at Faking on Personality Questionnaires?" *Personality and Individual Differences,* 32 (2002), pp. 247–56.

27. *Karraker v. Rent-a-Center,* 2005 WL 1389443 (7th Cir. June 14, 2005).

28. 42 U.S.C. § 12112(d)(3)(C)-(4)(A).

29. F. Schmidt and J. Hunter, "General Mental Ability in the World of Work: Occupational Attainment and Job Performance," *Journal of Personality and Social Psychology* 86 (2004), pp. 162–73; Sara L. Rynes et al., "The Very Separate Worlds of Academic and Practitioner Periodicals in Human Resource Management: Implications for Evidence-Based Management," *Academy of Management Journal* 50, no. 5 (2007), pp. 987–1008; F. Schmidt, "The Orphan Area for Meta-Analysis: Personnel Selection" (2006), http://www.siop.org/tip/Oct06/05schmidt.aspx.

30. Schmidt and Hunter, "General Mental Ability."

31. *Baughman v. Wal-Mart Stores, Inc.,* 592 S.E.2d 824 (W. Va. 2003); *Twigg v. Hercules Corporation,* 406 S.E.2d 52 (W. Va. 1990).

32. Paul Rountree, "Drug Testing and Workplace Accidents," http://www.aiha.org/aihce04/handouts/rt227rountree1.pdf.

33. 868 F.2d 74 (3d Cir. 1989).

34. 490 U.S. 228 (1989).

35. K. Dion, E. Berscheild, and E. Walster, "What Is Beautiful Is Good," *Journal of Personality and Social Psychology* 24 (1986), pp. 285–90; D. Landy and H. Sigall, "Beauty Is Talent: Task Evaluation as a Function of the Performer's Physical Attractiveness," *Journal of Personality and Social Psychology* 29 (1974), pp. 299–304, in R. Brown, *Social Psychology,* 2nd ed. (New York: Free Press, 1986), pp. 393–94.

36. 411 U.S. 792 (1973).

37. 102 Mich. App. 606 (1980).

38. 457 F.2d 348 (5th Cir. 1972).

39. Ibid.

40. Note, however, that there is long-standing arbitral precedent that the decision as to the severity of a penalty is a matter of management discretion and that the exercise of that

discretion should not be disturbed unless it can be shown that it was exercised in an arbitrary, capricious, or discriminatory fashion. See, e.g., *Stockham Pipe Fittings,* 1 LA 160 (1945).

41. *Chertkova v. Connecticut General Life Insurance,* 71 FEP Cases 1006 (2d Cir. 1996).
42. See *Hanchard v. Facilities Development Corporation,* 10 IER Cases 1004 (N.Y. App. 1995); *Gipson v. KAS Snacktime Company,* 71 FEP Cases 1677 (E.D. Mo. 1994).
43. 42 LA 555, 557–59 (1964).
44. 268 F.3d 1095 (D.C. Cir. 2001), cert. denied, 122 S. Ct. 2356 (2002).

Cases

EEOC v. Consolidated Service System
989 F.2d 233 (7th Cir. 1993)

Defendant is a small janitorial firm in Chicago owned by Mr. Hwang, a Korean immigrant, and staffed mostly by Koreans. The firm relied mainly on word-of-mouth recruiting. Between 1983 and 1987, 73 percent of the applicants for jobs and 81 percent of the hires were Korean, while less than 1 percent of the workforce in the Chicago area is Korean. The district court found that these discrepancies were not due to discrimination and the circuit court agreed.

Posner, J.

***

Consolidated is a small company. The EEOC's lawyer told us at argument that the company's annual sales are only $400,000. We mention this fact not to remind the reader of David and Goliath, or to suggest that Consolidated is exempt from Title VII (it is not), or to express wonderment that a firm of this size could litigate in federal court for seven years (and counting) with a federal agency, but to explain why Mr. Hwang relies on word of mouth to obtain employees rather than reaching out to a broader community less heavily Korean. It is the cheapest method of recruitment. Indeed, it is practically costless. Persons approach Hwang or his employees—most of whom are Korean too—at work or at social events,

and once or twice Hwang has asked employees whether they know anyone who wants a job. At argument the EEOC's lawyer conceded, perhaps improvidently but if so only slightly so, that Hwang's recruitment posture could be described as totally passive. Hwang did buy newspaper advertisements on three occasions—once in a Korean-language newspaper and twice in the *Chicago Tribune*—but as these ads resulted in zero hires, the experience doubtless only confirmed him in the passive posture. The EEOC argues that the single Korean newspaper ad, which ran for only three days and yielded not a single hire, is evidence of discrimination. If so, it is very weak evidence. The Commission points to the fact that Hwang could have obtained job applicants at no expense from the Illinois Job Service as further evidence of discrimination. But he testified that he had never heard of the Illinois Job Service and the district judge believed him.

If an employer can obtain all the competent workers he wants, at wages no higher than the minimum that he expects to have to pay, without beating the bushes for workers—without in fact spending a cent on recruitment—he can reduce his costs of doing business by adopting just the stance of Mr. Hwang. And this is no mean consideration to a firm whose annual revenues in a highly competitive business are those of a mom and pop grocery store. Of course if the employer is a member of an ethnic community, especially an immigrant one, this stance is likely to result in the perpetuation of an ethnically imbalanced workforce. Members of these communities tend to work and to socialize with each other rather than with people in the larger community. The social and business network of an immigrant community racially and culturally distinct from the majority of Americans is bound to be largely confined to that community, making it inevitable that when the network is used for job recruitment the recruits will be drawn disproportionately from the community.

No inference of *intentional* discrimination can be drawn from the pattern we have described, even if the employer would prefer to employ people drawn predominantly or even entirely from his own ethnic or, here, national-origin community. Discrimination is not preference or aversion; it is acting on the preference or aversion. If the most efficient method of hiring adopted *because* it is the most efficient (not defended because it is efficient—the statute does not allow an employer to justify intentional discrimination by reference to efficiency) just happens to produce a workforce whose racial or religious or ethnic or national-origin or gender composition pleases the employer, this is not intentional discrimination. The motive is not a discriminatory one. "Knowledge of a disparity is not the same thing as an intent to cause or maintain it." Or if, though, the motives behind adoption of the method were a mixture of discrimination and efficiency, Mr. Hwang would have adopted the identical method of recruitment even if he had no interest in the national origin of his employees, the fact that he had such an interest would not be a "but for" cause of the discriminatory outcome and again there would be no liability. There is no evidence that Hwang is biased in favor of Koreans

or prejudiced against any group underrepresented in his workforce, except what the Commission asks us to infer from the imbalance in that force and Hwang's passive stance.

If this were a disparate-impact case (as it was once, but the Commission has abandoned its claim of disparate impact), and, if, contrary to *EEOC v. Chicago Miniature Lamp Works,* word of mouth recruitment were deemed an employment practice and hence was subject to review for disparate impact, as assumed in *Clark v. Chrysler Corp.,* then the advantages of word-of-mouth recruitment would have to be balanced against its possibly discriminatory effect when the employer's current workforce is already skewed along racial or other disfavored lines. But in a case of disparate treatment, the question is different. It is whether word-of-mouth recruitment gives rise to an inference of intentional discrimination. Unlike an explicit racial or ethnic criterion or, what we may assume without deciding amounts to the same thing, a rule confining hiring to relatives of existing employees in a racially or ethnically skewed workforce, as in *Thomas v. Washington County School Board,* word-of-mouth recruiting does not compel an inference of intentional discrimination. At least it does not do so where, as in the case of Consolidated Services Systems, it is clearly, as we have been at pains to emphasize, the cheapest and most efficient method of recruitment, notwithstanding its discriminatory impact. Of course, Consolidated had some non-Korean applicants for employment, and if it had never hired any this would support, perhaps decisively, an inference of discrimination. Although the respective percentages of Korean and of non-Korean applicants hired were clearly favorable to Koreans (33 percent to 20 percent), the EEOC was unable to find a single person out of the 99 rejected non-Koreans who could show that he or she was interested in a job that Mr. Hwang ever hired for. Many, perhaps most, of these were persons who responded to the ad he placed in the *Chicago Tribune* for a contract that he never got, hence never hired for.

The Commission cites the statement of Consolidated's lawyer that his client took advantage of the fact that the Korean immigrant community offered a ready market of cheap labor as an admission of "active" discrimination on the basis of national origin. It is not discrimination, and it is certainly not active discrimination, for an employer to sit back and wait for people willing to work for low wages to apply to him. The fact that they are ethnically or racially uniform does not impose upon him a duty to spend money advertising in the help-wanted columns of the *Chicago Tribune.* The Commission deemed Consolidated's "admission" corroborated by the testimony of the sociologist William Liu, Consolidated's own expert witness, who explained that it was natural for a recent Korean immigrant such as Hwang to hire other recent Korean immigrants, with whom he shared a common culture, and that the consequence would be a work-force disproportionately Korean. Well, of course. People who share a common culture tend to work together as well as marry together and socialize together. That is not evidence of illegal discrimination.

In a nation of immigrants, this must be reckoned an ominous case despite its outcome. The United States has many recent immigrants, and today as historically they tend to cluster in their own communities, united by ties of language, culture, and background. Often they form small businesses composed largely of relatives, friends, and other members of their community, and they obtain new employees by word of mouth. These small businesses—grocery stores, furniture stores, clothing stores, cleaning services, restaurants, gas stations—have been for many immigrant groups, and continue to be, the first rung on the ladder of American success. Derided as clannish, resented for their ambition and hard work, hated or despised for their otherness, recent immigrants are frequent targets of discrimination, some of it violent. It would be a bitter irony if the federal agency dedicated to enforcing the anti-discrimination laws succeeded in using those laws to kick these people off the ladder by compelling them to institute costly systems of hiring. There is equal danger to small black-run businesses in our central cities. Must such businesses undertake in the name of non-discrimination costly measures to recruit non-black employees?

Although Consolidated has been dragged through seven years of federal litigation at outrageous expense for a firm of its size, we agree with the Commission that this suit was not frivolous. The statistical disparity gave the Commission a leg up, and it might conceivably have succeeded in its disparate-impact claim but for our intervening decision in *EEOC v. Chicago Miniature Lamp Works,* supra. Had the judge believed the Commission's witnesses, the outcome even of the disparate-treatment claim might have been different. The Equal Access to Justice Act was intended, one might have thought, for just such a case as this, where a groundless but not frivolous suit is brought by the mighty federal government against a tiny firm; but Consolidated concedes its inapplicability. We do not know on what the concession is based— possibly on cases like *Escobar Ruiz v. INS,* on rehearing, holding the Act inapplicable to statutes that have their own fee-shifting statutes—but other cases, such as *Gavette v. Office of Personnel Management,* are contra. It may not be too late for Consolidated to reconsider its concession in light of our holding in *McDonald v. Schweiker,* supra, regarding the deadline for seeking fees under the Act.

AFFIRMED.

Case Questions

1. If the court in Consolidated ruled that, even though the statistics told another story, there was no evidence of "intentional" discrimination, would an unbalanced workforce due to word-of-mouth recruiting alone ever constitute disparate treatment?

2. Consider your and the court's response to the above question. Would your decision be different if it could be shown that, in a certain small, all-white firm, recruiting was done only using word of mouth and this effort resulted in only white applicants. Would your decision remain the same?

3. If this case were tried as a disparate impact case, as discussed by the court, how would you balance the advantages of word-of-mouth recruiting against the possibility of a discriminatory impact?

National Treasury Employees Union v. Von Raab
489 U.S. 656 (1989)

Case 2

The U.S. Customs Service implemented a drug-screening program that required urinalysis tests of service employees who wanted to be transferred or promoted to positions where there might be some contact with drugs, such as confiscation, or where the employee might have to carry a firearm or handle classified material. The program provides that the results of the test may not be turned over to any other agency without the employee's written consent. The petitioners, a federal employees' union and one of its officials, sued claiming a violation of the Fourth Amendment. The district court agreed and enjoined the program because the plan was overly intrusive without probable cause or reasonable suspicion. The court of appeals vacated the injunction, holding that this type of search was reasonable in light of its limited scope and the service's strong interest in detecting drug use among employees in certain positions. The Supreme Court affirmed in connection with positions involving contact with drugs and/or firearms but vacated and remanded the decision in regard to those positions that require handling of classified materials.

Kennedy, J.

***

In *Skinner v. Railway Labor Executives Assn.*, decided today, we held that federal regulations requiring employees of private railroads to produce urine samples for chemical testing implicate the Fourth Amendment, as those tests invade reasonable expectations of privacy. Our earlier cases have settled that the Fourth Amendment protects individuals from unreasonable searches conducted by the Government, even when the Government acts as an employer and, in view of our holding in *Railway Labor* that urine tests are searches, it follows that the Customs Service's drug testing program must meet the reasonableness requirement of the Fourth Amendment.

While we have often emphasized and reiterate today that a search must be supported, as a general matter, by warrant issued upon probable cause, our decision in *Railway Labor* reaffirms the longstanding principle that neither a warrant nor probable cause, nor, indeed, any measure of individualized suspicion, is an indispensable component of reasonableness in every circumstance. As we note in *Railway Labor*, our cases establish that where a Fourth Amendment intrusion serves special governmental needs, beyond the normal need for law enforcement, it is necessary to balance the individual's privacy expectations against the Government's interests to determine whether it is impractical to require a warrant or some level of individualized suspicion in the particular context.

It is clear that the Customs Service's drug testing program is not designed to serve the ordinary needs of law enforcement. Test results may not be used in criminal prosecution of the employee without the employee's consent. The purposes of the program are to deter drug use among those eligible for promotion to sensitive positions within the Service and to prevent the promotion of drug users to those positions. These substantial interests, no less than the Government's concern for safe rail transportation at issue in *Railway Labor*, present a special need that may justify departure from the ordinary warrant and probable cause requirements.

Petitioners do not contend that a warrant is required by the balance of privacy and governmental interests in this context, nor could any such contention withstand scrutiny. We have recognized that requiring the Government to procure a warrant for every work-related intrusion "would conflict with 'the common sense realization that government offices could not function if every employment decision became a constitutional matter.'"

Even where it is reasonable to dispense with the warrant requirement in the particular circumstances, a search ordinarily must be based on probable cause. . . . We think Customs employees who are directly involved in the interdiction of illegal drugs or who are required to carry firearms in the line of duty likewise have a diminished expectation of privacy in respect to intrusions occasioned by a urine test. Because successful performance of their duties depends uniquely on their judgment and dexterity, these employees cannot reasonably expect to keep from the Service personal information that bears directly on their fitness.

In sum, we believe that the Government has demonstrated that its compelling interests in safeguarding our borders and the public safety outweigh the privacy expectations of employees who seek to be promoted to positions that directly involve the interdiction of illegal drugs or who are required to carry a firearm. We hold that the testing of these employees is reasonable under the Fourth Amendment.

Case Questions

1. An approved drug use test must be conducted within reasonable parameters. In *Capua,* the court determined that a urine collection process may not be reasonable if

"done under close surveillance of a government representative [as it] is likely to be a very embarrassing and humiliating experience." Courts will generally balance the employee's rights against the employer's stated basis for the test and determine whether the cause of the test is reasonable and substantial. For instance, in *Skinner v. Railway Labor Executives Assn.,* the Supreme Court stated that the railway employees had a reduced expectation of privacy due to the highly regulated nature of the industry. In addition, societal interests, such as safety and security of the railways, may outweigh the individual employee's privacy interests. When might this be the case?

2. Why do you think the Court made a distinction between positions involving contact with drugs and firearms and positions that require handling of classified materials?

Regulation of Discrimination in Employment

Hi. Yes, we're speaking to you. Yes, we actually *do* know you're there. We think about you all the time. With each and every word we write. From the very beginning of this textbook more than 15 years ago, our *constant* thought in writing this text for you has always been: How can we say this so they "get it"? What information do they need to know in order to prevent workplace liability? What interesting cases can we choose that will best illustrate our point? What cases can we choose that will not only give them insight into how the court thinks so they will know what to consider when making workplace decisions themselves, but that will also demonstrate how a manager or supervisor should act (or not act) in this situation, so he or she will not cause liability for the employer? All for you.

We have read thousands of cases, hundreds of studies, and zillions of journal, newspaper, and magazine articles. Perhaps just as important, we have spoken with thousands of employers, managers, supervisors, employees, and students. We do this all with an eye toward how we can better tell you what you need to know to avoid unnecessary and preventable workplace liability.

What we've found over the years is that when it comes to the subject matter covered in this section, telling you the law is simply not enough. The subject matter of this section is much more personal than just the laws, per se. It calls upon you as managers and supervisors to make decisions that call into play your own personal narratives—that is, your worldview based on your experiences, upbringing, family, friends, and so on. As such, we would be remiss if we did not approach this area a bit differently—a way that is not geared to giving you all you need to make defensible workplace decisions. We have found through our extensive experience that it is necessary to give you not only the law, but also a solid grounding in the background and history of certain areas so you will understand the issues more thoroughly and thus avoid liability because you will make better, more informed workplace decisions.

For nearly 30 years we have been on a quest to deconstruct how workplace managers make the decisions that cause liability for the employer so that we can share that information with you and prevent you from making the same mistakes when you are in that position. We hate to see employers pay out money in judgments or settlements for unnecessary, avoidable liability. We hate the thought of our students or readers being the cause of actions in the workplace that result in liability for the employer. All could have been so easily avoided.

The things you see in the chapters in this section reflect that. We understand that in choosing to take our approach, we may come off as being "preachy." What we are actually doing is stepping outside of the pure law to give you better information and more context because we know from our extensive experience that this is how decisions are made and how the courts will judge them.

So, as you read the chapters in this section, keep in mind that what appears to be outside of the pure law is included in order to give you what you need to be able to make better decisions in the workplace. If it seems like we're preaching, maybe we are. We are passionate about teaching you what you need to know to avoid unnecessary workplace liability about these issues. If it takes sounding preachy, we'll own it—just so you understand that the preaching comes straight from the law and research and is put there to help you better do your job for your employer.

Chapter 5

Affirmative Action

Learning Objectives

After reading this chapter, you should be able to:

LO1 Discuss what affirmative action is and why it was created.

LO2 Provide the results of several studies indicating why there continues to be a need to take more than a passive approach to equal employment opportunity.

LO3 Name and explain the three types of affirmative action.

LO4 Explain when affirmative action plans are required and how they are created.

LO5 List the basic safeguards put in place in affirmative action plans to minimize harm to others.

LO6 Define "reverse discrimination" and tell how it relates to affirmative action.

LO7 Explain the arguments of those opposed to affirmative action and those who support it.

LO8 Explain the concept of valuing diversity/inclusion/multiculturalism and why it is needed, and give examples of ways to do it.

Opening Scenarios

SCENARIO 1

1) A union has not permitted African-Americans to become a part of its ranks because of opposition from white union members. Black employees win when they sue to join. The court orders appropriate remedies. The union still resists African-Americans as members. Eventually the court orders that the union admit a certain number of African-Americans by a certain time or be held in contempt of court. Is this a permissible remedy under Title VII?

SCENARIO 2

2) An employer is concerned that her workplace has only a few African-Americans, Hispanics, and women in upper-level management and skilled-labor jobs. Most unskilled-labor and clerical positions are held by women and minorities. Employer decides to institute a program that will increase the numbers of minorities and women in management and skilled-labor positions. Is this permissible? Do you have all relevant facts needed to decide? Explain.

SCENARIO 3

3) An employer is found by a court to have discriminated. As part of an appropriate remedy, employer is ordered to promote one female for every male that is promoted, until the desired goal is met. Male employees who would have been next in line for promotions under the old system sue the employer, alleging reverse discrimination in that the new promotees are being hired on the basis of gender, and the suing employees are being harmed because of their gender. Who wins and why?

Statutory Basis

Except in the contracts exempted in accordance with Section 204 of this Order, all Government contracting agencies shall include in every Government contract hereafter entered into the following provisions:

During the performance of this contract, the contractor agrees as follows:

(1) The contractor will not discriminate against any employee or applicant for employment because of race, color, religion, sex, or national origin. The contractor will take affirmative action to ensure that applicants are employed, and that employees are treated during employment, without regard to their race, color, religion, sex, or national origin. Such action shall include, but not be limited to, the following: employment, upgrading, demotion, or transfer; recruitment or recruitment advertising; layoff or termination; rates of pay or other forms of compensation; and selection for training, including apprenticeship. [202, Executive Order 11246.]

If the court finds that respondent has intentionally engaged in or is intentionally engaging in an unlawful employment practice charged in the complaint, the court may enjoin the respondent from engaging in such unlawful employment practice, and order such affirmative action as may be appropriate, which may include, but is not limited to, reinstatement or hiring of employees . . . or any other equitable relief as the court deems appropriate. [Section 706(g) of Title VII of the Civil Rights Act of 1964, 42 U.S.C. § 2000e, sec. 706(g).]

*2035 (a) (1) Any contract in the amount of $100,000 or more entered into by any department or agency of the United States for the procurement of personal property and nonpersonal services (including construction) for the United States, shall contain a provision requiring that the party contracting with the United States take affirmative action to employ and advance in employment qualified covered veterans. This section applies to any subcontract in the amount of $100,000 or more entered into by a prime contractor in carrying out any such contract. [Jobs for Veterans Act of 2002, 38 U.S.C.A. § 4212(a)(1).]

Other pieces of more limited protective employment legislation, such as the Americans with Disabilities Act (which encourages, but does not mandate, affirmative action), the Rehabilitation Act, and the Vietnam Era Veterans' Readjustment Assistance Act, as amended by the Jobs for Veterans Act of 2002, also address affirmative action.

The Design and Unstable History

Note: Several pieces of legislation contain affirmative action provisions, but we are here primarily devoting coverage to areas covered by Title VII of the Civil Rights Act of 1964 and Executive Order 11246.

Introduction

affirmative action
Intentional inclusion of women and minorities in the workplace based on a finding of their previous exclusion and/or to address existing discrimination.

Noise. There is a lot of it around the concept of **affirmative action**. It can be difficult to turn off the noise and determine what is real and what is not. Did you ever hear someone say, "We *have* to hire an African-American" or "We *have* to hire a woman"? Such a statement is likely rooted somewhere in the concept of affirmative action. While there may be truth somewhere in the statement, it is probably far from what it appears to be. Many, mistakenly, think affirmative action is a law that takes qualified whites or males out of their jobs and gives the jobs to unqualified minorities or females, or that affirmative action is an entitlement program that provides unqualified women or minorities with jobs while qualified whites or males, or both, are shut out of the workplace. According to the EEOC Compliance manual, affirmative action is "actions appropriate to overcome the effects of past or present practices, policies, or other barriers to equal employment opportunity."[1]

Imagine sitting at a nice upscale restaurant enjoying a great meal. At the table next to yours is what appears to be a mother and a daughter in her early twenties. Suddenly the mother raises her hand and slaps the daughter hard across the face. Everything stops. Everyone in the restaurant is shocked. You are appalled. You think the mother must be crazy for doing such a thing and you find yourself being angry with the mother for such a violent, heartless, embarrassing spectacle.

Imagine your surprise when you learn that from birth, from time to time, the daughter has suffered violent seizures that put her life in danger. She has managed to live a fairly normal life and is an honor student in her senior year of college, but occasionally, for no particular reason that doctors can discern, she will have one of these seizures. She gets a certain look in her eyes when the seizure is about to occur, and the only way it can be prevented is to immediately slap her hard across the face.

What a difference knowledge and context make. What may appear as one thing without knowing the facts and context can seem quite different if you do. We find that our students, and most employees we meet during consulting, dislike affirmative action. However, they rarely know what it actually is, and they know even less about its context. Seen from their experience of living in a post–Title VII world, where people think everyone is operating by the same rules in employment and not giving a lot of thought to discrimination, it makes no sense at all to have race or gender play any part whatsoever in an employment or any other decision. However, once they learn what it is, why it was created, and the reality of the relevant issues, they have a better foundation upon which to base their opinion. Whether it changes their opinion is up to them, but at least now they are basing that opinion on fact and reality rather than misconceptions. This is extremely important for making workplace decisions.

Affirmative Action's Misunderstandings Based on Race

Most of the anger around affirmative action stems from the issue of race. Despite the fact that white women have made the most gains under affirmative action, there is still the basic view that African-Americans are getting something others are not, just because they are African-American, and this makes people angry. Perhaps, as with our students and attendees at our consulting sessions, viewing affirmative action in the context of a rough racial timeline will give you more information and a context for the law and thus a clearer view. It puts what nowadays appears to be a ridiculously unfair legal requirement into its proper context, thus making it more understandable. Some of this you will recall from our discussion on the history leading up to Title VII, but it bears repeating where necessary, in this context. Keep in mind that this is history, not a judgment of history.

> *1619—First slaves arrive in America.* As we discussed in the Title VII chapter 3, slavery is a way of life for African-Americans who have virtually no other role in American society for the next 246 years. Personnel are not available to constantly watch over slaves every minute of the day, so methods are developed to keep them in line without the need for constant supervision. Slave Codes, policies and actions that make them aware of their subjugation every minute of every day, accomplish this mental and physical enslavement.

> *1865—The Civil War ends.* The war had begun four years earlier in 1861 to prevent the South from leaving the Union and establishing its own country in which slavery was permitted.

> *1865—The Thirteenth Amendment to the Constitution abolishes slavery.*
> - Shortly thereafter, Slave Codes are replaced by Black Codes.
> - After federal troops, which came to the South to make sure slavery actually ended, leave 11 years later (the period called Reconstruction), the Ku Klux Klan (KKK) rises and enforces Jim Crow laws keeping blacks in very much the same position they had been in during slavery.
> - This continues for the next 100 years, except for public school segregation, which is outlawed by the U.S. Supreme Court in 1954.
> - Segregation is so strict that, in 1959, Alabama state librarian Emily Reed is fired for refusing to remove from the library the children's book *A Rabbit's Wedding,* despite demands of state senators who say it (and other books like it) should be removed and burned because the groom was a black bunny and the bride was a white bunny.

1964—Civil Rights Act of 1964 is passed, prohibiting discrimination on the basis of race, color, gender, religion, and national origin in employment, education, receipt of federal funds and public accommodations.

- The country is in turmoil over African-Americans not being able to vote because of remaining restrictive measures instituted after Reconstruction. (See Exhibit 5.1, "Voting under Jim Crow.")

Exhibit 5.1 *Voting under Jim Crow*

In 1962, Fannie Lou Hamer, a sharecropper who worked on a plantation in Ruleville, Mississippi, tried to register to vote and could not. Hamer became a field organizer for the Student Nonviolent Coordinating Committee (SNCC), trying to register African-Americans to vote in the South. Hamer ran for Congress in 1964 with the help of the Mississippi Freedom Democratic Party formed by the SNCC to expand African-American voter registration and challenge the legitimacy of the state's all-white Democratic Party. The MFDP attended the Democratic National Convention in Atlantic City in 1964 and Hamer appeared before the credentials committee in an attempt to unseat the Mississippi delegation or be seated with them. This is an excerpt from the speech she gave before the committee. It provides insight into how deeply race was ingrained in our culture at the time the Civil Rights Act was passed, and how deep-seated the prejudice against African-Americans was, which in turn necessitated taking more than a passive approach to prohibiting workplace discrimination.

> Mr. Chairman, and the Credentials Committee, my name is Mrs. Fannie Lou Hamer, and I live at 626 East Lafayette Street, Ruleville, Mississippi, Sunflower County, the home of Senator James O. Eastland and Senator Stennis [staunch Southern segregationists].
>
> It was the 31st of August in 1962 that eighteen of us traveled twenty-six miles to the county courthouse in Indianola to try to register to become first-class citizens.
>
> We was met in Indianola by policemen, High way Patrolmen, and they only allowed two of us to take the literacy test at the time. After we had taken this test and started back to Ruleville, we

was held up by the City Police and the State Highway Patrolmen and carried back to Indianola where the bus driver was charged that day with driving a bus of the wrong color.

After we paid the fine among us, we continued on to Ruleville, and Reverend Jeff Sunny carried me four miles in the rural area where I had worked as a timekeeper and sharecropper for eighteen years. I was met there by my children, who told me that the plantation owner was angry because I had gone down to try to register.

After they told me, my husband came, and said the plantation owner was raising Cain because I had tried to register. Before he quit talking the plantation owner came and said, "Fannie Lou, do you know—did Pap tell you what I said?"

And I said, "Yes, Sir."

He said, "Well I mean that." He said, "If you don't go down and withdraw your registration, you will have to leave." Said, "Then if you go down and withdraw," said, "you still might have to go because we are not ready for that in Mississippi."

And I addressed him and told him and said, "I didn't try to register for you. I tried to register for myself."

I had to leave that same night.

On the 10th of September 1962, sixteen bullets was fired into the home of Mr. and Mrs. Robert Tucker for me. That same night two girls were shot in Ruleville, Mississippi. Also, Mr. Joe McDonald's house was shot in.

And June the 9th, 1963, I had attended a voter registration workshop; was returning back to Mississippi. Ten of us was traveling by the Continental Trailways bus. When we got to Winona,

continued

Exhibit 5.1 *continued*

Mississippi, which is Montgomery County, four of the people got off to use the washroom, and two of the people—to use the restaurant—two of the people wanted to use the washroom.

The four people that had gone in to use the restaurant was ordered out. During this time I was on the bus. But when I looked through the window and saw they had rushed out I got off of the bus to see what had happened. And one of the ladies said, "It was a State Highway Patrolman and a Chief of Police ordered us out."

I got back in the bus and one of the persons had used the washroom got back on the bus, too.

As soon as I was seated on the bus, I saw when they began to get the five people in a highway patrolman's car. I stepped off of the bus to see what was happening and somebody screamed from the car that the five workers was in and said, "Get that one there." When I went to get in the car, when the man told me I was under arrest, he kicked me.

I was carried to the county jail and put in the booking room. They left some of the people in the booking room and began to place us in cells. I was placed in a cell with a young woman called Miss Ivesta Simpson. After I was placed in the cell I began to hear sounds of licks and screams, I could hear the sounds of licks and horrible screams. And I could hear somebody say, "Can you say, 'yes, sir,' nigger? Can you say 'yes sir'."

And they would say other horrible names.

She would say, "Yes, I can say 'yes sir.'"

"So, well, say it."

She said, "I don't know you well enough."

They beat her, I don't know how long. And after a while she began to pray, and asked God to have mercy on those people.

And it wasn't too long before three white men came to my cell. One of these men was a State Highway Patrolman and he asked me where I was from. I told him Ruleville and he said, "We are going to check this."

They left my cell and it wasn't too long before they came back. He said, "You are from Ruleville all right," and he used a curse word. And he said, "We are going to make you wish you was dead."

I was carried out of that cell into another cell where they had two Negro prisoners. The State Highway Patrolmen ordered the first Negro to take the blackjack.

The first Negro prisoner order me, by orders from the State Highway Patrolman, for me to lay down on a bunk bed on my face.

I laid on my face and the first Negro began to beat. I was beat by the first Negro until he was exhausted. I was holding my hands behind me at that time on my left side, because I suffered from polio when I was six years old.

After the first Negro had beat until he was exhausted, the State Highway Patrolman ordered the second Negro to take the blackjack.

The second Negro began to beat and I began to work my feet, and the State Highway Patrolman ordered the first Negro who had beat me to sit on my feet—to keep me from working my feet. I began to scream and one white man got up and began to beat me in my head and tell me to hush.

One white man—my dress had worked up high—he walked over and pulled my dress—I pulled my dress down and he pulled my dress back up.

I was in jail when Medgar Evers was murdered.

All of this is on account of we want to register, to become first-class citizens. And if the Freedom Democratic Party is not seated now, I question America. Is this America, the land of the free and the home of the brave, where we have to sleep with our telephones off the hooks because our lives be threatened daily, because we want to live as decent human beings, in America? Thank you.

Fannie Lou Hamer and the MFDP were not seated at the convention. Four years later, at the Democratic National Convention in Chicago, they were. Hamer received a standing ovation as she became the first African-American official delegate at a national party convention since Reconstruction, and the first ever woman from Mississippi.

Source: Catherine Ellis and Stephen Drury Smith, eds., *Say It Plain: A Century of Great African American Speeches* (New York: The New Press, 2005).

- To put this in perspective, 1964 is the year the Beatles burst onto the U.S. music scene.

1965—Civil Rights Act of 1964 becomes effective; the Voting Rights Act of 1965 is passed, allowing African-Americans to vote for the first time since Reconstruction.

- The country is to go from 346 years of treating African Americans as separate and inferior to being required by law to treat them as equals.
- The Temptations' "My Girl" is a Billboard chart-topper.

1971—First important Title VII case decided by the U.S. Supreme Court, Griggs v. Duke Power Co.[2]

- The case is significant because African-Americans had never been equal in the United States, so few know what this picture of equality under Title VII was actually supposed to look like. Is it enough to simply take down the omnipresent "Colored" and "White" signs?
- Six years after the law takes effect, *Griggs* made clear that the new law meant equality in every way. Now the country understands that it must take Title VII seriously.
- For perspective, Janis Joplin's "Me and Bobby McGee" is a top hit for the year.

1979—First workplace affirmative action case decided by the U.S. Supreme Court.

- The Court determines that affirmative action is a viable means of effectuating the law and addressing present-day vestiges of the 346-year system that kept African-Americans subjugated.
- Perspective: The Village People's hit single "Y.M.C.A." sweeps the country.

1980s—Affirmative action is hotly debated between the presidents, who are opposed, and federal agencies responsible for enforcement of the laws, some of which oppose the law. (See Exhibit 5.2, "1980s Media Statements Regarding Affirmative Action.")

- Employers, seeing these very public disagreements, were confused about what they were required to do, but knew they were supposed to do something to have African-Americans and women in the workplace.
- Employers often simply did what they thought they needed to do to try to protect themselves from violating the new law: determined how many minorities and women they needed to prevent a disparate impact and hired that number.
- This became transformed into the idea of a quota in society's eyes.
- Note that this was not imposed by the government but came about as a result of employers trying to protect themselves and thinking this was the right way to go about it.
- At the same time, politicians took advantage of the disorganization by using tactics such as depictions of whites being fired from jobs in order to hire African-Americans—something that was always illegal under the law but that fed into constituents' worst fears.[3]

Exhibit 5.2 *1980s Media Statements Regarding Affirmative Action*

After the seminal U.S. Supreme Court cases on affirmative action in 1978 and 1979, the concept of affirmative action was really shaped and molded by fallout from the Court's decisions in the 1980s. You can gather from the statements below how divisive the issue was during that time when policy was being formed. This was true even for the federal administrators and others with responsibility in the area. You can imagine why employers who were to implement the law were so confused. Think about how recent this was—there are reruns on TV that go back much further!

3/4/85. "Department of Justice is asking public sector employers to change their negotiated consent decrees [which DOJ had previously pressed for] to eliminate preferential treatment to nonvictims of discrimination." (*BNA Daily Labor Report,* No. 42.)

4/4/85. "Dept. of Justice moves to eliminate quotas called 'betrayal' by Birmingham mayor, in testimony before the Subcommittee on Civil and Constitutional Rights of the House Judiciary Committee. Cites 'remarkable progress' made in bringing blacks into the city's fire and police departments." (*BNA Daily Labor Report,* No. 74.)

5/6/85. "Challenges Mount to Department of Justice's Anti-Quota Moves." (*BNA Daily Labor Report,* No. 87.)

9/16/85. "Congress recently ordered an audit of the U.S. Civil Rights Commission and the EEOC, headed by Clarence Pendleton, Jr., and Clarence Thomas, respectively, to find out if financial and personnel troubles are hurting the way both federal panels are enforcing civil rights laws." (*Jet* magazine, p. 16.)

10/17/85. "Attorney General Meese acknowledges that review of Executive Order 11246 is

proceeding at Cabinet level, but dismisses charges that Administration officials are at odds over question of affirmative action." (*BNA Daily Labor Report,* No. 201.)

11/29/85. "Majority of Senate is on record as opposing efforts by Attorney General Meese and others in Administration to alter Executive Order 11246 to prohibit goals and timetables for minority hiring." (*BNA Daily Labor Report,* No. 230.)

5/12/86. "Business Applauded for Opposing Changes in Affirmative Action Order." (*BNA Daily Labor Report,* No. 91.)

7/7/86. "Civil Rights Groups Applaud Supreme Court [for *Cleveland Firefighters and Sheet Metal Workers* decisions upholding affirmative action]; Department of Justice Vows to Continue Bid to Revise Executive Order 11246." (*BNA Daily Labor Report,* No. 129.)

7/7/86. "Labor Department says 'we don't see anything in these cases to suggest a legal necessity to change either the executive order or the OFCCP program.'" (*BNA Daily Labor Report,* No. 129.)

6/4/87. "OFCCP Enforcement Activity Scored by House Labor Staff: Alleged Lack of OFCCP Enforcement Activity Criticized by House Labor Staff." (*BNA Daily Labor Report,* No. 106.)

6/5/87. "DOL Official Defends OFCCP's Performance Against Charges of Declining Enforcement." (*BNA Daily Labor Report,* No. 107.)

7/2/89. "Civil Rights: Is Era Coming to an End? Decades of Change Called into Question by [Supreme Court] Rulings." (*Atlanta Journal and Constitution,* p. A-1.)

- For perspective: This is the time of Madonna's "Like a Virgin," Michael Jackson's worldwide blockbuster "Thriller," and Cindy Lauper's "Girls Just Wanna Have Fun."

2008—The last Civil War widow dies.

2008—U.S. House of Representatives apologizes for slavery, Jim Crow, and its aftermath, joining five states that had already issued such resolutions.

Two things should become apparent in viewing this timeline: (1) affirmative action has not been around for nearly as long as we may think, and (2) the 30 years or so it has been on the country's radar screen is not a very long time compared to the 346-year history that created the present-day vestiges of racial discrimination that the concept seeks to remedy.

Clearing the Air

Many people *hate* affirmative action. Most who do generally make that determination based on misconceptions about what it is. (See Exhibit 5.3, "Affirmative Action Realities.") Others simply believe it is ineffective.[4] Several points

---

Exhibit 5.3 *Affirmative Action Realities*

Here are realities based on common misconceptions about affirmative action gathered from students, employees, managers, supervisors, and business owners over the years. See if you recognize any of them.

- Affirmative action does not require employers to remove qualified whites and males from their jobs and give these jobs to minorities and women whether or not they are qualified.
- Affirmative action does not prevent employers from hiring white males who are more qualified for the job.
- Under affirmative action, an applicant need not simply be a female or a minority to be placed in a job.
- The law takes the position that any employee who obtains a job under an affirmative action plan be qualified for the job.
- Workplace productivity and efficiency do not suffer under affirmative action plans.
- We believe we have always lived in a meritocracy in which the best person gets the job. That

simply has not always been true and operated to disadvantage minorities and women.

- There are workplaces where affirmative action is still needed to make sure job applicants have more of a level playing field.
- If a female or minority is in an applicant pool with other nonminority or female candidates, the female or minority need not automatically be hired.
- Employers are to apply to females and minorities the same job requirements they apply to males and nonminorities.
- Affirmative action is not about punishment, reparations, or slavery. It is about present-day exclusion of minorities and women from the workplace.
- Minorities and females can and should be terminated from their jobs if they do not perform as required. However, their race or gender may not be the reason for the termination—their actions should be.

are of interest here that routinely arise in affirmative action discussions. We will address them up front, then discuss the background and need for the law, as well as its provisions.

1. As you will see shortly, it is no secret in history that our system was created for the benefit of whites and has done well in that regard. It is illogical, given the 346-year history, that without intervention of some sort by the government, things would not continue to proceed as they always had. Taking a *laissez-faire,* or hands-off, approach did not work in the 99 years before Title VII was passed, and more than 40 years after its passage, there are still significant differences in all facets of society, including employment, based on race and gender.[5]

2. One of the most persistent arguments about affirmative action has little logic. The argument is that affirmative action is a bad idea because it undermines the belief that women and minorities are competent. First of all, that is not consistent with affirmative action dictates that applicants be qualified. Also, it ignores the fact that without affirmative action, it was clear that those traditionally excluded from the workplace would continue to be. To take steps to address this and then say that those who must use such steps are perceived with suspicion is self-serving. Each of us has control over what we think. If we wish to think they are, we can, but it is not an inevitable consequence of affirmative action. This is like slapping someone and then complaining about the noise when they cry.[6]

3. As President Lyndon Johnson said in endorsing the Civil Rights Act of 1964, "You do not take a person who, for years, has been hobbled by chains and liberate him, bring him up to the starting line of a race and then say, 'you are free to compete with all the others,' and still justly believe that you have been completely fair"[7] Conveniently forgetting this history and simply calling affirmative action that seeks to bridge that gap of more discrimination is to ignore the difference between the two very different relative positions. Blacks and women are simply not in the same position as those who benefitted from a 346-year head start.[8]

4. Affirmative action is not a great idea for anyone concerned, but it is the best the country has managed to come up with. Colorblindness is the goal of many, but the country is simply not in that place yet. To act as if it is, is to continue the status quo that ensures it will not be reached.

5. If a person breaks a leg, it is impossible for a doctor to repair it without causing the patient additional pain (without the use of anesthesia). Trying to repair the vestiges of a 346-year system is the same way. There will be people who feel imposed upon by it. But, as a society, it is a necessary evil if we are to get to a place of equality, just as the further pain in repairing the leg is necessary to repair it. Those who believe affirmative action is only fixing discrimination by more discrimination ignore the fact that there are laws in place that severely limit the negative impact of affirmative action. This is akin to believing that the pain from being beat up for no reason is the same as the pain from having your

ruptured appendix removed. Yes, both hurt, but one at least has a good reason, while the other does not. Everyone wants to have an equal society, but to do so we must be willing to take the steps necessary to make sure it happens, and that will not always feel good to everyone. The solace comes in knowing it is addressing the problem rather than continuing to ignore it.

6. Affirmative action was created to address societal, endemic, persistent, systemic discrimination the country had engaged in for centuries. Interpreting it in an individual context is inappropriate. It is not the single person who believes he or she is affected that the law is about. It is the millions who will continue to suffer if something is not done.[9]

Yet and still, you are absolutely entitled to your feelings about affirmative action, whatever they are, but:

• You need to know what it actually is, rather than what you may have been told or gathered here and there.
• You need to know how and why it applies to the workplace.

In this chapter we will clear up the misconceptions. We will learn what affirmative action is, what it is not, what the law requires, and whom it affects. If you are like most of our students, what you learn may surprise you. As we go through learning what affirmative action is and what it is intended to do, try to think of what you would do if you were charged with finding a solution for the problem it was created to solve. Even the proponents of affirmative action would prefer that it be unnecessary at all and tend to agree that it is far from a perfect solution. However, given what we have to deal with in ridding the workplace of the vestiges of a 346-year system that still results in discrimination, it is at least the law's attempt. Given all the factors involved, what would be your solution?

Affirmative action does not apply to all employers. For the most part, it applies to those with 50 or more employees who have contracts with the federal government to provide the government with goods or services worth $50,000 or more. This means it covers just over 20 percent of the workforce. As a part of that contract, the government requires the employer to agree not to discriminate in the workplace and, further, to engage in affirmative action if a need is established (discussed later in the chapter). Contracts are completely voluntary agreements that we can choose to enter or not. Just as each of us has the choice to contract or not with businesses whose policies we like or dislike, so too does the federal government. It has decided that it does not want to contract with businesses that discriminate against employees in violation of the Title VII categories.

Despite what you think or may have heard, affirmative action does not require anyone to give up his or her job to someone who is not qualified to hold it. In fact, it generally does not require anyone to give up his or her job at all. It also does not require quotas. In fact, they are, for the most part, illegal. If you are like most of our students, this goes against everything you've ever heard.

(**LO1**) # What Is Affirmative Action?

At its simplest, affirmative action involves the employer taking steps to ensure job opportunities to traditionally excluded groups by bringing qualified women and minorities or other statutorily mandated groups into a workplace *from which it has been determined that they are excluded,* in order to make the workplace more reflective of their availability in the workforce from which the employees are drawn. This would ordinarily happen on its own in the absence of discrimination or its vestiges. However, in order for the plan to withstand a lawsuit by those who feel wrongly impacted by it, this intentional inclusion must be premised on one of several bases we will discuss in this chapter.

The actions an employer can take to make an effort to include those historically underrepresented in the workplace include:

- Expanded outreach to groups the employer has not generally made an effort to reach.
- Recruitment of groups the employer generally has not made an attempt to recruit.
- Mentoring, management training, and development.
- Hiring, training, and other attempts to bring into the workplace groups that have tended to be left out of the employment process.

The absence generally stems from attitudes about, or actions toward, such groups that resulted in their absence from the workplace or presence in very low numbers, at odds with their availability in the workforce. The absence can just as likely have come from simply letting the status quo continue unabated, with no particularly negative feelings or even thoughts about excluded groups. Given the history of systemic discrimination we have discussed, it is clear why this would occur. (See Exhibit 5.4, "Life under Jim Crow.") If you always do what you have always done, the status quo is maintained and things remain the same, It is only through making an effort to do things differently that change occurs.

Intentionally including employees previously excluded from a workplace is quite different from saying that workplace discrimination is prohibited. The former is the active approach required by Executive Order 11246; the latter, Title VII's passive approach.

You may wonder in this day and time, decades removed from the Civil Rights Act of 1964 prohibiting discrimination, why we would still need something like affirmative action. In order to understand why such a thing would still be needed, you must understand the basis for the law in the first place. To do so, we cannot look at the law from the perspective of today, which is how most students view it, as they sit in classrooms in which they may be surrounded by women and minorities. That is not what was going on when the law was created. It is important to look at the law in terms of what existed at the time, what the law was created to accomplish and why.

The reason we include the" slice of life" boxes for you is to give you a flavor of what life was actually like when these laws were created. With our students we have always found that it is one thing to say, for instance, "blacks and whites were segregated before Title VII." It is quite another for them to see a video

Exhibit 5.4 *Life under Jim Crow*

In '64 we had a public hospital constructed, and at that hospital, blacks were segregated by rooms. Blacks in one room, Whites in another. Health, Education and Welfare came down and inspected the hospital and found out that it was segregated by race. [They] wrote a letter to the hospital telling them that they were violating federal law, and if they didn't correct the problem and admit patients to rooms regardless of color, federal funds would be withdrawn. Finally they were forced to integrate the rooms at the hospital, but the feds had to make a grand stand before that happened.

Nash General over in Nash County got around the problem by building a new hospital with all private rooms. There were no semi-private rooms in Rocky Mount. People have forgotten it now, but the reason was to get around integration. So health care was terrible.

There were two clinics staffed by white physicians and blacks could go to those clinics to see white doctors but the rules were different. You had to sit in a very, very small room bunched up together with very poor ventilation. You couldn't see out of the room very much. There was maybe an 18" by 18" hole that the receptionist would talk to you through. You were called by your first name. Whereas whites had this spacious, beautiful waiting room with plants and windows and the light. Black patients would always be last.

— George Kenneth Butterfield Jr.

I volunteered to go into the service. It was well segregated. We went one way and the whites went another. Each outfit was equipped with the same equipment and whatnot. After I went overseas we could see the segregated part. As a black soldier, you had truck drivers and laborers. I found it was much easier to stay out of trouble because they would court martial you if you didn't. The first trouble I really had was in London. We were getting ready for the invasion of North Africa, so the people were trying to show their appreciation toward black servicemen.

So they made up the passes to go to the dance that night, and I put them on [the commanding officer's] desk. He had signed four or five of them before he read the first one. So he looked and asked the first sergeant of the outfit, "What are these passes for?"

Sergeant Johnson said, "They are passes for the men to go to a party in Birmingham, England."

He says, "Birmingham, England?"

He said, "Yes."

My company commander was from Mississippi, and he didn't want his black boys fraternizing with the white girls in the area. He said, "Well, there ain't no black girls in Birmingham, England. None of my black boys are going to dance with no white girls." And so he began to tear the passes up. He tore all of them up.

—Henry Hooten

Source: William H. Chafe, Raymond Gavins, and Robert Korstad, eds., *Remembering Jim Crow: African-Americans Tell about Life in the Segregated South* (New York: The New Press, 2001), pp. 22, 25.

of the 101st Airborne, with rifles at the ready, holding back crowds of screaming angry whites as nine black teenagers surrounded by military escorts walked into a public high school being integrated three years after the *Brown v. Board of Education* decision. It can be easy to gloss over the underpinnings of the law, and if you do, you will not have any real idea of why the law was created or why we are still dealing with these issues long after their original creation. That is why we go into the historical detail we do. None of this makes sense if we don't.

It is essential to understand how divided this country was along the issues of race and gender at the time the law was passed; how thoroughly separated races and genders were (for instance, with classified ads divided into gender and race);

how deeply held the negative views about minorities and African-Americans in particular were by many in society, even legislators. It is important to understand how these issues came together and resulted in there not being the instant total embrace of groups long ostracized by society after the laws passed. (See Exhibits 5.1 and 5.4.) While you, personally, may not hold them, negative attitudes about those covered by affirmative action ran/run exceedingly deep and were/are closely held. You probably saw some of them surface during the 2008 presidential election resulting in the first black president of the U.S. If you are like most students in your age group, you wondered what all the race fuss was about because you thought all of that was over and done with long ago. Here, you get to see the genesis of the positions and why one need only scratch the surface to find them.

Given society's history with race and gender, it was going to take more than simply telling people not to discriminate to move the country toward what the anti-discrimination laws were created to do. Evidence of these attitudes held both then and now lies in the statistics reflected in Exhibit 5.5 ("Employment Research Findings") and other information provided in this chapter.[10]

Exhibit 5.5   *Employment Research Findings*

Take a look at the items below and think about whether research indicates that affirmative action has outlived its usefulness.

- Research shows that people who hire tend to notice value more quickly in someone who looks like them.[11]
- In the suburbs, equally qualified blacks are hired about 40 percent less than whites because of negative assumptions.[12]
- Almost 90 percent of jobs are filled through word-of-mouth rather than advertising, resulting in fewer minorities and women being able to take advantage of those networks.[13]
- In one experiment, retailers consistently chose slightly less qualified white women over more qualified black women in entry-level positions.[14]
- When black and white discrimination testers who are similar in qualifications, dress, and so on applied for jobs, whites were 45 percent more likely to receive job offers and 22 percent more likely to be granted interviews.[15]

- When made-up résumés were sent out in response to classified ads, with only names changed to sound more or less ethnic and addresses changed to more likely be in predominantly black areas, white applicants were not only more likely to be granted interviews, but employers tried harder to reach them. Whites were 50 percent more likely to be chosen based only on their résumés, when the blacks were more qualified in terms of experience and credentials.[16]
- In 2006, white women's median weekly earnings were 77 percent those of white men. African-American women's earnings were 66 percent of the earnings of white men, and Latina women's earnings were 55 percent those of white men's earnings.
- African-American women with bachelor's degrees make only $1,545 more per year than white males who have only completed high school.
- In an important longitudinal study of black and white women ages 34 to 44, only one-fifth of the gap between their wages could be explained by education and experience. The study

continued

found that while women are segregated into lower-paying jobs, the impact is greater on African-American women than white women.[17]

- After a comprehensive GAO study in 2003 showed a 20 percent gap in wages between males and females even when the researchers held steady for the usual factors that would cause such a difference, such as education, job tenure, race, industry, and so on. In 2008 it reported that enforcement agencies should do a better job monitoring the situation.[18]

- Women of color—African-American, Latina, and Asian—are overrepresented in institutional service work, in occupations such as private household workers, cleaners, nurses' aides and licensed practical nurses, typists, file clerks, kitchen workers, hospital orderlies, and some occupations in the food packaging and textile industries. Other jobs that have disproportionate numbers of women and men of color include guards and corrections officers, mail and postal clerks, social workers, telephone operators, bus drivers, taxi drivers and chauffeurs, and some operator or laborer jobs within manufacturing.[19]

- Research indicates that as the percentage of females and the percentage of minorities in a job increase, average pay falls, even when all other factors are held steady.

- African-American men with professional degrees receive 79 percent of the salary paid to white men with the same degrees and comparable jobs. African-American women earn 60 percent.

- A study conducted by the U.S. Department of Labor found that women and minorities have made more progress breaking through the glass ceiling at smaller companies. Women constitute 25 percent of the managers and corporate officers in smaller establishments, while minorities represent 10 percent. But among Fortune 500 companies, women held 18 percent of the managerial jobs, with minorities holding 7 percent.

- The federal Glass Ceiling Commission found that white women made up close to half the workforce, but held only 5 percent of the senior-level jobs in corporations. African-Americans and other minorities account for less than 3 percent of top jobs (vice president and above).[20]

- The Glass Ceiling Commission found that a majority of chief executives acknowledge that the federal guidelines have been crucial in maintaining their commitment to a diverse workforce. It is estimated that only 30 to 40 percent of American companies are committed to affirmative action programs purely for business reasons, without any federal pressure. Most medium-sized and small companies, where job growth is greatest and affirmative action the gains biggest, have adopted affirmative action only grudgingly, and without guidelines, they are most likely to toss it overboard.

- Studies show that there is little correlation between what African-American and white workers score on employment tests and how they perform in the workplace.

- A Census Bureau survey of 3,000 businesses asked them to list the things they consider most important when hiring workers. The employers ranked test scores as 8th on a list of 11 factors. Generally speaking, job testing did not come into wide usage in the United States until after Title VII.

- The Glass Ceiling Commission research reported that stereotyping and prejudice still rule many executive suites. Women and minorities are frequently routed into career paths like customer relations and human resources, which usually do not lead to the top jobs.

- Cecelia Conrad, associate professor of economics at Barnard College in New York, examined whether affirmative action plans had hurt worker productivity. She found "no evidence that there has been any decline in productivity due to affirmative action." She also found no evidence of improved productivity due to affirmative action.

- A study of Standard and Poor's 500 companies found firms that broke barriers for women and minorities reported stock market records nearly 2.5 times better than comparable companies that took no action.

As an example of the attitudes prevalent at the time, as you will see in the gender chapter, Howard W. Smith, a segregationist Democrat from Virginia and chairman of the powerful House Committee on Rules, promised that the civil rights bill would never emerge from his committee. Eventually it did, for reasons unrelated to the substance of the law. During the floor debate, however, Smith introduced an amendment to add the word "sex" to the bill.[21] In doing so, he said to his colleagues, who interrupted him with howls of laughter, that he was very serious about this amendment. He explained that he had received a letter from a woman in Nebraska who wanted Congress to equalize the gender ratio in the population by helping the "surplus of spinsters" obtain their "right" to happiness.[22]

At the time laws for workplace equality were instituted, women and minorities were simply not an accepted part of the workplace. Congress now legislating that women and minorities were not to be subjected to discrimination was going to take more than a little getting used to—especially when Congress itself was having trouble with the idea.

LO2 As you will see, however, affirmative action is used only when there is a *demonstrated* underrepresentation or a finding of discrimination. It is designed to remedy *present-day* employment inequities based on race or gender. It is about the past only in the sense that what happened in the past has present-day vestiges. Affirmative action is about remedying discrimination, not about punishing anyone.

It makes little sense that if a system existed for 346 years, as slavery and Jim Crow did, there would be no vestiges of it 40+ years after the system ended. A seven-volume study released on October 1, 1999, by Harvard University and the Russell Sage Foundation found that racial stereotypes and attitudes "heavily influence the labor market, with blacks landing at the very bottom."[23] The researchers found that "race is deeply entrenched in the country's cultural landscape—perhaps even more than many Americans realize or are willing to admit."[24] Attitudes such as those found by the Harvard study find their way into the workplace and lessen the chances of minority and female applicants being chosen as employees. That, in turn, leads to the need for assistance such as affirmative action to remedy the situation.

If we could think of one thing that bothers us the most about affirmative action, it is that we believe our country is a meritocracy. We view our country as being one based on fairness and our achievement as based on the effort we put forth. Affirmative action seems to fly in the face of this because it appears that women and minorities get something without any effort when everyone else has to work for it. All they have to do is be born female or a minority, show up, and they get the job or get into schools or are granted contracts. Based on this premise, it makes perfect sense to resent affirmative action. However, as we have seen, research demonstrates this is far from reality. Despite anti-discrimination laws, minorities and women still lag in pay, jobs, and promotions.

This makes sense since, as we have discussed, our history with race and gender was one of institutionalized prejudices that were manifested in laws, regulations, policies, and funding. Congress recognized as much for race when, after many failed chances to do so, on July 29, 2008, it finally apologized for slavery and recognized that "African-Americans continue to suffer from the complex interplay between slavery and Jim Crow—long after both systems were formally abolished—through enormous damage and loss, both tangible and intangible, including the loss of human dignity, the frustration of careers and professional lives, and the long-term loss of income and opportunity." (See Exhibit 5.6, "U.S. House of Representatives Resolution Apologizing for Slavery.")

Before deciding if affirmative action has outlived its usefulness, keep in mind the timeline discussed earlier and the deep-seated attitudes that result in the imbalance of one group's presence in the workplace versus another's. Also keep in mind that while African-Americans, women, and other minorities were being excluded from the workplace for 346 years, those who were in the workplace gained 346 years' worth of advantages that benefited them whether they wanted them or not. The system worked the way it was intended. It was simply the way society was at the time.

We often hear that affirmative action is unfair because it seems like whites today are being punished for something they had nothing to do with since it happened so long ago. This is the "sins of the father" argument. Again, affirmative action is not about punishing anyone, but rather, about remedying discrimination. To have credibility, the sins-of-the-father position also must take into consideration the benefits and privileges the fathers provided for their progeny, many of which still exist today. When a parent disciplines a child, is the parent "being mean" or is the parent training the child? It depends on perspective. The child will think the parent is being mean. The parent will see it as a parent's duty to train his or her child. Perspective makes all the difference.

Since Title VII, it has become fashionable to think we treat everyone the same. What we may forget is that before that law came into existence, a law that has been around less than 50 years, a system was in place that provided advantages based on race and gender for 346 years. (See Exhibits 5.1 and 5.4.) That system did not disappear as soon as Title VII was passed. (See Exhibit 5.7, "Institutionalizing Prejudice: The Mississippi Sovereignty Commission.") We are still struggling with it today. Recognition of this is why the courts uphold the concept of affirmative action.

For instance, the primary laws that set the stage for the middle class many of us now enjoy, including even things like suburbs, malls, college educations, business ownership, and so on, received its start after the Great Depression under the New Deal with passage of legislation like the National Labor Relations Act in 1935, the Fair Labor Standards Act in 1938, and later the GI Bill (Selective Service Readjustment Act) in 1944. The NLRA allowed for the power of collective bargaining by employees to gain employees more equitable, stable working wages and conditions. The FLSA, for the first time, guaranteed a minimum wage that could lift employees out of poverty. The GI Bill provided returning veterans of World War II the right to receive financial assistance to go to college (something the vast majority of people could not afford to do) and low-interest loans for homes and businesses. It was a big part of the post–World War II boom in housing and business that created the middle class as we know it. In fact, it helped to create a housing demand so strong that suburbs were born. And, of course, malls (and, thus, life as many of us know it) were not far behind.

Exhibit 5.6   *U.S. House of Representatives Resolution Apologizing for Slavery*

This is the actual text of the 2008 Congressional Resolution apologizing for slavery. The House was several times presented with the opportunity to pass such a resolution over the years, but it refused, out of fear of a call for reparations. Congress had apologized for its actions toward Native Americans, to Hawaiians for overthrowing their government, and to Japanese interred in World War II internment camps, including paying them money. The Resolution was presented by Rep. Steve Cohen (D-TN), the only white legislator to represent the 60 percent black congressional district in the past 30 years.

Whereas millions of Africans and their descendants were enslaved in the United States and the 13 American colonies from 1619 through 1865; (Engrossed as Agreed to or Passed by House)

HRES 194 EH

H. Res. 194
In the House of Representatives, U.S.,
July 29, 2008

Whereas millions of Africans and their descendants were enslaved in the United States and the 13 American colonies from 1619 through 1865;

Whereas slavery in America resembled no other form of involuntary servitude known in history, as Africans were captured and sold at auction like inanimate objects or animals;

Whereas Africans forced into slavery were brutalized, humiliated, dehumanized, and subjected to the indignity of being stripped of their names and heritage;

Whereas enslaved families were torn apart after having been sold separately from one another;

Whereas the system of slavery and the visceral racism against persons of African descent upon which it depended became entrenched in the Nation's social fabric;

Whereas slavery was not officially abolished until the passage of the 13th Amendment to the United States Constitution in 1865 after the end of the Civil War;

Whereas after emancipation from 246 years of slavery, African-Americans soon saw the fleeting

political, social, and economic gains they made during Reconstruction eviscerated by virulent racism, lynchings, disenfranchisement, Black Codes, and racial segregation laws that imposed a rigid system of officially sanctioned racial segregation in virtually all areas of life;

Whereas the system of de jure racial segregation known as 'Jim Crow,' which arose in certain parts of the Nation following the Civil War to create separate and unequal societies for whites and African-Americans, was a direct result of the racism against persons of African descent engendered by slavery;

Whereas a century after the official end of slavery in America, Federal action was required during the 1960s to eliminate the de jure and de facto systems of Jim Crow throughout parts of the Nation, though its vestiges still linger to this day;

Whereas African-Americans continue to suffer from the complex interplay between slavery and Jim Crow—long after both systems were formally abolished—through enormous damage and loss, both tangible and intangible, including the loss of human dignity, the frustration of careers and professional lives, and the long-term loss of income and opportunity;

Whereas the story of the enslavement and de jure segregation of African-Americans and the dehumanizing atrocities committed against them should not be purged from or minimized in the telling of American history;

Whereas on July 8, 2003, during a trip to Goree Island, Senegal, a former slave port, President George W. Bush acknowledged slavery's continuing legacy in American life and the need to confront that legacy when he stated that slavery 'was . . . one of the greatest crimes of history . . . The racial bigotry fed by slavery did not end with slavery or with segregation. And many of the issues that still trouble America have roots in the bitter experience of other times. But however long the journey, our destiny is set: liberty and justice for all.';

Whereas President Bill Clinton also acknowledged the deep-seated problems caused by the

continued

continuing legacy of racism against African-Americans that began with slavery when he initiated a national dialogue about race;

Whereas a genuine apology is an important and necessary first step in the process of racial reconciliation;

Whereas an apology for centuries of brutal dehumanization and injustices cannot erase the past, but confession of the wrongs committed can speed racial healing and reconciliation and help Americans confront the ghosts of their past;

Whereas the legislature of the Commonwealth of Virginia has recently taken the lead in adopting a resolution officially expressing appropriate remorse for slavery and other State legislatures have adopted or are considering similar resolutions; and

Whereas it is important for this country, which legally recognized slavery through its Constitution and its laws, to make a formal apology for slavery and for its successor, Jim Crow, so that it can move forward and seek reconciliation, justice, and harmony for all of its citizens: Now, therefore, be it

Resolved, *That the House of Representatives—*

(1) acknowledges that slavery is incompatible with the basic founding principles recognized in the Declaration of Independence that all men are created equal;

(2) acknowledges the fundamental injustice, cruelty, brutality, and inhumanity of slavery and Jim Crow;

(3) apologizes to African-Americans on behalf of the people of the United States, for the wrongs committed against them and their ancestors who suffered under slavery and Jim Crow; and

(4) expresses its commitment to rectify the lingering consequences of the misdeeds committed against African-Americans under slavery and Jim Crow and to stop the occurrence of human rights violations in the future.

Attest:
Clerk.

Exhibit 5.7 *Institutionalizing Prejudice: The Mississippi Sovereignty Commission*

This is America and we have the right to feel however we want to about whomever we want to for whatever reasons we want to. We don't have to like everyone. Prejudice is prejudging someone before you know them and deciding you don't feel positively about them based on that prejudgment. We have a right to be prejudiced if we want to. Racism, however, is institutionalized prejudice. Racism goes beyond the realm of mere personal feelings, becomes actualized in policies and laws that effectuate that prejudice, and acts to exclude or harm a particular group. Knowing in your head that you do not like a particular group is one thing. Acting in ways to harm or exclude that group is quite another. Prejudice is personal; racism is not. This is particularly harmful when it is the government that is doing the harming or excluding. For instance, in 1924 Virginia passed laws for involuntary sterilization aimed primarily at African-Americans, and the government administrator in charge of enforcing the law was in contact with, and a great admirer of, German eugenics officials of Hitler's Third Reich who were exterminating blacks as well. He even wrote to the German official about the official's work, "I hope this work is complete and not one has been missed. I sometimes regret that we have not the authority to put some measures in practice in Virginia." Virginia's involuntary sterilization law was not repealed until 1979. Yes, you read it correctly—1979.[25] California's law was repealed the same year.[26] We know it may be hard for you to believe this could ever happen in America, but it did. In many ways. But we will here give you one example so that you can understand for yourself how deeply rooted the issues are that led legislators to believe that affirmative

continued

Exhibit 5.7   *continued*

action was necessary if the purpose of Title VII was to be fully effectuated.

In 1954 the U.S. Supreme Court outlawed racial segregation in public education. Two years later, in 1956, the Mississippi Sovereignty Commission was created to preserve segregation in the eleven southern states. The commission was charged to "protect the sovereignty of the State of Mississippi and her sister states from federal government interference." The commission, primarily an information-gathering agency, outwardly espoused racial harmony, but secretly paid spies and investigators to report on civil rights activists or anyone even remotely thought to be sympathetic to the cause of racial equality. Such people were branded as racial agitators and communist infiltrators (a huge issue after the McCarthy era and during the Cold War with Russia). In addition, the commission contributed money to segregationist causes, acted as a clearinghouse for segregation and anti–civil rights information, and circulated segregationist rhetoric and ideals. The commission was a state government commission like any other, with members of the commission appointed by the governor. The governor served as chair of the commission, and among the ex-officio members (members by reason of their office) were the lieutenant governor, the speaker of the house of representatives, and the attorney general. Commission members included state legislators and other high officials.

The commission had a budget, an executive director, and clerical staff, and its first investigators were a former FBI agent and a former chief of the Mississippi Highway Patrol. The public relations director devised projects to portray Mississippi in a favorable light. The commission was given subpoena power and had the authority to gather information and keep its files and records secret. There was a fine and jail time for divulging the commission's secrets. Information was gathered through spying, informants, and law enforcement agencies and by working with the Citizens Counsel, a white supremacist organization.

In 1973—nearly 10 years after Title VII was passed—Governor Bill Waller vetoed funding for the commission and it officially became defunct four years later. When the commission was officially closed in 1977, the legislature decreed that its records be sealed for 50 years, until 2027. The ACLU sued to open them and eventually won, and they were opened in 1998.* The files contained over 132,000 documents. Among them were documents that shed light on the murders of the three voting rights activists Schwerner, Chaney, and Goodman, whose story is the basis of the popular movie *Mississippi Burning.* The three were killed and buried in an earthen dam while trying to register black voters in Mississippi.

Sources: Mississippi History Now, http://mshistory.k12. ms.us/features/feature35/sovereignty.html; Facts about Mississippi Sovereignty Commission, http://www. mdcbowen.org/p2/bh/badco/missSov.htm.

*The records of the Mississippi Sovereignty Commission can be found online at http://mdah.state.ms.us/arlib/contents/er/sovcom/.

What does all of this have to do with institutionalized racism that serves as a foundation for the necessity of affirmative action to counteract its effects? All of this legislation was passed with the help of a very powerful southern voting bloc in Congress that was interested primarily in keeping the South as it had been since after the Civil War—segregated and in the throes of Jim Crow. The southern legislators had wide and varied views, but they were all in accord on one: the South was to remain segregated and their way of life untouched by these new laws.

In return for their votes, they received provisions in the law that guaranteed what they wanted. Seventy-five percent of African-Americans in the South, and 60 percent nationwide, were agricultural workers at the time. Virtually the same was true of domestics. Those were the two top jobs African-Americans were permitted to hold in the Jim Crow years. Excluding these two jobs from the minimum wage laws was the price exacted by the southern legislators for their vote to pass the legislation. This meant that African-Americans working as domestics and agricultural workers—the vast majority of African-Americans—would not receive minimum wages and therefore would be kept in low wages that did not put them on par with whites.

We know it is probably hard for you to imagine, but at that time in our history, the idea of an African-American in the South making the same wages as whites would have been unthinkable. Since many southern legislators employed agricultural workers, housekeepers, cooks, laundresses, and nannies to support their way of life, largely unchanged since the Civil War ended, not only would minimum wages and overtime be against their own economic interests, but it would have put the African-American employees on a par with white workers and that was, in the minds of southern legislators, unacceptable. As Martin Dies (D-TX) said, in debating the bill, "What is prescribed for one race must be prescribed for the others, and you cannot prescribe the same wages for the black man as for the white man."[27] Even if they had wanted to do it, which they did not, their constituents would never have accepted it. Minimum wages and overtime under FLSA was designed for whites.[28]

As for the labor laws, the South has always had a notoriously low rate of unionization, and now you can understand part of what accounts for that, given the political and social landscape. Since, of course, agricultural workers and domestics were not unionized, this meant the vast majority of African-Americans also would not benefit from the improved working and wage provisions of the labor laws.

The GI Bill granting a host of benefits to veterans was proposed as a federally administered law. Southerners knew that if this happened, everyone would be governed by the same rules, which would mean African-Americans had the same rights under the law as whites. The trade-off for the southern bloc vote was that administration of the law would be local. In this way, when the African-American veteran wanted to use the college benefits to attend college, he could be told that he was not allowed to attend the college because it was for whites only. When he went to borrow money from the local bank for a home mortgage or business loan at the favorable GI Bill rates, the local southern bank could deny the loan based on Jim Crow policies.

The Davis-Bacon Act of 1931 requiring that prevailing local wage rates be paid to workers on projects receiving federal funds of over $2,000 is another important piece of legislation born of racial protectiveness. Though historians have debated the matter and dismiss the racially derogatory statement made in Congress during the legislative debates on the bill, the reality is that it was created after Bacon of New York learned that "colored" workers had been brought to New York from Alabama to build a Veterans Administration hospital in his district because they would work for less, Of course, not only did that mean that white workers were left out of the project, but also that the projects he managed to get Congress to fund for his district would not employ local voters.[29]

The super boost these laws gave to create the American middle class as we know it today left the vast majority of African-Americans well out of the loop. The prejudices of the southern legislators found their way into the laws and there they remain to this day.[30] That, combined with societal attitudes and mores, virtually ensured that when the Civil Rights Act of 1964 was passed, African-Americans would need more than a passive approach to realizing the law's promise. This was provided by affirmative action.

Efforts to eliminate affirmative action in employment, government contracts, university admissions, and other areas come primarily from those who feel it has outlived its usefulness and causes only ill will among majority employees and students. Many think of it as "punishment" to redress slavery and feel they should not have to bear the burden of something for which they had no responsibility. And whites are not the only ones who complain about affirmative action. African-American University of California regent and outspoken affirmative action critic Ward Connerly suggested in a *60 Minutes* interview that "Black Americans are not hobbled by chains any longer. We're free to compete. We're capable of competing. It is an absolute insult to suggest that we can't."

The first workplace affirmative action case did not reach the U.S. Supreme Court until 1979. Throughout the 1980s, government agencies and officials argued about it, and employers were confused. Note too that while many changes have come about since the passage of Title VII, statistics still show African-Americans and other minorities lagging behind in jobs, and even farther behind in promotions and pay. Think about the information we have discussed and the research items in Exhibit 5.5, and ask yourself if it appears that everything is now equal.

Throughout the chapter, keep this thought in mind: If Alaska is 99 percent Inuit (Eskimo), then, all things being equal, that will be reflected at all or most levels of their employment spectrum. All things being equal, it would look odd if Alaska is 99 percent Inuit but the Inuit hold only 5 percent of managerial-level jobs but 100 percent of the unskilled labor jobs. Of course, the reality is that it is rare to have a workforce that has so little diversity. Among other things, there also will be differing skill levels and interests within the workforce from which the employees are drawn. However, the example is instructive for purposes of illustrating how a workplace should reflect the available workforce from which its employees are drawn. If there is a significant difference that cannot be accounted for otherwise, the difference between availability and representation in the workplace should be addressed. In essence, this is affirmative action. We believe that the more you understand what affirmative action actually is and what it is used for, the more likely you are to help your employer more effectively meet affirmative action obligations.

We should note that while we have given you a good deal of background on the reasons for affirmative action, we have done so because our experience shows that lack of information about the history and context of the concept is the single biggest reason for the common misconceptions about it. It is time well spent to give you the thorough grounding we have. You should also note that as we have discussed and you probably know well, not everyone believes affirmative action should exist. Since affirmative action is the law and our goal is to tell you how to comply with the law in order to avoid workplace liability, we have not delved into the other side of the issue. This is not a debate. Affirmative action is presently the law and must be obeyed or the employer runs the risk of liability.[31]

Affirmative action also arises in other contexts such as college admissions, granting of government contracts, and set-asides. However, except for historical development purposes, these are beyond the scope of this text's employment context.

LO3

There are three ways in which affirmative action obligations arise:

1. Through Executive Order 11246.
2. Judicially as a remedy for a finding of discrimination under Title VII.
3. Voluntary affirmative action established by an employer.

Each will be discussed in turn.

Affirmative Action under Executive Order 11246

Though people tend to think of affirmative action as a part of Title VII, and in fact, Title VII has an affirmative action component as part of its remedies, affirmative action actually stems from a requirement imposed by Executive Order 11246 and its amendments. Under the executive order, those employers who contract to furnish the federal government with goods and services, called *federal contractors,* must agree not to discriminate in the hiring, termination, promotion, pay, and so on of employees on the basis of race, color, religion, gender, or national origin.

The first forerunner to E.O. 11246 was Executive Order 8802, signed by President Franklin D. Roosevelt on June 25, 1941. It applied only to defense contracts and was issued to combat discrimination during World War II "as a prerequisite to the successful conduct of our national defense production effort."[32] This executive order underwent several changes before the present version was signed into law by President Lyndon B. Johnson on September 24, 1965. Each president thereafter has allowed it to remain.

E.O. 11246 Provisions

In addition to prohibiting discrimination in employment, for certain contracts the executive order requires that contractors who have underrepresentations of women and minorities in their workplace agree to take steps to ensure adequate representation. In cases where the employer refuses to remedy disparities found,

debar
Prohibit a federal contractor from further participation in government contracts.

he or she is **debarred** from further participation in government contracts. This is a rare occurrence since most employers eventually comply with the OFCCP's suggestions for remedying disparities.

The executive order is enforced by the Office of Federal Contract Compliance Programs (OFCCP) in the Employment Standards Administration Office of the U.S. Department of Labor. The OFCCP issues extensive regulations implementing the executive order.[33] OFCCP's enforcement addresses only the employer's participation in federal government contracts and contains no provisions for private lawsuits by employees. Employees seeking redress must do so through their state's fair employment practice laws, Title VII, or similar legislation previously discussed. However, employees may file complaints with the OFCCP, which the secretary of labor is authorized to receive and investigate, and may sue the secretary to compel performance of executive order requirements.

Employers who contract with the federal government to provide goods and services of $10,000 or more must agree to comply with the executive order. In addition, contractors and subcontractors agree to

- Post in conspicuous places, available to employees and applicants, notices provided by the contracting officer setting forth the provisions of the non-discrimination clause. You may have seen these in your workplace or university/college.
- Include in all the contractor's solicitations or advertisements for employees a statement that all qualified applicants will receive consideration for employment without regard to race, color, religion, gender, or national origin (although research shows that employers with such notices are just as likely to discriminate in employment as those without such notices).
- Include a statement of these obligations in all subcontracts or purchase orders, unless exempted, which will be binding on each subcontractor or vendor.
- Furnish all information and reports required by the executive order and the implementing regulations, and permit access to the contractor's or subcontractor's books, records, and accounts by the contracting agency and the Secretary of Labor for purposes of investigation to ascertain compliance with the executive order and its regulations.

LO4

Under the implementing regulations, Executive Order 11246 increases compliance requirements based on the amount of the contract. For the smallest contracts, the employer agrees that, in addition to not discriminating in employment, it will post notices that it is an equal opportunity employer. If a contractor or subcontractor has 50 or more employees and a nonconstruction contract of $50,000 or more, the contractor must develop a written affirmative action plan for each of his or her establishments within 120 days of the beginning of the contract.

affirmative action plan
A government contractor's plan containing placement goals for inclusion of women and minorities in the workplace and timetables for accomplishing the goals.

Affirmative Action Plans

Affirmative action plans must be developed according to the rules set forth in the Code of Federal Regulations (C.F.R.) part 60-2 that effectuates the executive order. According to the regulations, "an affirmative action plan should be considered a management tool—an integral part of the way a corporation conducts its business . . . to encourage self-evaluation in every aspect of an employment by establishing systems to monitor and examine the contractor's employment decisions and compensation systems to ensure that they are free of discrimination."[34] (See Exhibit 5.8, "More Than a 'Numbers Game.'")

underrepresentation or underutilization
Significantly fewer minorities or woman in the workplace than relevant statistics indicate are available or their qualification indicate they should be working at better jobs.

Affirmative action plans have both quantitative and qualitative aspects. The quantitative part of the plan examines the contractor's workplace to get a snapshot, of sorts, of who works there and in what capacity, as it relates to minorities and women. Minority categories include African-American, Hispanic, Asian/Pacific Islander, and American Indian/Alaskan Native. The qualitative part of the plan sets out a course of action for how to address any **underrepresentation, underutilization**, or other problems found.

Exhibit 5.8 *More Than a "Numbers Game"—Major Affirmative Action Regulation Overhaul: The Dog Now Wags the Tail, Rather Than Vice Versa*

Most people tend to think of affirmative action as a "numbers game" in which an employer tries to hire a certain magic number of minorities and women in order to avoid running into trouble with the "feds." That is *so* not the case. Actually, there may have been some basis for that view when set against the background of the 1980s discussed earlier. When much of the policy was hammered out, OFCCP may have seemed more interested in the bottom-line figures. But as affirmative action evolved, it became clear that numbers, alone, were not sufficient to accomplish what the law was designed to do. After all, it is equal employment *opportunity* that the law wanted to ensure, confident that if the opportunities were equal, that would be reflected in the bottom-line figures. With the numbers approach, OFCCP obviously found that managerial policies suffered in an attempt to achieve numbers and the intent of the law was not being met. The tail was wagging the dog, rather than vice versa.

In 2000, OFCCP issued the most comprehensive set of changes to its regulations since the 1970s. Not only did the new regulations make changes in a few significant ways affirmative action plans are to be developed, such as decreasing the number of availability factors it will consider from eight to two and permitting employers to replace the previously required workforce analysis with an organization profile that is usually simpler, but it also clarified and reaffirmed basic foundations of affirmative action. In recognizing this more balanced approach, OFCCP said that "affirmative action programs contain a diagnostic component which includes a number of quantitative analyses designed to evaluate the composition of the workforce of the contractor and compare it to the composition of the relevant labor pools. Affirmative action programs also include action-oriented programs."

Probably most important, it was clear that OFCCP was moving from an approach that was perceived as being interested primarily in the mechanics of affirmative action plans submitted by employers, to one in which the plan is viewed as "a management tool to ensure equal employment opportunity." The agency said that "a central premise underlying affirmative action is that, absent discrimination, over time a contractor's workforce, generally, will reflect the gender, racial and ethnic profile of the labor pools from which the contractor recruits and selects. If women and minorities are not being employed at a rate to be expected given their availability in the relevant labor pool, the contractor's affirmative action program includes specific practical steps designed to address this underutilization. Effective affirmative action programs also include internal auditing and reporting systems as a means of measuring the contractor's progress toward achieving the workforce that would be expected in the absence of discrimination."

Rather than being a numbers game, OFCCP envisions affirmative action plans as a way for contractors to take the opportunity to look at their

continued

Exhibit 5.8 *continued*

workforces and see if they are reflective of the relevant population they are drawn from, and if they determine they are not, to make a plan to work toward making that happen. This reflects the understanding that given the country's racial, ethnic, and gender history, without taking the time and opportunity to actually step back and look at the larger picture, employers may not be aware of the underrepresentation, and thus it will continue. In addressing its preferred approach, OFCCP noted that this analysis should not just be done in anticipation of reporting to OFCCP, but on a regular basis as part of management of the workplace in all aspects. "An affirmative action program also ensures equal employment opportunity by institutionalizing the contractor's commitment to equality in every aspect of the employment process. Therefore, as part of its affirmative action program, a contractor monitors and examines its employment decisions and compensation systems to evaluate the impact of those systems on women and minorities."

In this more holistic view OFCCP pronounced in its regulatory revisions, it said that "an affirmative action program is, thus, more than a paperwork exercise. An affirmative action program includes those policies, practices, and procedures that the contractor implements to ensure that all qualified applicants and employees are receiving an equal opportunity for recruitment, selection, advancement, and every other term and privilege associated with employment. Affirmative action, ideally, is a part of the way the contractor regularly conducts its business. OFCCP has found that when an affirmative action program is approached from this perspective, as a powerful management tool, there is a positive correlation between the presence of affirmative action and the absence of discrimination.

"Pursuant to these regulatory changes, OFCCP will focus its resources on the action undertaken to promote equal employment opportunity, rather than on the technical compliance."

Sources: Department of Labor, Office of Federal Contract Compliance Programs, "41 CFR Parts 60-1 and 60-2; Government Contractors, Affirmative Action Requirements; Final Rule," 165 Fed. Reg. 68021, 68021–47 (November 13, 2000), http://frwebgate.access.gpo.gov/cgi-bin/getdoc.cgi?dbname=2000_register&docid=00-28693-filed

organizational profile
Staffing patterns showing organizational units; their relationship to each other; and gender, race, and ethnic composition.

job group analysis
Combines job titles with similar content, wage rates, and opportunities.

In order to get the snapshot of what the contractor's workplace looks like as it relates to minorities and/or females, employers must prepare an **organizational profile**. An organizational profile shows staffing patterns within a workplace, much like an organizational chart, showing each of the organizational units, their relationship to one another, and the gender, race, and ethnic composition of each unit. It is "one method contractors use to determine whether barriers to equal employment opportunity exist in their organization."

Another part of the snapshot is the contractor's **job group analysis**. Job group analysis combines job titles in the contractor's workplace that have similar content, wage rates, and opportunities. The job group analysis must include a list of the job titles for each job group and the percentage of minorities and the percentage of women it employs in each job group. This information is then compared to the availability of women and/or minorities for these job groups.

Now that the contractor has this snapshot of the workplace, the foundation of the affirmative action plan is laid. The purpose of the snapshot is to see if there is an underrepresentation of women and/or minorities based on the difference

availability
Minorities and women in a geographic area who are qualified for a particular position.

between their **availability** in the workforce from which employees are hired and their presence in the workplace. According to the regulation, availability is important in order to "establish a benchmark against which the demographic composition of the contractor's employees can be compared in order to determine whether barriers to equal employment opportunity may exist within particular job groups."

Availability is not based on the mere presence of women and minorities in a given geographic area. Rather, it is based on the availability of women and minorities qualified for the particular job under consideration. Simply because women are 35 percent of the general population for a particular geographic area does not mean that they are all qualified to be doctors, professors, skilled craft workers, or managers. Availability for jobs as, for instance, managers would only consider those qualified to fill the position of managers, rather than all women in the geographic area. The regulations contain resources for finding out availability for various jobs in a given geographic area.

The two factors to be used in determining availability of employees (separately for minorities and women for each job group) are (1) the percentage of minorities or women with requisite skills in the reasonable recruitment area, defined as the geographic areas from which the contractor usually seeks or reasonably could seek workers to fill the positions in question, and (2) the percentage of minorities or women among those promotable, transferable, and trainable within the contractor's organization.

If the percentage of women and/or minorities employed in a job group is less than would reasonably be expected based on their availability in the area from which employees are drawn, the contractor must establish a **placement goal** that reflects the reasonable availability of women and/or minorities in the geographic area.

placement goal
Percentage of women and/or minorities to be hired to correct underrepresentation, based on availability in the geographic area.

By regulation, placement goals, which serve as objectives "reasonably attainable by means of applying every 'good faith effort' to make all aspects of the entire affirmative action program work," do not mean that the underrepresentation is an admission or a finding of discrimination. They are designed to measure progress toward achieving equal employment opportunity and "may not be rigid and inflexible quotas which must be met," nor a ceiling or floor for employing certain groups. "*Quotas are expressly forbidden.*"[35] In making decisions, employers are expressly *not* required "to hire a person who lacks qualifications to perform the job successfully, or hire a less qualified person in preference to a more qualified one."[36] In all employment decisions, the contractor must make selections in a non-discriminatory manner.[37]

Once this quantitative part of the affirmative action plan is in place, if an underrepresentation or other problem has been found, the contractor must then develop and execute "action-oriented" programs designed to correct them. OFCCP believes that in order for the programs to be effective, they must be more than the contractor's "business as usual," which, of course, led to the underrepresentation in the first place. (See Exhibits 5.9, "Affirmative Actions," and 5.10, "Voluntary Affirmative Action Plan Considerations.")

Exhibit 5.9 *Affirmative Actions*

While there are guidelines as to what may or may not be legally acceptable as affirmative action designed to intentionally include women and minorities in the workplace, there are no specific requirements about what affirmative action must be taken. As a result, employers' means of addressing affirmative action have varied greatly. Keep in mind the Supreme Court's characterization of plans that are acceptable when viewing the following ideas employers have used. Just because employers have used these methods does not mean they are always legal. Sometimes they may simply be convenient.

- *Advertising for applicants in nontraditional sources.* Employers solicit minority and female applicants through resources such as historically African-American colleges and universities; women's colleges; and minority and female civic, educational, religious, and social organizations, including the NAACP, National Urban League, La Raza, American Indian Movement, National Organization for Women, and other such groups.

- *One-for-one hiring, training, or promotion programs.* One minority or female is hired, trained, or promoted for every white or male until a certain desired goal is reached. This is usually only used in long-standing, resistant cases of underrepresentation and is rarely used anymore.

- *Preferential layoff provisions.* As in *Wygant v. Jackson Board of Education*,[1] in recognition of the reality that recently hired female and minority employees would be lost if layoffs are conducted based on seniority and, thereby, affirmative action gains lost, employers institute plans that are designed to prevent the percentage of minorities and women from falling below a certain point. Some minorities and women with less seniority may be retained, while those with more are laid off. While the U.S. Supreme Court did not prohibit this approach, it did indicate an employer would have to overcome a very rigorous analysis to ensure protection of the adversely impacted employees.

- *Extra consideration.* Women and minorities are considered along with all other candidates, but extra consideration is given to their status as women and minorities, and all other factors being equal, they may be chosen for the job.

- *Lower standards.* Women and minorities may be taken out of the regular pool of candidates and given different, usually less stringent, standards for qualifying for the position. Natural questions are why the higher standards are imposed if the job can be performed with lesser qualifications and why someone who is not qualified under the higher, "normal" standards should be given the job. This is *not* a good approach, and would probably *not* pass judicial muster.

- *Added points.* Much like with a veteran's preference, the employer has a rating system giving points for various criteria, and women and minorities receive extra points because they are women or minorities. This was not permitted by the U.S. Supreme Court in the undergraduate admissions program at the University of Michigan.

- *Exam discarding.* In an effort to avoid liability for the disparate impact of an objective examination, some employers have discarded the results when minority or female candidates did not score as well as whites or males. The US. Supreme Court in *Ricci v. DeStefano*[2] struck down this approach.

- *Minority or female "positions."* In an effort to meet affirmative action goals, employers create and fund positions that are designed to be filled only by women or minorities. These positions may or may not be needed by the employer. This is not a smart approach for an employer and would not stand up in court.

Some of the approaches are more desirable than others because they are less likely to result in "reverse discrimination" suits or more likely to result in qualified minority or female employees. Affirmative action plans walk a fine line between not holding

[1]476 U.S. 267 (1986).

[2]129S.Ct.2658 (2009).

continued

women and minorities to lower standards than other employees while, at the same time, not permitting the standards to be arbitrary and likely to unnecessarily or unwittingly screen out female or minority candidates. The 1991 Civil Rights Act made it unlawful to "adjust the scores of, use different cut-off scores for, or otherwise alter the results of, employment related tests" on the basis of race, color, religion, gender, or national origin. Since there are few rules, employers can be creative, within the guidelines provided by law. Now that you have seen some of the affirmative action schemes employers have used, which seem most suited to accomplish the goals of affirmative action, while having the least adverse impact on other employees? How would you design an affirmative action plan?

OFCCP may perform audits of contractors to determine if they are complying with the regulations and providing equal employment opportunity. To withstand an OFCCP audit, contractors must show that they have made good-faith efforts to remove any identified barriers to equal employment opportunity, expand employment opportunities, and produce measurable results. As part of an action program, contractors must

- Develop and implement internal auditing systems that periodically measure the effectiveness of their affirmative action plans, including monitoring records of all personnel activity to ensure that the contractor's non-discriminatory policy is being carried out.
- Require internal reporting on a scheduled basis as to the degree to which equal employment opportunity and organizational objectives are attained.
- Review report results with all levels of management.
- Advise top management of the program's effectiveness and submit recommendations for improvement, where necessary.

corporate management compliance evaluation
Evaluations of mid- and senior-level employee advancement for artificial barriers to advancement of women and minorities.

In an effort to combat the glass ceiling, the regulations also require **corporate management compliance evaluations** designed to determine whether employees are encountering artificial barriers to advancement to mid- and senior-level corporate management. During such evaluations, special attention is given to those components of the employment process that affect advancement into these upper-level positions. The Glass Ceiling Commission found that it was easier for women and minorities to enter a business at the entry level than to progress up once there. This tool is used to address this phenomenon.

Each year, OFCCP conducts an Equal Opportunity Survey to provide the agency with compliance data early in the evaluation process so that it can more effectively and efficiently identify contractors for further evaluation, as well as acting as a self-evaluation tool for contractors. The survey requests brief information that will allow OFCCP to have an accurate assessment of contractor personnel activities, pay practices, and affirmative action performance. Employers are required to submit data on applicants, hires, promotions, terminations, compensation, and tenure by race and gender. (See Exhibit 5.10.)

In fiscal year 2010, OFCCP began developing a predictive statistical model to more accurately identify potential violators. Since the model would allow the

Exhibit 5.10   *Voluntary Affirmative Action Plan Considerations*

According to the federal regulations governing voluntary affirmative action plans:

PART 1608 AFFIRMATIVE ACTION APPROPRIATE UNDER TITLE VII OF THE CIVIL RIGHTS ACT OF 1964

Sec. 1608.3   Circumstances under which voluntary affirmative action is appropriate.

(a) Adverse effect. Title VII prohibits practices, procedures, or policies which have an adverse impact unless they are justified by business necessity. In addition, title VII proscribes practices which "tend to deprive" persons of equal employment opportunities. Employers, labor organizations and other persons subject to title VII may take affirmative action based on an analysis which reveals facts constituting actual or potential adverse impact, if such adverse impact is likely to result from existing or contemplated practices.

(b) Effects of prior discriminatory practices. Employers, labor organizations, or other persons subject to title VII may also take affirmative action to correct the effects of prior discriminatory practices. The effects of prior discriminatory practices can be initially identified by a comparison between the employer's work force, or a part thereof, and an appropriate segment of the labor force.

(c) Limited labor pool. Because of historic restrictions by employers, labor organizations, and others, there are circumstances in which the available pool, particularly of qualified minorities and women, for employment or promotional opportunities is artificially limited. Employers, labor organizations, and other persons subject to title VII may, and are encouraged to take affirmative action in such circumstances, including, but not limited to, the following:

(1) Training plans and programs, including on-the-job training, which emphasize providing minorities and women with the opportunity, skill, and experience necessary to perform the functions of skilled trades, crafts, or professions;

(2) Extensive and focused recruiting activity;

(3) Elimination of the adverse impact caused by unvalidated selection criteria (see sections 3 and 6, Uniform Guidelines on Employee Selection Procedures (1978), 43 FR 30290; 38297; 38299 (August 25, 1978));

(4) Modification through collective bargaining where a labor organization represents employees, or unilaterally where one does not, of promotion and layoff procedures.

Source: 29 C.F.R. ch. XIV (7-1-04 Edition), § § 1608.1, 1608.3, http://www.access.gpo.gov/nara/cfr/waisidx_04/29cfr1608_04.html.

agency to maximize limited resources and focus on the contractors and industries most likely to be found not complying with the law, it makes even more sense for employers with federal contracts to comply with the law.[38]

Again, there is no requirement of quotas under Executive Order 11246 or under Title VII. In fact, as we saw previously, the law specifically says it is not to be interpreted as such. Virtually the only time quotas are permitted is when there has been a long-standing violation of the law and there is little other recourse. The *Sheet Metal Workers* case, discussed shortly, demonstrated this with the union's resistance over an 18-year period, resulting in the imposition of quotas.

Case 1

Placement goals to remedy underrepresentation should not be confused with quotas. As long as an employer can show a legitimate, good-faith effort to reach affirmative action placement goals, quotas are not required and will not be imposed as a remedy for underrepresentation.

Penalties for Noncompliance

The secretary of labor or the appropriate contracting agency can impose on the employer a number of penalties for noncompliance, including

- Publishing the names of nonconforming contractors or labor unions.
- Recommending to the EEOC or the Department of Justice that proceedings be instituted under Title VII.
- Requesting that the attorney general bring suit to enforce the executive order in cases of actual or threatened substantial violations of the contractual EEO clause.
- Recommending to the Department of Justice that criminal proceedings be initiated for furnishing false information to a contracting agency or the secretary of labor.
- Canceling, terminating, or suspending the contract, or any portion thereof, for failure of the contractor or subcontractor to comply with the non-discrimination provisions of the contract (this may be done absolutely, or continuance may be conditioned on a program for future compliance approved by the contracting agency).
- Debarring the noncomplying contractor from entering into further government contracts until the contractor has satisfied the secretary that it will abide by the provisions of the order.

The secretary of labor must make reasonable efforts to secure compliance by conference, conciliation, mediation, and persuasion before requesting the U.S. attorney general to act or before canceling or surrendering a contract. While a hearing is required before the secretary can debar a contractor, it may be granted before any other sanction is imposed, if appropriate. As a practical matter, the more severe penalties are rarely used because contractors are generally not so recalcitrant toward OFCCP orders.

In making its compliance determinations for contractors' affirmative action plans, OFCCP will not make the judgment solely on whether the contractor's affirmative action goals are met, that is, "the numbers game." (See Exhibit 5.7.) That alone will not serve as a basis for sanctions under the executive order. What is important to OFCCP is the nature and extent of the contractor's good-faith affirmative action activities and the appropriateness of those activities to the problems the contractor has identified in the workplace. An assessment of compliance will be made on both statistical and nonstatistical information indicating whether employees and applicants are being treated without regard to the prohibited categories of the executive order. This is far from the law blindly requiring a certain number of places to be filled by a certain gender or race, as many think it does.

The affirmative action plan regulations clearly state that they prefer to have contractors perform ongoing monitoring of their workplaces to ensure that their policies and practices are consistent with non-discriminatory hiring, promotions, termination, pay, and other workplace considerations. An employer would do well to heed that advice and catch any small problems before they become larger ones. Careful monitoring will address this quite well.

Judicial Affirmative Action

judicial affirmative action

Affirmative action ordered by a court as a remedy for discrimination found by the court to have occurred, rather than arising from Executive Order 11246.

Rather than an affirmative action plan imposed by Executive Order 11246, an employee may sue alleging an employer violated Title VII, and the affirmative action arises in response to a finding of workplace discrimination that must be remedied. Title VII gives courts fairly wide latitude in redressing wrongs. The courts' imposition of affirmative action as the means of redress is known as **judicial affirmative action**.

In addition to agency rules and regulations, courts have played an important role in shaping the concept of affirmative action. While there are no specific requirements as to what form an affirmative action plan must take (see Exhibit 5.9), if the plan is in keeping with the requirements set forth below, the employer has little to fear from suits challenging implementation of the plan, although the monetary and energy costs in dealing with them are great.

The first affirmative action case to reach the U.S. Supreme Court, *Regents of the University of California v. Bakke,*[39] involved affirmative action in medical school admissions, rather than employment; however, the case is viewed as the one that opened the affirmative action debate, and much of its reasoning was used in subsequent employment cases. While endorsing the concept of affirmative action to further the educational goal of a diverse student body, the Court struck down the University of California's affirmative action plan because it set aside a certain number of places for "disadvantaged students," who also could compete for the other spaces. The Court said it was not fair to have the disadvantaged group have additional spaces open to them that were not available to others.

In *Local 28, Sheet Metal Workers v. EEOC,* included at the end of the chapter, the Court imposed one of the stiffer judicial affirmative action plans ever developed, but only after the Court's orders had repeatedly been ignored by the union. In the case, the question arose as to who can receive the benefit of affirmative action plans. Can the plan benefit individuals who were not the actual victims of the employer's discriminatory practices? The Supreme Court held that there need not be a showing of discrimination against the particular individual (employee, applicant, promotion candidate, and the like) as long as the affirmative action plan meets appropriate requirements (see Exhibit 5.10) and the individual fits into the category of employees the plan was designed to benefit. This approach recognizes that the employer's policy may result in discouraging certain people from even applying for a job because they know it would be futile, given the employer's history.

While the notion of providing relief for nonspecific victims of discrimination may appear questionable, the *Sheet Metal Workers* is exactly the type of situation that justifies such action. As you read the case, in addition to thinking about what the union or employer should have done, think of how you would have handled the situation if you were the court imposing the remedy. Also, think of whether you would have allowed the situation to go on for so long if you were the court. This case is the basis for Opening Scenario 1.

Scenario

Would you believe that on January 15, 2008, 22 years after this case was decided, the EEOC announced that a federal court had granted final approval for a $6.2 million partial settlement in this case? Twenty-two years later, after it had already been nearly 20 years when this case was heard and the above decision issued. This most recent settlement covers only lost wages from 1984 to 1991 for black and Hispanic workers, but the litigation covering post-1991 discrimination is still ongoing. "We hope that these developments are an indication with the recent changes in leadership, the union has decided, after many years of costly litigation, to work with the court and the plaintiffs in obeying the court orders and begin to resolve outstanding claims against it," said Spencer Lewis, the district director of the EEOC's New York office.[40] Considering the litigation has been going on for 40+ years, good luck with that.

Voluntary Affirmative Action

After the Court for the first time dealt with the issue of affirmative action in the *Bakke* case, the next big questions were whether a similar analysis applied (1) if the affirmative action plan involved private rather than state action, (2) if the plan involved a workplace rather than a university admissions program, and (3) whether voluntary affirmative action plans are permissible rather than only those required by Executive Order 11246 or imposed by a court to remedy prior discrimination that was found to have existed. The opportunity to have those important Title VII developmental questions answered came the year after *Bakke,* in the *United Steelworkers of America, AFL-CIO v. Weber*[41] case. The answer to all three questions was yes.

In *Weber,* a white employee sued under Title VII alleging race discrimination, in that the union and employer adopted a voluntary affirmative action plan reserving for African-American employees 50 percent of the openings in a training program until the percentage of African-American craft workers in the plant approximated the percentage of African-Americans in the local labor force. The Supreme Court held that the program was permissible, in that Title VII did not prohibit voluntary race-conscious affirmative action plans undertaken to eliminate a manifest racial imbalance, the measure is only temporary, and it did not unnecessarily trample the rights of white employees.

Based on *Weber,* in addition to affirmative action plans required by Executive Order 11246 and those imposed by a court to remedy discrimination found in the workplace pursuant to a Title VII claim, there is also the possibility of voluntary affirmative action. Here, the employer decides to institute an affirmative action plan on his or her own, regardless of whether the employer is required to do so under the executive order, and despite the fact that no one has brought a Title VII case. Employers generally engage in voluntary affirmative action as a proactive measure to avoid discrimination claims after making a determination that there is an underrepresentation of minorities and women in the workplace, generally based on previous exclusionary policies or practices. However, an employer cannot simply unilaterally decide to institute a plan out of the goodness of his or her heart and run with it. Based on *Weber,* there are strict guidelines that must be followed if the plan is to withstand a reverse discrimination challenge by an affected employee alleging discrimination because of the plan's implementation. (See Exhibit 5.10.)

Many employers were surprised by *Weber* since the year before the Court struck down a voluntary affirmative action plan in *Bakke.* While both concerned affirmative action plans, there were considerable differences, beyond even employment versus school admissions. Some of these differences and the Court's reasoning got lost in news coverage. Both decisions endorsed the concept of affirmative action, but the requirements were not met in *Bakke* and were in *Weber,* thus giving different, though not inconsistent, outcomes. *Weber* is the basis for Opening Scenarios 1 and 3.

2)
Scenario

After *Weber,* you now realize that in Opening Scenario 2, it is permissible for an employer to have a voluntary affirmative action plan, but certain factors must be present in order to justify the plan to a court. In Opening Scenario 2, we do not have all the relevant facts to determine if the employer can take the affirmative action measures the employer wishes. For instance, we do not know why there are such small numbers of minorities and women in upper-level management and skilled-labor jobs. We do not know if it is because there is a history of discrimination and exclusion, or that there simply are not sufficient numbers of women and minorities available in the workforce from which employees are drawn.

3)
Scenario

In Opening Scenario 3, we know from *Weber* that an employer can have a one-for-one affirmative action promotion plan as part of a remedy for past discrimination, and if the *Weber* requirements are met, the employer is protected from liability for discrimination against employees alleging reverse discrimination; that is, that they are adversely impacted by implementation of the plan.

Seven years later, in the case of *Wygant v. Jackson Board of Education,*[42] and consistent with the language in *Bakke* and *Weber,* the Supreme Court again upheld the concept of affirmative action, this time for protection against lay-offs for public employees, though it held that the requirements of demonstrating a compelling state interest and narrowly tailoring the plan to meet the objective had not been met in this case. This answered the question of whether the Court's decision in *Bakke,* involving the admissions policy for a public university, also applied to an affirmative action plan in a public workplace. It did. It also answered the question left after *Weber* as to whether the acceptance of voluntary affirmative action in private employment also applied to public employment. It did.

Johnson v. Transportation Agency, Santa Clara County, California,[43] a 1987 Supreme Court decision discussed later, relied heavily on *Weber* to determine that, under circumstances similar to those in *Weber* but involving a public employer rather than private, and gender rather than race, the employer could appropriately take gender into account under its voluntary affirmative action plan as one factor of a promotion decision. The Court said the plan, voluntarily adopted to redress a "conspicuous imbalance in traditionally segregated job categories," represented a "moderate, flexible, case-by-case approach to effecting a gradual improvement in the representation of minorities and women." Consistent with *Weber,* the plan was acceptable because

LO5

1. It did not unnecessarily trammel male employees' rights or create an absolute bar to their advancement.
2. It set aside no positions for women (as did *Bakke*) and expressly stated that its goals should not be construed as quotas to be met.
3. It unsettled no legitimate, firmly rooted expectation of employees.
4. It was only temporary in that it was for purposes of attaining, not maintaining, a balanced workforce.
5. There was minimal intrusion into the legitimate, settled expectations of other employees.

"Reverse Discrimination"

LO6

reverse discrimination
Claim brought by a majority member who feels adversely affected by the use of an employer's affirmative action plan.

So-called **reverse discrimination**[44] has often been considered the flip side of affirmative action. When an employer is taking race or gender into account under an affirmative action plan in order to achieve an affirmative action placement goal, someone not in the excluded group alleges she or he is harmed by the employer's consideration of race or gender, or both, in hiring or promotion decisions.

For example, an employer finds an underrepresentation of women in managerial positions in the workplace and develops an affirmative action plan for their inclusion. As part of that plan, one qualified female employee is to be chosen for a managerial training program for each male chosen. The employer chooses one male, then one female. The male employee who feels he would have been chosen next if there were no affirmative action plan requiring a woman to be chosen sues the employer, alleging reverse discrimination. That is, but for his gender, he would have been chosen for the position the female received.

Despite what you may have heard, "reverse discrimination" is not the flip side of affirmative action. It accounts for only about 3 percent of the charges filed with the EEOC, and most of those claims result in no-cause findings. Most employees have a fundamental misunderstanding of what reverse discrimination is and how it operates.

As you learned in our discussion of the requirements for an employer to have an affirmative action plan, once the plan is deemed necessary because there is an underrepresentation that cannot be accounted for in virtually any way other than exclusion of certain groups, even unwittingly, then consideration of race or gender becomes a necessary part of the remedy. The law builds in protections for employees who feel they may be adversely affected by ensuring that the plan is only given protection if it complies with the legal requirements.

One of the arguments frequently made in reverse discrimination cases is that affirmative action requires the "sons to pay for the sins of the fathers" and that "slavery is over—why can't we just forget it and move on?" Affirmative action is not about something that happened nearly 150 years ago. It is about underrepresentation in the workplace *today.* Also keep in mind that it is not punishment in any way, but rather a *remedy* for discrimination, or its vestiges, *that has been found to exist.* As for the "sins of the fathers," keep in mind the extent to which African-Americans and women were *legally* excluded from the workplace from the beginning of this country's existence until passage of the Civil Rights Act in 1964. Their intentional inclusion only began to become a significant issue in the late 1970s to early 1980s. This gave those groups who were in the workplace for all those years before a huge head start on experience, training, presence, trustworthiness, seniority, perception of appropriateness for the job, and so on.

These factors come into play each time an applicant or employee applies for a job, promotion, training, or other benefit. Without the applicant's intentionally doing anything that may ask for more favorable or less favorable consideration (depending on the group to which the applicant belongs) because of more than 345 years of ingrained history, as shown by study after study, it happens. While it may not be intentional, or even conscious, it has a definite harmful impact on groups traditionally excluded from the workplace—an impact that research has proved to be present time and again. For instance, despite the anecdotal evidence of seemingly omnipresent reverse discrimination situations we may hear about from our friends or colleagues, the U.S. Department of Labor's 1995 Glass Ceiling Report found that, though anti-discrimination laws have made a significant impact in bringing women and minorities into the workplace in entry-level positions, there are still significant workplace disparities. Given that, it should come as no surprise that, according to the Glass Ceiling Commission Report, white men are only 43 percent of the Fortune 2000 workforce but hold 95 percent of the senior management jobs. Women are only 8.6 percent of all engineers, less than 1 percent of carpenters, 23 percent of lawyers, 16 percent of police, and 3.7 percent of firefighters. White men are 33 percent of the U.S. population but 65 percent of physicians, 71 percent of lawyers, 80 percent of tenured professors, and 94 percent of school superintendents. This was later borne out again in the Harvard study mentioned earlier.

LO7

Case 3

While we would all love to live in a color-blind society, where merit is the only factor considered in the workplace, research shows that we are not there yet. Affirmative action steps in as a measure to help remedy this situation. (For pro and con views, see Exhibit 5.11, "Opposing Views of Affirmative Action.") Nevertheless, as you can see from the *Ricci v. DeStefano* case, included at the end of the chapter, claims by those who feel they were unjustly impacted by an employer's efforts to be inclusive remain an important tool in effectuating rights under Title VII for everyone, as well as further defining its parameters.

In *Ricci,* the city of New Haven, Connecticut, took great pains to have a test developed for the promotion of firefighters to lieutenant and captain. Since these promotions did not happen often and were a great source of pride and upward mobility for the firefighters, it was important to the city to get it right. After the test was given, the percentage of blacks and Hispanics passing the exams was considerably lower than that of whites, and under existing rules, none of the blacks qualified for promotion, though several passed the exam. The city was concerned that the promotions based on the exam scores would be challenged by

Exhibit 5.11   *Opposing Views of Affirmative Action*

Affirmative action has been in place for years as the law, but for some reason, people still feel the need to debate it or to take sides, as if it is not actually the law. Despite the years, these two pieces still do one of the best jobs we've seen pinpointing the basic positions of those who are for or against affirmative action. Given what you now know about affirmative action, which side makes the most sense to you? Keep in mind that we said given what you *now* know because you should now have much more insight into what affirmative action actually is than before you read this chapter and only had what you had gathered from other, usually nonlegal, sources.

CON—CLARENCE PENDLETON, CHAIR OF THE U.S. COMMISSION ON CIVIL RIGHTS

Human resource management departments are "the major force companies have for getting rid of preference (hiring) plans and for not letting the 'new racism' take hold," Clarence Pendleton told his packed luncheon-time audience at a recent monthly meeting of the Metropolitan New York City American Society of Personnel Administrators.

"New racism," Pendleton explained, is a lot like old racism. New racists typically are vociferous supporters of civil rights, but want different treatment for minorities, such as goals, timetables and quotas. "New racists think of blacks as a commodity," he commented, "and, therefore, they set numbers as goals."

Preferential treatment, which Pendleton characterized as "neo-slavery," leads automatically to different results for classes of people. With no equality of results, he said.

Pendleton, who is often and loudly criticized for his conservative Republican beliefs, made no apologies for his work with the Reagan administration. He defended the civil rights record of the administration, claiming that "we are not turning our backs on civil rights. Discriminatory affirmative action programs are dead, but those who have been discriminated against should be made whole."

He suggested that a best-selling book could be a compendium of the Civil Rights Act of 1964. "Read it," he challenged his audience, "and you will find that nowhere does the Act call for preferential treatment. The faster we get preferential treatment out of politics, the faster we are going to get to a color-blind society."

Too many black leaders "are peddling pain with federal preference programs, but they don't demand education," Pendleton charged.

And that is where HR professionals come into Pendleton's plan. He challenged the audience to "develop a profile on what it takes to move into corporate America without preferences. Let us know what training and support is necessary to get minorities into the economic system. Tell us—'Here's what it takes to get prepared.' Pass that information on to educators."

He asked that professionals support schools and fight for a reduced minimum wage for teens. "Affirmative action without jobs isn't doing a thing for the 59 percent of black youth who are unemployed and are not qualified for jobs which exist."

"It's time to remove all the chains," he said. "And you in human resources play a major role in the development of public policy. We need a majestic national river of employees, and not these ethnic creeks."

PRO—RICHARD WOMACK, DIRECTOR, OFFICE OF CIVIL RIGHTS FOR THE AFL-CIO

It is all well and good to promote the concept of equality in hiring and promotion, but centuries of discrimination against minorities and women have put them at a disadvantage in the workplace that must first be corrected through aggressive action.

Addressing a June 5 plenary session of the 15th annual American Association of Affirmative Action conference, Womack told several hundred conferees that the challenge facing equal employment and affirmative action officers today is to decide

continued

Exhibit 5.11   *continued*

how to proceed "until we reach the day when we can say we have a color-blind society."

Womack likened the state of today's workforce to a football game where the dominant team, which has mounted a huge lead by cheating and putting 15 players on the field, decides to stop cheating and pare its team down to 11 players with just three minutes left to play. "For those three minutes the two teams may be equal, but the cheating that preceded the equality will doom the other team to certain failure," Womack said.

White males have had the advantage of preference in the workplace for years. "Now it's time to do the same thing for women and minorities." Noting that his remarks may be viewed by some as "harsh," Womack said that protected groups must be given preference in order to put all workers on the same level playing field. "After whites used race as a basis for slavery and a standard for the exclusion to education and advancement, why now should we be color-blind? There is too much damage to undo."

Womack urged the EEO officers to provide opportunity to minorities and women in the same manner that white males have in the past. "White males have historically taken care of other whites," Womack said.

Affirmative action is an "imperfect tool" to be used to correct past discrimination and suffers from a perception problem, Womack said. "You mention affirmative action to whites and they conjure up images of incompetent blacks who have been given jobs that should have gone to qualified whites," Womack told the conference. Blacks, on the other hand, view affirmative action as "a paltry effort of reduced bias—a dent in whites favoring whites," he said.

The concept and use of goals and timetables also face perception problems, Womack said. The federal government and corporations alike set goals and timetables for everything from collection of taxes to the implementation of new products or procedures, he noted. "So why are goals and timetables so horrible in the employment context?" Womack asked.

Sources: *Con*—reprinted with the permission of *HR Magazine,* published by the Society for Human Resource Management, Alexandria, VA; *pro*—reprinted with permission from *Daily Labor Report,* No. 107 (June 6, 1989), pp. A-10–A-11. Copyright 1989 by the Bureau of National Affairs, Inc. (800/372-1033), http://www.bna.com.

the black firefighters as having a disparate impact upon them, so the city discarded the exam scores, and those who would have been promoted were not. These firefighters sued and their position was upheld by the U.S. Supreme Court.

As you will see when you read the case, it is a perfect example of why an employer should simply do the right thing and let the chips fall where they may. It is why fair and consistent rules, evenly applied, are an employer's best protection against discrimination lawsuits. The city had already done a great deal to make sure its exam was fair and reflective of what was needed for the positions. If it had simply given the exam and allowed the scores to be used, even if the black firefighters sued based on disparate impact, they would not have been able to make their case. The city had done all it could to make sure the exam was valid.

Though the case was brought based on the disparate treatment of the firefighters, we include it here in the affirmative action chapter because what the city did was, in essence, treat the situation as an affirmative action plan. As managers and supervisors, do not simply do what you think will avoid liability because you think you might be sued. Make defensible legal workplace policies and decisions. Not only will employees be less likely to bring lawsuits, but when they do, you will be in a better position to successfully defend against them.

Affirmative Action and Veterans

In November of 2002, President George W. Bush signed into law the Jobs for Veterans Act of 2002 (JVA), amending the Vietnam Era Veterans' Readjustment Assistance Act of 1974 (VEVRAA). The law applies to all contracts entered into on December 1, 2003, or thereafter. Contracts entered into prior to that date are still covered by VEVRAA. JVA raised the minimum contract threshold that required affirmative action for veterans from $25,000 to $100,000 and changed the veteran categories of the act. Contractors are required to take affirmative action demonstrating an active effort to hire and promote qualified disabled veterans, other protected veterans, armed forces service medal veterans, and recently separated veterans.

Contractors must disseminate all promotion information internally regarding promotion activities, including agreements to lease workers from temp agencies. JVA also requires federal contractors to report the total number of all current employees in each job category and at each hiring location, and it is mandatory that contractors immediately list all job openings with state employment agencies or other employment outlets. Exemptions from such postings include positions that are to be filled in top management or executive staff, positions lasting three days or less, or positions that are to be filled from within the contractor's organization. In addition, veterans have priority service in Department of Labor job-training programs, allowing them to be given priority over nonveterans for receiving employment, training, and placement services provided in the program.

Federal contractors must file VETS-100 forms (termed VETS-100A for contracts after December 3, 2003) annually, verifying that their plans have been followed and no discrimination has occurred against veterans or other covered groups; demonstrating active recruitment of veterans and that information regarding promotion activities within their organization has been disseminated; and stating the numbers of veterans in their workforce by job category and hiring location and the total number of employees and the number of veterans hired during the reporting period.

Unlike the affirmative action requirements we have been discussing for Title VII categories that primarily require an employer to make an effort to be inclusive of heretofore excluded categories of employees, veteran affirmative action contains provisions for priorities for referring veterans for employment. That is, under the law, generally, "qualified targeted veterans are entitled to priority for referral to federal contractor job openings." This does not mean they must be hired, but they are given priority in job openings.

Valuing Diversity/Multiculturalism/Diversity and Inclusion

LO8

Once affirmative action plans accomplished (at least to a limited degree) their purpose of bringing heretofore excluded employees into the workplace, employers discovered that this, in and of itself, was not enough to provide equal opportunity conditions. Employees coming into workplaces not used to their presence found the workplace often hostile in subtle, but very real ways. As you can see from simply the title of this section, as the workplace evolves, concepts change accordingly. The newest version of how to address the issue of making workplaces more inclusive for everyone is diversity and inclusion, or D&I. Some also call it I&D. Whatever name is used, the goal is to work on ensuring that everyone in the workplace feels free to make a contribution and flourish.

The Society for Human Resource Management, a nonpartisan human resources organization, is currently working on creating both national and international voluntary standards for workplace diversity programs (similar to ISO standards for business) as well as measuring workplace diversity initiatives. Until now, there has been no standard and employers were simply left on their own to figure out what might work best. The new standards would enable employers to have some idea of what to look for and how best to go about creating the workplace they wish to have.

While the hostility may have been subtle, the impact on female and minority work lives was not. These employees found they did not move up as quickly as other, more traditional, employees. Many were not included in workplace activities, were reprimanded more often, did not receive the same opportunities, and thus had higher turnover rates. Even subtle differences in their treatment meant the difference between progressing in the workplace and remaining stagnant.

Faced with workplaces filled with new kinds of people, employers sought answers. The search became even more immediate after the release of the Hudson Institute's "Workforce 2000" study for the U.S. Department of Labor in 1987. According to the study, the United States was about to face its largest wave of immigration since World War II, and unlike the last big wave that was 90 percent European, this one would be about 90 percent Asian and Latin American.

valuing diversity
Learning to accept and appreciate those who are different from the majority and value their contributions to the workplace.

The idea of **valuing diversity** began to take root. Valuing diversity means being sensitive to and appreciative of differences among groups outside the mainstream and using those differences, coupled with basic human similarities, as a positive force to increase productivity and efficiency and to avoid liability for discrimination. For the past several years, employers all over the country have sponsored workplace programs to sensitize employees to differences among people in the workplace. Being made aware of these differences in various racial, ethnic, religious, and other groups has helped employees learn to better deal with them. Chances are, at some point in your career, you will be exposed to the concept of valuing diversity. It will greatly increase your value to the employer to do so. (See Exhibits 5.12, "Cultural Differences," and 5.13, "Valuing Diversity.")

As the concept of valuing diversity has evolved, it has recently also been paired with the concept of inclusion. As our ideas expand to include more groups, more bases for differences heretofore not addressed in the workplace, it has become clear that even simply valuing diversity is not enough. Making employees feel included by realizing the myriad of ways in which they are subtly excluded is an important tool for avoiding liability and being more productive.

Again, what employers can choose to do to bring more people into their workplace who have traditionally been left out (and, without some measure to include

Exhibit 5.12   *Cultural Differences*

Did you ever think about how much culture affects us, and how we differ culturally? Not only does it impact big things like our holidays, clothing, and so on, but it shapes much smaller things.

A list of tips to travelers abroad issued by the Chinese government warned:

Don't squat when waiting for a bus or a person. Don't spit in public. Don't point at people with your fingers. Don't make noise. Don't laugh loudly. Don't yell or call to people from a distance. Don't pick your teeth, pick your nose, blow your nose, pick at your ears, rub your eyes, or rub dirt off your skin. Don't scratch, take off your shoes, burp, stretch or hum.

Exhibit 5.13   *Valuing Diversity*

Make a circle with your thumb and forefinger. What does it mean? In America we know it primarily as meaning "okay." But how many of us know that it may also mean the equivalent of "flipping someone the bird," "give me coin change," "I wish to make love with you," or "I wish you dead, as my mortal enemy"? The objective act has not changed, yet the meaning has. The interpretation the act is given depends on the cultural conditioning of the receiver. Welcome to multiculturalism. Knowing what is meant becomes a necessity in processing the act, otherwise the act has little meaning. Culture is what provides that information and, thus, meaning for virtually everything we do, say, wear, eat, value, and where and in what we live, sit, and sleep. Imagine how many other acts we engage in every day which can be misinterpreted based upon differences in cultural conditioning. Yet our cultural conditioning is rarely given much thought. Even less is given to the culture of others. That will not be true much longer.

In the fall 1992 issue of the magazine of the American Assembly of Collegiate Schools of Business, the accrediting body of schools of business, the cover story and lead article was "Teaching Diversity: Business Schools Search for Model Approaches." In the article, it stated that "without integrating a comprehensive diversity message into the entire curriculum, the most relevant management education cannot occur." *Multiculturalism* is learning to understand, appreciate, and value (not just "tolerate") the unique aspects of cultures different from one's own. The end product is learning to value others who may be different, for what they contribute, rather than rejecting them simply because they are different.

The concept of "culture" encompasses not only ethnicity, but also gender, age, disability, affinity orientation, and other factors which may significantly affect and in many ways, define, one's life. Multiculturalism is learning that "different from" does not mean "less than." It is getting in touch with one's cultural conditioning and working toward inclusion, rather than conformity.

Learning to value diversity opens people up to more. A major workplace concern is maximizing production and minimizing liability. Multiculturalism and valuing diversity contribute to this. To the extent that each person, regardless of cultural differences, is valued as a contributor in the workplace, he or she is less likely to sue the employer for transgressions (or perceived transgressions) stemming from not being valued. To the extent they are valued for who they are and what they can contribute in society, they are much less likely to end up engaging in acts such as the Los Angeles riots

continued

Exhibit 5.13   *continued*

causing death and destruction in the spring of 1992 after the Rodney King verdict.

The U.S. Department of Labor's Workforce 2000 study conducted by the Hudson Institute and released in 1987 held a few surprises that galvanized America into addressing the issue of multiculturalism. According to the widely cited study, by the year 2000 we will experience the greatest influx of immigrants since World War II. At the same time, the percentage of women entering the workforce is increasing. The net result, according to the study, is that 85% of the net growth in the workforce will be comprised of women and non-Europeans. For the first time, white males will be a minority in the workforce. This need not be viewed as a threatening circumstance, but rather an opportunity for innovation and progress.

These factors, alone, reveal that the workplace (and by implication, schools, universities, recreational facilities and everything else) will be very different from before. It will no longer do to have a white, European, male, standard of operation. Others will be pouring into the workplace and will come with talent, energy, ideas, tenacity, imagination and other contributions the U.S. has always held dear as the basis for the "American Dream." They will come expecting to be able to use those qualities to pursue that dream. They will come feeling that they have much to offer and are valuable for all their uniqueness and the differences they may have from "the norm." And what will happen? There is no choice but to be prepared. It is a simple fact that the workplace cannot continue to operate in the same way and remain productive.

Studies have shown that when the same problem is given to homogeneous groups and heterogeneous groups to solve, the heterogeneous groups come up with more effective solutions. When people feel valued for who they are and

what they can contribute, rather than feeling pressed into conformity as if who they are is not good enough, they are more productive. Energy and creativity can be spent on the task at hand, rather than on worrying about how well they fit into someone's idea of who they should be. A significant number of the problems we face as a society and on which is spent millions in precious tax dollars comes from rejecting multiculturalism and not valuing diversity. If people were judged for who they are and what they contribute, there would not be a need for a civil rights act, affirmative action plans, riot gear, human rights commissions, etc.

There are, of course, naysayers on the topic of multiculturalism such as those who think it is just an attempt at being "politically correct." It has been said that the term "politically correct" is an attempt to devalue, trivialize, demean, and diffuse the substantive value of the issues spoken of; that once something is deemed to be an issue of "political correctness," then there is no need to worry about the real import or impact of it, because it is only a passing fad which need not be taken seriously, as it will die its own natural death soon enough.

Multiculturalism is here to stay. People have evolved to the point where it will not go away. Self-worth and valuing oneself is a lesson that it takes many a long time to learn. Once learned, it is hard to give up. And, of course, why should it be given up? Again, "different from" does not mean "less than." Learning to value others as unique human beings whose culture is [sic] an integral part of who they are, rather than something to be shed at the work or school door, and learning to value the differences rather than to try to assimilate them, will benefit everyone.

Source: Reprinted with permission from the University of Georgia's *Columns.*

them, would continue to be left out) is not defined in the law. But as employers have warmed up to the idea of going beyond the status quo, they have been quite innovative. Sometimes, like with the NFL's Rooney Rule (see Exhibit 5.14, "The Rooney Rule: Affirmative Action Comes to Professional Football?"), all it takes is bringing into the consideration process someone who might not necessarily otherwise be

Exhibit 5.14 *The Rooney Rule: Affirmative Action Comes to Professional Football?*

Ever wonder why so many African-American football players are on the field playing extremely well, yet so few end up in the front office or as coaches? The NFL eventually did. In an attempt to provide more opportunities to minorities in the consideration of NFL football coaches, the NFL adopted the Rooney Rule (named for the Pittsburgh owner Dan Rooney, head of the NFL's Workplace Diversity Committee). The Rooney Rule requires a team with a vacant head coaching position to interview at least one minority candidate. The intent of the rule is to provide an opportunity for teams to look at candidates they might otherwise not interview. They are not required to hire, only to interview. The Pittsburgh Steelers interviewed former Vikings defensive coordinator Mike Tomlin when they were searching for a head coach. Tomlin ended up being the best candidate for the job, and got it, becoming the youngest head coach in the league. The Rooney Rule is still debated, with some saying it is too little to simply require that a minority candidate be interviewed, and some saying it is forcing the situations and making teams just go through the motions. Tomlin received his offer the same day that, for the first time ever, two African-American NFL head coaches made it to the Super Bowl. At the historic Super Bowl XLI, on February 4, 2007, Coach Tony Dungy of the Indianapolis Colts beat out Coach Lovie Smith of the Chicago Bears in what most fans referred to as one of the best games ever. Coincidentally, the BCS national championship college football game between the University of Florida Gators and the unbeaten Ohio State Buckeyes also featured a historic matchup: two African-American quarterbacks. Florida's Chris Leak beat out Heisman trophy winner Troy Smith, 41–14. In June of 2009, the Rooney Rule was extended to cover general managers.

included. In an effort to value diversity and ensure that, once employees are hired, the employer maximizes the opportunity, employers do such things as:

- Organize workplace affinity groups for gays, female employees, Hispanic employees, and so on.
- Include diverse actors in advertising and commercials.
- Hold workshops for high-potential diverse employees.
- Institute formal procedures to handle complaints from diverse employees.
- Closely monitor the progress of diverse employees along the way.
- Tie performance reviews of managers to their measurable support for diversity inclusion.
- Organize business networking groups.
- Hold management diversity training.
- Provide for mentors for diverse employees.
- Have a chief diversity officer who reports directly to the chief executive officer (CEO).
- Focus on single diversity issues such as diversity in philanthropy, recruiting, retention, supply contractors, and so on.
- Have diverse board of directors members have a "road show" to meet with diverse employees for networking.
- Take the direct approach, like Walmart did when, in 2007, it notified its 100 outside-counsel law firms that it was only going to retain firms that made

Management Tips

Affirmative action can be a bit tricky. Keeping in mind these tips can help avoid liability for instituting and implementing an affirmative action plan.

- Ensure that the hiring, promotion, training, and other such processes are open, fair, and available to all employees on an equal basis.
- If an affirmative action plan is to be adopted voluntarily, work with the union (if there is one) and other employee groups to try to ensure fairness and get early approval from the constituencies affected to ward off potential litigation.
- Make sure voluntary affirmative action plans meet the judicial requirements of

    —Being used to redress a conspicuous imbalance in traditionally segregated job categories.

    —Being moderate, flexible, and gradual in approach.

    —Being temporary in order to attain, not maintain, a balanced workforce.

    —Not unnecessarily trammeling employees' rights or creating an absolute bar to their advancement.

    —Unsettling no legitimate, firmly rooted expectations of employees.

    —Presenting only a minimal intrusion into the legitimate, settled expectations of other employees.

- Provide training about the plan so that all employees understand its purpose and intent. Try to allay fears from the outset to ward off potential litigation. The more employees know and understand what is being done, the less likely they are to misunderstand and react adversely. Even so, keep in mind that some employees will still dislike the plan. Reiterating top-level management's commitment to equal employment opportunity will stress the seriousness of management's commitment.
- Implement periodic diversity and related training. This not only provides a forum for employees to express their views about diversity issues, but it also provides information on learning how to deal with their co-workers as diversity issues arise.

a concerted effort to be inclusive of women and minorities, as evidenced by them being on the liaison committee for business with Walmart.

- Build diversity into everything the employer does, not just Mexican food on Cinco de Mayo or remembrance of Dr. Martin Luther King during Black History Month.
- Institute scholarship and internship programs to groom diverse employees for eventual hire.
- Make personal phone calls and follow-ups with diverse applicants to assure them of the seriousness of inclusion.
- Notify employees of inappropriate or exclusionary workplace behaviors toward others.
- Review workplace policies and practices and their impact on diversity.
- Make sure white males are included in the employer's concept of diversity.
- Seek the input of diverse groups in developing a workplace approach to diversity and inclusion.

Chapter Summary

- Affirmative action is intentional inclusion of women, minorities, and others traditionally excluded in the workplace after demonstrated underrepresentation of these historically disadvantaged groups.

- Affirmative action plans may arise voluntarily, as a remedy in a discrimination lawsuit, or as part of an employer's responsibilities as a contractor or subcontractor with the government.

- Understanding the historical background of why affirmative action exists is critical to a true understanding of the concept and how to avoid pitfalls in its implementation.

- Employers should conduct voluntary periodic equal employment opportunity audits to monitor their workforce for gender, minority, and other inclusion. If there is underrepresentation, the employer should develop a reasonable, nonintrusive, flexible plan within appropriate guidelines.

- Such plans should not displace nonminority employees or permit people to hold positions for which they are not qualified, simply to meet affirmative action goals. This view should not be encouraged or tolerated.

- A well-reasoned, flexible plan with endorsement at the highest levels of the workplace, applied consistently and diligently, will greatly aid in diminishing negativity surrounding affirmative action and in protecting the employer from adverse legal action.

- Diversity and inclusion have become important concepts as employers move past simply bringing women and minorities into the workplace and instead try to ensure that they are provided with the environment and tools they need to fully contribute to the workplace. Programs that promote diversity and inclusion can be an effective basis for creating a workplace that does not have affirmative action issues resulting in litigation.

Chapter-End Questions

1. What is the monetary floor an employer/federal government contractor must meet to have Executive Order 11246 imposed?

2. Anne is employed by Bradley Contracting Company. Bradley has a $1.3 million contract to build a small group of outbuildings in a national park. Anne alleges that Bradley Contracting has discriminated against her, in that she has not been promoted to skilled craft positions with Bradley because it thinks that it is inappropriate for women to be in skilled craft positions and that most of the male skilled craftworkers are very much against having women in such positions. Knowing that Bradley Contracting has a contract with the federal government, Anne brings suit against Bradley under Executive Order 11246 for gender discrimination. Will she be successful? Why or why not?

3. Can employers lawfully consider race or gender when making hiring or promotion decisions? Explain.

4. If so, may it only be used to remedy identified past discrimination? Discuss.

5. Must such discrimination have been committed by the employer or can the discrimination have been committed by society in general? Explain.

6. Can affirmative action be used to benefit those who did not actually experience discrimination? Discuss.

7. Can race or gender be the only factor in an employment decision? Explain.

8. If race or gender can be the only factor in an employment decision, how long can it be a factor?

9. What is the difference between an affirmative action goal and a quota? Is there a difference? Explain.

10. What is the proper comparison to determine if there is an underrepresentation of women or minorities in the workplace?

End Notes

1. *EEOC Compliance Manual,* Section 15, VI (c), http://www.eeoc.gov/policy/docs/race-color.html#VIC.

2. 401 U.S. 424 (1971).

3. See Charlton D. McIlwain and Stephen M. Caliendo, *Race Appeal: How Candidates Invoke Race in U.S. Political Campaigns* (Philadelphia: Temple University Press, 2011).

4. In Kaler, Doblin, Kelly, "Best Practices or Best Guesses: Assessing the Efficacy of Corporate Affirmative Action and Diversity Policies," *American Sociological Review* 71, August 2006, pp. 589–617, the authors' rigorous analysis of various policies and their effectiveness.

5. See Thomas Ross, *Just Stories: How the Law Embodies Racism and Bias* (Boston: Beacon Press, 1996).

6. Ibid, p. 20, "The Awful Magic of Rhetoric."

7. President Lyndon B. Johnson's Commencement Address at Howard University: "To Fulfill These Rights," June 4, 1965, http://www.lbjlib.utexas.edu/johnson/archives.hom/speeches.hom/650604.asp.

8. For a very insightful video on this point, see Tim Wise in "Affirmative Action Debate," by Intelligence Squared, http://open.salon.com/blog/edward_rhymes/2009/05/08/affirmative_action_its_a_white_thing_part_two.

9. For a look at how the workplace is still significantly impacted by discrimination, see The American Values Institute's "Hiring," http://americansforamericanvalues.org/issues/hiring/; Tim J. Wise, *Affirmative Action: Racial Preference in Black and White* (New York: Routledge, 2005); Joseph Barndt, *Understanding and Dismantling Racism: The Twenty-First Century Challenge to White America* (Minneapolis: Fortress, 2007); Barbara Trepagnier, *Silent Racism: How Well-Meaning White People Perpetuate the Racial Divide* (Boulder, CO: Paradigm, 2006); Pierre L. van den Berghe, *Race and Racism: A Comparative Perspective* (New York: John Wiley & Sons, 1967); Louis L. Knowles and Kenneth Prewitt, eds., *Institutional Racism in America* (Upper Saddle Rive, NJ: Prentice-Hall, 1969); Stephen L. Carter, *Reflections of an Affirmative Action Baby* (New York: Basic Books, 1991); Claude M. Steele, *Whistling Vivaldi and Other Clues to How Stereotypes Affect Us* (New York: W.W. Norton, 2010), Sabina E. Vaught, *Racism, Public Schooling, and the Entrenchment of White Supremacy: A Critical Race Ethnography* (New York: State University of New York Press, 2011).

10. See also "The U.S. Today—Racial Discrimination Is Alive and Well: Interview with Maria Krysan and Amanda Lewis," *Challenge* 48, no. 3, pp. 33–49, May–June 2005,

http://www.challengemagazine.com/Challenge%20interview%20pdfs/Krysan%
20Lewis.pdf, "What We Know about Mortgage Lending Discrimination in America,"
U.S. Department of Housing and Urban Development, http://archives.hud.gov/
news/1999/newsconf/biblio.html; Lane Kenworthy, "Incarceration and Inequality,"
Socio-Economic Review 5, no. 3, pp. 569–584, (2007); *Measuring Racial Discrimination,* Common National Statistics (CNSTAT) (The National Academies Press, 2004).

11. Barbara R. Bergman, *In Defense of Affirmative Action* (New York: Basic Books,
1996), 44.

12. Philip Moss and Chris Tilly, *Stories Employers Tell: Race, Skill and Hiring in America*
(New York: Russell Sage Foundation, 2001).

13. Gertrude Exrosky, *Racism and Justice: The Case for Affirmative Action* (Ithaca, N.Y.:
Cornell University Press, 1991).

14. LeAnn Lodder et al., *Racial Preference and Suburban Employment Opportunities*
(Chicago: Legal Assistance Foundation of Metropolitan Chicago and the Chicago
Urban League, April 2003).

15. Marc Benedick, Charles W. Jackson, and Victor Reinoso, "Measuring Employment
Discrimination through Controlled Experiments," *Review of Black Political Economy*
25 (Summer 1994).

16. Marianne Bertrand and Sendhil Mullainathan, "Are Emily and Brendan More Employable Than Lakisha and Jamal? A Field Experiment on Labor Market Discrimination," http://www.economics.harvard.edu/faculty/mullainathan/files/emilygreg.pdf.

17. Valerie A. Rawslton and William E. Spriggs, *"Pay Equity 2000: Are We There Yet?"*
(Washington, DC: National Urban League Institute for Opportunity and Equality,
SRR-02-2001, April 2001).

18. *Women's Earnings: Federal Agencies Should Better Monitor Their Performance in
Enforcing Anti-Discrimination Laws,* U.S. Government Accounting Office 8/11/08,
http://www.gao.gov/products/A83444.

19. National Committee on Pay Equity, Race and Pay Policy Brief, http://www.pay-
equity.org/info-racebrief.html.

20. Report of the Federal Glass Ceiling Commission, *Good for Business: Making Full
Use of the Nation's Human Capital,* March 1995, http://www.dol.gov/oasam/
programs/history/reich/reports/ceiling.pdf.

21. There is serious debate as to whether Smith introduced gender into the bill to help
women or to kill the bill altogether, knowing such a bill would never pass. Smith had
apparently been a supporter of women, but, given the societal norms at the time, it is
doubtful whether this was intended as an extension of that support. Clearly, with his
colleagues' reaction to his amendment, and the response by his female colleagues
who accused him of trying to kill the bill by inserting this amendment, the amendment
was not taken seriously as a blow for women's equality. See Bruce Dierenfield, "Howard W. Smith (1883–1976)," *Encyclopedia Virginia,* ed. Brendan Wolfe (Virginia
Foundation for the Humanities, 2011), http://www.encyclopediavirginia.org/
Smith_Howard_Worth_1883–1976.

22. For a more descriptive and in-depth account of this matter, see Taylor Branch, *Pillar
of Fire: America in the King Years, 1963–65* (New York: Simon & Schuster, 1998),
pp. 231–34.

23. *Multi-City Study on Urban Inequality* (Russell Sage Foundation Publications, 2001);
http://www.icpsr.umich.edu/icpsrweb/ICPSR/studies/02535.

24. Robin Estrin for the Associated Press, "Study: Race Is Still Key to Chances for Success," *The Philadelphia Inquirer,* October 2, 1999.

25. House Joint Resolution No. 607, Expressing the General Assembly's Regret for Virginia's Experience with Eugenics, 2/2/01 (House), 2/14/01 (Senate), http://leg1.state.va.us/cgi-bin/legp504.exe?011+ful+HJ607ER

26. Alexandra Minna Stern, "Sterilized in the Name of Public Health: Race, Immigration and Reproductive Control in Modern California," *American Journal of Public Health,* July 2005, pp. 1128–38, http://www.ncbi.nlm.nih.gov/pmc/articles/PMC1449330/.

27. Congressional Record, 75th Cong., 2d sess. (1937), 82:1388.

28. See, Ira Katznelson, *When Affirmative Action Was White: An Untold History of Racial Inequality in Twentieth-Century America* (New York: W. W. Norton, 2005).

29. See David E. Bernstein, *Only One Place of Redress: African Americans, Labor Regulations and the Court from Reconstruction to the New Deal* (Durham: Duke University Press, 2001)

30. See Ira Katznelson, *When Affirmative Action Was White: An Untold History of Racial Inequality in Twentieth-Century America* (New York: W.W. Norton, 2005).

31. For fun and informative exercises about affirmative action, see http://www.understandingprejudice.org/demos/.

32. Executive Order 8802, Prohibition of Discrimination in the Defense Industry, 5/25/41, http://docs.fdrlibrary.marist.edu/od8802t.html.

33. OFCCP's regulations can be found at 41 Code of Federal Regulations part 60, http://www.ogc.doc.gov/ogc/contracts/cld/regs/65fr26087.html.

34. http://www.ogc.doc.gov/ogc/contracts/cld/regs/65fr26087.html.

35. 41C.F.R. § 60-2.16(e)(1).

36. 41C.F.R. § 60-2.16(e)(4).

37. 41C.F.R. § 60-2.16(e)(2).

38. See U.S. Department of Labor's Fiscal Year 2010 Annual Performance Report at 68, http://www.dol.gov/dol/budget/2012/PDF/CBJ-2012-V1-01.pdf.

39. 438 U.S. 265 (1978).

40. "Judge Grants Final Approval of $6.2 Million Partial Settlement of Historic Union Discrimination Case," EEOC Press Release, 1/15/08, http://www.eeoc.gov/eeoc/newsroom/release/1-15-08a.cfm.

41. 443 U.S. 193 (1979).

42. 476 U.S. 267 (1986).

43. 480 U.S. 616 (1987).

44. The reason the term "reverse discrimination" is put in quotation marks is because it is not actually a legal concept, but rather an outgrowth of the implementation of affirmative action plans. *Everyone* is protected from workplace discrimination by the anti-discrimination laws. There is only one type of discrimination recognized by law and it applies to everyone. That discrimination is the unlawful use of prohibited criteria for making job decisions. Whether it is done in the context of an affirmative action plan or not, if it is illegal discrimination, the law does not see it as different simply because of the type of person involved or the way it arose. See EEOC Compliance Manual, Section 15, at 5. We do not use the quotation marks after the first usage.

Local 28, Sheet Metal Workers v. EEOC *478 U.S. 421 (1986)*

The union and its apprenticeship committee were found guilty of discrimination against Hispanics and African-Americans and were ordered to remedy the violations. They were found numerous times to be in contempt of the court's order, and after 18 years the court eventually imposed fines and an affirmative action plan as a remedy. The plan included benefits to persons not members of the union. The Supreme Court held the remedies to be appropriate under the circumstances.

Brennan, J.

***

Local 28 represents sheet metal workers employed by contractors in the New York City metropolitan area. The Local 28 Joint Apprenticeship Committee (JAC) is a labor–management committee which operates a 4-year apprenticeship training program designed to teach sheet metal skills. Apprentices enrolled in the program receive training both from classes and from on-the-job work experience. Upon completing the program, apprentices become journeyman members of Local 28. Successful completion of the program is the principal means of attaining union membership.

In 1964, the New York State Commission for Human Rights determined that the union and JAC had excluded African-Americans from the union and apprenticeship program in violation of state law. The Commission, among other things, found that the union had never had any black members or apprentices, and that "admission to apprenticeship is conducted largely on a nepot[is]tic basis involving sponsorship by incumbent union members," creating an impenetrable barrier for nonwhite applicants. The union and JAC were ordered to "cease and desist" their racially discriminatory practices. Over the next 18 years and innumerable trips to court, the union did not remedy the discrimination.

To remedy the contempt and the union's refusal to comply with court orders, the court imposed a 29 percent nonwhite membership goal to be met by a certain date, and a $150,000 fine to be placed in a fund designed to increase nonwhite membership in the apprenticeship program and the union. The fund was used for a variety of purposes, including:

- Providing counseling and tutorial services to non-white apprentices, giving them benefits that had traditionally been available to white apprentices from family and friends.

- Providing financial support to employers otherwise unable to hire a sufficient number of apprentices.

- Providing matching funds to attract additional funding for job-training programs.

- Creating part-time and summer sheet metal jobs for qualified nonwhite youths.

- Extending financial assistance to needy apprentices.

- Paying for nonwhite union members to serve as liaisons to vocational and technical schools with sheet metal programs in order to increase the pool of qualified nonwhite applicants for the apprenticeship program.

The union appealed the remedy. Principally, the parties maintain that the Fund and goal exceeds the scope of remedies available under Title VII because it extends race-conscious preferences to individuals who are not the identified victims of their unlawful discrimination. They argue that section 706(g) authorizes a district court to award preferential relief only to actual victims of unlawful discrimination. They maintain that the goal and Fund violates this provision since it requires them to extend benefits to black and Hispanic individuals who are not the identified victims of unlawful discrimination. We reject this argument and hold that section 706(g) does not prohibit a court from ordering, in appropriate circumstances, affirmative race-conscious relief as a remedy for past discrimination. Specifically, we hold that such relief may be appropriate where an employer or a labor union has engaged in persistent or egregious discrimination, or where necessary to dissipate the lingering effects of pervasive discrimination.

The availability of race-conscious affirmative relief under section 706(g) as a remedy for a violation of Title VII furthers the broad purposes underlying the statute. Congress enacted Title VII based on its determination that racial minorities were subject to pervasive and systematic discrimination in employment. It was clear to Congress that the crux of the problem was "to open employment opportunities for Negroes in occupations which have been traditionally closed to them and it was to this problem that Title VII's prohibition against racial discrimination was primarily addressed." Title VII was designed to achieve equality of employment opportunities and remove barriers that have operated in the past to favor an identifiable group of white employees over other employees. In order to foster equal employment opportunities, Congress gave the lower courts broad power under section 706(g) to fashion the most complete relief possible to remedy past discrimination.

In most cases, the court need only order the employer or union to cease engaging in discriminatory practices, and award make-whole relief to the individuals victimized by those practices. In some instances, however, it may be necessary to require the employer or union to take affirmative steps to end discrimination effectively to enforce Title VII. Where an employer or union has engaged in particularly longstanding or egregious discrimination, an injunction simply reiterating Title VII's prohibition against discrimination will often prove useless and will only result in endless enforcement litigation. In such cases, requiring a recalcitrant employer or unions to hire and to admit qualified minorities roughly in proportion to the number of qualified minorities in the workforce may be the only effective way to ensure the full enjoyment of the rights protected by Title VII.

Further, even where the employer or union formally ceases to engage in discrimination, informal mechanisms may obstruct equal employment opportunities. An employer's reputation for discrimination may discourage minorities from seeking available employment. In these circumstances, affirmative race-conscious relief may be the only means available to assure equality of employment opportunities and to eliminate those discriminatory practices and devices which have fostered racially stratified job environments to the disadvantage of minority citizens. Affirmative action promptly operates to change the outward and visible signs of yesterday's racial distinctions and thus, to provide an impetus to the process of dismantling the barriers, psychological or otherwise, erected by past practices.

Finally, a district court may find it necessary to order interim hiring or promotional goals pending the development of non-discriminatory hiring or promotion procedures. In these cases, the use of numerical goals provides a compromise between two unacceptable alternatives: an outright ban on hiring or promotions, or continued use of a discriminatory selection procedure.

We have previously suggested that courts may utilize certain kinds of racial preferences to remedy past discrimination under Title VII. The Courts of Appeals have unanimously agreed that racial preferences may be used, in appropriate cases, to remedy past discrimination under Title VII. The extensive legislative history of the Act supports this view. Many opponents of Title VII argued that an employer could be found guilty of discrimination under the statute simply because of a racial imbalance in his workforce, and would be compelled to implement racial "quotas" to avoid being charged with liability. At the same time, supporters of the bill insisted that employers would not violate Title VII simply because of racial imbalance, and emphasized that neither the EEOC nor the courts could compel employers to adopt quotas solely to facilitate racial balancing. The debate concerning what Title VII did and did not require culminated in the adoption of section 703(j), which stated expressly that the statute did not require an employer or labor union to adopt quotas or preferences simply because of a racial imbalance.

Although we conclude that section 706(g) does not foreclose a court from instituting some sort of racial preferences where necessary to remedy past discrimination, we do not mean to suggest such relief is always proper. The court should exercise its discretion with an eye towards Congress' concern that the measures not be invoked simply to create a racially balanced workforce. In the majority of cases the court will not have to impose affirmative action as a remedy for past discrimination, but need only order the employer or union to cease engaging in discriminatory practices. However, in some cases, affirmative action may be necessary in order effectively to enforce Title VII, such as with persistent or egregious discrimination or to dissipate the effects of pervasive discrimination. The court should also take care to tailor its orders to fit the nature of the violation it seeks to correct.

Here, the membership goal and Fund were necessary to remedy the union and JAC's pervasive and egregious discrimination and its lingering effects. The goal was flexible and thus gives a strong indication that it was not being used simply to achieve and maintain racial balance, but rather as a benchmark against which the court could gauge the union's efforts. Twice the court adjusted the deadline for the goal and has continually approved changes in the size of apprenticeship classes to account for economic conditions preventing the union from meeting its targets. And it is temporary in that it will end as soon as the percentage of minority union members approximates the percentage of minorities in the local labor force. Similarly the fund is scheduled to terminate when the union achieves its membership goal and the court determines it is no longer needed to remedy past discrimination. Also, neither the

goal nor the fund unnecessarily trammels the interests of white employees. They do not require any union members to be laid off, and do not discriminate against existing union members. While whites seeking admission into the union may be denied benefits extended to nonwhite counterparts, the court's orders do not stand as an absolute bar to such individuals; indeed a majority of new union members have been white. Many of the provisions of the orders are race-neutral (such as the requirement that the JAC assign one apprenticeship for every four journeymen workers) and the union and JAC remain free to adopt the provisions of the order for the benefit of white members and applicants. Accordingly, we AFFIRM.

Case Questions

1. Is it clear to you why a court would be able to include in its remedies those who are not directly discriminated against by an employer? Explain.

2. If you were the court and were still trying to get the union to comply with your order 18 years after the fact, what would you have done?

3. As an employer, how could you avoid such a result?

Johnson v. Transportation Agency, Santa Clara County, California   *480 U.S. 616 (1987)*

A female was promoted over a male pursuant to an affirmative action plan voluntarily adopted by the employer to address a traditionally segregated job classification in which women had been significantly underrepresented. A male employee who also applied for the job sued, alleging it was illegal discrimination under Title VII for the employer to consider gender in the promotion process. The U.S. Supreme Court upheld the promotion under the voluntary affirmative action plan. It held that since it was permissible for a public employer to adopt such a voluntary plan, the plan was reasonable, and since the criteria for the plan had been met, gender could be considered as one factor in the promotion.

Brennan, J.

***

In December 1978, the Santa Clara County Transit District Board of Supervisors adopted an Affirmative Action Plan (Plan) for the County Transportation Agency. The Plan implemented a County Affirmative Action Plan, which had been adopted because "mere prohibition of discriminatory practices is not enough to remedy the effects of past practices and to permit attainment of an

equitable representation of minorities, women and handicapped persons." Relevant to this case, the Agency Plan provides that, in making promotions to positions within a traditionally segregated job classification in which women have been significantly underrepresented, the Agency is authorized to consider as one factor the sex of a qualified applicant.

In reviewing the composition of its workforce, the Agency noted in its Plan that women were represented in numbers far less than their proportion of the County labor force in both the Agency as a whole and in five of seven job categories. Specifically, while women constituted 36.4 percent of the area labor market, they composed only 22.4 percent of Agency employees. Furthermore, women working at the Agency were concentrated largely in EEOC job categories traditionally held by women: women made up 76 percent of Office and Clerical Workers, but only 7.1 percent of Agency Officials and Administrators, 8.6 percent of Professionals, 9.7 percent of Technicians, and 22 percent of Service and Maintenance Workers. As for the job classification relevant to this case, none of the 238 Skilled Craft Worker positions was held by a woman. The Plan noted that this underrepresentation of women in part reflected the fact that women had not traditionally been employed in these positions, and that they had not been strongly motivated to seek training or employment in them "because of the limited opportunities that have existed in the past for them to work in such classifications." The Plan also observed that, while the proportion of ethnic minorities in the Agency as a whole exceeded the proportion of such minorities in the County workforce, a smaller percentage of minority employees held management, professional, and technical positions.

The Agency stated that its Plan was intended to achieve "a statistically measurable yearly improvement in hiring, training and promotion of minorities and women throughout the Agency in all major job classifications where they are underrepresented." As a benchmark by which to evaluate progress, the Agency stated that its long-term goal was to attain a workforce whose composition reflected the proportion of minorities and women in the area labor force. Thus, for the Skilled Craft category in which the road dispatcher position at issue here was classified, the Agency's aspiration was that eventually about 36 percent of the jobs would be occupied by women.

The Agency's Plan thus set aside no specific number of positions for minorities or women, but authorized the consideration of ethnicity or sex as a factor when evaluating qualified candidates for jobs in which members of such groups were poorly represented. One such job was the road dispatcher position that is the subject of the dispute in this case.

The Agency announced a vacancy for the promotional position of road dispatcher in the Agency's Roads Division. Twelve County employees applied for the promotion, including Joyce and Johnson. Nine of the applicants, including Joyce and Johnson, were deemed qualified for the job, and were interviewed by a two-person board. Seven of the applicants scored above 70 on this interview, which meant that they were certified as eligible for selection by the appointing authority. The scores awarded ranged from 70 to 80. Johnson was tied for second with a score of 75, while Joyce ranked next with a score of 73. A second interview was conducted by three Agency supervisors, who ultimately recommended that Johnson be promoted.

James Graebner, Director of the Agency, concluded that the promotion should be given to Joyce. As he testified: "I tried to look at the whole picture, the combination of her qualifications and Mr. Johnson's qualifications, their test scores, their expertise, their background, affirmative action matters, things like that . . . I believe it was a combination of all those."

The certification form naming Joyce as the person promoted to the dispatcher position stated that both she and Johnson were rated as well qualified for the job. The evaluation of Joyce read: "Well qualified by virtue of 18 years of past clerical experience including 3½ years at West Yard plus almost 5 years as a [road maintenance worker]." The evaluation of Johnson was as follows: "Well qualified applicant; two years of [road maintenance worker] experience plus 11 years of Road Yard Clerk. Has had previous outside Dispatch experience but was 13 years ago." Graebner testified that he did not regard as significant the fact that Johnson scored 75 and Joyce 73 when interviewed by the two-person board.

Johnson filed a complaint with the EEOC alleging that he had been denied promotion on the basis of sex in violation of Title VII.

In reviewing the employment decision at issue in this case, we must first examine whether consideration of the sex of applicants for Skilled Craft jobs was justified by the existence of a "manifest imbalance" that reflected underrepresentation of women in "traditionally segregated job categories." In determining whether an imbalance exists that would justify taking sex or race into account, a comparison of the percentage of minorities or women in the employer's work force with the percentage in the area labor market or general population is appropriate in analyzing jobs that require no special expertise or training programs designed to provide expertise. Where a job requires special training, however, the comparison should be with those in the labor force who possess the relevant qualifications. The requirement that the "manifest imbalance" relate to a "traditionally segregated job category" provides assurance both that sex or race will be taken into account in a manner consistent with Title VII's purpose of eliminating the effects of employment discrimination, and that the interests of those employees not benefitting from the plan will not be unduly infringed.

It is clear that the decision to hire Joyce was made pursuant to an Agency plan that directed that sex or race be taken into account for the purpose of remedying underrepresentation. The Agency Plan acknowledged the "limited opportunities that have existed in the past," for women to find employment in certain job classifications "where women have not been traditionally employed in significant numbers." As a result, observed the Plan, women were concentrated in traditionally female jobs in the Agency, and represented a lower percentage in other job classifications than would be expected if such traditional segregation had not occurred. Specifically, 9 of the 10 Para-Professionals and 110 of the 145 Office and Clerical Workers were women. By contrast, women were only 2 of the 28 Officials and Administrators, 5 of the 58 Professionals, 12 of the 124 Technicians, none of the Skilled Craft Workers, and 1— who was Joyce—of the 110 Road Maintenance Workers. The Plan sought to remedy these imbalances through "hiring, training and promotion of . . . women throughout the Agency in all major job classifications where they are underrepresented."

The Agency adopted as a benchmark for measuring progress in eliminating underrepresentation the long-term goal of a workforce that mirrored in its major job classifications the percentage of women in the area labor market. Even as it did so, however, the Agency acknowledged that such a figure could not by itself necessarily justify taking into account the sex of applicants for positions in all job categories. For positions requiring specialized training and experience, the Plan observed that the number of minorities and women "who possess the qualifications required for entry into such job classifications is limited." The Plan therefore directed that annual short-term goals be formulated that would provide a more realistic indication of the degree to which sex should be taken into account in filling particular positions. The Plan stressed that such goals "should not be construed as 'quotas' that must be met," but as reasonable aspirations in correcting the imbalance in the Agency's workforce. These goals were to take into account factors such as "turnover, layoffs, lateral transfers, new job openings, retirements and availability of minorities, women and handicapped persons in the area workforce who possess the desired qualifications or potential for placement." The Plan specifically directed that, in establishing such goals, the Agency work with the County Planning Department and other sources in attempting to compile data on the percentage of minorities and women in the local labor force that were actually working in the job classifications constituting the Agency workforce. From the outset, therefore, the Plan sought annually to develop even more refined measures of the underrepresentation in each job category that required attention.

As the Agency Plan recognized, women were most egregiously underrepresented in the Skilled Craft job category, since none of the 238 positions was occupied by a woman. In mid-1980, when Joyce was selected for the road dispatcher position, the Agency was still in the process of refining its short-term goals for Skilled Craft Workers in accordance with the directive of the Plan. This process did not reach fruition until 1982, when the Agency established a short-term goal for that year of 3 women for the 55 expected openings in that job category—a modest goal of about 6 percent for that category.

The Agency's Plan emphasized that the long-term goals were not to be taken as guides for actual hiring decisions, but that supervisors were to consider a host of practical factors in seeking to meet affirmative action objectives, including the fact that in some job categories women were not qualified in numbers comparable to their representation in the labor force.

By contrast, had the Plan simply calculated imbalances in all categories according to the proportion of women in the area labor pool, and then directed that hiring be governed solely by those figures, its validity fairly could be called into question. This is because analysis of a more specialized labor pool normally is necessary in determining underrepresentation in some positions. If a plan failed to take distinctions in qualifications into account in providing guidance for actual employment decisions, it would dictate mere blind hiring by the numbers, for it would hold supervisors to "achievement of a particular percentage of minority employment or membership . . . regardless of circumstances such as economic conditions or the number of available qualified minority applicants . . . ."

The Agency's Plan emphatically did not authorize such blind hiring. It expressly directed that numerous factors be taken into account in making hiring decisions, including specifically the qualifications of female applicants for particular jobs. The Agency's management had been clearly instructed that they were not to hire solely by reference to statistics. The fact that only the long-term goal had been established for this category posed no danger that personnel decisions would be made by reflexive adherence to a numerical standard.

Furthermore, in considering the candidates for the road dispatcher position in 1980, the Agency hardly needed to rely on a refined short-term goal to realize that it had a significant problem of underrepresentation that required attention. Given the obvious imbalance in the Skilled Craft category, and given the Agency's commitment to eliminating such imbalances, it was plainly not unreasonable for the Agency to determine that it was appropriate to consider as one factor the sex of Ms. Joyce in making its decision. The promotion of Joyce thus satisfies the first requirement since it was undertaken to further an affirmative action plan designed to eliminate Agency workforce imbalances in traditionally segregated job categories.

We next consider whether the Agency Plan unnecessarily trammeled the rights of male employees or created an absolute bar to their advancement. The Plan sets aside no positions for women. The Plan expressly states that "[t]he 'goals' established for each Division should not be construed as 'quotas' that must be met." Rather, the Plan merely authorizes that consideration be given to affirmative action concerns when evaluating qualified applicants. As the Agency Director testified, the sex of Joyce was but one of numerous factors he took into account in arriving at his decision. The Plan thus resembles the "Harvard Plan" approvingly noted in *Regents of University of California v. Bakke,* which considers race along with other criteria in determining admission to the college. As the Court observed: "In such an admissions program, race or ethnic background may be deemed a 'plus' in a particular applicant's file, yet it does not insulate the individual from comparison with all other candidates for the available seats." Similarly, the Agency Plan requires women to compete with all other qualified applicants. No persons are automatically excluded from consideration; all are able to have their qualifications weighed against those of other applicants.

In addition, Johnson had no absolute entitlement to the road dispatcher position. Seven of the applicants were classified as qualified and eligible, and the Agency Director was authorized to promote any of the seven. Thus, denial of the promotion unsettled no legitimate, firmly rooted expectation on the part of Johnson.

Furthermore, while Johnson was denied a promotion, he retained his employment with the Agency, at the same salary and with the same seniority, and remained eligible for other promotions.

Finally, the Agency's Plan was intended to attain a balanced workforce not to maintain one. The Plan contains 10 references to the Agency's desire to "attain" such a balance, but no reference whatsoever to a goal of maintaining it. The Director testified that, while the "broader goal" of affirmative action, defined as "the desire to hire, to promote, to give opportunity and training on an equitable, non-discriminatory basis," is something that is "a permanent part" of "the Agency's operating philosophy," that broader goal "is divorced, if you will, from specific numbers or percentages." The Agency acknowledged the difficulties that it would confront in remedying the imbalance in its workforce, and it anticipated only gradual increases in the representation of minorities and women. It is thus unsurprising that the Plan contains no explicit end date, for the Agency's flexible, case-by-case approach was not expected to yield success in a brief period of time.

Express assurance that a program is only temporary may be necessary if the program actually sets aside positions according to specific numbers. This is necessary both to minimize the effect of the program on other employees, and to ensure that the plan's goals "[are] not being used simply to achieve and maintain . . . balance, but rather as a benchmark against which" the employer may measure its progress in eliminating the underrepresentation of minorities and women. In this case, however, substantial evidence shows that the Agency has sought to take a moderate, gradual approach to eliminating the imbalance in its workforce, one which establishes realistic guidance for employment decisions, and which visits minimal intrusion on the legitimate expectations of other employees. Given this fact, as well as the Agency's express commitment to "attain" a balanced workforce, there is ample assurance that the Agency does not seek to use its Plan to maintain a permanent racial and sexual balance.

In evaluating the compliance of an affirmative action plan with Title VII's prohibition on discrimination, we must be mindful of "this Court's and Congress's consistent emphasis on 'the value of voluntary efforts to further the objectives of the law.'" The Agency in the case before us has undertaken such a voluntary effort, and has done so in full recognition of both the difficulties and the potential for intrusion on males and nonminorities. The Agency has identified a conspicuous imbalance in job categories traditionally segregated by race and sex. It has made clear from the outset, however, that employment decisions may not be justified solely by reference to this imbalance, but must rest on a multitude of practical, realistic factors. It has therefore committed itself to annual adjustment of goals so as to provide a reasonable guide for actual hiring and promotion decisions. The Agency earmarks no positions for anyone; sex is but one of several factors that may be taken into account in evaluating qualified applicants for a position. As both the Plan's language and its manner of operation attest, the Agency has no intention of establishing a workforce whose permanent composition is dictated by rigid numerical standards.

We therefore hold that the Agency appropriately took into account as one factor the sex of Diane Joyce in determining that she should be promoted to the road dispatcher position. The decision to do so was made pursuant to an affirmative action plan that represents a moderate, flexible, case-by-case approach to effecting a gradual improvement in the representation of minorities and women in the Agency's workforce. Such a plan is fully consistent with Title VII, for it embodies the contribution that voluntary employer action can make in eliminating the vestiges of discrimination in the workplace. Accordingly, the judgment of the Court of Appeals is AFFIRMED.

Case Questions

1. What do you think of the Court's decision in this case? Does it make sense to you? Why or why not?

2. If you disagree with the Court's decision, what would you as the employer have done instead?

3. Are the Court's considerations for how to institute an acceptable affirmative action program consistent with how you thought affirmative action worked? Explain.

Ricci v. DeStefano, *129 S. Ct. 2658 (2009)*

The City of New Haven administered an objective exam for firefighter promotions to captain and lieutenant. Whites performed better than blacks, and rather than risk a lawsuit by blacks based on violation of Title VII due to disparate impact, the City discarded the results of the exam. White and Hispanic employees who thought they would be able to be promoted based on their test performance sued the city for violation of, among other things, Title VII. The U.S. Supreme Court sided with the firefighters and held that fear of a disparate impact claim is not a viable basis for discriminating against the white and Hispanic firefighters unless the employer can demonstrate a strong evidentiary basis that it would have been liable for disparate impact if it had not taken such action. Though the case actually is based on a disparate impact analysis, it is included here in reverse discrimination since the employer took the action it did in an effort to be more inclusive and not have the exam have a disparate impact upon black candidates.

Kennedy, J.

***

Our analysis begins with this premise: The City's actions would violate the disparate-treatment prohibition of Title VII absent some valid defense. All the evidence demonstrates that the City chose not to certify the examination results because too many whites and not enough minorities would be promoted were the lists to be certified. Without some other justification, this express, race-based decisionmaking violates Title VII's command that employers cannot take adverse employment actions because of an individual's race.

Writing for a plurality in *Wygant* and announcing the strong-basis-in-evidence standard, Justice Powell recognized the tension between eliminating segregation and discrimination on the one hand and doing away with all governmentally imposed discrimination based on race on the other. The plurality stated that those "related constitutional duties are not always harmonious," and that "reconciling them requires . . . employers to act with extraordinary care." The plurality required a strong basis in evidence because "evidentiary support for the conclusion that remedial action is warranted becomes crucial when the remedial program is challenged in court by nonminority employees." An amorphous claim that there has been past discrimination . . . cannot justify the use of an unyielding racial quota."

Congress has imposed liability on employers for unintentional discrimination in order to rid the workplace of "practices that are fair in form, but discriminatory in operation. But it has also prohibited employers from taking adverse employment actions "because of" race. Applying the strong-basis-in-evidence standard to Title VII gives effect to both the disparate-treatment and disparate-impact provisions, allowing violations of one in the name of compliance with the other only in certain, narrow circumstances. The standard leaves ample room for employers' voluntary compliance efforts, which are essential to the statutory scheme and to Congress's efforts to eradicate workplace discrimination. And the standard appropriately constrains employers' discretion in making race-based decisions: It limits that discretion to cases in which there is a strong basis in evidence of disparate-impact liability, but it is not so restrictive that it allows employers to act only when there is a provable, actual violation.

Resolving the statutory conflict in this way allows the disparate-impact prohibition to work in a manner that is consistent with other provisions of Title VII, including the prohibition on adjusting employment-related test scores on the basis of race. Examinations like those administered by the City create legitimate expectations on the part of those who took the tests. As is the case with any promotion exam, some of the firefighters here invested substantial time, money, and personal commitment in preparing for the tests. Employment tests can be an important part of a neutral selection system that safeguards against the very racial animosities Title VII was intended to prevent. Here, however, the firefighters saw their efforts invalidated by the City in sole reliance upon race-based statistics.

If an employer cannot rescore a test based on the candidates' race, then it follows that it may not take the greater step of discarding the test altogether to achieve a more desirable racial distribution of promotion-eligible candidates—absent a strong basis in evidence that the test was deficient and that discarding the results is necessary to avoid violating the disparate-impact provision. Restricting an employer's ability to discard test results (and thereby discriminate against qualified candidates on the basis of their race) also is in keeping with Title VII's express protection of bona fide promotional examinations. For the foregoing reasons, we adopt the strong-basis-in-evidence standard as a matter of statutory construction to resolve any conflict between the disparate-treatment and disparate-impact provisions of Title VII.

Nor do we question an employer's affirmative efforts to ensure that all groups have a fair opportunity to apply for promotions and to participate in the process by which promotions will be made. But once that process has been established and employers have made clear their selection criteria, they may not then invalidate the test results, thus upsetting an employee's legitimate expectation not to be judged on the basis of race. Doing so, absent a strong basis in evidence of an impermissible disparate impact, amounts to the sort of racial preference that Congress has disclaimed, and is antithetical to the notion of a workplace where individuals are guaranteed equal opportunity regardless of race.

We hold only that, under Title VII, before an employer can engage in intentional discrimination for the asserted purpose of avoiding or remedying an unintentional disparate impact, the employer must have a strong basis in evidence to believe it will be subject to disparate-impact liability if it fails to take the race-conscious, discriminatory action.

On the record before us there is no evidence—let alone the required strong basis in evidence—that the tests were flawed because they were not job-related or because other, equally valid and less discriminatory tests were available to the City. Fear of litigation alone cannot justify an employer's reliance on race to the detriment of individuals who passed the examinations and qualified for promotions. The City's discarding the test results was impermissible under Title VII.

The record in this litigation documents a process that, at the outset, had the potential to produce a testing procedure that was true to the promise of Title VII: No individual should face workplace discrimination based on race. Respondents thought about promotion qualifications and relevant experience in neutral ways. They were careful to ensure broad racial participation in the design of the test itself and its administration. As we have discussed at length, the process was open and fair.

The problem, of course, is that after the tests were completed, the raw racial results became the predominant rationale for the City's refusal to certify the results. The injury arises in part from the high, and justified, expectations of the candidates who had participated in the testing process on the terms the City had established for the promotional process. Many of the candidates had studied for months, at considerable personal and financial expense, and thus the injury caused by the City's reliance on raw racial statistics at the end of the process was all the more severe. Confronted with arguments both for and against certifying the test results—and threats of a lawsuit either way—the City was required to make a difficult inquiry. But its hearings produced no strong evidence of a disparate-impact violation, and the City was not entitled to disregard the tests based solely on the racial disparity in the results.

If, after it certifies the test results, the City faces a disparate-impact suit, then in light of our holding today it should be clear that the City would avoid disparate-impact liability based on the strong basis in evidence that, had it not certified the results, it would have been subject to disparate-treatment liability.

REVERSED AND REMANDED

Chapter 6

Race and Color Discrimination

Learning Objectives

By the time you finish this chapter, you should be able to:

LO1 Discuss and give details on the history of race discrimination and civil rights in the United States.

LO2 Explain the relevance of the history of civil rights to present-day workplace race discrimination issues.

LO3 Set forth the findings of several recent studies on race inequalities.

LO4 Identify several ways that race and color discrimination are manifested in the workplace.

LO5 Explain why national origin issues have recently been included under race discrimination claims by the EEOC.

LO6 Describe ways in which an employer can avoid potential liability for race and color discrimination.

Opening Scenarios

SCENARIO 1

1) Mary, an Asian employee with light skin tone, reports that her manager, Joan, who is a darker skin-toned Asian, is saying negative things to Mary about the color of Mary's lighter skin. The comments include statements such as that Mary thinks she (Mary) is better than other employees, Mary is not as special as Mary thinks she is, and so on. Joan also constantly calls Mary "Sunshine" in a sarcastic way, which Mary takes as a reference to Mary's lighter skin. Mary is afraid that Joan will give her a bad evaluation. Mary is also embarrassed about having this constantly happen in front of other employees. Are Joan's actions more than just unprofessional behavior, are they Illegal?

SCENARIO 2

2) A black female employee is terminated during a downsizing at her place of employment. The decision was made to terminate the two worst employees, and she was one of them. The employer had not told the employee of her poor performance nor given her any negative feedback during evaluations to enable her to assess her performance and govern herself accordingly. In fact, there were specific orders not to give her any negative feedback. The employee sues for racial discrimination, alleging it was a violation of Title VII for the employer not to give her appropriate negative feedback during evaluations to prevent her from being put in the position of being terminated. Does the employee win? Why or why not?

SCENARIO 3

3) An employer has a "no-beard" policy, which applies across the board to all employees. A black employee tells the employer he cannot shave without getting severe facial bumps from ingrown hairs. The employer replies that the policy is without exception and the employee must comply. The employee refuses and is later terminated. The employee brings suit under Title VII on the basis of race discrimination. Does he win? Why? Why not?

Statutory Basis

It shall be an unlawful employment practice for an employer—

(1) to fail or refuse to hire or to discharge any individual, or otherwise to discriminate against any individual with respect to his compensation, terms, conditions, or privileges of employment, because of such individual's race, color . . . or

(2) to limit, segregate, or classify his employees or applicants for employment in any way which would deprive or tend to deprive any individual of employment opportunities or otherwise adversely affect his status as an employee, because of such individual's race, color . . . [Title VII of the Civil Rights Act of 1964, as amended, 42 U.S.C. § 2000e-2(a).]

Note: Not a semester goes by that white students do not ask: "Which term should we use: 'black' or 'African-American'?" They are unsure which term to use for fear of offending. You may have noticed that the terms are used interchangeably throughout the text. If in doubt, simply ask. This is particularly important for managers and supervisors, as it indicates a respect for the employee's feelings. Even if you do not ask, our experience has been that it rarely matters and most blacks are not offended by the choice of one or the other.

Surprised?

LO1

LO2

Race is the first of the prohibited categories in Title VII, the main reason for passage of the law, and it remains, even today, a factor in the lives of many employees. At the same time we can point to having elected President Barack Obama the country's first African-American president, having had two black secretaries of state, and Oprah Winfrey topping the Forbes list of the wealthiest Americans, the Southern Poverty Law Center issued a report in February 2011 that, for the first time since it began tracking hate groups in the United States, the number of groups has risen to over 1,000.[1] Race still matters more than many may realize. So much so that it might surprise you to discover the following:

LO3

- Research showed that employers would rather hire a white man who had served time in prison than a black man who had not.[2]

- When researchers sent out identical résumés for jobs listed in the newspaper, with the only difference being the names of the applicants, those with "ethnic" names like Jamal or Lakiesha received 50 percent fewer callbacks for jobs than the identical résumés with traditionally white names like Megan or Brad. This remained true even when the ethnic applicants were given zip codes that indicated that the applicant lived in an area of higher socioeconomic status.[3]

- In addition to visual profiling, researchers have found linguistic profiling— African-Americans who leave messages in response to ads often never receive return calls, while whites almost always do.[4]

- In 2008, blacks were making about $.62 for every dollar whites made. In 2007 it was $.60. In the mid-1970s it had narrowed to about $.50 on the dollar.[5]

- During oral arguments in the *Lopez v. Gonzales*[6] and *Toledo-Flores v. United States*[7] cases that could impact thousands of immigrants, U.S. Supreme Court Justice Antonin Scalia made a reference to one of the parties in a case, a Mexican who had been deported back to his country, as someone unlikely to keep from drinking tequila on the chance he could return to the United States.[8]

- In the 2004 elections in Alabama, voters voted to keep the Alabama constitution's language that says "separate schools shall be provided for white and colored children, and no child of either race shall be permitted to attend a school of the other race."[9]

- A full-time paid intern hired over the phone to work at an Iowa cosmetics company as a cosmetics formulator because she was in England at the time, arrived in Iowa, only to be told by her supervisor that everyone would be "surprised" that she was black. She was given no work as other white interns were, despite her continually asking for it. She was fired shortly thereafter.[10]

- At Charapp Ford South, a car dealership near Pittsburgh, two black employees who complained about constant racial harassment in the workplace allegedly found a document that suggested "ten ways to kill" African-Americans. When they complained, a manager told them that "people [around here] wanted to see blacks washing cars, not selling them."[11]

- A temp agency used code words to supply Jamestown Container Co. and Whiting Door Mfg. Co. with the white male employees they requested, denying placements to minorities and women.[12]

- The president of a staffing services company allegedly told Carolyn Red Bear, a Native American employee, many derogatory statements that had been made about her "ethnic" appearance, alleging that she did not "fit in" with the white community and should seek employment more consistent with the skills of Native Americans. She was terminated for refusing to comply with a directive to cut her hair, change her last name, and stop "rubbing in" her heritage.[13]

- A congressionally commissioned study by the Institute of Medicine found that "bias, prejudice, and stereotyping on the part of health care providers" contributes to African-Americans being less likely than whites to receive appropriate heart medication, coronary artery bypass surgery, and kidney transplants, as well as being more likely to receive a lower quality of basic clinical services such as intensive care.[14]

- Nearly half of white Bostonians surveyed said that African-Americans and Hispanics are less intelligent than whites and that African-Americans are harder to get along with than other ethnic groups.[15]

- A five-year, seven-volume study by the Russell Sage Foundation found that "racial stereotypes and attitudes heavily influenced the labor market, with blacks landing at the very bottom."[16]

- A survey of new recruits and minority firefighters at the Los Angeles Fire Department found that 87 of them had either experienced or were aware of discrimination and that hazing and discrimination are rampant. In one case, a black firefighter said white firefighters mixed dog food into his spaghetti dinner. After reporting it, he experienced verbal slurs and insults by firefighters "barking like dogs."[17]

- In DeKalb County, GA, three white and one black employee sued for race discrimination. The black employee alleged he was terminated because he refused to discriminate against white managers when he was told to withhold information from white employees so they would appear incompetent. The white employees alleged they were replaced with black employees in an effort to create a "darker administration" to reflect DeKalb's racial makeup.[18]

- The EEOC settled a case in which supervisors routinely used "egregious" ethnic slurs for African-Americans, Hispanics, and Asians and said things like "It should not be against the law to shoot Mexican men, women, and children or to shoot African-Americans and Chinese people," and "If I had my way I'd gas them [referring to African-American employees] like Hitler did the Jews."[19]

Unfortunately, there are many more items that could be added to this list. We gave you this sampling of wide-ranging race-related news items so that you can see how much racism is still a factor of life in the United States and in how many ways it can be manifested by individuals of any status. We included so many, and such varied, items because unless these issues are on your radar screen, you may be totally unaware of them. This is a luxury that a manager, supervisor, or business owner cannot afford. A 2008 *USAToday*/Gallup poll found that a majority of Americans say racism against blacks is widespread, including 51 percent of whites, 59 percent of Hispanics, and a whopping 78 percent of blacks.[20] After the election of the first black U.S. president, the numbers went up somewhat,[21] but by the next year, they had gone back to pre-Obama levels.[22]

If any of this surprises you, you are not alone. As you can see from the 2008 poll above, there is a large gap between what whites and Hispanics believe about race and what blacks believe (51 and 59 percent vs. 78 percent). This is consistent with a 2001 Gallup poll reporing that 76 percent of whites, *including 9 out of 10 under 30* (emphasis added because our experience shows most students think it is only older people who discriminate), thought African-Americans were now being treated fairly or somewhat fairly, compared to only 38 percent of African-Americans who thought so.[23] It also makes sense given that much of our attitude stems from our own personal experience as well as history. The history of slavery and its aftermath represented quite a different experience for whites and Hispanics than blacks. Hispanics, and whites of course, have their own history here also, and you can see that reflected in the numbers.

You can see what a problem these findings would present in the workplace. Not only could discrimination be occurring, but, as a manager, you could possibly not realize it. Much of the race discrimination now occurring in the workplace is not as overt as it was before Title VII (see Exhibit 6.1, "Classified Ads, 1961"), but it is still very much a factor in employment. (See Exhibits 6.2, "Equal Income?" and 6.7, "EEOC's Revised Rule Guidance.") And, as you can also see from some of the items in our sampling, race discrimination in the workplace does not occur in a vacuum. It is part of a much larger picture of race-based discrimination in the greater society.

Working to get future managers and supervisors to see this larger picture is a big part of what this chapter is about. The more you can see the bigger picture, the less likely you are to be a part of unnecessary claims of workplace race discrimination. That is why we can't simply tell you the law and leave it at that. The law has been in place for over 40 years and race discrimination claims are still very much a part of Title VII. They have risen every decade since the law was passed and still account for over one-third of the EEOC's total claims filed. This is consistent with the research findings. What we are seeing as the Title VII system is still being fine-tuned through litigation, legislation, and regulatory efforts is that supervisors and managers often do not recognize race discrimination or its effects when they occur. We do not want that to happen to you. We want to provide you with an effective and basic background in the area of race discrimination so you have the tools you need to protect your employer from liability for workplace discrimination.

Exhibit 6.1 *Classified Ads, 1961*

The exhibit below, taken from an actual newspaper classified ad section from 1961, is typical of want ads found in newspapers before Title VII was passed in 1964. For publication purposes, names and phone numbers have been omitted. It now illegal to advertise for males, females, or racial groups.

Male Help Wanted

SOUTH ATLANTA
PERMANENT position for 2 young men 18-35, must be ambitious, high school graduate, and neat appearing. $85 week guaranteed, plus bonus. Opportunity to earn in excess of $100 per week. Must have desire to advance with company. For interview call...

ATTN YOUNG MEN
18-25, SINGLE, free to travel, New York and Florida, returns for clearing house for publishers. New car, transportation furnished. Expense account to start. Salary plus commission. We train you. Apply...

10 BOYS
14 OR OVER. Must be neat in appearance to work this summer. Salary 75 cent per hour. Will be supervised by trained student counselor. Apply...

MAN experienced in selling and familiar with the laundry and dry cleaning business needed to sell top brands of supplies to laundries and dry cleaning plants. This is an excellent opportunity for a man who is willing to work for proper rewards. Salary and comm. Reply to...

EXPERIENCED dairy man to work in modern dairy in Florida. Must be married, sober, and reliable. Salary $60 per week for 6 days with uniform, lights and water—furnished. Excellent house. Write...

SALESMEN
THIS corporation provides its salesmen with a substantial weekly drawing account. New men are thoroughly trained in the field with emphasis directed toward high-executive income bracket. Men experienced in securities, encyclopedias, and other intangibles who can stand rigid investigation, are dependable, and own late-model car. Reply to...

Situations Wanted, Female   24

SECRETARY—RECEPTIONIST (experienced). Ex-Spanish teacher desires diversified permanent position. Responsible, personable, like people, unencumbered. Can travel.

EXPERIENCED executive secretary with college degree, top skills, currently employed—seeks better position with opportunity for advancement and good salary.

SECRETARY desires typing at home, evenings, and weekends.

COLORED EMPLOYMENT

Help Wanted Male, Colored   26

CURB BOYS
DAY or night shift. No experience necessary. Good tips. Apply in person only.

HOUSEMAN, chauffeur. Must be experienced. Recent references, driver's license, health card required. Must be sober, reliable. Write...

RESTAURANT COOK
FOR frying and dinner cooking. Age 22-35. Must be sober, dependable and well-experienced. Salary $250-$275 for good man. Apply...

SOBER, experienced service station porter. No Sundays. Top pay.

PART-TIME lawn and yard maintenance man.

EXP service station porter, 6-day wk. Good sal.

KITCHEN porters, also ware washers. Apply...

Situations Wanted, Male, Col.   28

YOUNG man wants job. Short order and plain cooking, experienced.

Help Wanted, Female, Col.   29

MAID, free to travel with family, $35 to $50 week. Free room and board.

LAUNDRY MARKER—Experienced. 40 hours—pay hourly basis.

SHIRT girl. Experienced.

SHIRT girl, Experienced. Good pay. Good hours. Apply in person.

WAITRESS, experienced, for lunch counter. Over 40. Call...

Situation Wanted, Female, Col.   31

COOK-MAID (experienced)—desires Monday, Wednesday, Friday. References and health card.

MAID wants 5 days week. References.

GIRL WANTS 5 DAYS

MAID wants 5 days work. Will live-in.

MID-TEEN girl desires maid or office work.

Exhibit 6.2 *Equal Income?*

According to 2006 U.S. Census data, Asian Americans had higher personal income than any other racial demographic except holders of graduate degrees. Whites with advanced degrees had the highest median income. African-Americans earned 22 percent less than whites. Hispanics/Latinos had the lowest overall median income, with 28.51 percent less than whites and 35 percent less than Asian Americans.

Source: U.S. Census Bureau, http://pubdb3.census.gov/macro/032006/perinc/new03_000.htm.

According to WCBS radio:

U.S. Census data indicate that Queens, New York, is the only U.S. county of 65,000 or more residents where the median income of African-Americans is greater than that of whites. Black median income was $51,000, while white median income was $50,900. Asian American income was nearly $53,000, while Hispanic income was $44,000. Across the river in Manhattan, the situation is quite different, with the largest gap of any other large county in the country, white median income was $86,000 and African-American income was $28,000.

Source: "Median Income for Blacks Greater Than Whites in Queens," October 2, 2006, http://forum.dvdtalk.com/archive/t-480980.html.

Evolving Definitions of Race

When someone says the word *race,* what do you think of? Chances are, most of us think of black or white. We find ourselves at a rather interesting juncture regarding race claims at this point in time. For virtually the entire time Title VII has been in existence, race has been almost exclusively about African-Americans and whites, with discrimination against other groups considered primarily under the national origin category. (See Exhibits 6.3, "EEOC's Revised Race/National Origin Guidance," and 6.4, "Hispanic: Race or National Origin—and Who Is Included?") As you have seen in previous chapters, the long and extensive history leading up to the passage of the Civil Rights Act and the court interpretations of it afterward bear this out.

Exhibit 6.3 *EEOC's Revised Race/National Origin Guidance*

New forms of discrimination are emerging. With a growing number of interracial marriages and families and increased immigration, racial demographics of the workforce have changed and the issue of race discrimination in America is multidimensional. Over the years, EEOC has received an increasing number of race and color discrimination charges that allege multiple or intersecting prohibited bases such as age, disability, gender, national origin, and religion.

Source: http://eeoc.gov/initiatives/e-race/why_e-race.html.

Exhibit 6.4 *Hispanic: Race or National Origin—and Who Is Included?*

Ever wonder where racial categories come from? In this interesting exhibit, you get to see (1) how a court addresses certain groups being left out of a definition of Hispanic (note especially footnote 1) and (2) how the government comes up with racial classifications and how they find their way into the mainstream. The first is an excerpt from a discrimination case; the second is a document from the U.S. Census Bureau about how Asians will be added to the minimum categories and how Hispanics will be classified in the census. While reading the document and noting all the effort and energy given to this issue, ponder the necessity of having such classifications at all.

(1)

Rocco Luiere, Jr., "the son of a Spanish mother whose parents were born in Spain," owns seventy-five percent of the shares in Jana-Rock Construction, Inc. Luiere and Jana-Rock bring a challenge under the Equal Protection Clause of the Fourteenth Amendment to New York's "affirmative action" statute for minority-owned businesses, because the law does not include in its definition of "Hispanic" people of Spanish or Portuguese descent unless they also come from Latin America. The plaintiffs allege that by distinguishing among different subclasses of Hispanics, Article 15-A contains an explicit classification on the basis of national origin that should be subjected to strict scrutiny, and that under strict scrutiny New York's definition of "Hispanic" would fail. Applying rational basis review rather than strict scrutiny, the district court entered judgment in favor of the defendants and dismissed the complaint.

When a plaintiff challenges "racial classifications, imposed by whatever federal, state, or local governmental actor, [the classifications] must be analyzed by a reviewing court under strict scrutiny. In other words, such classifications are constitutional only if they are narrowly tailored measures that further compelling governmental interests."[1]

"The purpose of strict scrutiny is to 'smoke out' illegitimate uses of race by assuring that the legislative body is pursuing a goal important enough to warrant use of a highly suspect tool."

But once the government has shown that its decision to resort to explicit racial classifications survives strict scrutiny by being narrowly tailored to achieve a compelling interest, its program is no longer presumptively suspect. We do not think that it is appropriate to apply automatically strict scrutiny a second time in determining whether an otherwise valid affirmative action program is underinclusive for having excluded a particular plaintiff. In order to trigger strict scrutiny, such a plaintiff—like other plaintiffs with equal-protection claims—must demonstrate that his or her exclusion was motivated by a discriminatory purpose. Because the plaintiffs do not otherwise challenge the constitutional propriety of New York's race-based affirmative action program, and because Luiere and Jana-Rock cannot show that New York adopted its chosen definition of "Hispanic" for a discriminatory purpose or that its definition lacks a rational basis, we agree with the district court's judgment for the defendants and affirm.

Source: *Jana-Rock Construction, Inc. v. New York State Department of Economic Development, Division of Minority & Women's Business Development,* 438 F.3d 195 (2d Cir. 2006).

(2) RACIAL AND ETHNIC CLASSIFICATIONS USED IN CENSUS 2000 AND BEYOND

Introduction. The purpose of this document is to provide information about changes to the questions on race and Hispanic origin that have occurred for the Census 2000. These changes conform to the revisions of the standards for the classification of federal data on race and ethnicity

[1] The classifications that are the subject of this appeal are based on national origin rather than race. It is undisputed, however, that principles of analysis applicable to race-based affirmative action programs are the same as those applicable to national-origin-based affirmative action programs. We therefore use the terms interchangeably.

continued

Exhibit 6.4 *continued*

promulgated by the Office of Management and Budget (OMB) in October 1997.

Old Standards. In response to legislative, programmatic, and administrative requirements of the federal government, the OMB in 1977 issued Statistical Policy Directive Number 15, "Race and Ethnic Standards for Federal Statistics and Administrative Reporting." In these standards, four racial categories were established: American Indian or Alaskan Native, Asian or Pacific Islander, Black, and White. In addition, two ethnicity categories were established: Hispanic origin and Not of Hispanic origin. Although the Census Bureau has traditionally used more categories for decennial censuses, those categories collapsed into the four minimum race categories identified by the OMB, plus the category Some Other Race.

Reason for Changing the Old Standards. The racial and ethnic makeup of the country has changed since 1977, giving rise to the question of whether those standards still reflected the diversity of the country's present population. In response to this criticism, the OMB initiated a review of the Directive. This review included (1) organizing a workshop to address the issues by the National Academy of Science, (2) convening four public hearings, and (3) appointing an Interagency Committee for the Review of Racial and Ethnic Standards, which later developed a research agenda and conducted several research studies. The result of the Committee's efforts was a report describing recommended changes to the Directive. The members of the Committee included representatives of more than 30 agencies that covered the many diverse federal requirements for data on race and ethnicity. In 1997, the OMB accepted almost all of the recommendations of the Interagency Committee, resulting in changes to the standards.

What Are the New Standards and When Do They Take Effect?

In October 1997, the Office of Management and Budget (OMB) announced the revised standards for federal data on race and ethnicity. The minimum categories for race are now: American Indian or Alaska Native; Asian; Black or African-American; Native Hawaiian or Other Pacific Islander; and White. Instead of allowing a multiracial category as was originally suggested in public and congressional hearings, the OMB adopted the Interagency Committee's recommendation to allow respondents to select one or more races when they self-identify. With the OMB's approval, the Census 2000 questionnaires also include a sixth racial category: Some Other Race. There are also two minimum categories for ethnicity: Hispanic or Latino and Not Hispanic or Latino. Hispanics and Latinos may be of any race.

How Should Hispanics or Latinos Answer the Race Question?

People of Hispanic origin may be of any race and should answer the question on race by marking one or more race categories shown on the questionnaire, including White, Black or African-American, American Indian or Alaska Native, Asian, Native Hawaiian or Other Pacific Islander, and Some Other Race. Hispanics are asked to indicate their origin in the question on Hispanic origin, not in the question on race, because in the federal statistical system ethnic origin is considered to be a separate concept from race.

What Racial Categories Will Be Used in Current Surveys and Other Data Collections by the Census Bureau?

By January 1, 2003, all current surveys must comply with the 1997 revisions to the Office of Management and Budget's standards for data on race and ethnicity, which establish a minimum of five

continued

categories for race: American Indian or Alaska Native, Asian, Black or African-American, Native Hawaiian or Other Pacific Islander, and White. Respondents will be able to select one or more of these racial categories. The minimum categories for ethnicity will be Hispanic or Latino and Not Hispanic or Latino. Tabulations of the racial categories will be shown as long as they meet agency standards for data quality and confidentiality protection. For most surveys, however, tables will show data at most for the White, Black, and Asian populations.

Source: U.S. Census Bureau, Population Division, Special Population Staff, http://www.census.gov/population/www/socdemo/race/racefactcb.html.

But as the United States takes in more immigrants and they join the workforce and bring claims involving workplace discrimination, what constitutes race discrimination is changing. The term *race,* in the context of employment discrimination, is being used differently than it had been. For instance, on April 16, 2007, you will likely recall that Virginia Tech University senior Cho Seung-Hui shot and killed 32 people and wounded 25 others on the university campus. It was a while before police could identify the gunman. Three days later, the *Atlanta Journal and Constitution* ran a headline: "Tragedy strikes; then race enters the picture." Seung-Hui was born in Korea but was a permanent resident of the United States. According to the article, the first official identification of the Virginia Tech gunman was of his race and gender: "We do know that he was an Asian male," the university president said. It surprised us to see race (rather than national origin) used in this context. However, especially since the events of September 11, 2001, with its resulting backlash against Middle Easterners, and the simultaneous growing, visible presence of Hispanics, Southeast Asians, and other ethnicities in this country, it is clear that there is a trend toward negative treatment of these groups that we should address.

While the editions of this book prior to the last one reflected the situation existing at the times they were published, our last edition expanded and updated the chapter on racism to include discrimination against people other than the traditional groups of black and white. Keep in mind that we always addressed workplace discrimination on the basis of ethnicity or national origin; it was simply dealt with in a separate chapter because that is the way the law generally handled it. There will continue to be a separate chapter on national origin discrimination, as the issues called upon in such cases have their own history and legal interpretation to which attention must be given. However, in keeping with the changing times and our rapidly changing American demographics, we also will address other ethnicities in this chapter.

In expanding our race coverage, however, it is important that we preserve the history and background of the Civil Rights Act of 1964 so that the law can continue to be understood in its proper context; that is, the context of slavery, Jim Crow, and the fight for civil rights (and the lingering effects of each) in

Exhibit 6.5   *Reality of Intentional Job Discrimination*

In 2002, Alfred W. Blumrosen and Ruth G. Blumrosen, well-respected lawyers, law professors, and civil rights researchers, released an unprecedented, comprehensive, groundbreaking study of workplace discrimination called *The Reality of Intentional Job Discrimination in Metropolitan America—1999.* The objective of the Ford Foundation–funded study was "to advance the public 'sense of reality' concerning the present extent of intentional job discrimination." The study examined 160,297 EEO-1 reports (discussed in Chapter 4) supplied to the federal government by private employers with 100 or more employees and federal contractors with 50 or more employees, for the period 1975–1999. It identified intentional employment discrimination by applying legal standards to statistics of the race, gender, and ethnic composition of large and medium-sized employers in the private sector. The report contained statistical information on 40 individual states, as well as the nation as a whole.

The report concluded that "a substantial part of the public has erroneously assumed that intentional job discrimination is either a thing of the past, or the acts of individual 'bad apples' in an otherwise decent work environment . . . Meanwhile, thousands of employers have continued systematic restriction of qualified minority and female workers, and these workers have lost opportunities to develop and exercise the skills and abilities that would warrant higher wages." The report found that African-Americans "still bear the severest brunt of this discrimination . . . Thirty-five thousand business establishments discriminated against 586,000 African-Americans. Ninety percent of these black workers were affected by establishments that were so far below the average utilization that there was only a 1 in 100 chance that this happened by accident and half by 'hard core' employers who had been discriminating for at least nine years."

Source: Alfred W. Blumrosen and Ruth G. Blumrosen, *The Reality of Intentional Job Discrimination in Metropolitan America—1999* (2002), http://www.eeo1.com/1999_NR/Title.pdf.

which it occurred. It is important that we not marginalize what has been, and continues to be, a long-standing, persistent, and maddeningly stubborn issue in this country: discrimination against African-Americans (see Exhibit 6.5, "Reality of Intentional Job Discrimination"). This is not a value judgment as to the relative importance of discrimination against one group versus another. Rather, it is a recognition of the long, tortuous, and lingering history and impact of traditional notions of race discrimination in the United States and the role that the fight for equality and civil rights for African-Americans has played in all groups now expecting to be treated equally. The expanded notion of race will not neglect either the important basis for the law that birthed the legislation in the first place, or the present-day effects that continue to persist even as other groups come into the United States and rise to become accepted as a part of our country rather than "outsiders." This is a factor that the Russell Sage/Harvard study on race discussed.

In taking the approach we now do, we want to recognize that the willingness of other groups to exercise their rights under the law by using the race category rather than, or in addition to, the national origin category is a trend

Exhibit 6.6 *EEOC's E-RACE Initiative*

THE E-RACE INITIATIVE (ERADICATING RACISM AND COLORISM FROM EMPLOYMENT)

Why Do We Need E-RACE?

The most frequently filed claims with the EEOC are allegations of race discrimination, racial harassment, or retaliation arising from opposition to race discrimination. In Fiscal Year 2006, 27,238 charges alleged race-based discrimination, accounting for 36 percent of the charges filed that year.

In a 2005 Gallup poll, 31 percent of Asian Americans surveyed reported having witnessed or experienced incidents of discrimination, the largest percentage of any ethnic group, followed closely by 26 percent of African-Americans, the second largest group. A December 2006 CNN poll conducted by Opinion Research Corporation revealed that 84 percent of 328 Blacks/African-Americans and 66 percent of 703 non-Hispanic Whites/Caucasians think racism is a "very serious" or "somewhat serious" problem in America.

Color discrimination in employment seems to be on the rise. In Fiscal Year 1992, the EEOC received 374 charges alleging color-based discrimination. By Fiscal Year 2006, charge-filings alleging color discrimination increased to 1,241. A recent study conducted by a Vanderbilt University professor "found that those with lighter skin earn on average 8 to 15 percent more than immigrants with the darkest skin tone—even when taking into account education and language proficiency. This trend continued even when comparing people of the same race or ethnicity." Similarly, a 2006 University

of Georgia survey revealed that a light-skinned black male with only a bachelor's degree and basic work experience would be preferred over a dark-skinned black male with an MBA and past managerial positions. However, in the case of black female applicants seeking a job, "the more qualified or experienced darker-skinned woman got it, but if the qualifications were identical, the lighter-skinned woman was preferred."

Meanwhile, overt forms of race and color discrimination have resurfaced. In the past decade, some of the American workforce have witnessed nooses, KKK propaganda, and other racist insignia in the workplace. Racial stereotypes and cultural distortions continue to influence some decisions regarding hiring, discipline, evaluations, and advancement.

Finally, some facially neutral employment criteria are significantly disadvantaging applicants and employees on the basis of race and color. Studies reveal that some employers make selection decisions based on names, arrest and conviction records, employment and personality tests, and credit scores, all of which may disparately impact people of color. Further, an employer's reliance on new technology in job searches, such as video résumés, could lead to intentional race or color discrimination based on appearance or a disproportionate exclusion of applicants of color who may not have access to broadband-equipped computers or video cameras.

Collectively, these data show that racial inequality may remain a problem in the 21st century workplace.

Source: http://eeoc.gov/initiatives/e-race/index.html.

we see, note, and here reflect. The EEOC also has seen this trend and, in part because of it, launched a new initiative called E-RACE (Eradicating Racism and Colorism from Employment) intended to address these changes. (See Exhibit 6.6, "EEOC's E-RACE Initiative.") As part of their revised Compliance Manual, issued in 2006, the EEOC outlined the differences between the categories of race, color, and national origin. (See Exhibits 6.7, "EEOC's Revised Race Guidance"; 6.8, "EEOC's National Origin Guidance"; and

Exhibit 6.7 *EEOC's Revised Race Guidance*

WHAT IS "RACE" DISCRIMINATION?

Title VII prohibits employer actions that discriminate, by motivation or impact, against persons because of race. Title VII does not contain a definition of "race," nor has the Commission adopted one. For the collection of federal data on race and ethnicity, the Office of Management and Budget (OMB) has provided the following five racial categories: *American Indian or Alaska Native; Asian; Black or African-American; Native Hawaiian or Other Pacific Islander;* and *White;* and one ethnicity category, *Hispanic or Latino.* The OMB has made clear that these categories are "social-political constructs . . . and should not be interpreted as being genetic, biological, or anthropological in nature."

Title VII's prohibition of race discrimination generally encompasses:

- **Ancestry:** Employment discrimination because of racial or ethnic ancestry. Discrimination against a person because of his or her ancestry can violate Title VII's prohibition against race discrimination. Note that there can be considerable overlap between "race" and "national origin," but they are not identical. For example, discrimination against a Chinese American might be targeted at her Asian ancestry and not her Chinese national origin. In that case, she would have a claim of discrimination based on race, not national origin.

- **Physical Characteristics:** Employment discrimination based on a person's physical characteristics associated with race, such as a person's color, hair, facial features, height, and weight.

- **Race-Linked Illness:** Discrimination based on race-linked illnesses. For example, sickle cell anemia is a genetically-transmitted disease that affects primarily persons of African descent. Other diseases, while not linked directly to race or ethnicity, may nevertheless have a disproportionate impact. For example, Native Hawaiians have a disproportionately high incidence of diabetes. If the employer applies facially neutral standards to exclude treatment for conditions or risks that disproportionately affect employees on the basis of race or ethnicity, the employer must show that the standards are based on generally accepted medical criteria.

- **Culture:** Employment discrimination because of cultural characteristics related to race or ethnicity. Title VII prohibits employment discrimination against a person because of cultural characteristics often linked to race or ethnicity, such as a person's name, cultural dress and grooming practices, or accent or manner of speech. For example, an employment decision based on a person having a so-called black accent, or "sounding white," violates Title VII if the accent or manner of speech does not materially interfere with the ability to perform job duties.

- **Perception:** Employment discrimination against an individual based on a belief that the individual is a member of a particular racial group, regardless of how the individual identifies himself. Discrimination against an individual based on a perception of his or her race violates Title VII even if that perception is wrong.

- **Association:** Employment discrimination against an individual because of his or her association with someone of a particular race. For example, it is unlawful to discriminate against a white person because he or she is married to an African-American or has a multiracial child, or because he or she maintains friendships or otherwise associates with persons of a certain race.

- **Subgroup or "Race Plus":** Employment discrimination against a subgroup of persons in a racial group because they have certain attributes in addition to their race. Thus, for example, it would violate Title VII for an employer to reject black women with preschool-age

continued

children, while not rejecting other women with preschool age children.

- **"Reverse" Race Discrimination:** Title VII prohibits race discrimination against all persons, including Caucasians. A plaintiff may prove a claim of discrimination through direct or circumstantial evidence. Some courts, however, take the position that if a white person relies on circumstantial evidence to establish a reverse

discrimination claim, he or she must meet a heightened standard of proof. The Commission, in contrast, applies the same standard of proof to all race discrimination claims, regardless of the victim's race or the type of evidence used. In either case, the ultimate burden of persuasion remains always on the plaintiff.

Source: EEOC Compliance Manual, Section 15-II, http://www.eeoc.gov.

Exhibit 6.8 *EEOC's National Origin Guidance*

NATIONAL ORIGIN DISCRIMINATION

Whether an employee or job applicant's ancestry is Mexican, Ukrainian, Filipino, Arab, American Indian, or any other nationality, he or she is entitled to the same employment opportunities as anyone else.

ABOUT NATIONAL ORIGIN DISCRIMINATION

National origin discrimination means treating someone less favorably because he or she comes from a particular place, because of his or her ethnicity or accent, or because it is believed that he or she has a particular ethnic background. National origin discrimination also means treating someone less favorably at work because of marriage or other association with someone of a particular nationality.

- **Employment Decisions.** Title VII prohibits any employment decision, including recruitment, hiring, and firing or layoffs, based on national origin.
- **Harassment.** Title VII prohibits offensive conduct, such as ethnic slurs, that creates a hostile work environment based on national origin. Employers are required to take appropriate steps to prevent and correct unlawful harassment.

Likewise, employees are responsible for reporting harassment at an early stage to prevent its escalation.

- **Accent Discrimination.** An employer may not base a decision on an employee's foreign accent unless the accent materially interferes with job performance.
- **English Fluency.** A fluency requirement is only permissible if required for the effective performance of the position for which it is imposed.
- **English-only Rules.** English-only rules must be adopted for non-discriminatory reasons. An English-only rule may be used if it is needed to promote the safe or efficient operation of the employer's business.

COVERAGE OF FOREIGN NATIONALS

Title VII and the other anti-discrimination laws prohibit discrimination against individuals employed in the United States, regardless of citizenship, or those working for American companies in other countries. However, relief may be limited if an individual does not have work authorization.

Source: EEOC Compliance Manual, http://www.eeoc.gov.

6.11, "EEOC's Color Guidance.") The EEOC noted that the Civil Rights Act did not define race (it was understood at the time of the passage of the law, given our country's history and the recent and painful civil rights activity leading up to passage of the law, to include African-Americans and whites), but in light of recent trends, the EEOC undertook to bring some understanding to the matter in a world in which things had changed since passage of the act.

We now think of race under Title VII as a more inclusive concept. We applaud the EEOC's recognition of this trend and have modified our approach accordingly. In the *Alonzo v. Chase Manhattan Bank, N.A* case, provided at the end of the chapter, you can see for yourself the struggle the courts had dealing with this issue when a Hispanic employee sued for national origin discrimination, then amended his complaint to include a claim for race discrimination. Compare the court's analysis about Hispanics and race in *Alonzo* to the discussion of race versus ethnicity in Exhibit 6.4, "Hispanic: Race or National Origin—and Who Is Included?" Do they seem consistent to you?

Things have certainly changed dramatically in the 40-odd years since passage of the Civil Rights Act. But keep the previously mentioned poll in mind: 9 out of 10 whites under 30 believe African-Americans and whites are treated equally. With this mind-set, employers would be less likely to respond appropriately to claims of racial discrimination from nonwhite employees and thus increase the likelihood of liability under Title VII. This is only one of many such polls with similar results. Even in the midst of legalized segregation and Jim Crow, polls showed that whites thought blacks were treated equally. It demonstrates one of the reasons that the disappearance of race discrimination may not necessarily be as realistic in the near future as we would like to think, as per the 2009 poll mentioned above.

In fact, researchers refer to the idea that whites think everything is fair for everyone, so nothing need be done to ensure equal opportunity anymore, as the "new racism."[24] As Congress noted in its resolution apologizing for slavery, because our unique racial history involved systemic, institutionalized, legal, and social race discrimination, we are left with enough of the vestiges to account for much of the racial differences we see reflected in the items above. If managers and supervisors do not realize that vestiges remain, they are likely to run afoul of

the law. We see it in case after case after case. Keep in mind that employers do not need to engage in deliberate, intentional racial discrimination in order to violate the law and the law does not require this in order to find liability. That is why providing information here to address these matters is so important for making workplace decisions that avoid liability.

Despite this, clearly much progress has been made in the area of race discrimination in the workplace since Title VII was enacted. However, as mentioned earlier, the extremely comprehensive, four-year, 1,400-page study of intentional workplace discrimination between 1975 and 1999, released by Alfred and Ruth Blumrosen in 2002,[25] found that workplace discrimination against African-Americans is still the worst of all groups; "the seriousness of intentional job discrimination against black workers by major and significant industries is evident; and the 'playing field' is far from level. However, minorities increased their participation in the labor force by 4.6 million workers beyond the increase resulting from economic growth and increased their share of 'better jobs' as officials, managers, professionals, technical, and sales workers." The study showed that 15 percent of African-Americans experience intentional workplace discrimination.

In addition, there are, in fact, companies that are doing just fine and understand the impact of race in the workplace and work to make sure they do not violate the law. *The Wall Street Journal* reported that after a study of 31,000 of their U.S. jobs showed discrepancies, Eastman Kodak Co. agreed to pay about $13 million in retroactive and current pay raises to 2,000 female and minority employees in New York and Colorado. The pay raise was not in response to a threatened lawsuit, as is generally the case. Employees had complained about it to supervisors the year before, so Kodak conducted the study and determined it would make the correction.[26]

One of the best ways we have found to address this gap in awareness that can lead to employer liability is to give you some of the history of race in our country. We have found in our own classrooms that most of our students fit quite neatly into that "9 out of 10" category. They come into the course thinking everyone is treated equally and see little reason to still have Title VII in force. Until, that is, we show them documentaries on historical events like slavery, the Jim Crow era, and school desegregation riots leading up to its passage and discuss this and the information in this introduction. Then they get it. They are astonished at how clueless (their term, not ours) they were about it all and how little they really knew about this history, yet how important it is to know in order to understand the law, where we are today, and how it impacts their actions in the workplace. It would take volumes to do it any real justice, but we will give you the most significant highlights leading up to passage of Title VII, primarily to address racial discrimination in the workplace, so that you can see what contributes to some of the workplace situations resulting in employer liability.

Before we do this, however, we want you to read the *Jones v. Horseshoe Casino & Hotel* case, included at the conclusion of the chapter. It is a case in which you get to see how racial discrimination can play out in the workplace. We want you to read it before you proceed to the "Background" section below so you can have some sense of why the next section is such an important one for you to be aware of.

Background of Racial Discrimination in the United States

Chances are, the *Jones* case doesn't make a lot of sense to you. You probably can't figure out why, in this day and time, an employer would do such a thing and be so open and blatant about it. You likely think that if Jones was as good as the court said, a casino would be glad to get him. This makes perfect sense if you've never really thought about or been confronted with race discrimination. That's why a bit of background is helpful. None of this makes any sense unless you understand where it comes from. The fact that this took place in Mississippi is not surprising, given its racial history.

LO2

History and its present-day effects account for much of the race discrimination we see manifested today. And make no mistake about it, our history regarding race has been a long, complex, and tortured one. Six months after the death of the erstwhile staunch segregationist, South Carolina Senator Strom Thurmond, in 2003, it was a national media event when a black woman announced she was his daughter and had been privately, but not publicly, acknowledged by him all her life. She had been the result of a union between Thurmond, then a 22-year-old lawyer living with his parents, and her mother, a 16-year-old maid in the household.[27] Despite the fact that the hallmark of Thurmond's career had been supporting racial segregation, including running for president on a segregationist "Dixiecrat" ticket, he had an acknowledged daughter by a black woman and was one of the first southern legislators to hire a black aide in the early 1970s. Complex indeed.

As you recall from the Title VII and affirmative action chapter, Africans arrived in this country in 1619, before the *Mayflower*. Their initial experience was as free people who were contracted as indentured servants. After the first 40 years or so, this changed as the need for cheap labor grew with America's rapid expansion, and slavery came into existence. While a very small number of African-Americans were free, slavery as an integral and defining part of American life lasted for well over 200 years, until after the Civil War ended in 1865. With a slight pause (11 years) for Reconstruction after the Civil War, the next 99 years saw Black Codes and Jim Crow laws legalize and codify racial discrimination.

In many places, there were many more slaves than whites (South Carolina had an 80 percent slave population), so absolute control was necessary in order to prevent slave uprisings, which were a *major* concern for whites. Without having sufficient manpower to exercise this control physically, such control had to be imposed psychologically, as well. This was done quite systematically and with the intention of keeping the system of slavery in place forever. Each of the rules and regulations contained in the Slave Codes, and later, after Reconstruction, in the Black Codes, was designed to do this.

To give you an idea of the detail into which such measures went, a 2002 *USA Today* news article excerpted a quote from an 1822 South Carolina grand jury in response to complaints about slaves wearing clothes made from ordinary cloth. The grand jury said: "Negroes should be permitted to dress only in coarse stuffs [called "Negro cloth" and manufactured by WestPoint Stevens, today the United States' largest producer of bed and bath textiles]. . . . Every distinction should be created between whites and the Negroes, calculated to make the latter feel the superiority of the former."[28] "Drapetomania" was an actual "medical condition" doctors ascribed to slaves who wanted to run away and be free.[29] Clearly the control was comprehensive, all-encompassing, and minutely detailed to accomplish this purpose. It is important to understand this so that you can recognize how insinuated into every aspect of life racism was in this country, and why there were bound to be vestiges long after slavery ended.

When Reconstruction ended, about 11 years after the Civil War was over, the Slave Codes were simply renamed "Black Codes" and used virtually as if slavery had never ended. This system of laws governing black and white relations was based on both law and social custom that was as ironclad as any law ever was. The system, adopted by either law or social custom all over the country, remained in place until the Civil Rights Act of 1964, and in some places well into the 1970s, constantly reasserting the institutionalized role of race in the United States. If you think this was a terribly long time ago, you'd probably be surprised to know that there are audio recordings of actual former slaves telling their stories of what life was like under slavery.[30]

But what do we really mean by "a system" and "the institutionalized role of race"? And why can't we just all forget it and move on? Think back to the information in the prior chapters about how every facet of life was based on race. Doing so is helpful in trying to figure out why race is still such a persistent and pervasive issue in the workplace today.

Race governed every facet of life. In addition to the ways we have already set forth in earlier chapters, blacks were routinely discriminated against by being forced to sit in the balconies of movie theaters or made to attend on days different from those when whites attended. Some fairs had "Negro days" on which African-Americans could attend, and some towns had "Negro days" for African-Americans to shop. Rather than be seated in restaurants, they were generally sent to the back door, where they ordered their food on a take-out basis long before take-out came to be. Staying in hotels was virtually out of the question, even if they had the funds to do so (keep in mind they were relegated to menial labor).

Although they paid full bus fare, in the South, African-Americans had to sit in the back of the bus. They could not simply pay their fare and walk to the back of the bus, as this would mean they were in close contact with whites. Rather, they were required to pay their fare in the front, get off the bus, and reenter through the back, rain or shine. If whites wanted or needed blacks' seats, African-Americans had to give up their seats even though they were full-fare-paying passengers.

African-Americans could not testify against whites in court; look whites in the eye; stay on the sidewalk when whites passed by; be called "Mr.," "Mrs.," or "Miss"; or contradict anything a white person said. The simple act of registering to vote could cost an African-American his or her job, family, home, or life. It was not until the Voting Rights Act of 1965 that African-Americans received full voting rights in the United States. Breach of Jim Crow law or social policy by African-Americans resulted in swift retribution, up to and including death—generally by lynching for males—an event that was often attended by whole families of whites, including children, and treated as a festive family outing, complete with picnic baskets.

In historical terms, this was not that long ago. If you were not alive during that time, then most certainly your parents or grandparents were. Remember that the system officially ended only in 1964, and in many places it, or its effects, lingered on long after—in some places, even until today. For instance, in Atlanta, retiring black police officers are suffering right now because of the police department's racial policy that lingered until the 1970s, which prevented black officers from contributing to a whites-only pension fund. This has resulted in hundreds of dollars a month less in pension payouts to retiring black officers. Along with the difference in pensions, black officers were not permitted to partner with white officers, were made to dress in separate dressing rooms in separate buildings, and were not permitted to arrest white suspects.[31] There are other examples of present-day vestiges:

- Between 2000 and 2004, 16 major insurance cases were settled, covering about 14.8 million policies sold by 90 insurance companies between 1900 and the 1980s to African-Americans who were charged more, as was the custom of the day, simply because they were black. The settlements amounted to more than $556 million. During the high-water mark for burial insurance, as it was known, American insurance companies held policies worth more than $40 billion. According to the Federal Trade Commission, some companies, like Metropolitan Life, built their businesses largely on such policies, which not only charged African-Americans higher premiums, but were specifically targeted to poor African-Americans and often paid out less in benefits than the premiums paid in.

- In 2006, the U.S. Supreme Court unanimously held that the term "boy" used by white managers at an Alabama Tyson Foods plant to refer to black employees could, alone, be used as evidence of workplace race discrimination. The term is one used in the slave and Jim Crow era to refer to black men.[32]

- In 2006, the Delaware Masons fraternal organization signed a compact to end 150-plus years of racial separation. In 12 southern states, white Masons still do not officially recognize black Masons as their brothers.

- In early 2007, nearing the 400th anniversary of the founding of Jamestown, America's first permanent English settlement and an entry point for those coming from Africa to be enslaved, the Virginia House of Delegates expressed "profound regret" for its role in the slave trade and other injustices against African-Americans and Native Americans. Nine members did not cast ballots. In 2001, the Virginia legislature had expressed "profound regret" for its role in the discredited "science" of eugenics that led to the sterilization of well over 6,000 Virginians between 1924 and 1979 under the Racial Integrity Act and the Sterilization Act, in the name of purifying the white race. Virginia's apology was later joined by apologies in Florida, Alabama, North Carolina, and New Jersey. The U.S. Congress is also considering such a proposal.

- In 2008—after years of refusing to do so, but after doing so for Native Americans, Japanese detention camp detainees, and Hawaiians for the overthrow of their government—the U.S. House of Representatives passed a resolution apologizing for slavery, Jim Crow, and its present-day impact on blacks. The Senate passed a similar resolution the next year.

Notice that this is not dull, dry history from eons ago. This is now. We are living the history as we speak. In fact, the last widow of a Civil War veteran just died in May 2004, which is certainly in your lifetime.[33]

We again provided this picture of pre-1964 life in this chapter and in this context because in order to understand why the issue still persists today, it is important to get a picture of what it meant in everyday life for all concerned. It was not until passage of the Civil Rights Act of 1964 that this country was first forced to deal with African-Americans on anything even approaching an equal basis. For virtually their entire history in this country, African-Americans were dealt with as inferiors, with societal laws and customs totally built around that approach. Then came the Civil Rights Act of 1964, attempting to change this 300+-year history overnight. You might now understand a bit better why we have been struggling with the issue ever since.

While African-Americans were visibly fighting for civil rights and an end to segregation, their struggle for civil rights highlighted for other groups that they also had received poor treatment in this country. The struggle for civil rights, in part, helped some of those permitted to realize their full potential and become the successful and productive members of society they longed to be. The Irish went from being so reviled that store windows had signs saying "No Dogs, No Irish," to having John F. Kennedy become a revered first Irish and Catholic president of the United States. Other groups, like Native Americans, Hispanics, and Asians were, for various reasons, castigated, vilified, ostracized, marginalized, and discriminated against by the greater society. They dealt with it in different ways. Asian Americans are now the minority with the highest income, but also with an increasing number of discrimination claims.[34]

But a rising tide lifts all boats, so once the Civil Rights Act was passed, it benefited all groups by protecting them from discrimination. As was stated about Supreme Court Justice Thurgood Marshall, who argued, and won, the *Brown v. Board of Education* case that began to dismantle racial segregation in our country by outlawing segregated public schools, "He created a new legal landscape, where racial equality was an accepted principle. He worked in behalf of black Americans but built a structure of individual rights that became the cornerstone of protections for all Americans."[35] (See Exhibit 6.9, "Profile: Thurgood Marshall.")

Exhibit 6.9 *Profile: Thurgood Marshall (1908–1993), Associate Justice of the U.S. Supreme Court, 1967–1992*

You probably had no idea how different your life would be had it not been for Justice Thurgood Marshall.

Thurgood Marshall was born in Baltimore, Maryland, the son of a steward and a school teacher. He graduated from Lincoln University and from Howard University Law School in 1933. While at Howard, Marshall attracted the attention of Dean Charles Houston, a noted black lawyer and chief legal planner for the NAACP. When he met Marshall, Houston was about to begin a campaign challenging the constitutionality of racial segregation laws in the United States. After law school, Marshall practiced law for a brief period, joined the NAACP as a staff attorney, then took over as chief counsel after Houston in 1938.

When Marshall assumed leadership of the NAACP legal program, racial segregation pervaded every aspect of life in the United States—its legality was hardly questioned, and blacks were not considered full partners in the American republic. The Thirteenth, Fourteenth, and Fifteenth Amendments and the laws enacted to give meaning to their promise of black equality had been emptied of content by decisions of the U.S. Supreme Court. The most influential decision, *Plessy v. Ferguson,* 1896, was understood to give broad approval to providing separate public facilities and services for blacks. The political power of the southern states was such that neither Congress nor the president would support legislation to outlaw lynching, much less to end racial segregation. Marshall and his colleagues determined, therefore, to concentrate their efforts on the courts. Their early cases aimed at documenting the inequalities—for example, in per-pupil spending and teacher pay—that made the segregated public facilities and education offered to blacks by the southern and border states not equivalent to those provided to whites. It was thought that such litigation might lead to significant short-term improvement in the facilities with which blacks were provided. However, the NAACP's ultimate goal and grand design were to persuade the Supreme Court that racial segregation as such was unconstitutional, that regardless of the facilities offered to blacks, it inevitably relegated them to a position of inferiority and second-class citizenship.

After World War II, the pace of litigation quickened, and the Supreme Court struck down particular instances of racial discrimination in interstate travel, primary elections, housing, and criminal justice. Eventually litigation efforts were concentrated on education. By 1954 when Marshall argued *Brown v. Board of Education,* dealing with public school segregation, extensive documentation had been accumulated demonstrating that, as the Court ultimately found, "separate educational facilities are inherently unequal." Soon after, civil rights lawyers won a series of cases that made clear that *Brown* had undermined any constitutional basis for the government to make invidious distinctions in the allocation of goods, services, or benefits on the basis of race.

During his years with the NAACP, Marshall earned a reputation as a tough, shrewd legal tactician with a deceptively easygoing personal style. Southern senators attempted to block his appointment to the U.S. Court of Appeals in 1961, but the nomination was confirmed in 1962. In 1965, President Lyndon B. Johnson named Marshall solicitor-general, and in 1967 Johnson appointed him an associate justice of the Supreme Court.

On the Supreme Court, Marshall usually supported positions taken by civil libertarians, equal rights advocates, and those who construe the procedural guarantees of the Bill of Rights to protect criminal defendants. In the 1970s when many ground-breaking liberal decisions of the later 1950s and the 1960s were restricted by a new conservative majority of justices appointed by President Richard M. Nixon, Marshall became one of the Court's more vocal dissenters, especially in cases such as the *Bakke* decision outlawing reverse racial quotas, where he believed the Court had retreated from a commitment to eliminate racism in public life.

Source: Adapted from Michael Meltsner, "Thurgood Marshall," *Collier's Encyclopedia,* vol. 15. Copyright © 1983 by Macmillan Educational Company. Reprinted by permission of the publisher.

Race: Putting It All Together

LO2

When race has been as ingrained in a culture as it has been in the United States, it is predictable that it is taking a rather long while to rid the workplace of the vestiges of race discrimination. The effects of racially based considerations and decisions linger long after the actual intent to discriminate may have dissipated.

As we saw earlier the U.S. Department of Labor Glass Ceiling Studies in 1991 and 1995 of barriers to full management participation in the workplace by women and minorities found that minorities had made strides in entering the workplace, but a "glass ceiling" exists beyond which minorities rarely progress. The study found that minorities plateau at a lower corporate level than women, who plateau at a lower level than white males.

According to the studies, monitoring for equal access and opportunity was almost never considered a corporate responsibility or a part of the planning and developmental programs and policies of the employer, nor as part of participation with regard to senior management levels. Neither employee appraisals nor total compensation systems were usually monitored. Most companies had inadequate records regarding equal employment opportunity and affirmative action responsibilities in recruitment, employment, and developmental activities for management-level positions.

Such factors militate against serious consideration of full participation by all sectors of the work population and prevent the employer from being presented in the best light should lawsuits arise. If an employer analyzed and monitored workplace information based on the Glass Ceiling considerations, much race discrimination could be discovered and addressed long before it progressed to the litigation stage. As you saw in the affirmative action chapter, that is the approach that the law would prefer employers to take so that liability can be avoided altogether.

The cases in this chapter are specifically chosen to help you learn to recognize race discrimination claims when you see them coming, before they turn into litigation. Pay particular attention to the facts in the cases and the case questions following them. They are specifically developed to make you think about the issue as a manager would so that you will be able to practice analyzing situations for potential liability as they arise and become familiar with issues in this area with which you may not have experience. After thoroughly reading and thinking about the cases, you should feel much more comfortable about being a manager or supervisor who is able to spot trouble in this area and do what needs to be done to avoid it.

General Considerations

Title VII was enacted primarily in response to discrimination against African-Americans in this country, but the act applies equally to all. Though, as we saw in the chapter on affirmative action, there are times when it *appears* the law does not equally protect rights of nonminorities; this is done only in a remedial context with strict safeguards in place. The *McDonald v. Santa Fe Transportation*[36] case demonstrated that racial discrimination may occur against whites also and is equally prohibited under Title VII. In that case, both black and white employees stole merchandise that was being transported by the company they worked for. The white employee was terminated, while the black employee was disciplined. The white employee sued for race discrimination and won. It may seem strange to think that it took a U.S. Supreme Court case to determine that Title VII protects whites as well as blacks, but keep in mind the history we discussed leading up to passage of the Civil Rights Act. Discrimination against whites was never contemplated since it was not an issue.

We have often heard the perception from our students and employees in the business world that "all someone has to do is yell discrimination, and they win a case." This is not so. It takes far more than alleging discrimination to win a case under Title VII. It is necessary to present credible evidence of discrimination in order to succeed. This can be done directly, by presenting evidence that the employer did or said something racially negative, or indirectly, by way of the disparate impact requirements discussed in the toolkit chapter. In *Phongsavane v. Potter,*[37] an Asian employee was unable to prove the discrimination she alleged, and thus lost her case. She complained that she was not given as much overtime as she had wanted, and she alleged it was because she was Asian, but she gave no evidence to support the allegation, and the employer could show that the decision was not based on race. This is one of the reasons that employers should not fear Title VII claims. Either there is a viable basis for discrimination or there is not. If there is not, the employee's alleging discrimination does not make it true and no liability will attach to the employer. Of course, an employer still must use resources to counter the claim, which is another reason why a "best practices" approach is always best. It lessens the likelihood that employees will file claims because they perceive fairness by the employer on an ongoing basis.

Recognizing Race Discrimination

Often, one of the most difficult things for a manager is recognizing race discrimination when it presents itself. The latest EEOC statistics for FY 2010 indicated that race remains one of the most frequent types of claim filed with the agency, with 35.890 percent of the total claims filed being on the basis of race. Many of these claims involve systemic race discrimination affecting hundreds of employees. That is, the glass ceiling is still at work, denying full workplace participation to minorities. Just within the past couple of years, the EEOC has settled class action suits with Abercrombie & Fitch ($50 million), Consolidated Freightways ($2.75 million), Milgard Windows ($3.37 million), Home Depot ($5.5 million), Carl Buddig ($2.5 million), Local 28 Steelworkers' Union ($6.4 million), and Supercuts ($3.5 million). All of these cases involve widespread workplace discrimination in hiring, promotions, training, and other aspects of work life. Cases of systemic glass ceiling–type discrimination that actually go to trial are becoming increasingly rare. Even if, as was the case with Abercrombie & Fitch, the employer settles with the EEOC for a whopping $50 million, they still may be better off than taking the case to trial where higher compensatory damages and punitive damages are possible.

Often employers are held liable for race discrimination because they treated employees of a particular race differently without even realizing that they was building a case of race discrimination for which they could ultimately be liable. Sometimes it is something seemingly small or subtle, but given the stage we are playing on, with the history we presented to you, it can be perceived as discriminatory. Remember Sen. Joseph Biden's January 2007 statement about his 2008 presidential opponent Barack Obama as the "first mainstream African-American who is articulate and bright and clean and a nice-looking guy"? Though he said he did not mean to offend, because of the history we provided in this and other chapters, you should be able to recognize why his statement would cause a stir. At the very least it offered insight into his questionable perception of blacks—keep in mind these are people who had run for the highest office in our government. As the *Vaughn v. Edel* case demonstrates, provided for your review, intent may be established by direct evidence of discrimination by an employer even when the employer may discriminate for what it considers to be justifiable reasons. In *Vaughn,* a manager told a supervisor not to have any confrontations with a black female employee about her work after she asked a member of the legal staff if she thought a conversation she had with her supervisor sounded discriminatory. Two years later when she was terminated for poor performance, she sued and alleged race discrimination in that she was not given proper feedback that would have allowed her to better her performance. As you read the *Vaughn* case, think about whether you would have handled things differently to avoid the result the court reached here. *Vaughn* is the basis for Opening Scenario 2.

An employer who has not considered the issue of race may well develop and implement policies that have a racially discriminatory impact without ever intending to do so. The *Bradley v. Pizzaco of Nebraska, Inc., d/b/a Domino's Pizza*[38] "no-beard" case is a good example of this. As you may recall from an earlier chapter, in *Bradley,* the employer had a "no-beard" policy requiring employees to be clean shaven. The employee, a black pizza delivery driver, told the employer he could not shave without severe discomfort. The employer told him he must shave, and when he did not, he was terminated. The employee sued for race discrimination and won. The court determined that the condition the employee had was pseudofolliculitis barbae (PFB), which occurs in about 50 percent of the black male population, and about 4 percent of the white male population. Thus, the policy had a disparate impact on black males and had to be proved to be a business necessity if the employer was to keep the policy. The employer could not show this since being clean shaven is not a requirement for being able to drive a pizza delivery truck.

Bradley is also a good example of why disparate impact cases must be recognized if Congress's legislative intent of ridding the workplace of employment discrimination is to be at all successful. *Bradley* is the basis for Opening Scenario 3.

Bradley also clearly demonstrates why the more an employer knows about diverse groups, the better. Here, where the employer was not aware of the impact of PFB on at least 50 percent of the black male population and less than 4 percent of the white male population, it could have saved the employer from liability. *Bradley* demonstrates just how important it is to simply be able to recognize race discrimination when you see it. If you, as a manager, never had to deal with PFB (as 95 percent of the white male population and certainly all of the white female population and other ethnicities need not do), you would be blissfully unaware of the impact of your policy on 50 or so percent of the black male population (and only about 5 percent of the white male population).

How would you avoid this situation? As a manager faced with an unfamiliar situation, your favorite eight words should be, "Let me get back to you on that." This informs the employee that you have heard her or his concern and will take it seriously. It then gives you time to find out what you need to know to make an informed decision. If it is something you do not know, ask the employee for more information, check the Internet, use resources around you, but do not simply react. If time is not a factor, there is no need to rush into making a decision on something about which you may be clueless.

If the employer in *Bradley* had simply asked the employee to provide documentation for his condition from a reputable and reliable source, such as a dermatologist or barber, the outcome might have been different. Simply taking the time to treat the employee's concern as legitimate (rather than merely dismissing it because it was not something with which the manager was familiar) and trying to seek alternatives would have made all the difference.

The employer would have had a basis for providing an exception to the rule in these particular circumstances, while still maintaining the general rule for other employees. While not satisfied that everyone does not have to obey the policy, the employer at least would feel satisfied that sufficient justification was provided to excuse this employee. Other employees seeing the employee treated differently would be less likely to be resentful, knowing that the difference in treatment was based on justifiable medical reasons available to anyone with the same condition.

If the employer had been flexible, rather than dismissing the employee's assertions out of hand simply because it was not familiar to him, he undoubtedly could have avoided the result in this case. As a manager, make sure you try to consider all angles before making a decision. It is especially important to consider the realities of those who belong to groups with which you may not be familiar. Again, don't be afraid to seek help or information from those in a better position to know—starting with the employee for whom it is an issue. It may help you avoid a much bigger problem later. (For more examples of manifestations of discrimination, see Exhibit 6.10, "Names and 'Hello' Can Keep You Out.")

Chandler v. Fast Lane, Inc., provided for your review, is another unusual manifestation of racial discrimination that might well slip by a manager, just as it did in this case. In *Chandler,* the action was brought by a white manager who was trying *not* to discriminate when her company wanted her to do so. You should be aware that this also is covered by Title VII.

Exhibit 6.10   *Names and "Hello" Can Keep You Out*

Two research studies have shown just how pervasive, yet subtle, race discrimination can be for employees and job applicants.

In the first, researchers from the University of Chicago and MIT conducted a study in which they sent out nearly 5,000 fictional résumés in response to 1,300 newspaper ads for jobs in Chicago and Boston. To each ad they sent two sets of two résumés: one identical set had a résumé with a "traditionally black" name and one with a "traditionally white" name; the other set of résumés had more experience, and again, one had a "traditionally black" name and the other a "traditionally white" name. "Traditionally black" names included Rasheed, Kareem, Leroy, Tyrone, Ebony, Kenya, LaTonya, Tanisha, Keisha, Hakim, Aisha, and Tamika. "Traditionally white" names included Greg, Jill, Allison, Emily, Laurie, Sarah, Brendan, Brad, Meredith, Kristen, Matthew, and Brett.

Applicants with "traditionally white" names received 50 percent more callbacks than those with "traditionally black" names. The researchers found that increasing credentials resulted in a better chance of whites being called back more often, but not African-Americans. Applicants with "traditionally white" names were called back at a rate comparable to having eight additional years of experience. The result was the same across occupations, industries, and employer size. Federal contractors or others who indicated they were equal employment opportunity employers were just as likely to discriminate as other employers, according to the researchers. Having more upscale addresses helped whites, but not African-Americans. The researchers concluded that "differential treatment by race still appears to be prominent in the U.S. labor market."

In the second study, Dr. John Baugh, a professor of education and linguistics at Stanford University, presented over 300 university students recordings of voices saying a single word. The students were asked to identify the ethnicity of the speaker. Over 80 percent were able to do so correctly, based solely on hearing the single word, "hello."

Baugh, black, became interested in linguistic profiling when he placed several calls in response to newspaper ads for housing, but when he showed up at the property, he was always given reasons why it could not be rented to him. He suspected that the phenomenon was because he used his professional voice on the phone and the landlords thought he was white, but he showed up and was black. He set out to investigate his suspicions. Dr. Baugh is particularly adept at voices, having grown up in Philadelphia and Los Angeles with many different dialects. He placed over 100 calls inquiring about a rental property, some using his professional voice, and others his "ethnic dialects." He used the exact same sentence each time he called, and only varied his voice and intonation. Dr. Baugh found that when using his "white" voice, he received 50 percent more callbacks.

After James Johnson suspected that the same thing happened to him while looking for an apartment in San Francisco, he reported it to the local fair housing agency, the Eden Council for Hope and Opportunity. Eden used five callers to inquire about housing, leaving messages. Three of the callers "sounded white" and two "sounded black." The "white" callers' calls were returned within hours. The "black" callers' calls were not returned. The counselor who ran the investigation said it was "pretty blatant." Shanna Smith, executive director of the National Fair Housing Alliance, says it is a familiar practice for housing, banking, and other industries, such as insurance.

Sources: Marianne Bertrand and Sendhil Mullainathan, "Are Emily and Greg More Employable Than Lakisha and Jamal? A Field Experiment on Labor Market Discrimination," 2004, http://economics.harvard.edu/faculty/mullainathan/files/emilygreg.pdf; Patrice D. Johnson, "Linguistic Profiling," *The Black Commentator* 1 (April 5, 2002), http://www.blackcommentator.com/linguistic_profiling_pr.html; Steve Osunsami, "When Voice Recognition Leads to Bias" *ABC News.com*, December 6, 2001, http://abcnews.go.com/WNT/story?id=130504&page=1; "The Color of Voice: How Inferring Race Can Become Discrimination," ABC News.com, February 6, 2002, http://abcnews.go.com/sections/Downtown/2020/downtown_linguisticsprofiling_020205.html.

Racial Harassment

In addition to an employer being liable for race discrimination under Title VII, the employer also can be liable for workplace racial harassment. Harassment claims filed with the EEOC have been increasing, particularly incidents involving nooses, the "n-word," and other racial epithets. "It is shocking that such egregious and unlawful conduct toward African-American employees is still occurring, even increasing, in the 21st century workplace, more than 40 years after enactment of the landmark Civil Rights Act of 1964," said David Grinberg of the EEOC.[39] The Louisiana House and Senate recently unanimously passed a bill outlawing public display of a hangman's noose with the intent to intimidate someone. The bill was signed into law by Governor Jindal in 2008. According to the EEOC, harassment claims have more than doubled since the early 1990s, from 3,075 in fiscal year 1991 to about 7,000 in 2007, with race the most frequently alleged basis.[40] As EEOC general counsel Eric Dreiband said, "As blatant discrimination decreases, other areas like harassment increase."

To hold an employer liable for racial harassment, the employee must show that the harassment was (1) unwelcome, (2) based on race, and (3) so severe or pervasive that it altered the conditions of employment and created an abusive environment, and that (4) there is a basis for imposing liability on the employer. The employer is responsible for such activity if the employer himself or herself is the one who perpetrates the harassment, or if it is permitted in the workplace by the employer or supervisory employees. For instance, in January 2008, the EEOC announced a settlement with Lockheed Martin for $2.5 million for claims that it allowed a black electrician to be "severely harassed," including, among other things, threatened with lynching and called the "n-word" while working on military aircraft at various places he was assigned all over the country. One of the harassers was a supervisor, and though the employer knew, no discipline was imposed and the harassment continued unabated.[41] This is the largest settlement the EEOC has ever obtained for a single employee in a racial harassment case, and one of the largest for any single employee.

Actions for racial harassment, like those of race discrimination under Title VII, may be brought under the same alternative statutes as race discrimination, as appropriate—that is, the post–Civil War statutes, state human rights or fair employment practice laws, or constitutional provisions.

In *Daniels v. WorldCom Corp.*,[42] the two black employees reported being sent racially charged e-mails through their work computer. The court said that racial harassment has as its basis the employer imposing on the harassed employee different terms or conditions of employment based on race. The employee is required to work in an atmosphere in which severe and pervasive harassing activity is directed at the employee because of the employee's race or color. However, the employer took prompt, corrective remedial action to address the situation, so the court found no liability.

As *Daniels* demonstrates, the employer's best approach to racial harassment is to maintain a workplace in which such activity is not permitted or condoned in any way, to take all racial harassment complaints seriously, and to take immediate corrective action, if necessary, after investigation. An employer must do this to avoid liability. The case also demonstrates how important it is for a manager to keep up with changes that result in new and different ways to harass. In *Daniels,* the harassment was accomplished by e-mail., but because the employer took immediate corrective action, liability was avoided.

Keep in mind that an employer's prompt response to harassment is important. In a recent case in which the EEOC sued the employer for workplace racial harassment, the employer ended up paying a $1.8 million settlement despite the fact that in responding to the racial harassment it had called the police, photographed the "racist graffiti," offered rewards, placed undercover employees in the plant, hired handwriting analysts, sent employees to diversity training, increased plant security, and sought the help of the FBI. The graffiti continued to appear, yet declined to a large extent "after the company started taking the remedial steps and the litigation was in full swing." The EEOC said that the company could have stopped the harassment earlier if it had wanted to. The company also was required to take preventive measures including adopting a policy against racial harassment and instituting camera monitoring of its facilities, training managers and employees, and periodic reporting to the EEOC on racial harassment complaints.[43]

In the *Henderson v. Irving Materials, Inc.* case,[44] it is clear that racial harassment may be established by piecing together many things that in and of themselves may seem insignificant but, when taken together, as they must be for racial harassment, create for the harassee a very different workplace than for those not being harassed. This is extremely important for employers to keep in mind, as it may not be one big harassing act that causes liability, but rather, many small ones. That is why staying on top of things and dealing with them as they arise is so very important. In *Henderson*, a black employee was subjected to a number of incidents at work, including racial epithets, threats, greasing of his truck, dead mice placed in his truck, and the buttons cut off his uniform, by two of his white co-workers. Several of the incidents were witnessed by their supervisor. The court found that though some of the events, in isolation, may not qualify as harassment, when taken in the total context of the employee's experience as the first black hired to work there and in the greater context of race in our country, they constituted racial harassment.

A Word about Color

LO5

Detroit DJ and promoter Ulysses "DJ Lish" Barnes was totally surprised when a furor erupted over the "Light Skin Libra Birthday Bash" at Club APT he scheduled for October 2007. The plan was to allow light-skinned African-American women to get into the party for free. An Internet blitz led him to change his mind and he canceled the event. "I made a mistake," Barnes said. "I didn't think there would be a backlash."

We can't imagine why not. As an African-American, very brown at that, Barnes would certainly have been aware that skin color has a long and painful

Exhibit 6.11 *EEOC's Color Guidance*

WHAT IS "COLOR" DISCRIMINATION?

Title VII prohibits employment discrimination because of "color" as a basis separately listed in the statute. The statute does not define "color." The courts and the Commission read "color" to have its commonly understood meaning—pigmentation, complexion, or skin shade or tone. Thus, color discrimination occurs when a person is discriminated against based on the lightness, darkness, or other color characteristic of the person. Even though race and color clearly overlap, they are not synonymous. Thus, color discrimination can occur between persons of different races or ethnicities, or between persons of the same race or ethnicity.

EXAMPLE 1. COLOR-BASED HARASSMENT

James, a light-complexioned African-American, has worked as a waiter at a restaurant for over a year. His manager, a brown-complexioned African-American, has frequently made offensive comments and jokes about James's skin color, causing him to lose sleep and dread coming in to work. James's requests that the conduct stop only intensified the abuse. James has been subjected to harassment in the form of a hostile work environment, based on his color.

EXAMPLE 2. COLOR-BASED EMPLOYMENT DECISIONS

Melanie, a brown-complexioned Latina, works as a sales clerk for a major department store. She applies for a promotion to be the Counter Manager for a major line of beauty products, but the employer denies her the promotion because the vendor prefers a "light skinned representative" to manage its product line at this particular location. The employer has unlawfully discriminated on the basis of color.

Source: EEOC Compliance Manual, section 15-III, http://www.eeoc.gov/policy/docs/race-color.pdf.

history in the African-American culture, stretching back to a time when lighter blacks were given jobs in the slave owner's home, while darker blacks worked the fields. This often resulted in better treatment and the pitting of one group against the other. Later, after slavery ended, the division stuck and "the paper bag test" was used as a basis for allowing entrée to everything from schools to social organizations. If your skin was any darker than a brown paper bag, you were excluded.

Color has been a divisive issue for as long as African-Americans have been in this country, and it is still with us today. As other ethnicities have joined the mix, it is clear that color is an issue with them also. Lighter-toned Hispanics, East Asians, and Asians, among others, all have experienced serious color issues within their cultures. While you may not think that you care about color, research indicates that we tend to feel more comfortable with those most like ourselves, and one of the ways this is manifested is through color discrimination.

Now you have an idea of why color is one of the five categories included in Title VII as a prohibited basis for discrimination. (See Exhibit 6.11, "EEOC's Color Guidance.") However, despite the findings reflected in Exhibit 6.12, "Light and Dark," the first color discrimination case was not decided under Title VII until 1990.[45] The number of cases has since steadily grown.

Exhibit 6.12 *Light and Dark*

- The National Survey of Black Americans across the country, published in the *American Journal of Sociology,* found that "the fairer one's pigmentation (skin color), the higher his or her occupational standing." Researchers found that a light-complexioned black, on average, had a 50 percent higher income than darker African-Americans, regardless of educational, occupational, or family background.[1]

- We are proud to say that one of our students, psychology doctoral student (now a newly minted PhD!) Matthew Harrison, received national attention (including by the EEOC; see Exhibit 6.6) when he presented at the national meeting of the Academy of Management results of a first-of-its-kind study indicating that dark-skinned African-Americans face a distinct disadvantage when applying for jobs even if their résumés are better than those of lighter-skinned African-Americans. Other studies had been conducted on colorism,

  Keith, V.M. and C. Herring, "Skin Tone and Stratification in the Black Community," American Journal of Sociology, v. 97, no. 3 (Nov. 1991), pp. 760–778.

  but Harrison was the first to specifically examine how colorism operates in workplace hiring. He used the same photo, but had the skin tone manipulated to dark, medium, or light with Adobe Acrobat. A light-skinned man with a bachelor's degree and minimal experience was consistently chosen for a job over a dark-skinned man with an MBA and managerial experience when evaluators were presented with their résumés.

- A law and economics professor at Vanderbilt University looked at a government survey of 2,084 legal immigrants to the United States from around the world and found that even taking into consideration virtually all other factors that could affect wages, those with the lightest skin earned an average of 8 to 15 percent more than similar immigrants with much darker skin. Economics professor Shelly White-Means of the University of Tennessee at Memphis said the study shows there is a growing body of evidence that there is a preference for whiteness in America that goes beyond race.

After Title VII was enacted, the country started out with such severe race issues that it was not until later that the fine-tuning of looking at color discrimination came along—even though the color issues had been around as long as race had. Be aware that while we tend to be faced with race discrimination where the discriminator is one race and the discriminatee another, with color discrimination that is not necessarily the case. Often the discrimination is by people of the same race. In several cases, both the party alleging discrimination and the alleged perpetrator of the discrimination have been black. Employers should not miss the possibility of this legal liability by thinking there can be no discrimination since two people of the same race are involved. This is why in Opening Scenario 1, Joan is doing more than acting unprofessionally toward Mary by constantly making comments about Mary's skin color. Joan is violating Title VII.

1) Scenario

If you think color doesn't matter, think about whether it was a coincidence that the first-ever black Miss America, in 1984, Vanessa Williams, was light brown, with green eyes and long hair. As recently as 1984, America was not ready for Miss America to be a darker brown with short, kinky natural hair. It didn't appeal to the nation's cultural sensibilities of beauty. That is why African-Americans and other ethnic groups began, and still hold, their own beauty pageants (e.g., "Miss Black America" pageant, "Miss Latina America" pageant, "Miss Asian America" pageant). It is not for purposes of self-segregation. Rather, it is to have a pageant that reflects the standards of beauty and talent that arise from, and are appreciated by, the group itself rather than those of the larger society that may not reflect the group's own standards.

However, the reality is that it was also against the rules for nonwhites to be in the main pageants. African-Americans were not allowed into the Miss America pageant until after the Civil Rights Movement in the 1960s. It was not until 1945 that they even had someone Jewish, and it was a *very* big deal when Bess Myerson won the crown.

You may recall the brouhaha during the 2008 presidential election when several comments were made about candidate Barack Obama only getting as far as he did as an African-American presidential candidate because he was light skinned. One of the statements was made by Senator Harry Reid, who was the majority leader of Obama's own Democratic Party.[46]

When several of the Hemmings who claimed to be the descendants of the 38-year-long relationship between revered U.S. President Thomas Jefferson and his slave Sally Hemmings appeared in public and looked just as white as many of their white Jefferson kin, there was initially widespread public disbelief. If color did not matter, this simply would not have occurred.

In his book *Ace of Spades,*[47] David Matthews, who has a Jewish mother and African-American father and who looks white, gives a vivid and gut-wrenching portrayal of growing up in Baltimore, Maryland, with his dad (his mother left when he was an infant), walking the tightrope of race by passing for white. He did this because even as a child, he could clearly see how much better whites were treated than African-Americans, even by teachers.

If you don't think you ever notice color, think about who comes to mind when I ask you about African-American actresses (Halle Berry?) or performers (Beyoncé?) Both are light. There are certainly other famous actresses and entertainers, but chances are, these quickly came to mind. Not only that, we would likely agree that they are both beautiful (or, as my male students would say, "hot"). Whoopi Goldberg was the first black actress to win an Oscar since 1939, but chances are, that is not who came to mind.

Also, notice how different your thoughts are when you think of black actors. Chances are, you are more likely to think of a browner (and older) male. JayZ? Lawrence Fishburne? Denzel Washington? Just keep in mind that we do notice color, whether it registers consciously or not.

Don't misunderstand. There is nothing *wrong* with this, per se, but just keep it in mind as you make decisions in the workplace. As we see in Exhibit 6.12, research shows that color can matter a great deal. Whether or not you agree with the idea that color matters, the point is that skin color exists and has a value (negative or positive) in our society that may be reflected in the workplace. Make sure you are aware that Title VII prohibits discrimination on the basis of color and be mindful of the subtle, though not necessarily conscious, role it may play in how we deal with others.

Management Tips

Race discrimination can seem elusive. Many of us tend to think it no longer exists, or that others feel as neutral as we do about race. That is not necessarily so. Because a manager can be unaware of the presence of race discrimination, he or she can miss it until litigation arises. Think back to the *Patterson* case discussed in the toolkit chapter. Recall that Patterson worked for the bank for 10 years without a promotion and finally sued for race discrimination when she was laid off. Remember that many of the things Patterson alleged as part of a discriminatory pattern of treatment toward her would have been insignificant in and of themselves. However, taken together, the list becomes quite significant. Be aware of what goes on in the workplace and "don't miss the forest for the trees." The following tips may prove useful:

LO6
- Believe that race discrimination occurs and be willing to investigate it when it is alleged.
- Make sure that there is a top-down message that the workplace will not tolerate race discrimination in *any* form.
- Don't shy away from discussing race when the issue arises. Be open to learning and sharing. There are many resources you can use, including the Internet and books on race.
- Provide a positive, nonthreatening, constructive forum for the discussion of racial issues. Don't let the only time a discussion of race arises be in the midst of an allegation of racial discrimination.
- Be aware of cultural differences that may be connected, at least in part, to race, when doing things as simple as deciding how to celebrate special events in the workplace. Be inclusive regarding what music will be played, what food will be served, what recreation will be offered, what clothes will be worn, and other factors. These all form a part of the atmosphere in which an employee must work and experience workplace leisure. If people do not see themselves reflected in the workplace culture, they will not feel a part of it and will feel isolated. If they feel isolated, they are more likely to experience other factors leading to discrimination and ultimately to litigation. If this seems like a small matter to you, imagine yourself showing up at a gathering at work, and the music, decorations, food, and clothing were all Japanese. There's sushi to eat sake to drink, and everyone is speaking Japanese. You'd probably feel a bit out of your element and would quickly realize how those seemingly simple things make a big impact. Now imagine that happening at *every* workplace party.
- When an employee reports discrimination based on race, don't let the first move be telling the employee he or she must be mistaken. Investigate it as any other workplace matter would be investigated.
- Be willing to treat the matter as a misunderstanding if it is clear that is what has taken place. There is no use in making a federal case (literally) out of a matter that could be handled much more simply. Do not, however, underplay the significance of what occurred.
- Offer support groups if there is an expressed need.
- Offer training in racial awareness and sensitivity. Courts have offered language indicating they will look more favorably on employers who do so.
- Constantly monitor workplace hiring, termination, training, promotion, raises, and discipline to ensure that they are fair and even-handed. If there are differences in treatment among races, be sure they are explainable and legally justifiable.

Exhibit 6.13   *Still Not Convinced?*

We know it is difficult to imagine that race discrimination is still an issue of grave importance when you may live in a world in which race doesn't seem to matter. Just in case you're still having trouble believing it, we ask you to consider the following.

A 2007 survey conducted by TheLadders.com, the world's largest online executive job search service, concluded that racial discrimination in the workplace is as bad now as it was 10 years ago.

According to the research, 81 percent of executives had witnessed discriminatory actions in their companies, with race accounting for 42 percent of the discrimination; 54 percent say there has been no improvement in the past 10 years, and 77 percent say discrimination starts at the top.

Source: "Workplace Discrimination Starts at the Top; Found to Be Commonplace in American Business," February 28, 2007, http://www.theladders.com/press/job_search_engine/workplace_discrimination_2007.2.28.

Employees also can sue under the state or federal Constitution for a denial of equal protection if they work for the government or under state tort laws for defamation, intentional infliction of emotional distress, assault, or any other tort the facts support.

An employer who must remedy racial discrimination may not avoid doing so because of the possibility of a reverse discrimination suit by employees alleging they were adversely affected. If an employer institutes a judicially imposed or voluntary affirmative action plan that can withstand judicial scrutiny for the reasons set forth in the affirmative action chapter, the employer will not be liable to employees for reverse discrimination. (See Exhibit 6.13, "Still Not Convinced?")

Chapter Summary

- Title VII prohibits discrimination on the basis of race and color. This also may intersect with national origin discrimination.
- Employers must ensure that every employee has an equal opportunity for employment and advancement in the workplace, regardless of race, color, or national origin.
- Employers must be vigilant in guarding against the more stubborn, subtle manifestations of race and color discrimination.
- Racial discrimination may be by way of disparate treatment or disparate impact.
- Disparate treatment may be shown by direct or indirect evidence of discrimination.
- Disparate impact may be more difficult to discern, so employers need to closely scrutinize workplace policies and procedures to prevent unintended disparate impact leading to liability.
- Race cannot be used as a bona fide occupational qualification.

Chapter-End Questions

1. A black firefighter alleges that each time he is transferred from one fire station to another, he must take his bed with him, on orders of the fire chief. The chief defends on the basis that it is a legitimate decision because white firefighters would not want to sleep in the same bed in which a black firefighter slept. Is this illegal under Title VII? Explain. [Georgia newspaper article]

2. A white college receptionist is fired when it is found that she told a black college applicant that the applications for admissions are distinguished by race by the notation of a small *RH* in the corner of black applicants' applications. "RH," she says, is her supervisor's term for "raisin heads," which he calls African-Americans. Is the employee entitled to reinstatement? [*Jet* magazine article]

3. It is discovered that, at a health club, the owner has been putting a notation on the application of black membership applicants that reads "DNWAM," which means "do not want as member." In addition, the black membership applicants are charged higher rates and are much less likely to be financed as other nonblack applicants. Can the black applicants bring a successful action under Title VII?

4. A black female employee is told that she cannot come to work with her hair in decorative braids traditionally worn in Africa, and if she continues to do so, she will be terminated. Does the employee have a claim under Title VII?

5. Bennie's Restaurant chain routinely hires Hispanics, but it only assigns them to the lower-paying jobs as kitchen help, rather than as higher-paid servers, salad bar helpers, or managers. Bennie's says it does not discriminate because it has many Hispanic employees. If suit is brought by the Hispanic employees, who will likely win? [Based on Denny's restaurants]

6. Five white and one black canine unit officers sued for race discrimination when the operating procedures for their unit were drastically changed, they alleged, because the unit was "too white." Can the black officer bring suit for race discrimination on these facts even though he is not white? [*Ginger v. District of Columbia*, 477 F. Supp. 2d 41 (D. D.C. 2007).]

7. Ken recruits applicants for several prominent companies. Often when the companies call for Ken's services, they strongly hint that they do not wish to hire Southeast Asians, so Ken never places them with those companies. Is Ken liable for illegal discrimination?

8. José and César, both Hispanic, are carpenters employed by a contractor to help build an office building in Maryland. While working, José and César discover that they are being paid less than non-Hispanic employees. In addition, they allege a hostile work environment and discriminatory terms and conditions of employment, including anti-Hispanic statements by managers and employees, segregated eating areas, and an "English-only" rule imposed by the contractor. José and César sue for race discrimination. Will they win? [*Aleman v. Chugach Support Services*, 485 F.3d 206 (4th Cir. 2007).]

9. Jill, the owner of a construction business, says her construction crew will not work if she hires Hispanic crew members, so Jill does not do so. Is this a defense to a Title VII action?

10. Sam has worked at Allied for several years with no problems. Avril is transferred into Sam's unit. Sam immediately begins having a strong allergic reaction to the perfume Avril wears each day. After having to take days off work because of his allergies, Sam asks Avril if she can tone down her perfume. Avril does so for a few

days, then resumes her usual amount. Sam does not complain any further but is thinking of quitting because his allergies are so bad. He doesn't want to go any further with Avril about it because Sam is white and Avril is Asian, and Sam thinks it might lead to race discrimination liability for his employer. Is Sam correct? [Based on student's parent's dilemma]

End Notes

1. "Number of Hate Groups on the Rise, Report Says," CNN.com, 2/23/11, http://articles.cnn.com/2011-02-23/us/splc.hate.groups_1_patriot-groups-southern-poverty-law-center-mark-potok?_s=PM:US.

2. Devah Pager, "The Mark of a Criminal Record," *American Journal of Sociology,* 108, 5 (March 2003), pp. 937–75.

3. Marianne Bertrand and Sendhil Mullainathan, "Are Emily and Brendan More Employable Than Lakisha and Jamal? A Field Experiment on Labor Market Discrimination," http://www.economics.harvard.edu/faculty/mullainathan/files/emilygreg.pdf.

4. Patricia Rice, "Linguistic Profiling: The Sound of Your Voice May Determine If You Get That Apartment or Not," Washington University in St. Louis Newsroom, 2/2/2006. For a fun test originally given on ABC TV's *20/20,* take a look at this Web site: http://www.uiowa.edu/~c103112/lingprof.html.

5. Derdrick Muhammad, senior organizer and research associate for the Institute for Policy Studies, "Census Shows Lingering Racial Wage Gap," *New Pittsburgh Courier,* 10/11/10, http://www.blackvoicenews.com/news/news-wire/45111-census-shows-lingering-racial-income-gap.html. In an interesting article on the racial wage gap, Amitabh Chandra of Darmouth College's Department of Economics argues that the decrease shown in the wage gap over the years is actually greater than it appears to be because of the failure to include black men who have left the labor market due to factors such as incarceration. See Amitabh Chandra, "Is the Convergence of the Racial Wage Gap Illusory?" NBER Working Paper # 9476, 1/2003.

6. 127 S. Ct. 625 (2006).

7. 127 S. Ct. 638 (2006).

8. 2006 U.S. TRANS LEXIS 48.

9. DeWayne Wichkham, "Alabama Segregation Vote Stirs Memories of Wallace," *USA Today,* 12/6/2004, http://www.usatoday.com/news/opinion/columnist/wickham/2004-12-06-wickham_x.htm.

10. *EEOC v. Northwest Cosmetic Labs LLC,* consent decree Civil Action No. 10-608-CWD, (D Idaho, 2011).

11. *EEOC v. Charapp Ford South,* consent decree No. 03-0171 (WD Pa. 2003), http://archive.eeoc.gov/litigation/settlements/settlement11-03.html.

12. Consent decree, *EEOC v. SPS Temporaries, Inc., Jamestown Container Lockport, Inc, and Whiting Door Manufacturing Corp.,* No. 04-CV-0052E (SC) (WDNY 2005), http://archive.eeoc.gov/litigation/settlements/settlement11-05.html.

13. *EEOC v. Wisconsin Staffing Services, Inc., d/b/a Nicolet Staffing, Inc.,* Case No. 3:10-cv-543 (WD WI 2010).

14. "Unequal Treatment: Confronting Racial and Ethnic Disparities in Health Care," National Academies' Institute of Medicine, 3/20/2002, http://www8.nationalacademies.org/onpinews/newsitem.aspx?RecordID=10260.

15. *Boston Globe,* October 2, 1999, p. B1, http://www8.nationalacademies.org/onpinews/newsitem.aspx?RecordID=10260.

16. *Multi-City Study on Urban Inequality,* (Russell Sage Foundation Publications, 2001), http://www.icpsr.umich.edu/icpsrweb/ICPSR/studies/02535.

17. Lisa Richardson, "History of Racism and Sexism Chronicled in LAFD," *Los Angeles Times,* 3/13/2006.

18. Jeffry Scott, "Jones Ordered to Pay $185,000," *Atlanta Journal and Constitution,* 4/1/2010, http://www.ajc.com/news/dekalb-discrimination-suit-jones-426095.html.

19. *EEOC v. Professional Transit Management, d/b/a Springs Transit,* Case No. 06-cv-01915 (D. Colo. May 17, 2007).

20. "Majority of Americans Say Racism against Blacks Widespread," Gallup, 8/4/2008, http://www.gallup.com/poll/109258/Majority-Americans-Say-Racism-Against-Blacks-Widespread.aspx.

21. "In U.S., Views on Race Relations Return to Pre-Obama Levels," Gallup, 10/20/2009, http://www.gallup.com/video/123935/Views-Race-Relations-Return-Pre-Obama-Levels.aspx.

22. Ibid.

23. "Gallup Poll Social Audit: Black-White Relations in the U.S.," http://www.gallup.com/poll/4627/gallup-social-audit-blackwhite-relations-us.aspx; http://media.gallup.com/GPTB/specialReports/sr010711.PDF.

24. Eduardo Bonilla-Silva, *Racism without Racists: Color-Blind Racism and the Persistence of Racial Inequality in the U.S.* (Lanham, MD: Rowman & Littlefield, 2003); Eduardo Bonilla-Silva, *White Supremacy and Racism in the Post-Civil Rights Era,* (Boulder, CO: Lynne Rienner, 2001).

25. Alfred Blumrosen and Ruth Blumrosen, *The Reality of Intentional Job Discrimination in Metropolitan America—1999* (Jersey City, NJ: EEO1, 2002).

26. http://www.adversity.net/Kodak/02_non-lawsuit.htm.

27. David Mattingly, "Strom Thurmond's Family Confirms Paternity Claim," 12/16/2003, http://articles.cnn.com/2003-12-15/us/thurmond.paternity_1_thurmond-family-essie-mac-washington-williams-carrie-butler?_s=PM:US.

28. "Textile Firm Linked to "Negro Cloth" for Slaves, *USA Today,* 2/21/02, http://www.usatoday.com/money/general/2002/02/21/slave-westpoint-stevens.htm.

29. *Diseases and Peculiarities of the Negro Race: by Dr. Cartwright (in Debow's Review),* "Africans in America," PBS.org, http://www.pbs.org/wgbh/aia/part4/4h3106t.html.

30. Ira Berlin, Marc Favreau, and Steven F. Miller, *Remembering Slavery: African Americans Talk about Their Personal Experiences of Slavery and Emancipation* (with MP3 Audio CD) (New York: The New Press, 1998).

31. "Retired Black Police Seek Pension Parity: Retired Black Officer Lobbying to Gain Credit, Compensation for Lost Years," MSNBC, 3/2/2008, http://www.msnbc.msn.com/id/23426196/ns/us_news-life/.

32. *Ash v. Tyson Foods, Inc.,* 546 U.S. 454 (2006).

33. "Civil War Widow, Final Link to Old Confederacy, Dies," *USA Today,* 5/31/2004, http://www.usatoday.com/news/nation/2004-05-31-war-widow_x.htm.

34. "Usual Weekly Earnings of Wage and Salary Workers, Fourth Quarter 2010," U.S. Bureau of Labor Statistics. "Among the major race and ethnicity groups, median weekly earnings for black men working at full-time jobs were $629 per week or 73.4 percent of the median for white men ($857). The difference was less among women, as black women's median earnings ($605) were 87.1 percent of those for white women ($695). Overall, median earnings of Hispanics who worked full time ($539) were lower than those of blacks ($614), whites ($772), and Asians ($828). http://www.bls.gov/news.release/wkyeng.nr0.htm.

35. Juan Williams, *Thurgood Marshall: American Revolutionary* (New York: Three Rivers Press, 1998), p. xiv.

36. 427 U.S. 273 (1976).

37. 2006 U.S. Dist. LEXIS 70103 (W.D. Tex. 2006).

38. 7 F3d 795 (8th Cir. 1993).

39. Eve Tahmincioglu, "Racial Harassment Still Infecting the Workplace," *MSNBC.com,* January 13, 2008, http://www.msnbc.com/id/22575581/from/ET/print/1/displaymode/1098/ (last visited January 15, 2008).

40. "Lockheed Martin to Pay $2.5 Million to Settle Racial Harassment Lawsuit," http://www.eeoc.gov/press/1-2-08.html (last visited February 6, 2008).

41. *EEOC v. Lockheed Martin,* CV-05-00479 (D. Hawaii 2008).

42. 1998 US Dist LEXIS 2335 (N.D. Tex. 1998).

43. *EEOC v. Scientific Colors, Inc., d/b/a Apollo Colors,* No. 99 C 1959 (N.D. Ill. 2002).

44. 329 F. Supp.2d 1002 (S.D. Indianapolis Div. 2004).

45. *Walker v. Secretary of the Treasury, Internal Revenue Service,* 742 F. Supp. 670 (N.D. Ga., Atl. Div. 1990).

46. Jeff Zeleny, "Reid Apologizes for Remarks on Obama's Color and Dialect," 1/9/10, *The New York Times,* http://www.nytimes.com/2010/01/10/us/politics/10reidweb.html. See also the comment by then-Sen. Joe Biden widely understood to imply color, "Biden's Description of Obama Draws Scrutiny," CNN, 1/13/2007, http://articles.cnn.com/2007-01-31/politics/biden.obama_1_braun-and-al-sharpton-african-american-presidential-candidates-delaware-democrat?_s=PM:POLITICS.

47. David Matthews, *Ace of Spades: A Memoir* (New York: Henry Holt, 2007).

Cases

Alonzo v. Chase Manhattan Bank, N.A 25 F. Supp. 2d 455 (S.D.N.Y. 1998)

Case 1

A Hispanic employee sued his employer for national origin discrimination, alleging he was the only Hispanic in his unit and the only person subjected to name calling and racial slurs because of it. After the EEOC's determination and before bringing the case to court, the employee amended the complaint to include race discrimination. The employer argued that race was not included in the original EEOC complaint; therefore, the court had no jurisdiction to hear it at this point. In holding that it was permissible to include the new category because it was within the scope of what could reasonably have been expected to grow out of the EEOC investigation, the court discussed the uncertainty of race versus national origin discrimination.

Sweet, J.

***

Whereas the term "black," or even "Asian," does not trigger the concept of national origin or an affiliation to a particular country, the term "Hispanic" may trigger the concept of race. Thus, the allegations contained in Alonzo's EEOC charge would reasonably cause the EEOC to investigate discrimination based both on national origin and race, thereby satisfying the "reasonably related" requirement, even though he only checked the box labeled "national origin" on his EEOC charge.

Alonzo stated his belief that he was discriminated against because he is Hispanic. While the term "black" is not associated with national origin, some courts have treated "Hispanic" as a racial category. In an oft-cited passage, the court in *Budinsky v. Corning Glass Works*, 425 F. Supp. 786 (W.D. Pa. 1977), reasoned that:

> The terms "race" and "racial discrimination" may be of such doubtful sociological validity as to be scientifically meaningless, but these terms nonetheless are subject to a commonly-accepted, albeit sometimes vague, understanding . . . On this admittedly unscientific basis, whites are plainly a "race" susceptible to "racial discrimination." Hispanic persons and Indians, like African-Americans, have been traditional victims of group discrimination, and, however inaccurately or stupidly, are frequently and even commonly subject to a "racial" identification as "non-whites."

Whether being Hispanic constitutes a race or a national origin category is a semantic distinction with historical implications not worthy of consideration here. Thus, submits Alonzo, neither he nor the EEOC employee who filled out his EEOC charge should be penalized for not checking the box marked "race". Alonzo points out that because he did not state that he was the only Hispanic from a particular country treated in a discriminatory manner, he did not confine his claim to one of national origin discrimination.

Due to Alonzo's pronouncement that he was discriminated against because he is an Hispanic, because it has not been established that the designation of being an Hispanic precludes a claim of racial discrimination, and given the uncertainty among courts as to whether "Hispanic" is better characterized as a race or a national origin, Alonzo's claims of racial discrimination are reasonably related to his claims of national origin discrimination as they fall within the reasonable scope of EEOC investigation. Accordingly, Defendants' MOTION for judgment on the pleadings regarding the claims premised on racial discrimination is DENIED.

Case Questions

1. What do you think of the court's quote from the *Budinsky* case about classification of race being stupid and inaccurate? Explain.

2. Do you think it matters whether someone's category is called "race" vs. "ethnicity"? Explain.

3. Do you agree with the court that the employee should not be penalized for checking the race box? Explain.

Jones v. Robinson Property Group, L.P., d/b/a Horseshoe Casino & Hotel   *427 F.3d 987 (5th Cir. 2005)*

Case 2

A better-than-average black poker dealer with a good deal of experience sued a casino for refusing to hire him over an eight-year period, alleging it was only because of his race. Based on the facts, the court agreed.

Stewart, J.

***

Ralph Jones is an African-American male living in Tunica County, Mississippi. He is a certified poker dealer who has worked in various casinos as a poker dealer and in other capacities. He has also dealt in several major poker tournaments, including the World Poker Open held at the Horseshoe Casino. It is undisputed that Jones is a well qualified poker dealer, whose dealing skills are better than the average poker dealer in Tunica County, Mississippi.

Robinson Property Group (RPG) first opened the Horseshoe Casino and Hotel in Tunica, Mississippi, in 1995. Ken Lambert has served as the poker room manager at the Horseshoe since that time.

Jones alleges that he has repeatedly sought and been refused a position with RPG. Jones first applied for a position at Horseshoe in late 1994, before the casino opened. In May 1995, Jones applied for a poker floor person and a poker dealer position at Horseshoe. Jones was not hired for either position. Two weeks later, Jones complained to Anna West, Horseshoe's Director of Human Resources, that his non-hiring was due to racism. Jones asked her whether the casino had a problem with hiring blacks as poker dealers because he observed that there were no African-Americans working at the Horseshoe as poker dealers at that time. Lambert was summoned to respond to Jones' question. Lambert responded to Jones' complaint by stating that there were no qualified African-American poker dealers in Tunica County. Jones informed him that there were at least five qualified African-Americans in the area, including himself. Lambert testified that he became indignant at Jones' accusation, and he felt "misjudged" and "embarrassed." He claims that he nonetheless offered Jones a position as a poker dealer again. When Jones refused and he persisted in his racial allegations, Lambert testified that his feelings became hurt and he ended the conversation. Jones denies that he was offered a position as a poker dealer.

Between 1995 and 2002, Jones submitted applications for a poker dealer position no less than 10 times. Horseshoe has employed Jones in other departments and on a temporary basis as a poker dealer during high profile poker tournaments; however, Jones has never been hired by Horseshoe on a permanent basis. The record reveals that during the relevant time period the Horseshoe was hiring poker dealers for permanent positions. The Horseshoe generally employs a staff of 40–45 poker dealers.

***

Under Title VII, an employer cannot "fail or refuse to hire or to discharge any individual, or otherwise to discriminate against any individual with respect to his compensation, terms, conditions, or privileges of employment, because of such individual's race[.]" An employee can prove discrimination through direct or circumstantial evidence. If an employee presents credible direct evidence that discriminatory animus at least in part motivated, or was a substantial factor in the adverse employment action, then it becomes the employer's burden to prove by a preponderance of the evidence that the same decision would have been made regardless of the discriminatory animus.

***

We have previously held that "statements or documents which show on its face that an improper criterion served as a basis—not necessarily the sole basis, but a basis—for the adverse employment action are direct evidence of discrimination." When a person or persons with decision making authority evinces [sic] racial animus that may constitute direct evidence of discrimination. [sic] ("This court has implied that calling an employee a 'nigger' would be direct evidence of race discrimination.") We have also previously observed that racial epithets undoubtably demonstrate racial animus.

***

. . . Upon extensive review of the parties' arguments and the record in this case, we find that Jones has demonstrated direct evidence of discrimination.

Mims [a poker dealer and part-time supervisor] stated that she inquired why an African-American poker dealer was not hired and was told, by either Lambert or his assistant, that "they hired who they wanted to hire and there [sic] were not going to hire a black person unless there were extenuating circumstances." She was then told by Lambert, or his assistant, that "good old white boys don't want blacks touching their cards in their face." Sam Thomas [a former Horseshoe employee] testified that in 1995, that Lambert told him that "maybe I've been told not to hire too many blacks in the poker room." It is incontrovertible that Lambert made the hiring decisions at Horseshoe and Presley as his assistant would have provided input, therefore, viewing the evidence in the light most favorable to Jones, the aforementioned evidence proves, without inference or presumption, that race was *a* basis in employment decisions in the poker room at Horseshoe. The evidence need not show that race was the sole basis in order to constitute direct evidence. . . . Mims' and Thomas' testimony clearly and explicitly indicates that decision maker(s) in the poker room used

race as a factor in employment decisions, which is by definition direct evidence of discrimination. Thus, we find that Jones has presented direct evidence of discrimination and accordingly, he has established a *prima facie* case of discrimination. The district court erred in granting summary judgment for RPG. We thus REVERSE and REMAND this case back to the district court for further proceedings consistent with this opinion.

Case Questions

1. Are you surprised that this is a 2005 case? Explain.
2. Given the evidence, do you understand why the lower court would have found that no race discrimination had taken place? Explain.
3. What do you think of the statements that management allegedly made? Do they seem like appropriate bases for making workplace decisions? Explain.

Vaughn v. Edel *918 F.2d 517 (5th Cir. 1990)*

During a retrenchment, a black female was terminated for poor performance. She alleged race discrimination in that her employer intentionally determined not to give her necessary feedback about her performance that would have helped her perform better and perhaps avoid dismissal. The court upheld the employee's claim.

Wiener, J.

***

Emma Vaughn, a black female attorney, became an associate contract analyst in Texaco's Land Department in August of 1979. Her supervisors were Robert Edel and Alvin Earl Hatton, assistant chief contract analyst. In Vaughn's early years with Texaco, she received promotions and was the highest ranked contract analyst in the department.

The events leading to this dispute began on April 16, 1985, the day after Vaughn returned from a second maternity leave. On that day, Edel complained to Vaughn about the low volume of her prior work and the excessive number of people who visited her office. Vaughn later spoke with Roger Keller, the head of the Land Department, about Edel's criticism of her.

In a memorandum concerning this discussion, Keller wrote that he had told Vaughn that he had been told that Vaughn's productivity "was very low"; that he "had become aware for some time of the excessive visiting by predominantly blacks in her office behind closed doors"; and that "the visiting had a direct bearing on her productivity." Keller then told Vaughn, as he noted in his memo, that "she was allowing herself to become a black matriarch within Texaco" and "that this role was preventing her from doing her primary work for the company and that it must stop."

Keller's remarks offended Vaughn, so she sought the advice of a friend who was an attorney in Texaco's Legal Department. Keller learned of this meeting and of

Vaughn's belief that he was prejudiced. To avoid charges of race discrimination, Keller told Vaughn's supervisor, Edel, "not [to] have any confrontations with Ms. Vaughn about her work." Keller later added that "if he [Edel] was dissatisfied, let it ride. If it got serious, then see [Keller]."

Between April 1985 and April 1987 when Vaughn was fired, neither Edel nor Hatton expressed criticism of Vaughn's work to her. During this period all annual written evaluations of Vaughn's work performance (which, incidentally, Vaughn never saw) were "satisfactory." Vaughn also received a merit salary increase, though it was the minimum, for 1986. Keller testified that for several years he had intentionally overstated on Vaughn's annual evaluations his satisfaction with her performance because he did not have the time to spend going through procedures which would result from a lower rating and which could lead to termination.

In 1985–86 Texaco undertook a study to identify activities it could eliminate to save costs. To meet the cost-reduction goal set by the study, the Land Department fired its two "poorest performers," one of whom was Vaughn, as the "lowest ranked" contract analyst. The other employee fired was a white male.

In passing Title VII, Congress announced that "sex, race, religion, and national origin are not relevant to the selection, evaluation, or compensation of employees."

When direct credible evidence of employer discrimination exists, employer can counter direct evidence, such as a statement or written document showing discriminatory motive on its face, "only by showing by a preponderance of the evidence that they would have acted as they did without regard to the [employee's] race."

Vaughn presented direct evidence of discrimination. Keller testified that to avoid provoking a discrimination suit he had told Vaughn's supervisor not to confront her about her work. His "black matriarch" memorandum details the events that led Keller to initiate this policy. Keller also testified to deliberately overstating Vaughn's evaluations in order not to start the process that might eventually lead to her termination. This direct evidence clearly shows that Keller acted as he did solely because Vaughn is black.

Although Vaughn's race may not have directly motivated the 1987 decision to fire her, race did play a part in Vaughn's employment relationship with Texaco from 1985–1987. Texaco's treatment of Vaughn was not color-blind during that period. In neither criticizing Vaughn when her work was unsatisfactory nor counselling her how to improve, Texaco treated Vaughn differently than it did its other contract analysts because she was black. As a result, Texaco did not afford Vaughn the same opportunity to improve her performance and perhaps her relative ranking, as it did its white employees. One of those employees was placed on an improvement program. Others received informal counselling. The evidence indicates that Vaughn had the ability to improve. As Texaco acknowledges, she was once its highest ranked contract analyst.

Had her dissatisfied supervisors simply counselled Vaughn informally, such counselling would inevitably have indicated to Vaughn that her work was deficient. Had Keller given Vaughn the evaluation that he believed she deserved, Texaco's regulations would have required his placing her on a ninety-day work improvement program, just as at least one other employee—a white male—had been placed. A Texaco employee who has not improved by the end of that period is fired.

When an employer excludes black employees from its efforts to improve efficiency, it subverts the "broad overriding interest" of Title VII—"efficient and trusty workmanship assured through fair and racially neutral employment and personnel decisions." Texaco has never stated any reason, other than that Vaughn was black, for treating her as it did. Had Texaco treated Vaughn in a color-blind manner from 1985–1987, Vaughn may have been fired by April 1987 for unsatisfactory work; on the other hand, she might have sufficiently improved her performance so as not to be one of the two lowest ranked employees, thereby avoiding termination in April 1987.

Because Texaco's behavior was race-motivated, Texaco has violated Title VII. Texaco limited or classified Vaughn in a way which would either "tend to deprive [her] of employment opportunities or otherwise adversely affect [her] status as an employee" in violation of the law.

Case Questions

1. Do you agree with the court's decision? Why or why not?

2. How would you have handled this matter if you were the manager?

3. What do you think of Keller's remarks about Vaughn becoming the "black matriarch" of Texaco, "meeting behind closed doors," and "excessive meetings with predominantly blacks"? What does it signify to you? What attitudes might it reflect that may be inappropriate in the workplace? What concern, if any, might be appropriate?

Case 4   Chandler v. Fast Lane, Inc.   *868 F. Supp. 1138 (E.D. Ark., W. Div. 1994)*

A white employee brought suit against her employer for constructive dismissal under Title VII and other statutes, alleging that she was forced to leave her job when the employer would not allow her to hire and promote African-Americans. The employer argued that since its policies discriminated only against African-Americans, the white employee had no right to sue under Title VII. The court disagreed and permitted the case to be brought.

Eisele, J.

***

In the complaint filed with the Court, Chandler (who is white) alleges that she was the victim of a discriminatory employment practice at the hands of her employers. Chandler, a former manager of employer's restaurant, claims that her employer thwarted her efforts to employ and promote African-American employees, and that as a result the conditions of her employment became so intolerable that she was forced to resign. The employer argues that because they are alleged to have adopted discriminatory hiring and promotional practices targeted only at African-Americans, a white person has no standing to assert a Title VII claim premised upon these policies.

It is true that only individuals whom employers are claimed to have failed or refused to hire or promote were African-Americans. However, by focusing on the "fail or refuse to hire" provision of 2000e-2(a)(1), employer's argument misperceives the unlawful employment practice alleged by Chandler. Chandler does not claim that she was a target of employer's allegedly anti–African-American employment practices. Rather, Chandler argues that employer's insistence that she enforce these practices violated her fundamental right to associate with African-Americans, and as a consequence employer committed a separate violation by engaging in an unlawful employment practice that "otherwise discriminate[d] against an individual," namely Chandler.

Although the Court recognizes that Chandler's Title VII claim is somewhat novel, it is of the opinion that such a claim, if proven, would state a cause of action under Title VII. A white person's right to associate with African-Americans is protected by Sec. 1981. Therefore, the Court concludes that an employer's implementation of an employment practice that impinges upon this right is actionable under Title VII.

Additionally, Chandler's allegations are sufficient to establish a Title VII claim under a separate provision of the statute. The relevant provision of Title VII is found in 42 U.S.C.A. § 2000e-3(a), which provides in pertinent part:

> It shall be an unlawful employment practice for an employer to discriminate against any of his employees . . . because [s]he has opposed any practice made an unlawful employment practice by [Title VII].

In order to establish a *prima facie* case under the "opposition" clause of § 2000e-3(a), an employee must show: (1) that she was engaged in an opposition activity protected under Title VII; (2) that she was a victim of adverse employment action; and (3) that a causal nexus exists between these two events. The Court has no doubt that an employee who exercises her authority to promote and employ African-Americans engages in protected "opposition" to her employer's unlawful employment practice which seeks to deprive African-Americans of such benefits. Thus, Chandler's allegations are clearly sufficient to meet the first requirement of a § 2000e-3(a) claim. The Court further concludes that employer's insistence that Chandler enforce such an employment practice, if proven, would certainly cause an "adverse employment action" to be visited upon her. Title VII forbids an employer from requiring its employees "to work in a discriminatorily hostile or abusive environment," and included within this prohibition is the right of white employees to a work environment free from discrimination against African-Americans, or any other class of persons. Indeed, subjecting an employee to such a hostile working environment may result in an actionable constructive discharge, a result that is especially likely under facts similar to those presently alleged. Under Title VII, a constructive discharge occurs whenever it is reasonably foreseeable that an employee will resign as a result of her employer's unlawful employment practice, and it is plainly foreseeable that an employee might choose to resign rather than to acquiesce in or enforce her employer's discriminatory and illegal employment practice.

The Court is therefore satisfied that employer's efforts to hinder Chandler from hiring and promoting African-Americans, and their insistence that she discriminate against such persons, if proven, would result in an actionable Title VII claim. Indeed, "[u]nder the terms of § 2000e-3(a), requiring an employee to discriminate is itself an unlawful employment practice." Accordingly, it is therefore ordered that employer's motion to dismiss is DENIED.

Case Questions

1. What do you think of the employer's argument that since its policies discriminated against African-Americans, the white employee should not be able to bring a suit for discrimination? Explain.

2. Do you understand the court's reasoning that the white employee was being discriminated against by not being able to hire and promote black employees? Explain.

3. What reason can you think of as to why the employer had the policy of not hiring or promoting African-Americans? Do you think it makes good economic sense? (Consider all facets of economics, including the possibility of litigation over the policies.)

Chapter 7

National Origin Discrimination

Learning Objectives

By the time you finish studying this chapter, you should be able to:

LO1 Describe the impact and implications of the changing demographics of the American workforce.

LO2 Define the *prima facie* case for national origin discrimination under Title VII.

LO3 Explain the legal status surrounding "English-only policies" in the workplace.

LO4 Describe a claim for harassment based on national origin and discuss how it might be different from one based on other protected classes.

LO5 Identify the difference between citizenship and national origin.

LO6 Explain the extent of protection under the Immigration Reform and Control Act.

Opening Scenarios

SCENARIO 1

1 Kayla, a supervisor, recently hired a new
Scenario manager, Alex, but has received complaints
from customers that they cannot understand him when they speak to him on the telephone. Alex is a Romanian employee visiting from
the company's Romanian office and is scheduled to
remain with the firm for two years. Kayla is concerned that if she allows Alex to perform duties
similar to other managers, the firm will lose customers; however, she is unsure about the firm's liability
for decreasing Alex's responsibilities as a result of
his foreign accent.

SCENARIO 2

2 Muhammad, an Arab-American Muslim high
Scenario school student, had a job after school at a
fast-food restaurant. A few co-workers
started asking him why his "cousins" bombed the
World Trade Center. Muhammad ignored their
taunts. Then a manager began to add comments such
as "Hey, Muhammed, we're going to have to check
you for bombs." Muhammed felt humiliated and
angry. Soon after, he was terminated for accidentally
throwing away a paper cup that the manager was
using. Muhammed suspects that his religious and
ethnic background was the reason he was fired.

Statutory Basis

The statutory basis for protection against national origin discrimination is
presented in Exhibit 7.1, "Legislation Prohibiting National Origin Discrimination."
These statutes include section 703(a) of Title VII of the Civil Rights Act of 1964
and the Immigration Reform and Control Act of 1986.

Chez/Casa/Fala/Wunderbar Uncle Sam

America has always considered itself to be a melting pot. Under this theory,
different ethnic, cultural, and racial groups came together in America, but
differences were melted into one homogeneous mass composed of all cultures.
Recently, this characterization has been revisited and other, more accurate terms
have been proposed. They include such terms as a *salad bowl,* in which all the
ingredients come together to make an appetizing, nutritious whole but each
ingredient maintains its own identity, or a *stew,* in which the ingredients are
blended together but maintain their distinct identity, with the common thread of
living in America acting as the stew base that binds the stew's ingredients
together.

While the words on the Statue of Liberty—"Give me your tired, your poor,
your huddled masses yearning to breathe free"—have always acted as a beacon to
citizens of other countries to find solace on our shores, the reality once they get
here, even sometimes after being here for generations, is that they are often
discriminated against, rather than consoled. National origin was included in Title
VII's list of protected classes to ensure that employers did not base employment
decisions on preconceived notions about employees or applications based on their
country of origin. Note that section 1981 of the Civil Rights Act of 1964 also may

Exhibit 7.1 *Legislation Prohibiting National Origin Discrimination*

TITLE VII, CIVIL RIGHTS ACT OF 1964

Sec. 703(a)

It shall be an unlawful employment practice for an employer—

(1) to fail or to refuse to hire or to discharge any individual, or otherwise to discriminate against any individual with respect to his compensation, terms, conditions, or privileges of employment, because of such individual's . . . national origin.

IMMIGRATION REFORM AND CONTROL ACT OF 1986

Sec. 274A(a)

(1) It is unlawful for a person or other entity:

    (A) to hire or to recruit or refer for a fee for employment in the United States an alien knowing the alien is an unauthorized alien with respect to such employment, or

    (B) to hire for employment in the United States an individual without [verification of employment eligibility].

(2) It is unlawful for a person or other entity, after hiring an alien for employment in accordance with paragraph (1), to continue to employ the alien in the United States knowing the alien is (or had become) an unauthorized alien with respect to such employment.

(3) A person or entity that establishes that it has complied in good faith with the [verification of employment eligibility] with respect to hiring, recruiting or referral for employment of an alien in the United States has established an affirmative defense that the person or entity has not violated paragraph (1)(A).

Sec. 274(B)(a)

(1) It is an unfair immigration-related practice for a person or other entity to discriminate against any individual (other than an unauthorized alien) with respect to the hiring, or recruitment or referral for a fee, of the individual for employment or the discharging of the individual from employment—

    (A) because of such individual's national origin, or

    (B) in the case of a protected individual [a citizen or authorized alien], because of such individual's citizenship status.

apply in those circumstances where national origin is a proxy for or equivalent to race (discussed later in this chapter).[1]

Speaking of race, as was mentioned in the introduction to the chapter on race discrimination, recently there has been a sort of blending of the race and national origin categories, with employees bringing as race discrimination cases those that had traditionally been brought as national origin claims. The traditional distinctions in the law are becoming blurred; but the significant thing is that, for instance, whether being Hispanic is considered race discrimination or national origin discrimination, it is, in fact, illegal to make workplace decisions on the basis of this attribute. What is critical to understand is that a decision based on either attribute is illegal; and national origin is a distinct category in this textbook because it is the way that such claims are traditionally handled, and because we are reluctant to blend completely the two areas when they have quite different histories, implications, and analyses for today's employment arena.

Exhibit 7.2   *REALITIES about National Origin Discrimination*

1. "Citizenship" and "national origin" are not synonymous.
2. No matter the national origin of a restaurant, it likely will still be required strictly to abide by

   Title VII non-discrimination principles in hiring its waitstaff.
3. It is illegal discrimination for an employer to require that employees speak only English at work.

The Changing Workforce

LO1

The 1990s saw a dramatic increase in the number of immigrants to the United States, particularly from Latino and Asian countries, which continued throughout the first decade of the 21st century. By 2010, the United States was growing by one person every 8 seconds, about the amount of time it takes to read the beginning of this paragraph.[2] Census figures released in 2010 show that the number of Latinos has risen to 48 million people, representing 15.8 percent of the population.[3] In 2009, foreign-born workers represented more than 15.5 percent of U.S. workers, which has remained roughly constant, although their unemployment rate was higher than that of native-born workers for the first time since 2003.[4]

In 2004, African-Americans made up 11.3 percent of the workforce; Latinos made up 13.1 percent (the first time Latinos comprised a higher percentage than African-Americans); and Asians, Pacific Islanders, Native Americans, and Alaska Natives made up 4 percent.[5] By 2006, Latinos, the largest minority group, numbered 44.3 million and accounted for almost half the nation's growth of 2.9 million over that past year.[6] Between 2008 and 2018, the number of African-Americans in the workforce is expected to increase by 14.1 percent; Asians, Pacific Islanders, Native Americans, and Alaska Natives by 29.8 percent; and Latinos by 33.1 percent.[7] By 2018, the U.S. workforce is expected to be comprised of 17.6 percent Hispanics, 12.1 percent African-Americans, and 5.6 percent Asians.

However, as of 2007, the median weekly earnings of foreign-born full-time workers was significantly less than for non-foreign-born workers, $532 compared with $698 for other groups (among men only, the difference is $563 versus $782!).[8]

On its face, national origin discrimination appears to be relatively simple to determine; however, it has surprising complexities. Employers have always been uncertain of the scope of Title VII's coverage in this area and what could be used as a defense against decisions based on national origin. (See Exhibit 7.2, "REALITIES about National Origin Discrimination.") Notwithstanding its complexity, however, complaints to the EEOC based on alleged national origin discrimination have been on the rise since 1999 and represent the fastest-growing source of complaints submitted to the EEOC,[9] which received 9,369 charges of national origin discrimination in 2007, 12 percent more than received in 2006.[10]

Regulatory Overview

LO2

national origin discrimination protection
It is unlawful for an employer to limit, segregate, or classify employees in any way on the basis of national origin that would deprive them of the privileges, benefits, or opportunities of employment.

The **national origin discrimination protection** offered by Title VII is similar to that of gender or race and is used somewhat synonymously with *ethnicity*, though they are distinguishable. That is, it is an unlawful employment practice for an employer to limit, segregate, or classify employees in any way that would deprive them of employment opportunities because of national origin. An employer may not group its employees on the basis of national origin, make employment decisions on that basis, or implement policies or programs that, though they appear not to be based on an employee's or applicant's country of origin, actually affect those of one national origin differently than those of a different group.

An employee may successfully claim discrimination on the basis of national origin if it is shown that

1. He or she is a member of a protected class (i.e., articulate the employee's national origin).
2. He or she was qualified for the position for which he or she applied or in which he or she was employed.
3. The employer made an employment decision against this employee or applicant.
4. The position was filled by someone who was not a member of the protected class.

Each of the above will be discussed in turn.

Member of the Protected Class

In connection with the first requirement, what is meant by national origin? While the term is not defined in Title VII, the EEOC guidelines on discrimination define **national origin** discrimination as "including, but not limited to, the denial of equal employment opportunity because of [an applicant's or employee's] or his or her ancestor's place of origin; or because an applicant has the physical, cultural, or linguistic characteristics of a national origin group."

national origin
Individual's, or her or his ancestor's, place of origin (as opposed to citizenship), or physical, cultural, or linguistic characteristics of an origin group.

Note that the law provides protection against discrimination based only on country of origin, not on country of *citizenship*. Title VII protects employees who are not U.S. citizens from employment discrimination based on the categories of the act, but it does not protect them from discrimination based on their status as aliens, rather than as U.S. citizens. That is, it protects a Somali woman from gender discrimination, but not from discrimination on the basis of the fact that she is a Somali citizen, rather than an American citizen. The issue of citizenship as it relates to national origin is discussed later in this chapter.

Many national origin cases under Title VII involve claims of discrimination by those who were not born in America; however, American-born employees also are protected against discrimination on the basis of their *American* origin. For example, a court has held that the employer's conscious decision about whom to dismiss on the basis of the national origin of its employees (in an effort to promote "affirmative action") was not acceptable because that method tended to disfavor Americans, in favor of other nationalities.

In addition to national origin encompassing the employee's place of birth, it also includes ethnic characteristics or origins, as well as physical, linguistic, or cultural traits closely associated with a national origin group. For instance, it has been held that Cajuns, Gypsies, and Ukrainians are protected under Title VII. It also may serve as the basis for a national origin discrimination claim if the employee

- Is identified with or connected to a person of a specific national origin, such as when someone suffers discrimination because he or she is married to a person of a certain ethnic heritage.
- Is a member of an organization that is identified with a national group.
- Is a participant in a school or religious organization that is affiliated with a national origin group.
- Has a surname that is generally associated with a national origin group.
- Is perceived by an employer to be a member of a particular national origin group, whether or not the individual is in fact of that origin.

Qualification/BFOQs

The second factor that must be present for an employee to claim national origin discrimination is that the applicant or employee is *qualified* for the position. That is, the claimant must show that he or she meets the job's requirements.

Contrary to situations involving disability or religion, the employee in a national origin case must show that she or he is qualified for the position without the benefit of accommodation. No accommodation of one's national origin is required of employers. For example, while an employer would be required to reasonably accommodate an employee's religious attire, there is no similar responsibility to accommodate an employee's attire of national origin, such as traditional African dress, unless it can be shown to overlap with one's religion.

The employer may counter the employee's claim that she or he is otherwise qualified by showing that national origin is actually a bona fide occupational qualification (BFOQ) (discussed in Chapter 3) for the job. That is, the employer may explain why a specific national origin is necessary for the position applied for, why it is a legitimate job requirement that is reasonably necessary for the employer's particular business. However, it is important to note that customer, client, or co-worker *discomfort or preference may not be relied upon by the employer.* However, consider the following example. In one case, national origin was allowed as a BFOQ involving a subsidiary of a Japanese company. The court found that the firm could impose a preference for Japanese nationals based on the unique requirements of international trade.[11] In addition, where the provisions of an international treaty apply and the BFOQ is *citizenship* rather than national origin, a foreign-based multinational may be allowed to express a preference for its own citizens.[12]

English Fluency and Speaking Native Languages in the Workplace

LO3

Some employers choose to maintain policies requiring all employees either to be fluent in English or to speak only English while in the workplace, even when employees are speaking only among themselves. "English-only" policies have become increasingly relevant. In 2005, 19.4 percent of the U.S. population five years and older spoke a language other than English in the home, with 8.6 percent of these same people speaking English less than "very well."[13] While these policies may raise challenges related to national origin discrimination, those employers who maintain the policies contend that fluency in English is a BFOQ and, therefore, they should not be required to hire someone who is not fluent in English because of his or her national origin.

Diversity in the workplace brings many benefits, including a greater breadth of skills and life experiences among the workforce. It also may present unique challenges to employers, particularly in the form of poor communication among those who may prefer to speak in their native tongue, which might be not English but Spanish, Hindi, or Tagalog. While such communication problems may cause confusion, severe English-only restrictions may create frustration and resentment among employees for whom English is a second language. To avoid alienating these employees, to ensure realistic and reasonable job qualifications, and to decrease the risk of litigation, employers should not permit managers to arbitrarily impose language restrictions.[14]

To best be protected from possible Title VII liability, the employer must be able to show that English fluency is required for the job and that the requirement is necessary to maintain supervisory control of the workplace. Perhaps it may be required of an employee who has significant communication with clients, or it may be justified as a BFOQ where the employee could not speak or understand English sufficiently to perform required duties.

For example, where a teacher was fluent in English but spoke with such a thick accent that her students had a difficult time understanding her, her discharge was upheld. On the other hand, if the employee is in a job requiring little speaking and the employee can understand English, the requirement may be more difficult to defend—for instance, requiring English fluency for a janitor who talks little, has little reason to speak to carry out the duties of the job, and who understands what is said to him or her. In fact, in *In re Rodriguez,*[15] the court found that an employment decision based on an employee's accent and speech characteristics (where due to the employee's national origin) was *direct evidence* of employment discrimination sufficient to shift the burden of proof to the defendant to articulate a legitimate non-discriminatory reason for the decision that the employer "would have terminated the [employee] had it not been motivated by discrimination." The court noted that "accent and national origin are inextricably intertwined."

1)
Scenario

Unlike the teacher above, in Scenario 1 Kayla is considering *decreasing* Alex's responsibilities due to his foreign accent, not terminating him. However, like the teacher, it is quite possible in this scenario to show that speaking clear English is a BFOQ, especially if it can be shown that customers have been complaining that they cannot understand him.

As mentioned above, closely related is the employer's policy requiring employees capable of speaking English to speak only English in the workplace. These policies may be based in well-intentioned employer efforts aimed at decreasing workplace tension where multiple languages have segregated a workplace, improving employees' English, or promoting a safe and efficient workplace. Courts have gone both ways on this issue. Some have held the policy to be discriminatory, excessively prohibitive, and a violation of Title VII. Others have held that it is not national origin discrimination if all employees, regardless of ancestry, were prohibited from speaking anything but English on the job and that there is no statutory right to speak other languages at work. It has been held that the right to speak one's native language when the employee is bilingual is not an immutable characteristic that Title VII protects.

In general, though, English-only rules have been upheld (see *Garcia,* discussed below and included at the end of the chapter). In *EEOC v. Sephora USA, L.L.C.,*[16] the court specifically held that a policy at a cosmetics store that required salespeople to speak English when customers were present served a legitimate business necessity. The court did not find that the policy had a disparate impact on the Latino employees who worked there. However, challenges to these rules increased fivefold between 1996 and 2006 and some resulted in large awards and settlements to affected employees.[17]

The EEOC takes the position that English-only rules *applied at all times* or only applied to certain foreign speakers are presumptively discriminatory, although the courts have not always agreed with that approach.[18] When a rule is applied only at certain times, the EEOC recommends that it be justified by a business purpose in order to avoid discrimination claims. Rules applied during work time *only* are less likely to be considered harassment and more likely to show a business purpose. When an employer is considering an English-only rule, it should take into consideration the legal implications as well as the fact that such a rule can create an atmosphere of inferiority, isolation, and intimidation that may result in a discriminatory work environment.

According to the EEOC, an employer may justify the business necessity of an English-only rule

- For communications with customers, co-workers, or supervisors who only speak English.
- In emergencies or other situations in which workers must speak a common language to promote safety.
- For cooperative work assignments in which the English-only rule is needed to promote efficiency. For example, a taxi company was permitted to maintain an English-only policy for main office employees to prevent miscommunications during dispatch.[19]
- To enable a supervisor who only speaks English to monitor the performance of an employee whose job duties require communication with co-workers or customers.

Garcia v. Spun Steak Co., given at the conclusion of the chapter, is one of the most important cases on the subject. In that case, the court ruled against the EEOC's guidelines but mentioned that an English-only policy may be discriminatory if it "exacerbate[s] existing tensions, combine[s] with other discriminatory behavior to contribute to discrimination, [or is] enforced in a 'draconian manner' [such] that the enforcement itself amounts to harassment." In 2006, however, the EEOC's position was supported in *Maldonado v. City of Altus,*[20] where the court held that a hostile work environment might exist based solely on the employer's adoption of an English-only policy in the workplace.

An employer, therefore, may properly enforce a limited, reasonable, and business-related English-only rule against an employee who can readily comply. However, if the practice of requiring only English on the job is mere pretext for discrimination on the basis of national origin (i.e., the employer imposes the rule *in order to* discriminate, or the rule produces an atmosphere of ethnic oppression), such a policy would be illegal. This might be the case where an employer requires English to be spoken in all areas of the workplace, even on breaks or in discussions between employees during free time.

Adverse Employment Action and Dissimilar Treatment

The third and fourth requirements will be addressed together because they often arise together. The third element of the *prima facie* case for national origin discrimination is that the employee has suffered an **adverse employment action** by the employer's employment decision. This may include a demotion, termination, or removal of privileges afforded to other employees. The adverse effect may arise either because employees of different national origin are treated differently (disparate treatment) or because the policy, though neutral, adversely impacts those of a given national origin (disparate impact).

The fourth element requires that the employee show that her position was filled by someone who is not a member of her protected class or, under other circumstances, that those who are not members of her protected class are treated differently than she. For example, assume an Asian employee is terminated after the third time he is late for work. There is a rule that employees will be terminated if they are late for work more than twice. However, the employer does not enforce the rule against the other employees, only against Asian employees. This would be a case of disparate treatment because the employee could show that he was treated differently from other employees who were similarly situated but not members of his protected class.

Alternatively, disparate impact has been found, for example, with physical requirements such as minimum height and weight. Such requirements may have a disparate impact on certain national origin groups as a result of genetic differences among populations and these requirements disproportionately precluded the groups from qualifying for certain jobs. These requirements violate Title VII and must be justified by business necessity. For instance, a requirement that a firefighter be at least 5 feet 7 inches tall was found to be unlawful where the average height of an Anglo man in the United States is 5 feet 8 inches, Spanish-surnamed

adverse employment action
Any action or omission that takes away a benefit, opportunity, or privilege of employment from an employee.

American men average 5 feet 4½ inches, and females average 5 feet 3 inches. On the other hand, if the rule can be shown to be a business necessity, it may be allowed (such as some English fluency requirements, as discussed earlier).

Once the employee has articulated a *prima facie* case of discrimination based on national origin, the burden falls to the employer to identify either a BFOQ or a legitimate nondiscriminatory reason (LNDR) for the adverse employment action. In the *Alvarado-Santos v. Department of Health of the Commonwealth of Puerto Rico* case, included at the end of the chapter, the employer offers two such LNDRs but, to its detriment in the case, cannot explain on which of them the decision was based. (For more detailed discussions of *prima facie* cases, BFOQs, and LNDRs, please see Chapter 2.)

Harassment on the Basis of National Origin

In addition to providing protection against traditional types of discrimination, Title VII also protects employees against harassment on the basis of national origin. Unfortunately, claims of national origin harassment have been on a sharp increase, rising from 7,792 charges filed with the EEOC in 2000 to 11,134 in 2009. In fact, in 2009, almost 12 percent of all claims filed with the EEOC included a claim for national origin discrimination.

Not all harassment is prohibited under Title VII. Similar to claims of sexual harassment, claims of national origin harassment are only actionable if the harassment was so severe or pervasive that the employee reasonably finds the workplace to be hostile or abusive. Common concerns include ethnic slurs, workplace graffiti, or other offenses based on traits such as an employee's birthplace, culture, accent, or skin color. In considering employer liability, the court will look to whether the conduct was physically threatening or intimidating, its severity, pervasiveness throughout the working environment, whether a reasonable person would find the conduct offensive and/or hostile, and how the employer responded. The EEOC offers the following examples of conduct that do and do not satisfy this review:[21]

Offensive Conduct Based on National Origin That Violates Title VII

Muhammad, an Arab-American, works for XYZ Motors, a large automobile dealership. His coworkers regularly call him names like "camel jockey," "the local terrorist," and "the ayatollah," and intentionally embarrass him in front of customers by claiming that he is incompetent. Muhammad reports this conduct to higher management, but XYZ does not respond. The constant ridicule has made it difficult for Muhammad to do his job. The frequent, severe, and offensive conduct linked to Muhammad's national origin has created a hostile work environment in violation of Title VII.[22]

Offensive Conduct Based on National Origin That Does Not Violate Title VII

Horia, a Romanian emigrant, was hired by XYZ Shipping as a dockworker. On his first day, Horia dropped a carton, prompting Bill, the foreman, to yell at him. The same day, Horia overheard Bill telling a coworker that foreigners were stealing jobs from Americans. Two months later, Bill confronted Horia about an argument with a coworker, called him a "lazy jerk," and mocked his accent. Although Bill's conduct was offensive, it was not sufficiently severe or pervasive for the work environment to be reasonably considered sufficiently hostile or abusive to violate Title VII.

Employers have the responsibility to prevent and correct any national origin harassment that may take place within its working environment. However, that responsibility is limited to occurrences of harassment of which the employer knows or should have known. Consequently, if an employee is consistently subject to abuse but never informs the employer and the supervisors at her or his workplace have no other way of knowing the abuse is taking place, the employer may not be liable. In addition, if the employer is aware of or is made aware of the harassment and takes reasonable steps to prevent and correct it, the employer may likewise be relieved of any liability.

WC&M is included in this chapter in order to demonstrate that many forms of discrimination and harassment may satisfy a *prima facie* case under Title VII, not only the most obvious ones. It is important for workers to know that they are protected, even if the adverse working conditions might not fit the traditional model under Title VII, and for employers to ensure that they are diligent in their training and sensitivity to unique cross- (and even within) cultural phenomena.

Guidelines on Discrimination Because of Religion or National Origin

Guidelines on Discrimination Because of Religion or National Origin
Federal guidelines that apply only to federal contractors or agencies and that impose on these employers an affirmative duty to prevent discrimination.

Federal agencies or employers who enter into contracts with a government agency are required by the **Guidelines on Discrimination Because of Religion or National Origin** to ensure that individuals are hired and retained without regard to their religion or national origin. These guidelines impose on the federal contractor an affirmative obligation to prevent discrimination. The provisions include the following ethnic groups: Eastern, Middle, and Southern European ancestry, including Jews, Catholics, Italians, Greeks, and Slavs. Blacks, Spanish-surnamed Americans, Asians, and Native Americans are specifically excluded from the guidelines' coverage because of their protection elsewhere in Office of Federal Contract Compliance Rules.

The guidelines provide that, subsequent to a review of the employer's policies, the employer should engage in appropriate outreach and positive recruitment activities to remedy existing deficiencies (i.e., affirmative action). Various approaches to this outreach requirement include the following:

1. Internal communication of the obligation to provide equal employment opportunity without regard to religion or national origin.
2. Development of reasonable internal procedures to ensure that the equal employment policy is fully implemented.
3. Periodic informing of all employees of the employer's commitment to equal employment opportunity for all persons, without regard to religion or national origin.

4. Enlistment of the support and assistance of all recruitment sources.

5. Review of employment records to determine the availability of promotable and transferable members of various religious and ethnic groups.

6. Establishment of meaningful contacts with religious and ethnic organizations and leaders for such purposes as advice, education, technical assistance, and referral of potential employees (many organizations send job announcements to these community groups when recruiting for positions).

7. Significant recruitment activities at educational institutions with substantial enrollments of students from various religious and ethnic groups.

8. Use of the religious and ethnic media for institutional and employment advertising.

Middle Eastern Discrimination after September 11, 2001

In the aftermath of September 11, hate crimes against individuals of Middle Eastern descent dramatically increased. Workplace discrimination complaints brought by Muslims and those of Middle Eastern descent also rose sharply. From September 11, 2001, to February 2002, the EEOC received 260 such claims, an increase of 168 percent over the same period a year earlier. The EEOC even created a special classification, "Code Z," to designate complaints tied to September 11.[23] Although the number of complaints by Muslims dropped thereafter, reaching a low of 694 in 2004, the number spiked upward for five consecutive years between 2005 and 2009, reaching a high of 1,490 by 2009.[24]

Scenario

Opening Scenario 2 presents one post–September 11 incident. Further examples include a California employee who was allegedly fired without explanation after being told by her boss not to reveal to anyone that her husband was Palestinian and a New York City nurse who was ordered to take some time off and then was given a lesser position "for her own safety" after she reported that a co-worker threatened to "kill Muslims."[25]

The U.S. Department of Justice (DoJ), through its National Origin Working Group, initiative is working proactively to combat civil rights violations against Arab, Sikh, and South-Asian Americans, as well as those who are perceived to be members of those groups. The group is battling these crimes and acts of discrimination by identifying cases involving bias crimes, conducting outreach, and working with other DoJ offices. As of June 2010, the initiative had helped to respond to more than 800 incidents of bias crime alone, resulting in federal charges against 48 defendants, with 44 convictions. In addition, DoJ attorneys have worked with state and local prosecutors in 150 nonfederal criminal prosecutions. In one case, *EEOC v. Fairfield Toyota*,[26] two auto dealerships agreed to pay seven former workers $550,000. The suit was filed by workers of Afghani national origin and Muslim faith as a result of harassment they suffered on the job. One worker claimed constructive discharge and others suffered retaliation after complaining about the harassment.

Issues of concern and questions that have arisen from these cases have centered on a few key issues. Employers may not treat workers differently because of their religious attire, such as a Muslim *hijab* (head scarf). Employers also need to be sensitive to possible instances of ethnic harassment, especially that which may unfairly relate to security concerns. Finally, employers may not require individuals of one ethnic background to undergo more significant security checks or other preemployment requirements unless all applicants for that position are required to do so.

In the post–September 11 era, employers actually have a unique opportunity to raise awareness of and sensitivity to cultural diversity in the workplace. Elmer Johnson, head of the Aspen Institute, which seeks to improve corporate leadership, has stated that corporate leaders should inspire employees and inculcate a sense of shared values.[27] Perhaps this can be achieved by reaching out to employees of Middle Eastern descent who may be experiencing fear of discrimination. Jaffe Dickerson, a partner in the Littler, Mendelson law firm, had a client's Middle Eastern employee confide that he no longer wants to travel by air or go out to clubs after work out of fear of being victimized by bias.[28] Remaining sensitive to such employees' concerns in job assignments and work-related activities is key to their effective resolution. "Quick fixes," such as compulsory transfer to another position, must be avoided. To further promote a healthy environment at work, employers also should consider the post–September 11 issues in diversity training.

It should be noted that, under certain limited circumstances, employers may reach decisions on the basis of national origin by relying on security requirements, where the security requirements are imposed "in the interest of national security under any security program in effect pursuant to federal statute or executive order."[29]

Citizenship and the Immigration Reform and Control Act

LO5

As mentioned earlier in this chapter, Title VII's prohibition against discrimination on the basis of national origin does not necessarily prohibit discrimination on the basis of citizenship; this only occurs where citizenship discrimination "has the purpose or effect" of national origin discrimination or where it is pretext for national origin discrimination. In fact, legal aliens (noncitizens residing in the United States) are often restricted from access to certain government or other positions by statute. For instance, in *Foley v. Connelie,*[30] the Supreme Court held that a rule requiring citizenship was valid in connection with certain nonelected positions held by officers who participate directly in the formulation, execution, or review of broad public policy. This is called the "political function" exception for positions that are intimately related to the process of self-government. In cases where the restricted position satisfies this exception, discrimination against legal aliens is permitted. *Espinoza v. Farah Manufacturing Co.,* included for your review, is the seminal case by the U.S. Supreme Court in the area of discrimination on the basis of citizenship.

LO6

The Immigration Reform and Control Act (IRCA), *in contrast to Title VII,* does prohibit employers in certain circumstances from discriminating against employees on the basis of their citizenship or intended citizenship, and from hiring those not legally authorized for employment in the United States. However, IRCA does allow discrimination in favor of U.S. citizens as against legal aliens. While aliens are guaranteed various rights pursuant to the Constitution, the law confers certain benefits only to those who are citizens and not to those who are legal aliens in the United States. For instance, while rights pursuant to the National Labor Relations Act and Fair Labor Standards Act are provided to citizens and aliens alike, some government-provided benefits are limited to citizens. Also, the IRCA allows employers to enact a preference for U.S. citizens if the applicants are all equally qualified. Employers may not act on this preference if the foreign national is more qualified for the position than the U.S. citizen.

Employers not subject to Title VII's prohibitions because of their small size may still be sufficiently large to be covered by IRCA's anti-discrimination provisions; those employers with 4 to 14 employees are prohibited from discriminating on the basis of national origin; and employers with 4 or more employees may not discriminate on the basis of citizenship.

Two acceptable BFOQs are statutorily allowed under IRCA:

1. English-language skill requirements that are reasonably necessary to the normal operation of the particular business or enterprise.
2. Citizenship requirements specified by law, regulation, executive order, or government contracts, along with citizenship requirements that the U.S. attorney general determines to be essential for doing business with the government.

The main difference between a proof of discrimination under Title VII and IRCA is that, in proving a case of disparate impact, Title VII does not require proof of discriminatory intent, while IRCA requires that the adverse action be knowingly and intentionally discriminatory. Therefore, innocent or negligent discrimination is a complete defense to a claim of discrimination under IRCA.

For example, consider a hypothetical firm that is interviewing for customer service representatives in their large order-processing department. They require all applicants to speak fluent English. Ching Lee applied and was denied employment due to his accent, which some thought was heavy. It turns out that only 3 applicants out of 20 of Asian descent obtained jobs at the firm. The employer explained to Lee that not many Chinese applicants apply and those who do have had strong accents. It claims that customers have complained of not understanding these individuals. Does Lee have a claim under Title VII? Under IRCA? Without evidence of knowledge and intentional discrimination, the employer could survive the IRCA claim if Lee could not prove that it discriminated against him intentionally; however, such knowledge and intention are not required under Title VII and Lee might prevail in that case.

Undocumented Workers

Approximately 12 million undocumented workers made up about 5 percent of the U.S. workforce in 2007.[31] The number has since dropped for the first time in

20 years, to 11.1 million, according to the Pew Hispanic Center.[32] The decline has been attributed to some combination of a weak U.S. economy and increased border enforcement.[33] A section of the IRCA was established to correct an unfair double standard that prohibited these individuals from working in the United States but permitted employers to hire them. In other words, originally, the unauthorized worker had committed a legal wrong, but the employer who hired the worker had not! Among other things, IRCA now makes it unlawful for any person knowingly to hire, recruit, or refer for a fee any alien not authorized to work. "Knowingly" includes that which "may be fairly inferred through notice of certain facts and circumstances which would lead a person . . . to know about a certain condition."[34] Employers are thereby denied the "ostrich" defense where they simply ignore obvious evidence to a violation. Employers are instead required to verify all newly hired employees by examining documents that identify the individual and show his or her authority to work in the United States using a Form I-9. (See Exhibit 7.3, "INS Employment Form and Document List.") Further, employers, recruiters, and those who refer individuals for employment are required to keep records pertaining to IRCA requirements. (For a list of employer responsibilities under IRCA, see Exhibit 7.4, "Employer Responsibilities under IRCA.") A violation of this provision can mean *personal liability* for corporate officers, so it is not a requirement to be taken lightly.

In 2007, in an effort to further implement these provisions, the Department of Homeland Security (DHS) announced that employers would be required to terminate all workers who used false social security numbers, otherwise known as a "no-match" (based on the 140,000 no-match letters received annually by employers from the Social Security Administration notifying them that the names and social security numbers of employees do not match the agency's records). Employers were to have 90 days in which to reconcile the no-match letters; if they could not, they were going to be forced to fire the worker or face fines of up to $10,000. With an estimated 6 million unauthorized aliens currently employed, the impact on both the workforce and the economy would have been monumental, notwithstanding the claim by the Social Security Administration that 12.7 million of its records contained errors that could lead to terminations.[35] The impact in the agricultural industry alone would have been overwhelming, where estimates by the growers' associations place undocumented workers at about 70 percent.[36] However, only five days before its implementation, a California federal judge issued an order blocking the implementation of the no-match rule based on a suit filed jointly by the American Federation of Labor and Congress of Industrial Organizations (AFL-CIO), the American Civil Liberties Union, and the National Immigration Law Center. In late 2007, the Bush administration suspended its defense of the rule, preferring to go back to the drawing board in order to respond to the judicial concerns.

The DHS issued a Supplemental Proposed Rule in March 2008 and a Supplemental Final Rule in October 2008 that required employers to clear up the discrepancy within 93 days or fire the employees in question. Neither the Supplemental Proposed Rule nor the Supplemental Final Rule, however, was ever enforced.

Exhibit 7.3 *INS Employment From and Document List*

OMB No. 1615-0047; Expires 06/30/08

Department of Homeland Security
U.S. Citizenship and Immigration Services

**Form I-9, Employment
Eligibility Verification**

Please read instructions carefully before completing this form. The instructions must be available during completion of this form.

ANTI-DISCRIMINATION NOTICE: It is illegal to discriminate against work eligible individuals. Employers CANNOT specify which document(s) they will accept from an employee. The refusal to hire an individual because the documents have a future expiration date may also constitute illegal discrimination.

Section 1. Employee Information and Verification. To be completed and signed by employee at the time employment begins.

Print Name: Last	First	Middle Initial	Maiden Name

Address *(Street Name and Number)*	Apt. #	Date of Birth *(month/day/year)*

City	State	Zip Code	Social Security #

I am aware that federal law provides for imprisonment and/or fines for false statements or use of false documents in connection with the completion of this form.

I attest, under penalty of perjury, that I am (check one of the following):
☐ A citizen or national of the United States
☐ A lawful permanent resident (Alien #) A _____
☐ An alien authorized to work until _____
(Alien # or Admission #) _____

Employee's Signature	Date *(month/day/year)*

Preparer and/or Translator Certification. *(To be completed and signed if Section 1 is prepared by a person other than the employee.)* I attest, under penalty of perjury, that I have assisted in the completion of this form and that to the best of my knowledge the information is true and correct.

Preparer's/Translator's Signature	Print Name

Address *(Street Name and Number, City, State, Zip Code)*	Date *(month/day/year)*

Section 2. Employer Review and Verification. To be completed and signed by employer. Examine one document from List A OR examine one document from List B and one from List C, as listed on the reverse of this form, and record the title, number and expiration date, if any, of the document(s).

List A	OR	**List B**	**AND**	**List C**
Document title:				
Issuing authority:				
Document #:				
Expiration Date *(if any)*:				
Document #:				
Expiration Date *(if any)*:				

CERTIFICATION - I attest, under penalty of perjury, that I have examined the document(s) presented by the above-named employee, that the above-listed document(s) appear to be genuine and to relate to the employee named, that the employee began employment on *(month/day/year)* _____ **and that to the best of my knowledge the employee is eligible to work in the United States.** (State employment agencies may omit the date the employee began employment.)

Signature of Employer or Authorized Representative	Print Name	Title

Business or Organization Name and Address *(Street Name and Number, City, State, Zip Code)*	Date *(month/day/year)*

Section 3. Updating and Reverification. To be completed and signed by employer.

A. New Name *(if applicable)*	B. Date of Rehire *(month/day/year) (if applicable)*

C. If employee's previous grant of work authorization has expired, provide the information below for the document that establishes current employment eligibility.

Document Title:	Document #:	Expiration Date (if any):

I attest, under penalty of perjury, that to the best of my knowledge, this employee is eligible to work in the United States, and if the employee presented document(s), the document(s) I have examined appear to be genuine and to relate to the individual.

Signature of Employer or Authorized Representative	Date *(month/day/year)*

LISTS OF ACCEPTABLE DOCUMENTS

LIST A		LIST B		LIST C
Documents that Establish Both Identity and Employment Eligibility	**OR**	**Documents that Establish Identity**	**AND**	**Documents that Establish Employment Eligibility**
1. U.S. Passport (unexpired or expired)		1. Driver's license or ID card issued by a state or outlying possession of the United States provided it contains a photograph or information such as name, date of birth, gender, height, eye color and address		1. U.S. Social Security card issued by the Social Security Administration *(other than a card stating it is not valid for employment)*
2. Permanent Resident Card or Alien Registration Receipt Card (Form I-551)		2. ID card issued by federal, state or local government agencies or entities, provided it contains a photograph or information such as name, date of birth, gender, height, eye color and address		2. Certification of Birth Abroad issued by the Department of State *(Form FS-545 or Form DS-1350)*
3. An unexpired foreign passport with a temporary I-551 stamp		3. School ID card with a photograph		3. Original or certified copy of a birth certificate issued by a state, county, municipal authority or outlying possession of the United States bearing an official seal
4. An unexpired Employment Authorization Document that contains a photograph (Form I-766, I-688, I-688A, I-688B)		4. Voter's registration card		4. Native American tribal document
		5. U.S. Military card or draft record		5. U.S. Citizen ID Card *(Form I-197)*
5. An unexpired foreign passport with an unexpired Arrival-Departure Record, Form I-94, bearing the same name as the passport and containing an endorsement of the alien's nonimmigrant status, if that status authorizes the alien to work for the employer		6. Military dependent's ID card		6. ID Card for use of Resident Citizen in the United States *(Form I-179)*
		7. U.S. Coast Guard Merchant Mariner Card		
		8. Native American tribal document		7. Unexpired employment authorization document issued by DHS *(other than those listed under List A)*
		9. Driver's license issued by a Canadian government authority		
		For persons under age 18 who are unable to present a document listed above:		
		10. School record or report card		
		11. Clinic, doctor or hospital record		
		12. Day-care or nursery school record		

Illustrations of many of these documents appear in Part 8 of the Handbook for Employers (M-274)

Form I-9 (Rev. 06/05/07) N Page 2

Note: The INS provides document M-274, "A Handbook for Employers," which can be found at http://www.uscis.gov/files/nativedocuments/m-274.pdt.

Exhibit 7.4 *Employer Responsibilities under IRCA: Do's and Don'ts*

Subject	Do	Don't
Completion of Form I-9, Section 1	New employees must complete Section 1 in full before the end of their first day of work if expected to work fewer than three days; otherwise they have until the end of their third day of work. Applies to all workers hired to perform labor or services in return for wages or other remuneration.	Do not require only certain employees to comply before the end of their first day of work.
Completion of Form I-9, Section 2	Employer must examine proper documentation (one from List A or one each from Lists B and C). Employer must accept the documents if they reasonably appear to be genuine. This must be completed by the end of the new employee's third day of work. Employer must refuse acceptance of documents that do not reasonably appear to be genuine.	Do not accept copies or faxes of documents. (Note: The only exception is for a certified copy of a birth certificate.) Do not require more or different documentation than the minimum necessary to avoid an unfair immigration-related employment practice. Do not require completion of the I-9 in the preoffer stage.
Genuineness of documents and reporting	If a document does not reasonably appear to be genuine, employer may ask for assistance from INS.	[If a document that reasonably appeared to be genuine is in fact not genuine, the employer will not be held responsible by the INS.]
Discovering unauthorized employees	Employer should question the employee and provide another opportunity for review of proper I-9 documentation.	If the employee is not able to provide satisfactory documentation after an opportunity to do so, the employer should not retain the employee. Do not make threats of reporting the employee to the INS in retaliation for discrimination complaints or other protected activity.
Discovering false documentation	If an employee gains employment with false documentation but then later obtains and presents proper work authorization, the employer should correct the relevant information on Form I-9.	Employers do not have to terminate an employee who presents subsequent work authorization.

continued

Subject	Do	Don't
	Personnel policies regarding provision of false information to the employer may apply.	
"Green cards"	Resident Alien card, Permanent Resident card, Alien Registration Receipt card, and Form I-551 grant permanent residence in the United States. Proof of this status may expire. Alien cardholders must obtain new cards. Employers should check that unexpired "green cards" used for Form I-9 appear genuine and establish identity of the cardholder.	Employers should not accept an expired card for purposes of Form I-9. Employers are neither required nor permitted to reverify the employment authorization of aliens who have presented one of these cards to satisfy I-9 requirements.
Social Security cards	For purposes of payroll, employers may accept SSA cards that bear the restriction "Not Valid for Employment" from employees who satisfy I-9 requirements. Often those who initially got such a restricted SSA card proceed to permanent residence or U.S. citizenship.	Employers must not accept restricted SSA cards for purposes of I-9 requirements. Employers must not accept Individual Taxpayer Identification numbers for purposes of I-9 requirements.
Retention of I-9 forms	Generally, retain during an employee's employment and the longer of either three years past the hire date or one year past the termination date.	While not prohibited from doing so, private employers should not store I-9 records in employee personnel files.
Official inspection of I-9 records	Generally, all I-9 forms of current employees must be made available in their original form or on microfilm or microfiche to an authorized official upon request. The official will give employers at least three days' advance notice before the inspection.	Employers should not leave preparation for such an inspection to the last minute! Storing I-9 records in employee personnel files makes this task unduly difficult.

Sources: INS, "IRCA and Employer Sanctions," http://www.uscis.gov/graphics/aboutins/history/sanctions.htm, last modified February 28, 2003; INS, "About Form I-9, Employment Eligibility Verification," http://www.uscis.gov/graphics/howdoi/faqeev.htm, last modified February 9, 2004; INS, "Frequently Asked Questions about Employment Eligibility," http://www.uscis.gov/graphics/howdoi/EEV.htm, last modified February 19, 2003.

President Obama's Secretary of Homeland Security, upon taking office in early 2009, ordered a review of the no-match policy. On July 8, 2009, the DHS announced that it was rescinding the no-match rule.

Whereas the Bush administration focused its worksite employment strategy on the arrest and deportation of undocumented workers, the Obama administration focused instead on civil and criminal actions against employers that knowingly hired undocumented workers. In July 2009, Immigration and Customs Enforcement (ICE), the DHS's enforcement unit, issued 652 Notices of Inspection (NOIs) to businesses around the country (by comparison, 503 NOIs were issued for the entire year in 2008). ICE's enforcement strategy is to investigate employers' compliance with the Form I-9 rules. Under federal law, a Form I-9 (Employment Eligibility Verification) must be filed for every new employee regardless of citizenship, and it must be retained for three years after the date of hire or one year after the date of discharge. Once an employer receives an NOI, it has three days to provide the Form I-9s for all employees working for that employer during the stated audit period.

IRCA also established civil and criminal penalties for hiring illegal aliens. Employers are selected at random for compliance inspections under the General Administrative Plan (GAP) developed by the Immigration and Naturalization Services (INS), the administrative agency charged with some elements of oversight of IRCA, along with the Immigration and Customs Enforcement (ICE) Division of the Department of Homeland Security. Generally, fines are not imposed for paperwork violations alone or for employment of aliens whose illegal status was unknown, unless the employer refused to comply or other egregious factors existed. However, employers who knowingly employed illegal aliens after receiving education regarding IRCA, visits, or GAP inspections will receive a Notice of Intent to Fine.[37]

However, in its October 1999 "Enforcement Guidance on Remedies Available to Undocumented Workers," the EEOC emphasized that workers' undocumented status does not justify workplace discrimination. The EEOC also set forth that employers' liability for monetary remedies irrespective of a worker's unauthorized status promotes the goal of deterring unlawful discrimination without undermining the purposes of IRCA. The EEOC's position on available remedies is that unauthorized workers are entitled to the same remedies as any other worker, including back pay and reinstatement. In fact, a U.S. district court held in a 2006 ruling that discovery regarding the immigration status of plaintiffs in civil rights cases would be generally prohibited since it would otherwise have a chilling effect on filings and it could result in "countless acts of illegal and reprehensible conduct" being unreported.[38] The National Labor Relations Board took a similar position with respect to discrimination based on union activity.

However, in *Hoffman Plastic Compounds Inc. v. NLRB,*[39] the U.S. Supreme Court held that the NLRB could not award back pay to unauthorized workers who had been unlawfully discriminated against for engaging in union-organizing activities. According to the Court, to do so would contravene federal immigration policy embodied in IRCA. *Hoffman* opens the possibility that back pay will not be available to unauthorized workers who have been illegally discriminated against under Title VII, the Americans with Disabilities Act (ADA), and the Age Discrimination in Employment Act (ADEA).[40] The Court offers an extensive review of the pre-*Hoffman* history and then discusses important implications in *Singh v. Jutla & C.D. & R's Oil, Inc.*

Case 5

Unauthorized workers are particularly vulnerable to threats to report them to the INS. In every case in which the employer asserts that the worker is unauthorized and the employer appears to have acquired that information *after* the worker complained of discrimination, the EEOC will determine whether the information was acquired through a retaliatory investigation. If the investigation is retaliatory, the employer will be liable for equitable relief as well as monetary damages without regard to the worker's actual work status. However, a worker's unauthorized status may serve as a legitimate reason for an adverse employment action, although employers who knowingly employ unauthorized workers could not assert this defense in a discrimination claim.[41]

The Fair Labor Standards Act also protects unauthorized workers from abuse. In a dramatic 2001 case, a group of mostly Mexican workers in New Jersey claimed that the operators of a bargain retail chain subjected them to "inhumane" working conditions and failed to pay them fair wages and overtime compensation when performing such tasks as building and stocking new stores. Workers generally received $230 for a seven-day workweek of about 12 hours per day, which amounted to $2.74 an hour. These workers also were often forced to work in stores without heat, access to meals, adequate water, proper ventilation, or adequate bathroom facilities. Bosses also called workers derogatory names.[42] The case was settled when the defendants apologized, agreed to ensure future compliance, and agreed to pay damages to the workers.[43]

Alternate Basis for National Origin or Citizenship Discrimination: Section 1981

While it is probably the most popular basis for the claim of discrimination based on national origin, Title VII is not the only basis for such a claim. In *St. Francis College v. Al-Khazraji*,[44] the Supreme Court held that 42 U.S.C. § 1981 addressed national origin also. In this case, a U.S. citizen who was born in Iraq sued under section 1981 alleging discrimination when he was denied tenure. The Court held that, though originally designed to prohibit racial discrimination, the law also applied to "identifiable classes of persons who are subjected to intentional discrimination solely because of their ancestry or ethnic characteristics." The requirement for section 1981 actions is that employees show they were discriminated against because of what they are (in this case, Arabic) and not just because of their place of origin or religion. In other words, they must show some nexus between their national origin and the major concern of section 1981, their ethnic characteristics or race.

Management Tips

- While a specific national origin may be a BFOQ, make sure that only individuals of that origin can do the specific job since courts have a high standard for BFOQs in this area.
- An employee may have a claim for national origin discrimination if the worker is simply *perceived* to be of a certain origin, even if the individual is not, in fact, of that origin.
- While English fluency may be required, you are not allowed to discriminate because of an accent (unless the accent makes it impossible to understand the individual). However, be cautious in evaluating the requirement of the job since there may be positions that do not actually require speaking English.
- An employer may not point to customer, client, or co-worker preference, comfort, or discomfort as the source of BFOQ.
- If you are a federal contractor, remember that you have additional responsibilities to engage in outreach and positive recruitment activities under the Guidelines on Discrimination Because of Religion or National Origin.
- While you are not prohibited from discriminating on the basis of citizenship under Title VII, you may be prohibited from discriminating on this basis under IRCA. Before instituting a policy, consider the implications of both statutes.
- Recognize the concerns of Middle Eastern employees in the post–September 11 era: Include the topic of ethnic diversity in any workplace diversity training. Intervene promptly in incidents of harassment. Remain sensitive and flexible. Refrain from mandatory transfers and other short-term solutions to harassment, intimidation, and discrimination.

Since *St. Francis College,* however, several courts have declined to extend section 1981 to more traditional claims of national origin discrimination. In *King v. Township of East Lampeter,*[45] for instance, plaintiffs sought section 1981 protection on the basis of their "Amish ethnic culture." The court denied the plaintiffs protection on this basis, distinguishing a New York case that found Orthodox Jews were indeed protected under section 1981. The court in *King* found that Jews are a distinct race for civil rights purposes but did not find the Amish to be a similarly distinct racial group and, without evidence that they have an independent, separate ethnic identity beyond religious observance, they were not protected under section 1981. Interestingly, the court was persuaded by the contention that one could fail to "practice" Judaism but still be a Jew, while "there is no proof of a similar population of 'non-practicing' Amish." Perhaps an argument could be made that the door therefore remains open on this issue.

If the increases are anywhere near the projections, then entry, development, or promotion barriers to diversity of the workplace will likely result in reductions in the business's effectiveness and productivity. For any business wishing to be on the cutting edge, or simply to effectively use its resources and encourage the best performance from employees, adherence to Title VII's requirements regarding race and national origin should be viewed as a business imperative and not merely as compliance with the law.

The significance to managers of this protection is that there must be a complete review of all policies that may have an impact on employees or applicants of diverse national origin. As stated above, this impact may not be obvious.

Employers must be cognizant of the varying needs of employees from different backgrounds. For instance, employers may address the perceived problem of bilingual employees in a number of ways, such as offering English-as-a-second language classes or tutors for semibilingual employees. Not only would this foster less isolation and exclusion of the employee, but it also would create greater confidence and less intimidation when the employees are speaking English. This type of proactive approach may prevent problems in this area before they emerge.

Chapter Summary

- Title VII, the Civil Rights Act of 1964, makes it an unlawful employment practice for employers to limit, segregate, or classify employees in any way that would deprive them of employment opportunities based on their national origin.
- An employee or applicant must show the following to be successful in a claim of discrimination based on national origin:
  1. The individual was a member of a protected class.
  2. The individual was qualified for the position at issue.
  3. The employer made an employment decision against the individual.
  4. The position was filled by someone not in a protected class.
- "National origin" refers to an individual's ancestor's place of origin or physical, cultural, or linguistic characteristics of an origin group.
- An employer has a defense against a national origin discrimination claim if it can show that the national origin is a bona fide occupational qualification. However, in general, this is very difficult to do. An exception to the difficulty is the requirement of English fluency, if speaking English is a substantial portion of the individual's job.
- No accommodation of a worker's national origin is required, as it would be in situations involving disability or religion.
- English-only rules applied at all times are presumptively discriminatory, according to the EEOC. If the employer is considering an English-only rule, it is recommended that the employer should
  1. Consider whether the rule is necessary.
  2. Determine if the rule is a business necessity.
  3. Consider if everybody is fluent in English.
  4. Communicate the rule to employees.
  5. Enforce the rule fairly.
- An alternative basis for national origin or citizenship discrimination is 42 U.S.C. § 1981.

- Guidelines on Discrimination Because of Religion or National Origin are federal guidelines that apply to federal contractors or agencies and impose on those employers an affirmative duty to prevent discrimination.
- The Immigration Reform and Control Act, unlike Title VII, prohibits, in certain circumstances, discrimination on the basis of citizenship. The act does allow for discrimination in favor of U.S. citizens where applicants are equally qualified.
- Two statutorily allowed BFOQs under IRCA are
  1. English-language skill requirements that are reasonably necessary.
  2. Citizenship requirements specified by law, regulation, executive order, government contracts, or requirements established by the U.S. attorney general.

Chapter-End Questions

1. Which, if any, of the following scenarios would support an employee's claim of discrimination on the basis of national origin?

   a. Applicant with a speech impediment is unable to pronounce the letter "r." The applicant therefore often has difficulty being understood when speaking and is denied a position.

   b. The owner of a manufacturing facility staffed completely by Mexicans refuses employment to a white American manager because the owner is concerned that the Mexicans will only consent to supervision by and receive direction from another Mexican.

   c. An Indian restaurant seeks to fill a server position. The advertisement requests applications from qualified individuals of Indian descent to add to the authenticity of the restaurant. In the past, the restaurant found that its business declined when it used Caucasian servers because the atmosphere of the restaurant suffered. An Italian applies for the position and is denied employment.

   d. A company advertises for Japanese-trained managers, because the employer has found that they are more likely to remain at the company for an extended time, to be loyal and devoted to the firm, and to react well to direction and criticism. An American applies for the position and is denied employment in favor of an equally qualified Japanese-trained applicant, who happens to also be Japanese.

2. A pipefitter in a Chrysler assembly plant, a Cuban-born Jew, was subjected from his co-workers to hate graffiti on his locker, such as "Heil Hitler," and other harassment, such as slashed car tires. Can he recover damages for national origin discrimination? Is being Jewish a "national origin"? Can harassment and other abuse from co-workers rather than from management constitute national origin discrimination? [*May v. Chrysler Group,* LLC, No. 02-cv-50440 (N.D. Ill. 2010).]

3. An Egyptian-born doctor, who was a naturalized U.S. citizen, was subjected to harassment from his supervisor at a Texas hospital because of his national origin, including statements such as "middle easterners are lazy." He ultimately left the hospital but was denied a position at a second hospital because of a poor referral from the first hospital. Can the poor referral constitute national origin discrimination? Another doctor at the original hospital refused to support the supervisor against the

Egyptian-born doctor when asked to do so. Can the second doctor sue for national origin discrimination if he suffers retaliation because of his refusal, even if the retaliation against him is not based on *his* national origin, but instead because of the underlying case? [*Nassar v. University of Texas Southwest Medical Center,* No. 3:08-cv-1337 (N.D. Texas 2008).]

4. In 1998, the Human Resources Director at Colorado Central Station Casino (CCSC) implemented a blanket English-only language policy in the housekeeping department: any employee caught violating the policy would be disciplined. Housekeeping had the highest concentration of Latino employees, and while some employees on staff were bilingual, others were monolingual Spanish speakers. The reason offered for implementing the language policy was that a non–Spanish-speaking employee thought that other employees were talking about her in Spanish, and CCSC believed that it needed the policy in defense for undefined "safety reasons." Higher-level managers or other non-Latino employees would shout "English, English" at the Latino employees when encountering them in the halls in order to remind them of the policy. Is this English-only rule in violation of Title VII or is it acceptable? [*EEOC v. Anchor Coin d/b/a Colorado Central Station Casino, Inc.,* No. 01-B-0564 (D. Colo. July 21, 2003).]

5. Mamdouh El-Hakem was employed by BJY, Inc., for more than a year. His manager repeatedly called Mamdouh, an Arabic employee, "Manny" or "Hank," instead of his given name. His manager explained that he believed that Mamdouh would have a better opportunity for success with the firm's clients with a more Western-sounding name. However, Mamdouh made it clear during his entire time with BJY that he objected to the westernization of his name and requested repeatedly that the manager call him by his rightful moniker. Mamdouh finally sued for national origin discrimination. Does he have a claim? [*El-Hakem v. BJY, Inc.,* 415 F.3d 1068 (9th Cir. 2005).]

6. Hannoon, a Kuwaiti employee who worked as an information systems manager, requested Friday afternoons off to observe weekly Muslim prayer services. His supervisor noted in his personnel file, "first week on job requested Fri. off." In fact, Hannoon was permitted to take the time off and to work at other times to make up for those afternoons. Hannoon was terminated for poor performance and he filed an action claiming national origin and race discrimination. What flaws can you find in his claim? [*Hannoon v. Fawn Eng'g Corp.,* 84 EPD ¶ 41,370 (8th Cir. 2003).]

7. A white, non-Latino meat cutter was fired by his supermarket employer and replaced with a Latino worker for reasons he believes were racially motivated. Can he sue the company for national origin discrimination? Is it possible to commit national origin discrimination by favoring a Latino person over a white, non-Latino person? If so, what would he need to prove to satisfy a *prima facie* case and then to succeed overall? [*EEOC v. West Front Street Foods, LLC d/b/a Compare Foods,* No. 5:08-cv-102 (W.D. N.C. 2008).]

8. Maria Cardenas, a Latina woman, worked for Aramark as a housekeeper at McCormick Place convention center for over 20 years. It was a long-standing rule for employees that they could not remove any items from a trade show for personal use, even if an exhibitor gave them away. Employees found in violation of this rule would be immediately fired. In October 2004, Cardenas and a co-worker, Juanita Williams, were stopped by a security guard who noticed them carrying food items away from a convention that had just ended. Both employees were discharged, but Williams was

later reinstated because she was a newer employee and allegedly had been told by Cardenas that it was okay to take the items in question. Cardenas filed a national origin discrimination suit against Aramark. What does Cardenas need to show to prove that her termination was in violation of Title VII, and how might Aramark defend its decision if she states a *prima facie* case? [*Cardenas v. Aramark,* 101 FEP Cases 1114 (N.D. Ill. 2007).]

9. Latino managers of a Florida-based tomato growing, packing, and distributing company harassed and intimidated Haitian production workers. When the Haitians complained about their treatment, the managers retaliated against them. Do the national origin anti-discrimination laws prohibit national origin discrimination by *any* group against *any* other group? Or do the laws require that the discrimination be committed by a group that is considered to represent the majority in that environment against people of color? Could the Haitians recover if their managers had been Haitian? Similarly, would the Latinos have similar liability if the workers involved had been Latino? [*EEOC v. LFC Agricultural, Inc., Six L's Packing Company, and Custom Pak, Inc.,* No. 2:09-cv-00636-JES-DNF, (M.D. Fl. 2009).]

10. In 2002, Sami Elestwani worked for Nicolet Biomedical and was a key account manager. He was informed that he would be reassigned due to concerns about his ability to adequately perform his job because of his Arab heritage. His boss told him that the fact that he was Muslim, was from the Middle East, and had to travel extensively to meet with customers were "not good for the company." Nicolet offered him a lower-level position in a different part of the country. When he complained to human resources about his boss's remarks and the reassignment, he was fired. He was subsequently replaced by a non-Arab employee. Elestwani sued Nicolet for national origin discrimination, claiming that the company wanted to transfer him simply because of his religion, ethnicity, and cultural heritage. What result? [*Elestwani v. Nicolet Biomedical,* No. 04-C-0947-S (W.D. Wis. Aug. 23, 2005).]

11. A nursing home instituted an English-only policy for its employees. Latino employees were disciplined for violating the policy. Is the policy void on its face, or are some English-only policies acceptable under the law? Does the policy's legality depend on the type of conversation involved (i.e., whether the employee is speaking to customers or speaking to co-employees on a break)? Does the policy's legality depend on how it is enforced (i.e., Spanish-speaking employees disciplined but those speaking other foreign languages not disciplined)? [*EEOC v. Skilled Healthcare Group, Inc.,* C. D. Cal., settled in 2009; www.eeoc.gov/eeoc/newsroom/release/4-14-09.cfm.]

End Notes

1. See, for example, *DeSalle v. Key Bank,* 47 F.E.P. Cas. 37 (D. Me. 1988).
2. U.S. Census Bureau, "U.S. POPClock Projection," www.census.gov/population/www/popclockus.html.
3. *Hispanically Speaking News,* "U.S. Census Highlights: Latinos Drive Population Growth, Number of Undocumented Remains Unknown," December 22, 2010.
4. Bureau of Labor Statistics, U.S. Department of Labor, "Labor Force Characteristics of Foreign-Born Workers Summary," USDL 10-0319 (March 19, 2010), http://www.bls.gov/news.release/forbrn.nr0.htm.

5. Library Index, "Minorities in the Labor Force—Workforce Projections for 2010" (2007), http://www.libraryindex.com/pages/2910/Minorities-in-Labor-Force-WORKFORCE-PROJECTIONS-2010.html.

6. Haya El Nasser and Paul Overberg, "Nation's Minority Numbers Top 100MM," *USA Today*, March 2007, http://www.usatoday.com/news/nation/census/2007-05 17-minority-numbers_N.htm.

7. Bureau of Labor Statistics, U.S. Department of Labor, "Employment Projections: 2008–2018 Summary," http://stats.bls.gov/news.release/ecopro.nr0.htm, December 10, 2009.

8. Bureau of Labor Statistics, U.S. Department of Labor, "Labor Force Characteristics of Foreign-Born Workers Summary," USDL 07-0603 (April 25, 2007), http://www.bls.gov/news.release/forbrn.nr0.htm.

9. Karyn-Siobhan Robinson, "English-Only Rule Costs Casino $1.5 Million in EEOC Settlement" (2003), http://www.shrm.org/hrnews_published/archives/CMS_005129.asp.

10. EEOC, "Job Bias Charges Rise 9% in 2007, EEOC Reports," *Press Release* (March 5, 2008), http://www.eeoc.gov/press/3-5-08.html.

11. *Avigliano v. Sumitomo Shoji America, Inc.*, 638 F.2d 552 (2d Cir. 1981).

12. *Bennett v. Total Minatome Corp.*, 138 F.3d 1053 (5th Cir. 1998).

13. U.S. Census Bureau, American Community Survey Office, "R1601. Percent of People 5 Years and Over Who Speak a Language Other Than English at Home" (2005), http://factfinder.census.gov/servlet/GRTTable?_bm=y&-geo_id=01000US&-_box_head_nbr=R1601&-ds_name=ACS_2005_EST_G00_&-_lang=en&-redoLog=true&-format=US-30&-mt_name=ACS_2004_EST_G00_R1603_US30&-CONTEXT=grt and http://factfinder.census.gov/servlet/GRTSelectServlet?ds_name=ACS_2005_EST_G00_&_lang=en.

14. See "English-Only Rules May Spell Trouble for Employers," special to law.com, October 11, 2001, http://www.law.com.

15. 487 F.3d 1001 (6th Cir. 2007).

16. 419 F. Supp. 2d 408 (S.D.N.Y. 2005)

17. John Cunningham, "English-Only Complaints on the Rise," *Lawyers Weekly USA*, January 30, 2006.

18. *See Garcia v. Spun Steak Co.*, 998 F.2d 1480 (9th Cir. 1993). For the contrary opinion supporting EEOC's contention, see *EEOC v. Premier Operator Services, Inc.*, 75 F. Supp. 550 (N.D. Tex. 1999), and *EEOC v. Synchro-Start*, 29 F. Supp. 2d 911 (N.D. Ill. 1999).

19. *Gonzalo v. All Island Transportation,* No. CV-04-3452 (BMC), 2007 WL 642959, at *7 (E.D.N.Y. Feb. 26, 2007).

20. 433 F.3d 1294 (10th Cir. 2006).

21. http://www.eeoc.gov/policy/docs/national-origin.html.

22. The EEOC based this example on *Amirmokri v. Baltimore Gas & Electric Co.*, 60 F.3d 1126 (4th Cir. 1995) (finding that the Iranian emigrant employed as an engineer at a nuclear power plant established a *prima facie* case of national origin harassment).

23. See Eric Lichtblau, "Bias against U.S. Arabs Taking Subtler Forms," *Los Angeles Times,* February 10, 2002, p. A20.

24. See the September 15, 2010, posting on the Employment Lawyer blog at www.employment-lawyer-blog.com/2010/09/number-of-muslim-employment-di.html.

25. Ibid.

26. No. Civ-S-03-657 (E.D. Calif. Apr. 6, 2004).

27. See "CEOs: Human and Humane," *Corporate Counsel,* October 19, 2001.

28. See "Employment Counsel Tackle Anxieties and Problems after September 11," *National Law Journal,* October 29, 2001.

29. 42 U.S.C. § 2000e-2(g).

30. 435 U.S. 291 (1978).

31. Gregory Begg and Lorraine D'Angelo, "Immigration Law Developments," July 12, 2007, http://www.mondaq.com/article.asp?articleid=50104.

32. Pew Hispanic Center, pewhispanic.org/reports/report.php?ReportID=126.

33. See, for example, an Associated Press report of December 9, 2010, at abcationnews.com/dpp/news/national/number-of-undocumented-workers-in-us-now-declining-EWS-AP-WPTV-NTW-201009011283396192439.

34. 8 C.F.R. § 274a.1(1)(1).

35. J. Preston, "Revised Rule for Employers That Hire Immigrants," *The New York Times,* November 26, 2007, http://www.nytimes.com/2007/11/25/washington/25immig.html.

36. J. Preston, "U.S. Set for a Crackdown on Illegal Hiring," *The New York Times,* August 8, 2007.

37. See http://www.ins.gov/graphics/aboutins/history/sanctions.htm.

38. *EEOC v. The Restaurant Company, d/b/a Perkins Restaurant & Bakery,* 490 F. Supp. 2d 1039 (D. Minn. 2006).

39. 122 S. Ct. 1275 (2002).

40. See Donna Y. Porter, "Undocumented Workers Have NLRA Rights, but Not Monetary Remedies," *Employment Law Strategies,* June 6, 2002.

41. See "Workforce Online," *CCH,* November 1999, citing "Policy Guidance: Remedies Available to Undocumented Workers under Federal Employment Discrimination Laws," October 26, 1999, Appendix B of sec. 622, vol. II of *EEOC Compliance Manual.*

42. See Associated Press, "Mexican Workers Claim U.S. Bargain Store Chain Exploited Them," http://www.law.com, January 10, 2001.

43. Internet Bankruptcy Library, *Class Action Reporter III,* no. 67 (April 5, 2001), http://bankrupt.com/CAR_Public/010405.MBX.

44. 481 U.S. 604 (1987), *cert. denied,* 483 U.S. 1011 (1987).

45. 17 F. Supp. 2d 394 (E.D. Pa 1998).

Cases

Case 1

Garcia v. Spun Steak Co. *998 F.2d 1480 (9th Cir. 1993)*

Defendant, Spun Steak Co., employs 33 workers, 24 of whom are Spanish-speaking. Two of the Spanish-speakers speak no English. Plaintiffs Garcia and Buitrago are production line workers for the defendant and both are bilingual. After receiving complaints that some workers were using their second language to harass and to insult other workers, Spun Steak enacted an English-only policy in the workplace in order to (1) promote racial harmony, (2) enhance worker safety because some employees who did not understand Spanish claimed that they were distracted by its use, and (3) enhance product quality because the USDA inspector in the plant spoke only English. The two plaintiffs received warning notices about speaking Spanish during working hours, and they were not permitted to work next to each other for two months. They filed charges with the EEOC, which found reasonable cause to believe that the defendant had violated Title VII. The district court found in favor of the employees and Spun Steak appealed. The appellate court reversed, finding that Spun Steak did not violate Title VII in adopting the English-only rule.

O'Scannlain, J.

***

The Spanish-speaking employees do not contend that Spun Steak intentionally discriminated against them in enacting the English-only policy. Rather, they contend that the policy had a *discriminatory impact* on them because it imposes a burdensome term or condition of employment exclusively upon Hispanic workers and denies them a privilege of employment that non-Spanish-speaking workers enjoy.

The employees argue that denying them the ability to speak Spanish on the job denies them the right to cultural expression. It cannot be gainsaid that an individual's primary language can be an important link to his ethnic culture and identity. Title VII, however, does not protect the ability of workers to express their cultural heritage at the workplace. Title VII is concerned only with disparities in the treatment of workers; it does not confer substantive privileges. It is axiomatic that an employee must often sacrifice individual self-expression during working hours. Just as a private employer is not required to allow other types of self-expression, there is nothing in Title VII which requires an employer to allow employees to express their cultural identity.

Next, the Spanish-speaking employees argue that the English-only policy has a disparate impact on them because it deprives them of a privilege given by the employer to native-English speakers: the ability to converse on the job in the language with which they feel most comfortable. It is undisputed that Spun Steak allows its employees to converse on the job. The ability to converse—especially to make small talk—is a privilege

of employment, and may in fact be a significant privilege of employment in an assembly-line job. It is inaccurate, however, to describe the privilege as broadly as the Spanish-speaking employees urge us to do.

The employees have attempted to define the privilege as the ability to speak in the language of their choice. A privilege, however, is by definition given at the employer's discretion; an employer has the right to define its contours. Thus, an employer may allow employees to converse on the job, but only during certain times of the day or during the performance of certain tasks. The employer may proscribe certain topics as inappropriate during working hours or may even forbid the use of certain words, such as profanity.

Here, as is its prerogative, the employer has defined the privilege narrowly. When the privilege is defined at its narrowest (as merely the ability to speak on the job), we cannot conclude that those employees fluent in both English and Spanish are adversely impacted by the policy. Because they are able to speak English, bilingual employees can engage in conversation on the job. It is axiomatic that "the language a person who is multilingual elects to speak at a particular time is . . . a matter of choice." The bilingual employee can readily comply with the English-only rule and still enjoy the privilege of speaking on the job. "There is no disparate impact" with respect to a privilege of employment "if the rule is one that the affected employee can readily observe and nonobservance is a matter of individual preference."

The Spanish-speaking employees argue that fully bilingual employees are hampered in the enjoyment of the privilege because for them, switching from one language to another is not fully volitional. Whether a bilingual speaker can control which language is used in a given circumstance is a factual issue that cannot be resolved at the summary judgment stage. However, we fail to see the relevance of the assertion, even assuming that it can be proved. Title VII is not meant to protect against rules that merely inconvenience some employees, even if the inconvenience falls regularly on a protected class. Rather, Title VII protects against only those policies that have a *significant* impact. The fact that an employee may have to catch himself or herself from occasionally slipping into Spanish does not impose a burden significant enough to amount to the denial of equal opportunity. This is not a case in which the employees have alleged that the company is enforcing the policy in such a way as to impose penalties for minor slips of the tongue. The fact that a bilingual employee may, on occasion, unconsciously substitute a Spanish word in the place of an English one does not override our conclusion that the bilingual employee can easily comply with the rule. In short, we conclude that a bilingual employee is not denied a privilege of employment by the English-only policy.

By contrast, non-English speakers cannot enjoy the privilege of conversing on the job if conversation is limited to a language they cannot speak. As applied "[t]o a person who speaks only one tongue or to a person who has difficulty using another language than the one spoken in his home," an English-only rule might well have an adverse impact. Indeed, counsel for Spun Steak conceded at oral argument that the policy would have an adverse impact on an employee unable to speak English. There is only one employee at Spun Steak affected by the policy who is unable to speak any English. Even with regard to her, however, summary judgment was improper because a genuine issue of material fact exists as to whether she has been adversely affected by the policy. She stated in her deposition that she was not bothered by the rule because she preferred not to make small talk on the job, but rather preferred to work in peace. Furthermore, there is some evidence suggesting that she is not required to comply with the policy when she chooses to speak. For example, she is allowed to speak Spanish to her supervisor. Remand is necessary to determine whether she has suffered adverse effects from the policy. It is unclear from the record whether

there are any other employees who have such limited proficiency in English that they are effectively denied the privilege of speaking on the job. Whether an employee speaks such little English as to be effectively denied the privilege is a question of fact for which summary judgment is improper.

We do not foreclose the prospect that in some circumstances English-only rules can exacerbate existing tensions, or, when combined with other discriminatory behavior, contribute to an overall environment of discrimination. Likewise, we can envision a case in which such rules are enforced in such a draconian manner that the enforcement itself amounts to harassment. In evaluating such a claim, however, a court must look to the totality of the circumstances in the particular factual context in which the claim arises.

In holding that the enactment of an English-only while working policy does not inexorably lead to an abusive environment for those whose primary language is not English, we reach a conclusion opposite to the EEOC's long standing position. The EEOC Guidelines provide that an employee meets the *prima facie* case in a disparate impact cause of action merely by proving the existence of the English-only policy. Under the EEOC's scheme, an employer must always provide a business justification for such a rule. The EEOC enacted this scheme in part because of its conclusion that English-only rules may "create an atmosphere of inferiority, isolation and intimidation based on national origin which could result in a discriminatory working environment."

We do not reject the English-only rule Guideline lightly. We recognize that "as an administrative interpretation of the Act by the enforcing agency, these Guidelines . . . constitute a body of experience and informed judgment to which courts and litigants may properly resort for guidance." But we are not bound by the Guidelines. We will not defer to "an administrative construction of a statute where there are 'compelling indications that it is wrong.'"

In sum, we conclude that the bilingual employees have not made out a *prima facie* case and that Spun Steak has not violated Title VII in adopting an English-only rule as to them. Thus, we reverse the grant of summary judgment in favor of Garcia, Buitrago, and Local 115 to the extent it represents the bilingual employees, and remand with instructions to grant summary judgment in favor of Spun Steak on their claims. A genuine issue of material fact exists as to whether there are one or more employees represented by Local 115 with limited proficiency in English who were adversely impacted by the policy. As to such employee or employees, we reverse the grant of summary judgment in favor of Local 115, and remand for further proceedings. REVERSED and REMANDED.

Case Questions

1. Do you agree with the contention that denying a group the right to speak their native tongue denies them the right to cultural expression?

2. Do employees have a "right" to cultural expression in the workplace?

3. Do you agree with the court that an English-only rule is not abusive per se to those whose primary language is not English? Do you believe that it creates a "class system" of languages in the workplace and therefore inherently places one group's language above another's?

Case 2

Alvarado-Santos v. Department of Health of the Commonwealth of Puerto Rico, *No. 08-2027, 2010 U.S. App. LEXIS 18759 (1st Cir., 2010).*

Ana Alvarado-Santos is a native of Puerto Rico who worked as a doctor with a specialization in family medicine. In 2002, Dr. Alvarado-Santos was hired as an Admissions Director at the Rio Piedras Correctional Complex with the Correctional Health Services Program of the Department of Health to supervise a team of medical and support staff and oversee the medical screening and evaluation of inmates admitted to the correctional complex. After a year and a half, her location was closed and all of the personnel who had worked at the Rio Piedras Admissions Center, including Alvarado-Santos, were transferred to Bayamón.

After the transfer, Bayamón had two Admissions Centers for inmate health services: Admissions Center 308 and Admissions Center 705.[1] Alvarado-Santos directed the provision of health services at Admissions Center 705, while Marcos Devarie, a male physician also originally from Puerto Rico, directed Admissions Center 308. Devarie had first begun working for the Correctional Health Services Program in 1991 and had been the director of Admissions Center 308 in Bayamón since 1997.

Alvarado-Santos' direct supervisor, Dr. Francisco Rodríguez-Pichardo, a native of the Dominican Republic, was overheard saying that "Dominican doctors were better" than "the other physicians who were there, who were Puerto Rican." One physician working at Admissions Center 705 described him as a "hard" and "aggressive" person.

After her transfer, Alvarado-Santos had much difficulty with her supervisor. He removed some of her responsibilities when conflicts occurred, rather than speaking with her about them; he took away some of her direct reports; did not invite her to all of the staff meetings; and dismissed her complaints about some of her workers falsifying time sheets without consulting with her. A year later, she was notified that her contract would not be renewed, upon the recommendation of Rodríguez-Pichardo, while Devarie would be retained and oversee both admissions centers.

At trial, the court learned that the decision not to renew the contract was based on a combination of two factors. First, the Department claimed that there was a need to restructure the Bayamón Correctional Complex so that both Admissions Centers were under the authority of one Admissions Director. Second, according to

---

[1]The Admissions Centers were so-named because Admissions Center 308 could accommodate 308 inmates as patients, while the larger Admissions Center 705 could accommodate 705 inmates.

monthly reports, Alvarado-Santos' Admission Center 705 routinely had much lower compliance rates in treating inmates according to certain time tables and standards than Devarie's Admission Center 308. These compliance reports reflected how well the Admissions Center met established goals related to the provision of health services to inmates.

The jury found in favor Alvarado-Santo on both her claims of national origin and gender discrimination under Title VII. Department of Health appeals and Alvarado-Santos cross-appeals, arguing that she was entitled to an award of front pay in addition to compensatory damages and back pay. The First Circuit concludes that the evidence is insufficient to support a finding of discrimination and reverses, entering judgment for the Department of Health.

LIPEZ, Circuit Judge.

* * *

The jury was instructed to evaluate Alvarado-Santos' claims of gender and national origin discrimination under the *McDonnell Douglas* burden-shifting framework. *McDonnell Douglas Corp.* v. *Green.* Under this framework, the plaintiff must first establish a *prima facie* case of discrimination. *See Lockridge* v. *Univ. of Me. Sys.* The *prima facie* case varies according to the nature of the plaintiff's claim but it requires, among other things, a showing of an adverse employment action. *Id.* After the plaintiff has made this *prima facie* showing, the burden of production shifts to the employer to articulate a legitimate, non-discriminatory reason for the adverse employment action. *Id.* If the employer meets its burden, the focus then shifts back to the plaintiff to show, "by a preponderance of the evidence, that the employer's articulated reason for the adverse employment action is pretextual and that the true reason for the adverse action is discriminatory." *Id.*

As to both the gender and national origin discrimination claims, we assume arguendo that Alvarado-Santos met her burden to establish a *prima facie* case. At trial, the Department of Health, in turn, met its burden to articulate a legitimate non-discriminatory reason for the contract nonrenewal. The Department of Health offered evidence that it needed to place both Admissions Centers in Bayamón under the authority of one Admissions Director to achieve greater uniformity and efficiency, and it chose Devarie for that position over Alvarado-Santos due to the better compliance record at the center run by Devarie. Our focus is therefore on the ultimate question: whether the evidence set forth at trial would enable a reasonable jury to find that the Department of Health's proffered non-discriminatory reasons are pretextual and Alvarado-Santos' contract was in fact not renewed because of her gender and/or national origin.

* * *

A. National Origin Discrimination

As we described above, the Department of Health offered testimony from both Mena-Franco and Rodríguez-Pichardo that they needed to consolidate the two Admissions Centers in Bayamón under the leadership of one Admissions Director, and that they chose Devarie to fill that role rather than Alvarado-Santos because his Admission Center had a better compliance record. In an effort to meet her burden to show that, in fact, discriminatory animus based on her national origin motivated the employment decision, Alvarado-Santos relied entirely on evidence of two facts: (1) the supervisors who participated in the decision to not renew her contract, Mena-Franco and Rodríguez-Pichardo, are both originally from the Dominican Republic, whereas she was born in Puerto Rico, and (2) at some point after the October 1, 2003 transfer to Bayamón, Rodríguez-Pichardo commented that Dominican doctors are better than Puerto Rican doctors. Importantly, however, Alvarado-Santos conceded at trial that Devarie, the person that Mena and Rodríguez-Pichardo chose to direct both Admissions Centers in Bayamón, was Puerto Rican, not Dominican.

In addition, Alvarado-Santos offered no evidence that Rodríguez-Pichardo's isolated remark about Dominican doctors was close in time to the decision not to renew her employment contract,[2] was related to her, or was otherwise related to the employment decision. *See Straughn* v. *Delta Air Lines, Inc.* (reasoning that although "'stray remarks' may be material to the pretext inquiry,

---

[2]Alvarado-Santos received notice that her contract would not be renewed at the end of May 2004. Rodríguez-Pichardo's comment was described at trial as having been made some time "after October 1, 2003."

'their *probativeness is circumscribed* if they were made in a situation temporally remote from the date of the employment decision, *or* . . . were not related to the employment decision in question'" (quoting *McMillan* v. *Mass. Soc'y for the Prevention of Cruelty to Animals*)). Based on this evidence, no reasonable jury could conclude that Alvarado-Santos met her burden to show that the decision to not renew her contract was motivated by national origin discrimination rather than by legitimate, non-discriminatory reasons.

* * *

C. Comments During Closing Argument

The Department of Health also claims that it is entitled to a new trial based on the improper remarks of plaintiff's counsel during closing arguments. Because judgment is being entered for the Department of Health, there is no need to resolve that question. Nevertheless, if we had to reach the closing argument issue on the merits, the Department would have a good argument that it was entitled to a new trial. It may well be that the jury was influenced by the entirely improper and inflammatory closing argument by plaintiff's counsel, pitting people from Puerto Rico against people from the Dominican Republic.

Counsel made the following comments during closing argument:

All these people care is about their cronies from the Dominican Republic. They don't care about Puerto Ricans, except that they want to take their money. That's all they care about.

They came to this service with one specific purpose: It wasn't to take care of the inmates; it was to profit, and not let others, such as women, and non-Dominicans, to work with your money.

Later in closing, plaintiff's counsel stated:

Your verdict has to be sufficient to show these individuals that in Puerto Rico we do not discriminate. ... The number I submit to you should be herein no less than $2.5 million. That is an amount that is gonna give them respect, it's gonna show them what ball game we are about. . . .

You have to send a message to Dr. Pichardo and his cronies that this doesn't happen in Puerto Rico. , , , What amount, if any, do you adequately say? I submit to you that the number here is 2.5 million. Nothing less will clear this event.

Ladies and gentlemen, don't let it happen in Puerto Rico. You opened your arms to these people. They came in. You treated them fairly. And what do they do?— They stab you in the back. They stabbed her in the back because she's a woman. They stabbed her in the back because she's Puerto Rican.

That is not what Dr. Martin Luther King convinced a nation to do.

We are dismayed that, even while calling on the jury to uphold principles of equality and anti-discrimination, plaintiff's counsel made inflammatory arguments to the jury based on the Dominican nationality of some individual defendants. Such arguments are "clearly prohibited conduct" and have no place in a court of law. *Smith* v. *Kmart Corp.*

III.

For the foregoing reasons, we reverse the judgment of the district court and order the entry of judgment in favor of the Department of Health. The parties shall bear their own costs on appeal.

Case Questions

1. Who has to prove a company discriminated against an employee? Do you agree with the burden of this obligation?

2. Do you believe that Dr. Alvarado-Santos could not possibly have experienced discrimination on the basis of national origin as long as the individual who assumed her responsibilities was of the same national origin as she was? In other words, since she and Dr. Devarie were both Puerto Rican, was it not possible that Dr. Rodríguez-Pichardo was discriminating against her on the basis of her national origin?

3. As an employer, what is the best way for you to protect the company from charges accusing one of your supervisors of discrimination such as the one involved in this case?

Case 3

EEOC v. WC&M Enterprises, Inc., *496 F. 3d 393,* (*9th Circuit, 2007*)

Mohommed Rafiq, born in India and a practicing Muslim, worked as a car salesman for WC&M. Rafiq's co-workers and supervisors implied that he was involved in the September 11, 2001, terrorist attacks, called him "Taliban" everyday, and told him that this was America and, if he did not like it, he could go back to where he came from. They also often referred to Rafiq as an "Arab," even though Rafiq told them on numerous occasions that he was from India. The court held that Rafiq could pursue a national origin harassment claim; although none of the harassing comments referred to India, several of the comments made to the employee referred to national origin generally.

***

... [T]he district court made two findings that essentially disposed of the EEOC's hostile work environment claim on the merits: (1) that the EEOC had not shown that Rafiq lost sales as a result of the alleged harassment that he suffered; and (2) that the EEOC could not bring a claim based on Rafiq's national origin because none of the harassing comments specifically referred to the fact that Rafiq was from India. The EEOC argues that the district court erred in each respect. We agree.

To state a hostile work environment claim under Title VII, the plaintiff must show that: (1) the victim belongs to a protected group; (2) the victim was subjected to unwelcome harassment; (3) the harassment was based on a protected characteristic; (4) the harassment affected a term, condition, or privilege of employment; and (5) the victim's employer knew or should have known of the harassment and failed to take prompt remedial action. Only elements (3) and (4) are seriously contested in this case.

***

For harassment to be sufficiently severe or pervasive to alter the conditions of the victim's employment, the conduct complained of must be both objectively and subjectively offensive. Thus, not only must the victim perceive the environment as hostile, the conduct must also be such that a reasonable person would find it to be hostile or abusive. To determine whether the victim's work environment was objectively offensive, courts consider the totality of the circumstances, including (1) the frequency of the discriminatory conduct; (2) its severity; (3) whether it is physically threatening or humiliating, or merely an offensive utterance; and (4) whether it interferes with an employee's work performance. No single factor is determinative. In short, a

showing that the employee's job performance suffered is simply a factor to be considered, not a prerequisite. As the Supreme Court stated, "even without regard to ... tangible effects, the very fact that the discriminatory conduct was so severe or pervasive that it created a work environment abusive to employees because of their race, gender, religion, or national origin offends Title VII's broad rule of workplace equality."

***

Here, the district court held that even if Rafiq could prove that any harassment occurred, "he has not shown that it was so severe that it kept him from doing his job." In so holding, the district court applied an incorrect legal standard. Whether Rafiq lost sales as a result of the alleged harassment is certainly relevant to his hostile work environment claim; but it is not, by itself, dispositive. The district court erred in concluding otherwise.

***

With respect to national origin, the district court found that the EEOC could not prevail on its claim that Rafiq was harassed on the basis of national origin because none of the alleged harassment related to the fact that Rafiq is from India. The district court is correct that none of the harassing comments directly referred to Rafiq's actual national origin. However, a party is able to establish a discrimination claim based on its own national origin even though the discriminatory acts do not identify the victim's actual country of origin.

Indeed, the EEOC's guidelines on discrimination define "discrimination based on national origin" broadly, to include acts of discrimination undertaken "because an individual has the physical, cultural or linguistic characteristics of a national origin group." Nothing in the guidelines requires that the discrimination be based on the victim's actual national origin. The EEOC's final guidelines make this point clear:

In order to have a claim of national origin discrimination under Title VII, it is not necessary to show that the alleged discriminator knew the particular national origin group to which the complainant belonged. . . . [I]t is enough to show that the complainant was treated differently because of his or her foreign accent, appearance, or physical characteristics. Guidelines on Discrimination Because of National Origin, 45 Fed. Reg. 85,632, 85,633 (Dec. 29, 1980); see also *Langadinos v. Appalachian Sch. of Law*, No. 1:05CV00039, 2005 U.S. Dist. LEXIS 20958, 2005 WL 2333460, at *1 n.6 (W.D. Va. Sept. 25, 2005) ("The plaintiff may still establish a cause of action under the Civil Rights Act despite the defendant's mistaken belief that his ethnic characteristics are those of a person of Italian, rather than Greek, descent."); *Kanaji v. Children's Hosp. of Philadelphia*, 276 F. Supp. 2d 399, 401-04 (E.D. Pa. 2003) ("Defendant fails to cite a single case where a court has held that a plaintiff alleging 'national origin' discrimination must specify a 'country' or 'nation' of origin."); *LaRocca v. Precision Motorcars, Inc.*, 45 F. Supp. 2d 762, 770 (D. Neb. 1999) ("The fact that [co-worker] ignorantly used the wrong derogatory ethnic remark toward the plaintiff is inconsequential.").

In this case, the evidence that the EEOC presented supports its claim that Rafiq was harassed based on his national origin. Indeed, several of the challenged statements refer to national origin generally (even though they do not accurately describe Rafiq's actual country of origin): (1) Kiene's comment to Rafiq, "Why don't you just go back where you came from since you believe what you believe?"; (2) Swigart's statement, "This is America. That's the way things work over here. This is not the Islamic country where you come from"; and (3) Kiene's and Argabrite's practice of referring to Rafiq as "Taliban" and calling him an "Arab."

Accordingly, we conclude that the EEOC has submitted sufficient evidence to support its claim that Rafiq was subjected to a hostile work environment both on the basis of religion and on the basis of national origin.

***

For the foregoing reasons, we reverse the district court's grant of summary judgment in favor of the defendant-appellee and remand this matter to the district court for proceedings consistent with this opinion.

Case Questions

1. Do you agree that harassment based upon an inaccurate portrayal of a worker's national origin is as unethical or wrongful as harassment based on the worker's actual national origin?

2. Does the conduct described seem sufficiently connected to national origin to meet the requirements of the Guidelines on Discrimination Because of National Origin? How would you decide if you were on the jury?

3. Can you make any argument that the definition of religion and of harassment based on national origin should be different?

Case 4

Espinoza v. Farah Manufacturing Co. *414 U.S. 86 (1973)*

Cecilia Espinoza, a lawful Mexican alien, applied for a position at Farah Manufacturing's San Antonio Division. She was denied the position, however, as a result of Farah's policy to hire only U.S. citizens. The issue to be decided by the court is whether Title VII's proscription against discrimination on the basis of national origin protects against discrimination on the basis of citizenship. The Court determines that it does not.

Marshall, J.

***

The term "national origin" on its face refers to the country where a person was born, or, more broadly, the country from which his or her ancestors came.

There are other compelling reasons to believe that Congress did not intend the term "national origin" to embrace citizenship requirements. Since 1914, the federal government itself, through Civil Service Commission regulations, has engaged in what amounts to discrimination against aliens by denying them the right to enter competitive examination for federal employment. But it has never been suggested that the citizenship require-ment for federal employment constitutes discrimination because of national origin. To interpret the term "national origin" to embrace citizenship requirements would require us to conclude that Congress itself has repeatedly flouted its own declaration of policy. This Court cannot lightly find such a breach of faith. Certainly Title VII prohibits discrimination on the basis of citizenship when-ever it has the purpose or effect of discriminating on the basis of national origin. However, there is no indication in the record that Farah's policy against employment of aliens had the purpose or effect of discriminating against persons of Mexican national origin.

Douglas, J., dissenting

It is odd that the Court which holds that a State may not bar an alien from the practice of law or deny employment to aliens can read a federal statute that prohibits discrimination in employment on account of "national origin" so as to per-mit discrimination against aliens.

Alienage results from one condition only: being born outside the United States. Those born within the country are citizens from birth. It could not be clearer that Farah's policy of excluding aliens is *de facto* a policy of prefer-ring those who were born in this country.

Case Questions

1. Which argument, the majority's or the dissent, do you find more compelling?

2. What implications does this case have for hiring prac-tices in parts of the United States where aliens are prevalent?

3. If Espinoza could show that this policy, while argu-ably "facially neutral," actually impacts people of Mexican origin differently than people of American origin, wouldn't Espinoza have a claim for disparate impact?

Centeno-Bernuy, et al. v. Perry, *302 F. Supp. 2d 128 (2003)*

The plaintiffs in this case are workers from Peru who entered the United States legally as H-2A agricul-tural workers. An H-2A worker is only permitted to remain in the United States as long as the worker is employed by a particular employer. The workers left the farm unannounced in the middle of the night and the defendant notified the Immigration and Naturalization Service (INS) but did not at that time claim that the workers were terrorists. The workers subsequently filed an action against the farm owners under the FLSA and the MSAWPA. Immediately after he learned of the suit, the defendant went to the local INS office and told agents that the workers were part of a Peruvian terrorist group. Despite having no proof, he repeated that charge to several government agencies and officials. The court granted a pre-liminary injunction since the workers would suffer irreparable harm if the defendant's action were not enjoined because his conduct had negatively affected the workers' ability to enforce their rights and also held that the workers had established a *prima facie* case of retaliation.

***

Plaintiffs have demonstrated a likelihood of success on the merits of their FLSA retaliation claim. The FLSA provides that it is "unlawful for any person . . . to dis-charge or in any other manner discriminate against any employee because such employee has filed any com-plaint or instituted or caused to be instituted any proceed-ing under [the FLSA] . . . ." . . .

To establish a *prima facie* claim of retaliation in viola-tion of the FLSA, a plaintiff must show "(1) participation in protected activity known to the defendant; (2) an employ-ment action disadvantaging the plaintiff; and (3) a causal connection between the protected activity and the adverse employment action." The Court finds that the plaintiffs have established a *prima facie* case of retaliation in this case.

Plaintiffs have undertaken a protected activity under the FLSA in filing the Becker Farms litigation and Perry knew of the lawsuit within a few days after it was filed. Perry's actions after learning of the lawsuit, *i.e.,* reporting plaintiffs to the INS and making baseless allegations to the government that plaintiffs are terrorists, constitute an adverse employment action. Further, there is sufficient evidence to support a finding of a causal connection between plaintiffs' protected activity under the FLSA and Perry's adverse employment action. As stated above, the evidence shows that Perry asserted the sensational yet unfounded claims that plaintiffs are terrorists to government authorities for the sole purpose of preventing or dissuading plaintiffs from pursuing the Becker Farms litigation. Both the timing and nature of Perry's accusations support such a finding. Perry's first contact with the INS, before the Becker Farms litigation was filed, did not involve the sort of accusations that Perry has made about plaintiffs since learning of the lawsuit. The escalating accusations all occurred after the Becker Farms litigation was filed.

***

For the reasons stated, the Court denies Perry's motion to dismiss and grants the plaintiffs' motion for a preliminary injunction.

Case Questions

1. In your opinion, is there a conundrum created by legal protection against retaliation offered to the individuals in this case? They were working in the United States legally and then "absconded" (the legal term for the circumstances of the case), and the court held that they suffered a form of retaliation and sought protection of the court system. What is your impression of the dicta and holding in this case?

2. Would it be relevant to your above response if the defendants had recruited the workers to work for them in the United States?

3. Do you agree with the Court in Patel that protecting undocumented aliens by requiring that employers treat them the same as other workers will discourage illegal immigration?

Chapter **8**

Gender Discrimination

Learning Objectives

When you finish this chapter, you should be able to:

LO1 Recite Title VII and other laws relating to gender discrimination.

LO2 Understand the background of gender discrimination and how we know it still exists.

LO3 List the different ways in which gender discrimination is manifested in the workplace.

LO4 Analyze a situation and determine if there are gender issues that may result in employer liability.

LO5 Define fetal protection policies, gender-plus discrimination, workplace lactation issues, and gender-based logistical concerns.

LO6 Differentiate between legal and illegal grooming policies.

LO7 List common gender realities at odds with common bases for illegal workplace determinations.

LO8 Distinguish between equal pay and comparable worth and discuss proposed legislation.

SCENARIO 1

1 A discount department store has a policy requiring that all male clerks be attired in coats and ties and all female clerks wear over their clothing a smock provided by the store, with the store's logo on the front. A female clerk complains to her supervisor that making her wear a smock is illegal gender discrimination. Is it? Why or why not?

SCENARIO 2

2 A male applies for a position as a server for a restaurant in his hometown. The restaurant is part of a well-known regional chain named for an animal whose name is a colloquial term for a popular part of the female anatomy. Despite several years of experience as a server for comparable establishments, the male is turned down

for the position, which remains vacant. The applicant is instead offered a position as a kitchen helper. The applicant notices that all servers are female and most are blonde. All servers are required to wear very tight and very short shorts, with T-shirts with the restaurant logo on the front, tied in a knot below their, usually ample, breasts. All kitchen help and cooks are male. The applicant feels he has been unlawfully discriminated against because he is a male. Do you agree? Why or why not?

SCENARIO 3

3 An applicant for a position of secretary informs the employer that she is pregnant. The employer accepts her application but never seriously considers her for the position because she is pregnant. Is this employment discrimination?

Statutory Basis

LO1

It shall be an unlawful employment practice for an employer—

(1) to fail or refuse to hire or to discharge any individual, or otherwise to discriminate against any individual with respect to his compensation, terms, conditions, or privileges of employment, because of such individual's . . . sex [gender] . . . [Title VII of the Civil Rights Act of 1964, as amended. 42 U.S.C. § 2000e-2 (a).]

(1) No employer . . . shall discriminate between employees on the basis of sex by paying wages to employees . . . at a rate less than the rate at which he pays wages to employees of the opposite sex . . . for equal work on jobs the performance of which requires equal skill, effort, and responsibility, and which are performed under similar working conditions, except where such payment is made pursuant to (i) a seniority system; (ii) a merit system; (iii) a system which measures earnings by quantity or quality of production; or (iv) a differential based on any other factor other than sex . . . . [Equal Pay Act, 29 U.S.C.A. § 206(d).]

(k) The term "because of sex" or "on the basis of sex" includes, but is not limited to, because of or on the basis of pregnancy, childbirth, or related medical conditions; and women affected by pregnancy, childbirth, or related medical conditions shall be treated the same for all employment-related purposes, including receipt of benefits under fringe benefit programs, as other persons not so affected but similar in their ability or inability to work.... [Pregnancy Discrimination Act, 42 U.S.C. § 2000e.]

Note: Reread the Preface regarding the use of gender terminology before reading this chapter.

Does It Really Exist?

What does a group of 25 attorney-mediators have to do with a swimsuit calendar? Good question. The Miami-based Florida Mediation Group has probably been asking itself that same question ever since it received a good deal of flack for having its name emblazoned across one of several themed calendars given away as gifts to clients.

Of all the bases for employment discrimination we cover in class and in consulting, gender seems to be the one that is most difficult for students to believe exists. This, despite that fact that a 2010 Harris Poll of 2,227 adults surveyed online found that 7 in 10 Americans say women often do not receive the same pay as men for doing exactly the same job, 63 percent agreed the United States still has a long way to go to reach complete gender equality, and 74 percent believe there are more pressing issues to fix first.[1] As Stuart J. Ishimaru, then-acting chairman of the EEOC stated: "Sex discrimination against males and females alike continues to be a problem in the 21st century workplace."[2]

We understand that if you are not used to thinking that it exists, sometimes it can be difficult to recognize gender discrimination when it plays itself out in the workplace. Gender is a part of our everyday life and so much related to it is based on stereotypes, customs, mores, and ideas that we learn from birth. Gender discrimination comes in so many different forms. That is why in this chapter we will provide many different manifestations of gender discrimination for you to look at so you can gain exposure. As a manager, supervisor or business owner, we want you to be able to analyze fact situations in the workplace as they occur in order to determine if there is potential liability.

Suppose a woman is required by her employer to wear two-inch heels to work. Doing so causes her to develop bunions, which can only be removed by surgery. After surgery she is ordered by her doctor to wear flat shoes for two months. Her employer refuses to permit her to do so. Left with no alternative, she quits. The employer imposes no such requirement on male employees. When you realize that the employer's two-inch-heels policy cost the woman her job and that had she been male this would not have happened, it becomes more obvious that the policy is discriminatory on the basis of gender.

Remember the wires of the bird cage in the piece at the opening of this section of the text. Those wires are probably what the members of the executive board of the Miami-Dade chapter of the Florida Association of Women Lawyers were thinking of when they registered their objection to the calendar. "We believe this type of advertising, whether picturing men or women, does not promote dignity in the law and is inappropriate when circulated by an organization that serves the legal community."[3]

It is not difficult to discriminate on the basis of gender if an employer is not sensitive to the issues involved. (See Exhibit 8.1, "Gender-Neutral Language?") Once again, as with race discrimination, vigilance pays off. This chapter will address gender discrimination in general, including pregnancy discrimination, lactation policies, fetal protection policies, and equal pay. Sexual harassment, another type of gender discrimination, will be considered in the next chapter.

Exhibit 8.1 *Gender-Neutral Language?*

Attorney Harry McCall, arguing before the U.S. Supreme Court, stated, "I would like to remind you gentlemen" of a legal point. Associate Supreme Court Justice Sandra Day O'Connor asked, "Would you like to remind me, too?" McCall later referred to the Court as "Justice O'Connor and gentlemen." Associate Justice Byron White told McCall, "Just 'Justices' would be fine."

Source: *Newsweek,* November 25, 1991, p. 17.

Gender discrimination covers both males and females, but because of the unique nature of the history of gender in this country, it is females who feel the effects of gender discrimination in the workplace more so than men, and the vast majority of EEOC gender claims are filed by women. However, during the recent economic downturn, more men than women lost their jobs,[4] with 78 percent of the jobs lost in the recession held by males.[5] The reason given is that the jobs women hold tend to be more stable, but lower paying, and the male-dominated sectors such as construction, investment banking, and manufacturing tended to be hardest hit.[6] However, by March of 2011, the Bureau of Labor Statistics reported that 90 percent of the jobs gained in the recovery went to men.[7]

Women are the single largest group of beneficiaries under affirmative action. They seem to be gaining in all facets of life. As we write this, three of the U.S. Supreme Court justices are women. Hillary Rodham Clinton made an unprecedented run for president of the United States as the first female candidate with a serious chance of winning. Nancy Pelosi was the first female speaker of the U.S. House of Representatives. Women head corporations and states, own businesses, and are members of the president's cabinet. Even the Navy now allows women to serve on submarines.[8] Things seem OK. You think to yourself, who would be dumb enough to discriminate against women these days? It can be hard to believe that gender discrimination still exists when you go to school and work with so many people of both genders; you don't feel like *you* view gender as an issue, and it just seems like everything is OK. However, the EEOC reports that gender suits account for the second highest percentage of substantive claims brought under Title VII, behind race.[9]

As a reality check, just recently, one of our female master's students was told by an employer that if she were a man with her qualifications, he would pay her 50 percent more. Another was told she had a full-time job upon graduation in a company in which she had experienced a very successful internship, but only if she allowed the very prominent president of the company to set her up in an apartment so she could be available to him whenever he wished to have sex with her. She did not take him up on his offer. She was, however, put in the unenviable position of starting her job hunt all over again and not finding another job in her field until five months after she graduated. Gender discrimination is real and is not just something that happens to other people. It is real and must be addressed in the workplace. But, first you have to be able to recognize it.

Even professionals can be caught off guard. In 1999 a gender-discrimination charge that started with eight female stockbrokers at Merrill Lynch alleging various forms of gender inequality, particularly economic discrimination, ballooned to 900 women and was still growing. "It's been a flood. I've been stunned. We were expecting 200–300 claims, but the calls are still coming in," said one of the lawyers representing the women. In 2004, arbitrators determined that it was standard operating procedure at Merrill Lynch to discriminate against women. It was the first time a Wall Street firm had been found to have engaged in systematic gender discrimination. Merrill Lynch spent more than $100 million settling close to 95 percent of the 900 or so claims. In subsequent press releases, the firm said this is not an accurate picture of the firm today.

Unfortunately, that was only the beginning of Wall Street's gender-based litigation. Cases continue to be brought by female employees against several Wall Street firms for the same types of discrimination that cost Merrill Lynch so much. In 2010 women filed EEOC claims against Goldman Sachs investment bank, alleging systematic discrimination against women including pay and promotions.[10] At least 58 women have joined in a 2009 suit filed by the EEOC against financial services and media company Bloomberg, founded by New York mayor Michael Bloomberg, claiming pregnancy discrimination.[11] Women at Citigroup, Inc. filed a class action for gender discrimination alleging they were laid off in the 2008 recession as part of the firm's "glass ceiling," and lesser qualified or under-performing males were retained.[12] Morgan Stanley settled a gender-bias class action suit for $46 million in 2007; Putnam Investments was sued for its "ingrained culture of chauvinism," leading to demotions and firings based on gender; Smith Barney was sued for a pattern and practice of gender discrimination against its female financial consultants; and Wall Street bank Dresdner Kleinwort Wasserstein Securities, LLC, was sued for $1.4 billion by female employees who alleged they were hired as "eye candy," subjected to *Animal House*–like antics, passed over for promotions, and generally treated like second-class citizens.

Clearly, Merrill Lynch's $100 million message was not heard by all. In fact, it was not even heard by Merrill Lynch. In 2009 another group of women sued Bank of America, which acquired Merrill Lynch, alleging Bank of America had paid them substantially lower bonuses than men based on information from Merrill Lynch that BOA knew was discriminatory.[13] The next year, three female financial advisors filed a class action lawsuit against BOA Merrill Lynch alleging a pattern and practice of gender discrimination in account distributions, partnership opportunities, up-front money, pay-out rate, other benefits in its compensation plan and opportunities for brokers to increase their income.[14]

But Wall Street is hardly alone. Recent cases have been filed for everything from a female animal handler terminated for refusing to expose her breasts to a 300-pound gorilla who had a "nipple fetish"; to a female attorney suing her firm because she alleged she was not being paid the same as similarly situated men and there was a separate, lower track for female lawyers with children or who took maternity leave; to the Clearwater, Florida, Fire & Rescue chief being charged by the EEOC with gender discrimination for ordering the department's six female firefighters to stay away from structure fires amid reported threats that their male colleagues might not protect them; to a man suing in California because there is no convenient, easy, comparable way for him to take his wife's name when they marry as it is for her to take his. Add race to the gender mix and it gets even worse. An American Bar Association study on women of color in law firms, commissioned after a National Association for Law Placement study found that 100 percent of female minority lawyers left their jobs in law firms within eight years of being hired, 44 percent of the women reported being passed over for desirable assignments (compared to 2 percent for white men), 62 percent said they had been excluded from formal and informal networking opportunities (compared to 4 percent of white men), and 49 percent reported being subjected to demeaning comments or other types of harassment at their firms.[15]

Gender equality in the workplace is an ever-evolving area and does not occur in a vacuum. The issues in the workplace are only one part of a much larger environment of different, often unequal, treatment of individuals based on gender. Imagine the swimsuit calendar having bikini-clad males instead of females. Do you think it would have been received the same way? Manifestations of gender differences in society are the basis for differences in treatment in the workplace. They can be as diverse as the group of Massachusetts teens suing the Selective Service System, arguing it is an unconstitutional violation of the Fifth and Fourteenth Amendments' Equal Protection Clause for females not to be subject to the draft just as men are, asserting that "if people want women's rights, they should want it wholeheartedly, including for women to have to fight in wars,"[16] to the protest over General Nutrition Center (GNC) dropping women from its GNC Show of Strength bodybuilding competition and replacing it with the International Federation of Body Builders (IFBB) Pro Figure competition[17]; from males suing bars for offering "Ladies' Night" discounts to women because such promotions discriminate against men,[18] to the Congressional House Oversight and Government Reform Committee expressing support for the 2010 Restroom Gender Parity in Federal Building Act (H.R. 4869)[19]; from *Playboy* magazine running an article titled "Ten Conservative Women I'd Like to F—," to *Right Wing News* compiling a list of the "hottest conservative women in the news media"[20]; from Lawry's restaurant chain not allowing men to be servers because of a 1938 policy,[21] to a female construction flag worker feeling compelled to wear a diaper to work because she was not allowed to find a bathroom in time at remote sites[22]; from female police officers being called "overtime whores,"[23] to an athletic club charging men more than women[24]; and from female playwrights in New York complaining at a standing-room-only town hall meeting with producers that men's plays in the 2008-9 season were produced at four times the rate theirs were,[25] to Club Med's "Ladies Fly Free" travel promotion.[26]

Of course, it goes without saying that gender differences also find their way into the workplace through lower pay for women; women being consigned to lower-paid jobs (pink-collar jobs); women being hassled, not promoted, or not given the same assignments and training as men in jobs traditionally held by men; or men not being hired for traditionally female jobs such as Hooters' servers.

New types of gender claims are constantly evolving. In the past few years, at least 24 states have passed "contraceptive equity" laws requiring that any health plan that provides coverage for prescription drugs also must provide coverage for FDA-approved contraceptive drugs. When employers' health plans routinely covered the cost of Viagra for male employees but not the cost of birth control for females, which the EEOC determined violated Title VII, at least 28 states passed "contraceptive equity" laws requiring that any health plan that provides coverage for prescription drugs also must provide coverage for FDA-approved contraceptive drugs.[27] As a result of state mandates, the number of employers allowing coverage for both tripled from 1993 to 2002. A 2004 Guttmacher Institute report found that by 2002, 86 percent of employers covered both.[28]

Despite federal and, in some cases, state law, the need for lactation facilities for nursing mothers has become a growing area of workplace concern. Increasing male employee interest in balancing work and family also has found its way into the workplace. The first gender-based Family and Medical Leave Act (FMLA) claim involved a new father who won $40,000 after being denied appropriate FMLA leave to take care of his premature baby and seriously ill wife.[29]

In 2007, the EEOC issued guidelines on "caregiver responsibility" discrimination, also known as "caregiver bias" or "family responsibility discrimination" (FRD).[30] The EEOC issued the guidelines because it realized the growing issue of the disparate impact that the conflict between work and family had on both male and female employees though it noted that since most caregiving responsibilities fall on women, such discrimination has a disparate impact on them. That is, because of their caregiving responsibilities, women are more likely to suffer adverse employment actions taken against them such as diminishing workplace responsibilities, failure to promote or train, exclusion from decision-making channels, or other actions coming from the idea that if employees have caregiving responsibilities, then they are less likely to be dependable, competent employees who can live up to their full workplace potential.

As women have increasingly entered the workforce since passage of Title VII, the focus of claims of gender discrimination has more recently shifted away from hiring discrimination toward on-the-job issues such as equal pay, promotions, harassment, and pregnancy leave and lactation policies. Eric S. Dreiband, EEOC general counsel, recently said this reflects "new issues erupting in a diverse workforce. As blatant discrimination decreased, other areas like harassment increase."

Viewed in this context, it then comes as no surprise that in the past few years, in addition to the substantial sums paid out by Wall Street for gender discrimination:

- Novartis Pharmaceutical Corporation was ordered to pay $250 million in compensatory damages and $3.3 million in punitive damages to female sales representatives for discrimination in pay and promotions, and because of pregnancy, despite the fact that for the past 10 years it had been declared one of the 100 best companies by *Working Mother* magazine.[31]

- Toshiba's U.S. unit was sued by its female employees for $100 million in February 2011, alleging systemic discrimination in pay and promotions and a pervasive atmosphere of women being required to be submissive to men.[32]
- A court upheld a $2 million award against Walmart to a female pharmacist who was fired for asking to be paid the same as her male colleagues.[33]
- Outback Steakhouse was made to pay $19 million to thousands of women at hundreds of its restaurants nationwide because they hit a glass ceiling and were denied favorable job assignments that were required for them to be considered for top management positions, and they could not get into the higher profit-sharing positions.[34]
- Wachovia Bank reached a settlement with the Office of Federal Contract Compliance Programs (OFCCP) to pay $5.5 million compensation for discrimination against women.[35]
- Home Depot agreed to pay $5.5 million to resolve a class action suit alleging, among other things, gender discrimination in its Colorado stores.
- The Palm Steak House agreed to a $500,000 settlement for failing to hire women to wait tables at its 29 restaurants because males, who could make up to $80,000 per year, including tips, were viewed as more prestigious.[36]
- Washington is the only state in the country that can boast that its governor is female, both of its U.S. senators are female, four of its nine state supreme court justices are female, and roughly a third of its state legislators are female, yet Seattle-based aeronautical giant Boeing agreed to pay $72.5 million compensation for gender-based discrimination against its female employees.
- A University of California lab agreed to pay $9.7 million to 3,200 women to whom it had paid less wages and whom it had promoted less often than male employees.
- Costco Wholesale Corp., with a workforce of 78,000, was sued by about 650 women in a class action suit alleging that the company did not announce openings for higher-paying managerial jobs, relying instead on a "tap the shoulder" policy of choosing managers. That is, top-level male managers would pick other males for high-level positions. Fewer than one in six of Costco's managers were women, while nearly 50 percent of its workforce is female.[37]
- Then, of course, there is Walmart, whose size alone puts it nearly in a class by itself. With sales of $405 billion for fiscal year 2010,[38] it is the world's largest retailer and the largest private employer in the United States. More than 70 percent of its hourly sales employees are women. In *Dukes v. Wal-Mart Stores, Inc.,*[39] potentially about 1.6 million present and former female employees (roughly the population of Dallas/Fort Worth) were certified for a class action suit against Walmart for gender bias and the court of appeals upheld the class certification.[40] The employees allege that Walmart systematically mistreats women in a variety of ways, including paying them less even though they may have more experience or outrank men, prohibiting women from advancing by denying them training, prohibiting them from working in departments

traditionally staffed by men (positions that usually pay more), and not posting all management position openings.

Damages could run into the billions if Walmart is found liable for gender discrimination. Walmart denies any wrongdoing, A study done at the request of the employees' attorney found that of Walmart's top 20 competitors, 56 percent of the managers are women, compared with about one-third of that for Walmart. Only about 14 percent of the top managers at its 3,000 stores are female. In response to the media coverage of the lawsuit, Walmart took out more than 100 full-page newspaper ads across the country, outlining its wages and benefits and the good the company brings to its communities.[41]

The Walmart case has been going on for 10 years and in 2011, it went to the U.S. Supreme Court on the issue of whether it should be certified as a class action.[42]

Let's take a look at some of the statistics that might underlie these cases to see if they support the overall picture.

- Forty-seven percent, nearly half the workforce, is female.[43]
- Forty-three percent of female employees work in the four most common female occupations: secretary, registered nurse, teacher and cashier.[44] Paradoxically, a 2004 EEOC report[45] found that women have the lowest odds of being managers in nursing care facilities.,
- A 2007 report by the U.S. Census Bureau found that the median income for a male working full time, year-round was $41,965, while for females the median was $32,168, or 29 percent less. The gender-based wage gap is present in every profession. For instance, female doctors on average earn 58 percent less than male doctors.
- A March 2011 report released by the White House Commission on Women and Girls was the most comprehensive federal report on the status of women in the United States since 1963. Its statistical snapshot of women indicated that women earn 75 percent as much as men at all levels of educational attainment, with Hispanic women making 62 percent and black women 71 percent. This is despite the fact that women have now passed men in education and are more likely than men to have college or graduate degrees. Women are also more likely to live in poverty, do more housework, and suffer depression and chronic health problems.[46]
- Across the workforce the gap between what men and women earn has shrunk over the last few decades. Full-time women workers closed the gap to 80.2 cents for every dollar earned by men in 2009, up from 62.3 cents in 1979 and 59 cents when the Equal Pay Act was passed in 1963.[47]
- A study by Stephen J. Rose, an economist at the consulting firm of Macro International, Inc., and Heidi I. Hartmann, president of the Institute for Women's Policy Research, found that while the Bureau of Labor Statistics (BLS) reports that women earn about 77 percent of men's pay over the course of their careers, it is actually more like 44 percent. The researchers say the

BLS statistics consider only full-time, year-round employees—a category only about 25 percent of women fit into over the course of their work life—and do not account for the roughly 75 percent of those who work only part time at some point and dip in and out of the labor force to care for children or elderly parents. When the more accurate reality is used for calculation, the figure becomes 44 percent.[48] These differences in the way the determinations are made may account for the variations above between 75 percent and 80 percent.

- A longitudinal study released in February 2010 by Catalyst, a global nonprofit organization, titled "Pipeline's Broken Promise," found that despite company-implemented diversity and inclusion programs instituted with the expectation of creating a talent pipeline where women would be poised to make rapid gains to the top, inequality remains entrenched. In the study of 4,143 MBA graduates from elite programs in the United States, Canada, Europe, and Asia, those that companies count on for future leadership, women lagged behind men in advancement and compensation. Unless they are part of the 10 percent of women who begin their post-MBA career at mid-management or above, they do not achieve parity in position with men. They make on average $4,600 less on their initial jobs and continue to be outpaced by men in rank and salary. Men are twice as likely to hold CEO or senior executive positions and less likely to be in the lower positions where women are overrepresented. The findings held even when considering men and women without children as well as those who aspired to senior leadership positions. Needless to say, they found that, in general, men were more satisfied with their careers overall than women were.[49]

- According to a 2010 Government Accounting Office report commissioned by the Joint Economic Council of Congress, as of 2007, the latest year for which comprehensive data on managers were available, women accounted for about 40 percent of managers in the U.S. workforce. In 2000 it was 39 percent.[50]

- On the other hand, women earn more high school diplomas, BAs, MAs, and doctorates than men, yet it is generally recognized that campuses are still predominantly male when it comes to professors, department heads, and other high-level administrators.[51]

- U.S. Department of Education data show that a year out of school, despite having earned a higher grade point average in every subject, young women will take home, on average, across professions, just 80 percent of what their male co-workers do.[52]

- A 2010 American Association of University Professors' study of decades of research to cull recommendations for drawing more women into the science and technology fields found that though women have made gains, stereotypes and cultural biases are still in the way of their progress. In "Why So Few?" they found, for instance, that a female post-doctoral applicant had to publish 3 more papers in prestigious journals or 20 more in less prestigious journals to be judged as productive as a male applicant. The report showed that even as women earned a growing share of doctorates in the science and technology fields, they do not show up a decade later in a proportionate number of tenured faculty positions. Harvard just tenured its first female after 375 years.[53]

- Women are less than 25 percent of law partners and politicians.[54]

- Women were 2.8 percent of Fortune 500 chief executives in 2010, In the FTSE 500, they were 1.8 percent.[55]

- On the other hand, the Fortune 500 corporate counsels grew to 92 from 44 in the nine years since the minority Corporate Counsel Association began keeping records in 1999.[56]

- According to a report by Deloitte Global Center for Corporate Governance, women make up 15.2 percent of Fortune 500 corporate boards. The chief executive of Germany's largest bank, Deutsche Bank, recently said a woman on his board (there were none) would make the board "more colourful and prettier." Several European countries have instituted quotas and others are considering it.[57]

- In a historic move in 2004, Susan Hockfield was tapped to be the new president of the prestigious Massachusetts Institute of Technology. Shortly thereafter, in January 2005, the then-president of Harvard University, Lawrence Summers, created quite a stir when he suggested at an academic conference that women represent such a small percentage of math and science faculties because they lack innate ability in math and science. He subsequently apologized, saying, in part, "The human potential to excel in science is not somehow the province of one gender or another." In February 2007, he was replaced by Drew Gilpin Faust, the first female president in Harvard's then 371-year history.

- The Global Gender Gap Index, a ranking of women's health, education, political, and financial standing by the World Economic Forum, found that from 2006 to 2009, the United States had fallen from 23rd to 31st place, behind Cuba and just above Namibia. Women still rank "masculine or patriarchal corporate culture" as the highest impediment to success.[58]

- An American Association of University Professors study found that men who are a year out of college make 20 percent more than their female counterparts.[59]

Given the statistics and situations we see reflected in the above items, the workplace discrimination litigation listed before it makes sense. The 1991 Civil Rights Act called for the establishment of a Glass Ceiling Commission to investigate the barriers to female and minority advancement in the workplace and suggest ways to combat the situation. In 1995, the U.S. Department of Labor released a study by the bipartisan commission. Findings were based on information obtained from independent studies, existing research, public hearings, and focus groups. The commission reported that while women have gained entry into the workforce in substantial numbers, once there they face all but invisible barriers to promotion into top ranks. "Glass ceilings" prevent them from moving up higher in the workplace. "Glass walls" prevent them from moving laterally into areas that lead to higher advancement. Research indicates that many professional women hold jobs in such areas as public relations, human resources management, and law—areas that are not prone to provide the experience management seeks when it determines promotions to higher-level positions. This was further supported by the study by Professor Blumrosen mentioned in the previous chapter.

The Glass Ceiling report found that segregation by both race and gender among executives and management ranks is widespread. A survey of top managers in Fortune 1000 industrial and Fortune 500 service firms found that 97 percent are white males. As part of their findings, a survey by Korn/Ferry International found that 3 to 5 percent of top managers are women. Of those, 95 percent are white, non-Hispanic. Further, women and minorities are trapped in low-wage, low-prestige, and dead-end jobs, the commission said. It is therefore not difficult to see why, in a *New York Times* poll of women about "the most important problem facing women today," job discrimination won overwhelmingly. Things have changed in the years since the comprehensive report was issued, but as you can see, the situation is still far from what most of us think of as a level playing field.

Our country, like many others, has a history in which women's contributions to the workplace have historically been precluded, denied, or undervalued. Prior to the 1964 Civil Rights Act, it was common for states to have laws that limited or prohibited women from working at certain jobs, under the theory that such laws were for the protection of women. Unfortunately, those jobs also tended to have higher wages. The effect was to prevent women from entering into, progressing within, or receiving higher wages in the workplace. In *Muller v. Oregon*,[60] which upheld protective legislation for women and justified them being in a class of their own for employment purposes, the U.S. Supreme Court stated that a woman must "rest upon and look to her brother for protection . . . to protect her from the greed as well as the passions of man." This is precisely the view our laws took until the Civil Rights Act of 1964.

After women came into the workplace in unprecedented numbers out of necessity during World War II and performed traditional male jobs admirably, it became more difficult to maintain the validity of such arguments. This type of protective legislation was specifically outlawed by Title VII, and the glass ceiling and walls notwithstanding, women have made tremendous strides in the workplace in the fifty-plus years since the Civil Rights Act was passed. In evaluating those strides, keep in mind that women were virtually starting from scratch since there was little or nothing to prevent workplace discrimination before Title VII, so gaining entry into the workplace and the statistics reflected by that should, of course, be high.

Despite the fact that many of the strides made by women were made with the help of male judges, employers, legislators, and others, much of the cause of the inequity given is attitudinal. (See Exhibit 8.2, "Sexist Thinking.") Workplace policies generally reflect attitudes of management. In a national poll of chief executives at Fortune 1000 companies, more than 80 percent acknowledged that discrimination impedes female employees' progress, yet less than 1 percent regarded *remedying* gender discrimination as a goal that their personnel departments should pursue. In fact, when the companies' human resources

---

Exhibit 8.2 *Sexist Thinking*

An *Esquire* magazine poll asked men: "If you received $1.00 for every sexist thought you had in the past year, how much richer would you be today?" The median answer was $139.50. (We have never had a male student who didn't think the figure should be *much* higher.)

Source: *Parade Magazine,* December 1991, p. 5.

---

officers were asked to rate their departments' priorities, women's advancement ranked last. Keep in mind that this attitude was also reflected in the 2010 Harris Poll in which, even though 70 percent said women do not receive the same pay as men for the same job, and 63 percent agreed the United States still has a long way to go to reach complete gender parity, 75 percent of women and 74 percent of men believed there were more pressing issues to deal with first. With women's income now being critical to the well-being of more than 40 percent of American families, this is not a trivial issue.[61]

While the pay gap between men and women has been stubbornly resistant to closing, not all of it can be attributed to discrimination. In general, women tend to be acculturated differently, which causes differences in how they approach the workplace. A Girl Scouts study found that young women avoid leadership roles for fear they'll be labeled bossy; women are four times less likely than men to negotiate a starting salary. A Harvard study found that women who demand more money are perceived as "less nice."[62]

Interestingly enough, while the biggest gains under protective employment legislation in the last nearly 50-years have been made by women, the truth is, gender was not even originally a part of the Civil Rights Act. Gender was inserted into the civil rights bill at the last moment by Judge Howard Smith, a southern legislator and civil rights foe desperate to maintain segregation in the south, who was confident that, if gender was included in the bill legislating racial equality, the bill would surely be defeated. He was wrong. However, because of the ploy, there was little legislative debate on the gender category, so there is little to guide the courts in interpreting what Congress intended by prohibiting gender discrimination. To date, courts have determined that gender discrimination also includes discrimination due to pregnancy and sexual harassment, but not because of affinity orientation or being transgender.

The goal of a manager, supervisor, human resources employee, or business owner is to have workplace policies that maximize the potential for *every* employee to contribute to the productivity and growth of the workplace, while minimizing or eliminating irrelevant, inefficient, and nonproductive policies that prevent them from doing so. The underlying consideration to keep in mind when developing, enforcing, or analyzing policies is that, no matter what we may have been taught about gender by family or cultural and societal mores, gender, alone, is considered by the law as irrelevant to one's ability to perform

Exhibit 8.3 *Career Stereotyping*

Dear Abby: As I begin my second year of medical school, I need some advice on how to respond to those ignorant people who assume that, since I am female, I am studying to be a nurse. Men and women alike are guilty of this.

Please don't get me wrong, I have just as much respect for nurses—they work as hard as some physicians, but women are seldom given the credit they deserve. I once heard this statement: "Oh, so you're in medical school? My sister is a nurse, too!"

I cannot tell you how angry this makes me. Many of my female classmates also feel this way. Do you have a response that expresses our feelings without offending the speaker?—Ms. Future Doctor in L.A.

Dear Future Doctor: Anyone who is confused about the role of a student in medical school should be told that future physicians are trained in medical schools, and future nurses are trained in nursing schools.

Dear Abby: After reading the letter from "Ms. Future Doctor," I felt the need to write and give another view on career sexual stereotypes.

I am 27, a registered nurse for four years, and I am a MALE. I am frequently asked, "When will you become a doctor?" Or, "You're doing this just to put yourself through medical school, right?" Also, "What's the matter, couldn't you get into medical school?"

When I first started my schooling to become a nurse, I considered medical school, but the further I got into nursing, the more I enjoyed being a nurse. I enjoy comforting a patient in pain, teaching my patients about their diseases, and holding the hand of someone who is frightened and hurting. These feelings are experienced by every nurse, and being male did not exclude me from doing them. (Most doctors are too busy.) I still work hard being a competent and compassionate nurse.

More males are choosing nursing as a career, and we need to shed our preconceived notions about who nurses are and what they look like.— Mr. Nurse in Tampa

Source: "Dear Abby" columns by Abigail Van Buren. Dist. by Universal Press Syndicate. Reprinted with permission. All rights reserved

a job. By law, it is the person's *ability* to perform, *not* his or her *gender,* that must be the basis of workplace decisions. (See Exhibits 8.3, "Career Stereotyping," and 8.4, "Gender Realities.") As we shall see, there may be very limited exceptions to this rule if a bona fide occupational qualification (BFOQ) exists. It is not only the law, but it is in the best interest of any employer who is serious about maximizing production, efficiency, and profits, as well as minimizing legal liability for workplace discrimination, to recognize that gender discrimination, whether subtle or overt, is just plain bad business. After all, workplace turnover, morale, and defending against lawsuits cost the employer money, time, and energy better spent elsewhere. (See Exhibit 8.5, "Discrimination: Bad for Business and Employees.")

The aim of this chapter is to provide information about obvious gender discrimination and what factors must be considered in making determinations about the policies in "gray areas." This chapter provides the tools to use when developing, applying, or analyzing policies that may result in gender discrimination claims.

Exhibit 8.4 *Gender Stereotypes*

Due to the particular historical development of gender in our country, there are many stereotypes about gender that affect how those of a given gender are perceived. Here are some of the stereotypes we have actually heard from managers and supervisors. These stereotypes impact how we view employees of a given gender in the workplace. See if any are familiar.

- Women are better suited to repetitive, fine-motor-skill tasks.
- Women are too unstable to handle jobs with a great deal of responsibility or high pressure.
- Men make better employees because they are more aggressive.
- Men do not do well at jobs requiring nurturing skills such as day care, nursing, elder care, and the like.

- When women marry, they will get pregnant and leave their jobs.
- When women are criticized at work, they will become angry or cry.
- A married woman's income is only extra family income.
- A woman who changes jobs is being disloyal and unstable.
- A woman cannot have a job that requires her to have lunch or dinner meetings with men.
- Women cannot have jobs that require travel or a good deal of time away from home.

Exhibit 8.5 *Discrimination: Bad for Business and Employees*

JURY TELLS NBA TO PAY FEMALE REFEREE $7.85 MILLION

Read what happened when a female rose to number two on the list of those in line to officiate in the NBA, only to be repeatedly passed over:

Sandra Ortiz-Del Valle sued the National Basketball Association (NBA) for gender discrimination for passing her over as a referee and handed the NBA its first discrimination case loss when the federal jury awarded Ortiz-Del Valle $7.85 million, $7 million of which was punitive damages (the award was later reduced by a judge to $350,000). Ortiz-Del Valle had dreamed of being an NBA referee for years but kept getting passed over. Despite documents praising Ortiz-Del Valle as being "very knowledgeable about the rules" and having "excellent basketball officiating skills," and although the evaluator said, "I would not hesitate to recommend that at sometime

in the near future she be considered to enter our training program," the NBA kept giving her varying reasons for denying her the position. The NBA denied any discrimination and said she was not hired because she failed to upgrade the level of competition in her officiating schedule despite being asked to, and said she was out of shape. Ortiz-Del Valle claimed she had all the qualifications to be an NBA referee, including officiating in top men's amateur and professional basketball leagues for 17 years. She was the first woman in history to officiate a men's professional basketball game. Ortiz-Del Valle said she finally sued after continuously doing everything the league asked of her, and not being promoted, then seeing men she trained hired by the league. "It was like they kept moving the basket," she said.

Source: *Ortiz-Del Valle v. NBA,* 42 F. Supp. 2d 334 (S.D.N.Y. 1999).

Exhibit 8.6   *Pre–Title VII Newspaper Want Ads for Females*

This classified ad excerpt, taken from an actual newspaper, is typical of those found in newspapers in the United States before Title VII was passed in 1964. For publication purposes, all names and phone numbers have been omitted. Title VII made it illegal to advertise for jobs based on gender.

FEMALE EMPLOYMENT

Female Help Wanted   23

ATTRACTIVE, NEAT APPEARING, RELIABLE YOUNG LADIES
FOR permanent employment as food waitresses. Interesting work in beautiful surroundings. Good salary plus tips. UNIFORMS FURNISHED. Vacation with pay. Age 21-35 years. For interview appointment phone…

SETTLED white woman who needs home to live in.

LADY to run used furniture store on…

GIRL FRIDAY
If you are a qualified executive secretary, dependable, and would like a solid connection with a growing corporation, write me your qualifications in confidence…

A REFRESHING CHANGE
FROM your household chores! Use those old talents of yours and become a part-time secretary. You can earn that extra money you have been needing by working when you want. XXX has temporary positions open in all locations in town and you can choose what and where you want. TOP HOURLY RATES…NO FEE

Opening Soon…WAITRESSES…NO EXPERIENCE NECESSARY
Will train neat, trim, and alert applicants to be coffee house and cocktail waitresses. Apply at once.

CLERK FOR HOTEL
CLERK for medium-size, unusually nice motor hotel. 6-day wk. Hours 3-11. Experience not necessary. Must be mature, neat, and refined. Call…

Gender Discrimination in General

LO3

Title VII and state fair-employment-practice laws regarding gender cover the full scope of the employment relationship. Unless it is a BFOQ, gender may not be the basis of any decision related to employment. This includes the following, taken from actual situations:

- *Advertising* for available positions and specifying a particular gender as being preferred (see Exhibit 8.6, "Pre–Title VII Newspaper Want Ads for Females").

- Asking questions on an *application* that are only asked of one gender. For example, for background-check purposes asking the applicant's maiden name, rather than simply asking all applicants if there is another name they may have used.

- Asking questions in an *interview* that are only asked of one gender. For example, asking female interviewees if they have proper day care arrangements for their children and not asking male interviewees who also have children. Or asking female applicants about reproductive plans and not asking males. (Yes, people actually do such things. Quite frequently, as a matter of fact.)

- *Requiring one gender to work different hours or job positions* for reasons not related to their ability or availability for the job. For example, not permitting women to work at night or not giving a promotion to a woman because it involves travel.

- *Disciplining* one gender for an act for which the other gender is not disciplined. For example, chastising a female employee who is late for work because of reasons related to her children while not similarly chastising a male employee who is late because of a sick dog, or chastising a female employee for cursing but not a male.

- Not taking into consideration legitimate differences between genders that can mean that treating them exactly the same may produce an undue hardship for the other, such as refusal to provide proper restroom facilities for all employees on construction sites.

LO7
- Providing or not providing *training* for one gender, while doing so for another. For example, requiring all female employees to be trained on word processing equipment, no matter what position they hold in the company, while not requiring that males undergo the same training. Or, alternatively, providing training opportunities for career advancement to male employees and not to similarly situated female employees.

- Establishing *seniority systems* specifically designed to give greater seniority to one gender over another. For example, instituting a new seniority system that bases seniority on how long an employee has been working for the employer, rather than how long the employee has been working in a particular department with the intent that, if the employer ever needs to lay off employees for economic reasons, more males will be able to retain their positions because females have been in the workplace a shorter time and thus have less seniority.

- *Paying* employees different wages based on gender, though the job one employee performs is the same or substantially the same as another. This may also violate the Equal Pay Act, which prohibits discrimination in compensation on the basis of gender for jobs involving equal skill, effort, or responsibility.

- Providing different *benefits* for one gender than for another. For example, providing spouses of male employees with coverage for short-term disabilities, including pregnancy, while not providing female employees with similar coverage for short-term disabilities for their spouses, or providing prescription coverage for Viagra for men, but not birth control for women.

- Subjecting one gender to different *terms or conditions of employment.* For example, requiring female associates in an accounting firm to dress, talk, or act "feminine," when no comparable requirement is imposed on males aspiring to partnership.

- Subjecting one gender to continual unwanted teasing, joking, comments, angry statements, or general hassling to which the other gender is not subjected.

• *Terminating* the employment of an employee of one gender for reasons that would not serve as the basis for termination for an employee of the other gender. For example, terminating a female employee for fighting on the job, when males engaged in similar activity are retained.

Clearly the anti-discrimination provisions are comprehensive. The law is broad enough to cover virtually every decision or policy that could possibly be made in the workplace. The scope of anti-discrimination laws is intentionally undefined so that decisions can be made on a case-by-case basis. Some of the examples above are not illegal per se. Rather, they elicit gender or gender-related information that can form the basis of illegal gender-based employment decisions—or at least make it appear as if that is the case.

The law takes a case-by-case approach to gender discrimination, so it is imperative to know what factors will be considered in analyzing whether gender discrimination has occurred. To the extent that these factors are considered when developing or implementing policies, it is less likely that illegal considerations or criteria will be used in making workplace decisions and policies. (See Exhibits 8.7, "Appearance-Based Discrimination," and 8.8, "On the Lighter Side.")

Recognizing Gender Discrimination

When analyzing employment policies or practices for gender discrimination, first check to see if it is obviously so. See if the policy excludes members of a particular gender from the workplace or some workplace benefit. An example is a policy that recently appeared in a newspaper story on local restaurants. One owner said that he did not hire males as servers because he thought females were more pleasant and better at serving customers. As *Wedow v. City of Kansas, Missouri,* demonstrates, employers may engage in obvious gender discrimination and claim to be unaware of their policies' negative legal repercussions, even though it is a workplace held in high regard such as a fire department. This case is available at the conclusion of the chapter.

Not all cases may be as easy to recognize as gender discrimination when making workplace decisions or policies. (See Exhibit 8.9, "Illegal or Unfair?") It is easier to realize there is gender discrimination when the policy says "no women hired as guards" than when, as with the *Dothard v. Rawlinson* case (given at the end of the chapter), there is a policy, neutral on its face, saying all applicants must meet certain height and weight requirements to be guards, yet due to their genetic differences, statistically, most women do not generally meet the requirements. In the *Dothard* case, for the first time, the U.S. Supreme Court was faced with whether Title VII's gender discrimination provision applied to the seemingly neutral criteria of height and weight restrictions, which had long been an accepted basis for screening applicants for certain types of jobs such as prison guards, police officers, and firefighters, even

Exhibit 8.7   *Appearance-Based Discrimination*

We often discriminate against others without even realizing it. Since only those things prohibited by law are considered illegal, not all discrimination is actionable. However, look at the items below and note the gender differences:

- Very attractive men and women earn at least 5 percent more per hour than people with average looks.
- Plain women earn an average of 5 percent less than women with average looks.
- Plain men earn 10 percent less than average men.
- Most employers pay overweight women 20 percent less per hour than women of average weight.
- Overweight males earn 26 percent more than underweight co-workers.
- Of men with virtually identical résumés, the taller man will be hired 72 percent of the time.
- Men who are 6 feet 2 inches or taller receive starting salaries 12 percent greater than men under 6 feet.
- Married men earn, on average, 11 percent more per hour than men who have never married.
- White women 65 pounds overweight earn 7 percent less than those of median weight; there is little effect of weight on the earnings of Hispanic women, none on black women, and virtually none on the wages of men.
- Better-looking men get more job offers, higher starting salaries, and better raises; good-looking women get better raises but not usually better jobs or starting salaries.
- Plain women tend to attract the lowest-quality husbands (as measured by educational achievement or earnings potential); beautiful women do no better in marriage than average women; looks don't seem to affect men's marriage prospects.
- The less attractive you are, the more likely you are to receive a longer prison sentence, a lower damage award, and a lower salary.
- Over his career, a good-looking man will make about $250,000 more than his least-attractive counterpart.
- In a *Newsweek* survey, 61 percent of hiring managers said it is advantageous for a woman to show off her figure in the workplace.
- In the same survey, 57 percent of corporate managers said landing a job is harder for an unattractive candidate.
- Beauty can also be a hindrance. A study in the *Journal of Social Psychology* found that attractive women are discriminated against when applying for jobs that are considered more traditionally male, such as director of finance, mechanical engineer, prison guard, tow-truck driver, construction worker, or hardware salesperson. Attractive men were not subjected to the same discrimination.

Sources: Taken from *The Paranoid's Pocket Guide,* by Cameron Tuttle, Chronicle Books, 1997, reprinted with permission; Professors Jeff Biddle and Daniel Hamermesh, "Beauty and the Labor Market," *American Economic Review* 83, no. 1174 (December 1994); John Cawley, *Body Weight and Women's Labor Market Outcomes* 2, no. 1, Joint Center for Poverty Research, 2000: Dahlia Lithwick, "Our Beauty Bias Is Unfair," *Newsweek*, 6/14/2010 , p. 20; Jessica Bennett, "The Beauty Advantage," *Newsweek*, 7/26/2010, p. 47; Lisa Johnson Mandrell, "Workplace Discrimination: Beauty Can Be a Beast at Work," AOL Jobs Original, 8/9/2010, http://jobs.aol.com/articles/2010/08/09/discrimination-gender-beauty-study/.

though there was little or no legitimate reason for the criteria. The Court decided that Title VII did, in fact, apply to such facially neutral policies when they screened out women (later cases extended this standard to shorter and slighter ethnicities as well) at an unacceptable rate and were not shown to be directly correlated to ability to do the job.

Exhibit 8.8 *On the Lighter Side**

Women are often accused of being humorless when it comes to gender issues. While the issue of gender discrimination is far from funny, it doesn't mean we can't laugh at ourselves. To wit, the following e-mail:

IS YOUR COMPUTER A HE OR A SHE?

A college professor who was previously a sailor was very aware that ships are addressed as "she" and "her." He often wondered [by] what gender computers should be addressed.

To answer that question, he set up two groups of computer experts. The first was composed of women, and the second of men. Each group was asked to recommend whether computers should be referred to in the feminine gender, or the masculine gender. They were asked to give four reasons for their recommendations.

The group of women reported that the computers should be referred to in the masculine gender because:

1. In order to get their attention, you have to turn them on.

2. They have a lot of data, but they are still clueless.

3. They are supposed to help you solve problems, but half the time they are the problem.

4. As soon as you commit to one, you realize that if you had waited a little longer, you could have had a better model.

The men, on the other hand, concluded that computers should be referred to in the feminine gender because:

1. No one but the Creator understands their internal logic.

2. The native language they use to communicate with other computers is incomprehensible to everyone else.

3. Even your smallest mistakes are stored in long-term memory for later retrieval.

4. As soon as you make a commitment to one, you find yourself spending half your paycheck on accessories for it.

*Thanks to Dr. Andy Walters, Northern Arizona University. Used with permission.

Exhibit 8.9 *Illegal or Unfair?*

Several courts have wrestled with the issue of what constitutes gender discrimination under Title VII. One issue that has arisen several times is whether it is illegal gender discrimination under Title VII if a female who is having a relationship with a supervisor receives a job or promotion over a qualified male who applies for the position. In *Womack v. Runyon,* 77 FEP Cases 769 (11th Cir. 1998), Paul Womack, having excellent credentials, experience, and training, applied for a carrier supervisor position in Waycross, Georgia. He was unanimously selected as the best-qualified candidate by a review board, but O. M. Lee, the newly appointed postmaster of Waycross, instead appointed Lee's paramour, Jeanine Bennett. In rejecting Womack's Title VII claim of gender discrimination, the court held that Title VII did not cover claims of favoritism, saying that such decisions may not be fair, but they are not illegal under Title VII. According to an EEOC policy guidance, "Title VII does not prohibit . . . preferential treatment based upon consensual romantic relationships. An isolated instance of favoritism toward a paramour . . . may be unfair, but it does not [amount to] discrimination against women or men in violation of Title VII, since both [genders] are disadvantaged for reasons other than their genders."

Exhibit 8.10 *Breast-Feeding: A Gender-Plus Issue?*

A federal judge in New York dismissed a gender discrimination and disability suit brought by Alicia Martinez, a cable television producer, alleging that after returning from maternity leave, her employer, MSNBC cable, failed to provide her with a "safe, secure, sanitary and private" place to pump breast milk during work breaks and harassed her for complaining. [*Martinez v. NBC, Inc. and MSNBC*, 49 F. Supp. 2d 305 (S.D.N.Y. 1999).]

Regarding the ADA claim, Judge Kaplan said it was "preposterous to contend a woman's body is functioning abnormally because she is lactating." As to the Title VII claim, the court said this was not "sex plus" discrimination because "to allow a claim based on sex-plus discrimination here would elevate breast milk pumping—alone—to a protected status," and that could only be done by Congress. It was not plain gender discrimination under Title VII because "the drawing of distinctions among persons of one gender on the basis of criteria that are immaterial to the other, while in given cases perhaps deplorable, is not the sort of behavior covered by Title VII."

Note that a similar argument was struck down by Congress in enacting the Pregnancy Discrimination Act, where the court determined it was not illegal gender discrimination to treat pregnant employees differently, since only females could become pregnant. Keep an eye on what happens with breast-feeding in the workplace. On March 23, 2010, President Obama signed into law the Patient Protection and Affordable Care Act of 2010. Among its provisions was an amendment to the Fair Labor Standards Act of 1938 that requires an employer of more than 50 employees to provide reasonable break time for an employee to express breast milk for her nursing child for one year after birth each time the employee has a need to express milk. The employer need not compensate the employee unless she is expressing milk on a regular paid break. The employer must also provide a private functional space other than a bathroom in which the employee may express the milk. If the employer has less than 50 employees and these requirements present an undue hardship, then the employer need not comply with this law. If state law provides stronger provisions, then the employer must comply with state law.

Twenty-four states, the District of Columbia and Puerto Rico have laws related to breastfeeding in the workplace (Arkansas, California, Colorado, Connecticut, Georgia, Hawaii, Illinois, Indiana, Maine, Minnesota, Mississippi, Montana, New Mexico, New York, North Dakota, Oklahoma, Oregon, Rhode Island, Tennessee, Texas, Vermont, Virginia, Washington and Wyoming). The number keeps growing. Even in the absence of legislation, many employers are taking this issue quite seriously and creating policies to address lactation.

See National Conference of State Legislatures, http://www.ncsl.org/default.aspx?tabid=14389.

"Gender-Plus" Discrimination

LO5

"gender-plus" discrimination
Employment discrimination based on gender and some other factor such as marital status or children.

There are some situations in which the employer may permit the hiring of women but not if there are other factors present—for example, no hiring of women who are pregnant, are married, are over a certain age, have children under a certain age, or are unmarried with children. This is **"gender-plus" discrimination**. Of course, the problem is that such policies are not neutral at all because males are not subject to the same limitations. (See Exhibit 8.10, "Breast-Feeding: A Gender-Plus Issue?")

Phillips v. Martin Marietta Corp.[63] was the first Title VII case to reach the U.S. Supreme Court and is still widely cited. *Martin Marietta* involved an employer's policy of not hiring women with preschool-aged children. No such policy applied to men with such children. The Court determined that unless the employer showed a legitimate basis for making the gender-based distinction, the policy could not stand. The case is interesting in that the employer did not keep all women out of the workplace, but only those with preschool-aged children. That is the "plus" involved. The dissent in the *Martin Marietta* case filed by Justice Thurgood Marshall refused to believe there could be any basis for proof of a justification for the policy. The Court evidently took Justice Marshall's dissent seriously because in the years after *Martin Marietta* the Court has not permitted BFOQs to be used in the way he warned against. Keep in mind that, while BFOQs are permitted as a lawful means of discriminating based on gender, they are *very* narrowly construed. The employer is under a heavy duty to show that the gender requirement is reasonably necessary for the employer's particular business.

Gender Issues

LO4

As we have seen, many issues are included under the umbrella of illegal gender discrimination. Following are some that are most prevalent. Keep in mind that many things we take for granted and dismiss as "that's just the way things are" may actually be illegal in the workplace. That is what Justice Marshall alluded to in his dissent in the Phillips case, which has been fully accepted by subsequent courts. It is extremely important to keep this in mind as managers make workplace decisions and to guard against letting such thoughts be the basis of illegal Title VII decisions that result in employer liability.

Gender Stereotyping

gender stereotypes
The assumption that most or all members of a particular gender must act a certain way.

Much discrimination on the basis of gender is in some way based on **gender stereotypes**. That is, workplace decisions are based on ideas of how a particular gender should act or dress, or what roles they should perform or jobs they should hold. An employer may terminate a female employee who is too "abrasive," or not hire a female for a job as a welder because it is "men's work." Stereotypes generally have little or nothing to do with an individual employee's qualifications or ability to perform. Workplace decisions based on stereotypes are prohibited by Title VII. (See Exhibits 8.5, "Discrimination: Bad for Business and Employees"; 8.11, "Stereotyped Humor"; and 8.12, "Stereotypes.")

Exhibit 8.11 *Stereotyped Humor*

"Hey, didja hear the one about the blond bimbo?" Well, you won't hear it here. Whether or not jokes playing on stereotypes of women make you laugh, they might affect your judgments of women. About 100 male and female college students who heard sex-stereotyped jokes before watching female lecturers later rated the women in a more stereotyped fashion than did students who heard nonsexist jokes. "This study suggests we should be on guard about [stereotyped humor]," says co-author Christine Weston, Boston University.

Source: *USA Today,* August 24, 1993, p. D-1

Exhibit 8.12   *Stereotypes*

Do any of the stereotypes below, taken from actual cases, sound familiar? Note that they are not limited to gender.

- "Older employees have problems adapting to changes and to new policies."
- One had to be wary around "articulate black men."
- Would not consider "some woman" for the position, questioned plaintiff about future pregnancy plans, and asked whether her husband would object to her "running around the country with men."

- Female employee who spent time talking to other black employees was becoming "the black matriarch" within the company.
- A lesser job position was sufficient for women and no woman would be named to the higher position.
- If it were his company, he would not hire any black people.
- He was "not going to hire a black leasing agent."

Case 3

As *Price Waterhouse v. Hopkins* (included at the end of the chapter) demonstrates, stereotyping frequently leads to actions that form the basis of unnecessary liability for the employer. It is senseless for employers to allow managers and supervisors who hold such views to cause liability that costs the entire company unnecessary loss of revenue. Gender stereotyping began as stereotyping about females, but recent cases also have used the *Price Waterhouse* case to prohibit gender stereotyping of males, particularly as it relates to effeminacy. See the *Azteca* case in the affinity orientation chapter.

Grooming Codes

LO6

The issue of gender stereotypes may be closely linked to that of grooming codes since the issue often arises in a gender context (e.g., men being prohibited from wearing earrings at work or women being required to wear makeup). Courts recognize that employers need to be able to control this aspect of the workplace, and a good deal of flexibility is permitted. In *Harper v. Blockbuster Entertainment Corporation*[64] male employees sued for gender discrimination based on not being allowed to wear long hair, since there was no such limitation on female employees. In rejecting their claim, the court said that "distinctions in employment practices between men and women on the basis of something other than immutable or protected characteristics do not inhibit employment *opportunity* in violation of Title VII. Congress sought only to give all persons equal access to the job market, not to limit an employer's right to exercise his informed judgment as to how best to run his shop." Title VII does not prohibit an employer from using gender as a basis for reasonable grooming codes.

Note, however, that we here address grooming codes only in the context of gender discrimination. The more recent workplace issue of, for example, applicants or employees with numerous body piercings, tattoos, and the like is generally not a gender issue but, rather, one of pure dress code–based appropriate business attire as determined by the employer. Again, employers are given a good deal of leeway in setting workplace dress codes. The codes can be pretty much whatever the employer wants, unless a policy violates the law, such as being illegally discriminatory on the basis of gender. In making this determination, employers can use reasonable standards of what is generally thought to be male- or female-appropriate attire in a business setting. For instance, a Florida city council in 2009 wanted to "clean up" and instituted a dress code requiring employees to wear underwear and use deodorant. It also prohibited exposed underwear, clothing with "foul" language, "sexually provocative" clothes, and piercings anywhere except the ears. The one city council member who opposed the measure did so because he believed the underwear rule "takes away freedom of choice."[65]

Courts also have upheld grooming codes that required, among other things, male supermarket clerks to wear ties, female employees to not wear pants, a female attorney to "tone down" her "flashy" attire, and male and female flight attendants to keep their weight down. Not permitted was a weight restriction policy applied only to the exclusively female category of flight attendants, but not the category of male directors of passenger service, when both were in-flight employees. Also not permitted was requiring male employees to wear "normal business attire" and women to wear uniforms, though both performed the same duties. The court found "there is a natural tendency to assume that the uniformed women have a lesser professional status than their male colleagues attired in normal business clothes. This is the basis for Opening Scenario 1, and the reason the female clerk made to wear the smock would have a viable claim for gender discrimination.

The wearing of the smock (picture the loose-fitting, coverall-type, button down overdress that hairdressers often wear) may seem like a small thing to you, and you might say to yourself, "What's the big deal? Why would anybody complain about such a little thing?" Think back to the wires of the cage at the opening of the discrimination section of the text. It is not the smock itself that presents the problem. Rather, as the court said above, it is how that smock positions the employee to be perceived in the workplace. That perception is a large part of what happens in that employee's work life, affecting whether that employee receives promotions, training, raises, and so on.

When you think of business attire (keep in mind that the males with the same jobs were required to wear the "normal business attire" of coats and ties), a smock does not generally come to mind. If both genders were performing the same job, a female wearing a smock would not qualify as comparable to a male wearing a coat and tie. If you think she would, just turn the facts around and require the males to wear the blousy-looking smock and the females to wear "normal business attire." Not the same picture, is it? And when you think of who should get a promotion, the employee in the smock probably doesn't come to mind. Like the wires, each requirement, in and of itself, may not make a big difference, but taken together, the policies create a picture that is likely to keep the female employee on the low end of the workplace ladder and be more likely to lead to unnecessary litigation.

As a managerial exercise for yourself, try to think of why the employer would have required the smock. Why not require it for all employees if they really are all the same? What is the difference between males wearing them and females wearing them? Once you come up with a reason, ask yourself if it makes sense. Chances are, it doesn't. For instance, if the smock was required to keep the employees' clothes clean, then why not protect the clothing of males also?

Being able to see and really understand the smock case goes a long way toward being able to truly grasp the big picture of how gender discrimination works and how you can think about avoiding liability when faced with your own situations as a manager.

A gender-based grooming policy that subjects one gender to different conditions of employment also would not be allowed, for instance, where the scant uniform the female lobby attendant was required to wear made her the object of lewd comments and sexual propositions from male entrants,[66] or where a manager required female employees to wear skirts when the "head honcho" visited because he "liked to look at legs." It is not a defense for an employer to argue that the employee knew about the grooming code when he or she came into the workplace. If the code is illegal, it is illegal, period. Agreeing to it makes it no less so, particularly given the unequal bargaining positions of the employer and job applicant/employee.

An interesting case arose when Harrah's Casino in Reno, Nevada, instituted a new dress code that required female employees to wear makeup. The "Personal Best" program "specified the makeup as foundation or powder, blush, lipstick and mascara, applied precisely the same way every day to match a photograph held by the supervisor." The only requirement for men was that they not wear makeup of any kind and keep their hair and nails trimmed. Darlene Jespersen, a bartender who had been employed by the casino for 21 years and had an excellent work history, was "highly offended she had to doll herself up to look like a hooker." She was terminated for failing to comply with the policy. Jespersen argued that the cosmetics cost hundreds of dollars per year and took a good deal of time to apply and therefore created an unequal burden on female employees. The Ninth Circuit Court of Appeals upheld the policy, saying "there is no evidence in the record in support of [Jespersen's] contention that cosmetics can cost hundreds of dollars per year and that applying them requires a significant investment of time."

Can you reconcile the court's position with that of the U.S. Supreme Court in the *Price Waterhouse* decision, which held that gender stereotyping violated Title VII? Remember that the Court found gender discrimination when, among other things, Hopkins was told she must "walk more femininely, talk more femininely, dress more femininely, wear make-up, have her hair styled and wear jewelry." The Ninth Circuit said its decision did not run afoul of *Price Waterhouse* because *Price Waterhouse* did not address the specific question of whether an employer can impose sex-differentiated appearance and grooming standards on its male and female employees (presumably because the more direct issue before the Court was Hopkins's assertive/aggressive behavior, which her employers used as a large part of their rejection of her as a partner).

The full Ninth Circuit reheard the case again *en banc* (i.e., with all the judges present, not just a three-judge panel) in *Jespersen v. Harrah's Operating Co.*[67] the next year and issued its decision in 2006. Given the queries put to you about the reconciling the case with *Price Waterhouse,* you can imagine the controversy it caused when the full court upheld the prior decision for the employer.

A couple of cases have arisen lately that will again test the parameters of employers' dress codes. In one case, a Hooters server, 20 years old, 5′8″ 132 pounds, which is 13 pounds less than she weighed when she was recruited by Hooters in 2008, was told she must agree to be put on 30-day probation to be able to fit into an extra-small uniform, or lose her job. She resigned and is suing for weight discrimination. She happens to live in the only state that has a weight discrimination policy, so she may have a case under Michigan's weight law. The employer says it did nothing wrong.[68]

In another case, Atlantic City servers at Harrah's Casino were terminated when the manager decided to try to draw a younger clientele. All the servers were sent into a room to try on the new size 2 and 4 uniforms and were photographed from all angles. Later, 16 of them, all between the ages of 40 and 60, were called and notified they were terminated. The manager said that while he empathized, all were given individual consideration and the selection process was fair and objective.[69]

It will be interesting to see if the court agrees with the employers. What do you think *should* happen? What do you think *will* happen? Is there a difference between the two? Think about why or why not.

Customer or Employee Preferences

Frequently an employer uses gender as a basis for assigning work because of the preference of customers, clients, or other employees. You saw this in the Harrah's Casino suit just discussed, where younger, presumably smaller, servers were kept on in the workplace in an effort to attract a younger clientele. Often the work to which one gender is not privy represents a loss of valuable revenue or a professionally beneficial opportunity for that employee. Such considerations may be formidable in client-driven businesses such as law, brokerages, accounting, sales, and other professions. If a customer does not wish to have a female audit his or her books, can her accounting firm legally refuse to let her service the client? Is an employer in violation of Title VII if the employer does not permit an employee of a certain gender to deal with a customer because the customer does not wish to deal with someone of that gender and the employee is thereby denied valuable work experience or earning potential? What if male employees on a construction site don't want a female to work with them?

The answer is yes, the employer is in violation of Title VII and can be held liable to the employee for gender discrimination. Customer preference is *not* a legitimate and protected reason to treat otherwise-qualified employees differently based on gender.

Hooters, mentioned above, is an Atlanta-based restaurant chain known for its buffalo wings and scantily clad (very short shorts and T-shirts tied around the middle, revealing a bare midriff), generally well-endowed, female servers. It came to light that Hooters refuses to hire males as servers. The conventional wisdom is that despite Hooters' claims that it is a family restaurant and "Hooters" refers to its owl logo, "Hooters" is a not-so-subtle reference to female breasts, and the servers are likely more important than the food it serves. This is further supported by the servers' outfits, the fact that Hooters is known for its "Hooters' Girls," complete with pin-up calendars and a 10-page *Playboy* magazine spread, and its "more than a mouthful" logo, which few believe refers to chicken wings or owls.

Hooters alleges that customers want only female servers. In 1996, Hooters launched a "no to male servers" billboard campaign featuring husky, hairy male servers clad in the Hooters' attire. Today, Hooters' serving staff is still female, despite the lawsuits brought by the EEOC and class action suits by males in Chicago and Maryland. Hooters has chosen to settle cases rather than litigate them, which, of course, it has the right to do as long as it is willing to foot the bill.

 The Hooters situation is the basis for Opening Scenario 2. Not a semester goes by that one of our students doesn't ask how Hooters can "get away with" hiring only female servers. The short answer is, it can't. At least not legally, in its present incarnation. Hooters has the right to use gender as a BFOQ to protect its female-only server policy if it can show that the gender of its servers is a bona fide occupational qualification reasonably necessary to the particular job done by the servers.

For instance, the BFOQ would be defensible if Hooters declared itself to be in the business of entertainment by use of its servers—rather like Playboy Club bunnies. It has chosen, instead, to classify itself otherwise. This means either gender can serve its food and its female-only server policy violates Title VII's prohibition against gender discrimination. The way Hooters "gets away with" hiring only female servers is to settle lawsuits brought by males challenging its exclusionary policy. Obviously, (1) Hooters does not want to classify itself as adult entertainment and allow the BFOQ defense and (2) Hooters has concluded that it is worth more to keep its female-only server policy and settle claims by male applicants than to change its policy. Again, that approach is something it has every right to take as long as it is willing to foot the bill for that choice. To see the fine line Hooters walks in trying to characterize itself to avoid liability, visit their Web site and read the "about Hooters" section.

This issue of customer preference may cause special problems now that the Civil Rights Act of 1991 applies Title VII to U.S. citizens employed by American-owned or -controlled companies doing business outside the United States. An employer in a country whose mores may not permit women to deal with men professionally must still comply with Title VII unless doing so would cause the company to actually violate the law of the country in which the business is located.

Logistical Considerations

LO5

 In some workplaces, males and females working together can present logistical challenges—for instance, female sports reporters going into male athletes' locker rooms, female firefighters sleeping at a fire station, or lack of bathrooms at a construction site. This issue arose in the context of construction workers in the *Lynch v. Freeman* case, which is included at the conclusion of the chapter, when a female employee was told to use the same portable toilet as males. The court determined that the unclean (to put it mildly) toilets presented different challenges to males and females, resulting in gender discrimination. Note how the employer can take little for granted in making workplace decisions, as even the seemingly smallest decisions can be the basis of a time-consuming and expensive lawsuit.

A growing logistical concern in recent years has been the matter of female employees breast-feeding or expressing their milk at work. While the benefits of breast-feeding are clear as providing the best means of giving infants, among other things, natural immunities and nutrients, women who needed to, or chose to, return to work before their babies were weaned from the breast had little means of continuing to provide them with the benefits of their milk when they were not available to feed them. It was even illegal in many states to breast-feed in public.

In 2006, a national "nurse-in" was held to protest the treatment of Emily Gillette of Santa Fe, New Mexico. Gillette was sitting aboard a Freedom Airlines (a regional airline for Delta) plane that was three hours late in taking off, when she began to breast-feed her daughter. A flight attendant who told Gillette that Gillette was offending her had Gillette removed from the plane when Gillette refused to cover herself with a blanket. Now, at least 44 states have passed lactation laws that make it permissible for women to breastfeed in public places without being cited for public indecency (see Exhibit 8.10, "Breast-Feeding: A Gender-Plus Issue?"). Federal legislation was reintroduced by U.S. Rep. Carolyn Maloney in May 2007 to amend the Civil Rights Act of 1964 to protect breast-feeding and provide tax incentives to businesses that establish lactation areas (Breastfeeding Promotion Act). This did not pass, but as you saw in Exhibit 8.10, as of March 23, 2010, under the Fair Labor Standards Act of 2010, federal law does now require employers with 50 or more employees to provide a reasonable and private place other than a restroom and breaks for new mothers to express their milk. The breaks need not be paid unless they are normal paid breaks, and if the employer has fewer than 50 employees and the requirement presents an undue hardship, the employer need not comply. If state law provides more rights, the employer must comply with those. The right is given to employees who qualify for overtime under Fair Labor Standards Act laws discussed in a later chapter. A growing number of employers had already begun to provide lactation rooms for employees to be able to express milk at work and a means to keep it cool until they can take it home.

Initially women were consigned to workplace bathrooms when they needed to express milk and had no or inadequate refrigeration facilities to store the milk they cooled and bottled for their breast-feeding babies. Of course, the idea of expressing their milk in a public restroom was less than ideal. With lactation rooms and refrigeration facilities, female employees are able to have a safe, private place to take care of this issue. A popular route recently is for the employer to draw up a lactation agreement setting forth the parameters of the workplace lactation provisions, and the responsibilities of both the employer and the employee, and have the employee understand and sign it.

Employers may not forgo hiring those of a certain gender because of logistical issues unless it involves an unreasonable financial burden—usually a matter difficult for an employer to prove. These challenges must be resolved in a way that does not discriminate against the employee based on gender. Generally it is not exceedingly difficult, although it may take thinking about the workplace in a different way. In one situation, the employer said he could not hire females because there was only one restroom on the premises. However, if there is no state sanitation or building code prohibiting it, there is no requirement that males and females use separate restrooms as long as privacy is maintained.

Equal Pay and Comparable Worth

LO8

(1) No employer . . . shall discriminate between employees on the basis of sex by paying wages to employees . . . at a rate less than the rate at which he pays wages to employees of the opposite sex . . . for equal work on jobs the performance of which requires equal skill, effort, and responsibility, and which are performed under similar working conditions, except where such payment is made pursuant to (i) a seniority system; (ii) a merit system; (iii) a system which measures earnings by quantity or quality of production; or (iv) a differential based on any other factor other than sex. . . . [Equal Pay Act, 29 U.S.C.A § 206(d).]

Despite the statute quoted above, according to the March 2011 White House report on the status of women's wages, discussed earlier, women earn on average 75 cents for every dollar earned by men. This is up from 60 cents in 1979. Younger women make 80 cents for every dollar a man makes in the same age group. At the rate the gender wage gap is closing, widely cited AFL-CIO research shows that women's salaries will not be equal until the year 2050.[70] A 2003 General Accounting Office report found that the gender wage gap exists because of less education or experience or because women get on a "mommy track" or choose low-paying professions. Instead, they concluded that discrimination is the biggest factor in the wage gap between genders.[71] While Title VII prohibits discrimination in employment including in the area of compensation, even before Title VII there was legislation protecting employees against discrimination in compensation solely on the basis of gender. The year before Title VII was passed, the Equal Pay Act (EPA), actually part of the Fair Labor Standards Act (FLSA) governing wages and hours in the workplace, became law.

Under the act, employers subject to the minimum wage provisions of the FLSA may not use gender as a basis for paying lower wages to an employee for equal work "on jobs the performance of which requires equal skill, effort, and responsibility, and which are performed under similar working conditions." There are exceptions. Differences in wages are permitted if based on seniority or merit systems, on systems that measure earnings by quantity or quality of production, or on a differential based on "any other factor other than [gender]."

To comply with the Equal Pay Act, the employer may not reduce the wage rate of the higher-paid employees. According to Bureau of Labor Statistics figures, the pay gap that was supposed to be closed by the legislation actually widened at least nine times from one year to the next since passage of the EPA.

The EPA overlaps with Title VII's general prohibition against discrimination in employment on the basis of gender. Title VII's Bennett Amendment was passed so that the exceptions permitted by the EPA also would be recognized by Title VII. The EPA also has a longer statute of limitations (two years from the time of the alleged violation, which may be raised to three years for willful violations, rather than 180 days under Title VII). Perhaps due to the fact that Title VII was passed very soon after the EPA, and more generally proscribed discrimination in employment, there has been less activity under the EPA than under Title VII. However, the prohibitions on pay discrimination should be considered no less important. (See Exhibit 8.13, "Equal Pay: Hardly a Dead Issue.")

Exhibit 8.13 *Equal Pay: Hardly a Dead Issue*

A national study undertaken by the AFL-CIO and the Institute for Women's Policy Research reveals very interesting insights into the issue of pay equality among American workers. Almost two-thirds of all working women responded to the survey. When looking at the findings and thinking about the issue of wage equality, keep in mind that the women responding provided half or more of their families' incomes.

- Ninety-four percent of working women described equal pay as "very important"; two of every five cited pay as the biggest problem women face at work.

- Working families lose $200 billion of income annually to the wage gap—an average yearly loss of more than $4,000 for each working woman's family because of unequal pay, even after accounting for differences in education, age, location, and the number of hours worked.

- If married women were paid the same as comparable men, their family income would rise by nearly 6 percent, and their families' poverty rates would fall from 2.1 percent to 0.8 percent.

- If single working mothers earned as much as comparable men, their family incomes would increase by nearly 17 percent, and their poverty rates would be cut in half, from 25.3 percent to 12.6 percent.

- If single women earned as much as comparable men, their incomes would rise by 13.4 percent and their poverty rates would be reduced from 6.3 percent to 1 percent.

- Working families in Ohio, Michigan, Vermont, Indiana, Illinois, Montana, Wisconsin, and Alabama pay the heaviest price for unequal pay to working women, losing an average of roughly $5,000 in family income each year.

- Family income losses due to unequal pay for women range from $326 million in Alaska to $21.8 billion in California.

- Women who work full time are paid the least, compared with men, in Indiana, Louisiana, Michigan, Montana, North Dakota, Wisconsin, and Wyoming, where women earn less than 70 percent of men's weekly earnings.

- Women of color fare especially poorly in Louisiana, Montana, Nebraska, Oregon, Rhode Island, Utah, Wisconsin, and Wyoming, earning less than 60 percent of what men earn.

- Even where women fare best compared with men—in Arizona, California, Florida, Hawaii, Massachusetts, New York, and Rhode Island—women earn little more than 80 percent as much as men.

- Women earn the most in comparison to men—97 percent—in Washington, DC, but the primary reason women appear to fare so well is the very low wages of minority men.

- For women of color, the gender pay gap is smallest in Washington, DC; Hawaii; Florida; New York; and Tennessee, where they earn more than 70 percent of what men overall in those states earn.

- The 25.6 million women who work in predominantly female jobs lose an average of $3,446 each per year; the 4 million men who work in predominantly female occupations lose an average of $6,259 each per year.

Sources: "Equal Pay for Working Families: National and State Data on the Pay Gap and Its Costs," http://www.aflcio.org/issues/jobseconomy/women/equalpay/EqualPayForWorkingFamilies.cfm.

Exhibit 8.14 *Staying on Top of Gender-Based Pay Inequities*

The Catalyst research on MBAs discussed earlier was sponsored by many big corporations including American Express. These CEOs offered insights and suggestions on the study's findings. They included the following and if you have been reading the chapter carefully should sound quite familiar:

- Don't assume that the playing field has been leveled.
- Redesign systems to correct early inequities.

- Collect and review salary growth metrics.
- Build in checks and balances against unconscious bias.
- Make assignments based on qualifications, not presumptions.

Source: Nancy M. Carter, Christine Silva, "Pipeine's Broken Promise," Catalyst, 2/24/2010, http://www.catalyst.org/publication/372/pipelines-broken-promise.

In *Pollis v. The New School for Social Research*[72] a professor sued her university for gender discrimination in pay because she not only made less than her similarly situated male colleagues, but the employers knew it and would not do anything about it. As you saw in many of the cases mentioned in the beginning of the chapter, not only is unequal pay the basis of many gender discrimination lawsuits, but often the cases are class action suits that reflect a systemic issue in the workplace. As we mentioned then, discrimination may not account for all of the wage differential, but research shows that much of it is based on gender-based ideas. That is within the employer's control and is thus something the employer can do something about to avoid liability. (See Exhibit 8.14, "Staying on Top of Gender-Based Pay Inequities.")

Under the EPA, it is the content of the job, not the job title or description, that controls the comparison of whether the jobs are substantially the same. For instance, if a hospital's male "orderlies" and female "aides" perform substantially the same job, they should receive the same pay, despite the difference in job titles.

In *County of Washington v. Gunther,*[73] the Court held that Title VII's Bennett Amendment only incorporated the four EPA exceptions into Title VII, not the "substantially equal" requirement; therefore, the jobs compared in a Title VII unequal pay action need not be substantially equal.

comparable worth
A Title VII action for pay discrimination based on gender, in which jobs held mostly by women are compared with comparable jobs held mostly by men in regard to pay to determine if there is gender discrimination.

Thus, under Title VII, employees have attempted to bring **comparable worth** cases in which higher-paid predominantly male jobs with similar value to the employer are compared in order to challenge lower wage rates for jobs held mostly by women. For instance, Minnesota has a gender pay equity law and uses outside consultants to help set wage levels. In 1982 it was determined that van drivers (predominantly male) and clerk typists (predominantly female) were comparable, yet the men earned $1900 per month and the women $1500 per month.[74]

Federal courts, however, have generally rejected Title VII claims based on comparable worth.

The historic *AFSCME v. State of Washington*[75] case was the first significant statewide case to challenge gender-based pay differences on the basis of the comparable worth theory. The state of Washington conducted studies of prevailing market rates for jobs and wages in order to determine the wages for various state jobs and found that female-dominated jobs paid lower wages than male-dominated jobs. The state then compared jobs for comparable worth and, after finding that female-dominated job salaries were generally about 20 percent less than wages in male-dominated jobs, legislated that it would begin basing its wages on comparable worth rather than the market rate, over a 10-year period. State employees wanting the scheme to go into effect immediately brought a Title VII suit against the state alleging it was a violation of Title VII for the state to know of the wage differences and not remedy the situation immediately. The court held that since the state was not responsible for the market rates, it did not violate Title VII.

You can imagine the impact of the *AFSCME* decision on employers. The state had basically gotten burned by trying to do the right thing in taking it upon itself to determine if there were pay inequities based on market rates and comparable worth. When it discovered the 20 percent differential benefitting men, it made a workable plan to correct the discrepancies it found. It was then sued for not correcting the discrepancies quickly enough. If you were an employer would you have then taken it upon yourself to go seeking discrepancies? We think not. There was no way they were going to wade into this morass of comparable worth unless they absolutely had to. Based on the court's decision, since the differential was caused by market forces rather than discrimination by the state, the state had no responsibility for the pay differential. This pretty much brought the idea of comparable worth to a halt for a long while.

Prompted by the flap over pay disparities in women's soccer in January 2000, there was a flurry of activity surrounding the issue of gender-based wage differences in the American workplace. Twenty members of the U.S. Women's Soccer Team refused to play in an Australian tournament and demanded pay equal to that of the U.S. Men's Soccer Team. The women were scheduled to be paid $3,150 per month for the most experienced player and about $250 per game. Men were to receive $5,000 per month and an additional $2,000 for the 18 players going to Australia. In the wake of the incident, at least two pieces of legislation were introduced into Congress (the Fair Pay Act and the stronger Paycheck Fairness Act) to amend the Fair Labor Standards Act to address the issue of gender-based wage disparities. In February 2000, President Clinton, accompanied by women's soccer player Michelle Akers, announced that he was seeking an Equal Pay Initiative of $27 million to close the gap between men's and women's pay, of which $10 million would be allocated to the EEOC to deal with the issue of gender-based wage violations. However, nothing much came of the flurry of activity and the laws have not yet been enacted by Congress.

The Paycheck Fairness Act would amend the Equal Pay Act to allow, in addition to the compensatory damages now permitted by the law, punitive damages for wage discrimination; prohibit employers from retaliating against employees for disseminating wage information to other employees; create training programs to help women strengthen their negotiation skills[76]; enforce equal pay laws for federal contractors; and require the Department of Labor to work with employers to eliminate pay disparities. The Fair Pay Act seeks to end wage discrimination in female- or minority-dominated jobs by ensuring equal pay for equivalent work. This proposed law is aimed at female- and minority-dominated employees and would establish equal pay for equivalent work. Employees would be protected on the basis of race and national origin. Wage differentials would be permitted based on seniority, merit, or quantity or quality of work and there would be exemptions for small business. The proposed law would not allow employers to pay predominantly female jobs less than predominantly male jobs if they are equivalent in value to the employer.

In May 2007, the U.S. Supreme Court issued its decision in the case of *Ledbetter v. Goodyear Tire and Rubber Co., Inc.*[77] The case once again reignited the issue of women and wages in a serious way. In the case, Lilly Ledbetter had been the victim of illegal pay discrimination over a long period of time. The employer had a policy prohibiting discussion of salaries, so Ledbetter did not discover the pay discrimination until she was given an anonymous note near her retirement. She then sued the employer for gender discrimination. The issue came down to whether the 180-day statute of limitations in the Civil Rights Act began to run 180 days after the initial act of discrimination, in which case the employee was foreclosed from bringing her cause of action, or whether it ran anew each time she was given a lower paycheck based on the discriminatory pay. The Supreme Court held that she could not sue because the statute of limitations was 180 days after the original act. The decision was roundly criticized by employees and lauded by business. Congress immediately took issue with the Court's decision and the next month introduced the Lilly Ledbetter Fair Pay Act (H.R. (June 22, 2007)) to amend Title VII to allow the statute of limitations to start each time a paycheck is issued based on the discriminatory pay.

This case, in which Justice Ruth Bader Ginsburg took the unusual step of reading her spirited dissent from the bench, also reignited the two other laws above and they began receiving attention once again. Neither has yet been passed, but in the meantime, President Obama made the Lilly Ledbetter Fair Pay Act the first legislation he signed into law, in January 2009. When pay discrimination occurs, the statute of limitations begins to run anew with each paycheck. Both the Fair Pay Act and the Paycheck Fairness Act continue to be reintroduced in Congress. Their passage does not look promising any time soon.

However, since taking office, President Obama has introduced a stronger gender equity agenda than any in recent memory. Among other things, in 2009 he created the White House Council on Women and Girls to assess whether government programs do enough to benefit women and to make sure women were treated fairly in all matters of public policy; in February 2010, his administration announced a task force to coordinate enforcement of equal pay law, including an education campaigned aimed at businesses to let them know that "equal work

Exhibit 8.15 *Not All Women Are Paid Less . . . But What a Choice*

According to a study of 2008 census data by Reach Advisors, single, childless women in their twenties working full time who live in 39 out of the 50 biggest cities in the U.S earn more than comparable men, and they match them in 8 other cities. Women 22 to 30 with no husband or children earn a median of $27,000 per year. This is 8 percent more than comparable men in the top 366 metropolitan areas. In Atlanta the difference is most pronounced, with women earning 21 percent more than comparable men. Women in their twenties who do not meet this criteria earn only 90 percent of what men do. [Notice the difference in the 90 percent figure and the 75–80 percent earnings gap figure given earlier in the chapter. The overall figure includes all women, not just those in their twenties, and thus is lower.] Researchers believe the shift is because women go to college in bigger numbers. Three-fourths of women go to college from high school, but only two-thirds of men. In addition, women are one and a half times more likely to go on to graduate school. It is also due to the loss of well-paying manufacturing jobs for men who did not go to college. The trend is most apparent in cities with more than a 50 percent minority population since black and Hispanic women are more than twice as likely to earn college degrees.

The trend has interesting implications for society and the economy. Not only are male-oriented businesses such as cars and sporting goods increasingly targeting women, but builders who expected this generation to drive demand for apartments is disappointed since these women increasingly live at home with their parents.

Source: Paul Wiseman, "Young, Single, Childless Women Out-earn Male Counterparts," *USA Today*, 9/1/2010, http://www.usatoday.com/money/workplace/2010-09-01-single-women_N.htm?csp=usat me.

means equal pay"; and in March 2011, the most comprehensive report on the status of women since 1963 was released by his office. In addition, for the first time, there is an advisor on domestic violence and an ambassador for women's issues around the world. All of this taken together means that, while these two laws that would greatly facilitate reaching gender-based pay equity have not passed, employers still have pressure from other quarters to comply with the law. Despite all of this, there is a segment of the female population that is not experiencing a pay gap. Single women with no children sometimes actually make more than men. (See Exhibit 8.15, "Not All Women Are Paid Less . . . But What a Choice")

Under existing law, employers should be aware of any pay differentials between specific males and females, as well as between jobs that are held primarily by males and those held primarily by females. As mentioned in Exhibit 8.14, employers should perform periodic audits to ensure that they are not operating under gender-based pay differentials, which may lead to preventable wage discrimination litigation against the employer.

Gender as a BFOQ

Title VII permits gender to be used as a bona fide occupational qualification (BFOQ) under certain limited circumstances. Under EEOC guidelines, a BFOQ may be used when there is a legitimate need for authenticity such as for the part of a female in a theater or film production. More often than not, when employers have attempted to use BFOQ as a defense to gender discrimination, courts have found the defense inapplicable. This makes sense when you consider that in the EEOC's view, the guideline for determining the appropriateness of a BFOQ is that it would be necessary for a male acting as a sperm donor or a female acting as a wet nurse (a woman who nurses someone else's baby from her own breast). That is a pretty strict guideline and provides insight into how irrelevant the EEOC considers the matter of gender in the workplace to be.

That does not only hold true for women. As we have discussed, it includes men also. In *EEOC v. Audrey Sedita, d/b/a Women's Workout World,*[78] the employer refused to hire males as managers, assistant managers, or instructors in the employer's exercise studio, even though they were used as instructors on an occasional basis. The employer alleged that since it was a women's exercise studio, being female is reasonably necessary to the employer's business. In its view, clients would want women personnel and there were privacy issues involved in seeing nudity when taking new clients around to tour the facilities. The court did not agree and said that the purpose of the operation is to provide individualized fitness and exercise instruction to the club's women members. Therefore, the employer would have to prove that it could not achieve its business purpose without engaging in single-gender hiring. The assertion that the alternatives were not feasible because of the views of its clientele, and the difficulties of accommodating men in the health club, were not strong enough to prove that no alternatives were feasible.

Pregnancy Discrimination

Scenario

The Pregnancy Discrimination Act (PDA) prohibits an employer from using pregnancy, childbirth, or related medical conditions as the basis for treating an employee differently than any other employee with a short-term disability if that employee can perform the job. This is why in Opening Scenario 3, it is illegal for the employer to evaluate the pregnant employee differently than it would any other. Employers illegally treat employees differently in many ways. For instance, the employer

- Refuses to hire pregnant applicants.
- Terminates an employee on discovering the employee's pregnancy.
- Does not provide benefits to pregnant employees on an equal basis with short-term disabilities of other employees.
- Refuses to allow a pregnant employee to continue to work even though the employee wishes to do so and is physically able to do so.
- Does not provide the employee with lighter duty if needed, when such accommodations are made for employees with other short-term disabilities.
- Terminates the pregnant employee by moving her to a new job title with the same pay, then eliminates the position in a job restructuring or a reduction in force.

- Evaluates the employee as not having performed as well or as much as other employees when the basis for the evaluation is the employer's own refusal or hesitation to assign equal work to the employee because the employee is pregnant and the employer feels the need to "lighten" the employee's load, though the employee has not requested it.

- Does not permit the pregnant employee to be a part of the normal circle of office culture so she becomes less aware of matters of importance to the office or current projects, resulting in more likelihood that the employee will not be able effectively to compete with those still within the circle.

The Supreme Court determined in *General Electric Co. v. Gilbert*[79] that discrimination on the basis of pregnancy was not gender discrimination under Title VII. Two years later, Congress passed the PDA, amending Title VII's definitions to include discrimination on the basis of pregnancy. Despite the fact that women comprise nearly 50 percent of the workforce, and statistics show that about 75 percent of those of childbearing age will have children sometime during their work life, pregnancy discrimination is still a serious workplace concern.

Many employers have maternity leave policies to address this more-than-likely event, but others, particularly smaller employers, do not. Based on traditional notions about the inappropriateness of women in the workplace in general, or pregnant women in particular, some employers are actually hostile to pregnant employees and run the very real risk of being sued for pregnancy discrimination.

> It didn't bother me at all that she was pregnant. But whether or not she was going to be able to spend the time to actually perform the job and to be a mom and do all that, yeah, we factored it in, sure. We were concerned.

This statement by Robert DiFazio, head of Smith Barney's equities division regarding why someone other than the pregnant applicant was promoted to head the over-the-counter sales desk, is typical of many employers' views about pregnant employees. The employee here filed a claim and the arbitration panel said, "It is hard to imagine sentiments more universally regarded as symbolic of illegal gender bias" and ruled that the remarks constituted evidence of gender discrimination. A study in the *Journal of Personality and Social Psychology* found that while "business women" were rated similar in competence to "business men" or "millionaires," women who became mothers were rated as similar in competence to the "elderly," "blind," "retarded," or "disabled." That's pretty startling.

The EEOC recently reported that there has been at least a 182 percent increase in the filing of pregnancy discrimination charges over the past 10 years. While the EEOC says the most common scenario in pregnancy discrimination claims is termination of the pregnant employee (like the car dealer who fired the employee for fear she'd have morning sickness and throw up in the vehicles), employers take all kinds of measures. Walmart rejected pregnant job applicants, thousands of female Verizon Wireless employees lost benefits during maternity leave, Delta Airlines fired one pregnant ramp attendant and forced another to take unpaid leave, a producer on Spelling Entertainment's *Melrose Place* fired pregnant actress Hunter Tylo on the grounds that she was "unable to play the role of a seductress," a Dallas attorney at the law firm of Jenkins & Gilchrist claimed she was constructively discharged due to her pregnancy, and a New York City police commander claims she was passed over because of her pregnancies, as does the first woman promoted within the Annapolis Fire Department, the education reporter for television station WLOX in Biloxi, a bartender at a topless bar in Long Island, a dry cleaning presser in Minneapolis, and two pregnant teachers in Atlanta.

In the *Asmo v. Keane, Inc.*[80] the court concluded there was pregnancy discrimination when, on a conference call with other employees and the supervisor, the employee announced being pregnant with twins and the supervisor said nothing, though everyone else congratulated her. The employee was terminated by the supervisor two months later. We specifically included these facts and some of the quick blurbs above to demonstrate to you that as a manager or supervisor, your actions matter. The court held in *Asmo* that it was clear under the circumstances, when everyone else was congratulating the employee and wishing her well, that the supervisor's silence was a clear message that the pregnancy was not acceptable. Pregnant bartender in a topless bar, you say? When making workplace decisions, just make sure to think about the law first, and not preconceived notions all of us tend to have in our minds.

If the employee is temporarily unable to perform the duties of the job because of pregnancy, then the law requires that the inability to perform be the issue, not the fact that the employee is pregnant. The employee therefore should be treated just as any other employee who is temporarily unable to perform job requirements. Whatever arrangements the employer generally makes in such circumstances must be extended to the pregnant employee. Note, however, that the EEOC has ruled that an employer's adherence to a facially neutral sick leave policy and its consequent refusal to provide pregnant employees with a reasonable leave of absence, in the absence of a showing of business necessity, discriminates on the basis of gender because of its disproportionate impact on women.[81] Pregnancy can, of course, be used as a BFOQ.

As a manager, you should be aware of the ingrained ideas people hold about pregnancy and work and be sure to ward off any trouble. According to a recent Jury Verdict Research study, if job applicants or employees with pregnancy discrimination claims go to jury trial, they win 54 percent of the time. On the other hand, while the study shows that pregnancy discrimination claimants are more likely than other kinds of discrimination claimants to recover from a jury, the amount they recover is substantially less. The median jury award in a pregnancy discrimination case was $56,360, while for others it was $146,468. But since the discrimination is avoidable, even a verdict of $56,360 is unnecessary.

Management Tips

As you have seen from the chapter, gender discrimination can manifest itself in many forms, some of which may take the employer by surprise. Following these tips can help keep the surprises to a minimum.

- Let employees know from the beginning that gender bias in the workplace will not be tolerated in any way. Give them examples of unacceptable behavior.
- Back up the strong gender message with appropriate enforcement.
- Take employee claims of gender discrimination or bias seriously.
- Promptly and thoroughly investigate all complaints, keeping privacy issues in mind.
- Don't go overboard in responding to offenses substantiated by investigation. Make sure the "punishment fits the crime."
- Conduct periodic training to keep communication lines open and to act as an ongoing reminder of the employer's antibias policy.
- Conduct periodic audits to make sure gender is not adversely affecting hiring, promotion, and raises.
- Review workplace policies to make sure there are no hidden policies or practices that could more adversely impact one gender than another.
- In dealing with gender issues, keep in mind that none of the actions need make the workplace stilted and formal. Employees can respect each other without discriminating against each other.

Fetal Protection Policies

fetal protection policies
Policies an employer institutes to protect the fetus or the reproductive capacity of employees.

The issue of **fetal protection policies** will be given attention here because of the unique gender employment problems involved. Fetal protection policies are policies adopted by an employer that limit or prohibit employees from performing certain jobs or working in certain areas of the workplace because of the potential harm presented to pregnant employees, their fetuses, or the reproductive system or capacity of employees.

The problem with these policies is that, as in the seminal case of *UAW v. Johnson Controls, Inc.,*[82] they say they are for the protection of the unborn child, but that is not the employer's duty under Title VII. In addition, they tend to only protect one group and leave the other vulnerable. In *Johnson Controls,* a group of employees challenged the employer's policy barring all women except those whose infertility was medically documented from jobs involving actual or potential lead exposure exceeding Occupational Safety and Health Administration (OSHA) standards. Included in the group was a male who wished to transfer out of the facility in order to bring up his sperm count so he and his wife could conceive. The exposure to lead lowers sperm count. Scientific evidence showed that the lead exposure had an adverse impact on the reproductive capacity of both males and females, yet the employer only limited the females from the higher-paying jobs. Thus, the Court found the policy to be illegal gender discrimination. Where fetal protection policies apply only to women and not men, when both are shown to be adversely affected by the conditions calling for the policy, they will considered to be a violation of Title VII.

Chapter Summary

- Discrimination on the basis of gender is illegal and not in keeping with good business practices of efficiency, maximizing resources, and avoiding unnecessary liability.

- Gender discrimination has many manifestations, including discrimination in hiring, firing, compensation, training, pregnancy, lactation issues, fetal protection policies, client preferences, dress codes, and child care leave.

- In determining whether employment policies are gender biased, look at the obvious, but also look at the subtle bias that may arise from seemingly neutral policies adversely impacting a given gender, such as height and weight requirements. Both types of discrimination are illegal.

- Where employees must be treated differently, ensure that the basis for differentiation is grounded in factors not gender-based but, instead, address the actual limitation of the employee's or applicant's qualifications.

- Dress codes are not prohibited under Title VII, but dress code differences based on gender should be reasonable and not based on limiting stereotypical ideas about gender.

- Logistical concerns of bathrooms, lactation rooms, and other such matters should be handled in a way that does not overly burden or unnecessarily exclude either gender.

- Under the PDA, employers must treat a pregnant employee who is able to perform the job just as they treat any other employee with a short-term disability.

- Because of health and other considerations, an employer may use pregnancy as a BFOQ and may have policies excluding or limiting pregnant employees if there is a reasonable business justification for such policies.

- If there are legitimate bases for treating pregnant employees differently, an employer has ample flexibility to make necessary decisions.

- Outmoded ideas regarding pregnant employees may not be the basis of denying them equal employment opportunities.

- Fetal protection policies may not operate to discriminate against employees and fail to extend to them equal employment opportunities.

Chapter-End Questions

1. A female restaurant employee is on the phone in the kitchen talking to her mother. The chef of the restaurant comes up to the employee, throws off his chef's hat, grabs both the employee's arms, and begins shaking her violently and screaming at her. She reports this to the police. She is later terminated and sues for gender discrimination. Will she win? Why or why not? [*Labonia v. Doran Assoc., LLC,* 2004 U.S. Dist. LEXIS 17025 (D. Conn. 2004).]

2. An employee says she was forced to quit her job because of her status as a mother of young children. She claimed that her female supervisor created a hostile work environment that violated Title VII. She was replaced by another mother. Does she win? [*Fuller v. GTE Corp./Contel Cellular, Inc.,* 926 F. Supp. 653 (M.D. Tenn. 1996).]

3. An employer had only one promotion to give, but he was torn between giving it to the single female and the male who had a family and, the employer thought, most needed and could best use the money. He finally decided to give the promotion to the male and told the female he gave it to the male because the male was a family man and needed the money. If the female employee sues, will she win? [*Taylor v. Runyon*, 175 F.3d 861 (11th Cir. 1999).]

4. An accounts receivable supervisor was laid off by her employer after taking an extended disability leave for pregnancy. She claimed that the employer discriminated against her on the basis of gender and ability to bear children, stating that two male employees were retained and her replacement was a childless, 40-year-old unmarried female. She files suit, alleging gender discrimination. The employer said it was a legitimate layoff. What should the court consider in determining whether the employer's argument is true? [*Leahey v. Singer Sewing Co.*, 694 A.2d 609 (N.J. Super. 1996).]

5. A female police officer becomes pregnant and, after a scuffle with an arrestee, is told by her doctor to request a light-duty assignment. The police department says it has no such positions available and that the officer must take leave until she can return to full duty, which ends up being from September to June. The female cites two male officers who were injured and did not stop working. Is this discrimination? [*Tysinger v. Police Department of the City of Zanesville*, 463 F.3d 569 (6th Cir. 2006).]

6. A cable company closed its door-to-door sales department and released all employees of that department after settling a discrimination complaint by one of the department's employees. The employee's mother, sister, and two close friends also had been employed in the department. Eighteen months later, the company resumed its door-to-door sales but refused to rehire three of the former employees connected with the employee who had previously sued. The former employees sue, alleging gender discrimination. Will they be successful in their suit? Explain. [*Craig v. Suburban Cablevision, Inc.*, 660 A.2d 505 (N.J. 1995).]

7. A power company began employing women as meter readers, and the job classification went from all-male to all-female within a few years. The labor union that represented bargaining-unit employees negotiated a new collective bargaining agreement that froze wages in the meter reader classification and lowered the wage for new hires. There was evidence that the company president made comments concerning the desirability of housewives to read meters and that he admitted the contract was unfavorable to women. A number of women in the meter reader category filed a state court lawsuit against the employer and union for gender discrimination on the basis of state law and wage discrimination under federal law. The employer argued that the federal labor law preempted the state law gender discrimination complaint; therefore, the gender complaint should be dismissed. Is the state law preempted? [*Donajkowski v. Alpena Power Co.*, 556 N.W.2d 876 (Mich. App. 1996).]

8. A female employee is terminated for slapping a male employee. The male employee is not disciplined. Is this gender discrimination? Do you know all you need to know? [*Gamboa v. American Airlines*, 170 Fed. Appx. 610, 2006 U.S. App. LEXIS 3649 (11th Cir. 2006).]

9. An employer decides to shut down one of its three plants because the employees at that plant are almost exclusively women. The males who worked at the plant and lost their jobs as a result of the closing wish to sue for gender discrimination under Title VII. If they do, will they be successful? [*Allen v. American Home Foods, Inc.*, 644 F. Supp. 1553 (N.D. Ind. 1986).]

10. During an interview, an employer asks a female applicant questions such as whether she had children, what her child care responsibilities were, and how her family felt about her weekly commute between the business's headquarters in Virginia and the family home in New York. The employer also asked the applicant "how her husband handled the fact that [she] was away from home so much, not caring for the family" and said he had "a very difficult time" understanding why any man would allow his wife to live away from home during the workweek. Is this employer's line of questioning a violation of Title VII? Explain. [*Lettieri v. Equant, Inc.,* 478 F.3d 640 (4th Cir. 2007).]

End Notes

1. "Three in Five Americans Say U.S. Has Long Way to Go to Reach Gender Equality: Seven in 10 Americans Say Women Often Do Not Receive the Same Pay as Men for Doing Exactly the Same Job," *Harris Interactive,* 8/16/2010, http://www.harrisinteractive.com/NewsRoom/HarrisPolls/tabid/447/ctl/ReadCustom%20Default/mid/1508/ArticleId/452/Default.aspx.

2. "Lawry's Restaurants, Inc. to Pay $1 Million for Sex Bias Against Men in Hiring," EEOC press release, 11/2/2009, http://www.eeoc.gov/eeoc/newsroom/release/11-2-09.cfm.

3. Jessica M. Walker, "Bikini Lines in the Sand: Attorney-Mediators' Swimsuit Calendar Makes Waves in Legal Community," *Miami Daily Business Review,* 12/23/2004, http://www.law.com/jsp/article.jsp?id=1103549729332.

4. Barbara Hagenbaugh, "Men Losing Jobs at Higher Rate Than Women in Recession," *USA Today,* 1/12/2009, http://www.usatoday.com/money/economy/2009-01-11-unemployment-rate-sexes_N.htm. Apparently, there were more than simply economic consequences to men being out of work. The *London Daily Mail* Online reported that the traffic at websites offering opportunities for infidelity for married men rose 25% during the recession. Sadie Nicholas, "Infidelity, Inc.: The Boom in Websites Offering Illicit Encounters for Out-of-Work Highfliers and How Their Partners Cope," *London Daily Mail,* 4/7/2009, http://www.dailymail.co.uk/femail/article-1167718/Infidelity-Inc-The-boom-websites-offering-illicit-encounters-work-high-fliers.html.

5. Elizabeth Eaves, "In This Recession, Men Drop Out," *Forbes.com,* 4/10/2009, http://www.forbes.com/2009/04/09/employment-men-women-recession-opinions-columnists-gender-roles.html.

6. See Barbara Hagenbaugh, "Men Losing Jobs at Higher Rate Than Women in Recession," *USA Today,* 1/12/2009, http://www.usatoday.com/money/economy/2009-01-11-unemployment-rate-sexes_N.htm; Bradley Blackburn, "Women Lag behind Men in Economic Recovery: New Government Numbers Show 90 Percent of Newly-Created Jobs Go to Men," ABC World News, 3/21/11, http://abcnews.go.com/US/unemployment-recession-men-return-work-women-left-economic/story?id=13185406.

7. Bradley Blackburn, "Women Lag Behind Men in Economic Recovery: New Government Numbers Show 90 Percent of Newly-Created Jobs Go to Men," ABC World News, 3/21/11, http://abcnews.go.com/US/unemployment-recession-men-return-work-women-left-economic/story?id=13185406.

8. Russ Bynum, "Navy to Allow Women to Serve on Submarines: Military Orders an End to One of Its Few Remaining Gender Barriers," Associated Press, 4/29/2010, http://www.msnbc.com/id/36854592/ns/us_news-militry/print/1/displaymode/1098.

9. EEOC Charge Statistics FY 2010, http://www.eeoc.gov/eeoc/statistics/enforcement/charges.cfm. The single highest group of charges are for retaliation claims.

10. Peter Lattman, "3 Women Claim Bias at Goldman," *The New York Times,* 9/15/2010, http://www.nytimes.com/2010/09/16/business/16bias.html?_=ref=business&pagewanted=print.

11. David W. Chen, "Bloomberg Is Deposed in Bias Suit Against Firm," *The New York Times,* 5/15/2009, http://www.nytimes.com/2009/05/15/nyregion/15bloomberg.html?_r=1.

12. "Thompson Wigdor & Gilly LLP; Class Action Gender Discrimination Charges Filed by Five Female Former Employees of Citigroup," *Women's Health Weekly,* 3/12/2009, Document WHWK000020090306e53c000fp.

13. "Bank of America Accused of Gender discrimination at Merrill Lynch," *Workforce Management,* 7/10/2009, http://www.workforce.com/section/news/article/bank-america-accused-gender-discrimination-merrill.php.

14. Bank of America and Merrill Lynch sex discrimination lawsuit, http://bofagenderlawsuit.com/.

15. *Visible Invisibility: Women of Color in Law Firms,* http://www.abanet.org/women/woc/wocinitiative.html.

16. Thanassis Cambanis, "Military Challenge," *Boston Globe,* 1/10/2003, http://nl.newsbank.com/nl-serch/we/Archives?p_action=print.

17. Bill Dobbins, "GNC Show of Strength 2003 to Exclude Female Bodybuilding: Boycott Threatened?" November 2003, http://billdobbins.com/PUBLIC/pages/coolfree/GNC-nofbb/main.html.

18. "No Longer 'Ladies Night' in New Jersey Bars," Associated Press, Fox News, 6/2/2004, http://www.foxnews.com/printer_friendly_story/0,3566,121579,00.html; Dunstan McNichol, "Nothing Makes Up for Ladies Night Loss," *The Star–Ledger,* 9/27/2004, http://www.nj.com/news/ledger/jersey/index.ssf?/base/news-7/1096260705323880.xml.

19. Dawn Lim, "Lawmakers Push Potty Parity," 5/12/2010, GovernmentExecutive.com. The bill called for requiring new or renovated federal buildings to have an equal number of restrooms for both genders. About half the states and many municipalities already have such laws. John Branch, "New Ballpark Statistics: Stadium's Toilet Ratio," *The New York Times,* 4/13/2009. Many of the laws require two female restrooms for every male restroom. However, when some facilities opened up, it was found that males were waiting in line while women did not have to do so. Some laws, therefore, revised the ratio of men to women bathrooms upward. In case you think that the "potty parity" laws are silly, keep in mind that the long waits women have for bathrooms exacerbate things like urinary tract infections. In passing the laws, legislatures noted the longer time women spent in the restroom because of things like having to take their clothes up, or down, having to use toilet paper, being more likely to have children with them, and so on. Note that when men had to stand in lines, how laws were quickly changed to address this inconvenience women had suffered forever.

20. Julia Baird, "Too Hot to Handle: Stop Ogling Republican Women," *Newsweek,* 7/12/2010, p. 37.

21. "Lawry's Restaurant Chain Settled an EEOC Suit for over $1M," EEOC press release, eeoc.gov.

22. Katharine Gray, NBCPhiladelphia.com, "Woman Felt Forced to Wear Diapers to Work," 11/12/2009.

23. Roger Dupis II, "Pa. Dept. Sued for 'Overtime Whores' Remark," *The Times-Tribune* (Scranton, PA), 10/25/2009, http://www.officer.com/publication/printer.jsp?id=49020.

24. Steve Friess, "Lower Rates for Women Are Ruled Unfair," *The New York Times*, 8/13/2008, p. A17.

25. Patricia Cohen, "Charging Bias by Theaters, Female Playwrights to Hold Meeting," *The New York Times,* 10/25/2008 http://nytimes.com/2008/10/25/theater/25women.html

26. Diane Bell, "Men Win in Gender Discrimination Suit," *The San Diego Tribune,* 3/25/2008, http://www.signonsandiego.com/uniontrib/20080325/news_1m25bell.html.

27. The 28 states that have passed comprehensive laws or regulations ensuring equity in private insurance coverage for prescription contraception are: AZ, AR, CA, CO, CT, DE, GA, HI, IL, IA, ME, MD, MA, MI, MO, MT, NV, NH, NJ, NM, NY, NC, OR, RI, VT, WA, WV, WI. http://www.prochoiceamerica.org/what-is-choice/fast-facts/insurance_contraception.html.

28. http//www.factcheck.org/elections-2008/mccains_viagra_moment.html; Adam Sonfield, Rachel Benson Gold, "A New Study Documents Major Strides in Drive for Contraceptive Coverage," *The Guttmacher Report on Public Policy,* 2004, 7(2):4–7, http://www.guttmacher.org/pubs/tgr/07/2/gr070204.pdf. For the impact of the new health care plan on contraceptive equity, see the National Women's Law Center's "Guaranteeing Contraceptive Coverage in All New Health Insurance Plans,"11/18/2010, http://www.nwlc.org/resource/guaranteeing-contraceptive-coverage-all-new-health-insurance-plans.

29. Geraldine Sealey, "Parent Trap: Moms and Dads Starting to Sue, and Win, for Discrimination," ABC News.com, 8/29/2004, http://abcnews.go/sections/us/dailynews/discrimination020829.html.

30. http://www.eeoc.gov/policy/docs/caregiving.html.

31. Reuters, "Novartis Fined $250 M in Sex Discrimination Suit," *The New York Times,* 5/9/2010.

32. Chad Bray, "Toshiba's U.S. Unit Faces $100 Million Gender-Discrimination Suit," *The Wall Street Journal,* 2/1/2011, http://online.wsj.com/article/SB10001424052748703439504576116040649121656.html.

33. "Court Upholds $2M Award to WalMart Pharmacist," *The New York Times,* 10/5/2009.

34. "Outback Steakhouse to Pay $19M for Sex Bias Against Women in 'Glass Ceiling' Suit by EEOC," EEOC press release, http://www1.eeoc.gov//eeoc/newsroom/releas/12-29-09a.cfm?renderforprint=1.

35. 9/27/2004.

36. Gersh Kuntzman, "Steakhouse Sexism: At Risk of Litigation, a Steakhouse Chain Has Agreed to Implement Gender Training and Hire Female Servers. Could This Mean the End of Meat-Filled Men's Clubs?" *Newsweek,* 1/5/2004, http://www.msnbc.com/id/3880701/.

37. Brooke A. Masters and Amy Joyce, "Costco Is the Latest Class Action Target," *The Washington Post,* 8/18/2004, http://www.washingtonpost.com/ac2/wp-dyn/A8646-2004Aug17?language=printer.

38. "WalMart Reports Fourth Quarter and FY 2010 Results," 2/18/10, http://investors .walmartstores.com/phoenix.zhtml?c=112761&p=irol-newsArticle&ID=1392384& highlight=.

39. 474 F.3d 1214 (9th Cir. 2007).

40. *Dukes v. WalMart Stores, Inc.* 603 F.3d 571 (9th Cir. 2010), http://www.ca9.uscourts. gov/datastore/opinions/2010/04/26/04-16688.pdf.

41. Chuck Bartels, "Stung by Bias Suits, Wal-Mart Turns to Ads," The Associated Press, 1/14/2005, http://www.law.ocm/jsp/printerfriendly.jsp?c=LawArticle.

42. *Wal-Mart Stores, Inc. v. Dukes.* Docket No. 10-277 (2010), http://www.supremecourt .gov/qp/10-00277qp.pdf. For a comprehensive website of the documents filed in the case, see the Supreme Court of the U.S. Blog at http://www.scotusblog.com/case-files/cases/wal-mart-v-dukes/.

43. *Women in the Labor Force: A Databook* (2010 Edition), U.S. Bureau of Labor Statistics, http://www.bls.gov/cps/wlf-intro-2010.htm.

44. Jessica Bennett, Jesse Ellison, Sarah Ball, "Are We There Yet?" *Newsweek,* 3/29/10, http://www.newsweek.com/2010/03/18/are-we-there-yet.html.

45. Equal Employment Opportunity Commission, *Glass Ceilings: The Status of Women as Officials and Managers in the Private Sector,* http://www.eeoc.gov/stats/reports/ glassceiling/index.html.

46. http://www.whitehouse.gov/sites/default/files/rss_viewer/Women-in-America.pdf.

47. "Women in Management: Analysis of Female Managers' Representation, Characteristics and Pay," U.S. Government Accounting Office, 9/28/2010; Leezel Tanglao, "Gender Pay Gap Report: Women Managers Still Lag Behind Men: More Women Have Higher Degrees but are Still Earning Less," ABC News, 9/28/2010, http:// abcnews.go.com/print?id=11742405; Jeniffer Ludden, "Despite New Law, Gender Salary Gap Persists," NPR, 4/19/2010.

48. Stephen J. Rose and Heidi I. Hartmann, *Still a Man's Labor Market: The Long-Term Earnings Gap,* http://www.nd.edu/ hlrc/documents/Hartmann-StillManLaborMkt.pdf (last visited February 7, 2008).

49. Nancy M. Carter, Christine Silva, "Pipeline's Broken Promise," Catalyst, 2/24/2010, http://www.catalyst.org/publication/372/pipelines-broken-promise

50. "Still a Slow Climb for Women in Management, Federal Report Says," *The New York Times,* 9/27/2010, http://www.nytimes.com/2010/09/28/business/28gender/html/ ?_r=1&hp.

51. George F. Will, "A New Project for the Gender Police: Gallant Government Will Protect the Weaker Sex," *Newsweek,* 10/4/2010; *AAUP Faculty Gender Equity Indicators 2006,* http://www.aaup.org/NR/rydonlyres/ 63396944-44BE-4ABA-9815-5792.

52. Jessica Bennett, Jesse Ellison, Sarah Ball, "Are We There Yet?" *Newsweek,* 3/29/2010, http://www.newsweek.com/2010/03/18/are-we-there-yet.html.

53. Tamar Lewin, "Bias Called Persistent Hurdle for Women in Sciences," *The New York Times,* 3/21/2010. See also Joya Misra, Jennifer Hickes Lundquist, Elissa Holmes, Stephanie Agiomavritis, "The Ivory Ceiling of Service Work: Service Work Continues to Pull Women Associate Professors Away from Research, What Can Be Done? *Academe Online,* Jan.-Feb. 2011, http://www.aaup.org/AAUP/pubsres/academe/2011/JF/feat/misr.htm.

54. Jessica Bennett, Jesse Ellison, Sarah Ball, "Are We There Yet?" *Newsweek,* 3/29/2010 http://www.newsweek.com/2010/03/18/are-we-there-yet.html

55. Ginka Toegel, "Business Benefits from Authentic Women: Women Are Still Rare at the Upper Reaches of Business and Politics, but Companies Need Their Talent—and Their Non-Male *Modus Operandi*," *Bloomberg BusinessWeek,* 9/17/2010.

56. Katheryn Hayes Tucker, "Fortune 500 Sees Growth in Female GCs," *Fulton County Daily Reporter,* 8/7/2008.

57. "A Push for More Women on Corporate Boards," National Public Radio's *Morning Edition,* 2/24/2011, http://www.wbur.org/npr/133875785/a-push-for-more-women-on-corporate-boards.

58. "Women Leaders and Gender Parity," http://www.weforum.org/women-leaders-and-gender-parity; Jessica Bennett, Jesse Ellison, Sarah Ball, "Are We There Yet?," *Newsweek,* 3/29/2010, http://www.newsweek.com/2010/03/18/are-we-there-yet.html.

59. Hannah Seligman, "Girl Power in School But Not in the Office," *The New York Times,* 9/1/2008.

60. 208 U.S. 412 (1908).

61. Kathleen Deveny, "Families Need to Man Up: The Recession's Silver Lining," *Newsweek,* 12/14/2009, p. 30.

62. Jessica Bennett, Jesse Ellison, Sarah Ball, "Are We There Yet?" *Newsweek,* 3/29/2010, http://www.newsweek.com/2010/03/18/are-we-there-yet.html; See also, Linda Babcock, Sara Laschever, *Women Don't Ask: Negotiation and the Gender Divide* (Princeton, NJ: Princeton University Press, 2003); Lois P. Frankel, *Nice Girls Don't Get the Corner Office:101 Unconscious Mistakes Women Make That Sabotage Their Careers* (New York: Warner Business Books, 2004).

63. 400 U.S. 542 (1971).

64. 139 F.3d 1385 (11th Cir. 1998).

65. "City to Workers: Wear Underwear, Deodorant: New Dress Code Instructs Employees to Observe 'Strict Personal Hygiene'," Associated Press, 6/18/2009, http://www.msnbc.msn.com/id/31424512/ns/us_news-weird_news/.

66. *EEOC v. Sage Realty Corp.,* 507 F. Supp. 599 (S.D.N.Y. 1981).

67. 444 F3d 1104 (9th Cir. 2006) (*en banc*).

68. Jeff Engel, "Rare Michigan Law May Help Waitress Win Weight Discrimination Lawsuit against Hooters," *The Grand Rapids Press,* 5/26/2010, http://www.mlive.com/news/index.ssf/2010/05/rare_michigan_law_may_help_wai.html.

69. "Atlantic City Hotel Accused of Discrimination Over Skimpy Uniforms," Foxnews.com, 4/2/2011 http://www.foxnews.com/us/2011/04/02/atlantic-city-hotel-charged-discrimination-skimpy-uniforms/.

70. http://www.pay-equity.org/PDFs/payequitysummarytable.pdf.

71. "Women's Earnings: Work Patterns Partially Explain Difference between Men's and Women's Earnings," http://www.maloney.house.gov/documents/olddocs/womenscaucus/2003EarningsReport.pdf.

72. 132 F3d 115 (2d Cir. 1997).

73. 452 U.S. 161 (1981).

74. Jennifer Ludden, "Despite New Law, Gender Salary Gap Persists," *Morning Edition,* National Public Radio, http://www.npr.org/templates/story/story.php?storyId=125998232.

75. 770 F.2d 1401 (9th cir. 1985).

76. Men are more than four times more likely than women to negotiate salary, which generally means higher salaries for men. This can lead women to lose more than $500,000 by age 60. Linda Babcock and Sara Laschever, *Women Don't Ask: Negotiation and the Gender Divide* (Princeton, NJ: Princeton University Press, 2003). See also Lee E. Miller and Jessica Miller, *A Woman's Guide to Successful Negotiating: How to Convince, Collaborate, & Create Your Way to Agreement"* (New York: McGraw-Hill, 2001); Phyllis Mindell, *How to Say It for Women: Communicating with Confidence and Power Using the Language of Success* (Upper Saddle River, NJ: Prentice-Hall, 2001). Online tools for researching salary data preparatory to negotiating include salary.com and payscale.com. Tory Johnson, "Take Control: How to Negotiate Your Salary," ABC News, April 24, 2007, http://www.abcnews.go.com/GMA/TakeControlOfYourLife/story?id(3071603&page(1.

77. 550 U.S. __, 127 S. Ct. 2162 (2007).

78. 755 F. Supp.808(N.D. IL. E.D 1991)

79. 429 U.S. 125 (1976).

80. 471 F.3d 588 (6th Cir. 2006).

81. EEOC Dec. No. 74-112, 19 FEP Cases 1817 (April 15, 1974); EEOC Guidelines, 29 C.F.R. § 1604.10(c).

82. 499 U.S.187 (1991).

Cases

Wedow v. City of Kansas City, Missouri   *442 F.3d 441 (8th Cir. 2006)*

Female firefighters were not given proper firefighting uniforms (while male firefighters were given two uniforms), which put them at risk for years; were not given restroom or shower facilities; and were otherwise not treated comparably to male firefighters. The court found that despite the fire department's arguments to the contrary, this was gender discrimination.

Hansen, J.

***

Firefighters are each issued two sets of personalized protective clothing called bunker gear, consisting of a coat, pants, boots, helmet, gloves, a tool belt, and a self-contained breathing apparatus. Two sets are necessary because if protective gear becomes wet or soiled with chemicals at one fire, there is a danger of injury from steam when the same gear must be worn at another fire that day. The protective clothing must fit properly to ensure that the body is protected from injury due to smoke, water, heat, gasoline, and chemicals and to ensure the mobility needed while fighting a fire. The City issued and required Ms. Wedow and Ms. Kline to wear ill-fitting male firefighting clothing, although female clothing and gear were available and management officials knew of sources from which female gear could be obtained. Because the protective clothing did not fit Ms. Wedow and Ms. Kline properly, they suffered injuries from fire and chemicals when the coats would not close properly, or too large hats and boots would fall off while fighting a fire. Ms. Wedow's and Ms. Kline's movements were cumbersome and restricted by pants that caused them to trip or prevented them from easily climbing ladders. Excess length in the fingers of gloves made it difficult to grip objects such as the fire hose. The City's failure to procure protective clothing tailored for women and its provision of only male-sized protective clothing to Ms. Wedow and Ms. Kline made their jobs more difficult and more hazardous than was necessary.

Despite their complaints, no one in the Fire Department made any effort to provide Ms. Kline and Ms. Wedow with adequately fitting protective clothing from 1990 through October 1998. In October 1998, the Fire Department provided Ms. Kline with one set of female-sized protective clothing, although each male firefighter is given two sets of properly fitting clothing. In late 1998, Ms. Wedow received a female-sized pair of bunker pants and a male-sized coat; she never received a complete set of adequately fitting protective clothing during the relevant time period.

Ms. Kline and Ms. Wedow also complained of a lack of adequate restrooms, showers, and private changing facilities (referred to collectively as "facilities"). Showering at the station after fighting a fire is necessary to maintain good health when serving in 24-hour shifts. At a number of stations that Ms. Wedow and Ms. Kline visited on a daily basis as battalion chiefs, the restrooms were located in the male locker rooms with the male shower room, doors were not secure, males had the keys, and where female restrooms existed, they were unsanitary and often used as storage rooms. Food and water for the station's pet dog were kept in the women's room in two stations and sexually explicit magazines and a poster were kept in the female restroom in station 23. Most of the female restrooms that existed did not contain shower rooms and in some stations, the women's shower could be accessed only through the male bunkroom.

Department officials were aware of complaints about the facilities as early as 1993. From 1994 through 2000, the Fire Department submitted yearly budgets to the City requesting money for female locker room upgrades, and every year the City allocated money for this purpose, but the money was diverted to a whole-station upgrade at station 4, which already had a female restroom.

The City argues that it is entitled to judgment as a matter of law on the claim of disparate treatment in protective clothing and facilities because the plaintiffs failed to demonstrate that they suffered an adverse employment action. "An adverse employment action is a tangible change in working conditions that produces a material employment disadvantage." "Mere inconvenience without any decrease in title, salary, or benefits" or that results only in minor changes in working conditions does not meet this standard.

We cannot say as a matter of law that being required to work as a firefighter with inadequate protective clothing and inadequate restroom and shower facilities is a mere inconvenience. Title VII makes it unlawful to discriminate on the basis of sex with regard to the "terms, conditions, or privileges of employment" and prohibits an employer from depriving "any individual of employment opportunities or otherwise adversely affecting his status as an employee" on the basis of sex. The record amply demonstrates that the terms and conditions of a female firefighter's employment are affected by a lack of adequate protective clothing and private, sanitary shower and restroom facilities, because these conditions jeopardize her ability to perform the core functions of her job in a safe and efficient manner. The danger inherent in the job of a firefighter compounded by the need to move and work efficiently in those dangerous circumstances, to quickly change in and out of gear, to shower for health reasons following a fire, and the need to serve in 24-hour shifts, combine to make the provision of adequate protective clothing and facilities integral terms and conditions of employment for a firefighter. JUDGMENT FOR PLAINTIFF AFFIRMED.

Case Questions

1. Are you surprised that this is a 2006 case? Why or why not?

2. How do you think the fire department should have responded when the women registered complaints about their uniforms? Explain.

3. Why do you think the fire department treated the female employees as it did?

Dothard v. Rawlinson *433 U.S. 321 (1977)*

After her application for employment as an Alabama prison guard was rejected because she failed to meet the minimum 120-pound weight, 5-foot-2-inch height requirement of an Alabama statute, the applicant sued, challenging the statutory height and weight requirements as violative of Title VII of the Civil Rights Act of 1964. The Supreme Court found gender discrimination.

Stewart, J.

***

At the time she applied for a position as a correctional counselor trainee, Rawlinson was a 22-year-old college graduate whose major course of study had been correctional psychology. She was refused employment because she failed to meet the minimum 120-pound weight requirement established by an Alabama statute. The statute stated that the applicant shall not be less than five feet two inches nor more than six feet ten inches in height, shall weigh not less than 120 pounds nor more than 300 pounds. Variances could be granted upon a showing of good cause, but none had ever been applied for by the Board and the Board did not apprise applicants of the waiver possibility.

In considering the effect of the minimum height and weight standards on this disparity in rate of hiring between genders, the district court found that when the height and weight restrictions are combined, Alabama's statutory standards would exclude 41.13% of the female population while excluding less than 1% of the male population.

In enacting Title VII, Congress required "the removal of artificial, arbitrary, and unnecessary barriers to employment when the barriers operate invidiously to discriminate on the basis of racial or other impermissible classification." The District Court found the minimum height and weight requirements constitute the sort of arbitrary barrier to equal employment opportunity that Title VII forbids. This claim does not involve an assertion of purposeful discriminatory motive. It is asserted, rather, that these facially neutral qualification standards work in fact disproportionately to exclude women from eligibility for employment by the Alabama Board of Corrections.

We turn to Alabama's argument that they have rebutted the *prima facie* case of discrimination by showing that the height and weight requirements are job related. These requirements, they say, have a relationship to strength, a sufficient but unspecified amount of which is essential to effective job performance as a correctional counselor. In the district court, however, they failed to offer evidence of any kind in specific justification of the statutory standards.

If the job-related quality that the Board identifies is bona fide, their purpose could be achieved by adopting and validating a test for applicants that measures strength directly. But nothing in the present record even approaches such a measurement.

The district court was not in error in holding that Title VII of the Civil Rights Act of 1964 prohibits application of the statutory height and weight requirements to Rawlinson and the class she represents. AFFIRMED in part, REVERSED in part, and REMANDED.

Case Questions

1. What purpose did the height and weight requirements serve? Do you think they were made to intentionally discriminate against women?

2. How could management have avoided this outcome?

3. Does your view of illegal discrimination change now that you have seen how disparate impact claims work? Would you have been able to foresee this outcome? Explain.

Price Waterhouse v. Hopkins   *490 U.S. 228 (1989)*

Case 3

Ann Hopkins, a female associate who was refused admission as a partner in an accounting firm, brought a gender discrimination action against the firm. The U.S. Supreme Court determined that it is a violation of Title VII for gender stereotyping to play a significant role in evaluating an employee's work performance

Brennan, J.

***

In a jointly prepared statement supporting her candidacy, the partners in Hopkins' office showcased her successful 2-year effort to secure a $25 million contract with the Department of State, labeling it "an outstanding performance" and one that Hopkins carried out "virtually at the partner level." None of the other partnership candidates had a comparable record in terms of successfully securing major contracts for the partnership.

The partners in Hopkins' office praised her character and her accomplishments, describing her as "an outstanding professional" who had a "deft touch," a "strong character, independence, and integrity." Clients appeared to have agreed with these assessments. Hopkins "had no difficulty dealing with clients and her clients appeared to be very pleased with her work" and she "was generally viewed as a highly competent project leader who worked long hours, pushed vigorously to meet deadlines, and demanded much from the multidisciplinary staffs with which she worked."

Virtually all of the partners' negative comments about Hopkins—even those of partners supporting her—had to do with her "interpersonal skills." Both supporters and opponents of her candidacy indicate she was sometimes "overly aggressive, unduly harsh, difficult to work with, and impatient with staff."

There were clear signs, though, that some of the partners reacted negatively to Hopkins' personality because she was a woman. One partner described her as "macho"; another suggested that she "overcompensated for being a woman"; a third advised her to take "a course at charm school." Several partners criticized her use of profanity; in response, one partner suggested that those partners objected to her swearing only "because it['s] a lady using foul language." Another supporter explained that Hopkins "ha[d] matured from a tough-talking somewhat masculine hard-nosed manager to an authoritative, formidable, but much more appealing lady partner candidate." But it was the man who bore responsibility for explaining to Hopkins the reasons for the Policy Board's decision to place her candidacy on hold who delivered the coup de grace; in order to improve her chances for partnership, Thomas Beyer advised, Hopkins should "walk more femininely, talk more femininely, dress more femininely, wear makeup, have her hair styled, and wear jewelry."

Dr. Susan Fiske, a social psychologist and Associate Professor of Psychology at Carnegie-Mellon University, testified at trial that the partnership selection process at Price Waterhouse was likely influenced by gender stereotyping. Her testimony focused not only on the overtly gender-based comments of partners but also on gender-neutral remarks, made by partners who knew Hopkins only slightly, that were intensely critical of her. One partner, for example, baldly stated that Hopkins was "universally disliked" by staff and another described her as "consistently annoying and irritating"; yet these were people who had had very little contact with Hopkins. According to Fiske, Hopkins's uniqueness (as the only woman in the pool of candidates) and the subjectivity of the evaluations made it likely that sharply critical remarks such as these were the product of gender stereotyping.

An employer who acts on the basis of a belief that a woman cannot be aggressive or that she must not be has acted on the basis of gender. Although the parties do not overtly dispute this last proposition, the placement by Price Waterhouse of "sex stereotyping" in quotation marks throughout its brief seems to us an insinuation either that such stereotyping was not present in this case or that it lacks legal relevance. We reject both possibilities. A number of the partners' comments showed gender stereotyping at work. As for the legal relevance of gender stereotyping, we are beyond the day when an employer could evaluate employees by assuming or insisting that they matched the stereotype associated with their group, for "[i]n forbidding employers to discriminate against individuals because of their gender, Congress intended to strike at the entire spectrum of disparate treatment of men and women resulting from sex stereotypes." An employer who objects to aggressiveness in women but whose positions require this trait places women in the intolerable and impermissible Catch-22: out of a job if they behave aggressively and out of a job if they don't. Title VII lifts women out of this bind.

Remarks at work that are based on gender stereotypes do not inevitably prove that gender played a part in a particular employment decision. The plaintiff must show that the employer actually relied on her gender in making its decision. In making this showing, stereotyped remarks can certainly be evidence that gender played a part. REVERSED and REMANDED.

Case Questions

1. What were Price Waterhouse's fatal flaws?
2. Does Hopkins's treatment here make good business sense? Explain.
3. How would you avoid the problems in this case?

Lynch v. Freeman *817 F.2d 380 (6th Cir. 1987)*

A female carpenter's apprentice sued her employer for gender discrimination, alleging the failure to furnish adequate sanitary toilet facilities at her worksite. The court found the unsanitary facilities violated Title VII.

Lively, J.

***

The portable toilets were dirty, often had no toilet paper or paper that was soiled, and were not equipped with running water or sanitary napkins. In addition, those designated for women had no locks or bolts on the doors and one of them had a hole punched in the side.

To avoid using the toilets, Lynch began holding her urine until she left work. Within three days after starting work she experienced pain and was advised that the practice she had adopted, as well as using contaminated toilet paper, frequently caused bladder infections.

The powerhouse, which had large, clean, fully equipped restrooms, was off limits to construction workers. Lynch testified that some of the men she worked with used them regularly and were not disciplined. Knowing the restrooms were off limits, Lynch began using the powerhouse restrooms occasionally, after her doctor diagnosed her condition as cystitis, a type of urinary infection. When the infection returned Lynch began using a restroom in the powerhouse regularly and she had no further urinary tract infections. Lynch was eventually fired for insubordination in using the powerhouse toilet.

The lower court found that the toilets were poorly maintained. The cleaning was accomplished by pumping out the sewage. This process often left the toilets messy, with human feces on the floors, walls, and seats. The contractors were to scrub down the toilets afterwards, but it appears they often failed to do so. Paper covers were not provided, and the toilet paper, if any, was sometimes wet and/or soiled with urine. No running water for washing one's hands was available near the toilets, although a chemical hand cleaner could be checked out from the "gang-boxes."

The lower court found it credible that most women were inhibited from using the toilets. Further, the inhibitions described were not personal peculiarities, but that Lynch and others reasonably believed that the toilets could endanger their health. Lynch introduced credible medical expert testimony to demonstrate that women are more vulnerable to urinary tract infections than are men.

On the basis of that evidence, the court concluded that all increased danger of urinary tract infections may be linked to the practice of females holding their urine and to the use of toilets under the circumstances where the female's bacteria-contaminated hands came into contact with her external genitalia or where a female's perineal area comes into direct contact with bacteria-contaminated surfaces.

Few concerns are more pressing to anyone than those related to personal health. A *prima facie* case of disparate impact is established when a plaintiff shows that the facially neutral practice has a significantly discriminatory impact. Any employment practice that adversely affects the health of female employees while leaving male employees unaffected has a significantly discriminatory impact. The burden then shifts to the employer to justify the practice which resulted in this discriminatory impact by showing business necessity; that is, that the practice of furnishing unsanitary toilet facilities at the work site substantially promotes the proficient operation of business.

Title VII is remedial legislation, which must be construed liberally to achieve its purpose of eliminating discrimination from the workplace. Although Lynch was discharged for violating a rule, she did so in order to avoid the continued risk to her health which would have resulted from obeying the rule. The employer created an unacceptable situation in which Lynch and other female construction workers were required to choose between submitting to a discriminatory health hazard or risking termination for disobeying a company rule. Anatomical differences between men and women are "immutable characteristics," just as race, color, and national origin are immutable characteristics. When it is shown that employment practices place a heavier burden on minority employees than on members of the majority, and this burden relates to characteristics which identify them as members of the protected group, the requirements of a Title VII disparate impact case are satisfied. REVERSED and REMANDED.

Case Questions

1. Are you surprised by this outcome? Why or why not?
2. Does the outcome make sense to you? Explain.
3. What would you have done if you were the employer in this situation?

Chapter 9

Sexual Harassment

Learning Objectives

By the time you have studied this chapter, you should be able to:

LO1 Discuss the background leading up to sexual harassment as a workplace issue.

LO2 Explain quid pro quo sexual harassment and give the requirements for making a case.

LO3 Explain hostile environment sexual harassment and give the requirements for making a case.

LO4 List and explain employer defenses to sexual harassment claims.

LO5 Define the reasonable victim standard and how and why it is used in sexual harassment cases.

LO6 Differentiate the sex requirement and anti-female animus in sexual harassment actions.

LO7 Explain employer liability for various types of sexual harassment claims.

LO8 Describe proactive and corrective actions an employer can take to prevent or lessen liability.

Opening Scenarios

SCENARIO 1

1 A female employee tells her supervisor that she is disturbed by the workplace display of nude pictures, calendars, and cartoons. He replies that, if she is bothered, she should not look. The employee suspects this is a form of sexual harassment. Do you agree? Why or why not?

SCENARIO 2

2 An employee routinely compliments colleagues about their appearance, hair, and body. Is this sexual harassment? Why or why not?

SCENARIO 3

3 A male and female employee have engaged in a two-year consensual personal relationship, which ends. The male continues to attempt to get the female to go out with him on dates. When she does not, she is eventually fired by the male, who is her supervisor. She sues, alleging sexual harassment. Who wins and why?

Statutory Basis

It shall be unlawful employment practice for an employer—

(1) to fail or refuse to hire or to discharge any individual, or otherwise to discriminate against any individual with respect to his compensation, terms, conditions, or privileges of employment, because of such individual's . . . sex [gender]. . . . [Title VII of the Civil Rights Act of 1964, as amended. 42 U.S.C. § 2000e2(a).]

Unwelcome sexual advances, requests for sexual favors, and other verbal or physical conduct of a sexual nature constitute sexual harassment when (1) submission to such conduct is made either explicitly or implicitly a term or condition of an individual's employment, (2) submission to or rejection of such conduct by an individual is used as the basis for employment decisions affecting such individual, or (3) such conduct has the purpose or effect of unreasonably interfering with an individual's work performance or creating an intimidating, hostile, or offensive working environment. [29 C.F.R. § 1604.11 (a) (EEOC Sexual Harassment Guidelines).]

Since Eden . . . and Counting

Introduction

Imagine your boss whacking you over the head with his naked penis, then the same day, lifting your shirt and masturbating on you while he held you down, and ejaculating on you. That is precisely what happened in a St. Louis case in June 2011. The jury awarded employee Ashley Alford $95 million against Aaron Rentals, the national rent-to-own chain. It is one of, if not the largest, sexual harassment awards in history.[1] Experience tells us that of all the chapters you will read in this book, this is probably the single most perplexing. Why in the world would someone engage in such an unnecessary act that can have such wide-ranging negative consequences for the employer? Why would an employer permit it? You will probably find yourself asking this over and over as you read this chapter. You will likely find yourself asking how this could ever be worth it to an employer when it is so *purely* personal?

No matter what the workplace, whether employees are practicing law, serving customers, hosting a television show, being the president of the United States, running a medical clinic, or being a professor, the fact that it is a workplace means we presume a certain standard for our interaction with co-workers. It may be loosely defined, but we know it is there. Just picture what you think your workplace will be like when you graduate. You worked long and hard to get that diploma; you schlep from one interview to another in a race to obtain a job before graduation; you step out into the workplace feeling a degree of trepidation and uncertainty but knowing that, if given a chance, you'll be able to work hard and make your dreams come true. You take a job where you will have dignity and respect and be allowed to contribute your time and energies to the productivity of your employer. Without even giving it much thought, you may expect there to be some unpleasant personalities and even jerks in your workplace, but you still expect a certain level of decorum.

With this picture in mind, we guarantee that the following situations do not comport with your idea of a workplace you would like to step into. Keep in mind that these incidents are only from the last few years. They are provided in order for you to see the many ways in which this issue is manifested in the workplace so you will recognize it when you see it. These are not easy issues to talk about, and they are not always for the faint of heart. This is especially so sitting in a class with others. But, as someone who will likely be faced with this issue as a manager, you cannot afford to be shy. Sexual harassment in the workplace happens and more frequently than you would think. Backing away from it will not help you learn what you need to in order to prevent liability. These cases are not provided for purposes of sensationalism or titillation. They are cases that arise in the workplace and cause great consternation and distress not only to the harassee, but also to those who witness it, those who must address it, those who must pay for it, and those who are employed at the workplace and are embarrassed by the negative publicity. The impact on the workplace in terms of embarrassment, loss of time in dealing with the issue, the cost of litigation and judgments or settlements, and loss of productivity is simply not worth it. Not even for us, as taxpayers who have to pay out about $1 million a year to sexually harassed staffers of legislators on Capitol Hill.[2]

- A Chicago court found for a female employee in a suit against Custom Companies, a trucking company in Northlake, Illinois, when it determined that the founder and top managers in the company engaged in "reprehensible conduct" against three female sales representatives by repeatedly touching; groping; making sexually explicit comments using lewd language; and exposing them to pornography, jokes, sexual advances, and a sexually charged atmosphere, which included making them take clients to strip clubs and other places of adult entertainment. In sharply criticizing the harassers in a 50-page memorandum opinion, among other things, the court enjoined Custom from further engaging in such activity and ordered them to send a letter to their clients notifying them of the court's decision.[3]

- A male lawyer sued his ex-firm for trying to bully him into going to an all-male weekend retreat that could involve naked participants passing around a wooden phallus in a circle and describing their sexual experiences, and becoming "extremely hostile" and refusing to pay him because of his refusal.[4]

- A female employee was awarded $1.7 million after her employer spanked her in front of co-workers in what the employer called a "camaraderie-building exercise" that pitted sales teams against each other, with winners throwing pies at the losers, feeding them baby food, making them wear diapers, and spanking them.[5]

- Lutheran Medical Center in Brooklyn, New York, agreed to pay nearly $5.5 million to settle a sexual harassment case in which a hospital doctor allegedly subjected more than 50 female employees to invasive touching and intrusive questions about their sex life during mandatory physical exams. He threatened to delay or deny their employment if they did not cooperate.[6]

- The city of Richmond, Virginia, agreed to pay $100,000 to settle a suit by a female employee claiming police administrators ignored sexual harassment complaints against a high-ranking official and, for months after she formally complained, allowing him to continue to supervise her. She claimed he repeatedly made sexually explicit comments to her and asked her out, used derogatory language to describe female employees, and engaged in unwelcome, offensive, or other unwanted conversations of a sexual or personal nature.

- Airguide Corporation and Pioneer Metals, Inc., entered into a consent decree with the EEOC, agreeing to pay $1 million for sexual harassment and retaliation to three former female employees allegedly subjected to sexually explicit slurs and comments by their supervisors. Though they complained repeatedly, the harassment persisted.

- Burger King entered into a consent decree with the EEOC to pay $400,000 to settle a claim for sexual harassment of seven female employees, *six of whom were high school students,* after the manager subjected them to repeated groping, vulgar sexual comments, and demands for sex. Nothing was done when this was reported to assistant managers at the restaurant or to the district manager.

- A New Hampshire judge resigned from the bench after groping five female victim advocates of his court at a conference on sexual assault and domestic violence. Late-night partying at the conference also led to the attorney general's resignation after an investigation into his inappropriate touching of a woman while dancing.

- Donald D. Thompson, a federal district court judge, married and the father of three grown children, was disbarred and sentenced to four years in prison after allegations that he habitually masturbated with a penis pump under his robe at trial. The claim was bolstered by semen samples on his robe, chair, and carpet;

samples collected from behind the bench; as well as witnesses such as the court reporter, lawyers who heard the "whooshing" sound made by the pump, and police officers who took photos of the pump under the desk during a break in a murder trial after seeing a piece of plastic tubing disappear under the judge's robe. It was expected that a number of defendants would appeal, alleging the judge was not paying sufficient attention while presiding over their trials. It was reported, "During one trial, the judge seemed so distracted that some jurors thought he was playing a handheld video game or tying fishing lures behind the bench."[7]

We could go on, but we will stop here. You get the message. From *The Price Is Right* game show host Bob Barker,[8] to governor and actor Arnold Schwarzenegger (who, after being dogged by allegations of sexual misconduct with up to 16 women during his campaign for governor of California, underwent a voluntary course in preventing sexual harassment after his election)[9]; from the founder of Habitat for Humanity, to conservative talk show host Bill O'Reilly,[10] to a president, no one seems to be immune from engaging in sexual harassment. (See Exhibit 9.1, "Even

---

Exhibit 9.1 *Even a Professor . . .*

No doubt you have heard about President Bill Clinton's sexual encounter with White House intern Monica Lewinsky. This situation involved a student who evidently resembled Ms. Lewinsky and her professor who kept reminding her of that fact in front of other students.

Inbal Hayut, a female student of political science professor Alex Young at the University of New York at New Paltz, sued Professor Young for nicknaming her "Monica" and subjecting her to harassment about it over the course of the semester. Hayut apparently resembled Monica Lewinsky, the White House intern who had an affair with then-President Bill Clinton and was much in the news at the time. Professor Young opened virtually every class session by asking Hayut in front of the entire class, "How was your weekend with Bill?" Hayut alleged that twice in class Professor Young told her, "Be quiet, Monica. I'll give you a cigar later." She asked Professor Young to stop referring to her as "Monica" but was ignored. Classmates mockingly addressed Hayut as "Monica" outside class.

Hayut said the comments affected her deeply, humiliated her in front of her classmates, and made it difficult for her to sleep or concentrate at school or

work. She barely passed her courses that semester, received failing grades the next term, withdrew from the school, and had to complete a year of remedial work before she could transfer to another school.

Hayut sued the university, the professor, and several school administrators for, among other things, violating the Title IX Educational Amendments of 1972, which prohibit gender discrimination in any education program or activity receiving federal financial assistance. Professor Young, who had been teaching for 30 years, admitted making the statements, but said they were a joke. He retired a month after school administrators met to decide what to do about the situation.

In the lawsuit, the school claimed the actions by Professor Young did not amount to sexual harassment. The court ruled that Professor Young, as "a teacher at a state university, was a state actor vested with considerable authority over his students." His comments were severe and pervasive enough to transcend the bounds of propriety and decency and became actionable harassment, and Hayut's academic performance suffered as a result. [*Hayut v. SUNY at New Paltz, et al.*, 352 F.3d 733 (2d Cir. 2003).]

a Professor. . . .") Sexual harassment suits are still far more frequent an occurrence than we would like them to be, if for no other reason than they cost the employer totally unnecessary time, effort, energy, bad press, and money.

In 1991, the first sexual harassment class action was approved in *Jenson v. Eveleth Taconite, Inc.*[11] Leading up to the class action certification proceedings there was much speculation in the legal community as to whether such a thing could be done, or even if it really needed to be done. How frequently could there possibly be a case with so many charges that a class action suit was necessary? Unfortunately, in the years since, many such cases have been brought, involving both men and women. Few are brought to trial. The risk to the employer is too great. Sexual harassment class action trials (actual trials, not lawsuits filed) have been called "a white buffalo" by one lawyer because so few are seen.[12] Many cases are filed, but they are settled rather than litigated as a means of avoiding bad publicity and the possibility of even greater damages if the matter goes to trial. Keep in mind that at trial the jury would hear employee after employee take the witness stand and under oath tell similar stories, generally of a grossly inappropriate-for-the-workplace, graphic sexual nature, often from the employer's offices all over the country. To think that there would be enough employees experiencing sexual harassment at a workplace to even be certified as a class action (no small feat!) ought to give you cause for concern as a future manager, supervisor, or business owner.

The *Eveleth* case became the inspiration for the 2005 Academy Award–nominated movie *North Country,* starring Charlize Theron, detailing the very ugly situation the employee faced in trying to do something about the sexual harassment of herself and other female employees. The film was based on the book *Class Action* by Clara Bingham and Laura Leedy Gansler.[13] In addition to the class action suits set forth above, consider these:

- CB Richard Ellis, a $1.6 billion, publicly traded commercial real estate brokerage firm with 17,000 employees in 300 offices around the world, was sued by female employees whose affidavits alleged management condoned and perpetuated discrimination and sexual harassment against women through such things as its decades-old, much-touted, annual "Fight Night" event in Atlanta. This was characterized as a "rowdy, black-tie Vegas-style boys night out of cigar smoke, boxing, and women on display." Female employees were chosen to wear evening clothes and serve them and their clients drinks and cigars. At work, female employees across the country alleged they were subjected to groping, degrading comments, and vulgar discussions about sex and women's body parts. Male employees also exposed themselves to female employees. The plaintiffs alleged daily circulation of offensive, lewd, and pornographic e-mails; granting or withholding permission to interface with customers based on a female employee's looks; viewing of pornographic Web sites and videos in the office; and the display of offensive, lewd, and pornographic pictures and calendars in the office. The real estate brokerage firm eventually settled the case for an undetermined amount that included, among other things,

$3.4 million in attorney fees and a $400,000 donation to a women's real estate trade group for scholarships.[14]

- Dial Corporation, maker of Dial soap, entered into a consent decree with the EEOC to settle a class action by 91 women who alleged that the Dial Corporation's soap factory in Montgomery, Illinois, had a sexually abusive environment for years and management either participated in the activities or did nothing when it was reported. Harassing activity included everything from grabbing female employees and fondling their breasts, to sexual comments and propositions, to placing a sanitary napkin doused with ketchup beside a female employee's tool box, as well as a life-sized penis carved from pink soap.[15]

- Thirty-two female employees at the U.S. Mint's Denver plant, nearly one-third of the females, filed suit alleging they were subjected to sexist comments, treated more favorably if they had sex with some managers, disciplined more harshly than men, discouraged from complaining about the treatment, and ignored after they met with Mint officials. Until they met with higher authorities at the U.S. Treasury Department, the harassment continued. The Mint director was female.

- In 2010, nearly 50,000 male veterans screened positive for "military sexual trauma" at the Department of Veterans Affairs, up from just over 30,000 in 2003. The Pentagon has begun to acknowledge the rampant problem of sexual violence as both males and females and men are coming forward in unprecedented numbers. Experts say that male-on-male assault in the military is not motivated by sexual orientation, but by power, intimidation, and domination.[16]

- The EEOC sued Kraft on behalf of a class of male employees who were subjected to "egregious" same-sex harassment and retaliation by their male supervisor in Birmingham, Alabama. The employees were the subject of sexual comments, propositioned for sex, touched, grabbed, and sexually assaulted by a male supervisor for Nabisco.

- The EEOC filed for class action certification in an action against Federal Express Corp. for same-gender sexual harassment in Kankakee, Illinois. One of the employees alleged that he repeatedly complained to management about the harassment by another male employee, but he was told to "act like a man" and that "nothing can be done."

Can you think of a good reason an employer would watch millions of hard-earned dollars go out of a business's coffers for such unnecessary, avoidable, and totally useless actions? Impeachment of a president, resignation of multi-starred generals and other high-level military personnel, resignation of company and university presidents and long-term legislators, and embarrassing televised hearings of a U.S. Supreme Court nominee all have been a part of our national consciousness and abrupt introduction to, and education in, the area of sexual harassment. It is frustrating to see the same thing over and over again, while liability is so avoidable if employers will only take a few steps we will discuss.

LO1

But before we do that, let's get a bit of context. Sexual harassment may have been something you are used to realizing existed, but it really is of pretty recent vintage. It seems like such a short time ago that most of us were blissfully unaware that the legal cause of action of sexual harassment even existed. Though it had been around for more than 10 years, most people knew very little about it. Until, that is, it was thrust into the limelight when then–University of Oklahoma law professor Anita Hill took her seat at a table before the Senate Judiciary Committee in the confirmation hearings for associate justice of the U.S. Supreme Court, Clarence Thomas. Hill had worked for Thomas when he was head of the EEOC about 10 years before. When Thomas came up for confirmation, friends of Hill reported to the Judiciary Committee that she had at one time revealed to them details of unprofessional exchanges with Thomas that could have amounted to sexual harassment. The committee contacted Hill and made clear that she would either testify about the matter and set the record straight herself or leave them to their own devices of discovery. Hill very reluctantly chose to testify, and the country hasn't been the same since.

Hill's testimony over the next several days, and Thomas's barely concealed anger about it, were painful for the millions of Americans who sat glued to their television sets during those unbelievable autumn days in 1991. People who had never even heard the term *sexual harassment* now had implacable opinions about it. From barber shops to executive suites, and everywhere in between, *everyone* discussed the pros and cons of not only Hill's and Thomas's assertions, but also the concept of sexual harassment itself. Men who had thought nothing of what they considered harmless sexually suggestive jokes, comments, gestures, and even touching suddenly felt themselves looked upon as virtual lechers. Women who had found themselves on the uncomfortable receiving end of such unwanted attentions now discovered that those attentions might be not just uncomfortable, but actually illegal under Title VII. Eight months after the Hill–Thomas hearings, sexual harassment complaints filed with the EEOC increased by more than 50 percent. Ninety percent of the charges were from women. In the elections of 1992, called the "Year of the Woman," unprecedented numbers of female politicians rode the backlash wave of women who wanted to change "politics as usual" after witnessing what they perceived as the Senate's poor treatment of Hill during the hearings and Thomas's confirmation despite Hill's revelations. Ironically, at the time he engaged in the alleged activity, Thomas was head of the EEOC, the very agency charged with enforcing sexual harassment claims.

Much happened in the wake of the Hill–Thomas fiasco. (See Exhibit 9.2, "Maine Has First Sexual Harassment Law.") Almost overnight, the country's offices and workplaces went from friendly to foul. Sexual harassment captivated the national consciousness, much like watching the recent North African and Middle East quests for freedom unfold, in Tunisia and Egypt, only there was an immediate, acerbic, often acrimonious air to it. Lines were drawn in offices, bars, schools, universities, churches, and homes all across the country, and people took their places on one side or the other and held their ground.

Exhibit 9.2 *Maine Has First Sexual Harassment Law*

26 MAINE REVISED STATUTES SECTIONS 806, 807

In an effort to ensure a workplace free of sexual harassment, Maine was the first state to pass a sexual harassment law. There are now at least 22 states with such laws. The laws can be, as Maine's is, stricter than the federal law, but not less strict. Maine's law, which took effect in 1991, imposes affirmative duties on all employers, whether or not they have been found to have violated Maine's human rights law. The law, which in large part tracks the EEOC guidelines, requires employers to provide employees with information regarding sexual harassment, including

- A statement that it is illegal.
- The definition of sexual harassment under the state law.
- Descriptions of sexual harassment using examples.
- Descriptions of the internal complaint process available to employees.
- The availability of legal recourse and complaint process through the state's Human Rights Commission.
- Directions on how to contact the commission.
- The availability of protection against retaliation for invoking rights under the discrimination law.

The employer must provide this information in three ways:

- The employer must display a poster (which cannot exceed a 6th grade literacy level and may be purchased from Maine's Human Rights Commission) in a prominent and accessible location in the workplace.

- The employer must provide employees each year with an individual written notice about sexual harassment delivered in a manner to ensure its receipt, such as with employees' pay.
- If the employer has 15 or more employees, the employer must conduct an education and training program for all new employees within one year of the employee starting work. Additional training is required for supervisory and managerial employees within a year of commencing work to ensure that those employees take immediate and appropriate corrective action addressing sexual harassment complaints.

In an interesting note, in March 2001, after several sexual harassment complaints against the U.S. Postal Service (USPS) in Maine, Senator Olympia Snow (R-Maine) requested that the federal office of the inspector general (IG) conduct an investigation. In March 2002, the IG's office reported, among other things, that while there were strong sexual harassment policies in place, they were not well enforced. Supervisors who knew of sexual harassment complaints had routinely been given promotions, and one employee even committed suicide, leaving a note blaming sexual harassment for her despair. Based on the findings in Maine, the USPS ordered a nationwide investigation of its facilities. The lesson here is vigilance. Even though Maine was the first state to enact sexual harassment regulations into law, including requirements for training, the legislation is useless without vigorous enforcement.

Source: CBC Employment Alert, August 15, 1991, pp. 2–3, © 1994 by Clark Boardman Callahan, a division of Thomson Legal Publishing, Inc. For a list of other states and their provisions, see *The Business Owner's Toolkit* at http://www.toolkit.com/small_business_guide/sbg.aspx?nid=P05_5190.

As you can see, sexual harassment law is not something that has been around forever or that we've grown accustomed to and learned to live with over hundreds of years or even in the 40+ years since Title VII was born. Even though it may seem like old hat today, it is still pretty new in the legal sense. It is still evolving. The U.S. Supreme Court did not hear its first sexual harassment case until 1986, and the next one did not come until six years later in 1992. And of course, as we saw earlier, there are still many who don't yet "get it."

We also told you the background of sexual harassment because there is a lot of baggage that comes with the issue. Often, managers, supervisors, and employees don't recognize sexual harassment when it occurs. Our society preaches sexual permissiveness on the one hand, through music, movies, television, advertising, acculturation, and so forth, but when it comes to the workplace, the rules are different and some people don't make the transition very well.

Despite this, is sexual harassment something with which we really should be concerned? Is it that big a deal? Well, let's take a look. In one of the first and still one of the most comprehensive studies ever conducted on the issue, the U.S. Merit Systems Protection Board in 1980 found that over 40 percent of federal employees had reported incidents of sexual harassment; seven years later, the results were nearly the same (42 percent). A survey by *Working Woman* magazine of 160 of the Fortune 500 companies showed that nearly 40 percent of the companies had received at least one sexual harassment complaint in the previous 12 months. A *New York Times* poll found that 4 of every 10 women reported having experienced sexual harassment. The *National Law Journal* reported that 60 percent of female attorneys nationally said they had experienced some form of sexual harassment. A *Parade Magazine* poll discovered that 70 percent of the women polled who served in the military said they had been sexually harassed, as had 50 percent of the women who worked in congressional offices on Capitol Hill. Despite the numbers, only about 5 percent of the incidents of sexual harassment were reported. Those who experience sexual harassment "pay all the intangible emotional costs inflicted by anger, humiliation, frustration, withdrawal, [and] dysfunction in family life."[17]

In *Robinson v. Jacksonville Shipyards, Inc.,*[18] the court found, based on expert testimony, that

> [v]ictims of sexual harassment suffer stress effects from the harassment. Stress as a result of sexual harassment is recognized as a specific, diagnosable problem by the American Psychiatric Association. Among the stress effects suffered is "work performance stress," which includes distraction from tasks, dread of work, and an inability to work. Another form is "emotional stress," which covers a range of responses, including anger, fear of physical safety, anxiety, depression, guilt, humiliation, and embarrassment. Physical stress also results from sexual harassment; it may manifest itself by sleeping problems, headaches, weight changes, and other physical ailments. A study by the Working Women's Institute found that 96 percent of sexual harassment victims experienced emotional stress, 45 percent suffered work performance stress, and 35 percent were inflicted with physical stress problems.
>
> Sexual harassment has a cumulative, eroding effect on the victim's well-being. When women feel a need to maintain vigilance against the next incidence of harassment, the stress is increased tremendously. When women feel that their individual complaints will not change the work environment materially, the ensuing sense of despair further compounds the stress.

Regarding tangible costs, according to the classic 1988 MSPB update study, sexual harassment cost the federal government $267 million from May 1985 to May 1987 for losses in productivity, sick leave costs, and employee replacement costs.

The *Working Woman* magazine survey found the actual cost of sexual harassment in the responding companies to be $6.7 million in low productivity, absenteeism, and employee turnover. In addition, along with the nontangible price they pay, the MSPB found that employees who are sexually harassed pay medical expenses, litigation expenses, and job search expenses, and lose valuable sick leave and annual leave.

Whether it occurs through joking, e-mails, touching, gestures, staring, unwanted requests for dates, denials of job opportunities, or some other means, sexual harassment is not just kidding or a joke or workplace fraternization. It is an illegal form of gender discrimination that violates Title VII of the 1964 Civil Rights Act. But it is not only illegal: Given the toll it takes on the workplace, it is simply not good business. Since it is purely personal on the part of the harasser, it makes little sense for an employer not to take simple steps to prevent this totally unnecessary liability. It has become even less justifiable in the face of the 1991 Civil Rights Act amending Title VII to permit jury trials and compensatory and punitive damages.

The Civil Rights Act was passed in 1964, but it was the mid-to-late 1970s before courts began to seriously recognize sexual harassment as a form of gender discrimination under Title VII. In 1980, soon after the first few significant sexual harassment cases were decided, the EEOC issued guidelines on sexual harassment. The guidelines, quoted in the opening of this chapter, are not law in the sense of Title VII but carry a great deal of weight when it comes to how courts will view and analyze the issue.

Where Do Sexual Harassment Considerations Leave the Employer?

The letter to Ann Landers in Exhibit 9.3, "Employer Confusion over Harassment Issues," evidences a common frustration with and ignorance of sexual harassment issues. The intent of the law is *not* that the workplace either become totally devoid of sexuality on the one hand or be given completely over to employees who would

---

Exhibit 9.3 *Employer Confusion over Harassment Issues*

Dear Ann Landers: I am married. I am also the boss. I have several competent women employees who come on to me in subtle ways. They wear see-through blouses in the office, which I consider in poor taste. I do not wear see-through pants to work. Their thigh-high short skirts may be fashionable but when they sit down I am afraid to look for fear of what might be showing.

If I were to bring up this subject, they might charge me with "sexual harassment," so once they are hired and their work skills are up to par, there is very little I can do. The law is now on their side.

I often wonder if these women are trying to trap me into making passes at them. When I once mentioned "appropriate clothing" in the office, they pointed out that they dress like everyone else in the building—which is true.

I am proud to say that in the 28 years I've been married, cheating never once crossed my mind. Why, then, do these women come on to me? I don't flirt and am very businesslike. Of course, I could not ask my secretary to type this letter, so please excuse the mistakes.—Business Man, USA.

Source: Permission to reprint granted by Ann Landers/Creators Syndicate.

misuse the law on the other. Consensual relationships are not forbidden under the law, and employees may date consistent with company policy. It is only when the activity directed toward an employee is *unwelcome* and imposes terms or conditions different for one gender than another that it becomes a problem. For instance, a female employee might be required as a condition of employment to date her supervisor, while male employees have no such condition imposed. Most workplaces have now adopted sexual harassment policies (see Exhibit 9.4, "Example of a Sexual Harassment Policy") to govern this workplace issue. Recently, California joined Maine and Connecticut and took it a step further and mandated at least two hours of training every other year for supervisors in any U.S. firm with 50 or more employees if it has at least one supervisor based in California.[19]

Exhibit 9.4   *Example of a Sexual Harassment Policy*

Often the employer doesn't really know what is appropriate to include in a sexual harassment policy. In the *Jacksonville Shipyards* case, as part of the court's order, it required the employer to adopt a sexual harassment policy, which it included in an appendix. In order for you to see what one actually looks like and make the theoretical more practical for you, it is reproduced below, with changes as appropriate to generalize the policy (rather than have it be specific to JSI). It is important to check state laws in your area, as they may vary from the federal. For instance, some state laws mandate postings, some do not, many begin coverage if the employer has only one employee while others track the federal law's 15, and some specify what must be in any posting that is provided by the employer.

XYZ COMPANY SEXUAL HARASSMENT POLICY

Statement of Policy

Title VII of the Civil Rights Act of 1964 prohibits employment discrimination on the basis of race, color, gender, religion, or national origin. *Sexual harassment is included among the prohibitions.*

Sexual harassment, according to the federal Equal Employment Opportunity Commission (EEOC), consists of unwelcome sexual advances, requests for sexual favors, or other verbal or physical acts of a sexual or sex-based nature where (1) submission to such conduct is made either explicitly or implicitly a term or condition of an individual's employment; (2) an employment decision is based on an individual's acceptance or rejection of such conduct; or (3) such conduct interferes with an individual's work performance or creates an intimidating, hostile, or offensive working environment.

It is also unlawful to retaliate or take reprisal in any way against anyone who has articulated any concern about sexual harassment or discrimination, whether that concern relates to harassment of or discrimination against the individual raising the concern or against another individual.

Examples of conduct that would be considered sexual harassment or related retaliation are set forth in the Statement of Prohibited Conduct, which follows. These examples are provided to illustrate the kind of conduct proscribed by this policy; the list is not exhaustive.

XYZ Company and its agents are under a duty to investigate and eradicate any form of sexual harassment, gender discrimination, or retaliation. To further that end, XYZ Company has issued a procedure for making complaints about conduct in violation of this policy and a schedule for violation of this policy.

Sexual harassment is unlawful, and such prohibited conduct exposes not only XYZ Company but

continued

individuals involved in such conduct to significant liability under the law. Employees at all times should treat other employees respectfully and with dignity in a manner so as not to offend the sensibilities of a coworker. Accordingly, XYZ's management is committed to vigorously enforcing its Antisexual Harassment Policy at all levels within the company.

Statement of Prohibited Conduct

The management of XYZ Company considers the following conduct to represent some of the types of acts which violate XYZ's Antisexual Harassment Policy:

A. Physical assaults of a sexual nature, such as:

(1) rape, sexual battery, molestation, or attempts to commit these assaults; and

(2) intentional physical conduct, which is sexual in nature, such as touching, pinching, patting, grabbing, brushing against another employee's body, or poking another employee's body.

B. Unwanted sexual advances, propositions, or other sexual comments, such as:

(1) sexually oriented gestures, noises, remarks, jokes, or comments about a person's sexuality or sexual experience directed at or made in the presence of any employee who indicates or has indicated in any way that such conduct in his or her presence is unwelcome;

(2) preferential treatment or promise of preferential treatment to an employee for submitting to sexual conduct, including soliciting or attempting to solicit any employee to engage in sexual activity for compensation or reward; and

(3) subjecting, or threats of subjecting, an employee to unwelcome sexual attention or conduct or intentionally making performance of the employee's job more difficult because of that employee's gender.

C. Sexual or discriminatory displays or publications anywhere in XYZ's workplace by XYZ's employees, such as:

(1) displaying pictures, posters, calendars, graffiti, objects, promotional materials, reading materials, or other materials that are sexually suggestive, sexually demeaning, or pornographic, or bringing into the XYZ work environment or possessing any such material to read, display, or view at work.

A picture will be presumed to be sexually suggestive if it depicts a person of either gender who is not fully clothed or in clothes that are not suited to or ordinarily accepted for the accomplishment of routine work in and around the workplace and who is posed for the obvious purpose of displaying or drawing attention to private portions of his or her body;

(2) reading or otherwise publicizing in the work environment materials that are in any way sexually revealing, sexually suggestive, sexually demeaning, or pornographic; and

(3) displaying signs or other materials purporting to segregate an employee by gender in any area of the workplace (other than restrooms and similar semiprivate lockers/changing rooms).

D. Retaliation for sexual harassment complaints, such as:

(1) disciplining, changing work assignments of, providing inaccurate work information to, or refusing to cooperate or discuss work-related matters with any employee because that employee has complained about or resisted harassment, discrimination, or retaliation; and

(2) intentionally pressuring, falsely denying, lying about, or otherwise covering up or attempting to cover up conduct such as that described in any item above.

E. Other acts:

(1) The above is not to be construed as an all-inclusive list of prohibited acts under this policy.

(2) Sexual harassment is unlawful and hurts other employees. Any of the prohibited conduct described here is sexual harassment of anyone at whom it is directed or who is otherwise subjected to it. Each incident of harassment,

continued

Exhibit 9.4 *continued*

moreover, contributes to a general atmosphere in which all persons who share the victim's gender suffer the consequences. Sexually oriented acts or gender-based conduct have no legitimate business purpose; accordingly, the employee who engages in such conduct should be and will be made to bear the full responsibility for such unlawful conduct.

Schedule of Penalties for Misconduct

The following schedule of penalties applies to all violations of this policy, as explained in more detail in the Statement of Prohibited Conduct.

Where progressive discipline is provided for, each instance of conduct violating the policy moves the offending employee through the steps of disciplinary action. In other words, it is not necessary for an employee to repeat the same precise conduct in order to move up the scale of discipline.

A written record of each action taken pursuant to the policy will be placed in the offending employee's personnel file. The record will reflect the conduct, or alleged conduct, and the warning given, or other discipline imposed.

A. Assault:

Any employee's first proven offense of assault or threat of assault, including assault of a sexual nature, will result in dismissal.

B. Other acts of harassment by coworkers:

An employee's commission of acts of sexual harassment, other than assault, will result in nondisciplinary oral counseling upon alleged first offense; written warning, suspension, or discharge upon the first proven offense, depending upon the nature and severity of the misconduct; and suspension or discharge upon the second proven offense, depending upon the nature and severity of the misconduct.

C. Retaliation:

Alleged retaliation against a sexual harassment complainant will result in nondisciplinary oral counseling. Any form of proven retaliation will result in suspension or discharge upon the first proven offense, depending upon the nature and severity of the retaliatory acts, and discharge upon the second proven offense.

D. Supervisors:

A supervisor's commission of acts of sexual harassment (other than assault) with respect to any employee under that person's supervision will result in nondisciplinary oral counseling upon alleged first offense, final warning or dismissal for the first offense, depending upon the nature and severity of the misconduct, and discharge for any subsequent offense.

Procedures for Making, Investigating, and Resolving Sexual Harassment and Retaliation Complaints

A. Complaints:

XYZ Company will provide its employees with convenient, confidential, and reliable mechanisms for reporting incidents of sexual harassment and retaliation. Accordingly, XYZ designates at least two employees in supervisory or managerial positions to serve as investigative officers for sexual harassment issues. The names, responsibilities, work locations, and phone numbers of each officer will be routinely and continuously posted so that an employee seeking such name can enjoy anonymity and remain inconspicuous to all of the employees in the office in which he or she works.

The investigative officers may appoint "designees" to assist them in handling sexual harassment complaints. Persons appointed as designees shall not conduct investigations until they have received training equivalent to that received by the investigative officers. The purpose of having several persons to whom complaints may be made is to avoid a situation where an employee is faced with complaining to the person, or a close associate of the person, who would be the subject of the complaint.

continued

Complaints of acts of sexual harassment or retaliation that are in violation of the sexual harassment policy will be accepted in writing or orally, and anonymous complaints will be taken seriously and investigated. Anyone who has observed sexual harassment or retaliation should report it to a designated investigative officer. A complaint need not be limited to someone who was the target of harassment or retaliation. Only those who have an immediate need to know, including the investigative officers and/or his/her designee, the alleged target of harassment or retaliation, the alleged harasser(s) or retaliator(s), and any witnesses will or may find out the identity of the complainant. All parties contacted in the course of an investigation will be advised that all parties involved in a charge are entitled to respect and that any retaliation or reprisal against an individual who is an alleged target of harassment or retaliation, who has made a complaint, or who has provided evidence in connection with a complaint is a separate actionable offense as provided in the schedule of penalties. This complaint process will be administered consistent with federal labor law when bargaining unit members are affected.

B. Investigations:

Each investigative officer will receive thorough training about sexual harassment and the procedures herein and will have the responsibility for investigating complaints or having an appropriately trained and designated XYZ investigator do so.

All complaints will be investigated expeditiously by a trained XYZ investigative officer or his/her designee. The investigative officer will produce a written report, which, together with the investigation file, will be shown to the complainant upon request within a reasonable time. The investigative officer is empowered to recommend remedial measures based upon the results of the investigation, and XYZ management will promptly consider and act upon such recommendation. When a complaint is made, the investigative officer will have the duty of immediately bringing all sexual harassment and retaliation complaints to the confidential attention of the office of the president of XYZ, and XYZ's EEO officer. The investigative and EEO officers will each

maintain a file on the original charge and follow up investigation. Such files will be available to investigators, to federal, state, and local agencies charged with equal employment or affirmative action enforcement, to other complainants who have filed a formal charge of discrimination against XYZ, or any agent thereof, whether that formal charge is filed at a federal, state, or local law level. The names of complainants, however, will be kept under separate file.

C. Cooperation:

An effective antisexual harassment policy requires the support and example of company personnel in positions of authority. XYZ agents or employees who engage in sexual harassment or retaliation or who fail to cooperate with company-sponsored investigations of sexual harassment or retaliation may be severely sanctioned by suspension or dismissal. By the same token, officials who refuse to implement remedial measures, obstruct the remedial efforts of other XYZ employees, and/or retaliate against sexual harassment complainants or witnesses may be immediately sanctioned by suspension or dismissal.

Procedures and Rules for Education and Training

Education and training for employees at each level of the workforce are critical to the success of XYZ's policy against sexual harassment. The following documents address such issues: the letter to be sent to all employees from XYZ's chief executive officer/president; the Antisexual Harassment Policy; Statement of Prohibited Conduct; the Schedule of Penalties for Misconduct; and Procedures for Making, Investigating, and Resolving Sexual Harassment Complaints. These documents will be conspicuously posted throughout the workplace at each division of XYZ, on each company bulletin board, in all central gathering areas, and in every locker room. The statements must be clearly legible and displayed continuously. The antisexual harassment policy under a cover letter from XYZ's president will be sent to all employees. The letter will indicate that copies are available at no cost and how they can be obtained.

continued

Exhibit 9.4 *continued*

XYZ's antisexual harassment policy statement will also be included in the Safety Instructions and General Company Rules, which is issued in booklet form to each XYZ employee. Educational posters using concise messages conveying XYZ's opposition to workplace sexual harassment will reinforce the company's policy statement; these posters should be simple, eye-catching, and graffiti resistant.

Education and training include the following components:

1. *For all XYZ employees:* As part of the general orientation, each recently hired employee will be given a copy of the letter from XYZ's chief executive officer/president and requested to read and sign a receipt for the company's policy statement on sexual harassment so that they are on notice of the standards of behavior expected. In addition, supervisory employees who have attended a management training seminar on sexual harassment will explain orally at least once every six months at general meetings attended by all employees the kind of acts that constitute sexual harassment, the company's serious commitment to eliminating sexual harassment in the workplace, the penalties for engaging in harassment, and the procedures for reporting incidents of sexual harassment.

2. *For all female employees:* All women employed at XYZ will participate on company time in annual seminars that teach strategies for resisting and preventing sexual harassment. At least a half-day

in length, these seminars will be conducted by one or more experienced sexual harassment educators, including one instructor with work experience in the trades for skilled employees in traditionally male-dominated jobs.

3. *For all employees with supervisory authority of any kind over other employees:* All supervisory personnel will participate in an annual, half-day-long training session on gender discrimination. At least one-third of each session (of no less than one and one-half hours) will be devoted to education about workplace sexual harassment, including training (with demonstrative evidence) as to exactly what types of remarks, behavior, and pictures will not be tolerated in the XYZ workplace. The president of XYZ will attend the training sessions in one central location with all company supervisory employees. The president will introduce the seminar with remarks stressing the potential liability of XYZ and individual supervisors for sexual harassment. Each participant will be informed that they are responsible for knowing the contents of XYZ's antisexual harassment policy and for giving similar presentations at meetings of employees.

4. *For all investigative officers:* The investigative officers and their designees, if any, will attend annual full-day training seminars conducted by experienced sexual harassment educators and/or investigators to educate them about the problems of sexual harassment in the workplace and the techniques for investigating and stopping it.

Sexual Harassment in General

There are two theories on which an action for sexual harassment may be brought: **quid pro quo sexual harassment** and **hostile environment sexual harassment.** The first generally involves the employer requiring some type of sexual activity[20] from the harassee as a condition of employment or workplace benefits. The second addresses an offensive work environment to

Exhibit 9.5   *Wanted?*

One of the requirements of sexual harassment is that the activity be unwelcome. Take a look at these cases and see if this is what you think the law had in mind.

EEOC v. Bon Secours DePaul Med. Ctr., Civil Action No. 2:02cv728 (E.D. Va. 2002)
A jury awarded over $4 million to a hospital administrator who sued for retaliation under Title VII for being forced to resign when she attempted to prevent sexual harassment in the hospital's operating room. There were complaints of a nurse hugging, kissing, embracing, and rubbing doctors and other staff. The administrator verbally warned the nurse that this was inappropriate behavior. The nurse complained to doctors and staff about unfair treatment and quit. Several doctors complained about the administrator and a prominent doctor threatened to leave the hospital unless the administrator was terminated and the nurse reinstated. The administrator, given the choice to resign or be terminated for "breach of confidentiality," left. Six days later the nurse returned.

Miller v. Department of Corrections, 36 Cal. 4th 446, 115 P.3d 77 (2005)
The California Supreme Court held that an employee can sue a supervisor engaging in consensual sexual conduct with other employees when it has the effect of creating a "widespread atmosphere of sexual favoritism in the workplace." This decision forces employers to closely monitor employee relationships.

quid pro quo sexual harassment
Sexual harassment in which the harasser requests sexual activity from the harassee in exchange for workplace benefits.

hostile environment sexual harassment
Sexual harassment in which the harasser creates an abusive, offensive, or intimidating environment for the harassee.

which one gender is subjected but not the other. (See Exhibit 9.5, "Wanted?") While there are two different types of sexual harassment and each has its own requirements, the U.S. Supreme Court has said that the distinction need not be rigid. In *Burlington Industries, Inc. v. Ellerth,* the supervisor made threats to the harassee but did not carry them out. The harassee brought suit on the theory of *quid pro quo sexual harassment,* but rather than deny relief because there had been no loss of a tangible job benefit necessary for quid pro quo sexual harassment, the Court said that the terms *quid pro quo* and *hostile environment* are not controlling for purposes of determining employer liability for harassment by a supervisor. Rather, they are helpful in making rough demarcations between Title VII cases in which sexual harassment threats are carried out and where they are not or are absent altogether (see *Burlington Industries Inc. V. Ellerth* at the end of this chapter).

Most sexual harassment takes place between males and females, with the male as the harasser and the female as the harassee. But the gender of the harasser need not be male and the gender of the harasser does not matter. Males can be sexually harassed also. (See Exhibit 9.6, "Playing Catch Up.") Unfortunately, because society views males and sex so differently from females and sex, many males do not bring cases for fear of ridicule. Males who are being sexually harassed and wish to put a stop to it often find themselves the object of workplace jokes, teasing, and questioned sexuality, so they forgo filing claims. Even so, EEOC statistics show that claims by men have been increasing, particularly during the recent recession.[21]

Exhibit 9.6 *Playing Catch Up*

In 1993 when a 10-woman, 2-man jury awarded Sabino Gutierrez more than $1 million in damages for sexual harassment by his boss, Maria Martinez of Cal-Spas, a hot tub manufacturing company in California, it was the largest award in history for a male sexual harassee. Given the rarity of men bringing sexual harassment suits at the time (the harassing events of fondling, kissing, pressure for sex and eventually demotion, began in 1986 and continued for six years), it is almost certain that the novelty of a male suing for sexual harassment played some role in the case and jury award amount.

In the years since, however, such cases have been on the rise and are becoming more common. According to the EEOC, male victims accounted for 12 percent of claims in 1999. By 2009, a decade later, they accounted for 16.4 percent of sexual harassment claims filed with the EEOC. This uptick has been even greater since the country's recent financial crisis resulted in a higher percentage of men losing their jobs. According the Bureau of Labor Statistics, from September of 2008 to January of 2010, women lost 2.3 million jobs, versus 4.4 million for men. While male victims of sexual harassment may have previously simply quit and found another job, that is not as possible in this economy.

As a result, the data indicate that sexual harassment claims rose more in states with higher unemployment rates.

For years, men were hesitant to come forward about sexual harassment in the workplace because it often made them the butt of jokes. There were questions about their affinity orientation, loyalty, character, and toughness once they brought such claims forward. However, once the U.S. Supreme Court ruled in *Oncale v. Sundowner Offshore Drilling, Inc.* that males could be the victims of sexual harassment by other males in violation of Title VII's proscription on gender discrimination via sexual harassment, claims by males being sexually harassed began to increase.

Overall, only about 6 percent of sexual harassment cases are ever actually litigated in court, and the harassee wins about one-third of the time, according to a study by the American Bar Foundation.

Sources: Bill Hewitt and Nancy Matsumoto, People Weekly, 1993. Alissa Figueroa, "Workplace Harassment: Same-Sex Sexual Harassment Cases Are on the Rise," The Christian Science Monitor, 7/21/2010, http://www.cs-monitor.com/Business/new-economy/2010/0721/Work-place-harassment-Same-sex-sexual-harassment-cases-are-on-the-rise Sarah Herman, "Male Sexual Harassment on the Rise," HRM, 6/21/10, http://www.hrmreport.com/news/male-sexual-harassment-claims-rising/

As a final preliminary matter, Title VII does not protect employees from discrimination on the basis of affinity orientation, but the U.S. Supreme Court held in *Oncale v. Sundowner Offshore Services, Inc.*,[22] that even though both the harasser and the harassee are the same gender, a harassee can still bring a sexual harassment claim and be protected by Title VII. Since affinity orientation is not covered by Title VII, the basis for the harassment cannot be because the harassee is gay or lesbian, but there is no longer a presumption that if both parties are the same gender the claim is not covered by Title VII, as was the case with many courts before. As you saw in the information on the military, according to experts, the increase in sexual harassment and assaults of males is not related to affinity orientation but instead to power, control and violence.

Exhibit 9.7 *Jones v. Clinton**

Demonstrating that no one seems to be exempt from claims of sexual harassment, in what is probably the most famous sexual harassment case in history, Paula Jones, a former Arkansas state employee, filed suit against a state trooper and a sitting president of the United States. Jones claimed that she was the victim of a sexual advance from President Bill Clinton while he was serving as governor of Arkansas prior to his presidency. The decision of whether the sexual harassment case could be brought against a sitting president went all the way to the U.S. Supreme Court, and the Court saw no impediment to Jones's bringing the suit. In the end, the Eighth Circuit Court of Appeals affirmed the district court's dismissal of Jones's case. The court held that the facts alleged by Jones, even if taken to be true, were insufficient to establish a basis for either quid pro quo or hostile work environment sexual harassment. In the court's view, the president's dropping his trousers, fondling his penis, and asking Jones to kiss it, and then backing off when she said no, while boorish, was not sufficiently severe or pervasive to constitute a violation of the statute.

*138 F.3d. 758 (8th Cir. 1998).

Quid Pro Quo Sexual Harassment

LO2

In quid pro quo sexual harassment, the employee is required to engage in sexual activity in exchange for workplace entitlements or benefits such as promotions, raises, or continued employment. This is the more obvious type of sexual harassment and is not generally difficult to recognize. (See Exhibit 9.7, "*Jones v. Clinton.*") In order for there to be an exchange for some workplace benefit, the harasser generally must have some sort of workplace power or position. The exchange of sex for workplace benefits will often leave a paper trail that can be followed. For instance, if an employee receives a raise, there is usually a basis for it and the paper trail should show whether it was justified or not. The same with a promotion, or more favorable hours or benefits. An employer can limit a supervisor's ability to abuse power by choosing supervisory employees carefully and having in place a system with adequate monitors and checks. It greatly decreases morale, and thus lowers workplace productivity, for other employees to witness quid pro quo harassment by the supervisor. In fact, it has even been held that the other employees witnessing such activity may bring a cause of action of their own.

Hostile Environment Sexual Harassment

LO3

The more difficult sexual harassment issues have been in the area of hostile environment because there remains confusion about what activity constitutes the offense. Part of the difficulty lies in the fact that many of the causes that may serve as a basis for liability have until recently gone unchallenged. However, a closer look at what courts have held to constitute a hostile environment lends more predictability.

To sustain a finding of hostile environment sexual harassment, it is generally required that

- The harassment be unwelcome by the harassee.

- The harassment be based on gender.

- The harassment be sufficiently severe or pervasive to create an abusive working environment.

- The harassment affects a term, condition, or privilege of employment.

- The employer had actual or constructive knowledge of the sexually hostile working environment and took no prompt or adequate remedial action.

Scenario

Case 2

In light of these requirements, it becomes clear why simply giving polite compliments as in Opening Scenario 2 is not, in and of itself, sexual harassment. Sexual harassment involves much more.

Meritor Savings Bank, FSB v. Vinson was the first sexual harassment case to reach the U.S. Supreme Court. In the case, which is provided at the conclusion of the chapter, the branch manager of a bank engaged in sexually harassing activity with the harassee, up to and including sex in the bank vault. The harassee finally took a leave of absence and was terminated for excessive leave. When she sued for sexual harassment, the employer argued that since she engaged in the sexual activity, the activity did not meet the "unwanted" requirement of the guidelines. The Supreme Court disagreed. In addition, the employer argued that since the harassee lost no raises or promotions, she lost no tangible job benefits, so it was not quid pro quo sexual harassment. Read the case and see if you can now distinguish between quid pro quo and hostile environment sexual harassment.

In *Meritor* it is clear that the supervisor's actions changed the terms and conditions of Vinson's employment. There is a big difference between the ongoing, pervasive actions of Vinson's supervisor and merely giving someone an occasional nonsexual compliment. In a hostile environment action, the activity must be more than someone committing a boorish, stupid, inappropriate act. The act must come up to the standards the courts and the EEOC have set forth for the cause of action. Contrary to what you may have been led to believe by the press or other information you've received, not every act, even if it is unwanted or offensive, will meet that standard; thus, not every act, though considered offensive by the employee, constitutes sexual harassment as set forth by law. (See Exhibit 9.7, "*Jones v. Clinton.*")

Unwelcome Activity

The basis of hostile environment sexual harassment actions is unwanted activity by the harasser. (See Exhibit 9.8, "Comparison between Quid Pro Quo and Hostile

Exhibit 9.8 *Comparison between Quid Pro Quo and Hostile Environment Sexual Harassment*

QUID PRO QUO SEXUAL HARASSMENT

- Workplace benefit promised, given to, or withheld from harassee by harasser
- In exchange for sexual activity by harassee
- Generally accompanied by a paper trail (for example, promotion, raise, or termination paperwork).

HOSTILE ENVIRONMENT SEXUAL HARASSMENT

Activity by harasser, toward harassee that

- Is unwanted by the harassee.
- Is based on harassee's gender.
- Creates for harassee a hostile or abusive work environment.
- Unreasonably interferes with harassee's ability to do his or her job.
- Is sufficiently severe and/or pervasive.
- Affects a term or condition of harassee's employment.

Scenario

Environment Sexual Harassment.") If the activity is wanted or welcome by the harassee, there is no sexual harassment. Even if the activity started out being consensual, if one employee calls a halt to it and the other continues, it can become sexual harassment at the time the activity is no longer consensual, as in Opening Scenario 3.

In making the determination of whether the harasser's activity was welcome, the actions used as a basis for the determination can be direct or indirect. For instance, in *McLean v. Satellite Technology Services, Inc.,*[23] the court had no trouble in determining that the harassee welcomed the activity of the harasser, if, in fact, it took place at all. The female employee engaged in a good deal of sexually tinged behavior at work such as pulling up her shirt to show a scar, having sexual conversations on the phone with clients even after being asked not to do so, and being away from her desk at a business conference having sex with people she met there. After being terminated upon return from the conference, she alleged that her supervisor tried to touch her leg and kiss her while they were on the business trip and she was in his room dressed in a bikini. It also demonstrates that there is more to winning a sexual harassment case than simply alleging that sexual harassment occurred.

Of course, there also may be a finding that the harassee did not welcome the activity by the harasser. Evidence can be direct, such as the harassee telling the harasser to discontinue the offending activity, or indirect, such as the harassee using body language, eye signals, and the like to show disapproval of the harasser's actions. Employees should be told to make it clear to a harasser that the activity is unwelcome; otherwise, the signals may become confused and the harasser may think his or her actions are wanted by the harassee. In Exhibit 9.9, "Wanna Fool Around?" you can see how some employers are trying to address the issue in novel ways.[24]

Exhibit 9.9 *Wanna Fool Around? Sign on the Dotted Line, Please . . .*

In the face of increasingly expensive and embarrassing sexual harassment litigation, there have been all sorts of attempts to lessen employer liability. See how you like this workplace idea. You may recall hearing about a similar plan imposed on the students by the administration at a large midwestern university a few years ago to prevent date rape.

"LOVE CONTRACTS" HELP FEND OFF HARASSMENT SUITS

No matter how many training sessions or awareness workshops they conduct, companies still find themselves facing sexual harassment claims. Alarmingly, claims keep going higher up the chain of command, increasingly hitting CEOs. And when such a suit reaches a top executive, it's not just a department in trouble, but the entire company itself.

The latest trend in fending off sexual harassment suits is a "love contract." Teresa Butler, managing partner in the Atlanta office of employment law firm Littler Mendelson, explains.

Can You Talk about the "Love Contract" and How It Works?
It's really only intended for higher-level executives. This isn't something we advise employers to put in their handbooks, and we don't recommend that all supervisors issue them to subordinates. We talk about this for CEOs and officers, top-level executives, and maybe directors; that's a judgment call for the company. It's basically for people who have broad power in the workplace—not the average first-level supervisor.

What's Included in the Contract?
The love contract does three things. First, it restates the voluntary nature of the relationship. The CEO, or whoever is in this situation, issues the agreement to a subordinate employee, basically explaining to the individual, "I want to have this relationship with you. My understanding is you want to have this relationship with me. But I'm concerned that over time you might believe that the continuation of this relationship—even though you don't want it

anymore—might be necessary for you to be successful here. As you know, we have a harassment policy, and I want you to understand that I'm aware of that policy and would never allow [the end of the relationship] to influence my decision making with regard to your employment." So the agreement is actually a formal contract. It restates the voluntary nature of the relationship.

What Else Should a Love Contract Do?
Second, it affirms that the parties will use the company's sexual harassment policies if a problem arises, and it confirms the existence of those policies and [procedures]. It also states that if the policies aren't used, it's fair to assume there isn't a problem. And third, the parties agree if work-related disputes arise, they'll resolve their differences using alternative dispute resolution (ADR) rather than resorting to the courts. Some might want to use that third piece and some might not, but we recommend ADR from a legal standpoint.

How Are These Contracts Useful?
Often these relationships go bad at some point; one party wants to end it and the other doesn't. And then there's retaliatory conduct by the other, sometimes by the subordinate in the form of a sexual harassment complaint. So this contract is a method for the top-level executives to just say out loud what is actually the case. It's assurance for the company and the individuals that everybody understands what the rules are.

How Legally Defensible Is a Love Contract?
The first response we typically hear, especially from lawyers, is: How could this possibly be enforceable? The idea is this person can always come back and say this was coerced, that he or she was forced to sign this agreement. That's a risk you take with any contractual relationship because an employee is always in a subordinate role to the employer. If you take that to its logical end, you might as well say you could never have an enforceable contract with an employee.

continued

So Can They Raise That Issue?

Of course they can. But are you better off with the contract than without it? Yes. I think it's a pretty tough argument for an individual who signs this agreement to say that he or she was coerced into having this consensual relationship that you'll be able to [prove] the person had. There's usually evidence in these cases of a consensual relationship: You've got birthday cards, receipts for dinner, letters and other types of communications that the subordinate employee has clearly engaged in on a voluntary basis.

"LOVE CONTRACT" SAMPLE LETTER

Dear [Name of Object of Affection]:

As we discussed, I know that this may seem silly or unnecessary to you, but I really want you to give serious consideration to the matter as it is very important to me. [Add other materials as appropriate]

I very much value our relationship and I certainly view it as voluntary, consensual, and welcome, and I have always felt that you feel the same. However, I know that sometimes an individual may feel compelled to engage in or continue in a relationship against their will out of concern that it may affect the job or working relationships.

It is very important to me that our relationship be on an equal footing and that you be fully comfortable that our relationship is at all times fully voluntary and welcome. I want to assure you that under no circumstances will I allow our relationship or, should it happen, the end of our relationship, to impact on your job or our working relationship. Though I know you have received a copy of [our company's name] sexual harassment policy, I am enclosing a copy [Add specific reference to policy as appropriate] so that you can read and review it again. Once you have done so, I would greatly appreciate your signing this letter below, if you are in agreement with me.

[Add personal closing]

Very truly yours,

[Name]

I have read this letter and the accompanying sexual harassment policy, and I understand and agree with what is stated in both this letter and the sexual harassment policy. My relationship with [name] has been (and is) voluntary, consensual, and welcome. I also understand that I am free to end this relationship any time, and doing so will not adversely impact on my job.

[Signature of Object of Affection]

Source: Teresa Butler, Littler Mendelson, Atlanta, 888-LITTLER; Gillian Flynn, *Workforce Magazine,* March 1999, pp. 106–108. Used with permission.

In another type of welcomeness issue, the Hooters restaurant chain was involved in several cases that, among other things, brought up the question of unwelcomeness parameters. As discussed in the previous chapter, Hooters is an Atlanta-based chain of over 435 restaurants in 44 states and 20 countries. It is noted for its buffalo chicken wings and scantily clad female servers. Several lawsuits have been filed by female servers who were allegedly illegally fired or forced to quit because of sexual harassment.

The suits alleged that the environment created by management for female servers was hostile, starting with the name "Hooters," which is a slang term for women's breasts. Servers (a position for which Hooters only hires females), who are required to wear uniforms of revealing shorts and T-shirts, alleged that they were required to endure an atmosphere of sexually offensive remarks, touching, and other conduct by both management and customers. For example, the sign on entering Hooters reads, "Men: no shirt, no shoes: no service. Women: no shirt: free food."

An important issue in the lawsuits was whether, as the company argued, the women assumed the risk of the activities directed at them by agreeing to work for the company—that is, whether the conduct was welcomed by the fact that the servers worked for a company whose concept encouraged such behavior. What do you think? Should it matter if, as it turns out, the requirement is illegal under Title VII? Check out the Hooters Web site and see if you agree, as Hooters argued, that it is merely a neighborhood restaurant (previously it had argued it was a family restaurant), complete with a children's menu. There is at least some truth to this. One of our students said his Little League baseball coach took the all-male team to Hooters to celebrate the student's 12th birthday and they *loved* it. The coach was his dad.

Severe and Pervasive Requirement

severe and/or pervasive activity
Harassing activity that is more than an occasional act or is so serious that it is the basis for liability.

One of the most troublesome problems with hostile environment is determining whether the harassing activity is **severe and/or pervasive** enough to amount to an unreasonable interference with an employee's ability to perform. (See Exhibit 9.5, "Wanted?") Built into the elements of hostile environment sexual harassment is a requirement that the offending activity be sufficiently severe and/or pervasive. That is, the activity is not an isolated occurrence that is not serious enough to warrant undue concern. The more frequent or serious the occurrences, the more likely it is that the severe and/or pervasive requirement will be met. If it is egregious enough, one time may meet the severity requirement, for example, in the case of rape.

In *Ross v. Double Diamond, Inc.*,[25] events over a two-day period were determined to meet the requirement for severity. Within hours of being hired, a female employee endured groping, sexually suggestive comments and jokes, a demand that she allow her legs to be photographed as she pulled up her dress, and a photo being taken up her dress as she delivered a message into an all-male meeting.

Regarding the "unreasonable interference" requirement, in *Harris v. Forklift Systems*[26] the company owner constantly infused sexual comments and actions into the workplace by, for instance, making female employees dig in his front pockets for change, or throwing it on the floor and making them bend down and pick it up so he could see their backsides. The claimant finally left after he promised not to continue this behavior; then after she made a profitable deal, he said in front of other employees that she must have negotiated it in the Holiday Inn. The U.S. Supreme Court decided that sexual harassment claims do not require findings of severe psychological harm to be actionable. The Court said that "so long as the environment would reasonably be perceived, and is perceived, as hostile or abusive, there is no need for it also to be psychologically injurious."

Whether an environment is hostile or abusive can be determined only by looking at all the circumstances. These may include the frequency of the discriminatory conduct, its severity, whether it is physically threatening or humiliating or a mere offensive utterance, and whether it unreasonably interferes with an employee's work performance. According to the Court, no single factor is determinative. (See Exhibit 9.10, "Is 'Discomfort' Enough?")

Exhibit 9.10 *Is "Discomfort" Enough?*

Students often think that merely feeling uncomfortable about something going on in the workplace is sufficient to sustain a claim under Title VII for hostile environment sexual harassment. As you can see from this situation, this is far from the case—or is it?

A male sales representative for Canon, Inc., had, as part of his territory, a store owned by a woman, his client. At a Christmas party, the female store owner/client was inappropriately touched, hugged, and kissed on the face and forehead by the sales rep's immediate supervisor. The client decided she did not want to complain about it. The sales rep complained to the company anyway. When the supervisor to whom the complaint was made called the client to discuss it as part of the investigation of the claim, the client again said she did not want to pursue the matter. When the sales rep was told this, he called the client and left a voice mail message expressing his anger at her refusal to corroborate his claims against his supervisor. In a "loud, rapid" voice, he used abusive language, told her he was "pissed off," accused her of lying to Canon, and said that he was going to "lose his f-ing job" and she needed to back up his claim of the harassment against her. Because of the message, the client was so afraid of the sales rep that she would no longer allow him in her store. When the company found out about the voice mail message, the sales rep was fired. Canon, Inc., told him his conduct toward the client was unprofessional and

unacceptable and would not be tolerated under any circumstances. The employee filed suit for retaliation under Title VII, claiming that the company terminated his employment because he complained about the sexual harassment of his client. Canon said the termination was for sufficient cause based on his actions toward the client.

As part of his claim, the employee alleged that the sexual harassment action against the client presented a hostile environment for him because he was "made uncomfortable" by his boss's alleged advances toward his client.

The court did not agree. The court said "feelings of 'discomfort' cannot support a hostile environment claim. Instead, such a claim is stated only where plaintiff alleges that the conditions of his workplace were so permeated with discriminatory intimidation, ridicule, and insult that is sufficiently severe or pervasive as to alter the conditions of the victim's employment and create an abusive working environment." [*Kunzler v. Canon, USA, Inc.,* 257 F. Supp. 3d 574 (E.D.N.Y. 2003).]

On the other hand, in August 2003, the Minneapolis Public Library entered into a settlement agreement with its employees for $435,000 after the employees accused the library administration of subjecting them to a hostile environment by leaving them exposed to patrons' displays of explicit Web sites.

Do the two square for you?

Perspective Used to Determine Severity

reasonable person standard
Viewing the harassing activity from the perspective of a reasonable person in society at large (generally tends to be the male view).

Until recently the determination of whether the harasser's activity was sufficiently severe and pervasive was generally based on a **reasonable person standard,** which is supposed to be a gender-neutral determination. That is, the activity would be judged as offensive (or not) based on whether the activity would offend a reasonable person under the circumstances. Since this "neutral" standard generally turned out to be instead a male standard, the EEOC issued a policy statement by which it required that the victim's perspective also must be considered so as not to perpetuate stereotypical notions of what behavior is acceptable to those of a given gender. This notion, labeled the "reasonable

reasonable victim standard
Viewing the harassing activity from the perspective of a reasonable person experiencing the harassing activity including, gender-specific sociological, cultural, and other factors.

LO6

woman" or **reasonable victim standard**, has been used increasingly by courts and should be given serious consideration when evaluating harassing activity. If the victim is a male, it would, of course, be a reasonable man standard.

In *Ellison v. Brady,* provided for your review, the court adopted a reasonable woman standard for analyzing whether the harasser's behavior was severe and pervasive enough to create a hostile work environment. It explains why viewing severity and pervasiveness from this perspective may render different results. The U.S. Supreme Court has not addressed the reasonable victim versus reasonable person dichotomy as a direct issue, but in *Oncale v. Sundowner Offshore Services Inc.,*[27] the Court's first case involving same-gender sexual harassment, it said "the objective severity of harassment should be judged from the perspective of a reasonable person *in the plaintiff's position.*" The *Ellison v. Brady* case was the basis for the movie *Hostile Advances,* starring Rena Sofer and Victor Garber.

"Sexual" Requirement Explained

While the harassment of the employee must be based on gender, it need not involve sex, requests for sexual activity, sexual comments, or other similar activity. Even today, a female entering a workplace with few or no other females is often verbally harassed about "doing men's work," "taking away the job a man should have," or simply inappropriately working at a traditionally male job. Despite the lack of sexual overtones (though the comments are obviously based on gender), this could well constitute sexual harassment. In the case of *Andrews v. City of Philadelphia,*[28] the sexual activity was only a small part of what the females who came into the traditionally male job of police officers were subjected to. They were called very derogatory names, their property was vandalized, their files were stolen or ripped, officers who were supposed to help them would not, their cars were vandalized, soda was poured into their typewriters, obscene phone calls were made to their unlisted numbers, a caustic substance was poured into one officer's locker and she received severe burns on her back when she put on a shirt from the locker, and pornographic material was put in their desks and male officers would gather around to see their reaction. When they reported it to their supervisor, he did nothing.

Notice how little of what they went through conforms to what we usually think of as sexually based hostile environment. This "non sex" requirement is also one of the reasons it is better to use the term *gender* in sexual harassment discussions so that sex in the traditional sense, and gender, meaning whether one is male or female, are clearly differentiated and the discussion less confusing. The *Andrews* case gives you a good example of how serious hostile sentiments can become.

A common element of hostile environment sexual harassment cases that may lack an actual sexuality factor is **anti-female animus** exhibited by the harasser toward those of the harassee's gender. This is manifested through, for instance, the use of derogatory terms when referring to women. Courts also have found anti-female animus in derogatory statements to or about women in the context of their jobs, such as "women have shit for brains," "should be barefoot and pregnant," "should not be surgeons because it takes them too long to bathe and put on makeup," "could never stand up to union representatives," "are unstable when

anti-female animus
Negative feelings about women and/or their ability to perform jobs or functions, usually manifested by negative language and actions.

Exhibit 9.11 *All in Good Fun? Just Joking . . .*

A number of sexual harassment cases arise from situations having nothing to do with "sex" as we ordinarily think of it. It has to do instead with gender—more specifically, anti-female animus, or feelings against women who are in male-dominated or traditionally male jobs such as truck driving, construction, firefighting, trash collection, and so on. Even when males are in traditionally female jobs, they rarely are subjected to the same kind of actions directed toward them that women in traditionally male fields are. And often, when men in a traditionally female job are subjected to harassing activity, it is by other males who tease, joke, make derogatory comments, and more. Case law indicates that male nurses generally do not get hassled by female nurses or male kindergarten teachers by female kindergarten teachers.

Students, and even managers and supervisors in the workplace, often comment that "it's only joking" and that women who complain are being "overly sensitive." What they don't understand is that rarely is the ribbing or joking an isolated event. Rather, it is usually accompanied by other indicators in the workplace that one gender is being treated differently, less well, than another. Rarely will you find women progressing as they should in a workplace when the atmosphere exhibits anti-female animus through jokes, ribbing, and derogatory gender-based comments. It all goes together and creates a certain environment that is less likely to allow women to progress. The thought is parent to the act. Anti-female animus manifested through jokes, comments, and ribbing is very likely also to be manifested in lack of full participation in the workplace for women through pay, training, discipline, and advancement. It's never "just jokes." That is why it is such a serious matter.

As a manager or supervisor, how you handle these events as they occur can make all the difference in the world for your employer. It may seem like only joking, ribbing, or all in good fun, but as a manager, you ignore it at the peril of your company. Heaped on an employee day after day, this harassing activity places upon them different terms or conditions of employment than it does other employees of the other gender who do not have to contend with this hostile environment.

In November 2008, the Los Angeles City Council awarded a female member of the city's canine unit $2.25 million for the harassment she suffered in the unit. She alleged the men took items from her desk and the women's locker room, used her shower and hygiene products, exposed their genitalia, made offensive and sexually explicit remarks, excluded her from training exercises and other opportunities, barred her from "cigar" meetings held to discuss training issues and practices, blew cigar smoke in her face, and was told another officer rubbed his penis on her phone. When she reported these events, the harassment worsened. The week before her settlement, an officer who was demoted and suffered retaliation when he defended her was awarded $3.6 million.

Source: Joanna Linn, "LAPD Officer Awarded $2.25 Million in Harassment Case," *The Los Angeles Times,* 11/20/2008, http://articles.latimes.com/2008/nov/20/local/me-harass20.

they are 'in heat' [having their menstrual cycle, said to a female doctor]," or "all she needs is a good lay." Often anti-female animus is accompanied by sexually based activity, but need not be. A manager should not dismiss a harassee's complaint simply because it does not involve sexually related activity. (See Exhibit 9.11, "All in Good Fun? Just Joking. . . .")

In analyzing hostile environment claims, keep in mind that it can be accomplished also by electronic means. Claims involving sexual harassment through workplace e-mail, bulletin boards, chat rooms, and social Web sites have increased dramatically in the past few years. It is best to be aware of the potential for liability. Again, there need not be a sexual element involved in order for it to constitute sexual harassment. It is a good idea to have a well-enforced workplace policy giving guidelines for this kind of activity and to keep up with any changes that may result in new ways for liability to occur.

Employer Liability for Sexual Harassment

The U.S. Supreme Court has been wrestling with the issue of employer liability for sexual harassment since it decided the first case on the subject in 1986 *(Meritor,* discussed earlier in the chapter). In its *Ellerth* case, also discussed in this chapter, the Court said that it was hearing the case in order to assist in defining the relevant standards of employer liability since "Congress has left it to the courts to determine controlling agency law principles in a new and difficult area of federal law." Without trying to drag you into the legal mire that has surrounded the issue, we will give you some general rules with which to operate and leave the intricacies for the courts to continue to unravel.

Supervisor toward Employee (Tangible Employment Action)

This is generally going to be quid pro quo sexual harassment (for instance, the employee's supervisor denies the employee an expected raise or promotion because she refuses to have sex with him), but the courts have said that the categories are not cast in stone. An employer is strictly liable for the tangible acts of its supervisors regardless of whether the specific acts complained of were authorized or even forbidden by the employer and regardless of whether the employer knew or should have known of their occurrence. Since the supervisor is, in effect, the employer, the supervisor's acts are considered those of the employer.

The employer has control of the situation by carefully choosing supervisory employees. As discussed, in a tangible job action there is usually a paper trail involved, so it also gives the employer a measure of control by keeping up with what is going on in the workplace and monitoring for actions that may violate the law. For instance, if an employee is precipitously terminated or demoted, not given a raise if it is expected, or given a raise if none is expected, there will be a paper trail and the law holds the employer responsible for knowing what is going on in the employer's workplace. The law says the employer cannot engage in sexual harassment, so doing so through a supervisor is tantamount to the employer doing it and the employer is strictly liable for the harassment.

Supervisor toward Employee (No Tangible Employment Action)

If there is no tangible employment act by a supervisor, such as termination, and instead there is activity by a supervisor causing a severe and/or pervasive hostile environment resulting in harm to the harassed employee (for instance, the supervisor may constantly ask the employee out on dates and make sexual comments, but still give the employee her usual raises and promotions), the employer is not strictly liable. This is also true of a constructive discharge. As you will see below, in constructive discharge, the workplace becomes so unbearable, objectively speaking, that the employee has no real option except to leave. In these situations, the harassed employee can bring a claim, but there is no virtually automatic liability like there is for strict liability offenses. Here, the employer has an affirmative defense available. The employer can use the *Ellerth/Faragher* defense to show that the employer had a reasonable sexual harassment policy to prevent and address sexual harassment and the harassed employee unreasonably failed to use it. This defense is not permitted in a case where there is a tangible unfavorable job action by a supervisor.

Co-worker Harassment or Third-Party Harassment of Employee

When the harassment is by (1) one employee toward another on the same level (rather than by a supervisory employee to a subordinate) or (2) someone who is not employed by the employer, such as a client or someone who comes in to service the machinery at the employer's business, the employer is liable if the employer knew or should have known of the acts of the harasser and took no immediate corrective action.

For instance, if the computer repairer comes to service computers and regularly feels the employee's legs while working with wires under the desk or makes suggestive sexual comments, the employer would be liable even though the repairer does not work for the employer. The employee would usually have to make the employer aware of the situation and the employer would have to take no steps to remedy the situation before liability would attach. If the employer saw what was happening and saw that the employee was clearly upset by the situation, the employer would be put on notice that something should be done and liability could attach. The same is true with co-workers. That is why it is so important for managers and supervisors to be aware of what is going on around them in the workplace and deal with it effectively. The law will hold the employer responsible through the acts of the supervisory employees who were aware and took no action to rectify the situation.

In *Faragher v. City of Boca Raton,* included for your review, the U.S. Supreme Court discussed employer liability for sexual harassment. The case involved sexual harassment of lifeguards who were stationed in a remote (from the main office) location, which resulted in less supervision of what was occurring. The Court provided employers not only with a defense they could use when sued by an employee who had not acted reasonably in seeking to avoid harm (the *Ellerth/Faragher* affirmative defense) but also with ammunition for an employee who could allege that the employer did not use reasonable measures to prevent sexual harassment.

Sometimes the employee is not terminated but instead believes the harassment is so unbearable that he or she must quit his or her job without going through the employer's sexual harassment complaint process. This is constructive discharge.

In *Pennsylvania State Police v. Suders,*[29] the Supreme Court addressed what to do if a supervisor's actions result in a constructive discharge for an employee and whether such a discharge is loss of a tangible job benefit, resulting in strict liability for the employer. The Court said that when there is no official act resulting in the constructive discharge, and thus, no way for an employer to be made aware that there was an issue resulting in the constructive discharge, rather than strict liability attaching to the employer, the employer is able to use the *Ellerth* and *Faragher* affirmative defense to show how it tried to avoid liability.

Scenario

In *Robinson v. Jacksonville Shipyards, Inc.,* which we mentioned earlier, the court provided important information as to how sexual harassment cases should be handled. It is the basis for Opening Scenario 1. The case involved nude pictures, magazines, plaques, and posters in the workplace. When the employee complained, she was told she simply should not look. The court said this was not an appropriate response by the employer, as this type of paraphernalia creates a hostile environment for which the law will hold the employer liable.

Remember that it is a defense to liability if an employer can show that the harassee unreasonably failed to avail himself or herself of a mechanism the employer had in place for preventing or correcting sexual harassment. Likewise, it is helpful to a harassee if he or she can show that the employer had unreasonable means of preventing or correcting sexual harassment (for instance, the only one to whom claims are reported is the harasser). This makes it more important than ever for an employer to have strong sexual harassment policy as well as effective training, monitoring, and reporting of sexual harassment. The EEOC has determined that since harassment of any kind is the only type of discrimination carried out by a supervisor for which an employer can avoid liability, that limitation is to be narrowly construed.

Other Important Considerations

There are several other important miscellaneous matters you should be aware of that are often at issue in sexual harassment claims.

Determining the Truth of Allegations

The number-one problem managers have in responding to sexual harassment complaints (other than their discomfort in dealing with such matters) is determining the truth of sexual harassment allegations. We cannot tell you how many times we have heard employers and managers say, "We don't know who to believe! How are we supposed to know who is telling the truth?" Appropriate investigation should provide the employer a basis on which to decide and to appropriately respond. Both parties, as well as any witnesses, should be questioned. The investigator's objective is to find out the "who," "what," "when," "where," and "how" of the allegations as quickly and as discreetly as possible. Employees should be involved only on a "need to know" basis. When all appropriate evidence is gathered, much like the members of a jury, the employer must determine the facts. The employer bases the determination on who seems most credible, whose version of the alleged incidents is more likely to be closer to the truth, what interests the parties have in telling their version of the events, and any credible corroboration presented. The common problem of the employer's discomfort with making judgments should not, as it so often does, prevent moving quickly and appropriately on complaints.

The EEOC's Policy Guidance on Harassment provides insight into how credibility determinations are to be made. According to the EEOC, while none of the following is necessarily determinative, factors to consider in deciding credibility include

- *Inherent plausibility.* Is the testimony believable on its face? Does it make sense?
- *Demeanor.* Did the person seem to be telling the truth or lying?
- *Motive to falsify.* Did the person have a reason to lie?
- *Corroboration.* Is there *witness testimony* (such as testimony of eyewitnesses, people who saw the person soon after the alleged incidents or people who discussed the incidents with him or her at or around the time that they occurred) or *physical evidence* (such as written documentation) that corroborates the party's testimony?
- *Past record.* Did the alleged harasser have a history of similar behavior in the past?

We wish there was more we could tell you, but the truth is, there isn't much more that can be said. It can be uncomfortable, but investigating and making a decision must be done, and there are no special tools to do it, much like a jury has no special tools when deciding a murder case. They just come in, listen carefully to the evidence, observe carefully, and make a determination using their best judgment based on what they have taken in. There is no magic, no easy way to do it. Responding quickly, taking the matter seriously, using your best judgment to evaluate what you find, and going where the information leads you are the best tools you can use in determining the truth of the matter.

Retaliation and Employee Privacy

LO8

Often harassees report sexual harassment and, out of fear of retaliation, want the employer to provide relief without informing the alleged harasser of the complaint or of the harassee's identity. Harassees should be informed that the alleged harasser must be told of the complaint for the employer to effectively address it but that retaliation will not be tolerated, as the law has separate retaliation provisions. Even alleged harassers are not required to play hide-and-seek with claims and claimants. As uncomfortable as the claimant may be in coming forward, the alleged harasser must be notified.

According to the EEOC, there has been a dramatic increase in the number of retaliation claims in recent years. The EEOC has been clear in reiterating that it takes such cases very seriously. Courts and juries have been clear in sending the message that they do not like retaliation by employers for employees pursuing their legal rights under the law. Punitive damages are likely to be granted in such cases since retaliation, in a manner of speaking, adds insult to injury and is much more deliberate.

Corrective Action

The guidelines state that the employer must take "immediate and appropriate corrective action" to remedy sexual harassment. The most appropriate thing to do under the specific circumstance depends on the facts. Consideration should be given to such factors as the employment position of the employees, the activity involved, the duration of the actions, the seriousness of the actions, the employer's sexual harassment policy and other methods used to deter sexual harassment, the alleged harasser's prior history of sexual harassment, and so on. While the remedy must be calculated to stop the harassment and must not have the effect of punishing the harassee, neither should it be out of proportion to the act. Make sure the punishment fits the crime. Every act of sexual harassment need not result in automatic termination, the "capital punishment" of the workplace.

With all this in mind, the good news is that there is now a more formalized purpose to all this. For years, courts admonished employers to take claims seriously and respond accordingly, but this had no consistent, formalized result for the employer. Employers could do the best they could and still get into trouble with the law. That is no longer so for certain cases. Through two cases you have already been introduced to in this chapter, *Faragher* and *Ellerth,* the U.S. Supreme Court created the *Ellerth/Faragher* affirmative defense we spoke of earlier, which employers can use to protect themselves from liability when they have tried to consistently obey the law. In *Burlington Industries, Inc. v. Ellerth,* the Court outlines that defense and provides employers with a good deal of control over avoiding and/or limiting liability for violations of Title VII when there is no loss of tangible job benefits because of a harasser's action. Keep in mind that the defense can only be used where there was no tangible employment action by a supervisor.

Damages and Jury Trials

We discussed these issues in Chapter 2, "The Employment Law Toolkit," but due to the sensitive nature of this area, we thought it was worth reiterating. Under the Civil Rights Act of 1991, an employee suing for sexual harassment can ask for up to $300,000 in compensatory and punitive damages (and unlimited medical damages) and request a jury trial. Both these factors greatly increase the employer's potential liability for sexual harassment and make avoiding liability for this unnecessary activity even more imperative.

As you can imagine, after the 1991 amendments allowed damages and jury trials, Title VII claims increased dramatically. It finally made economic sense to go through the time-consuming, arduous process of suing, for both claimants and their attorneys. Of course, this was not a welcome event for employers. In sexual harassment in particular, jury trials can be very damaging. The nature of the activities constituting the claim can be quite emotional for a jury to hear. That is why it is even more important not to let things get that far unless the employer is certain of victory—which is virtually unknown since juries are unpredictable.

In response to our country's exploding litigation dockets, the use of alternative dispute resolution, or ADR, for settling disputes went from a backwater alternative to litigation to one of the most-used methods. As we discussed in the chapter on Title VII, EEOC has now institutionalized the use of ADR in its proceedings in several ways and has gotten employers to do the same, using their own extensive, in-house ADR resources. Among other things, the EEOC conducts mediation on appropriate claims filed with them, and in 2003, it began pilot or start-up programs for handling its own internal complaints, a program to have Fair Employment Practice Agencies mediate private-sector claims, and a program in which national employers handle claims of their employees informally before handing it over to the EEOC (if it is necessary to do so). Many attorneys and court systems now also offer ADR as a part of their services.

ADR is a much less acrimonious, expensive, time-consuming alternative that also has the bonus of not being on the public record, for the most part, or precedent setting, in the formal sense. If you are an employer or employee, it would probably be in your best interest to try this route before going to court. You have little to lose and a host of benefits to gain.

Tort and Criminal Liability

In addition to bringing an action under Title VII, harassees also may bring civil actions in state court—or, if permitted, federal court—based on state laws that also may be violated by the actions of the alleged harasser. Recall that in *Meritor,* the first sexual harassment case to come before the U.S. Supreme Court, the bank manager was alleged to have fondled the plaintiff in public, followed her to and entered the ladies' restroom with her, and engaged in unwelcome sexual intercourse, including while in the bank's vault. These acts, while constituting sexual harassment under Title VII, also could form the basis for the tort actions of:

Assault: Intentionally putting the victim in fear or apprehension, or both, of immediate unpermitted bodily touching.

Battery: Intentional unpermitted bodily touching.

Infliction of emotional distress: An intentional outrageous act that goes outside the bounds of common decency, for which the law will provide a remedy.

False imprisonment: Intentionally preventing the harassee's exit from a confined space.

Interference with contractual relations: Intentionally causing the harassee to be unable to perform her employment contract as agreed upon.

These cases are generally heard by juries, with the possible result of unlimited compensatory and punitive damages. In addition, the harasser's action could form the basis of criminal prosecution for, at a minimum, criminal assault, battery, and rape. Of course, the criminal cases would be against the harasser, rather than the employer, and would result in punishment for the harasser, rather than money damages to the harassee (unless the state has a victim assistance or restitution program). In *Miller v. Washington Workplace,*[30] the employee was assaulted and battered by her boss after simply asking for the company's sexual harassment policy!

Management Tips

Sexual harassment doesn't have to be the employer's worst nightmare. Don't ever expect to have absolute control over every employee in the workplace, but following the tips below can substantially decrease the chances of a recalcitrant employee causing liability.

Zero tolerance, both in word and deed, should be the rule. The EEOC and courts take the position that the best thing an employer can do to effectively keep sexual harassment complaints to a minimum—and to minimize liability for sexual harassment complaints that do occur—is to take a preventive approach. This may include the following:

- Adopt an anti-sexual harassment policy discouraging such activity. This should be separate from the general anti-discrimination policy, and every employee should be aware of it.

- Make sure, from the top down, that all employees understand that sexual harassment in the workplace simply will not be tolerated. *Period.*

- Create and disseminate information about an effective reporting mechanism for harassees.

- After adopting the policy, don't let it sit in a drawer somewhere. Use it.

- Provide employees with training and/or information apprising them of what sexual harassment is and of what specific activities are appropriate and inappropriate in the workplace. This will go a very long way toward decreasing potential liability for the employer.

- Ensure that reported incidents of sexual harassment are taken seriously by supervisors and others involved in reporting. Do not tell the employee to "get over it," or that it is to be expected.

- Ensure that the training employees receive is effective and answers their questions and concerns.

- Keep in mind that creating an atmosphere in which sexual harassment is not tolerated is a big part of what the EEOC and courts want employers to do. Operationalize this on a real-life basis. That is, when employees engage in activity that helps to create an atmosphere that accepts harassing activity, challenge it. Don't tolerate the jokes, sneers, leers, teasing, gestures, and so forth.

- Promptly investigate all sexual harassment claims and circulate information only on a need-to-know basis.

- Keep an eye out for anti-female animus that also may constitute sexual harassment.

- If investigation warrants discipline for the harasser, ensure that immediate, appropriate corrective action is taken. Make sure the corrective action is commensurate with the policy violation. Termination is not the response to every sexual harassment claim.

- Work to keep the workplace friendly and open. Having a workplace free of sexual harassment does not mean employees can't still work in a pleasant, respectful atmosphere.

Chapter Summary

- Consensual activity is not a violation of Title VII.
- Unwelcome sexual advances that cause one gender to work under conditions or terms of employment different from those of the other gender constitute sexual harassment for which the employer may be liable.
- Employers will be responsible only if the sexual harassment is severe and pervasive.
- Activity need not be sexual in nature to constitute sexual harassment.
- Employers should treat all sexual harassment complaints seriously and act on them quickly.
- Prevention is imperative to avoid sexual harassment claims and lessen liability. The employer must make it clear that sexual harassment will not be tolerated. This should be clearly stated and followed up and monitored by appropriate mechanisms.
- Employers need a strong anti-sexual harassment policy that is vigorously enforced.

Chapter-End Questions

1. Employer uses the "f***" word frequently in the workplace and makes statements to employee such as, in regard to an installer, he was always confused and bet that as a baby he "probably didn't know which tit to suck"; and in discussing a motorcycle seat, cupped his hands and said he would be "glad to fit employee's ass for the right size seat." Is this likely to be successful as a sexual harassment suit? [*LaPorte v. Fireplace and Patio Center, Inc.*, 2004 U.S. Dist. LEXIS 2113 (W.D. Ill. 2004).]

2. Employee, a 33-year-old unmarried male, is frequently teased by the other males in his plant about being unmarried and still living at home with his mother. Is this sexual harassment? [*Goluszek v. Smith*, 697 F. Supp. 1452 (N.D. Ill. 1988).]

3. Employee sues employer for sexual harassment because her supervisor once touched her on her back and made an "untoward" statement to her. Will she win? Explain. [*Strickland v. Sears, Roebuck and Co.*, 693 F. Supp. 403 (E.D. Va. 1988).]

4. Two employees, Marge and Ben, are having a relationship that later turns sour. When Marge does not get the promotion she goes up for, she sues the employer for sexual harassment, alleging it was committed by her ex-boyfriend Ben, who has, since their breakup, left Marge alone. Will Marge win her suit? [*Koster v. Chase Manhattan Bank*, 687 F. Supp. 848 (S.D.N.Y. 1988).]

5. Dennis comes up to his supervisor, Mae, at a Christmas party and tells Mae he wants to sue for sexual harassment. Mae asks what happened. Dennis says that Linda came over to him and tweaked his cheek and called him sweetie. Dennis pursues the case. Does he win? Why or why not? [Facts from business consulting session attendee]

6. An employer asks an employee to go to dinner and drinks and said they could "see what happen(ed) after that." Is this enough for a sexual harassment claim? [*Mireault v. Northeast Motel Assocs., LP*, 20 Mass. L. Rep. 614; 2006 Mass. Super. LEXIS 65 (2006).]

7. A female employee has an operation on her breast, and when she returns to work, a male employee "jokingly" asks to see the scar. Actionable sexual harassment? [*Keziah v. W. M. Brown Son, Inc.,* 683 F. Supp. 542 (W.D.N.C. 1988).]

8. Joan, a female manager, asks Margaret, one of her subordinates, out on a date. When Margaret refuses, Joan becomes mean to her at work and rates Margaret's work poorly on her next evaluation. Margaret wants to bring a sexual harassment claim but feels she cannot do so since her boss is female. Is Margaret correct?

9. A truck driver trainer sexually harassed a trainee and she brought suit for sexual harassment. The trainer claimed to have power over the trainee, but in reality, the trainer was not a supervisory employee. Is it possible for her to make her claim of quid pro quo sexual harassment if the trainer actually is not a supervisor? [*Vernarsky v. Covenant Transport, Inc.,* 2003 U.S. Dist. LEXIS 18330 (E.D. Tenn. 2003).]

10. Trudy comes to Pat, her supervisor, and tells her that Jack has been sexually harassing her by making suggestive remarks, comments, and jokes; constantly asking her for dates; and using every available opportunity to touch her. Pat has been friends with Jack for a long time and can't imagine Jack would do such a thing. Pat is hesitant to move on Trudy's complaint. What should Pat do?

End Notes

1. Nina Mandell, "St. Louis Woman Awarded $95 Million after Former Boss Allegedly Masturbated on Her," *The New York Daily News,* 6/10/11, http://articles.nydailynews.com/2011-06-10/news/29663292_1_verdict-harassment-runaway-jury.

2. *Newsweek,* 7/26/2010, p. 16.

3. "Final Judgment in EEOC Sexual Harassment Case against Custom Companies Tops $1.1M: Federal Judge Cites Involvement of Top Management in Permitting Harassment and in Retaliating Against Victims," EEOC press release, 3/8/2007; *EEOC v. Custom Companies, Inc., et al,* Nos. 02-C-3768, 03-C2293, Mem. Op. & Order (N.D. Ill. March 8, 2007).

4. "Lawyer Sues Ex-firm for Naked Male Retreat," News.com, 9/28/2010, http://www.news.com.au/business/business-smarts/lawyer-sues-ex-firm-for-naked-male-retreat/story-e6frfm9r-1225930875532.

5. "Woman Spanked at Work Awarded $1.7M: Alarm Company Employee Found Camaraderie-Building Exercise Humiliating," MSNBC, 4/28/2006, http://www.msnbc.msn.com/id/12534543/ns/us_news-life/.

6. Tamara Loomis, "Record $5.5M Accord Reached in Doctor Harass Case," Law.com, 4/10/2003, http://www.law.com/jsp/article.jsp?id=900005534973&slreturn=1&hbxlogin=1.

7. "Penis Pump Judge Gets 4-Year Jail Term," *USA Today,* 8/18/2006, http://www.usatoday.com/news/nation/2006-08-18-judge-sentenced_x.htm.

8. William Keck, "The Time Is Right for Barker," *USA Today,* 5/14/2007, http://www.usatoday.com/life/people/2007-05-13-bob-barker_N.htm.

9. "Arnold Apologizes for 'Bad Behavior'," Fox News, 10/3/2003 http://www.foxnews.com/story/0,2933,98883,00.html.

10. Lauren Johnson, "O'Reilly Settles Sex Harass Suit: Lawyer for Fox News Announces Settlement with Fox Producer," CBS News, 10/28/2004, http://www.cbsnews.com/stories/2004/10/20/entertainment/main650282.shtml.

11. 139 F.R.D. 657 (D. Minn. 1991).

12. David Hechler, *A White Buffalo,* March 31, 2003, at p. A1.

13. Clara Bingham and Laura Leedy Gansler, *Class Action: The Story of Lois Jenson and the Landmark Case That Changed Sexual Harassment Law* (New York: Doubleday, 2002).

14. Parke Chapman, "C B Richard Ellis Denies Sexual Harassment Claims," *National Real Estate Investor,* 11/1/2004, http://nreionline.com/mag/real_estate_cb_richard_ellis_16/; "Settlement: Real Estate Brokerage Harassment," 10/16/2007, http://www.lawyersandsettlements.com/settlements/09555/real-estate-brokerage-harassment.html.

15. "Dial Settles Sexual Harassment Lawsuit for $10M," H.R. BLR.com, 5/1/2003, http://hr.blr.com/HR-news/Discrimination/Sexual-Harassment/Dial-Settles-Sexual-Harassment-Lawsuit-for-10M/.

16. Jesse Ellison, "The Military's Secret Shame," *Newsweek,* April 11, 2011, p. 40.

17. *Ellison v. Brady,* 924 F.2d 872, 881, n.15 (9th Cir. 1991), quoting from the MSPB update study, U.S. Merit Systems Protection Board, *Sexual Harassment in the Federal Government: An Update,* (Washington, DC: U.S. Government Printing Office, 1988), p. 42.

18. 760 F. Supp. 1486, 1506–07 (M.D. Fla. 1991).

19. California Government Code § 12950.1 (AB 1825).

20. Notice that we do not use the term "sexual favors." It hardly makes sense to do so when the activity is unwanted. Making the "request" sound more palatable only masks the truth. We choose to simply call it what it is: a request for sexual activity of some kind.

21. Dana Mattioli, "More Men Make Harassment Claims," *The Wall Street Journal,* 3/23/2010, http://online.wsj.com/article/SB10001424052748704117304575137881438719028.html.

22. 523 U.S. 75 (1998).

23. 673 F. Supp (1458 E.D. Mo 1987).

24. Susan M. Heathfield, "The Scoop on Love Contracts: Do Dating Co-workers Need to Sign Love Contracts?" http://humanresources.about.com/od/glossaryl/qt/love_contract.htm.

25. 672 F. Supp. 1205 (D.R.I. 1991).

26. 510 U.S. 17 (1993).

27. 523 U.S. 575 (1998).

28. 895 F.2d 1469 (3d Cir. 1990).

29. 542 U.S. 129 (2004).

30. 298 F. Supp. 2d 364 (E.D. Va 2004).

Cases

and the person who hired Vinson. Vinson alleged that in the beginning Taylor was "fatherly" toward her and made no sexual advances, but eventually he asked her to go out to dinner. During the course of the meal Taylor suggested that he and Vinson go to a motel to have sexual relations. At first she refused, but out of what she described as fear of losing her job, she eventually agreed. Taylor thereafter made repeated demands upon Vinson for sexual activity, usually at the branch, both during and after business hours. She estimated that over the next several years she had intercourse with him some 40 or 50 times. In addition, she testified that Taylor fondled her in front of other employees, followed her into the women's restroom when she went there alone, exposed himself to her, and even forcibly raped her on several occasions. These activities ceased in 1977 when Vinson started going with a steady boyfriend.

Courts have applied Title VII protection to racial harassment and nothing in Title VII suggests that a hostile environment based on discriminatory *sexual* harassment should not be likewise prohibited. The Guidelines thus appropriately drew from, and were fully consistent with, the existing case law.

Of course, not all workplace conduct that may be described as "harassment" affects a "term, condition, or privilege" of employment within the meaning of Title VII. For instance, mere utterance of an ethnic or racial epithet which engenders offensive feelings in an employee would not affect the condition of employment to a sufficiently significant degree to create an abusive working environment. For sexual harassment to be actionable, it must be sufficiently severe or pervasive to alter the conditions of the victim's employment and create an abusive working environment. Vinson's allegations in this case—which include not only pervasive harassment, but also criminal conduct of the most serious nature—are plainly sufficient to state a claim for hostile environment sexual harassment.

The District Court's conclusion that no actionable harassment occurred might have rested on its earlier finding that if Vinson and Taylor had engaged in intimate or sexual relations, that relationship was a voluntary one. But the fact that sex-related conduct was "voluntary" in the

sense that the complainant was not forced to participate against her will, is not a defense to a sexual harassment suit brought under Title VII. The gravamen of any sexual harassment claim is the alleged sexual advances were "unwelcome." While the question whether particular conduct was indeed unwelcome presents difficult problems of proof and turns largely on credibility determinations committed to the trier of fact, the District Court in this case erroneously focused on the "voluntariness" of Vinson's participation in the claimed sexual episodes. The correct inquiry is whether Vinson, by her conduct, indicated that the alleged sexual advances were unwelcome, not whether her participation in sexual intercourse was voluntary.

The district court admitted into evidence testimony about Vinson's "dress and personal fantasies." The court of appeals stated that testimony had no place in the litigation, on the basis that Vinson's voluntariness in submitting to Taylor's advances was immaterial to her sexual harassment claim. While "voluntariness" in the sense of consent is not a defense to such a claim, it does not follow that a complainant's sexually provocative speech or dress is irrelevant as a matter of law in determining whether she found particular sexual advances welcome. To the contrary, such evidence is obviously relevant. The EEOC Guidelines emphasize that the trier of fact must determine the existence of sexual harassment in light of "the record as a whole" and the "totality of circumstances," such as the nature of the sexual advances and the context in which the alleged incidents occurred.

In sum we hold that a claim of "hostile environment" sexual harassment gender discrimination is actionable under Title VII. AFFIRMED.

Case Questions

1. As a manager, what would you have done if Vinson had come to you with her story?
2. Under the circumstances, should it matter that Vinson "voluntarily" had sex with Taylor? That she received her regular promotions? Explain.
3. As a manager, how would you determine who to believe?

Ellison v. Brady *924 F.2d 872 (9th Cir. 1991)*

Case 3

An employee brought a sexual harassment suit because, among other things, her co-worker, whom she barely knew, kept sending her personal letters. The court found that while some may think it only a small matter, viewed from the employee's perspective as a female in a society in which females are often the victims of violence, the action was offensive and a violation of Title VII.

Beezer, J.

***

The case presents the important issue of what test should be applied to determine whether conduct is sufficiently severe or pervasive to alter the conditions of employment and create a hostile working environment.

Ellison worked as a revenue agent for the IRS in San Mateo, California. During her initial training in 1984 she met Sterling Gray, another trainee also assigned to that office. The two never became friends and did not work closely together. Gray's desk was twenty feet from Ellison's, two rows behind and one row over.

In June of 1986 when no one else was in the office, Gray asked Ellison to go to lunch. She accepted. They went past Gray's house to pick up his son's forgotten lunch and Gray gave Ellison a tour of his house. Ellison alleges that after that June lunch, Gray began to pester her with unnecessary questions and hang around her desk.

On October 9, when Gray asked Ellison out for a drink after work, she declined, but suggested lunch the following week. Ellison did not want to have lunch alone with him and she tried to stay away from the office during lunch time. The next week Gray asked her out to lunch and she did not go.

On October 22, 1986 Gray handed Ellison a note written on a telephone message slip which read: "I cried over you last night and I'm totally drained today. I have never been in such constant termoil [sic]. Thank you for talking with me. I could not stand to feel your hatred for another day." Ellison was shocked at the note, became frightened and left the room. Gray followed Ellison into the hallway and demanded that she talk to him. Ellison left the building. While Gray reported this to her supervisor and asked to try to handle it herself, she asked a male co-worker to talk to Gray and tell him she was not interested in him and to leave her alone. The next day, Gray called in sick. Ellison did not work the following day, Friday, and on Monday started a four-week training session in Missouri.

While Ellison was at the training session, Gray mailed her a card and a three-page, typed, single spaced letter. Ellison described the letter as "twenty times, a hundred times weirder" than the prior note. In part, Gray wrote:

> I know that you are worth knowing with or without sex. . . . Leaving aside the hassles and disasters of recent weeks, I have enjoyed you so much over these past few months. Watching you. Experiencing you from O so far away. Admiring your style and elan. . . . Don't you think it odd that two people who have never even talked together, alone, are striking off such intense sparks . . . I will [write] another letter in the near future.

Ellison stated that she thought Gray was "crazy. I thought he was nuts. I didn't know what he would do next. I was frightened." Ellison immediately called her supervisor and reported this and told her she was frightened and wanted one of them transferred. Gray was told many times over the next few weeks not to contact Ellison in any way. On November 24 Gray transferred to the San Francisco office. Ellison returned from Missouri in late November. After three weeks in San Francisco, Gray filed a grievance to return to San Mateo and as part of the settlement in Gray's favor, he agreed to be transferred back provided he spend four more months (a total of six months) in San Francisco and promise not to bother Ellison. When Ellison learned of Gray's request to return in a letter from her supervisor indicating Gray would return after a six-month separation, she said she was "frantic" and filed a formal sexual harassment complaint with IRS. The letter to Ellison also said that they could revisit the issue if there was further need.

Gray sought joint counseling. He wrote another letter to Ellison seeking to maintain the idea that he and Ellison had a relationship.

We do not agree with the standard set forth in *Rabidue*. We believe that Gray's conduct was sufficiently severe and pervasive to alter the conditions of Ellison's employment and create an abusive working environment. We believe that, in evaluating the severity and pervasiveness of sexual harassment, we should focus on the perspective of the victim. If we examined whether a reasonable person would engage in allegedly harassing conduct, we would run the risk of reinforcing the prevailing level of discrimination. Harassers could continue to harass merely because a particular discriminatory practice was common, and victims of harassment would have no remedy.

We therefore prefer to analyze harassment from the victim's perspective. A complete understanding of the victim's view requires, among other things, an analysis of the different perspectives of men and women. Conduct that many men consider unobjectionable may offend many women. See, e.g., *Lipsett v. University of Puerto Rico,* 864 F.2d 881, 898 (1st Cir. 1988) ("A male supervisor might believe, for example, that it is legitimate for him to tell a female subordinate that she has a 'great figure' or 'nice legs.' The female subordinate, however, may find such comments offensive"); Yates, 819 F.2d at 637, n.2 ("men and women are vulnerable in different ways and offended by different behavior"). See also, Ehrenreich, Pluralist Myths and Powerless Men: The Ideology of Reasonableness in Sexual Harassment Law, 99 Yale L. J. 1177, 1207–1208 (1990) (men tend to view some forms of sexual harassment as "harmless social interactions to which only overly-sensitive women would object"); Abrams, Gender Discrimination and the Transformation of Workplace Norms, 42 Vand. L. Rev. 1183, 1203 (1989) (the characteristically male view depicts sexual harassment as comparatively harmless amusement).

We realize that there is a broad range of viewpoints among women as a group, but we realize that many women share common concerns which men do not necessarily share. For example, because women are disproportionately victims of rape and sexual assault, women have stronger incentives to be concerned with sexual behavior. Women who are victims of mild forms of sexual harassment may understandably worry whether a harasser's conduct is merely a prelude to violent sexual assault. Men, who are rarely victims of sexual assault, may view sexual conduct in a vacuum without a full appreciation of the social setting or the underlying threat of violence that a woman may perceive.

In order to shield employers from having to accommodate the idiosyncratic concerns of the rare hypersensitive employee, we hold that a female plaintiff states a *prima facie* case of hostile environment sexual harassment when she alleges conduct that a reasonable woman would consider sufficiently severe or pervasive to alter the conditions of employment and create an abusive working environment. Of course, where male employees allege that co-workers engage in conduct which creates a hostile environment, the appropriate victim's perspective would be that of a reasonable man.

We adopt the perspective of a reasonable woman primarily because we believe that a gender-blind reasonable person standard tends to be male-biased and tends to systematically ignore the experiences of women. The reasonable woman standard does not establish a higher level of protection for women than men. Instead, a gender-conscious examination of sexual harassment enables women to participate in the workplace on an equal footing with men. By acknowledging and not trivializing the effects of sexual harassment on reasonable women, courts can work towards ensuring that neither men nor women will have to "run a gauntlet of sexual abuse in return for the privilege of being allowed to work and make a living."

We note that the reasonable woman victim standard we adopt today classifies conduct as unlawful sexual harassment even when harassers do not realize that their conduct creates a hostile working environment. Well-intentioned compliments by co-workers or supervisors can form the basis of a sexual harassment cause of action if a reasonable victim of the same gender as plaintiff would consider the comments sufficiently severe or pervasive to alter a condition of employment and create an abusive working environment. That is because Title VII is not a fault-based tort scheme. Title VII is aimed at the consequences or effects of an employment practice and not the motivation of co-workers or employers.

The facts of this case illustrate the importance of considering the victim's perspective. Analyzing the facts from the alleged harasser's viewpoint, Gray could be portrayed as a modern-day Cyrano de Bergerac wishing no more than to woo Ellison with his words. There is no evidence that Gray harbored ill-will toward Ellison. He even offered in his "love letter" to leave her alone if she wished [though he said he would not be able to forget her]. Examined in this light, it is not difficult to see why the district court characterized Gray's conduct as isolated and trivial.

Ellison, however, did not consider the acts to be trivial. Gray's first note shocked and frightened her. After receiving the three-page letter, she became really upset and frightened again. She immediately requested that she or Gray be transferred. Her supervisor's prompt response suggests that she too did not consider the conduct trivial. When Ellison learned that Gray arranged to return to San Mateo, she immediately asked to transfer and she immediately filed an official complaint.

We cannot say as a matter of law that Ellison's reaction was idiosyncratic or hyper-sensitive. We believe that a reasonable woman could have had a similar reaction. After receiving the first bizarre note from Gray, a person she barely knew, Ellison asked a co-worker to tell Gray to leave her alone. Despite her request, Gray sent her a long, passionate, disturbing letter. He told her he had been "watching" and "experiencing" her; he made repeated references to sex; and he said he would write again. Ellison had no way of knowing what Gray would do next. A reasonable woman could consider Gray's conduct, as alleged by Ellison, sufficiently severe and pervasive to alter a condition of employment and create an abusive working environment.

Sexual harassment is a major problem in the workplace. Adopting the victim's perspective ensures that courts will not "sustain ingrained notions of reasonable behavior fashioned by the offenders." Congress did not enact Title VII to codify prevailing sexist prejudices. To the contrary, "Congress designed Title VII to prevent the perpetuation of stereotypes and a sense of degradation which serve to close or discourage employment opportunities for women." We hope that over time both men and women will learn what conduct offends reasonable members of the other gender. When employers and employees internalize the standard of workplace conduct we establish today, the current gap in perception between the genders will be bridged. REVERSED and REMANDED.

Case Questions

1. Do you agree with the court's use of the "reasonable victim" standard? Explain.

2. Do you think the standard creates problems for management? If so, what are they? If not, why not?

3. Do you think Ellison was being "overly sensitive"? What would you have done if you had been the supervisor to whom she reported the incidents?

Faragher v. City of Boca Raton *524 U.S. 775 (1998)*

A former city lifeguard sued the city under Title VII for sexual harassment based on the conduct of her supervisors. The Supreme Court held that an employer is subject to vicarious liability under Title VII for actionable discrimination caused by a supervisor, but the employer may raise an affirmative defense that looks to the reasonableness of the employer's conduct in seeking to prevent and correct harassing conduct and to the reasonableness of the employee's conduct in seeking to avoid harm. The Court held that the employer was vicariously liable here because it failed to exercise reasonable care to prevent harassing behavior.

This case calls for identification of the circumstances under which an employer may be held liable under Title VII of the Civil Rights Act for the acts of a supervisory employee whose sexual harassment of subordinates has created a hostile work environment amounting to employment discrimination. We hold that an employer is vicariously liable for actionable discrimination caused by a supervisor, but subject to an affirmative defense looking to the reasonableness of the employer's conduct as well as that of a plaintiff victim.

Souter, J.

***

Between 1985 and 1990, while attending college, petitioner Beth Ann Faragher worked part time and during the summers as an ocean lifeguard for the Marine Safety Section of the Parks and Recreation Department of respondent, the City of Boca Raton, Florida (City). During this period, Faragher's immediate supervisors were

Bill Terry, David Silverman, and Robert Gordon. In June 1990, Faragher resigned. In 1992, Faragher brought an action against Terry, Silverman, and the City, asserting claims under Title VII, and Florida law. The complaint alleged that Terry and Silverman were agents of the City, and that their conduct created a "sexually hostile atmosphere" that amounted to discrimination in the "terms, conditions, and privileges" of her employment at the beach by repeatedly subjecting Faragher and other female lifeguards to "uninvited and offensive touching," by making lewd remarks, and by speaking of women in offensive terms.

Throughout Faragher's employment with the City, Terry served as Chief of the Marine Safety Division, with authority to hire new lifeguards (subject to the approval of higher management), to supervise all aspects of the lifeguards' work assignments, to engage in counseling, to deliver oral reprimands, and to make a record of any such discipline. Silverman and Gordon were captains and responsible for making the lifeguards' daily assignments, and for supervising their work and fitness training. The lifeguards and supervisors were stationed at the city beach. The lifeguards had no significant contact with higher city officials like the Recreation Superintendent.

In February 1986, the City adopted a sexual harassment policy, which it stated in a memorandum from the City Manager addressed to all employees. In May 1990, the City revised the policy and reissued a statement of it. Although the City may actually have circulated the memos and statements to some employees, it completely failed to disseminate its policy among employees of the Marine Safety Section, with the result that Terry, Silverman, Gordon, and many lifeguards were unaware of it.

Faragher did not complain to higher management about Terry or Silverman. In April 1990, however, two months before Faragher's resignation, Nancy Ewanchew, a former lifeguard, wrote to Richard Bender, the City's Personnel Director, complaining that Terry and Silverman had harassed her and other female lifeguards. Following investigation of this complaint, the City found that Terry and Silverman had behaved improperly, reprimanded them, and required them to choose between a suspension without pay or the forfeiture of annual leave.

Since our decision in *Meritor,* Courts of Appeals have struggled to derive manageable standards to govern employer liability for hostile environment harassment perpetrated by supervisory employees. While indicating the substantive contours of the hostile environments forbidden by Title VII, our cases have established few definite rules for determining when an employer will be liable for a discriminatory environment that is otherwise actionably abusive.

A "master is subject to liability for the torts of his servants committed while acting in the scope of their employment." Restatement § 219(1). This doctrine has traditionally defined the "scope of employment" as including conduct "of the kind [a servant] is employed to perform," occurring "substantially within the authorized time and space limits," and "actuated, at least in part, by a purpose to serve the master," but as excluding an intentional use of force "unexpectable by the master."

A justification for holding the offensive behavior within the scope of Terry's and Silverman's employment was well put in Judge Barkett's dissent: "[A] pervasively hostile work environment of sexual harassment is never (one would hope) authorized, but the supervisor is clearly charged with maintaining a productive, safe work environment. The supervisor directs and controls the conduct of the employees, and the manner of doing so may inure to the employer's benefit or detriment, including subjecting the employer to Title VII liability."

It is by now well recognized that hostile environment sexual harassment by supervisors (and, for that matter, co-employees) is a persistent problem in the workplace. An employer can, in a general sense, reasonably anticipate the possibility of such conduct occurring in its workplace, and one might justify the assignment of the burden of the untoward behavior to the employer as one of the costs of doing business, to be charged to the enterprise rather than the victim. As noted, developments like this occur from time to time in the law of agency.

We agree with Faragher that in implementing Title VII it makes sense to hold an employer vicariously liable for some tortious conduct of a supervisor made possible by abuse of his supervisory authority. The agency relationship affords contact with an employee subjected to a supervisor's sexual harassment, and the victim may well be reluctant to accept the risks of blowing the whistle on a superior. When a person with supervisory authority discriminates in the terms and conditions of subordinates' employment, his actions necessarily draw upon his superior position over the people who report to him, or those under them, whereas an employee generally cannot check a supervisor's abusive conduct the same way that she might deal with abuse from a co-worker. When a fellow employee harasses, the victim can walk away or tell the offender where to go, but it may be difficult to offer such responses to a supervisor, whose "power to supervise—[which may be] to hire and fire, and to set work schedules and pay rates—does not disappear . . . when he chooses to harass through insults and offensive gestures rather than directly with threats of firing or promises of promotion." Recognition of employer liability when discriminatory misuse of supervisory authority alters the terms and conditions of a victim's employment is underscored by the fact that the employer has a greater opportunity to guard against misconduct by supervisors than by common workers; employers have greater opportunity and incentive to screen them, train them, and monitor their performance.

In order to accommodate the principle of vicarious liability for harm caused by misuse of supervisory authority, as well as Title VII's equally basic policies of encouraging forethought by employers and saving action by objecting employees, we adopt the following holding in this case and in *Burlington Industries, Inc. v. Ellerth,* also decided today. An employer is subject to vicarious liability to a victimized employee for an actionable hostile environment created by a supervisor with immediate (or successively higher) authority over the employee.

When no tangible employment action is taken, a defending employer may raise an affirmative defense to liability or damages, subject to proof by a preponderance of the evidence. The defense comprises two necessary elements: (a) that the employer exercised reasonable care to prevent and correct promptly any sexually harassing behavior, and (b) that the plaintiff employee unreasonably failed to take advantage of any preventive or corrective opportunities provided by the employer or to avoid harm otherwise.

While proof that an employer had promulgated an antiharassment policy with complaint procedure is not necessary in every instance as a matter of law, the need for a stated policy suitable to the employment circumstances may appropriately be addressed in any case when litigating the first element of the defense. And while proof that an employee failed to fulfill the corresponding obligation of reasonable care to avoid harm is not limited to showing an unreasonable failure to use any complaint procedure provided by the employer, a demonstration of such failure will normally suffice to satisfy the employer's burden under the second element of the defense. No

affirmative defense is available, however, when the supervisor's harassment culminates in a tangible employment action, such as discharge, demotion, or undesirable reassignment.

Applying these rules here, it is undisputed that these supervisors "were granted virtually unchecked authority" over their subordinates, "directly controll[ing] and supervis[ing] all aspects of [Faragher's] day-to-day activities." It is also clear that Faragher and her colleagues were "completely isolated from the City's higher management."

While the City would have an opportunity to raise an affirmative defense if there were any serious prospect of its presenting one, it appears from the record that any such avenue is closed. The City entirely failed to disseminate its policy against sexual harassment among the beach employees and its officials made no attempt to keep track of the conduct of supervisors like Terry and Silverman. The City's policy did not include any assurance that the harassing supervisors could be bypassed in registering complaints. Under such circumstances, we hold as a matter of law that the City could not be found to have exercised reasonable care to prevent the supervisors' harassing conduct. Unlike the employer of a small workforce, who might expect that sufficient care to prevent tortious behavior could be exercised informally, those responsible for city operations could not reasonably have thought that precautions against hostile environments in any one of many departments in far-flung locations could be effective without communicating some formal policy against harassment, with a sensible complaint procedure. REVERSED and REMANDED.

Case Questions

1. How could the city have avoided this outcome? Explain.

2. Do you think that it would have made sense for the city to consider the particulars of the circumstances here, such as that these were lifeguards, in a remote location, who by the nature of the job would be dressed in fairly little clothing, and who, because of the environment (the beach and recreational facilities) might need a different approach to sexual harassment than, say, office employees? Explain.

3. What do you think of the Court's affirmative defense given to employers and employees? What are the pros and cons?

Chapter 10

Affinity Orientation Discrimination

Learning Objectives

When you finish studying this chapter, you should be able to:

LO1 Relate the history of the modern gay rights movement.

LO2 Name the states that include gays and lesbians in their anti-discrimination laws as well as Title VII's position.

LO3 Give the pros and cons of employers being inclusive of gay and lesbian employees.

LO4 Discuss how some courts have circumvented the exclusion of gays and lesbians from Title VII coverage.

LO5 Identify whether same-gender sexual harassment is covered by Title VII.

LO6 Discuss the workplace issues involving transgenders.

LO7 Identify some of the employment benefits issues for gays and lesbians.

LO8 List some ways that employers can address gay and lesbian issues in the workplace.

Opening Scenarios

SCENARIO 1

1 | Scenario

A third-year female law student is given an offer to come to work for a law firm after graduation. She accepts the offer. Later, the lawyers at the law firm find out that the law student is planning on engaging in a symbolic ceremony of commitment with another female. The ceremony is private and does not have the legal effect of marriage. The law firm takes back its "offer" (actually now a contract) after it discovers the law student is a lesbian. The law student sues for employment discrimination. Does she win? Why or why not?

SCENARIO 2

2 | Scenario

A male airline pilot is terminated after he puts in a request for medical leave, in accordance with company policy, to have sexual reassignment surgery to change anatomically from male to female. Is this illegal discrimination? Why or why not?

SCENARIO 3

3 | Scenario

Sylvio's immediate supervisor, Leroy, has been giving Sylvio sexually suggestive looks and making sexually suggestive comments. Sylvio is feeling extremely uncomfortable about it and fears for his job. However, Sylvio thinks that because both he and Leroy are males, there can be no sexual harassment. Is Sylvio correct?

Statutory Basis

It shall be an unlawful employment practice for an employer—

(1) to fail or refuse to hire or to discharge any individual, or otherwise to discriminate against any individual with respect to his compensation, terms, conditions, or privileges of employment, because of such individual's . . . sex. [Title VII of the Civil Rights Act of 1964, as amended. 42 U.S.C. § 2000e-2(a).]

affinity orientation
Whom one is attracted to for personal and intimate relationships.

The above does *not* prohibit discrimination on the basis of **affinity orientation**.

[N]or shall any State deprive any person of life, liberty, or property, without due process of law; nor deny to any person within its jurisdiction the equal protection of the laws. [Amendment XIV of the U.S. Constitution.]

Out of the Closet

See Exhibit 10.1, "Terms to Know."

"Look!" the angry gentleman in the audience said gruffly as the diversity consultant walked into the room and up to the stage in preparation for conducting a training session. "Does this diversity training mean that I have to deal with homosexuals? Because if it does, I'm not doing it! Homosexuality is against my religion and I just don't think it's right!"

This employee's attitude is not unique. Some of the social trends that are provoking such reactions include

- An Arkansas farmer acknowledges spreading three tons of manure along the route of a gay rights parade, saying he was exercising his constitutional right to free speech.[1]

433

Exhibit 10.1 *Terms to Know*

TERMS TO KNOW

Terms may evolve over time to reflect changes in thinking and/or preferences within the LGBT community.

Catalyst offers these definitions but encourages readers to recognize that different language may be used by different people, companies, and countries. Also, it is important to respect the language individuals use to identify themselves, regardless of how they are labeled by others.

Bisexual: A person whose emotional, sexual, or romantic attractions are to both women and men. Bisexuals need not be "equally" attracted to, or have had equal sexual experience with, both sexes. Nor do they need to have attractions toward both sexes at the same time.

Closeted/In the closet: LGBT individuals who do not openly disclose their sexual orientation to others.

Coming out of the closet: The process of self-acceptance and/or disclosure of LGBT identity to others. People can disclose to none, some, or all of the people they know.

Gay/Homosexual: A woman or a man whose emotional, sexual, or romantic attractions are primarily to members of the same gender.

Gender expression: How an individual manifests a sense of femininity or masculinity through appearance, behavior, grooming, and/or dress.

Gender identity: One's inner sense of being a woman or a man, regardless of biological sex; different from sexual orientation.

Heterosexism: The attitude that heterosexuality is the only valid sexual orientation. Heterosexism denies, denigrates, and stigmatizes any non-heterosexual form of behavior, relationship, or community.

Homophobia: Disapproval of, fear of, hatred of, or hostility toward people who are identified as, or assumed to be, LGBT.

Intersex: Individuals with sex chromosomes or biological/physical characteristics that are neither exclusively female nor male.

Lesbian: A woman whose emotional, sexual, or romantic attractions are primarily to other women.

LGBT: The acronym most commonly used in Canada and the United States to refer to the lesbian, gay, bisexual, and transgender community. The acronym can vary in a number of ways, including GLBT and GLB, and can include additional letters, such as Q (queer; also questioning), I (intersex), and A (straight ally).

Non-LGBT: Anyone who does not identify as LGBT; most commonly refers to straight/heterosexual individuals.

Out employee: An employee who discloses his or her LGBT identity to a few, some, or all of his or her co-workers.

Queer: A fluid term with numerous meanings. It is commonly used to describe sexual orientation and/or gender identity or gender expression that does not conform to heterosexual norms. The term is often used to refer to the LGBT community in general. It can be either a positive or a negative term, depending on the context in which it is used.

Questioning: Someone who is questioning their gender, sexual identity, or sexual orientation.

Sexual orientation: A term commonly used to refer to a person's emotional, romantic, or sexual attraction to individuals of a particular gender (women or men).

Straight/Heterosexual: A person whose emotional, sexual, or romantic attractions are primarily to members of the opposite sex.

Straight ally/LGBT supporter: An individual who identifies as non-LGBT and who supports the LGBT community in a direct way, such as attending LGBT ERG activities, acting as an executive sponsor, or volunteering at LGBT events.

Transgender: People who identify with the characteristics, roles, behaviors, or desires of a gender different from the one they were assigned at birth. This is an umbrella term that can be used to include transsexuals, cross-dressers, and other gender-variant people; some may use the umbrella term *trans-identified*.

Transsexual: Transsexuals change (or seek to change) their physical characteristics to a gender

continued

different from the one they were assigned at birth—for example, individuals born as males seek to change their sex to female. These changes can include sex reassignment surgery and/or hormone therapy.

Two-spirit. The term used by contemporary Native Americans and Aboriginal people in Canada to describe a masculine spirit and a feminine spirit living in the same body.

Source: Christine Silva and Anika K. Warren, *Building LGBT-Inclusive Workplaces: Engaging Organizations and Individuals in Change*, Catalyst.org, June 2009, http://www.catalyst.org/publication/328/building-lgbt-inclusive-workplaces-engaging-organizations-and-individuals-in-change.

- A Mississippi high school cancels its prom after a female student wanted to bring a female date.[2]
- Republican California governor Arnold Schwarzenegger causes an uproar when he calls Democratic legislators who oppose his budget "girlie men."[3]
- Hofstra Law School creates three $25,000 scholarships for the Equality of Lesbian, Gay, Bisexual and Transgender People in response to the university's decision to allow the military to recruit on campus, despite objections from faculty and students that the military's "Don't Ask, Don't Tell" policy is discriminatory.[4]
- A seven-year-old is scolded and forced to write repeatedly "I will never use the word 'gay' in school again" after he told a classmate about his lesbian mom in response to a question during recess by a classmate about the boy's parents.[5]
- Congress repeals "Don't Ask, Don't Tell" for gays in the military after 17 years.[6]
- As part of "dirty" recruiting tactics, parents of highly sought-after female high school basketball players are told that female coaches of competing teams are lesbian in what is called the "fear of a gay boogeyman who will make their daughters choose a lesbian sexual orientation" (partly in response, the NCAA is studying whether homophobia is a reason that the number of female head basketball coaches dropped from 79 percent in 1977 to 63 percent in 2002).
- The American Psychological Association issues a statement that mental health professionals should not tell gay clients they can become straight through therapy.[7]
- The U.S. Supreme Court rules in 2011 that anti-gay protests at funerals of American soldiers are protected by the First Amendment's freedom of speech. The Court affirms the appellate court's decision that the protests were "utterly distasteful" but protected because they were related to "matters of public concern." The protests were by members of the Westboro Baptist Church in Topeka, Kansas, who contend that the death of American soldiers is God's punishment for the country's tolerance of homosexuality. They have held over 43,000 such protests since 1991.
- The Episcopal Church consecrates its first openly lesbian bishop in 2010.[8]
- Two days after unanimously requesting that the county attorney find a way to enact an ordinance banning gays and lesbians from living in the county (saying, "We need to keep them out of here"), the Rhea County, Tennessee, commissioners withdraw the request because of the outcry outside the county.[9]

- The 2010 Census reports the number of married same-gender couples for the first time.[10]
- On April 15, 2010, President Obama issues a memorandum for the secretary of health and human services requesting that she initiate appropriate rulemaking and other relevant provisions of law to ensure that hospitals that participate in Medicare or Medicaid respect the rights of patients to designate visitors and not deny visitation privileges on the basis of, among other things, affinity orientation or gender identity.[11] The move came after a lesbian and the three children of her and her partner were denied visitation to see her partner, who suffered a brain aneurysm. The partner died the next day.[12]
- New York then-gubernatorial candidate Carl Paladino calls gay pride parades "disgusting," but lesbian sex "awesome."[13]
- A Georgia man believes his bedroom was set on fire because he was gay.[14]
- Connecticut, Massachusetts, Iowa, Vermont, New Hampshire, and the District of Columbia pass laws allowing same-gender marriage. New York's governor issues an edict that same-gender marriages legal in other states will be recognized as such for state employees.

As you can see from this sprinkling of recent items, same-gender affinity orientation[15] pushes a lot of buttons in society in general, and the workplace is just a microcosm of society. Though a bit gruff, the employee's assertion that homosexuality was against his religion, as stated in the opening sentences of the chapter, was a manifestation of that. This employee spoke for many others when he made his statement. The good thing is that he got it out onto the table where it could be discussed, put into perspective, and fitted into what his employer wanted the program to accomplish: less exposure to liability for violations of the law on this and other bases of discrimination. Since we understand that this sentiment is a fairly common one, let's take a bit of time up front to discuss it and give you some things to keep in mind as you go through the chapter.

From the battle with the Boy Scouts of America over whether the Philadelphia chapter could continue to discriminate against gays and stay in the city-owned building it had been in for 80 years, paying $1 annual rent rather than the $200,000 fair market value when the city had an anti-discrimination policy, to celebrity and adoptive mother Rosie O'Donnell announcing that she is a lesbian and taking up the issue of Florida law not permitting adoptions by gays and lesbians, to whether a transgender employee can lawfully sue for the use of certain toilet facilities, to the fining of basketball superstar Kobe Bryant for calling a referee a "faggot" in the heat of a game, the issue of affinity orientation is being debated and discussed not only in the United States, but all across the world, in every conceivable context. From whether gays and lesbians can marry and have children or can visit a partner in a hospital when only "family" members are permitted, to whether they can be terminated from a job because of being gay or lesbian or whether their partners can receive job benefits as spouses do, the issue has vast implications for people's everyday lives. And, of course, anything that is of any great social importance generally ends up finding its way into the workplace. The issue of affinity orientation is no different. The increasing prominence of the issue in the workplace and the legal implications arising therefrom make it essential that we include coverage here, despite the fact that Title VII does not prohibit discrimination on this basis.

Again, discrimination on the basis of affinity orientation is not included in Title VII. You may wonder, then, why we include a chapter on the topic. We do so because the fact that 21 state laws and the District of Columbia (see Exhibit 10.2,

---

Exhibit 10.2 *State Laws Banning Workplace Discrimination on the Basis of Affinity Orientation or Gender Identity*

- State laws prohibiting discrimination based on affinity orientation, gender identity, or both:

California (1992)*	New Hampshire (1998)
Colorado (2007)*	New Jersey (1992)*
Connecticut (1991)*	New Mexico (2003)*
Delaware (2009)	New York (1992)
Hawaii (1991)	Nevada (1999)
Illinois (2006)*	Oregon (2008)*
Iowa (2007)*	Rhode Island (1995)
Maine (2005)*	Vermont (1991)*
Maryland (2001)	Washington (2006)*
Massachusetts (1989)*	Wisconsin (1982)*
Minnesota (1993)*	Washington, D.C. (1977)*

- An executive order prohibits discrimination in the federal civilian workforce and mandates that security clearances not be denied based on affinity orientation.
- State courts, commissions, agencies, or attorney generals have interpreted the existing law to include some protection against discrimination against transgender individuals in

Florida	Hawaii	New York

- At least 532 cities or counties prohibit discrimination in public and/or private employment. Jurisdictions include

Fayetteville, AR	Lawrence, KS	Portland, OR
Phoenix, AZ	Louisville, KY	Philadelphia, PA
Boulder, CO	New Orleans, LA	Charleston, SC
Wilmington, DE	Detroit, MI	Minnehaha County, SD
Broward County, FL	St. Louis, MO	Austin, TX
Atlanta, GA	Durham, NC	Salt Lake County, UT
Ames, IA	Albuquerque, NM	Alexandria, VA
Chicago, IL	New York, NY	Seattle, WA
Bloomington, IN	Toledo, OH	Morgantown, WV

*Law also includes protection based on gender identity
Source: Human Rights Campaign, www.hrc.org.

Exhibit 10.3 *Numbers and Percentages of Employers with Non-discrimination Policies That Include Sexual Orientation, Gender Identity, or Expression*

	Fortune 100	Fortune 500	Fortune 1000	AmLaw 200	Raw Totals
2009	69	207	254	112	804
Interim	69%	41%	25%	56%	(−)

(Data from the *State of the Workplace for LGBT Americans 2007–2008* report and *How Fortune-Ranked Companies Stack Up on LGBT Workplace Issues,* September 2009.)

Source: HRC.org: http://www.hrc.org.

"State Laws Banning Workplace Discrimination on the Basis of Affinity Orientation or Gender Identity), hundreds of local ordinances, and thousands of workplaces, including nearly 90 percent of Fortune 500 companies (87 percent as of March 2011),[16] include it as part of their employment discrimination laws and policies[17] dictates that we include coverage here. (See Exhibit 10.3, "Numbers and Percentages of Employers with Non-discrimination Policies That Include Sexual Orientation, Gender Identity or Expression.") As we write this, 10 more states have laws pending that would prohibit workplace discrimination based on orientation or gender identity.[18] As exhibited by the gentleman in the opening paragraph (one of your authors was actually the consultant involved), affinity orientation discrimination is also one of the types of discrimination that may call into question ideas we hold dear and wish to protect. As a result we may think of this type of discrimination differently—as more justifiable—than we do others. In order to prevent those thoughts from turning into actions that lead to litigation and liability for the employer, we must learn to view the costly and avoidable matter in its proper workplace perspective.

As you read the chapter, keep this thought in the front of your mind: The intent of this chapter is not to get you to "accept" homosexuality. This chapter is not about going against your religious dictates, moral values, or conscience. As with our other chapter topics, you are free to believe whatever you wish. Rather, this chapter is about what the law requires in this area and what will lessen or prevent costly workplace liability from attaching for violations of the law. This is especially important as things in this area are changing so rapidly to include new rights.

Before choosing to engage in activity that may cause the employer liability for discrimination and result in your termination, keep in mind that this is the *employer's* workplace, not yours. Employees don't have the right to engage in activities that will cause unnecessary liability or embarrassing publicity for their employer. Since this is the employer's workplace, the employer is the one in charge of such things. If the employer has hired someone you don't like, for whatever reason, you have to decide what it's worth to you. Do you create trouble for the employer and run the risk of getting fired, or do you conduct yourself in a professional manner and keep your personal issues to yourself and collect a check? If you feel like you can't do the latter, then you are free to seek employment elsewhere. But if you choose to stay, you have no right to impose your purely personal beliefs on the workplace in a way that increases the employer's liability.

If you think your religious beliefs do not "permit" homosexuality, then don't be gay or lesbian. Don't take your gay or lesbian co-worker to lunch. Don't take him or her home for dinner. But refusing to work with him or her as required or otherwise treating the co-worker in ways that discriminate and expose the employer to liability is simply not an option.

It might help to think about whether you discriminate against other employees who do things that are against your religion. If you also refuse to deal with co-workers who are alcoholics, fornicators, or adulterers; had an abortion; or engage in other activity against your religious beliefs, at least the religious justification is consistent. For most, it rarely is. Working with someone who is gay or lesbian does not mean you "accept homosexuality" any more than working with alcoholics means you "accept alcoholism." Many people put affinity orientation into another category that permits them to treat it differently. That may be fine for your personal life, but work is work, and your personal life is your personal life, and the considerations for one are not always the same as the considerations for the other. When it is a matter of business and someone else's finances that will suffer, you have to rein in your personal feelings. Again, if all else fails, and you simply cannot bring yourself to think of this differently for work purposes, you should find another job where you would be more comfortable. If this sounds like we have an agenda, then you heard us correctly. Our agenda is to protect the employer from unnecessary costly, and avoidable liability.

With that out of the way, let's explore this area and see what's here.

Despite the stereotypes of gay males as florists, designers, or interior decorators, a survey by the Chicago marketing research firm Overlooked Opinions[19] found that more gay males work in science and engineering than in social services, 40 percent more are employed in finance and insurance than in entertainment and the arts, and 10 times as many work in computers as in fashion. (See Exhibit 10.4, "Heterosexual Realities.") Once, gays and lesbians in the workplace were virtually invisible, but diverse circumstances have begun to change that in dramatic ways.

You have the blessing (or curse, depending on your view) of actually living history as it relates to this issue. There have been dramatic changes in just the past 15 years or so. From never speaking the word *gay* on TV, to having award-winning TV shows like *Will and Grace, Queer Eye for the Straight Guy, The L Word,* or *Glee* be top performers, the landscape has changed. You may wonder how it happened.

Exhibit 10.4   *Heterosexual Realities*

QUESTIONNAIRE

The questions below provide a somewhat humorous yet insightful look at some of the more frequent assumptions surrounding gays and lesbians, which affect how they may be perceived in the workplace and society at large. The approach of reversing the questions subtly challenges commonly held heterosexually based notions.

1. What do you think caused your heterosexuality?

2. When and how did you first decide you were heterosexual?

3. Is it possible your heterosexuality is just a phase you may grow out of?

4. Is it possible your heterosexuality stems from a neurotic fear of others of the same gender?

5. Heterosexuals have histories of failures in gay relationships. Do you think you may have turned to heterosexuality out of fear of rejection?

6. If you've never slept with a person of the same gender, how do you know you wouldn't prefer that?

7. To whom have you disclosed your heterosexual tendencies? How do they react?

8. Your heterosexuality doesn't offend me as long as you don't try to force it on me. Why do you people feel compelled to seduce others into your sexual orientation?

9. Why do you insist on being so obvious and making a public spectacle of your heterosexuality by holding hands or kissing in public? Can't you just be what you are and keep it quiet?

10. How would the human race survive if everyone were heterosexual like you, considering the menace of overpopulation?

11. Why do heterosexuals place so much emphasis on sex?

12. How can you be heterosexual if you've never had sex?

Source: Adapted from Martin Rochlin, Ph.D., by Dr. Miranda Pollard, University of Georgia.

These changes have all been a function of a confluence of events including recent issues such as

- The impact of AIDS in society and in the workplace.
- The military's "Don't Ask, Don't Tell" policy.
- The 1993 March on Washington for Lesbians, Gays, and Bisexuals, which brought together unprecedented numbers of participants to call for non-discrimination in employment and equity.
- The 1992 presidential election in which President Bill Clinton voiced support for gays. It was the first time a presidential candidate had dealt with the issue.
- Clinton's later support for the Employment Non-discrimination Act (ENDA) prohibiting workplace discrimination against gays and lesbians, which has not yet passed.
- Clinton's appointment of over 150 gays and lesbians in his administration, including an ambassador and cabinet-level positions (see Exhibit 10.5, "Lesbian Confirmed for No. 2 HUD Post").

Exhibit 10.5 *Lesbian Confirmed for No. 2 HUD Post*

On May 24, 1993, President Clinton's nominee for assistant secretary of housing and urban development, Roberta Achtenberg, was confirmed by the Senate 58–31 after a three-day debate. Ms. Achtenberg was a member of the San Francisco Board of Supervisors who had won numerous awards for her community service, and the Senate's vote made her the first open lesbian appointed to such a high government position.

During the Senate debate, Senator Jesse Helms (R-N.C.) brought up that Ms. Achtenberg was seen with her partner, municipal court judge Mary Morgan, kissing and hugging while leading a 1992 Gay Pride parade. The Christian Action Network sent a copy of the videotape to every member of the Senate, and senators received thousands of calls from opponents after being urged to call by TV shows like Reverend Pat Robertson's *700 Club*.

During the Senate debate, Senator Dianne Feinstein (D-Calif.), former mayor of San Francisco, said, "Today we have a chance to turn our back to prejudice. Today we can vote down the politics of hate and take a small step to make sure our government is representative of all the people it seeks to serve."

Note: Achtenberg resigned in 1995 to run for elected office in San Francisco.

- Colorado's attempted constitutional ban on protection for gays and lesbians, which the U.S. Supreme Court struck down, and many other events put the issue of gays and lesbians on the national agenda for the first time.

After President Clinton became the first president to ever address the issue of gays and lesbians, and in such a public way, 1993 was a watershed year and a turning point for gay and lesbian issues. On April 25, 1993, the Cable News Network (CNN) provided day-long national television coverage of the convergence of nearly a million people, gay and straight, on Washington, D.C., for the March on Washington for Lesbian, Gay, and Bisexual Equal Rights and Liberation. It was clear that it was one of the largest marches ever held, and that gays and lesbians could no longer be ignored.

Since that time, states have seen a good deal of legislation about gays and lesbians, and courts have seen cases on issues ranging from parental rights to military discharges, from domestic partner benefits to gay marriage, and from hate crimes to workplace discrimination. Things change very quickly in this area, in historical terms, so employers must work diligently to make sure their policies are consistent with legal and other changes. For instance, in April 2011, a CNN poll showed that for the first time, a majority of Americans favored allowing gays and lesbians to have the same right to marry as anyone else. In 2009 the majority of Americans were against it.[20]

Earning a living is a necessity for most people, so the issue of gays and lesbians is increasingly surfacing in the workplace and has become one an employer must deal with. There is a growing realization that gays and lesbians are everywhere and should be judged for who they are as people and what they bring to the table, not for the singular measure of the private matter of sex. With the rules changing almost daily, and more state and local legislation both for and against civil rights for gays, it has become necessary for employers to know what their potential legal liability is in this area.

A fairly recent development has been the emergence of non-discrimination policies and gay and lesbian employee support groups within the workplace. There are well over 2,000, including groups in over 300 Fortune 500 companies, many colleges and universities, nonprofits, unions, and state and local governments. Now listed among such employers are Apple Computer, Digital Equipment, AT&T, Coca-Cola, IBM, Kodak, Du Pont, Hewlett-Packard, Lucent Technologies, Sun Microsystems, Pacific Gas and Electric Company, Walt Disney Co., J. P. Morgan, Chase & Co., Goldman Sachs, Merrill Lynch, and United Parcel Service, to name a few.

The groups tackle such issues as workplace hostility, extending employee benefits to domestic partners, making sure that partners are welcome at company social functions, and generally making the workplace less threatening to the worklife and workplace progress of gays and lesbians and thus more productive for the employees and, ultimately, the employer. After a recent spate of gay teen suicides due to bullying caused Fort Worth City Councilman Joel Burns to give an impassioned city council speech on the matter urging teens to know that things do get better, the YouTube video of the speech went viral.[21] Price Waterhouse Coopers, a top accounting firm, made its own video of its gay and lesbian employees urging struggling teens to know that things do get better. Other companies did it also, such as Google and Facebook. This should give you some idea of companies' approach to this area; not only are they trying to support their employees regarding this matter, but they are also reaching beyond the workplace to their communities. For that reason, it is an issue anyone involved with employment law should be aware of.

Some companies sponsor their gay and lesbian employees at events like Gay Pride Month, a nationwide celebration each June, culminating in a parade comprised of many types of contingents, including businesses. Companies provide employees with information and novelty items to be passed out to attendees or T-shirts with slogans such as "ABC Company Supports Its Gay and Lesbian Employees." (See Exhibit 10.6, "AT&T's Support for Its Gay Employees.") A recent poll showed that this type of workplace support is important to 71 percent of the gays and lesbians polled.

LO1   Gay Pride Month is not just a fun time. And despite what your local news coverage may choose to show, it involves not just parade participants with their behinds hanging out of leather clothing or "freaky" looking characters. It is actually the commemoration of the historic events of June 1969. Being gay or lesbian is often a life-threatening proposition, but it was even more so then. As a result, most gays and lesbians led an extremely closeted existence and often congregated in gay bars just to be sure of the safety of their surroundings. Since gays and lesbians were considered social outcasts of the highest order, they did not want to risk their own lives, or embarrass their families and friends, by being honest about who they were. Fearing discovery made them a very vulnerable group that rarely

Exhibit 10.6 *AT&T's Support for Its Gay Employees*

This is part of a full-color brochure handed out at the 1993 March on Washington for Gay, Lesbian, and Bisexual Equal Rights and Liberation. The 1987 march referred to is the first national gay and lesbian march that had been held in Washington, D.C., six years before.

IT'S GREAT TO BE GAY AT AT&T

PROVIDED

BY THE

LESBIAN,

BISEXUAL &

GAY UNITED

EMPLOYEES

AT AT&T

LEAGUE

HISTORY OF LEAGUE

In 1987 a handful of AT&T employees returned home from the March on Washington inspired, energized and convinced that they could change their part of the world . . . that they could make AT&T a place that welcomed ALL its employees!

Meeting in restaurants and private homes, they formed an informal support group called LEAGUE. In 1988, these brave people brought LEAGUE to the corporation where it was recognized as the two-way communication vehicle between the decision-makers and the AT&T gay community. Soon, word about LEAGUE came out on informal gay bulletin boards across the country . . . chapters sprang up in Denver, then New Jersey, then Ohio and Illinois! In 1992, LEAGUE National was created and bound the loosely associated chapters together to form a common voice, with a common vision: To share the AT&T values, we commit ourselves to advancing changes that will help people respect and value lesbian, bisexual and gay employees and further AT&T's quest for excellence and customer satisfaction. Today there are over 20 LEAGUE chapters across the country that provide its members:

- Advocacy and access to all levels of management
- Professional development courses and conferences
- Workplace community support via electronic mail and regular meetings
- The "Safe Place"™ program
- Help with community service projects
- Social and networking opportunities
- Resources for solving workplace issues
- Opportunities to educate the AT&T community via homophobia workshops and speaking engagements.

LEAGUE has become a proud and visible leader in the global business community, offering an example for other gay employee resource groups to follow.

continued

I LOVE WORKING FOR AT&T BECAUSE...

...I have something special here: a non-discrimination policy, the respect of my management, the support of fellow lesbian, bisexual, gay and straight co-workers, the empowerment to help make AT&T a better place for everyone and the freedom to bring my partner to Family Day at my office.

Rich Mielke, Network Systems, LEAGUE, N. Illinois

...I can aspire toward my professional goals without compromising my personal values or pretending to be someone I'm not. It's inspiring to see gay role models and rewarding to be one in a corporation that takes valuing the diversity of its workforce as seriously as its other business imperatives.

Linda Escalante, Mgr.-Int'l Sales Support, LEAGUE, N. Jersey

...I can finally be open about who I am. I feel very supported by AT&T knowing that if anyone gives me a hard time because of my sexual orientation, more education will take place. I am a much more powerful manager now that I am open about who I am. My personal and professional relationships are moving to deeper levels as I share more of myself with others.

Don Shuart, Programmer/Analyst, LEAGUE, Atlanta

...I believe that our management is honestly committed to understanding our issues and to promoting a healthy, diverse work place and that this will give us a competitive advantage in the decades to come.

Bill Thacker, Quality Engineer, LEAGUE, Columbus

...while recognizing that this is not a perfect place to work, AT&T is committed to making it an attractive, supportive place for all employees. I feel safe being out at work because people around me make it a supportive, caring place.

Terry Teeter, QA Specialist, LEAGUE, Central Florida

...it has taught me the true value of a supportive community on the job. When my life partner became ill with AIDS seven years ago, I "came out" to my boss and my co-workers in order to help them understand why I might suddenly be absent to deal with a health crisis at home. My boss cried and offered me her complete support. When my partner died a year later, about half of the workers in our office—secretaries, paralegals and attorneys—came to his memorial service. I knew then that I was "at home" and "with family" here at AT&T and have felt even closer to my colleagues in the years since.

Glenn Stover, Senior Attorney, LEAGUE, At-Large

...since my involvement with LEAGUE-Atlanta, I've gained a deeper self-respect and found that the people I work with respect me more as a person. I used to live my life in fear of what a few people may have thought of me rather than accepting the positive support that I now know was out there all along. After 25 years with the company, I now know that AT&T really is its people.

Jane Darby, Quality Specialist, LEAGUE, Atlanta

Source: Reprinted with permission of AT&T.

fought against their circumstances. Gay bars, often the only place gays and lesbians could go and feel accepted for who they were, were routinely raided by police officers for no apparent reason, and the patrons hauled off to jail for one minor infraction or another. Fearing publicity, most patrons just went quietly.

In June 1969, this changed. When plainclothes police officers raided the Stonewall Inn in New York's Greenwich Village, there was uncharacteristic resistance by the bar patrons and people on the street that resulted in a weekend of riots. The next year in New York, the first legislative hearings on gay issues were held, as was the first parade to commemorate the events at Stonewall the year before. The resistance at Stonewall in 1969 is considered the beginning of the modern gay rights movement. Over the years, the commemoration has grown and spread as more people, gay and straight, determine that being gay should not equal being vulnerable to discrimination or death. Each June there are now Gay Pride Month celebrations across the country and around the world. While in office, President Clinton issued proclamations declaring June Gay Pride Month, as do many state governors. President Bush broke with this tradition, saying he considers affinity orientation a personal matter.

The Clinton administration's first U.S. Department of Transportation secretary, Federico Peña, held a lunch-hour Gay Pride Day ceremony for department employees, stating, "We need to draw on the talents of everyone. It's not about special privileges. It's about equal treatment." In June 2002, among others, the U.S. Environmental Protection Agency's director of the Office of Administration and Resource Management, William E. Laxton, issued a memo setting forth support for, and listing, Gay Pride Month activities and encouraging managers and supervisors to do likewise. AT&T handed out slick, three-color brochures during the 1993 march on Washington (see Exhibit 10.6) providing information for gay and lesbian AT&T employees about AT&T and its policies and attitudes regarding them. Each year there is a National Conference on Gay Issues in the Workplace held for human resources professionals needing guidance in this area. Each October 11 is National Coming Out Day, the purpose of which is to bring attention to the forced invisibility of gays and lesbians and the importance of their being open about who they are in an effort to help dispel the myths and stereotypes society holds that have resulted from their historical silence and invisibility. The question often arises as to why a gay person has to let people know of his or her affinity orientation. "I don't go around telling people I'm straight, so why do they have to say they are gay?" The reason is that there is an overriding presumption that virtually everyone is heterosexual, and if the gay person does not say otherwise, he or she ends up feeding into it and living a lie. Being honest and letting people know takes away the presumption that forces the gay employee into complicity.

The issue of gays in the workplace can surface in some surprising ways, making it all the more compelling for an employer to be aware of the possibilities and take them into consideration when making policy in this area. Apple (the computer company) was thinking of moving its operations to Williamson County, Texas. The city council refused to vote Apple concessions as an incentive to move there after it discovered that Apple had domestic partnership benefits for its employees. Apple refused to take away these benefits, and the city council finally voted to give Apple the concessions. The Walt Disney Company took a real beating from conservatives when it extended benefits to domestic partners of its employees. The company chose to continue the benefits. Anheuser-Busch took flak for its ads featuring two men holding hands, but the ads continued. In 2005, two weeks after dropping the protection for gays and lesbians from its legislative agenda due to threats of boycotts from religious groups, Microsoft's CEO, Steve Ballmer, said, "After looking at the question from all sides, I've concluded that diversity in the workplace is such an important issue for our business that it should be in our legislative agenda." Microsoft also, issued an "It's Getting Better" video.[22]

Based on the potential for increased productivity and the possibility of litigation or other business problems, some employers conclude that the safer practice is to base workplace decisions solely on an employee's ability to effectively perform the job, rather than on his or her affinity orientation. If the employee's *conduct* interferes with the workplace, it may be the basis for a disciplinary action, but this is not the same as the employee's affinity orientation. The focus should not be on the employee's status as gay or lesbian but rather, on the employee's workplace performance.

Again, the above notwithstanding, affinity orientation is *not* a protected category under Title VII of the Civil Rights Act. It has been judicially and administratively determined that gender discrimination under Title VII does not include discrimination on the basis of same-gender affinity orientation, **gender/sexual reassignment surgery (transgenders)**, or **bi-gender affinity orientation** (bisexuality). Note that the transgendered may or may not have actually had reassignment surgery for reasons of economics or personal preference, However, they identify as the gender opposite their original gender. Those who are terminated or not hired solely on the basis of affinity orientation have no claim for relief under this law. This is reaffirmed each time Congress fails to pass the Employment Non-discrimination Act (ENDA). The bill has missed passage by as little as one vote. When gender identity was added to the bill, they realized that they did not have enough votes for passage if discrimination on the basis of gender identity was included. It is again before Congress.[23]

ENDA would basically extend Title VII's reach to include discrimination on the basis of affinity orientation. Hundreds of corporations have formally endorsed ENDA, including NYNEX Corp., Polaroid, Bethlehem Steel Corp., Xerox, Yahoo, Kaiser Permanente, Harley-Davidson, Merrill Lynch, Quaker Oats, and Microsoft, to name a few.[24]

A U.S. Government Accounting Office report on states with anti-discrimination laws protecting gays and lesbians found that the laws had not generated a significant amount of litigation. Separate nationwide polls by Gallup and Harris found widespread public support (85 percent and 61 percent, respectively) for protective legislation. Interestingly, the Harris poll showed that 42 percent of those surveyed already thought such a law existed.[25]

As you can see from the number of state and local jurisdictions with protective legislation, having no federal legislation protecting gays and lesbians from workplace discrimination does not mean that employers are totally free to discriminate against them. As we said earlier, to date, legislation has been passed protecting gays and lesbians from workplace discrimination in over 500 municipalities and 21 states and the District of Columbia, and 10 states have such laws pending. Between state laws and local ordinances or executive orders, every single state in the union now has *some* form of job discrimination protection for gays and lesbians. In addition, more than 73 local jurisdictions, 12 states (California, Colorado, Illinois, Iowa, Maine, Minnesota, New Jersey, New Mexico, Oregon, Rhode Island, Vermont, and Washington), and Washington, D.C., provide workplace protection for transgenders, called **gender identity statutes**. The GAO study previously mentioned, of states with job discrimination laws for gays and lesbians, found little, if any, increase in the number of affinity orientation job discrimination lawsuits filed.

In addition to rights that may be provided by state and local legislation, gay and lesbian public employees adversely affected by an employment decision

---

gender/sexual reassignment surgery
The surgery required to change a person's gender due to gender dysphoria, the condition of one's physical gender not matching the emotional/psychological gender.

transgender
Someone whose physical gender does not match his or her emotional/psychological gender; may or may not undergo gender reassignment surgery.

bi-gender affinity orientation
Someone attracted to both genders.

LO2

gender identity statutes
Laws providing protection for transgenders.

based on affinity orientation may, under appropriate circumstances, use state constitutions or the First, Fifth, or Fourteenth Amendments of the U.S. Constitution as a basis for suit, as well as the constitutional right to privacy. This applies to federal, state, and local employees. These lawsuits have traditionally been decided in the employer's favor, but recent decisions have impacted this trend and increasingly recognize the rights of gays and lesbians. This means employers should take note.

Gay and lesbian employees also may bring civil tort actions such as intentional infliction of emotional distress, intentional interference with contractual relations, invasion of privacy, or defamation. The outcome depends on the particular circumstances, but employers should be mindful of the possibility of civil suits with unlimited damages.

Employers also should be aware of the possibility of several closely related matters that may arise in affinity orientation cases and cause liability based on the protected category of gender—for instance, gender stereotyping as discussed in the gender chapter. Judging employees based on stereotypical ideas about a given gender (that is, females who are "too aggressive" or "too macho" or males who are "too effeminate"), rather than on legitimate job requirements, may result in liability for gender discrimination, rather than affinity orientation, and should be avoided. Similarly, if an employer knowingly hires lesbians but not gay men, this could be the basis for gender discrimination. In such a case, under Title VII, affinity orientation is clearly not an issue for the employer, since the employer knowingly hired lesbians.

So, unlike the rest of the categories we have discussed, affinity orientation is not nearly as settled as other types of employment discrimination. However, the vast patchwork quilt of constitutional guarantees, state and local laws and ordinances, and employer policies, as well as the public relations aspects of the issue, make it one in which giving careful thought to policy is critical. We are in the rare position of seeing an entirely new area of law unfold. As exciting as this is from a legal standpoint, it can have traps for the unwary employer. Sticking with only relevant qualifications and watching trends in case law and legislation at all levels will greatly aid in making policy decisions much less likely to result in liability.

Seeing how the court handles this issue in the case *Weaver v. Nebo School District,* included at the end of the chapter, is instructive in trying to shape policies consistent with its pronouncements. When a high school teacher said she was a lesbian, in response to being asked, her coaching job was taken away and a notation was put in her personnel file. The court held that this was an unconstitutional denial of equal protection of the law.

The *Weaver* decision was mentioned the *Romer* case,[26] in which the state of Colorado passed a constitutional provision that would have prohibited any government subdivision from passing laws protecting gays and lesbians from discrimination. This was one of the first major U.S. Supreme Court cases that challenged states' rights to pass laws restricting rights of gays and lesbians. As such, it sent an important message to states regarding their ability to exclude certain groups from constitutional protections. To some extent, this paved the way for much of what was to come, as you can see from the *Weaver* case. Note, too, that as the court mentioned, Title VII did not protect Weaver on the basis of affinity orientation, and the state did not have a law protecting her, but because she was a public school teacher, and thus a government employee, she had a cause of action for an unconstitutional denial of equal protection under the law.

Affinity Orientation as a Basis for Adverse Employment Decisions

As you will see from the case, not all affinity orientation issues arise in the same contexts. The employee may be the basis of employer concern because the employee, among other things:

- Is gay or lesbian (i.e., status or orientation).
- Has primary relationships with those of the same gender (activity rather than status).
- Exhibits inappropriate workplace behavior such as detailed discussions of intimate sexual behavior or improperly propositioning others in the workplace (this is certainly not *presumed* of gays and lesbians, and as you saw in Chapter 8 this is not solely a gay or lesbian phenomenon).
- Wears clothing, jewelry, or makeup in violation of workplace grooming codes.
- Is in the presurgery adjustment stages of such gender reassignment surgery.
- Undergoes gender reassignment surgery.

Note that some of the activity presents a problem no matter who the employee is. An employer should not tolerate from any employee inappropriate workplace behavior such as improperly propositioning other employees. A distinction also should be made between *status* or *orientation* as a gay or lesbian, on the one hand, and, on the other, *activity* that may be inappropriate. Basing decisions and policies on actions is more defensible than basing them on status. But even then the action should not be singled out solely based on the actor's orientation. Each of the above contexts of gay or lesbian issues presents its own unique issues.

DeSantis v. Pacific Telephone and Telegraph Co., Inc.,[27] is one of the earliest cases about gays and Title VII. In that case, several telephone company employees brought Title VII claims when the employer terminated them because they were gay or lesbian or perceived to be so. The court's reasoning for not allowing the Title VII claims is based on the employees' status of being gay or lesbian rather than something the employees did. It is this basic approach that underlies why the employee would not be protected in Opening Scenario 1. In the *Nichols* case provided at chapter's end, this same court reversed itself to some extent, but *DeSantis* is an important historical case setting forth that Title VII did not provide protection for gays and lesbians at a time when few such cases had been brought. On the other hand, look at Exhibit 10.7, "New Push to Recruit Gay Students," to see how much the workplace is changing.

Scenario 1

Case 2

Exhibit 10.7 *New Push to Recruit Gay Students*

In a February 2000 *Wall Street Journal* article, Rachel Emma Silverman reported that Wall Street financial firms were, for the first time, targeting their recruitment toward gay and lesbian business students. Firms such as Goldman Sachs Group, Inc., J. P. Morgan & Co., and American Express Co. have gone to great lengths to woo gay students. According to the employers, the tightening labor market as well as the increasingly vocal employees of the firms caused them to use this as a tool to be or remain competitive in their recruiting efforts. The recruitment efforts include wining and dining the students at posh restaurants, co-hosting dinners for gay students, having gay and lesbian support groups in the workplace, having gay recruiting events with well-known speakers, and having discussion groups about being gay in the workplace.

Other firms, in an effort to thwart the criticism from students that they ought to be chosen for their qualifications, not their affinity orientation, declined to target gays and lesbians in recruiting. Students were clear, however, that it was important for them to feel comfortable in their workplace, including feeling comfortable about their affinity orientation. Since this time, there also have been gay and lesbian job fairs and college fairs, among other things, organized to ensure that gays and lesbians would be able to seek opportunities in settings in which they would be comfortable, given the usual hostile environment they can encounter.

Realizing the effect of *DeSantis,* which has been widely used as precedent in other jurisdictions to deny gay and lesbian employees workplace discrimination protection for being gay or lesbian, employees have tried to get around the Title VII limitation by alleging some other recognized basis for discrimination under Title VII. For instance, in *Williamson v. A.G. Edwards & Sons, Inc.*[28] a black male employee was terminated for wearing makeup in the workplace. He sued the employer for race discrimination, rather than affinity orientation. The employee alleged the employer treated him differently than white males who were allowed to wear such things. However, the court found no evidence that he had been treated differently based on race. The evidence the employee provided was not comparable; therefore, the comparison made was inappropriate.

Sometimes an employer terminates an employee who fits into more than one category, or perceived category, of Title VII. One category may be protected and the other not. Liability may still ensue. For instance, if an employer terminates a black (protected) female (protected) after the employer finds that she is a lesbian (not protected), the employee is not able to use her status as a lesbian as the basis for a Title VII claim. However, if the employee can show that white lesbians were not terminated, this would be discrimination based on her race and would be actionable. However, as *Williamson* demonstrates, the claim must be more than a mere allegation; it must be proved. To be fully protected in the decision to terminate, an employer must be certain there are no facts that will support the other categories the employee may allege as a basis for workplace discrimination.

Regarding the makeup issue in *Williamson,* as we discussed in the gender chapter, employers are able to have workplace dress codes as long as they do not violate Title VII. There is nothing in Title VII to prevent an employer from prohibiting men from wearing makeup in the workplace. Note that this is generally more of a transgender issue than a gay issue. The Washington State Supreme Court ruled that Boeing Company had sufficient basis for terminating a male engineer who was undergoing gender reassignment surgery. Boeing attempted to accommodate the employee by permitting him to wear "unisex" clothing; but the employee was terminated when he added pink pearls to such an outfit and insisted on using the women's bathroom. (*Boeing,* is Case 3, discussed later.)

For years male employees also tried to argue that their effeminacy should not be a basis on which employers can refuse to hire them or can terminate them from their jobs. Until recently, this argument rarely succeeded and courts routinely sided with the employer, usually using *DeSantis* for precedent. The court in *DeSantis* had stated:

> Employee Strailey contends he was terminated by the Happy Times Nursery School because the school felt that it was inappropriate for a male teacher to wear an earring to school. He claims that the school's reliance on a stereotype—that a male should have a virile, rather than an effeminate, appearance—violates Title VII. This does not fall within Title VII. We hold that discrimination because of effeminacy, like discrimination because of [affinity orientation], does not fall within the purview of Title VII.

LO4

However, in the *Nichols* case discussed shortly, the *DeSantis* court reversed itself as it related to the issue of stereotyping and determined that under certain circumstances, Title VII permits employees claiming discrimination based on failing to fit a certain gender-based stereotype (usually effeminate men) to bring a claim based on gender stereotyping. In doing so, the court interpreted the U.S. Supreme Court's *Price Waterhouse v. Hopkins* case, discussed in the gender chapter, as being inconsistent with its *DeSantis* holding. The court said:

> *Price Waterhouse* sets a rule that bars discrimination on the basis of sex stereotypes. That rule squarely applies to preclude the harassment here. We do not imply that all gender-based distinctions are actionable under Title VII. For example, our decision does not imply that there is any violation of Title VII occasioned by reasonable regulations that require male and female employees to conform to different dress and grooming standards.
>
> The only potential difficulty arises out of a now faint shadow cast by our decision in *DeSantis* holding that discrimination based on a stereotype that a man "should have a virile rather than an effeminate appearance" does not fall within Title VII's purview. This holding, however, predates and conflicts with the Supreme Court's decision in *Price Waterhouse*. And, in this direct conflict, *DeSantis* must lose. To the extent it conflicts with *Price Waterhouse,* as we hold it does, *DeSantis* is no longer good law.

A Note about Same-Gender Sexual Harassment

LO5

We are addressing this issue here instead of in the sexual harassment chapter because of the special development of the area and the way the law looks at this in light of Title VII not covering gays and lesbians. We also do it here because the background for the issue was not provided until this chapter.

Since Title VII does not include a prohibition against discrimination on the basis of affinity orientation, an important question had been whether an employee sexually harassed by someone of the same gender could bring an action under Title VII. Some courts said no because they considered any sexual harassment between employees of the same gender to be based on same-gender affinity orientation (regardless of the nature of the harassment), and since Title VII excluded affinity orientation coverage, a harassee had no cause of action.

Other courts looked at the nature of the harassment and allowed a cause of action if it was not based on affinity orientation (rather than presuming that because it was between employees of the same gender it *must* be). And there were many other variations on the theme. In the *Oncale v. Sundowner Offshore Services, Inc.,* case[29] the U.S. Supreme Court finally made sense of it all by saying there could be a cause of action for sexual harassment even if both parties are of the same gender, as long as it is clear that the basis for the harassment is not because the harassee is gay or lesbian.

Oncale was a *huge* case. Not only had courts across the country been absolutely splintered in their approaches to the same facts, but legal scholars and employers, as well as the public, debated the issue at length. The U.S. Supreme Court finally came down on the side of the intent of Title VII in striking at the full spectrum of gender-based employment discrimination. It made sense that if the issue involved was workplace harassment and discrimination, then the gender or affinity orientation of either party should not matter. That inquiry is not made in other harassment cases, and it made little sense to make it in this instance. As the Court determined, the important inquiry is whether "the workplace is permeated with discriminatory intimidation, ridicule, and insult that is sufficiently severe or pervasive to alter the conditions of the victim's employment and create an abusive working environment." If so, then Title VII is violated. Clearly that happened in *Oncale.* There have been several similar cases since the *Oncale* decision, including the two class action suits in the introductory material. This analysis is the basis for Opening Scenario 3.

3
Scenario

Under the *Oncale* decision, the Court preserved Title VII's exclusion of discrimination on the basis of affinity orientation by holding that the sexual harassment of an employee by someone of the same gender is prohibited unless it can be shown that it was actually based on affinity orientation. That is, if a female employee can show that a female harassed her by calling her negative names, undermining her work productivity, spreading lies about her, or negatively commenting on her personality, actions, friends, speech, or clothing, as it relates to gender, and so on, then she can bring a claim under Title VII. If, however, the harassee is a lesbian and the harassment is in the form of something such as constantly calling her a lesbian, "dyke," or other terms related to her orientation; directing teasing, joking, and comments on homosexuality toward her; or persistently asking for dates or making sexual comments, then the harassee would not have a cause of action under Title VII.

The first situation is plain old sexual harassment even though the parties are both the same gender, and it is covered by Title VII. The second is harassment based on affinity orientation and it is not covered. What the Supreme Court did is to not presume that every harassment between employees of the same gender is based on same-gender affinity orientation. See if you can make the distinction in the *Nichols v. Azteca Restaurant Enterprises, Inc.* case, supplied for your review, in which the court permitted a cause of action for gender harassment by an employee who was constantly harassed by his co-workers for being effeminate.

Gender Identity Discrimination

LO6

Closely related to affinity orientation, but actually quite separate, is the matter of gender identity. As you saw earlier in the chapter, some state and local laws protect affinity orientation but do not also protect gender identity. Gender identity involves how an individual identifies with gender. It encompasses several different manifestations, including the transgendered. This is quite different from the issue of affinity orientation. Gays and lesbians do not feel that their body and mind are at odds. They simply have an affinity for their same gender.

According to the Human Rights Campaign, the largest gay rights advocacy group in the United States, the term *transgender* encompasses cross-dressers, intersexed people (formerly called hermaphrodites, or those born with both sex organs), transsexuals, and people who live substantial portions of their lives as other than their birth gender. Our students usually have a pretty hard time wrapping their heads around this issue. Unlike the other types of discrimination we have discussed, most of them are not aware of knowing anyone in this category, so they have no frame of reference for it. To them, it seems bizarre and unsettling. "Why in the world would somebody want to change their gender?" they wail plaintively. The biggest surprise for them is realizing that transgenders do not just decide on a whim to change their gender. The condition of feeling like your mind is one gender and your body is the opposite is a medical condition recognized by the American Medical Association as gender dysphoria. The term *transsexual* is traditionally used to describe a person who has undergone gender reassignment surgery. Though it may seem drastic to us, for transsexuals, changing their body is easy compared to living with a body that does not represent who they feel themselves to be. For them, changing their body is simply making the outside conform to the inside.

Most of us do not realize just how mental our gender is. We just take for granted that we are the way we are, period. We're male and that's it. We're female and that's it. The truth is, a lot of what we think of as our gender is mental, due to both acculturation as well as physiology.

If I said to males reading the text, "Paint your toes red and go out wearing sandals," most of you would howl in protest. It doesn't change your toes. It doesn't change who you are. It's just fingernail polish. Yet you don't want to do it because it just doesn't feel like you. For most of you, it would be feminine and you feel masculine. So much so, that you would never do it. For individuals with gender dysphoria, their body looks like one gender, but their mind feels like the opposite gender and always has. For the most part, until they transition, they have an overriding sense that they are in the wrong body.

While the term *transgender* has traditionally been used for those who have undergone gender reassignment surgery, with a growing awareness of the issues of transgenders and a greater sense of themselves than historically, has come a change in the use of the term. It is now often used more loosely to include those who may not yet have had surgery but are living as the opposite gender. Within the transgender community are those who may have had surgery to change their gender, or those who cannot afford such surgery or for other reasons may not wish to have surgery, but they still feel like the gender opposite their outward appearance and they wish to present that to the world. They may have had some surgery and not other surgery. Whether they have or have not is totally irrelevant to their ability to do their job, and it is inappropriate to ask. Those who are transgender simply want to be treated as the gender they feel themselves to be.

This may all sound like a strange conversation to have in an employment law text. Again, we do so because many people have little or no understanding of these issues; thus, when they are faced with them as managers or supervisors, they have no idea how to make legally defensible decisions. It is important to recognize that because you do not understand or "accept" gender identity issues does not mean (1) that they do not exist, or (2) that you can afford to ignore the reality of handling these workplace issues.

Think the issue of transsexuals is isolated and far-fetched? In the *Boeing* case mentioned earlier, the Boeing Corporation was faced with requests for accommodating transsexual employees so frequently (at least nine times) that it finally developed a carefully crafted policy. As managers and supervisors, you will encounter all types of employees and it helps to have some knowledge to try to draw on. Don't be afraid to seek information on what may not be familiar to you.

Due in part to the activity surrounding issues of affinity orientation, transgender discrimination became really active and is now one of the fastest-growing issues in workplace discrimination. As a result, it is presenting itself more and more frequently as a workplace issue. As we saw earlier, several state and local laws now include transgenders within their protection for workplace discrimination. According to the Human Rights Campaign, the number of Fortune 500 companies that include gender identity protection in their workplace anti-discrimination policies has quadrupled just since 2003. The last time the Employment Non-discrimination Act was before Congress, it was clear that it would have passed except that some wanted to include gender identity in the law and Congress was not ready for that. Since most people are not familiar with this issue, you can imagine that it presents rather interesting, confusing, and, at times, complicated workplace challenges that must be addressed.

As a matter of information, once someone has changed his or her gender identity and complies with state laws to do so, he or she is now legally considered to be the gender to which he or she has changed. None of that "he/she" stuff as if you don't know what to consider them. They are the gender they have transitioned to, again, whether you understand it or not. They generally can have their identity documents reissued to be consistent with their new gender and can even have their birth certificate reissued in some jurisdictions. After surgery, they are, for all intents and purposes, the opposite gender and wish to be treated that way by society.

Again, we tell you this because we have taught thousands of students and had thousands of attendees at consulting and training sessions, and they routinely ask these questions in order to better grasp this alien issue. It may seem a bit strange to do this in a textbook. However, we care about giving you the right tools to make decisions in the workplace. Since so many of our students and attendees asked the questions, we thought you might have the same ones. We also believe that providing a thumbnail sketch here gives you some means of analyzing the cases in this section.

Like affinity orientation, gender identity is not a protected category under Title VII. However, again like affinity orientation, there are several state and local laws—and more pending—and workplace non-discrimination policies that provide protection and the number is growing; therefore, we need to make sure it is covered.

Scenario

The argument has been made by trangenders, particularly those who have had gender reassignment surgery, that they should be afforded the protection of Title VII because they have changed their gender status from male to female or vice versa and now are being discriminated against in employment because they have changed genders. Courts have not upheld this position. As stated in *Ulane v. Eastern Airlines, Inc.,*[30] the basis for Opening Scenario 2, it is not the status of the employee as a member of the gender to which he or she has been reassigned that has created the issue. That is, a male who is terminated on becoming a female is not discriminated against because he is a female as contemplated by Title VII. Rather, she is discriminated against because she changed from male to female. These are considered two very different arguments, with the former being provided Title VII protection, but not the latter.

Ulane v. Eastern Airlines, Inc.[31] was the first significant case to address the matter of transgender discrimination and still remains the general approach to transgender discrimination in the workplace under Title VII. As mentioned, the employee argued that she was discriminated against because of gender, but the court held this was not the case; it held that the basis for discrimination was changing her gender from male to female, and that was not protected by Title VII.

Employees also have argued that being a transgender is a disability that must be accommodated. The "pink pearls" case, as *Jane Doe v. Boeing Company* became known, rejected that view in Washington State. It also provides great insight into how an employer can approach these issues to best provide protection against liability for discrimination. Keep in mind, while you review the case at the conclusion of the chapter, that Washington enacted a law protecting transgenders from workplace discrimination in 2006, but Boeing had put a policy in place several years before.

Employment Benefits

LO7

In the past few years, one of the most active issues regarding affinity orientation and the workplace has been that of employment benefits. Benefits that other employees take for granted are major hurdles for gays and lesbians. For instance, bereavement leave routinely granted for the death of a loved one is often not provided to gays and lesbians when their life partners die. Sick leave routinely granted to take care of a family member is often not given when the family is the gay or lesbian employee's life partner. (See Exhibits 10.8, "Workplace Issues for Gays and Lesbians," and 10.9, "Domestic Partner Law Debate.")

Exhibit 10.8 *Workplace Issues for Gays and Lesbians*

- *Non-discrimination policies.* Corporate anti-discrimination policies are a primary concern for lesbians, gays, and transgenders who don't have state or local civil rights ordinances protecting them. A basic statement that employees are given the same opportunity to enter, advance, and succeed in an organization sets the tone for how that organization relates to lesbians and gays.

- *Bereavement leave for domestic partners.* Many corporations have policies granting employees paid leave to attend the funerals of spouses and immediate members of the family. These policies don't help unmarried domestic partners of gays or straights. This was a particularly important issue, given the devastating impact of the AIDS crisis.

- *Vacation leave transfer.* Another issue is the enormous financial burden placed on employees with AIDS. Other employees often want to help these employees by donating their earned vacation time. Gay and lesbian groups are lobbying companies to consider allowing employees to offer support in this way. A great many have been successful, and the number continues to grow.

- *Benefits for domestic partners.* Earning health care benefits for their partners is an important goal for lesbian and gay employees. They're asking corporations to respect alternative families and recognize their benefit needs, and they argue that the family partner of an unmarried employee is just as likely to need health insurance as is the spouse of a married employee. Gays and lesbians also are asking for parental leave benefits when appropriate. Thousands of companies have granted such benefits, and the number continues to increase.

Source: Adapted from G. K. Kronenberger, "Out of the Closet," *Workforce Magazine,* June 1991, p. 40.

Exhibit 10.9 *Domestic Partner Law Debate: Domestic Partner Law Protects Personal Wishes*

Though this editorial debate is from 1994—eons ago in this quickly changing area of the law (for instance, California now permits same-gender marriage though, as you can see from the article, such was not then the case), it still does a good job of laying out the fundamentals of the debate on domestic partnerships.

USA TODAY EDITORIAL: OUR VIEW

Shouldn't you be able to decide who should care for you in crisis or [should] benefit if you die?

Unmarried couples should keep an eye on California. A bill awaiting the governor's signature would bring some needed changes to Californians' lives. The concept could, and should, spread to other states.

There's nothing earthshaking about the bill. In fact, it's surprising no state yet offers three basic protections to unmarrieds:

- The right to have your partner visit if you're hospitalized.

- The right to have your partner act as guardian if you're incapacitated.

- And the right to leave your money and property to whom you wish in your will, avoiding nasty court battles with relatives.

Spouses, of course, already have these rights. But there are plenty of couples—nearly half a million in California alone—who aren't married, 93 percent of them heterosexual. Many will marry later; some never will, for a variety of reasons. And for gay couples, marriage is out of the question.

Domestic partner programs have expanded rapidly in the past decade. Two states and several cities grant full health benefits to employees' partners.

Others offer domestic partner registration, which offers varying degrees of legal protection. Ordinances in Minneapolis, Minn., and West Hollywood, Calif., for example, allow hospital visitation. In other places, registration provides psychological benefits but not legal ones.

continued

Exhibit 10.9 *continued*

How important is legal recognition of a partnership? Anyone who pooh-poohs it could use a lesson from Karen Thompson and Sharon Kowalski. The two women, teachers in Minnesota, began living together in 1979. In 1983, Kowalski was injured in an accident caused by a drunken driver. She was brain damaged and comatose for five months.

Thompson battled Kowalski's parents over guardianship, and when the parents won in 1985, they banned Thompson from even visiting their daughter. The case went to the Minnesota Court of Appeals, and Thompson, who had built a wheelchair-accessible home for Kowalski, finally gained custody in 1991.

When it comes to the law, spouses and blood relatives come first regardless of the wishes of the victim. That's why legislation such as the one in California [is] so important.

[It allows] people to say, in effect, "Hey, world. This is my life partner. This is the person I want when I'm sick or need to be taken care of, and it's the person I want taken care of if I die first."

The California proposal is such a little step in the legal scheme of things, but it's an important one.

Growth of Benefits

More than 2,800 firms and organizations offer some type of domestic partner benefits. Two states, Vermont and New York, have granted health and dental benefits to domestic partners of state employees. Some cities with similar provisions:

Health benefits: Ann Arbor and East Lansing, Mich.; Berkeley, Calif.; Cambridge, Mass.; Seattle, Wash.; New York, N.Y.

Registration and/or sick and bereavement leave: Atlanta, Ga.; Madison, Wis.; Takoma Park, Md.; Los Angeles, Calif.; West Palm Beach, Fla.

OPPOSING VIEW

This law isn't necessary. Stop this campaign to legitimize cohabitation.

Hold on to your checkbook, because the liberal/left is pushing another nearsighted social experiment called "domestic partners," which will cost taxpayers and redefine the institution of marriage.

The goal of the homosexual special interest lobby is to change the public policy of this nation by expanding the definition of marriage and family to include two homosexuals or heterosexuals living together. This new quasi-marital union impacts the way our judges make their rulings on issues that relate to marriage and family, and it devalues the concept of marriage.

So far, courts have denied marital status to cohabiting homosexuals. But this could change. If government expands the definition of marriage, the courts will then be compelled to force businesses to pay benefits for the domestic partners of employees just like benefits for employees' spouses. And governments could be forced to use scarce tax dollars for benefits for domestic partners of government employees. Most states allow consenting adults to live together, but that doesn't mean taxpayers should have to subsidize this arrangement.

Also, domestic partnerships weaken the institution of marriage and encourage relationships without the responsibility of marriage. Some may argue this new legislation promotes monogamous relationships, but these laws typically allow for a new "partner" every six months and erode the cultural support for the permanency of marriage.

Homosexual activists are good at marketing. They have tried to mainstream themselves by garnering some senior citizens' support. But domestic partners is an unnecessary shotgun approach to remedy some senior-citizen concerns.

Moreover, medical facilities already allow visitation in intensive care units and hospital rooms by friends or relatives. Existing law allows a testator to will property to anyone—friend or stranger. Existing law allows any "interested person" to file petitions or receive notice regarding conservatorship or guardianship.

The man/woman marriage relationship is best for society.

Source: "Our View"—Copyright 1994, *USA Today,* reprinted with permission; "Opposing View"—courtesy of the Rev. Louis P. Sheldon, chairman of Traditional Values Coalition, Anaheim, Calif.

In recent years, in addition to the five states that allow same-gender marriages, mentioned in the opening blurbs, cities like Atlanta, Georgia; Ithaca, New York; Madison, Wisconsin; and West Hollywood, California, and many others, provided for the registration of unmarried couples (gay or straight) as domestic partners. (See Exhibit 10.10, "Marriage, Civil Union, and Domestic Partnership Jurisdictions.") Domestic partners generally must be able to prove that for a specified length of time they have lived together and given mutual aid and support. Upon proof of the jurisdiction's requirements, domestic partners may qualify for certain benefits. For instance, Delta Airlines expanded its definition of "family" to whom frequent flyer miles can be transferred to include registered gay partners. In June 1994, Vermont became the first state to offer health benefits to domestic partners of state workers. Other jurisdictions followed. More than 5,000 private companies and city governments now permit their employees to include domestic partners in their health insurance coverage. Included among them are Goldman Sachs and J. P. Morgan, both major Wall Street investment firms generally considered rather staid and conservative.

As the labor market continues to tighten, such benefits are used as a marketing tool to attract and retain gay and lesbian employees. (See Exhibit 10.7, "New Push to Recruit Gay Students.") As an example of what partnership recognition legislation does, in 2002, the state of Connecticut passed legislation extending many rights to same-gender partners, such as allowing them to name someone to make their medical decisions, allowing private visits in nursing homes, and requiring employers to allow emergency calls from a legally designated person. These are things that heterosexuals generally take for granted, but they are rights that are not present for gays and lesbians except through legislation permitting it. Connecticut later enacted a gay marriage law. In those states that allow same-gender marriages, there is still a question as to benefits to be granted to a spouse by the federal government. The Defense of Marriage Act (DOMA) defines marriage as between a man and a woman. Therefore, even in states that permit same-gender marriages, legally married same-gender couples may not take advantage of the federal rights that come with that institution such as tax benefits. There has been a move to repeal DOMA. On February 23, 2011, U.S. Attorney General Eric Holder announced that the U.S. Department of Justice would no longer defend DOMA in cases challenging its constitutionality.[32] On their own, businesses have increasingly extended benefits to same-gender couples.

What might seem like purely social issues have workplace implications that are quite far-reaching. For instance, a San Francisco UPS employee sued after the employer denied his request for an out-of-state transfer so he could follow his male life partner's move to Chicago. The ongoing gay marriage debate has many implications for employers. In response to mounting concerns that gay marriage could result in mandatory domestic partner benefits or mandatory family leave for domestic partners, employers have already begun to address the issue of gay families in significant ways, regardless of what states or Congress choose to do. Nearly half of the Fortune 500 companies offer domestic partner benefits. Many companies go beyond. Of companies that provide such benefits, 90 percent cover

Exhibit 10.10   *Marriage, Civil Union, and Domestic Partnership Jurisdictions*

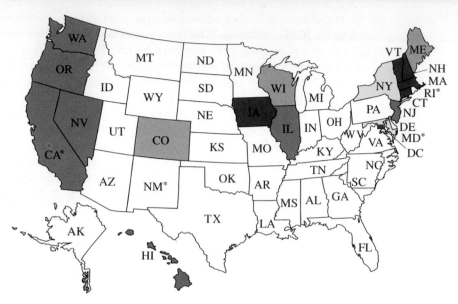

■ State issues marriage licenses to same-sex couples (5 states and the District of Columbia): Connecticut (2008), District of Columbia (2010), Iowa (2009), Massachusetts (2004), New Hampshire (2010) and Vermont (2009).

☐ State recognizes marriages by same-sex couples legally entered into in another jurisdiction (2 states): Maryland (2010) and New York (2008).

■ Statewide law providing the equivalent of state-level spousal rights to same-sex couples within the state (7 states and Washington, DC): California (domestic partnerships, 1999, expanded in 2005), Hawaii (civil unions, effective Jan. 1, 2012), Illinois (civil unions, effective June 1, 2011), Nevada (domestic partnerships, 2009), New Jersey (civil unions, 2007), Oregon (domestic partnerships, 2008) and Washington (domestic partnerships, 2007/2009).

■ Statewide law providing some statewide spousal rights to same-sex couples within the state (3 states): Colorado (designated beneficiaries, 2009), Maine (2004), and Wisconsin (domestic partnerships, 2009).

*California: Same-sex marriages that took place between June 16, 2008 and Nov. 4, 2008 continue to be defined as marriages. On Oct. 12, 2009, Gov. Schwarzenegger signed into law a bill that recognizes out-of-jurisdiction same-sex marriages that occurred between the June to Nov. 2008 time frame as marriages in California, and all other out-of-jurisdiction same-sex marriages as domestic partnerships.
*Maine: Gov. John Baldacci signed marriage equality legislation May 6, 2009. However, the new law was repealed by a ballot measure in November 2009.
*Maryland: Does not have a registry but does provide certain benefits to statutorily defined domestic partners. Also, in 2010, the Maryland Attorney General issued an advisory opinion declaring that the state can recognize out-of-jurisdiction marriages.
*New Mexico: In Jan. 2011, the New Mexico Attorney General issued an advisory opinion declaring that the state can recognize out-of-jurisdiction same-sex marriages. At this time, it is unclear what effect this opinion will have.
*Rhode Island does not have a registry but does provide certain benefits to statutorily defined domestic partners. In Feb. 2007, the Rhode Island Attorney General issued an advisory opinion declaring that the state can recognize out-of-jurisdiction marriages. However, in Dec. 2007 the Rhode Island Supreme Court refused to grant a divorce to a same-sex couple legally married in Massachusetts.

Source: Human Rights Campaign, 1649 Rhode Island Avenue, N.W., Washington, DC 20036. http://www.hrc.org/documents/Relationship_Recognition_Laws_Map.pdf, from www.hrc.org/state_laws. Updated February 25, 2011.

a domestic partner's dependents or children, 60 percent extend adoption assistance to domestic partners, and 72 percent also allow employees to take extended family leave to care for a domestic partner or their dependents.

According to the U.S. Census, the National Adoption Information Clearinghouse, and the Urban Institute, the number of children who have a gay or lesbian parent could be anywhere from 6 to 14 million. The most conservative estimates, based on underreported census data, puts the number of children growing up in single-gender-parent households at over 1 million. This has a significant impact on the workplace and an employee's willingness to fight for workplace pay and benefits.

Over the past several years, particularly as the gay marriage debate heated up, local jurisdictions began passing laws to allow gays and lesbian couples to register as domestic partners and receive some of the same benefits as married couples. (See Exhibit 10.10, "Marriage, Civil Union, and Domestic Partnership Jurisdictions.")[33]

- Below are states that have cities that provide procedures for registering as domestic partners:

Arizona	Michigan
Arkansas	Minnesota
California	Missouri
Colorado	North Carolina
Connecticut	New York
Florida	Ohio
Georgia	Oregon
Iowa	Pennsylvania
Illinois	Texas
Kansas	Utah
Louisiana	Washington
Massachusetts	Wisconsin
Maine	

- Same-gender marriages are legal in Massachusetts, New Jersey, Connecticut, Vermont, New Hampshire, Iowa, and the District of Columbia.
- Same-gender civil unions are permitted in Hawaii, Illinois, and New Jersey.
- Other states allow variation such as recognition of marriages legal in other states (Maryland and New York) or designated beneficiary rights (Colorado).

This means that workplace leave policies, adoption policies, and flexible schedule issues will become more pronounced as gay families continue to seek workplace rights provided to others. According to the Urban Institute, in 1990, 1 in 20 male single-gender couples had children under 18. By the year 2000, that number was 1 in 5. For women, 1 in 5 rose to 1 in 3 by 2000. Data indicate that gay dads are as likely to have one stay-at-home partner as heterosexual couples with children.[34] Gay and lesbian parents are quitting their jobs and moving to part-time work in order to deal with their children, and many employers are responding by offering work–life programs and benefits to gay parents.

Since research shows that gay couples with children are more likely to settle where there are more families with children, rather than in areas considered more "gay-friendly," this is not an issue for only a limited area of the country. Would it surprise you to know that the Urban Institute's research shows that the state where gay couples are most likely to raise children is—are you ready for this?—*Mississippi?*[35]

While there are employers who treat gay, lesbian, and transgender employees much like any other employees when it comes to these issues, others do not. More gay, lesbian and transgender employees have been fighting back. In *Alaska Civil Liberties Union v. State of Alaska*[36] gay and lesbian couples sued their state employer to have the right to include their long-term life partners in their workplace benefits. They won. The employers can make whatever policies they think are best for the workplace, but must keep in mind that there are many different sources of law to consider in this area. In addition, competition may well have an impact as more and more employers use the issue of creating a more welcoming workplace as a recruitment and retention tool to give themselves a competitive edge.

Management Considerations

Since affinity orientation is not a protected category under Title VII, employers have more flexibility in making workplace policies and decisions on this issue. The approach the employer takes will depend in large part on the employer's own views and preferences. Those employers who prefer the benefits of a diverse workplace—and who wish to maximize the potential the employee has for growth and contribution within the workplace and who wish to avoid legal wrangling—will likely choose to deal with the affinity orientation issue in a less restrictive manner.

Such employers will likely not have policies that have a hard-and-fast rule of "no transgenders, gays, or lesbians allowed." Rather, they will judge all employees on the basis of work-related criteria.

If some action of the transgender, lesbian, or gay employee presents an issue, it should be dealt with as a legitimate workplace issue, rather than one that arose solely because of the employee's affinity orientation or gender identity. The fact that the employee happens to be transgender, gay, or lesbian should not be treated as the "why," any more than it would be if the employee were not transgender, gay, or lesbian. It is irrelevant to the activity. The focus is on the conduct itself, not on the affinity orientation or gender identity of the employee. It greatly reduces the potential for liability to deal with all employees this way.

Employers who decide to have a policy that treats transgenders, gays, and lesbians as full contributors to the workplace should ensure that the message goes out from the very top. It is more likely to be accepted, appreciated, and understood and therefore will be more likely to accomplish its purpose. Other employees will be more likely to comport themselves consistently with the policy if it comes from the top of the hierarchy. It should be made clear that not only will the employer not discriminate on the basis of affinity orientation or gender identity, but it will not be tolerated from other employees, particularly in the form of harassment of transgenders, gays, and lesbians.

The employer who does not prefer this approach may have more latitude under the law (depending on the jurisdiction in which the employer is located) not to take this view than it would, say, about having women in the workplace, or having Jews, or blacks, or Hispanics. Some employers may even wish to take an adverse workplace decision involving a transgender, gay, or lesbian employee to court to maintain maximum control over areas not as heavily regulated as the other protected categories. That is the employer's personal choice, but at least the employer now knows both sides of the issue. (See Exhibit 10.9, "Domestic Partner Law Debate.")

Some employers take a middle-ground position. That is, they do not have a specific policy of either support or prohibition, but they deal with issues as they arise on a case-by-case basis. Again, because the law is not as restrictive for this category of employees as it is for others and does not extend the same Title VII protections, the employer potentially (again, depending on the state the employer is in) has more leeway to choose the management approach that best suits his or her needs or desires.

The caution to be heeded is that simply because Title VII or the majority of state fair-employment practice laws do not prohibit discrimination on the basis of affinity orientation or gender identity does not mean that it is not prohibited by relevant state or local laws relating to closely connected issues such as privacy, right to free speech, interference with contractual relations, and so on. And the laws are changing every day. Employers concerned about workplace decisions should, at the very least, check such laws or case law in their jurisdiction before making final decisions. Remember that every single state has either a state or local law protecting transgenders, gays, and lesbians in some way or another.

Even if the law is on the employer's side, the employer may wish to consider other possible repercussions of restrictive employment policies in this area. An example of this is the Cracker Barrel restaurant chain, headquartered in Tennessee. Cracker Barrel operates a number of restaurants around the country. With no apparent motivating event, in 1991 the company announced that it would no longer employ people "whose sexual preferences fail to demonstrate normal heterosexual values which have been the foundation of families in our society." Pursuant to this policy, Cracker Barrel summarily dismissed its gay and lesbian employees.

After doing so, it was the subject of vigorous opposition, mainly by the gay and lesbian community. Many of Cracker Barrel's restaurants were picketed and denounced by vocal protesters. Gays and lesbians bought stock in order to have a say in its policies. Cracker Barrel later revoked the policy as overreactive. Even though the law permitted Cracker Barrel's actions, some employers may wish to avoid the controversy exhibited here, particularly if there is no pressing need to address the issue. In a complete about-face, in 2002, Cracker Barrel's board of directors voted to include gays and lesbians in its anti-discrimination policy.[37]

Management Tips

LO8

Policies and decisions in the affinity orientation and gender identity areas are rapidly evolving. The patchwork of state, federal, local, public, and private laws and policies we have discussed present the employer with the challenge of trying to do what is required for each jurisdiction, when, in fact, the requirements may be quite different. However, conclusions can be drawn about creating policy in the midst of such seeming chaos. In order to provide the maximum protection from liability for affinity orientation–related issues, an employer can do several things:

- Hire using only relevant, work-related criteria.
- Keep inquiries about applicants' personal lives at a minimum and make sure the information is relevant.
- Have a policy ensuring all employees respect in the workplace, and ensure that all employees are aware of the policy and what it means.
- No matter what the employer's policy about lesbians, gays, or transgenders, in the workplace, be sure the respect policy protects everyone from things like unsolicited negative statements about immutable and other characteristics such as race, religion, gender, and affinity orientation.
- Take prompt action whenever there are complaints of violations of the policy or it sends the message that the policy is meaningless.
- Decide what position to take on affinity orientation–related issues for policy purposes either proactively, before the issue arises, or defensively to meet the issue when it comes about; the latter has the benefit of specificity, the former the advantage of deliberate, strategic thinking.
- Be aware of the potential impact on transgenders, gays, and lesbians of workplace policies regarding issues like bereavement leave, benefits, bringing significant others to office functions, accepting personal calls during work hours, and displaying personal items at work (photos, cards, political buttons, and so forth).
- If the employer decides to institute policies inclusive of transgenders, gays and lesbians, ensure that they are fair and evenly handled.

Case 4

Despite all the information in this chapter, it is still up to the employer how the issue of gays and lesbians in the workplace is to be handled. A word of caution should be given, however. If the employer decides to create a workplace inclusive of transgenders, gays, and lesbians, he or she should be aware of the religious conflicts employees have alleged based on diversity policies. As *Buonanno v. AT&T Broadband, LLC* demonstrates, at the conclusion of the chapter, the employer should not trample over the rights of other employees in order to address the issue of diversity and avoiding liability. In *Buonanno*, an employee was terminated for refusing, based on his religious objection to same-gender affinity orientation, to sign a workplace document pledging him to value diversity. The court agreed that it was wrong for the employer to terminate the employee without trying to accommodate his religious beliefs.

Chapter Summary

- Affinity orientation and gender identity discrimination is not protected by Title VII.
- Washington, DC, 21 states, and hundreds of municipalities have passed protective legislation. Constitutional protection also may apply to public employees and thousands of workplaces have included affinity orientation and gender identity in their non-discrimination policies.
- Employers in most jurisdictions have more leeway in this area to make employment decisions without regard to the same legal strictures applicable to other categories of employees included within Title VII.
- The safer approach is to base employment decisions on the person's qualifications and fitness for the job, rather than on questionably relevant characteristics about his or her personal life.

Chapter-End Questions

1. Applicant applies for a position with Ace Corporation. During the interview, Ace suspects that the applicant is gay. When asked why the suspicion, Ace says that the male applicant acted effeminately. Ace decides not to hire the applicant, who is otherwise qualified. Does the applicant have a cause of action against Ace? [*Jantz v. Muci,* 759 F. Supp. 1543 (D. Kan. 1991).]

2. When the FBI learns that Mary, its FBI agent, is a lesbian, Mary is fired. Mary goes to an attorney to find out about the possibility of suing to get her job back. What does the attorney likely tell her?

3. As a manager, an employee comes to you and tells you that he has a hunch that one of the other employees is probably gay. What do you do?

4. Charlie, the manager, does not like it that Chester wears an earring and orders Chester to get rid of it or be terminated. Chester refuses. Can Charlie terminate Chester?

5. Employee sues his employer, saying that he is being sexually harassed by gay males, who only harass young male employees. Does he have a cause of action? [*Wrightson v. Pizza Hut of America, Inc.,* 99 F.3d 138 (4th Cir. 1996).]

6. Maureen brings her same-gender partner of 14 years to a company picnic. One of the other employees treats Maureen poorly after realizing she is a lesbian. Does Maureen have any recourse?

7. A male firefighter is diagnosed with gender dysphoria seven years after coming onto the force and having no negative incidents with co-workers. As he begins to exhibit a more feminine demeanor, he begins to have administrative troubles, which he attributes to his failing to conform to gender stereotypes. Does he have a cause of action under Title VII? [*Smith v. City of Salem, Ohio,* 378 F.3d 566 (6th Cir. 2004).]

8. A female assistant at a hair salon is terminated. She brings suit under Title VII, alleging that it is because she is a lesbian whose overall appearance is more male than female. The employer counters that the termination was due to poor performance; there was no dress code, and the employee was allowed to wear her hair in a Mohawk cut as long as it was styled by someone at the salon. Is the employee likely to win? [*Dawson v. Bumble & Bumble,* 398 F.3d 211 (2d Cir. 2005).]

9. Employee was designated male at birth and on her driver's license, but considered herself a woman. When she used both the male and female bathrooms at work, her

employer asked her to supply a letter from her doctor indicating her gender. Her attorney wrote saying that she was not entirely male or female, and was, instead, intersexed. The employer tells the employee she can only use the men's restroom. If the employee had not notified the employer that she was intersexed, and possibly within Title VII, would employer be held liable for discrimination? [*Johnson v. Fresh Mark, Inc.,* 337 F. Supp. 2d 996 (N.D. Ohio 2003).]

10. Employee is harassed by a male co-worker, who makes repeated statements to him in the men's locker room such as "your hands are so soft—what are you doing after work?" and "why don't you come strip for me?" The employee complains to management. Does management have to respond? [*Jones v. Pacific Rail Services,* 85 Fair Empl. Prac. Cas. (BNA) 90 (N.D. Ill. 2001).]

End Notes

1. "Farmer Spreads Manure along Gay Parade Route," *Shortnews,* 8/2/2004, http://www.shortnews.com/start.cfm?id=41710.

2. Suzi Parker, Michael Rozman, "Constance McMillen Case: Proms as Gay-rights Battleground," *The Christian Science Monitor,* 3/23/2010, http://www.csmonitor.com/USA/Justice/2010/0323/Constance-McMillen-case-proms-as-gay-rights-battleground.

3. John M. Broder, "Schwarzenegger Calls Budget Opponents "Girlie Men," *The New York Times,* 7/19/2004, http://www.nytimes.com/2004/07/19/us/schwarzenegger-calls-budget-opponents-girlie-men.html?src=pm.

4. http://www.qrd.org/qrd/usa/legal/lgln/2003/09.03.

5. Lauren Johnson, "Boy, 7, Scolded for Saying 'Gay': La. Student Says Mother Is a Lesbian, Sent to Principal for Saying 'Bad Word,'" CBS News, 12/1/2003, http://www.cbsnews.com/stories/2003/12/01/national/main586293.shtml.

6. "Obama Signs Repeal of 'Don't Ask, Don't Tell' Policy, CNN.com, 12/22/2010, http://articles.cnn.com/2010-12-22/politics/dadt.repeal_1_repeal-openly-gay-men-president-barack-obama?_s=PM:POLITICS.

7. Sharon Jayson, "APA Meeting: Being Gay Isn't a Mental Illness," *USA Today,* 8/10/2009, p. 5D.

8. "Episcopal Church Consecrates First Openly Lesbian Bishop," CNN.com, 5/15/2010, http://articles.cnn.com/2010-05-15/us/episcopal.lesbian.bishop_1_gay-bishops-canterbury-rowan-williams-consecrated?_s=PM:US.

9. Ellen Barry, "County Rescinds Vote to Ban Gay Residents, In the Courtroom of the 1925 'Monkey Trial,' Commissioners Retreat Amid Ideological Furor," *The L.A. Times,* 3/19/2004, http://www.commondreams.org/headlines04/0319-10.htm.

10. Haya El Nasser, "Same-sex Unions Challenge Census," *USA Today,* 7/6/2009, p 3A.

11. Presidential Memorandum—Hospital Visitation, 4/15/2010, http://www.whitehouse.gov/the-press-office/presidential-memorandum-hospital-visitation.

12. "Lesbian's Case against Jackson Memorial Hospital Tossed," *The Miami Herald,* 9/30/2009, http://www.miamiherald.co/news/miami-dade/stor/1258772.html.

13. *Newsweek,* 10/25/2010 p. 16.

14. Alexis Stevens, "Man Says His Room Set on Fire Because He's Gay," *The Atlanta Journals-Constitution,* 1/24/2011, http://www.ajc.com/news/man-says-his-room-813704.html.

15. Also included in this general discussion are persons of bigender affinity orientation and transgenders. Since workplace issues generally stem from exercise of their same-gender component, they are not specifically delineated here separately except as necessary, and for convenience only, are generally referred to as gays and lesbians. However, because of the unique workplace issues they present, there is a later section in the chapter on transgenders. Gender identity issues also included the intersexed (formerly hermaphrodites).

16. http://www.hrc.org/issues/workplace/enda.asp.

17. Human Rights Campaign http://www.hrc.org/laws_and_elections/enda.asp.

18. http://www.hrc.org/issues/workplace/equal_opportunity/equal_opportunity_legislation.asp.

19. Now defunct.

20. "Poll: More Americans Favor Same-Sex Marriage," 4/19/2011, http://politicalticker.blogs.cnn.com/2011/04/19/poll-more-americans-favor-same-sex-marriage/; Dan Gilgoff, "CNN Poll: Most Americans Oppose Gay Marriage, but Those Under 35 Back It," 5/5/2009, http://www.usnews.com/news/blogs/god-and-country/2009/05/05/cnn-poll-most-americans-oppose-gay-marriage-but-those-under-35-back-it.

21. Ft. Worth City Council Representative Joel Burn, http://www.youtube.com/watch?v=ax96cghOnY4&feature=related; Price Waterhouse Coopers PwC, It Gets Better http://www.youtube.com/watch?v=fffI4TzuIk0 Google's video http://www.youtube.com/watch?v=pYLs4NCgvNU&feature=related Facebook's video http://www.youtube.com/watch?v=iPg02qjL40g&feature=related.

22. http://www.youtube.com/watch?v=DmvV-E1LEXo.

23. http://www.hrc.org/issues/workplace/5636.htm.

24. http://www.hrc.org/documents/Business_Coalition_for_Workplace_Fairness_-_Members.pdf.

25. http://www.gao.gov/new.items/d10135r.pdf.

26. *Romer v. Evans,* 517 U.S. 620 (1996).

27. 608 F.2d 327 (9th Cir. 1979).

28. 876 F.2d 69 (8th Cir. 1998).

29. 523 U.S. 75 (1998).

30. 742 F.2d 1081 (7th Cir. 1984).

31. 742 F.2d 1081 (7th Cir. 1984).

32. Eric Holder's statement regarding DOJ no longer defending DOMA can be found at http://www.justice.gov/opa/pr/2011/February/11-ag-222.html.

33. http://www.hrc.org/documents/Relationship_Recognition_Laws_Map.pdf.

34. Stephanie Armour, "Gay Parents Cheer a Benefit Revolution," *USA Today,* 1/9/2005, http://www.usatoday.com/money/workplace/2005-01-09-gay-parents_x.htm#.

35. Ibid.

36. 122 P.3d 781 (Alaska 2005).

37. Ronald Smothers, "Company Ousts Gay Workers, Then Reconsiders," *The New York Times,* 2/28/1991, http://www.nytimes.com/1991/02/28/us/company-ousts-gay-workers-then-reconsiders.html.

Cases

Weaver v. Nebo School District *29 F. Supp. 2d 1279 (D. Utah 1998)*

A schoolteacher was reprimanded when she said yes when asked by a student if she was gay. Her coaching job was taken away and a notation put in her personnel file. The court held that treating her this way based on affinity orientation was an unconstitutional denial of equal protection.

Jenkins, J.

***

For the past 19 years, plaintiff Wendy Weaver has been a teacher at Spanish Fork High School in the Nebo School District. Ms. Weaver, a tenured faculty member since 1982, teaches psychology and physical education. Her reputation as an educator at Spanish Fork is unblemished: she has always been considered an effective and capable teacher, her evaluations range from good to excellent, and she has never been the subject of any disciplinary action. In addition to her teaching responsibilities, Ms. Weaver has served as the girl's volleyball coach since 1979. She has been effective in this endeavor, leading the team to four state championships.

Unlike her teaching position, however, Ms. Weaver's position as coach was not tenured. Instead, as is the case with all coaching positions at Spanish Fork High School, Ms. Weaver was hired as volleyball coach on a year-to-year basis. For each year she was hired as coach, Ms. Weaver received a stipend, which in her most recent year of coaching was $1,500. The practice of hiring coaches, however, is somewhat informal. It is the policy of the School District that Principal Wadley has final decision-making authority in selecting a coach. Generally, Principal Wadley finds out who has an interest, selects a coach from the interested candidates, and notifies the coach that he or she has the position. No written contract is prepared. In practice, the coach from the previous year is routinely offered the position for the following year, or, as Principal Wadley

stated, "you assign them once and they stay assigned until you assign someone else."

In the late spring and early summer of 1997, Ms. Weaver began preparing for the upcoming school volleyball season—as she did in the past—by organizing two summer volleyball camps for prospective team players. As usual, these camps were to be held at Spanish Fork High School in June and July of 1997. Ms. Weaver telephoned prospective volleyball team members to inform them of the camp schedules. One of the calls went to a senior team member. During the conversation, the team member asked Ms. Weaver, "Are you gay?" Ms. Weaver truthfully responded, "Yes." The team member then told Ms. Weaver that she would not play on the volleyball team in the fall. On July 14, 1997, the team member and her parents met with defendants Almon Mosher, Director of Human Resources for the Nebo School District, and Larry Kimball, Director of Secondary Education for the Nebo School District, and told them that Ms. Weaver told them that she is gay and that the team member decided she would not play volleyball.

In April of 1997, Gary Weaver, Ms. Weaver's ex-husband and a school psychologist for the Nebo School District, spoke with Principal Wadley about Ms. Weaver's sexual orientation. In May of 1997, Nedra Call, the Curriculum Coordinator for the School District, received two calls concerning Ms. Weaver's "lifestyle and her actions." She related the substance of these calls to defendant Mosher. Defendant Dennis Poulsen, Superintendent of the Nebo School District, also received calls about Ms. Weaver. In addition, several adults affiliated or formerly affiliated with the school contacted Principal Wadley with comments or questions about Ms. Weaver's sexual orientation. Principal Wadley held a meeting with his two assistant principals to discuss Ms. Weaver's sexual orientation. On May 22, 1997, before the phone conversation with Ms. Weaver, the team member and her mother telephoned Principal Wadley to let him know that the team member would not be playing volleyball because she was uncomfortable playing on the team knowing that Ms. Weaver is gay. On May 22nd, Principal Wadley discussed Ms. Weaver's sexual orientation with defendant Larry Kimball. Even the School Advisory Council wanted to discuss Ms. Weaver's sexual orientation.

In response to these reports, and after meeting again with the team member's family on July 14, 1997, defendants Mosher and Kimball discussed taking some action against Ms. Weaver because they felt Ms. Weaver's comments about her sexual orientation were in "violation of district policy." Several days later, on July 21, 1997, Ms. Weaver met with Principal Wadley, who informed her that she would not be assigned to coach volleyball for the 1997–98 school year. This discussion was memorialized in a letter to Ms. Weaver dated the same day but sent subsequently. The following day, Ms. Weaver was called to a meeting at the School District office and presented a letter, printed on the School District letterhead. The letter was drafted by defendant Mosher, signed by him and Larry Kimball, was reviewed by defendant Dennis Poulsen, delivered to Ms. Weaver, and placed in her personnel file. On August 8, 1997, a similar letter was issued to Gary Weaver. This letter was delivered to Mr. Weaver and placed in his personnel file.

Despite mounting evidence that gay males and lesbians suffer from employment discrimination and, as recent events in Wyoming [the brutal murder of gay college student Matthew Shepard] remind us, other more life-threatening expressions of bias, courts, including the Supreme Court, have not yet recognized a person's sexual orientation as a status that deserves heightened protection. The deep-seated prejudice on the part of some persons against the gay and lesbian community can be summed up in a single quote from ardent anti-gay activist and former entertainer Anita Bryant: "I'd rather my child be dead than be a homosexual." See Millie Ball, "I'd Rather My Child Be

Dead Than Homo," *The Times-Picayune*, June 19, 1977, at 3 (quoting Ms. Bryant). To date, Congress has expressly prohibited employment discrimination on the basis of race, religion, national origin, gender, age, and disability, but not sexual orientation. As of this year, eleven states and the District of Columbia offer statutory protection against discrimination on the basis of sexual orientation; thirty-nine states, including Utah, do not.

Nevertheless, the Fourteenth Amendment of the United States Constitution entitles all persons to equal protection under the law. It appears that the plain language of the Fourteenth Amendment's Equal Protection Clause prohibits a state government or agency from engaging in intentional discrimination—even on the basis of sexual orientation—absent some rational basis for so doing.

The Supreme Court has recognized that an "irrational prejudice" cannot provide the rational basis to support a state action against an equal protection challenge. "A bare desire to harm a politically unpopular group" is not a legitimate state interest. Indeed, mere negative attitudes, or fear, unsubstantiated by factors which are properly cognizable in [the circumstances], are not permissible bases for differential treatment by the government.

Supreme Court precedent has recognized that when state action reflects an animus directed at a defined minority, it cannot be supported under the Equal Protection Clause. More recently, in *Romer v. Evans*, 517 U.S. 620 (1996), the Court was called upon to examine whether an amendment to Colorado's state constitution, prohibiting any legislation or judicial action designed to protect the status of a person based on sexual orientation violated the Fourteenth Amendment. It had no trouble finding that it did. In *Romer*, the Court noted that under the ordinary deferential equal protection standard—that is, rational basis—the Court would "insist on knowing the relation between the classification adopted and the object to be obtained." It is this search for a "link" between classification and objective, noted the Court, that "gives substance to the Equal Protection Clause." In *Romer*, such a "link" was noticeably absent. Noting that the "inevitable inference" that arises from a law of this sort is that it is "born of animosity toward the class of persons affected," the Court described the amendment as "a status-based enactment divorced from any factual context from which we could discern a relationship to legitimate state interests."

The question then is whether bias concerning Ms. Weaver's sexual orientation furnishes a rational basis for the defendants' decision not to assign her as volleyball coach. The "negative reaction" some members of the community may have to homosexuals is not a proper basis for discriminating against them. So reasoned the Supreme Court in the context of race. See, e.g., *Brown v. Board of Education,* 347 U.S. 483 (1954) (declaring that racial school segregation is unconstitutional despite the widespread acceptance of the practice in the community and in the country). If the community's perception is based on nothing more than unsupported assumptions, outdated stereotypes, and animosity, it is necessarily irrational and under *Romer* and other Supreme Court precedent, it provides no legitimate support for the School District's decisions.

The record now before the court contains no job-related justification for not assigning Ms. Weaver as volleyball coach. Nor have the defendants demonstrated how Ms. Weaver's sexual orientation bears any rational relationship to her competency as teacher or coach, or her job performance as coach—a position she has held for many years with distinction. As mentioned earlier, it is undisputed that she was an excellent coach and apparently, up until the time her sexual orientation was revealed, the likely candidate for the position. Principal Wadley's decision not to assign Ms. Weaver (a decision reached after consulting with the other defendants) was based solely on her sexual orientation. Absent some rational relationship to job performance, a decision not to assign Ms. Weaver as coach because of her sexual orientation runs afoul of the Fourteenth Amendment's equal protection guarantee.

Although the Constitution cannot control prejudices, neither this court nor any other court should, directly or indirectly, legitimize them. The private antipathy of some members of a community cannot validate state discrimination. Because a community's animus towards homosexuals can never serve as a legitimate basis for state action, the defendants' actions based on that animus violate the Equal Protection Clause. Because this perceived negative reaction arose solely from Ms. Weaver's sexual orientation, and not from her abilities as coach, it does not furnish a rational job-related basis for the defendants' decision. Therefore, Ms. Weaver's motion for summary judgment is granted as to this claim.

In Ms. Weaver's second equal protection claim, she asserts that the defendants violated her rights to equal protection by imposing a viewpoint and content-based restriction on her speech. She argues that she was prohibited from discussing her sexual orientation only because she would have discussed her homosexuality, and points

out that other teachers were free to discuss their heterosexual orientations.

Ms. Weaver was threatened with disciplinary action for discussing her intimate associations and sexual orientation. At the same time, no other teacher in the School District was prohibited from discussing these topics. Indeed, as the School District conceded at the hearing, no similar restriction was placed on heterosexual teachers at all. Clearly then, the School District wanted to silence Ms. Weaver's speech because of its expected pro-homosexual viewpoint. Such viewpoint-based restriction is constitutionally impermissible.

Simple as it may sound, as a matter of fairness and evenhandedness, homosexuals should not be sanctioned or restricted for speech that heterosexuals are not likewise sanctioned or restricted for. Because the School District has not restricted other teachers in speaking out on their sexual orientation, the School District has not only violated the First Amendment, but also the Fourteenth Amendment's Equal Protection Clause. In such an instance, when an equal protection claim is based on a person's exercise of a fundamental constitutional right, the proper standard of review is strict scrutiny—that is, is the restriction supported by a compelling state interest. Because the Court has concluded that the School District's actions cannot be supported on any rational basis, the District's actions obviously fail the strict scrutiny test. Ms. Weaver is granted summary judgment on this claim as well.

For the foregoing reasons, it is ordered that plaintiff's motion for summary judgment is GRANTED and defendants' motion is DENIED; that the School District shall remove the letters from plaintiff's personnel file; the School District is directed to offer the plaintiff the Spanish Fork High School girl's volleyball coaching position for the 1999–2000 school year; and the School District pay damages to the plaintiff in the sum of $1,500.

Case Questions

1. What would you have done if you had been the school administrator receiving calls in this situation?

2. Do you think the school was correct in ignoring the teacher's record?

3. Does it make a difference that this matter did not arise at the teacher's instigation, but in response to a question from a student? Explain.

Nichols v. Azteca Restaurant Enterprises, Inc.
256 F.3d 864 (9th Cir. 2001)

Employee brought suit under Title VII for gender harassment directed toward him at work that employer did little to stop. The court agreed with the employee that this constituted a violation of Title VII even though the employee was gay.

Gould, J.

⁂

Throughout his tenure at Azteca, Sanchez was subjected to a relentless campaign of insults, name-calling, and vulgarities. Male co-workers and a supervisor repeatedly referred to Sanchez in Spanish and English as "she" and "her." Male co-workers mocked Sanchez for walking and carrying his serving tray "like a woman," and taunted him in Spanish and English as, among other things, a "faggot" and a "f**king female whore." The remarks were not stray or isolated. Rather, the abuse occurred at least once a week and often several times a day.

This conduct violated company policy. Since 1989, Azteca has expressly prohibited sexual harassment and retaliation and has directed its employees to bring complaints regarding such conduct directly to the attention of the corporate office. Upon receipt of a complaint, Azteca's policy is to conduct a thorough investigation, the results of which are reviewed by the company's EEO Board, which is then responsible for implementing an appropriate remedy.

In addition to this policy, Azteca has a bilingual (English and Spanish) training program about sexual harassment. This training, which all employees attend when hired, and annually thereafter, defines sexual harassment and instructs employees how to report complaints.

Under Title VII, it is unlawful for an employer "to discriminate against any individual with respect to his compensation, terms, conditions, or privileges of employment, because of . . . sex." It is by now clear that sexual harassment in the form of a hostile work environment constitutes sex discrimination.

To prevail on his hostile environment claim, Sanchez was required to establish a "pattern of ongoing and persistent harassment severe enough to alter the conditions of employment." To satisfy this requirement, Sanchez needed to prove that his workplace was "both objectively and subjectively offensive, one that a reasonable person would find hostile or abusive, and one that the victim in fact did perceive to be so." In addition, Sanchez was required to prove that any harassment took place "because of sex." The district court ruled against Sanchez on each of these elements, concluding that: (1) Sanchez's workplace was not objectively hostile; (2) Sanchez did not perceive his workplace to be hostile; and (3) the alleged conduct did not occur because of sex. We disagree with each of these conclusions and, where applicable, the clearly erroneous findings upon which they are based.

Having reviewed the record, we hold that a reasonable man would have found the sustained campaign of taunts, directed at Sanchez and designed to humiliate and anger him, sufficiently severe and pervasive to alter the terms and conditions of his employment. Indeed, even Azteca does not contend otherwise on appeal.

Assuming that a reasonable person would find a workplace hostile, if the victim "does not subjectively perceive the environment to be abusive, the conduct has not actually altered the conditions of the victim's employment, and there is no Title VII violation." We must determine whether Sanchez, by his conduct, indicated that the alleged harassment was "unwelcome."

The district court concluded that the frequent verbal abuse was not unwelcome. Although the court made no factual finding directly on point, its determination may have been influenced by its findings that: (1) Sanchez made no complaint of sexual harassment to Serna, or anyone else from the corporate office; (2) Sanchez never sought mental health treatment; and (3) Sanchez engaged in horseplay with his male co-workers. We see the evidence another way.

The first of these findings by the district court, which forms the crux of Azteca's appeal, is clearly erroneous. It is undisputed that in May 1995 Sanchez told Serna, in considerable detail, about the fact and nature of the verbal abuse. Sanchez also complained to the South-center general manager and an assistant manager, though in less detail. That Sanchez complained about the frequent, degrading verbal abuse supports our conclusion that the conduct was unwelcome, as does Sanchez's unrebutted testimony to that effect. We hold that Sanchez perceived his workplace to be hostile.

Nor do the other potentially relevant findings noted above—that Sanchez never sought mental health treatment, and that he engaged in horseplay with some of his harassers—warrant a different result. As to the first, the scope of Title VII is not limited to conduct that affects a victim's psychological well-being. As to the second, the fact that not all of Sanchez's interactions with his harassers were hostile does not mean that none of them was. As any sensible person would, Sanchez drew a distinction between conduct he perceived to be objectionable, and conduct that was not. He viewed horseplay as "male bonding" and excluded it from his hostile environment claim; he viewed relentless verbal affronts as sexual harassment, and sought legal recourse for that conduct. And, in complaining to Serna about the verbal abuse, he demonstrated a subjective belief that he was being harassed.

Sexual harassment is actionable under Title VII to the extent it occurs "because of" the employee's gender. Sanchez asserts that the verbal abuse at issue was based upon the perception that he is effeminate and, therefore, occurred because of gender. In short, Sanchez contends that he was harassed because he failed to conform to a male stereotype.

At its essence, the systematic abuse directed at Sanchez reflected a belief that Sanchez did not act as a man should act. Sanchez was attacked for walking and carrying his tray "like a woman"—i.e., for having feminine mannerisms. Sanchez was derided for not having sexual intercourse with a waitress who was his friend. Sanchez's male co-workers and one of his supervisors repeatedly reminded Sanchez that he did not conform to their gender-based stereotypes, referring to him as "she" and "her." And, the most vulgar name-calling directed at Sanchez was cast in female terms. We conclude that this verbal abuse was closely linked to gender.

We hold that the verbal abuse at issue occurred because of gender. Because we hold that Sanchez has established each element of his hostile environment claim, we further hold that the conduct of Sanchez's co-workers and supervisor constituted actionable harassment under Title VII. AFFIRMED IN PART, REVERSED IN PART, and REMANDED.

Case Questions

1. Title VII does not prohibit discrimination on the basis of affinity orientation. How would you characterize this case? Do you see the discrimination as being based on affinity orientation and thus not protected by Title VII, or as based on gender and thus protected by Title VII?

2. Why do you think the managers did not address the employee's complaints?

3. What would you have done differently here if you had been Sanchez's manager?

Jane Doe v. Boeing Company *121 Wash. 2d 8 (1993)*

A biological male employee who was planning to have gender reassignment surgery sued his employer, Boeing, for employment discrimination, alleging an unaccommodated disability. He was discharged by Boeing for wearing "excessively" feminine attire (pink pearls) in violation of company directives. The Washington Supreme Court found that Boeing had done enough to reasonably accommodate the employee, even though it had no duty to do so under Washington's law against discrimination.

Guy, J.

                      ***

Jane Doe was hired as a Boeing engineer in 1978. At the time of hire, Doe was a biological male and presented herself as such on her application for employment. In 1984, after years of struggling with her sexual identity,

Doe concluded that she was a transsexual. Transsexualism is also known in the psychiatric and medical communities as gender dysphoria.

Doe's treating physician confirmed Doe's self-assessment and diagnosed Doe as gender dysphoric. In April 1984, Doe began hormone treatments, as prescribed by Dr. Smith, as well as electrolysis treatments. In December 1984, Doe legally changed her masculine name to a feminine name.

In March 1985, Doe informed her supervisors, management and co-workers at Boeing of her transsexualism and of her intent to have gender reassignment surgery. Doe informed Boeing of her belief that in order to qualify for gender reassignment surgery, she would have to live full time, for 1 year, in the social role of a female. Doe based her belief on discussions with her treating psychologist and her physician about a treatment protocol for transsexuals known as the Harry Benjamin International Gender Dysphoria Standards (Benjamin Standards). Benjamin Standard 9 states: "Genital sex reassignment shall be preceded by a period of at least 12 months during which time the patient lived full-time in the social role of the genetically other sex."

Upon being notified of Doe's intentions, Boeing informed Doe that while Doe was an anatomical male, she could not use the women's rest rooms or dress in "feminine" attire. Boeing informed Doe that she could dress as a woman at work and use the women's rest rooms upon completion of her gender reassignment surgery.

While Doe was an anatomical male, Boeing permitted Doe to wear either male clothing or unisex clothing. Unisex clothing included blouses, sweaters, slacks, flat shoes, nylon stockings, earrings, lipstick, foundation, and clear nail polish. Doe was instructed not to wear obviously feminine clothing such as dresses, skirts, or frilly blouses. Boeing applied its unwritten dress policy to all employees, which included eight other transsexuals who had expressed a desire to have gender reassignment surgery while working for Boeing. Both Doe's psychologist and treating physician testified that what Doe was allowed to wear at Boeing was sufficiently feminine for Doe to qualify for gender reassignment surgery.

Between June and late September 1985, Boeing management received approximately a dozen anonymous complaints regarding Doe's attire and use of the women's rest rooms. On October 25, 1985, following the receipt of a complaint about Doe using the women's rest room, Boeing issued Doe a written disciplinary warning. The warning reiterated Boeing's position on acceptable attire

and rest room use and stated that Doe's failure to comply with Boeing's directives by November 1, 1985, would result in further corrective action, including termination. During this "grace" period, Doe's compliance with Boeing's "acceptable attire" directive was to be monitored each day by Doe's direct supervisor. Doe was told that her attire would be deemed unacceptable when, in the supervisor's opinion, her dress would be likely to cause a complaint were Doe to use a men's rest room at a Boeing facility. No single article of clothing would be dispositive. Doe's overall appearance was to be assessed.

Doe's transsexualism did not interfere with her ability to perform her job duties as a software engineer at Boeing. There was no measurable decline in either her work group's performance or in Doe's own job performance. There was no testimony to indicate that Boeing's dress restrictions hindered Doe's professional development.

On November 4, 1985, the first day Doe worked after the grace period, Doe wore attire that her supervisor considered acceptable. Doe responded that she was disappointed that her attire was acceptable, and that she would "push it" the next day. By "push it," Doe testified that she meant she would wear more extreme feminine attire. The next day, Doe came to work wearing similar attire, but she included as part of her outfit a strand of pink pearls which she refused to remove. This outfit was similar to one she had been told during the grace period was unacceptable in that the addition of the pink pearls changed Doe's look from unisex to "excessively" feminine. Doe was subsequently terminated from her position at Boeing as a result of her willful violation of Boeing's directives. Doe filed a handicap discrimination action against Boeing pursuant to Washington's Law Against Discrimination (hereafter Act) RCW49.60. The trial court held that Doe was "temporarily handicapped" under its construction of the law. The Court of Appeals reversed, finding Boeing failed to accommodate Doe. We reverse the Court of Appeals.

This case presents two issues for review. First, is Jane Doe's gender dysphoria a "handicap" under RCW 49.60.180? We hold that Doe's gender dysphoria is not a handicap under the Act. The definition of "handicap" for enforcement purposes in unfair practice cases under RCW 49.60.180, as defined in WAC 162-22-040, requires factual findings of both (1) the presence of an abnormal condition, and (2) employer discrimination against the plaintiff because of that condition. While gender dysphoria is an abnormal condition, we hold that Doe was not "handicapped" by her gender dysphoria because Boeing did not discharge her because of that condition.

Second, did Boeing have to provide Doe's preferred accommodation under RCW 49.60.180? We hold that the scope of an employer's duty to reasonably accommodate an employee's abnormal condition is limited to those steps necessary to enable the employee to perform his or her job. We hold that Boeing's actions met this standard and did not discriminate against Doe by reason of her abnormal condition.

It is uncontested that gender dysphoria is an abnormal, medically cognizable condition with a prescribed course of treatment. Assuming the presence of an abnormal condition, the next inquiry is whether the employer discriminated against the employee because of that condition. Boeing did not discriminate against Doe because of her condition. Boeing discharged Doe because she violated Boeing's directives on acceptable attire, not because she was gender dysphoric. Doe was treated in a respectful way by both her peers and supervisors at Boeing. Doe's supervisor consistently rated her work as satisfactory on her performance evaluations. While complaints were filed with Boeing management about Doe's use of the women's rest room, the record is void of any evidence that Doe suffered harassment because of her use of the rest room or because of her attire.

Inasmuch as Boeing did not discharge Doe based on her abnormal condition but on her refusal to conform with directives on acceptable attire, we must turn our attention to whether Boeing discriminated against Doe by failing to reasonably accommodate her condition of gender dysphoria.

We recognize that employers have an affirmative obligation to reasonably accommodate the sensory, mental, or physical limitations of such employees unless the employer can demonstrate that the accommodation would impose an undue hardship on the conduct of the employer's business. The issue before us is whether Boeing had a duty to accommodate Doe's preferred manner of dress prior to her gender reassignment surgery. We hold that the scope of an employer's duty to accommodate an employee's condition is limited to those steps reasonably necessary to enable the employee to perform his or her job.

Doe contends that Boeing's dress code failed to accommodate her condition and thus was discriminatory. We disagree. The record substantially supports the trial court's findings that Boeing reasonably accommodated Doe in the matter of dress by allowing her to wear unisex clothing at work. Despite this accommodation, Doe determined unilaterally, and without medical confirmation, that she needed to dress as a woman at her place of employment in order to qualify for gender reassignment surgery. We find substantial support for the trial court's finding that Doe had no medical need to dress as a woman at work in order to qualify for her surgery.

[P]laintiff's experts declined to state that any particular degree of feminine dress was required in order for plaintiff to fulfill any presurgical requirements. In fact, the evidence was uncontradicted that the unisex dress permitted by Boeing . . . would not have precluded plaintiff from meeting the Benjamin Standards presurgical requirement of living in the social role of a woman. The trial court's findings are well supported by the testimony of Doe's own treating physician and psychologist, as well as other medical evidence.

Doe argues, however, that the trial court's findings on this point are irrelevant since Boeing did not have the benefit of such medical testimony prior to enforcing its dress policy. We disagree. The trial court found that Boeing's policy on accommodation of transsexuals was developed with input from Boeing's legal, medical, personnel and labor relations departments. The Boeing medical department consulted with outside experts in the field and reviewed the literature on transsexualism. The trial court also held that Boeing has a legitimate business purpose in defining what is acceptable attire and in balancing the needs of its work force as a whole with those of Doe. The record supports the trial court's findings of fact and conclusions of law that Boeing developed and reasonably enforced a dress policy which balanced its legitimate business needs with those of its employees.

Doe further argues that, as a gender dysphoric, her perceived needs should have been accommodated. We disagree. The Act does not require an employer to offer the employee the precise accommodation he or she requests. Her perceived need to dress more completely as a woman did not impact her job performance. Doe's condition had no measurable effect on either Doe's job performance or her work group's performance. That is not to say that Doe did not have emotional turmoil over the changes that were taking place in her life, but that turmoil did not prevent her from performing her work satisfactorily. Based on the record, there was no need for any further action by Boeing to facilitate Doe in the performance of job-related tasks.

Doe also argues that Boeing failed to accommodate her unique condition because its dress policy was uniformly applied.

In determining what is a reasonable accommodation, the evaluation must begin with the job specifications and how those tasks are impacted by the abnormal condition.

In the case of trauma or physical deterioration, the answers are generally apparent and the issue becomes one of whether the accommodation is reasonable, not what is the accommodation. In Doe's case, the analysis is not so simple. Doe's job performance was unchanged by reason of her condition. Based on the record, there was no accommodation that Boeing could have provided that would have aided Doe in the performance of her work. How she dressed or appeared had no impact on the physical or mental requirements of her employment responsibilities.

Doe's gender dysphoria did not impede her ability to perform her engineering duties. Therefore, Boeing had no duty to provide any further accommodation to Doe beyond what it provided for all employees. REVERSED.

Case Questions

1. What do you think the real problem was here? If you say that it was Jane trying to push too hard, explore what that really means. How responsible should the employer be for the discomfort of other employees? What about when the discomfort arises from long-held beliefs based on misinformation, which society may have taken for granted until now? Would it be different if the issue was race instead of affinity orientation (that is, employees did not want to deal with employees of other races in the workplace and were uncomfortable doing so)? Explain.

2. Are you surprised that Boeing had eight other employees to deal with on this issue? Explain. Are you surprised that an employer dealt with this issue with the depth that Boeing did? Why do you think it did so?

3. Doe evidently kept going to the female toilet, but it was the pink pearls that got her fired. Any thoughts as to why? Explain.

Buonanno v. AT&T Broadband, LLC *313 F. Supp. 2d 1069 (D. Colo. 2004)*

Employee was terminated for refusing to sign a workplace document containing language that he would "value" diversity, under the employer's diversity policy. His refusal was based on his religion rejecting homosexuality. The employee sued the employer for terminating him without trying to reasonably accommodate the employee's religious belief or practice. The court sided with the employee.

Krieger, J.

***

Buonanno is a Christian who believes that the Bible is divinely inspired. He attempts to live his life in accordance with its literal language. Because the Bible requires that he treat others as he would like to be treated, Buonanno values and respects all other AT&T employees as individuals. He never has nor would he discriminate against another employee due to differences in belief, behavior, background, or other attribute. However, his religious beliefs prohibit him from approving, endorsing, or esteeming behavior or values that are repudiated by Scripture.

In January 2001, AT&T promoted a new "Employee Handbook" that addressed "How We Work: Employee Guidelines" and "Doing What's Right: Business Integrity & Ethics Policies." AT&T maintains a "Certification Policy," which provides that "each AT&T Broadband employee must sign and return the Acknowledgment of Receipt and Certificate of Understanding form indicating that you have received a copy of the handbook and the AT&T Code of Conduct and that you will abide by our employment policies and practices." The parties agree that one of the "employment policies and practices" to which Buonanno was required to adhere is AT&T's "Diversity Policy." The Handbook, however, does not contain a single policy clearly denoted as such; instead, it contains numerous references in various locations to AT&T's philosophy and goals with regard to diversity in the workplace. The parties' references to a "Diversity Policy" appear to be primarily referring to a section of the Handbook entitled "A Summary of Our Business

Philosophy," a subsection of which is entitled "Diversity." It reads as follows:

> The company places tremendous value on the fresh, innovative ideas and variety of perspectives that come from a diverse workplace. Diversity is necessary for a competitive business advantage—and the company is competing for customers in an increasingly diverse marketplace. To make diversity work to our advantage, it's our goal to build an environment that:
>
> • Respects and values individual differences.
>
> • Reflects the communities we serve.
>
> • Promotes employee involvement in decision making.
>
> • Encourages innovation and differing perspectives in problem solving.
>
> • Allows our diverse employee population to contribute richly to our growth.
>
> We want to create a team that is diverse, committed and the most talented in America. To that end, AT&T Broadband has a "zero tolerance" policy toward any type of discrimination, harassment, or retaliation in our company. Each person at AT&T Broadband is charged with the responsibility to fully recognize, respect and value the differences among all of us. This is demonstrated in the way we communicate and interact with our customers, suppliers and each other every day.

There was no uniform understanding at AT&T as to what comprised the company's "Diversity Policy," or, more importantly, what an employee was required to do or not do to comply with it. Buonanno questioned the meaning of the third sentence in the second paragraph of the Diversity Philosophy, which reads "Each person at AT&T Broadband is charged with the responsibility to fully recognize, respect and value the differences among all of us." (The Court will hereinafter refer to this phrase as "the challenged language.") He believed that some behavior and beliefs were deemed sinful by Scripture, and thus, that he could not "value"—that is hold in esteem or ascribe worth to—such behavior or beliefs without compromising his own religious beliefs. Buonanno was fully prepared to comply with the principles underlying the Diversity Philosophy; he recognized that individuals have differing beliefs and behaviors and he would not discriminate against or ha-

rass any person based on that person's differing beliefs or behaviors. However, he could not comply with the challenged language insofar as it apparently required him to "value" the particular belief or behavior that was repudiated by Scripture. Accordingly, if the challenged language literally required him to do so, he could not sign the Certificate of Understanding, agreeing to "abide by" such language.

No AT&T representative explored or explained the intended meaning (or any of the various interpretations) of the challenged language to Buonanno. No AT&T employee inquired as to the particulars of Buonanno's concerns, sought to devise ways to accommodate Buonanno's religious beliefs, or reassured him that the challenged language did not require him to surrender his religious beliefs. At all relevant times, Buonanno was presented with a choice between accepting the language of the Handbook without any additional clarification and signing the Certificate, or losing his employment.

AT&T's Diversity Philosophy reflects a legitimate and laudable business goal. The Court accepts AT&T's contention that allowing employees to strike piecemeal portions of the Handbook or Certification could pose an undue hardship on its business, making uniform application of company policies much more difficult. Nevertheless, had AT&T gathered more information about Buonanno's concerns before terminating his employment, it may have discovered that the perceived conflict between his beliefs and AT&T's policy was not an actual conflict at all, or that if a true conflict existed, it was possible to relieve that conflict with a reasonable accommodation.

Had [Human Resources Manager] Batliner sought more details about Buonanno's concerns, rather than steadfastly insisting that he had to agree with the ambiguous "Diversity Policy" to retain his job, she would have discovered that, but for the challenged language, Buonanno agreed with the entirety of the Handbook, including the Diversity Philosophy, the non-discrimination policy, and all other aspects of AT&T's policies and practices. His only objection was to a literal interpretation of the challenged language that required him to "value" particular behavior and beliefs of co-workers. Had Batliner followed [vice president of Human Resources for Colorado operations] Davis' instructions and engaged in a conversation through which she gathered information about Buonanno's concerns, based on her interpretation of the challenged language, she would have discovered no actual conflict between the challenged language and

Buonanno's religion. If Batliner had, as directed, reported these findings back to Davis, based on Davis' interpretation of the challenged language, Buonanno's religious beliefs would not have been in conflict with the challenged language. Had Batliner reported this information to [Senior Vice President for Human Resources] Brunick, he would have observed that, like the Jewish employee who must recognize—but not adopt—the differing beliefs of his Muslim co-worker, the challenged language did not require Buonanno to actually "value" the particular conduct of his co-workers that he considered sinful. Had [Director of Employee Relations] Wilson been consulted, Buonanno's promise to recognize that there were differences between what he believed and did and what his co-workers believed and did and to treat everyone with respect regardless of their beliefs and behavior would have been sufficient to accomplish the goals of the challenged language. Had Batliner, Davis, Brunick, or Wilson ever explained that they understood the challenged language to have a figurative, rather than literal, meaning and listened to his concerns, the issue could have been resolved without any need for accommodation. Accordingly, AT&T has failed to show that it could not have accommodated Buonanno's beliefs without undue hardship.

Even assuming that—despite the testimony of Batliner, Davis, and, at times, Brunick and Wilson—AT&T intended that the challenged language be applied literally and that all employees were affirmatively required to ascribe value in the various beliefs and behaviors of their co-workers, AT&T could nevertheless have accommodated Buonanno without suffering undue hardship. Although AT&T's Diversity Philosophy confers a business advantage, AT&T did not show that the literal application of the challenged language was necessary to obtain such advantage. For example, Wilson explained the advantages conferred by the "Diversity Policy" by relating an anecdote in which homosexual employees at American Express, sensing a need for estate-planning services in the gay community, proposed the creation of a successful new targeted product. In such example, no employee at American Express was required to ascribe any "value" to the practice of homosexuality in order to capitalize on the opportunity. Rather, American Express officials simply recognized that homosexual employees had a unique perspective on ways to market the company's product. Thus, as Wilson admitted, a minor revision of the challenged language, requiring all employees company-wide to "fully recognize, respect and value that there are differences among all of us" would have "accomplished [AT&T's] goals" as set forth in the Diversity Philosophy, without imposing any apparent hardship on AT&T. Whether such a change is characterized as clarifying AT&T's interpretation of the existing Handbook language or a reasonable accommodation for Buonanno is irrelevant.

AT&T violated Title VII by failing to engage in the required dialogue with Buonanno upon notice of his concerns and by failing to clarify the challenged language to reasonably accommodate Buonanno's religious beliefs. Accordingly, Buonanno is entitled to damages.

Case Questions

1. If you were Buonanno's manager, how would you have handled this situation?

2. Think about the issue of an employee deciding not to accept a co-worker because of religious reasons. If you were the manager, how would you balance the two (workplace requirements versus religion)? What if, as in Chapter 10, the employee's religion teaches him or her to hate blacks and Jews? Is it the same? Explain.

3. What considerations should an employer be concerned with when coming up with approaches to promote workplace cohesion and avoidance of discrimination claims?

Chapter **11**

Religious Discrimination

Learning Objectives

By the time you finish studying this chapter, you should be able to:

LO1 Discuss the background of religious discrimination and give some contemporary issues.

LO2 Give Title VII's definition of religion for discrimination purposes.

LO3 Explain religious conflicts under Title VII and give examples.

LO4 Define religious accommodation and guidelines to its usage.

LO5 Define undue hardship as it allows an employer defense to religious discrimination claims.

LO6 Describe religious harassment and give examples.

LO7 Identify the ways in which unions and religious conflicts occur.

LO8 List some ways in which management can avoid religious discrimination conflicts.

Opening Scenarios

SCENARIO 1

1 Mohammed, a member of the Sikh religion, wears a turban as part of his religious man-
Scenario date, including at work. His supervisor tells him the turban makes his co-workers uncomfortable. Must he stop wearing it?

SCENARIO 2

2 In his preemployment interview, Mosley stated that he would not work on Saturdays
Scenario because that is the day of his Sabbath. As a result, he is not hired. Is this religious discrimination?

SCENARIO 3

3 Three months after coming to work for Steel Bank, Jon joins a religious group whose Sab-
Scenario bath is on Tuesdays. Members of the religion are not to work on the Sabbath. Jon refuses to work on Tuesdays. He is terminated. Jon sues the employer, alleging religious discrimination. The employer defends by saying that (1) Jon was not of this religion when he was hired, (2) Tuesday is not a valid Sabbath day, and (3) any religious group that celebrates a Sabbath on Tuesday is not a valid religion and the employer does not have to honor it. Are any of the employer's defenses valid?

Statutory Basis

It shall be an unlawful employment practice for an employer—

(1) to fail or refuse to hire or to discharge any individual, or otherwise to discriminate against any individual with respect to his compensation, terms, conditions, or privileges of employment, because of such individual's . . . religion . . . or

(2) to limit, segregate, or classify his employees or applicants for employment in any way which would deprive or tend to deprive any individual of employment opportunities or otherwise adversely affect his status as an employee, because of such individual's religion . . . [Title VII of the Civil Rights Act of 1964, as amended; 42 U.S.C. § 20002-2(a).]

Congress shall make no law respecting an establishment of religion, or prohibiting the free exercise thereof . . . [First Amendment to the U.S. Constitution.]

This Is Not Your Forefather's Religious Discrimination

LO1

- Grammy-winning musician Carlos Santana ("You've Got to Change Your Evil Ways") is sued for unjust dismissal by a former personal assistant who claims Santana and his wife made the employee visit a chiropractor to be tested for his "closeness to God." Mrs. Santana said that when prospective employees were being evaluated for hire, she had the chiropractor "calibrate" them, as the more the chiropractor "enlightened" employees through treatments, the closer to God they became and the better employees they become.[1]

- An employee sues to have the court impose an injunction allowing her to say "have a blessed day" in written communications to clients and customers.[2]

- A Starbucks server sues Starbucks for retaliation after she refuses to remove her Wiccan symbol necklace and her hours are reduced, she is not promoted or transferred, and her tardiness is scrutinized.[3] The same thing happens at Google.[4]

- An employee sues after being terminated for eating a bacon, lettuce, and tomato sandwich (BLT) at work, in violation of the "no pork or pork products" rule put in place in deference to Muslim employees and clients.[5]

- Seven female employees at Belmont Abbey College, a small Catholic institution in North Carolina, claim discrimination against them due to the college's refusal to cover prescription contraceptives in its health insurance plan.[6]

- A Muslim trucker is fired for refusing to pick up a load of beer from a brewer because Muslims are forbidden from handling alcohol. In Minnesota, the Metropolitan Airports Commission cracks down on Muslim taxi drivers (about one-third) for refusing to pick up passengers carrying alcohol they say violates their religion.[7]

- General Motors wins a lawsuit by an employee who wants to form a Christian group at work like other affinity groups, claiming it is religious discrimination to allow those and not the Christian one. The court held that GM had no religious groups, so refusal to have a Christian one was not religious discrimination.[8]

- Pharmacists with religiously based objections to premarital sex or abortion are disciplined for refusing to fill prescriptions for birth control pills or the morning after pill.[9]

- An Indiana state police officer is terminated for refusing a casino detail, saying gambling or being around it is against his religion.[10]

- Employees whose religion requires them to "witness" or proselytize sue for the right to do so to their fellow employees in the workplace.[11]

- The New York Police Department is found guilty of religious discrimination for banning the wearing of a turban on the job by a Sikh.[12]

- Alabama Supreme Court Chief Justice Roy S. Moore is removed from office for refusing a court's order to remove a 5,280-pound granite carving of the Ten Commandments from the courthouse rotunda.[13]

- Oklahoma City agrees to pay $20,000 in attorney fees for two employees who filed a lawsuit over Christmas decoration policies requiring them to remove a religious decoration on a filing cabinet, remove a Bible from a break room, and cancel an annual break-room Christmas party that included an opening prayer.[14]

- A television producer is fired for complaining about the company including biblical scriptures inside paycheck envelopes and promoting office Bible study.[15]

- Muslim Target cashiers in Minneapolis are shifted to other jobs as a religious accommodation after refusing to scan pork products because it conflicts with their religion's ban on pork.[16]

- A soldier sues the Army, saying that his atheism led to threats in a culture that tilts heavily toward evangelical Christianity.[17]

- An AT&T employee is terminated for refusing to sign a "Certificate of Understanding" requiring him to adhere to the company's diversity policy that conflicted with the employee's religious beliefs about homosexuality.[18]

- At Hewlett-Packard, in the same situation, an employee is terminated for refusing to remove biblical scriptures he placed on an overhead bin in his workplace cubicle, hoping his gay and lesbian co-workers would see them, be hurt, repent, and be saved.[19]

- Minnesota employees who bring their Bibles to the diversity session on working with gays and lesbians sue their employers, saying punishing them for this was a violation of their constitutional rights.[20]

- The EEOC sues Grand Central Partnerships on behalf of four Grand Central Station security guards who said the policy requiring them to tuck their dreadlocks under their uniform caps discriminates against their Rastafarian beliefs.[21]

- An employee belonging to the World Church of the Creator that teaches that "all people of color are savages who should go back to Africa and the Holocaust never happened and if it did, Nazi Germany would have done the world a tremendous favor" sues his employer after being terminated for giving a newspaper interview espousing these views. He wins.[22]

The face of religious discrimination has changed dramatically in just the past few years. Of course, in each of these situations, the employer argued that he or she had a workplace policy against religious discrimination and that they never engaged in such discrimination. Without guidance, it can be difficult to know. And those were just examples of religious issues in the workplace. That doesn't even include recent issues outside the workplace that also form a part of the religious landscape. Examples include the armed forces settling a lawsuit by agreeing to add to the 38 existing religious symbols it permits on military burial monuments the Wiccan pentagram symbol; the Supreme Court case challenging the pledge of allegiance phrase "One nation under God"; the Supreme Court's decision on the exhibition of Ten Commandment monuments on federal or state premises; the Pennsylvania Amish winning a suit allowing them to use, for safety purposes, retroreflective tape to outline their buggies rather than the bright orange triangles, whose color and shape deeply offend their religious sensibilities; the University of Georgia Jewish cheerleader (one of our students) who alleged that the Christian cheerleading coach did not appoint her to the prestigious football cheering squad because she did not participate in pregame prayers or attend Bible studies held in the coach's home; the female Muslim University of South Florida basketball player who voluntarily resigned from the team after the coach refused to allow her to wear a uniform with long pants, long sleeves, and a head scarf in conformity with her religious dictates; or the Muslim sixth-grader who caused a stir in Oklahoma when she refused to remove her *hijab,* the head covering required by her religion, which the school said violated its dress code. There are many more we could add, but one thing is for sure: religious discrimination is no longer the backwater issue of Title VII that it once may have been perceived to be.

Religious discrimination has certainly come a long way from what was likely envisioned by our forefathers when they wrote its protection into our Constitution. As a nation of immigrants, the United States has always had a diversity of religions among its people. However, with the growing influx of even more types of people from around the world, each expecting the freedom of religion that America felt strongly enough about to include in its constitution, it has changed the face of what many of us have come to expect when we think of religious discrimination. (See Exhibits 11.1, "Major Religions of the World—Ranked by Number of Adherents," and 11.2, "Major Religions and Denominations in the United States.")

Religion has unique significance in our country's creation and development. In the 16th century, when the Catholic Church did not allow King Henry VIII to divorce his wife Catherine of Aragon and to marry Anne Boleyn, Henry broke with Rome. This led to the establishment of a separate national church in England under

---

Exhibit 11.1 *Major Religions of the World—Ranked by Number of Adherents*

Sizes shown are *approximate estimates* and are here mainly for the purpose of ordering the groups by size, not to provide a definitive number. (This list is sociological/statistical in perspective.)

Christianity: 2.1 billion

Islam: 1.5 billion

Secular/Nonreligious/
Agnostic/Atheist: 1.1 billion

Hinduism: 900 million

Chinese traditional
   religion: 394 million

Buddhism: 376 million

Primal-indigenous:
   300 million

African traditional
   & diasporic:
   100 million

Sikhism: 23 million

Juche: 19 million

Spiritism: 15 million

Judaism: 14 million

Baha'i: 7 million

Jainism: 4.2 million

Shinto: 4 million

Cao Dai: 4 million

Zoroastrianism: 2.6 million

Source: www.adherents.com.

Note: Total adds up to more than 100% due to rounding and because upper bound estimates were used for each group.
© 2005 www.adherents.com

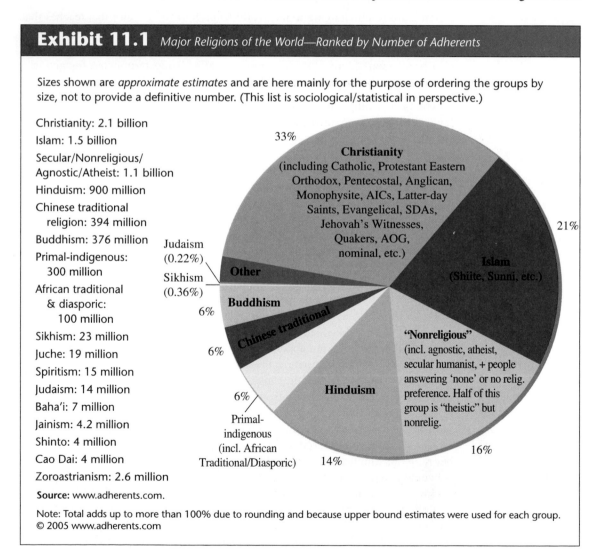

Exhibit 11.2 *Major Religions and Denominations in the United States*

Top Organized Religions

Christianity	76.5%
Judaism	1.3
Islam	0.5
Buddhism	0.5
Hinduism	0.4
Unitarian Universalist	0.3
Wiccan/Pagan/Druid	0.1

Largest Denominational Families

Catholic	24.5%
Baptist	16.3
Methodist	6.8
Lutheran	4.6
Pentecostal	2.1
Presbyterian	2.7
Mormon	1.3
Nondenominational Christians	1.2
Church of Christ	1.2
Episcopal/Anglican	1.7
Assemblies of God	0.5
Congregational/United Church of Christ	0.7
Seventh Day Adventist	0.3

Source: www.adherents.com

the supreme headship of the king. Henry VIII was allowed to divorce Catherine (he eventually took six wives) and marry Anne, whom he ordered beheaded in 1536.

The aftermath of Henry's maneuvers was that the church became inextricably woven into the government, and religious freedom was virtually nonexistent in the government from which America was born. The right to practice religion freely and not be required to blindly accept the government's state-imposed religious beliefs was a large part of what made America break away from Great Britain and its Church of England more than a century later.

Of course, this is only a simplified version of a very long and complex developmental process for our relationship as a country with religion. But the end product was that, rejecting the tyranny of this state-imposed religion, religious freedom was included in the U.S. Constitution, and freedom of religion has since always been highly valued and closely held, and has enjoyed a protected position in American law.

Title VII embodies this protection in the employment arena by prohibiting employment discrimination based on religious beliefs or practices. While litigation on the basis of religious discrimination may not occur as frequently as some of the other categories, or have as high a profile, it is just as important a concern for employers. The percentage of claims may seem small, but the more important factor is that there has been a steady increase in claims since 1993 and an absolute spike after September 11, 2001. In FY 2010, religious discrimination accounted for 3.8 percent of charges filed with the EEOC. That was 3,790 charges. In 1997, the percentage was 2.1 with 1,709 charges. In 13 years the number of charges has more than doubled.[23]

However, religious discrimination is no less important. It is clear that this issue has taken on an even more pressing note since the tragic events of September 11, 2001. Though we will have experienced the 10th anniversary of that event by the time you see this, according to the EEOC, federal, state, and local fair employment practice agencies have documented a significant increase in the number of charges of workplace harassment and discrimination claims based on national origin (with those perceived to be of Arab and South Asian descent being the target) and religion (Muslims, Sikhs). Employment discrimination claims increased by 4.5 percent from 2001 to 2002, with much of that increase coming from ethnicity and religion after 9/11. In fact, in issuing a new comprehensive directive on religious discrimination for the EEOC Compliance Manual on July 22, 2008, the EEOC noted that claims of religious discrimination had doubled between 1992 and 2007 and that as religious pluralism has increased, questions about religious discrimination have increased.[24]

Actually, the increase in litigation involving religious issues began when issues of workplace activities and harassment issues surrounding religious practices became more prominent in the late 1980s and early 1990s with the rising popularity of Fundamentalist Christianity and televangelism. Many of the Fundamentalists, commonly referred to as "born-again Christians," ran into trouble when, as an article of faith, they attempted to share their religion with others in the workplace, sometimes whether the co-worker wished to have it so or not. On the other hand, Fundamentalists experienced trouble when they were mocked, teased, or otherwise singled out for their religious beliefs at work.

These religious discrimination issues have now extended into areas surrounding the practices and dictates—and harassment—involving those of primarily Middle Eastern religions. Can a Sikh be required to remove his religiously dictated turban at work? Can a Muslim woman be terminated for wearing a religiously dictated head covering? Must a Muslim employee be allowed to attend a midday Friday religious service or have a place provided for religion-required prayer five times a day? Can a Muslim taxi driver refuse to pick up fares that have liquor? Can a grocery store cashier refuse to touch pork, saying it is against her religion? All of these issues and those mentioned at the beginning of the chapter have been a part of the post–September 11, 2001, landscape and must be addressed consistent with Title VII and other legal dictates.

Federal and state constitutional guarantees of due process, equal protection, and freedom of religion also provide protection for federal, state, and local government employees. If the employer is a governmental entity, the employer must avoid workplace policies that have the effect of tending to establish or to interfere with the practice of the employee's religion. In determining whether the employer has discriminated on the basis of religion, the court must sometimes first address whether even deciding the issue entangles the government excessively in the practice of religion. Title VII is the only legislation specifically prohibiting religious discrimination in employment, and consideration is given to constitutional issues where necessary.

duty to reasonably accommodate

The employer's Title VII duty to try to find a way to avoid conflict between workplace policies and an employee's religious practices or beliefs.

undue hardship

Burden imposed on an employer, by accommodating an employee's religious conflict, that would be too onerous for the employer to bear.

Unlike the other categories included in Title VII, there is not an absolute prohibition against discrimination on the basis of religion. Rather, under Title VII, we see for the first time a category that has built into it a **duty to reasonably accommodate** the employee's religious conflict unless to do so would cause the employer **undue hardship**. There is no such reasonable accommodation requirement for race, gender, color, or national origin, but there is under the Americans with Disabilities Act (ADA) as we shall see in that chapter. However, the nature of the accommodation in the ADA is quite different.

To a great extent, religious organizations are exempt from the prohibitions in Title VII. As a general rule, they can discriminate so that, for instance, a Catholic church may legitimately refuse to hire a Baptist minister as its priest. Section 703(e)(2) of Title VII states that it is not an unlawful employment practice for a school, college, university, or other educational institution to hire or employ employees of a particular religion if the institution is in whole or in substantial part owned, supported, controlled, or managed by a particular religion or by a religious corporation, association, or society or if its curriculum is directed toward the propagation of a particular religion. That is, religion is recognized as a basis for a BFOQ reasonably necessary to the normal operation of that particular business or enterprise under section 703(e)(1) of Title VII. If the church has non-sectarian activities such as running a day care center, bookstore, or athletic club, it may enjoy the same broad type of freedom to discriminate on the basis of religion since these activities may have religion or propagation of the religion as an integral part of their purpose. Employers should be cautioned that the specific facts play an important role in making this determination. In *Corporation of the Presiding Bishop of the Church of Jesus Christ of Latterday Saints v. Amos*,[25] the U.S. Supreme Court upheld the church's termination of a janitor in the church-owned gym for not paying his dues and keeping current his church affiliation card. In the Court's determination, the gym had been conceived as a manifestation of dedication to their religious beliefs and terminating the janitor for his failure to maintain his membership in the denomination did not violate the law.

Before Title VII, it was fairly routine for employers to be nearly as adamant about not hiring those of certain religious faiths, such as Jews, as it was about not hiring people of a certain race, ethnic background, or gender. Universities routinely imposed quotas on the number of Jewish students they would accept, just as restrictive covenants in real estate contracts routinely prohibited the sale of property to Jews. The issue has usually been more covertly handled, but it existed extensively, nonetheless. Title VII was enacted to remedy such practices in the workplace, just as fair housing legislation now prohibits restrictive covenants.

Some have still not gotten the message. In 2011 a Jewish hockey player for the National Hockey League's Anaheim Ducks sued the organization for what he called a "barrage of anti-Semitic, offensive and degrading verbal attacks regarding his Jewish faith" from the head coach. The coach said he did not intend the comments to insult or hurt him in any way.[26] In 2010 the EEOC settled a case with Administaff, Inc. on behalf of two Jewish brothers for $115,000. They were called "dirty Jew" and "dumb Jew" and subjected to other anti-Semitic comments. They also had their work vehicle defaced with a swastika and were forced into a trash bin for the amusement of managers watching on surveillance cameras, calling it "throw the Jew in the Dumpster."[27] A 2009 lawsuit by two Jewish teachers contained dozens of pages describing religious discrimination by their colleagues and former principal.[28] And in 2008 two Army drill sergeants were reprimanded for religious discrimination against a Jewish soldier who they called "Juden," the German word for Jews. They also made him remove his yarmulke religious head covering. The soldier was later beaten so badly by other soldiers that he was treated at a hospital.[29]

The more frequent basis for lawsuits today is that an employee is not hired or is terminated because of some religious practice that comes into conflict with the employer's workplace policies. The employee may refuse to work on a particular day because it is the employee's Sabbath. Or the employee may dress a certain way for religious reasons, or wish to take certain days off for religious holidays or observances. When it conflicts with the employer's policies and the employee refuses to attempt to accommodate the conflict, the employee is terminated and Title VII comes into play.

For instance, Ivy Hall Assisted Living paid an employee $43,000 in a settlement after she sued when they refused to allow her to wear her Muslim hijab. In fact, the employer insisted that she remove the hijab and refrain from wearing it as a condition of continued employment.[30] This issue has arisen in several different contexts, including an applicant who was told by Abercrombie & Fitch that the hijab violated the Abercrombie & Fitch "Look Policy."[31] The EEOC sued Convergys Corporation because an applicant who was a Hebrew Israelite and could not work on his Sabbath (Saturday) from sunup to sundown was told by the interviewer that unless he could work on Saturdays, the interview was over.[32]

Frequently the employer discovers religious information through questions on an employment application or during a preemployment interview, either of which generally relates to notifying a religious figure or taking the employee to a particular hospital in the event of on-the-job injury. If the question is asked, the applicant has a right to think it is asked for a reason and will be taken into consideration. The employer may have the question for totally different reasons than the applicant thinks, but once the question is there, it can be left up to unintended interpretations. To eliminate the appearance of illegal consideration of religion in hiring, employers should, instead, ask such questions after hire and then simply ask who should be notified or what hospital the employee prefers.

In this chapter, we will learn what is meant by religious discrimination, what the duty to accommodate involves, and how far an employer can go in handling management considerations when religious conflict is at issue.

In *Tyson v. Clarian Health Partners, Inc.*[33] the court addressed one of the growing post-9/11 areas of religious conflict: employers accommodating religious conflicts of those practicing the Muslim faith. As mentioned, the number of claims in this area has increased dramatically since 9/11. In *Tyson*, the employer was faced with what to do with a Muslim employee working in the hospital who used an empty hospital room to perform her ablutions (ritual washing up) before praying, in violation of hospital rules.

What Is Religion?

Title VII originally provided no guidance as to what it meant by the word *religion*. In the 1972 amendments to Title VII, Congress addressed the issue. In section 701, providing definitions for terms within Title VII, section (j) states: "The term 'religion' includes all aspects of religious observance and practice, as well as belief, unless an employer demonstrates that he is unable to reasonably accommodate an employee's or prospective employee's religious observance or practice without undue hardship on the conduct of the employer's business."

The question frequently arises: "What if I never heard of the employee's religion? Must I still accommodate it?" The answer is based on two considerations: whether the employee's belief is closely held and whether it takes the place of religion in the employee's life. The latter requirement means that even atheism has been considered a "religion" for Title VII purposes. If the answer to both queries is yes, then the employer must accept the belief as a religious belief and attempt accommodation for conflicts.

The religious belief need not be a belief in a religious deity as we generally know it. However, courts have determined that groups like the Ku Klux Klan are political, not religious, organizations, even though their members have closely held beliefs. The employer need not previously know of, or have heard of, or approve of the employee's religion in order to be required to accommodate it for Title VII purposes. Also, the employer cannot question the sincerity of the belief merely because the employer thinks the religion is strange. In *Frazee v. Illinois Department of Employment Security*[34] the employee asserted he could not work on the Sabbath because he was a Christian even though he did not attend church. The U.S. Supreme Court held that the employee need not be a member of an organized religion at all. The case involves the Free Exercise Clause of the First Amendment to the U.S. Constitution, made applicable to the states by the Fourteenth Amendment, but the considerations are similar to those of Title VII. This is why in Opening Scenario 1 the Sikh need not stop wearing his religiously mandated turban simply because other employees are "uncomfortable." That is to say,

Scenario

they are unfamiliar with the employee's religion and religious dictates and his wearing of a turban seems strange to them.

Perhaps the single most-asked question in this area is: "Must I accommodate the employee's religious conflict if the conflict did not exist when the employee was hired?" The answer is yes. The duty attaches to the conflict itself, not to when the conflict arises. The idea behind the question is that if the employer had known of the conflict, then he or she would not have hired the employee in the first place. It is illegal to use the religious conflict, alone, as a basis for not hiring the applicant. So, legally, it does not matter whether the conflict was present when the applicant was hired or arose later; there is still a duty on the employer to attempt to accommodate the religious conflict. The duty to accommodate, however, is only to the extent that it does not cause the employer undue hardship. What constitutes undue hardship will be discussed shortly.

The duty to accommodate only applies to religious *practices,* not religious *beliefs.* An employer is only required to accommodate a religious practice to the extent that it does not present an undue hardship on the employer, but religious beliefs do not have that limitation. That is, no matter how unorthodox, or even outrageous, an employee's religion may seem to the employer, the employer cannot take an adverse employment action against the employee simply because the employee holds that religious belief. In *Peterson v. Wilmur Communications, Inc.,* given at the end of the chapter, the employer was called upon to deal with a religion espousing racial separation much like the Ku Klux Klan. The court determined that the religion, as unorthodox, and even as repulsive, as it was, was required by Title VII to be treated just like any other religion for Title VII purposes.

Religious Conflicts

Imagine mass firings of Muslim employees who walk off the job over prayer disputes. The workers ask management to adjust their evening break time so they can pray at sunset as required; management agrees, then reverses its decision when non-Muslim employees protest. This occurred in Colorado and Nebraska and about 200 employees were fired.[35]

Workplace conflict between employee religious practices at odds with workplace policies is probably the most frequent type of religious discrimination case there is, and as we discussed earlier, the numbers are growing. That is, it is not so much that the employer dislikes a particular religion and refuses to hire members of that religion; rather, it is that the employee may engage in some religious practice that is not perceived to be compatible with the workplace. For instance, the employer may have a no-beard policy, but the employee's religion forbids shaving; the employer may have a policy forbidding the wearing of headgear, but the employee's religion requires the wearing of some sort of head cover; the employer may have a policy forbidding the wearing of long hair on males, but the employee's religion forbids the cutting of male hair except in certain limited circumstances; the employer may have a policy that all employees must work on

Saturdays, but the employee's religious Sabbath may be on Saturday and followers may be forbidden to work on the Sabbath.

In fact, sometimes the conflict comes not with the employee's religion, but with that of the employer. In Exhibit 11.3, "The Lord at Work," the atheist employee is upset at having to attend mandatory Fundamentalist Christian workplace church services at the manufacturing plant in which he is employed.

In order for an employee to proceed with a claim of religious discrimination, he must first establish a *prima facie* case by establishing that

1. He holds a sincere religious belief that conflicts with an employment requirement.
2. He has informed the employer of the conflict.
3. He was discharged or disciplined for failing to comply with the conflicting employment requirement.

If an employee establishes a *prima facie* case, the burden shifts to the employer to show that it offered a reasonable accommodation to the employee or that it could not reasonably accommodate the employee without incurring undue hardship.

Exhibit 11.3 *The Lord at Work*

MANDATORY PRAYER MEETINGS PIT CHRISTIAN BOSS AGAINST ATHEIST WORKER

Jake Townley can't understand it—why this atheist from Arizona complained about these weekly devotional meetings, why anyone would. It's *paid* work time. Nobody's asking him to do anything except show up, just like all Townley Manufacturing employees are required to do. The meetings only last half an hour. They're harmless. They've been a Townley tradition for 25 years.

Until this Louis Pelvas came along.

Pelvas, a machinist in the Townley plant in Arizona, objected to the prayer meetings. He filed a complaint of religious discrimination with the Equal Employment Opportunity Commission raising questions about religion in the workplace. Questions Jake Townley thinks the government has no right asking.

Townley is seated on one of about 50 metal folding chairs in the Townley Manufacturing Company workshop in Candler [Florida]. It is 7 A.M. Tuesday, time for the weekly devotional meeting held at this and five other Townley Manufacturing plants in the United States.

The working men file through the door slow and easy, the way people amble into church on Sundays. The preacher sits, Bible in hand, by the welding station. The meeting begins. A man strums a red electric guitar and sings: "I won't walk without Jesus and I won't talk without Jesus."

After the song, one manager speaks briefly about production schedules. Another manager talks just as quickly about safety regulations. Then the preacher rests his large hands on the lectern.

"Good morning," he says. "Praise the Lord."

He points out "Brother and Sister Townley," the company owners, and speaks of their blessed mission of gospel-sharing and toolmaking. He begins

continued

Exhibit 11.3 *continued*

conversationally, as if he were addressing the family at the dinner table, but then picks up steam. "God is the one that breathes in us the breath of life, he made us, he created us, he loves us. . . . " The preacher's words rise from his belly, his voice swells. He cups his arms toward the ceiling. Tears moisten his cheeks.

The workers sit motionless, a sea of wooden faces. Twenty minutes pass. The preacher closes with a prayer. The men bow their heads.

Seconds later, the men are at their stations and Townley looks proud: That wasn't so bad, now was it?

The Townleys think they have a right to keep it that way.

But that may not be possible. The EEOC sued Townley Manufacturing, charging its policy of requiring attendance at devotional meetings violates Title VII of the Civil Rights Act of 1964.

Townley says the case will determine whether owners of private, for-profit companies can operate their businesses according to their religious beliefs.

The EEOC says Title VII requires employers to accommodate an employee's religious beliefs and practices unless it presents undue hardship.

All newly hired employees must read and sign an employee handbook, which states that all employees must attend weekly "non-denominational" services; missing them is grounds for termination. Profanity is also prohibited, and the handbook encourages employees to keep track of "how our politicians stand on various issues and to vote for those candidates who support a realistic and stable government policy toward business."

"We run the business according to Christian principles," Townley says. "Everyone may not agree with it, but we feel the Lord gave us the business and it's inseparable from what we do."

Pelvas says his family never went to church. "I was always brought up to the fact that religion and politics should never enter industry."

If he had known the meetings would start in Eloy [Arizona], he says, "I don't believe I would ever have taken the job."

Townley pressured the manager to comply with company policy, and pretty soon one atheist and a roomful of Hispanic Catholics got weekly doses of Bible readings. Pelvas asked to be allowed to work, instead, but was told to show up, even if he didn't pay attention.

Pelvas acquiesced. He listened to music from an ear plug attached to a radio. Sometimes he read. Company business was never discussed, he says. Nor were the services "nondenominational."

"It was strictly born-again services. There were three different preachers. All three of 'em would start off with what a bad person they was—alcohol, woman chaser—and they must have seen the light because they're all different now. I'm 60-some years old, and I haven't seen the light yet."

"I went along with 'em for quite a while until I got disgusted with the whole thing."

The other employees wouldn't object because they were afraid of being fired, Pelvas said. Besides, they didn't mind "listening to some yo-yo blabber away as long as they're gettin' paid for it—I can't blame 'em for that."

Two men, two views: America means freedom of religion; America means freedom *from* religion.

Note: The EEOC decided in favor of Pelvas, 859 F.2d 610 (9th Cir. 1988).

Source: *St. Petersburg Times,* April. 24, 1988, p. 1F.

As more and more employees come into the workplace who are not of the "traditional" religions with which an employer may be more familiar, and these employees have an expectation of being accommodated in accordance with the law, employers will need to learn to effectively handle the religious conflicts that arise. The religious conflicts serving as the basis for discrimination claims have become more and more fascinating over the years. Recent conflicts have included such diverse situations as a woman suing for religious discrimination because her religion does not allow her to wear men's clothing (i.e., pants), but her employer required pants as part of her uniform;[36] a Jehovah's Witness who sued Chi-Chi's Mexican restaurant for religious discrimination after being fired for not adhering to Chi-Chi's policy of all employees singing birthday songs to patrons on their birthday because the policy conflicted with her religion, which does not observe personal birthdays, believing they arise out of pagan celebrations;[37] a Jehovah's Witness suing Belk department store for being terminated when she refused to wear a Santa hat and apron because, again, her religion prohibited recognizing holidays;[38] an employee refusing to answer the telephone with the hotel's required "happy holidays" (rather than "Merry Christmas") greeting during the Christmas season, claiming her religious beliefs prohibited her from doing so;[39] a strict vegetarian bus driver who was fired for refusing to hand out coupons to riders for free hamburgers as part of a promotion between the bus company and a hamburger chain;[40] and an employee who sued Walmart for religious discrimination when it fired her for screaming at a lesbian employee that God does not accept gays, they should not "be on earth," and they will "go to hell" because they are not "right in the head."[41] We are giving you so many of these examples because we want you to be prepared; religious conflicts come into the workplace in an awful lot of ways, and the more examples you see, the better equipped you are to make defensible workplace decisions.

The key is for an employer to make sure that the basis for the conflict is a religious one and then to try to work out an accommodation. Once the employer is aware of the conflict, the employer must attempt a good-faith accommodation of the religious conflict and the employee must assist in the attempted accommodation. If none can be worked out and the employer has tried everything available that does not present an undue hardship, then the employer has fulfilled his or her Title VII obligation and there is no liability, even if the employee's religious conflict cannot be accommodated. Of course, because of the diversity of religious conflicts that are possible, there is no single set of rules that can be provided that will cover all religious conflicts.

In *Goldman v. Weinberger,*[42] for example, the issue of conflict arose in the context of the military where a rabbi's wearing of the Jewish yarmulke head covering under his military uniform violated military dress regulations. The regulation was upheld by the U.S. Supreme Court. We mention this case for several reasons. First, it presents a conflict between religious practice (wearing a yarmulke) and work (being a member of the military). It also allows you to understand the U.S. Supreme Court's position on matters military and how they interact with Title VII and other protective legislation. As we are discussing Title VII, students frequently ask how the military can have the rules it has, which seem to be at odds with Title VII.

Our answer is that the Court tends to view the military as being in a class all its own for most purposes. The military's need for "good order," cohesion, instant and unquestioning obedience, esprit de corps, morale, and other such interests usually results in the Court deferring to the military when there are conflicts. We also wanted to reiterate that the right to be free of religious discrimination is not absolute. There are limitations to the right where there may be overriding considerations such as the military cohesion in *Goldman* or the undue hardship on the employer under Title VII.

Not every conflict involving religion will necessarily be a religious conflict recognized by the law. Think about the description of the Walmart employee who was terminated for violating Walmart's Discrimination and Harassment Prevention Policy by screaming at the lesbian employee. She was not terminated because of her religious beliefs, as she argued, but instead for violating Walmart's policy by harassing an employee. The decision to terminate was based on the employee's conduct, not on her religious beliefs.[43] In *Lumpkin v. Jordan*[44] the legitimate non-discriminatory basis for termination was not deemed a religious conflict at all, even though it involved religion to an extent. In *Jordan,* a member of the San Francisco Human Rights Commission, who was also a minister, had religious beliefs in conflict with same-gender affinity orientation that put him at odds with the Commission's work in enforcing non-discrimination laws, including on the basis of affinity orientation. The court upheld his termination, despite the minister's religious beliefs, since it conflicted with the very purpose of his job and its duties.

Employer's Duty to Reasonably Accommodate

LO4

Again, unlike the other categories under Title VII, the prohibition against religious discrimination is not absolute. An employer can discriminate against an employee for religious reasons if to do otherwise causes the employer undue hardship. When the employer discovers a religious conflict between the employer's policy and the employee's religion, the employer's first responsibility is to attempt accommodation. If accommodation is not possible, the employer can implement the policy even though it has the effect of discriminating against the employee on the basis of religion.

The duty to reasonably accommodate is not a static concept. Due to the nature of religious conflicts and the fact that they can arise in all types of contexts and in many different ways, there is no one single action an employer must take to show that she or he has reasonably accommodated. It depends on the circumstances and will vary from situation to situation. For example:

- The employer owns a sandwich shop. The employer's policy entitles employees to eat all the restaurant food they wish during their meal break, free of charge. An employee's religion does not allow eating meat. Aside from the meat used for sandwiches, the employer has little else, other than sandwich trimmings like lettuce and tomatoes. The employee alleges it is religious discrimination to provide the benefits of free meals that the employee cannot eat for religious reasons while other employees receive full free meals. The duty to accommodate may be as simple as the employer arranging to have peanut butter and jelly, eggs, or a variety of vegetables or pasta available for the employee.

- The employer requires employees to work six days per week. An employee cannot work on Saturdays due to a religious conflict. The accommodation may be that the employee switches days with an employee who does not wish to work on Sundays—a day that the employee with the religious conflict is available to work.

- Employer grocery store has a policy requiring all counter clerks to be clean-shaven, to present the employer's view of a "clean-cut" image to the public. An employee cannot shave for religious reasons. The accommodation may be that the employer switches the employee to a job the employee can perform that does not require public contact such as stocking shelves or handling paperwork.

If it can be shown that the employer reasonably accommodated or attempted to accommodate the employee, then the employer is relieved of liability. In *Wilson v. U.S. West Communications*[45] the Catholic employee believed she should be "an instrument of God like the Virgin Mary," and wear a button showing a color photo of an 18-week fetus until abortion was outlawed. The button was offensive and disturbing to other employees for reasons unrelated to abortion such as infertility, miscarriages, and the death of a premature infant. The employer considered it a "time robber" since employees were upset and gathered to discuss it. The employer gave her the option of only wearing it in her cubicle or covering it. This was unacceptable to the employee and she sued. The court found the employer's accommodation to be reasonable, but also found that the employee's claim of the problematic activity of "needing" to wear an antiabortion button with a graphic picture of a fetus on it was not based on religious requirements.

Similarly, in *EEOC v. Firestone Fibers & Textiles Company*[46] the Fourth Circuit found that an employer met the accommodation requirements for the employee's religious beliefs prohibiting him from working on his Sabbath from sundown Friday to sundown Saturday and on seven religious holidays during the year. The employer sought an accommodation by altering his Friday work shift where it could and using the collective bargaining agreement's seniority system. But the employee requested 11 additional days to observe two religious holidays and was terminated when he violated the company's attendance policy prohibiting taking over 60 hours of unpaid leave. So, too, when a Home Depot employee who wore a "One nation under God" button on his work apron, in violation of the store's policy against wearing religious buttons, was given the option to wear a company pin saying United We Stand.[47]

If an accommodation cannot be found, as *Williams v. Southern Union Gas Company*[48] demonstrates, the employer's duty is discharged. The *Williams* case involved an employee who was terminated for not working on Saturday, his Sabbath. The court upheld the termination because it found that the employer had tried to accommodate the employee's religious conflict, but the only way it could have been done would have caused the employer undue hardship. This case is the basis for Opening Scenarios 2 and 3. The important factor is for the employer to make a good-faith attempt at an accommodation rather than simply dismissing the

2) Scenario

3) Scenario

conflict without even trying to do so. Remember the case mentioned previously where the Hebrew Israelite was told by the interviewer that if he could not work on Saturdays (because it was his Sabbath), the interview was over. That sort of refusal to even try to accommodate is what the law prohibits.

Even where an employee's activity is religiously based, it need not be accommodated if doing so presents real problems for the employer. In the very interesting *Chalmers v. Tulon Company of Richmond* case, included at the end of the chapter, the employee believed it to be her religious duty to write letters to her co-workers telling them what she perceived as their religious shortcomings. When one letter led to an employee's wife thinking he had an affair, the court refused to find a basis for accommodation, even though the employee claimed she was doing what her religion dictated she do.

There have been other types of manifestations of religious dictates employers and others have had to address. In one case, a Wisconsin woman's religious leader of the Order of the Divine Will told her that a 90-year-old woman who died would come back alive if she allowed the corpse to sit on the toilet in her home. The homeowner's children were told by the religious leader that demons were destroying the corpse's appearance as she decayed in the bathroom to make it look like she would not rise from the dead. Police officers finally discovered the rotting body in the "stench filled" home.[49] A North Carolina teen's nose piercing got her suspended from school in violation of the county dress code even though she said she and her mother belonged to the Church of Body Modification, which had a clergy, statement of beliefs, and formal process for accepting new members.[50]

Employee's Duty to Cooperate in Accommodation

The U.S. Supreme Court has held that, in attempting to accommodate the employee, all that is required is that the employer attempt to make a reasonable accommodation. If one can be made, then any reasonable accommodation will do and it need not necessarily be the most reasonable accommodation or the one the employee wants. The employee also must be reasonable in considering accommodation alternatives. The protection Title VII provides for employment discrimination on the basis of religion does not mean that the employer must resolve the conflict in the way the employee wants. In *Vargas v. Sears, Roebuck & Company,*[51] the employer attempted to accommodate the Hispanic employee's Native American religious belief involving letting his hair grow. The employee's wearing his hair in a pony tail violated the employer's appearance policy. The employer suggested tucking the pony tail inside the employee's shirt or jacket, but the employee refused to even consider it and provided no suggestions of his own. The court held that the employee had not shown that the employer failed to attempt to accommodate the religious conflict and the employee's termination was upheld.

The employer's only alternative may involve demoting or even terminating the employee, depending on the circumstances. This is not prohibited if all other alternatives present the employer with an undue hardship. The EEOC and the courts will look to the following factors in determining whether the employer has successfully borne the burden of reasonably accommodating the employee's religious conflict:

- Whether the employer made an attempt at accommodation.
- The size of the employer's workforce.
- The type of job in which the conflict is present.
- The employer's checking with other employees to see if anyone was willing to assist in the accommodation.
- The cost of accommodation.
- The administrative aspects of accommodation.

Each factor will be considered and weighed as appropriate for the circumstances. If on balance the employer has considered the factors appropriate for the employer's particular circumstances and accommodation was not possible, there is usually no liability for religious discrimination.

What Constitutes Undue Hardship?

LO5

Just as reasonable accommodation varies from situation to situation, so, too, does what constitutes undue hardship. There are no set rules about what constitutes undue hardship since each employer operates under different circumstances. What may be hardship for one employer may not be for another. What constitutes an undue hardship is addressed by the EEOC and courts on an individual basis.

It is clear, however, that the undue hardship may not be a mere inconvenience to the employer. The EEOC has provided guidelines as to what factors it will consider in deciding whether the employer's accommodation would cause undue hardship.[52] Such factors include

- The nature of the employer's workplace.
- The type of job needing accommodation.
- The cost of the accommodation.
- The willingness of other employees to assist in the accommodation.
- The possibility of transfer of the employee and its effects.
- What is done by similarly situated employers.
- The number of employees available for accommodation.
- The burden of accommodation on the union (if any).

The factors are similar to those used to determine if the employer has made reasonable accommodation. Generally, the EEOC's interpretation of what constitutes undue hardship and reasonable accommodation has been more stringent than the interpretation of undue hardship by the courts. However, since the EEOC's guidelines are simply guidelines (though strong, well-respected ones) and thus not binding, and court decisions are, employers must look to the interpretation by courts in their own jurisdictions. Courts have found, among other things, that it would be an undue hardship if an employer had to violate the seniority provision of a valid collective bargaining agreement, to pay out more than a "de minimis" cost (in terms of money or efficiency) to replace a worker who has religious conflicts, or to force other employees who do not wish to do so to trade places with the employee who has a religious conflict. The U.S. Supreme Court's determination of what constitutes undue hardship was established in *Trans World Airlines v. Hardison,* which still stands today. As you can see, after reviewing the case at the end of the chapter, it did not place an unduly heavy burden on the employer.

Case 3

Religion as a BFOQ

Title VII permits religion to be a bona fide occupational qualification if it is reasonably necessary to the employer's particular normal business operations. It also specifically permits educational institutions to employ those of a particular religion if they are owned in whole or in substantial part by a particular religion. In *Pime v. Loyola University of Chicago*[53] the court looked at whether a historically Jesuit university could have Jesuit membership as a BFOQ for philosophy professors. A Jewish professor applied to teach philosophy in a department that had passed a resolution saying the professors needed to be Jesuits. The court determined that the university could impose such a measure because essential to the mission of the university was to have not just the subject matter presented to students, but to have them exposed to the particular attributes that the Jesuits trained as Jesuits had that was part of the basis of the university. Exhibit 11.4, "Catholic Bishops Split on Women Priests," discusses the issue of being male as a BFOQ for being a Catholic priest.

Religious Harassment

LO6

One of the most active areas under religious discrimination lately has been religious harassment. Several factors have come together and caused many employees to decide that expressing their religious views in some way in the workplace is something they are compelled to do, either by their religious dictates or their own interpretation of them.

For instance, employees may feel they must, or wish to, display crosses or other religious artifacts at work; display religious brochures or material on their desk or pass them out to co-workers; hold Bible or other religious study groups during the workday; preach, teach, testify, or "witness" to their co-workers in order to practice their religion; or engage in other such activities. As mentioned earlier, after the events of September 11, 2001, there was an increase in the number of claims of religious harassment. In one incident cited by the EEOC, a Muslim employee who had experienced no workplace problems before September 11, 2001, reported that afterward none of his co-workers would speak to him and that when they did, they referred to him as "the local terrorist" or "camel jockey." This was an extremely frequent occurrence across the country for not only Muslims,

Exhibit 11.4 *Catholic Bishops Split on Women Priests*

In this piece, the use of gender as a BFOQ for a religious position is under discussion—more particularly, whether women can be ordained as priests in the Catholic Church. The exhibit gives you some idea of the varying points of view on the subject, all of which would be considered internal religious affairs and, thus, off limits to the use of Title VII.

DOCUMENT ON WOMEN'S ROLE IN CHURCH, SOCIETY REJECTED

WASHINGTON—Nine years of sharp debate and soul searching over the ordination of women priests ended Wednesday as the United States' Roman Catholic bishops rejected a controversial statement on the role of women in society and the church.

On a 137–110 vote, 53 short of the required two-thirds of eligible voters needed for passage, the prelate sealed a tumultuous chapter in the history of the American church over the ordination of women.

But it did not close the book on the debate over admitting women to the priesthood.

While the letter, which was repeatedly revised, strongly reaffirmed the church's ancient tradition of an all-male priesthood, many advocates of women's ordination said the mere fact that the bishops were debating the issue was a victory.

Some bishops stressed that the vote against the letter was not a vote against banning women priests.

Those bishops, including Cardinal Joseph Bernardin of Chicago, said the missive was rejected because it was either too insensitive in dealing with the subject of women's ordination, or too weak in advancing a rationale for upholding a male priesthood.

Others said the letter had strayed from the bishops' original intent to address pressing social concerns affecting women, such as sexism and domestic violence, and had become too political and divisive.

It marked the first time that a proposed pastoral letter, an authoritative teaching of bishops, had been defeated in the United States.

The letter's defeat came on the eve of the Episcopal Church's plans tonight to consecrate the Rev. Jane Holmes Dixon as the second woman bishop in its history and the third in the 70 million member worldwide Anglican Communion.

Last week, the Church of England—mother church of the Anglican Communion, which broke with Rome in the 16th century—voted to admit women to its priesthood.

Source: L. B. Stammer, *Palm Beach Post,* November. 19, 1992, p. 1A. Copyright 1992, *Los Angeles Times.* Reprinted by permission.

Note: On June 29, 2002, seven women were ordained as Catholic priests near Passau, Germany. Less than two weeks later, the Vatican threatened to excommunicate them unless they admitted that the ceremony was invalid and expressed repentance. www.womenpriests.org/called/woc_usa.htm.

---

but for anyone who even appeared to be of Middle Eastern descent. Unfortunately, such incidents still frequently occur in the workplace.

An article in *The New York Times* reported that a survey of 743 human resource professionals by the Society for Human Resource Management indicated that the most common religion-related issues among employees are employees proselytizing (20 percent), employees feeling harassed by co-workers' religious expressions (14 percent), employees objecting to job duties (9 percent), and employees harassing co-workers for their religious beliefs (6 percent).[54]

This activity surrounding the issue of religious harassment is due, in part, to matters peripheral to workplace religious discrimination. In 1990, the U.S. Supreme Court rejected Native Americans' argument that they should be permitted the ritual use of the hallucinogenic drug peyote in their tribal religious ceremonies as a part of their First Amendment right to freedom of religion. With tremendous support from many quarters, in 1993 Congress passed the Religious Freedom Restoration Act (RFRA) in order to ensure the free exercise of religious practices. RFRA was an attempt to restore the previous status quo under which religious practices must be accommodated unless a compelling governmental interest can be demonstrated and advanced in the least restrictive manner. In 1997, the U.S. Supreme Court overturned RFRA as giving a governmental preference for religion, in violation of the First Amendment to the Constitution.[55]

While the matter of religious practices in the workplace was not at issue in these cases or this legislation, the national attention and debate about it, along with a growing religious presence in political issues and the media, extended the religious practices issue to the workplace by extrapolation. When the religious practices were challenged, religious harassment claims rose.

Of course, with all different types of religions in the workplace, it is predictable that there would be religious conflicts and that those with religions considered out of the ordinary or with religious practices that co-workers consider extreme would be the subject of religious harassment. In addition, it is often the nonreligious employees who allege they are being harassed by religious employees. For instance, in a case filed by information systems manager Rosamaria Machado-Wilson of DeLand, Florida, the employee alleged that she was fired after less than six months on the job after reporting religious harassment to the human resources office of her employer, BSG Laboratories. According to Machado-Wilson, a simple walk to the coffeepot sometimes meant "weaving past prostrate, praying co-workers and stopping for impromptu ceremonies spoken in tongues." She says she was forced to attend company prayer meetings and be baptized, employees were subjected to inquiries into and comments about their religious beliefs, and those found to be nonbelievers were fired.[56]

Of course, since Title VII prohibits religious discrimination, it also prohibits religious harassment. EEOC guidelines on liability for workplace harassment explicitly cover religious harassment. In the wake of the RFRA situation, in 1997 President Clinton issued guidelines for the religious freedom of federal employees. The purpose of the guidelines is to accommodate religious observance in the workplace as an important national priority by striking a balance between religious observance and the requirements of the workplace. Under the guidelines, employees

- Should be permitted to engage in private religious expression in personal work areas not regularly open to the public to the same extent that they may engage in nonreligious private expression.
- Should be permitted to engage in religious expression with fellow employees, to the same extent that they may engage in comparable nonreligious private expression, subject to reasonable restrictions.
- Are permitted to engage in religious expression directed at fellow employees, and may even attempt to persuade fellow employees of the correctness of their religious views. But employees must refrain from such expression when a fellow employee asks that it stop or otherwise demonstrates that it is unwelcome.

In order to best prevent liability for religious harassment, employers should be sure to protect employees from those religious employees who attempt to proselytize others who do not wish to be approached about religious matters, as well as to protect employees with permissible religious practices who are given a hard time by those who believe differently. Making sure that employees are given comparable opportunities to use workplace time and resources for religious practices if given for secular ones is also an important consideration, as otherwise it may appear that the employer is discriminating on the basis of religion.

The *Peterson v. Hewlett-Packard Co.* case, included at the end of the chapter, sets forth the very interesting issue of what to do when an employer's workplace diversity policy is at odds with an employee's religious beliefs, to the extent that the employee who opposes the policy feels harassed. The court upheld his termination after the employer posted diversity posters that included affinity orientation and the employee placed biblical passages on the overhead bins in his office for all to see, with the goal of hurting gay and lesbian employees "so they would repent."

Keep in mind here that as an employer, the employer gets to make the determinations about religion in the workplace within the confines of the law. Hopefully, they are consistent with law and promote workplace productivity. Employees who decide, for whatever reason, that they cannot abide the employer's lawful and legal policies always have the choice of either toughing it out or looking for a job that presents no such conflict. While the employer has no right to make employees choose between their religion and work, where a religious conflict does not pose an undue hardship, the employee also has no right to dictate to the employer what workplace policies must be. And, of course, harassment on the basis of religion is illegal under Title VII.

Union Activity and Religious Discrimination

As the earlier *Hardison* case discussed, at times the religious conflicts that arise between the employee and the employer are caused by collective-bargaining agreement provisions, rather than by policies unilaterally imposed by the employer. It has been determined that, even though Title VII defines the term *religion* with reference to an employer having a duty to reasonably accommodate, unions are also under a duty to reasonably accommodate religious conflicts.

The most frequent conflicts are requirements that employees be union members or pay union dues. Union membership, payment of union dues, or engaging in concerted activity such as picketing and striking conflicts with some religious beliefs. Employees also have objected to the payment of union dues as violating their First Amendment right to freedom of religion and Title VII's prohibition against religious discrimination. Unions have claimed that applying the religious proscription of Title VII violates the Establishment Clause of the First Amendment to the U.S. Constitution, ensuring government neutrality in religious matters.

Courts have ruled that union security agreements requiring that employees pay union dues within a certain time after the effective date of their employment or be

LO8 One of the primary reasons employers run into trouble in this area is because they simply fail to recognize the religious conflict when an employee notifies them, or they refuse to adequately address it if they do. Many of the conflicts can be avoided by following a few basic rules:

- Take all employee notices of religious conflicts seriously.
- Once an employee puts the employer on notice of a religious conflict, immediately try to find ways to avoid the conflict. An employer doesn't have to accommodate if doing so would cause an undue hardship, but there *must* be an attempt at accommodation.
- Ask the employee with the conflict for suggestions on avoiding the conflict. Employers need not take the suggestion, but allow the employee to provide input and knowledge in an area about which he or she may have more information.
- Ask other employees if they can be of assistance in alleviating the conflict (such as switching days off), but make it clear that they are not required to do so.
- Keep workplace religious comments and criticisms to a minimum.
- Make sure all employees understand that they are not to discriminate in any way against employees on the basis of religion.
- Once an employee expresses conflict based on religion, do not challenge the employee's religious beliefs, though it is permissible to make sure of the conflict.
- Make sure undue hardship actually exists if it is claimed.
- Revisit issues such as "Christmas" bonuses and "Christmas" parties, and giving out Christmas turkeys or other gifts to see if it is more appropriate to use more inclusive language such as "holiday" to cover employees who do not celebrate the Christian holiday of Christmas. Further, revisit the issue of whether all employees are being fairly covered by such policies and events.
- Revisit the issue of granting leave for religious events and make sure it does not favor one religion over another, such as giving employees paid leave for Christmas but requiring them to take their own leave for other religious holidays such as Rosh Hashanah, Yom Kippur, or Ramadan. "Floating holidays" that they can use for whatever holiday they celebrate may make more sense and be less exclusionary.
- Make sure food at workplace events is inclusive of all employees, regardless of religion, such as having kosher (or at least nonpork or nonseafood) items for Jewish employees, having alternatives to alcoholic beverages for those who do not drink for religious reasons, having nonpork items for Muslims, and so on. Asking employees what religious dietary limitations they have or having employees bring a dish to share is an easy way to handle this. It may seem like a small, bothersome thing to deal with, but for those whose religions dictate these things, it is *very* significant. These types of things help to create (or not) a workplace that employees feel truly adheres to both the letter as well as the spirit of the law and this, in turn, impacts an employee's perception of discrimination.

discharged does not violate an employee's First Amendment rights. However, it violates Title VII for an employer to discharge an employee for refusal to join the union because of his or her religious beliefs.

Employees with religious objections must be reasonably accommodated, including the possibility of the alternative of keeping their job without paying union dues. However, the union could prove undue hardship if many of the employees chose to have their dues instead paid to a nonunion, nonsectarian charitable organization chosen by the union and the employer since the impact on the union would not be insubstantial.

In *Tooley v. Martin-Marietta Corp,*[57] Seventh Day Adventists who were prohibited by their religion from becoming members of, or paying a service fee to, a union offered to pay an amount equal to union dues to a mutually acceptable charity. The union refused and argued that to accommodate the employees violated the Establishment Clause ensuring governmental neutrality in matters of religion. The court said that the government could legitimately enforce accommodation of religious beliefs when the accommodation reflects the obligation of neutrality in the face of religious differences and does not constitute sponsorship, financial support, or active involvement of the sovereign in religious activities with which the Establishment Clause is mainly concerned. The Establishment Clause, typically applied to state legislation, such as in *Frazee,* discussed earlier, requires that the accommodation reflect a clearly secular purpose, have a primary effect that neither inhibits nor advances religion, and avoid excessive government entanglement with religion.

Whether the objection under Title VII is directed toward the employer or the union, a government employer still has a duty to reasonably accommodate the employee's religious conflict unless to do so would cause undue hardship or excessive entanglement with religion or violate the Establishment Clause.

Chapter Summary

- Employees are protected in the workplace in their right to adhere to and practice their religious beliefs, and the employer cannot discriminate against them on this basis unless to do so would be an undue hardship on the employer.

- The employer cannot question the acceptability of an employee's religion or when or why the employee came to believe.

- The employer should be conscious of potential religious conflicts in developing and implementing workplace policies.

- The prohibition on religious discrimination is not absolute, as the employer has only the duty to reasonably accommodate the employee's religious conflict unless to do so would cause the employer undue hardship.

- While the employer must make a good-faith effort to reasonably accommodate religious conflicts, if such efforts fail, the employer will have discharged his or her legal duties under Title VII.

Chapter-End Questions

1. *The Christian Science Monitor* refused to hire Feldstein because he was not a Christian Scientist. The newspaper said they only hired those who were of the Christian Science religion, unless there are none qualified for a position. Is the newspaper's policy legal? Explain. [*Feldstein v. EEOC,* 547 F. Supp. 97 (D. Mass. 1982).]

2. Cynthia requested a two-week leave from her employer to go on a religious pilgrimage. The pilgrimage was not a requirement of her religion, but Cynthia felt it was a "calling from God." Will it violate Title VII if Cynthia's employer does not grant her the leave? Explain. [*Tiano v. Dillard Department Stores, Inc.,* 1998 WL 117864 (9th Cir. 1998).]

3. At the end of all her written communications, employee writes "have a blessed day." One of employer's most important clients requests that employee not do so and employer asks employee to stop. Employee refuses, saying it is a part of her religion. If employee sues the employer for religious discrimination, is she likely to win? [*Anderson v. USF Logistics (IMC), Inc.,* 274 F.3d 470 (7th Cir. 2001).]

4. Employee is terminated for refusal to cover or remove his confederate flag symbols as requested by his employer. He sues the employer, claiming discrimination on the basis of his religion as a Christian and his national origin as a "Confederate Southern American." Is he likely to win? [*Storey v. Burns International Security Service,* 390 F.3d 760 (3d Cir. 2004).]

5. A Michigan Holiday Inn fired a pregnant employee because the "very Christian" staff members were very upset by her talk of having an abortion. Has the employer violated Title VII? [*Turic v. Holland Hospitality, Inc.,* No. 1-93-CV-379 (W.D. Mich. 1994).]

6. A police officer who is assigned to a casino refuses the assignment, claiming his Baptist religion prohibits him from gambling or being around gambling. Is he legitimately able to do so? [*Endres v. Indiana State Police,* 349 F.3d 922 (7th Cir. 2003).]

7. Employer has a strict policy of not allowing employees with beards to work in public contact positions. All managerial positions are public contact positions. Employer does not make exceptions to its policies for those with religious objections to shaving, but it reasonably accommodates them by offering them other positions within the company. When employee applies for a driver position and is turned down, he sues employer. Does he win? [*EEOC v. UPS,* 94 F.3d 314 (7th Cir. 1996).]

8. Employee, a Muslim, is a management trainee at an airport car rental office. As part of her religious practice, employee wears a *hijab* (headscarf). She is told by her supervisor that the *hijab* does not match the uniforms she is required to wear, so she must stop wearing it or be transferred to another position with less customer interaction. Employee was later terminated as a part of a company cutback. She sues for religious discrimination. Does she win? Explain. [*Ali v. Alamo Rent-A-Car,* 246 F.3d 662 (4th Cir. 2001).]

9. A Pentecostal nurse claims she was constructively discharged after refusing, because of her religious beliefs, to assist in medical procedures she considered to be abortions. She was initially transferred from labor and delivery to the newborn intensive care unit. Employee found this unacceptable because she says she would once again be forced to refuse tasks that involved allowing infants to die. The hospital invited the employee to meet with human resources and to investigate available positions, but she refused. Employee says the duty to assist in an accommodation never arose because a transfer to any other department is not a viable option since it would require her to

give up her eight years of specialized training and education and undertake retraining. Employee is terminated and sues for religious discrimination. Does she win? Explain. [*Shelton v. University of Medicine & Dentistry of New Jersey*, 2000 U.S. App. LEXIS 19099 (3d Cir. 2000).]

10. A Baptist-run home for troubled youngsters terminates an employee for being a lesbian. Can it do so? [*Pedreira v. Kentucky Baptist Home for Children*, 186 F. Supp. 2d 757 (W.D. Ky. 2001).]

End Notes

1. Donna Horowitz, "Ex-Santana Employee Sues Over Firing: Aide to the Musician and His Wife Says They Dismissed Him for Spiritual Shortcomings. He Also Alleges Age and Gender Discrimination," *L.A. Times*, 10/11/2005, http://articles.latimes.com/2005/oct/11/local/me-santana11.

2. *Anderson v. U.S.F. Logistics, Inc.*, 274 F.3d 470 (7th Cir. 2001).

3. *Hedum v. Starbucks Corp.*, 546 F. Supp. 1017 (D. Or. 2008).

4. Thomas Claburn, "Google Sued for Sexual, Religious Discrimination," 11/3/2009, *InformationWeek*, http://www.informationweek.com/news/services/saas/showArticle.jhtml?articleID=221600072.

5. James Joyner, "Woman Fired for Eating 'Unclean' Meat," Orlando Local6 TV, 8/4/2004, http://www.outsidethebeltway.com/_woman_fired_for_eating_unclean_meat/.

6. Patrick J. Reilly, "Look Who's Discriminating Now," *The Wall Street Journal*, 8/13/2009, http://online.wsj.com/article/SB10001424052970203863204574346833989489154.html.

7. "Minnesota's Muslim Cabdrivers Face Crackdown," Reuters, 4/17/2007, http://www.reuters.com/article/2007/04/17/us-muslims-taxis-idUSN1633289220070417.

8. *Moranski v. General Motors Corp.*, 433 F.3d 537 (7th Cir. 2005).

9. Rob Stein, "Pharmacists' Rights at Front of New Debate: Because of Beliefs, Some Refuse to Fill Birth Control Prescriptions," *The Washington Post*, 3/28/2005, http://www.washingtonpost.com/wp-dyn/articles/A5490-2005Mar27.html.

10. *Endres v. Indiana State Police*, 349 F.3d 922 (7th Cir. 2003). The U.S. Supreme Court declined to hear the officer's appeal.

11. *Knight v. State of Connecticut, Department of Public Health*, 275 F.3d 156 (2d Cir. 2001).

12. Anne Castellani, "Judge Rules in Favor of Turban-Wearing Officer," CNNJustice, 5/3/2004, http://articles.cnn.com/2004-04-30/justice/turban.cop_1_turban-judge-rules-sikh?_s=PM:LAW.

13. "Ten Commandments Judge Removed from Office," CNNJustice, 11/4/2003, http://articles.cnn.com/2003-11-13/justice/moore.tencommandments_1_ethics-panel-state-supreme-court-building-ethics-charges?_s=PM:LAW.

14. "City Agrees to Pay $20,000 in Fees, Clarify Rules After 2 Employees Claim Christmas Discrimination," Fox News, 2/20/2008, http://www.foxnews.com/story/0,2933,331431,00.html?sPage=fnc/us/lawcenter.

15. "Florida TV Producer Sues over Firing," 1/29/2003, http://www.highbeam.com/doc/1P1-71355459.html.

16. John Gibson, "Some Muslim Cashiers at Minnesota Target Refuse to Scan Pork Products," Fox News, 3/20/2007, http://www.foxnews.com/story/0,2933,259914,00.html.

17. Neela Banerjee, "Soldier Sues Army, Saying His Atheism Led to Threats," *The New York Times*, 4/26/2008, http://www.nytimes.com/2008/04/26/us/26atheist.html.

18. "Worker Opposed to Gays Wins Suit," *The Washington Times*, 4/7/2004, http://www.washingtontimes.com/news/2004/apr/7/20040407-124312-3261r/.

19. *Peterson v. Hewlett-Packard, Co.*, 358 F.3d 599 (9th Cir. 2004).

20. *Altman v. Minn. Dept. of Corr.*, 251 F.3d 1199 (7th Cir. 2001).

21. Martin Espinoza, "Order to Tuck in Dreadlocks Leads to Civil Rights Lawsuit," *The New York Times*, 9/18/2008, http://www.nytimes.com/2008/09/18/nyregion/18dreads.html.

22. *Peterson v. Wilmur Communications, Inc.* 205 F. Supp. 1014 (E.D. Wis. 2002).

23. http://www.eeoc.gov/eeoc/statistics/enforcement/charges.cfm.

24. http://eeoc.gov/policy/does/religion.html.

25. 483 U.S. 327 (1987).

26. "Jewish Hockey Player Claims He Was Harassed," 1/25/2011, CNN.com http://www.cnn.com/2011/US/01/25/hockey.player.lawsuit/index.html?iref=allsearch.

27. "Brothers' Religious Discrimination Suit Settled," JTA.org, 3/18/2010. http://www.jta.org/news/article-print/2010/03/18/1011187/lawsuit-filed-by-the-eeoc-on-behalf.html.

28. "Teachers File Discrimination Lawsuit against School District," *Bakersfield News*, 5/21/2009, http://www.turnto23.com/news/19533316/detail.html.

29. "Drill Sergeants Reprimanded for Bias, Calling Trainee 'Juden',"10/18/2008, www.usatoday.com/news/religion/2008-10-06-jewish-soldier-n.html.

30. "Ivy Hall Assisted Living Pays $43,000 to Settle Religious Discrimination Lawsuit," EEOC press release, 1/29/2010, http://www.eeoc.gov/newsroom/release/12-18-09.cfm.

31. Bob Egelko, "Abercrombie & Fitch Sued over Muslim Scarf," SFGate.com, 9/2/2010, http://www.sfgate.com/cgi-bin/article.cgi?f=/c/a/2010/09/02/BATJ1FBVC.DTL&type=printable.

32. "EEOC Sue Covergys Corporation for Religious Discrimination," EEOC press release, 3/3/2011, http://www.eeoc.gov/eeoc/newsroom/release/3-3-11.cfm.

33. 2004 U.S. Dist. LEXIS 3973 (S.D. Ind. 2004).

34. 489 U.S.829 (1989).

35. Phred Dvorak, "Religious-Bias Filings Up," *The Wall Street Journal*, 10/16/2008, http://online.wsj.com/article/SB122411562348138619.html.

36. "Brinks to Pay $30,000 to Peoria Area Woman for Failure to Accommodate Religious Beliefs: EEOC Suit Said Pentecostal Employee Fired for Refusal to Wear Pants as Part of Uniform," EEOC press release, 1/2/2003, http://www1.eeoc.gov//eeoc/newsroom/release/1-2-03b.cfm?renderforprint=1.

37. *EEOC v. Chi Chi's Restaurant,* http://archive.eeoc.gov/abouteeoc/annual_reports/annrep96-98.html.

38. "Belk, Inc. to Pay $55,000 to Settle EEOC Religious Discrimination Suit," EEOC press release, 3/16/2011, http://www.eeoc.gov/eeoc/newsroom/release/3-16-11.cfm.

39. "Employee's Refusal to Say 'Happy Holidays' Leads to EEOC Complaint," *Business Management Daily*, 4/19/2009, http://www.businessmanagementdaily.com/articles/17858/1/Refusal-to-say-Happy-holidays-leads-to-EEOC-complaint/Page1.html#.

40. David Haldane, "Dismissed Bus Driver Files Federal Complaint: Labor: The Vegetarian Who Refused to Hand Out Hamburger Coupons to Riders for OCTA Cites Religious Discrimination," *The L.A. Times*, 6/11/1996, http://articles.latimes.com/1996-06-11/local/me-13909_1_bus-driver.

41. *Tanisha Matthews v. WalMart*, 10-2242 (7th Cir. 2011) (unpublished opinion); "Court: Wal-Mart Firing of Anti-Gay Employee Not Religious Harassment," *Chicago Sun Times*, 4/6/2007, http://www.suntimes.com/4693324-417/court-wal-mart-firing-of-anti-gay-employee-not-religious-harassment.html.

42. 475 U.S. 503 (1986).

43. *Tanisha Matthews v. WalMart*, 10-2242 (7th Cir. 2011).

44. 49 Cal. App. 4th 1223 (1996).

45. 58 F.3d 1337 (8th Cir. 1995).

46. 515 F.3d 307 (4th Cir. 2008).

47. Brian Skoloff, "Fla. Man Says Home Depot Fired Him Over God Button," *Atlanta Journal & Constitution*, 10/28/2009, http://www.ajc.com/business/fla-man-says-home-175481.html.

48. 529 F.2d 483 (10th Cir. 1976).

49. "Wis. Woman Pleads No Content in Toilet Corpse Case," 11/18/2008, http://www.comcast.net/articles/news-general/20081117/Decaying.Corpse/.

50. Tom Breen, "NC Teen: Nose Ring More Than Fashion, It's Faith," 9/16/2010, http://news.yahoo.com/s/ap/us_rel_piercing_church/print.

51. 1998 U.S. Dist. LEXIS 21148 (E.D. Mich. 1998).

52. 29 C.F.R. § 1605.1.*City of Boerne, Texas v. Flores*, 521 U.S. 507 (1997).

53. 803 F.2d 351 (7th Cir. 1986).

54. Sabra Chartrand, "Protecting Freedom of Religion in the Workplace," *The New York Times*, 6/8/1997, http://partners.nytimes.com/library/jobmarket/060897sabra.html.

55. *City of Boerne, Texas v. Flores,* 521 U.S. 507 (1997); *Rosamaria D. Machado-Wilson v. BSG Laboratories, Inc.,* Case No. 98-106601 CIDL (Cir. Ct., 7th Jud. Cir., Volusia County, Fla., 1998).

56. *Rosamaria D. Machado-Wilson v. BSG Laboratories, Inc.,* Case No. 98-106601 CIDL (Cir. Ct., 7th Jud. Cir., Volusia County, Fla., 1998).

57. 648 F.2d 1239 (9th Cir. 1981).

Cases

Case 2

Chalmers v. Tulon Company of Richmond *101 F.3d 1012 (4th Cir. 1996)*

The supervisory employee sued for religious discrimination and a failure to accommodate after being terminated for sending employees letters at home about their personal and religious lives. One employee received the letter while ill at home on leave after delivering a baby out of wedlock, and the other employee's wife opened the letter and became distraught because she thought the references in the letter meant her husband was having an affair. The court held that there was no duty to accommodate the terminated employee's religious practice of sending such letters.

Motz, J.

***

Chalmers, a supervisor, has been a Baptist all of her life, and in June 1984 became an evangelical Christian. At that time, she accepted Christ as her personal savior and determined to go forth and do work for him. As an evangelical Christian, Chalmers believes she should share the gospel and looks for opportunities to do so.

Chalmers felt that her supervisor, LaMantia, respected her, generally refraining from using profanity around her, while around other employees who did not care, "he would say whatever he wanted to say." She felt that she and LaMantia had a "personal relationship" and that she could talk to him. Chalmers stated that "in the past we have talked about God." Chalmers further testified that "starting off" she and LaMantia had discussed religion about "everytime he came to the service center . . . maybe every three months" but "then, towards the end maybe not as frequently." LaMantia never discouraged these conversations, expressed discomfort with them, or indicated that they were improper. In one of these conversations, LaMantia told Chalmers that three people had approached him about accepting Christ.

Two or three years after this conversation, Chalmers "knew it was time for [LaMantia] to accept God." She believed LaMantia had told customers information about the turnaround time for a job when he knew that information was not true. Chalmers testified that she was "led by the Lord" to write LaMantia and tell him "there were things he needed to get right with God, and that was one thing that . . . he needed to get right with him."

Accordingly, on Labor Day, September 6, 1993, Chalmers mailed the following letter to LaMantia at his home:

Dear Rich:

The reason I'm writing you is because the Lord wanted me to share somethings [sic] with you. After reading this letter you do not have to give me a call, but talk to God about everything.

One thing the Lord wants you to do is get your life right with him. The Bible says in Romans 10:9vs that if you confess with your mouth the Lord Jesus and believe in your heart that God hath raised him from the dead, thou shalt be saved. vs 10—For with the heart man believeth unto righteousness, and with the mouth confession is made unto salvation. The two verse are [sic] saying for you to get right with God now.

The last thing is, you are doing somethings [sic] in your life that God is not please [sic] with and He wants you to stop. All you have to do is go to God and ask for forgiveness before it's too late.

I wrote this letter at home so if you have a problem with it you can't relate it to work.

I have to answer to God just like you do, so that's why I wrote you this letter. Please take heed before it's too late.

In his name,
Charita Chalmers

On September 10, 1993, when Chalmers' letter arrived at LaMantia's home, he was out of town on Tulon business and his wife opened and read the letter in his absence. Mrs. LaMantia became distraught, interpreting the references to her husband's improper conduct as indicating that he was committing adultery. In tears, she called Chalmers and asked her if LaMantia was having an affair with someone in the New Hampshire area where

LaMantia supervised another Tulon facility. Mrs. LaMantia explained that three years before she and LaMantia had separated because of his infidelity. Chalmers told Mrs. LaMantia that she did not know about any affair because she was in the Richmond area. When Mrs. LaMantia asked her what she had meant by writing that there was something in LaMantia's life that "he needed to get right with God," Chalmers explained about the turnaround time problem. Mrs. LaMantia responded that she would take the letter and rip it up so LaMantia could not read it. Chalmers answered, "Please don't do that, the Lord led me to send this to Rich, so let him read it." The telephone conversation then ended.

Mrs. LaMantia promptly telephoned her husband, interrupting a Tulon business presentation, to accuse him of infidelity. LaMantia, in turn, called the Richmond office and asked to speak with Chalmers; she was in back and by the time she reached the telephone, LaMantia had hung up. Chalmers then telephoned the LaMantias' home and, when she failed to reach anyone, left a message on the answering machine that she was sorry "if the letter offended" LaMantia or his wife and that she "did not mean to offend him or make him upset about the letter."

LaMantia also telephoned Craig A. Faber, Vice President of Administration at Tulon. LaMantia told Faber that the letter had caused him personal anguish and placed a serious strain on his marriage. LaMantia informed Faber that he felt he could no longer work with Chalmers. LaMantia recommended that Tulon management terminate Chalmers' employment.

While investigating LaMantia's complaint, Faber discovered that Chalmers had sent a second letter, on the same day as she sent the letter to LaMantia, to another Tulon employee. That employee, Brenda Combs, worked as a repoint operator in the Richmond office and Chalmers was her direct supervisor. Chalmers knew that Combs was convalescing at her home, suffering from an undiagnosed illness after giving birth out of wedlock. Chalmers sent Combs the following letter:

Brenda,

You probably do not want to hear this at this time, but you need the Lord Jesus in your life right now.

One thing about God, He doesn't like when people commit adultery. You know what you did is wrong, so now you need to go to God and ask for forgiveness.

Let me explain something about God. He's a God of Love and a God of Wrath. When people sin against Him, He will allow things to happen to them or their family until they open their eyes and except [sic] Him. God can put a sickness on you that no doctor could ever find out what it is. I'm not saying this is what happened to you, all I'm saying is get right with God right now. Romans 10:9;10vs says that is [sic] you confess with your mouth the Lord Jesus and believe in your heart that God has raised him from the dead thou shalt be saved. For with the heart man believeth unto righteousness; and with the mouth confession is made unto salvation. All I'm saying is you need to invite God into your heart and live a life for Him and things in your life will get better.

That's not saying you are not going to have problems but it's saying you have someone to go to.

Please take this letter in love and be obedient to God.

In his name,

Charita Chalmers

Upon receiving the letter Combs wept. Faber discussed the letter with Combs who told him that she had been "crushed by the tone of the letter." Combs believed that Chalmers implied that "an immoral lifestyle" had caused her illness and found Chalmers' letter "cruel." Combs, in a later, unsworn statement, asserted that although the letter "upset her" it did not "offend" her or "damage her working relationship" with Chalmers.

Faber consulted with other members of upper management and concluded that the letters caused a negative impact on working relationships, disrupted the workplace, and inappropriately invaded employee privacy. On behalf of Tulon, Faber then sent Chalmers a memorandum, informing her that she was terminated from her position. The memorandum stated in relevant part:

We have decided to terminate your employment with Tulon Co. effective today, September 21, 1993. Our decision is based on a serious error in judgment you made in sending letters to LaMantia and Combs, which criticized their personal lives and beliefs. The letters offended them, invaded their privacy, and damaged your work relationships, making it too difficult for you to continue to work here.

We expect all of our employees to show good judgment, especially those in supervisory positions, such as yours. We would hope you can learn from this experience and avoid similar mistakes in the future.

As a result of the preceding events, Chalmers filed suit, alleging that Tulon discriminated against her based on her religion, in violation of Title VII. She contended that her letter writing constituted protected religious activity that Tulon, by law, should have accommodated with a lesser punishment than discharge.

In a religious accommodation case, an employee can establish a claim even though she cannot show that other (unprotected) employees were treated more favorably or cannot rebut an employer's legitimate, non-discriminatory reason for her discharge. This is because an employer must, to an extent, actively attempt to accommodate an employee's religious expression or conduct even if, absent the religious motivation, the employee's conduct would supply a legitimate ground for discharge.

Tulon's proffered reasons for discharging Chalmers—because her letters, which criticized her fellow employees' personal lives and beliefs, invaded the employees' privacy, offended them and damaged her working relationships—are legitimate and non-discriminatory.

To establish a *prima facie* religious accommodation claim, a plaintiff must establish that: "(1) he or she has a bona fide religious belief that conflicts with an employment requirement; (2) he or she informed the employer of this belief; (3) he or she was disciplined for failure to comply with the conflicting employment requirement."

Chalmers has alleged that she holds bona fide religious beliefs that caused her to write the letters. Tulon offers no evidence to the contrary. The parties agree that Tulon fired Chalmers because she wrote the letters. Accordingly, Chalmers has satisfied the first and third elements of the *prima facie* test. However, in other equally important respects, Chalmers' accommodation claim fails.

Chalmers cannot satisfy the second element of the *prima facie* test. She has forecast no evidence that she notified Tulon that her religious beliefs required her to send personal, disturbing letters to her co-workers. Therefore she did not allow the company any sort of opportunity to attempt reasonable accommodation of her beliefs.

Chalmers concedes that she did not expressly notify Tulon that her religion required her to write letters like those at issue here to her co-workers, or request that Tulon accommodate her conduct. Nonetheless, for several reasons, she contends that such notice was unnecessary in this case.

Initially, Chalmers asserts that Tulon never explicitly informed her of a company policy against writing religious letters to fellow employees at their homes and so she had "no reason to request an accommodation." However, companies cannot be expected to notify employees explicitly of all types of conduct that might annoy co-workers, damage working relationships, and thereby provide grounds for discharge. Chalmers implicitly acknowledged in the letters themselves that they might distress her co-workers. Moreover, she conceded that, as a supervisor, she had a responsibility to "promote harmony in the workplace."

Although a rule justifying discharge of an employee because she has disturbed co-workers requires careful application in the religious discrimination context (many religious practices might be perceived as "disturbing" to others), Chalmers, particularly as a supervisor, is expected to know that sending personal, distressing letters to co-workers' homes, criticizing them for assertedly ungodly, shameful conduct, would violate employment policy. Accordingly, the failure of the company to expressly forbid supervisors from disturbing other employees in this way provides Chalmers with no basis for failing to notify Tulon that her religious beliefs require her to write such letters.

Alternatively, Chalmers contends that the notoriety of her religious beliefs within the company put it on notice of her need to send these letters. In her view, Chalmers satisfied the notice requirement because Tulon required "only enough information about an employee's religious needs to permit the employer to understand the existence of a conflict between the employee's religious practices and the employer's job requirements."

Knowledge that an employee has strong religious beliefs does not place an employer on notice that she might engage in any religious activity, no matter how unusual. Chalmers concedes that she did not know of any other employee who had ever written distressing or judgmental letters to co-workers before, and that nothing her co-workers had said or done indicated that such letters were acceptable. Accordingly, any knowledge Tulon may have possessed regarding Chalmers' beliefs could not reasonably have put it on notice that she would write and send accusatory letters to co-workers' homes.

Chalmers appears to contend that because Tulon was necessarily aware of the religious nature of the letters after her co-workers received them and before her discharge, Tulon should have attempted to accommodate her by giving her a sanction less than a discharge, such as a warning. This raises a false issue. There is nothing in Title VII that requires employers to give lesser punishments to employees who claim, after they violate company rules (or at the same time), that their religion caused them to transgress the rules.

Part of the reason for the advance notice requirement is to allow the company to avoid or limit any "injury" an employee's religious conduct may cause. Additionally, the refusal even to attempt to accommodate an employee's religious requests, prior to the employee's violation of employment rules and sanction, provides some indication, however slight, of improper motive on the employer's part. The proper issue, therefore, is whether Chalmers made Tulon aware, prior to her letter writing, that her religious beliefs would cause her to send the letters. Since it is clear that she did not, her claims fail.

In sum, Chalmers has not pointed to any evidence that she gave Tulon—either directly or indirectly—advance notice of her need for accommodation. For this reason, Chalmers has failed to establish a *prima facie* case of discrimination under the religious accommodation theory.

If we had concluded that Chalmers had established a *prima facie* case, Chalmers' religious accommodation claim would nonetheless fail. This is so because Chalmers' conduct is not the type that an employer can possibly accommodate, even with notice.

Chalmers concedes in the letters themselves that she knew the letters to her co-workers, accusing them of immoral conduct (in the letter to Combs, suggesting that Combs' immoral conduct caused her illness), might cause them distress. Even if Chalmers had notified Tulon expressly that her religious beliefs required her to write such letters, i.e. that she was "led by the Lord" to write them, Tulon was without power under any circumstances to accommodate Chalmers' need.

Typically, religious accommodation suits involve religious conduct, such as observing the Sabbath, wearing religious garb, etc., that result in indirect and minimal burdens, if any, on other employees. An employer can often accommodate such needs without inconveniencing or unduly burdening other employees.

In a case like the one at hand, however, where an employee contends that she has a religious need to impose personally and directly on fellow employees,

invading their privacy and criticizing their personal lives, the employer is placed between a rock and a hard place. If Tulon had the power to authorize Chalmers to write such letters, and if Tulon had granted Chalmers' request to write the letters, the company would subject itself to possible suits from Combs and LaMantia claiming that Chalmers' conduct violated their religious freedoms or constituted religious harassment. Chalmers' supervisory position at the Richmond office heightens the possibility that Tulon (through Chalmers) would appear to be imposing religious beliefs on employees.

Thus, even if Chalmers had notified Tulon that her religion required her to send the letters at issue here to her co-workers, Tulon would have been unable to accommodate that conduct.

We do not in any way question the sincerity of Chalmers' religious beliefs or practices. However, it is undisputed that Chalmers failed to notify Tulon that her religious beliefs led her to send personal, disturbing letters to her fellow employees accusing them of immorality. It is also undisputed that the effect of a letter on one of the recipients, LaMantia's wife, whether intended or not, caused a co-worker, LaMantia, great stress and caused him to complain that he could no longer work with Chalmers. Finally, it is undisputed that another employee, Combs, told a company officer that Chalmers' letter upset her (although she later claimed that her working relationship with Chalmers was unaffected). Under these facts, Chalmers cannot establish a religious accommodation claim. Accordingly, the district court's order granting summary judgment to Tulon is AFFIRMED.

Case Questions

1. Is there any way the employer could have avoided this situation? Explain.

2. If the employee had initially told the employer of her plan to write the letters and the employer had told her not to send them, would the outcome be any different if she had done so anyway?

3. What would you have done if your employee's wife called as Mrs. LaMantia did?

Trans World Airlines, Inc. v. Hardison *432 U.S. 63 (1977)*

Case 3

Employer was unable to accommodate employee's religious conflict of working on the Sabbath, without undue hardship. The Court set forth the guidelines for determining what constitutes undue hardship.

White, J.

***

The employee, Hardison, was employed by Trans World Airlines (TWA), in a department that operated 24 hours a day throughout the year in connection with an airplane maintenance and overhaul base. Hardison was subject to a seniority system in a collective bargaining agreement between TWA and the International Association of Machinists & Aerospace Workers (union), whereby the most senior employees have first choice for job and shift assignments as they become available, and the most junior employees are required to work when enough employees to work at a particular time or in a particular job to fill TWA's needs cannot be found.

Because Hardison's religious beliefs prohibit him from working on Saturdays, attempts were made to accommodate him, and these were temporarily successful mainly because on his job at the time he had sufficient seniority regularly to observe Saturday as his Sabbath. But when he sought, and was transferred to, another job where he was asked to work Saturdays and where he had low seniority, problems began to arise. TWA agreed to permit the union to seek a change of work assignments, but the union was not willing to violate the seniority system, and Hardison had insufficient seniority to bid for a shift having Saturdays off. After TWA rejected a proposal that Hardison work only four days a week on the ground that this would impair critical functions in the airline operations, no accommodation could be reached, and Hardison was discharged for refusing to work on Saturdays.

We hold that TWA, which made reasonable efforts to accommodate Hardison's religious needs, did not violate Title VII, and each of the Court of Appeals' suggested alternatives would have been an undue hardship within the meaning of the statute as construed by the EEOC guidelines. The employer's statutory obligation to make reasonable accommodation for the religious observances of its employees, short of incurring an undue hardship, is clear, but the reach of that obligation has never been spelled out by Congress or by EEOC guidelines. With this in mind, we turn to a consideration of whether TWA has met its obligation under Title VII to accommodate the religious observances of its employees.

The Court of Appeals held that TWA had not made reasonable efforts to accommodate Hardison's religious needs. In its view, TWA had rejected three reasonable alternatives, any one of which would have satisfied its obligation without undue hardship. First, within the framework of the seniority system, TWA could have permitted Hardison to work a four-day week, utilizing in his place a supervisor or another worker on duty elsewhere. That this would have caused other shop functions to suffer was insufficient to amount to undue hardship in the opinion of the Court of Appeals. Second, also within the bounds of the collective-bargaining contract the company could have filled Hardison's Saturday shift from other available personnel competent to do the job, of which the court said there were at least 200. That this would have involved premium overtime pay was not deemed an undue hardship. Third, TWA could have arranged a "swap between Hardison and another employee either for another shift or for the Sabbath days." In response to the assertion that this would have involved a breach of the seniority provisions of the contract, the court noted that it had not been settled in the courts whether the required statutory accommodation to religious needs stopped short of transgressing seniority rules, but found it unnecessary to decide the issue because, as the Court of Appeals saw the record, TWA had not sought, and the union had therefore not declined to entertain, a possible variance from the seniority provisions of the collective-bargaining agreement. The company had simply left the entire matter to the union steward who the Court of Appeals said "likewise did nothing."

We disagree with the Court of Appeals in all relevant respects. It is our view that TWA made reasonable efforts to accommodate and that each of the suggested alternatives would have been an undue hardship within the meaning of the statute as construed by the EEOC guidelines.

It might be inferred from the Court of Appeals' opinion and from the brief of the EEOC in this Court that TWA's efforts to accommodate were no more than negligible. The findings of the District Court, supported by the record, are to the contrary. In summarizing its more detailed findings, the District Court observed:

"TWA established as a matter of fact that it did take appropriate action to accommodate as required by Title VII. It held several meetings with plaintiff at which it attempted to find a solution to plaintiff's problems. It did accommodate plaintiff's observance of his special religious holidays. It authorized the union steward to search for someone who would swap shifts, which apparently was normal procedure."

It is also true that TWA itself attempted without success to find Hardison another job. The District Court's view was that TWA had done all that could reasonably be expected within the bounds of the seniority system.

We are also convinced, contrary to the Court of Appeals, that TWA itself cannot be faulted for having failed to work out a shift or job swap for Hardison. Both the union and TWA had agreed to the seniority system; the union was unwilling to entertain a variance over the objections of men senior to Hardison; and for TWA to have arranged unilaterally for a swap would have amounted to a breach of the collective-bargaining agreement.

Hardison and the EEOC insist that the statutory obligation to accommodate religious needs takes precedence over both the collective-bargaining contract and the seniority rights of TWA's other employees. We agree that neither a collective-bargaining contract nor a seniority system may be employed to violate the statute, but we do not believe that the duty to accommodate requires TWA to take steps inconsistent with the otherwise valid agreement. Collective bargaining, aimed at effecting workable and enforceable agreements between management and labor, lies at the core of our national labor policy, and seniority provisions are universally included in these contracts. Without a clear and express indication from Congress, we cannot agree with Hardison and the EEOC that an agreed-upon seniority system must give way when necessary to accommodate religious observances.

The Court of Appeals also suggested that TWA could have permitted Hardison to work a four-day week if necessary in order to avoid working on his Sabbath. Recognizing that this might have left TWA short-handed on the one shift each week that Hardison did not work, the court still concluded that TWA would suffer no undue hardship if it were required to replace Hardison either with supervisory personnel or with qualified personnel from other departments. Alternatively, the Court of Appeals suggested that TWA could have replaced Hardison on his Saturday shift with other available employees through the payment of premium wages. Both of these alternatives would involve costs to TWA, either in the form of lost efficiency in other jobs or higher wages.

To require TWA to bear more than a de minimis cost in order to give Hardison Saturdays off is an undue hardship. Like abandonment of the seniority system, to require TWA to bear additional costs when no such costs are incurred to give other employees the days off that they want would involve unequal treatment of employees on the basis of their religion. By suggesting that TWA should incur certain costs in order to give Hardison Saturdays off the Court of Appeals would in effect require TWA to finance an additional Saturday off and then to choose the employee who will enjoy it on the basis of his religious beliefs. While incurring extra costs to secure a replacement for Hardison might remove the necessity of compelling another employee to work involuntarily in Hardison's place, it would not change the fact that the privilege of having Saturdays off would be allocated according to religious beliefs. While the cost may seem small for one employee compared to TWA's resources, TWA may have many employees who need such accommodation.

Case Questions

1. In your opinion, were the alternatives suggested by the court of appeals viable for TWA? Why or why not?

2. Does it seem inconsistent to prohibit religious discrimination yet say that collective bargaining agreements cannot be violated to accommodate religious differences? Explain.

3. If you had been Hardison's manager and he came to you with this conflict, how would you have handled it? Does that change now that you have seen the Court's decision? If so, how?

Case 4

Peterson v. Hewlett-Packard Co. *358 F.3d 599 (9th Cir. 2004)*

Employee sued employer for religious discrimination and alleged religious harassment after being terminated for repeatedly refusing to remove biblical passages he posted in his workplace cubicle, easily seen by all, in response to employer's workplace diversity posters that included affinity orientation. The court upheld the termination, concluding that the employer was not required to go along with employee's admitted goal of hurting gay and lesbian employees in an effort to get them to "repent and be saved."

Reinhardt, J.

***

In this religious discrimination action under Title VII of the Civil Rights Act of 1964, Richard Peterson claims that his former employer, the Hewlett-Packard Company, engaged in disparate treatment by terminating him on account of his religious views and that it failed to accommodate his religious beliefs.

The conflict between Peterson and Hewlett-Packard arose when the company began displaying "diversity posters" in its Boise office as one component of its workplace diversity campaign. The first series consisted of five posters, each showing a photograph of a Hewlett-Packard employee above the caption "Black," "Blonde," "Old," "Gay," or "Hispanic." Posters in the second series included photographs of the same five employees and a description of the featured employee's personal interests, as well as the slogan "Diversity is Our Strength."

Peterson describes himself as a "devout Christian," who believes that homosexual activities violate the commandments contained in the Bible and that he has a duty "to expose evil when confronted with sin." In response to the posters that read "Gay," Peterson posted two Biblical scriptures on an overhead bin in his work cubicle. The scriptures were printed in a typeface large enough to be visible to co-workers, customers, and others who passed through an adjacent corridor.

***

Peterson's direct supervisor removed the scriptural passages after consulting her supervisor and determining that they could be offensive to certain employees, and that the posting of the verses violated Hewlett-Packard's policy prohibiting harassment. Throughout the relevant period, Hewlett-Packard's harassment policy stated as follows: "Any comments or conduct relating to a person's race, gender, religion, disability, age, sexual orientation, or ethnic background that fail to respect the dignity and feeling [sic] of the individual are unacceptable."

Over the course of several days after Peterson posted the Biblical materials, he attended a series of meetings with Hewlett-Packard managers, during which he and they tried to explain to each other their respective positions. Peterson explained that he meant the passages to communicate a message condemning "gay behavior." The scriptural passages, he said, were "intended to be hurtful. And the reason [they were] intended to be hurtful is you cannot have correction unless people are faced with truth." Peterson hoped that his gay and lesbian co-workers would read the passages, repent, and be saved.

In these meetings, Peterson also asserted that Hewlett-Packard's workplace diversity campaign was an initiative to "target" heterosexual and fundamentalist Christian employees at Hewlett-Packard, in general, and him in particular. Ultimately, Peterson and the managers were unable to agree on how to resolve the conflict. Peterson proposed that he would remove the offending scriptural passages if Hewlett-Packard removed the "Gay" posters; if, however, Hewlett-Packard would not remove the posters, he would not remove the passages. When the managers rejected both options, Peterson responded: "I don't see any way that I can compromise what I am doing that would satisfy both [Hewlett-Packard] and my own conscience." He further remonstrated: "as long as [Hewlett-Packard] is condoning [homosexuality] I'm going to oppose it. . . ."

Peterson was given time off with pay to reconsider his position. When he returned to work, he again posted the scriptural passages and refused to remove them. After further meetings with Hewlett-Packard managers, Peterson was terminated for insubordination.

Following receipt of a right to sue notice from the EEOC, Peterson filed a complaint alleging religious discrimination in violation of Title VII and the Idaho Human Rights Act. Both parties moved for summary judgment. The district court granted Hewlett-Packard's motion and denied Peterson's. We affirm.

Title VII makes it unlawful for an employer "to discharge any individual ... because of such individual's ... religion[.]" "The term 'religion' includes all aspects of religious observance and practice, as well as belief, unless an employer demonstrates that he is unable to reasonably accommodate to an employee's ... religious observance or practice without undue hardship on the conduct of the employer's business." Our analysis of Peterson's religious discrimination claims under the Idaho Human Rights Act is the same as under Title VII.

A claim for religious discrimination under Title VII can be asserted under several different theories, including disparate treatment and failure to accommodate. In arguing that Hewlett-Packard discriminated against him on account of his religious beliefs, Peterson relies on both these theories.

Peterson has the burden of establishing a *prima facie* case by showing that (1) he is a member of a protected class; (2) he was qualified for his position; (3) he experienced an adverse employment action; and (4) similarly situated individuals outside his protected class were treated more favorably, or other circumstances surrounding the adverse employment action give rise to an inference of discrimination. It is with respect to the fourth requirement that Peterson's case fails.

Initially, we address Peterson's argument that Hewlett-Packard's workplace diversity campaign was "a crusade to convert fundamentalist Christians to its values," including the promotion of "the homosexual lifestyle." The undisputed evidence shows that Hewlett-Packard carefully developed its campaign during a three-day diversity conference at its Boise facility in 1997 and subsequent planning meetings in which numerous employees participated. The campaign's stated goal—and no evidence suggests that it was pretextual—was to increase tolerance of diversity. Peterson may be correct that the campaign devoted special attention to combating prejudice against homosexuality, but such an emphasis is in no manner unlawful. To the contrary, Hewlett-Packard's efforts to eradicate discrimination against homosexuals in its workplace were entirely consistent with the goals and objectives of our civil rights statutes generally.

In addition to Peterson's allegations about the general purposes of the diversity initiative, he asserts that the campaign that Hewlett-Packard conducted, as well as "the entire disciplinary process" that it initiated in response to his posting of the scriptural passages, constituted "an inquisition serving no other purpose than to ferret out the extremity of Peterson's views on homosexuality." According to Peterson, Hewlett-Packard managers harassed him in order to convince him to change his religious beliefs. However, the evidence that Peterson cites in support of this theory shows that Hewlett-Packard managers acted in precisely the opposite manner. In numerous meetings, Hewlett-Packard managers acknowledged the sincerity of Peterson's beliefs and insisted that he need not change them. They did not object to Peterson's expression of his anti-gay views in a letter to the editor that was published in the *Idaho Statesman*— a letter in which Peterson stated that Hewlett-Packard was "on the rampage to change moral values in Idaho under the guise of diversity," and that the diversity campaign was a "platform to promote the homosexual agenda." Nor did the Hewlett-Packard managers prohibit him from parking his car in the company lot even though he had affixed to it a bumper sticker stating, "Sodomy is Not a Family Value." All that the managers did was explain Hewlett-Packard's diversity program to Peterson and ask him to treat his co-workers with respect. They simply requested that he remove the posters and not violate the company's harassment policy—a policy that was uniformly applied to all employees. No contrary inference may be drawn from anything in the record.

Peterson also maintains that the disciplinary proceedings and his subsequent termination stand in marked contrast to Hewlett-Packard's treatment of three other groups of similarly situated employees. Peterson compares himself, first, to the employees who hung the diversity posters. He argues that these posters were intended "to make people uncomfortable so they would think again about diversity and change their actions to be more positive." He likens these actions to his own intentions to make his "scriptures [] hurtful so that people would repent (change their actions) and experience the joys of being saved." This comparison fails because the employees who hung the diversity posters were simply communicating the views of Hewlett-Packard as they were directed to do by management, whereas Peterson was expressing his own personal views which contradicted those of management. Moreover, unlike Peterson's postings, the company's workplace diversity campaign did not attack any group of employees on account of race, religion, or any other important individual characteristic. To the contrary, Hewlett-Packard's initiative was intended to promote tolerance of the diversity that exists in its workforce. Hewlett-Packard's failure to fire employees for following management's instructions to hang the posters prepared by management provides no evidence of disparate treatment.

Second, Peterson compares himself with other employees who posted religious and secular messages and symbols in their work spaces. Yet Peterson failed to present any evidence that the posters in other Hewlett-Packard employees' cubicles were intended to be "hurtful" to, or critical of, any other employees or otherwise violated the company's harassment policy. In fact, the only posters in other employees' work spaces that Peterson identified were of "Native American dream catchers," "New Age pictures of whales," and a yinyang symbol.

Third, Peterson argues that he was similarly situated to the network group of homosexual employees that Hewlett-Packard permitted to organize in the workplace and advertise in the company's email and its newsletter. Yet Peterson failed to present any evidence that communications from this network group were, let alone were intended to be, hurtful to any group of employees. Nor does anything in the record indicate that Hewlett-Packard permitted or would have permitted any network group or any individual employee to post messages of either a secular or religious variety that demeaned other employees or violated the company's harassment policy.

In short, we conclude that Peterson's evidence does not meet the threshold for defeating summary judgment in disparate treatment cases. Peterson offered *no* evidence, circumstantial or otherwise, that would support a reasonable inference that his termination was the result of disparate treatment on account of religion. Viewing the record in the light most favorable to Peterson, it is evident that he was discharged, not because of his religious beliefs, but because he violated the company's harassment policy by attempting to generate a hostile and intolerant work environment and because he was insubordinate in that he repeatedly disregarded the company's instructions to remove the demeaning and degrading postings from his cubicle.

Peterson also appeals the district court's rejection of his failure-to-accommodate theory of religious discrimination. An employee who fails to raise a reasonable inference of disparate treatment on account of religion may nonetheless show that his employer violated its affirmative duty under Title VII to reasonably accommodate employees' religious beliefs. To establish religious discrimination on the basis of a failure-to-accommodate theory, Peterson must first set forth a *prima facie* case that (1) he had a bona fide religious belief, the practice of which conflicts with an employment duty; (2) he informed his employer of the belief and conflict; and (3) the employer discharged, threatened, or otherwise subjected him to an adverse employment action because of his inability to fulfill the job requirement. If Peterson makes out a *prima facie* failure-to-accommodate case, the burden then shifts to Hewlett-Packard to show that it "initiated good faith efforts to accommodate reasonably the employee's religious practices or that it could not reasonably accommodate the employee without undue hardship."

As we explain below, it is readily apparent that the only accommodations that Peterson was willing to accept would have imposed undue hardship upon Hewlett-Packard. Therefore, we will assume *arguendo* that Peterson could establish a *prima facie* case that his posting of the anti-gay scriptural passages stemmed from his religious beliefs that homosexual activities "violate the commandments of God contained in the Holy Bible" and that those same religious beliefs imposed upon him "a duty to expose evil when confronted with sin." We make that assumption with considerable reservations, however, because we seriously doubt that the doctrines to which Peterson professes allegiance compel any employee to engage in either expressive or physical activity designed to hurt or harass one's fellow employees.

An employer's duty to negotiate possible accommodations ordinarily requires it to take "some initial step to reasonably accommodate the religious belief of that employee." Peterson contends that the company did not do so in this case even though Hewlett-Packard managers convened at least four meetings with him. In these meetings, they explained the reasons for the company's diversity campaign, allowed Peterson to explain fully his reasons for his postings, and attempted to determine whether it would be possible to resolve the conflict in a manner that would respect the dignity of Peterson's fellow employees. Peterson, however, repeatedly made it clear that only two options for accommodation would be acceptable to him, either that (1) both the "Gay" posters and anti-gay messages remain, or (2) Hewlett-Packard remove the "Gay" posters and he would then remove the anti-gay messages. Given Peterson's refusal to consider other accommodations, we proceed to evaluate whether one or both of the "acceptable" accommodations would have imposed undue hardship upon Hewlett-Packard, or to determine whether Hewlett-Packard carried its burden of showing that no reasonable accommodation was possible.

As we explain further below, Peterson's first proposed accommodation would have compelled Hewlett-Packard to permit an employee to post messages intended to demean and harass his co-workers. His second proposed accommodation would have forced the company to exclude sexual orientation from its workplace diversity program. Either choice would have created undue hardship for Hewlett-Packard because it would have inhibited its efforts to attract and retain a qualified, diverse workforce, which the company reasonably views as vital to its commercial success, thus, neither provides a reasonable accommodation.

With respect to Peterson's first proposal, an employer need not accommodate an employee's religious beliefs if doing so would result in discrimination against his co-workers or deprive them of contractual or other statutory rights, Nor does Title VII require an employer to accommodate an employee's desire to impose his religious beliefs upon his co-workers.

That is not to say that accommodating an employee's religious beliefs creates undue hardship for an employer merely because the employee's co-workers find his conduct irritating or unwelcome. Complete harmony in the workplace is not an objective of Title VII. If relief under Title VII can be denied merely because the majority group of employees, who have not suffered discrimination, will be unhappy about it, there will be little hope of correcting the wrongs to which the Act is directed. While Hewlett-Packard must tolerate some degree of employee discomfort in the process of taking steps required by Title VII to correct the wrongs of discrimination, it need not accept the burdens that would result from allowing actions that demean or degrade, or are designed to demean or degrade, members of its workforce. Thus, we conclude that Peterson's first proposed accommodation would have created undue hardship for his employer.

The only other alternative acceptable to Peterson— taking down all the posters—would also have inflicted undue hardship upon Hewlett-Packard because it would have infringed upon the company's right to promote diversity and encourage tolerance and good will among its workforce. The Supreme Court has acknowledged that "the skills needed in today's increasingly global marketplace can only be developed through exposure to widely diverse people, cultures, ideas, and viewpoints." These values and good business practices are appropriately promoted by Hewlett-Packard's workplace diversity program. To require Hewlett-Packard to exclude homosexuals from its voluntarily adopted program would create undue hardship for the company.

Because only two possible accommodations were acceptable to Peterson and implementing either would have imposed undue hardship upon Hewlett-Packard, we conclude that the company carried its burden of showing that no reasonable accommodation was possible, and we therefore reject Peterson's failure-to-accommodate claim.

Peterson failed to raise a triable issue of fact that his termination from employment at Hewlett-Packard was on account of his religious beliefs. The ruling of the district court is therefore AFFIRMED.

Case Questions

1. Do the employer's actions here seem reasonable to you (both those in response to diversity and those in response to the employee's reaction)?

2. Would you have balanced the two sides here the same as the court? Explain.

3. How would you design a diversity program that no employee would have problems with?

Chapter 12

Age Discrimination

Learning Objectives

When you finish studying this chapter, you should be able to:

LO1 Distinguish the perception of older workers from the reality of their impact in the workplace.

LO2 Describe the history of the protection of older workers in the United States.

LO3 Distinguish the ADEA and state-based age discrimination laws.

LO4 Identify the legal options available to an employee who believes that he or she is a victim of age discrimination.

LO5 Explain the *prima facie* case of discrimination based on age.

LO6 Describe the *bona fide occupational qualification* defenses available to employers under the ADEA.

LO7 Distinguish circumstances where disparate impact and disparate treatment apply in connection with age discrimination.

LO8 Analyze factual circumstances when employer economic concerns may justify adverse action against particular groups of workers.

LO9 Recognize necessary elements to establish pretext under the ADEA.

LO10 Define the parameters of a valid waiver of ADEA rights.

Opening Scenarios

SCENARIO 1

1 In an effort to reduce costs across the board,
Pilchard wishes to hire recent graduates of
Scenario MBA programs who have little experience.
His firm would be paying them above competitive salaries even if it offered them one-half the salaries of its present staff members who are over age 40. Should Pilchard terminate the older employees in favor of the younger, less-expensive workers? What if one or more of the older employees were willing to accept a 50-percent pay cut? Can Pilchard make the 50-percent pay cut a condition on older employees for remaining employed?

SCENARIO 2

2 Beth, an employer, wants to hire someone
for a strenuous job that requires a great deal
Scenario of training, which will take place over the
course of several years. The applicant who appears most qualified is 58 years old; however, Beth is concerned that the applicant will not be able to handle the physical demands of the position in the long run. Further, she is concerned that the applicant will only continue working for several more years before she retires. Does Beth hire the applicant anyway? What advice would you give Beth?

SCENARIO 3

3 Mary had worked as an accountant for
Andrew Arthurson, a once prestigious
Scenario accounting firm, for over 20 years before she
was laid off after the firm suffered a great loss of clients due to a scandal. Fifty-year-old Mary applies for a position as an accountant at Knott Hower Phault, an accounting firm with 25 employees in Chicago, Illinois. Thirty-eight-year-old senior partner Dan Knott is impressed by Mary's credentials and understands that Mary had no involvement in the Arthurson scandal. Still, he fears that Mary's years of experience make her overqualified for the accountant position at his firm. Dan thinks that a professional at Mary's stage would not care to take direction from him or his partners, who are either Dan's age or younger. What advice would you give Dan?

Statutory Basis

The statutory basis is presented in Exhibit 12.1, "Age Discrimination in Employment Act."

Oldie . . . but Goldie?

America is a culture in which youth is valued. It must be very strange indeed to those of other cultures, like the Japanese, who revere age and believe that with it comes wisdom and insight unobtainable by the young. In our culture, the general perception is that with youth comes energy, imagination, and innovation. With age comes decreasing interest, lack of innovation and imagination, and a lessening of the quality of the person. Television networks, studios, and talent agencies have been accused of stereotyping "older" television writers as not having the energy and ability to write for the younger demographic group they want to attract.[1] In 2010, to prove the point, 17 major networks and production studios paid $70 million to settle an age discrimination suit brought by 165 writers, who had alleged that they were tossed aside in Hollywood's pursuit of younger audiences.[2]

LO1 The scenarios at the beginning of this chapter are mere generalizations, or perhaps even stereotypes, but they are omnipresent in the workplace. While statistics show that older workers are more reliable, harder working, and more committed

517

Exhibit 12.1 *Age Discrimination in Employment Act*

Sec. 4 (a) It shall be unlawful for an employer—

(1) to fail or refuse to hire or to discharge any individual or otherwise discriminate against any individual with respect to his compensation, terms, conditions, or privilege of employment, because of such individual's age;

(2) to limit, segregate, or classify his employees in any way which would deprive or tend to deprive any individual of employment opportunity or otherwise adversely affect his status as an employee, because of such individual's age; or

(3) to reduce the wage rate of any employee in order to comply with this chapter.

Source: 20 U.S.C. § 623.

Scenario

and have less absenteeism than younger workers—all characteristics that employers say they value—the general perception of them as employees is exactly the opposite. A Government Accountability Office report to Congress[3] evidences a continuing bias against older workers. When asked how their organizations view older workers, 42 percent of respondents answered that older workers were an "issue to be dealt with." Less than one-fourth viewed older workers as a leveraging opportunity. This attitude adversely affects employees who may not be treated as well because they are perceived as less-desirable employees.

This perception is not limited to the United States, of course. Until 2007, lawyers were not permitted to be admitted to practice for the first time in the Indian state of Delhi if they were over the age of 45. This prohibition was based on the general understanding that "lawyers above 45 just get into the profession [to pass time]. They don't contribute anything, engage in malpractice and crowd in."[4] The constraint was recently lifted.

Contrary to those perceptions, older workers are actually now more likely to remain on the job than their counterparts earlier in this century. Between 1999 and 2009, the share of the workforce that was 55 and older grew from 12 percent to 19 percent, marking the largest proportion ever recorded in that age bracket.[5] If the same pace continues, this age group will constitute 25 percent of the workforce in 2019. In addition, a study by Pew Research found that more than 75 percent of workers today *expect* to continue to work for pay after they retire.[6] In contrast, the number of workers between the ages of 35 and 44 is expected to increase between 2010 and 2030, but at a much slower pace than the rate for older workers.[7] This eventuality presents a workforce challenge since more than 50 percent of companies do not actively recruit or work to retain older workers[8] and since a large proportion of the workforce will be eligible to retire within five years.[9] As a result, for many employers, the number one concern is how to attract and retain new talent.

Many employers feel that older employees may be more expensive to retain because they have greater experience and seniority. They may receive a raise each year until their salary becomes a burden on the firm. Management realizes that it could reduce costs by terminating older employees, who have more experience than may be necessary to perform the requirements of the position, and by hiring younger, less-experienced employees. However, the economic bias against older workers is not well founded in fact. (See Exhibit 12.2, "Realities about Older Workers and Age Discrimination.") A report issued by the American Association of Retired People (AARP) demonstrates that, contrary to popular beliefs that older workers impose higher costs on employers than younger workers, any additional costs are minimal, at best. With regard to retention, offsetting costs are actually related to turnover. In other words, the costs are based on the value that older workers have brought to the workplace through their "deep institutional knowledge and job-related know-how."[10] In connection with hiring, age-based compensation cost differences are exceptionally low. The same report found that older workers are more motivated to exceed expectations on the job than are younger counterparts.

While there certainly is an argument that *some* younger workers might be better qualified than older workers for certain types of positions at the moment the younger workers enter the workforce, employers might instead choose to rely on generalizations about groups of workers when they make hiring decisions. They may opt only to choose employees from those groups that they perceive as

---

Exhibit 12.2 *Realities about Older Workers and Age Discrimination*

1. In a reduction in force caused by economic factors, employers should be aware of the impact of terminations based on salary since older workers may be higher paid than others on average, due to job seniority.

2. Just because most people in a certain age group might have a common weakness, it cannot be generalized that *all* in that group have the weakness; so age may not be used as a job qualification.

3. Employees have no claim under the Age Discrimination in Employment Act for discrimination on the basis of their youth, only on the basis of age 40 and older.

4. Under most circumstances, employees are not required to retire at age 65 in the United States.

5. As workers, the following are **mere myths about older employees: They**

   - Are not hard workers.
   - Will get tired more easily than younger workers.
   - Are less able to perform than younger workers.
   - Do not understand technology.
   - Do not want to travel too much and are generally more stubborn and uninterested in learning.
   - Make too much money since it often is based on seniority and not performance.
   - Are just marking time before they can retire.

6. The following are **mere myths about younger employees: They**

   - Have it easy; they never suffer discrimination.
   - Always win the job when competing against older workers.
   - Have a lower unemployment rate than older workers.
   - Can easily find jobs since older workers are retiring all the time.

more likely to be successful as opposed to making a time-consuming individualized determination of the abilities of each applicant. While some of these generalizations may be grounded in their past experiences, it is the act of generalizing, rather than the individualized conclusions, that constitutes the wrongful discrimination. In this chapter, we will discuss older employees, their legal rights under the laws that protect them, and the most effective way for employers to end up with the most qualified workforces while respecting those laws.

Regulation: Age Discrimination in Employment Act

Age Discrimination in Employment Act
Prohibits discrimination in employment on the basis of age; applies to individuals who are at least 40 years old. Individuals who are not yet 40 years old are not protected by the act and *may* be discriminated against on the basis of their age.

Baseless discrimination against older workers occurs with such consistency that Congress was compelled to enact legislation to protect older workers from discrimination to prevent increased unemployment for those over 40. In 1967, Congress enacted the **Age Discrimination in Employment Act (ADEA)** for the express purpose of "promot[ing the] employment of older people based on their ability rather than age [and prohibiting] arbitrary age discrimination in employment." The act applies to employment by public and private employers and by unions and employment agencies, as well as by foreign companies with more than 20 workers located in the United States. Age discrimination complaints filed with the EEOC rose dramatically in recent years. Between 1999 and 2008, age-based complaints increased by almost 74 percent, to 24,582.[11] The percentage of all EEOC complaints based on age also grew substantially, by 7.5 percent, to 25.8 percent of all complaints filed. In 2009, however, the number of age-based complaints actually dropped 7 percent, to 22,778, surprising many analysts.[12] Among the reasons offered were (1) a prolonged economic downturn in which fewer age discrimination-eligible workers were still employed, (2) greater reliance on state age discrimination laws, which sometimes allow a wider range of damages than the federal law, (3) greater reliance on arbitration, and (4) a recent U.S. Supreme Court decision that tightened the screws on certain types of age discrimination suits (more on that later in this chapter).

On its effective date, the act covered employees between the ages of 40 and 65. The upper limit was extended to 70 in 1978 and later removed completely. There is no longer an upper age limit, in recognition that an 80-plus-year-old may be just as qualified for a position as a 30-year-old and should have the opportunity to prove her or his qualifications and to obtain or retain employment based on them. With few exceptions, mandatory retirement has now become a dinosaur (discussed below). It is also important to recognize that the act will become all the more critical as health care advances allow people to live more vital lives to older ages. Many people today feel healthy enough to work long beyond the age at which most people used to retire.

LO2   Courts and Congress have recognized there is a trade-off for the required employment of qualified older workers. In *Graefenhain v. Pabst Brewing Co.,*[13] the court said:

> Although the ADEA does not hand federal courts a roving commission to review business judgments, the ADEA *does* create a cause of action against business

decisions that merge with age discrimination. Congress enacted the ADEA precisely because many employers or younger business executives act as if they believe that there are good business reasons for discriminating against older employees. Retention of senior employees who can be replaced by younger lower-paid people frequently competes with other values, such as profits or conceptions of economic efficiency. The ADEA represents a choice among these values. It stands for the propositions that this is a better country for its willingness to pay the costs for treating older employees fairly.

Distinctions between ADEA and Title VII

You may wonder why age was not merely included as an amendment to Title VII since the laws have several similarities. Both are enforced by the EEOC, as well as through private actions. However, discrimination based on age is substantively different from discrimination based on factors covered by Title VII in three important ways. First, the ADEA is more lenient than Title VII regarding the latitude afforded employers' reasons for adverse employment decisions. The ADEA allows an employer to rebut a *prima facie* case of age discrimination by identifying any "reasonable factor other than age" that motivated the decision. (For a more general discussion of a *prima facie* case, please see Chapter 3.)

Second, an employee is not barred from pursuing a claim simply because the employer treated another older worker better. In other words, a 62-year-old is not barred from a claim when terminated simply because her replacement was 55 (that is, also in the protected class).

Third, the act only protects employees over 40 from discrimination. Unlike Title VII, there is no protection from "reverse" discrimination. In other words, an individual under 40 cannot file a claim under the act based on the claim that she was discriminated against because of her youth. Moreover, in a 2004 decision, the Supreme Court held that the ADEA does not protect workers over 40 who were discriminated against (in this case) in favor of workers over 50 with regard to benefits. As Justice Souter noted in *General Dynamics Land Systems, Inc. v. Cline,* "The law does not mean to stop an employer from favoring an older employee over a younger one . . . The enemy of 40 is 30, not 50."[14]

LO3

Note, however, that certain state laws or precedents allow for what might be considered a youth's "reverse-discrimination" claim under state age discrimination statutes. One New Jersey man who claimed he was fired from a bank vice president position because of his young age (25) was allowed to proceed in court in that state. In direct response to the *Cline* case, the EEOC modified its regulations to remove language that prohibited discrimination against younger workers, opening the doors to what some consider affirmative action in favor of an older generation.

It is interesting to note that, in recent years, there has been somewhat of an upward trend in seeking to hire and retain older workers. (See Exhibit 12.3, "The Times, They Are a' Changin', or Not?" for an alternate perspective.) The AARP reports that some businesses, particularly in health care and retail, are increasingly focusing on hiring and retaining older workers as the nation's 78 million

Exhibit 12.3   *The Times, They Are a' Changin', or Not?*

Age discrimination became illegal in Britain as of October 2006. Perhaps you thought it might have occurred earlier?

As a *Financial Times* article pointed out, "[M]ost people instinctively know that [age discrimination] is nonsense," but, as you will see throughout cases and examples in this chapter, perhaps that conclusion is not so universally accepted. As the language in the article suggests, perhaps gender discrimination persists as well; "[w]omen in lap-dancing clubs will still be young, men in boardrooms old. Employers can still make workers retire at age 65, at least for the moment."[1] [*Note: See below for U.S. differences in the law.*]

Examples are not difficult to find, though perhaps they are difficult to prove. In a 2007 case involving

global law firm Akin Gump, Donald Gross filed an age discrimination claim alleging he was terminated less than two years after being hired as senior counsel for its practice in Korea. He contends that he was told that it was not due to performance but instead because he was too senior due to his age and therefore "not a good fit." The firm denies the claims entirely.[2] The court ultimately granted Akin Gump's motion for summary judgment on the ground that, though Gross was able to meet the requirements of a *prima facie* case of age discrimination, the law firm was able to establish a legitimate non-discriminatory reason for firing him (poor performance).

[1] J. Kay, "A Subtler Approach Is Needed Than Laws Against Ageism," *Financial Times,* October 3, 2006, p. 13.

[2] E. Schwartz, "Former Akin Gump Attorney Accuses Firm of Age Discrimination," *Legal Times,* March 6, 2007.

baby boomers age. CNBC adds, "With the prospect of shortfalls in funding for Social Security and the potential for a real labor shortage when the economy expands, employment forecasters say the country can't afford to lose older workers in the years ahead."[15]

Another restriction on the ADEA's protection came from the U.S. Supreme Court's 2000 decision in *Kimel v. Florida Board of Regents.*[16] In *Kimel,* state employees alleged that their state employers had discriminated against them on the basis of age in violation of the ADEA. Under the U.S. Constitution's Eleventh Amendment, states cannot be sued by citizens of another state. Federal courts have interpreted the Eleventh Amendment to extend immunity to states not consenting to being sued by their citizens. The U.S. Supreme Court determined that while Congress intended to allow state employees to sue their state employers under the ADEA, this attempt exceeded congressional authority. Therefore, in almost half the states, specifically those that have not waived sovereign immunity, state employees are not able to sue their state employers under the ADEA.

To ensure that appropriate and adequate information exists as to hiring practices in connection with age, the act has specific record-keeping provisions for employers. Employers are required to maintain the following information for *three years* for each employee and applicant, where applicable:

- Name.
- Address.
- Date of birth.

- Occupation.
- Rate of pay.
- Compensation earned each week.

Employers are required to maintain the following information for *one year* for each employee and for both regular and temporary workers:

- Job applications, résumés, or other employment inquiries in answer to ads or notices, plus records about failure or refusal to hire.
- Records on promotion, demotion, transfer, selection for training, layoff, recall, or discharge of any employee.
- Job orders given to agencies or unions for recruiting personnel for job openings.
- Test papers.
- Results of physical exams that are considered in connection with any personnel action.
- Ads or notices relating to job openings, promotions, training programs, or opportunities for overtime.

The ADEA also addresses discrimination in the provision of benefits. Specifically, employers are held to an equal-benefit/equal-cost rule. Under the rule, employers can comply with the ADEA by either providing equal benefits to workers of all ages or spending an equal amount to purchase the benefits. In recognizing that it may cost more to provide equivalent benefits to older workers, Congress was striving to encourage the hiring of older workers.

State Law Claims

Most states, and some municipalities, have laws that protect older workers and, in some cases, provide protections greater than those provided by the ADEA. These state laws vary widely. Some states, principally in the South, have no age discrimination laws, which means that employees in those states are limited to the remedies provided by the ADEA. A few other states have age discrimination laws that track the ADEA. A large third group, however, has laws that provide greater protections than those afforded by the ADEA (because federal law applies to all states, of course, no state can have protections less protective than the ADEA).

Employees who live in states with state age discrimination protections greater than those provided by the ADEA can choose to file a state law claim rather than a federal law claim. Laws in those states that provide greater protections typically may provide for the following:

1. State age discrimination laws apply to a wider range of employers. The ADEA applies to employers with 20 or more employees. Some state laws, however, apply to all employers in the state, while others apply to employers with 2, 5, 10, or 15 employees. Thus, employees who may be prevented from filing an ADEA claim because the law does not apply to their employee might still have a remedy under state law.

2. State age discrimination laws sometimes allow a wider range of damages. For example, an employee can recover back wages and attorney's fees under the ADEA. However, under some state laws, an employee can also recover damages for emotional distress, as well as punitive damages, both of which are not permitted under the ADEA. Punitive damages are those designed to punish the employer for its actions. Thus, an employee who believes that the employer's actions were particularly horrible might want to file a state law claim to try to collect punitive and/or emotional distress damages.

3. States often provide longer filing periods. In an age discrimination case, two filing deadlines are important. The first is the 180 days after the discrimination occurs that the employee has to file a complaint with the EEOC. Where state or local age discrimination laws exist, the deadline can be pushed back to 300 days. The second deadline is the amount of time to file a suit once the regulatory body evaluates the claim and gives the go-ahead to file suit, which is 90 days in complaints involving the EEOC. Many state laws give employees a longer time to file suit after getting the go-ahead. Thus, an employee who has waited too long to file a claim under the ADEA might still be able to file a state law claim.

Some also contend that a fourth benefit is that state law claims are processed more quickly than federal law claims, but that cannot be verified. Most likely, some are and some are not. One final point to note about state law claims: as you know, age discrimination only applies to those 40 and older. No state is permitted to extend the protection to someone younger than 40.

Employee's Options

LO4   An employee who believes that his or her employer has engaged in age discrimination has several options to try to correct the wrong. The option most often used is to file a complaint with the employer, using the employer's internal grievance procedures. Some companies have extensive internal grievance procedures, which may involve arbitration or some other type of mediation, though some employers do not have these procedures.

If filing a grievance does not bring satisfaction, the employee has several legal options: file a complaint with the federal Equal Employment Opportunity Commission, file a complaint with the state equivalent of the EEOC (if one exists), file a lawsuit in federal court under the ADEA, or file a lawsuit in state court under state age discrimination laws. These legal options are not exclusive—pursuing one option does not prevent the employee from later pursuing one or more of the other options.

As previously mentioned, the deadline for filing a complaint with the EEOC is 180 days from when the discrimination occurred, which is extended to 300 days if the state has age discrimination laws and an administrative agency to oversee age discrimination complaints. Note, however, that using the employer's internal grievance procedure does not affect the EEOC timing. Thus, if the grievance procedure drags out, the employee might be forced to file within the 180 days even if the employer's grievance procedure has not run its course. So, the employee could file an internal grievance, then file a complaint with the state agency (within however many days the state allows), then file an EEOC complaint within 300 days. Or the employee could have skipped the complaint process entirely and filed suit right away; employees are not required to go through the grievance process before filing suit.

Upon receiving the complaint, the EEOC has several possible responses (state procedures are generally similar). It could dismiss the complaint if it believes that the charges have no merit, or it could investigate the charges. If it investigates the charges, the EEOC can either bring suit on the employee's behalf if it believes that the charges have merit or give the employee what is called a right-to-sue letter, if it believes that the charges lack the merit needed to file suit. Once the employee receives the right-to-sue letter, she or he has 90 days to file suit against the employer in her or his own name.

Employee's *Prima Facie* Case: Disparate Treatment

LO5

Suppose that an employee believes that she or he has suffered age discrimination based on an adverse employer action (a pay cut, bad performance review, demotion or otherwise). For our purposes, let us assume that the employee has gone through the complaint process and has decided to file a federal lawsuit under the ADEA. Two types of discrimination exist under the ADEA: disparate treatment and disparate impact. As is discussed in greater detail in Chapter 3, disparate treatment occurs when the discrimination is directed at the employee, to the exclusion of other employees. The employee is treated differently from other employees because of age. The employee does not have to be the only one affected; but the action must be directed at that employee. Choosing not to hire the employee because of her or his age is one example. Disparate treatment, on the other hand (discussed in more detail later in this chapter), involves actions that are not directed at the employee because of her or his age but that have an unfair impact on older workers.

The employee filing an action against the employer under the ADEA based on disparate treatment must prove age discrimination by utilizing the method of proof for Title VII cases originally set forth in *McDonnell Douglas Corp. v. Green* and later adapted to age discrimination claims under the ADEA. Under this approach, an employee must establish the following four elements to persuade the court that she or he even has a claim for age discrimination:

adverse employment action
Any action or omission that takes away a benefit, opportunity, or privilege of employment from an employee.

1. The employee is in the protected class.
2. She or he suffered an **adverse employment action** (was terminated or demoted).
3. The employee was doing her or his job well enough to meet her or his employer's legitimate expectations.
4. Others not in the protected class were treated more favorably.

Member of the Protected Class

To satisfy the first requirement of the *prima facie* case, the employee must merely show that she or he is 40 years old or older.

Adverse Employment Action

The second requirement is proof that the employer made an employment decision that adversely affected the employee. This may include a decision not to hire the applicant or to terminate the employee.

Qualified for the Position

qualified for the position
Able to meet the employer's legitimate job requirements.

With the third requirement, the applicant must prove that he or she was **qualified for the position**. If the applicant is not qualified, then the employer's decision would be justified and the applicant's claim fails. The position requirements, however, must be legitimate requirements and not merely devised for the purpose of terminating or refusing to hire older workers. Courts have allowed this requirement to be met by the employee simply by showing that the employee was never told that performance was unacceptable. The qualifications requirement is not a difficult one. Courts have even held that the fact that the employee was hired initially indicates that he or she has the basic qualifications.

Dissimilar Treatment

In connection with the fourth requirement for a *prima facie* case of age discrimination, which is almost always the most difficult element to prove, the employee or applicant must show that he was treated differently from other employees who are not in the protected class. This might require an employer to explain its actions if it terminates (or refuses to hire) an older qualified employee, while simultaneously hiring younger employees. For instance, where an employer terminates a 57-year-old worker and hires, in her place, a 34-year-old employee, and the 57-year-old employee can show that she remains qualified for her position, the employer must defend its decision.

The courts have struggled to develop consistent rules that can be applied in these situations. What if an 80-year-old is fired and replaced by a 78-year-old? Is this discriminatory action? The basic ADEA case is filed where an employee is replaced by or not hired in favor of an employee who is not a member of the protected class. However, the Supreme Court has held, in *O'Connor v. Consolidated Coin Caterers,*[17] that a plaintiff can state a claim as long as she or he is replaced by someone younger, even if the replacement is 40 years old or older. Of interest is a 2008 Supreme Court case, *Sprint/United Management Co. v. Mendelsohn,* which held that evidence of other older workers terminated from the same company should be evaluated on a case-by-case basis. Called "me, too" evidence, the court explained that "[t]he question whether evidence of discrimination by other supervisors is relevant . . . is fact-based and depends on many factors, including how closely related the evidence is to the plaintiff's circumstances."[18]

One other provision of the ADEA merits special attention: section 4(e) makes it unlawful to "print or publish or cause to be printed or published, any notice or

---

Exhibit 12.4 *EEOC Guidance*

The EEOC Interpretive Rules offer the following guidance:

> When help wanted notices or advertisements contain terms and phrases such as "age 25 to 35," "young," "boy," "girl," "college student," "recent college graduate," or others of a similar nature, such a term or phrase discriminates against the employment of older people, and will be considered

in violation of the act. Such specifications as "age 40 to 50," "age over 50," or "age over 65" are also considered to be prohibited. Where such specifications as "retired person" or "supplement your pension" are intended and applied so as to discriminate against others within the protected group, they, too, are regarded as prohibited unless one of the exceptions applies.

---

advertisement . . . indicating any preference, limitation, specification, or discrimination, based on age." The court in *Hodgson v. Approved Personnel Serv., Inc.*[19] found that, in determining whether an advertisement had a discriminatory effect on older individuals, "the discriminatory effect of an advertisement is determined not by 'trigger words' but rather by its context." That is, the ad is not considered discriminatory because of a word or words but rather because of the intent of the ad to discriminate against older individuals.

The use of certain trigger words like "girl" or "young" may establish an ADEA violation under most circumstances, so the context of the statement is important to determine its discriminatory effect. For instance, the use of "recent college graduate" is not discriminatory if a personnel agency merely intended to identify those *services* that it offered to that specific class of individuals. (See Exhibit 12.4, "EEOC Guidance.") The EEOC specifically explains as follows:

> The ADEA generally makes it unlawful to include age preferences, limitations, or specifications in job notices or advertisements. A job notice or advertisement may specify an age limit only in the rare circumstances where age is shown to be a "bona fide occupational qualification" (BFOQ) reasonably necessary to the normal operation of the business.[20]

Burden Shifting No More

Prior to the summer of 2009, once the employee presented evidence of the employer's wrongful actions, the burden of proof shifted to the employer to present a legitimate nondiscriminatory reason (LNDR) for its actions. The motivations behind employment actions, such as a dismissal, are often difficult to determine. Discrimination cases involving more than one potential motivation for the employment action are referred to as mixed-motives cases. Because the employee only has to prove that age discrimination was a *motivating factor* (one of many, perhaps), the employer in a mixed-motives case has always been given the opportunity to prove that it would have come to the same decision even if there were no discrimination present because of some non-discriminatory motivation, such as poor performance or a legitimate business necessity, the LNDR.

However, in *Gross v. FBL Financial Servs. Inc.,* No. 08-441, June 18, 2009, included at the end of this chapter, the court ruled that age discrimination cases under the ADEA require proof that age was the "but for" cause of the adverse employment action. Critical to the court's decision was the fact that Title VII had been amended in 1991 to include "motivating factor" language but that the ADEA had not.

As a result, the court said, no burden shifting occurs in ADEA cases. In fact, the decision means that mixed-motives age discrimination claims do not exist under the ADEA for disparate treatment claims, although burden shifting still applies to Title VII cases. Henceforth, the employee could recover *only if the employment action would not have taken place but for age discrimination.*

The decision caused quite a stir, with commentators interpreting the ruling to mean that disparate treatment age discrimination claims would be more difficult to prove. Whether that comes to pass remains to be seen, but efforts were launched in the aftermath of *Gross* to undo the decision. Jack Gross was called to testify before Congress, and bills have been introduced in both the House and Senate to legislatively overturn the decision. To date, however, *Gross* remains the law of the land on ADEA-based age discrimination claims alleging disparate treatment.

Meanwhile, as the legislative process continued, the lower courts were left to implement *Gross* and to answer related questions not raised in the case. Generally speaking, subsequent lower court answers to open questions have softened the impact. For example, does *Gross* require that age discrimination be the *only* factor? The 10th Circuit has said no; *Gross* can be interpreted to mean that other factors can be present as long as age is the factor that made the difference.[21] Does the *McDonnell Douglas* burden-shifting approach still have any relevance in ADEA disparate treatment cases? Surprisingly, perhaps, eight circuits—the 1st, 2nd, 3rd, 4th, 5th, 6th, 7th, and 10th—have all said yes. According to the 10th Circuit,[22] summarizing the opinions of the other seven circuits, *Gross* held only that the burden of *persuasion* never shifts. *McDonnell Douglas*, on the other hand, shifts only the burden of *production.* Under those appellate court opinions, at some point after the employee has met the "but for" requirement, the burden shifts to the employer to produce evidence of a non-discriminatory justification for the action. The burden of persuading the judge or jury that the employer is guilty of age discrimination, however, always rests with the employee. The distinction between burden of proof and burden of production can be difficult to draw. We will have to wait to see if the Supreme Court agrees with those lower court interpretations.

LO6 Employer's Defenses

Bona Fide Occupational Qualification

Scenario

If an employer is sued for age discrimination, the defense of BFOQ is available. (See Chapter 2 for a more general discussion of BFOQs.) In fact, age is one of the most consistently applied BFOQs. The employer's proof of a bona fide occupational qualification under the ADEA is slightly different and less exacting than under Title VII. Title VII requires that the employer demonstrate that the essence of the business requires the exclusion of the members of a protected class and all or substantially all of the members of that class are unable to perform adequately in the position in question. The EEOC follows the requirements of Title VII in connection with the ADEA but adds one further possibility for the employer's proof, included as item 3, below. The EEOC identifies what the employer must prove in an age discrimination case brought under the ADEA as

1. The age limit is reasonably necessary to the essence of the employer's business; and either
2. All or substantially all of the individuals over that age are unable to perform the job's requirements adequately; or
3. Some of the individuals over that age possess a disqualifying trait that cannot be ascertained except by reference to age.

The third element of the proof allows an employer to exclude an older worker from a position that may be unsafe to *some* older workers. This defense would only be accepted by a court where there is no way to individually assess the safety potential of a given applicant or employee.

For example, assume there existed a medical disorder that was prevalent among those over 80 and was not discoverable under standard medical investigation. Assume also that this medical condition caused its sufferers to lose consciousness without warning. An employer who refused to place those over 80 in the position of a school bus driver would satisfy the proof of a BFOQ. Note that it is not enough for an employer to simply think there is a condition related to age that supports a BFOQ. The decision must be based on competent expert evidence of a connection between age and the component of the job affected (see Exhibit 12.5 "Employer's Defenses").

mandatory retirement
Employee must retire upon reaching a specified age. Deemed illegal by the 1986 amendments to the ADEA, with few exceptions.

When Congress passed the 1986 amendments to the ADEA prohibiting **mandatory retirement** on the basis of age for most workers, it included several temporary exemptions, notably one for tenured faculty in higher education. That exemption expired December 31, 1993. Mandatory retirement has been limited to two circumstances. First, a small number of high-level employees with substantial executive authority can be subjected to compulsory retirement

---

Exhibit 12.5 *Employer's Defenses*

The employer may defend its actions in one of several ways. The act states:

It shall not be unlawful for an employer
(1) to take any action otherwise prohibited where age is a bona fide occupational qualification reasonably necessary to the normal operation of the particular business, or where the differentiation is based on reasonable factors other than age.
(2) to observe the terms of a bona fide seniority system or any bona fide employee benefit plan such as a retirement, pension, or insurance plan.
(3) to discharge or otherwise discipline an individual for good cause.

at age 65 or beyond if the individual will receive a company pension of $44,000 or more. This exception is a very narrow one and does not allow for compulsory retirement policies for midlevel managers. Perhaps this exception is narrowly confined to those with decision-making authority based on stereotypes that the majority of powerful executives tend to be over 40, with wealth and opportunity that make a mandatory retirement policy less burdensome. Second, persons in two specific occupations, police officers and firefighters, have been subject to mandatory retirement. However, age is not necessarily a BFOQ in these occupations. Voluntary retirement plans are, however, permitted and are discussed later in this chapter.

The employer cannot simply base employment decisions on age-related stereotypes; the employer must base such decisions on credible evidence. As demonstrated in *Western Airlines, Inc. v. Criswell,* provided at the end of the chapter, an airline attempted to defend its mandatory retirement policy for flight engineers over the age of 60 as a BFOQ. This defense ultimately failed because individual determinations of health could help achieve the airline's goal of safe transportation of passengers in a less restrictive manner.

Scenario

The policy was apparently based on the Federal Aviation Administration's original "Age 60 Rule," which prohibited people at or over the age of 60 from acting as pilots or co-pilots.[23] Interestingly, while the FAA requires individual pilot medical certifications and a semiannual exam of pilots, it maintained the Age 60 Rule until 2007, when then-President Bush signed a bill raising the mandatory retirement age to 65, bringing the United States into alignment with international rules. At the time of its passage, the legislation was praised for keeping more experienced pilots in the cockpit longer, for easing the challenge brought on by a pilot shortage but also for its requirement that pilots over 60 be accompanied by a younger co-pilot on international flights.

Employee's *Prima Facie* Case: Circumstances Involving Claims of Disparate Impact

We now turn to disparate impact. Disparate treatment, as discussed in Chapter 2, occurs where an employee is treated differently from other employees because she or he is a member of a protected class. Disparate impact, on the other hand, exists where a policy or rule of an employer, though not discriminatory on its face, has an effect on one group different from that on another. For example, a rule that requires all bus drivers to have 20/20 vision may have the effect of limiting the number of older workers who can be bus drivers. Now, this rule is indeed discriminatory in that it distinguishes between those who have good vision and those who do not. The question is whether the rule is discriminatory. In the example, perhaps it is justified by business reasons, and thus perfectly acceptable. Because of the close connection between the *prima facie* cases and the employer defenses, we will discuss the case of disparate impact at this juncture and then return to the employee's burden of evidencing pretext shortly; but let us review where we are in the case process for navigational purposes (see Exhibit 12.6, "Proving a Case of Age Discrimination").

Exhibit 12.6 *Proving a Case of Age Discrimination*

DISPARATE TREATMENT

Step One: Employee's *prima facie* case

1. The employee is in the protected class.
2. She or he was terminated or demoted.
3. The employee was doing her or his job well enough to meet her employer's legitimate expectations.
4. Others not in the protected class were treated more favorably.

Step Two: Employer defenses

1. Bona fide occupational qualification.

Step Three: Employee may evidence pretext for employer actions.

DISPARATE IMPACT

Step One: Employee's *prima facie* case

1. A facially neutral policy or rule is imposed by an employer,
2. Which has a different effect on an older group of workers.
3. No intent to discriminate is necessary.

Step Two: Employer defenses

1. Reasonable factor other than age (RFOA):
   a. Economic concerns.
   b. Seniority.

---

reasonable factor other than age (RFOA)

May include any requirement that does not have an adverse impact on older workers, as well as those factors that do adversely affect this protected class but are shown to be job-related. For example, if an employee is not performing satisfactorily and is terminated, her failure to meet reasonable performance standards would constitute a reasonable factor other than age.

In mid-2005, the Supreme Court reached a decision in *Smith v. City of Jackson*[24] that resolved this issue—one that had caused a distinct split in the circuit courts. In that case, police and public safety officers employed by the city of Jackson, Mississippi, argued that the city had given senior officers lower salary increases than those offered to younger officers. The city had adopted this salary plan "to attract and retain qualified people, provide incentive for performance, maintain competitiveness with other public sector agencies and ensure equitable compensation to all employees regardless of age, sex, race and/or disability." The appellate court held that disparate impact claims are categorically unavailable under the ADEA.

While holding that disparate impact claims are actionable under the ADEA, the Supreme Court ended up finding against the officers because the city based its decision on **reasonable factors other than age (RFOA)**. "The RFOA provision provides that it shall not be unlawful for an employer 'to take any action otherwise prohibited under [the Act] . . . where the differentiation is based on reasonable factors other than age discrimination. . . .' In most disparate treatment cases, if an employer in fact acted on a factor other than age, the action would not be prohibited under [the Act] in the first place." One of the important elements of the decision is that the Court found that the disparate impact provision is to be interpreted much more *narrowly* for disparate impact claims under the ADEA compared to Title VII. First, there is no RFOA defense in Title VII; under Title VII, the employer can justify a practice that has been shown to have a disparate impact by evidencing that it is job-related and consistent with business necessity.

In evaluating the city's salary plan, the Supreme Court concluded that reliance on seniority and rank is unquestionably reasonable given the city's goal of raising employees' salaries to match those in surrounding communities. The court explained again that the analysis in this ADEA case was different from an analysis under Title VII: "While there may have been other reasonable ways for the City to achieve its goals, the one selected was not unreasonable. Unlike the business necessity test, which asks whether there are other ways for the employer to achieve its goals that do not result in a disparate impact on a protected class, the reasonableness inquiry includes no such requirement." The court therefore decided that the city's decision was based on a "reasonable factor other than age" that responded to the city's legitimate goal of retaining police officers.

2)
Scenario

In Opening Scenario 2, the applicant's age appears to be of some concern; however, the real issue is whether the applicant can do the strenuous job. If it can be shown that the applicant can perform all the necessary job functions, he should be hired because he is the most qualified. In the future, if he becomes unable to meet the demands of the job, his termination would be a result of his lack of ability, not his age. Furthermore, regarding the concerns about the applicant leaving after a few years, *any* employee can leave an employer at any time unless there is a contract. This is not a concern with older individuals only.

LO8   *Economic Concerns*

1)
Scenario

Would a company's desire to cut payroll costs constitute a reasonable factor other than age? Given the above decision, cases that arise based on economic justifications may spell some bad news for older workers who were relying on the decision to strengthen their footing with regard to facially neutral termination plans. Often, a reduction in force may adversely impact older workers since their seniority may reward them with higher salaries. To reduce costs, a firm may opt to reduce its workforce based in part on salary amounts in order to have the greatest impact. Based on *City of Jackson,* above, it is crucial that the discharges be made on the basis of an objective standard so that the RFOA defense remains available to the employer.

This issue is unique to ADEA discrimination claims because it is not more costly, for instance, to hire an Asian employee than a Caucasian employee. However, in many cases, it is more expensive to hire or to retain older workers since, among other reasons, they have more experience and thereby command a higher wage. Courts disfavor this justification for the termination of older workers. As stated by the Illinois district court in *Vilcins v. City of Chicago,* "[n]othing in the ADEA prohibits elimination of a protected employee's position for budgetary reasons. In fact, the case law establishes that economic or budgetary factors may provide valid reasons for discharging a protected employee. A termination allegedly based on economic factors may constitute impermissible discrimination, however, *when the economic reasons proffered serve merely to obscure the fact that age was the true determinant.*"[25]

With regard to reductions in force, courts generally absolve the employer from liability where the employer follows a specified procedure for the terminations, where objective criteria are used to determine the individuals to be discharged, and where the entire position is eliminated. In one example of a pre–*City of Jackson* case, the Second Circuit did find that the ADEA allowed disparate impact claims during a reduction in force. Its dicta are relevant as the case offers some insight into the ways in which a court may evaluate such claims in the future. In the Supreme Court's 2008 decision, *Meacham v. Knolls Atomic Power Laboratory*, it further clarified that the burden of proving the RFOA is on the employer in these cases since it is an affirmative defense. In other words, the employer must prove that age was *not* a factor in the decision.

This brings to mind one of the most interesting case opinions in this area: *Metz v. Transit Mix, Inc.*[26] In that case, the appellate court noted that salary is often a direct function of seniority. Individual salary increases may occur yearly with no regard to the financial condition of the employer; consequently, those who have been employed for the longest times, and have accrued the most seniority, are also the highest-paid employees. In disallowing the termination of older workers for financial reasons, the court then cited Willie Loman, the salesman who was fired after working for his boss for 34 years (in Arthur Miller's *Death of a Salesman*): "You can't eat the orange and throw the peel away—a man is not a piece of fruit." Courts have emphatically rejected business practices in which the "plain intent and effect was to eliminate older workers who had built up, through years of satisfactory service, higher salaries than their younger counterparts."

Scenario

The court stated that where salary is tied directly to seniority (and therefore age), seniority then serves as a "proxy" for age, supporting a claim of age discrimination. The court of appeals noted that one possible solution to the high-pay quandary for the continued employment of older workers is to offer the older worker the option of accepting a pay cut in lieu of termination. The pay cut, of course, must be warranted by business necessity such as economic difficulties, but at least the older worker would be retained and not replaced by a younger worker who would be willing to accept the lower salary offered. Such an offer to the older worker would be evidence of the intent to reduce costs, as opposed to the intent to relieve the firm of its older workforce. In addition, terminations pursuant to bona fide reductions in force, bankruptcy, or other legitimate business reasons are generally legal, even if the economic considerations that have necessitated the reduction in force require the termination of more older workers than younger employees. Of course, if the true reason for the pay cut is economic, it would be an unfortunate result if an older worker is fired and a younger worker is hired, only to avoid a discrimination suit by not offering the older worker a lower salary instead. If the employer actually wanted to get rid of the older worker (i.e., had discriminatory intent), it would not make this offer in the first place. (See discussion, below, on this option.)

In 2004, that court upheld a lower court's decision in *Meacham v. Knolls Atomic Power Laboratory,*[27] finding that a reduction in force (RIF) program had a disparate impact on older workers, even though the employer did not intend to discriminate. To state a cause of action, the Second Circuit explained that the employee would need to identify the actual, specific policy that resulted in harm (such as particular selection criteria). Next, the employee would need to show that this policy resulted in a disparity in the retention rates of younger and older employees "sufficiently substantial to raise an inference of causation" (using statistical data, discussed below). The employer is then given the opportunity to explain the business necessity of the challenged employment practice. The burden then shifts back to the employee, who may prevail "only if they can show that the employer's explanation was merely a pretext for discrimination." The court suggests that the employee could point to another practice that would achieve the same result at comparable cost without causing a disparate impact on older workers.

In *Meacham,* the Second Circuit found that the employee had satisfied this burden by showing that the selection procedures were extremely imprecise, allowing for excessive subjectivity to impact the results. If an employer seeks to use subjective criteria to make decisions such as these, and if adequate alternative methods exist by which to make the same determination, the court warns that these criteria will need to be validated or audited to ensure that a disparate impact does not result. Employers may instead opt for more effective, job-related, objective criteria when reaching these decisions.

In *Schuster v. Lucent Technologies, Inc.*, provided for your review, the Seventh Circuit revisits the issue of age discrimination in the face of economic duress and, under the facts of this case, finds the employer's arguments persuasive. In *Hazen Paper Co. v. Biggins*, included at the end of the chapter, the employee claimed that he was fired in order to prevent his pension from vesting, rather than for a bona fide reason. The Supreme Court was asked to determine whether a firing decision based on number of years served is "age-based." The case is an important one in this area since the Court holds that there is no disparate treatment under the ADEA when the factor motivating the employer is some feature "*other than the employee's age*" (emphasis added).

Interestingly, one challenge to stating a claim for discrimination based on a reduction in force is the fourth prong of the traditional *prima facie* case—where an RIF occurs, no one replaces the employee so there is no one similarly situated. Therefore, in the event of an RIF, age discrimination may be proven where

- The employer refuses to allow the discharged (or demoted) employee to bump others with less seniority, and
- The employer hires younger workers when the jobs become available after the employee was discharged (or demoted) at the prior salary of the older worker.

The question mentioned at the end of the *Metz* discussion, above, then arises: in an effort not to terminate the employee but to continue to cut costs, can an employer unilaterally reduce the salary of a protected employee to respond to its economic challenges? While this may seem a creative option, section 4(a)(3) of the ADEA specifically states that it is "unlawful for any employer . . . to reduce the wage rate of any employee in order to comply with this Act." Strangely, though striving to be clear, in light of *City of Jackson,* this prohibition remains vague since an employer may argue that it was not reducing the wage rate to comply with the ADEA but instead for some RFOA such as reducing costs.

What if an employee told he is to be laid off for economic reasons voluntarily offers to reduce his salary? The law is unsettled, but the Second Circuit reversed a lower court decision and held instead that rejecting such an offer might indeed constitute age discrimination. In *Carras v. MGS 728 Lex*,[28] a chief financial officer was told that he was being terminated for financial reasons. He then offered to take a severe pay cut, to $60,000. The company rejected his offer, laid him off, replaced him with a younger person, and paid the new person more than $60,000. The former CFO convinced the appellate court that rejection of his offer might be an indication that economic reasons were not the real motivation.

There is no consensus in the federal courts on the question of whether there is a "high correlation" between compensation and age in any generic manner that would imply that compensation-based decisions would have a disparate impact on older workers as a general rule. An employer's decision based on salary that disproportionately affected older workers because of the high correlation between age and salary would be actionable age discrimination under a number of federal circuit court decisions.[29] On the other hand, federal courts that have examined the issue more recently, particularly in the wake of *Hazen Paper Co. v. Biggins,* have tended to hold that economic decisions do not give rise to liability for age discrimination, despite the disparate impact of such decisions on older workers.[30]

The split among courts on whether economic factors can be considered when terminating older workers can be traced to two fundamentally differing views about the goal of the age discrimination statutes. If the goal of the age discrimination statutes is to preclude decisions based on generalities about older workers that may have no basis as to individuals, then they certainly do not extend to decisions based on relative compensation rates between individual workers. In this view, age discrimination statutes were enacted to prevent employers from assuming that just because an individual attained a certain age, he or she no longer could do the job, or do it as well. This view was best articulated by the dissent in *Metz v. Transit Mix, Inc.,* which stated, "The Act prohibits adverse personnel actions based on myths, stereotypes, and group averages, as well as lackadaisical decisions in which employers use age as a proxy for something that matters (such as gumption) without troubling to decide employee-by-employee who can still do the work and who can't."

The other view is that age discrimination statutes were enacted to protect older workers because of their status as older workers, since older workers, generally speaking, face unique obstacles late in their careers. Age discrimination law is thus seen as a kind of protective legislation designed to improve the lot of people who are vulnerable as a class. If this view is correct, then holding that decisions based solely on salary may contravene laws precluding discrimination based on age makes sense.

Defenses Based on Benefit Plans and Seniority Systems

The ADEA specifically excludes bona fide retirement plans that distinguish based on age but are "not a subterfuge to evade the purpose of [the] Act." "Subterfuge" in this definition denotes those plans that are mere schemes for the purpose of evading the ADEA or the Older Workers' Benefit Protection Act (discussed below). The effect of the 1978 and 1986 amendments to the ADEA was to completely prohibit involuntary retirement plans when they are imposed on the sole basis of an employee's age.

To qualify as a bona fide voluntary retirement plan allowed by the act, the plan must be truly voluntary. Some employees have contended that there is no voluntary decision when they are given only a short time in which to reach a decision about whether to accept the retirement option. But a short time period in which to reach a decision does not necessarily render the decision involuntary. The determination of what qualifies as a bona fide plan must be made on a case-by-case basis.

It has been held that early retirement plans offered by employers are not bona fide pursuant to the act if a reasonable person would have felt compelled to resign under similar circumstances. However, even after several court decisions relating to the issues of voluntariness, and whether a plan was a subterfuge, employers are left without much direction in terms of the formulation of early retirement programs and other means of providing benefits.

"Same Actor" Defense

A number of appellate courts, including the First, Second, Fourth, Fifth, Sixth, Seventh, Eighth, Ninth, and Eleventh Circuits, have adopted a defense called the "same actor" defense to age discrimination claims. The circuit courts have applied various weights of strength or value of the defense when the hirer and firer are the same actor. These courts have held that when the same "actor" both hires and fires a worker protected by the ADEA, there is a permissible inference that the employee's age was not a motivating factor in the decision. After all, if someone held discriminatory beliefs about older workers, why would that person have hired the worker in the first place? The Fourth Circuit reasoned that "claims that the employer animus exists in termination but not in hiring seem irrational. From the standpoint for the putative discriminator, it hardly makes sense to hire workers from a group one dislikes (thereby incurring the psychological costs of associating with them), only to fire them once they are on the job."[31]

Retaliation

The ADEA prohibits retaliation,[32] which usually occurs when an employer takes an employment action against an employee, such as a dismissal, a denial of a promotion, a demotion, or a suspension, in response to an age discrimination complaint filed by that employee. The protection is quite broad and protects not only the person filing the complaint but also includes any other employee who might have participated in the claim. As a result, the ADEA protects an employee who, for example, is a witness in support of the employee's position. If the employer retaliates against that employee, the employer violates the ADEA.

punitive damages
Punitive damages are designed to punish the party being sued rather than compensate the injured party. Punitive damages can be quite high, especially if the actions are especially offensive, the defendant is a large company, and the jury is angry. They are paid to the injured party, which some have criticized as an unearned windfall.

While, originally, some legal analysts thought that the ADEA might not protect federal employees from retaliation because the public sector language in the ADEA was different from the private sector language,[33] the Supreme Court dispelled any confusion on that issue in *Gomez-Perez v. Potter.*[34] In that case, the U.S. Supreme Court ruled that federal and private sector employees have the same protection from retaliation under the ADEA, reversing the First Circuit, which had previously found no similar rights.

Interestingly, punitive damages, which are generally unavailable in ADEA-based claims, are available for retaliation claims.[35] **Punitive damages** are those designed to punish the employer (rather than compensating the employee), and often significantly higher in amount. The ADEA requires that the employer's conduct be willful,[36] which the U.S. Supreme Court has said means "the employer either knew or showed reckless disregard for the matter of whether its conduct was prohibited by the statute."[37]

Employee's Response: Proof of Pretext

LO9

Let us return to the standard *prima facie* case of discrimination. Assume that the employee has demonstrated the required four elements of that case and that the employer has demonstrated a bona fide occupational qualification (BFOQ). The next step in proving a case of discrimination is for the employee to show that that reason or defense is *pretextual*. When a claim is pretextual, it means that it is not the true reason for the action, that there is some underlying motivation to which the employer has not admitted. To prove that the offered reason is pretext for an actual case of age discrimination, the employee need not show that age was the *only* factor motivating the employment decision, but only that age was a determining factor.

Where there is direct evidence of discrimination, proof of pretext is not required. This may occur where the employer admits to having based the employment decision on the employee's age, or when a representative of the employer says that it would be cheaper to hire younger applicants. You would not think that an employer would actually admit something so directly; but in *Mauer v. Deloitte & Touche, LLP,* a supervisor gave a speech where he explained that the firm would get rid of poor performers just like you prune a blueberry bush. He explained that you cut off "older branches to make room for younger ones." The court held that the supervisor's statement was direct evidence of age discrimination.[38]

The question of what constitutes direct evidence is not always clear. Despite the similarity between statements made by employers, however, statements regarding an applicant's or employee's race are taken more seriously than those about age. For instance, most courts would rule in the employee's favor if it were determined that she was not hired pursuant to the manager's statement "I don't want any more blacks in my unit." But it is questionable whether this same employer would be held guilty if the manager states, "We need some new ideas in this unit. Let's hire younger analysts." The statement may be viewed as merely descriptive.

An employee also can show pretext by proving that the offered reasons for the adverse employment action have no basis in fact, the offered reasons did not actually motivate the adverse employment action, or the offered reasons are insufficient to motivate the adverse action taken. In addition, in a 2004 case, the First Circuit held that an adverse action taken by a nonbiased decision maker, but based on information from another worker who has a discriminatory motive, still satisfies a *prima facie* case. In other words, if someone takes an adverse action against an employee based on what appears to be a reasonable factor, the employer will be liable if the basis of that decision is actually grounded in bias and a discriminatory motive.[39] The employee also may show that pretext exists where the employer presents conflicting rationales for the adverse employment action.[40]

In its 2000 decision in *Reeves v. Sanderson Plumbing Products,*[41] the U.S. Supreme Court held that a jury may infer discriminatory intent behind an adverse employment action based on the falsity of the employer's explanation. In October 1995, 57-year-old Reeves, who had worked for Sanderson Plumbing for 40 years, was terminated. As a supervisor, Reeves was responsible for keeping attendance records of his employees. After the department reportedly suffered a downturn in productivity due to tardiness and absenteeism, the records were audited. The audit revealed that Reeves and two other managers had made numerous errors in timekeeping. One other manager was discharged along with Reeves. Reeves brought a claim under the ADEA against his former employer, claiming that he had kept accurate attendance records. Further, Reeves argued that the employer's reasons for firing him were merely a pretext for age discrimination that was demonstrated through age-related comments made to him by his supervisor. The U.S. Supreme Court stated in its opinion that once the employer's rationalization has been eliminated, discrimination may well be the most likely alternative explanation for the adverse employment action.[42]

The *Reeves* decision, therefore, rejected what has become known as the "pretext plus" standard. Courts cannot require employees both to show pretext and to produce additional evidence of discrimination. No additional evidence is necessary to show discrimination because, once the pretext has been shown, an inference can be made that the action was done for discriminatory reasons.[43]

Employee's *Prima Facie* Case: Hostile Environment Based on Age

The Sixth Circuit recognizes a cause of action under the ADEA based on hostile environment age harassment. In *Crawford v. Medina General Hosp.,*[44] Crawford claimed hostile environment based on ageist remarks consistently made by her supervisor such as "old people should be seen and not heard" and "I don't think women over 55 should be working." Crawford also alleged that, in addition to the disparaging remarks, the older women are "not included in anything," such as parties, as well as information about minor changes in office procedures, and that the supervisor would customarily call the young people into her office to question them about what the older people were doing "and then she encourages them to go out and confront those people."[45]

The Sixth Circuit found that it was a "relatively uncontroversial proposition that such a theory is viable under the ADEA"[46] and, since that time, the Eighth and Eleventh Circuits and some district courts have applied the same theory.[47] The court then articulated the *prima facie* case for hostile environment under the act:

1. The employee is 40 years old or older.
2. The employee was subjected to harassment, either through words or actions, based on age.
3. The harassment had the effect of unreasonably interfering with the employee's work performance and creating an objectively intimidating, hostile, or offensive work environment.
4. There exists some basis for liability on the part of the employer.[48]

Though it denied the claim based on the facts of that case, the Northern District of Illinois also upheld a cause of action under the ADEA for hostile environment age harassment.[49] The claim will most likely be recognized as well by the Seventh Circuit, which stated one year prior "[plaintiff] asserts that he was subjected to a hostile work environment because of his age. This circuit has assumed, without deciding, that plaintiffs may bring hostile environment claims under the ADEA. See *Halloway v. Milwaukee County,* 180 F.3d 820, 827 (7th Cir. 1999). We will do likewise here because we conclude that, even if such a hostile work environment claim could be brought under the ADEA, Bennington could not prevail."[50] While several other circuits and districts also have so allowed,[51] the remaining courts have refused to expand the ADEA to include a hostile environment claim without express statutory language to the contrary.

Note that, if a hostile environment age harassment claim becomes more universally recognized, the impact may go significantly further than a solely age discrimination claim. Consider the impact on constructive discharge. A worker subject to age harassment may be reasonable in quitting, based on the intolerable working condition, which could then give rise to a claim of constructive discharge based on age harassment.

Waivers under the Older Workers' Benefit Protection Act of 1990

In 1990, Congress enacted the Older Workers' Benefit Protection Act (OWBPA), amending section 4(f) of the ADEA. The OWBPA concerns the legality and enforceability of early retirement incentive programs (called "exit incentive programs" in the act) and of waivers of rights under the ADEA, and it prohibits age discrimination in the provision of employee benefits. What this act really involves are those situations where employees are offered amounts of money through retirement plans as incentives for leaving a company. In that way, the company is not terminating an older worker and, thereby, cannot in theory be held liable under the ADEA.

LO10

Many companies also request that older workers sign a waiver whereby they relinquish the right to later question the plan by filing an age discrimination action. Once the waiver is signed and the worker accepts the benefits under the plan, the company would like to believe it is safe from all possible claims of discrimination. Where a waiver is valid under the ADEA/OWBPA, the employer can use it as an affirmative defense to an ADEA claim. The burden, however, is on the employer to prove validity. This is not necessarily always the case, as will be discussed.

The OWBPA codifies the EEOC's "equal cost principal," requiring firms to provide benefits to older workers that are at least equal to those provided to younger workers, unless the cost of their provision to older workers *greatly* exceeds the cost of provision to younger workers. Therefore, a firm may only offer different benefits to older and younger workers if it costs a significant amount more to provide those benefits to older workers. This section amends section 4 of the ADEA, which provides that adverse employment actions taken in observance of the terms of a bona fide employee benefit plan are partially exempt from question.

waiver
The intentional relinquishment of a known right.

In connection with employee waivers of their rights to file discrimination actions under the ADEA, the OWBPA requires that every **waiver** must be "knowing and voluntary" to be valid. In order to satisfy this requirement, the waiver must meet all of the following requirements:

1. The waiver must be written in a manner calculated to be understood by an average employee.
2. The waiver must specifically refer to ADEA rights or claims (but may refer to additional acts, such as Title VII or applicable state acts).
3. The waiver only affects those claims or rights that have arisen prior to the date of the waiver (i.e., the employee is not waiving any rights that will be acquired after signing the waiver).
4. The waiver of rights to claims may only be offered in exchange for some consideration in addition to anything to which the individual is already entitled (this usually involves inclusion in an early retirement program).
5. The employee must be advised in writing to consult with an attorney prior to execution of the waiver (this does not mean that the employee must consult with an attorney, but must merely be advised of the suggestion).
6. The employee must be given a period of 21 days in which to consider signing a waiver, and an additional 7 days in which to revoke the signature. Note that where a waiver is offered in exchange for an early retirement plan, as opposed to some other consideration, the individual must have 45 days in which to consider signing the agreement.
7. If the waiver is executed in connection with an exit incentive (early retirement) or other employment termination program, the employer must inform the

employee in writing of the exact terms and inclusions of the program. This information must be sufficient for the employee to test the impact of the selection decision made; in other words, does the decision about inclusion in the program have any discriminatory impact?[52]

The waiver may not bar the employee from filing a claim with the EEOC or participating in investigations by the EEOC. Therefore, the employee may testify on another's behalf if requested. The purpose of these provisions is basically to ensure that the employee entered into the agreement that waived her or his rights knowingly and voluntarily based on the "totality of the circumstances." Courts are serious about enforcing these provisions in order to protect stridently the rights of workers, which was the original intent of the act. In one case, *Ruehl v. Viacom, Inc.,*[53] the court held that an ADEA waiver was completely invalid based on the fact that the employer did not give adequate and written notice to the employee of the relevant information, or how to obtain it. In another, the court tossed out waivers where the employer simply misstated the number of workers terminated in the RIF (154 instead of 152) and did not properly disclose job titles.[54]

Based on the court's decision in *Oubre v. Entergy Operations, Inc.,* if an employee signs a defective waiver, the employee is *not* required to give back any benefits received under the defective waiver. In addition, if the employer offers to individually negotiate the waiver (as opposed to offering a standard form to the employee on a take-it-or-leave-it basis), this may be able to serve as proof to the court that the employee knew what he was doing when he signed the document. Because the court's explanation of this holding is so critical, it has been included at the end of the chapter.

Employers may use general waivers as an attempt to avoid all employment-related liability in contexts other than layoffs. For example, Allstate Insurance decided to transform its 15,200-member sales force from regular employees to independent contractors. To remain as contractors, the agents were required to sign a release stating that they would not sue Allstate. Those agents who refused to sign the waivers were dismissed. Ninety percent of these agents were over the age of 40. In December 2001, the EEOC filed a suit against Allstate alleging it engaged in age discrimination against its agents.[55] However, employers must beware of asking employees to sign waivers that are considered *too general,* such as a document that contains a general release and a covenant not to sue, since courts may find that they are so ambiguous that they do not constitute a knowing and voluntary waiver of the employee's right to sue under the ADEA.[56] In *Thomforde v. International Business Machines Corp.,* the court found the agreement unclear because it failed to explain how the release and the covenant not to sue were related since it used the terms interchangeably, and because it failed to explain the agreement sufficiently to the employee.

After the Supreme Court decision in *Oubre,* the EEOC issued a notice of proposed rule making to address the issues raised in that case. After receiving comments, the EEOC published its final regulation setting forth its interpretation of the waiver provisions of the OWBPA. This regulation became effective on January 10, 2001.[57] The regulation makes clear that employees cannot be required to "tender back" the consideration received under an ADEA waiver agreement before being permitted to challenge the waiver in court. Further, the contract principle of ratification does not apply to ADEA waivers. The EEOC also recognized that covenants not to sue operate as waivers in the ADEA context. Therefore, the OWBPA's requirements and these rules apply to such agreements as well.[58]

A firm must be cautious because individual negotiations may lead to slightly different agreements with various employees, and varying benefits among similar employees may constitute a violation of the Employee Retirement Income Security Act (ERISA).

The OWBPA also contains the following provisions in connection with early retirement plans, 29 U.S.C. § 623:

1. Employers may set a minimum age as a condition of eligibility for normal or early retirement benefits.
2. A benefit plan may provide a subsidized benefit for early retirement.
3. A benefit plan may provide for Social Security supplements in order to cover the time period between the time when the employee leaves the firm and the time when the employee is eligible for Social Security benefits.
4. While severance pay cannot vary based on the employee's age, the employer may offset the payments made by the value of any retiree health benefits received by an individual eligible for immediate pension.

Thus, while an employer may not actually discriminate in the amount of the payments offered by the retirement plan on the basis of age, these provisions actually seem to allow for inconsistent payments to older and younger workers, under certain circumstances.

Note that no provision of the OWBPA prohibits an employer from revoking a retirement offer *while* the employee is considering it. So, for example, a firm could offer an employee a retirement package in a separation agreement; then, while the employee considers it, the firm could revoke it and offer a less attractive package. This could be abused, of course, if it is interpreted as a threat to encourage the worker to decide earlier than the 21-day limit.

The Use of Statistical Evidence

Courts allow the use of statistical evidence to prove discrimination on the basis of age, though it is generally more useful in disparate impact cases than it is in disparate treatment cases. However, the court in *Heward v. Western Electric Co.* explained the similarities in the application of statistics in disparate impact cases as compared to disparate treatment cases:

> The significance of companywide statistics is heightened in disparate *impact* cases because plaintiffs need only demonstrate statistically that particular companywide practices in actuality operate or have the effect of excluding members of the protected class. However, even in a disparate *treatment* class action or "pattern and practice" suit, only gross statistical disparities make out a *prima facie* case of discrimination.

In either case, statistical evidence is meticulously examined to ensure that the statistics shed some light on the case. There is a great deal of skepticism relating to statistical evidence in age discrimination cases precisely because of the fact that older workers are likely to be replaced by younger workers, merely as a result of attrition of the workforce. This is not true in cases brought under Title VII based on race or gender discrimination; therefore, statistics may be slightly more relevant to a determination under Title VII because they may represent pure discrimination.

Where statistics are used to prove discriminatory effect, the Supreme Court has offered some guidance about their use. The Supreme Court has considered percentage comparisons and standard deviation analyses of those comparisons: "As a general rule, . . . if the difference between the expected value and the observed number is greater than two or three standard deviations, then the hypothesis that the [selection process] was random would be suspect." In addition, the Court cautioned that the usefulness or weight of statistical evidence depends on all of the surrounding facts and circumstances, and, specifically, "when special qualifications are required to fill particular jobs, comparisons to the general population (rather than to the smaller group of individuals who possess the necessary qualifications) may have little probative value."

Remedies

equitable relief
Relief that is not in the form of money damages, such as injunctions, reinstatement, and promotion. Equitable relief is based on concepts of justice and fairness.

The court may award a variety of remedies to a successful employee/plaintiff in an age discrimination action. However, where money damages such as back pay (what the employee would have received but for the violation) or front pay (which includes a reasonable and expected amount of compensation for work that the employee would have performed until the time of her expected retirement) are ascertainable and adequately compensate the employee for damages incurred, the court may *not* grant other **equitable relief**. Compensation for pain and suffering or emotional distress is not available under the ADEA.[59] Forms of equitable relief include reinstatement, promotions, and injunctions.

liquidated damages
Liquidated damages limit awards to a predetermined amount. As used in the ADEA, liquidated damages are equal to the unpaid wage and are available in cases involving "willful violations" of the statute.

If an employee-plaintiff proves that the employer-defendant "willfully violated" the ADEA, then the court is also allowed to award **liquidated damages** in an amount equal to unpaid wage liability.[60] Suffice it to say that, by contrast, violations of the ADEA need not, therefore, be otherwise willful. As one has often heard, "ignorance of the law is no excuse," and the same holds true here. In fact, it has been tested in court. The employer's defense that its hiring managers had not been trained concerning bias and admitted their ignorance on the issues was no defense to an ADEA action in *Mathis v. Phillips Chevrolet, Inc.*[61]

Employee Retirement Income Security Act

In 1974, Congress passed the Employee Retirement Income Security Act, which regulates private employee benefit plans. While ERISA specifically governs the operation of retirement plan provisions and other benefits and is therefore relevant to the issue of age discrimination, a complete discussion of its implications is found in Chapter 16.

In short, ERISA's purpose is to protect employees from wrongful denial of all types of benefits, including retirement or pension benefits. Prior to ERISA's enactment, employers were able to discriminate against certain employees in their determination of eligibility for pension benefits and the amount of time one must work for the employer to be eligible for benefits. In addition, many employees suffered from the loss of their benefits when companies underwent management reorganizations, or when the company decided to terminate the plan only a short time before the employees' benefits were to vest. Other employees lost their benefits when they became sick and were forced to quit their job prior to the time at which their pension rights vested.

ERISA prevents these problems by regulating the determination of who must be covered by pension plans, vesting requirements, and the amount that the employer must invest for the benefit of its employees. In an effort to encourage compliance with this provision, ERISA also requires complete disclosure of the administration of the plan. Further, ERISA stipulates that an employee may not be excluded from a plan on account of age, as long as she or he is at least 21 years of age and is a full-time employee with at least one year of service.

ERISA does have some negative side effects. It has made the provision of benefit plans more costly for employers. In addition, no federal law requires that employers offer retirement plans.

Distinctions among Benefit Plans

Can an employer simply decide to lower the amounts of benefits it offers its employees? Yes, as long as it is in line with requirements of ERISA. However, those reductions must be made across the board; the OWBPA limits the distinctions that an employer may make on the basis of age to only those that are justified by "age-based cost differences."

Many firms also have seniority systems that award benefits on the basis of seniority. Because experience seniority is often balanced in favor of older workers, not as many problems arise as a result of these systems. Those not themselves based in age discrimination are valid. In other words, those systems that disadvantage employees as they age are not protected by the ADEA.

Management Considerations

Generalizations such as "older people have poorer vision" or "workers over 50 are less motivated than younger workers" may appear to be grounded in fact, based on the experiences of many firms. But adherence to these prejudiced principles during recruitment or retention of employees may cause more problems for the company than it prevents. As with other areas of protection against wrongful discrimination, managers are not precluded by the ADEA from hiring or retaining the most qualified individual; the act specifically requires that the employer do just that.

The employer may be losing a valuable and completely qualified employee simply because it incorrectly believes that all individuals over a certain age are not qualified for the available position. Instead of relying on vague generalizations concerning all individuals of advanced years, employers would do better to reevaluate the true requirements of the position then test for those characteristics.

For instance, if an employee must have 20/20 vision to safely drive a taxicab, the taxi company will hire the most qualified individuals if it chooses the most competent and experienced from the pool of applicants and subjects these individuals to a vision test. In that way, the employer is sure to locate those workers who are, actually, the most *qualified* for the position, while not excluding an older worker based on a preconceived idea about failing vision. Or, if a position on an assembly line requires great dexterity and speed of movement, the employer should choose the most qualified applicants and allow them to perform the functions required of the position. If the older worker performs adequately, that applicant should be evaluated with no regard to age.

In addition, employers may inadvertently discriminate against older workers and, in doing so, hurt themselves and their firm by failing to train and develop their older workers. Often older workers are not considered for continuous learning or other development because "they're on their way out, anyway." Managers should pay attention to the basis for decision making and selection in connection with training and development opportunities.

In addition, several problems are unique to the employer's defense of a claim of discrimination as a result of an RIF. These problems arise as a result of the difficulty of complete documentation of employee performance.

First, employers generally do not retain intricate written analyses of performance. Consequently, when asked what are the particular problems associated with the employment of this individual, the employer must rely on the subjective oral reports of its supervisors or managers. The jury is then not only faced with the question of whether the adverse action was justified but also with whether the recollection of the managers is correct or merely fabricated for purposes of the litigation. In addition, the employer should ensure that the performance appraisals that *are* recorded reflect an objective evaluation of the employee's performance at that time. The evaluator must exercise caution in the area of the employee's future potential because this is an area that may be related to age and comments may be suspect.

Second, managers and supervisors will likely evaluate an employee as compared to other employees. Therefore, a rating of "good" may be the worst rating given in a department. When the RIF later requires that certain employees be discharged, the employer is left with the obligation to justify the termination of an individual who, in fact, never received a poor evaluation. This is not a sympathetic position.

Finally, the employer may make a decision based on some factor other than performance, such as the fact that a retained employee's wife is in the hospital or that the discharged worker had the opportunity to participate in an early retirement program,

Management Tips

- Any job requirement on the basis of age must be subject to your highest scrutiny. There are extremely few BFOQs allowed on the basis of age alone. Instead, consider what you are actually concerned about and test for that characteristic. For instance, if you are concerned about the eyesight of your applicants or workers, conduct vision tests rather than follow a presumption that older workers will always be disqualified because of their eyesight.

- Reductions in force are prone to problems in connection with age discrimination as a result of higher salaries paid to older and more experienced workers. Review all termination decisions carefully in order to ensure fair and balanced procedures.

- Prior to implementing an RIF, study and document the forces that led to the decision and consider using an employee committee to help plan for the RIF.

- Terminating an older worker and replacing her or him with another worker who is over 40 does not protect you from a charge of age discrimination.

- Even though "accommodation" is most often associated with disability discrimination, it can apply to age discrimination claims. Managers should be trained to understand that failing to consider possible accommodations to age could be evidence of age discrimination.

- Review all recruiting literature to remove all age-based classifications like "looking for young upstarts to help build growing business."

- You may not terminate an older worker on the basis of age; if you must terminate a worker who is 40 or over, ensuring that you have appropriate documentation to justify dismissal creates a safe harbor.

- In drafting a waiver of discrimination claims for older workers to sign upon termination, review the form to ensure compliance with the OWBPA.

- Employers should neither permit nor encourage age-based remarks, comments, or jokes to avoid liability under the ADEA for age-related harassment. Antiharassment policies and procedures should encompass age and all prohibited factors.

- Employers should be sensitive about the inclination in the past to single out workers over 40 for medical exams.

- Beware the situation where an older worker laid off for economic reasons offers to take a pay cut, especially if the offered pay cut is less than what would be paid to a younger replacement. The law is unsettled as to whether these circumstances constitute age discrimination.

- Remember that retaliation for filing a claim of age discrimination is forbidden, not just against the employee filing the claim, but against anyone who supported the claim, such as by testifying.

- The chances of retaliation occurring can be reduced by proper management training and by making sure that all employee handbooks adequately address the issue.

while the retained worker could not. Superior care should be exercised in reaching a conclusion regarding terminations where these issues serve as the bases for retention and discharge because many determining factors could be viewed as age based.

It is in both the employer's and the employee's interest to ensure that the employee periodically receives an objective, detailed performance appraisal. In this way, the employer protects against later claims that the employee was not informed of the employer's dissatisfaction with her or his work, and the employee can guarantee that the employer may only use valid justifications for its discharge decisions.

Chapter Summary

- Employees are protected against discrimination on the basis of their age under the ADEA, unless age is a bona fide occupational qualification.
- Employees who believe that they are victims of age discrimination have available to them a wide array of choices under both state and federal law.
- To prove a case of age discrimination, the employees must show that

  1. They are 40 years of age or older.
  2. They suffered an adverse employment decision.
  3. They are qualified for the position (either that they meet the employer's requirements or that the requirements are not legitimate).
  4. They were replaced by someone younger.

- Once the employee has presented this information, the employer may defend its decision by showing that

  1. Age requirement of a job is a bona fide occupational qualification. This can be done by showing
     a. The age limit is reasonably necessary to the employer's business and
     b. All or a substantial number of people over that age are unable to perform the requirements of the job adequately; or
     c. Some of the people over that age possess a trait that disqualifies them for the position and it cannot be ascertained except by reference to age.
  2. The decision was made based on some reasonable factor other than age.
  3. The employee was not qualified for the position.
  4. The decision to leave was because of a voluntary retirement plan.
  5. The "same actor" defense may be used in some courts. The presumption is that when the same person hires and fires a worker protected by the ADEA, there is a permissible inference that the employee's age was not a motivating factor in the decision to terminate.

- Once the employer presents its defense, the employee will have the opportunity to prove that this defense is mere pretext for the actual discrimination that exists.

- The *Gross* decision seemingly altered the burden-shifting requirement, but subsequent lower court rulings have suggested that the shifting does still apply in age discrimination cases.
- The ADEA prohibits retaliation, both against the employee who alleges age discrimination and any other employee who assists the employee in her or his claim.
- Federal courts are split as to whether an employer can terminate an older employee due to economic considerations.
- Benefit plans and seniority systems cannot be created for the purpose of evading the ADEA or the OWBPA.
- The OWBPA amended section 4(f) of the ADEA and places restrictions where employers offer employees amounts of money through retirement plans as incentives for leaving the company.
- The Employee Retirement Income Security Act (ERISA) regulates private employee benefit plans. It governs the operation of welfare and retirement plan provisions. (See Chapter 16 for a further discussion of ERISA.)
- A variety of remedies are available to those discriminated against due to their age.
- A reduction in force (RIF) occurs when a company is forced to downscale its operations to address rising costs or the effects of a recession. When an individual is terminated pursuant to a bona fide RIF, the employer's actions are protected. In the event of an RIF, age discrimination may be proven when

1. The employer refuses to allow a discharged or demoted employee to bump others with less seniority.
2. The employer hires younger workers when jobs become available.

Chapter-End Questions

1. Calder, age 60, worked as an account executive for TCI Cable, selling advertising time. Calder believed that she had a number of negative experiences at TCI because of her age. She bases this contention on several facts, including several discriminatory comments made by management at TCI. During one of Calder's individual meetings with an executive, he told her that she should walk faster, comparing her to a younger account executive. Another manager told her that he did not understand why, "at this time in [her] life," she did not want free time to travel. Another referred to a job applicant as "grandma" and hired a younger candidate. Is this evidence of discrimination sufficient to support a claim? [*Calder v. TCI Cablevision of Missouri, Inc.*, 298 F.3d 723 (8th Cir. 2002).]

2. Eugene Kilpatrick, who worked for Tyson Foods for 27 years, was terminated at age 68 and replaced by a much younger employee. His only evidence of age discrimination is an email from the manager stating that he understood how long Kilpatrick had worked for Tyson, but that Kilpatrick was not effectively doing his job. Is this enough to establish age discrimination? [*Kilpatrick v. Tyson Foods, Inc.*, 268 Fed. Appx. 860 (11th Cir. 2008).]

3. John Van Voorhis, a pilot over 50 years of age, applied to the county for a job as a helicopter pilot. Although Van Voorhis was clearly the most qualified applicant, the county chose not to interview anyone because, as the supervisor explained, they did not want to hire "an old pilot." The position was later reopened, with reduced minimum requirements, but the previous applicants were not notified. The county hired a younger woman who had previously applied but who had not been considered because she did not meet the earlier minimum standards. Has Van Voorhis presented sufficient direct evidence to establish age discrimination? [*Van Voorhis v. Hillsborough County Board of County Commissioners,* No. 07-12672 (11th Cir. 2008).]

4. Allstate Insurance established a corporate restructuring plan in which it fired employee-agents, then rehired them either one year after they were fired or at the end of the severance they received, whichever was longer. Statistical evidence showed that, of the 6,000 employees affected by the policy, 90 percent were older than 40 and that the over-40 group constituted only 23 percent of Allstate's total workforce. Does the policy have a disparate impact in violation of the ADEA because older employees generally received severance for longer than younger employees? [*EEOC v. Allstate Ins. Co.,* 528 F.3d 1042 (8th Cir. 2008).]

5. Richard Hopkins, a 61-year-old employee of the city of Independence, Missouri, was diagnosed with a heart condition that prevented him from driving for six months. Driving was an essential function of his job, so it was impossible for him to work for six months. Under the city's "Leave Donation Program," employees of the city were permitted to donate up to 40 hours of vacation, personal-business, and sick leave to other employees. When his co-workers learned of Hopkins's condition, they began to donate leave time to him under the Leave Donation Program. Shortly after the donations began, however, the city's Human Resources Administrator told Hopkins that he was ineligible for the program because he was over 60, also saying, "I didn't know you were that old." Among several other requirements, the Leave Donation Program stipulated that, in order to be eligible, the recipient employee must "not be eligible for regular retirement." Eligibility for retirement is defined in the city's Personnel Policies and Procedures manual as "age sixty (60)" and "vested" in the city's pension plan (requiring five years of service). Does the city's Leave Donation Program violate the ADEA? [*United States Equal Employment Opportunity Commission (EEOC) v. City of Independence, Missouri,* 471 F.3d 891 (8th Cir. 2006).]

6. Can an employer be liable under any anti-discrimination statute for refusing to hire someone whom the employer thinks is overqualified? [*Taggart v. Time, Inc.,* 924 F.2d 43 (2d Cir. 1991).]

7. The oldest or nearly oldest in each department happened to be the employee chosen by each unit supervisor to be laid off in a cutback. An employee filed suit and the employer claimed that (1) it had the right to terminate the oldest employees because they cost the most to the company and (2) there was no discrimination or intent to do so because each unit supervisor made her or his own decisions, so there was no concerted effort or decision to get rid of older employees. Are you persuaded by this defense?

8. Tommy Morgan was a 20-year employee of New York Life Insurance Company. At age 52, his career at New York Life included a promotion, high marks for job performance, and a good reputation among his colleagues. One co-worker described Morgan as the best managing partner he had seen in 40 years. In September 2005, the

company sent out an email announcing a "new generation of managers." Within three weeks of that email, Morgan was fired. He sued New York Life for age discrimination. Does he have any basis for a legitimate claim? Why or why not? [*Morgan v. New York Life Ins. Co.,* 101 FEP Cases 657 (N.D. Ohio 2007).] Would the situation be different if the employer simply said that Morgan was no longer "compatible" with the company's corporate culture? [*Brian Reid v. Google,* 155 Cal. App. 4th 1342, 66 Cal. Rptr. 3d 744 (2007).]

9. Fifty-five-year-old Merriweather had worked for 14 years as a benefits coordinator before he was laid off by his employer. The employer contended that it eliminated Merriweather's job for economic reasons. To support its strategic goals, the employer had decided to hire new workers instead of training Merriweather to handle projected additional tasks. The employer chose not to retain an employee who is seven months older than Merriweather as the only full-time benefits coordinator. Two new workers, ages 42 and 50, were hired to divide their time between benefits coordination and the added tasks. Merriweather claimed that he was qualified to handle the added responsibilities, but he did not offer evidence to support this claim. You be the judge. Do the employer's actions violate the ADEA? Explain. [*Merriweather v. Philadelphia Federation of Teachers Health & Welfare Fund,* 2001 U.S. Dist. LEXIS 18511 (E.D. Pa. 2001).]

End Notes

1. See Erin Carroll, "Television Writers' Age-Bias Case Moves to State Court," *Los Angeles Daily Journal,* February 27, 2002, p. 3.

2. Richard Verrier, "Hollywood Writers' Age-Discrimination Case Settled," *Los Angeles Times* website, January 23, 2010, articles.latimes.com/2010/jan/23/business/la-fi-ct-writers23-2010jan23.

3. U.S. Government Accountability Office, "Older Workers: Labor Can Help Employers and Employees Plan Better for the Future," GAO-06-80, December 2005, p. 12.

4. R. Ambrogi, "Delhi Abolishes Lawyer Age Cap," Legal Blog Watch, November 19, 2007, http://legalblogwatch.typepad.com/legal_blog_watch/2007/11/delhi-abolishes.html; "Age Bar on Bar Enrolment Goes," *The Hindu,* November 13, 2007, http://www.hindu.com/2007/11/13/stories/2007111366890400.htm.

5. Richard W. Johnson, "Older Workers: Opportunities and Challenges," Urban Institute, July 2010, www.urban.org/uploadedpdf/412166-older-workers.pdf.

6. Pew Research, "Working after Retirement: The Gap Between Expectations and Reality," September 21, 2006, http://pewresearch.org/pubs/320/working-after-retirement-the-gap-between-expectations-and-reality.

7. Ibid., p. 8.

8. J. Collison, *Older Workers Survey.* Alexandria, VA: Society for Human Research Management (SHRM/NOWCC/CED), 2003.

9. Ernst and Young, *The Aging of the U.S. Workforce.*

10. AARP, "The Business Case for Workers Age 50+: Planning for Tomorrow's Talent Needs in Today's Competitive Environment," December 2005, http://www.aarp.org/research/work/employment/workers_fifty_plus.html.

11. See the EEOC charge statistics at www.eeoc.gov/eeoc/statistics/enforcement/charges.cfm.

12. See, for example, a November 12, 2009, blog post on the Workplace Prof Blog (lawprofessors.typepad.com/laborprof_blog/2009/11/new-eeoc-statistics-show-age-discrimination-complaints-are-down.html).

13. 827 F.2d 13, n.8 (7th Cir. 1987), overruled on other grounds, 860 F.2d 834 (7th Cir. 1988).

14. *General Dynamics Land Systems, Inc. v. Cline,* 540 U.S. 581, 124 S. Ct. 1236 (2004).

15. Bertha Coombs, "Demand Grows for Older Workers: Firms Focus on Hiring and Retaining Baby Boomers," CNBC TV, May 7, 2004.

16. 528 U.S. 62 (2000).

17. 517 U.S. 308, 116 S. Ct. 1307 (1996).

18. *Sprint/United Management Co. v. Mendelsohn,* 552 U.S.___, 128 S. Ct. 1140 (2008), http://www.law.cornell.edu/supct/html/06-1221.ZS.html.

19. 529 F.2d 760 (4th Cir. 1975).

20. http://www.eeoc.gov/types/age.html.

21. *Jones v. Oklahoma City Public Schools,* No. 09-6108 (10th Cir. 2010).

22. Ibid., at p. 10, "[T]he rule articulated in *Gross* has no logical effect on the application of *McDonnell Douglas* to age discrimination cases."

23. See 14 C.F.R. § 121.383(c).

24. 351 F.3d 183 (2005), affirmed, *Smith v. City of Jackson,* 544 U.S. 228 (2005).

25. 1991 WL 74610 (N.D. Ill. 1991) (emphasis added).

26. 828 F.2d 1202 (7th Cir. 1987).

27. 381 F.3d 56 (2d Cir. 2004).

28. No 07-4480 (2d Cir. 2008).

29. See *Caron v. Scott Paper Co.,* 834 F. Supp. 33 (D. Me. 1993); *Camacho v. Sears, Roebuck de Puerto Rico,* 939 F. Supp. 113 (D.P.R. 1996).

30. See *Ellis v. United Airlines, Inc.,* 73 F.3d 999, 1009 (10th Cir. 1996): "Of those courts that have considered the issue since *Hazen,* there is a clear trend toward concluding that the ADEA does not support a disparate impact claim."

31. *Proud v. Stone,* 945 F.2d 796 (4th Cir. 1991).

32. Section 623(d) of the ADEA says, "It shall be unlawful for an employer to discriminate against any of his employees . . . because such individual . . . has made a charge, testified, assisted, or participated in any manner in an investigation, proceeding, or litigation."

33. Section 633(a) says only that personnel "shall be made free from any discrimination based on age." No mention is made of individuals who participate in an investigation, as there is in section 623(d).

34. No. 06-1321 553 U.S. ___, 128 S.Ct. 1931 (May 27, 2008).

35. See, for example, "Punitive Damages in Employment Discrimination Law," by Louis Malone (www.bna.com/bnabooks/ababna/annual/2000/malone.pdf.), in which he says, "No punitive damages are permitted under the ADEA, except for retaliation claims."

36. See section 7(b).

37. See *Hazen Paper Company v. Biggins,* 507 U.S. 604, 113 S. Ct. 1701 (1993).

38. Kline, Susan and John Gaidoo, "Labor & Employment-Recent Federal Court Decisions Highlight ADEA Pitfalls" (Nov. 8, 2010), http://www.bakerdaniels.com/newsandevents/articlesalerts/detail.aspx?id=EEB7BB948D184A6D968E01706733C482.

39. *Cariglia v. Hertz Equipment Rental Corporation,* 363 F.3d 77 (1st Cir. 2004).

40. *Christensen v. Titan Distribution, Inc.,* 481 F.3d 1085 (8th Cir. 2007).

41. 530 U.S. 133 (2000).

42. See "Have Discrimination Cases Gotten More Difficult?" *Texas Lawyer,* September 27, 2000.

43. See, for example, *Jones,* the 2010 10th Circuit decision, supra, at pp. 13–14.

44. 96 F.3d 830 (6th Cir. 1996).

45. Ibid. at 833.

46. Ibid. at 834.

47. *Smith v. Kmart Corporation,* 1996 WL 780490 (E.D. Wash. 1996); *Lewis v. Federal Prison Industries, Inc.,* 786 F.2d 1537 (11th Cir. 1986); *Kelewae v. Jim Meagher Chevrolet, Inc.,* 952 F.2d 1052 (8th Cir. 1992); *City of Billings v. State Human Rights Commission,* 209 Mont. 251 (1984).

48. *Crawford,* 96 F.3d at 834–35.

49. *Alexander v. CIT Technology Financing Services,* 217 F. Supp. 2d 867 (N.D. Ill. 2002).

50. *Bennington v. Caterpillar Inc.,* 275 F.3d 654 (7th Cir. 2001).

51. *Jones v. SmithKline Beecham Corp.,* 309 F. Supp. 2d 343 (N.D.N.Y. 2004); *Lacher v. West,* 147 F. Supp. 2d 538 (N.D. Tex. 2001); *Jackson v. R.I. Williams & Associates, Inc.,* Civ. A. No. 98-1741, 1998 WL 316090 (E.D. Pa. 1998); *Tumolo v. Triangle Pacific Corp.,* 46 F. Supp. 2d 410, 412 (E.D. Pa. 1999); *Burns v. AAF-McQuay, Inc.,* 166 F.3d 292, 294 (4th Cir. 1999); *Ricci v. Applebee's Northeast, Inc.,* 301 F. Supp. 81 (D. Me. 2004); and *Lacher v. Principi,* 2002 WL 1033089 (W.D. Tex. 2002). In addition, while the Tenth Circuit has not expressly recognized a cause of action for hostile work environment under the ADEA, it has decided a case where the plaintiff raised the issue before the district court. See *McKnight v. Kimberly Clark Corp.,* 149 F.3d 1125, 1129 (10th Cir. 1998) (deciding a hostile work environment claim under the ADEA, but not addressing the apparent lack of authority for raising such a theory). In light of the *McKnight* case, the court in *Ellison v. Sandia National Laboratories,* 192 F. Supp. 2d 1240 (D.N.M. 2002), assumed without deciding that employee may assert a hostile work environment claim under the ADEA.

52. *Burlison v. McDonald's Corp.,* 455 F.3d 1242 (11th Cir. 2006).

53. 500 F.3d 375 (3d Cir. 2007).

54. *Peterson v. Seagate US LLC,* 534 F.Supp. 2d 996 (D.MN 2008).

55. See "U.S. Sues Allstate over Age Discrimination," Reuters, http://news.findlaw.com/legalnews/s/20011228/n28194796.html, December 28, 2001.

56. *Thomforde v. International Business Machines Corp.,* 406 F.3d 500 (8th Cir. 2005).

57. 29 C.F.R. § 1625.

58. See Kiren Dosanjh, "Old Rules Need Not Apply: The Prohibition of Ratification and 'Tender Back' in Employees' Challenges to ADEA Waivers," *Journal of Legal Advocacy and Practice* 3, no. 5 (2001).

59. *Commissioner of Internal Revenue v. Schleier,* 515 U.S. 323, 115 S. Ct. 2159 (1995).

60. 29 U.S.C. § 626(b).

61. 269 F.3d 771. (7th Cir. 2001).

Cases

Western Air Lines, Inc. v. Criswell *472 U.S. 400 (1985)*

Western Air Lines requires that its flight engineers, who are members of the cockpit crew but do not operate flight controls unless both the pilot and the co-pilot become incapacitated, retire at age 60. The Federal Aviation Administration prohibits anyone from acting as a pilot or co-pilot after they have reached the age of 60. The respondents in this case include both pilots who were denied reassignment to the position of flight engineers at age 60 and flight engineers who were forced to retire at that age. The airline argued that the age 60 retirement requirement is a BFOQ reasonably necessary to the safe operation of the business. The lower court instructed the jury as follows: The airline could establish age as a BFOQ only if "it was highly impractical for [petitioner] to deal with each [flight engineer] over age 60 on an individualized basis to determine his particular ability to perform his job safely" and that some flight engineers "over 60 possess traits of a physiological, psychological or other nature which preclude safe and efficient job performance that cannot be ascertained by means other than knowing their age." The Supreme Court evaluated whether this instruction was appropriate and determined that it correctly stated the law.

Stevens, J.

***

The evidence at trial established that the flight engineer's "normal duties are less critical to the safety of flight than those of a pilot." The flight engineer, however, does have critical functions in emergency situations and, of course, might cause considerable disruption in the event of his own medical emergency.

The actual capabilities of persons over age 60, and the ability to detect diseases or a precipitous decline in their faculties, were the subject of conflicting medical testimony. Western's expert witness, a former FAA [Federal Aviation Administration] deputy federal air surgeon, was especially concerned about the possibility of a "cardiovascular event," such as a heart attack. He testified that "with advancing age the likelihood of onset of disease increases and that in persons over age 60 it could not be predicted whether and when such diseases would occur."

The plaintiff's experts, on the other hand, testified that physiological deterioration is caused by disease, not aging, and that "it was feasible to determine on the basis of individual medical examinations whether flight deck crew members, including those over age 60, were physically qualified to continue to fly." Moreover, several large commercial airlines have flight engineers over age 60 "flying the line" without any reduction in their safety record.

Throughout the legislative history of the ADEA, one empirical fact is repeatedly emphasized: the process of psychological and physiological degeneration caused by aging varies with each individual. "The basic research in the field of aging has established that there is a wide range of individual physical ability regardless of age." As a result, many older workers perform at levels equal or superior to their younger colleagues.

In 1965, the secretary of labor reported to Congress that despite these well-established medical facts, "there is persistent and widespread use of age limits in hiring that in a great many cases can be attributed only to arbitrary discrimination against older workers on the basis of age and regardless of ability." Two years later, the president recommended that Congress enact legislation to abolish arbitrary age limits on hiring. Such limits, the president declared, have a devastating effect on the dignity of the individual and result in a staggering loss of human resources vital to the national economy.

The legislative history of the 1978 amendments to the ADEA makes quite clear that the policies and substantive provisions of the act apply with especial force in the case of mandatory retirement provisions. The House Committee on Education and Labor reported: "Increasingly, it is being recognized that mandatory retirement based solely upon age is arbitrary and that chronological age alone is a poor indicator of ability to perform a job."

In *Usery v. Tamiami Trail Tours, Inc.,* the court of appeals for the Fifth Circuit was called upon to evaluate the merits of a BFOQ defense to a claim of age discrimination. Tamiami Trail Tours had a policy of refusing to hire persons over age 40 as intercity bus drivers. At trial, the bus company introduced testimony supporting its theory that the hiring policy was a BFOQ based upon safety considerations—the need to employ persons who have a low risk of accidents. The court concluded that "the job qualifications which the employer invokes to justify his discrimination must be *reasonably necessary* to the essence of his business—here, the safe transportation of bus passengers from one point to another. The greater the safety factor, measured by the likelihood of harm and the probable severity of that harm in case of an accident, the more stringent may be the job qualifications designed to insure safe driving."

In the absence of persuasive evidence supporting its position, Western nevertheless argues that the jury should have been instructed to defer to "Western's selection of job qualifications for the position of flight engineer that are reasonable in light of safety risks." This proposal is plainly at odds with Congress's decision, in adopting the ADEA, to subject management decisions to a test of objective justification in a court of law. The BFOQ standard adopted in the statute is one of "reasonable necessity," not reasonableness.

In adopting that standard, Congress did not ignore the public interest in safety. That interest is adequately reflected in instructions that track the language of the statute. When an employer establishes that a job qualification has been carefully formulated to respond to documented concerns for public safety, it will not be overly burdensome to persuade a trier of fact that the qualification is "reasonably necessary" to safe operation of the business. The uncertainty implicit in the concept of managing safety risks always makes it "reasonably necessary" to err on the side of caution in a close case. . . . Since the instructions in this case would not have prevented the airline from raising this contention to the jury in closing argument, we are satisfied that the verdict is a consequence of a defect in Western's proof, rather than a defect in the trial court's instructions.

Case Questions

1. What is the basis for the determination that an employer should or should not be required to test applicants on an individual basis?

2. Should an employer have available as a defense that the cost of the tests would impose a great burden on the employer? Why or why not?

3. What is the distinction the Criswell opinion makes between "reasonable necessity" and "reasonableness"?

Case 2

Gross v. FBL Financial Services, Inc. *No. 08-441* *(S.Ct. 2009)*

Gross began working for FBL in 1971. In 2003, when Gross was 54, he was reassigned from his position as claims administration director to the position of claims project coordinator. His previous position was renamed to claims administration manager and was given to a younger employee whom Gross had previously supervised. Although his pay remained the same, Gross considered the change a demotion and sued FBL for age discrimination. Gross introduced evidence at trial that the decision was at least partly based on age. FBL's defense was that the move was part of a restructuring and that the new position was a better fit for Gross's skills. The trial court gave the jury an instruction that it should find for Gross if it found that "age was a motivating factor." It also instructed the jury that it should find for FBL if it found, by a preponderance of the evidence, that FBL would have demoted him regardless of age. The jury found in Gross's favor and FBL appealed. The 8th Circuit reversed the decision and sent the case back for trial. The U.S. Supreme Court reviews the 8th Circuit's ruling.

Thomas, J.

***

The parties have asked us to decide whether a plaintiff must "present direct evidence of discrimination in order to obtain a mixed-motive instruction in a non-Title VII discrimination case." . . . Before reaching this question, however, we must first determine whether the burden of persuasion ever shifts to the party defending an alleged mixed-motives discrimination claim brought under the ADEA. We hold that it does not. Petitioner relies on this Court's decisions construing Title VII for his interpretation of the ADEA. Because Title VII is materially different with respect to the relevant burden of persuasion, however, these decisions do not control our construction of the ADEA.

***

In *Price Waterhouse* . . . the Court . . . determined that once a "plaintiff in a Title VII case proves that [the plaintiff's membership in a protected class] played a motivating part in an employment decision, the defendant may avoid a finding of liability only by proving by a preponderance of the evidence that it would have made the same decision even if it had not taken [that factor] into account." . . . But as we explained in *Desert Palace, Inc. v. Costa*, 539 U. S. 90, 94–95 (2003), Congress has since amended Title VII by explicitly authorizing discrimination claims in which an improper consideration was "a motivating factor" for an adverse employment decision.

***

This Court has never held that this burden-shifting framework applies to ADEA claims. And, we decline to do so now. When conducting statutory interpretation, we "must be careful not to apply rules applicable under one statute to a different statute without careful and critical examination."

***

We cannot ignore Congress' decision to amend Title VII's relevant provisions but not make similar changes to the ADEA . . . As a result, the Court's interpretation of the ADEA is not governed by Title VII decisions such as *Desert Palace* and *Price Waterhouse*.

***

Our inquiry therefore must focus on the text of the ADEA to decide whether it authorizes a mixed-motives age discrimination claim. It does not . . . The words

"because of" mean "by reason of: on account of." . . . Thus, the ordinary meaning of the ADEA's requirement that an employer took adverse action "because of" age is that age was the "reason" that the employer decided to act. . . . It follows, then, that under §623(a)(1), the plaintiff retains the burden of persuasion to establish that age was the "but-for" cause of the employer's adverse action.

***

We hold that a plaintiff bringing a disparate-treatment claim pursuant to the ADEA must prove, by a preponderance of the evidence, that age was the "but-for" cause of the challenged adverse employment action. The burden of persuasion does not shift to the employer to show that it would have taken the action regardless of age, even when a plaintiff has produced some evidence that age was one motivating factor in that decision.

Justice Stevens, with whom Justice Souter, Justice Ginsberg, and Justice Breyer join, dissenting

The "but-for" causation standard endorsed by the Court today was advanced in Justice Kennedy's dissenting opinion in *Price Waterhouse v. Hopkins*, 490 U. S. 228, 279 (1989), a case construing identical language in Title VII of the Civil Rights Act of 1964 . . . Not only did the Court reject the but-for standard in that case, but so too did Congress when it amended Title VII in 1991. Given this unambiguous history, it is particularly inappropriate for the Court, on its own initiative, to adopt an interpretation of the causation requirement in the ADEA that differs from the established reading of Title VII. I disagree not only with the Court's interpretation of the statute, but also with its decision to engage in unnecessary lawmaking. I would simply answer the question presented by the certiorari petition and hold that a plaintiff need not present direct evidence of age discrimination to obtain a mixed-motives instruction.

The Court asks whether a mixed-motives instruction is ever appropriate in an ADEA case. As it acknowledges, this was not the question we granted certiorari to decide.

***

Unfortunately, the majority's inattention to prudential Court practices is matched by its utter disregard of our precedent and Congress' intent.

***

We recognized [in *Price Waterhouse*] that the employer had an affirmative defense: It could avoid a finding of liability by proving that it would have made the same decision even if it had not taken the plaintiff's sex into account. . . . But this affirmative defense did not alter the meaning of "because of." As we made clear, when "an employer considers both gender and legitimate factors at the time of making a decision, that decision was 'because of' sex.". . . We readily rejected the dissent's contrary assertion. "To construe the words 'because of' as colloquial shorthand for 'but-for' causation," we said, "is to misunderstand them." . . . Today, however, the Court interprets the words "because of" in the ADEA "as colloquial shorthand for 'but-for' causation."

***

The Court's resurrection of the but-for causation standard is unwarranted. *Price Waterhouse* repudiated that standard 20 years ago, and Congress' response to our decision further militates against the crabbed interpretation the Court adopts today. The answer to the question the Court has elected to take up—whether a mixed-motives jury instruction is ever proper in an ADEA case—is plainly yes.

***

The Court's endorsement of a different construction of the same critical language in the ADEA and Title VII is both unwise and inconsistent with settled law. The but-for standard the Court adopts was rejected by this Court in *Price Waterhouse* and by Congress in the Civil Rights Act of 1991. Yet today the Court resurrects the standard in an unabashed display of judicial lawmaking. I respectfully dissent.

Case Questions

1. Do you agree with the dissent that the majority opinion in *Gross* completely alters the burden-shifting framework adopted in *Price Waterhouse?*

2. Is the *Gross* opinion likely to make recovery by employees more difficult in age discrimination cases, as many commentators have suggested?

3. Appellate court decisions subsequent to *Gross* have drawn a distinction between a burden of proof, which does not shift, and a burden of production, which does. In your opinion, what is the difference and how is it relevant to the employee's age discrimination case?

Case 3

Hazen Paper Co. v. Biggins   *507 U.S. 604 (1993)*

The Hazens hired Walter Biggins in 1977 and fired him in 1986 when he was 62 years old. Biggins sued, alleging a violation of the ADEA. The Hazens claimed instead that they terminated him because he did business with their competitors. A jury decided in favor of Biggins and the appellate court agreed, relying on evidence that the Hazens really fired him in order to prevent his pension benefits from vesting (which would have happened in the few weeks following his termination). In this case, the Supreme Court determines whether a firing decision based on number of years served is "age-based."

O'Connor, J.

***

The Courts of Appeals repeatedly have faced the question whether an employer violates the ADEA by acting on the basis of a factor, such as an employee's pension status or seniority, that is empirically correlated with age . . . . We now clarify that there is no disparate treatment under the ADEA when the factor motivating the employer is some feature other than the employee's age.

***

In a disparate treatment case, liability depends on whether the protected trait (under the ADEA, age) actually motivated the employer's decision. The employer may have relied upon a formal, facially discriminatory policy requiring adverse treatment of employees with that trait. Or the employer may have been motivated by the protected trait on an ad hoc, informal basis. Whatever the employer's decision-making process, a disparate treatment claim cannot succeed unless the employee's protected trait actually played a role in that process and had a determinative influence on the outcome.

Disparate treatment, thus defined, captures the essence of what Congress sought to prohibit in the ADEA. It is the very essence of age discrimination for an older employee to be fired because the employer believes that productivity and competence decline with old age.

"Although age discrimination rarely was based on the sort of animus motivating some other forms of discrimination, it was based in large part on stereotypes unsupported by objective fact. . . . Moreover, the available empirical evidence demonstrated that arbitrary age lines were in fact generally unfounded and that, as an overall matter, the performance of older workers was at least as good as that of younger workers."

Thus the ADEA commands that "employers are to evaluate [older] employees . . . on their merits and not their age." The employer cannot rely on age as a proxy for an employee's remaining characteristics, such as productivity, but must instead focus on those factors directly.

When the employer's decision is wholly motivated by factors other than age, the problem of inaccurate and stigmatizing stereotypes disappears. This is true even if the motivating factor is correlated with age, as pension status typically is. Pension plans typically provide that an employee's accrued benefits will become nonforfeitable, or "vested," once the employee completes a certain number of years of service with the employer. On average, an older employee has had more years in the workforce than a younger employee, and thus may well have accumulated more years of service with a particular employer. Yet an employee's age is analytically distinct from his years of service. An employee who is younger than 40, and therefore outside the class of older workers as defined by the ADEA, may have worked for a particular employer his entire career, while an older worker may have been newly hired. Because age and years of service are analytically distinct, an employer can take account of one while ignoring the other, and thus it is incorrect to say that a decision based on years of service is necessarily "age based."

The instant case is illustrative. Under the Hazen Paper pension plan, as construed by the Court of Appeals, an employee's pension benefits vest after the employee completes 10 years of service with the company. Perhaps it is true that older employees of Hazen Paper are more likely to be "close to vesting" than younger employees. Yet a decision by the company to

fire an older employee solely because he has nine-plus years of service and therefore is "close to vesting" would not constitute discriminatory treatment on the basis of age. The prohibited stereotype ("Older employees are likely to be—") would not have figured in this decision, and the attendant stigma would not ensue. The decision would not be the result of an inaccurate and denigrating generalization about age, but would rather represent an accurate judgment about the employee—that he indeed is "close to vesting."

We do not mean to suggest that an employer lawfully could fire an employee in order to prevent his pension benefits from vesting. Such conduct is actionable under § 510 of ERISA. But it would not, without more, violate the ADEA. That law requires the employer to ignore an employee's age (absent a statutory exemption or defense); it does not specify further characteristics that an employer must also ignore. . . .

We do not preclude the possibility that an employer who targets employees with a particular pension status on the assumption that these employees are likely to be older thereby engages in age discrimination. . . . Finally, we do not consider the special case where an employee is about to vest in pension benefits as a result of his age, rather than years of service, and the employer fires the employee in order to prevent vesting. That case is not presented here. Our holding is simply that an employer does not violate the ADEA just by interfering with an older employee's pension benefits that would have vested by virtue of the employee's years of service.

Case Questions

1. Do you agree with the court that age and years of service are sufficiently distinct to allow for terminations based on years of service and to find no violation of the ADEA where the terminations result in a greater proportion of older workers being fired?

2. Aren't workers close to vesting more likely to be older workers? And, if so, then do you believe that an employer can use the category "close to vesting" to avoid liability under the ADEA?

3. If an employer did terminate a group of individuals on the basis of their being close to vesting with the intention of getting rid of older workers, what type of evidence would the employees/plaintiffs be able to use to prove the unlawful intent?

Oubre v. Entergy Operations, Inc. *522 U.S. 422, 118 S. Ct. 838 (1998)*

Case 4

Dolores Oubre worked as a scheduler at a power plant in Louisiana run by Entergy Operations, Inc. In 1994, she received a poor performance rating. Oubre's supervisor met with her on January 17, 1995, and gave her the option of either improving her performance during the coming year or accepting a voluntary arrangement for her severance. She received a packet of information about the severance agreement and had 14 days to consider her options, during which time she consulted with attorneys. On January 31, Oubre decided to accept. She signed a release, in which she "agree[d] to waive, settle, release, and discharge any and all claims, demands, damages, actions, or causes of action . . . that I may have against Entergy. . . . " In exchange, she received six installment payments over the next four months, totaling $6,258.

Kennedy, J.

***

Oubre filed this suit against Entergy alleging constructive discharge on the basis of her age in violation of the ADEA and state law. She has not offered or tried to return the $6,258 to the employer, nor is it clear she has the means to do so. The lower court agreed with the employer that Oubre had ratified the defective release by failing to return or offer to return the monies she had received. The Court of Appeals affirmed judgment for the employer and the Supreme Court reverses.

***

The statutory command [of the OWBPA] is clear: An employee "may not waive" an ADEA claim unless the waiver or release satisfies the OWBPA's requirements. The policy of the Older Workers' Benefit Protection Act is likewise clear from its title: It is designed to protect the rights and benefits of older workers. The OWBPA implements Congress' policy via a strict, unqualified statutory stricture on waivers, and we are bound to take Congress at its word. Congress imposed specific duties on employers who seek releases of certain claims created by statute. Congress delineated these duties with precision and without qualification: An employee "may not waive" an ADEA claim unless the employer complies with the statute. Courts cannot with ease presume ratification of that which Congress forbids.

. . . The statute creates a series of prerequisites for knowing and voluntary waivers and imposes affirmative duties of disclosure and waiting periods. The OWBPA governs the effect under federal law of waivers or releases on ADEA claims and incorporates no exceptions or qualifications. The text of the OWBPA forecloses the employer's defense, notwithstanding how general contract principles would apply to non-ADEA claims.

The rule proposed by the employer (that the employee must first give back monies received before avoiding the release) would frustrate the statute's practical operation as well as its formal command. In many instances a discharged employee likely will have spent the monies received and will lack the means to tender their return. These realities might tempt employers to risk noncompliance with the OWBPA's waiver provisions, knowing it will be difficult to repay the monies and relying on ratification. We ought not to open the door to an evasion of the statute by this device.

Oubre's cause of action arises under the ADEA, and the release can have no effect on her ADEA claim unless it complies with the OWBPA. In this case, both sides concede the release the employee signed did not comply with the requirements of the OWBPA. Since Oubre's release did not comply with the OWBPA's stringent safeguards, it is unenforceable against her insofar as it purports to waive or release her ADEA claim. As a statutory matter, the release cannot bar her ADEA suit, irrespective of the validity of the contract as to other claims.

In further proceedings in this or other cases, courts may need to inquire whether the employer has claims for restitution, recoupment, or setoff against the employee, and these questions may be complex where a release is effective as to some claims but not as to ADEA claims. We need not decide those issues here, however. It suffices to hold that the release cannot bar the ADEA claim because it does not conform to the statute. Nor did the employee's mere retention of monies amount to a ratification equivalent to a valid release of her ADEA claims, since the retention did not comply with the OWBPA any more than the original release did. The statute governs the effect of the release on ADEA claims, and the employer cannot invoke the employee's failure to tender back as a way of excusing its own failure to comply. REVERSED and REMANDED.

Case Questions

1. Do you think the fact that an attorney was consulted before the acceptance of the offer is relevant in this case to determine whether the waiver was knowing and voluntary?

2. As an employer, what should you do to ensure the waiver an individual will be signing is valid?

3. Why do you think an employer must follow such strict guidelines when creating a waiver? Do you think the guidelines are correct? How would you change them?

Chapter 13

Disability Discrimination

Learning Objectives

When you finish this chapter, you should be able to:

LO1 Identify the current environment for disabled workers in today's workplaces.

LO2 Identify the challenges inherent in drafting, interpreting, and enforcing a disability anti-discrimination statute.

LO3 Outline the *prima facie* case for discrimination under the Americans with Disabilities Act, paralleled by section 504 of the Vocational Rehabilitation Act of 1973.

LO4 Describe the term *disability* as it is defined by the ADA and offer examples of covered disabilities or disabilities that may not be covered.

LO5 Define *major life activity* and *substantially limited* according to court decisions under the ADA.

LO6 Explain how someone could be covered by the ADA when they are not at all disabled, under the provision for "*perception* of impairment."

LO7 Describe how employers can determine the reasonableness of any proposed accommodation.

LO8 Outline the burden-shifting framework of the ADA.

LO9 Describe the defenses available to employers under the ADA.

LO10 Describe how the law treats mental or intellectual disabilities under the ADA.

LO11 Identify the distinctions between employer liability based on workers' compensation and liability based on the ADA.

Opening Scenarios

SCENARIO 1

1 Scenario

A sales manager in a large security systems company was terminated soon after his co-workers learned that he is homosexual and that his life partner has HIV, the virus that causes AIDS. The sales manager himself is HIV-negative. Has the employer violated the Americans with Disabilities Act?

SCENARIO 2

2 Scenario

At 41, Taylor is the most senior accounting clerk in his department, making roughly $40,000 per year in a firm of about 200 employees. It has been a lean year for his firm. Product orders from customers have slowed down and commodity prices for the firm's materials are up. Alexis, the human resources director, is considering laying off Taylor. Because Taylor is the senior accounting clerk, he makes about $5,000 more than the next-highest-paid clerk. Alexis knows that laying off Taylor instead of one of the other clerks will save the company money.

However, Taylor is the parent of three children. His spouse does freelance work from home, but business has been way down this year and the loss of income has put a severe strain on the family finances. If Taylor loses his job, he will probably lose his home. In addition, his youngest daughter has cerebral palsy and his family depends on his job for health insurance benefits. Alexis knows of Taylor's situation but also that Taylor's circumstances are sending the company's health insurance premiums through the roof. Alexis is trying to be careful not to let that affect the decision. What decision should be made?[1]

SCENARIO 3

3 Scenario

Thekla Tsonis is responsible for filling a vacant position at her firm. The position requires good interpersonal and communication skills and the ability to type, file, and travel on an as-needed basis. An applicant sits before her during an interview for the vacant position. Tsonis is relatively confident that the applicant satisfies the first three criteria. However, Tsonis is concerned about the fourth requirement, traveling on an as-needed basis, because the applicant is bound to a wheelchair due to a muscular disorder. The disorder does not affect the applicant's cognitive skills or her use of her arms and hands. A second applicant's performance evaluations come from her previous employer and are slightly lower than those received by the first applicant, but the second applicant informs Tsonis that she is looking forward to the traveling. Does Tsonis hire the first applicant, even though she believes that the wheelchair will pose a problem with travel and other areas, or does she hire the second?

Statutory Basis

Americans with Disabilities Act of 1990, ¶ 602, § 102

No covered entity shall discriminate against a qualified individual with a disability because of the disability of such individual in regard to job application procedures, the hiring, advancement, or discharge of employees, employee compensation, job training, and other terms, conditions, and privileges of employment.

Vocational Rehabilitation Act of 1973, ¶ 504 § 794

No otherwise qualified individual with a disability in the United States . . . shall, solely by reason of her or his disability, be excluded from the participation in, be denied the benefits of, or be subjected to discrimination under any program or activity receiving Federal financial assistance or under any program or activity conducted by any Executive agency.

Removing Old Barriers

While Title VII assured certain groups of protection from discrimination in employment decisions, workers with disabilities continued to face the frustration of physical and attitudinal employment barriers long after the passage of Title VII—employers refused to hire the disabled for fear that they would not be able to perform at the same level as other employees, or employers had concerns about challenges based on the attitudes of co-workers. Disabled applicants found that they were required to prove themselves and their abilities to a much greater extent than did able-bodied applicants.

LO1

Approximately 54 million Americans, or about one in five, have one or more physical or mental disabilities.[2] In 2007, more than 15 years after the American with Disabilities Act (ADA) was signed into law, only 36.9 percent of working-age individuals with disabilities were employed, compared to 79.7 percent for those without disabilities (they tend to be the "last hired and first fired").[3] However, research has shown that the performance of a disabled worker, when properly placed, equals that of an able-bodied worker. It also has been shown that a disabled employee may in fact surpass co-workers as he or she overcomes the effects of his or her disability—both real and perceived (see Exhibit 13.1, "What Is in a Name?").

These numbers have a real impact on the rest of the population, of course. The poverty rate among working-age individuals without disabilities is 10 percent, while the rate among individuals living with disabilities jumps to 25 percent.[4] Since research shows that this latter population is often able to work but kept out of the workplace because of misperceptions, the burden of supporting those living in poverty could be reduced.[5]

Exhibit 13.1   *What Is in a Name?*

Throughout this chapter, we will use the word *disabled* to refer to individuals who have different abilities than the norm in the workplace. In the past, these individuals have been called handicapped, among other terms. The origins of that word were originally mistakenly connected to the term "cap in hand," referring to those who begged in the streets with their caps in hand on behalf of disabled veterans after a brutal war in England in 1504 during the reign of King Henry VII.

However, the correct etymology, in fact, is a lottery game from the 1600s, "hand-in-cap." The game involved a comparison between two items to be bartered between traders. Where the items were of unequal value, the amount of difference was placed into a cap, shortened to "hand i'cap." The term later came to reference any means by which people created an equalization such as in balancing wagers at horse tracks or casinos.

Today, *handicap* has been seen by some as offensive because it stresses a lack of ability or area in need of compensation, thus perpetuating discrimination or discriminatory perception. Indeed, even the term *disability* has been criticized in favor of *less abled.* However, because that latter term seems to accentuate further an absence or exclusion rather than a neutral or positive perception, we have opted for the currently common usage, "disabled."

Employers have yet to recognize the potential lost by their underutilization of this valuable resource. Instead, many employment decisions regarding disabled applicants are grounded in naïve prejudice. Often, managers reach inaccurate conclusions related to the scope of the disabled applicant's abilities and are apprehensive regarding the perceived costs of employing a disabled person. For instance, an employer who invites an applicant to her office for an interview based on a stellar résumé may be surprised to discover that the applicant is blind. The employer may immediately jump to the conclusion that this blind applicant is not qualified for the position, which requires a great deal of reading. If it overlooks this candidate, however, the employer may be losing an excellent worker merely because it failed to recognize possible ways in which it might be able to accommodate the disability, allowing the applicant to make a meaningful contribution to the staff. In fact, many disabled workers are capable of performing the essential requirements of their position with little or no accommodation on the part of their employer. (See Exhibit 13.2, "Innovations Break Stereotypes.")

To ensure that an employer is reaping the greatest benefit from its applicant pool, the employer should be "disability-blind" and evaluate each applicant on the basis of her or his competence. This is true during all stages of employment, including the interview, hiring, employee relations, transfer requests, performance reviews, disciplinary decisions, and termination decisions.

Exhibit 13.2 *Innovations Break Stereotypes*

A distribution center opened by Walgreens in 2007 is performing at 20 percent greater efficiency than the firm's older facilities. While this would not otherwise be remarkable, this situation is particularly noteworthy in that 40 percent of the workers in that center are either mentally or physically disabled. The center is part of an innovative program established by Walgreens (and now also in place at Home Depot, McDonald's, Walmart, and elsewhere) to design positions and tasks that can be performed by individuals with disabilities. "'One thing we found is they can all do the job,' says Randy Lewis, a senior vice president of distribution and logistics at Walgreens, which is based in Deerfield, Ill. 'What surprised us is the environment that it's created. It's a building where everybody helps each other out.'"[1]

The context for the idea began when Walgreens was evaluating new technology that could make Walgreens' next round of distribution centers far more automated than in the past. Could Walgreens make the work simple enough to employ people with cognitive disabilities? It realized that employing disabled people was not going to affect the distribution center's costs or efficiency at all. Therefore, "[i]t didn't move the needle on the business decision," said David Bernauer, then chief executive and now its chairman.

[1] Amy Merrick, "Erasing 'Un' from 'Unemployable': Walgreens Program Trains the Disabled to Take on Regular Wage-Paying Jobs," *The Wall Street Journal*, August 2, 2007, http://www.psycport.com/showArticle.cfm?xmlFile=ap_2007_08_02_ap.ds.dsf.all_D8QP0OEO1_news_ap_org.anpa.xml&provider=Associated%20Press.

Regulation

Section 503 of the Vocational Rehabilitation Act

In an effort to stem discrimination against disabled employees and applicants, Congress enacted the Vocational Rehabilitation Act of 1973, which applies to the government and any firm that does business with the government. Section 504 of the act prohibits discrimination against otherwise qualified individuals with disabilities by any program or activity receiving federal assistance. The Rehabilitation Act . . . seeks to remove those burdens that people with disabilities confront specifically because they have disabilities, so that they are left facing only the challenges normally faced by employees or applicants who are not disabled. **Section 503** of the act further requires that, where a federal department or agency enters into a contract that exceeds $10,000 annually, the contractor is required to take *affirmative action* to employ and promote qualified disabled individuals.[6] Where a contractor or subcontractor has 50 or more employees and contracts of $50,000 or more, it is required to have an affirmative action program at each establishment. Federal contractors, therefore, must take proactive steps to change their hiring policies, to recruit disabled employees, to train disabled employees so they are likely to advance, and to assist in their accommodation should they experience surmountable difficulties in their position.

The Rehabilitation Act's additional requirement of federal employers or contractors to employ and to advance disabled workers may include proactive steps to recruit disabled employees; modification of personnel practices to meet the needs of the disabled workforce such as special training for individuals who will be interviewing disabled applicants; and/or the training of supervisors and managers to provide a strong internal support and an environment in which a disabled employee would feel welcome.

Unfortunately, since it only applies to the government and federal contractors, the Vocational Rehabilitation Act was insufficient to prevent discrimination against private-sector employees and was inconsistently enforced against federal employers. Congress passed other statutes relating to discrimination against the disabled after the Rehabilitation Act, but on a segmented basis. Disabled veterans were protected by one statute and mine workers who had contracted black lung disease were protected by another; private-sector employers remained virtually immune from prosecution in this regard.

Americans with Disabilities Act

As the 1990s began, prior to passage of the **Americans with Disabilities Act (ADA)**, some legal protection against disability discrimination did exist. Congress had passed the Vocational Rehabilitation Act of 1973, but that law applied only to federal employees and those who contracted with the federal government. Title VII of the Civil Rights Act of 1964, which prohibited employment discrimination, was on the books, but disability was not one of the listed protected classes. On the other hand, however, most states had laws that explicitly prohibited

Section 503 of the Rehabilitation Act
Prohibits discrimination against otherwise-qualified individuals with disabilities by any program or activity receiving federal assistance. Requires affirmative action on the part of federal contractors and agencies to recruit, hire, and train disabled workers.

Americans with Disabilities Act
Extends Rehabilitation Act protection to employees in the private sector, with few modifications.

Exhibit 13.3 *Not Just* Americans *with Disabilities*

Significant not only as the first major human rights treaty of the 21st century, but also because it is expected to impact the 650 million people living with disabilities (10 percent of the world's population) and to provide benefits to more than 470 million disabled workers worldwide, the UN unanimously adopted the *Convention on Rights of Persons with Disabilities* on December 13, 2006. The convention prohibits discrimination against disabled workers in all forms of employment and also requires proactive efforts to create opportunities for people with disabilities in mainstream workplaces. At its adoption, outgoing United Nations Secretary-General Kofi Annan stressed, "Today promises to be the dawn of a new era—an era in which disabled people will no longer have to endure the discriminatory practices and attitudes that have been permitted to prevail for all too long. This convention is a remarkable and forward-looking document."[1]

The UN estimates that social exclusion of otherwise able workers costs the global economy an astronomical $1.9 trillion each year.[2]

[1] United Nations, press release, "Lauding Disability Convention as 'Dawn of a New Era,' UN Urges Speedy Ratification," December 13, 2006, http://www.un.org/apps/news/story.asp?NewsID=20975&Cr=disab&Cr1.

[2] Convention on the Rights of Persons with Disabilities, http://www.un.org/disabilities/convention/.

disability discrimination, so those in the private sector who were victims of disability discrimination could seek legal protection in state court if their state had such laws, but that was their only recourse. Congress passed other statutes relating to discrimination against the disabled after the Rehabilitation Act, but on a piecemeal basis. For example, disabled veterans were protected by one statute and mine workers who had contracted black lung disease were protected by another; private-sector employers remained virtually immune from prosecution at the federal level in this regard.

In 1992, however, Congress passed the ADA, which was seen by many disability advocates as the "Declaration of Independence" or "Emancipation Proclamation" for the disabled because it applied nationwide and because it extended legal protections to private employers. As it exists today, the ADA applies to all employers with at least 15 employees (25, originally) and its protections extend to private, state, and local government employees. Because the approach taken by the ADA was largely borrowed from the Vocational Rehabilitation Act of 1973, the protections are now similar for private, federal, state, and local disabled employees. (See also Exhibit 13.3, "Not Just *Americans* with Disabilities.") Even today, however, a majority of employers are unsure about many applications of the act. (See Exhibit 13.4, "Realities about Disability Discrimination.")

In 1998, however, the first report of the Presidential Task Force on the Employment of Adults with Disabilities released some disturbing findings on the effects of the ADA. The Task Force concluded that "enforcement mechanisms of the ADA have not proven sufficient to begin narrowing the gap in employment rates between people with and without disabilities. Enforcement of existing legislation . . . is clearly inadequate."[7]

Exhibit 13.4   *Realities about Disability Discrimination*

1. Employers may not question applicants about specific disabilities, only about their ability to engage in specific business-related activities.

2. An employer may have to alter the working environment in order to accommodate a disabled applicant or employee.

3. Employees with disabilities have no more rights to their jobs than do non-disabled applicants.

4. If someone does not have a disability but others believe she or he does, that person is protected against discrimination based on that misperception.

5. HIV status may be considered a disability under the ADA.

6. The definition of disability under the ADA is not limited only to physical disabilities.

7. Employers are not required to provide *any possible* accommodations requested by employees with disabilities.

8. The need for a reasonable accommodation for a preemployment test does not automatically disqualify an applicant from a job.

In an executive order later in 1998, President Clinton allocated funding to implement the Task Force's recommendations to help disabled adults find jobs.[8] In furtherance of these initiatives, in 2004, President George W. Bush established the New Freedom Initiative, designed to "help Americans with disabilities by increasing access to assistive technologies, expanding educational opportunities, increasing the ability of Americans with disabilities to integrate into the workforce, and promoting increased access into daily community life."[9] For example, the New Freedom Initiative established the Workforce Recruitment Program for college students with disabilities, an effort to help employers identify qualified temporary and permanent employees from a variety of fields.

While Congress and the White House were busy trying to implement effective anti-discrimination rules, employers were similarly busy trying to figure out how to comply with the ADA; and the courts were at work trying to interpret it. For employers, the ADA has proven to be different from any other anti-discrimination law because the ADA is the only such law that imposes a duty on employers to accommodate the protected class. The accommodation requirement, as we will discuss in more detail later in this chapter, has caused a great deal of confusion about what the law expects from employers. Meanwhile, the courts have for the most part narrowly interpreted the protections afforded by the ADA,[10] which is opposite from how courts have responded to other anti-discrimination laws, where they have basically interpreted protections as broadly as possible. As a result, the success rates of disabled employees who sue their employers have been generally lower than success rates for other types of employees.[11]

In 2008, largely in response to the general dissatisfaction with progress for disabled workers, Congress passed the ADA Amendments Act (ADAAA),[12] which sought to right some of the perceived wrongs in the way the law was written and the way it was being interpreted. In essence, by broadening and clarifying definitions of terms used in the ADA, the ADAAA mandates that the ADA be broadly rather than narrowly interpreted.[13]

Why Prohibiting Disability Discrimination Is So Difficult

LO2

To understand why the disability discrimination laws have been so difficult to implement, imagine you are the staff attorney on a subcommittee charged with writing a new law to prohibit disability discrimination. Your first step would be to define a "disability." When most people think of a disabled person, they think of someone who is sightless, hearing-impaired, or in a wheelchair. Those are easy enough but, under your definition, would you include any of the following conditions: depression, nicotine addiction, a disfiguring birthmark, neuroses, perfume allergy, AIDS, obesity, alcoholism, carpal tunnel syndrome, post-traumatic stress disorder, chronic fatigue syndrome, Internet addiction, migraine headaches, mild epilepsy with rare seizures, or being really short? What about someone who is denied a job because she has to care for a disabled person at home? What about someone who is perceived to be disabled by fellow workers, but who is otherwise healthy? How do you define "disability" neither too narrowly nor too broadly?

These definitional hurdles are just the beginning of the difficulties, as we shall see. The ADAAA contains a surprisingly long list of new terms, each of which has spawned its own debate about what that particular term means.

There is the additional challenge of how to manage employers who prefer to deny a job to a disabled person if hiring that person will cause the employer to spend extra money, perhaps to acquire specially equipped bathrooms, modified computer monitors, or even on additional health care costs. Do you create a statute that requires employers to make the accommodation? If so, what extent of accommodation is fair to expect of employers? Accommodations can involve facilities—bathroom modifications, entrance ramps, special parking spaces, computer equipment—but what about the myriad other types of accommodations, such as time off for medical treatments, guide dogs, paid human assistants, and asking fellow employees to cover some job tasks for the disabled employee? How much accommodation is too much accommodation and where do you draw the line?

When you begin to consider all the implications of disability discrimination laws, you begin to get a sense of why all the parties involved—those who wrote the laws, the administrative bodies that handle employee discrimination complaints, the courts that interpret the laws, disabled advocates, the disabled, and employers—have struggled mightily to understand and define what constitutes disability discrimination.

The Statutory Structure of the ADA

The ADA combines some features of other anti-discrimination laws with some entirely new features. Similar to other anti-discrimination statutes, the ADA prohibits both disparate treatment discrimination and disparate impact discrimination.[14] (For a more detailed discussion of both disparate treatment and disparate impact, please see Chapter 2.)

hostile work environment
A work environment in which harassment of an employee exists to such an extent that a reasonable employee would dread or fear going to work.

A third type of discrimination, also found in other anti-discrimination laws, is based on a **hostile work environment**. Typically, however, discrimination is not found unless the employer takes some employment action against the protected person, such as firing, demoting, or refusing to hire. Some courts, however, have found an implied right of the employee to be free from a hostile work environment, even in the absence of any employment action. For example, a hostile work environment could be created if fellow employees made fun of an employee's disability or otherwise created an intolerable situation at work. Some courts have imposed a duty on employers to end the teasing and to create an environment that is free from the hostility. With regard to the ADA, whether the hostile work environment exists depends upon the circuit in which you work. Some circuits have recognized the right, while others have not. (For more on the hostile work environment, see "Disability Harassment", below.)

To further complicate matters, employees can allege a pattern or practice of discrimination. Pattern-or-practice cases are tried in two stages. Stage one requires proof that the discrimination has been a regular procedure or policy. The employer must then prove that the evidence provided by the employees was inaccurate or insignificant. Proof can be met by showing numerous examples of discrimination, by using statistics, or by using anecdotal evidence from which discrimination can be inferred. For example, the party filing suit against a charter school for allegedly discriminating against disabled students was able to show a pattern and practice by providing 12 examples of disabled children who were either disenrolled or denied enrollment.[15] At this point, if the employees succeed, the court will grant equitable relief, usually ordering that the policy be stopped. Stage two consists of individual employees proving individual harm, armed with the stage-one finding that the policy was discriminatory.

If, on the other hand, an employment policy is facially discriminatory, the proof is different. In that case, the employee needs to prove only that the policy was illegal because the employer is not contesting the fact that it is discriminatory.

With those basic ideas in mind, let us turn to the actual requirements necessary to prove disability discrimination.

ADA and Rehabilitation Act protection
As long as an individual with a disability is otherwise qualified for a position, with or without reasonable accommodation, the employer may not make an adverse employment decision solely on the basis of the disability.

The *Prima Facie* Case for Disability Discrimination

LO3   **ADA and Rehabilitation Act protection** means that, generally, as long as the applicant or employee is otherwise qualified for the position, with or without reasonable accommodation, the employer is prohibited from making any adverse employment decision solely on the basis of the disability. An employer may not terminate an employee, for example, who is able to adequately perform merely because the employee uses a walker to assist in his or her mobility. An employee may be able to claim discrimination on the basis of her or his disability if the employee can prove, in addition to the fact that the ADA applies to her or his employer, the following (see also Exhibit 13.5, "Proving a Case of Disability Discrimination"):

1. She or he is disabled.
2. She or he is otherwise qualified for the position.
3. If an accommodation is required, the accommodation is reasonable.
4. She or he suffered an adverse employment decision such as a termination or demotion.

Employers should keep in mind that there are state laws as well as the federal laws that protect employees from discrimination. Employees filing claims based on a disability may find greater relief in state courts, applying state laws. In some states, damages are higher for disability discrimination under state laws, and claims are easier to prove than in federal courts applying the federal laws.[16]

The key to understanding the *prima facie* approach established by the ADA is to have clarity surrounding the definitions of the terms used in the act. As we shall see shortly, the definition of "disabled" creates two new terms that must be defined: "major life activity" and "substantially limits." The second element, that the employee be otherwise qualified for the position, requires an understanding of what is meant by "otherwise qualified." That definition will in turn, as we shall see, require an understanding of the definition for "essential functions." And, finally, the third element requires that the employer "reasonably accommodate" the employee, the ADA term that probably has caused the most trouble in terms of its definition and one that, in turn, requires an understanding of what is meant by "undue hardship." It can get complicated. Let us tackle the terms one at a time.

Disability

disability
"A physical or mental impairment that substantially limits one or more of the major life activities of an individual; a record of such impairment; or being regarded as having such an impairment." [From the ADA regulations.]

In our earlier analysis, we touched on the difficulties inherent in defining the term "disability." The drafters of the ADA defined **disability** as "(a) a physical or mental impairment that substantially limits one or more of the major life activities of an individual; (b) a record of having such impairment; or (c) being regarded as having such an impairment." Three important points are worth noting about the choice the drafters made when defining disability. First, there are three separate possibilities for triggering ADA protection. Second, disability is determined, not on the basis of the name or diagnosis of the employee's impairment but, instead, on the basis of the *effect* the impairment has on the disabled person's life. Third, the definition contains no definitive list of impairments that are considered to be disabilities (although some states have laws that mandate that certain conditions be considered disabilities). Courts are directed to reach determinations on a case-by-case basis. Examples of impairments that subsequently have been considered *not* to be disabilities include normal pregnancy, predisposition to an illness or disease, personality traits such as a quick temper (unless part of an underlying psychological disorder), or advanced age.

The first definition of disability refers to a physical or mental impairment that substantially limits one or more of the major life activities of an individual. This

Exhibit 13.5 *Proving a Case of Disability Discrimination*

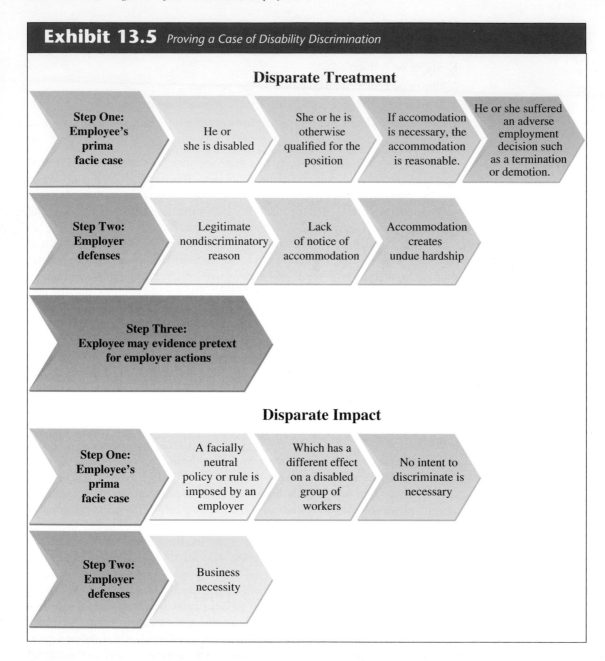

Disparate Treatment

Step One: Employee's prima facie case → He or she is disabled → She or he is otherwise qualified for the position → If accomodation is necessary, the accommodation is reasonable. → He or she suffered an adverse employment decision such as a termination or demotion.

Step Two: Employer defenses → Legitimate nondiscriminatory reason → Lack of notice of accommodation → Accommodation creates undue hardship

Step Three: Exployee may evidence pretext for employer actions

Disparate Impact

Step One: Employee's prima facie case → A facially neutral policy or rule is imposed by an employer → Which has a different effect on a disabled group of workers → No intent to discriminate is necessary

Step Two: Employer defenses → Business necessity

definition of disability itself opens up the need for further definitions. What is meant by "substantially limits"? And what constitutes a "major life activity"? The drafters of the ADA left those definitions to the courts and to the Equal Employment Opportunity Commission.

Before we move forward to examine the terms "major life activities" and "substantially limits" found in the first definition, let us address the second and third definitions of disability. One of the most well-known cases discussing a "record" of impairment is *School Board of Nassau County v. Arline,* decided under the Vocational Rehabilitation Act.[17] In the *Arline* case, the record of impairment was found in the employee's 1957 hospitalization for tuberculosis. Tuberculosis was such a serious illness in 1957 that anyone who had it was acknowledged to have an illness that interfered with a major life activity, namely, breathing.

The third definition is being regarded as having such an impairment, which is a curious part of the definition of disability because it suggests that someone who is not disabled can still be covered under the ADA as long as she or he is perceived by the employer as being disabled. For example, an employee with hepatitis C might be perceived incorrectly as being incapable of functioning while, in fact, no symptoms of the disease are manifested or inhibiting.

Congress included an employee who is perceived as being disabled in the definition of disability because it was concerned with discrimination stemming from simple prejudice, and also from "archaic attitudes and laws" and from "the fact that the American people are simply unfamiliar [with] and insensitive to the difficulties confront[ing] individuals with disabilities." (See Exhibit 13.6, "Attitudinal Barriers.")

In 2008, the ADAAA clarified that a plaintiff is regarded as having an impairment if she or he can demonstrate that "he or she has been subjected to an action prohibited under [the ADA] because of an actual or perceived physical or mental impairment, whether or not the impairment limits or is perceived to limit a major life activity." However, individuals who are "regarded as" having a transitory or minor impairment with an actual or expected duration of six months or less are not covered by the act.

In one particularly interesting case, a telemarketer who was missing 18 teeth was fired from his position after only three days of training. Even though he had generally positive evaluations in the training program, the trainers reported that the gentleman mumbled on the phone. The worker claimed that he did not have a disability and that his missing teeth did not cause him to mumble; he filed an ADA claim based on his employer's *perception* that he was disabled. The district court held that, since the worker did not actually have a disability, he could not sustain a claim that his employer perceived him as disabled. Without finding whether mumbling would be considered a disability, the Seventh Circuit reversed, holding that, "[i]f, for no reason whatsoever, an employer regards a person as disabled—for example, because of a blunder in reading medical records, it imputes to him a heart condition he has never had—and takes an adverse action, it has violated the [ADA]."[18] (Note that, on remand, the district court found that mumbling would not substantially limit a major life activity. Therefore, a decision based on a *perception* of mumbling could not be considered a violation of the ADA.)

In *Justice v. Crown Cork and Seal Company, Inc.,*[19] the employee, after working for his employer for 10 years, suffered a stroke that affected his vision, speaking, walking, and balance. He mostly recovered from his conditions and was able to work under certain restrictions for a couple of years. Following a strike, however, the employee was reassigned, ultimately being reassigned as a janitor, a position

Exhibit 13.6 *Attitudinal Barriers*

People with disabilities encounter many different forms of attitudinal barriers:

Inferiority. Because a person may be impaired in one of life's major functions, some people believe that individual is a "second-class citizen." However, most people with disabilities have skills that make the impairment moot in the workplace.

Pity. People feel sorry for the person with a disability, which tends to lead to patronizing attitudes. People with disabilities generally don't want pity and charity, just equal opportunity to earn their own way and live independently.

Hero worship. People consider someone with a disability who lives independently or pursues a profession to be brave or "special" for overcoming a disability. But most people with disabilities do not want accolades for performing day-to-day tasks. The disability is there; the individual has simply learned to adapt by using his or her skills and knowledge, just as everybody adapts to being tall, short, strong, fast, easy-going, bald, blonde, etc.

Ignorance. People with disabilities are often dismissed as incapable of accomplishing a task without the opportunity to display their skills. In fact, people with quadriplegia can drive cars and have children. People who are blind can tell time on a watch and visit museums. People who are deaf can play baseball and enjoy music. People with developmental disabilities can be creative and maintain strong work ethics.

The Spread Effect. People assume that an individual's disability negatively affects other senses, abilities or personality traits, or that the total person is impaired. For example, many people shout at people who are blind or don't expect people using wheelchairs to have the intelligence to speak for themselves. Focusing on the person's abilities rather than his or her disability counters this type of prejudice.

Stereotypes. The other side of the spread effect is the positive and negative generalizations people form about disabilities. For example,

many believe that all people who are blind are great musicians or have a keener sense of smell and hearing, that all people who use wheelchairs are docile or compete in paralympics, that all people with developmental disabilities are innocent and sweet-natured, that all people with disabilities are sad and bitter. Aside from diminishing the individual and his or her abilities, such prejudice can set too high or too low a standard for individuals who are merely human.

Backlash. Many people believe individuals with disabilities are given unfair advantages, such as easier work requirements. Employers need to hold people with disabilities to the same job standards as co-workers, though the means of accomplishing the tasks may differ from person to person. The Americans with Disabilities Act (ADA) does not require special privileges for people with disabilities, just equal opportunities.

Denial. Many disabilities are "hidden," such as learning disabilities, psychiatric disabilities, epilepsy, cancer, arthritis and heart conditions. People tend to believe these are not bona fide disabilities needing accommodation. The ADA defines "disability" as an impairment that "substantially limits one or more of the major life activities." Accommodating "hidden" disabilities which meet the above definition can keep valued employees on the job and open doors for new employees.

Fear. Many people are afraid that they will "do or say the wrong thing" around someone with a disability. They therefore avert their own discomfort by avoiding the individual with a disability. As with meeting a person from a different culture, frequent encounters can raise the comfort level.

Breaking Down Barriers

Unlike physical and systematic barriers, attitudinal barriers that often lead to illegal discrimination cannot be overcome simply through laws. The best remedy is familiarity, getting people with and without disabilities to mingle as co-workers, associates, and

continued

social acquaintances. In time, most of the attitudes will give way to comfort, respect, and friendship.

Tips for interacting with people with disabilities:

- Listen to the person with the disability. Do not make assumptions about what that person can or cannot do.

- When speaking with a person with a disability, talk directly to that person, not through his or her companion. This applies whether the person has a mobility impairment or a mental impairment, is blind or is deaf and uses an interpreter.

- Extend common courtesies to people with disabilities as you would anyone else. Shake hands or hand over business cards. If the person cannot shake your hand or grasp your card, they will tell you. Do not be ashamed of your attempt, however.

- If the customer has a speech impairment and you are having trouble understanding what he or she is saying, ask the person to repeat rather than pretend you understand. The former is respectful and leads to accurate communication; the latter is belittling and leads to embarrassment.

- Offer assistance to a person with a disability, but wait until your offer is accepted before you help.

- It is okay to feel nervous or uncomfortable around people with disabilities, and it's okay to admit that. It is human to feel that way at first. When you encounter these situations, think "person" first instead of disability; you will eventually relax.

Source: Office of Disability Employment Policy, http://www.dol.gov/odep/pubs/ek99/barriers.htm.

far below the jobs he previously held. The Tenth Circuit Court of Appeals held that the employee qualified as disabled under the "regarded as" definition, which the court said focuses on the employer's subjective state of mind. Does the employer mistakenly believe that the employee is substantially limited in performing a major life activity? In this case, the court determined that the employer regarded the employee as disabled from a major life activity, namely, working, despite the fact that his doctor released him to work subject to a few restrictions.

In another case, a woman with a dark purple birthmark covering her face was repeatedly denied promotions at the fast food restaurant where she worked.[20] After being told by her manager that she would never be promoted because she "would scare the customers off," she filed a complaint with the EEOC, which found that she had been discriminated against because her employer regarded her as disabled even though she was perfectly capable of performing the job.

Violations where the employer perceives the employee as disabled are somewhat confusing because they seem counterintuitive to the real world; the courts seem to be asking employers to accommodate disabilities that do not actually exist. But, when viewed in light of the effort to remove stereotypes so that they do not negatively impact otherwise able employees, the decisions make more sense. If an employer insists on pursuing a faulty prejudice, then it cannot later claim the employee is not disabled and have it both ways. In fact, in a 2006 case, *Gelfo v. Lockheed Martin,*[21] the court held that, where an employee suffers an adverse employment action because of a disability or perceived disability, the employee need not even prove the disability in the first place. That element of the *prima facie* case is taken as established.

Scenario

One final element of the "perceived as" disability relates to someone who is perceived as disabled based on her or his association or relationship with someone who has a disability, whether or not the employee or applicant has a disability herself or himself. Again, the purpose of this extension of the ADA protection is to prevent stereotypes from adversely impacting individuals who associate with disabled individuals, such as a child, partner, or parent. The EEOC guidelines on the issue offers the following example:

> An employer is interviewing applicants for a computer programmer position. The employer determines that one of the applicants is the best qualified, but is reluctant to offer him the position because he learns that the applicant has a child with a disability. The employer violates the ADA if it refuses to hire the applicant based on its belief that the applicant's need to care for his child will have a negative impact on his work performance or attendance.

Interestingly, the ADA does *not* require that the employer reasonably accommodate the worker since it is not the worker who has the disability. Therefore, if, in the end, the association with the disabled child does, in fact, have a negative impact on performance or attendance that interferes with the essential functions of the position, then the employer is permitted to terminate the worker. However, it cannot prejudge the worker based on a stereotype beforehand.[22]

LO5

impairment
"Any physiological disorder or condition . . . affecting one or more of the following body systems: neurological; musculoskeletal; special sense organs; respiratory, including speech organs; cardiovascular; reproductive; digestive; genitourinary; hemic and lymphatic; skin; and endocrine; or any mental or psychological disorder" that substantially limits one of life's major activities. [From the EEOC regulations.]

major life activities
"[F]unctions such as caring for one's self, performing manual tasks, walking, seeing, hearing, speaking, breathing, learning and working." [From the EEOC regulations.]

Major Life Activity

Not surprisingly, the Supreme Court originally interpreted the term **impairment** or **major life activity** narrowly, including only those activities that are of "central importance to most people's daily lives."[23] Then the ADAAA came along and expanded what is meant by a major life activity, although it did not provide its own definition. Instead, the ADAAA provided the following list of examples of major life activities: caring for oneself, performing manual tasks, seeing, hearing, eating, sleeping, walking, standing, lifting, bending, speaking, breathing, learning, reading, concentrating, thinking, communicating, communicating, and working.[24] Importantly, the ADAA also extended the definition of major life activities to include bodily functions, such as immune system functions, reproductive functions, respiratory and circulatory functions, normal cell growth, and bladder and bowel functions.[25]

In *Wright v. CompUSA, Inc.,*[26] Stephen Wright claimed discrimination on the basis of his attention deficit disorder (ADD). The court disagreed, holding that Wright failed to present evidence that he "could not perform some usual activity compared with the general population, or that he had a continuing inability to handle stress at all times, rather than only episodically." Though Wright claimed limitation in reading, spelling, concentrating, and hearing, among other activities, these impairments only occurred when Wright worked for a manager with a particularly demanding management style. Though these activities, if significantly impaired, would constitute major life activities, Wright's ADD was deemed episodic and therefore not a substantial limitation.[27] Under the ADAAA, however, Wright's claim would likely have prevailed.

While some employees have argued a "bootstrap" theory of coverage—that if an employer denies a position to an applicant on the basis of his impairment, such denial may be just the act necessary for the employee to prove that the impairment constitutes a disability—this argument has not been traditionally accepted by the courts. However, this particular area is where the impact of the ADAAA—both financial and otherwise—might be felt in the near future, warn some commentators. The act specifically encourages that the term *disability* shall be construed broadly in favor of coverage of individuals. In addition, the amendments also modify current holdings in that "an impairment that substantially limits one major life activity need not limit other major life activities in order to be [considered to be] a disability."

Therefore, the dilemma faced by some courts involves an impairment that substantially limits interactivity with others. Several circuits have been asked to rule on whether that would constitute a major life activity. Though one might think otherwise by virtue of human nature, the First Circuit has held that "getting along with others" is not a major life activity under the ADA, whereas the Ninth Circuit has found that "interacting with others" is a major life activity. The Second Circuit agrees with the First, holding that "getting along" is too subjective to be enforceable, but did find that "interacting with others" is essential to major life activity. Confusing? Yes. In *Jacques v. DiMarzio, Inc.,* the Second Circuit imposed a new test for the standard, finding that a worker is substantially limited in the major life activity of interacting with others when the

> mental or physical impairment severely limits the individual's fundamental ability to communicate with others, when the impairment severely limits the individual's ability to connect with others, i.e. to initiate contact with other people and respond to them, or to go among other people.[28]

Substantially Limits

Case 1

The standard to be applied in determining whether a worker is disabled is whether she or he is **substantially limited** in a major life activity. The courts have defined *substantially limited* to mean something that "prevents or severely restricts,"[29] which is a restrictive interpretation when you consider that employers could use it to deny disability status to any employee who is not *entirely* prevented from a major life activity. The U.S. Supreme Court, in *Sutton v. United Air Lines, Inc.,*[30] has also imposed what has become known as the "mitigating measures" rule, which means that the determination of whether a person has a disability must consider any mitigating or corrective measures that can be used to offset the impairment. The most obvious example, and the one involved in *Sutton,* is considering that an employee with poor vision is not disabled because the vision can be corrected with glasses. The rule seems reasonable—until you move to questions such as whether an employer can consider various medications in determining whether an employee is disabled. Can an employer, for example, declare that an employee is not disabled because a particular drug on the market has been shown to normalize the employee's condition? Most troublingly, the Supreme

substantially limited

"[U]nable to perform a major life activity that the average person in the general population can perform; or significantly restricted as to the condition, manner, or duration under which an individual can perform a major life activity." [From the EEOC regulations.]

Court also extended the "mitigating measures" rule to include systems at work inside the employee's own body.[31] As a result, employers have used the mitigating factor of an employee's faulty internal system to deny disability under the ADA to those with severe physical and mental impairments.[32]

The ADAAA, however, completely invalidated the "mitigating measures" rule and its extensions,[33] although it also specifically stated that employers are allowed to consider the mitigating effects of eyeglasses and contact lenses. Where that left us is not entirely clear, other than to say that the courts are no longer supposed to interpret the definition of disability narrowly.

In *Thomas v. Avon Prods., Inc.,*[34] the court held that migraine headaches caused by exposure to chemicals in the working environment did not constitute a disability. In *Thomas,* the employee worked at a perfume manufacturing plant and found that the "perfumed ambiance" caused her migraine headaches. Since her condition only prevented her from participating in those jobs surrounded by those odors, rather than "a broad range of jobs in various classes," she was "not substantially limited in a major life activity" and therefore was not disabled under the ADA.

Scenario

In 1986, the Department of Justice issued an opinion that stated that, if fear of contagion is the basis for the termination, the employee is not considered disabled and is not protected under the Rehabilitation Act because the ability to communicate the disease to another is not a disability. The opinion made no distinction based on whether the fear of contagion is reasonable or unreasonable on the part of the employer. However, the Department of Justice opinion was in direct contravention of the Supreme Court's later determination in *Arline,* which specifically stated that chronic contagious diseases are considered to be protected disabilities. The Department of Justice thereafter issued a second memorandum that reversed its earlier analysis in connection with HIV after then-Surgeon General Koop informed the Justice Department that physical impairment is almost always present. Do you believe that someone who is contagious due to a congenital disease, but who exhibits no physical impairment, is considered disabled under the act? We will discuss HIV again with regard to the question of *direct threat* later in this chapter.

The ADA Amendments Act of 2008 specifically overruled the Supreme Court's decision in *Toyota Motor Manufacturing, Kentucky, Inc. v. Williams.*[35] In that case, the Court articulated a demanding standard for the terms "substantially" and "major" in the definition of disability under the ADA. It held that, to be substantially limited in performing a major life activity under the ADA, "an individual must have an impairment that prevents or severely restricts the individual from doing activities that are of central importance to most people's daily lives." To the contrary, however, in enacting the ADAAA, Congress explained that "the question of whether an individual's impairment is a disability under the ADA should not demand extensive analysis."[36]

Otherwise Qualified

The acts state that an employer may not terminate or refuse to hire an employee with a disability who is "otherwise qualified" to perform the essential requirements of his or her position. The determination of a position's essential functions ensures that disabled persons are not disqualified simply because they may have difficulty in performing tasks that bear only a marginal relationship to a particular job. In that way, employers protect themselves from liability and are able to most effectively utilize their human resources.

In one case, the court held that a civilian employee of the Navy failed to establish that she was qualified for her position due to her chronic fatigue syndrome. The court noted that "the accommodation plaintiff seeks is simply to be allowed to work only when her illness permits." The court held that the employee was not otherwise qualified because she was not prepared to pull her full weight. In addition, an employer may not consider the possibility that an employee or applicant will become disabled or unqualified for the position in the future. If the applicant or employee is qualified *at the time the adverse employment action is taken,* the employer has violated the acts.[37]

It is important to note that the ADA Amendments prohibit the use of any qualification test or other selection criteria to determine whether someone is "otherwise qualified" based on that individual's unmitigated or uncorrected disability, unless it can be shown that it is a business necessity.

Direct Threat

Where the claim of disability is based on a disease, the court in the *Arline* case (discussed earlier) held that the determination of whether an individual is "otherwise qualified" should be based on the following factors:

- The nature of the risk (how the disease is transmitted).
- The duration of the risk (how long the carrier is infectious).
- The severity of the risk (potential harm to third parties).
- The probability that the disease will be transmitted and will cause varying degrees of harm.

Scenario

HIV and AIDS have presented questions to employers, and therefore to the courts, over the past few decades with regard to the ADA. The Supreme Court's decision in the *Arline* case is important because it serves, by implication, as a proclamation that the act safeguards the rights of employees with HIV or AIDS. Subsequent to *Arline,* the Supreme Court decided *Bragdon v. Abbott,*[38] in which it held that that HIV represented an impairment that *substantially limits* reproduction, and that reproduction is a *major life activity* under the ADA. The Court stated, "HIV infection must be regarded as a physiological disorder with a constant and detrimental effect on the infected person's hemic and lymphatic systems from the moment of infection." The Court also noted that HIV substantially limited reproduction, a major life activity. This case challenges many lower court decisions that have held a condition must more or less visibly interfere with the person's public life or economic life on a fairly consistent basis to be a disability under the ADA. However, the Court in *Bragdon* states, in effect, that there are some conditions that are inherent disabilities if they so greatly affect the human biological system, in this case the HIV virus. This is especially significant, given the fact that there are as many as 950,000 HIV-positive employees in the work-force today.[39]

The issue of the *level of risk* the disabled employee poses to herself or to others is crucial to the determination of whether the applicant is otherwise qualified for the position. The standard for balancing the risk of harm to others against the employer's duties under the acts is whether the employer can show there is a *direct threat* to the health and safety of the potential employee or others. For example, as it has been shown that HIV is not transmitted through casual but only through intimate contact, it is extremely unlikely that a showing of reasonable probability of infection can be made. Therefore, employers who take adverse employment actions based on the unreasonable complaints or fears of co-employees or customers relating to HIV would violate either the Rehabilitation Act or the ADA. Such was the case when the performance company Cirque du Soleil terminated Matthew Cusick, an HIV-positive gymnast, after he concluded preparations for an aerial act in the Las Vegas show "Mystere." Prior to a later settlement, Renée-Claude Ménard, a Cirque spokesperson, explained, "the reasons that motivated our decision have nothing to do with discrimination, but safety," claiming that the company couldn't risk infection of other performers or patrons.[40] However, as this flies in the face of common knowledge about the means of infection discussed above, the parties reached a $600,000 settlement through the EEOC. The settlement included a provision by which Cirque du Soleil agreed to waive confidentiality surrounding the settlement, as well as requirements that Cirque appoint an EEO officer to oversee EEO training of all employees and post a notice about the resolution of this case in its workplace.[41]

The question of *direct threat* is not only whether the employee poses a threat to others, but also whether continued work will pose a direct threat to the employee. This was the question faced by the Supreme Court in *Chevron USA v. Echazabal*,[42] where Chevron refused to employ Echazabal because exposure to toxins at its refinery would have aggravated Echazabal's hepatitis C. Chevron defended itself on the basis of the direct threat that employment would pose to Echazabal's health. The Ninth Circuit disagreed with Chevron, holding that this was an inappropriate inquiry in the context of hiring and was only relevant to the context of ongoing employment.[43] The Supreme Court reversed the Ninth Circuit, rejecting the restrictive language and reaffirming the direct-threat defense for the employer. The Court warned employers, however, that the defense is *only available* when based on "reasonable medical judgment and an individualized assessment" of the circumstances.

A 2006 case that involved a Type II diabetic reinforced the requirement of reasonableness on the part of employers. The court in that case explained in exceptionally strong language that the employer's "blanket policy of refusing to hire what it characterizes as 'uncontrolled' diabetics violates [a] fundamental tenet of ADA law; it embraces what the ADA detests: reliance on 'stereotypes and generalizations' about an illness when making employment decisions. . . . [A]n employer cannot slavishly defer to a physician's opinion without first pausing to assess the objective reasonableness of the physician's conclusions."[44]

Essential Functions

essential functions
Those tasks that are fundamental, not marginal or unnecessary, to the fulfillment of the position's objectives. The employer may not take an adverse employment action against a disabled employee based on the disability where the individual can perform the essential functions of the position.

For an employer to determine whether a worker or applicant is otherwise qualified for a position, the employer must first ascertain the **essential functions** of that position. For example, some companies require that all employees have a driver's license, "in case of emergencies." While this is a meritorious request, the ability to drive is not always a basic requirement of the positions themselves but, instead, is marginal to the objectives of each position. An applicant who cannot drive because of a disability is otherwise qualified for the position, unless the position specifically has driving as its integral purpose, such as a taxi driver or delivery person.

The term *essential* refers to those tasks that are fundamental, and not marginal or unnecessary, to fulfillment of the position's objectives. Often this determination depends on whether removing the function would fundamentally change the job. Disabled persons may not be disqualified simply because they may have difficulty in performing tasks that bear only a marginal relationship to a particular job. How does an employer determine what job tasks are considered essential? Employers may not include in their job descriptions responsibilities that are incidental to the actual job or duties that are not generally performed by someone in this position. The employer must look not to the means of performing a function but, instead, to the function desired to be accomplished. Some employers are shocked to find that an individual with disabilities may discover innovative and novel means to accomplish the same task. On the other hand, some individuals cannot perform the essential functions of their jobs no matter what accommodation they might request. For instance, in one case, as a result of his disability, a corrections officer did not have the physical ability to restrain inmates during an emergency. The court held that this ability was an essential function of his position and therefore he was not qualified under the ADA.[45]

Can a job function be *essential* where someone was in the position for 16 years and never performed this task? Is the frequency with which the function must be performed relevant to determining whether it is essential? In one case, the Fourth Circuit Court of Appeals determined that frequency is just one factor that a manager should look to in determining the essential functions of the position. *Champ v. Baltimore County, MD*[46] involved a police officer who sustained an arm injury and was put on light duty. Whole officers were not supposed to remain on light duty for more than 251 days; this officer continued to work in this capacity for 16 years. The chief of police then determined that all officers must be able to perform the full duties of a police officer. The court held that this officer could not perform the job's essential functions with or without reasonable accommodation and upheld the officer's termination.

One of the more perplexing issues to have developed since the ADA's inception is attendance. While the EEOC has viewed attendance as being an important but not an essential function of a job, allowing for a waiver of attendance policies as a reasonable accommodation, some courts have disagreed. In addition, courts have held that employees with erratic, unexplained absences are not protected, even if the attendance issues are due to a disability.[47]

You will have a chance to read, in the *Pickens v. Soo Line Railroad Co.* case at the end of the chapter, the Eighth Circuit Court of Appeals' important analysis of whether attendance is an essential element of the plaintiff's position and whether a sporadic lack of attendance (whenever the plaintiff's back injury flared up) was sufficient for termination. Though the case is from 2001, it continues to be cited[48] for its holding that "regular and reliable attendance is a necessary element of most jobs. Even though the railroad's system of scheduling appears quite flexible, the railroad's policy requires regular, reliable attendance, and Pickens' conductor's job was full-time. . . . An employee who is unable to come to work on a regular basis is unable to satisfy any of the functions of the job in question, much less the essential ones."

The concept of essential functions under the ADA and the Rehabilitation Act differs slightly from the job-relatedness requirement for selection criteria under Title VII. Under Title VII, an employer has a defense to a claim of discrimination if it can show that the basis for the discrimination was the employee's failure to satisfy job-related requirements. Under the ADA and the Rehabilitation Act, however, the court will look one step further. The requirement may be job-related, but the court will look to whether that requirement is also consistent with business necessity. In addition, courts disfavor employers who make general exclusions on the basis of business necessity, unless it can be shown that all or substantially all of the individuals who satisfy that category of disability could not do the job, or the exclusion is justified by the high personal or financial risk involved, which cannot be protected against. For example, in *Davis v. Bucher,*[49] a categorical exclusion of methadone program participants and those with a history of drug addiction was ruled unlawful, as was a general prohibition against epileptics in the workforce in *Duran v. City of Tampa.*[50]

Reasonable Accommodation

Scenario

reasonable accommodation
An accommodation to the individual's disability that does not place an undue burden or hardship (courts use the language interchangeably) on the employer.

An applicant or employee is otherwise qualified for the position if, with or without **reasonable accommodation**, the worker can perform the essential functions of the position. Reasonable accommodation in this context generally means the removal of unnecessary restrictions or barriers. Reasonable accommodation is further defined as a modification that does not place an *undue burden* or *hardship* on the employer. Therefore, as one commentator wrote, "reasonable accommodation is but one side of the coin; undue hardship . . . is the other side." The reasonableness of the accommodation may be determined by looking to the size of the employer, the cost to the employer, the type of employer, and the impact of the accommodation on the employer's operations. It is important to understand that each case will be determined by looking to the *particular* job responsibilities as they are impacted by the employee's or applicant's *particular* disability. Courts have referred to this inquiry as one that is "fact intensive and case specific."

Exhibit 13.7 *Reasonable Accommodation*

How far does the employer have to go for the disabled employee or applicant? The EEOC has defined "reasonable accommodation" in its regulations as follows:

1. The term "reasonable accommodation" means:
   (i) Any modification or adjustment to a job application process that enables a qualified individual with a disability to be considered for the position such qualified individual desires, and which will not impose an undue hardship on the covered entity's business; or
   (ii) Any modification or adjustment to the work environment, or to the manner or circumstances under which the position held or desired is customarily performed, that enables a qualified individual with a disability to perform the essential functions of that position, and which will not impose an undue hardship on the operation of the covered entity's business; or
   (iii) Any modification or adjustment that enables a covered entity's employee with a disability to enjoy the same benefits and privileges of employment as are enjoyed by its other similarly situated employees without disabilities, and which will not impose an undue hardship on the operation of the covered entity's business.

2. Reasonable accommodation may include but is not limited to:
   (i) Making facilities used by employees readily accessible to and usable by individuals with disabilities, and
   (ii) Job restructuring; part-time or modified work schedules; reassignment to a vacant position; acquisition or modification of equipment or devices; appropriate adjustment or modification of examinations, training materials, or policies; the provision of readers or interpreters; and other similar accommodations for individuals with disabilities.

Source: 29 C.F.R. § 1630.2(o).

It is generally believed that these types of accommodation expenses are normally quite low, with almost one-third costing nothing at all, 19 percent costing between $1.00 and $50.00, and 50 percent costing less than $500.00.[51] (See also Exhibits 13.7, "Reasonable Accommodation," and 13.8, "Cost Guidelines for Reasonable Accommodations.") Consider the economic balance between those costs and the following. About one-third of ADA complaints filed with the EEOC allege failure to provide reasonable accommodation and it is estimated that the average cost to an employer to defend these suits is approximately $30,000.[52]

An example of a reasonable accommodation is the adaptation of a work space for someone who uses a wheelchair. In a situation where an employer has two applicants for an open position, one who requires the use of a wheelchair and another who has no disability, the employer is not permitted to choose the applicant without a disability solely because of the need to modify the work space for the other applicant (that is, the obligation to provide a reasonable accommodation). But, referring to Scenario 1 at the introduction of this chapter, what if the wheelchair poses a significantly greater burden than merely adapting a work space?

In that situation, the position for which the disabled applicant applied required a great deal of traveling. Unless there is some reason to believe that the disabled

Exhibit 13.8 *Cost Guidelines for Reasonable Accommodations*

The Job Accommodation Network is a free service of the Office of Disability Employment Policy of the U.S. Department of Labor. JAN identifies possible disabilities and then makes suggestions for possible accommodations. The following are just two examples of accommodations for workers with various disabilities. *Please check JAN's Web site for an extensive list of disabilities and proposed accommodations.*[1]

RESPIRATORY AILMENTS (ALLERGIES)

Avoiding Environmental Triggers

It may be helpful to:

- Maintain a clean and healthy work environment.
- Provide air purification.
- Condition, heat, dehumidify, or add moisture to the air as appropriate.
- Provide additional rest breaks for the individual to get fresh air or take medication.
- Create a smoke- and fragrance-free work environment.
- Consider an alternative work arrangement such as work from home.
- Allow for alternative work arrangements when construction is taking place.
- Use alternative pest management practices.
- Implement a flexible leave policy.
- Allow for alternative means of communication such as telephone, e-mail, instant messaging, fax, or memos.

Accessibility Accommodations

It may be necessary to address access concerns for an individual who has difficulty approaching the work facility, moving around the facility, getting to work, or traveling as an essential job function.

- Modify the work site to make it accessible.
- Provide an accessible parking space with an unobstructed and easily traveled path into the workplace.

- Provide an entrance free of steps with doors that open automatically or that have a maximum opening force of five pounds.
- Provide an accessible route of travel to and from work areas used by the individual throughout the work environment.
- Consider providing a scooter or motorized cart for the employee to use for long distances if the employee does not already use a mobility aid.
- Move the individual's workstation closer to equipment, materials, and rooms the individual uses frequently.
- Modify the workstation to accommodate a wheelchair, scooter, or the use of oxygen therapy equipment.
- Arrange the workstation so materials and equipment are within reach range.
- Provide restrooms that are easily accessed from the individual's workstation.
- Review emergency evacuation procedures.

DEPRESSION[2]

Maintaining Stamina

- Allow flexible scheduling.
- Allow longer or more frequent work breaks.
- Provide additional time to learn new responsibilities.
- Provide self-paced workload.
- Provide backup coverage for when the employee needs to take breaks.
- Allow time off for counseling.
- Allow use of supported employment and job coaches.
- Allow employee to work from home during part of the day or week.

[1] http://www.jan.wvu.edu/media/atoz.htm (last visited July 31, 2007).

[2] The material is excerpted from JAN's Web site and is not a complete list of possible accommodations mentioned there.

continued

Maintaining Concentration

- Reduce distractions in the work area.
- Provide space enclosures or a private office.
- Allow for use of white noise or environmental sound machines.
- Allow the employee to play soothing music using a cassette player and headset.
- Increase natural lighting or provide full spectrum lighting.
- Allow the employee to work from home and provide necessary equipment.
- Plan for uninterrupted work time.
- Allow for frequent breaks.
- Divide large assignments into smaller tasks and goals.
- Restructure job to include only essential functions.

Interacting with Coworkers

- Educate all employees on their right to accommodations.
- Provide sensitivity training to coworkers and supervisors.

- Do not mandate that employees attend work-related social functions.
- Encourage all employees to move non-work-related conversations out of work areas.

Difficulty Handling Stress and Emotions

- Provide praise and positive reinforcement.
- Refer to counseling and employee assistance programs.
- Allow telephone calls during work hours to doctors and others for needed support.
- Allow the presence of a support animal.
- Allow the employee to take breaks as needed.

Attendance Issues

- Provide flexible leave for health problems.
- Provide a self-paced work load and flexible hours.
- Allow employee to work from home.
- Provide part-time work schedule.
- Allow employee to make up time.

Source: Reprinted with permission, Job Accommodation Network, Office of Disability Employment Policy, U.S. Department of Labor, http://www.jan.wvu.edu.

applicant would not be able to travel, the employer must afford her the opportunity. While accommodation may be necessary to allow her to travel, such as a modified schedule to allow her more time to get from one place to another, such accommodation would generally be considered reasonable and required.

Importantly, as noted previously, each case will be determined by looking to the *particular* job responsibilities as they are impacted by the employee or applicant's *particular* disability. Courts have referred to this inquiry as one that is "fact intensive and case specific." An accommodation need not be the best possible solution, but it must be sufficient to meet the needs of the individual with the disability. An employee who suffers from a congenital upper respiratory disease may be unable to maintain consistent stamina or a high degree of effort throughout an entire workday. The requirement of reasonable accommodation does not mean that the employer must create a new job, modify a full-time position to create a part-time position, or modify the essential functions of the job. However, the fact that a proposed accommodation conflicts with an employer's other workplace rules and policies does not necessarily mean that it is unreasonable.

Employers are not expected to accommodate employees by eliminating an essential function of the job, lowering a production standard that applies to all employees, or providing personal use items such as a prosthetic limb or a hearing aid. Employers are certainly permitted to make those accommodations; but they are not required to do so under the ADA.

With regard to workplace policies on reassignments, courts have held that an employer does not have to reassign a qualified disabled employee to a vacant position when the employee is not the *most* qualified worker for the job and the reassignment would violate the employer's legitimate non-discriminatory policy of hiring the *most* qualified candidate. In reaching this conclusion in a 2007 case included in the text, *Huber v. Wal-Mart Stores, Inc.,* the Eighth Circuit *overruled* the EEOC enforcement guidance that originally stipulated that a disabled employee should be entitled to reassignment if he or she is qualified to fill a vacant position, *even if he or she can no longer perform the essential functions of her or his own position.* In other words, even if the worker is not actually qualified for her or his own position, if she or he is qualified for some position within the organization, and even if she or he was not the most qualified, the EEOC advocated protection and reassignment. Moreover, the burden was originally on the employer to notify the worker of open positions for which she or he was qualified. However, as you will see when you review the *Huber* case, the Eighth Circuit, which is joined by the Seventh but opposed by the Tenth, has now diverted drastically from the EEOC's original suggestion. With split circuits, employers are left to follow guidance by jurisdiction until the Supreme Court resolves the dilemma.

Scenario 3 presents an issue of reasonable accommodation and concerns the definition of essential functions of a position. Our earlier discussion of the scenario in this chapter presumed that travel was simply part of the job requirements. If travel is an *essential function* of the position, Thekla Tsonis may be able to justify "ability to travel" as a qualification for employment. Even if it is a valid requirement, the wheelchair-bound applicant may be perfectly able and willing to travel. Tsonis should simply lay out the requirements of the position, then ask both applicants if there is any reason why they would not be able to perform these functions, with or without reasonable accommodation. The wheelchair-bound applicant may need some accommodation, such as assistance getting to and from the airport or, as discussed previously, schedules that allow her or him to have extra time to arrive at the airport. These would probably be viewed as reasonable accommodations.

Undue Hardship

Employers are not required to accommodate disabled employees if the accommodation would impose an undue hardship on the employer. The concept of undue hardship is not limited to financial difficulty but also may include any accommodation that would be unduly extensive, substantial, or disruptive, or that would fundamentally alter the nature or operation of the business. While employers also may attempt to show that they took an adverse employment action based on their fears relating to future absences or higher insurance costs, an undue hardship, or more than a *de minimis* cost that the employer should not have to bear, these are not acceptable defenses to a claim of discrimination. In fact, courts have gone out of their way to explain the nature of the concept of undue hardship. In *Kilcullen v. New York State Department of Transportation*,[53] the court explained that it means more than the term *readily achievable,* which is used in Title III governing the requirement to alter existing public accommodations. Readily achievable means "easily accomplishable and able to be carried out without much difficulty or expense," the court said. "The duty to provide reasonable accommodation, by contrast, is a much higher standard than the duty to remove barriers in existing buildings (if removing the barriers is readily achievable) and creates a more substantial obligation on the employer."

Undue hardship may be determined by examining the following factors:

- Nature and cost of the accommodation.
- Overall financial resources of the facility involved in the accommodation.
- Overall size of the employer.
- Type of operation of the employer.[54]

The EEOC guidelines add another requirement: the impact of the accommodation on the ability of the other employees to do their jobs and on the facility to conduct its business.[55]

Undue hardship under the ADA is distinct from the duty to provide reasonable accommodation under Title VII in cases of religious discrimination such as *TWA v. Hardison,* discussed earlier in the text. In that case, the court held that accommodations to religious beliefs need not be provided if the cost was more than a *de minimis* expense to the employer. Thus, the court held, "the definition of undue hardship in the ADA is intended to convey a significant, as opposed to a *de minimis,* or insignificant, obligation on the part of employers." As an example, in a case dealing with an employer's concern that an obese employee would cost the employer higher health care amounts in the future, the New York high court held that this was not a valid defense even though obese people, as a class, *are* at a greater risk for certain health problems than others. The case, *EEOC v. Convergys Customer Management Group, Inc.,* at the end of the chapter, examines whether permitting breach of a punctuality policy constitutes reasonable accommodation or undue hardship for an employer.

The appendix to the EEOC's ADA regulations suggests the following hypothetical situations as examples of the weight to be given to each of the factors in an "undue hardship" determination:

> [A] small day care center might not be required to expend more than a nominal sum, such as that necessary to equip a telephone for use by a secretary with impaired hearing, but a large school district might be required to make available a teacher's aide to a blind applicant for a teaching job. Further, it might be considered reasonable to require a state welfare agency to accommodate a deaf employee by providing an interpreter while it would constitute an undue hardship to impose that requirement on a provider of foster care services.

Exhibit 13.9 *Factors in Undue Hardship*

In connection with the definition of "undue hardship," the EEOC regulations direct the following:

In determining whether an accommodation would impose an undue hardship on the employer, factors to be considered include:

(i) The nature and cost of the accommodation needed under this part.

(ii) The overall financial resources of the facility or facilities involved in the provision of the reasonable accommodation, the number of people employed at such site, and the effect on expenses and resources.

(iii) The overall financial resources of the employer, the overall size of the business of the employer with respect to the number of its employees, and the number, type, and location of its facilities.

(iv) The type of operation or operations of the employer, including the composition, structure, and functions of the workforce of such entity, and the geographic separateness and administrative or fiscal relationship of the site or sites in question to the employer.

(v) The impact of the accommodation upon the operation of the site, including the impact on the ability of other employees to perform their duties, and the impact on the site's ability to conduct business.

In addition, where the cost of the accommodation would result in an undue hardship and outside funding is not available, the disabled employee or applicant should be given the option of paying the portion of the cost that constitutes an undue hardship. (See Exhibit 13.9, "Factors in Undue Hardship.")

Reasonable Accommodation and the Contingent Worker

Employment through staffing firms and temporary agencies offers individuals with disabilities unique opportunities to move into the workforce. During the employee shortage in early 2000, temporary agencies such as Manpower Inc. turned to workers with disabilities to fill their needs.[56] In December 2000, the EEOC issued its Enforcement Guidance "Application of the ADA to Contingent Workers Placed by Temporary Agencies and Other Staffing Firms." Only the staffing firm must provide reasonable accommodations for the application process before any client has been identified as a prospective employer. However, if an employer requests an applicant through the staffing firm, both the staffing firm and the prospective employer must provide reasonable accommodation.

When a staffing firm and its clients are joint employers of an individual with a disability, both are obligated to provide reasonable accommodation at the workplace. Of course, this obligation does not extend to undue hardship. Further, the staffing firm and its clients must have notice of the need for accommodation.

In order to ease the financial burden of providing accommodation, the Internal Revenue Service offers several federal tax incentives to eligible small businesses (those with either 30 or fewer full-time employees or $1 million or less in gross receipts in the preceding tax year) that make these accommodations.

First, they can take advantage of the Disabled Access Tax Credit—50 percent of eligible expenditures over $250 (but not over $10,250) made to provide access to the workplace for disabled workers. Second, any business may be eligible for a deduction for removing architectural or transportation barriers to disabled workers in the firm, up to $15,000 per year. (Eligible small businesses can take *both* of these deductions.) Finally, firms that hire workers who are "vocational rehabilitation referrals" certified by local employment agencies will be allowed a tax credit under the Work Opportunity Tax Credit (Internal Revenue Code, 26 U.S.C. § 51).

The Legal Process

If an employee believes that she or he is the subject of discrimination on the basis of disability, the typical first step is to file a complaint with the employer, using the employer's internal grievance procedures. If the employee expects the employer to make accommodations for his or her disability, as we will discuss in greater detail later, notice to the employer is essential. Employers are under no obligation to accommodate until they have been notified. If the internal grievance process does not resolve the problem, the employee has several legal options: file a complaint with the federal Equal Employment Opportunity Commission, file a complaint with the state equivalent of the EEOC (if one exists), file a lawsuit in federal court under the ADA, or file a lawsuit in state court under state disability discrimination laws. For a more complete discussion on the employee's options, see the equivalent process discussed in greater detail with regard to age discrimination in Chapter 11.

Burden of Proof

In disparate treatment cases, assuming that suit is filed under the ADA, the courts analyze the case based on the same burden-shifting analysis used in other types of discrimination. For a detailed discussion of this analysis, see Chapter 3. First set forth by the U.S. Supreme Court in *McDonnell Douglas Corp. v. Green*,[57] the burden-shifting analysis provides that once the employee meets her or his requirements for establishing a *prima facie* case of disability discrimination, the employer has the opportunity to establish a legitimate non-discriminatory reason (LNDR) for the employment action. Once the employer meets that requirement, the analysis shifts back to the employee, who has the right to establish that the non-discriminatory reason was merely a pretext for discrimination.

For example, in *Wilson v. Phoenix Specialty Manufacturing*,[58] which is reproduced at the end of this chapter, an employee offered evidence that his firing was based on disability discrimination. The employer then countered with an LNDR for his firing, namely, that his job had been replaced by a new computer system. The Fourth Circuit Court of Appeals, however, affirmed the lower court's ruling that the LNDR was a pretext for discrimination, based on the fact that the employer used a different LNDR with the EEOC than the new-computer-system justification it offered later to the court.

Employment actions are often driven by a combination of motives. In these so-called mixed-motives cases, employees historically have been required only to establish that discrimination was one of the motivating factors. In the summer of 2009, however, the U.S. Supreme Court, in *Gross v. FBL Financial Servs., Inc.*,[59] raised the ante on employees in age discrimination cases by ruling that they had to prove that the employment action would not have taken place *but for the discrimination* (for a more complete discussion of the *Gross* case, see Chapter 11).

In 2010, the Seventh Circuit ruled that the language of the ADA and the ADEA (the Age Discrimination in Employment Act) were similar enough to justify extending the *Gross* analysis to disability discrimination cases. *Serwatka v. Rockwell Automation Inc.*[60] involved an employee's claim that she was fired from her job because her employer regarded her as disabled even though she contended that she was able to perform the essential functions of the job. The trial court, in finding for the employee, treated the case as a mixed-motives case that combined both legitimate and discriminatory reasons for the firing. The Seventh Circuit, however, reversed the lower court's decision and ordered judgment in favor of the employer on the ground that the *Gross* decision means that mixed-motives cases no longer exist under the ADA.

Efforts are underway legislatively to overturn *Gross*. For the time being, at least in the Seventh Circuit, which encompasses Wisconsin, Illinois, and Indiana, mixed-motives cases do not exist under the ADA. Employees must prove that discrimination was *the* reason for the employment action.

Requests for Accommodation and Employer Responses: Process

As mentioned previously, an employee who needs the employee to make an accommodation must notify the employer of that need. The EEOC offers lengthy Enforcement Guidance to provide assistance to employers to help them better navigate and understand the EEOC's and the courts' perceptions and expectations concerning the employment of disabled individuals. The guidance clarifies how a disabled individual can request reasonable accommodations and how employers can reasonably accommodate such requests.

According to the Enforcement Guidance, when an ADA situation first arises, the disabled employee must provide notice to the employer of her or his disability and any resulting limitations. Courts have recognized that an employee has the initial duty to inform her or his employer of a disability before ADA liability is triggered for failing to provide an accommodation. An employee cannot keep secret her or his disability and then later sue for failure to accommodate. Nor are employers expected to be clairvoyant.

What suffices as a request for an accommodation? A key reasonable accommodation request, according to this guidance, "does not require the employee to speak any magic words . . . the employee need not mention the ADA or even the term accommodation."[61] The courts also have concluded that an employee who merely tells his supervisor that "his pain prevented him from working and that he requested leave under the Family and Medical Leave Act (FMLA)" is protected by the ADA.[62] A request simply asking for continued employment can be a sufficient request for accommodation; the employee does not need to request a specific accommodation.[63] Nothing in the ADA requires an individual to use legal terms or to anticipate all of the possible information an employer may need in order to provide a reasonable accommodation. The ADA avoids a formulaic approach in favor of an interactive discussion between the employer and the individual with a disability, after the individual has requested a change due to a medical condition. However, some courts have required that individuals initially provide detailed information in order to trigger protection under the act.

In addition, the EEOC encourages employers to be receptive to any relevant information or requests they receive from a third party acting on the disabled individual's behalf because the reasonable accommodation process presumes open communication (in order to help the employer make an informed decision). The essence of the reasonable accommodation concept requires an employer to go out of its way to maintain a disabled employee's employment. It is an interactive process; it requires participation by both the employee and the employer. As part of that interactive process, once the employer's responsibilities are triggered by appropriate notice from the employee, the employer may want to take the lead. The employer may want to initiate informal discussions about the need for and the scope of any possible accommodation. Communication is essential. The object is to identify the precise limitations resulting from the disability and potential reasonable accommodations that could overcome those limitations.

The EEOC and the courts have been tough on employers who have not been promptly receptive and responsive to disability situations. When determining whether or not there has been an unnecessary delay in responding to ADA situations, the courts consider these relevant factors: (1) the reason(s) for the delay, (2) the length of the delay, (3) how much the individual with a disability and the employer each contributed to the delay, (4) what the employer was doing during the delay, and (5) whether the required accommodation was simple or complex to provide. Employers who do not respond expeditiously to an employee's requests tend to suffer greater legal consequences.

Employee's Responsibility for "Interactive Process": Identification and Request for Reasonable Accommodation

Once an employee learns that she or he will need some form of accommodation in order to perform the essential functions of her or his position, the burden is on the employee to make a request for the accommodation. As mentioned above, except in unusual circumstances, an employee does not have a claim under the ADA for an employer's failure to accommodate unless that employee has made a request for reasonable accommodation that has been denied. Once the employee has made the request for accommodation, she or he has the responsibility to work with the employer to determine the most effective and efficient means by which to meet these needs. "The federal regulations implementing the ADA envision an interactive process that requires participation by both parties."[64] This requirement of interaction would usually include meeting with the worker, obtaining as much information as possible about the condition, discussing alternatives, considering accommodations, and documenting the process.

In one case where an employer requested a medical form from a worker's doctor, the worker refused to provide the form. The worker claimed that she was concerned that the company would misuse the information provided in the form, while the employer asserted that it needed the requested information in order to determine her accommodation needs and to comply with insurance requirements. The Tenth Circuit Court held that the worker's ADA claim was barred because she failed to engage in the interactive process with her employer to determine a reasonable accommodation for her disability: "Even assuming such conduct by Neodata could support a claim under the ADA for failure to provide reasonable accommodation, that claim would only arise after Mrs. Templeton satisfied her duty to notify the employer of the nature of her disability."[65]

In fact, the EEOC's Enforcement Guidance on reasonable accommodations specifically states that employers have a right to request medical documentation of disabilities in order to best satisfy their duty to reasonably accommodate. The Enforcement Guidance, however, does not place *too* large a burden on workers for such "interaction." The request [for accommodation] may be in "plain English" and need not explicitly mention the ADA or the term "reasonable accommodation."

Employer Defenses

Once the employee puts forth a *prima facie* case of disability discrimination, the burden shifts to the employer under the *McDonnell Douglas* analysis to establish an LNDR for the employment action. The burden to prove disability discrimination always remains with the employee;[66] but the employer now has an opportunity to present evidence of an LNDR for the employment action. (See Chapter 2 for a more detailed discussion of LNDRs.)

In a disparate treatment case, one of the employer's defenses is to establish that the employment action was taken for a reason other than disability discrimination. LNDRs might include the employee's poor performance or economic necessity. In hiring and promotion cases, the employer can try to establish that the employee was unqualified for the position. (For more on what constitutes being unqualified, see the discussion above on the definition of "otherwise qualified.")

Disability discrimination cases present employers with two additional defenses that do not exist in other types of discrimination because of the accommodation requirement. Employees are required to give notice to their employers of the need for accommodation. An employer's first defense, therefore, is that it did not receive notice from the employee of a need to accommodate the disability. Because no specific requirements apply to the notice, employers must be extremely careful in evaluating whether they received notice. Even a casual remark by an employee to a supervisor might constitute notice under the right circumstances.

For example, in *Enica v. Principi*,[67] a case brought against the Department of Veterans Affairs under the Rehabilitation Act, the First Circuit evaluated whether a nurse disabled from polio met her notice requirements with regard to her claim that her employer failed to accommodate her disability. At some point during her employment, she told her employer that she was having trouble walking long distances. That communication, which triggered a series of conversations back and forth about possible solutions, did satisfy the ADA notice requirement, the court said. But her claim for failure to accommodate her disability that related to actions *prior* to that communication was dismissed because she suffered in silence without ever letting her employer know of her need for accommodation.

Certain types of disabilities do not require notice if, by their nature, they are so obvious that the employer should be on notice that the employee might need an accommodation. An employee who uses a wheelchair would be one example.

If an employer receives notice of the need for accommodation, the employer is obligated to provide reasonable accommodation. Now that we have defined the terms used in the ADA in detail, this concept should be more clear. Examples of reasonable accommodation might therefore include modifying the work schedule, restructuring the job, providing leave, and reassigning the employee to a different position.[68] The second accommodation-related defense available to an employer, therefore, is that the proposed accommodation is unreasonable because it places an undue hardship or burden on the employer. (For more detail, see the preceding sections, which discuss the definitions of "reasonable accommodation" and "undue hardship.")

qualification standards
The EEOC regulations define qualification standards as "the personal and professional attributes, including the skill, experience, education, physical, medical, safety and other requirements established . . . as requirements which an individual must meet in order to be eligible for the position held or desired."[72]

Disparate impact cases, on the other hand, will involve a **qualification standard**, a rule that applies across the board to all employees. In those cases, the employer may defend with a claim of business necessity,[69] by explaining that the qualification standard was dictated by business requirements. Note that this is different from the bona fide occupational qualification (BFOQ) defense, which applies in some other anti-discrimination cases, and which *does not apply* in disability discrimination cases.[70]

The business necessity defense requires the employer to demonstrate all of the following:

1. The qualification standard is job related (it fairly measures the individual's actual ability to perform the essential functions of the job).

2. The standard is consistent with business necessity (it substantially promotes the business's needs).

3. Performance cannot be accomplished by reasonable accommodation (no reasonable accommodation would cure the deficiency *or* the accommodation would pose an undue hardship on the employer).[71]

Therefore, whenever an employer implements a qualification standard for a job, it must make sure that the standard is tied to the job and is necessary. A trucking company, for example, has every right to demand that applicants for truck driving positions have the required trucker's license and the necessary truck driving experience. But employers need to be careful to ensure that the qualification standard is related to an essential job function.

As another example, the IRS maintained the following qualification standard for its criminal investigators: investigators could not have any condition that would prevent them from full performance of their duties or would cause the individual to be a hazard to himself or others. An applicant, who was denied a job as a criminal investigator because his diabetes might place him at risk, sued the IRS.[73] The Seventh Circuit ruled that the employee need prove only that he was qualified for the job because he met the job's essential functions. If the qualification standard raised a safety issue, the burden was on the IRS to prove that the employee was a safety threat. The burden was not on the employee to prove that he was *not* a safety threat.

Similarly, UPS instituted a requirement that all drivers pass a federally mandated hearing test. The federal mandate, however, applied only to those who drove trucks weighing more than 10,000 pounds, but UPS applied it to all drivers. When hearing-impaired employees who drove or wanted to drive smaller trucks sued, the court said that the employees had to prove that they were able to perform the essential job functions.[74] Once they did, the court then shifted the burden to UPS to prove that the hearing test was relevant to the essential job function of being a safe driver of smaller trucks.

Mental or Emotional Impairments

LO10 The issue of how to handle mental impairments has been a concern for employers and employees alike because of the increased possibility for fraudulent claims (due to the challenge of verification). In October 2004, the EEOC published "Questions & Answers about Persons with Intellectual Disabilities in the Workplace and the Americans with Disabilities Act"[75] to address specific issues raised in connection with the 2.5 million people in the United States with an intellectual disability. The National Institute for Mental Health estimates that 26 percent of adults in the United States have some type of diagnosable mental disorder, and for those individuals between the ages of 15 and 44, mental disorders represent the leading disability.[76]

Individuals who are subject to mental impairments that may give rise to violence as a result of their disability may be subject to protection under the ADA. In addition, employers have a general duty under the Occupational Safety and Health Act to provide a place of employment "free from recognized hazards that are causing or are likely to cause death or serious physical harm to . . . employees." For a more detailed discussion of the growing issue of violence in the workplace, please see Chapter 16.

The EEOC guidelines on Intellectual Disabilities in the Workplace are essential to employers since they offer examples and information about how to apply the standards discussed in this chapter to situations involving individuals with intellectual disabilities and can be particularly relevant to many of these issues. The EEOC explains that its guidelines follow the model of the President's Committee on Intellectual Disabilities (formerly known as the President's Committee on Mental Retardation) in using this particular terminology. The committee adopted this term to "update and improve the image of people with disabilities who were formerly referred to as people with mental retardation and to help reduce discrimination against these citizens." The committee also "sought to reduce the public's confusion between the terms 'mental illness' and 'mental retardation' and to remove the use of terms that resulted in faulty name-calling."[77]

The EEOC defines intellectual disability as anyone with an IQ of below 70–75, with significant limitations in adaptive skill areas as expressed in conceptual, social, and practical adaptive skills; and with a disability that originated before the age of 18. "Adaptive skill areas" refers to basic skills needed for everyday life, including communication, self-care, home living, social skills, leisure, health and safety, self-direction, functional academics (reading, writing, basic math), and work. This is similar to the ADA's concept of major life activities, discussed elsewhere in this chapter. The individual also must meet the traditional requirements of the ADA in that the impairment must limit major life activities, the individual must have had a record of such an impairment, or the individual must be perceived as having such an impairment.

The guidelines offer examples of reasonable accommodations that may be offered to an intellectually disabled applicant or employee, including providing a reader or interpreter, demonstrating what the job requires, replacing a written test with an expanded interview or other measurement technique, restructuring a position, providing slower-paced training, job coaching, modifying a work schedule, providing modified equipment, or relocating a workstation to reduce distractions. Employers are cautioned to be on the lookout for harassment of individuals with intellectual disabilities since about 20 percent of discrimination claims involve this type of concern.

The following are examples of individuals who would be covered under the ADA for intellectual disabilities:

- A person with an intellectual impairment is capable of living on his own but requires frequent assistance from family, friends, and neighbors with cleaning his apartment, grocery shopping, getting to doctors' appointments, and cooking. He is unable to read at a level higher than the third grade, and so needs someone to read his mail and help him pay bills. This person is substantially limited in caring for himself and therefore has a disability under the ADA.

- A person may have two or more impairments that are not substantially limiting by themselves, but that taken together substantially limit one or more major life activities. In that situation, the person has a disability.

- An employee has a mild intellectual disability and a mild form of ADHD. Neither impairment, by itself, would significantly restrict any major life activity. Together, however, the two impairments substantially limit the employee's ability to concentrate, learn, and work. The employee is a person with a disability.

- A person was erroneously diagnosed as having an intellectual disability that substantially limited his ability to learn when he was attending high school. The applicant has a past record or history of a disability.

- An applicant with a facial deformity that affects her speech applies for a position as a secretary. The applicant is denied employment because the interviewer believes she has an intellectual disability and that the condition will make her unable to communicate with clients effectively. The employer has regarded the applicant as a person with a disability.

- The parent of a child with an intellectual disability applies for a position as an attorney at a law firm and mentions during a discussion with one of her interviewers that she has a child with an intellectual disability. She is denied employment because the employer believes the child's disability will cause her to be absent from work and will affect her productivity. The parent is protected under the ADA.

- An individual who has an effective performance record but who experiences a traumatic event and subsequently suffers from post-traumatic stress disorder that causes him to erupt with anger at a superior may have a covered disability.

Accordingly, employers should have a process in place to obtain and to evaluate appropriate medical information. The employer can request further information, beyond a doctor's note, from an employee claiming a mental impairment by requesting permission from the employee to have the company doctor review his or her medical records. The company can then verify that the accommodation is medically necessary to enable the employee to do the job.

In one case involving mental impairments, Don Perkl, who was autistic and diagnosed with mental retardation, was hired as a janitor for a Chuck E. Cheese restaurant in Madison, Wisconsin. His job duties included mopping floors, cleaning bathrooms, and vacuuming carpets. A district manager fired Perkl after telling one of the store's managers that it was the employer's policy not to hire "those kind of people." Perkl's foster mother described Perkl as "devastated" by the termination. The EEOC brought an action under the ADA on behalf of Perkl. The jury awarded Perkl $70,000 in compensatory damages and $13 million in punitive damages. The judge upheld the jury's verdict and ordered that Perkl be reinstated to his former position at the restaurant.[78]

Does a mere "inability to get along with others" constitute a disability? The First Circuit originally said that it does not,[79] but the Ninth Circuit later disagreed, contending that a disability exists where the employee can evidence a pattern of withdrawal, consistently high levels of hostility, and failure to communicate when necessary.[80] Amidst this inconsistency among the circuits, the Second Circuit then decided *Jacques v. DiMarzio, Inc.,*[81] in which it agreed with the First Circuit that such a determination might be subjective. However, the court also held that a disability exists where the employee is severely limited in the fundamental ability to communicate with others, connect with others, or "go among other people" at the most basic level of activity. Therefore, the court strived to make a distinction between a basic "office nuisance" and someone with a more substantial interpersonal limitation.

Disability Harassment

The ADA prohibits workplace harassment when it creates a hostile environment against disabled workers. While there have not been a great number of cases brought on this basis, there is evidence of a trend toward greater reporting and enforcement of the prohibition.[82] The *prima facie* case should be an easy one to

Exhibit 13.10 *Prohibitions under the ADA*

Employers may not reach any employment decision on the basis of individual's disability.

Employers may not classify an applicant or employee because of a disability in a way that adversely affects her or his opportunities or status.

Employers may not make persumptions about what a class of disabled individuals may or may not be able to do.

Employers may not impose standards or criteria that discriminate against or screen out employees or applicants on the basis of their disability, unless those criteria can be shown to be job-related and consistent with business necessity.

Employers may not discriminate against qualified disabled applicants or employees in recruitment, hiring, promotion, training, layoff, pay, termination, position assignment, leave policies, or benefits.

figure out by now, given all we have discussed about the law of sexual harassment, coupled with protection for disabled workers under the ADA (see Exhibit 13.10 for protections through prohibitions):

- The plaintiff is a qualified individual with a disability protected by the ADA.
- The plaintiff was subject to unwelcome harassment.
- The harassment was based on plaintiff's disability.
- The harassment was sufficiently severe or pervasive to alter a term, condition, or privilege of employment.
- The employer knew or should have known of the harassment and failed to take prompt, remedial action).

In cases under the Rehabilitation Act, the plaintiff must show that the employer was the recipient of federal funds.

The fourth element in the *prima facie* case, as with sexual harassment cases, is often the most challenging to prove. In cases where there is some tangible injury, courts are more likely to find that harassment has occurred. In a federal case, *Lanni v. State of New Jersey Department of Environmental Protection*,[83] the plaintiff-employee claimed that he was subject to harassment and teasing as a result of his dyslexic learning disability. Co-workers reportedly made faces at Lanni and derogatory sounds when speaking to him, as well as committing some physical abuse. The jury awarded Lanni $277,030, finding an ADA violation.[84]

A second important federal case on the issue is *Fox v. General Motors Corp.,*[85] which involved an employee, Fox, who had sustained a back injury and was restricted to light-duty work. Even though Fox's foreman was aware of the restriction, the foreman asked Fox to engage in work that Fox was not permitted to do. When Fox refused, the foreman teased him, calling him and others with disabilities "hospital people," "handicapped MFs," and "911 hospital people." The foreman told co-workers to ostracize workers with disabilities and discouraged them from speaking with those with disabilities, among other activities. The foreman required Fox to work at a table in a hazardous area that was too low and Fox re-aggravated his injury. The Fourth Circuit upheld a finding for hostile environment based on disability discrimination. In fact, the court supported compensation for both physical and emotional injury, based on testimony that Fox's increased pain and suffering from his back injury may have been triggered solely by the harassment Fox experienced at work.

Additional Responsibilities of Employers in Connection with Health-Related Issues

"No Fault" Liability: Workers' Compensation

LO11

In addition to liability under the ADA, employer liability with regard to health issues also can arise in connection with workers' compensation. It is important to keep in mind that liability based on workers' compensation is distinct from liability based on the ADA: Just as an injury at work does not necessarily lead to workers' compensation liability, workers' compensation liability does not instantaneously result in an employer's obligation under the ADA. The purpose of the two statutes are distinct, as well. Workers' compensation is a statutory scheme to provide no-fault insurance for lost wages and medical expenses resulting from work-related injuries. The ADA is a federal anti-discrimination statute designed to protect individual rights to equal employment opportunity.

A Remedial History: Purpose of Workers' Compensation

Suppose you work in an office and one morning you come in, turn on the computer, and receive an electrical shock that severely jolts you, nearly knocking you off your chair.

Think of the repercussions of this, financial and otherwise. Now imagine adding this: suing your employer to recover for the losses you suffered as a result of the injury on the job. Among other things, you must find a suitable attorney; find a means of paying the attorney at a time when you are least able because of your injury; take time away from work to deal with the attorney and your injuries; wait for a court date, which may be a year or more away; and have the attorney gather evidence to support your claim that the employer is responsible for your injury.

When you finally get to court, you are subject to the results of the more formidable resources that the employer can probably afford and also defenses that would prevent the employer from being liable for your injuries. Among other

negligence
Failure to meet the appropriate standard of care for avoiding unreasonable risk of harm to others.

no-fault
Liability for injury imposed regardless of fault.

things, the employer may allege it was your **negligence** that caused the injury, or that it was the fault of some other employee.

In the end, after all of your time, energy, and expense, you may lose. Or you may get much less of a judgment than you anticipated. Just when you need it most, you also could lose your job because you sued your employer. You would lose benefits to which your job may entitle you, such as health insurance.

Bleak scenario, isn't it? That is the reason for a system of state and federal workers' compensation statutes. That scenario was the reality in the workplace before such **no-fault** statutes were enacted to address primarily the issues of lost wages and medical expenses incurred in work-related injuries. The main reason for the statutes was to reduce the troublesome scenario the employee had to go through at such a difficult time, but the statutes are not unbalanced. There are benefits for employers also.

With workers' compensation statutes, employees trade off potentially higher damages awarded after litigation against the certainty of smaller benefits provided immediately. Also included in the statutory scheme is the guarantee of protection from employer retaliation for filing workers' compensation claims and the employer's inability to use the usual defenses against the employee to avoid liability for workplace injuries. The employee gets less in terms of benefits, but the benefits they are allowed are certain if the workers' compensation requirements are met. The employer gains freedom from lawsuits for workplace injuries and the certainty of how much such injuries will cost.

The overall effect is intended to make the workplace more efficient and to assist in the marketplace, since increased accidents mean lost time and lower production. Since workers' compensation statutes are remedial in nature, they are usually broadly construed to permit recovery where possible.

General Statutory Scheme

Workers' compensation plans basically provide compensation for time away from work and medical expenses related to on-the-job injuries. Employers pay into the system, which is administered by a state workers' compensation agent. Each state has a *schedule of benefits,* which tells how long an employee is to receive benefits (generally for a certain number of weeks) and the amount of benefits for a particular injury. The schedules also provide for the employee's death or loss of the use of a limb. Employers usually arrange the payment of their workers' compensation contributions by taking out insurance or self-insuring. Self-insuring involves employers paying into a private fund of their own, while taking out insurance may be done through private or state insurance policies.

The amounts and time periods of benefit coverage vary from state to state. Nonpermanent injury benefit schedule amounts are usually based on some percentage of the employee's weekly wages. There is a limitation on the amount to be received; and, once it is reached, the employer's statutory duty is fulfilled. Generally, in exchange for this immediate nonlitigated payment benefit, the employee does not sue the employer. However, there are states where employees may (under limited circumstances) sue the employer in addition to receiving workers' compensation benefits.

For instance, Florida has determined that, in sexual harassment cases, the workers' compensation statute will not be the exclusive remedy because of the overwhelming public policy against workplace sexual harassment. In *Ramada Inn Surfside and Adjusto, Inc. v. Swanson,*[86] the court, referring to *Byrd v. Richardson-Greenshields Securities, Inc.,*[87] stated that "[a]pplying the exclusivity rule of workers' compensation to preclude any and all tort liability effectively would abrogate this policy, undermine the Florida Human Rights Act, and flout Title VII of the Civil Rights Act of 1964."[88]

In concluding that workers' compensation should no longer be the exclusive remedy for workplace sexual harassment injuries, the court noted that

> workers' compensation is directed essentially at compensating a worker for lost resources and earnings. This is a vastly different concern than is addressed by the sexual harassment laws. While workplace injuries rob a person of resources, sexual harassment robs the person of dignity and self esteem. Workers' compensation addresses purely economic injury; sexual harassment laws are concerned with a much more intangible injury to personal rights. To the extent these injuries are separable, we believe that they both should be, and can be, enforced separately.

Workers' compensation statutes in some form or another have now been adopted in all states. A small minority of states have made them optional but, in doing so, generally prohibit employers who do not become a part of the state's workers' compensation plan from using the common-law defenses if the employer is sued by the employee for negligence.

There is also federal coverage under other legislation, including the Federal Employers' Liability Act of 1908. This act limited the common-law defenses an employer could use, rather than replacing virtually the entire common-law approach to on-the-job injuries with a no-fault system. Later, the Federal Employee's Compensation Act of 1916 provided a workers' compensation scheme for U.S. civil employees. The Longshore and Harbor Workers Service Compensation Act supplements state workers' compensation laws by providing benefits for employees in maritime employment.

Coverage in this arena is of vital importance as unsafe working conditions are not simply vestiges of days long ago or workplaces one reads about in *other* countries but instead remain present and current throughout the United States. (For a comparison of workplace fatalities between men and women, see Exhibit 13.11, "Workplace Fatalities Discriminate.")

"Out of or in the Course of" Employment

One of the most frequently litigated areas of workers' compensation is whether the accident injuring an employee arose out of or in the course of employment. An injury that occurs at work is not necessarily work-related. For instance, if a diabetic employee goes into a coma while at work, this may have nothing whatsoever to do with work except that it occurred there. Though workers' compensation statutes are remedial, and generally an attempt is made to find compensation for injured employees, the statutory requirements must still be met.

Exhibit 13.11   *Workplace Fatalities Discriminate*

In 2005, men comprised 54 percent of the American workforce. However, out of 5,702 workplace fatalities in that same year, men comprised 93 percent of those workplace fatalities.

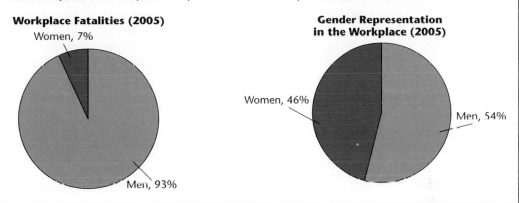

"Arising out of or in the course of" employment generally requires the employee's injury to be one that has a causal connection with the employee's employment ("arise out of employment") and may involve the time, place, and circumstances of the accident ("sustained in the course of employment"), or both, depending on the state. An employee can be injured off the premises and still have a valid workers' compensation claim if the employee was in the course of employment, just as she may receive an injury on the work premises and not be covered because it did not arise out of employment.

For the most part, the system works. However, it is not without flaws. A common problem employers have is that they may routinely respond to inquiries from the workers' compensation office without giving them the closer inspection they deserve. Contributions for larger employers are based on their injury record, so premium contributions, which must be paid by the employer, increase when claims are filed. Without investigation of claims, unwarranted claims slip through, and this unnecessarily increases the employer's contribution. However, it is the experience of the industry as a whole that serves as the basis for premiums; thus, this may not be as crucial for smaller companies. Employer attention to workplace safety can greatly reduce accidents and resulting premiums and claims.

Workers' compensation is big business. An employer must be vigilant about providing a safe workplace and training so preventable workplace accidents are minimized. Some states are taking this very seriously. The California Corporate Criminal Liability Act may impose fines of up to $1 million on corporations for failure to notify employees of a "serious concealed danger" in the workplace. In addition, managers also may be fined and criminally prosecuted if they actually knew of a workplace condition that created a substantial probability of death, great bodily harm, or serious exposure to a hazardous substance. Again, employers also should keep a close watch on claims to ensure that only valid claims are permitted.

Protection of Co-Workers

tort
A private (civil) wrong against a person or her or his property.

The employer of an employee with a contagious disability may be liable to co-workers of the employee based on a variety of common-law **tort** theories. While the only remedy available to the employee for common workplace injury is workers' compensation (discussed above), the employer may be additionally liable to its employee for any intentional torts. The employer has both a statutory duty to provide a safe work environment according to federal regulations, and a similar common-law duty to refrain from an intentional wrong against the employee. This type of tort liability may arise based on the response of the employer to the news that an employee has a contagious disease. If the employer reacts in a manner that causes the employee severe emotional distress by its outrageous conduct, the employer would be liable in tort. In addition, unwarranted invasions of privacy, breaches of confidentiality, and defamation have been held to be bases for actions against employers. A tortious invasion of privacy occurs where the employer intentionally intrudes into an employee's private affairs, and the court finds that the intrusion would be highly offensive to a reasonable person.

Scenario

How does this issue arise? Predictably, several cases have been filed by employees who work with HIV-positive employees. Usually, the case will surface after the employee has made requests for additional protections. Pursuant to the Occupational Safety and Health Act, an employer must provide a safe workplace for its employees, free from conditions reasonably believed in good faith to be hazardous. Where an employer knowingly and willfully disregards the safety of its employees, the employer will be liable.

In California, for instance, a group of nurses requested gloves and masks when treating AIDS patients. The nurses were denied protection based on the California Labor Commission's finding that there was no health danger from working in an AIDS ward without protective clothing. The employees' fears must be based on an honest, good faith, and reasonable belief that their safety is threatened. Since the employer is therefore required to protect both the employee, by virtue of the ADA, and the complaining employees, by virtue of the National Labor Relations Act and the Occupational Safety and Health Act, the only answer must be complete education of the workforce to preclude any "good-faith" belief that the employee with AIDS presents a health danger.

Retaliatory Discharge and Remedies Available

The ADA prohibits discrimination against anyone who "made a charge, testified, assisted, or participated in any manner in an investigation, proceeding, or hearing."[89] Interference, coercion, and intimidation are similarly forbidden.[90]

To establish a retaliation claim, the employee must demonstrate three elements:

1. A protected activity (such as opposition to discrimination or participation in a complaint process).
2. An adverse action by the employer against the employee.
3. Some causal connection between the protected activity and the adverse action.[91]

No jury trial and no punitive or compensatory damages are allowed in an ADA retaliation suit, which means that the remedy is limited to equitable relief, such as reinstatement if you were fired.[92]

Genetic Testing

genetic testing
"The analysis of chromosomes, genes or gene products to determine whether a mutation is present that is causing or will cause a certain disease or condition."

Advances in technology now allow employers to discover a great deal of information about their employees through the process of genetic screening and often more with information than the employee actually wants to know about herself or himself. **Genetic testing** involves "the analysis of chromosomes, genes or gene products to determine whether a mutation is present that is causing or will cause a certain disease or condition."[93] Genetic tests exist for more than 1,000 diseases and research is underway for hundreds more. Though many people express a desire to learn about their genetic information, a majority (92 percent) also prefer that it is not collected because of fears of discrimination on the basis of what is uncovered. In this way, genetic information differs from other medical information in that society has historically justified discrimination on this basis and the information gathered also includes data about one's blood relatives in addition to one's self.[94] Only 16 percent of workers would trust their employers with the information.[95] (See Exhibit 13.12, "How Much Do You Trust Each of the Following to Have Access to Your Genetic Test Results?")

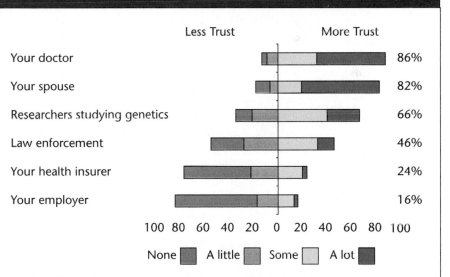

Exhibit 13.12 *How Much Do You Trust Each of the Following to Have Access to Your Genetic Test Results?*

Source: © Genetics and Public Policy Center, "U.S. Public Opinion on Uses of Genetic Information and Genetic Discrimination," April 24, 2007, http://www.dnapolicy.org/resources/GINAPublic_Opinion_Genetic_Information_Discrimination.pdf. Reprinted with permission.

In one of the most notable cases on the subject, 36 railroad workers shared a $2.2 million settlement in the case of *EEOC v. Burlington Northern Santa Fe Railroad.*[96] The EEOC alleged that the railroad had secretly conducted genetic tests to determine whether workers' compensation claims based on carpal tunnel syndrome were work-related or the result of a genetic predisposition. In April 2001, two months after the lawsuit was filed, the railroad agreed to stop the testing pending the EEOC's investigation of whether the test violated the ADA. While a court did not rule on the issue, the size of the settlement, which also requires the railroad to update the training of its medical personnel regarding the ADA, indicates that employers engage in genetic testing at their own risk.

In addition, at least 35 states have passed laws against genetic discrimination in the workplace and 46 have laws against genetic discrimination in health insurance.[97] According to an American Management Association survey, less than 1 percent of the companies polled admitted to engaging in genetic testing. Perhaps employers realize that the potential for liability is too great to support such testing.[98]

In 2008, Congress passed the Genetic Information Nondiscrimination Act (GINA), which prohibits employers with 15 or more employees from both requesting genetic testing and considering someone's genetic background in taking any employment action, such as hiring, firing, or promoting. GINA's stated purpose was to free employees to seek genetic counselling without having to worry that their employers might use the results against them.

Because "genetic information" is broadly defined in GINA, employers generally are forbidden from asking employees about their family histories for reasons other than certification. Thus, for example, a supervisor could run afoul of GINA if she or he asked an employee why the employee is requesting family medical leave. In fact, in its final regulations under GINA, the EEOC clarifies that no specific intent is required to violate GINA—a violation may occur unintentionally.[99] However, there is an exception for "inadvertent discoveries," that is, those bits of information that the employer might learn simply by overhearing them or in response to a general question of the employee.

In addition to its protection against discrimination on the basis of an individual's genetic information, GINA provides a series of privacy provisions that prohibit the collection of genetic information except where health or genetic services are offered by the employer; where an employer needs certain information to comply with the certification provisions of the Family and Medical Leave Act of 1993 or with state family and medical leave laws; where an employer learns the information through publicly available documentation; or where necessary to monitor the effects of toxic substances in the workplace (when authorized by the employee or as required by law). Moreover, group health plans and individual health insurance providers would not be permitted to differentiate between insured individuals in terms of premiums or eligibility based on the information either.

Though advocates argue that protecting individuals in this manner provides benefits of genetic testing without fear of the discriminatory implications, opponents of the bill are concerned that employers would now be prohibited from protecting workers with a genetic predisposition to certain diseases from accepting certain dangerous positions. This specific issue was not addressed in GINA and courts will have to negotiate whether a legitimate business necessity would allow employers to make decisions base on genetic information.[100]

Family and Medical Leave Act and the ADA: Distinctions

As discussed in Chapter 16, the Family and Medical Leave Act provides eligible employees with leave based on certain circumstances. The FMLA intersects with the ADA in that both require a covered employer to grant leave based on medical reasons. The ADA's reach is slightly broader as the ADA applies to private employers of 15 or more employees while the FMLA covers private employers with 50 or more employees.

In addition, the coverage provided by the two acts differs slightly in terms of the circumstances under which each applies. Under the FMLA, an employee may take advantage of the act in connection with a "serious health condition." This is defined as "an illness, injury or physical or mental condition that involves . . . inpatient care . . . or continuing treatment by a health care provider." Of course, those conditions that are covered by this definition might not constitute disabilities under the ADA. The clearest example of this divergence is in the case of pregnancy. Pregnant women qualify for leave under the FMLA, but normal circumstances of pregnancy are not considered disabilities under the ADA.

Another distinction between the two acts is the extent of the leave. The FMLA provides for up to 12 weeks of leave per year for covered conditions. The ADA does not identify a specific duration for leaves due to disabilities. In some cases, where leaves for more than 12 weeks would not constitute an undue burden on the employer, a leave for an extended period may be considered to be reasonable accommodation. Under the FMLA, an employee is entitled to return to the same or equivalent position as that which she or he left when taking the leave. Under the ADA, the employee may request additional leave even after an employer informs the employee that her or his position may no longer be available (or that it would constitute an undue burden to keep it available). If this happens, the employer is obligated to try to find a vacant position for the worker at an equivalent level or, if not available, at a lower level.

Management Considerations

As discussed in Chapter 3, employers are restricted in their preemployment inquiries with regard to disabilities and those restrictions should now be much clearer in their origins and implications. Medical examinations may only be required after the employment offer has been extended, and only where all employees in that position category are subject to similar examinations. Employment may then be conditioned on passing the test. However, as previously stated, where the withdrawal of the offer is based on the discovery of a disability, that disability must be related to adequate performance of the job or business necessity and there must exist no reasonable accommodation. All information obtained through medical examinations must be kept confidential by the employer. The employer should therefore establish separate files for this information and restrict access to them.

The ADA apparently treats testing differently based on when the test is given. As mentioned above, no medical testing is allowed preoffer unless it relates specifically to job performance. Once the offer has been made, but prior to employment, some testing might be acceptable. Once hired and employed, employers are far more restricted in terms of testing and the decisions that may be based on the results of testing. In *Rowles v. Automated Production Systems, Inc.,*[101] the plaintiff was a worker who had been given an offer conditioned on a drug test. The worker, an epileptic, took medication to prevent seizures. Upon learning that this particular medication was on the list of prohibited drugs for which he would be tested, he refused to take the drug test and was fired. Rowles filed a claim under the ADA asserting a violation since the firm prohibited the use of legally prescribed drugs without any showing that testing for these drugs was job-related or a business necessity.

The district court judge in *Rowles* held that since the policy prohibited the use of physician-prescribed medication, the policy was in direct violation of the ADA. In so holding, the judge granted partial summary judgment but still required the employee to show that the termination resulted from the illegal policy.

Not all preemployment inquiry issues are so clear. Imagine a situation where the interviewer notices an apparent disability that might interfere with the applicant's job performance. However, when asked if he can perform the essential functions of the position, the applicant replies that he can. The ADA is unclear as to whether the interviewer can inquire further about the applicant's disability given this response. (See Exhibit 13.13, "Preemployment Questions.")

Many firms have adopted educational programs so their managers become more aware of the needs of the disabled. In this way, firms can better prevent problems from arising once the disabled employee joins the workforce. This is of even greater necessity given the ADA's prohibition on preoffer medical examinations. A company may not require a medical examination before an offer has been extended, though it may make a verbal inquiry about whether the applicant is capable of performing the essential functions of the position in question. Only after that time may a company

Exhibit 13.13 *Preemployment Questions*

Examples of questions that may *not* be asked of an applicant for a position:

1. Please list any disabilities.
2. Have you ever filed a workers' compensation claim, and on what basis?
3. Do you have any disability(ies) that may prevent you from performing the requirements of this position?
4. How did you become disabled?
5. How often do you expect to miss work as a result of this disability?

Examples of questions that *may* be asked:

1. This job requires that you [be present for eight hours a day, five days a week], [lift 150-pound bags], [stand for long periods of time]. Can you meet this requirement?
2. If the employer is aware of the disability, the employer may ask how the applicant intends to perform the essential functions of the position with or without accommodation.
3. The employer may request documentation of the need for a requested accommodation.

require an examination. Because of this prohibition, many firms employ disabled employees who did not appear to be disabled at the time the offer was extended.

Firms are also developing policies of direct referral of disabled employees to specially designated personnel directors. This director or counselor is aware of job possibilities and would be in the best position to suggest job content modifications and redesign potential. After assignment or reassignment, the counselor usually checks on the employee to ensure that the requirements of the position are appropriate to the needs of the employee and that the employee is satisfying the needs of the firm. In addition, many firms conduct periodic reviews of their position descriptions to ensure that they encompass the essential functions of the position, as well as a review of their job application forms and procedures, facilities, personnel programs, and policies.

Employers should be aware that the Internal Revenue Service offers a Targeted Jobs Tax Credit to employers against five-year wages paid to newly hired workers with disabilities, among others who have difficulty obtaining employment. The program is administered by the U.S. Department of Labor.

Employers should also be aware of ADA regulations enacted by the Department of Justice, and which went into effect in 2012. The new regulations require employers to continue to remove barriers of access within employee work areas, if readily achievable. The rules apply to work areas only, and not to areas such as bathrooms and break rooms. In essence, employers are required to make all "circulation paths," which are those areas for getting into and out of cubicles, desks, and other work areas, accessible to the disabled.

For many employers, an important concern in interpreting the ADA is not necessarily how to respond in connection with applicants or employees who have disabilities that our society currently recognizes as substantially limiting major life activities, such as some impairments to sight, hearing, or access. Instead, the concern may be how to create an integrated response to common conditions that might not readily be considered disabilities but that might qualify as such under some circumstances, including obesity, alcoholism, smoking, drug abuse, and allergies.

Obesity

Obesity as a disability has caused confusion among some employers and courts. While obesity has cost employers an estimated $45 billion a year in the United States (when one combines both medical costs and costs due to absenteeism),[102] it is also the cause of unlawful discrimination on the basis of disability. Morbid obesity, defined by the Centers for Disease Control and Prevention as being 100 pounds over the normal weight for one's frame, may be considered a disability under the ADA. In addition, obesity may lead to a condition resulting in a disability. In the evolution of case law under the ADA, courts have begun to make a distinction between "physiologically caused" obesity (such as a condition that is caused by a genetic disorder or gland dysfunction) and obesity that is not physiologically caused.

In one case, an employee who was morbidly obese due to a genetic condition suffered from related physical problems. The employer fired her after four days of work at its small business in New Jersey, allegedly for having a poor work ethic. A jury awarded the employee a large sum in her discriminatory discharge action, which alleged pretextual reasons for the firing.[103] In another case, *EEOC v. Watkins Motor Lines, Inc.,*[104] the Sixth Circuit clarified the standard of proof, holding that a morbidly obese employee will not be protected if the condition is "transitory," due to a lack of fitness or eating habits. To the contrary, the employee will only qualify as disabled under the ADA if the obesity is due to a physiological condition, *and will only be protected* if the employee is also substantially limited or perceived by an employer as being substantially limited because of the obesity.

Title VII protections against discrimination based on gender may be relevant where an overweight woman is subject to different treatment or standards than overweight men. In addition, employers who stereotype the morbidly obese and who then base employment decisions on these assumptions also may be found liable under the ADA, subject to the *Watkins Motor Lines* standard, above. In addition, while the mildly obese are not considered impaired, related medical conditions may be considered impairments within the meaning of the ADA.

Additionally, if an employer merely regards an overweight employee or applicant as morbidly obese, that individual would be protected from disparate treatment based on that perception.

Substance Use and Abuse

Alcohol

It is evident that employers must establish cohesive guidelines to ensure their compliance in the area of disability discrimination. (See Exhibit 13.14, "Self-Audit for ADA Compliance.") Alcoholism is a covered disability under both the ADA and the Rehabilitation Act, and guidelines were established by the courts several decades ago in connection with claims by alcoholic employees who alleged a disability due to their alcoholism, including a five-step directive designed to assist employers in responding to alcoholic employees (see Exhibit 13.15).[105]

It is important to separate *alcoholism* from *alcohol-related misconduct,* which is not universally protected under the statutes by the courts. Employers have every

---

Exhibit 13.14 *Self-Audit for ADA Compliance*

James Frierson, a professor in the College of Business at East Tennessee State University, suggests that companies conduct a 50-question self-audit in order to identify ADA compliance problem areas and to preclude any potential hazards. Here are some of the questions that Frierson suggests a manager or owner should ask of his or her business:

1. Does the company have a written policy concerning disabled job applicants and employees?

2. Does the company have a system to encourage employees to report their disabilities in order that accommodations can be provided?

3. Has the company notified unions and professional organizations with whom they have a contract of the company's disability policies?

4. Are procedures in place to ensure that all contractors who come into contact with company employees are complying with the ADA?

5. Have all written job descriptions been reviewed and revised to omit outdated or nonessential

continued

tasks and, where possible, to describe required job results, rather than methods?

6. Has the company designated individuals to be responsible for making reasonable accommodations? Does the designated individual understand the legal definition of a disabled person? Does the designated individual understand the legal duty of accommodation?

7. How are decisions documented when disabled individuals are not hired, retained, or promoted because the needed accommodation creates an undue hardship?

8. Do all managers who make employment decisions understand the A-B-C-D-E rule? (Frierson contends that disability lawsuits that are settled unfavorably for employers are most likely to occur when people with AIDS, bad backs, cancer, diabetes, and epilepsy are denied jobs because of a risk of future injury.)

9. Is the company's HR department or any other location where job applicants must go fully accessible to disabled people, including those who use wheelchairs?

10. Have all employment tests and procedures for taking the tests been reviewed to ensure that they accurately measure necessary skills and aptitudes?

11. Has the company created a separate, confidential file for employee health and medical information?

12. Are disabled and nondisabled employees who are in the same job classifications provided with the same fringe-benefit coverage?

Source: James Frierson, "A Fifty-Question Self-Audit on ADA Compliance," *Employment Relations Today* 19, no. 2 (1992), pp. 151–66. Reprinted by permission of John Wiley & Sons, Inc.

Exhibit 13.15 *Five-Step Directive to Respond to Alcoholic Employees*

1. If the employer suspects alcoholism, she must inform the employee of counseling services.

2. If the alcoholism continues, the employer must give the employee a "firm choice" between treatment and discipline.

3. The employer must then provide the employee the opportunity to complete outpatient treatment

4. If this is unsuccessful, the employer must provide the employee the opportunity to complete an inpatient treatment.

5. Only if the first four steps fail can the employer legally discharge the employee. Employers are advised to follow similar directives in connection with the hiring, retention, and termination of employees with other addiction disabilities.

right to establish workplace policies and to discipline workers who fail to meet those standards. If the alcoholic cannot meet the basic requirements of the job, the employer has the right to fire the alcoholic, although drawing the line between alcoholism and alcohol-related misconduct is not always easy. Consider, for instance, the employee who oversleeps and misses work because of her or his alcoholism. Some courts would consider an adverse action because of this "alcoholic-related misconduct," *not "because of the disability."*[106] Other courts find to the contrary and instead hold that firing the employee for being late, for instance, would be *"because of the disability."*[107] In that case, the employer could not fire the employee for being late because that would be the same as firing the employee for being an alcoholic. This conflict between the circuits has not yet been resolved.

On the other hand, a police chief was fired from his job after injuring two people in a drunken driving accident.[108] He sued under the ADA, but lost on the ground that the accident violated workplace rules. Similarly, a nurse who got into a drunken altercation with a security guard at the hospital while on vacation was properly fired for violating workplace rules.[109]

Conditions that occur as a result of the alcoholism may also qualify for ADA protection. Thus, someone who has cirrhosis of the liver because of the alcoholism may qualify for protection. Also, remember that while alcoholism is covered by the ADA, some state disability statutes explicitly exempt alcoholism from legal protection.[110]

Smoking

The issue of smoking in the workplace also presents some questions. Many, if not all, states have enacted legislation banning smoking in the workplace environment. An employer is forced to balance the rights of smokers without violating the laws intended to protect nonsmokers. But is nicotine dependence or withdrawal a disability? Is the addiction a substantial impairment of major life activities? Does smoking create a physiological or a psychological dependency requiring the employer to provide a reasonable accommodation for smokers? The answer has not been fully decided but one is hard-pressed to imagine a case with a strong employee argument. Congress remains silent on this issue, and the Supreme Court has not had a case on point.

Drug Use and Abuse

Drug addiction is also an issue that employers are now facing with regard to disabilities, but it is treated somewhat differently from alcoholism. Current drug users are not protected by the ADA; but *former* illicit drug users as well as those who use prescription medications unlawfully, including individuals who either are participating in or have completed a drug rehabilitation program, are protected by the ADA. Courts have recognized that, under certain circumstances, drug addiction *may* constitute a disability under the ADA and the federal Rehabilitation Act. As with all disabilities, the former drug users must demonstrate they have a disability; that is, they must show that the past drug use limits a major life activity and it must have been sufficiently severe to be considered a drug addiction. An employee who is a recovering addict no longer using drugs may use the past drug addiction to argue that he or she has a disability based on a record of such an impairment or perception of impairment. This perception may be due to stereotypes about past drug use that lead someone to believe that someone is a current user (stereotypes such as "once a user, always a user") or erroneous beliefs based on false positives during employer drug testing. Recovered drug abusers can also be expected to meet performance and behavior standards.

The best an employer can do at this time is to amend its drug and alcohol policies to require disclosure of medical marijuana use in the same way it requires disclosure of the side effects of prescription drugs. Perhaps the worker also could be moved to a position that is less sensitive to its effects. Finally, the employer could grant the worker a leave during the time she or he requires use of the drug. If an employer suspects impairment that could make the worker unqualified for the position, the worker can be tested based on that reasonable suspicion (such as slurred speech, attitude, involvement in an accident, or odor).

It is also important to recall the Supreme Court's decision in *Raytheon Co. v. Hernandez,* discussed earlier in this chapter, which held that disparate impact claims are available to workers who test positive for illegal drug use. In that case, the worker was fired after a positive result on a drug test. The employer had a no-rehire policy, but the Court left open the possibility that individuals with disabilities may be entitled to differential treatment under facially neutral policies. Accordingly, recovering drug addicts and/or recovering alcoholics may claim that they should not be covered by such a policy. Based on *Raytheon,* policies may be suspect if they automatically bar reemployment after a positive drug or alcohol test, or for other possible consequences of a covered disability, or if they change the conditions of work for those who have tested positive or exhibit these effects. On the other hand, as long as the employer can justify decisions based on business necessity or job-relatedness, their decisions are more likely to be defensible.

Allergies

Those with allergies can be disabled under the ADA, if their allergy interferes with a major life activity. An allergy can also include sensitivity to certain chemicals, such as perfumes. The difficulty in these cases usually involves a question of how far employers must go to accommodate the allergy.

In one case, a Michigan employee brought an ADA action on the ground that she experienced a severe reaction to a co-employee's perfume, to a plug-in air freshener, and to potpourri in the bathroom.[111] The court agreed with the employee that her allergies interfered with a major life activity, namely, breathing. The court also said, however, that a scent-free workplace is an undue burden on the employer, but it noted that some other accommodation, such as a transfer to a different part of the building, might be reasonable. The case was ultimately settled without a trial in 2010, with the employer paying the employee a lump sum.

A similar case in Pennsylvania had a different result.[112] After an employee experienced severe allergic reactions to co-workers' perfume, the employer instituted a no-perfume policy. The employer also moved her desk, changed air filters, and gave her a desktop air filter and fan. The employer eventually fired her for poor performance because her attendance was erratic. Her ADA suit against the employer was dismissed on the ground that the employer met its accommodation obligations under the ADA. This case serves as another reminder for employers of the importance of having in place solid workplace rules that can be applied evenly to all employees.

Management Tips

- Never assume the physical or intellectual limitations of a worker or applicant with a disability. If you assume that someone cannot perform certain functions, you may be creating limitations where none actually exist.

- Review all job descriptions to make sure that the job requirements are actually required to complete the job; remove extraneous requirements that are not truly essential to job performance.

- Ensure that all decision-makers understand what constitutes notice of a request for accommodation and what rights are triggered by that request. In some cases, offhand comments such as "I'm having a hard time pushing this cart" can constitute notice that an accommodation is needed.

- Be sure to explore all possible reasonable accommodations for otherwise qualified applicants or employees with a disability. Failure to do so might result not only in legal liability but also in costs connected with identifying and training alternative candidates. Often, a small accommodation will allow you to retain qualified and experienced individuals with disabilities.

- Engage in frank and open discussions. Determining the appropriate reasonable accommodation is a collaborative process. Candid communication is the key ingredient leading to successfully handling ADA matters.

- Consult with the employee. Ask questions. Ask the employee to offer suggestions. Asking the employee to provide additional information will lead you to more opportunities for the most effective way to identify and to handle the accommodation.

- Document that dialogue. These are negotiations. They may or may not lead to litigation. Do not let the employee say that you remained silent once the employee asked for an accommodation if you did not. Confirm in writing your efforts to accommodate. This documentation is one of the best defenses against a possible failure in memory.

- Be proactive. Reasonable accommodation obligations require action and effort on the employer's part. Flexibility is critical to management's efforts.

- Negotiate. Make counterproposals. Be sure they are fair and reasonable. Remember, an employer is not required to provide the best accommodation, only a reasonable accommodation.

- Be clear on the rules for when medical examinations can be required of a disabled person. Pre-hiring examinations are never allowed. Post-hiring examinations are allowed, but only if all other employees are required to submit to the examination. Employees with disabilities can be subject to an individual, post-hiring examination in limited situations, such as where it relates to job performance or safety issues.

- Review all application materials to ensure that there are no inappropriate questions concerning irrelevant abilities.

- Since "disability" under the statutes includes someone who is perceived as being disabled, as well as those associated with individuals who are disabled, conduct training sessions with all management to educate them regarding what is actually a disability and what is not. All decision-makers should understand that they can violate the ADA, even if the employee has no disability, if they *treat the employee as disabled.*

- You are not required to accommodate all disabilities. Consider all costs involved with providing accommodation and consider whether it would be an undue burden under the courts' precedents.

- If an employee is on leave, you may request documentation or a medical examination prior to her or his return to work. However, the request should only be made if you have a reasonable belief that the employee may be unable to perform her or his job or might pose a direct threat to herself, himself, or others. In addition, you may only ask about the employee's present ability to perform the work and to do so safely.

- Post information on the Genetic Information Nondiscrimination Act, which includes significant changes such as no longer asking employees about family medical history, including when they make FMLA leave requests or engage in a workplace wellness program. The EEOC publishes "EEO is the Law" posters, which include up-to-date information on GINA, the ADAAA, and many federal laws in English, Arabic, Chinese and Spanish.[113]

- All Equal Employment Opportunity statements and manuals should be amended to include references to genetic discrimination and the ADAAA.

Chapter Summary

- Statutory protections against disability discrimination in employment strike a balance between the right of individuals with disabilities to have job opportunities and the need of employers to have an "able" workforce. This balance is achieved by several measures. First, the determination of whether an individual has a disability is made on a case-by-case basis, examining whether the impairment substantially limits one or more of the individual's major life activities. "Major life activities" are defined as activities that have central importance to daily life. "Substantial limitation" is determined by taking into account mitigating measures such as medication and medical devices.

- Not every impairment will lead to protection as a disability. However, those who have a record of such an impairment, who have been perceived as having such an impairment, and who are associated with individuals who are disabled also are protected. This prevents employers from defending discriminatory actions on the basis that the individual is not covered under the statute.

- The balance between employees' rights and employers' needs is further maintained by the concept of reasonable accommodation. An applicant or employee with a disability who meets the basic job requirements regarding education, experience, skills, and abilities may need accommodation to perform the essential job functions. The applicant or employee is required to notify the employer of the need for accommodation. If the accommodation places an undue hardship on the employer, the employer is not required to provide it. This determination is fact intensive and case specific. Further, if the applicant or employee with a disability poses a direct threat to the health and safety of others that cannot be reasonably accommodated, then that individual is not "qualified" for the position.

- Employers are well advised to ensure that they fairly and equitably analyze these issues in addressing all disability-related situations arising in the workplace.

Chapter-End Questions

1. Thomas Larimar was fired from his position as an IBM salesman not long after his wife gave birth prematurely to twin girls. Unfortunately, the babies suffered from several serious medical conditions. Larimar contended that his termination was motivated by IBM's desire to rid itself of potentially large future medical expenses for the two girls. What additional information do you need in order to determine whether IBM violated the ADA? [*Larimar v International Business Machines Inc.,* 370 F. 3d 698 (7th Cir. 2004).]

2. Rehrs was a warehouse technician for Iams Company (a pet food manufacturer) who suffered from Type I diabetes. Iams ran its plant on a straight shift schedule—three shifts that ran for eight hours each throughout 24-hour days. When Iams was purchased by Procter & Gamble, P&G instituted shifts of 12 hours each for warehouse technicians, which rotated every two weeks. After two years of rotating shifts, Rehrs suffered a heart attack and was then medically restricted from working a rotating shift. P&G claims that a rotating shift is an essential function of the job because all of its facilities operate under this "high performance work system." P&G contends shift rotation exposes employees to management and to more resources, suppliers, and outside customers with whom the company only interfaces during the day shift. P&G believes this type of exposure provides all employees with additional opportunities for training and development to further their career opportunities in the company and, in turn, increases productivity. Plus, if Rehrs did not rotate, someone else would lose their rotation option as well. Are you persuaded by P&G's arguments? Is shift rotation an essential job function? [*Rehrs v. The Iams Company,* 486 F.3d 353 (8th Cir. 2007).]

3. Squibb was a nurse who had suffered three back injuries over a seven-year period while lifting patients in her work. She was placed on light duty, followed by an administrative leave. Following the leave, her doctor imposed a lifting restriction of 25–30 pounds, so the hospital offered her a job as a clinical case manager. Squibb declined the position and was fired. Squibb sued the hospital under the ADA for failure to accommodate her disability. The hospital claimed that she was not disabled because she could still perform a large number of jobs, both within and outside of the hospital, even with the restriction. Does Squibb have a case? [*Squibb v. Memorial Medical Center,* 497 F.3d 775 (7th Cir. 2007).]

4. A disabled employee identifies vacant positions to which he can transfer but fails to formally apply for those positions. Is the employer still responsible for engaging in an interactive process with the worker to identify a reasonable accommodation? [*Shapiro v. Township of Lakewood,* 292 F.3d 356 (3d Cir. 2002).]

5. Wood suffered permanent nerve damage at work and could no longer drive a ready-mix concrete truck, though he could drive other trucks. He asked for a reassignment, but since his employer did not have another job for him, he was terminated. He was somewhat limited in walking and in performing certain work functions. He also claimed discrimination based on the fact that his injury resulted in impotence, substantially limiting him in a major life activity. Is he covered? [*Wood v. Crown Redi-Mix, Inc.,* 339 F.3d 683 (8th Cir. 2003).]

6. Greenberg is a telephone installation and maintenance employee who works for BellSouth. He also is obese and suffers from other medical conditions. Under BellSouth's safe load limit policy, employees in certain jobs, such as Greenberg's, could weigh no more than the "safe load limit" of the equipment used in their work groups. Because Greenberg's weight exceeded the safe load limit for his position, his supervisor "would hand-pick Mr. Greenberg's job assignments to make sure he did not get any assignments that would require him to climb." However, when BellSouth hired an outside firm to track the weight of employees

governed by the safe load policy in order to ensure uniform implementation, Greenberg's supervisor informed him that he had to lose weight. After failing to lose the weight, Greenberg was terminated. Greenberg suffers from "diabetes, hypertension, hypothyroidism and a variety of disorders that affect his endocrinology and that such physiological disorders cause him to be overweight and prohibit him from losing weight." What additional information would you need in order to determine whether Greenberg suffered from discrimination in his termination? How can you determine whether he has sufficient facts on which to state a claim? [*Greenberg v. BellSouth Telecommunications, Inc.,* 498 F.3d 1258 (11th Cir. 2007).]

7. A Vietnam War veteran diagnosed with post-traumatic stress disorder was employed at the post office. After missing significant time at work for depression related to the PTSD, he requested an accommodation. The post office refused the request on the ground that his condition did not prevent him from engaging in any major life activity as required by the Rehabilitation Act. Has the post office violated the Rehabilitation Act? Is the post office correct in asserting that the depression does not prevent the employee from engaging in any major life activity? [*Zeigler v. Potter,* D.D.C., No. 06-1385, 2007 US Dist LEXUS 65329.]

8. Lucia Enica, who worked as a nurse for the Department of Veterans Affairs, suffered from poliomyelitis, which causes her to limp and prevents her from lifting heavy objects. The VA hospital where she worked accommodated her disability by placing a weight limit on what she had to pick up or push. She continued to experience difficulties over the years and was later reassigned to a position answering the telephone, which did not require walking or heavy lifting. With a master's degree and 16 years of nursing experience, Lucia was unhappy with the transfer. Has the hospital done enough under the Rehabilitation Act to accommodate her disability? Did it fail in its duty to accommodate? Did Enica properly request further accommodations? [*Enica v. Prinicipi,* 544 F. 3d 328 (1st Cir. 2008).]

9. The Department of Homeland Security rejected an employee's application to transfer to a position as a detention enforcement officer on the ground that he had limited vision in one eye because of an earlier injury. His request for an eye re-examination was also rejected. The DHS also noted that detention enforcement officers were required to have a commercial driver's license, which required better vision than the applicant demonstrated. Was the applicant disabled? Is the DHS guilty of disability discrimination? Were the vision rules job-related? [*Poquiz v. Homeland Sec. Dep't.,* EEOC Appeal No. 0720050095 (2008).]

10. An investigator for the Ohio Civil Rights Commission suffered from asthma and sarcoidosis, which affected her breathing. The Commission's workspace contained an outer ring of offices that were climate controlled and an inner ring that was not. The investigator was moved to an inner-ring office to be nearer her supervisor, at which point difficulties in keeping the temperature controlled triggered her breathing difficulties. Her request to be moved to an outer-ring office was denied. Is the investigator disabled? Was the Commission wrong to deny her request for a move? [*Benaugh v. Ohio Civil Rights Commission,* 6th Cir., No. 07-3825, unpublished opinion 5/11/2008.]

11. A dispatcher suffered from multiple sclerosis, which caused, among other things, incontinence and coordination difficulties. After having bowel accidents at work, the dispatcher was subjected to ridicule, which included name-calling, the posting of unflattering drawings and pictures on the office walls, and the theft of his cane. Has the employer created a hostile work environment? To what extent is the employer required to notify his supervisor of his belief that the work environment is hostile? [*Murphy v. Beavex,* Conn. D.C., No. 3:06CV01109 (DJS) (2008).]

End Notes

1. Scenario based on case studies by Richard Bales, "Taylor Smith, Alex(is) Miller" (2007), reprinted by permission of the author. © 2007 Richard Bales.

2. U.S. Department of Health and Human Services, Office on Disability, "Substance Abuse and Disability," December 12, 2006, http://www.hhs.gov/od/about/fact_sheets/substanceabuse.html (last visited July 30, 2007).

3. Amanda Ruggeri, "Recession's Bite Hits Americans with Disabilities Extra Hard," *U.S. News and World Report,* http://www.usnews.com/articles/news/national/2008/12/05/recessions-bite-hits-americans-with-disabilities-extra-hard.html?PageNr=1 (Dec. 5, 2008).

4. Livermore, Gina, "Poverty and Hardship Among Working-Age People with Disabilities," Mathematica Policy Research, Inc., Center for Studying Disability Policy (Dec. 3, 2009), http://www.disabilitypolicyresearch.org/Forums/20091203/livermore.pdf.

5. Meyer, Ann, "In Tough Job Market, Disabled Workers Need More Help Than Ever," *Chicago Tribune* (November 15, 2010), http://www.chicagotribune.com/business/columnists/ct-biz-1115-on-the-job-spr-20101115,0,3406657.column.

6. 41 C.F.R. § 60-741.1, http://www.dol.gov/dol/allcfr/Title_41/Part_60-741/41CFR60-741.1.htm.

7. "Re-charting the Course: First Report of the Presidential Task Force on Employment of Adults with Disabilities," November 15, 1998, http://www.workworld.org/ptfead/ptfead_1998.pdf.

8. The Task Force recommended that President Clinton (1) increase the number of disabled adults working for the federal government, (2) increase the employment options for person with psychiatric disabilities, and (3) support legislation allowing disabled adults to retain Medicare coverage when they return to work. See Employment Support Institute, Virginia Commonwealth University, "Presidential Task Force on the Employment of Adults with Disabilities," http://www.workworld.org/ptfead.html (accessed August 5, 2007).

9. U.S. Department of Health and Human Services, "New Freedom Initiative," http://www.hhs.gov/newfreedom/ (accessed August 5, 2007).

10. For example, the U.S. Supreme Court said in 2002 that the definition of disability should "be interpreted strictly to create a demanding standard for qualifying as disabled." *Toyota Motor Mfg. v. Williams,* 534 U.S. 184, 197 (2002).

11. See Ruth Colker, "Winning and Losing under the Americans with Disabilities Act," *Ohio State Law Journal* 62 (2001), pp. 240–41, where an analysis of 720 appellate ADA employment discrimination cases reported that the employer-defendant was the successful party in 93 percent of trial cases and 84 percent of appeals.

12. On March 25, 2011, the EEOC released final regulations on the ADAAA, "Regulations to Implement the Equal Employment Provisions of the Americans with Disabilities Act, as Amended," 29 CFR Part 1630 (2011), http://ofr.gov/OFRUpload/OFRData/2011-06056_PI.pdf. The EEOC has collected the ADAAA, these new regulations, an FAQ on the amendments, and a fact sheet at http://www.eeoc.gov/laws/statutes/adaaa_info.cfm.

13. The modifications enacted by the ADAAA were specifically extended to the Rehabilitation Act, as well. http://www.govtrack.us/congress/billtext.xpd?bill=s110-3406.

14. The U.S. Supreme Court recognized that both types apply to ADA cases in *Raytheon v. Hernandez,* 540 U.S. 44, 124 S.Ct. 513 (2003).

15. *United States v. Nobel Learning Communities, Inc.,* No. 09-1818 (E.D. Pa. 2009).

16. See *City of Moorpark v. Ventura County Superior Court,* 959 P.2d 752 (Cal. 1998), and *Dillard's v. Beckwith,* 989 P.2d 882 (Nev. 1999).

17. 480 U.S. 273, 107 S. Ct. 1123 (1987).

18. *Johnson v. American Chamber of Commerce Publishers, Inc.,* 108 F.3d 818 (7th Cir. 1997).

19. 527 F.3d 1080 (10th Cir. 2008).

20. See Steven Greenhouse, "Lifetime Affliction Leads to a U.S. Bias Suit," *New York Times,* www.nytimes.com/learning/teachers/featured_articles/20030331monday.html (March 31, 2003).

21. 140 Cal. App. 4th 34 (2006).

22. EEOC, "Questions and Answers about the Association Provision of the Americans with Disabilities Act," http://www.eeoc.gov/facts/association_ada.html.

23. *Toyota Motor Mfg. v Williams,* 534 U.S. 184, 198 (2002).

24. ADA Amendments Act §2(b)(4).

25. ADA Amendments Act §4(a).

26. 352 F.3d 472 (1st Cir. 2003).

27. A second interesting outgrowth of this case was the court's ruling on Mr. Wright's claim of retaliation based on his request for accommodation. The court ruled that the mere act of requesting an accommodation was "protected activity" under the ADA and therefore remanded the case for trial to determine whether CompUSA's proffered reason for discharge—insubordination—was pretextual.

28. *Jacques v. DiMarzio, Inc.,* 386 F.3d 192 (2d Cir. 2004).

29. *Toyota Motor Mfg. v Williams,* 534 U.S. 184, 198 (2002).

30. 527 U.S. 471 (1999).

31. *Albertson's, Inc. v. Kirkingburg,* 527 U.S. 555 (1999).

32. See Alex B. Long, "Introducing the New and Improved Americans with Disabilities Act: Assessing the ADA Amendments Act," 103 *Nw.U.L.Rev. Colloquy* __ (2008).

33. ADA Amendments Act §4(a).

34. No.1:05cv794 (S.D. Ohio, June 20, 2007).

35. 534 U.S. 184 (2002).

36. ADA Amendments Act of 2008, sec. 2(b)(5).

37. *Walders v. Garrett,* 765 F. Supp. 303 (DC. Va. 1991), *aff'd,* 956 F.2d 1163 (4th Cir. Va. 1992).

38. 524 U.S. 624 (1998).

39. U.S. Department of Health and Human Services, *A Guide to AIDS in the Workplace Resources* (September 1997), http://www.brta-lrta.org/tools/pdf_laborkit/resources.pdf (last visited July 31, 2007).

40. Chris Seeley, "HIV Discrimination Looms Large in U.S.," *Southernvoice.com,* November 28, 2003.

41. EEOC press release, "Cirque du Soleil to Pay $600,000 for Disability Discrimination against Performer with HIV," April 2, 2004, http://www.eeoc.gov/press/4-22-04.html.

42. 536 U.S. 73 (2002).

43. *Chevron USA v. Echazabal,* 226 F.3d 1063 (9th Cir. 2000).

44. *Rodriguez v. ConAgra Grocery Products, Inc.*, 436 F.3d 468 (5th Cir. 2006), quoting in part *Gillen v. Fallon Ambulance Service, Inc.*, 283 F.3d 11, 31 (1st Cir. 2002).

45. *Kees v. Wallenstein*, 161 F.3d 1196 (9th Cir. 1998).

46. 91 F.3d 129 (4th Cir. 1996).

47. *EEOC v. Yellow Freight Systems, Inc.*, 253 F.3d 943 (7th Cir. 2001); *Jovanovic v. In-Sink-Erator Division of Emerson Electric Co.*, 201 F.3d 894 (7th Cir. 2000).

48. *EEOC v. Ford Motor Credit Co.*, 531 F. Supp. 2d 930 (D.Ct. TN, 2008); *Spangler v. Federal Home Loan Bank of Des Moines*, 278 F. 3d 847 (8th Cir. 2002); *DeVito v. Chicago Park District*, 270 F. 3d 532 (7th Cir., 2001).

49. 451 F. Supp. 791 (E.D. Pa. 1978).

50. 430 F. Supp. 75 (M.D. Fla. 1977).

51. Terri Goldstein, "Succeeding Together: People with Disabilities in the Workplace," http://www.csun.edu/ sp20558/dis/reasonable.html (last visited July 29, 2007); AL-APSE, Network on Employment, "Employer Resources," http://www.al-apse.org/ employers/employers_ada.htm (last visited July 29, 2007).

52. J. L. Mueller, Inc., "Universal Design at Work: Why Universal Design?" in "Office and Workplace Design," *James Mueller Universal Design Handbook*, http://home.earthlink.net/~jlminc/workplace.html (last visited July 29, 2007).

53. 33 F. Supp. 2d 133 (N.D. N.Y. 1999), *vac'd on other grounds*, 205 F.3d 77 (2d Cir. 2000).

54. 42 U.S.C. §12111(10)(B).

55. 29 C.F.R. §1630.2(p)(2).

56. See Michelle Conlin, "The New Workforce," *BusinessWeek*, March 20, 2000.

57. 411 U.S. 792 (1973).

58. 513 F.3d 378 (4th Cir. 2008).

59. No. 08-441 (June 18, 2009).

60. *Serwatka v. Rockwell Automation Inc.*, No. 08-4010 (7th Cir. 2010).

61. *Schmidt v. Safeway Inc.*, 864 F. Supp. 991, 997, 3 Am. Disabilities Cas. (BNA) 1141, 1146–47 (D. Or. 1994).

62. *McGinnis v. Wonder Chemical Co.*, 5 Am. Disabilities Cas. (BNA) 219 (E.D. Pa. 1995).

63. *EEOC (Demirelli) v. Convergys Customer Management Group, Inc.*, 491 F.3d 790 (8th Cir. 2007).

64. *Templeton v. Neodata Services, Inc.*, 162 F.3d 617 (10th Cir. 1998).

65. Ibid.

66. See *Gross v. FBL Financial Servs., Inc.*, No. 08-441, June 18, 2009. For more on the *Gross* decision, see Chapter 11.

67. 544 F.3d 328 (1st Cir. 2008).

68. 42 U.S.C. §12111(9).

69. 42 U.S.C. §12113(a): "It may be a defense to a charge of discrimination . . . that an alleged application of qualification standards, tests, or selective criteria that screen out . . . an individual with a disability has been shown to be job-related and consistent with business necessity, and such performance cannot be accomplished by reasonable accommodation."

70. See *Bates v. United Parcel Service*, 511 F.3d 974 (9th Cir. 2007).

71. 42 U.S.C. §121112(a).

72. 29 C.F.R. §1630.2(q).

73. *Branham v. Snow,* 392 F.3d 896 (7th Cir. 2004).

74. *Bates v. United Parcel Service,* 511 F.3d 974 (9th Cir. 2007).

75. http://www.eeoc.gov/facts/intellectual_disabilities.html.

76. J. T. Neighbours, "Employee Interrupted: Managing Workers with Psychiatric Disabilities," *Law Letter* 17, no. 6 (June 2006).

77. http://www.acf.hhs.gov/programs/pcpid/index.html.

78. *EEOC v. CEC Entertainment, Inc.,* 2000 U.S. Dist. LEXIS 13934, 10 Am. Disabilities Cas. (BNA) 1593 (W.D. Wis. 2000).

79. *Soileau v. Guildford of Maine, Inc.,* 105 F.3d 12 (1st Cir. 1997).

80. *McAlindin v. County of San Diego,* 192 F.3d 1226 (9th Cir. 1999).

81. 386 F.3d 192 (2d Cir. 2004).

82. The Fourth, Fifth, Eighth, and Tenth Circuits explicitly recognize a cause of action for disability harassment under the ADA. *Fox v. General Motors Corp.,* 247 F.3d 169 (4th Cir. 2001); *Gowesky v. Singing River Hospital Systems,* 321 F.3d 503, 509–11 (5th Cir. 2003) (offensive comments were not sufficiently severe or pervasive to constitute disability harassment; found for defendant); *Shaver v. Independent Stave Co.,* 350 F.3d 716 (8th Cir. 2003) (found conduct merely rude, abrasive, unkind, and insensitive but not actionable); *Lanman v. Johnson County, Kansas,* 393 F.3d 1151 (10th Cir. 2004).

83. 177 F.R.D. 295 (D.N.J. 1998).

84. The district court awarded more than that amount in attorney fees and costs, though that award was vacated on appeal. *Lanni v. State of New Jersey Department of Environmental Protection,* 259 F.3d 146 (3d Cir. 2001).

85. 247 F.3d 169 (4th Cir. 2001).

86. 560 So. 2d 300 (Ct. App. Fla., 1st Dist. 1990).

87. 552 So. 2d 1099 (Fla. 1989).

88. *Swanson,* 560 So. 2d 300.

89. Section 12203(a).

90. Section 12203(b).

91. EEOC Compliance Manual. Volume 2, Section 614.

92. See *Alvarado v. Cajun Operating Company,* No. 08-15549 (9th Cir. 2009), and *Kramer v. Banc. of Am. Sec.,* 335 F.3d 961 (7th Cir. 2004).

93. National Institutes of Health, Secretary's Advisory Committee on Genetic Testing, "A Public Consultation on the Oversight of Genetic Tests," December 1, 1999–January 31, 2000, http://www4.od.nih.gov/oba/sacgt/reports/Public_Consultation_document.htm (last visited August 2, 2007).

94. Ashley Ellis, "Genetic Justice," *Texas Tech Law Review* 34 (2003), pp. 1071, 1074.

95. Genetics and Public Policy Center, "U.S. Public Opinion on Uses of Genetic Information and Genetic Discrimination," April 24, 2007, http://www.dnapolicy.org/resources/GINAPublic_Opinion_Genetic_Information_Discrimination.pdf.

96. Civ. No. 01-4013 MWB (N.D. Iowa Apr. 23, 2001).

97. National Human Genome Research Institute, "Genetic Discrimination in Health Insurance," November 21, 2007, http://www.genome.gov/10002328; see also Kathy Hudson,

"Prohibiting Genetic Discrimination," *New England Journal of Medicine* 356, no. 30 (May 17, 2007), pp. 2021–23.

98. See Darryl Van Duch, "EEOC Goes after Genetic Testing," *National Law Journal,* April 30, 2001.

99. The EEOC removed the term "deliberate acquisition" from Section 1635.1 and explained, "a covered entity may violate GINA without a specific intent to acquire genetic information." http://www.federalregister.gov/articles/2010/11/09/2010-28011/regulations-under-the-genetic-information-nondiscrimination-act-of-2008#p-20.

100. Sheppard Mullin, "The GINA of 2008: Civil Rights or Science Fiction?" (May 22, 2008), http://www.laboremploymentlawblog.com/discrimination-the-genetic-information-nondiscrimination-act-of-2008-civil-rights-or-science-fiction.html (accessed May 22, 2008).

101. 7992 F. Supp. 2d 424 (M.D. Pa. 2000).

102. M. Scott, "Obesity More Costly to U.S. Companies Than Smoking, Alcoholism," *Workforce Week* (April 9, 2008), http://www.workforce.com/section/00/article/25/46/91.html (accessed April 15, 2008).

103. *Viscik v. Fowler Equipment Co., Inc.,* 800 A.2d 826, 173 N.J. 14 (2002).

104. 463 F.3d 436 (6th Cir. 2006).

105. *Rodgers v. Lehman,* 869 F.2d 253 (4th Cir. 1989).

106. *Pernice v. City of Chicago,* 237 F.3d 783, 784 (7th Cir. 2001); *Little v. F.B.I.,* 1 F.3d 255, 256 (4th Cir. 1993); *Leary v. Dalton,* 58 F.3d 748, 750 (1st Cir. 1995).

107. *Teahan v. Metro-N. Commuter R.R.,* 951 F.2d 511, 513 (2d Cir. 1991).

108. *Budde v. Kane County Forest Preserve,* No. 09-2040 (7th Cir. 2010).

109. *Johnson v. New York Hospital,* 96 F.3d 33 (2nd Cir. 1996).

110. See, for example, Texas, Georgia, Tennessee, and others. Texas does extend coverage to recovering alcoholics.

111. *McBride v. City of Detroit,* No. 07-12794 (E.D. MI 2007).

112. *Kaufmann v. GMAC Mortg.,* No. 06-3019 (3rd Cir. 2007).

113. Available at http://www1.eeoc.gov/employers/poster.cfm (accessed November 3, 2010).

114. The railroad allocates conductors to job assignments based upon a list of employees ranked by seniority. Under the collective bargaining agreement, each employee may withdraw his name from the list or "lay off" if he chooses to use vacation, sick leave, or personal time.

Cases

Case 1

Wilson v. Phoenix Specialty Manufacturing Company, Incorporated, *513 F. 3d 378 (4th Cir. 2008)*

Jimmy Wilson was a shipping supervisor at a company that makes specialty washers used primarily in airplanes. He was diagnosed with Parkinson's disease after working at the company for 10 years. The disease caused Wilson to lose motor control in his right hand and to experience anxiety. Following a leave of absence triggered by the disease, Wilson returned to work without restrictions, and his condition was stabilized by medications. The company, however, treated him differently after his return and formed an opinion that he was unable to key information into a recently installed computer system. The company later reduced its work force by two salaried employees, including Wilson. It subsequently refused his request for an hourly position, even though it granted the same request for the other salaried employee who was dismissed at the same time. Wilson sued his former employer for violations of the ADA, and the court ruled that the employer treated him as disabled and terminated him because he was disabled. The company appealed, but the Fourth Circuit affirmed the trial court's decision.

Michael, C. J.

***

Phoenix contends that the record does not support the district court's ultimate finding that the company regarded Wilson as having an impairment that substantially limits a major life activity. We disagree because the district court made specific findings, which are not clearly erroneous, to support its ultimate finding that Phoenix regarded Wilson as having a disability.

First, the district court found that company president Hurst's statement in his June 2, 2001, e-mail to an assistant was evidence that Phoenix believed that Wilson was disabled. Hurst said pointblank that Wilson "qualifies for ADA designation." Phoenix argues that this statement should be discounted because it was made before Wilson's medication was adjusted, and it did not reflect what the company believed about Wilson's condition at the time he was terminated. The district court, however, cited Hurst's e-mail as an early example of Phoenix's erroneous perception that Wilson was disabled, a perception that continued, as the court found, until his termination in August 2002.

Second, the district court found that Phoenix's disability perception was evident when it ignored the May 24, 2001, opinion of Dr. Bergmann, the neurologist, who released Wilson to return to work without restrictions "and instead relied on the opinion of the company doctor who had not [re]examined" Wilson. In other words, the company's firm perception that Wilson was disabled led it to discount the specialist's medical opinion that Wilson was capable of returning to work.

Third, the district court credited Wilson's testimony that Phoenix's senior management treated him "like [he] was a handicapped person" after his panic attack. This testimony was accepted because Hurst and Wise avoided Wilson whenever possible, and Wise even refused to look at him. This treatment, the court noted, "shows [that] the very myths and fears about disability and disease" can result in a person being regarded as having a disability, one problem "Congress was trying to address with the ADA."

***

The court's determination that the company believed that Wilson could not effectively operate, or see well enough to make use of, a computer is supported by more specific findings: the company instructed Wilson not to perform tasks on the computer, such as the input of information, for fear of entry error; and the company did not make the effort to give Wilson adequate training on the new computer system. The district court found that the company believed Wilson could not write, and this finding is supported by the testimony of the human resources assistant who testified that she "couldn't really read" Wilson's handwriting. Finally, the court found that Phoenix believed that Wilson could not count washers (the company's product), and this finding is supported by the testimony of Wise, who instructed Wilson "not to do counting tasks," again because the company was afraid he would make errors.

These perceptions on Phoenix's part about the extent of Wilson's impairment were inaccurate. The company, in other words, believed that Wilson's Parkinson's symptoms were substantially more limiting than they actually were, as indicated in further findings by the district court and the record.

***

Two of the tasks Phoenix mistakenly believed Wilson could not do at work—use a computer effectively and write—transcend the work setting and qualify as activities that are of "central importance to people's daily lives." *Toyota,* 534 U.S. at 202. Likewise, the company's mistaken belief that Wilson could not count washers supports the district court's finding that "Wilson was perceived by Phoenix as unable to perform a variety of tasks central to most people's daily lives." *see Toyota,* 534 U.S. at 202. Moreover, as the district court found, after Wilson's Parkinson's symptoms flared up in May 2001, the company described him as disabled under the ADA, ignored a specialist's positive assessment of his ability to function, shunned him, and concocted a plan to eliminate his position and get rid of him. These factors, taken together, support the district court's ultimate finding that Phoenix regarded Wilson as having an impairment that substantially limited him in the major life activities of performing manual tasks and seeing.

***

The district court's disbelief of Phoenix's proffered reasons for Wilson's termination was based in part on the court's determination that the reasons the company

gave to the EEOC were different than the one advanced at trial. The company claimed for the first time at trial that the new computer system had "replaced Wilson's job functions," thereby prompting the company to terminate him . . . The court's more detailed findings about the company's false (or pretextual) reasons for terminating Wilson are . . . amply supported by the evidence.

***

The judgment of the district court is affirmed.

Case Questions

1. To what extent could Phoenix's liability have been avoided had it documented Wilson's alleged inability to perform required tasks on the new computer system? In your opinion, is Phoenix required to wait until Wilson makes a costly mistake before concluding that he cannot perform the functions of the job? Are there alternatives short of waiting for a mistake?

2. What could Phoenix have done to improve its handling of the medical diagnoses? Where did it go wrong?

3. What type of policy could you develop that would instruct your managers about how to handle an employee with Parkinson's disease or other serious medical condition that would have avoided the mistakes that Wilson's employer made?

Case 2

Pickens v. Soo Line Railroad Co. *264 F.3d 773 (8th Cir. 2001)*

Employee Dennis Pickens contends his former employer, Soo Line Railroad (Soo Line), terminated his employment in violation of the ADA after he suffered a back injury. Pickens found upon returning to work that he was only able to sustain full-time employment if he could take off some time when the back injury flared up. He did so on the basis of time off allowed by the collective bargaining agreement but did so in such a manner that it resulted in more than 20 absences in the course of a year. The jury found for Pickens; however, the court ruled in favor of Soo Line as a matter of law.

Hansen, C. J.

***

Pickens had worked for the Soo Line from 1973 until 1996 as a railroad conductor. On October 14, 1992, Pickens was injured while on the job. As a result, and after an unsuccessful five-month trial work period, Pickens was

unable to continue working for three years. Pickens returned to work in October 1995, but because of medical restrictions limiting his work time to no more than an eight-hour day, he was unable to resume his duties as a conductor. Soo Line offered Pickens a switchman's position to accommodate his medical limitations. Pickens worked as a switchman for three days before concluding the job was too strenuous and refusing to continue working in the position. Because Pickens wished to return to his "road" position as a conductor, he requested that his physician lift his medical restriction to allow for a twelve-hour work day, four days per week—the schedule that the job required. Two months after returning to his duties as a full-time conductor, Pickens found that working four days per week was too strenuous, and he sought another medical restriction. Pickens' physician refused to comply with his request. Consequently, Pickens regularly made himself unavailable for work by exercising his right to "lay off" under the railroad's collective bargaining agreement.]

After he chose to lay off in the spring of 1996, Soo Line required Pickens to obtain a medical status report from his physician prior to returning to work. This was the railroad's policy; however, it was the first time Soo Line had required Pickens to procure a release. One of the questions included in the release asked Pickens' physician whether he was able to return to full-time duty. Although his physician determined Pickens to be incapable of full-time employment, Pickens requested that his physician falsify his condition by answering affirmatively. His physician acquiesced to Pickens' deception of the railroad. Pickens continued his cyclical pattern of routinely laying off, obtaining a medical release, and returning to work when he chose. While waiting for clearance to return to work after a layoff in August 1996, Pickens wrote a letter to Soo Line's claims representative with copies sent to Soo Line's president and chief medical officer, expressing his frustration. He wrote in part: "I had my medical restrictions removed to get back to work before and I will do it again if this is required. I will totally disregard safety and common sense if this is required." Concerned both with the possibility that Pickens might act on his threat and that Pickens had misrepresented the status of his health, Soo Line held a hearing pursuant to the collective bargaining agreement and subsequently terminated him on August 16, 1996.

II.

***

Pickens asserts that he is qualified to perform the essential functions of his job regardless of his excessive absences given the nature of the railroad's scheduling structure. Pickens contends that because the railroad allows an employee to "lay off" of working any day of his choosing, this procedure makes his use of the practice a nonissue. We disagree. This court has consistently held that "regular and reliable attendance is a necessary element of most jobs." Even though the railroad's system of scheduling appears quite flexible, the railroad's policy requires regular, reliable attendance, and Pickens' conductor's job was full-time. Pickens' choice to lay off twenty-nine times from October 1995 to August 1996 is excessive and eviscerates any regularity in his attendance. "An employee who is unable to come to work on a regular basis [is] unable to satisfy any of the functions of the job in question, much less the essential ones."

Pickens' case is similar to *Buckles v. First Data Res., Inc.* In *Buckles,* a panel of this court reversed the district court's denial of judgment as a matter of law and remanded for entry of judgment in favor of the employer when an employee with acute sinusitis was chronically absent from his job. The employee contended that he was qualified to perform his duties with the accommodation of leaving work any time an air-borne irritant aggravated his condition. Our court disagreed, reasoning that "[u]nfettered ability to leave work at any time is certainly not a reasonable accommodation," and an employer is not required by the ADA to provide an unlimited absentee policy.

The ADA does cite a part-time or modified work schedule as a reasonable means of accommodation, but we view Pickens' suggested method—that he should be able to work only when he feels like working—as unreasonable as a matter of law. Soo Line accommodated Pickens by assigning him to do the switchman's job where he could work within his medical restrictions for two days per week but be paid for a full five-day work week. This effort proved unsuccessful when Pickens refused to perform as a switchman after only three days on duty. Additionally, he had his physician falsify that he was able to perform full-time work because he did not want to be limited to the part-time list of conductors. Furthermore, as the district court noted, when Pickens applied for disability benefits from the Railroad Retirement Board after Soo Line terminated him, he asserted under penalty of perjury that, as of August 1996, he was completely unable to work in the railroad industry because of his disability. Although Supreme Court precedent mandates that Pickens' admission of a total inability to work is not wholly inconsistent with inclusion under the ADA, this is true only if a reasonable juror could conclude he could perform the essential elements of his job with or without a reasonable accommodation. Our review of the record convinces us that as a matter of law, no reasonable juror could find Pickens to be a qualified individual because he was unable to perform the essential duties of his job with or without a reasonable accommodation.

Case Questions

1. Do you believe that attendance should be considered an essential function of most positions? Under what circumstances?

2. Should it matter that Pickens felt that he had no choice but to "go around" the system because he believed his employer was being unreasonable?

3. The court notes that the ADA does cite a part-time or modified work schedule as a reasonable means of accommodation. However, the court thought that Pickens' suggested method—that he should be able to work only when he feels like working—was unreasonable. If an employee is not sure when his disability will be more prohibitive with regard to work, a part-time schedule might not make sense. How can an employer appropriately accommodate a disabled worker who does not know when her or his disability will require an absence?

Huber v. Wal-Mart Stores, Inc.   *486 F.3d 480 (8th Cir. 2007)*

Huber worked for Wal-Mart as a dry grocery order filler earning $13.00 per hour, including a $0.50 shift differential. While working for Wal-Mart, she injured her right arm and hand and could no longer perform the essential functions of the order filler job. Because of her disability, Huber sought reasonable accommodation in the form of reassignment to a vacant router position, which was an equivalent position under the ADA. Wal-Mart, however, did not agree to reassign Huber automatically to the router position. Instead, pursuant to its policy of hiring the most qualified applicant for the position, Wal-Mart required that she apply and compete for the router position with other applicants. Ultimately, it filled the job instead with a nondisabled applicant. Wal-Mart explained that, although Huber was qualified with or without an accommodation to perform the duties of the router position, she was not the *most-qualified* candidate. Everyone involved agreed that the individual hired for the router position was the most-qualified candidate. Wal-Mart later placed Huber at another facility in a maintenance associate position (janitorial position), which paid $6.20 per hour.

Pam Huber brought an action against Wal-Mart Stores, Inc., claiming discrimination under the Americans with Disabilities Act of 1990. The parties filed cross-motions for summary judgment. The district court granted summary judgment in favor of Huber. Wal-Mart appealed and the Circuit Court reverses.

Riley, C. J.

***

We are faced with an unanswered question: whether an employer who has an established policy to fill vacant job positions with the most qualified applicant is required to reassign a qualified disabled employee to a vacant position, although the disabled employee is not the most qualified applicant for the position.

***

II. Discussion

. . . The ADA states the scope of reasonable accommodation may include:

[J]ob restructuring, part-time or modified work schedules, *reassignment to a vacant position,* acquisition or modification of equipment or devices, appropriate adjustment or modifications of examinations, training materials or policies, the provision of qualified readers or interpreters, and other similar accommodations for individuals with disabilities.

Huber contends Wal-Mart, as a reasonable accommodation, should have automatically reassigned her to the vacant router position without requiring her to compete with other applicants for that position. Wal-Mart disagrees, citing its non-discriminatory policy to hire the most qualified applicant. Wal-Mart argues that, under the ADA, Huber was not entitled to be reassigned automatically to the router position without first competing with other applicants. This is a question of first impression in our circuit. As the district court noted, other circuits differ with respect to the meaning of the reassignment language under the ADA.

The Tenth Circuit in *Smith v. Midland Brake, Inc.* (10th Cir. 1999) stated:

> [I]f the reassignment language merely requires employers to consider on an equal basis with all other applicants an otherwise qualified existing employee with a disability for reassignment to a vacant position, that language would add nothing to the obligation not to discriminate, and would thereby be redundant. . . .
>
> Thus, the reassignment obligation must mean something more than merely allowing a disabled person to compete equally with the rest of the world for a vacant position.

In the Tenth Circuit, reassignment under the ADA results in automatically awarding a position to a qualified disabled employee regardless whether other better qualified applicants are available, and despite an employer's policy to hire the best applicant.

On the other hand, the Seventh Circuit in *EEOC v. Humiston-Keeling, Inc.* (7th Cir. 2000) explained:

> The reassignment provision makes clear that the employer must also consider the feasibility of assigning the worker to a different job in which his disability will not be an impediment to full performance, and if the reassignment is feasible and does not require the employer to turn away a superior applicant, the reassignment is mandatory.

In the Seventh Circuit, ADA reassignment does not require an employer to reassign a qualified disabled employee to a job for which there is a more qualified applicant, if the employer has a policy to hire the most qualified applicant.

Wal-Mart urges this court to adopt the Seventh Circuit's approach and to conclude (1) Huber was not entitled, as a reasonable accommodation, to be reassigned automatically to the router position, and (2) the ADA only requires Wal-Mart to allow Huber to compete for the job, but does not require Wal-Mart to turn away a superior applicant. We find this approach persuasive and in accordance with the purposes of the ADA. As the Seventh Circuit noted in *Humiston-Keeling:*

> The contrary rule would convert a nondiscrimination statute into a mandatory preference statute, a result which would be both inconsistent with the nondiscriminatory aims of the ADA and an unreasonable imposition on the employers and coworkers of disabled employees. A policy of giving the job to the best applicant is legitimate and nondiscriminatory. Decisions on the merits are not discriminatory.

"[T]he [ADA] is not a mandatory preference act."

We agree and conclude the ADA is not an affirmative action statute and does not require an employer to reassign a qualified disabled employee to a vacant position when such a reassignment would violate a legitimate non-discriminatory policy of the employer to hire the most qualified candidate. This conclusion is bolstered by the Supreme Court's decision in *U.S. Airways, Inc. v. Barnett* (2002), holding that an employer ordinarily is not required to give a disabled employee a higher seniority status to enable the disabled employee to retain his or her job when another qualified employee invokes an entitlement to that position conferred by the employer's seniority system. We previously have stated in dicta that "an employer is not required to make accommodations that would subvert other, more qualified applicants for the job."

Thus, the ADA does not require Wal-Mart to turn away a superior applicant for the router position in order to give the position to Huber. To conclude otherwise is "affirmative action with a vengeance. That is giving a job to someone solely on the basis of his status as a member of a statutorily protected group."

***

III. Conclusion

We reverse the judgment of the district court, and we remand for entry of judgment in favor of Wal-Mart consistent with this opinion.

Case Questions

1. Are you more persuaded by the analysis of the Tenth Circuit or the Seventh and Eighth (current case)?

2. Does this case represent a clear win for the employer? What guidance would you give an employer after the holding in this case? What policies might be most effective?

3. What implications might this case have for determining the reasonableness of other forms of accommodation?

EEOC v. Convergys Customer Management Group, Inc., *491 F. 3d 790 (8th Cir. 2007)*

Case 4

Demirelli, who uses a wheelchair due to a rare condition commonly known as brittle bone disease, was hired by Convergys as a call representative to answer telephone calls from customers of Convergys' clients. To keep its call stations consistently attended, Convergys maintains a strict tardy policy and penalizes employees who are more than three minutes late to work or after lunch.

Demirelli was penalized for repeatedly arriving late to work and returning late from lunch. The company, however, didn't have assigned workstations, so employees had to find an open workstation when they arrived and when they returned from work. A jury found for the plaintiff, awarding Demirelli lost wages and compensatory damages. The district court denied Convergys's motions for judgment as a matter of law and Convergys appealed. The Eighth Circuit affirms.

Smith, C. J.

***

Records show that Demirelli was late reporting for work 37 times and late returning from lunch 65 times—far in excess of Convergys's 14 tardy allowance. Demirelli's tardiness reporting to work stemmed from the lack of adequate handicapped parking at Convergys's call center. The call center's large parking area only had two van-accessible, handicapped parking spaces—spaces large enough for a special-needs van to operate a ramp or motorized lift. These two spaces were usually occupied when Demirelli arrived, thus causing him to either wait for the space to become unoccupied or find an alternative parking space.

Demirelli made unsuccessful efforts to reduce his tardiness for work. Specifically, Demirelli tried arriving at work earlier—at one point arriving nearly an hour early—however, the two parking spots were still usually occupied. Demirelli then began parking at a nearby movie theater, but traveling via wheelchair from the theater's parking lot to the call center took over 10 minutes and caused Demirelli considerable physical pain. Finally, Demirelli requested different hours hoping that one of the two special-needs parking spaces might be available at a later hour. But even during a later work-shift, the two special-needs spots were still occasionally occupied.

Demirelli's condition and the layout of Convergys's call center hampered an on-time lunch return. Convergys's call center is a maze of hundreds of cubicles where individual call representatives answer customer calls. Cubicles are not assigned to specific call representatives; when call representatives report for work or return from lunch, they claim the first cubicle that they can find. Most employees simply look over the top of the rows of cubicles to find an available workstation. However, this option was not available to the wheelchair-confined Demirelli. He was forced to examine each workstation. . . .

. . . When his supervisors approached him to discuss his tardies, Demirelli explained that he was having problems finding a parking space and a workstation. He asked that he be given "a grace period"—a few extra minutes to return from lunch to work. Convergys denied this request. On June 27, 2002, Convergys terminated Demirelli's employment.

***

The matter proceeded to trial, and a jury found for the plaintiffs, awarding Demirelli $14,265.22 in lost wages and $100,000 in other compensatory damages.

II. Discussion

Convergys appeals the district court's denial of its motion for judgment as a matter of law, averring that it cannot be held liable for failure to accommodate Demirelli because he did not request a specific, reasonable accommodation. In the alternative, Convergys avers that Demirelli's proposed accommodations were unreasonable. Convergys also challenges the award and amount of compensatory damages.

A. Judgment as a Matter of Law

***

1. *The Interactive Process*

Convergys avers that, as a matter of law, an employer cannot be held liable for failing to accommodate a disabled employee who has not requested a specific, reasonable accommodation. Similarly, Convergys avers that the district court erred when it declined to instruct the jury that Demirelli was required to request a specific accommodation. We hold that the district court did not err.

Our case law has established a shared responsibility between employers and employees to resolve accommodation requests. A disabled employee must initiate the accommodation-seeking process by making his employer aware of the need for an accommodation. Additionally, the employee must provide relevant details of his disability and, if not obvious, the reason that his disability requires an accommodation.

Once the employer is made aware of the legitimate need for an accommodation, the employer must "make a reasonable effort to determine the appropriate accommodation." "This means that the employer should first analyze the relevant job and the specific limitations imposed

by the disability and then, in consultation with the individual, identify potential effective accommodations."

This division of responsibility is "only logical, as an employee will typically have better access to information concerning his limitations and abilities whereas an employer will typically have better access to information regarding possible alternative duties or positions available to the disabled employee."

Demirelli testified at trial that he requested an accommodation because of limitations created by his wheelchair, thus meeting his initial burden. The record does not show, however, that Convergys fulfilled its obligation to explore possible accommodations for Demirelli's disability. In fact, the record evidence shows that Demirelli assumed Convergys's responsibility by offering several potential accommodations, including a few extra minutes to return from lunch. Demirelli thus exceeded what disabled employees at the initial stage of the interactive process must do. Convergys's argument thus attempts to place the entire responsibility of fashioning an accommodation upon Demirelli.

***

We hold that Demirelli was not required to more specifically request accommodation. Accordingly, the district court did not err by denying Convergys's motion for judgment as a matter of law. Similarly, the district court did not err by declining to instruct the jury that Demirelli was required to request a specific accommodation.

2. *Reasonable Accommodation*

Convergys avers that any accommodation that provided Demirelli with extra time was unreasonable because it required Convergys to eliminate the essential punctuality requirement. We disagree. . . .

The district court determined that punctuality is an essential job function. In order to fulfill this essential job function, the record evidence is clear that Demirelli requested an extra 15 minutes to return from his lunch break. Viewing the evidence in a light most favorable to the jury verdict, we believe that an extra 15 minutes is a reasonable accommodation. First, Convergys puts forth no evidence showing that extending Demirelli's lunch break by 15 minutes would eliminate its punctuality requirement. An additional 15 minutes would merely create a different time for Demirelli to return from his lunch break. Contrary to Convergys's assertion, this modified work schedule would not create an open-ended schedule where Demirelli would be free to return from lunch at his pleasure or at unpredictable times. Second, the record evidence also shows that by granting Demirelli an extra 15 minutes, 62 of Demirelli's 65 lunch tardies would have been eliminated. . . .

III. Conclusion

After a careful review of the record, the judgment of the district court is affirmed.

Case Questions

1. Do you believe the employer made a good-faith effort to reasonably accommodate the employee?

2. Can you imagine other accommodations that may have been considered by the employer to be less disruptive to its three-minute punctuality requirement? From a relative perspective, do you agree with the court that fifteen minutes is a reasonable accommodation at the beginning of the work day and after lunch?

3. If increasing the number of special needs parking spaces would have allowed Demirelli to arrive at work on time, should the court have simply required that accommodation as an alternative? Cost was not discussed in this excerpted opinion; but do you think there should be a dollar limit on the price of a reasonable accommodation?

Part 3

Regulation of the Employment Environment

Chapter 14

The Employee's Right to Privacy and Management of Personal Information

Learning Objectives

When you finish this chapter, you should be able to:

LO1 Describe the nature of privacy as a fundamental right.

LO2 Explain the three general ways in which privacy is legally protected in the United States.

LO3 Define the legal concept of a "reasonable expectation of privacy" and its application to the workplace.

LO4 Identify and apply the standard for unreasonable searches and seizures under the Fourth Amendment.

LO5 Explain the distinctions between the protections for public- and private-sector privacy.

LO6 Describe the legal framework that applies to private sector privacy cases.

LO7 Identify and differentiate the *prima facie* cases for common-law claims of privacy invasions (intrusion into seclusion, public disclosure of private facts, publication in a false light, and breach of contract/defamation).

LO8 Explain the extent to which an employer can legally dictate the off-work acts of its employees.

LO9 Discuss how advances in technology have impacted employee privacy.

LO10 State the key business justifications for employee monitoring.

LO11 Explain the most effective means by which to design and implement a technology use policy.

LO12 Describe the legal environment that surrounds employee use of social media technologies.

Opening Scenarios

SCENARIO 1

1 Aravinda has been reading in the news lately of the skyrocketing costs of health care, particularly surrounding the HIV epidemic. She is concerned that her small 10-employee company would suffer a financial disaster if one of its workers contracted the virus since the company's insurance costs would increase. Therefore, she wants to conduct a confidential HIV test of each present employee and future applicant. Aravinda has several concerns. First, what if an individual refuses to take the test based on the grounds of invasion of privacy? Second, if someone tests positive, can Aravinda refuse to hire or can she discharge her or him without violating federal law protecting employees with disabilities? Third, how can she otherwise protect against rising costs? Fourth, if an employee tests negative, but Aravinda decides to terminate the employee anyway, is she liable for the *appearance* that the employee is HIV-positive and that Aravinda terminated her or him as a consequence of the test results? How can she ensure that the test results are kept confidential?

SCENARIO 2

2 Abraham, a real estate agent, has three children, two of whom are in college. In order to earn extra money to help with college tuition payments, Abraham (who studied modern dance during his college career) finds a job dancing in a club that caters specifically to women. While not exactly erotic dancing (he keeps all of his clothes on), it is not ballroom dancing either. Celebrating during a bachelorette party, one of the partners of the real estate firm for which Abraham works catches sight of him dancing. When he arrives at the office the next day, she calls him into her office and orders him to quit his night job. She claims that both clients and potential clients might see him there and he would lose all credibility as a real estate agent. Does she have a right to require Abraham to do this as a condition of future employment? (Presume that he is an employee and not an independent contractor.)

SCENARIO 3

3 Solange receives a spam email asking her to go look at a certain Web site. Since she does not know who it is from or why she is receiving it, she clicks on the link and finds herself at a Web site devoted to XXX-rated videos. She is so perturbed by this occurrence that she spends a few moments looking around the Web site trying to find its site administrator. She intends to send off a message to the administrator asking this person not to send her any more junk mail. After searching for several minutes with no luck, she leaves the Web site and goes back to reading her email. A few days later, she is called into her manager's office and reprimanded for using employer-owned computer equipment for personal interests such as this XXX-rated video site. It seems that her manager was using a program that alerted him any time an employee perused certain inappropriate Web sites. She tries to explain but leaves with a written reprimand in her hand and a copy in her files. She is furious, not only at her manager's unwillingness to understand, but also at the invasion of her privacy posed by this computer monitoring. Does her employer have a right to monitor her computer use in this way?

Are There Guarantees in Life?

Privacy is a surprisingly vague and disputed value in contemporary society. With the tremendous increase in computer technology in recent decades, calls for greater protection of privacy have increased. Yet, there is widespread confusion concerning the nature, extent, and value of privacy. Philosophers have argued that our society cannot maintain its core values without simultaneously guaranteeing the privacy of the individual. Edward Bloustein writes that "an individual deprived of privacy merges with the mass. His opinions, being public, tend never to be different; his aspirations, being known, tend always to be conventionally accepted ones; his feelings, being openly exhibited, tend to lose their quality of unique personal warmth and to become the feelings of every man. Such a being, although sentient, is fungible; he is not an individual."[1]

Recent inventions and business methods call attention to the next step that must be taken for the protection of the person and for securing to the individual what Judge Cooley calls the right "to be let alone." Instantaneous photographs and newspaper enterprises have invaded the sacred precincts of private and domestic life, and numerous mechanical devices threaten to make good the prediction that "what is whispered in the closet shall be proclaimed from the house-tops."[2]

Philosopher Chris MacDonald explains that privacy is about having a realm of personal control from which others can be excluded at will. In other words, it has to do with freedom of action, freedom from the prying eyes of neighbors, governments, or employers. The more such freedom we have, the more privacy we have.[3]

Europeans generally view employee rights using a different perspective from that in the U.S. While Americans view rights of employees in terms of the protection of their privacy, Europeans are more likely to perceive their protection with regard to human dignity, the employee's right to be free from embarrassment and humiliation.[4] The result of this distinction is that European employees generally enjoy a wider range of freedom from employer intrusion in the workplace than do U.S. employees. Indeed, some U.S. firms that engage in business internationally have found themselves in violation of EU standards, and subject to hefty fines, when they applied their privacy rules to employees who were located in the EU.

LO1

The concept of privacy as a fundamental right is certainly not limited to the United States and Europe. Privacy is protected in the Qur'an[5] and was recognized by Mohammed.[6] Ancient Greece already had laws protecting privacy, and the Jewish Talmud considers privacy an aspect of one's sanctity, providing rules for protecting one's home. In fact, the Talmud contains reference to "harm caused by seeing" (*hezeq re'iyyah*) when one intrudes upon another.

But do employees actually have a "fundamental right to privacy" as many believe? The answer to this question is not as easy as one might presume, given the wide recognition of employee rights in the workplace. The right to privacy may not be as fundamental as employees generally believe it to be, which makes it all the more important in these days of advancing information technology. Computer technology, though largely beneficial, can have a negative effect on employees if the easily obtained information is misused, incorrect, or misleading. Employers now have a greater capacity to invade an employee's privacy than ever before. Among other devices, there are chairs that can sense and record the time an employee spends at his or her desk, computer programs that measure employees' computer keystrokes to ensure they are as productive as they should be, phones that monitor employees' phone calls, and policies related to workplace communication to make sure all communications are work-related. Monitoring is only increasing in power, ability, and frequency. Sales of computer monitoring and surveillance software increased almost 500 percent to $622 million in 2006.[7] But perhaps there is presently a greater employer need for seemingly private information, with more than 75 percent of 14.8 million drug users in the United States employed.[8] Drug use in American industry costs employers approximately $82 billion per year in overall productivity due to absenteeism and attrition; theft of employer property by employees is estimated at $10 billion per year; and failure to perform an intensive reference and background check of an applicant may cost the employer enormous amounts in litigation fees defending claims of negligent hiring, easily outweighing the cost of a drug test, usually less than $50. In this time of increased competition in the global marketplace, each employee becomes all the more crucial to the workings of the company. An employer has a justified basis for attempting to choose the most appropriate and qualified person for the job; the means by which the employer obtains that information, however, may be suspect.

The right to privacy is not only balanced with the arguably legitimate interests of the employer but also with the employer's responsibility to *protect* the employees' personal information. A 2007 study of more than 800 North American privacy and security professionals reported that there is a strong likelihood of a security breach relating to personally identifiable information. In fact, 85 percent of those responding had experienced or observed a security breach within the past 12 months and 63 percent had experienced multiple breaches during that time— between 6 and 20 occurrences.[9]

Whereas erosion of at-will employment was the dominant issue of the 1980s, scholars predicted that privacy would be the main theme for the 1990s and beyond. This chapter will address the employee's rights regarding personal information and the employer's responsibilities regarding that information, as well as the employer's right to find out both job-related and nonrelated personal information about its employees. Chapter 3 previously addressed other issues regarding the legality of information gathering through testing procedures. This chapter will not address issues relating to consumer privacy since they fall outside the scope of the chapter's and the text's primary focus.

Background

There are three ways in which privacy may be legally protected: by the Constitution (federal or state), by federal and/or state statutes, and by the common law. The U.S. Constitution does not actually mention privacy, but privacy has been inferred as a necessary adjunct of other constitutional rights we hold. The right to privacy was first recognized by the Supreme Court in *Griswold v. Connecticut*,[10] when the Court held that a Connecticut statute restricting a married couple's use of birth control devices unconstitutionally infringed on the right to marital privacy.

The Court held a constitutional guarantee of various zones of privacy as a part of the **fundamental rights** guaranteed by the Constitution, such as the right to free speech and the right to be free from unreasonable searches and seizures. The latter right is that on which many claims for privacy rights are based; the Court

fundamental right
A right that is guaranteed by the Constitution, whether stated or not.

Exhibit 14.1 *Realities about Employee Privacy Rights*

1. Employees do not have an absolute right to privacy in their workplace.

2. It is not a breach of an employee's right to privacy for an employer to ask with whom the employee lives.

3. In the private sector, the Constitution does not protect employees' right to be free from unreasonable searches and seizures.

4. Without constitutional protection, employees are safeguarded to some extent by common law protections against invasions of privacy.

5. Though an employee may give information to an employer, the employer is still bound to use that information only for the purpose for which it was collected.

---

has held that under certain circumstances the required disclosure of certain types of personal information should be considered an unreasonable search. It has protected against the mandatory disclosure of personal papers, and it decided in favor of the right to make procreation decisions privately.

While baseless or unjustified intrusions, at first blush, may appear to be completely abhorrent in our society, proponents of the argument that employers can ask whatever they please argue that if an employee does not want to offer a piece of information, there is something the employee is trying to hide. For example, why would an employee refuse to submit to a drug test if that employee is not abusing drugs? Do **private sector** employers have the right to ask their employees any question they choose and take adverse employment actions against the employee if she or he refuses to answer since they are not necessarily constrained by constitutional protections? (See Exhibit 14.1, "Realities about Employee Privacy Rights.")

Additionally, employees are concerned about the type of information gathered in the course of applying for and holding a job. Who has access to that information? What information may be deemed "confidential," and what does that mean to the employee? Evidently, employers perceive challenging issues among these and others with regard to privacy; as of 2004, there were more than 2,000 chief privacy officers (CPOs) in businesses around the world, more than 10 times the estimate three years ago.[11]

private sector
That segment of the workforce represented by private companies (companies that are not owned or managed by the government or one of its agencies).

Workplace Privacy, Generally

Privacy protections in the workplace are a completely different animal than other types of workplace protections, such as those against discrimination on the basis of gender, disability, and age. Simply put, employees in the private sector workplace do not have broad rights to personal privacy. Why? To begin, unlike the other areas, no *comprehensive* federal workplace privacy legislation exists. The protections that do exist, as discussed previously, arise from a motley collection of inferences from the Constitution, limited-purpose federal laws, assorted state laws, and some **common law** (court-created through case law).

common law
Law made and applied by judges, based on precedent (prior case law).

Second, in almost every state, employees are hired at will, which means that employers can fire them for good reasons, for bad reasons, or for no reason at all (but not for an illegal reason), as we shall discuss in more detail later. If an employer legitimately can fire an employee for "bad reasons," you can see quite clearly why an employee is not going to be successful in stating a case against the employer for violating the employee's privacy unless the employee can fit his or her complaint specifically into one of the protections guaranteed by the federal, state, and common laws, thus turning a "bad reason" into an "illegal reason."

Perhaps the most effective way to understand workplace privacy protections is to examine where the protections do exist. Courts have recognized an employee's right to privacy in the workplace where there is a "reasonable expectation of privacy."[12] However, they have also held that a work area, unlike, for instance, a bedroom, is not a place of solitude or seclusion; so, there is no expectation of privacy in that environment.[13] In addition, anything that the employer provides to employees—a telephone, computer, desk, chair, or other business-related instrument—contains no expectation of privacy because it belongs to the employer, not to the employees. Thus, the content of emails, telephone calls, and computer activity conducted on employer-provided equipment is not private.

Is there *any* reasonable expectation of privacy in the workplace? (See Exhibit 14.2, "'Reasonable' Areas in Which to Expect Privacy in the Workplace, Subject to Exceptions.") Yes, employees have an expectation of privacy with regard to their body, including what they carry in their pockets. Their employer generally does not have the right to frisk them or to require them to disclose what they are carrying in their pockets; although, as we shall see later, there are situations in which such as invasion of privacy would be appropriate. This expectation extends to company-provided bathrooms, changing rooms, and showers. But, should this expectation cover drug testing? We will explore that question later in this chapter.

Second, employees have an expectation of privacy in connection with items that are contained in other normally private locations, such as a purse or briefcase;

Exhibit 14.2 *"Reasonable" Areas in Which to Expect Privacy in the Workplace, Subject to Exceptions*

1. One's body and physical space; one has a reasonable expectation to be free from a pat-down or body search.

2. Normally private locations, such as a purse or briefcase.

3. Personal information, accessed without permission.

however, these locations, also, are subject to exceptions under certain circumstances. For example, if an employee puts a purse in a company-provided desk drawer, the employer generally has the right to examine the desk drawer but likely not the contents of their purse. Similarly, employees have an expectation of privacy in the contents of their car that sits in the company parking lot, assuming that it is not a company car or that they are not using the car for company purposes other than to go to and from work. Their employer generally cannot go and search their car, with some exceptions.

Third, they have an expectation of privacy in their personal (not personnel) records and information. For example, they have the right to assume that their employer has no right to access their credit history, their driving record, or their family's medical records without their permission; but, we can all imagine situations in which that rule may not apply or may be excepted. Their employer, for example, could reasonably expect to access their driving history if they were applying for a job operating a company vehicle, although the employer needs their permission to do so.

Finally, workers have an expectation of privacy in what they choose to do in their free time, when they are away from work. However, this expectation is not quite as extensive as one might anticipate. Plenty of employers have tried to restrict what employees do in their free time, some successfully.

While the list may seem broad, the scope of workplace privacy rights is actually quite limited. The vast majority of the time during which employees are present at their employers' offices, they are subject to monitoring and other intrusions. Employers are free to monitor their movements, the keystrokes they make on their employer-provided computers, and the time they spend communicating with co-workers. Technological improvements have not only made their task that much easier but have also generated new ideas for intruding on employee privacy never before imagined (iris scans, voice prints, and face geometry, to name three).

Now we shall examine the specifics, first exploring public sector employee privacy, then continuing to private sector employee privacy.

Public Sector Employee Privacy

public sector
That segment of the workforce represented by governmental employers and governmental agency employers. In some situations, this term may include federal contractors.

With regard to the **public sector**, the Constitution protects individuals from wrongful invasions by the state or by anyone acting on behalf of the government. The personal privacy of federal, state, and local employees is therefore protected from governmental intrusion and excess. As we will see later in this chapter, private sector employees are subject to different—and often fewer—protections.

Constitutional Protection
The Fourth Amendment and Its Exceptions

For the Fourth Amendment's protection against unreasonable search and seizure to be applicable to a given situation, there must first exist a "search or seizure." The Supreme Court has liberally interpreted "search" to include a wide variety of activities such as the retrieval of blood samples and other bodily invasions, including urinalyses, as well as the collection of other personal information. One might imagine how this umbrella gets wider as technology advances.

For the search to violate the Fourth Amendment, that search must be deemed unreasonable, unjustified at its inception, and impermissible in scope. You will read in the seminal Supreme Court case, *O'Connor v. Ortega,* included at the end of the chapter, that a search is justified "at its inception" where the employer has reasonable grounds for suspecting that the search will turn up evidence that the employee is guilty of work-related misconduct, or where the search is necessary for a noninvestigatory work-related purpose such as to retrieve a file.

It is critical to review the *O'Connor* case to understand both the fundamental basis of public-sector search and seizure law as it applies to the workplace as well as much of current case law today. The Court held that a search is permissible in scope where "the measures adopted are reasonably related to the objectives of the search and not excessively intrusive in light of . . . the nature of the misconduct being investigated."

Generally, all searches that are conducted without a judicially issued warrant based on a finding of reasonable cause are held to be unreasonable. But there are several exceptions to this rule, including searches that happen as part of an arrest, some automobile searches, pat-down searches with probable cause to believe the subject is armed, and administrative searches of certain regulated industries.

One example of an exception occurred in *Shoemaker v. Handel*[14] where the Supreme Court held that a drug-related urine test of jockeys without a warrant was acceptable because it satisfied the court's two-pronged test. The Court held that (1) where there is a strong state interest in conducting the unannounced warrantless search and (2) where the pervasive regulation of the industry reduces the expectation of privacy, the search does not violate the Fourth Amendment. Similarly, in *Skinner v. Railway Labor Executives Association,*[15] decided three years after *Shoemaker,* the Court again addressed the question of whether certain forms of drug and alcohol testing violate the Fourth Amendment. While this case is discussed in this text in connection with testing, it is relevant here for the Court's analysis of the privacy right challenged. In *Skinner,* the defendant justified testing railway workers based on safety concerns: "to prevent accidents and casualties in railroad operations that result from impairment of employees by alcohol or drugs." The Court held that "[t]he Government's interest in regulating the conduct of railroad employees to ensure safety, like its supervision of probationers or regulated industries, or its operation of a government office, school, or prison, likewise presents 'special needs' beyond normal law enforcement that may justify departures from the usual warrant and probable-cause requirements."

It was clear to the Court that the governmental interest in ensuring the safety of the traveling public and of the employees themselves "plainly justifies prohibiting covered employees from using alcohol or drugs on duty, or while subject to being called for duty." The issue then for the Court was whether the means by which the defendant monitored compliance with this prohibition justified the privacy intrusion absent a warrant or individualized suspicion. In reviewing the justification, the Court focused on the fact that permission to dispense with warrants is strongest where "the burden of obtaining a warrant is likely to frustrate the governmental purpose behind the search," and recognized that "alcohol and other drugs are eliminated from the bloodstream at a constant rate and blood and breath samples taken to measure whether these substances were in the bloodstream when a triggering event occurred must be obtained as soon as possible." In addition, the Court noted that the railway workers' expectations of privacy in this industry are diminished given its high scrutiny through regulation to ensure safety. The Court therefore concluded that the railway's compelling interests outweigh privacy concerns since the proposed testing "is not an undue infringement on the justifiable expectations of privacy of covered employees." Consider the possible implications of this and related decisions on genetic testing in governmental workplaces or in employment in heavily regulated industries such as that involved in *Skinner.*

Finally, the employer may wish to conduct a search of employee lockers. Would this be acceptable? Under what circumstances is an employer allowed to conduct searches? A search may constitute an invasion of privacy, depending on the nature of the employer and the purpose of the search. The unreasonableness of a search is determined by balancing the extent of the invasion and the extent to which the employee should expect to have privacy in this area against the employer's interest in the security of its workplace, the productivity of its workers, and other job-related concerns.

Prior to any search of employer-owned property, such as desks or lockers, employees should be given formal written notice of the intent to search without their consent. Where the employer intends to search personal effects such as purses or wallets, employees should be forewarned, consent should be obtained prior to the search, and employees should be made well aware of the procedures involved.[16] Consent is recommended under these circumstances because an employee has a greater expectation of privacy in those personal areas. These rights are significantly diminished where the employer is not restrained by constitutional protections.

In an interesting combination of private/public workplace rights, the Ninth Circuit addressed these issues in the 2007 case *United States v. Ziegler.*[17] In that case, Ziegler worked for a private company that had a clear policy in technology use. It explained that equipment and software were company-owned, to be used for business purposes only, and that employees' emails would be constantly monitored. The FBI received a complaint from the firm's Internet provider that Ziegler had accessed child pornography from a company computer and requested access to his computer.[18] The employer consented to the request. The court held that the *employer* had the right to consent to the search because the computer was workplace property and the contents of Ziegler's hard drive were work-related items that contained business information and that were provided to, or created by, the employee in the context of a business relationship. Ziegler's downloading of personal items (pornography) did not destroy the employer's common authority over the computer given the company's policies that *informed employees that electronic devices were company-owned and subject to monitoring*—two key components necessary to the reasonable expectation element in any employment context.[19]

When an employee is detained during a search, the employee may have a claim for *false imprisonment,* which is defined as a total restraint on freedom to move against the employee's will, such as keeping an employee in one area of an office. The employee need not be "locked" into the confinement to be restrained; but when the employee remains free to leave at any time, there is no false imprisonment.

The Fifth and Fourteenth Amendments

The Fifth and Fourteenth Amendments also protect a government employee's right to privacy in that the state may not restrict one's rights unless it is justified. For instance, the Supreme Court has consistently held that everyone has a fundamental right to travel, free of government intervention. Where the state attempts to infringe on anything that has been determined to be a fundamental right, that infringement or restriction is subject to the *strict scrutiny* of the courts. For the restriction to be allowed, the state must show that the restriction is justified by a *compelling state interest.* Moreover, the restriction must be the least intrusive alternative available.

On the other hand, for those interests not deemed by the courts to constitute fundamental rights, a state may impose any restrictions that can be shown to be *rationally related to a valid state interest,* a much more lenient test.

To determine whether the state may restrict or intrude on an employee's privacy rights, it must first be determined whether the claimed right is fundamental. Two tests are used to make this determination. First, the court may look to whether the right is "implicit in the concept of ordered liberty, such that neither liberty nor justice would exist if [the rights] were sacrificed." Second is whether the right is "deeply rooted in this Nation's history and tradition."

While conception, child rearing, education, and marriage have been held to be within the area of privacy protected by the Constitution, other issues have not yet been addressed or determined by the Court, including the right to be free from mandatory preemployment medical tests. Moreover, the Court has found *no* general right of the individual to be left alone.

The Privacy Act of 1974

Governmental intrusion into the lives of federal employees is also restricted by the Privacy Act of 1974. Much of the discussion in the area of employee privacy is framed by governmental response to the issue, both because of limitations imposed on the government regarding privacy and because of the potential for abuse. The Privacy Act of 1974 regulates the release of personal information about federal employees by federal agencies. Specifically, but for 11 stated exceptions, no federal agency may release information about an employee that contains the

Exhibit 14.3 *Privacy Act of 1974*

PRIVACY ACT OF 1974

No Agency shall disclose any record which is contained in a system of records by any means of communication to any person, or to another agency, except pursuant to a written request by, or with the prior written consent of, the individual to whom the record pertains, unless disclosure of the record would be

1. To those officers and employees of the agency which maintains the record who have a need for the record in the performance of their duties.

2. Required under section 552 of this title; (*the Freedom of Information Act*). (*Note that this act does not apply to "personnel, medical, and similar files the disclosure of which would constitute a clearly unwarranted invasion of personal privacy."*)

3. Or a routine use as defined in subsection (a)(7) of this section and described under subsection (e)(4)(D) of this section; (*a purpose that is specifically compatible with the purpose for which the information was gathered*).

4. To the Bureau of the Census for purposes of planning or carrying out a census or survey or related activity. . . .

5. To a recipient who has provided the agency with advance adequate written assurance that the record will be used solely as a statistical research or reporting record, and the record is to be transferred in a form that is not individually identifiable.

6. To the National Archives of the United States as a record which has sufficient historical or other value to warrant its continued preservation by the United States Government, or for evaluation by the Administrator of General Services or his designee to determine whether the record has such value.

7. To another federal agency or to an instrumentality of any government jurisdiction within or under the control of the United States for a civil or criminal law enforcement activity if the activity is authorized by law, and if the head of the agency or instrumentality has made a written request to the agency which maintains the record specifying the particular portion desired and the law enforcement activity for which the record is sought.

8. To a person pursuant to a showing of compelling circumstances affecting the health or safety of an individual if upon such disclosure notification is transmitted to the last known address of such individual.

9. To either House of Congress, or, to the extent of matter within its jurisdiction, any committee or subcommittee thereof, any joint committee or subcommittee of any such joint committee.

10. To the Comptroller General, or any of his authorized representatives, in the course of the performance of the duties of the General Accounting Office.

11. Pursuant to the order of a court of competent jurisdiction.

means for identifying that employee without the employee's prior written consent. (See Exhibit 14.3, "Privacy Act of 1974.")

There are four basic principles that underlie the Privacy Act:

1. Employees should have access to their own personnel files, and there should be some way for them to find out the purposes for which the files are being used.

2. There should be some mechanism by which an employee may correct or amend an inaccurate record.

3. The employee should be able to prevent information from being inappropriately revealed or used without her or his consent, unless such disclosure is required by law.

4. The person who is in charge of maintaining the information must ensure that the files are not falling into the wrong hands and that the information contained within the files is accurate, reliable, and used for the correct reasons. By affording the employee with these rights, Congress has effectively put the right of disclosure of personal information in the hands of the employee, at least when none of the 11 specified exceptions applies.

When one of the Privacy Act exceptions applies, the act dismisses the employee consent requirement, which gives the agency total control over the use of the file. The right to privacy is not absolute; the extent of protection varies with the extent of the intrusion, and the interests of the employee are balanced against the interests of the employer. Basically, the information requested under either the Privacy Act or the Freedom of Information Act is subject to a balancing test weighing the need to know the information against the employee's privacy interest.

The Ninth Circuit Court of Appeals has developed guidelines to assist in this balancing test. The court directs that the following four factors be looked to in reaching a conclusion relating to disclosure:

1. The individual's interest in disclosure of the information sought.
2. The public interest in disclosure.
3. The degree of invasion of personal privacy.
4. Whether there are alternative means of getting the information.

Critics of the act suggest that it is enormously weakened as a result of one particular exemption that allows disclosure for "routine use" compatible with the reason the information was originally collected. In addition, certain specific agencies are exempted. For instance, in March 2003, the Department of Justice exempted the National Crime Information Center, which is a resource for 80,000 law enforcement agencies.

The Privacy Act grants employees two options for relief: criminal penalties and civil remedies, including damages and injunctive relief. The act also allows employees who are adversely affected by an agency's noncompliance to bring a civil suit against the agency in federal court.

Privacy Protection Study Commission

The Privacy Protection Study Commission was formed by Congress with the purpose of studying the possibility of extending the Privacy Act to the private sector. In 1977, the commission concluded that the Privacy Act should not be extended to private employers but that private sector employees should be given many new privacy protections. The suggested protections required a determination of current information-gathering practices and their reasons, a limitation on the information that may be collected to what is relevant, a requirement that the employer inform its employees to ensure accuracy, and a limitation on the usage of the information gathered both internally and externally.

The commission further found that certain issues demanded federal intervention and, for this reason, recommended that (1) the use of polygraph tests in employment-related issues be prohibited; (2) pretext interviews be prohibited; (3) the use of arrest or criminal records in employment decisions be prohibited except where otherwise allowed or required by law; (4) employers be required to use reasonable care in selection of their investigating agencies; and (5) the Federal Fair Credit Reporting Act provisions be strengthened. These recommendations have yet to be implemented by Congress, primarily due to private employers' vocal rejection of such an extension of federal law due to the cost of the implementation of the recommendations.

Federal Wiretapping—Title III

Title III of the Federal Wiretap Act,[20] as amended (particularly by the Electronic Communications Privacy Act of 1986, discussed below), provides privacy protection for and governs the interception of oral, wire, and electronic communications. Title III covers all telephone communications regardless of the medium, except that it does not cover the radio portion of a cordless telephone communication that is transmitted between the handset and base unit. The law authorizes the interception of oral, wire, and electronic communications by investigative and law enforcement officers conducting criminal investigations pertaining to serious criminal offenses, or felonies, following the issuance of a court order by a judge. The Title III law authorizes the interception of particular criminal communications related to particular criminal offenses. In short, it authorizes the acquisition of evidence of crime. It does not authorize noncriminal intelligence gathering, nor does it authorize interceptions related to social or political views.

Forty-four states, plus the District of Columbia and the Virgin Islands, have statutes permitting interceptions by state and local law enforcement officers for certain types of criminal investigations.[21] All of the state statutes are based upon Title III, from which they derive. These statutes must be at least as restrictive as Title III, and in fact most are more restrictive in their requirements. In describing the legal requirements, we will focus on those of Title III since they define the baseline for all wiretaps performed by federal, state, and local law enforcement agencies. In recent years, state statutes have been modified to keep pace with rapid technological advances in telecommunications.

Wiretaps are limited to the crimes specified in Title III and state statutes. Most wiretaps are large undertakings, requiring a substantial use of resources. In 2009, the average cost of installing intercept devices and monitoring communications was more than $52,000, up 10 percent from the 2008 costs.

The frequency of wiretap requests is also growing. In 2009, the number of federal and state wiretaps grew by 26 percent; none of the 2,376 federal and state applications for a wiretap were denied.

Electronic Communications Privacy Act (ECPA)

Title III was created to combat invasion by the government for eavesdropping, in large part due to the Watergate scandal in the 1970s. Originally the federal statutes targeted government eavesdropping on telephone discussion without the consent of the speakers. The federal statute required the government agents to obtain a warrant before they could intercept any oral discussions. In late 1986, Congress increased the coverage by broadening the range of electronic communications, resulting in the ECPA.

The ECPA covers all forms of digital communications, including transmissions of text and digitalized images, in addition to voice communications on the telephone. The law also prohibits unauthorized eavesdropping by all persons and businesses, not only by the government. However, courts have ruled that "interception" applies only to messages in transit and not to messages that have actually reached company computers. Therefore, the impact of the EPCA is to punish electronic monitoring only by third parties and not by employers. Moreover, the ECPA allows interception where consent has been granted. Therefore, a firm that secures employee consent to monitoring at the time of hire is immune from ECPA liability, which means that an employer does not violate the ECPA when it opens and reads employee emails on its own system.[22]

Private Sector Employee Privacy

LO5

Despite the fact that public and private employers have a similar legitimate need for information about applicants and employees to make informed decisions about hiring, promotion, security, discipline, and termination, privacy rights in the private sector of employment are limited; an employee who is arbitrarily treated, but who is without a union or contract, is generally left with fewer rights in the private sector environment.

Generally, employment actions by private employers do not trigger constitutional protections because the Constitution is designed to curb government excesses. The term used is *State action*, which includes actions by both state and federal governments. If no State action is involved, no constitutional protections are triggered. An employment action by a private employer is considered to be a private action.

Whether there should be a right to privacy in both the public and the private sectors, employers suggest that the employee has three choices when faced with objectionable intrusions by employers: quit, comply, or object and risk termination. Employees argue that they are defenseless because of their economic condition and that their privacy in the private sector is subject to greater abuse precisely because there are no protections and that the option to quit is unrealistic.

One explanation offered for the difference between public- and private-sector privacy protections is compliance-related costs. The implementation of the Privacy Act throughout its agencies costs the government relatively little because it is conducting self-regulation.

By contrast, ensuring compliance within the private sector requires administration of the compliance and adjudication of violations. The Privacy Protection Study Commission found that requiring an employer to change its manner of maintaining and using records can drastically increase the cost of operation.

These costs include the costs of changing employment record-keeping practices, removing relevant information from employment decisions, and implementing a social policy of employee privacy protection. These costs are not necessarily burdensome to the employer, however. One study found that protecting the rights of employees on a computer system could cost as little as $4 per person. Employers' concern for compliance costs may well be an unrealistic barrier to the development of regulations for privacy rights of private-sector employees.

A second distinction between public- and private-sector employers offered to justify different privacy standards is that more stringent regulation is needed for government employees because it is common for federal agencies to be overzealous in surveillance and information gathering. Private-sector employers, in contrast, do not generally have similar resources and, therefore, are unable to duplicate these invasive activities.

Legal Framework for Employee Rights in the Private Sector

In almost every state,[23] employment is considered to be "at will." **Employment-at-will** means that the employee serves at the will of the employer. Employers can therefore fire an employee for incompetence, insubordination, or any of the other reasons we might consider valid, as well as because the employee wore red shoelaces to work or because the manager's beloved Lakers lost an important game in double overtime the night before. The point is that employees serve at the whim of the employer. In the same manner, an employee at will may opt to leave a job at any time for any reason, without offering any notice at all. So the freedom is *theoretically* mutual; though, of course, the power balance is not always equal.

Even in at-will states, employees maintain a right to work (see Exhibit 14-4, *"Protecting the Right to Work in the At-Will Employment Context"*). First, as we

employment-at-will
Absent a particular contract or other legal obligation that specifies the length or conditions of employment, all employees are employed "at will." This means that, **LO6** unless an agreement specifies otherwise, employers are free to fire an employee—and employees are free to leave the position—at any time and for any reason. By virtue of the inherent imbalance of power in the relationship, this mutuality is often only in theory.

Exhibit 14.4   *Protecting the Right to Work in the At-Will Employment Context*

1. Federal and state statutory protections, such as anti-discrimination laws.

2. Employment contracts, where they exist.

3. Collective bargaining agreements, where applicable.

4. State law exceptions to employment-at-will, including violations of public policy, breaches of implied contracts, or other statutory exceptions.

have seen in other chapters, federal and state laws protect employees from certain employment actions, such as those based on discrimination against one of the protected classes, including gender or race. Second, an employee who signs an employment contract has those rights stated in the contract. Third, union employees have the protections guaranteed to them by the collectively bargained contract between the employer and the union.

Finally, employment at will is limited by certain exceptions created either by statute or case law. Some states recognize one or more exceptions, while others might recognize none at all. In addition, the definition of these exceptions may vary from state to state.

- Bad faith, malicious or retaliatory termination in violation of *public policy.*
- Termination in breach of the *implied covenant of good faith and fair dealing.*
- Termination in breach of some other *implied contract term*, such as those that might be created by employee handbook provisions (in certain jurisdictions).
- Termination in violation of the doctrine of *promissory estoppel* (where the employee reasonably relied on an employer's promise, to the employee's detriment).
- Other exceptions as determined by *statutes* (such as the Worker Adjustment and Retraining Notification Act [WARN]).

If an employee wishes to recover against an employer in an at-will relationship, the employee must be able to point to a law, court decision, or contractual provision that protects her or him. In the area of privacy, given the absence of any comprehensive national privacy law, that task might be quite difficult.

Bases for Right to Privacy in the Private Sector

Private-sector employers are not bound by constitutional structures. On a state-by-state basis, however, private-sector employees may be afforded protection either by the common law or by statute. All but two states provide common-law tort claims to protect individual privacy, such as intrusion into seclusion. Various torts described below have developed to protect individual solitude, the publication of private information, and publications that present personal information in a false light. (See Exhibit 14.5, "U.S. Companies with Operations in Europe Must Comply with Data Protection Laws," for the manner in which privacy protection is handled somewhat differently in the European context.)

Statutory Claims

State legislatures have responded to the issue of private-sector employee privacy in one of four ways:

1. Enacting legislation mirroring federal law regarding the compilation and dissemination of information.
2. Recognizing a constitutional right to privacy under their state constitutions, as in California, Illinois, and Arizona. For example, California appellate courts have found that employees terminated for refusing to submit to drug

Exhibit 14.5 *U.S. Companies with Operations in Europe Must Comply with Data Protection Laws*

The European Union's approach to data privacy is completely alien to American companies. But, as a recent decision from CNIL (Commission Nationale de l'Informatique et des Libertés, the French Data Protection Authority) makes clear, an American company with operations in Europe that does not learn how to play by European rules runs a serious risk of getting slapped with a hefty fine.

***

[T]he European Union's Directive governing the protection of individuals' personal data and the processing of such data mandates that the member nations adopt laws that cover all "processing" (defined to include even collection and storage) of data about personally-identifiable individuals. The EU Directive includes provisions addressing, among other things, limitations on the use of date [sic], data accuracy, and data destruction requirements. The Directive is not limited to electronic or computerized data, and therefore reaches written, Internet, and even oral communications.

The EU Directive offers a blueprint for data privacy laws across Europe but, in any given situation, the Directive itself is not legally binding. As to each specific data privacy issue arising within Europe, the *relevant country's* local statue [sic] that adopts ("transposes") the Directive will determine data privacy rights an[d] responsibilities.

The Extraterritorial Reach of the EU's Data Privacy Directive Means That *Any* Company with Operations in Europe Must Comply; Cross-Border Data Transfer Is Particularly Thorny

An important aspect of the directive for businesses headquartered outside of Europe, such as in the United States, is the directive's extraterritorial reach. The directive specifically prohibits sending personal data to any country without a "level of [data] protection" considered "adequate" by EU standards. Significantly, the EU has ruled that the United States, with its patchwork of privacy laws, does *not* possess an adequate level of data protection.

The directive authorizes a number of exceptions, legally permitting transmission of personal data outside of Europe even to a "third country" that fails to offer an "adequate level of protection."

Exceptions Permitting Cross-Border Transfers of Personal Data

The EU recognizes three "transborder data flow vehicles": (i) a company can self-certify with the U.S. Department of Commerce that it adheres to specified data protection principles (known as the "safe harbor" system); (ii) a company can enter into "model contracts" with its European subsidiaries, agreeing to abide by mandatory data protection provisions; or (iii) a company can develop a set of "binding corporate rules"—company-drafted data protection regulations that apply throughout the company, which must be ratified by each EU member state's data protection authority. Failure to implement at least one of these methods could result in significant liability.

Obtaining the data subject's free, unambiguous consent to transmit his or her data overseas is theoretically another permissible way in which to transfer data to a country outside the EU—even to a country without comparable data protection law—provided that the consent specifically lists the categories of data and the purposes for the processing outside the EU. Practically speaking, however, obtaining consent to legitimize a transfer overseas is often not an available alternative for employers; in the employment context, because of the imbalance in bargaining power between employer and employee, consents may be presumed *not* to have been freely given.

Also, of course, there is no prohibition against transmitting genuinely *anonymized* data out of the EU. Where the identity of the data subject is impossible to determine, the data transmission falls outside the scope of the directive.

***

Source: Labor & Employment Practice Group, Proskauer Rose LLP © 2008. Reprinted with permission.

tests were wrongfully discharged in violation of the state's constitutional guarantee of a right to privacy, which requires employers to demonstrate a compelling interest in invading an employee's privacy. In Pennsylvania, a court held that a drug test violates that state's policy against invasions of privacy where the methods used do not give due regard to the employee's privacy or if the test results disclose medical information beyond what is necessary. Other states that provide constitutional recognition and protection of privacy rights include Alabama, Florida, Hawaii, Louisiana, Montana, South Carolina, and Washington. However, in all states except California, application of this provision to private-sector organizations is limited, uncertain, or not included at all.

3. Protecting employees only in certain areas of employment, such as personnel records or the use of credit information.

4. Leaving private-sector employees to fend for themselves while the federal laws and the Constitution afford protection to federal employees and those subject to state action.

Tort Law Protections/Common Law

As mentioned above, courts in almost all states have developed case law, the "common law," which identifies certain torts in connection with private-sector invasion of privacy. Georgia was the first jurisdiction whose courts recognized a common-law right to privacy. As the court explained in *Pavesich v. New England Life Ins. Co.,*[24] "a right of privacy is derived from natural law, recognized by municipal law, and its existence can be inferred from expressions used by commentators and writers on the law as well as judges in decided cases. The right of privacy is embraced within the absolute rights of personal security and personal liberty." Though some states rely on statutory protections rather than common law, only two states—North Dakota and Wyoming—fail to recognize *any* of the four privacy torts discussed in this chapter.[25] A **tort** is a legal wrong, for which the law offers a remedy. The torts of particular interest in this chapter include intrusion into solitude or seclusion, the publication of private information, and publication that places another in a false light. Defamation also will be discussed.

Publication as used in these torts means not only publishing the information in a newspaper or other mass media but generally "bringing it to light" or disseminating the information. In addition, the concept of publication is defined slightly differently depending on the tort. Truth and absence of malice are generally not acceptable defenses by an employer sued for invasion of an employee's privacy. They are acceptable, however, in connection with claims of defamation.

tort
A private (that is, civil as opposed to criminal) wrong in which one person causes injury to another person, and which allows the injured person to sue the wrongdoer and to collect damages. The injury can be physical, mental, or financial.

LO7

Intrusion into Seclusion The *prima facie* case for the tort of intrusion into seclusion is listed in Exhibit 14.6. (For a more detailed discussion of *prima facie* cases, please see Chapter 3.)

Exhibit 14.6 *The* Prima Facie *Case for the Tort of Intrusion into Seclusion*

> To state a *prima facie* case for the tort of <u>intrusion into seclusion</u>, the plaintiff employee must show that

- The defendant employer intentionally intruded into a private area.

- The plaintiff was entitled to privacy in that area.

- The intrusion would be objectionable to a person of reasonable sensitivity.

The intrusion may occur in any number of ways. An employer may

- Verbally request information as a condition of employment.
- Require that its employees provide information in other ways such as through polygraphs, drug tests, or psychological tests.
- Require an annual medical examination.
- Ask others for personal information about its employees.
- Go into private places belonging to the employee.

Any of these methods may constitute a wrongful invasion that is objectionable to a reasonable person. On the other hand, if the employer can articulate a justifiable business purpose for the inquiry/invasion, the conduct is may be deemed acceptable.

Rogers v. Loews L'Enfant Plaza Hotel[26] was a case where the intrusion was found to be objectionable. In that case, an employee was continually sexually harassed by her supervisor, including bothersome telephone calls to her home, during which he made lewd comments to her about her personal sex life. The sexual harassment evolved into harassment in the workplace, where the supervisor verbally abused her in front of her co-workers, kept important business-related information from her, and refused to include her in meetings. Her employer, refusing to take formal action, suggested that she change positions. The court determined that the telephone calls were not of a benign nature but, instead, were unreasonably intrusive and not normally expected. Further, the harassment constituted an intrusion into a sphere from which the employee could reasonably exclude the defendant. On these bases, the court found in favor of the employee.

 Scenario

In connection with Opening Scenario 1, Aravinda's decision in connection with the HIV tests may be governed in part by the law relating to employment

Exhibit 14.7   *The Prima Facie Case for the Tort of Public Disclosure of Private Facts*

> To state a *prima facie* case for the tort of **public disclosure of private facts**, the plaintiff employee must show that

> • There was an intentional or negligent public disclosure

> • Of private matters, and

> • Such disclosure would be objectionable to a reasonable person of ordinary sensitivities.

testing as discussed in Chapter 3 and in part by the law relating to disability discrimination as discussed in Chapter 12 (since HIV is considered a disability under the Americans with Disabilities Act). On the other hand, the law relating to intrusion into seclusion also would have application here in terms of disclosure of the test results. If Aravinda discloses the results to anyone or, through her actions, leads someone to a belief about the employee's HIV status, she might be liable under this tort. In addition, it is important to consider that it is highly unlikely that Aravinda has any right to know any employee's HIV status as it is unlikely that the information would be job-related. (Can you imagine what employment position might warrant this type of information? Is HIV status ever considered job-related?)

Public Disclosure of Private Facts   The *prima facie* case for the tort of public disclosure of private facts is listed in Exhibit 14.7.

The information disclosed must not already be publicized in any way, nor can it be information the plaintiff has consented to publish. Therefore, in *Pemberton v. Bethlehem Steel Corp.,*[27] publication of an employee's criminal record did not constitute public disclosure of private facts because the criminal record did not contain private facts; it was information that was already accessible by the public.

As you shall see, at the end of the chapter, in the *Yoder v. Ingersoll-Rand Company a.k.a. ARO* case, the publication also must be made public, which involves more than mere disclosure to a single third party. The public disclosure must be communication either to the public at large or to so many people that the matter must be regarded as substantially certain to become one of public knowledge or one of knowledge to a particular public whose knowledge of the private facts would be embarrassing to the employee. Therefore, publication to all of the employees in a company may be sufficient, while disclosure to a limited number of supervisors may not.

Several states have enacted legislation codifying this common-law doctrine under the rubric of "breach of confidentiality." Connecticut, for instance, has passed legislation requiring employers to maintain employee medical records separate from other personnel records. Other states have limited an employer's ability to disclose personnel-related information or allowed a cause of action where, through the employer's negligent maintenance of personnel files, inaccurate employee information is communicated to a third party.

Publication in a False Light   The *prima facie* case of publication in a false light requires that there was a public disclosure of facts that place the employee in a false light before the public if the false light would be highly offensive to a reasonable person and the person providing the information had knowledge of or recklessly disregarded the falsity or false light of the publication.

Voluntary consent to publication of the information constitutes an absolute bar to a false-light action. This type of tort differs from defamation, where disclosure to even one other person than the employer or employee satisfies the requirements. The tort of publicizing someone in a false light requires that the general public be given a false image of the employee. In a false-light action, the damage for which the employee is compensated is the inability to be left alone, with injury to one's emotions and mental suffering, while defamation compensates the employee for injury to his or her reputation in the public's perception.

Note that any of the above claims may be waived by the employee if the employee also publishes the information or willingly or knowingly permits it to be published. For example, in *Cummings v. Walsh Construction Co.,*[28] the employee complained of public disclosure of embarrassing private facts, consisting of information relating to a sexual relationship in which she was engaged with her supervisor. The court held that, where the employee had informed others of her actions, she waived her right not to have her supervisor disclose the nature of their relationship.

As with defamation, an exception to this waiver exists in the form of compelled self-publication, where an employer provides the employee with a false reason as the basis for termination and the employee is compelled to restate this reason when asked by a future employer the basis of departure from the previous job. Therefore, where the employer intentionally misstates the basis for the discharge, that employer may be subject to liability for libel because it is aware that the employee will be forced to repeat (or "publish") that reason to others.

Breach of Contract   An employee also may contest an invasion of privacy by her or his employer on the basis of a breach of contract. The contract may be an actual employment contract, collective bargaining agreement, or one found to exist because of promises in an employment handbook or a policy manual.

Defamation   *Libel* refers to defamation in a written document, while *slander* consists of defamation in an oral statement. Either may occur during the course of a reference process. And, while the *prima facie* case of defamation requires a

Exhibit 14.8   *The* Prima Facie *Claim for Defamation*

To state a *prima facie* case for the tort of <u>defamation</u>, the plaintiff employee must show that

- There were false and defamatory words concerning the employee,

- Negligently or intentionally communicated to a third party without the employee's consent (publication), and

- Resulting harm to the employee defamed.

false statement, even a vague statement that casts doubt on the reputation of an individual by inference can cause difficulties for an employer if it cannot be substantiated.

The elements of a *prima facie* claim for defamation are included in Exhibit 14.8.

One cautious solution to this problem area is to request that all employees fill out an exit interview form that asks, "Do you authorize us to give a reference?" If the applicant answers yes, she or he should be asked to sign a release of liability for the company.

Ordinarily defamation arises from someone other than the defamed employee making defamatory statements about an employee; but one interesting form of defamation has evolved over the past decade where an employee is given a false or defamatory reason for her or his discharge. In that case, the employee is the one who is forced to publicize it to prospective employers when asked for the reason for her or his discharge. These circumstances give rise to a cause of action for defamation, termed *compelled self-disclosure,* because the employee is left with no choice but to tell the prospective employer the defamatory reasons for her or his discharge. Barring this result, the employee would be forced to fabricate reasons different from those given by the former employer and run the risk of being reprimanded or terminated for not telling the truth. This cause of action has been recognized, however, only in Colorado, Iowa, Minnesota, Connecticut, and California. (For a more detailed discussion, see Chapter 3.)

An employer may defend against an employee's claim of defamation by establishing the truth of the information communicated. While truth is a complete defense to defamation, it can be difficult to prove without complex paper management.

Employers also may be immune from liability for certain types of statements because of court-recognized privileges in connection with them. For example, in some states, an employer is privileged to make statements, even if defamatory, where the statement is made in the course of a judicial proceeding or where the statement is made in good faith by one who has a legitimate business purpose in making the communication (e.g., an ex-employer) to one who has a business interest in learning the information (e.g., a prospective employer).[29] This privilege would apply where a former employer offers a good-faith reference to an employee's prospective employer. (See additional discussion of liability for references, below.) "Good faith" means that the employer's statement, though defamatory, is not made with malice or ill will toward the employee.

Regulation of Employees' Off-Work Activities

Employers may regulate the off-work or otherwise private activities of their employees where they believe that the off-work conduct affects the employee's performance at the workplace. This legal arena is a challenging one since, in the at-will environment, employers can generally impose whatever rules they wish. However, as discussed earlier in this chapter, they may then run afoul of common-law privacy protections. In addition, some states have enacted legislation protecting against discrimination on the basis of various off-work acts. For instance, New York's lifestyle discrimination statute prohibits employment decisions or actions based on four categories of off-duty activity: legal recreational activities, consumption of legal products, political activities, and membership in a union.

Across the nation, there are other less-broad protections of off-work acts. Approximately 30 states have enacted protections specifically on the basis of consumption or use of legal products off the job, such as cigarettes.[30] These statutes originated from the narrower protection for workers who smoked off-duty. Currently, abstention from smoking cannot be a condition of employment in at least 29 states and the District of Columbia (and those states provide antiretaliation provisions for employers who violate the prohibition). In fact, instead of simply identifying the right to use lawful products outside of work, Rhode Island goes further by specifically prohibiting an employer from banning the use of tobacco products while not at work. Some states have responded a bit differently. In Georgia, for instance, certain state workers are charged an additional premium of $40 per month in connection with their state-provided health insurance if they or a covered family member use tobacco products. While the policy is based on an affirmative response to a simple survey question, any employee who misleads the system will lose her or his health coverage for an entire year. The State of Georgia is not alone; a survey by the Society for Human Resource Management found that 5 percent of firms charge a similar premium while 32 percent of firms offer smoking cessation programs as an alternate means by which to reduce costs.

You might be asking yourself, though, how do these firms know? What happens if employees *lie* about their habits? Alaska Airlines uses a preemployment urine screening and will not even hire candidates if they are smokers.[31] For an alternate approach, in what might seem like a program destined for problems, Whirlpool Corporation had imposed a $500 surcharge on employees who smoked—or at least those who admitted to being smokers—based on its increased benefits costs. When 39 individuals who had not paid the surcharge, thus claiming to be nonsmokers, were observed smoking in the firm's designated smoking areas, they were suspended by Whirlpool for lying. Presumably, they also owed the surcharge.[32]

On the other hand, the issue of weight is handled slightly differently than smoking. Employers are not prohibited from making employment decisions on the basis of weight, as long as they are not in violation of the Americans with Disabilities Act (ADA) when they do so (see Chapter 12). The issue depends on whether the employee's weight is evidence of or due to a disability. If so, the employer will need to explore whether the worker is otherwise qualified for the position, with or without reasonable accommodation, if necessary. If the individual cannot perform the essential functions of the position, the employer is not subject to liability for reaching an adverse employment decision. However, employers should be cautious in this regard since the ADA also protects workers who are not disabled but who are *perceived* as being disabled, a category into which someone might fall based on her or his weight.

One recent trend with regard to weight is to offer incentives to encourage healthy behavior. Some employers have adopted health plans with significantly lower deductibles for individuals who maintain healthier lifestyles (if an employee is not obese or does not smoke, and has yearly physicals). In one audacious statement along these lines, a hospital in Indiana has begun to require its employees to pay as much as $30 every two weeks unless they meet certain company-determined weight, cholesterol, and blood-pressure guidelines.[33]

Laws that protect against discrimination based on marital status exist in just under half of the states. However, though a worker might be protected based on marital *status,* she or he is not necessarily protected against adverse action based on *the identity of the person* to whom she or he is married. For instance, some companies might have an antinepotism policy under which an employer refuses to hire or terminates a worker based on the spouse working at the same firm, or a conflict-of-interest policy under which the employer refuses to hire or terminates a worker whose spouse works at a competing firm.

Because about 40 percent of workers have dated an office colleague, policies and attitudes on workplace dating have the greatest impact.[34] Though only about 9 percent of workplaces have policies prohibiting workplace dating,[35] a New York decision reaffirms the employer's right to terminate a worker on the basis of romantic involvement. In *McCavitt v. Swiss Reinsurance America Corp.,*[36] the court held that an employee's dating relationship with a fellow officer of the corporation was not a "recreational activity" within the meaning of a New York statute that prohibited employment discrimination for engaging in such recreational activities. The employee contended that, even though "[t]he personal relationship between plaintiff and Ms. Butler has had no repercussions whatever for the professional responsibilities or accomplishments of either" and "Swiss Re . . . has no written anti-fraternization or anti-nepotism policy," he was passed over for promotion and then discharged from employment largely because of his dating. The court agreed with the employer and found that dating was not a recreational activity.

Workplace policies on dating co-workers are largely a function of the employer's corporate culture. Some have banned all inter-office dating, while others permit it. The historical arguments for a ban usually are based on (1) reduced productivity, centered on a belief that such forms of socialization distract the parties involved, (2) potential liability, based on a concern that soured romances may result in harassment charges, or (3) moralistic concerns, particularly in encouraging extramarital affairs. However, to the contrary, some studies suggest that romantically linked employees may be actually more productive, while one study found that couples working in the same location have a divorce rate that is 50 percent lower than the average.[37] The trend today is toward more openness and fewer bans.

The majority of states protect against discrimination on the basis of political involvement, though states vary on the type and extent of protection. Finally, lifestyle discrimination may be unlawful if the imposition of the rule treats one protected group differently from another. For instance, as discussed elsewhere, if an employer imposes a rule restricting the use of peyote in Native American rituals that take place during off-work hours, the rule may be suspect and may subject the employer to liability. Similarly, the rule may be unlawful if it has a disparate impact on a protected group. (For a more detailed discussion of disparate impact and disparate treatment, please see Chapter 3.)

Most statutes or common-law decisions, however, provide for employer defenses for those rules that (1) are reasonably and rationally related to the employment activities of a particular employee, (2) constitute a bona fide occupational requirement, or (3) are necessary to avoid a conflict of interest or the appearance of conflict of interest. For example, drug testing in positions that affect the public safety, such as bus driver, would not constitute an unlawful intrusion because the employer's interest in learning of that information is justified. Where the attempted employer control goes beyond the acceptable realm, courts have upheld an exception to the employment-at-will doctrine based on public policy concerns for personal privacy or, depending on the circumstances, intentional infliction of emotional distress.[38]

Scenario 2

In connection with Opening Scenario 2, does Abraham have to quit his nighttime dancing job? Recall that Abraham is an at-will employee, making the answer somewhat easier. Since he can be terminated for any reason, as long as it is not a wrongful reason, the partner can impose this condition. But consider Abraham's arguments and the ethical, as well as the legal, implications. As long as Abraham can show that his dancing truly has no impact on his work (i.e., that the club is located in a different town from that of his clientele or that the club has an excellent reputation for beautiful, artistic dancing styles), then he would not have to quit his night job. On the other hand, if Abraham's reputation is soiled by his connection with this club and his boss can show that his work has a negative impact on his ability to perform, then she may be justified in her ultimatum.

In fact, in a case (albeit more extreme) from Arizona, a husband and wife who worked as nurses were fired from a hospital after hospital officials learned that they ran a pornographic Web site when not at work. The couple explained that they engaged in this endeavor in order to earn more money for their children's college education. "We thought we could just do this and it really shouldn't be a big deal," said the husband.[39] Though their dismissal attracted the attention of the American Civil Liberties Union for what it considered to be at-will gone awry, the nurses had no recourse. In another case, a police office was docked three days' pay when his wife posted nude pictures of herself on the Internet as a surprise to her husband. However, the pay suspension was justified by the department in that case since police officers could arguably be held to a higher standard of conduct than average citizens.

What about the well-intentioned employer who believes that employees who smoke cigarettes will benefit from a "no smoking anytime, anywhere" policy? The employer also may be concerned about the financial impact of disease and other health problems related to smoking. The employer may first encounter obstacles in applying this policy in the workplace itself: Some states specifically prohibit discrimination against smokers in employment. Other states regulate smoking in the workplace only in government agencies or public buildings that are also workplaces. Of course, there are other states, like California, that prohibit smoking in all enclosed places of employment and require employers to warn of any toxic substances in the workplace, including tobacco smoke.[40]

The problem in enforcement would grow as the employer tries to encourage or require employees to quit smoking altogether. How would the employer know whether the employees are smoking when not at the workplace? Would the employer's desire to have healthy employees support the intrusion into employees' decisions regarding their own health? Employers who seek to establish an exercise or "healthy eating" program may encounter similar issues. Emphasizing the work-related benefits of such a program and limiting its reach to the workplace (e.g., creating an exercise room at work where employees may take their breaks if they choose) may allow the employer to reach its goal of a healthier workforce. For more information about this issue, see Exhibit 14.9, "Legal Restrictions on Off-Duty Behavior of Private Employees."

U.S. Companies with Operations in Europe Must Comply with Data Protection Laws

The *City of San Diego v. Roe* case, provided for your review, explores the controversial topic of regulation of private activities away from work. In this case, the employer, the San Diego Police Department, believed that an officer's off-duty activities reflected poorly on the department and were entirely inappropriate. A critical component of the case was the fact that the officer's activities incorporated elements of his duties as a police officer. As you review the case, try to imagine where you would draw the line between appropriate and inappropriate behavior and whether you would have found the employer's actions proper even if no such incorporation of police activities had been involved.

Exhibit 14.9 *Legal Restrictions on Off-Duty Behavior of Private Employees*

Off-Duty Behavior of Private Employee	Business Justification	State Statutory Restrictions on Employer Policy
Illicit drug use	Concern that worker may come to work impaired, jeopardizing the worker's safety and the safety of other workers Quality of work of impaired worker may affect the product or service provided by the company, which, in turn, can affect the business's reputation and profitability Conduct is illegal and not deserving of legal protection	46 states allow employers to test for illicit drugs
Alcohol use	Same justifications as applied to those who use illicit drugs, except for the issue of legality	40 states allow employers to regulate off-duty alcohol consumption
Cigarette smoking	Smokers increase employer's healthcare costs and affect productivity by missing more work due to illness than nonsmokers	22 states allow employers to prohibit off-duty use of tobacco products
Use of weight standards	Same justifications as apply to smokers	49 states allow employers to establish weight standards that do not violate the ADA
Dating between employees	A romantic relationship between employees may affect their productivity The relationship could lead to sexual harassment charges against the employer, especially if one employee is a supervisor of the other Other employees may believe that an involved supervisor is showing favoritism and may then feel that they are victims of discrimination	48 states allow employers to regulate dating between employees
Moonlighting	Working too many hours may impair worker's productivity Working for a competitor could jeopardize privacy of employer information	48 states allow employers to regulate moonlighting
Social relationships with employees of a competitor	Concern that information could be exchanged that would cause harm to the business	48 states allow employers to regulate

Source: Reprinted with permission from John D. Pearce II and Dennis Kuhn, "The Legal Limits of Employees' Off-Duty Privacy Rights," *Organizational Dynamics* 32, no. 4 (2003), pp. 372–83, 376.

Employer's Information-Gathering Process/Justified Use/ Disclosure of Information

The above discussion focused on the scope of the privacy rights of the employee in connection with the dissemination of information. Privacy, however, can be invaded not only by a disclosure of specific types of information but also by the process by which the information has been obtained. An employer may be liable for its *process* of information gathering, storing, or utilization. Improper gathering of information may constitute an invasion where the process of collection constitutes harassment, where improper filing or dissemination of the information collected may leave the employer liable for defamation actions, and/or where inappropriate use of data for purposes other than those for which the information was collected may inflict other harms.

A final concern is called *function creep* and may begin with the voluntary transmission of information by an individual for one purpose for which the individual consents. For instance, an individual may offer personal information to her or his employer without understanding or intending that the employer then share more information than required with the Immigration and Naturalization Service. Similarly, information gathered during a preemployment physical for purposes of appropriate job placement may seem perfectly appropriate to share with an employer; but, the employee might have concerns if that information is later shared with her or his manager or co-workers for other purposes.

The collection or retrieval of information may occur in a variety of ways, depending on the stage of employment and the needs of the employer. For example, an employer may merely make use of the information provided by an applicant on her or his application form, or it may telephone prior employers to verify the data provided by the applicant. One employer may feel confident about an employee's educational background when she sees the employee's diplomas hung on the office wall, while a different employer may feel the need to contact prior educational institutions to verify attendance and actual graduation. On the more lenient end of the spectrum, the employer may rest assured that the employee is all that he states that he is on the application form, while, in more extreme situations, an employer may subject its employees to polygraph analyses and drug tests.

As is covered extensively in other chapters, employers are limited in the questions that may be asked of a potential employee. For example, an employer may not ask an applicant whether she or he is married or plans to have children, or the nature of her or his family's origin. These questions are likely to violate Title VII of the Civil Rights Act; in most cases this is not because the employer should not have the information, literally, but instead because an employer is prohibited from reaching any employment decision on the basis of the answers. In addition, employers are limited in their collection of information through various forms of testing, such as polygraphs or medical tests. These are discussed further in Chapter 3, but employers are constrained by a business necessity and relatedness standard or, in the case of polygraphs, by a requirement of reasonable suspicion. With regard to medical information specifically, employer's decisions are not only governed by the Americans with Disabilities Act but also restricted by the Health Insurance Portability and Accountability Act (HIPAA) (Public Law 104-191). HIPAA stipulates that employers cannot use "protected health information" in making employment decisions without prior consent. Protected health information includes all medical records or other individually identifiable health information. (See Exhibit 14.10, "Protecting Workers' Personal Data.")

Exhibit 14.10 *Protecting Workers' Personal Data*

In 1997, the International Labour Organization published a Code of Practice on the Protection of Workers' Personal Data. Though not binding on employers, it serves to help codify ethical standards in connection with the collection and use of employee personal information and is recognized as the standard among privacy advocates.[41] The code includes, among others, the following principles:

5. GENERAL PRINCIPLES

5.1 Personal data should be processed lawfully and fairly, and only for reasons directly relevant to the employment of the worker.

5.2 Personal data should, in principle, be used only for the purposes for which they were originally collected. . . .

5.4 Personal data collected in connection with technical or organizational measures to ensure the security and proper operation of automated information systems should not be used to control the behavior of workers.

5.5 Decisions concerning a worker should not be based solely on the automated processing of that worker's personal data.

5.6 Personal data collected by electronic monitoring should not be the only factors in evaluating worker performance. . . .

5.8 Workers and their representatives should be kept informed of any data collection process, the rules that govern that process, and their rights. . . .

5.10 The processing of personal data should not have the effect of unlawfully discriminating in employment or occupation. . . .

5.13 Workers may not waive their privacy rights.

6. COLLECTION OF PERSONAL DATA

6.1 All personal data should, in principle, be obtained from the individual worker.

6.2 If it is necessary to collect personal data from third parties, the worker should be informed in advance, and give explicit consent. The employer should indicate the purposes of the processing, the sources and means the employer intends to use, as well as the type of data to be gathered, and the consequences, if any, of refusing consent. . . .

6.5 An employer should not collect personal data concerning a worker's sex life; political, religious, or other beliefs; or criminal convictions. In exceptional circumstances, an employer may collect personal data concerning those in named areas above if the data are directly relevant to an employment decision and in conformity with national legislation.

6.6 Employers should not collect personal data concerning the worker's membership in a workers' organization or the worker's trade union activities, unless obliged or allowed to do so by law or a collective agreement.

6.7 Medical personal data should not be collected except in conformity with national legislation, medical confidentiality and the general principles of occupational health and safety, and only as needed to determine whether the worker is fit for a particular employment; to fulfill the requirements of occupational health and safety; and to determine entitlement to, and to grant, social benefits. . . .

continued

6.10 Polygraphs, truth-verification equipment or any other similar testing procedure should not be used.

6.11 Personality tests or similar testing procedures should be consistent with the provisions of this code, provided that the worker may object to the testing.

6.12 Genetic screening should be prohibited or limited to cases explicitly authorized by national legislation.

6.13 Drug testing should be undertaken only in conformity with national law and practice or international standards.

11. INDIVIDUAL RIGHTS

11.1 Workers should have the right to be regularly notified of the personal data held about them and the processing of that personal data.

11.2 Workers should have access to all their personal data, irrespective of whether the personal data are processed by automated systems or are kept in a particular manual file regarding the individual worker or in any other file which includes workers' personal data.

11.3 The workers' right to know about the processing of their personal data should include the right to examine and obtain a copy of any records to the extent that the data contained in the record includes that worker's personal data. . . .

11.9 Workers should have the right to demand that incorrect or incomplete personal data, and personal data processed inconsistently with the provisions of this code, be deleted or rectified. . . .

11.11 If the employer refuses to correct the personal data, the worker should be entitled to place a statement on or with the record setting out the reasons for that worker's disagreement. Any subsequent use of the personal data should include the information that the personal data are disputed and the worker's statement.

In connection with the storage of the information collected, employers must be careful to ensure that the information is stored in such a manner that it will not fall into the wrong hands. If an improper party has access to the personal information, the employer, again, may be subject to a defamation action by the employee based on the wrongful invasion of her personal affairs, as discussed above. In today's world of advanced computer data storage, new issues arise that have not been previously litigated. For instance, when an item is stored in a computer, it is crucial either to close the file to all but those who have a correct entry code or to delete private information. Access to computer terminals throughout an office creates a problem concerning the dissemination of the private information and the control of access.

The employer offering the reference is responsible for its dissemination only to appropriate parties. A fax machine or postcard would be unacceptable means of transmitting a reference since this would allow access by innumerable others. Similarly, an employer may get caught wrongfully disclosing information to an inappropriate individual in the case of a telephone reference. Failure to confirm the identity of the caller and purpose of the call may allow disclosure to one who otherwise should have no access to this information.

Electronic Monitoring or Surveillance of Employee Activities

With the dramatic increase in the use of technology in the workplace, several issues have recently arisen surrounding the use of email and the Internet. Many state and district courts have dealt with the issues differently or have not faced them at all. On the other hand, 84 percent of companies surveyed for a 2007 report have written policies concerning email use, 66 percent engage in some form of email monitoring, and 28 percent have terminated employees for inappropriate email use.[42]

Though, at first blush, blogs might seem an innocent environment in which employees can post comments regarding their employment situation, imagine the impact of a viral message when placed on the Web and then allowed to have the exponential impact generated by some blogs. Since it is estimated that blog readership is in the millions,[43] corporate reputations are at stake and legal consequences can be severe; 14 percent of U.S. publicly traded companies investigated a leak of material financial information via a blog in the past 12 months.[44] In one situation, a Google employee compared the firm's health plan to Microsoft's, and it did not fare too well. He also blogged about how the company's provision of free food was merely an incentive to work through the dinner hour. The employee was subsequently terminated. The term to be "dooced" refers to having lost one's job as a result of one's Web site.[45] Consider the challenges involved in the implementation of a companywide blogging policy, as discussed in Exhibit 14.11, "Bloggers Beware: New Rules for CBC Employees." For more on blogging and social media generally, see below.

Exhibit 14.11   *Bloggers Beware: New Rules for CBC Employees*

My name is Chris MacDonald, and I work for the Canadian Broadcasting Corporation. OK, that second part isn't true, but if it were, I might not be allowed to write this blog, or at least I wouldn't be allowed to tell you who I work for, according to a new "guideline" issued by the CBC's management. (CBC managers have asserted that it's a guideline, not a policy. As far as most of the concerns about the document are concerned, it's a spurious distinction.)

The document is not publicly available—in fact, it hasn't been officially distributed within the CBC yet—but it got leaked internally, and lots of CBC employees have seen it. It caught CBC-based bloggers off-guard; despite the fact that several of them had proactively written their own set of voluntary guidelines a few years ago, they weren't included or consulted in the process of devising the new official guideline.

According to the InsideCBC blog (an official, sanctioned, insider's blog), the new policy applies to a CBC employee's personal blog "if the content clearly associates them with CBC/Radio-Canada."

Among the requirements of the guideline/policy:

- Bloggers are "expected to behave in a way that is consistent with our journalistic philosophy, editorial values and corporate policies."

- "[T]he blog cannot advocate for a group or a cause, or express partisan political opinion. It should also avoid controversial subjects or contain material that could bring CBC/Radio-Canada into disrepute."

- To start and maintain a blog of this kind, you need your supervisor's approval.

continued

Note, also, that the guideline/policy applies to *all* employees, not just to journalists (whose blogs might reasonably be mistaken for news) or to marquee on-air personalities.

The guideline has caused a stir among CBC-employee-bloggers and beyond.

A lot of objections have already been raised in the Comments section of the InsideCBC blog. And while some elements of the document seem unproblematic and even constructive, I see a couple of *types* of problems with it. One has to do with content. The other has to do with process.

Content:

There are clearly a number of elements of the guideline/policy that are either unclear or unenforceable or both. For example, the stipulation that it applies to blogs "if the content clearly associates them with CBC/Radio-Canada." Several commentators have pointed out that there are lots of ways, intentional and unintentional, that a blog could associate itself with the CBC. The blogger might self-identify as a CBC employee, or merely imply or even just let slip that she or he is an employee. In terms of specific requirements, the one that has most angered those involved is the stipulation that employees must seek their supervisors' *permission* to write a *personal* blog. This seems on the face of it a pretty serious restriction on freedom of speech. Maybe (maybe) CBC has the right to make that stipulation as a matter of employment contract, but having a right to do so doesn't make it appropriate, or wise, to exercise that right.

Process:

It's pretty bad that bloggers at the CBC were caught off-guard by this guideline/policy, for at least 3 reasons

1) For policies and codes of all kinds, buy-in is crucial. Given how difficult this policy will be to enforce (i.e., very) it's utterly essential that the people to be governed by it accept it as legitimate and wise. Oops.

2) The CBC employees with blogs are a pretty smart bunch, who have thought a fair bit about what their obligations are. And, just through experience, they understand blogging better than anyone in CBC's editorial offices is going to. What a shame not to draw on that knowledge and experience. Serious error.

3) By drafting a document that doesn't reflect, acknowledge, or draw upon the bloggers' own manifesto, CBC management is neglecting the fact that some of their very bright employees have expended considerable effort on the very issue they're now seeking to regulate. At the very least, that seems disrespectful.

Now that the errors have been made, the serious ethics & leadership challenge lies in whether & how CBC managers can recover. "Recovery" here means ending up with a policy that is clear and enforceable, and retaining some semblance of moral authority in the eyes of their employees.

Disclosure of potential bias: I've got a friend among the CBC-employee-bloggers affected by this new guideline/policy.

Update

According to [an] update, the document referred to above was "only a proposed early draft." (Note that "proposed" doesn't make sense there: either it was a draft, or it wasn't.) Also according to the update, "There are currently no specific corporate policies in effect relating directly to blogging." (This update is brought to you by the nice Media Relations and Issues Management people at CBC, who asked me to correct the above posting.)

Source: Christopher MacDonald, "Bloggers Beware: New Rules for CBC Employees," August 6, 2007, http://www.businessethics.ca/blog/2007/08/bloggers-beware-new-rules-for-cbc.html. © Christopher MacDonald, reprinted with permission.

Author's note: The blog that includes the text of the CBC update mentioned above also includes the original text of the introduction to the blogging policy, which indicates nowhere that the document contained "proposed" guidelines. Instead, it said, "[a]ttached are personal blogging guidelines the Editor in Chief's office distributed a while back."

Exhibit 14.12 *Implications of New Technology*

Consider the implications of new technology on the following areas:

- Monitoring usage.
- Managing employee and employer expectations.
- Distinguishing between work use and personal use of technology.
- Managing flextime.
- Maintaining a virtual workplace.
- Protecting against medical concerns for telecommuters.
- Managing/balancing privacy interests.

- Monitoring use of the Web to spread information and misinformation.
- Managing fair use/disclosure.
- Responding to accessibility issues related to the digital divide.
- Managing temporary workforces.
- Adapting to stress and changing systems.
- Maintaining proprietary information.
- Measuring performance.
- Managing liability issues.

Of course, little did anyone anticipate what dilemmas would arise as a result of advances in technology over the past few decades. Who would have thought that one might begin her or his workday by placing a hand on a scanner to confirm her or his identity and time of arrival at work[46] or that location-based technologies would allow employers to know an employee's whereabouts at all times?[47] Notwithstanding issues in connection with production, marketing, finance, and other areas of a firm's operations, we now have countless issues that intersect law and ethics with which we were never before confronted. (See Exhibit 14.12.)

Where technology will take employer monitoring is anybody's guess, but a few recent trends may point the way. Global positioning systems (GPSs) are now ubiquitous, but employer use has so far been mostly confined to vehicle tracking such as on over-the-road trucks. Look for GPS to spread to employee tracking, for example, by including such devices in nametags, uniforms, key chains, or other devices that employees may carry.

A related technology involves radio frequency identification devices (RFIDs), which are microchips that can be planted anywhere, including under the skin. In 2006, Citywatcher.com became the first U.S. firm to ask employees to accept RFID bodily implants.[48] Those who refused the implant were required to carry a key chain with an RFID microchip. While one's first instinct might be a concern about privacy, consider the reasoning used by the attorney general in Mexico, who explained why he opted to implant the tiny devices under the skin of some of his workers. He wanted to be able to track them more effectively in case they were kidnapped because of their line of work. Companies uncomfortable with implementation are considering alternatives such as imbedding the microchips in clothing or employee IDs.

States are concerned enough about the possibility of the widespread use of RFID implants that they have begun to act. In 2006, Wisconsin became the first state to ban mandatory implants.[49] North Dakota, California, and Missouri have since followed course, with other states considering similar legislation.

Biometrics is an identification technology that includes fingerprints, voice recognition, and iris recognition. Proposals for a national identification card incorporate biometric technology in order to establish an individual's identity. Biometric Social Security cards and biometric employment cards have also been proposed.[50] Some employers see biometrics as a more modern version of the time clock, while employees tend to view it more ominously. It seems inevitable that most employers will ultimately incorporate some form of biometric technology into their employee-monitoring arsenal.

Though seemingly monumental on the surface, advances in the information-gathering abilities of these technologies are actually merely geometric rather than exponential. Employers have always gathered information about their employees; the only element that has changed in recent decades is how that information is collected, not the values that underlie the decision to do so.

For instance, Milton Hershey of Hershey's Chocolate used to tour Hershey, Pennsylvania, to see how well his employees maintained their homes. He hired detectives to spy on Hershey Park dwellers in order to learn who threw trash on their lawns. Henry Ford used to condition wages on his workers' good behavior *outside the factory,* maintaining a Sociological Department of 150 inspectors to keep tabs on workers. Technology, therefore, does not present us with new value judgments but, instead, simply presents new ways to gather the information on which to base them. Sorting through these issues is challenging nevertheless. Consider the impact of September 11, 2001, on an employer's decision to share personal employee information with law enforcement. Private firms may be more willing today to share private information than they would have been previously. Consider more specifically the issues raised above and the implications of technology on some of these traditional workplace challenges:

- Technology allows for in-home offices, raising issues of safety as well as privacy concerns; there are now more than 33.7 million U.S. telecommuters.[51] (Efforts by OSHA in the late 1990s to impose workplace safety standards on home offices received huge flack!)
- Technology allows for greater invasions by the employer but also allows for additional misdeeds by employees.
- Technology blurs the lines between personal and professional lives.
- Technology allows employers to ask more of each employee—each is capable of much greater production.
- What constitutes a "workday"? When is enough enough?
- Should the ability to find something out make it relevant (e.g., off-work activities)?
- Many of the new technologies (email, voice mail) allow for faceless communication.

- Research has shown that excessive exertion of power and authority over employees may actually lead to insecurity, feelings of being overwhelmed and powerless, and doubts about worthiness.[52]

"The psychological impact of constant observation is serious and represents a major assault on the ethical rights of workers. Furthermore, productivity may also be compromised as a by-product of the growth of surveillance in the workplace."[53]

Consider the following overview of the implications of the technology economy as reported in the *World Employment Report 2001,* issued by the International Labour Office:

> More and more, boundaries are dissolving between leisure and working time, the place of work and place of residence, learning and working. . . . Wherever categories such as working time, working location, performance at work and jobs become blurred, the result is the deterioration of the foundations of our edifice of agreements, norms, rules, laws, organizational forms, structures and institutions, all of which have a stronger influence on our behavioral patterns and systems of values than we are aware.[54]

Finally, intrusions may come from unexpected arenas. For instance, while employees perhaps are concerned about their rights with regard to employer monitoring in the workplace, they might contemplate the possibility of informal intrusions such as from their colleagues rather than their supervisors. In a 2007 survey of information technology employees, a security vendor found that one-third of 200 respondents admitted to having used their administrative passwords in order to access confidential employee information including compensation information. One of the survey respondents was quoted as saying, "Why does it surprise you that so many of us snoop around your files? Wouldn't you if you had secret access to anything you can get your hands on?"[55] Unfortunately, this same survey reported that access continued long after many of these respondents had left their employers. Further exploration into the subject only uncovers greater vulnerabilities. In a much larger survey of more than 16,000 IT practitioners, almost two-thirds reported that they had intruded into another employee's personal computer without permission, and this number includes one-third of respondents who were at the manager level or above!

Forms of Monitoring

Monitoring in the workplace can take several forms and occurs for numerous reasons. Privacy scholar Colin Bennett identifies four types of surveillance that can specifically impact workers.[56] The first is *surveillance by glitch,* in which information is uncovered by mistake. This occurred, for example, when Microsoft discovered that expired Hotmail accounts retained buddy lists, which were then shared with new subscribers who were given those accounts' email addresses. In the workplace, a glitch could occur when a technician checks to see if a computer's hard drive has been erased by the previous user for use by someone else. That technician might notice inappropriate content on the hard drive. A similar circumstance arose when the dean of Harvard's Divinity School asked a Harvard information management technician to do some work on his Harvard-owned laptop. The technician found inappropriate pornographic materials, and the media frenzy that erupted has only recently subsided. Oddly enough, the CFO of Mesa Airlines *defended* himself with pornography in a different case where he was accused of deleting company information from three computers. Instead, he claimed, he was simply trying to delete files of pornography he had downloaded and that he thought might embarrass him. Funny how our concepts of the "lesser evil" shift, depending on the nature of the harm done.[57]

In another example of a glitch or mistake, cheating by a worker in a government agency was discovered when the worker left a copy of a stolen promotion exam in the copying machine. Such glitches may uncover violations of a usage policy even when no systematic monitoring is being conducted.

Bennett's second form of surveillance is *surveillance by default*. This occurs when the default setting is "monitor," whereby all information that is sent through a system is caught and cataloged. An example of this type of monitoring would be the "Cue Cat." A Cue Cat is a mouse-like device that was sent to subscribers of certain magazines. They were told that they could scan bar codes in the magazine in order to gather more information on the accompanying topics later through their computers. What these users were not told was that each Cue Cat was individually coded to send subscriber information along with the information request. Therefore, the publishers or advertisers were able to surreptitiously collect data from anyone who used the device at all times. In the workplace, surveillance by default occurs when there is a video camera recording every transaction or activity by default, rather than recording only specific activities. Though they did not repeat the question on subsequent surveys, the American Management Association reported that 75 percent of firms surveyed in 2001 regularly recorded their employees' email transmissions by means of a default setting.[58]

The third form of monitoring is *surveillance by design,* where the entire purpose of the technology is to collect information and, generally, the user is aware of this purpose. Supermarkets often trade discounts on products in exchange for an individual's personal information on the application form for the encoded key chain device that allows the discount. The shopper is fully aware of the exchange when the information is collected, and the entire purpose of the key chain device is to provide information to the store. Often customer service representatives will be notified by an audible "beep" on the telephone that they are being monitored, and they understand that this monitoring will have implications for their performance evaluations. Another type of surveillance by design occurs when firms conduct either random or periodic keyword searches of email or other transmissions. One-fourth of firms surveyed by the American Management Association reported that they perform keyword searches, generally seeking sexual or scatological language to protect themselves from later liability.[59]

Surveillance by possession exists where the employer maintains employee information in a database or some other list. Bennett refers to this form of surveillance as gathering information that could be sold or acquired, such as employee personal information from application forms.

Much of the monitoring that occurs today in American firms is surveillance by design or by default. For instance, an email program that systematically sorts and saves all email that contains certain terms (such as those used in a job search or those that might be considered sexually harassing) would constitute surveillance by default. A monitoring program that tracks Internet accesses and blocks inappropriate Web sites would be surveillance by design.

How Does Monitoring Work?

Advances in information-gathering technology have allowed monitoring to an extent that was never before possible. Worldwide sales of monitoring technology are estimated at $140 million annually.[60] One example of this new technology is Raytheon's Silentrunner, which allows firms to track everything that occurs on a network, including not only email but also instant messaging ("IM," one of the ways employees thought they had foiled email monitoring).[61] Approximately 11 million people in the United States use IM at work.[62] While some firms may encourage its use since it can cut down on travel, in-person meeting, and conference call expenses, IM also poses a significant risk since there is no built-in security measure in IM systems.

Other products called location-based monitoring services allow trucking firms to track their vehicles across the nation using global positioning[63] or allow managers to test a worker's honesty by using a truth-telling monitor during telephone calls.[64] The most prevalent Internet-monitoring product in the United States is Websense, with 8.25 million users worldwide. While Websense merely *blocks* certain Web sites, Websense Reporter, an add-on, records all Web accesses—not only attempted accesses blocked by Websense but also all nonprohibited Web surfing (70 percent of Websense's customers install Reporter). MIMEsweeper is the most used email monitoring system in the United States, with 6,000 corporate customers and over 6 million ultimate users worldwide. In a less-publicized form of monitoring, SWS Security offers a product that allows managers to track the messages a worker receives on a portable paging device so that they can determine whether the employee is being distracted by outside messages. Another provider, www.tracingamerica.com, offers the following information at the listed prices:

- Social Security numbers, $25.
- General all-around background search, $39.
- Countywide search for misdemeanors and felonies, $35.
- Whether subject has ever spent time in prison, $25.
- Whether subject has ever served time in a federal prison, $50.
- National search for outstanding warrants for subject, $50.
- Countywide search for any civil filings filed by or against subject, $50.
- Subject's driving record for at least three years back, $30.

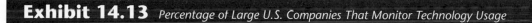

Exhibit 14.13   *Percentage of Large U.S. Companies That Monitor Technology Usage*

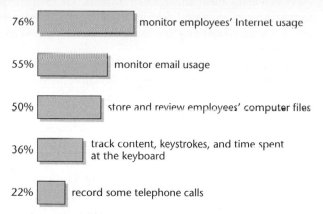

76%   monitor employees' Internet usage

55%   monitor email usage

50%   store and review employees' computer files

36%   track content, keystrokes, and time spent at the keyboard

22%   record some telephone calls

Source: Adapted by authors from data from the American Management Association, "2007 Electronic Monitoring & Surveillance Survey," March 13, 2008, www.amanet.org/training/articles/The-Latest-on-Workplace-Monitoring-and-Surveillance.aspx.

In the American Management Association's 2007 survey,[65] 43 percent of the respondents reported that they engaged in email monitoring as a result of their concerns for legal liability (see Exhibit 14.13, "Percentage of Large U.S. Companies That Monitor Technology Usage"). Monitoring does not stop with email and the Internet; the ACLU reports that employers monitor an estimated 400 million telephone calls annually.[66] Given the courts' focus in many cases on employer response to claims of sexual harassment or unethical behavior, among other complaints, firms believe that they need a way to uncover these inappropriate activities. More than 24 percent of firms have reported receiving a subpoena for employee email, and 26 percent of the firms reported firing employees for inappropriate email.[67] Without monitoring, how would companies know what occurs? Moreover, as courts maintain the standard in many cases of whether the employer "knew or should have known" of wrongdoing, the state-of-the-art definition of "should have known" becomes all the more vital. If most firms use monitoring technology to uncover such wrongdoing, the definition of "should have known" will begin to include an expectation of monitoring. Finally, some recent state cases have held that, where an employer provides notice to employees that email is the property of the employer and that it will be monitored, communications by the employee over that system cannot be privileged or confidential, *even if sent to a private attorney.*[68]

One of the most recent advances in monitoring technology involves the use of biometrics, including identification by fingerprint verification, iris and retinal scanning, hand geometry analysis, or facial feature scanning. Approximately 6 percent of employers in the United States use biometrics for a variety of purposes, from allowing customers to purchase goods and services to airline check-in. Those in favor of the technology contend that it will reduce the high economic and emotional costs of identity theft, among other benefits. Those opposed argue that it is subject to inaccuracies, provides more information than employers have a right to know, and is one additional way in which "big brother" can keep an eye on employees at all times.

Employee theft has led both public and private employers to increase monitoring of their employees by using video surveillance. According to the National Retail Security Survey, 47 percent of an annual retail loss to employers of almost $37.4 billion in 2005 was due to employee theft—more than $17 billion.[69] Another study conducted in 2005 by Hayes International reported that one out of every 26.5 employees was apprehended for theft from her or his employer in 2005. The survey also found that respondents caught 68,994 dishonest employees in 2005, which represented an increase of 11.49 percent over 2004's apprehensions, and that money gained by identifying dishonest employees totaled over $49.9 million.[70] Nevertheless, video surveillance may cost the employer through loss of morale. "Would you like to work in an environment where every time you blow your nose . . . it's on videotape?" asks Lewis Maltby, president of the National Workrights Institute in Princeton, New Jersey.[71]

While no case of employer monitoring has yet reached the Supreme Court, these actions have received lower-court attention. As early as 1990, Epson America survived a lawsuit filed by a terminated employee who had complained about Epson's practice of reading all employee email.[72] In that case, the court distinguished the practice of *intercepting* an email transmission from storing and reading email transmissions once they had been sent. However, relying on court precedent for protection is a double-edged sword. An employee-plaintiff in one federal action won a case against his employer where the employer had monitored the worker's telephone for a period of 24 hours in order to determine whether the worker was planning a robbery. The court held that the company had gone too far and had insufficient evidence to support its claims.[73] In another action, Northern Telecom settled a claim brought by employees who were allegedly secretly monitored over a 13-year period. In this case, Telecom agreed to pay $50,000 to individual plaintiffs and $125,000 for attorney fees.[74]

Courts have supported reasonable monitoring of employees in open areas as a method of preventing and addressing employee theft. For example, in *Sacramento County Deputy Sheriff's Association v. County of Sacramento*,[75] a public employer placed a silent video camera in the ceiling overlooking the release office countertop in response to theft of inmate money. The California Court of Appeals determined that the county had engaged in reasonable monitoring because employee privacy expectations were diminished in the jail setting.[76]

Though courts do not, per se, *require* notice in order to find that no reasonable expectation of privacy exists and to therefore allow monitoring by employers, notice of monitoring is favored by the courts.[77] The court in *Thygeson v. U.S. Bancorp*[78] held that an employer's specific computer usage policy precluded an employee's reasonable expectation of privacy.

While, as stated earlier, there is little legislation that actually relates to these areas specifically, there is some statutory protection from overt intrusions, though the statute does not apply in all circumstances. The federal wiretapping statute, Title III of the Omnibus Crime Control and Safe Streets Act of 1968, as amended by the Electronic Communications Privacy Act of 1986,[79] protects private- and public-sector employees from employer monitoring of their telephone calls and other communications without a court order.

There are two exceptions to this general prohibition. First, interception is authorized where one of the parties to the communication has given prior consent. Second, the "business extension" provision creates an exception where the equipment used is what is used in the ordinary course of business. An employer must be able to state a legitimate business purpose and there must be minimal intrusions into employee privacy such that they would not be objectionable to a reasonable person.

The employer's right to monitor private communications from an employee is not absolute, regardless of what the company policy might say.[80] Limits do exist. For example, in *Stengart v. Loving Care Agency, Inc.,*[81] the New Jersey Supreme Court ruled that communications between an employee and her attorney, which involved potential employment discrimination claims by the employee against the employer, were not subject to monitoring by the employer. Monitoring of those password-protected communications violated both the employee's right of privacy and the attorney-client privilege.

Similarly, in *Pietrylo v. Hillstone Restaurant Group,*[82] a federal court jury found in favor of employees who sued their managers for improperly accessing a password-protected MySpace page that contained criticisms of the managers without the employees' permission. The general rule that can be gleaned from these cases is that employers need permission from the employee to retrieve communications in password-protected areas. The approach taken by the city of Bozeman, Montana, is to require that all prospective employees disclose their user names and passwords for any profiles they have on Facebook, MySpace, Yahoo, Google and YouTube.[83] Whether that approach will hold up in court will have to wait for another day. However, in at least one case, a federal court required that an employee make available to an employer during a trial her complete Facebook and MySpace profiles, even though she had set various information to "private" using the online settings.[84] An interesting question arises as to the extent of an employer's responsibilities once it begins monitoring. If an employee's communications harm some third party, can the third party hold the employer legally responsible for failing to properly monitor the employee? The New Jersey Appellate Division said yes, because employers who tell employees that they will monitor communications have an affirmative duty to monitor and can be liable to a third party for failing to discover the improper behavior.

For example, in *Doe v. XYZ Corporation,*[85] the employee was visiting a pornographic Web site while at work. His manager knew about this activity, but never mentioned it to the IT department. It turned out that the Web site involved not just child pornography, but the employee's own stepdaughter. The stepdaughter was allowed to pursue a claim against the employer for failing to properly monitor the employee's online activities.

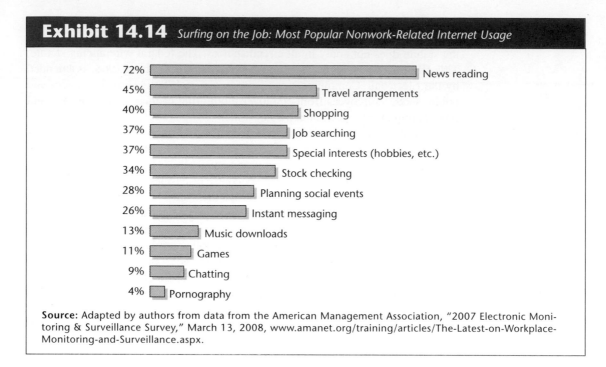

Exhibit 14.14 *Surfing on the Job: Most Popular Nonwork-Related Internet Usage*

- 72% News reading
- 45% Travel arrangements
- 40% Shopping
- 37% Job searching
- 37% Special interests (hobbies, etc.)
- 34% Stock checking
- 28% Planning social events
- 26% Instant messaging
- 13% Music downloads
- 11% Games
- 9% Chatting
- 4% Pornography

Source: Adapted by authors from data from the American Management Association, "2007 Electronic Monitoring & Surveillance Survey," March 13, 2008, www.amanet.org/training/articles/The-Latest-on-Workplace-Monitoring-and-Surveillance.aspx.

Business Justifications for Monitoring Employees' Technology Use

LO10

Web access at work may allow employees to be more creative and productive, but it also creates great risks. A survey by the Web site Vault.com found that 90 percent of employees surf nonwork-related Web sites while at work.[86] (See Exhibit 14.14, "Surfing on the Job: Most Popular Nonwork-Related Internet Usage.") Wasted time, over-clogged networks, and inappropriate material seeping into the workplace are all reasons why employers may seek to limit employees' Internet use at work. Of employers who monitor, almost half report that they restrict employees' Internet use.[87]

Scenario

As mentioned above, monitoring is made simpler through an employee's use of a computer. Employers now customarily provide many employees with personal computers that are linked either to the Internet or, at least, to an internal network. Employers can monitor the computer user's activities. As to the type of information that can be gathered, the Privacy Demonstration Page of the Center for Democracy and Technology can feed back to viewers information that it finds out merely because one has accessed the page. For instance, the page tells one individual viewer the type of computer that the viewer is using, the browser the individual is using, the server from which the viewer is operating, and some of the pages the viewer has recently visited. While this information may not necessarily seem personal to some, consider the facts of Scenario 2. The employer in that case seems to be within its rights to monitor the use of its computers.

The need to monitor employees' usage becomes clear when one focuses on five areas of potential employer liability: defamation, copyright infringement, sexual harassment, discrimination, and obscenity.

As discussed previously in this chapter, the guidelines that apply to a general defamation claim also apply to issues surrounding the Internet. However, some contend that the opportunity for harm is far greater. This is because employees and employers can easily disseminate information to a wide range of media. Not only can employers be subject to defamation claims by their own employees, but the far greater threat is the liability a company faces when an employee, as a representative of the employer, defames another individual using the Internet (with access provided by the employer) as the medium.

Further, firms are concerned about inappropriate use of Web software such as occurs when an employee downloads program files without compensating the creator or when employees use copyrighted information from the Web without giving credit to the original author, thereby exposing the firm to potentially significant copyright infringement liability. Finally, when an employee downloads software programs from the Web, the computer systems within the firm have the potential to be compromised by viruses or even unauthorized access.

Sexual harassment and discrimination by employees via the Web are governed by the same general guidelines that were previously discussed in the chapters addressing sexual harassment and discrimination. However, many employees believe that once an email message is deleted, it is permanently removed from the system. This is not the case. Because of this, email sent on company time, with content that constitutes sexual harassment, that might create a hostile working environment, or that contains other forms of discrimination, may easily be discovered, both by the employer and by opposing parties to litigation against the employer. In fact, in one survey, 24 percent of companies had been ordered by a court to produce employee email in the past 12 months.[88] For example, female warehouse employees alleged that a hostile work environment was created in part by inappropriate email, and they sought $60 million in damages in federal court. The case settled out of court.[89] In another case, *Zubulake v. UBS Warburg,* the plaintiff was awarded a jury verdict in the amount of $29.2 million.[90] The award ended up so large in part due to sanctions imposed by the trial judge as a result of the employer's failure to preserve emails for evidentiary purposes. Email is discussed in greater detail in the next section. Finally, obscenity becomes a critical issue, and the company may be placed at risk when employees download pornographic images while at the workplace.

Moreover, a firm might be concerned about the impression created when an employee visits various sites. Consider these scenarios: A customer service representative at an electronics store is surfing the Internet using one of the display computers. She accesses a Web site that shows graphic images of a crime scene. A customer in the store who notices the images is offended. Another customer service representative is behind the counter, using the store's computer to access a pornographic site, and starts to laugh. A customer asks him why he is laughing. He turns the computer screen around to show her the images that are causing him amusement.

Certainly, the employer would be justified in blocking employees' access to such Web sites. But what about sites of activist groups regarding sensitive issues such as abortion? Should an employer be allowed to block or restrict access to such sites? If such access may be restricted in order to promote efficiency and professionalism, then should employers be allowed to limit access to such innocuous sites as eBay or ESPN.com? The Vault.com survey mentioned above revealed that over half of the employees who make personal use of the Internet at work restrict their surfing to less than half an hour a day. By limiting or restricting access to Web sites, the employer may be creating an environment in which employees do not feel trusted and perhaps feel inhibited about using the Internet for creative, work-related purposes because they fear being reprimanded for misusing access.[91]

Employers seem to have business justification for other types of monitoring: "If [the employer] sees you doing something on the screen that they think you can do in a quicker way, they can tell you. They can even tell you ways to talk to people, or they can tell you ways to do things quicker to end your [customer service] call quicker," says Kathy Joynes, a travel agent for American Express who works out of her home, but whose supervisor can shadow her computer screen at any time.[92]

Because of the overall potential liability for their employees' actions, employers should develop a formal policy or program regulating employee usage of the Internet. In addition to having a formal policy, employers may choose to establish a process of monitoring their employee's Internet usage. This may involve tracking Web sites visited and the amount of time spent at each site using software programs designed for that specific purpose. However, employers need to consider the employees' rights to free speech and privacy when developing such policies and systems. (See Exhibits 14.15, "Monitoring Employees' Technology Usage," and 14.16, "Allowable Monitoring.")

The Case of Employee Email

An employer's need to monitor email must be weighed against an employee's right to privacy and autonomy. The employer is interested in ensuring that the email system is not being used in ways that offend others or harm morale, or for disruptive purposes—a significant concern when two-thirds of employees admit to using email, specifically, for personal reasons having nothing to do with work.[93] Likewise, an employer may choose to review email in connection with a reasonable investigation of possible employee misconduct. Also, companies that maintain sensitive data may be concerned about disclosure of this information by disloyal or careless employees, apparently justifying this type of intrusion.

In a well-publicized case, perhaps because the behavior rose to the highest levels of the organization, the CEO of Boeing resigned amid allegations of unethical conduct. In March 2005, Boeing officials discovered that its CEO, Harry Stonecipher, had transmitted sexually explicit emails to another Boeing executive. The case is instructive in that, apparently, Stonecipher and the executive were involved in a consensual relationship and no complaints had been received from

Exhibit 14.15 *Monitoring Employees' Technology Usage*

WHY DO FIRMS MONITOR TECHNOLOGY USAGE?

Managing the workplace:

- Ensuring compliance with affirmative action.
- Administering workplace benefits.
- Placing workers in appropriate positions.

Ensuring effective, productive performance:

- Preventing loss of productivity due to inappropriate technology use.

Protecting information and guarding against theft.

Protecting investment in equipment and bandwidth.

Protecting against legal liability, including possible

- Perceptions of hostile environments.
- Violations of software licensing laws.
- Violations regarding proprietary information or trade secrets.
- Inappropriate gathering of competitive intelligence.
- Financial fraud.
- Theft.
- Defamation/libel.
- Discrimination.

Maintaining corporate records (including email, voice mail, and so on).

Investigating *some* personal areas. (Consider Infoseek executive Patrick Naughton's pursuit of a tryst with an FBI agent posing as a 13-year-old girl in a chat room.)

ARGUMENTS IN FAVOR OF LIMITS ON MONITORING

Monitoring may create a suspicious and hostile workplace.

Monitoring constrains effective performance (employees claim that lack of privacy may prevent "flow").

It may be important to conduct *some* personal business at the office, when necessary.

Monitoring causes increased workplace stress and pressure, negatively impacting performance.

Employees claim that monitoring is an inherent invasion of privacy.

Monitoring does not always allow for workers to review and correct misinformation in the data collected.

Monitoring constrains the right to autonomy and freedom of expression.

Monitoring intrudes on one's right to privacy of thought. ("I use a company pen; does that mean the firm has a right to read my letter to my spouse?")

continued

Exhibit 14.15 *continued*

- Consider:

  — Surveys report alarming statistics about the use of the Internet while at work. Among them, up to 40 percent of workplace Internet use is not business-related, 64 percent of workers admit to using the Internet for personal purposes at some point during the workday, and the total amount of time spent on the Web can average more than 18 hours per week.[a]

  — It is estimated that 35 million workers, or approximately 25 percent of U.S. employees, spend an average of 3.5 hours a week on blogs.[b] Men spend a bit more time on nonwork-related Web surfing than women, 2.3 hours per week versus 1.5 hours among women.[c]

  — 13 percent of employees spend over two hours a day surfing nonbusiness sites.[d]

  — 24 percent of employees spend working hours at least one time each week watching or listening to streaming media.[e]

  — 70 percent of all traffic to Internet pornography Web sites is clocked during the traditional working hours of 9:00 a.m. and 5:00 p.m.[f]

[a]Deon Fair et al., "Internet Abuse Continues to Steal Workplace Productivity Despite the Use of Filters," April 27, 2005, http://www.minitrax.com/bw/whitepapers/AIWhitePaper.pdf.

[b]Ezra Palmer, "The Work Force Is Surfing," *I-Media Connection,* October 28, 2005, http://www.imediaconnection.com/content/7068.asp.

[c]Deborah Rothberg, "As Crucial as Coffee: Web Surfing at Work," *e-week,* May 17, 2006, http://www.eweek.com/article2/0,1895,1963997,00.asp. See also Websense, "Web @ Work Survey."

[d]Alan Cohen, "Worker Watchers: Want to Know What Your Employees Are Doing Online? You Can Find Out without Spooking Them," *Fortune/CNET Technology Review,* Summer 2001, pp. 70, 76.

[e]Rothberg, "As Crucial as Coffee."

[f]Staff Monitoring, "Staff Computer and Internet Abuse Statistics," 2007, http://staffmonitoring.com/P32/stats.htm.

Source: Adapted by authors from data from the American Management Association, "2007 Electronic Monitoring & Surveillance Survey," March 13, 2008, www.amanet.org/training/articles/The-Latest-on-Workplace-Monitoring-and-Surveillance.aspx.

Exhibit 14.16 *Allowable Monitoring*

Telephone calls	Monitoring is permitted in connection with quality control. Notice to the parties to the call is often required by state law, though federal law allows employers to monitor work calls without notice. If the employer realizes that the call is personal, monitoring must cease immediately.
Email messages	Under most circumstances, employers may monitor employee emails. Even in situations where the employer claims that it will not, its right to monitor has been held to persist. However, where the employee's reasonable expectation of privacy is increased (such as a password-protected account), this may impact the court's decision, though it is not determinative.
Voice mail system messages	Though not yet completely settled, it appears that voice mail system messages are analyzed in the same manner as email messages.
Internet use	Where the employer has provided the equipment and/or the access to the Internet, the employer may track, block, or review Internet use.

any individuals regarding the relationship. However, Stonecipher was originally hired after Boeing had experienced previous circumstances of alleged wrongdoings and after he, himself, had spearheaded the creation of an ethics policy in response. With notice of the emails and the possible later contention that a hostile environment existed for other workers, Boeing executives felt that they had no choice but to ask for his resignation.

While monitoring email transmissions over telephone lines is forbidden by the ECPA, communications within a firm do not generally go over the phone lines and therefore may be legally available to employers. In addition, there are numerous exceptions to the ECPA's prohibitions as discussed earlier in this chapter, including situations where one party to the transmission consents, where the provider of the communication service can monitor communications, or where the monitoring is done in the ordinary course of business. In order to satisfy the ECPA consent exception, however, the employer's interception must not exceed the scope of the employee's consent. Employers must be aware, as well, that an employee's knowledge that the employer is monitoring certain communications is insufficient to be considered implied consent. To avoid liability, employers must specifically inform employees of the extent and circumstances under which email communications will be monitored.

Despite the failure of legislative attempts to require employers to notify employees that their email is being monitored, such as the proposed Notice of Electronic Monitoring Act, employers should provide such notification, as described below.[94] In addition, some states, including Delaware and Connecticut, have now imposed notice requirements before monitoring.

Developing Computer Use Policies

An employer can meet its business necessity to monitor email, protect itself from liability, and, at the same time, respect the employees' legitimate expectation of privacy in the workplace in numerous ways. Moreover, research demonstrates that monitoring may be more acceptable to employees when they perceive that monitoring takes place within an environment of procedural fairness and one designed to ensure privacy.[95] Accordingly, employers should develop concise written policies and procedures regarding the use of company computers, specifically email. The Society for Human Resource Management strongly encourages companies both to adopt policies that address employee privacy and to ensure that employees are notified of such policies. Any email policy should be incorporated in the company policies and procedures manuals, employee handbooks, and instruction aids to ensure that the employee receives consistent information regarding the employer's rights to monitor employee email. Additionally, a company could display a notice each time an employee logs on to a company computer indicating the computers are to be used only for business-related communication or explaining that the employee has no reasonable expectation of privacy in the electronic messages. Employers also can periodically send memos reminding employees of the policy. For a sample email, voice mail, and computer systems policy, see Exhibit 14.17, "Sample Email, Voice Mail, and Computer Systems Policy."

Exhibit 14.17   *Sample Email, Voice Mail, and Computer Systems Policy*

Subject: Email, Voice Mail and Computer Systems Policy

Purpose: To prevent employees from using the Company computer and voice mail systems for harassing, defamatory, or other inappropriate communications. To preserve the Company's right to monitor and retrieve employee communications. To prohibit excessive personal use of the company's electronic systems.

Related Policies: Harassment Prevention, Rules of Conduct, Confidentiality of Company Information, Solicitations.

Background: Inappropriate employee use of Company computer, email, and voice mail systems can subject the Company to significant legal exposure. Due to the effervescent nature of computer communications, employees will often say things in email that they would never put in writing. Thus, it is important that all employers have a policy which strongly prohibits the inappropriate use of the Company's electronic systems, and puts employees on notice that the employer reserves the right to monitor such use.

Policy: The Company provides its employees with access to Company computers, network, Internet access, internal and external electronic mail, and voice mail to facilitate the conduct of Company business.

Company Property: All computers and data, information and software created, transmitted, downloaded, or stored on the Company's computer system are the property of Company. All electronic mail messages composed, sent, and received are and remain the property of Company. The voice mail system and all messages left on that system are Company property.

Business Use and Occasional Personal Use: The Company's computers, network, Internet access, electronic mail, and voice mail systems are provided to employees to assist employees in accomplishing their job responsibilities for the Company. Limited occasional personal use of such facilities is acceptable, provided such use is reasonable, appropriate, and complies with this policy. If you have any questions as to whether a particular use of such facilities is permissible, check with your supervisor before engaging in such use. The use of Company's computers, network, Internet access, electronic mail, and voice mail for personal use does not alter the facts that the foregoing remain Company property, and that employees have no reasonable expectation of privacy with respect to such use.

Privacy: Employees shall respect the privacy of others. Except as provided below, messages sent via electronic mail are to be read only by the addressed recipient or with the authorization of the addressed recipient. The data, information and software created, transmitted, downloaded, or stored on the Company's computer system may be accessed by authorized personnel only. Employees should understand that the confidentiality of electronic mail cannot be ensured. Employees must assume that any and all messages may be read by someone other than the intended recipient. Personal passwords are not an assurance of confidentiality. *There is no reasonable expectation of privacy in any email, voice mail, and/or other use of Company computers, network, and systems.*

Prohibited Conduct:

- Employees may not use the Company's computers, network, Internet access, electronic mail, or voice mail to conduct illegal or malicious activities.

continued

- Employees may not transmit or solicit any threatening, defamatory, obscene, harassing, offensive, or unprofessional material. Offensive content would include, but not be limited to, sexual comments or images, racial slurs, gender-specific comments or any comments that would offend someone on the basis of his or her race, religion, color, national origin, ancestry, disability, age, sex, marital status, sexual orientation, or any other class protected by any federal, state, or local law.
- Employees may not create, transmit, or distribute unwanted, mass, excessive or anonymous emails, electronic vandalism, junk email, or "spam."
- Employees may not access any Web site that is sexually or racially offensive or discriminatory.
- Employees may not display, download, or distribute any sexually explicit material.
- Employees may not violate the privacy of individuals by any means, such as by reading private emails or private communications, accessing private documents, or utilizing the passwords of others, unless officially authorized to do so.
- Employees may not represent themselves as being someone else, or send anonymous communications.
- Employees may not use the email, voice mail, or computer systems to solicit for religious causes, outside business ventures, or personal causes.
- Employees may not transmit any of Company's confidential or proprietary information including (without limitation) customer data, trade secrets, or other material covered by Company's policy re: Confidentiality of Company information.
- Employees may not install, run, or download any software (including entertainment software or games) not authorized by the Company.
- Employees may not disrupt or hinder the use of the Company computers or network, or infiltrate another computer or computing system.
- Employees may not damage software or propagate computer worms or viruses.

Only authorized employees may communicate on the Internet on behalf of the Company.

Monitoring: Company maintains the right to monitor and record employee activity on its computers, network, voice mail and email systems. Company's monitoring includes (without limitation) reading email messages sent or received, files stored or transmitted, and recording Web sites accessed.

Archiving: It is Company's practice to archive (i.e., make backup copies) all electronic documents, files, and email messages incident to the Company's normal back-up procedures. Employees should therefore understand that even when a document, file, or message is deleted, it may still be possible to access that message. Management and law enforcement agencies have the right to access these archives.

Copyright Laws: Any software or other material downloaded into the Company's computers may be used only in ways consistent with the licenses and copyrights of the vendors, authors, and owners of the material. No employee shall make illegal or unauthorized copies of any software or data.

Violations of this Policy: Any violation of this policy may result in disciplinary action up to and including immediate termination. Any employee learning of any violation of this policy should notify his or her [e.g., immediate supervisor] immediately.

continued

Exhibit 14.17 *continued*

Dates: Be sure to date policies when they become effective. Hang on to old policies and be sure to change the date on revised versions.

Source: Lee T. Paterson, ed., *Sample Personnel Policies* (El Segundo, CA: Professionals in Human Resources Association (PIHRA), 2002).

Some experts advocate policies that restrict the use of email to business purposes only and that explain that the employer may access the email both in the ordinary course of business and when business reasons necessitate. If the employer faithfully adheres to this policy 100 percent of the time, this process is certainly defensible. However, such a standard is one that is difficult to honor in every case and the employer may be subject to claims of disparate treatment if applied inconsistently. Therefore, a more realistic approach—and one that is generally accepted in both the courts and common practice—suggests that employees limit their use of technology to reasonable personal access that does not unnecessarily interfere with their professional responsibilities or unduly impact the workplace financially or otherwise (referring to bandwidth, time spent online, impact on colleagues, and so on).

Kevin Conlon, district counsel for the Communication Workers of America, suggests these additional guidelines that may be considered in formulating an accountable process for employee monitoring:

1. There should be no monitoring in highly private areas such as restrooms.
2. Monitoring should be limited to the workplace.
3. Employees should have full access to any information gathered through monitoring.
4. Continuous monitoring should be banned.
5. All forms of *secret* monitoring should be banned. Advance notice should be given.
6. Only information relevant to the job should be collected.
7. Monitoring should result in the attainment of some business interest.

Philosopher William Parent conceives the right to privacy more appropriately as a right to liberty and therefore seeks to determine the potential affront to liberty from the employer's actions. He suggests the following six questions to determine whether those actions are justifiable or have the potential for being an invasion of privacy or liberty:

1. For what purpose is the undocumented personal knowledge sought?
2. Is this purpose a legitimate and important one?
3. Is the knowledge sought through invasion of privacy relevant to its justifying purpose?

4. Is invasion of privacy the only or the least offensive means of obtaining the knowledge?

5. What restrictions or procedural restraints have been placed on the privacy-invading techniques?

6. How will the personal knowledge be protected once it has been acquired?[96]

Both of these sets of guidelines also may respect the personal autonomy of the individual worker by providing for personal space within the working environment, by providing notice of where that "personal" space ends, and by allowing access to the information gathered, all designed toward achievement of a personal and professional development objective.

As is apparent from the above discussion, it is possible to implement a monitoring program that is true to the values of the firm and accountable to those it impacts—the workers. Appropriate attention to the nature and extent of the monitoring, the notice given to those monitored, and the ethical management of the information obtained will ensure a balance of employer and employee interests.

In *City of Ontario v. Quon,* included at the end of the chapter, the court examines an employer's decision to monitor employee text message records. As you consider the case, ask yourself whether the employer could have used a less intrusive method for discovering whether the messages were work-related and whether you believe that its stated reason for requesting the records was legitimate.

Blogging and Other Social Media ("Web 2.0")

LO12

social media
User-created content, including text, video, audio, and other multimedia, published in a shared environment, such as a blog, wiki, or other similar site created to enable such sharing.

An estimated 200 million blogs were in existence in 2010,[97] a number growing so fast that it was out of date by the time this sentence was written.[98] **Social media** is now the number one activity on the Web (replacing pornography in 2010). But individuals are not the only ones embracing social media; an estimated 80 percent of companies use social media for recruitment, with 95 percent of those using LinkedIn, and more than 700,000 businesses with active pages on Facebook.

The enormous growth in blogging and other social media has created a dilemma for those businesses that have embraced these new technologies. While social media may offer new opportunities to reach a wider customer base in a variety of new ways, it also offers new arenas in which employees can harm the company image, share company information that should not be shared, harass fellow employees, or commit other acts that employers once worried about only with email. A 2007 study by Croner, a British consulting firm, found that an estimated 39 percent of bloggers have made inappropriate comments about their workplace.[99] In a separate survey, 12 percent of U.S. companies reported that they investigated the exposure of confidential or private information posted to a social media site in the previous year.[100]

For better or for worse, social media is here to stay. A 2009 report found a correlation between corporate profitability and engagement in social media, looking at 11 different online social media channels.[101] Generally, those that had a deeper involvement in social media saw revenues grow faster than those that did not.

The challenge for employers now is to find the right balance between embracing social media and discouraging employee misuse. As with email, employers have the right to control what is sent out through the various social media channels they own. The difficult part is trying to control what employees send out on their own time and through their own social media channels.

In a case included at the end of the chapter and discussed earlier, a San Diego police officer in his free time sold pornographic videos and other paraphernalia, including official police department uniforms, through an adults-only section of eBay. His superiors discovered the activity and ordered him to stop. When he did not, they dismissed him. He sued the department, alleging a violation of his First Amendment right to free speech. Although the appellate court accepted his argument, the U.S. Supreme Court reversed, concluding that the San Diego Police Department had legitimate and substantial interests of its own that were compromised by the employee's speech, especially because the policy officer linked his videos to his work (the videos depicted the police officer in a simulated police uniform).[102] Speech by a public employee that involves "public concern" is entitled to a balancing test, but those that are outside of public concern are subject to tighter restrictions.

The general rule is that bloggers (and other social media users) enjoy First Amendment protections for comments made on blogs and elsewhere, but that protection is not absolute.[103] First, it does not extend to unprotected speech, such as defamation. Second, unless a termination violates an exception, it does not protect employees from the at-will employment doctrine.

The other thing to note is that government employees have even fewer First Amendment rights than private employees. As the Supreme Court said in *Roe*, "a governmental employer may impose certain restraints on the speech of its employees, restraints that would be unconstitutional if applied to the general public."[104]

If employers want to punish employees for statements made in a blog written and posted on their free time, employees have little legal recourse. It has been suggested that they could claim protection under the National Labor Relations Act, if the blogging relates to wages, hours, or working conditions.[105] The fact that NLRA protection is the best that they can hope for illustrates how few protections they have.

Several states have laws that prevent employers from disciplining employees for engaging in lawful conduct away from work, as discussed previously.[106] Those statutes typically refer to "use of a lawful product" and were most often originally designed to prevent employers from punishing employees who smoke or drink *away* from work. Not all the laws are the same; New York, for example, specifically protects off-duty political and recreational activities.

Whether those state laws can be extended to protect blogging activities conducted away from work seems unlikely but remains an open question. Some commentators have suggested that states amend their laws to incorporate protections for off-duty blogging,[107] but none have yet to do so. Until Congress or state legislatures step in, employers will continue to have wide latitude in managing off-duty blogging.

Several cases illustrate the point. Ellen Simonetti was fired in 2004 by Delta Air Lines for an online journal post showing a photograph of her in her Delta uniform. Jessica Cutler was fired in 2004 from her job as a congressional aide after posting blogs detailing her sexual adventures and criticizing her boss. Chez Pazienza was fired in 2008 by CNN for operating a blog without permission. Others have been fired by Starbucks, Microsoft, Wells Fargo, Google, Friendster, the *Washington Post,* and Kmart; and the list goes on. Many of those were fired even though they did not blog in their own name and did not have prior notice that what they were doing would subject them to punishment.

What is an employee to do? The Electronic Frontier Foundation maintains a tutorial on blogging that includes tips on how to avoid getting fired.[108] One key recommendation is to blog anonymously. The Delaware Supreme Court, for example, refused to compel discovery of the identity of an anonymous blogger who published allegedly defamatory comments about a Smyrna, Delaware, city councilman.[109] The ultimate fate of anonymity remains to be seen; but, the court's assertions that "[b]logs and chat rooms . . . are not sources of facts or data upon which a reasonable person would rely," as well as "readers are unlikely to view messages posted anonymously as assertions of fact," already seem dated.

Until the legal boundaries become clearer, the best possible solution for employers and employees is probably a combination of a clear written policy, some tolerance of criticism, and more effective training. Companies that embrace social media need to find the right balance between encouraging employees to engage in open and honest communications with customers and protecting the company's interests. Therefore, a company social media policy should contain the following:[110]

- **Defined objectives that do not overreach.** A policy can range from restrictive—banning all employee comments on work-related matters, including on their own time—to permissive—allowing contact with customers but warning employees to avoid embarrassing the company.
- **A reminder that company policies apply.** Employers who embrace social media activities should remind employees that company policies continue to apply to off-work social media related activities, including those involving the sharing of company information, harassment, and discrimination.
- **Personal comment rules.** Employers should establish rules for employees who express opinions through social media; for example, employees who offer personal opinions may be required to identify themselves as employees of the company and provide a disclaimer that they have no authority to speak for the company and that the views are theirs, alone.
- **Disclosure reminders.** If the employer is publicly traded, the policy should include a reminder of the rules imposed by the Securities and Exchange Commission on information disclosures by publicly owned companies.
- **Monitoring reminders.** Employers should remind employees that they retain the right to monitor all social media activities, including the right to view Facebook and Twitter postings made while away from work; they may need to be

reminded that content sent through social media channels is not private and cannot be recalled.

- **Copyright reminders.** Employers may want to include a reminder to respect copyright law; social media users often mistakenly believe that anything they see on the Internet is fair game for copying and reusing.

Employers who embrace social media will have to decide how much criticism they are willing to tolerate. Employers that have been willing to tolerate some internal criticisms have sometimes been rewarded for that tolerance with a reputation for open-mindedness and a progressive embrace of social media technologies.

Social media technologies have democratized opinion-giving. Once upon a time, employers could control their message rather effectively by training the few top executives who were authorized to speak for the company. Today, however, any employee with a cell phone or a personal computer can publish her or his opinion any number of ways. Putting such a public microphone in the hands of employees who are untrained in the dangers of misstatements can be disastrous, potentially exposing the company to legal liability and possibly damaging the stock price. The answer is better employee training of the dangers inherent in social media and a clear social media policy that sets forth the employer's expectations of those who intend to use the technologies, including the risks for those who misuse them.

YouTube is another popular social media outlet. Because many cell phones now have not only cameras but also video capabilities, and because many employees carry cell phones, it is a short step between something an employee sees at work and YouTube, or another video-sharing site. Some employers, therefore, have implemented policies banning the use of cameras, cell phones, and any other devices used to take still pictures or video on the theory that employees may not fully appreciate the importance of not sharing the business's inner workings with the rest of the world. Although no cases exist that have challenged such bans, employers are likely within their rights to do so, especially if the ban is tied to a legitimate business reason.

Waivers of Privacy Rights

search
A physical invasion of a person's space, belongings, or body.

waiver
The intentional relinquishment of a known right.

On occasion, an employer may request that an employee waive her or his privacy rights as a condition of employment. This condition could be a **search**. A **waiver** would exempt the employer from liability for claims the employee may have as a result of privacy issues. While a valid waiver must be voluntarily given, requiring a waiver as an employment condition is a questionable approach. Employers maintain a superior bargaining position from which to negotiate such an arrangement, so voluntariness is questionable.

Waivers exist at all stages of employment, from preemployment medical screenings to a waiver of age discrimination claims when being bought out of one's job at a certain age. Courts are not consistent in their acceptance of these waivers, but one common link among those that are approved is that there exists some form of consideration in which the employee receives something in return for giving up rights.

It has thus been held that the waiver at least be accompanied by an offer of employment. No waiver that is given by an applicant prior to a job offer would be considered valid and enforceable. Other requirements articulated by the courts include that the waiver be knowingly and intelligently given and that it be clear and unmistakable, in writing, and voluntary.

Privacy Rights since September 11, 2001

The United States has implemented widespread modifications to its patchwork structure of privacy protections since the terrorist attacks of September 11, 2001. In particular, proposals for the expansion of surveillance and information-gathering authority were submitted and many, to the chagrin of some civil rights attorneys and advocates, were enacted.

The most public and publicized of these modifications was the adoption and implementation of the Uniting and Strengthening America by Providing Appropriate Tools Required to Intercept and Obstruct Terrorism (USA PATRIOT) Act of 2001, Public Law 107-56. The USA PATRIOT Act expanded states' rights with regard to Internet surveillance technology, including workplace surveillance and amending the Electronic Communications Privacy Act in this regard. The act also grants access to sensitive data with only a court order rather than a judicial warrant, among other changes, and imposes or enhances civil and criminal penalties for knowingly or intentionally aiding terrorists. In addition, the new disclosure regime increased the sharing of personal information between government agencies in order to ensure the greatest level of protection.

Title II of the act provides for the following enhanced surveillance procedures, among others, that have a significant impact on individual privacy and may impact an employer's effort to maintain employee privacy:

- Expanded authority to intercept wire, oral, and electronic communications relating to terrorism and to computer fraud and abuse offenses.
- Provided roving surveillance authority under the Foreign Intelligence Surveillance Act of 1978 (FISA) to track individuals. (FISA investigations are not subject to Fourth Amendment standards but are instead governed by the requirement that the search serve "a significant purpose.")
- Allowed nationwide seizure of voice mail messages pursuant to warrants (i.e., without the previously required wiretap order).
- Broadened the types of records that law enforcement may obtain, pursuant to a subpoena, from electronic communications service providers.
- Permitted emergency disclosure of customer electronic communications by providers to protect life and limb.
- Offered nationwide service of search warrants for electronic evidence.

Management Tips

- Develop and publish policies that reserve your right to monitor, gain access to, or disclose all emails in your system. Notify employees of the policy and train all managers (see Exhibit 14.18).

- When developing an email policy, do not overlook instant messaging (IM). Ensure that any policy that applies to emails also applies to IMs. IMs can pose a greater security risk than email if the IMs sent to employees are not subject to virus-checking software.

- The same warning applies for the so-called web 2.0 technologies, such as blogs, social networking, wikis, and similar technologies. Ensure that the privacy policy accounts for these social media technologies and strikes the right balance between appropriate and inappropriate uses.

- The privacy policy should be clear that employees have no expectation of privacy in all employer-provided equipment. Clear policies reduce the likelihood of future disputes.

- As an employer, you may search your employees' property where the employee does not have any expectation of privacy; the difficulty comes in determining where that expectation exists. Therefore, if you believe that searches are necessary, the policy should state clearly where the expectation of privacy ends and under what conditions searches will be permitted.

- Monitoring policies should be clearly stated and should explain that use of technology is subject to review, notwithstanding password protection. They should explain that passwords are provided for the user's protection from external intrusion, as opposed to the creation of an expectation that email is actually private with regard to the employer.

- In designing a monitoring process, avoid content-based and real-time monitoring as both give rise to subjective action rather than standardized procedures and may violate the Federal Wiretap Act.

- Since many privacy protections exist on a state-by-state basis, be sure to investigate the specific protections for which you are responsible in the states in which you do business.

- Your privacy policy should be targeted to protect your business interests. Therefore, consider prohibiting the following: (1) the use of cameras, cell phones, or other devices for taking pictures or making recordings on your property, (2) the use of emails for distributing illegal or improper content, (3) the use of company trademarks, logos, or other copyrighted material without permission, and (4) the disclosure of company materials to outside entities.

- While it may appear reasonable for you to want to regulate certain off-work activities of your employees, be wary of overrestricting since courts do not look on these regulations positively. Policies regulating off-work activities that have been upheld are generally those that are targeted to protect legitimate business interests, such as the company's reputation.

- On that note, if you do opt to regulate the off-work activities of your employees, you may wish to consider focusing the policy on the possible negative impact of off-duty conduct on the employer's business interests and on the public's perception of the employer, rather than on the specific off-duty conduct, in particular.

- You are less likely to find problems with a waiver of privacy rights where the waiver is accompanied by an offer of employment.
- Ensure that you comply with all privacy rules required by HIPAA, particularly involving the security of employee health records. Train the appropriate employees on those requirements.
- When you do collect personal information about your employees, be sure to regulate access to this information since unwarranted disclosure might constitute an invasion of privacy even where the original collection of information is allowed.
- Technology changes quickly. You should keep abreast of current developments and conduct periodic reviews of the privacy policy to ensure that emerging technologies are covered.
- Ensure that the privacy rules are enforced consistently.

Exhibit 14.18 *Toward Appropriate Information Collection from Employees*

Though it appears that employee privacy might be a moving target, there are steps that employers may take to be respectful of employee information and personal privacy while also maintaining a balanced management of its workplace:

- **First, conduct an information audit** for the purpose of determining those areas of the company's practices and procedures that have the potential for invasion, including what type of information is collected, how that information is maintained, the means by which the information is verified, who has access to the information, and to whom the information is disclosed. The audit should cover all facets of the organization's activities, from recruitment and hiring to termination. In addition, it may be helpful to ascertain what type of information is maintained by different sectors of the organization.

- **Second, in connection with sensitive areas where the company maintains no formal policy, develop a policy** to ensure appropriate treatment of data. It is recommended that a policy and procedure be maintained in connection with the acquisition of information, the maintenance of that information, the appropriate contents of personnel files, the use of the information contained therein, and the conduct of workplace investigations. For instance, in connection with

the maintenance of personnel files and the accumulation of personal information about company employees, the employer should request only information justified by the needs of the firm and relevant to employment-related decisions.

- **Third, the information collected should be kept in one of several files maintained on each employee:** (1) a personnel file, which contains the application, paperwork relating to hiring, payroll, and other nonsensitive data; (2) a medical file, which contains physicians' reports and insurance records; (3) evaluation files, which contain any evidence of job performance including, but not limited to, performance appraisals; and (4) a confidential file, which contains data relating to extremely sensitive matters that should not be disclosed except with express and specific authority, such as criminal records or information collected in connection with workplace investigations.

- **Fourth, information should be gathered from reliable sources,** rather than sources of questionable repute such as hearsay and other subjective indicators. Irrelevant or outdated material should periodically be expunged from these records as well.

- **Fifth, publicize privacy policies and procedures, and educate employees** regarding their rights as well as their responsibilities.

Pursuant to these provisions, the government is now allowed to monitor anyone on the Internet simply by contending that the information is "relevant" to an ongoing criminal investigation. In addition, the act provides anti-money-laundering provisions designed to combat money-laundering activity or the funding of terrorist or criminal activity through corporate activity or otherwise. All financial institutions must now report suspicious activities in financial transactions and keep records of foreign national employees, while also complying with anti-discrimination laws discussed throughout this text. It is a challenging balance, claim employers.

The USA PATRIOT Act, set to expire in February 2010, was renewed for one year without including many of the additional privacy measures sought by Democratic lawmakers. One extended provision does allow authorities greater access to certain personal and business records.

The USA PATRIOT Act was not the only legislative response. Both federal and state agencies have passed a number of new pieces of legislation responding to terrorism. Not everyone is comfortable with these protections. Out of concern for the USA PATRIOT Act's permitted investigatory provisions, some librarians now warn computer users in their libraries that their computer use could be monitored by law enforcement agencies (especially since reforms to the act were defeated in 2006 and certain provisions will stay in place for another four years). *The Washington Post* reports that some are even ensuring privacy by destroying records of sites visited, books checked out, and logs of computer use.[111] The American Civil Liberties Union reports that a number of communities have passed anti–USA PATRIOT Act resolutions.[112]

Employers have three choices in terms of their response to a governmental request for information. They may

1. Voluntarily cooperate with law enforcement by providing, upon request (as part of an ongoing investigation), confidential employee information.
2. Choose not to cooperate and ask instead for permission to seek employee authorization to release the requested information.
3. Request to receive a subpoena, search warrant, or FISA order from the federal agency before disclosing an employee's confidential information.[113]

Chapter Summary

- Privacy is a fundamental right that has been recognized as deserving constitutional protection.
- Public employers are subject to greater scrutiny because their actions are considered to be State actions, thus triggering constitutional protections that generally do not apply to private-sector employers.
- Employee privacy rights in the workplace originate from three sources: the Constitution, various state and federal laws, and the common law; those employees who have employment contracts, either individual or union-negotiated, also have whatever protections are provided in the contracts.
- Common law torts include intrusion into seclusion, public disclosure of private facts, publication in a false light, and defamation.

- Regulation of an employee's off-work activities is a controversial area, with the general rule being that employers have the right to regulate such activity as long as the regulation is connected to a legitimate business interest; some state legislatures have stepped in to limit what employers can regulate.
- Employers generally have the right to monitor employee activity while employees are on employer property; employers are generally on stronger footing if they develop a written policy, they notify employees of the policy, and they enforce the policy consistently.

Chapter-End Questions

1. Can a government employee state a claim for a violation of the constitutional right to privacy when she was required, as a job applicant, to sign an affidavit stating that she had not used tobacco products for one year prior to the application date?

2. A homosexual employee files a claim for invasion of privacy against his employer who shared with co-workers the fact that the employee's male partner was listed on his insurance policy and pension plan as his beneficiary. Does he have a claim?

3. An employee obtains permission to take a leave of absence to attend to a personal matter. A co-worker asks the manager why the employee is on leave. What information may the manager properly share with the co-worker?

4. In March and April 1998, John Doe, an employee of the U.S. Postal Service, missed several weeks of work because of an AIDS-related illness. Doe's supervisor told him that he had to submit an administrative form and a medical certificate explaining why he was sick or he would face disciplinary action for his unexplained absence. He was informed that he may qualify for coverage under FMLA and his supervisor provided him with the appropriate forms to fill out and return. Doe decided to pursue an FMLA request and his physician completed the forms, indicating that Doe had "AIDS related complex" and "chronic HIV infection." Doe submitted the request forms to his employer and, upon his return to work, discovered that his HIV status had become common knowledge among co-workers. Several co-workers made comments to him about his condition and many identified his supervisor as the source of the information. Doe filed a suit against the U.S. Postal Service for violation of the Privacy Act, alleging that Postal Service employees disclosed medical information contained in his FMLA forms. Can Doe prove his case? [*John Doe v. U.S. Postal Service,* No. 01-5395 (DC. Cir. Feb. 7, 2003).]

5. Marriott Resorts had a formal company party for more than 200 employees. At one point during the party, they aired a videotape that compiled employees' and their spouses' comments about a household chore that they hated. However, as a spoof, the video was edited to make it seem as if they were describing what it was like to have sex with their partner. For instance, though the plaintiff's husband (an employee) was actually responding to the question about housework, the plaintiff's husband was quoted on the video as seemingly responding to a provocative question by saying, "the smell. The smell, the smell. And then you go with the goggles. You have to put on the goggles. And then you get the smell through the nose. And as you get into it things start flying all over the place. And the smell. And you get covered in these things." The plaintiff herself was never mentioned by name, nor did she appear on the video. The plaintiff was terribly upset by the video and sued Marriott for intrusion into seclusion and portrayal of facts in a false light. Is Marriott liable? [*Stein v. Marriott Ownership Resorts, Inc.,* 944 P.2d 374 (UT. 1997).][114]

6. An employee submitted an expense report that included costs from a cell phone issued by his company. The company wanted to check the phone to verify information that the employee had provided and, because the employee was in the hospital, they obtained access to his office, as well as a key to his desk drawer, in order to look for the phone. Though they did not find the phone, they did find a pellet gun and ammunition. The employee was fired for violating the employer's weapons ban. Did the supervisors violate the employee's right to privacy? Is the fact that the employee shared the desk with other employees relevant? [*Ratti v. Service Management Systems*, No. 06-6034, DC NJ, 2008.]

7. A company institutes a no-fraternization policy that says that a manager will be fired for dating an hourly employee, regardless of whether the manager is the worker's supervisor. To some, the policy seems overbroad and unnecessary, but is it legal? [*Ellis v. UPS*, 523 F. 3d 823 (7th Cir. 2008).]

8. A trucking company installed in its terminal audio and video devices behind two-way mirrors in both the men's and women's bathrooms. The purpose of the devices was to detect and prevent drug use among the truckers. The devices were discovered when one day the mirror fell off of the wall. Are the tactics used by the trucking company legal because it has a right to restrict drug use? Or is its approach a violation of the truckers' right to privacy? [*Cramer v. Consolidated Freightways Inc.*, 255 F. 3d 683 (9th Cir. 2001).]

9. Two female employees of a 24-hour residential facility for abused and neglected children discovered video recording equipment hidden on a bookshelf in an office that they shared. They were able to lock the door and close the blinds to the office; and one of the women regularly changed clothes there. The California Supreme Court upheld the placement of the hidden video equipment by their employer, even though neither woman was suspected of any wrongdoing. How is that possible? Under what set of facts do you imagine that an employer could permissibly monitor employees who are not suspected of wrongdoing? [*Hernandez v. Hillsides, Inc.*, 47 Cal. 4th 272 (2009).]

10. State "sunshine" laws require the release of all documents relating to state business. Are employees' personal emails subject to public disclosure? Or do state employees retain privacy in personal emails? [*Schill v. Wisconsin Rapids School District*, No. 2008AP967-AC, Wis. Sup. Ct., July 16, 2010.]

11. A management employee had a private office with a locked door. Inside the office was an employer-provided computer, and the employee was told not to use the company computer for personal reasons. He was also warned that his computer use would be monitored. When the company discovered that the employee had child pornography on the computer, it authorized the FBI to go into the office and seize the computer. Given the company's policy, it clearly had the right to monitor the employee's use of the computer. But what about entering a locked office? Does the employee have an expectation of privacy in the locked office? [*U.S. v. Ziegler*, 474 F. 3d 1184 (9th Cir. 2007).]

12. In June of 1995, a hidden camera and VCR were installed at Salem State College in their off-campus Small Business Development Center. The camera was installed to investigate possible illegal entries into the center after regular business hours. The camera recorded 24 hours a day and was angled to view the entire length of the office, including private areas such as cubicles. During the summer of 1995, Gail Nelson, a secretary at the center, often brought a change of clothes to work and changed in a cubicle, either early in the morning before anyone else was in the office or after work

when the office was empty. These activities were recorded on the hidden camera. When Nelson later learned about the covert surveillance from a co-worker, she filed suit against the college and officials, arguing that they had violated her Fourth Amendment right to privacy. Was this an invasion of privacy? [*Gail Nelson v. Salem State College & others,* SJC-09519 (MA., Dec. 8, 2005–Apr. 13, 2006).] What if the video surveillance had taken place in a back room such as an employee locker area? [*Thompson v. Johnson County Community College,* 930 F. Supp. 501 (D. Kan. 1996), *aff'd,* 108 F.3d 1388 (10th Cir. 1997).]

13. A restaurant employee created a private MySpace page and invited fellow employees to the page for the purpose of sharing work-related frustrations and criticisms of their employer. A manager learned of the page, obtained the password from one of the invited employees, and read the postings. Ultimately, several managers went to the page and read the messages. The employee responsible for the MySpace page was fired. To what extent does an employee have an expectation of privacy in a private MySpace page? Does he have free speech rights to express his opinion to his fellow employees? Did the employer illegally invade his privacy? Is the method the manager used to obtain the password from the employee relevant? In other words, does it make any difference whether he coerced her into giving him the password? [*Pietrylo v. Hillstone Restaurant Group,* 2:06-5754-FSH-PS (D.N.J. 2008).]

End Notes

1. E. J. Bloustein, "Privacy as an Aspect of Human Dignity," in F. D. Schoeman (ed.), *Philosophical Dimensions of Privacy: An Anthology* (New York: Cambridge University Press, 1984), p. 188.

2. Samuel D. Warren and Louis D. Brandeis, "The Right to Privacy," *Harvard Law Review* 4, no. 193 (1890).

3. MacDonald, C., "Why Privacy Matters," *Management Ethics* (Fall/Winter 2010), http://www.ethicscentre.ca/EN/resources/Management_Ethics_FW10_dh.pdf.

4. See, for example, Avner Levin, "Dignity in the Workplace: An Enquiry into the Conceptual Foundation of Workplace Privacy Protection Worldwide," *ALSB Journal of Employment and Labor Law* 11, no. 1, p. 63 (Winter 2009).

5. an-Noor 24, pp. 27–28 (Yusufali); al-Hujraat 49, pp. 11–12 (Yusufali).

6. Vol. 1, Book 10, no. 509 (Sahih Bukhari); Book 31, no. 4003 (Sunan Abu Dawud).

7. R. L. Wakefield, "Computer Monitoring and Surveillance: Balancing Privacy with Security," *CPA Journal* 74, no. 7 (2004), pp. 52–55.

8. Delia Fahmy, "More U.S. Employers Testing Workers for Drug Use," *International Herald Tribune,* May 10, 2007, http://www.iht.com/articles/2007/05/10/business/drugtests.php (last visited August 5, 2007).

9. Deloitte & Touche, Poneman Institute, LLC, "Enterprise @ Risk: 2007 Privacy & Data Protection Survey," December 12, 2007, http://www.deloitte.com/dtt/article/0%2C1002%2Ccid%25253D182733%2C00.html.

10. 381 U.S. 479 (2965).

11. Steve Ulfelder, "CPOs on the Rise?" *Computerworld,* March 15, 2004, http://www.computerworld.com/securitytopics/security/story/0.10801.91166.00.html, quoting Alan F. Westin, president of the nonprofit Privacy & American Business organization.

12. See, for example, *Smyth v. Pillsbury*, 914 F.Supp. 97 (E.D. Penn. 1996). The standard was first enunciated by the U.S. Supreme Court in *Katz v. U.S.*, 389 U.S. 347 (1967), a Fourth Amendment search and seizure case involving a public telephone booth.

13. *Ulrich v. K-Mart*, 858 F.Supp. 1087 (D. Kan. 1994).

14. 795 F.2d 1136, 1141 (3d Cir. 1986).

15. 489 U.S. 602, 109 S. Ct. 1402 (1989), *aff'd,* 934 F.2d 1096 (9th Cir. 1991).

16. *U.S. v. Slanina,* 283 F.3d 670 (5th Cir. 2002); *Leventhal v. Knapek,* 266 F.3d 64 (2d Cir. 2001).

17. 474 F.3d 1184 (9th Cir. 2007), http://bulk.resource.org/courts.gov/c/F3/474/474.F3d.1184.05-30177.html.

18. As an interesting side note, though U.S. law considers child pornography illegal, most states have no legal obligation to report it. Only Arkansas, Missouri, Oklahoma, South Carolina, and South Dakota have laws that require workers in the information technology arena to report child pornography when it is found on workers' computers. Tam Harbert, "Dark Secrets and Ugly Truths: When Ethics and IT Collide," *Computerworld,* September 12, 2007.

19. *Ziegler,* 474 F.3d at 1199.

20. 18 U.S.C. §§ 2510–2521.

21. *Annual Report on Wiretapping in the U.S.*, Administrative Office of the United States Courts, p. 6, April 2010; www.scribd.com/doc/30800548/Annual-Report-on-Wiretapping-in-the-U-S.

22. *Fraser v. National Mutual Insurance,* 352 F.3d 107 (3d Cir. 2003). See also *United States v. Steiger,* 318 F.3d 1039 (11th Cir. 2003); *Konop v. Hawaiian Airlines, Inc.,* 302 F.3d 868 (9th Cir. 2002); and *Steve Jackson Games, Inc. v. U.S. Secret Serv.,* 36 F.3d 457 (5th Cir. 1994).

23. Montana is the one exception. Employees can be fired only for good cause under the Wrongful Discharge from Employment Act, Mont. Code Ann. §39-2-901, et seq. (2008).

24. 50 S.E. 68 (Ga. 1905).

25. *Lake v. Wal-Mart Stores, Inc.,* 582 N.W.2d 231 (Minn. 1998).

26. 526 F. Supp. 523 (D.D.C. 1981).

27. 66 Md. App. 133, 502 A.2d 1101, cert. denied, 306 Md. 289, 508 A.2d 488, cert. denied, 479 U.S. 984 (1986).

28. 561 F. Supp. 872 (S.D. Ga. 1983).

29. Certain states, however, provide no statutory protection, including Alabama, Connecticut, Mississippi, Nebraska, New Jersey, New York, Vermont, and Washington.

30. As of publication, these included Arizona, Connecticut, the District of Columbia, Illinois, Indiana, Kentucky, Louisiana, Maine, Mississippi, New Jersey, New Mexico, Oklahoma, Oregon, Rhode Island, South Carolina, South Dakota, Virginia, West Virginia, and Wyoming. See also John Pearce and Dennis Kuhn, "The Legal Limits of Employees' Off-Duty Privacy Rights," *Organizational Dynamics* 32, no. 4 (2003), pp. 372–83, and Ariana R. Levinson, "Industrial Justice: Privacy Protection for the Employed," *Cornell Journal of Law and Public Policy*, Vol. 18, p. 609 (2009).

31. R. Parekh, "States Hit Public Employees with Smoking Surcharge," *Business Insurance,* May 23, 2005.

32. M. McDonough, "Whirlpool Plant Suspends 39 Employees Caught Smoking," *ABA Journal,* April 23, 2008, http://www.abajournal.com/news/whirlpool_plant_suspends_39_employees_caught_smoking/; J. Wojcik, "Smoke Gets in Your Lies," *Workforce Week,* April 22, 2008, http://www.workforce.com/section/00/article/25/49/15.html.

33. D. Costello, "Workers Are Told to Shape Up or Pay Up," *Los Angeles Times,* July 29, 2007, http://www.latimes.com/news/nationworld/nation/la-fi-obese29jul29,1,7252935.story?coll=la-headlines-nation&ctrack=3&cset=true.

34. SHRM Research, "2006 Workplace Romance Poll Finding."

35. Ibid.

36. 237 F.3d 166 (2d Cir. 2001).

37. C. Boyd, "The Debate over the Prohibition of Romance in the Workplace," *Journal of Business Ethics* 97 (2010), p. 325.

38. J. T. A. Gabel and N. R. Mansfield, "The Information Revolution and Its Impact on the Employment Relationship: An Analysis of the Cyberspace Workplace," *American Business Law Journal* 40 (2003), pp. 301–51.

39. Mike Brunker, "Cyberporn Nurse: I Feel Like Larry Flynt," MSNBC, July 16, 1999.

40. CCH Human Resources Workforce Online, *Do Workplace Smoking Laws Regulate Your Business?* http://www.workforceonline.com/section/03/0005085.htm.

41. Electronic Privacy Information Center, "Workplace Privacy" (2010), http://epic.org/privacy/workplace/ (accessed November 27, 2010).

42. American Management Association, "Electronic Monitoring and Surveillance 2007 Survey."

43. Philip Gordon, and Katherine C. Franklin, "Blogging and the Workplace," *Law.com,* August 8, 2006.

44. Proofpoint, Inc., "Outbound Email and Data Loss Prevention in Today's Enterprise," 2008; survey conducted by Forrester Consulting.

45. *The Urban Dictionary,* http://www.urbandictionary.com/define.php?term=dooced.

46. Graeme Smith, "Is Big McBrother Invading Workplace Privacy?" *The Globe and Mail,* January 13, 2004, p. A8.

47. Philip Gordon, "It's 11 a.m. Do You Know Where Your Employees Are? Effective Use of Location-Based Technologies in the Workplace," 2005, http://library.findlaw.com/2005/Mar/10/163970.html.

48. See, for example, William A. Herbert and Amelia K. Tuminaro, "The Impact of Emerging Technologies in the Workplace: Who's Watching the Man (Who's Watching Me)?" *Hofstra Labor & Employment Law Journal* 25, p. 355 (2009).

49. Wis. Stat. Ann. §146.25.

50. Herbert and Tuminaro, supra, at p. 386.

51. According to "Telework Trendlines 2009," a survey by WorldatWork in conjunction with The Dieringer Research Group Inc.

52. Ashley Benigno, "Total Surveillance Is Threatening Your Health," *Asian Labour Update* (Hong Kong: Asia Monitor Resource Center, http://www.amrc.org.hk/Arch/3405.htm, last visited February 5, 2002).

53. Richard Rosenberg, "The Technological Assault on Ethics in the Modern Workplace," in *The Ethics of Human Resources and Industrial Relations,* ed. John W. Budd and James G. Scoville (Champaign, IL: Labor and Employment Relations Assn., 2005).

54. U. Klotz, "The Challenges of the New Economy," October 1999, cited in *World Employment Report 2001: Life at Work in the Information Economy,* p. 145 (Geneva: International Labour Office, 2001).

55. Tam Harbert, "Dark Secrets and Ugly Truths: When Ethics and IT Collide," *Computerworld,* September 12, 2007.

56. Colin Bennett, "Cookies, Web Bugs, Webcams and Cue Cats: Patterns of Surveillance on the World Wide Web," *Ethics and Information Technology* 3 (2001), pp. 197–210.

57. Ethisphere, "Mesa Airlines CFO Scrambled to Erase Porn," September 27, 2007, http://ethisphereblog.com/mesa-airlines-cfo-scrambled-to-erase-porn-not-valuable-evidence/#more-1273 (last visited September 28, 2007).

58. Dana Hawkins, "Lawsuits Spur Rise in Employee Monitoring," *U.S. News & World Report,* August 13, 2001.

59. Ibid.

60. Andrew Schulman, "One-Third of U.S. Online Workforce under Internet/Email Surveillance," *Workforce Surveillance Project* (Privacy Foundation), July 9, 2001, http://www.privacyfoundation.org/workplace/business/biz_show.asp?id=70&ac.

61. Jeffrey Benner, "Privacy at Work? Be Serious," *Wired Magazine,* March 2001, http://www.wired.com/news/business/0,1367,42029,00.html (accessed February 26, 2002).

62. Pew Internet and American Life Project, *How Americans Use Instant Messaging,* September 1, 2004, p. 2, http://www.pewinternet.org.

63. http://www.omnitracs.com.

64. http://www.spyzone.com.

65. American Management Association, "Electronic Monitoring and Surveillance 2007 Survey."

66. American Civil Liberties Union, "Privacy in America: Electronic Monitoring," December 31, 1997, http://www.aclu.org/privacy/workplace/15104res19971231.html (last visited July 26, 2007).

67. American Management Association and the ePolicy Institute, "2005 Electronic Monitoring & Surveillance Survey."

68. *Scott v. Beth Israel Medical Center, Inc.,* 847 N.Y.S.2d 436 (2007); but see, contra, *Curto v. Medical World Communications, Inc.,* 2006 WL 1318387 (E.D.N.Y. 2006).

69. R. Hollinger and L. Langton, "2005 National Retail Security Survey," 2005, http://www.crim.ufl.edu/research/srp/finalreport_2005.pdf.

70. Hayes International, 18th Annual Retail Theft Survey, http://www.hayesinternational.com/ts_emply_thft.html (last visited July 25, 2007).

71. Karen Robinson-Jacobs, "Retailers Taking Aim at Employee Pilferage," *Los Angeles Times,* February 16, 2002, p. C1.

72. *Shoars v. Epson America, Inc.,* No. SCW 112749 (Cal. Super. Ct., L.A. Cty., 1990), *appeal denied,* 994 Cal. LEXIS 3670 (Cal. 1994); James McNair, "When You Use Email at Work, Your Boss May Be Looking In," *Telecom Digest,* http://icg.stwing.upenn.edu/cis500/reading.062.htm, reprinted from the *Miami Herald,* February 9, 1994.

73. Winn Schwartau, "Who Controls Network Usage Anyway?" *Network World,* May 22, 1995, p. 71.

74. Bureau of National Affairs, "Northern Telecom Settles with CWA on Monitoring," *Individual Employment Rights,* March 10, 1992, p. 1.

75. 59 Cal. Rptr. 2d 834 (Cal. Ct. App. 1996).

76. See Ted Clark, "Legal Corner: Monitoring Employee Activities: Privacy Tensions in the Public Workplace," *NPLERA Newsletter,* June 1999, http://www.seyfarth.com/practice/labor/articles/II_1393.html.

77. Lisa Reed and Barry Freidman, "Workplace Privacy: Employee Relations and Legal Implications of Monitoring Employee Email Use," *Employee Responsibilities and Rights Journal* 19, no. 2 (June 2007), pp. 75–83.

78. 2004 U.S. Dist. LEXIS 18863 (D. Or. 2004).

79. 18 U.S.C. §§ 2510–2520.

80. See, for example, Galit Kierkut and Suzanne M. Cerra, "Monitoring Electronic Communications and Social Media Usage in the Workplace: What Are the Limits?" *New Jersey Labor and Employment Law Quarterly* 32, no.2 (2010).

81. 201 N.J. 300 March 30, 2010).

82. 2008 WL 3128429 (D.N.J. July 25, 2008).

83. See Frederic Lardinois, "Want to Work for the City of Bozeman, MT? Hand Over Your Social Network Logins and Passwords," ReadWriteWeb, June 18, 2009, www.readwriteweb.com/archives/want_to_work_for_the_city_of_bozeman_mt_hand_over_passwords_login_info.php.

84. *EEOC v. Simply Storage Management,* case no. 2010 U.S. Dist., LEXIS 527661, 1:09-cv-1223-WTL-DML (SD. IN., 5/11/2010), http://www.scribd.com/doc/31921843/EEOC-v-Simply-Storage-Mgmt-LLC.

85. 382 N.J. Super. 122, 887 A. 2d 1156 (App. Div. 2005).

86. Alan Cohen, "Worker Watchers: Want to Know What Your Employees Are Doing Online? You Can Find Out without Spooking Them," *Fortune/CNET Technology Review,* Summer 2001, p. 70.

87. Ibid.

88. Proofpoint, Inc., "Outbound Email and Data Loss Prevention in Today's Enterprise," 2008; survey conducted by Forrester Consulting.

89. *Harley v. McCoach,* 928 F. Supp. 533 (E.D. Pa. 1996), cited in "Cyberliability: An Enterprise White Paper," Elron Software, http://www.internetmanager.com.

90. 217 F.R.D. 309, 312 (S.D.N.Y. 2003); see also "Jury Awards $29.2 Million in Damages to Discharged Equities Saleswoman," *Daily Labor Report* (BNA), April 13, 2005, p. 449.

91. Cohen, "Worker Watchers," p. 76.

92. Dan Charles, "High-Tech Equipment in the Workplace," *All Things Considered,* National Public Radio, April 1, 1996.

93. Websense, "Web @ Work Survey," 2006, http://www.websense.com/global/en/PressRoom/PressReleases/PressReleaseDetail/?Release=0605161213.

94. Christopher A. Weals, "Workplace Privacy," *Legal Times,* March 6, 2002.

95. Reed and Freidman, "Workplace Privacy," pp. 75–83.

96. Miriam Schulman, "Little Brother Is Watching You," *Issues in Ethics* 9, no. 2 (Spring 1998).

97. See samswebguide.com/2010/07/13/60-amazing-blogging-social-media-statistics-facts-revealed.

98. Real Time Statistics project, http://www.worldometers.info/ (2010).

99. See Bloggers @ Work, www.justia.com/employment/docs/boggers-at-work.html.

100. Proofpoint, Inc., "Outbound Email and Data Loss Prevention in Today's Enterprise," 2008; survey conducted by Forrester Consulting.

101. The Altimeter Group, www.altimeter.com/2009/07/engagementdb.html. The 11 channels were blogs, branded social networks, content distribution to other sites, discussion forums, external social network presences (Facebook, MySpace), Flickr/Photobucket, innovation hubs, wikis, ratings and reviews, Twitter, and YouYube.

102. *City of San Diego v. Roe,* 543 U.S. 77 (2004).

103. See, for example, Tracie Watson and Elisabeth Piro, "Bloggers Beware: A Cautionary Tale of Blogging and the Doctrine of At-Will Employment," *Hofstra Labor & Employment Law Journal* 24, p. 358, Aug. 30, 2007.

104. *City of San Diego,* supra.

105. See Christine E. Howard, "Invasion of Privacy Liability in the Electronic Workplace: A Lawyer's Perspective," *Hofstra Labor & Employment Law Journal* 25, p. 517, Feb. 4, 2009.

106. See, for example, New York Consolidated Law §7-201-d (2009); Minn. Stat. §181.938 (2009); Mont. Code Ann. §39-2-313 (2009); Nev. Rev. Stat. §613.333 (2009); N.C. Gen. Stat. §95-28.2 (2009); Tenn. Code Ann. §50-1-304(e) (2009).

107. See, for example, Arianna R. Levinson, "Industrial Justice: Privacy Protection for the Employed," *Cornell Journal of Law and Public Policy,* 18, p. 609 (2009).

108. www.eff.org/wp/blog-safely.

109. *Doe v. Cahill,* 884 A.2d 451 (Del. 2005).

110. Adapted from Robert Barnes and Darya V. Pollak, "Employees Online: Protecting Company Interests in a Web 2.0 World," Bloomberg Finance L.P. (Nov. 10, 2008).

111. Rene Sanchez, "Librarians Make Some Noise over Patriot Act," *The Washington Post,* April 10, 2003, p. A20.

112. http://www.aclu.org/SafeandFree/SafeandFree.cfm?ID=11256&c=206.

113. Vance Knapp, "The Impact of the Patriot Act on Employers," 2003, http://www.rothgerber.com/newslettersarticles/le0024.asp.

114. http://caselaw.lp.findlaw.com/scripts/getcase.pl?court=ut&vol=appopin&invol=stien.

Cases

O'Connor v. Ortega *480 U.S. 709 (1987)*

The respondent, Dr. Ortega, was a physician and psychiatrist and an employee of a state hospital who had primary responsibility for training physicians in the psychiatric residency program. Hospital officials became concerned about possible improprieties in his management of the program. In particular, the officials thought that Dr. Ortega may have misled the hospital into believing that the computer had been donated when, in fact, the computer had been financed by the possibly coerced contributions of residents. Hospital officials were also concerned about charges that Dr. Ortega had sexually harassed two female hospital employees, and that he had taken inappropriate disciplinary action against a resident.

While he was on administrative leave pending investigation of the charges, hospital officials, allegedly in order to inventory and secure state property, searched Dr. Ortega's office and took personal items from his desk and file cabinets that later were used in administrative proceedings resulting in his discharge. The employee filed an action against the hospital officials, alleging that the search of his office violated the Fourth Amendment. The trial court found that the search was proper in order to secure state property. The court of appeals held that the employee had a *reasonable expectation of privacy* in his office, and thus the search violated the Fourth Amendment. The Supreme Court explains that a search must be reasonable both from its inception as well as in its scope, and remands the case to the district court for review of the reasonableness of both of those questions.

O'Connor, J.

***

Because the reasonableness of an expectation of privacy, as well as the appropriate standard for a search, is understood to differ according to context, it is essential first to delineate the boundaries of the workplace context. The workplace includes those areas and items that are related to work and are generally within the employer's control. At a hospital, for example, the hallways, cafeteria, offices, desks, and file cabinets, among other areas, are all part of the workplace. These areas remain part of the workplace context even if the employee has placed personal items in them, such as a photograph placed in a desk or a letter posted on an employee bulletin board.

Not everything that passes through the confines of the business address can be considered part of the workplace context, however. . . . The appropriate standard for a workplace search does not necessarily apply to a piece of closed personal luggage, a handbag or a briefcase that happens to be within the employer's business address.

***

Given the societal expectations of privacy in one's place of work, we reject the contention made by the Solicitor General and petitioners that public employees can never have a reasonable expectation of privacy in their place of work. Individuals do not lose Fourth Amendment rights merely because they work for the government instead of a private employer. The operational realities of the workplace, however, may make some employees' expectations of privacy unreasonable when an intrusion is by a supervisor rather than a law enforcement official. Public employees' expectations of privacy in their offices, desks, and file cabinets, like similar expectations of employees in the private sector, may be reduced by virtue of actual office practices and procedures, or by legitimate regulation. The employee's expectation of privacy must be assessed in the context of the employment relation. An office is seldom a private enclave free from entry by supervisors, other employees, and business and personal invitees. Instead, in many cases offices are continually entered by fellow employees and other visitors during the workday for conferences, consultations, and other work-related visits. Simply put, it is the nature of government offices that others—such as fellow employees, supervisors, consensual visitors, and the general public—may have frequent access to an individual's office. . . .

The undisputed evidence discloses that Dr. Ortega did not share his desk or file cabinets with any other employees. Dr. Ortega had occupied the office for 17 years and he kept materials in his office, which included personal correspondence, medical files, correspondence from private patients unconnected to the Hospital, personal financial records, teaching aids and notes, and personal gifts and mementos.

The files on physicians in residency training were kept outside Dr. Ortega's office. Indeed, the only items found by the investigators were apparently personal items because, with the exception of the items seized for use in the administrative hearings, all the papers and effects found in the office were simply placed in boxes and made available to Dr. Ortega. Finally, we note that there was no evidence that the Hospital had established any reasonable regulation or policy discouraging employees such as Dr. Ortega from storing personal papers and effects in their desks or file cabinets, although the absence of such a policy does not create an expectation of privacy where it would not otherwise exist.

On the basis of this undisputed evidence, we accept the conclusion of the Court of Appeals that Dr. Ortega had a reasonable expectation of privacy at least in his desk and file cabinets.

Having determined that Dr. Ortega had a reasonable expectation of privacy in his office, . . . we must determine the appropriate standard of reasonableness applicable to the search. A determination of the standard of reasonableness applicable to a particular class of searches requires "balanc[ing] the nature and quality of the intrusion on the individual's Fourth Amendment interests against the importance of the governmental interests alleged to justify the intrusion." In the case of searches conducted by a public employer, we must balance the invasion of the employees' legitimate expectations of privacy against the government's need for supervision, control, and the efficient operation of the workplace.

***

The governmental interest justifying work-related intrusions by public employers is the efficient and proper operation of the workplace. Government agencies provide myriad services to the public, and the work of these agencies would suffer if employers were required to have probable cause before they entered an employee's desk for the purpose of finding a file or piece of office correspondence. Indeed, it is difficult to give the concept of probable cause, rooted as it is in the criminal investigatory context, much meaning when the purpose of a search is to retrieve a file for work-related reasons. Similarly, the concept of probable cause has little meaning for a routine inventory conducted by public employers for the purpose of securing state property. To ensure the efficient and proper operation of the agency, therefore, public employers must be given wide latitude to enter employee offices for work-related, non-investigatory reasons.

We come to a similar conclusion for searches conducted pursuant to an investigation of work-related employee misconduct. Even when employers conduct an investigation, they have an interest substantially different from "the normal need for law enforcement." Public employers have an interest in ensuring that their agencies operate in an effective and efficient manner, and the work of these agencies inevitably suffers from the inefficiency, incompetence, mismanagement, or other work-related misfeasance of its employees. Indeed, in many cases, public employees are entrusted with tremendous responsibility, and the consequences of their misconduct or incompetence to both the agency and the public interest can be severe. . . . Public employers have a direct and overriding interest in ensuring that the work of the agency is conducted in a proper and efficient manner. In our view, therefore, a probable cause requirement for searches of the type at issue here would impose intolerable burdens on public employers. The delay in correcting the employee misconduct caused by the need for probable cause rather than reasonable suspicion will be translated into tangible and often irreparable damage to the agency's work, and ultimately to the public interest. Additionally, while law enforcement officials are expected to "schoo[l] themselves in the niceties of probable cause," no such expectation is generally applicable to public employers, at least when the search is not used to gather evidence of a criminal offense. It is simply unrealistic to expect supervisors in most government agencies to learn the subtleties of the probable cause standard. . . .

Balanced against the substantial government interests in the efficient and proper operation of the workplace are the privacy interests of government employees in their place of work which, while not insubstantial, are far less than those found at home or in some other contexts. . . . The employer intrusions at issue here "involve a relatively limited invasion" of employee privacy. Government offices are provided to employees for the sole purpose of facilitating the work of an agency. The employee may avoid exposing personal belongings at work by simply leaving them at home.

. . . We hold . . . that public employer intrusions on the constitutionally protected privacy interests of government employees for noninvestigatory, work-related purposes, as well as for investigations of work-related misconduct, should be judged by the standard of reasonableness under all the circumstances. Under this reasonableness standard, both the inception and the scope of the intrusion must be reasonable:

> Determining the reasonableness of any search involves a twofold inquiry: first, one must consider "whether the . . . action was justified at its inception,"

second, one must determine whether the search as actually conducted "was reasonably related in scope to the circumstances which justified the interference in the first place."

Ordinarily, a search of an employee's office by a supervisor will be "justified at its inception" when there are reasonable grounds for suspecting that the search will turn up evidence that the employee is guilty of work-related misconduct, or that the search is necessary for a noninvestigatory work-related purpose such as to retrieve a needed file. Because petitioners had an "individualized suspicion" of misconduct by Dr. Ortega, we need not decide whether individualized suspicion is an essential element of the standard of reasonableness that we adopt today. The search will be permissible in its scope when "the measures adopted are reasonably related to the objectives of the search and not excessively intrusive in light of . . . the nature of the [misconduct]."

***

On remand, therefore, the District Court must determine the justification for the search and seizure, and evaluate the reasonableness of both the inception of the search and its scope.

Accordingly, the judgment of the Court of Appeals is REVERSED and the case is REMANDED to that court for further proceedings consistent with this opinion.

Case Questions

1. Do you think the standard of the search articulated in this opinion is the correct standard for determining whether a search violates the Fourth Amendment? Think of arguments for both perspectives—the employer and employee.

2. How can an employer protect itself from a claim of an unreasonable search conducted in the workplace? Note the court stated that a policy regarding this issue was not a determinative factor in determining the constitutionality of the search.

3. What could you do as an employee to protect yourself from a company search?

Yoder v. Ingersoll-Rand Company a.k.a. ARO
31 F. Supp. 2d 565 (W.D. Ohio 1997)

Lavern Yoder sued his employer, Ingersoll-Rand Company, to recover for damages he alleged were caused as a result of the employer's failure to keep his medical records confidential. Yoder was employed as a tow motor driver. After he learned that he was HIV-positive, Yoder made every effort to keep his HIV-positive status confidential from his employer because he was concerned that he might suffer adverse employment consequences if his employer or co-workers learned of his condition. A year and a half later, his doctor recommended that he take a medical leave of absence because of stress-induced asthma. An employment disability form was sent by mistake through the employer's mail system, through inner office mail, and then finally to Yoder's home, where it was read by his mother. She learned from the Physician's Statement that he had AIDS. She had known her son was HIV-positive but did not know he had AIDS. Yoder brought a complaint against the firm for permitting the unauthorized disclosure of his medical condition. Count four alleged state common-law claim for invasion of privacy. Both sides moved for summary judgment.

Katz, J.

***

E. Invasion of Privacy

Yoder alleges an invasion of privacy under the theory, public disclosure of private facts about the plaintiff with which the public has no legitimate concern, which is also known as the "publicity" tort. In order successfully to

make out a claim under the "publicity" prong, Plaintiff must show five elements:

(1) there must be publicity, i.e., the disclosure must be of a public nature, not private;

(2) the facts disclosed must be those concerning the private life of an individual, not his public life;

(3) the matter publicized must be one which would be highly offensive and objectionable to a reasonable person of ordinary sensibilities;

(4) the publication must have been made intentionally, not negligently; and

(5) the matter publicized must not be a legitimate concern to the public.

Plaintiff can show neither the first nor the fourth element of this test. As to the first element, Plaintiff can prevail only if he shows that the matter has been communicated to "the public at large, or to so many persons that the matter must be regarded as substantially certain to become one of public knowledge." It is not enough to show merely that the matter was communicated by the defendant to a third person. The record evidence indicates that Plaintiff's HIV/AIDS status was actually communicated to only one unauthorized person. Even if the Court accepts Plaintiff's argument that mail clerk Kornrumpf and supervisor Chroninger should be treated as having received the information because they had the opportunity to read Plaintiff's medical report, the information was communicated to three people at most. Three people do not constitute "the public at large." Plaintiff cannot meet the publicity prong of the test.

As to the fourth element, Plaintiff cannot show that Defendant, or its authorized agents, made the disclosure intentionally, even as to Plaintiff's mother. It is undisputed that nothing on the outside of the envelope received in the ARO mail room indicated that it contained a confidential medical record. Kornrumpf's testimony that she did not read the form beyond Plaintiff's name, and did not know that it was a confidential medical record, is undisputed. Chroninger's testimony that he did not read the form, and did not know that it was a confidential medical record, is undisputed. It is a logical impossibility for a party intentionally to disclose information that it does not know it has. Furthermore, the disclosure would not have occurred without Plaintiff's mother's intervening act of opening and reading the medical records without authorization from Defendant. Plaintiff cannot meet the intent prong of the test. Defendant's motion for summary judgment on Count IV is granted.

***

Plaintiff's motion for summary judgment is DENIED. Defendant's motion for summary judgment is GRANTED.

Case Questions

1. Do you think Yoder should have prevailed on his state law claim of invasion of privacy? Why or why not?

2. Do you think this case would have been decided differently if the mail clerk and Yoder's supervisor did read the doctor's statements?

3. How many people would have to read a sensitive document such as this to meet the public disclosure requirement for an individual to prevail on his or her claim?

Case 3

City of San Diego v. Roe, *543 U.S. 77 (2004)*

The City of San Diego terminated a police officer for selling homemade, sexually explicit videotapes and related activities. Using an adults-only section of eBay, the officer sold not only videotapes of himself in a police uniform but also official San Diego Police Department uniforms and other police equipment. The officer sued the city, alleging a violation of his First Amendment right to free speech. The trial court found for the city on the ground that the speech was not entitled to protection because it was not of "public concern." The Ninth Circuit, however, reversed the trial court, finding that his conduct fell within the protected category of citizen commentary on matters of public concern because it took place off-duty, it was away from the employer's premises, and it did not involve a workplace grievance. The U.S. Supreme Court reversed.

Per Curiam

***

A government employee does not relinquish all First Amendment rights otherwise enjoyed by citizens just by reason of his or her employment. On the other hand, a governmental employer may impose certain restraints on the speech of its employees, restraints that would be unconstitutional if applied to the general public. The

Court has recognized the right of employees to speak on matters of public concern, typically matters concerning government policies that are of interest to the public at large, a subject on which public employees are uniquely qualified to comment. Outside of this category, the Court has held that when government employees speak or write on their own time on topics unrelated to their employment, the speech can have First Amendment protection, absent some governmental justification "far stronger than mere speculation" in regulating it. *United States v. Treasury Employees* (NTEU). We have little difficulty in concluding that the City was not barred from terminating Roe under either line of cases.

In concluding that Roe's activities qualified as a matter of public concern, the Court of Appeals relied heavily on the Court's decision in NTEU. In NTEU it was established that the speech was unrelated to the employment and had no effect on the mission and purpose of the employer. The question was whether the Federal Government could impose certain monetary limitations on outside earnings from speaking or writing on a class of federal employees. The Court held that, within the particular classification of employment, the Government had shown no justification for the outside salary limitations. The First Amendment right of the employees sufficed to invalidate the restrictions on the outside earnings for such activities. The Court noted that throughout history public employees who undertook to write or to speak in their spare time had made substantial contributions to literature and art, and observed that none of the speech at issue "even arguably [had] any adverse impact" on the employer.

The Court of Appeals' reliance on NTEU was seriously misplaced. Although Roe's activities took place outside the workplace and purported to be about subjects not related to his employment, the SDPD demonstrated legitimate and substantial interests of its own that were compromised by his speech. Far from confining his activities to speech unrelated to his employment, Roe took deliberate steps to link his videos and other wares to his police work, all in a way injurious to his employer. The use of the uniform, the law enforcement reference in the Web site, the listing of the speaker as "in the field of law enforcement," and the debased parody of an officer performing indecent acts while in the course of official duties brought the mission of the employer and the professionalism of its officers into serious disrepute.

The Court of Appeals noted the City conceded Roe's activities were "unrelated" to his employment. In the context of the pleadings and arguments, the proper interpretation of the City's statement is simply to underscore the obvious proposition that Roe's speech was not a comment on the workings or functioning of the SDPD. It is quite a different question whether the speech was detrimental to the SDPD. On that score the City's consistent position has been that the speech is contrary to its regulations and harmful to the proper functioning of the police force. The present case falls outside the protection afforded in NTEU. The authorities that instead control, and which are considered below, are this Court's decisions in *Pickering, Connick,* and the decisions which follow them.

To reconcile the employee's right to engage in speech and the government employer's right to protect its own legitimate interests in performing its mission, the Pickering Court adopted a balancing test. It requires a court evaluating restraints on a public employee's speech to balance "the interests of the [employee], as a citizen, in commenting upon matters of public concern and the interest of the State, as an employer, in promoting the efficiency of the public services it performs through its employees."

Underlying the decision in *Pickering* is the recognition that public employees are often the members of the community who are likely to have informed opinions as to the operations of their public employers, operations which are of substantial concern to the public. Were they not able to speak on these matters, the community would be deprived of informed opinions on important public issues. The interest at stake is as much the public's interest in receiving informed opinion as it is the employee's own right to disseminate it.

Pickering did not hold that any and all statements by a public employee are entitled to balancing. To require *Pickering* balancing in every case where speech by a public employee is at issue, no matter the content of the speech, could compromise the proper functioning of government offices. This concern prompted the Court in *Connick* to explain a threshold inquiry (implicit in Pickering itself) that in order to merit Pickering balancing, a public employee's speech must touch on a matter of "public concern."

In *Connick,* an assistant district attorney, unhappy with her supervisor's decision to transfer her to another division, circulated an intraoffice questionnaire. The document solicited her co-workers' views on, inter alia, office transfer policy, office morale, the need for grievance committees, the level of confidence in supervisors, and whether employees felt pressured to work in political campaigns.

Finding that—with the exception of the final question—the questionnaire touched not on matters of public concern but on internal workplace grievances, the Court held no Pickering balancing was required. To conclude otherwise would ignore the "common-sense realization that government offices could not function if every employment decision became a constitutional matter." *Connick* held that a public employee's speech is entitled to Pickering balancing only when the employee speaks "as a citizen upon matters of public concern" rather than "as an employee upon matters only of personal interest."

Although the boundaries of the public concern test are not well-defined, Connick provides some guidance. It directs courts to examine the "content, form, and context of a given statement, as revealed by the whole record" in assessing whether an employee's speech addresses a matter of public concern. In addition, it notes that the standard for determining whether expression is of public concern is the same standard used to determine whether a common-law action for invasion of privacy is present. That standard is established by our decisions in *Cox Broadcasting Corp. v. Cohn,* and *Time, Inc. v. Hill.* These cases make clear that public concern is something that is a subject of legitimate news interest; that is, a subject of general interest and of value and concern to the public at the time of publication. The Court has also recognized that certain private remarks, such as negative comments about the President of the United States, touch on matters of public concern and should thus be subject to Pickering balancing.

Applying these principles to the instant case, there is no difficulty in concluding that Roe's expression does not qualify as a matter of public concern under any view of the public concern test. He fails the threshold test and Pickering balancing does not come into play.

Connick is controlling precedent, but to show why this is not a close case it is instructive to note that even under the view expressed by the dissent in *Connick* from four Members of the Court, the speech here would not come within the definition of a matter of public concern. The dissent in *Connick* would have held that the entirety of the questionnaire circulated by the employee "discussed subjects that could reasonably be expected to be of interest to persons seeking to develop informed opinions about the manner in which . . . an elected official charged with managing a vital governmental agency, discharges his responsibilities." No similar purpose could be attributed to the employee's speech in the present case. Roe's activities did nothing to inform the public about any aspect of the SDPD's functioning or operation. Nor were Roe's activities anything like the private remarks at issue in *Rankin,* where one co-worker commented to another co-worker on an item of political news. Roe's expression was widely broadcast, linked to his official status as a police officer, and designed to exploit his employer's image.

The speech in question was detrimental to the mission and functions of the employer. There is no basis for finding that it was of concern to the community as the Court's cases have understood that term in the context of restrictions by governmental entities on the speech of their employees.

Case Questions

1. In your opinion, does the Ninth Circuit's conclusion that Roe's activities were protected by the First Amendment have merit?

2. Where do you think the line would have been drawn on Roe's free speech rights by the Supreme Court had he not tied his activities to the police department? What if Roe did not wear a police uniform but still sold police-related paraphernalia? What if he wore a police uniform but did not sell police-related paraphernalia?

3. Is the "public concern" requirement from the *Pickering* case a fair balancing of the rights involved? How might it be improved?

City of Ontario v. Quon, *130 S. Ct. 2619 (2010)*

The City of Ontario, California, acquired pagers that could send and receive text messages. The pagers were issued to Quon and other police officers, who were told that the city-provided service plan included a monthly limit on the number of characters sent and received each month. Overages had to be paid by the employees. When the employees exceeded their monthly limits for several months, the police chief sought to determine if the overages being paid by the police officers were for city-related business or personal messages. Based on transcripts sent by the service provider, the police chief discovered that Quon had been sending sexually explicit messages. He also learned that few of Quon's on-duty messages were related to police business, and he was disciplined. Quon and other officers sued, alleging violations of the Fourth Amendment search and seizure provisions.

The trial court ruled that Quon and the police officers had an expectation of privacy in the content of the messages, but it dismissed the Fourth Amendment claims because the jury found that the police chief's actions were motivated by the legitimate reason of determining whether the officers were unfairly paying for work-related overages. The Ninth Circuit, however, reversed, concluding that the police chief's motives were not determinative because he could have used less intrusive tactics than an audit of the messages. The U.S. Supreme Court reversed, holding that the search of the text messages was not excessive in scope.

Kennedy, J.

***

Though the case touches issues of far-reaching significance, the Court concludes it can be resolved by settled principles determining when a search is reasonable.

***

It is well settled that the Fourth Amendment's protection extends beyond the sphere of criminal investigations. *Camara v. Municipal Court of City and County of San Francisco.* "The Amendment guarantees the privacy, dignity, and security of persons against certain arbitrary and invasive acts by officers of the Government," without regard to whether the government actor is investigating crime or performing another function. The Fourth Amendment applies as well when the Government acts in its capacity as an employer. *Treasury Employees v. Von Raab.*

***

Before turning to the reasonableness of the search, it is instructive to note the parties' disagreement over whether Quon had a reasonable expectation of privacy. The record does establish that OPD, at the outset, made it clear that pager messages were not considered private. The City's Computer Policy stated that "[u]sers should have no expectation of privacy or confidentiality when using" City computers. Chief Scharf's memo and Duke's statements made clear that this official policy extended to

text messaging. The disagreement, at least as respondents see the case, is over whether Duke's later statements overrode the official policy. Respondents contend that because Duke told Quon that an audit would be unnecessary if Quon paid for the overage, Quon reasonably could expect that the contents of his messages would remain private.

At this point, were we to assume that inquiry into "operational realities" were called for, . . . it would be necessary to ask whether Duke's statements could be taken as announcing a change in OPD policy, and if so, whether he had, in fact or appearance, the authority to make such a change and to guarantee the privacy of text messaging. It would also be necessary to consider whether a review of messages sent on police pagers, particularly those sent while officers are on duty, might be justified for other reasons, including performance evaluations, litigation concerning the lawfulness of police actions, and perhaps compliance with state open records laws. These matters would all bear on the legitimacy of an employee's privacy expectation.

The Court must proceed with care when considering the whole concept of privacy expectations in communications made on electronic equipment owned by a government employer. The judiciary risks error by elaborating too fully on the Fourth Amendment implications of emerging technology before its role in society has become clear. See, e.g., *Olmstead v. United States,* overruled by *Katz v. United States.* In *Katz,* the Court relied on its own knowledge and experience to conclude that there is a reasonable expectation of privacy in a telephone booth. It is not so clear that courts at present are on so sure a ground. Prudence counsels caution before the facts in the instant case are used to establish far-reaching premises that define the existence, and extent, of privacy expectations enjoyed by employees when using employer-provided communication devices.

Rapid changes in the dynamics of communication and information transmission are evident not just in the technology itself but in what society accepts as proper behavior. As one amici brief notes, many employers expect or at least tolerate personal use of such equipment by employees because it often increases worker efficiency. Another amicus points out that the law is beginning to respond to these developments, as some States have recently passed statutes requiring employers to notify employees when monitoring their electronic communications. At present, it is uncertain how workplace norms, and the law's treatment of them, will evolve.

Even if the Court were certain that the O'Connor plurality's approach were the right one, the Court would have difficulty predicting how employees' privacy expectations will be shaped by those changes or the degree to which society will be prepared to recognize those expectations as reasonable. Cell phone and text message communications are so pervasive that some persons may consider them to be essential means or necessary instruments for self-expression, even self-identification. That might strengthen the case for an expectation of privacy. On the other hand, the ubiquity of those devices has made them generally affordable, so one could counter that employees who need cell phones or similar devices for personal matters can purchase and pay for their own. And employer policies concerning communications will of course shape the reasonable expectations of their employees, especially to the extent that such policies are clearly communicated.

A broad holding concerning employees' privacy expectations vis-à-vis employer-provided technological equipment might have implications for future cases that cannot be predicted. It is preferable to dispose of this case on narrower grounds. For present purposes we assume several propositions arguendo: First, Quon had a reasonable expectation of privacy in the text messages sent on the pager provided to him by the City; second, petitioners' review of the transcript constituted a search within the meaning of the Fourth Amendment; and third, the principles applicable to a government employer's search of an employee's physical office apply with at least the same force when the employer intrudes on the employee's privacy in the electronic sphere.

Even if Quon had a reasonable expectation of privacy in his text messages, petitioners did not necessarily violate the Fourth Amendment by obtaining and reviewing the transcripts. Although as a general matter, warrantless searches "are per se unreasonable under the Fourth Amendment," there are "a few specifically established and well-delineated exceptions" to that general rule . . . The Court has held that the "'special needs'" of the workplace justify one such exception.

Under the approach of the O'Connor plurality, when conducted for a "noninvestigatory, work-related purpos[e]" or for the "investigatio[n] of work-related misconduct," a government employer's warrantless search is reasonable if it is "'justified at its inception'" and if "'the measures adopted are reasonably related to the objectives of the search and not excessively intrusive in light of'" the circumstances giving rise to the search. The search here satisfied the standard of the O'Connor plurality and was reasonable under that approach.

The search was justified at its inception because there were "reasonable grounds for suspecting that the search [was] necessary for a noninvestigatory work-related purpose." As a jury found, Chief Scharf ordered the search in order to determine whether the character limit on the City's contract with Arch Wireless was sufficient to meet the City's needs. This was, as the Ninth Circuit noted, a "legitimate work-related rationale." The City and OPD had a legitimate interest in ensuring that employees were not being forced to pay out of their own pockets for work-related expenses, or on the other hand that the City was not paying for extensive personal communications.

As for the scope of the search, reviewing the transcripts was reasonable because it was an efficient and expedient way to determine whether Quon's overages were the result of work-related messaging or personal use. The review was also not "'excessively intrusive.'" Although Quon had gone over his monthly allotment a number of times, OPD requested transcripts for only the months of August and September 2002. While it may have been reasonable as well for OPD to review transcripts of all the months in which Quon exceeded his allowance, it was certainly reasonable for OPD to review messages for just two months in order to obtain a large enough sample to decide whether the character limits were efficacious. And it is worth noting that during his internal affairs investigation, McMahon redacted all messages Quon sent while off duty, a measure which reduced the intrusiveness of any further review of the transcripts.

Furthermore, and again on the assumption that Quon had a reasonable expectation of privacy in the contents of his messages, the extent of an expectation is relevant to assessing whether the search was too intrusive. Even if he could assume some level of privacy would inhere in his messages, it would not have been reasonable for Quon to conclude that his messages were in all circumstances immune from scrutiny. Quon was told that his messages were subject to auditing. As a law enforcement officer, he would or should have known that his actions were likely to come under legal scrutiny, and that this might entail an analysis of his on-the-job communications. Under the circumstances, a reasonable employee would be aware that sound management principles might require the audit of messages to determine whether the pager was being appropriately used. Given that the City issued the pagers to Quon and other SWAT Team members in order to help them more quickly respond to crises—and given that Quon had received no assurances of privacy—Quon could have anticipated that it might be necessary for the City to audit pager messages to assess the SWAT Team's performance in particular emergency situations.

From OPD's perspective, the fact that Quon likely had only a limited privacy expectation, with boundaries that we need not here explore, lessened the risk that the review would intrude on highly private details of Quon's life. OPD's audit of messages on Quon's employer-provided pager was not nearly as intrusive as a search of his personal email account or pager, or a wiretap on his home phone line, would have been. That the search did reveal intimate details of Quon's life does not make it unreasonable, for under the circumstances a reasonable employer would not expect that such a review would intrude on such matters. The search was permissible in its scope.

Case Questions

1. The Supreme Court and the Ninth Circuit reached different conclusions on the issue of the proper scope of the search. Which one do you think is the better approach? Why?

2. Both courts agreed that Quon did not have a reasonable expectation of privacy in the text messages, despite the fact that his boss told him that the messages would be private if he paid the overages. What statements or acts by an employee, in your opinion, would be necessary to create an expectation of privacy in the messages? Where is the line drawn?

3. Would this case, in your opinion, have been decided differently if it had involved an employer-supplied communication device other than a pager? If so, how?

4. Do you agree with the statement that an audit of text messages is less intrusive than a phone wiretap? Why or why not?

5. The Court decided the case on narrow grounds, purposefully stopping short of pronouncing broadly applicable rules for electronic communications. If they had taken on the task of a broadly applicable rule, what, in your opinion, should they have said?

Chapter 15

Labor Law

Learning Objectives

By the time you finish studying this chapter, you should be able to:

LO1   Discuss the history of unions in the United States.

LO2   Identify the Norris-LaGuardia Act of 1932 and what it covers.

LO3   Identify the National Labor Relations Act of 1935 (Wagner Act) and what it requires.

LO4   List and explain several collective bargaining agreement clauses.

LO5   Explain unfair labor practices and give examples.

LO6   Describe the Taft-Hartley Act of 1947 and its requirements.

LO7   Define the Landrum-Griffin Act of 1959 (Labor Management Reporting and Disclosure Act) and its provisions.

LO8   Discuss collective bargaining in the public sector and how it differs from the private sector.

Opening Scenarios

SCENARIO 1

1 *Scenario*

Plastico Corporation hears through the corporate grapevine that its employees are unhappy with working conditions at the manufacturing plant and are looking into bringing in a union. In an effort to stop the plant's unionization, Plastico posts a notice on the lunchroom bulletin board stating that anyone found to be sympathetic to the unions will be terminated. Is this strategy permissible as a way for Plastico to discourage unionization?

SCENARIO 2

2 *Scenario*

Zellico, Inc., is in the midst of a union fight and the employees eventually go on strike. The union later gives an unconditional request for reinstatement to the employer, but the employer refuses to reinstate them and give employees a wage increase without consulting the union. Did the employer commit an unfair labor practice?

SCENARIO 3

3 *Scenario*

A nonunion company offers to form a partnership with its employees in order to decide what it can do to cut costs because of declining profits. Is this legal?

Statutory Basis

Employees shall have the right to self-organization, to form, join, or assist labor organizations, to bargain collectively through representatives of their own choosing, and to engage in other concerted activities for the purpose of collective bargaining or other mutual aid or protection, and shall also have the right to refrain from any or all such activities. [National Labor Relations Act of 1935, 29 U.S.C. §§ 151–169, § 157, section 7.]

Coming Together on Issues

Think labor law doesn't affect you? Think back to the 2008 television season. Did you miss your favorite TV shows? Did you get tired of reruns? Did you hate the lame substitute shows put on in their place? That's because, as you may painfully recall, the television writers were on strike. The 13,500-member Writers Guild of America wanted a share of profits from the increasingly popular new technological outlets for their shows, such as the Internet. The 100-day strike ended just before the Academy Awards were to be telecast—much to the relief of everyone.

But the Writers Guild of America is hardly alone. The NFL is, as we speak, locked in collective bargaining negotiations with the NFL players. Things have gotten so bad that they are now resorting to litigation. Other recent events:

- Harley-Davidson wrapped up its labor negotiations with employees throughout its operations, including making an agreement in Pennsylvania to cut nearly 50 percent of jobs in exchange for the company's commitment to invest $90 million in the plant. In New York, the company threatened to move to a new plant in Kentucky if the contract was rejected.[1]
- Actor Danny Glover was arrested at the Montgomery County, Maryland, headquarters of Sodexo food service company in a labor protest he joined with the

705

Service Employees International Union (SEIU) over what SEIU called unfair and illegal treatment of workers. Sodexo said the union was spreading misinformation.[2]

- Concerned about being too taxed with extra responsibilities to do their jobs well, nurses have walked out at least 750 times in recent decades, making it the most strike-prone job in the country. A study published by the National Bureau of Economics shows that during 50 strikes at New York state hospitals between 1984 and 2004, patients were almost 20 percent more likely to die (about 140 patients).[3]
- After New Yorkers braced for a walkout by doormen, a strike was averted when a deal was reached.[4]
- The NBA "avoids the apocalypse" by reaching an interim labor agreement, thereby narrowly avoiding a walkout.[5]
- The National Hockey League loses its season to labor disputes, angering thousands of loyal fans; baseball lockouts threaten to cost revenues and crowds.[6]
- Disgruntled private-sector lawyers unionize over pay and working conditions for the first time.[7]

Though they have lost much of the numbers and clout that they once had, perhaps maybe even because they have done their job too well, as you can see from these recent issues, unions are still an important part of the American workplace landscape. (See Exhibit 15.1, "Who's in Unions?")

Labor law is actually a very different and discrete part of the law from employment law, but given its far-reaching impact on the workplace, it is important to be familiar with its basic history and provisions in order to have a more complete knowledge of issues in the workplace environment. Labor law involves **collective bargaining** between employers and employees about issues in the workplace. Rather than each employee striking his or her own deal with the employer, the law now permits employees to do so in an organized and collective way. This was not always so. The agrarian nature of the economy in the United States was such that until the middle of the 18th century, the majority of working Americans worked on farms. In 1820, only about 12 percent of workers were employed in manufacturing. By 1860, that number had increased to about 18 percent, and the location of manufacturing had shifted from private homes to factories. As this trend continued to grow, so did the size of the labor class, and the basis for modern labor issues was created. Compounding the competitive nature of industry during this time was the simultaneous improvement of the transportation system. This served to allow products from other markets to compete with local products, thus decreasing the local demand and the profit margin of production. This was often offset by decreasing the wage of the worker. It was in this atmosphere that the earliest labor strife leading to what most of us know as workers refusing to work unless their grievances are addressed—strikes—took place.

collective bargaining
Negotiations and agreements between management and labor about wages, hours, and other terms and conditions of employment.

A Historical Accounting

LO1

Labor law has a long and somewhat acrimonious history in this country. Central to an understanding of the struggle between labor and management is understanding

Exhibit 15.1 *Who's in Unions?*

According to the 2010 report of the U.S. Department of Labor's Bureau of Labor Statistics, released in January 2011:

- In 2010 the number of union members declined by 612,000 from the year before.
- There are 16.3 million union members in the United States. 14.6 percent are union members, while the rest are not union affiliated but have jobs covered by union contracts.
- 11.9 percent of wage and salary workers are union members, down from 20.1 percent in 1983, the first year such figures were kept.
- The median weekly earning for union members is $917; for nonunion workers, $717.
- Men are more likely to be union members (12.6 percent) than women (11.1 percent); when records were first kept in 1983, the gap between men and women was 10 points, but men's union membership declined more rapidly than women's and narrowed the gap.
- Blacks are more likely to be in a union (13.4 percent) than whites (11.7. percent), Asians (10.9 percent), or Hispanics (10 percent).
- Workers 55 to 64 are more likely to be union members (15.7 percent) than younger workers 16 to 24 (4.3 percent).
- Full-time workers are more likely to be union members (13.1 percent) than part-time workers (6.3 percent).
- All states in the Middle Atlantic and Pacific divisions had membership rates above the national average.
- All states in the East South Central and West South Central have rates below the national average.

- The state with the highest membership rate is New York (24.2 percent).
- The state with the lowest union membership rate is North Carolina (3.2 percent).
- About 1.6 million employees are represented by a union but are not members of the union. About half of these are government employees.
- Union membership rate has steadily declined from a high of 20.1 percent in 1983, the first year the data were available.
- 6.9 percent of private industry employees are union members (less than half of what it was in 1983), but 36.2 percent of public employees are union. Of the government workers, 42.3 percent are in local government, the group with the highest representation.
- Two occupational groups have the highest unionization rates (37.1 percent): (1) education, training, and library occupations and (2) protective service occupations such as police and firefighters (34.1 percent).
- In the private sector, transportation and utilities have the highest rate of union membership (21.8 percent), followed by telecommunications (15.8 percent) and construction (13.1 percent). Agriculture and related industries are lowest at 1.6 percent union membership, with the financial activities following closely at 2.0 percent.
- Union membership in 2010 was down in 33 states, and up in 17 states.

Source: U.S. Department of Labor, Bureau of Labor Statistics, *Union Members Summary,* http://www.bls.gov/news.release/union2.nr0.htm.

the role the courts played in shaping labor policy before the U.S. Congress enacted legislation that forms the basis for labor relationships today. There were four weapons of choice that business used to control early unionizing efforts: criminal conspiracy laws, injunctions, antitrust laws, and constitutional challenges. A brief examination of these early antiunion efforts helps to explain how the balance between workers' rights and management's rights was ultimately reached.

Criminal Conspiracy Laws

In the 1800s, many courts considered activity by workers such as striking and picketing to be common-law criminal conspiracies. Workers were convicted for trying to improve working conditions through union efforts. As early as 1806, employers in the shoemaking industry in Philadelphia discovered that they could enlist the aid of the courts by charging their unionized employees with criminal conspiracy. Thus, if a group of employees attempted to exert pressure on an employer to increase wages, they would be charged with criminal conspiracy and, if convicted, subject to imprisonment. Generally, the penalties imposed were fines rather than jail, but along with them came the threat of harsher sentences upon subsequent convictions. This acted to discourage and even eliminate union activity. This practice continued until 1842 when the landmark case of *Commonwealth v. Hunt,* included at the end of the chapter, severely criticized the use of criminal conspiracy charges to discourage unionization.

Despite *Commonwealth v. Hunt,* the criminal conspiracy trials retained some vitality until the 1890s. During this time, conspiracy trials were losing steam because of difficulty in getting juries to side with employers. Another method of discouraging unions was being developed that would prove equally difficult for labor.

Injunctions

injunction
A court order requiring individuals or groups of persons to refrain from performing certain acts that the court has determined will do irreparable harm.

Employers sought the use of **injunctions** to gain immediate relief from workers' attempted collective bargaining activities. This legal action was encouraged and proliferated after 1895. In that year, the U.S. Supreme Court issued a decision that upheld the constitutionality of the labor injunction.[8] Armed with this potent legal support, judges were quick to apply this remedy to quash strikes and protests. Judges often committed abuses by wielding their power in personal ways. For example, when an injunction was sought, a judge would have to decide whether a union's objectives were lawful or unlawful. Judges outlawed many union activities this way. This was not always an issue of improper motivation; judges were left without legislative directives and, in their absence, were free to use their own beliefs, attitudes, and prejudices to reach conclusions. Given the antilabor sentiment among the business class, which was the background of a good many judges of this period, the rulings were overwhelmingly against labor's attempt to organize.

yellow dog contract
Agreement employers require employees to sign stating they do not belong to a union and will not join one; now illegal.

This method came to a head in the case of *Hitchman Coal Company v. Mitchell,*[9] in which the Supreme Court declared that a labor injunction could be used to enforce a **yellow dog contract**. The yellow dog contract was a device used by antiunion employers to stop the progress of the union movement. It was the promise of a worker not to join a labor union while in the hire of an employer. Yellow dog contracts, used sparingly before *Hitchman,* proliferated afterward. Employees, often faced with no alternative employment options, were forced to sign yellow dog contracts. Later, if their employer was faced with a unionizing campaign, the employer could receive an injunction that would restrain anyone from encouraging these workers to join a union. This decision's hostile view toward organized labor dealt a harsh blow to workers seeking to organize. Its effects were felt until 1932, when yellow dog contracts were outlawed by Congress.

Antitrust Attacks

The early part of the 20th century saw declining competition and mammoth growth of industrialization. By 1930, nonagricultural occupations accounted for about 80 percent of the labor force. Business leaders saw the advantage of cooperation and began to establish price agreements, trusts, pools, and trade associations. These devices were intended to stamp out competition between rivals. Elimination of competition meant growth of huge and powerful corporations whose purpose was to monopolize an area. Once competition was eliminated, it was easy to control prices and make them whatever the corporation wanted them to be. Of course, this was a disaster for consumers, who were at the mercy of the monopolies.

Congress enacted the Sherman Antitrust Act in 1890 to eliminate monopolistic control of the nation's economy. After its passage, labor unions learned that the law limited a variety of their activities. Unions were prosecuted under various provisions that were interpreted to include them under the provisions that prohibited "every contract, combination . . . or conspiracy, in restraint of trade. . . ." When unions challenged the application of the Sherman Antitrust Act to their activities, the Supreme Court, in 1908,[10] held that the Sherman Act applied to labor unions, giving business a new weapon to combat unionism. In addition, the Court held that individual union members were responsible for the actions of their officers, making the rank and file liable for judgments against the union, and outlawed **secondary boycotts**. In response, unions organized themselves into a strong political force and in 1912 helped to elect Woodrow Wilson (who had pledged his support to the American Federation of Labor) as well as other Democratic candidates. The Democratic Party soon fulfilled its promise to organized labor, and in October 1914 the Clayton Act became law. Section 6 of that act provided that "nothing contained in the antitrust laws shall be construed to forbid the existence and operation of labor organizations" nor shall labor unions be held to be "illegal combinations or conspiracies in restraint of trade under the antitrust laws."

More importantly, the Clayton Act regulated the procedure by which a federal court could issue an injunction against labor. Some of the most important gains from labor's perspective were the requirement that an injunction not be issued without notice to the union, absent emergency circumstances; the requirement that a jury trial be held for those members who were charged with a violation under the injunction; the requirement that a bond be posted by the party seeking the injunction and indemnifying the union if they were found to have acted lawfully; and the requirement that specific acts be enjoined and not just the activity of the union wholesale.

secondary boycott
Union pressure on management by getting others who do business with management to cease.

Constitutional Challenges to Early Congressional Enactments

Early efforts by federal and state legislators to support organized labor were thwarted by the courts as a whole. Many state laws were declared unconstitutional by state supreme courts. Congress continued to recognize the rights of labor organizations and in 1898 passed the Erdman Act. The objective of the act was to set up a procedure by which conflicts in the railroad industry could be handled. Among other rights, it gave the railroad workers the right to self-organization and collective bargaining and outlawed the yellow dog contract. At this time, Congress targeted railroad workers for protection largely because of the Pullman strike, which had disrupted service in 1894. Feeling the need to ensure against further disruptions that had the effect of paralyzing the nation's transportation system, Congress thought it had found a way to make this issue one of constitutional dimension by making it one of interstate commerce. However, when confronted with the issue of whether Congress could regulate industry by regulating employer–employee relations in this way, the Supreme Court held that Congress could not and struck down this critical law. The Court was not partial to any laborers in particular. In 1918 and 1923, the Court struck down congressional laws that would have controlled the use of child laborers and legislation that would have given women a minimum wage when employed in industry.

Out of Necessity Comes Change

The start of World War I saw the first real movement away from antiunion sentiment. The need for uninterrupted production and for preventing wartime strikes was seen as critical for the greater national interest. President Woodrow Wilson formed the National War Labor Board for the purpose of peacefully resolving labor disputes. This precursor to the National Labor Relations Board (NLRB) embodied many of the tenets that were eventually adopted by the NLRB. While the war acted to create a moratorium on attacks on organized labor, it also served to show that peaceful efforts aimed at resolving labor disputes were possible. After World War I, the National War Labor Board was dismantled, but the unmistakable effect was that it was a stepping stone toward recognition of the organized labor movement.

Congress continued to enact piecemeal legislation aimed at limited pockets of laborers, but in 1932, responding to the harsh effects of the Depression, Congress enacted the National Industrial Recovery Act (NIRA). This law put business in charge of regulating prices and production. Because the regulation of the market in this way was a clear violation of the Sherman Antitrust Act, the NIRA exempted any price control measure (called "codes") from the reach of the Sherman Act. In addition, the NIRA established a minimum wage and gave workers collective bargaining and other rights. Under the NIRA, the ranks of organized labor began to increase. It was under the umbrella of the NIRA that President Roosevelt created the National Labor Board in 1933 and bolstered its enforcement provisions in 1934. Both the NIRA and the board operated successfully until a dispute with the automobile industry, which it could not settle, undermined labor's confidence in the board to such an extent that it was effectively dismantled. In 1935, the NIRA was declared unconstitutional by the Supreme Court because, the Court held, neither the president of the United States nor any private group (such as the business entities given the power under the NIRA to control prices) had the constitutional authority to do what was required of them under the act.

It is against this backdrop that the modern labor movement was born. After this, Congress was able to enact legislation that has formed the basis of what we know as organized labor. Through a series of enactments that have shifted the balance of power first to the unions and then to employers, the balance that has been created is subject today only to refinement. (See Exhibits 15.2, "Key Events in Labor–Management Relations," and 15.3, "Union Role in Services Expanding.")

Exhibit 15.2 *Key Events in Labor–Management Relations*

Chronology

1940s–1960s *The postwar economic boom establishes the model for middle-class Americans' expectations of ever-rising earnings and job security.*

1956
William H. Whyte Jr. describes the emerging ethos of the corporate employee in his best-selling book, *The Organization Man*. According to an often-unspoken pledge of reciprocal loyalty, the company offered job security, rising earnings and generous fringe benefits in return for the employee's commitment to stay with the firm for his entire career.

1970s *Rising labor costs and growing competition from overseas suppliers prompt U.S. corporations to step up automation and set up plants in low-cost countries.*

1973
The steady rise in workers' earnings that has marked the postwar period comes to a halt after the first of a series of oil crises sparks inflation and slows economic growth.

1979
In the first phase of corporate restructuring, manufacturers begin cutting production jobs. General Motors, Ford and Chrysler will eliminate 350,000 jobs over the next decade.

1980s *Corporations eliminate millions of blue-collar jobs in an attempt to "restructure" their operations to become more competitive with foreign producers.*

1981–82
The worst recession since the Great Depression of the 1930s takes its greatest toll on the manufacturing industries of the Midwest, pushing unemployment among blue-collar workers to double-digit levels.

1985
IBM hurt by mounting competition from foreign computer makers—begins cutting its work force.

1989
A wave of bank consolidations and closures begins, resulting in the loss of more than 100,000 jobs in that sector to date.

1990s *Restructuring begins to cut into white-collar employment as corporations eliminate many middle-management positions.*

July 1990
Recession begins, accelerating the pace of layoffs. While blue-collar workers continue to bear the brunt of unemployment, companies are for the first time cutting out entire layers of middle management to reduce labor costs and make their operations more flexible to changing economic conditions. As a result, white-collar unemployment spreads throughout U.S. industry.

August 1990
Sears, the nation's third largest retailer, begins a cost-reduction program that will cut about 33,000 positions by the end of 1991.

1991
Restructuring accelerates. U.S. corporations announce more than a half million permanent staff cuts affecting both production and white-collar workers.

Nov. 26, 1991
IBM announces it will cut 20,000 jobs next year.

Dec. 18, 1991
General Motors says it will close 21 of its 125 North American plants and pare 74,000 positions, or 18 percent of its work force, over the next four years.

Jan. 7, 1992
Sears announces it will eliminate an additional 7,000 positions by automating customer-service tasks.

Jan. 21, 1992
United Technologies Corp. announces it will cut 13,900 jobs in its defense and civilian industries.

Feb. 4, 1992
Congress approves legislation providing an additional 13 weeks of unemployment compensation. President Bush, who blocked or vetoed two similar measures in 1991, signs the bill into law Feb. 7.

Feb. 24, 1992
General Motors names the first 12 of 21 plants to be closed in the U.S. and Canada. GM also posts a $4.45 billion loss for 1991—the largest in American corporate history.

2000s *The global marketplace continues to transform American employment patterns.*

2005
According to the Labor Department, most of the 24.6 million new jobs that will be added to the U.S. economy over the 15-year period ending in 2005 will be high-skill positions requiring more training than most of the jobs they will replace.

Source: *Congressional Quarterly Researcher* 2, no. 8 (February 28, 1992), p. 171.

Exhibit 15.3   *Union Role in Services Expanding*

In a 1990 *New York Times* article on the sharp decline of union membership in the 1980s, the conclusion was that unions had to evolve or die. Suggestions for evolving included unions providing social and financial services such as drug and alcohol abuse prevention, reduced-fee credit cards, checking accounts, and so forth. It noted that the "Union, yes" television campaign to attract workers and the AFL-CIO's creation of a new membership category had been put in place to address these issues, but low private-sector unionization numbers weakened the union's bargaining position. Many experts were guardedly optimistic that unions would be revitalized, but with the downward decline in numbers, we can now see, 20 years later, this has not been realized.

At one point, labor unions enjoyed great popularity in the United States. According to the U.S. Department of Labor's Bureau of Labor Statistics, in 2010, about 11.9 percent of the workforce (about 16.3 million) were unionized, a decrease from former years, such as 1983, the first year for which comparable union data are available, when the number was 20.1 percent, or even 2009. In just the one-year period from 2009 to 2010, union representation went from 12.3 percent to 11.9 percent, a loss of 612,000 members. It rose by 311,000 from 2006 to 2007.

Due in part to such factors as the reduction in the labor force of traditionally heavily unionized industries such as steel manufacturing, international competition, aggressive nonunionizing campaigns by employers, union concessions during downturns in the economy, the enactment of legislation such as the North American Free Trade Agreement (NAFTA), and the loss of jobs to other countries with cheaper labor, the percentage has steadily decreased since the 1970s. (See Exhibit 15.4, "Maquiladoras: Mexico's Cheap Labor Lures Firms.") The economic downturn in the last few years, including the housing bust, accounted for heavy losses in areas like the construction industry and trades.

Yet with over 16 million members, labor unions remain an important part of the workplace. With the 2010 median weekly income of full-time wage and salary union members being $917 compared with $717 for nonunion employees (although union membership does not totally account for the difference), we can see at least some of the reason why unions still play an important part in the workplace landscape. One of the issues we may well see developing more frequently in the near future is unions increasing their membership by getting involved in issues such as low wages or immigrant workers. In the South, which is traditionally low in union membership, this occurred recently in the Koch Foods and Gold Kist poultry plants in Tennessee and Alabama. When employers engage in practices like refusing to allow employees to leave the processing line to go to the bathroom; heavy, unrealistic work quotas; wages so low that even employees working for 10 years can only make a maximum of $7.55 per hour; abusive treatment such as screaming, cursing, or not

Exhibit 15.4 *Maquiladoras: Mexico's Cheap Labor Lures Firms*

See an example of why labor complains about managements' moving jobs out of the United States.

TAKING JOBS SOUTH

In 1965 Mexico introduced the concept of maquiladoras as a way of encouraging foreign investment. They are plants just across the Mexican border to which U.S. companies such as Maytag, Nokia, Eaton, General Motors, and Zenith deliver raw materials and/or parts and receive finished goods. About 1 million Mexicans work at about 3,000 plants in Mexico. Not only are taxes and custom fees almost nonexistent because of NAFTA (the North American Free Trade Agreement), but Mexican workers work cheaper. Some employers may pay as much as $1 or $2 per hour for skilled labor, but most pay less—as little as 50 cents per hour—up to 10 hours per day, six days per week. Ten Mexican workers can be hired for the price of one American worker. There are virtually no unions for employers to worry about and working conditions required by

American laws such as the Occupational Safety and Health Act in the United States do not apply. Some employees may have air-conditioned, modern workplaces and employer-provided cheap lunches, health services, and housing aid, but that is generally not the case. Most maquiladoras are more like sweatshops that expose workers to dangerous conditions or chemicals without any of the protections they would have in the United States. Maquiladoras are also responsible for industrial pollution that would not be allowed if the company were operating just across the border in the United States. Because of foreign competition, American companies have used maquiladoras to stay competitive or even to remain in business at all. In recent years, due in large part to globalization, Mexico has been losing maquiladoras to places like Central America, China, and Taiwan. China, in particular, has been giving Mexican maquiladoras stiff competition and is trying hard to become the world's cheapest assembly destination. Maquildoras still account for 45 percent of Mexico's exports, however.

allowing sick employees to leave, even traditionally nonunion workplaces run the risk of workers uniting and resorting to collective bargaining. In this chapter, we will discuss the basic laws addressing collective bargaining, what the laws require, and how to lessen the likelihood of an employer running into union troubles.

Labor Laws

Four main federal laws constitute the statutory basis for labor law and unionization. The legislation initiating a move toward collective bargaining in the United States began with restricting court responses to union activity and establishing the right of employees to form labor organizations and to be protected against unfair labor practices at the hands of employers.

Until the Norris-LaGuardia Act of 1932 and the Wagner Act of 1935 (generally referred to as the National Labor Relations Act of 1935), employers had held virtually all the power. However, once that right to bargain collectively was created and unions were established, the matter took some rather sinister twists. Unions started feeling their power and often went overboard in using it.

This resulted in two other legislative measures to address the evolution of collective bargaining. The Taft-Hartley Act (also known as the Labor Management Relations Act) amended the Wagner Act in 1947 to establish unfair *union* practices, and the Landrum-Griffin Act of 1959 gave certain civil rights to union members and addressed corruption of union officials.

The Norris-LaGuardia Act of 1932

LO2

The Norris-LaGuardia Act was the first major labor law statute enacted in the United States. The opening section of the Norris-LaGuardia Act established that government recognized that the job is more important to a worker than a worker is to a corporation. It recognized that the only real power workers had was in impacting employers through numbers. An employer may not be disturbed when one worker walks out, but most certainly will be when all or most workers do so. The Norris-LaGuardia Act endorsed collective bargaining as a matter of public policy. To implement this policy, Congress sharply curbed the power of the courts to intervene in labor disputes, including curtailing use of the injunction. Norris-LaGuardia did not give labor unions any new legal rights; rather, it allowed them more freedom to operate free from court control and interference. This greatly facilitated labor unions acting as effective collective bargaining agencies.

Section 4 of the act declares that no federal court has the power to issue any form of injunctive relief in any case involving a labor dispute if that injunction would prohibit any person who was participating in such a dispute from doing certain acts. Judges cannot restrain any strike, regardless of its objective, and cannot restrain picketing activities. A labor union can provide relief funds to its strikers and publicize its labor disputes, and workers can urge other employees to join the conflict. Norris-LaGuardia allows a union to act in defense of a person prosecuted for his or her actions or to prosecute an action under the worker's contract. A union can conduct meetings to promote the interests of workers. Norris-LaGuardia protected any "labor dispute" even though parties did not stand as employer–employee with each other, further encouraging collective bargaining.

Most importantly, while it did not directly outlaw yellow dog contracts, the act declared that yellow dog contracts were inconsistent with U.S. public policy and not enforceable in any court in the United States. Later, the NLRB held that an employer engaged in an unfair labor practice if it demanded that an employee execute such an agreement.

The act also had a significant impact in curbing prosecution under the antitrust laws. In its statement of purpose, Congress claimed that the intent of the act was to give labor what it thought it had received under the Clayton Act. Given the broadly stated purpose of the act, the Supreme Court has broadly construed it, providing unions with the opportunity to engage in activities calculated to affect the collective bargaining process. When Norris-LaGuardia limited the enforcement of yellow dog contracts and removed the impediments of workers to organize in a concerted fashion, the way was paved for enactment of the National Labor Relations Act three years later.

The National Labor Relations Act of 1935 (Wagner Act)

Of the four pieces of seminal labor legislation, it is the National Labor Relations Act (NLRA) that most people consider to be the mainstay of union activity since it established the right of employees to form unions, to bargain collectively, and to strike. Recall that, at one time, it had been illegal—in fact, criminal—for employees to join together in an effort to collectively bargain with employers.

The National Labor Relations Act

In order to avoid the unconstitutional delegation of legislative power, Congress, in enacting the NLRA, placed the administration of the act in the hands of the National Labor Relations Board (NLRB), an independent federal administrative agency, rather than in the hands of an industrial group; set up standards to govern the exercise of power delegated to that administrative agency; and provided for the judicial enforcement of the orders of that agency. The board was empowered to issue remedial orders, enforceable in the courts, to prevent commission of unfair labor practices. Five such unfair practices were outlined in section 8 of the act. Under this section, it is an unfair labor practice to

- Interfere with, restrain, or coerce employees in the exercise of their rights.
- Interfere with the formation of a labor organization.
- Discriminate in the hiring or tenure of employment or discourage membership in a labor organization.
- Retaliate for filing charges or testifying under the act.
- Refuse to bargain with the representatives of the employees.

Notably absent from this act are unfair labor practices that might be committed by unions, although there were unfair labor practices listed that might be committed by employers. In the political climate that prevailed in 1935, the government placed its weight on the side of laborers because of the imbalance between corporate power and the labor market. The act was government's attempt to guarantee workers the right to organize so they would be able to bargain on a more equal basis with employers.

As you can imagine, given the history we discussed, creation of the NLRB did not rest well with business. For the first few years of its existence, the board survived a well-organized and concerted attack challenging its constitutionality and the scope of its authority. Finally, in 1937 and 1938, the U.S. Supreme Court brought the avalanche of injunction suits against the NLRB to a halt in a series of rulings that found the authority of the board to determine whether an employer had engaged in an unfair labor practice to be exclusive, subject only to subsequent judicial review after the board had issued its decision, and that detailed the scope of the NLRB's legal powers. These decisions form the foundations of the NLRB that are still effective today.

With the constitutionality of the NLRB settled and the injunctions halted, the judicial proceedings during the third year of the board's existence concerned the correctness of the NLRB's decisions and the power of the board to fashion remedies. Certain principles of law were established, including that employees on strike are still employees; that employees striking because of an unfair labor practice are entitled to reinstatement, even if reinstatement makes it necessary to discharge employees hired to replace them; and that threatened economic loss does not justify the commission of an unfair labor practice. From 1935 to 1947, the courts developed a vast body of law dealing with labor issues.

The National Labor Relations Board

The NLRB is the independent federal agency that enforces labor laws in the private sector. Once sufficient interest has been indicated by the employees (usually by signing union authorization cards), the NLRB conducts elections to determine what union, if any, will represent the employees in collective bargaining. The NLRB also decertifies unions that employees no longer wish to have represent them, issues labor regulations, hears unfair labor practice cases at the agency level, brings enforcement proceedings for unfair labor practice cases, and otherwise administers the NLRA. The board itself is composed of five members who, among other things, hear appeals from administrative law judge decisions of the agency on issues of unfair labor practices and union elections.

An interesting, unusual issue arose recently with far-ranging legal impact. Due to expiration of member terms and political stalemates in D.C., the National Labor Relations Board was down by three members for 27 months, beginning in January 2008 and lasting until President Obama's recess appointment on March 27, 2010. The two-member board issued nearly 600 decisions during that time, acting as a quorum of a three-member board delegated the power to do so. In June 2010, the U.S. Supreme Court held, in *New Process Steel, L.P., v. NLRB*,[11] that the board lacked the authority to issue decisions during this 27-month period. This effectively invalidated the nearly 600 cases addressed by the two-member board, leaving unclear how they would be resolved by the now fully functioning board. At the very least, the board had to reissue decisions in the 74 cases pending before the federal courts in which the losing party challenged the board's authority to act with only two members.[12]

community of interests
Factors employees have in common for bargaining purposes.

bargaining unit
The group of employees in a workplace that have the legal right to bargain with the employer.

In collective bargaining, employees with a **community of interests**—that is, similar workplace concerns and conditions—come together as a **bargaining unit** that the union will represent. The community of interests is based on such factors as similarity of the jobs the employees perform, similar training or skills, and so on. While the general rule is that at least two employees must be in a bargaining unit, an employer may agree to a one-person unit, such as for an on-site craftworker (e.g., a carpenter who belongs to a carpenter's union being employed at a worksite as the only carpenter).

Employees may unionize either by signing a sufficient number of authorization cards, by voting in a union during a union representation election, or, in some cases, by the NLRB ordering the employer to bargain with a union. The NLRB supervises the union election and certifies the results. The employer cannot interfere in any way with the employees' efforts to form a union, as was done in Opening Scenario 1.

Scenario

Concerted Activity

Section 7 of the NLRA guarantees employees the right to engage in concerted activities for mutual aid or protection. Typical protected concerted activities include union organizing, the discussion of unionization among employees, and the attempt by one employee to solicit union support from another employee. But concerted activity need not involve a union. Activities by groups of employees unaffiliated with a union to improve their lot in their workplace are deemed protected concerted activities.

Concerted activity also covers activity by a single employee, even if no other employee joins him or her. The reasoning is that the protected status of such activity should not turn on whether another employee decides to join the activity. Not all concerted activity is protected, however. Acts or threats of violence are not protected.

Unions

Unions are composed of nonsupervisory or nonmanagerial employees, including part-time workers. Specifically excluded from the NLRA are agricultural and domestic workers, independent contractors, and those employed by their spouse or parent. As we discussed in the chapter on affirmative action, agricultural and domestic workers were excluded from the law because these were the primary occupations to which blacks were consigned. The law was passed during the Jim Crow era of segregation as southern legislators refused to have blacks on par with whites.

The issue of supervisory employee inclusion in bargaining units has become heated recently. During the Bush administration, the definition of supervisor was clarified in *Oakwood Health Care, Inc.*[13] The terms *assign, responsible to direct,* and *independent judgment* in section 2(11) of the law were interpreted in a way that made it easier for an employer to consider an employee as a supervisory employee excluded from a bargaining unit for collective bargaining purposes. Unions were upset by this.

The Re-empowerment of Skilled and Professional Employees and Construction Tradeworkers (RESPECT) Act[14] was introduced in Congress in 2007 but has not been enacted into law. The law would essentially greatly increase the number of managers who could qualify to be a part of a bargaining unit. The law would remove from the definition of supervisor the duties of assigning the responsibility to direct other employees and would require that supervisors "hire, transfer, suspend, lay off, recall, promote, discharge, reward or discipline other employees" for a majority of their work time. This would have the effect of greatly reinvigorating unions, an idea of great concern to business. President Obama supports the law, but now has a Republican Congress, so passage is unlikely any time soon.

The union's **shop steward**, elected by the members, is the intermediary generally between the union and the employer. He or she may collect dues and recruit new workers, and, if a union member feels the **collective bargaining agreement** has been violated in some way, or an unfair labor practice has been committed, the shop steward is usually the first to contact the employer and discuss the issue, hopefully having it resolved.

shop steward
Union member chosen as intermediary between union members and an employer.

collective bargaining agreement
Negotiated contract between labor and management.

industrial union
Union organized across
an industry, regardless
of members' job type.

craft unions
Unions organized by the
employee's craft or trade.

business agent
The representative of a
union, usually craft.

Unions may be organized by industry or craft/trade. If all employees of a particular industry organize into a union, such as autoworkers, regardless of the job the members hold, this is an **industrial union**. The value of an industrial union from an employee's point of view is the solidarity and strength in a comprehensive group of workers—especially important in the event of a strike. Rather than being organized by industry, unions also may be organized around a particular craft or trade such as carpenters, sheet metal workers or pipefitters. These are **craft unions**. The value of a craft union is that the members all have the same issues specific to their craft or trade. Craft union members' interests are represented by a **business agent** of the craft union. You can imagine that management generally has an easier time trying to negotiate with one industrial union rather than a union for each craft/trade involved in management's enterprise. However, each type of union has its own advantages and disadvantages.

An interesting phenomenon in the past decade or so has been the unionization or attempted unionization of groups traditionally nonunion. For instance, since the early 1990s, registered nurses across the country sought to unionize and did so in record numbers. Before that time, nurses had considered unions to be for blue-collar workers, while nurses were considered professionals. One of the first projects President Clinton undertook when he came into office was to ask his wife, Hillary Rodham Clinton, to head up efforts to make health care more accessible and affordable to all. The health industry's response was unprecedented restructuring, and the resulting downsizing, among other things, displaced registered nurses. Registered nurses' perception of unions as being only for blue-collar workers changed, and they began to seek a collective voice purportedly to protect their profession and patient safety.

Even private attorneys are getting into the act. District attorneys had for some time been unionized in the public sector, but in 2003, in what is believed to be a first in the private legal profession, lawyers at the Phoenix office of the Los Angeles law firm of Parker Stanbury, which subcontracts with Pre-Paid Legal Service to provide easily accessible legal services, voted to unionize. Citing a lack of response by their employer to their complaints about low pay, few research materials, no law library, limited Internet access, hourly performance quotas, and working in open cubicles, they voted in representation by the local Teamsters union, which also represents truckers, grocery workers, bakery drivers, and UPS employees. There were allegations that management frequently tried to block the organizing effort, but the unionized lawyers said they were contacted by several other private attorneys interested in exploring unionizing.

There also have been organizing efforts for other nontraditional groups such as graduate students, college football players, medical interns and residents, and congressional researchers.

We cannot leave the area of organizing efforts without touching on another topic important to that area: the rise of the use of labor management consulting firms to thwart efforts at unionization. These organizations (often known as *union busters*) arose in the 1970s as primarily only a handful of law firms. Today, such firms have grown into a very sophisticated, billion-dollar industry. By 1989,

Exhibit 15.5 *Why Employers Don't Want Unions*

Union-busting is big business. You might wonder why a business would pay to have an organization come in to the workplace and stop employees' efforts to unionize. Here are a few of the reasons.

- Businesses prefer to make their own decisions, without the input of employees.
- Having to consult with the union means business is less likely to be able to make quick decisions.
- Bottom-line decisions such as outsourcing, subcontracting, or relocating to take advantage of cheaper labor or other costs would require union negotiation, thus making it less likely to be done smoothly, quickly, and efficiently.

- Unions often give the workplace a feeling of "us versus them," which can adversely impact morale and productivity.
- Union contracts requiring grievance proceedings and arbitration can be inefficient.
- Striking by workers, work stoppages, or slowdowns are a possible costly risk.
- The collective bargaining process is usually an adversarial affair, which does not help workplace morale.
- An employer looking to sell his or her business looks less appealing if a union is in place. This can lead to a lowering of the potential selling price for the business.

employers had hired antiunion consultants in 76 percent of all union organizing campaigns. To the extent that employers can stop organizing efforts by hiring help regarding how to discourage employees from voting to have union representation, they would consider the money spent as well worth the price. (See Exhibit 15.5, "Why Employers Don't Want Unions.")

The consulting firms' efforts may be successful in keeping unions out, but the employers may pay in other ways. For instance, nurses at Long Beach Memorial Hospital ran an organizing campaign to have the nurses join the California Nurses Association. A consulting firm was brought in to help keep the union out. The vote was eventually 591 to 581 to not have the nurses represented by a union, but the NLRB issued a complaint against the hospital alleging 26 violations of federal labor law. Many tactics are used to thwart unions during organizing efforts, some legal and some not. (See Exhibit 15.6, "Antiunionizing Tactics.") The best strategy is to have a workplace in which employees feel no need for a union because their reasonable needs are taken care of by the employer. However, if employers choose to make use of management consulting firms to keep unions out of the workplace, they should keep in close touch with the consultants and their tactics in order to avoid being left with the liability when the NLRB alleges an unfair management practices.

mandatory subject of bargaining
Wages, hours, and other conditions of employment, which, by law, must be negotiated between labor and management.

permissive subjects of bargaining
Nonmandatory subjects that can be negotiated between labor and management.

Good-Faith Bargaining

Under the NLRA, an employer is required to bargain in good faith with union representatives about wages, hours, and terms and conditions of employment. These are **mandatory subjects of bargaining**. While employers may actually bargain about other matters (**permissive subjects**), only a refusal to bargain

Exhibit 15.6 *Antiunionizing Tactics*

Below is a list of tactics used by employers over the years, both legal and illegal, to keep their employees from voting for union representation. As you will see, this is an extremely creative process, so the list is not exhaustive.

- Utilize scare tactics, including additional security guards and guard dogs, to create an atmosphere of fear and intimidation.
- Direct managers to disseminate misinformation about the union.
- Direct managers to disseminate antiunion flyers—one company passed out over 100 different flyers!
- Run newspaper ads against the union.
- Create antiunion videos and deliver them to employees' homes.
- Offer enticements such as improved working conditions and pay increases, and imply that they will not come about if the union is voted in.
- Plead for more time to try to make things better.
- Have supervisors interrogate employees to find out how they intend to vote.
- Pressure supporters not to talk to other employees about the union.
- Place managers in employee hangouts such as lounges, cafeterias, or break rooms to inhibit employees' discussion of the union vote.
- Have supervisors write letters to individual employees telling them things like the supervisor will lose his or her job if the union is voted in.

- Ignore and isolate pro-union employees.
- Use ethnicity as a wedge between various ethnic groups.
- Have supervisors call daily mandatory meetings.
- Have supervisors engage employees in one-on-one conversations about the union as much as possible.
- Disseminate antiunion buttons, flyers, posters, videos, bumper stickers, and T-shirts.
- Have an antiunion Web site.
- Install locked, glass-covered bulletin boards all over the workplace and post antiunion material on them.
- Make supervisors think they will lose their jobs if they do not get the employees to vote against the union.
- Have a few employees run an antiunion campaign.
- Spring last-minute surprises on employees, such as rumors of possible workplace shutdown, bonuses, or pay raises.
- Have payroll send out checks with an amount equal to union dues taken out, tell employees this is what their paychecks will look like if the union is voted in, and then put the money back in their next paychecks.
- Shut down part or all of operations and allege that the shutdown is because of union costs.

about mandatory subjects of bargaining may form the basis of an unfair labor practice. (See Exhibit 15.7, "Selected Collective Bargaining Agreement Clauses.")

At times, management and labor may differ on whether a particular matter is a mandatory subject of bargaining. If this disagreement is legitimate, it can form the basis of an unfair labor practice—for instance, a union may allege management has committed an unfair labor practice by refusing to bargain over a mandatory subject of bargaining such as wage increases. In *one* case, for example, the union demanded negotiations on the issue of the agency's new smoking ban.[15]

Exhibit 15.7 *Selected Collective Bargaining Agreement Clauses*

Wages—including cost-of-living increases, production increases, learners' and apprentices' overtime.

Benefits—including vacations, sick pay, holidays, insurance.

Hours—including overtime and determinations about assignment.

Seniority—setting forth how employee seniority is determined and used.

Management security—employers may make their own decisions about how to run the business as long as they are not contrary to the collective bargaining agreement or law.

Union security—the union's legal right to exist and to represent the employees involved.

Job security—how employees will maintain employment, including procedures for layoffs, downsizing, work sharing, and so on.

Dues checkoff—right of a union to have the employer deduct union dues from employees' wages and turn them over to the union.

Union shop—requires all employees to join the union within a certain time of coming into the bargaining unit.

Modified union shop—requires that all new employees must join the union after an agreement becomes effective, as must any employees who were already union members; but those already working who were not union members and do not wish to join need not do so.

Maintenance-of-membership—employees who voluntarily join a union may leave only during a short window period prior to agreement expiration.

Agency shop—requires all employees of the bargaining unit to pay union dues, whether union members or not.

Grievances—sets forth the basis for grievances regarding conflicts over the meaning of the collective bargaining agreement and procedures for addressing them.

Exclusive representation—the union representative will be the only party who can negotiate with the employer about matters affecting bargaining unit employees.

Arbitration—the matters that cannot be otherwise resolved will be submitted to arbitration to be resolved by a neutral third party whose decision is usually binding.

Midterm negotiations—permits agreed-on topics to be reopened to negotiation prior to contract expiration.

No-strike, no lockout—parties agree that the employees will not strike or will only do so under limited circumstances and that employers will not engage in lockouts. Instead, the grievance procedure will be used to handle labor disputes.

closed shop
Employer hires only union members.

If the matter proposed for negotiation is illegal, such as a proposal to have a **closed shop**, it is bad-faith bargaining even to bring it up as a proposal, and management's refusal to bargain cannot be the basis of an unfair labor practice.

The law requires only that the parties bargain in good faith about appropriate matters, not that one party necessarily agree with the other's position and include it in the collective bargaining agreement. The intent is to prevent management from unilaterally instituting workplace policies that closely affect workers without at least getting employee input and negotiating the matter. The fact that one side or the other does not receive what it wants in the contract is not just cause for an unfair labor practice. As long as good-faith bargaining takes place, there has been compliance with the statute.

A case of bargaining in bad faith might occur when, for instance, management comes to the bargaining table and denies a raise to employees without offering any evidence whatever as to why, and simply continues to reject the union's wage proposals. The 2011 National Football League negotiations with the National Football League Players Association experienced a stalemate where negotiation impasses and failure to agree on a new contract threatened to interrupt the start of the football season. Despite more than $9 billion in league revenues, owners asserted that stadium construction and other investments had driven their profits down to the single digits. They proposed that players should take 18 percent off the pool of money used to calculate salary caps. The players wanted to see league financial statements justifying the owners' claims, but the owners were reluctant to share.[16] Fortunately, an agreement was reached and the season salvaged.

It also could occur if one side rejects proposals out of hand without making counterproposals to the other side. Missing negotiation sessions and setting forth unsupported proposals could lead to an unfair labor practice charge. Of course, failing to show up for negotiations or refusing to sign the written agreement to which the parties orally agreed also would be bad-faith bargaining. The *Gimrock Construction, Inc. v. International Union of Operating Engineers, Local 487* case, provided for your review, demonstrates how extreme an employer can be in failing or refusing to bargain in good faith. Since 1999, Gimrock refused to bargain with the employees' union representative on the first collective bargaining agreement or to provide them with requested relevant information. The 11th Circuit Court of Appeals upheld and enforced two earlier board decisions finding a refusal to bargain. Finally, the NLRB general counsel took the extraordinary step of requesting remedies that included requiring the employer to bargain for a minimum of 16 hours per week and also to send written bargaining progress reports to the NLRB regional director every 30 days. Twelve years later, in a 2011 decision, the board agreed that because of the employer's extended reluctance, the remedies were appropriate. Delaying negotiating for 12 years gives you some idea of the resistance employers have to unions and the lengths to which they will go to avoid unions in the workplace.

The duty to bargain in good faith over terms and conditions of employment does not require agreement between the parties. As you witnessed with the NFL negotiations, if agreement is not reached with the union after good-faith bargaining is conducted, the union may then be free to advance to other alternatives it can exercise, up to and including strikes. Unions are also capable of engaging in refusals to bargain or bargaining in bad faith. These are not activities exclusive to management.

Duty of Fair Representation

Frequently when union members do not like the contract that results from collective bargaining negotiations, they will allege the union has breached its duty of fair representation. This duty, not formally defined in the statute and often used as a catchall allegation, requires the union to represent all employees fairly and non-discriminatorily. If employees feel that one group has come out better than another in a contract, they will use the duty of fair representation as a basis for challenging the contract. The U.S. Supreme Court spoke to this issue in *Air Line Pilots Association International v. O'Neill,*[17] when it held that since the final outcome was not "wholly irrational or arbitrary," the union had done its statutory job of upholding its duty of fair representation even though some members may not have liked the outcome.

Collective Bargaining Agreements

If all goes well, bargaining between labor and management results in a collective bargaining agreement. This is the term for the contract that is reached between the employer and the union about workplace issues. There is no set form that this agreement must take, and it may be any length and contain any provisions the parties decide. (See Exhibit 15.7, "Selected Collective Bargaining Agreement Clauses.") Job and union security is the main issue for employees, while freedom from labor strife such as strikes, slowdowns, and work stoppages is paramount for employers. Management will often wish to include a **management security clause**, stating that it has the power to run its business and make business decisions as long as it is not in violation of the collective bargaining agreement or the law.

management security clause
Parties agree that management has the right to run the business and make appropriate business decisions as long as applicable laws and agreements are complied with.

Toward that end, in addition to wages and hours, collective bargaining agreements often also contain provisions regarding strikes, arbitration of labor disputes, seniority, benefits, employment classifications, and so on. Because things change, the agreement is in effect only for a specified period. Prior to expiration of that period, the parties will negotiate a new contract to take effect when the old one expires. As you know from NFL negotiations discussed above, that does not always occur. The collective bargaining agreement between the NFL and the NFL Players Association expired on March 4, 2011, but that date came and went through summer 2011 with no agreement. Two extensions were agreed to, but to no avail. In fact, the NFLPA decertified its union on March 11, 2011, and was no longer represented by a union at the bargaining table. The NFLPA filed an antitrust suit against the NFL and the NFL responded with a lockout of the players as of March 12, 2011.[18] This first NFL work stoppage since 1987, of course, put the 2011 season in jeopardy as the situation moved from negotiation to litigation. On April 25, 2011, a federal judge granted the players' request for an injunction stopping the lockout.[19]

midterm negotiations
Collective bargaining negotiations during the term of the contract.

The collective bargaining agreement also may include a clause permitting **midterm negotiations**. These are negotiations during the life of the contract, rather than immediately prior to its expiration, about matters on which the parties have agreed they will permit interim negotiations. The parties may not be able to agree on a particular provision and, rather than allow it to hold up the entire contract, will agree to come back together later to negotiate it. Alternatively, the parties may agree to midterm negotiations because the contract may cover a fairly long period and the provision subject to midterm negotiation is one that may change quickly and need to be reviewed before the contract's expiration date.

Exhibit 15.8 *Management Unfair Labor Practices*

- Trying to control the union or interfering with union affairs, such as trying to help a certain candidate get elected to a union office.
- Discriminating against employees who join a union or are in favor of bringing in a union or who exercise their rights under the law (e.g., terminating, demoting, or giving poor working schedules to such employees).

- Interfering with, coercing, or restraining employees exercising their rights under the labor law legislation (e.g., telling employees they cannot have a union or they will be terminated if they do).
- Refusal to bargain or refusal to bargain in good faith.

Unfair Labor Practices

Refusal to bargain in good faith is not the only unfair labor practice that an employer can commit. Others include engaging in activities that would tend to attempt to control or influence the union, or to interfere with its affairs, and discriminating against employees who join or assist unions. Actual interference by the employer need not be proved for it to be considered an unfair labor practice. Rather, the question is whether the activity tends to interfere with, restrain, or coerce employees who are exercising rights protected under the law. (See Exhibit 15.8, "Management Unfair Labor Practices.") The *Columbia Portland Cement Co. v. National Labor Relations Board* case, which is provided at the conclusion of the chapter and is the basis for Opening Scenario 2, indicates the extent of possible unfair labor practices when the employer refused to reinstate striking employees and gave a unilateral wage increase without consulting the union.

Scenario

As mentioned previously, some employers are more aggressive in interfering with their employees' unionizing efforts. In *Davis Supermarkets, Inc. v. National Labor Relations Board,*[20] the company interfered with its employees' organizing efforts and even terminated some of its employees. The court found these acts to be unfair labor practices that violated the NLRA.

Sometimes, even though the employer may have the best of intentions, its other actions may amount to a violation of law. In *Electromation v. National Labor Relations Board,* included at the end of the chapter, what may have appeared to the company to be legitimate negotiations with nonunion employees was held to violate the NLRA. The nonunion employer attempted to resolve labor issues through "employee participation" or "employee–management" focus groups. When the court determined that the groups actually constituted labor organizations and were dominated by management, who had too much of a hand in administering these groups, it held that the employer's actions constituted an unfair labor practice. *Electromation* is the basis for Opening Scenario 3.

Scenario

In Exhibit 15.6, "Antiunionizing Tactics," we listed many of the antiunion organizing tactics that have been used by management over the years to thwart union efforts to organize, and in Exhibit 15.8, "Management Unfair Labor Practices," we

Exhibit 15.9 *Cans and Can'ts during Union Campaigns*

Often referred to as "NO TIPS" (threats, interrogation promises, or spying, along with several other things an employer cannot do), during a unionizing campaign, the employer can't

- Threaten to fire an employee for joining a union.
- Try to help the employees form a union.
- Lay off or terminate employees who support the union.
- Allow employees to copy antiunion leaflets at work and pass them out.
- Let employees hold antiunion meetings at work.
- Email, post, or circulate threatening or intimidating letters or leaflets.
- Try to question employees about their support of (or opposition to) the union.
- Terminate, discipline, transfer, or reassign union supporters to less desirable shifts, duties, or locations without some legitimate business cause other than their union support.
- Ask about union meetings or union activities.
- Spy on union activities or union supporters.
- Isolate all union supporters so that they cannot speak with other employees.

- Promise wage increases or other benefits if employees don't join the union.
- Threaten to take away job benefits if employees vote in a union.
- Ban pro union buttons if such things are generally permitted.

During a unionizing campaign, an employer *can*

- Send letters to employees' homes.
- Establish a suggestion box or complaint process.
- Give pay raises or benefits overall, not just to union supporters. (This can be limited after the union applies for its certificate or gives notice to bargain its first agreement.)
- Hold meetings in an effort to address or solve problems it becomes aware of.
- Tell employees how good the company is.
- Tell employees how good the company's benefits and working conditions are.
- Address issues that it may become aware of during the unionizing process.

listed some unfair labor practices. In Exhibit 15.9, "Cans and Can'ts during Union Campaigns," we list some specific acts employers can and cannot engage in during organizing efforts. It would be wise for employers to use these lists as guides in order to avoid unfair labor practice complaints.

Strikes and Lockouts

The NLRA permits certain strikes by employees as a legitimate bargaining approach that leverages economic and public pressure. (See Exhibit 15.10, "Types of Strikes.") When a union strikes, union members do not work but, instead, generally gather outside the employer's place of business and carry signs about the nature of the strike (**picketing**) and chant slogans. Engaging in such activity is for purposes of pressuring management to concede, bringing attention to the strikers' demands, gathering public support, and discouraging others who may support the employer. For instance, a picket line may encourage shoppers going into a grocery store not to patronize the store where the clerks are on strike because wages are too low.

picketing
The carrying of signs that tell of an unfair labor practice or strike, by union members in front of the employer's business.

Exhibit 15.10 *Types of Strikes*

- *Economic strike*—used to exert pressure on the employer regarding economic issues. Also used for strikes resulting from any other reason than an unfair labor practice. Protected activity.

- *Unfair labor practice strike*—called by union because of an employer's unfair labor practice. Protected activity.

- *Sympathy strike*—union not involved in strike also strikes to show solidarity and support for striking union.

- *Sitdown strike*—employees illegally take possession of workplace during strike. Not protected activity.

- *Wildcat strike*—strike not authorized by union. Generally not protected activity, but may be.

- *Intermittent strike*—strikes that occur from time to time and are not announced. Not protected activity.

- *Slowdown*—employees remain on the job and generally do not produce as much. Unprotected activity.

wildcat strike
A strike not sanctioned by the union.

Legitimate strikes may be called by the union either for economic reasons or because of unfair labor practices. For instance, the employees may strike when a collective bargaining agreement expires without a new one to take its place or if the employees are attempting to force economic concessions from the employer. If employees strike for legally recognized reasons, their actions are protected under the NLRA and they retain their status as employees. Strikes not authorized by the union are called **wildcat strikes** and are illegal if they force the employer to deal with the employees, rather than the union, or impose the will of the minority rather than the majority. They have been found not to be unlawful if they are merely to make a statement.

If the employer replaces the strikers with new employees, then once the strike is over, the strikers have a right to reinstatement if they offer an unconditional offer to return to work. If their jobs are occupied by replacement workers, then unfair labor practice strikers are entitled to be reinstated, but economic strikers are not.

lockout
Management does not allow employees to come to work.

Just as employees can stop working if they feel the need to strike to make their point, the employer can close the premises to employees and engage in a **lockout**. In a lockout, the employer curtails employment by either shutting down the plant or bringing in temporary nonunion employees after laying off striking workers. Under the NLRA, the employer may engage in lockouts not as a way of avoiding bargaining or unionizing but, rather, as with strikes, to bring pressure to bear on the other side for legitimate purposes. The pressure position is probably why the NFL chose to announce a lockout of the NFL players on March 11, 2011, effective at midnight that night.

no-strike, no-lockout clause
Labor and management agree that labor will not strike and management will not stage a lockout.

Many collective bargaining agreements contain **no-strike, no-lockout clauses**, which either prohibit or limit the availability of this action and, instead, call for the use of the grievance process to handle issues. In 2002, baseball commissioner Bud Selig pledged not to lock out players throughout the season and the World Series. His statement left open the possibility that team owners would come up with new work rules after that. Because the players' union had been working without a labor contract since November 7, 2001, they interpreted the commissioner's statement as a "veiled threat" to impose vast economic changes as soon as the postseason ended. In 1994, in its eighth walkout since 1972, the baseball players' union struck in order to fight management's plan to implement changes that included a salary cap. The walkout lasted 232 days and resulted in the cancellation of the World Series for the first time since 1904. In 2002, after fighting for months over changes imposed by club owners, the players entered into a new contract on August 30, avoiding the strike deadline by only hours.

In 2004–2005 there was the unfortunate National Hockey League fiasco where differences between the owners and players, primarily over the issue of salary caps, resulted in a five-month lockout by the owners and, eventually, cancellation of the entire season by the NHL commissioner—an event many hockey fans still think back on with much dismay. It was the first time a major North American professional sports league lost an entire season to a labor dispute.[21] The last time the NHL's Stanley Cup was not awarded was in 1919 because of a flu pandemic. The year before, the Boston Red Sox had won the World Series. Coincidentally, this time around, when the cup wasn't awarded because of labor disputes canceling the season, the Red Sox had once again, after over 80 years, won the World Series the year before.

In *Local 825, Int'l Union of Operating Engineers v. National Labor Relations Board*,[22] the union challenged the lockout and hiring of temporary workers as unfair labor practices, but the court held that the practices did not violate the law. The court discussed legitimate purposes for which an employer can stage a lockout and what happens if the workers are replaced with temporary employees during the lockout. It said that "if the adverse effect of the discriminatory conduct on employee rights is 'comparatively slight' an anti-union motivation must be proved to sustain the charge if the employer has come forward with evidence of legitimate and substantial business justifications for the conduct." Thus, the "slight" impact on employee rights (to organize, etc.) that the conduct at issue arguably had is negated if the employer has established a legitimate and substantial business justification for its conduct.

The Taft-Hartley Act of 1947

LO6

With the enactment of the NLRA and the subsequent gains made in unionism, the Taft-Hartley Act of 1947 was enacted as an amendment to the NLRA to curb excesses by unions. Most importantly, the Taft-Hartley Act changed the policies of the NLRA. No longer were all employers legislatively determined to be frustrating the organizational rights of their employees. Congress recognized that unions had grown so strong and powerful over the years that their activities required federal regulation. As such, unions were to have certain limitations placed on their activity. Congress wanted employers, employees, and labor organizations to recognize one another's legitimate rights and made the rights of all three subordinate to the public's health, safety, and interests.

Exhibit 15.11 *Union Unfair Labor Practices*

- Refusing to bargain or bargaining in bad faith—that is, not attending bargaining sessions, not providing proposals, not providing necessary information.

- Coercing or restraining employees in exercising their rights to join (or not join) a union. This is not a problem if the union and employer have a provision in their collective bargaining agreement that states a nonunion member coming into the bargaining unit must join the union within a certain amount of time.

- Charging discriminatory or very high dues or entrance fees for admittance into the union.

- Threatening, encouraging, or influencing employees to strike in an effort to pressure the employer to join an employer organization, to get the employer to recognize an uncertified union, or to stop doing business with an employer because of the employer not doing so.

- Influencing employers to discriminate against, or otherwise treat differently, employees who do not belong to the union or are denied union membership for some reason other than nonpayment of union dues or fees.

Section 7 was rewritten to recognize the right of an employee to refrain from concerted activity, including union activity. Like section 8 of the Wagner Act, which enumerates unfair labor practices that could be committed by employees, section 8 of the Taft-Hartley Act spells out six unfair labor practices that could be committed by organized labor (see Exhibit 15.11, "Union Unfair Labor Practices"), thereby bringing unions under the regulation of the federal law. Under this section, it is an unfair labor practice for unions to

1. Restrain or coerce employees in the exercise of their rights or employers in the selection of their representatives for collective bargaining.
2. Cause an employer to discriminate against an employee.
3. Refuse to bargain with an employer.
4. Engage in jurisdictional or secondary boycotts.
5. Charge excess or discriminatory initiation fees or dues.
6. Cause an employer to pay for goods or services that are not provided.

right-to-work laws
Permits employees to choose not to become a part of the union.

Before closed shops (where the employee must become a member of the union in order to obtain a job) were outlawed by the Taft-Hartley Act, states enacted right-to-work laws. (See Exhibit 15.12, "Right-to-Work States.") This was done in response to the use of closed shops by unions to control dissenters by severing their union membership, without which they could not work in a closed shop. The NLRA permits states to have **right-to-work laws**, and as of 2011, 22 of them do. In a right-to-work state, employment cannot be conditioned on union membership. Despite some employees' nonparticipation in the union, and thus their not being required to pay union dues, the union must still represent these employees as a part of the bargaining unit. If a state is not a right-to-work state, the union and employer may have as a part of their collective bargaining agreement union

Exhibit 15.12 *Right-to-Work States*

According to the U.S. Department of Labor, the following states had right-to-work laws in effect as of January 1, 2011:

Alabama	Nevada
Arizona	North Carolina
Arkansas	North Dakota
Florida	Oklahoma
Georgia	South Carolina
Idaho	South Dakota
Iowa	Tennessee
Kansas	Texas
Louisiana	Utah
Mississippi	Virginia
Nebraska	Wyoming

Indiana has a policy in effect, but it only applies to school employees.

Source: http://www.nrtw.org/d/rtwempl.htm.

union shop
Union and management agree that employees must be a member of the union.

union shop clause
Provision in a collective bargaining agreement allowing a union shop.

security devise a provision for a **union shop**. This provision, called a **union shop clause**, requires the employer to have all members or potential members of the bargaining unit agree that they will join the union within a certain amount of time (not less than 30 days) after becoming employed.

The issues involved in states having right-to-work laws versus not having them arose recently in the state of Michigan, which, with 19.6 percent of its workforce belonging to a union, is the fourth largest union membership state in the country. It is also the birthplace and home of the United Auto Workers union. Though job losses have decreased UAW membership from 1.5 million in 1979 to about 500,000 now, the union has been so successful in Michigan that even white-collar workers admit that their salaries would not be as high and their benefits as good if it were not for the unions. Due to union negotiations, among other things, union members enjoy good wages, extra days off, and rights such as the auto manufacturers' job bank preserving hourly workers' jobs even if there is nothing for them to do (earning UAW the nickname "U Ain't Working"). At the same time, for the past several years, Michigan has been losing jobs (336,000 from 2000 to 2006 alone) to places like Mexico, with its lower wages. In June 2007, at 7.2 percent, Michigan's unemployment rate was the highest in the nation. In an effort to attract more business to the state, in March of 2007, Michigan Republican Rep. Jack Hoogendyk introduced a right-to-work bill for the state to change its closed shop laws, which require that if there is a union in the workplace, employees must join, to an open shop where employees can decide for themselves if they wish to do so. In the view of some, the closed shop law in Michigan makes Michigan less attractive to businesses contemplating moving there because it means that the work environment is not employer-friendly. On the other hand, unions say such laws lead to lower wages and benefits and, because Michigan is such a strong union state, dismissed the idea of such legislation, saying they will fight any such moves. As of 2011, the debate was still ongoing, with Republicans making a concerted effort to pass the legislation.[23]

Oklahoma had the same fight before it passed its law in 2001. Since Oklahoma's law became effective in 2003, the impact has been "minimal," according to researchers. Personal income grew 7.6 percent in 2006, the third highest in the United States, but according to the Department of Commerce, that was because of growth in the preexisting oil and gas industry. On the other hand, several manufacturing plants closed, including General Motors, Bridgestone Firestone, and Wrangler jeans, which moved to Mexico. Union membership went from 8 percent to 5.4 percent.

agency shop clause
Requires nonunion members to pay union dues without having to be subject to the union rules.

It is also permissible for the collective bargaining agreement to contain an **agency shop clause**, which requires nonunion members to pay to the union the usual union dues and fees without joining the union and thereby becoming subject to union rules. Some right-to-work laws do not allow this and, instead, permit nonunion employees of the bargaining unit to be **free riders**—that is, to receive union benefits without having to pay union dues or fees. In the *National Football League Players Association v. Pro Football, Inc.* case, given for your review, the court addressed the issue of pro football players who did not want to pay union dues. The issue turned on whether the state law of the place where they played their games would govern, or the place where they held their practices. Virginia, where they primarily practiced, is a right-to-work state, while Washington, DC, where they played their games, is not. The court held that their primary workplace was in Virginia, and since it is a right-to-work state, the players were required to pay union dues.

free riders
Bargaining unit employees who do not pay dues but whom the union is still obligated to represent.

A frequent bone of contention with union members is the use of union dues for activities with which the members do not agree. This is a particularly interesting question when it involves the agency shop since employees who do not want to belong to the union must still pay to the union an amount equal to the union dues (often called a *service fee*). This is, of course, to prevent the problem of free riders who benefit from union activity but do not contribute to the union's resources.

In 1991 the U.S. Supreme Court addressed the issue of what the union could use this money for. In *Lehnert v. Ferris Faculty Association*,[24] the court determined that unions could use nonmember service fees for political activities. It said that that "chargeable activities must (1) be 'germane' to collective-bargaining activity; (2) be justified by the government's vital policy interest in labor peace and avoiding 'free riders,' and (3) not significantly add to the burdening of free speech that is inherent in the allowance of an agency or union shop." It used these guidelines to decide if the specific programs being challenged were within these rules.

In 2007, the Court addressed the agency shop nonmember funds' use issue when a public employee union asserted that Washington state's law prohibiting labor unions from using the agency shop fees of nonmembers for election-related purposes unless the nonmember affirmatively consents was an unconstitutional burden on the union's First Amendment right to free speech. In *Davenport v. Washington Education Association*,[25] the union asserted that the law was unconstitutionally restrictive of free speech because it put the burden on the union to find out if the nonmember objected to the use of the funds for election-related purposes. The court said that the public employee union being able to receive agency shop fees from government employees was much like the union being able to tax government employees for having a job. Under these circumstances, if the state of Washington wished to put the burden on the union to find out if the nonmembers wanted their funds used for election-related purposes, the Court did not think that was an unconstitutionally high price to pay.

In 2008, the High Court further refined the issue decided in *Lenhert* and addressed whether service fees could be used for litigation activities far removed from the workplace, a question upon which the Court had not reached a consensus in *Lenhert*. In *Locke v. Karass*,[26] the Court allowed such a use by the union for national union affairs such as litigation.

One of the other powers in the Taft-Hartley Act rarely comes into play, but it is an important provision when needed. The act gives the president of the United States the authority to halt a strike or lockout if it would imperil national health or safety. Under the act, the president can seek an injunction that would require an 80-day "cooling-off period" for the parties during which, hopefully, they would reach an agreement. If the union rejects management's terms after the cooling-off period, then the union can strike.

In the fall of 2002, not long after the tragic events of September 11, 2001, the 10,500 West Coast dockworkers of the International Longshore and Warehouse Union (ILWU) threatened to strike over issues involving the introduction of labor-saving technology and the outsourcing of union jobs. With the 29 ports handling about 50 percent of all ocean-borne cargo entering the United States or $300 billion in goods (about 7 percent of the gross domestic product) from San Diego to Seattle at about the rate of $1 billion per day, supporting about 1.4 million U.S. jobs, and at least 45 retailing giants like Walmart, Home Depot, Target, and The Gap, representing over $1 trillion in annual sales and 100,000 manufacturing, distribution, and retail centers, lobbying President George W. Bush to avert a strike or slowdown, the matter was serious. President Bush certainly thought so: he promised to use any means necessary to make sure troops received what they needed. Options floated included using U.S. Navy personnel to run the ports, trying to break up the union's coastwide bargaining unit, or introducing legislation that would restrict the union's ability to call a strike.

Management instituted a lockout after deciding the workers had engaged in a work slowdown. After eight days of the lockout, President Bush declared a national emergency, asserting the strike's potentially crippling effect on the national economy. On October 8, the U.S. Department of Justice took the case to a federal court in San Francisco to halt the lockout and requested a temporary restraining order under the Taft-Hartley Act. On behalf of President Bush they argued that the order was necessary to protect the economy because some businesses were reportedly running low on inventories and supplies and the strike was also jeopardizing the war on terrorism. Defense Secretary Donald Rumsfeld gave a sworn statement that the port dispute threatened to "degrade military readiness, hinder the department's ability to prosecute the global war on terrorism, and undercut other defense needs and worldwide commitments." The judge granted the restraining order and called an immediate halt to the lockout, ordering the West Coast ports to reopen immediately. More than 200 ships waited in the waters outside the ports, with an estimated unloading time of eight to nine weeks. On November 1, 2002, the union and management announced an agreement regarding the central technology issue.

The Landrum-Griffin Act of 1959

Also known as the Labor Management Reporting and Disclosure Act, this legislation was enacted in response to congressional investigations into union corruption from 1957 to 1959. After finding evidence of such corruption, Congress passed the legislation. Based on the investigative findings, the purpose of the law is to establish basic ways of unions operating to ensure a democratic process, to provide union members with a minimum bill of rights attached to union membership, and to regulate the activities of union officials and the use of union funds. (See Exhibit 15.13, "Union Members' Bill of Rights.")

The act provides a bill of rights for union members. Looking at some of the provisions of the bill of rights, one might think that they are so simplistic as to be taken as givens for an organization. However, keep in mind that the bill of rights was enacted in response to union abuses actually found during the two-year congressional investigation.

Exhibit 15.13   *Union Members' Bill of Rights*

Among other things, the Landrum-Griffin Act provides that

- Union members have the right to attend union meetings, vote on union business, and nominate candidates for union elections.

- Members may bring an agency or court action against the union after exhausting union procedures.

- Certain procedures must be followed before any dues or initiation fee increases.

- Except for the failure to pay dues, members must have a full and fair hearing when being disciplined by the union.

The Landrum-Griffin Act also set forth specific procedures to be followed when unions hold elections, including voting for officers by secret ballot, holding elections at least every three years (other times for different levels of the union, such as international officers), candidates being able to see lists of eligible voters, and procedures for having an election declared improper. Provisions also were enacted to safeguard union funds. Under the act, unions cannot use union funds for anything except benefiting the union or its members. Funds cannot be used to support union office candidates, and union officials, agents, employees, and so on cannot acquire financial interests that conflict with the union's. The law made stealing or embezzling union funds a federal crime.

Labor Relations in the Public Sector

 Much of what has been discussed relates to the private sector. Of more recent vintage is the matter of collective bargaining in the public sector.

Federal Employees

Historically, there has been little legislation affecting the labor relations of public employees (federal, state, and local government employees). The NLRA has always exempted these employees. There was no uniform federal policy on public labor–management relations. Currently, however, over half of the 50 states and the District of Columbia have collective bargaining statutes covering most, if not all, public employees.

Over time, federal employees formed associations, but only postal workers were not powerless to influence their workplace. In 1962, President Kennedy established the right of federal employees to form and join unions. Since that time, union ranks have increased in the public sector.

Federal restrictions prevent federal unions from conducting direct bargaining over wages and benefits and from striking. The Civil Service Reform Act of 1978 established the Federal Labor Relations Authority (FLRA) to administer federal sector labor law. This agency may be thought of as the federal counterpart to the private sector's National Labor Relations Board (NLRB).

State, County, and Municipal Public Employees

Most public employee organizations at the state, county, and municipal levels can be divided into three major categories: professional associations, craft unions, and industrial-type unions. *Professional associations* are composed of a wide variety of professionals. The largest professional employee organization is the National Education Association (NEA). This organization of school teachers has over 3 million members from kindergarten to college, and in addition to teachers, consists of principals, administrators, and other school specialists. The Fraternal Order of Police does not consider itself a union, but many local lodges engage in collective bargaining, handle grievances, and represent the interests of their members to their employers.

Craft unions consist of such groups as the International Association of Fire-fighters (IAFF), which is an affiliate of the AFL-CIO. Another teachers union that considers itself to be a craft union is the American Federation of Teachers (AFT), which limits its membership to classroom teachers only. While craft unions are too numerous to list, many of them are familiar and have been in existence for nearly a century, such as the United Mine Workers and International Brotherhood of Electrical Workers.

The union that typifies the *industrial-type union* is the American Federation of State, County, and Municipal Employees (AFSCME), an affiliate of the AFL-CIO. These local unions may represent an entire city or county, or they may represent a smaller unit of government, such as a department or a group of employees that cuts across many departments.

The AFL-CIO assists public workers' unions that affiliate with it through its Public Employees Department. This department, formed in 1974, has 33 affiliated unions that represent millions of federal, state, and local government employees. These unions represent workers in schools, courts, regulatory agencies, hospitals, transportation networks, police, and fire departments. The AFL-CIO believes that state and local employees are the only workers in the United States who do not enjoy the basic right to enter into collective bargaining agreements with their employers. That is, there is no national legislation that gives these workers the right to enter into collective bargaining agreements. If they have the right, it is because the state in which they operate has enacted state legislation that permits it.

To many, the most important difference between the public and private collective bargaining is that federal legislation and most state statutes do not contain the right of public employees to strike. This prohibition is grounded in the need to protect public health and safety (i.e., to prevent police officers or firefighters from being out on strike while crime rises or buildings burn), as well as the sovereignty doctrine deeming striking against a governmental employer as inconsistent with the government being the sovereign or highest authority.

State and federal employees have not always honored the prohibition on striking. While many ignored the prohibition, probably the most famous example occurred when the federal air traffic controllers, represented by the Professional Air Traffic Controllers Organization (PATCO), went on strike in 1981. One of the reasons the strike was so memorable was undoubtedly because newly elected President Ronald Reagan took a hard line and terminated 11,000 striking employees. The air traffic controllers were sued for their action in *United States v. Professional Air Traffic Controllers Organization.*[27]

There are also differences between the private and public sector about what may be negotiated. While the U.S. postal workers may do so, generally federal employees cannot bargain over wages, hours, or benefits. On the other hand, they can bargain about the numbers, types, and grades of positions; procedures for performing work or exercising authority; the use of technology; and alternatives for employees harmed by management decisions.

Management Tips

Dealing with unions can be an uncomfortable situation for an employer. The very idea is antithetical to many business owners who feel the business is theirs, and since they are taking all the risks and putting up all the money, they should have full control. Giving over any control to employees through the unions and the collective bargaining process is not easy for them. Like it or not, however, collective bargaining is the law. Following the tips below can help avoid problems resulting in liability for violating labor laws:

- If employees decide they wish to unionize, do not try to negatively influence the decision in impermissible ways.
- Do not assume any employee you speak to for the purpose of persuading him or her not to unionize will keep the conversation confidential.
- Know the kinds of things the employer can legally do to influence the unionizing decision, and do only those things that are permissible.
- Once the union is in place, conduct all negotiations only with the union representatives. Avoid making side deals with individual employees.
- Treat the collective bargaining process as you would any business activity. Do not invite unfair labor practice charges by engaging in activity that could be deemed a refusal to bargain in good faith.
- Know what the law requires—the employer need not do any more than the law requires in permitting the union to conduct its business. Know well what the employer can and need not do.
- Keep the lines of communication open between labor and management.
- Try to keep the "us versus them" mentality from having a negative impact on the collective bargaining process. It can be difficult to avoid, but if you can, it helps negotiations stay on an even keel, without letting egos get in the way.
- Play hardball without setting management up for an unfair labor practice charge.

Chapter Summary

- The four main labor law statutes form a framework within which employers and employees may address workplace issues with some modicum of predictability.
- Laws paved the way for unionism by preventing courts from prohibiting union activity. They also provided a statutory basis, with the Wagner or National Labor Relations Act, and they fine-tuned and addressed union abuses, with the Taft-Hartley Act and the Landrum-Griffin or Labor Management Recording and Disclosure Act.
- Private employers and employees are free to negotiate upon mandatory as well as permissive terms of bargaining to determine matters of wages, hours, and other terms and conditions of employment.

Chapter-End Questions

1. After a bitter strike and boycott that included strike-related violence and the use of "scabs" to replace workers in the walnut industry, a returning worker who had been a quality control supervisor prior to the strike was placed in a seasonal packing position, a job with less status, because the employer was afraid that the replacement workers, some of whom were still on the job, would try to instigate violence against the returning workers. The workers claimed that the employer refused to place them in their prior positions as retaliation for striking. After a strike, does the employer have an obligation to place striking workers back in their prestrike position if there might be violence aimed at them? [*Diamond Walnut Growers Inc. v. NLRB,* 113 F.3d 1259 (DC Cir. 1997).]

2. Bloom was hired to perform clerical work for Group Health Incorporated Office and Professional Employees International Union Local 12. Group Health had negotiated a collective bargaining agreement that contained a union security clause that stated employees must be "members in good standing," which Bloom interpreted as requiring that he pay union dues. Upon filing a grievance with the NLRB, what is the likely outcome? [*Bloom v. NLRB,* 30 F.3d 1001 (8th Cir. 1994).]

3. C. Tyler Williams Co. set up a committee called the Employee-Owners' Influence Council (EOIC). All employees were encouraged to become members. Of 150 employees who applied, 30 of Tyler Williams' 8,000 employees were selected by the company. They discussed such issues as medical insurance benefits, the Employee Stock Ownership Plan, and family and medical leave. Is this type of employee–management team in violation of the NLRA? [*Polaroid v. NLRB,* 329 NLRB No. 47 (Oct. 6, 1999).]

4. In its employee handbook, an employer stated that it would do "*everything possible* to maintain the company's union-free status for the benefit of both our employees and [the Company]." Is this an unfair labor practice under the NLRB? [*Aluminum Casting & Engineering Co. v. NLRB,* 328 NLRB No. 2 (Apr. 9, 1999).]

5. A truck driver who refused to drive a truck because he "smelled fumes" informed his co-worker of this fact. When the employee was disciplined for refusing to take the truck, he alleged that he was engaged in "concerted activity." What basis does he have for alleging this? [*NLRB v. PALCO,* 163 F.3d 662 (1st Cir. 1998).]

6. An employer was hiring employees after a strike. On employment applications, the employer asked potential employees whether they belonged to a union. Was the employer engaged in an unfair labor practice? [*Mathews Readymix, Inc. v. NLRB,* 165 F.3d 74 (DC. Cir. 1999).]

7. The employer engaged in the practice of photographing an employee engaged in picket-line activity. Is this illegal surveillance, even though the activity was "open and obvious," no action was taken against the employee, and the employer was preparing a defense regarding potential illegal secondary activity? [*Clock Electric, Inc. v. NLRB,* 162 F.3d 907 (6th Cir. 1998).]

8. What are the most important differences between public- and private-sector collective bargaining?

9. During contract negotiations, employer and union exchange information on the union's proposal for pay raises. The employer rejects the proposal. The employer is adamant and refuses to agree to the raises. The union alleges that this is an unfair labor practice in that the employer is not bargaining in good faith. Is it?

10. The union strikes the employer in an effort to receive higher wages. The employer brings in workers to replace the striking employees. Agreement is finally reached between the employer and employees. Must the employer dismiss the replacement workers?

End Notes

1. John Kell, "Harley-Davidson Wraps Up Labor Negotiations," *The Wall Street Journal*, 2/28/2011, http://online.wsj.com/article/SB1000142405274870461550457617285 16 67284040.html.

2. "Danny Glover and 11 Others Arrested During Union Protest in Maryland," *Access Hollywood*, 4/16/2010, http://www.accesshollywood.com/actor-danny-glover-11-others-arrested-in-md_article_31282.

3. Tony Dokoupil, "When Nurses Strike in New York," *Newsweek*, 5/3/2010, p.8.

4. Patrick McGeehan, "Deal Reached That Averts a Walkout by Doormen," *The New York Times*, 4/21/2010, http://community.nytimes.com/comments/www.nytimes.com/2010/04/21/nyregion/21strike.html; A.G. Sulzberger, "New Yorkers Brace for Doorman Strike," *The New York Times*, 4/18/2010, http://www.nytimes.com/2010/04/19/nyregion/19strike.html.

5. Howard Beck and Liz Robbins, "Pro Basketball; NBA and Players Union Agree to a Six-Year Deal," *The New York Times*, 6/22/2005, http://query.nytimes.com/gst/fullpage.html?res=9401EED9103EF931A15755C0A9639C8B63.

6. "Lockout over Salary Caps Shuts Down NHL," ESPN NHL, 2/16/2005, http://sports.espn.go.com/nhl/news/story?id=1992793.

7. Tresa Baldas, "Lawyers Unionize, Vote to Join the Teamsters," *The National Law Journal*, 4/8/2003, http://www.judicialaccountability.org/articles/lawyersunionize.htm.

8. *In re Debs*, 158 U.S. 564 (1895).

9. 245 U.S. 229 (1917).

10. *Loewe v. Lawlor* (a.k.a. the *Danbury Hatters* case), 208 U.S. 274 (1908).

11. 130 S. Ct. 2635 (2010).

12. http://www.jonesday.com/new_process_steel/.

13. 348 NLRB No. 37; Case 7-RC-22141, 9/29/2006.

14. H.R 1622 /S. 969 (110th Cong.).

15. *Department of Health and Human Services v. Federal Labor Relations Authority*, 920 F.2d 45 (DC. Cir 1990).

16. Daniel Kaplan, "NFL Labor Negotiations: The Issues," *Sports Business Journal*, 4/25/2011, http://aol.sportingnews.com/nfl/feed/2010-09/nfl-labor-talks/story/nfl-labor-negotiations-the-issues: http://sports.espn.go.com/nfl/news/story?id=6205936.

17. 499 U.S. 65 (1991).

18. Howard Fendrich, "NFLPA Decertifies As Talks Break Down," CBS Boston, 3/11/2011, http://boston.cbslocal.com/2011/03/11/report-nflpa-plans-to-decertify/.

19. Judy Battista, "Judge Grants Injunction to End N.F.L. Lockout Pending Appeal," *The New York Times*, 4/25/2011, http://www.nytimes.com/2011/04/26/sports/football/26nfl.html?_r=1&emc=na.

20. 2 F.3d 1162 (D.C.Cir. 1993).

21. "Lockout over Salary Cap Shuts Down NHL," Associated Press, ESPN-NHL, 2/16/2005, http://sports.espn.go.com/nhl/news/story?id=1992793; "NHL Lockout Chronology," *USA Today*, 7/13/2005, http://www.usatoday.com/sports/hockey/nhl/2005-07-13-lockout-chronology_x.htm.

22 829 F.2d 458 (3rd Cir. 1987).

23. Todd A. Heywood, "GOP Majority Eyes 'Right to Work' Legislation: Unions Call It an Assault on Workers' Rights," *The Michigan Messenger*, 2/22/2011, http://michiganmessenger.com/46725/gop-majority-eyes-right-to-work-legislation; Rolland Zullo, "What; Right to Work' Would Mean for Michigan," http://www.ilir.umich.edu/lsc/Publications/RightToWorkInMichigan.pdf; F. Vincent Vernuccio, "Michigan a Right to Work State?," *The American Spectator*, 7/16/2010, http://spectator.org/archives/2010/07/16/michigan-a-right-to-work-state.

24. 500 U.S. 501 (1991).

25. 127 S. Ct. 2372 (2007).

26. 129 S. Ct. 798 (2008).

27. 653 F.2d 1134 (7th Cir. 1981).

Cases

Commonwealth v. Hunt *45 Mass. (4 Metc.) 111 (Mass. 1842)*

A lower court found a group of seven shoemakers who belonged to a union guilty of conspiracy because they refused to work for an employer who hired a shoemaker who was not a member of their union. The Supreme Judicial Court of Massachusetts, in reversing the convictions, found not only that it was not an unlawful activity to unionize but that the object of unions may be "highly meritorious and public spirited."

Shaw, J.

***

Without attempting to review and reconcile all the cases, we are of the opinion, that as a general description, though perhaps not a precise and accurate definition, a conspiracy must be a combination of two or more persons, by some concerted action, to accomplish some criminal or unlawful purpose, or to accomplish some purpose, not in and of itself criminal or unlawful, by criminal or unlawful means. We use the terms criminal or unlawful, because it is manifest that many acts are unlawful, which are not punishable by indictment or other public prosecution; and yet there is no doubt, we think, that a combination by numbers to do them would be an unlawful conspiracy, and punishable by indictment.

Several rules upon the subject seem to be well established, to wit, that the unlawful agreement constitutes the gist of the offence, and therefore that it is not necessary to charge the execution of the unlawful agreement.

Another rule is a necessary consequence of the former, which is, that the crime is consummate and complete by the fact of unlawful combination, and, therefore, that if the execution of the unlawful purpose is averred, it is by way of aggravation, and proof of it is not necessary to conviction; and therefore the jury may find the conspiracy, and negative the execution, and it will be a good conviction.

And it follows, as another necessary legal consequence, from the same principle, that the indictment must—by averring the unlawful purpose of the conspiracy, or the unlawful means by which it is contemplated and agreed to accomplish a lawful purpose—set out an offense complete in itself; and that an illegal combination, imperfectly and insufficiently set out in the indictment, will not be aided by averments of acts done in pursuance of it.

From this view of the law respecting conspiracy, we think it an offence which especially demands the application of that wise and humane rule of the common law, that an indictment shall state, with as much certainty as the nature of the case will admit, the facts which constitute the crime intended to be charged. This is required, to enable the defendant to meet the charge and prepare for his defence, and, in case of acquittal or conviction, to show by the record the identity of the charge, so that he may not be indicted a second time for the same offence. It is also necessary, in order that a person, charged by the grand jury for one offence, may not be substantially convicted, on his trial, of another.

From these views of the rules of criminal pleading, it appears to us to follow, as a necessary legal conclusion, that when the criminality of a conspiracy consists in an unlawful agreement of two or more persons to compass or promote some criminal or illegal purpose, that purpose must be fully and clearly stated in the indictment; and if the criminality of the offence, which is intended to be charged, consists in the agreement to compass or promote some purpose, not of itself criminal or unlawful, by the use of fraud, force, falsehood, or other criminal or unlawful means, such intended use of fraud, force, falsehood, or other criminal or unlawful means, must be set out in the indictment.

We are here carefully to distinguish between the confederacy set forth in the indictment, and the confederacy or association contained in the constitution of the Boston Journeymen and Bootmakers' Society, as stated in the little printed book, which was admitted as evidence on the trial. Because, though it was thus admitted as evidence, it would not warrant a conviction for anything not stated in the indictment. It was proof, as far as it went to support the averments in the indictment. If it contained any criminal matter not set forth in the indictment, it is of no avail.

Now, it is to be considered, that the preamble and introductory matter in the indictment—such as unlawfully and deceitfully designing and intending unjustly to extort great sums, etc.—is mere recital, and not traversable, and therefore cannot aid an imperfect averment of the facts constituting the description of the offence. The same may be said of the concluding matter, which follows the averment, as to the great damage and oppression not only of their said masters, employing them in said art and occupation, but also of divers other workmen in the same art, mystery and occupation, to the evil example, &c. If the facts averred constitute the crime, these are properly stated as the legal inferences to be drawn from them. If they do not constitute the charge of such an offence, they cannot be aided by these alleged consequences.

Stripped then of these introductory recitals and alleged injurious consequences, and of the qualifying epithets attached to the facts, the averment is this: that the defendants and others formed themselves into a society, and agreed not to work for any person, who should employ any journeyman or other person, not a member of such society, after notice given to discharge such workman.

The manifest intent of the association is to induce all those engaged in the same occupation to become members of it. Such a purpose is not unlawful. It would give them a power which might be exerted for useful and honorable purposes, or for dangerous and pernicious ones. If the latter were the real and actual object, and susceptible of proof, it should have been specially charged. Such an association might be used to afford each other assistance in times of poverty, sickness and distress; or to raise their intellectual, moral, and social condition; or to make improvement in their art; or for other proper purposes. Or the association might be designed for purposes of oppression and injustice. But in order to charge all those, who become members of an association, with the guilt of a criminal conspiracy, it must be averred and proved that the actual, if not the avowed object of the association, was criminal. An association may be formed, the declared objects of which are innocent and laudable, and yet they may have secret articles, or an agreement communicated only to the members, by which they are banded together for purposes injurious to the peace of society or the rights of its members. Such would undoubtedly be a criminal conspiracy, on proof of the fact, however meritorious and praiseworthy the declared objects might be. The law is not to be hoodwinked by colorable pretenses. It looks at truth and reality, through whatever disguise it may assume. But to make such an association, ostensibly innocent, the subject of prosecution as a criminal conspiracy, the secret agreement, which makes it so, is to be averred and proved as the gist of the offence. But when an association is formed for purposes actually innocent, and afterwards its powers are abused by those who have the control and management of it, to purposes of oppression and injustice it will be criminal in those who thus misuse it, or give consent thereto, but not in the other members of the association.

Nor can we perceive that the objects of this association, whatever they may have been, were to be attained by criminal means. The means which they proposed to employ, as averred in this count, and which, as we are now to presume, were established by the proof, were, that they would not work for a person, who, after due notice, should employ a journeyman not a member of their society. Supposing the object of the association to be laudable and lawful, or at least not unlawful, are these means criminal? The case supposes that these persons are not bound by contract, but free to work for whom they please, or not to work, if they so prefer. On this state of things, we cannot perceive, that it is criminal for men to agree together to exercise their own acknowledged rights, in such a manner as best to subserve their own interests.

Suppose a baker in a small village had the exclusive custom of his neighborhood, and was making large profits by the sale of his bread. Supposing a number of those neighbors, believing the price of his bread too high, should propose to him to reduce his prices, or if he did not, that they would introduce another baker; and on his refusal, such other baker should, under their encouragement, set up a rival establishment, and sell his bread at lower prices; the effect would be to diminish the profit of the former baker, and to the same extent to impoverish him. And it might be said and proved, that the purpose of

the associates was to diminish his profits, and thus impoverish him, though the ultimate and laudable object of the combination was to reduce the cost of bread to themselves and their neighbors. The same thing may be said of all competition in every branch of trade and industry; and yet it is through that competition, that the best interests of trade and industry are promoted. It is scarcely necessary to allude to the familiar instances of opposition lines of conveyance, rival hotels, and the thousand other instances, where each strives to gain custom to himself, by which he may lessen the price of commodities, and thereby diminish the profits of others.

We think, therefore, that associations may be entered into, the object of which is to adopt measures that may have a tendency to impoverish another, that is, to diminish his gains and profits, and yet so far from being criminal or unlawful, the object may be highly meritorious and public spirited. The legality of such an association will therefore depend upon the means to be used for its accomplishment. If it is to be carried into effect by fair or honorable and lawful means, it is, to say the least, innocent; if by falsehood or force, it may be stamped out with the character of conspiracy. REVERSED.

Case Questions

1. Why do you think it was necessary to dissolve the relationship between criminal conspiracy and the labor movement? What was the relationship given by the court between criminal acts and employees' rights to control their environment at work?

2. Why do you think the court found that there was some good in organizing to affect the employer's policies? Explain.

3. Do you agree with the court's analysis in this case? Explain.

Gimrock Construction, Inc. and International Union of Operating Engineers, Local 487   *356 NLRB No. 83 (January 28, 2011)*

After repeatedly rejecting the union's request to engage in negotiations to create its first collective bargaining agreement, the board ordered the employer to engage in collective bargaining. The employer again refused, and the board eventually issued this order for the employer to engage in very specific activity in order to bargain collectively in good faith.

By Chairman Liebman
and Members Pearce and Hayes

***

For context, pursuant to a Stipulated Election Agreement, the International Union of Operating Engineers, Local 487, AFL-CIO (the Union) won an election on March 3, 1995, and was certified on March 20, 1995, as the bargaining representative of Respondent's equipment operators, oiler/drivers, and equipment mechanics employed in Miami-Dade and Monroe counties, Florida (the two counties). The Respondent's bargaining obligation arose from the Board's June 30, 2005 decision, finding that the Respondent violated Section 8(a)(5) and (1) of the Act by refusing—since October 27, 1999—to meet and bargain with the Union and provide it with requested relevant information. The board's order was enforced by the 11th Circuit on December 27, 2006. As explained in the judge's decision, the Respondent thereafter failed to respond to numerous requests to meet and bargain with the Union and to furnish it with the requested information.

In view of the Respondent's continuing refusal—over a period of years—to comply with the Board's bargaining order, the institution of a bargaining schedule and the submission of progress reports are necessary to ensure that (and gauge whether) the Respondent meaningfully complies with its bargaining obligations as set forth under the terms of the court-enforced Order. Because the General Counsel specifically sought these requirements in the compliance specification, we reject the Respondent's argument that it was denied due process.*

Further, as of September 2007, the Respondent had not posted the required notices to employees, and its

*Following the Court's enforcement of the Board's Orders in December 2006, the Board's Regional Office advised the Respondent of its remedial obligations, including the obligation to meet and bargain with the Union. Thereafter, and continuing through March 2008, the Union repeatedly requested bargaining with the Respondent pursuant to the terms of the court-enforced Order, sending five letters to the Respondent requesting that it provide dates to meet and bargain. The Union also requested the Respondent to furnish it with the requested information required under the terms of the Board's Order. The Respondent did not respond to any of these requests.

failure to post was one of the subjects of a proceeding in the United States District Court for the Southern District of Florida, wherein the Board sought to enforce certain investigative subpoenas requiring the Respondent to (a) demonstrate that it had posted the required notices, and (b) furnish requested information necessary to calculate the amount of back pay due under the terms of the Order in 344 NLRB 1033 (2005). By Order dated September 13, 2007, the District Court directed the Respondent to comply with the investigative subpoenas, and thereafter the Respondent posted the notices and provided certain payroll records to the Board's Regional Office.

Order

The National Labor Relations Board adopts the recommended Supplemental Order of the administrative law judge and orders that the Respondent, Gimrock Construction, Inc., Hialeah Gardens, Florida, its officers, agents, successors, and assigns, shall take the action set forth in the Order, including the payment to backpay claimants of the amounts set forth below, plus interest accrued to the date of payment minus tax and withholdings by Federal and State laws.

Murray R. Chinners $74,583.12
Alfred K. Duey $125,057.47
Joseph G. MacNeil $10,367.77
Joseph T. Robinson $580.83
Barney Sims $92,243.40
James K. Wilkerson $37,208.66
James L. Wolf $14,311.31
TOTAL $354,352.56

IT IS HEREBY ORDERED that Respondent Gimrock Construction, within 21 days of the Board's issuance of its Supplemental Decision in this matter, bargain upon request with the Union; meet and bargain for a minimum of 16 hours per week until an agreement is reached, the parties agree to a hiatus in bargaining, or they reach a lawful impasse; and prepare written bargaining progress reports every 30 days, submitting them to the Regional Director and serving copies on the Union to provide it with an opportunity to reply. The Administrative Law Judge's order is AFFIRMED.

Case Questions

1. Do you think the court made the right decision in this case?

2. Given that there is a statutory duty to bargain in good faith, why do you think management chose to do what it did?

3. Given how strict the final order to bargain was on the employer, does the employer's strategy make sense to you?

Case 3

Columbia Portland Cement Co. v. National Labor Relations Board *979 F.2d 460 (6th Cir. 1992)*

The employer engaged in unfair labor practices that eventually led employees to engage in an unfair labor practice strike. After the union gave an unconditional request for reinstatement to the employer, the employer refused to reinstate them, and also unilaterally gave a wage increase without consulting the union. The court found both to be unfair labor practices by the employer.

Contie, J.

***

Petitioner, Columbia Portland Cement Company (the "Company"), operates a limestone shale quarry and cement production facility in Zanesville, Ohio. Since at least September 1, 1984, Local Lodge D24 of the Cement, Lime, Gypsum & Allied Workers Division of the International Brotherhood of Boilermakers, Iron Shipbuilders, Blacksmiths, Forgers and Helpers, AFL-CIO (the "Union"), has represented the Company's employees. The most recent collective-bargaining contract between the Union and the Company's predecessor expired on May 1, 1984, but the predecessor company and the Union agreed to extend that contract during negotiations for a new contract.

The Company purchased the facility from the predecessor on August 28, 1984. The Company notified the Union on August 29, 1984, that it intended to terminate the extended contract and desired to negotiate a new one. The parties failed to reach agreement on a new contract, however, and on October 28, 1984, the Company unilaterally implemented the last offer it had made. On May 8, 1985, the employees went out on strike.

By letter dated April 29, 1987, the Union made an offer to return to work on behalf of the striking employees. The letter stated that the employees "unconditionally offer to return to work immediately." In response, the Company sent a letter dated May 7, 1987, informing the Union that, "with regard to [the] unconditional offer to return to

work," the Company would not reinstate the striking employees. The Company contended that some of the employees had been lawfully terminated, and that the remainder were permanently replaced economic strikers who would be kept on a list for future vacancies.

On April 20, 1988, the Company offered reinstatement, without back pay, to 62 of the striking employees; 33 eventually returned to work.

"A strike which is caused in whole or in part by an employer's unfair labor practices *is* an unfair labor practice strike." Employees who go out on strike in response to an employer's unfair labor practices may not be permanently replaced by other employees. Unfair labor practice strikers are entitled to immediate reinstatement by the employer upon their unconditional offer to return to work. Refusing to reinstate striking employees after their unconditional offer to return to work violates section 8(a)(3) and (1) of the Act.

The Company granted employees a wage increase of 20 cents per hour; replaced the retirement plan with a 401(k) plan; and changed the grievance procedure to bypass the union and deal directly with the grievant. These actions all violate the employer's duty to bargain with the employees' exclusive bargaining agent in contravention of section 8(a)(5) and (1). Accordingly, the Board's decision must be AFFIRMED.

Case Questions

1. Why do you think the employer refused to rehire the strikers after they gave an unconditional promise to return?

2. Do you think it is fair that employees striking because of an unfair labor practice are entitled to reinstatement? Explain.

3. Do you think the new owner of the business took this hard line in dealing with the union in order to try to initially establish its dominance over the union? Explain.

Case 4

Electromation v. National Labor Relations Board
35 F.3d 1148 (7th Cir. 1993)

A nonunion company negotiated with its workers to resolve labor issues through employee participation or employee–management focus groups rather than a union. The court held that these committees constituted labor organizations and were dominated by the employer, thus constituting an unfair labor practice.

Will, J.

***

At the time of the events which gave rise to this suit, Electromation's approximately 200 employees, most of whom were women, were not represented by any labor organization. To minimize the financial losses it was experiencing at the time, the company in late 1988 decided to cut expenses by revising its employee attendance policy and replacing the 1989 scheduled wage increases with lump sum payments based on the length of each employee's service at the company.

In January 1989, the company received a handwritten request signed by 68 employees expressing their dissatisfaction with and requesting reconsideration of the revised attendance bonus/wage policy. After meeting with the company's supervisors, the company President, John Howard, decided to meet directly with employees to discuss their concerns. Accordingly, on January 11, 1989, the company met with eight employees—three randomly selected high-seniority employees, three randomly selected low-seniority employees, and two additional employees who had requested that they be included—to discuss a number of matters, including wages, bonuses, incentive pay, tardiness, attendance programs, and bereavement and sick leave policy, all normal collective bargaining issues.

Following this meeting, Howard met again with the supervisors and concluded that management had "possibly made a mistake in judgment in December in deciding what we ought to do" . . . [and] "that the better course of action would be to involve the employees in coming up with solutions to these issues." The company determined that "action committees" would be an appropriate way to involve employees in the process. Accordingly, on January 18, 1989, the company met again with the same eight employees and proposed the creation of action committees to "meet and try to come up with ways to resolve these problems; and that if they came up with solutions that we believed were within budget concerns and they generally felt would be acceptable to the employees, that we would implement these suggestions or proposals." At the employees' suggestion, Howard agreed that, rather than having a random selection of employee committee members, sign-up sheets for each action committee would be posted.

On the next day, the company posted a memorandum to all employees announcing the formation of the following five action committees: (1) Absenteeism/Infractions; (2) No Smoking Policy; (3) Communication Network; (4) Pay Progression for Premium Positions;

and (5) Attendance Bonus Program. Sign-up sheets were also posted at this time.

On February 13, 1989, the International Brotherhood of Teamsters, Local Union No. 1049 (the "union") demanded recognition from the company. Until then, the company was unaware that any organizing efforts had occurred at the plant. In late February, Howard informed Employee Benefits Manager Loretta Dickey of the union's demand for recognition. Upon the advice of counsel, Dickey announced at the next meeting of each committee that, due to the union demand, the company could no longer participate in the committees, but that the employee members could continue to meet if they so desired.

Finally, on March 15, 1989, Howard formally announced to the employees that "due to the union's campaign, the Company would be unable to participate in the [committee] meetings and could not continue to work with the committees until after the [union] election." The union election took place on March 31, 1989; the employees voted 95 to 82 against union representation. On April 24, 1989, a regional director of the National Labor Relations Board (Board) issued a complaint alleging that Electromation had violated the Act by refusing to meet.

Section 2(5) of the Act defines a labor organization as:

> any organization of any kind, or any agency or employee representation committee or plan, in which employees participate and which exists for the purpose, in whole or in part, of dealing with employers concerning grievances, labor disputes, wages, rates of pay, hours of employment, or conditions of work.

Under this statutory definition, the action committees would constitute labor organizations if: (1) the Electromation employees participated in the committees; (2) the committees existed, at least in part, for the purpose of "dealing with" the employer; and (3) these dealings concerned "grievances, labor disputes, wages, rates of pay, hours of employment, or conditions of work."

With respect to the first factor, there is no question that the Electromation employees participated in the action committees. Turning to the second factor, which is the most seriously contested on appeal, the Board found that the activities of the action committees constituted "dealing with" the employer. We agree with the Board that the action committees can be differentiated only in the specific subject matter with which each dealt. Each committee had an identical relationship to the company:

the purpose, structure, and administration of each committee was essentially the same. We note, in addition, that even if the committees are considered individually, there exists substantial evidence that each was formed and existed for the purpose of "dealing with" the company. It is in fact the shared similarities among the committee structures which compels unitary treatment of them for the purposes of the issues raised in this appeal.

Given the Supreme Court's holding that "dealing with" includes conduct much broader than collective bargaining, the Board did not err in determining that the Electromation action committees constituted labor organizations within the meaning of Sections 2(5) and 8(a)(2) of the Act.

Finally, with respect to the third factor, the subject matter of that dealing—for example, the treatment of employee absenteeism and employee bonuses—obviously concerned conditions of employment. The purpose of the action committees was not limited to the improvement of company efficiency or product quality, but rather that they were designed to function and in fact functioned in an essentially representative capacity. Accordingly, given the statute's traditionally broad construction, there is substantial evidence to support the Board's finding that the action committees constituted labor organizations.

Section 8(a)(2) declares that it shall be an unfair labor practice for an employer: to dominate or interfere with the formation or administration of any labor organization or contribute financial or other support to it: Provided, that subject to rules and regulations made and published by the Board pursuant to Section 6, an employer shall not be prohibited from permitting employees to confer with him during working hours without loss of time or pay. Section 8(a)(1) provides that it shall be an unfair labor practice for an employer: to interfere with, restrain or coerce employees in the exercise of the rights guaranteed in section 157 of this title. Section 7 in turn provides that: [e]mployees shall have the right to self-organization, to form, to join, or assist labor organizations, to bargain collectively through representatives of their own choosing, and to engage in other concerted activities for the purpose of collective bargaining or other mutual aid or protection, and shall also have the right to refrain from any and all such activities except to the extent that such right may be affected by an agreement requiring membership in a labor organization as a condition of employment as authorized in section 158(a)(3) of this title.

Electromation argues that the Board's ruling in this case implies that an employer violates Section 8(a)(2) whenever it proposes a structure whereby the employees and employer "cooperate," or meet together to discuss topics of mutual concern. The company thus asserts that the Board may find a violation of Section 8(a)(2) only where it finds that the employer has actually undermined the free and independent choice of the employees.

The company played a pivotal role in establishing both the framework and the agenda for the action committees. Electromation unilaterally selected the size, structure, and procedural functioning of the committees; it decided the number of committees and the topic(s) to be addressed by each. The company unilaterally drafted the action committees' purposes and goal statements, which identified from the start the focus of each committee's work. Also, despite the fact that the employees were seriously concerned about the lack of a wage increase, no action committee was designated to consider this specific issue. In this way, Electromation actually controlled which issues received attention by the committees and which did not. Although the company acceded to the employees' request that volunteers form the committees, it unilaterally determined how many could serve on each committee, decided that an employee could serve on only one committee at a time, and determined which committee certain employees would serve on, thus exercising significant control over the employees' participation and voice at the committee meetings. Also, although it never became a significant issue because so few employees signed up for the committees, the initial sign up sheets indicated that the employer would decide which six employees would be chosen as committee members where more than six expressed interest in a particular committee. Ultimately, the company limited membership to five and determined the five to serve. Also, the company designated management representatives to serve on the committees.

Employee Benefits Manager Dickey was assigned to coordinate and serve on all committees. In the case of the Attendance Bonus Program Committee, the management representative—Controller Mazur—reviewed employee proposals, determined whether they were economically feasible, and further decided whether they would be presented to higher management. This role of the management committee members effectively put the employer on both sides of the bargaining table, an avowed proscription of the Act.

Finally, the company paid the employees for their time spent on committee activities, provided meeting space, and furnished all necessary supplies for the committees' activities. While such financial support is clearly not a violation of Section 8(a)(2) by itself, in the totality of the circumstances in this case such support may reasonably be characterized to be in furtherance of the company's domination of the action committees. We therefore conclude that there is substantial evidence to support the Board's finding of unlawful employer domination and interference in violation of Section 8(a)(2) and (1). NLRB ORDER ENFORCED.

Case Questions

1. Did the employer seem to intentionally violate the law? Explain.

2. What do you think would motivate an employer to prefer to deal directly with an employee participation group rather than a union?

3. Do you think it's harmful to put the employer on "both sides of the bargaining table"? Explain the pros and cons.

Chapter 16

Selected Employment Benefits and Protections

Learning Objectives

By the time you finish studying this chapter, you should be able to:

LO1 List the matters regulated by the Fair Labor Standards Act.

LO2 Discuss the requirements of the minimum wage laws and to whom they apply.

LO3 Explain the Family Medical Leave Act, including to whom it applies and under what circumstances.

LO4 Explain contributory negligence, assumption of risk, and the fellow servant rule, and their roles in the regulation of safety in the workplace, and determine how OSHA impacted this regulatory environment.

LO5 Set forth what OSHA requires of employers to create a safer workplace and how it is enforced.

LO6 Describe the reporting responsibilities of employers under the OSHA Act.

LO7 Explain the purposes of ERISA and identify who and what type of entities are covered.

LO8 Describe the minimum ERISA standards for employee benefit plans.

Opening Scenarios

SCENARIO 1

1 Drake, a new MBA graduate, is hired into a management position at $125,000 per year.
Scenario It is Drake's first job as a professional. After several months, Drake finds he is leaving work later and later. Drake begins to resent that he works late, putting in more and more hours, and is not receiving any more than the originally agreed-upon salary. He is contemplating legal action against his employer for violation of the Fair Labor Standards Act. Will it be worth his while to pursue this?

SCENARIO 2

2 Carly and Carl live with their two children and Carl's mom, who is in the advanced stages of
Scenario Alzheimer's. Carly works in pharmaceutical sales and has a lot of job flexibility. Carl is the chief financial officer for an investment firm and his job is very demanding. Carl's mom takes a turn for the worse and will need extra care for a few weeks. Carly knows she has the flexibility and time so she goes to her supervisor and requests time off under the Family and Medical Leave Act to take care of her ailing mother-in-law. Will it be granted?

SCENARIO 3

3 Singhie, an employee of Carterez, a contractor, is hospitalized due to the large number
Scenario of cement particles she inhaled while Bartow, a subcontractor, was laying the cement foundation for a structure. Carterez is cited by OSHA for violation of the protective gear requirements. Who is liable, Carterez, the contractor, or Bartow, the subcontractor?

Introduction

Beyond those laws that we have discussed in previous chapters, there are several other laws that do not contain anti-discrimination provisions but nevertheless significantly impact the workplace; this chapter will introduce you to some of them. These include the Fair Labor Standards Act of 1938 (FLSA), the Family and Medical Leave Act of 1993 (FMLA), the Occupational Safety and Health Act of 1970 (OSHA), and the Employee Retirement Income Security Act of 1974 (ERISA). Each is an important aspect of the workplace landscape.

Fair Labor Standards Act of 1938

Statutory Basis

Every employer shall pay to each of his employees who in any workweek is engaged in commerce or in the production of goods for commerce, or is employed in an enterprise engaged in commerce or in the production of goods for commerce, wages at the following rates: . . . not less than $6.55 an hour beginning July 24, 2008; and $7.25 per hour effective July 24, 2009. [Sec. 6(a), Fair Labor Standards Act of 1938, as amended, 29 U.S.C. § 201 et seq.]

. . . No employer shall employ any of his employees for a workweek longer than forty hours unless such employee receives compensation for his employment in excess of the hours above specified at a rate not less than one and one-half times the regular rate at which he is employed. [Sec. 7(a)(1), Fair Labor Standards Act of 1938, as amended, 29 U.S.C. § 201 et seq.]

747

Introduction: Show Me the Money!

Face it. If we were all rich and didn't have to work, many of us would not do so. Since we do have to work, we want to make sure that we get all that is coming to us. We don't want to have to work for whatever meager wages our employer wants to pay us, compete with 10-year-olds for our job, or work whatever number of hours our employer decides he or she wants us to work without extra pay. Under the broad constitutional powers that Congress has to regulate interstate commerce, in 1938 it passed a law to regulate pay and hours worked. The law, now amended several times, is called the Fair Labor Standards Act (FLSA). The act set standards for the minimum age for workers, **minimum wages** they can make, and the rate at which they must be paid if they work over a certain amount of time during a workweek. Much like the Equal Pay Act and Title VII, the act also prohibits pay differentials based solely on gender.

The FLSA is administered by the U.S. Department of Labor's Wage and Hour Division, which has authority to investigate, gather information, issue regulations, and enforce FLSA provisions. States also have wage and hour provisions administered by comparable state agencies. Violations, if willful, are crimes punishable by fines of up to $10,000, with second convictions resulting in possible imprisonment. Child labor violations carry civil penalties. The FLSA contains antiretaliation provisions to protect employees who use the FLSA, such as filing a complaint or participating in an FLSA proceeding.[1]

If an employer violates the FLSA by underpaying employees, the employees may recover back wages. The federal government recovered more than $176 million in back wages in fiscal year 2010 alone. The Wage and Hour Division reported that since FY 2001, it has recouped more than $1.4 billion for more than 2 million workers.[2] In December of 2008, Walmart paid $54.25 million to settle a lawsuit alleging Walmart cut Walmart and Sam's Club employees' break times short and worked employees while off the clock without paying them. The decision involves about 100,000 current and former hourly employees in Minnesota over the past decade.[3] The fines could have been much higher since Minnesota law allows a $1,000 fine to be imposed for each violation and the state district judge found that Walmart had violated the law more than 2 million times. Walmart has faced similar suits in at least 35 states, but rarely settles as it did this time.

The Obama administration is quite aggressive in making sure wage and hour laws are complied with and employees get what they have bargained for. It is expected that enforcement will become even more vigorous, with additional funding for agencies to handle the increased enforcement.[4] One of the issues that has seen growing interest has been unpaid student internships. The U.S. Department of Labor has said it is cracking down on firms that do not properly pay interns and increasing their education in the area to make employers aware of the law.[5] The Department of Labor issued new guidance to employers in 2010. (See Exhibit 16.1, "Fact Sheet on Internships under the Fair Labor Standards Act.")

According to the National Association of Colleges and Employers the number of graduating students who have held internships rose from 9 percent in 1992 to 83 percent in 2008,[6] so it is an area of increasing concern. Since most students

LO1

minimum wages
The least amount a covered employee must be paid in hourly wages.

Exhibit 16.1 *Factsheet on Internships under the Fair Labor Standards Act*

(April 2010) Fact Sheet #71: Internship Programs under the Fair Labor Standards Act

This fact sheet provides general information to help determine whether interns must be paid the minimum wage and overtime under the Fair Labor Standards Act for the services that they provide to "for-profit" private sector employers.

BACKGROUND

The Fair Labor Standards Act (FLSA) defines the term *employ* very broadly as including to "suffer or permit to work." Covered and nonexempt individuals who are "suffered or permitted" to work must be compensated under the law for the services they perform for an employer. Internships in the "for-profit" private sector will most often be viewed as employment, unless the test described below relating to trainees is met. Interns in the for-profit private sector who qualify as employees rather than trainees typically must be paid at least the minimum wage and overtime compensation for hours worked over forty in a workweek.*

THE TEST FOR UNPAID INTERNS

There are some circumstances under which individuals who participate in for-profit private sector internships or training programs may do so without compensation. The Supreme Court has held that the term *suffer or permit to work* cannot be interpreted so as to make a person whose work serves only his or her own interest an employee of another who provides aid or instruction. This may apply to interns who receive training for their own educational benefit if the training meets certain criteria. The determination of whether an internship or training program meets this exclusion depends upon all of the facts and circumstances of each such program.

The following six criteria must be applied when making this determination:

The internship, even though it includes actual operation of the facilities of the employer, is similar to training which would be given in an educational environment;

The internship experience is for the benefit of the intern;

The intern does not displace regular employees, but works under close supervision of existing staff;

The employer that provides the training derives no immediate advantage from the activities of the intern; and on occasion its operations may actually be impeded;

The intern is not necessarily entitled to a job at the conclusion of the internship;

The employer and the intern understand that the intern is not entitled to wages for the time spent in the internship.

If all of the factors listed above are met, an employment relationship does not exist under the FLSA, and the Act's minimum wage and overtime provisions do not apply to the intern. This exclusion from the definition of employment is necessarily quite narrow because the FLSA's definition of "employ" is very broad. Some of the most commonly discussed factors for for-profit private sector internship programs are considered below.

*The FLSA makes a special exception under certain circumstances for individuals who volunteer to perform services for a state or local government agency and for individuals who volunteer for humanitarian purposes for private non-profit food banks. WHD also recognizes an exception for individuals who volunteer their time, freely and without anticipation of compensation for religious, charitable, civic, or humanitarian purposes to non-profit organizations. Unpaid internships in the public sector and for non-profit charitable organizations, where the intern volunteers without expectation of compensation, are generally permissible. WHD is reviewing the need for additional guidance on internships in the public and non-profit sectors.

continued

Exhibit 16.1   *continued*

SIMILAR TO AN EDUCATION ENVIRONMENT AND THE PRIMARY BENEFICIARY OF THE ACTIVITY

In general, the more an internship program is structured around a classroom or academic experience as opposed to the employer's actual operations, the more likely the internship will be viewed as an extension of the individual's educational experience (this often occurs where a college or university exercises oversight over the internship program and provides educational credit). The more the internship provides the individual with skills that can be used in multiple employment settings, as opposed to skills particular to one employer's operation, the more likely the intern would be viewed as receiving training. Under these circumstances the intern does not perform the routine work of the business on a regular and recurring basis, and the business is not dependent upon the work of the intern. On the other hand, if the interns are engaged in the operations of the employer or are performing productive work (for example, filing, performing other clerical work, or assisting customers), then the fact that they may be receiving some benefits in the form of a new skill or improved work habits will not exclude them from the FLSA's minimum wage and overtime requirements because the employer benefits from the interns' work.

DISPLACEMENT AND SUPERVISION ISSUES

If an employer uses interns as substitutes for regular workers or to augment its existing workforce during specific time periods, these interns should be paid at least the minimum wage and overtime compensation for hours worked over forty in a workweek. If the employer would have hired additional employees or required existing staff to work additional hours had the interns not performed the work, then the interns will be viewed as employees and entitled compensation under the FLSA. Conversely, if the employer is providing job shadowing opportunities that allow an intern to learn certain functions under the close and constant supervision of regular employees, but the intern performs no or minimal work, the activity is more likely to be viewed as a bona fide education experience. On the other hand, if the intern receives the same level of supervision as the employer's regular workforce, this would suggest an employment relationship, rather than training.

JOB ENTITLEMENT

The internship should be of a fixed duration, established prior to the outset of the internship. Further, unpaid internships generally should not be used by the employer as a trial period for individuals seeking employment at the conclusion of the internship period. If an intern is placed with the employer for a trial period with the expectation that he or she will then be hired on a permanent basis, that individual generally would be considered an employee under the FLSA.

WHERE TO OBTAIN ADDITIONAL INFORMATION

This publication is for general information and is not to be considered in the same light as official statements of position contained in the regulations.

For additional information, visit our Wage and Hour Division Website: http://www.wagehour.dol.gov and/or call our toll-free information and helpline, available 8 a.m. to 5 p.m. in your time zone, 1-866-4USWAGE (1-866-487-9243).

Source: U.S. Department of Labor, http://www.dol.gov/whd/regs/compliance/whdfs71.htm.

want the experience, connections, and job possibilities that come from holding an internship, they are less likely to complain if they are unpaid or are used as a temporary employee, thus making them likely targets for exploitation.

Keep in mind that we discussed in the gender chapter that the FLSA was amended by the Patient Protection and Affordable Care Act to require that an employer provide reasonable unpaid breaks for nursing mothers to express milk for up to a year from the birth of their child. If the expressing is done during a regular paid break, the break is paid time. Unless the employer has less than 50 employees and it would cause an undue hardship to do so, the employer must also provide a private place other than a restroom in which the new mother can express her milk. The law does not preempt state laws requiring that such breaks be paid.

Another area of growing concern has been that of payment of employees' time for "donning and doffing" protective gear—that is, time spent before and after work putting on and taking off protective covering or equipment that is necessary for work. Generally, if the clothing and equipment are necessary for work, the time must be paid. It can, however, be negotiated otherwise in a collective bargaining agreement if employees wish to trade off something else with the employer, for instance, a higher hourly wage.

In 2010, the Fifth Circuit in *Allen v. McWane, Inc*,[7] joining the Third and Eleventh Circuits, held that if an employer has a custom and practice of not paying for time spent donning and doffing protective equipment and the employees never discussed it during collective bargaining negotiations, it is not a basis for claims of violation under the FLSA. In the court's view, "as long as there was a company policy of non-compensation for time spent changing for a prolonged period of time—allowing the court to infer that the union had knowledge of and acquiesced to the employer's policy—and a CBA existed, the parties need not have explicitly discussed such compensation when negotiating the CBA. McWane 'only need prove that the parties had a 'custom or practice' of non-compensation under the agreement.'"

Covered Employees

Since the FLSA was enacted pursuant to the powers of Congress to regulate interstate commerce, that requirement forms, in part, a basis for determining coverage. Actually, there are two types of coverage in the FLSA: individual coverage and enterprise coverage. If the individual employee's job involves interstate commerce directly, such as an over-the-road truck driver traveling from state to state, or moving or preparing goods for interstate commerce, including phoning and using the mail, then the individual is covered. For enterprise coverage, all employees of a business will be covered if the business is engaged in interstate commerce or in producing goods for interstate commerce and meets a minimum gross annual income requirement of $500,000. The law applies to both part-time and full-time employees. Federal, state, and local employees are also covered by the law, though there are some specific provisions for certain state and local employees.

If an employee works for certain types of businesses, the $500,000 minimum does not apply. That is, employees will be covered even if their employer does not make at least $500,000 per year. These organizations include hospitals and other institutions primarily engaged in the care of the sick, aged, mentally ill, or disabled who reside on the premises; schools for children who are mentally or physically disabled or gifted; preschools, elementary, and secondary schools and institutions of higher education; and federal, state, and local government agencies. The law also covers domestic service workers such as day workers, housekeepers, chauffeurs, cooks, valets, or full-time babysitters (defined as other than those babysitting on a casual basis; typically requiring at least 20 hours per week). State laws also may apply, and when both cover a situation, the law setting the higher standards must be the one used.

The FLSA contains exemptions from these rules for several groups, which vary depending on the area of the FLSA being addressed. As can be seen from *Reich v. Circle C Investment, Inc.,* given at the end of the chapter, even the threshold decision as to who is covered by the act is not always an easy one. In *Reich* the court was faced with deciding whether topless dancers who only received tips were, in fact, employees for purposes of the Fair Labor Standards Act provisions on minimum wages, overtime, and record-keeping requirements.

Minimum Wages

The minimum wage law was passed in 1938, nine years after the Wall Street crash of 1929, in hopes that it would avoid another Depression. The advocates of the law, primarily unions and other workers, believed that a minimum wage would provide everyone with sufficient money on which to live without causing economic harm to business owners.

LO2

Under the FLSA, employers are required to pay covered employees a certain minimum hourly wage. On July 24, 2007, pursuant to the Fair Minimum Wage Act signed by President George W. Bush on May 25, 2007, the minimum wage rose from $5.15 per hour, where it had been since September 1, 1997, to $5.85 per hour. On July 24, 2008, the minimum wage increased to $6.55, and on July 24, 2009, it increased to $7.25. In 1938, when the FLSA was enacted, it was 25 cents per hour. State wage laws may have higher minimums than the federal law. (See Exhibit 16.2, "State Minimum Wages.")

Wage rates may be lower if, in accordance with appropriate regulations, an industry wage order makes them so in Puerto Rico, the Virgin Islands, or American Samoa. The Fair Minimum Wage Act of 2007 provided for a 50-cent-per-hour industry-based increase in wages for American Samoa until the wage rate was generally the same as for the United States. If the covered employee is an apprentice, learner, or disabled worker, then, under certain circumstances, she or he may receive less than the minimum wage if the employer obtains a certificate issued by the Department of Labor's wage and hour administrator.

Tipped employees (defined in the regulations as those who regularly receive more than $30 a month in tips) may be paid direct wages of $2.13 per hour, but the employer must make up the difference if the tips do not equal the usual minimum wage.[8] Employees may be paid on a piece-rate rather than an hourly rate as long as they receive the equivalent of the minimum wage. (See Exhibits 16.3, "Exemptions from Both Minimum Wage and Overtime Pay," and 16.4, "Other FLSA Exemptions," for wage and overtime exemptions.) In *Kilgore v. Outback Steakhouse of Florida, Inc.,*[9] the court wrestled with the issue of whether it was permissible for an employer to require servers who receive tips to pool their tips and split them with other employees who do not receive tips. The court held that this was permissible for the employer to do. In 2008, a San Francisco superior

Exhibit 16.2 *State Minimum Wages*

Consolidated State Minimum Wage (MW) Update Table (Effective Date: 01/01/2011)

Federal MW	Equals Federal MW of $7.25	< Federal MW	No MW Required
AK: 7.75	DE	AR: 6.25	AL
AZ: 7.35	FL	GA: 5.15	LA
CA: 8.00	HI	MN: 6.15	MS
CO: 7.36	IA	WY: 5.15	SC
CT: 8.25	ID		TN
DC: 8.25	IN	**4 States**	
IL: 8.25	KS		**5 States**
MA: 8.00	KY		
ME: 7.50	MD		
MI: 7.40	MO		
MT: 7.35	NE		
NV: 8.25	NH		
NM: 7.50	NJ		
OH: 7.40	NY		
OR: 8.50	NC		
RI: 7.40	ND		
VT: 8.15	OK		
WA: 8.67	PA		
	SD		
17 States + DC	TX		
	UT		
	VA		
	WV		
	WI		
	24 states		

The state minimum wage rate requirements, or lack thereof, are controlled by legislative activities within the individual states. Federal minimum wage law supersedes state minimum wage laws where the federal minimum wage is greater than the state minimum wage. In those states where the state minimum wage is greater than the federal minimum wage, the state minimum wage prevails.

There are 4 states than have a minimum wage set lower than the federal minimum wage. There are 17 states (plus DC) with minimum wage rates set higher than the federal minimum wage. There are 24 states that have a minimum wage requirement that is the same as the federal minimum wage requirement. The remaining 5 states do not have an established minimum wage requirement.

The State of Washington has the highest minimum wage at $8.67/hour. The states of Georgia and Wyoming have the lowest minimum wage ($5.15) of the 45 states that have a minimum wage requirement.

Note: There are 10 states (AZ, CO, FL, MO, MT, NV, OH, OR, VT, and WA) that have minimum wages that are linked to a consumer price index. As a result of this linkage, the minimum wages in these states are normally increased each year, generally around January 1. On January 1, 2011, there were 7 states that increased their respective minimum wages. The three exceptions were Florida, Missouri and Nevada.

Source: Division of Communications, Wage and Hour Division, U.S. Department of Labor http://www.dol.gov/whd/minwage/america.htm.

Exhibit 16.3 *Exemptions from Both Minimum Wage and Overtime Pay*

- Executive, administrative, and professional employees (including teachers and academic administrative personnel in elementary and secondary schools), outside sales employees, and employees in certain computer-related occupations (as defined in Department of Labor regulations).
- Employees of certain seasonal amusement or recreational establishments, employees of certain small newspapers, seamen employed on foreign vessels, employees engaged in fishing operations, and employees engaged in newspaper delivery.
- Farm workers employed by anyone who used no more than 500 "man-days" of farm labor in any calendar quarter of the preceding calendar year.
- Casual babysitters and persons employed as companions to the elderly or infirm.

Source: http://www.dol.gov/esa/whd.

---

court held that Starbucks would have to pay $100 million ($86 million plus interest) to its 120,000 baristas (coffee servers) statewide because it had been Starbucks' policy to allow shift supervisors to share the tips received by the baristas, resulting in an average hourly wage of $1.71 for the baristas.[10] The California Court of Appeal, however, reversed the decision, saying that no law or court ruling prevents a service employee from sharing a collective tip.[11]

As mentioned, the FLSA has exemptions, so not everyone is covered under the statute. However some states cover FLSA-exempted employees under their state laws.

The following are the primary exemptions from both the wage and the overtime provisions of the FLSA. Note that under the FLSA, some employees are exempt from the overtime provisions but not the minimum wage provisions (see Exhibit 16.4, "Other FLSA Exemptions").

1. Outside salespeople; executive, administrative, and professional employees, including teachers, academic administrative employees in elementary and secondary schools; and certain employees in computer-related occupations if they are paid at least $27.63 per hour. (This is why it would not be worth Drake's time to pursue a claim in Opening Scenario 1; more below.)

Scenario

2. Employees of certain individually owned and operated small retail or service establishments not part of a covered enterprise.

3. Employees of certain seasonal amusement or recreational establishments, messengers, full-time students, employees of certain small newspapers, switchboard operators of small telephone companies, sailors employed on foreign vessels, and employees engaged in fishing operations.

4. Farm workers employed by anyone who used no more than 500 person-days of farm labor in any calendar quarter of the preceding calendar year.

5. Casual babysitters and people employed as companions to the elderly. (Recall our discussion in the affirmative action chapter about southern legislators at the time of enacting the law, specifically carving out the minimum wage and overtime exemption for farmworkers, domestics, and caretakers, predominantly black, who performed services for so many of them and their constituents.)

Exhibit 16.4 *Other FLSA Exemptions*

As you can see from the list below, there are many exemptions to the FLSA provisions. These do not include state exemptions that may exist.

(MW = minimum wage; OT = overtime; CL = child labor)

Aircraft salespeople—OT

Airline employees—OT

Amusement/recreational employees in national parks/forests/wildlife refuge system—OT

Babysitters on a casual basis—MW & OT

Boat salespeople—OT

Buyers of agricultural products—OT

Companions for the elderly—MW & OT

Country elevator workers (rural)—OT

Disabled workers—MW

Domestic employees who live in—OT

Farm implement salespeople—OT

Federal criminal investigators—MW & OT

Firefighters working in small (less than five firefighters) public fire departments—OT

Fishing—MW & OT

Forestry employees of small (less than nine employees) firms—OT

Fruit & vegetable transportation employees—OT

Homeworkers making wreaths—MW, OT, & CL

Houseparents in nonprofit educational institutions—OT

Livestock auction workers—OT

Local delivery drivers and drivers' helpers—OT

Lumber operations employees of small (less than nine employees) firms—OT

Motion picture theater employees—OT

Newspaper delivery—MW, OT, & CL

Newspaper employees of limited-circulation newspapers—MW & OT

Police officers working in small (less than five officers) public police departments—OT

Radio station employees in small markets—OT

Railroad employees—OT

Seamen on American vessels—OT

Seamen on other than American vessels—MW & OT

Sugar processing employees—OT

Switchboard operators—MW & OT

Taxicab drivers—OT

Television station employees in small markets—OT

Truck and trailer salespeople—OT

Youth employed as actors or performers—CL

Youth employed by their parents—CL

Source: http://www.dol.gov/elaws/esa/flsa/screen75.asp.

The FLSA overtime regulations underwent a major overhaul in August 2004 regarding their exemption for white-collar professionals, that is, primarily those in executive, administrative, and professional jobs. This matter had been debated for years and was accomplished under President George W. Bush. These rules are extremely important since they determine who must be paid overtime for working more than 40 hours per week. The general rule was that white-collar employees in the above categories were not entitled to overtime pay. Determinations as to who fit into these categories were made using a salary test and a duties test.

Prior to the rule change, the salary levels used in the wage and hour rules had not been updated for nearly 30 years. Under the old rules, the FLSA exempted from overtime pay workers who made more than $155 per week, or $8,060 per year, and who met certain other requirements that had been criticized as convoluted and confusing. For instance, the employee also had to devote at least 80 percent of his or her time to "exercising discretion" or other "intellectual" tasks that cannot be "standardized in . . . a given period of time." The new rules were designed to simplify application of the regulations to white-collar exemptions.

Under the new regulations, which required businesses to review their pay levels and jobs to make sure employees were being paid correctly under the new rules, employees earning up to $23,660 per year, or $455 per week, are automatically entitled to overtime pay, regardless of whether they are hourly or annual salaried employees. That is, regardless of the classification of the job, if the salary is at or below a certain level ($23,660 per year or $455 per week), the employee is entitled to overtime pay. For the most part, executive employees would be exempt if they manage two or more employees; if they have hiring, firing, and promotion authority or significant input; or if they have advanced degrees or similar training and work in a specialized field or the operations, finance, and auditing areas of a business. It was speculated that the jobs that would be most affected by the new overtime regulations would be assistant managers in stores, restaurants, and bars. Under the new regulations, an employer could boost salaries (that is, pay an employee more than $23,660) in order to avoid the new rules requiring overtime to be paid to those who earn up to $23,660.

Employees who earn at least $100,000 per year and perform some executive, professional (either learned or creative), or administrative job duties are automatically exempt from the overtime provisions of the FLSA. That is why in Opening Scenario 1, Drake would not be entitled to more pay for the additional hours he finds himself putting in. As with the prior regulations, the Department of Labor can collect back wages for overtime violations, and companies not in compliance run the risk of costly lawsuits by employees. Retaliation against employees filing claims or reporting an employer's violations is a separate violation of the law. Because FLSA class action lawsuits have increased by 70 percent since 2000, and the regulations may change employees' status from what it was before the new regulations, employers would do well to give considerable attention to these matters.

Overtime Provisions

In addition to minimum wages, covered employees working over 40 hours per week are entitled to overtime pay of at least time and a half—at least one and one-half times the covered employee's regular hourly wage rate. The FLSA does not limit the hours employees work but, rather, sets standards for the hours constituting a normal workweek for wage purposes. The statute then sets wage rates for hours worked over and above the normal week. It is a common misconception that the law prohibits an employer from requiring employees to work over 40 hours per week. The law does not dictate hours, but merely states that, if an employee works over 40 hours, he or she must be paid time and a half for the time worked in excess of 40 hours. (See Exhibit 16.5, "Full and Partial Overtime Pay Exemptions.") In January of 2011, CALNET, Inc. and two of its subcontractors were ordered to pay $1,060,554 in back wages for failing to pay employees for time that they were on call.[12]

Exhibit 16.5 *Full and Partial Overtime Pay Exemptions*

EXEMPTIONS FROM OVERTIME PAY ONLY

Certain commissioned employees of retail or service establishments; auto, truck, trailer, farm implement, boat, or aircraft salesworkers; or parts-clerks and mechanics servicing autos, trucks, or farm implements who are employed by non-manufacturing establishments primarily engaged in selling these items to ultimate purchasers.

Employees of railroads and air carriers, taxi drivers, certain employees of motor carriers, seamen on American vessels, and local delivery employees paid on approved trip rate plans.

Announcers, news editors, and chief engineers of certain nonmetropolitan broadcasting stations.

Domestic service workers living in the employer's residence.

Employees of motion picture theaters.

Farm workers.

PARTIAL EXEMPTIONS FROM OVERTIME PAY

Partial overtime pay exemptions apply to employees engaged in certain operations on agricultural commodities and to employees of certain bulk petroleum distributors.

Hospitals and residential care establishments may adopt, by agreement with their employees, a 14-day work period instead of the usual 7-day workweek, if the employees are paid at least time and one-half their regular rates for hours worked over 8 in a day or 80 in a 14-day work period, whichever is the greater number of overtime hours.

Employees who lack a high school diploma, or who have not attained the educational level of the 8th grade, can be required to spend up to 10 hours in a workweek engaged in remedial reading or training in other basic skills without receiving time and one-half overtime pay for these hours. However, the employees must receive their normal wages for hours spent in such training, and the training must not be job specific.

Source: http://www.dol.gov/esa/wpd.

Retaliation

The FLSA prohibits employers from retaliating against any employee who exercises his or her rights under the act, such as by filing suit to collect benefits wrongfully withheld. As we will see in *Mullins v. City of New York*, reproduced at the end of the chapter, retaliation can include acts of intimidation that fall short of firing or disciplining someone for exercising lawfully held rights.

Child Labor Laws

The FLSA sets minimum age standards for allowing children to work. Under the law, most cannot work before age 16, with 18 being the minimum age for hazardous jobs. The Department of Labor publishes a list of such occupations. Children between the ages of 14 and 16 may work at certain types of jobs that do not interfere with their health, education, or well-being. Certain agricultural work also is permitted. States may have child labor laws even stricter than the federal law, and, if so, the stricter rules apply. In 2008, as a part of the Genetic Information Non-discrimination Act of 2008, FLSA was amended to increase the civil penalties for child labor violations resulting in death or serious bodily injury.

The Family and Medical Leave Act of 1993

Statutory Basis

Leave Requirement

(a) (1) Entitlement to leave—an eligible employee shall be entitled to a total of 12 work-weeks of leave during any 12-month period for one or more of the following:

(A) Because of the birth of a son or daughter of the employee and in order to care for such son or daughter.

(B) Because of the placement of a son or daughter with the employee for adoption or foster care.

(C) In order to care for the spouse, or a son, daughter, or parent, of the employee, if such spouse, son, daughter, or parent has a serious health condition.

(D) Because of a serious health condition that makes the employee unable to perform the functions of the position of such employee. [The Family and Medical Leave Act of 1993, 29 U.S.C. § 2601 et seq.]

Introduction: It's All in the Family

The FMLA was previously in the gender chapter because it was enacted primarily in response to female employees' concerns about keeping their job or not being demoted or losing benefits after the birth or arrival of a child. Since its passage, however, the law has evolved into a much broader piece of legislation. With baby boomers playing such a large part in the national conscience and policies, it was inevitable that since the law also covers taking time off to care for parents, this would also become a fertile area under the law.

General Provisions

Scenario

On February 5, 1993, President Clinton signed into law the first piece of legislation of his administration: the Family and Medical Leave Act (FMLA). The act guarantees employees who have been on the job at least a year up to 12 weeks of unpaid leave per year for a birth; an adoption; or care of sick children, spouses, or parents (or their own serious illness) and the same or an equivalent job upon their return. This is why, in Opening Scenario 2, Carly will not be granted the FMLA leave she requests. She wishes to take time off for her husband's parent, not her own. This is not covered by the act. In January 2008, President George W. Bush signed into law an FMLA amendment that would allow an eligible employee to take up to 26 weeks unpaid leave in a 12-month period to care for a returning war veteran seriously injured in the line of duty. In addition the National Defense Authorization Act for FY 2008 (NDAA)[13] allows eligible employees to take up to 12 weeks of unpaid leave to deal with exigencies caused by a spouse, son, daughter, or parent either being called to active duty or being on active duty. The FMLA applies to employers with 50 or more employees within a 75-mile radius. Employees must have worked for their employer for at least one year and for at least 1,250 hours during the 12 months preceding the time off. They must give the employer at least 30 days' notice when practical (such as for a birth).

In 2010, the Department of Labor expanded leave rights under the FMLA and extended the right to care for a sick child to an employee who is acting as a parent, even if the employee does not have a legal or biological relationship to the child. In announcing the new guidance, Hilda Solis, Secretary of Labor, stated:

> No one who loves and nurtures a child day-in and day-out should be unable to care for that child when he or she falls ill. No one who steps in to parent a child when that child's biological parents are absent or incapacitated should be denied leave by an employer because he or she is not the legal guardian. No one who intends to raise a child should be denied the opportunity to be present when that child is born simply because the state or an employer fails to recognize his or her relationship with the biological parent. These are just a few of many possible scenarios. The Labor Department's action today sends a clear message to workers and employers alike: All families, including LGBT families, are protected by the FMLA.[14]

Employers may require employees to first use vacation or other leave before applying for the unpaid leave, but employees must be compensated for the vacation days as they normally would. Where both members of the couple work for the same employer, the employer can restrict the couple to a total of 12 weeks' leave per year. Employers must continue to provide employees with health insurance during their leave and may exclude the highest-paid 10 percent of their employees from FMLA coverage.

Employers also can require medical confirmation of an illness, which the U.S. Department of Labor defines as requiring at least one night in the hospital. Complaints may be filed with the Wage and Hour Division of the Labor Department, or the employee can file a lawsuit if he or she feels the employer violated the act.

In 1997, Congress declined to grant President Clinton's request to extend the FMLA to permit employees to take up to 24 hours of unpaid leave each year to fulfill certain family obligations such as attending parent-teacher conferences, taking a child to the doctor, finding child care, or caring for elderly relatives. Societal impediments also can be a factor, such as men feeling they will be viewed as disloyal if they take a leave of absence under the FMLA. However, the greatest impediment to full use of the law is the fact that the leave is unpaid. Though California recently provided that employees be paid 55 percent of their salary for up to six weeks of FMLA leave (in addition to whatever other leave employees may have), the United States is in the unique position of being the only industrially similar nation that does not provide at least some type of paid parental leave. This may, in fact, be remedied at some future point. In April 2008, the House Committee on Government Oversight and Reform passed a bill to provide federal employees at least a percentage of their income for four weeks when leave is taken to have or adopt a child.[15] Still pending in Congress, the bill proposes that employees and employers pay into a fund that will provide the source of the paid leave. Such legislation has been introduced before without success even though both parents work in 70 percent of American working households, and all other similar countries have such legislation.

The FMLA has been the subject of a great deal of uncertainty ever since its passage. The law, particularly the Department of Labor's regulations, has been a constant source of confusion for employers. There have been questions as to how serious an illness must be for the employee to qualify for the leave, assessment of eligibility requirements for the leave, what to do about intermittent leave, reinstatement after taking leave, and notification and certification requirements for leave, just to name a few issues.

These issues have resulted in a steadily increasing number of FMLA claims, causing it to develop into one of the most active areas of employment law. A July 2007 survey by the Society for Human Resource Management (SHRM), found that nearly 40 percent of human resource professionals reported that confusion over implementation of the FMLA has led to illegitimate leave being granted.[16] Two of the most challenging FMLA-related activities identified by organizations are tracking/administering intermittent FMLA leave and determining the overall costs incurred while complying with the requirements of the FMLA. According to the survey, many HR professionals noted that the timing of intermittent FMLA leave requests (e.g., around weekends, holidays, pleasant weather) raised suspicions of abuse.

The Wage and Hour Division of the Department of Labor heard these comments and on November 17, 2008, announced the first major overhaul of the FMLA in 10 years The new regulations became effective on January 16, 2009, and provided clarification and detailed new leave entitlements for the military, as mentioned earlier.[17] When the agency posted a request for comments on its proposed changes, over 15,000 were received.

If you think about the problems that can be presented for an employer if found to be in violation of the FMLA, and the many ways in which the law can be violated, you can see how the law would be such a frustrating one for employers. The *Spangler v. Federal Home Loan Bank of Des Moines*[18] case demonstrates why employers have such a problem with this law. A bank employee had a long history of depression that caused her to miss days of work. She had been given notice about her excessive absences and put on probation about her absenteeism, and yet she still took time off. She was terminated after calling in and leaving a voicemail message saying that she would not be in because of "depression again." The issue was whether this statement was sufficient to put the employer on notice that the employee was invoking the FMLA and taking FMLA leave. The court determined it well could be sufficient notice of a serious health condition as required by the FMLA because of the employer's extensive history with the employee taking absences because of depression. It did not mean the employer would be required to keep her on despite her absences, but it at least put the employer on notice that the employee was absent for FMLA reasons.

On the other hand, in *Righi v. SMC Corporation of America*,[19] the court upheld the termination of an employee who, discovering his mother had a medical emergency, emailed his supervisor that he would need the next couple of days off to arrange for her care. He was gone for nine days and during that time did not contact the employer to inform him of what was going on. When the employer repeatedly called the employee there was no answer. The court said that under the FMLA the employee had a duty to comply with the employer's policies for taking FMLA leave, including notifying the employer of plans to take such leave. Avoiding the employer's calls and not contacting the employer relieved the employer of liability for the termination.

In *Terwilliger v. Howard Memorial Hospital*,[20] the court said the employee's FMLA rights were interfered with when the employee, a hospital housekeeper off for back surgery, kept receiving phone calls from her supervisor asking when she was returning to work. The employee had already requested and been granted FMLA leave for her serious medical condition but felt pressured to return to work by the calls continually made to her by her supervisor during recuperation.

As you can see, there seem to be as many ways to violate the FMLA as there are employees, so it is in an employer's best interest to know the FMLA requirements and comply with them.

Occupational Safety and Health Act

Statutory Basis

Occupational Safety and Health Act

§ 654 (§ 5) Duties
  (a) Each employer—
    (1) shall furnish to each of his employees employment and a place of employment which are free from recognized hazards that are causing or are likely to cause death or serious physical harm to his employees;
    (2) shall comply with occupational safety and health standards promulgated under this Act.
  (b) Each employee shall comply with occupational safety and health standards and all rules, regulations and orders issued pursuant to this Act which are applicable to his own actions and conduct.

Introduction: Safety at Work

Workplace safety seems like it might not be such a big deal—that is, of course, until you slip on spilled salad dressing in the kitchen of the restaurant for which you work and you cannot continue to pay your tuition. Workplace safety is often perceived as the bailiwick of angry-looking union reps or blue-collar "working stiffs" who carry lunch pails to work. But it is a workplace issue that affects us all. *Each year,* more than 5,700 Americans die from workplace injuries; another 50,000 workers die from illnesses caused by workplace exposure; more than 83,000 work sites are found in violation of the Occupational Safety and Health Act's standards; and 4.7 million suffer nonfatal workplace injuries costing businesses over $170 billion—making health and safety one of the most vital workplace issues facing employers today.[21] (See Exhibit 16.6, "The Top Six Ethics-Related Global Workplace Issues.")

Exhibit 16.6   *The Top Six Ethics-Related Global Workplace Issues*

Forced labor, child labor, working hours

Health and safety in the workplace, working conditions

Discrimination, harassment

Financial malfeasance

Fraud, theft

Gift giving, bribes

Source: American Management Association, *The Ethical Enterprise: Doing the Right Things in the Right Ways, Today and Tomorrow* (New York: American Management Association/Human Resources Institute, 2006), http://www.amanet.org.

On December 29, 1970, President Richard Nixon signed into law the Occupational Safety and Health Act, attempting to ensure safe and healthful working conditions for all employees and to preserve the human resources of the United States. Since 1971, OSHA claims that the act has helped to cut workplace fatalities by more than 60 percent and injury/illness rates by 40 percent. More than 100,000 workers who might have died on the job did not because of improved safety and health.

OSHA specifically requires that an employer provide a safe and healthy workplace "to each of *its* employees. . . ." Does that language limit the liability of the employer only to those individuals who are actually employees of the employer? Under a concept called the "multiemployer doctrine," on multiemployer worksites, an employer who creates a safety hazard can be liable under the OSHA, regardless of whether the employees threatened are its own or those of another employer on the site. In Opening Scenario 3, Caterez could be found liable due to the multiemployer doctrine. An employer is liable as long as the government can show that the employee at a worksite was exposed to the risk by the contractor's safety violations. In Scenario 3, if it can be shown that Singhie was exposed to the cement dust due to the contractor's safety violation by not providing the mask, Caterez can be held liable and would be the responsible party to handle the OSHA violation.

Scenario

While the Occupational Safety and Health Review Commission ruled that the multiemployer worksite policy does not apply to a general contractor if the general contractor's own employees were not exposed to the hazard, the Eighth Circuit reversed that interpretation, ruling that the multiemployer worksite policy makes the general contractor, in effect, the guarantor of all construction work as long as it has employees present, regardless of whether they are similarly exposed.[22]

General Provisions

LO4

OSHA requires that an employer provide a safe workplace. Prior to passage of OSHA, there was no comprehensive national legislation about workplace safety, and state laws varied greatly. Employers could locate their workplaces in states with lax safety laws providing little protection for workers. Under such laws, employees were often limited in the damages they could recover due to injuries arising from the employer's unsafe workplace.

Several defenses were available to employers to escape liability for providing an unsafe work environment. **Contributory negligence** allowed the employer to defend against the employee's injury suit by claiming that the employee contributed to the injury through the employee's own negligence. The **assumption of risk** defense precluded the employee from recovering when the employee knew of a risk involved in the workplace, chose to chance not being injured, and was in fact injured. The **fellow servant rule** permitted the employer to escape liability when the negligence was the fault of an employee rather than the employer. As you can imagine, injured workers did not find much protection under these laws requiring that the employer provide a safe working environment.

Workers' compensation laws, however, are generally **no fault**, which means that workers injured on the job are entitled to recover for their injuries without having to prove who is at fault. The defenses became irrelevant. The trade-off for employers, in agreeing to be bound by a no-fault system, is that the injured workers are limited in their financial recovery to what they can obtain under workers' compensation laws.

Section 5(a) of the act imposes two basic requirements on all employers—regardless of size—to accomplish the goal of a safer workplace. First, the employer must comply with all the safety and health standards dictated by the Department of Labor, generally called the "compliance" requirements. Second, the employer must "furnish to each of [its] employees employment and a place of employment which are free from recognized hazards that are causing or are likely to cause death or serious physical harm." This broad requirement is called the "general duty" clause, and the traditional employer defenses noted above are not often available. The only exceptions to the reach of the act are self-employed people, family members employed by family farms, state and local government employees (except under an OSHA-approved plan), and work environments that are regulated by other federal agencies (such as mining or nuclear energy).

In furtherance of workplace safety, OSHA creates certain specific regulatory standards of safety (for example, how much flour dust is permitted to be in a wheat-processing plant) in addition to its general duty clause, which applies in the absence of specific standards. The law applies to any employer that has employees and is in a business affecting commerce (most employers!). In order to accomplish its mission of workplace safety, OSHA provides several tools, including unannounced workplace inspections by OSHA compliance officers, citations and penalties for violations, and continual safety training requirements. Complaints to OSHA may arise from employees, grievances filed by other sources, or reports of fatal or multiple injuries. OSHA protects from retaliation employees who file such complaints by prohibiting employers from discharging or discriminating against employees who exercise rights afforded by the act. OSHA also provided for the creation of the National Institute for Occupational Safety and Health (NIOSH), the research arm of OSHA, which conducts research on workplace

contributory negligence
A defense to a negligence action based on the injured party's failure to exercise reasonable care for her or his own safety.

assumption of risk
A defense to a negligence action based on the argument that the injured party voluntarily exposed herself or himself to a known danger created by the other party's negligence. **LO5**

fellow servant rule
An employer's defense to liability for an employee's injury where the injury occurred on the job and was caused by the negligence of another employee.

no-fault
The environment for workers compensation laws, which means that workers injured on the job are entitled to recover for their injuries without having to prove who is at fault.

health and safety and makes recommendations to the secretary of labor that, if approved, may become the standards of conduct in a certain industry.

Routine inspections in certain high-risk industries also are conducted by OSHA. The employer may consent to the inspection or may demand that the OSHA representatives obtain a search warrant. There may be reasons to use one strategy or the other that lie outside the scope of this text, so it is advisable to consult with legal counsel. The inspection is likely to proceed in either scenario. To ensure that the inspectors are viewing the workplace in the same condition as that experienced by the employees, inspections are conducted without prior notice to an employer. In fact, anyone giving unauthorized advance notice of the inspection to the employer can be punished by a fine of up to $1,000. The inspector will arrive at the worksite, ask to see the safety and accident records of the employer, conduct a "walk around" to visually inspect the site, and discuss with the employer any violations or concerns, as well as possible solutions to the problems. Because OSHA cannot inspect all 8.9 million worksites covered by the act, it has established an inspection priority system in order to have the most significant impact. Under this system, the agency inspects situations of imminent danger, catastrophes and fatal accidents, employee complaints involving serious harm, referrals, or planned inspections.

LO6

Penalties and "abatement orders" are assessed in connection with the inspection officer's report. A nonserious or a serious violation may require payment of a penalty ranging from $0 to $7,000, while repeated and/or willful violations have a price tag of up to $70,000 per violation or up to $500,000 plus prison time if the violation was willful and involved a fatality. Criminal sanctions and even higher fines are also possible where the employer acts willfully and causes the death of an employee. (See Exhibit 16.7, "Seven Main Categories of OSHA Violations and Resulting Penalties.") Congress is currently contemplating raising these fines. In fact, in 2008, it did so for child labor injuries.

As long as an employer is covered by the act, has more than 10 employees, and is not subject to one of the few exceptions (certain low-hazard industries in the retail, finance, insurance, real estate, and service sectors), it must maintain certain records for OSHA compliance. Where the injury or illness is work-related and meets the general recording criteria or falls into specific categories, reporting is mandated. It must be reported as long as it is an illness, a death, or an injury that involves (1) medical treatment, (2) loss of consciousness, (3) restriction of work or motion, or (4) transfer to a different position. Employers also must report workplace injuries due to assaults by family members or ex-spouses as a part of their recordkeeping requirements. The records must contain the following information, must be reported on OSHA Form 300,[23] and must be posted for the employees to see (i.e., it need not be filed with the government but, instead, must be kept throughout the year and compiled for the February posting): case number, employee's name, job title, date of injury or onset of illness, where the event occurred, description of the event, classification of the case, and number of days away from work.

Employees must be informed of their OSHA rights by their employer. This requirement may be met by displaying an OSHA poster in the workplace, but

Exhibit 16.7 *Seven Main Categories of OSHA Violations and Resulting Penalties*

1. **Other than serious violation:** A violation that has a direct relationship to job safety and health, but probably would not cause death or serious physical harm. A proposed penalty of up to $7,000 for each violation is discretionary.

2. **Serious violation:** A violation where there is substantial probability that death or serious physical harm could result and the employer knew, or should have known, of the hazard. A mandatory penalty of up to $7,000 for each violation is proposed.

3. **Willful violation:** A violation that the employer knowingly commits or commits with plain indifference to the law. Penalties of up to $70,000 may be proposed for each willful violation, with a minimum penalty of $5,000 for each violation. If an employer is convicted of a willful violation of a standard that resulted in the death of an employee, the offense is punishable by a court-imposed fine or by imprisonment for up to six months, or both. A fine of up to $250,000 for an individual, or $500,000 for a corporation, may be imposed for a criminal conviction.

4. **Repeated violation:** A violation of any standard, regulation, rule, or order where, upon re-inspection, a substantially similar violation can bring a fine of up to $70,000 for each such violation. The original violation must be final in order to be the basis for a repeated citation.

5. **Failure to abate prior violation:** Failure to abate a prior violation may bring a civil penalty of up to $7,000 for each day the violation continues beyond the prescribed abatement date.

6. **De minimis violation:** Violations of standards that have no direct or immediate relationship to safety or health.

7. **Additional violations:** Examples include falsifying record, reports, or applications; violations of posting requirements; assaulting a compliance officer; or otherwise resisting, opposing, intimidating, or interfering with a compliance officer while engaged in the performance of her or his duties.

Due to the expenses associated with these violations and considering the fact that each day represents a separate violation, employers often request variances in order to prevent citations or penalties. Employers may ask OSHA for a variance from a standard or regulation if they cannot fully comply by the effective date, due to shortages of materials, equipment, or professional or technical personnel, or can prove their facilities or methods of operation provide employee protection "at least as effective" as that required by OSHA. Employers can request a temporary variance, a permanent variance, an interim order, or an experimental variance in order to remain in compliance with OSHA standards. Variances are not retroactive, so an employer who has been cited for a standards violation may not seek relief from that citation by applying for a variance.

Source: U.S. Department of Labor, OSHA Office of Training and Education, Construction Safety and Health Outreach Program, "OSHA Act, OSHA Standards, Inspections, Citations and Penalties," May 1996, http:www.osha.gov/doc/outreachtraining/htmlfiles/introsha.html#.

displaying this poster is not mandatory. Employee rights also include requesting and participating in inspections, notice of an employer's violations or citations, access to monitoring procedures and results, and access to medical information. Employees who provide information to OSHA are protected from discharge and/or discrimination by the employer in retaliation for the reporting.

Responsibility for enforcing OSHA rests with the Department of Labor's Occupational Safety and Health Administration (OSHA). If an employer seeks to challenge a citation or penalty imposed, as opposed to simply demanding a warrant from the inspector to come onto the premises, it may submit an appeal to the Occupational Safety and Health Review Commission (OSHRC), an independent federal agency functioning as an administrative court created to decide issues of citations or penalties resulting from OSHA inspections.

An example of a relatively large penalty for willful violations would be the *Cintas* case in 2007, where OSHA proposed a penalty of $2.78 million after an inspection following the death of a worker who fell into a dryer while clearing a wet laundry jam.[24] Cintas, the largest industrial laundry company in the U.S., was subject to 42 willful, instance-by-instance citations for violations of the OSHA lockout/tagout standard, including the failures to shut down and to lock out power to the equipment before clearing jams. Cintas eventually settled with OSHA a year and a half later for $2.76 million, along with commitments to improve site safety. However, related unions claimed that the agreement had no teeth since Cintas was given two years to correct the severe safety violations and no follow-up inspections were planned. "On its way out the door, the Bush Labor Department has granted serial offender Cintas a despicable pardon for their failure to protect its workers from hazardous machinery," said Congressman Phil Hare (D-IL). Hare also noted that, as part of the settlement agreement, "the Department of Labor modified the willful citations to 'unclassified citations,' despite the fact that Cintas knew about these hazards and OSHA originally found the company to be negligent. There is nothing in the law that even allows unclassified citations and we are determined to take legislative action to prohibit the declassification of willful citations."[25]

Actually, the question of willfulness is one that remains somewhat open in the courts. It is an important one to answer because fines can be significantly increased where willfulness is shown. OSHA defines a willful violation as "a violation that the employer intentionally and knowingly commits or a violation that the employer commits with plain indifference to the law. The employer either knows that what he or she is doing constitutes a violation, or is aware that a hazardous condition existed and made no reasonable effort to eliminate it." In addition, the OSHRC has also interpreted willfulness to include a violation the employer should have known. In a case against Tyson Foods, Inc., an employee died after inhaling a poisonous gas while repairing equipment leaks. The gas was created by decaying chicken feathers, and the company was fined $436,000.[26]

Specific Regulations

Certain specific regulations seem to apply across the board to all types of employment environments. For instance, a number of specific requirements involve the physical layout of the worksite including proper ventilation, adequate means of emergency exit, safety nets, guard rails, and so on. Employees must be trained and informed (through classes, labels, signs) regarding protective measures, for everything from wearing protective devices, such as masks, to the proper use of chemicals. Medical examinations must be provided by the employer where an employee has been exposed to toxic substances.

OSHA can set standards on its own initiative or in response to petitions from other parties. If it is determined that a specific standard is needed, any of several advisory committees may be called upon to develop recommendations. Recommendations for standards also may come from NIOSH. Once OSHA has developed plans for a standard, it publishes them in the *Federal Register* as a "Notice of Proposed Rulemaking." A recent example is OSHA's recommendations for poultry processing facilities to reduce the number and severity of work-related musculoskeletal disorders. In preparing the recommendations, OSHA reviewed existing practices and programs as well as available scientific information on ergonomics and solicited comments from representatives of trade and professional associations, labor organizations, individual firms, and other interested parties. The final recommendations were announced in September 2004. The employer may be held liable for workplace hazards under the general duty clause even if specific regulations do not exist (see discussion of the general duty clause, below).

emergency temporary standards

Standards are imposed by OSHA without immediately going through the typical process where an employee is exposed to grave danger from exposure to substances and the standards are necessary to protect employees from the danger.

The secretary of labor may establish **emergency temporary standards** that will be effective immediately on publication in the *Federal Register* without having to go through the lengthy rule-making process otherwise required by the act where he or she "determines (a) that employees are exposed to grave danger from exposure to substances or agents determined to be toxic or physically harmful or from new hazards, and (b) that such emergency standard is necessary to protect employees from such danger." The emergency standard is effective until regular standards are approved through the regular procedures or for six months, whichever is shorter.

continual-training requirement

OSHA requires that the employer provide safety training to all new employees and to all employees who have been transferred into new positions.

One of the most burdensome requirements on employers is the **continual-training requirement**. OSHA requires that employers adopt a program of continual workplace safety training of employees. An employer is required to provide safety training every time an employee is hired or transferred into a new position, even if for just a day. This is generally the most frequently cited type of violation under the statute. As a result, OSHA has made an effort to simplify the requirement and now supplies employers with material safety data sheets regarding various types of chemicals and the surrounding hazards associated with them.

General Duty Clause

general duty clause

A provision of the act requiring that employers furnish to each employee employment and a place of employment free from recognized hazards that cause or are likely to cause death or serious physical harm to the employee.

The **general duty clause** protects employees against hazards in the workplace, *where no other OSHA standard would address the condition.* The general duty clause stems from the act's provision that "Each employer . . . shall furnish to each of his employees employment and a place of employment which are free from recognized hazards that are causing or are likely to cause death or serious physical harm to his employees." For instance, once it is found that a certain chemical used in an employer's manufacturing process causes reproductive harm, or perhaps damage to the employees' skin, then under the general duty clause the employer must take steps to protect employees and to provide a workplace free from this hazard. It is the employer's responsibility to be aware of these workplace hazards and to ensure that all employees are equally protected. A recognized hazard also may take the form of actual knowledge when the employer actually knows of the hazard or the form of constructive knowledge if the industry recognizes the hazard even if the employer doesn't actually know of the hazard.

It is not always easy for an employer to determine what constitutes a recognized hazard because we are constantly improving our knowledge; so, what we may think is all right today may prove harmful later. Whereas smokers were once free to puff away in the workplace, today OSHA has classified secondhand smoke as a potential cancer-causing agent. In fact, many states have regulations on the provision of smoke-free working conditions.

And what does the general duty clause's term *likely* mean in connection with those risks that an employer must protect against? If there is a chance that 1 person in 1,000 may be harmed, does that mean that the risk is likely, or must 5 people out of 10 be at risk for harm to be likely? The OSHRC has stated that the harm need not be likely but possible. In fact, the commission has said that "the proper question is not whether an accident is likely to occur, but whether, if an accident does occur, the result is likely to be death or serious physical harm."

Under OSHA, there are times when an employer or an employee may not comply with workplace rules or safety regulations and no violation results. For instance, where, based on a reasonable apprehension of death or serious injury and a reasonable belief that no less drastic alternative is available, an employee believes that the employer has violated its general duty to provide a safe working environment, the employees may refuse to work in that environment and the employer cannot punish them for doing so.

In *Whirlpool Corporation v. Marshall,*[27] the U.S. Supreme Court upheld an OSHA regulation protecting employees against retaliation for refusing to work under dangerous conditions. Two employees at a Whirlpool plant refused to perform maintenance work that would require them to walk on elevated mesh screens less than two weeks after a co-worker fell to his death through the screens. The employees were sent home, and written reprimands were placed in their personnel files. The Court held that Whirlpool had illegally retaliated against the employees.

As an example of the application of the general duty clause, as well as the enormous expense of pursuing the defense of an OSHA claim for an employer, consider the case of a Walmart employee in Valley Stream, Long Island, Jdimytai Damour, who was trampled to death in a Black Friday sales stampede early on the morning after Thanksgiving in 2008. OSHA determined that Walmart had committed a "serious violation" of the general duty clause. It ruled, in effect, that Walmart's failure to properly control the crowd, which had been foreseeable given previous Black Friday sales events, created a workplace hazard that was likely to cause death or serious physical injury to the employee. Although the proposed fine was only $7,000, the retail giant fought OSHA's citation in court—spending, so far, more than $2 million in legal fees—presumably because of the citation's future implications for any retailer when faced with large, unpredictable crowd surges. Although the case went to trial in the summer of 2010 and lasted only six days, no verdict had been returned as of early 2011. No matter which way the judge rules, appeals are expected, so this case should continue to drag through the courts for the foreseeable future. Meanwhile, no criminal penalties were ever brought against anyone at Walmart (Walmart settled the criminal case by agreeing to pay money to a victims' fund and to institute crowd management techniques), but a wrongful death suit brought against Walmart by Damour's family was still pending.

On the other hand, there may be workplace hazards or injuries for which the employer will *not* be held responsible under OSHA. The three most common of these circumstances include the following:

recklessness
Conscious disregard for safety; conscious failure to use due care.

1. Where the harm is the result of **reckless** behavior by an employee.
2. Where it is physically or economically impossible for the employer to comply with a safety requirement.
3. Where compliance with a requirement presents a greater harm than not complying (**greater hazard defense**).

greater hazard defense
An employer may use the greater hazard defense to an OSHA violation where the hazards of compliance are greater than the hazards of noncompliance, where alternative means of protection are unavailable, and where a variance was not available.

If any of the above three conditions exist, there will be no OSHA violation imposed on the employer. For example, a citation was issued because a construction company failed to install a cable railing on the perimeter of the top of a building it was constructing. The employer presented evidence that the risk involved in constructing the railing would subject its employees to a greater risk than if the railing were not there. To assert this defense, however, an employer must show

- The hazards of compliance with the standard are greater than the hazards of noncompliance.
- Alternative means of protection are unavailable.
- A variance from the secretary of labor was unavailable or inappropriate.

In *Horne Plumbing and Heating Co. v. OSHRC,*[28] the employer had taken precautionary measures; but two employees ignored the employer's instructions and warnings from co-workers, worked in an unsafe area of the site anyway, and were killed. The court noted: "[a] hazard consisting of conduct by employees, such as equipment riding, cannot be totally eliminated. A willfully reckless employee may on occasion circumvent the best conceived and most vigorously enforced safety regime. Congress intended to require elimination only of preventable hazards." The court found that the employer did everything possible to ensure compliance with the law, short of remaining at the worksite and directing the operations itself. This is slightly different from willfulness because it is simply whether a reasonable person would have recognized the hazard. Was this final effort required to protect the employee? The court responded that (citing a separate case):

> While close supervision may be required in some cases to avoid accidents, it is unrealistic to expect an experienced and well-qualified [worker] to be under constant scrutiny. Such a holding by the Commission, requiring that each employee be constantly watched by a supervisor, would be totally impractical and in all but the most unusual circumstances, an unnecessary burden.

Finally, if the injury or illness does not result from a work-related cause, no report need be made. An illness or injury is considered work-related if (1) it occurred on the employer's premises, (2) it occurred as a result of work-related activities, (3) the employee was required to be there by the employer, or (4) the employee was traveling to work or to a place he or she was required to be by the employer. If the activity does not fit into one of these categories, it was not work-related, and no report needs to be made. Accidents occurring in a tele-commuting employee's home are not covered, but those occurring in an employer's car are.

Intentional Acts

Although workers' compensation is the exclusive remedy available to injured employees, an exception exists for "intentional acts." If the workplace injury is caused by the employer's willful act, including the willful disregard of known dangers, the employee can sue the employer for compensatory (to compensate the injured party) and punitive (to punish the employer) damages.

Violence in the Workplace

Workplace violence is an often-overlooked component of on-the-job injuries, though it results in 2 million injuries and deaths each year. Under the OSH Act, an employer is required to protect employees against "recognized" workplace safety and health hazards that are likely to cause serious injury or death. OSHA takes the position that employers who do not take reasonable steps to prevent or abate a recognized workplace violence hazard could be found to be in violation of the general duty clause.

Although workplace violence is most often associated with a current or former disgruntled employee, it can also arise from customers, spouses, or relatives. To respond most effectively to potential violence and to head off any potential claim that the employee has failed in its duty to protect its employees, employers should develop a workplace violence policy that includes the following features:

- A "zero tolerance" policy toward threats or acts of violence.
- An established complaint process for employees to be able to warn the employer of potential violence.
- An established process for investigating complaints.
- A consistent application of disciplinary actions in response to violent acts.
- Training for managers and employees to recognize workplace violence.

The establishment of firm antiviolence policies, and consistent application of those policies, does not solve all the potential difficulties with workplace violence. Employers must also remember that perpetrators of the violence may also have rights. For example, the Americans with Disabilities Act protects employees with an emotional impairment that qualifies as a disability under the ADA. Those employees cannot be discriminated against as a result of that disability. Thus, an employer may be prevented from taking an employment action against the protected individual with mental or emotional impairments. Instead, the employer may have to accommodate the disability.

Bullying

Many workplace acts of violence are easy to recognize. Others, however, are subtler and harder to detect. Bullying, which has been defined as "the tendency of individuals or groups to use persistent aggressive or unreasonable behavior against a co-worker" is a prime example.

Workplace bullying is a serious problem. An estimated 54 million people have suffered from workplace bullying, about 45 percent of those targeted by bullies suffer stress-related health problems, and 40 percent of bullied workers voluntarily leave or otherwise lose their jobs to make the bullying stop. A study by the Workplace Bullying Institute (yes, there is such a place) found that 80 percent of the women and 20 percent of the men surveyed had been bullied in the workplace, and that 71 percent of the bullies are bosses.

Bullying can rise to the level of harassment and discrimination, and the creation of a hostile work environment, which can be especially difficult to prevent if the manager responsible for ensuring a safe work environment is the bully. In 2008, in *Raess v. Doescher*, the Indiana Supreme Court reinstated a $325,000 verdict in favor of an employee who was verbally assaulted by a surgeon during an altercation in the hospital's operating room. The decision is noteworthy because liability depended directly on the act of bullying rather than on any hostile work environment or anti-discrimination law. The decision, therefore, appears to have created a common-law tort of workplace bullying, making Indiana the first such state, but probably not the last.

Bullying can be difficult to detect. In addition to acts commonly associated with bullying, such as humiliating comments, intimidation, overly harsh criticism, excessive yelling, belittling remarks, and even physical assault, bullying can also involve setting impossible deadlines, undermining work productivity, and failing to give credit. Bullying can even be nonverbal and covert.

The *Raess* case is a warning to employers to get their workplace bullies under control. The fact that bullying may not involve serious physical harm, or constitute harassment and discrimination, does not mean that a workplace bully is not causing irreparable damage to the workplace, including high turnover costs and bad public relations, as well as creating serious legal liability, including higher workers' compensation costs.

Retaliation

Section 11(c) of the OSH Act prohibits retaliation against whistleblowers. To establish retaliation, an employee needs to prove (1) that he or she engaged in a protected activity (i.e., whistleblowing), (2) that the employer knew about that activity, (3) that the employer subjected him or her to an adverse action (which can include intimidation or threats), and (4) that the protected activity contributed to the adverse action. In addition to the OSH Act antiretaliation provision, federal whistleblowing provisions exist to protect 19 specific industries, including airline, commercial motor carrier, consumer product, environmental, financial reform, health care reform, nuclear, pipeline, public transportation agency, railroad, maritime, and securities laws. OSHA administers all 20 provisions.

Employee Benefits—ERISA, COBRA, and HIPAA

Statutory Basis

Employee Retirement Income Security Act (ERISA)

§ 1132. Civil Enforcement.

    (a) A civil action may be brought—

        (1) By a participant or beneficiary—

            (B) to recover benefits due to him under the terms of his plan, to enforce his rights under the terms of the plan, or to clarify his rights to future benefits under the terms of the plan.

§ 1140. Interference with protected rights.

It shall be unlawful for any person to discharge, fine, suspend, expel, discipline, or discriminate against a participant or beneficiary for exercising any right to which he is entitled under the provisions of an employee benefit plan, or for the purpose of interfering with the attainment of any right to which such participant may become entitled under the plan.

Introduction: Will It Be There When I Retire?

Although not required to provide such benefits, many firms offer employees retirement plans, health care, and other employee benefits. In most cases, through their employers, employees invest a portion of their salary in a plan that provides funding for the employee's retirement. But if the employer goes bankrupt, or the employee switches jobs, what happens to all of this money the employee paid into that plan? Or assume an employee has excellent medical benefits with his present company, benefits of which he often takes advantage of; is he tied to that company and discouraged from leaving because he is concerned that he will not find those benefits on his own or elsewhere? What about an employee who pays into a retirement fund through her employer, only to find there are insufficient funds for her to receive the benefits when she retires?

    Enron, WorldCom, Global Crossing, and United Airlines all filled the headlines of major newspapers in recent years with reports on their bankruptcies and accounting scandals. But Enron and WorldCom also contributed significantly to employee benefits law by adversely impacting the retirement benefits and health benefits of their employees, as well as the investments of other companies' and entities' retirement plans. For example, Enron employees whose retirement plans were heavily invested in Enron stock lost their retirement savings; and the University of California lost $145 million when Enron's stock collapsed, while the Florida State Board of Administration and New York City pension funds lost a combined $444 million.[29]

LO7   In 1974, as a result of concerns regarding the protection of pension benefits of workers who lost their jobs prior to retirement, Congress enacted the Employee Retirement Income Security Act (ERISA), a federal law that governs certain

---

Exhibit 16.8 *Realities about ERISA*

1. Your pension plans are not protected against the trustees who administer them.

2. Even if you put money into a retirement plan, it might not be there when you retire.

3. Even if your employer puts money into your retirement plan, depending on the type of plan, it might not be there when you retire.

4. ERISA applies beyond simply retirement or pension funds.

---

administrative aspects of employee benefit and retirement plans and that is enforced by the Department of Labor (DOL). Congress was concerned about the millions of employees and their dependents who were affected by employee benefit plans. ERISA was designed to encourage cautious, careful management of retirement funds by employers who were receiving tax benefits for doing so. As we will see, ERISA coverage is not restricted to merely retirement plans but covers many types of promised employee benefits. ERISA is a complex act that is multifaceted, and you will only be introduced to it in this text. (See Exhibit 16.8, "Realities about ERISA.")

General Provisions

LO8

An employer that offers welfare benefits (e.g., health, life, disability, or accident insurance) or retirement plans to its employees is subject to certain requirements under ERISA, which covers most private-sector employee benefit plans. In general, ERISA does not cover plans established or maintained by governmental entities or churches, plans maintained outside the United States primarily for the benefit of nonresident aliens, or plans maintained for nonemployees such as a director or independent contractors. The Department of Labor enforces the reporting and disclosure, and fiduciary requirements of ERISA. Individual plaintiffs may file actions based on ERISA violations, and ERISA preempts all state laws that relate to employee benefit plans, whether or not the situation contemplated by the state law is actually covered specifically in ERISA.

employee benefit plan (or plans)
A contractual obligation either through a plan, fund, or arrangement by which an employer or an employee organization such as a labor union agrees to provide retirement benefits or welfare benefits to employees and their dependents and beneficiaries.

ERISA technically applies to **employee benefit plans** and covers two basic types of plans. The first type of plan ERISA covers is welfare plans. A *welfare plan* is any plan, program, or fund that the employer maintains to provide the following: medical, surgical, or hospital care; benefits for sickness, accident, disability, or death; unemployment benefits; vacation benefits; apprenticeship and training programs; day care centers; scholarship funds; prepaid legal services; or severance pay. However, payroll practices from the employer's general assets are not welfare benefit plans covered by ERISA.

retirement or
pension plan
A plan that provides for
compensation at retire-
ment or deferral of
income to periods
beyond termination of
employment.

**defined
contribution**
Retirement plan where
the benefits payable to a
participant are based on
the amount of contribu-
tions and earnings on
such contributions.

defined benefit
Retirement plan where
the benefit payable to a
participant is defined up
front by a formula, the
funding of which is
determined actuarially.

The other type of plan ERISA covers is **retirement** or **pension plans**. There are two general forms of *pension plans:* those with **defined contributions** and those with **defined benefits**. The former involves plans in which each employee has her or his own account and the benefits received at retirement are based solely on the principal and income contributed. Contributions and defined contribution plans can come from employees, the employer, or both. Defined benefit plans comprise all other plans but generally refer to plans where the amount the employee receives at retirement is specifically designated at the time the employee enters the plan. Contributions to defined benefit plans generally only come from the employer, although some old plans also allow employee contributions. In defined contribution plans, the security comes from knowing the amount of principal that will be invested, while the security in defined benefit plans comes from knowing exactly how much will be paid in the end.

ERISA imposes the following requirements on a plan to ensure that employee benefit plans are created and maintained in a fair and financially sound manner:

- It must be in writing and communicated to all employees in a language they will understand within a specified period of time. Employees also must be notified in writing of plan changes.
- The assets of a plan must be held in trust.
- A plan must be for the exclusive benefit of the employees and their beneficiaries. An employer may have assets of the plan returned only after all plan liabilities have been satisfied.
- It must satisfy certain minimum participation, vesting, and distribution requirements.
- A plan may only be established and maintained by an employer, although funding of the plan may be from employer or employee contributions or both.

Also, ERISA establishes requirements for managing and administering pension and welfare plans. There are two main important issues arising from ERISA compliance: fiduciary duties, and reporting and disclosure.

Fiduciary Duty

Prior to the enactment of ERISA, plan coordinators routinely abused the funds entrusted to them, often at the expense of the employees. For instance, the funds may have been offered as loans to selected people, with little or no interest in return and little or no security for the loans, thereby interfering with employees' ability to earn income from the otherwise proper investment of funds.

fiduciary
Someone who has
discretionary authority
over the investment or
management of plan
assets on behalf of
others.

ERISA established a number of requirements, called *fiduciary standards,* to prevent these abuses. Those authorized to make decisions about the placement and investment of the pension plan or those who offer the plan investment advice are considered **fiduciaries** and are subject to the following fiduciary requirements:

- *Loyalty*—Fiduciaries must discharge their duties *solely in the interests of plan participants.* Although fiduciaries may have other concerns, they must ignore those concerns when making fiduciary decisions. They must have undivided loyalty to the participants in the plan.

- *Exclusive purpose*—Fiduciaries when making decisions must make them with the exclusive purpose of providing benefits under the plan and defraying the reasonable expenses under the plan. Accordingly, fiduciaries may not act for their personal benefit or for the benefit of their employer or any other party.

- *Prudence*—A fiduciary must exercise the care and judgment one would expect from a prudent person pursuing similar objectives under the same circumstance. In some instances, this requires a fiduciary to rely on the judgment of advisors, provided that such advisors are prudently selected and supervised. Prudence is determined at the time the investment decision is made and not retroactively with 20/20 hindsight.

- *Diversification*—When investing plan assets, a fiduciary must do so in a diversified manner so as to avoid large losses. This *diversification* standard is intended to limit the investment risk of a plan. The *prudence* standard generally would require that a fiduciary managing the investments of a plan maintain a diversified portfolio. However, the *diversification* standard in effect creates a presumption that an undiversified portfolio is not prudent.

- *Compliance with plan documents*—A fiduciary is required to administer the plan in a manner that is consistent with its governing documents.

If fiduciaries of retirement plans are required to diversify the plan's assets and act prudently, why did Enron, WorldCom, Global Crossing, and other large corporations have a significant concentration of plan assets in the company's stock? ERISA provides an exception to the fiduciary requirements for "individual account plans" that allow participants to direct the investment of their accounts. Individual account plans are defined contribution plans like popular 401(k) plans. However, the fiduciary is still responsible for selecting the menu of investment alternatives and providing adequate information concerning these choices. One such investment is often the employer's stock. Whether the employer's stock should be an investment and whether the amount of investment in employer stock should be limited is a question of prudence and diversification, as Enron, WorldCom, and Global Crossing have proven. In reaction to Enron, WorldCom, Global Crossing, and other instances where the value of employer stock has dropped, causing losses in retirement plans, Congress amended ERISA in 2006 to require public companies that allow for investment of employee contributions into an employer stock fund to notify them of their right to diversify into other nonemployer stock investments. In addition, public companies that match employee contributions in company stock must allow participants who have more than three years of service to diversify out of such investment and must provide for at least three alternative investments. Such companies also must provide notice of such diversification rights. Until employees are allowed to diversify out of employer stock, continued investment in such employer stock will be subject to the general fiduciary requirements of ERISA. *Varity Corp. v. Howe*, parts of which are reproduced at the end of this chapter, explores the nature of these fiduciary duties.

Certain transactions between an employee benefit plan and "parties in interest," which include the employer, fiduciaries, and others who may be in a position to exercise improper influence over the plan, are prohibited by ERISA and may suffer penalties. Most of these types of transactions also are prohibited by the tax code. However, there are some statutory exemptions from the prohibited transaction rules, and the DOL and IRS can authorize such exemptions through regulatory and individual exemptive procedures.

One holding that seems to be gaining steam as the dominant standard is the "presumption of prudence" approach, which is typified in this statement by the Third Circuit in *Moench v. Robertson*.[30] It "essentially shields the fiduciaries from such claims where the plan expressly authorizes employer stock as an investment unless the company and/or its stock value had been placed at extreme risk."[31] The standard is supported in the Third, Fifth, Sixth, Seventh and Ninth Circuits.[32]

Reporting and Disclosure

ERISA requires the employer or plan administrator to provide information to each participant and beneficiary about retirement plans and welfare plans; this information also must be provided to the federal government under certain circumstances. The required information includes a summary plan description (SPD), identifying in understandable terms the plan participants' eligibility for participation and benefits under the plan. Plan changes must be communicated in a timely manner through either a new SPD or a summary of material modification. The SPD is required to be furnished to each participant eligible for benefits under the plan, as well as other beneficiaries. The SPD is not required to be filed with the DOL, but it must be furnished when requested. An annual report must be filed with DOL containing financial and other information concerning the operation of the plan. Plan administrators also must furnish participants and beneficiaries with a summary of the information contained in the annual report. Certain plans may be exempt for the annual report requirement. For instance, the reporting and disclosure laws do not apply to insured welfare plans with fewer than 100 participants.

ERISA was amended by the Pension Protection Act (PPA) of 2006 to address the perceived abuses of Enron and WorldCom and the risks of having retirement investments heavily weighted in employer stock. Since Enron, participants in individually directed account plans have the following rights and must be notified of such rights:

- Participants must be notified in advance of any period in which they will be prohibited from trading in their plan accounts, or so-called blackout periods.
- Participants in defined contribution plans that invest in publicly traded stock of their employer must be allowed to diversify their accounts into at least three other investment options and must be notified of such rights.

Courts have taken ERISA's specific disclosure rules and crafted a broader and more general duty to disclose information. For example, as discussed in the *Varity Corp. v. Howe* case, provided at the end of the chapter, the Supreme Court ruled that a fiduciary has the duty not to mislead participants regarding their benefits. Many lower courts also have addressed cases alleging an affirmative duty to disclose information that may impact a participant's decisions regarding her or his benefits.

For example, several cases address whether or not a company has an affirmative duty to disclose to retiring employees whether or not enhanced early retirement benefits may be offered in the future. Claimants in these cases argue that the fiduciary had the duty to provide more or better information to the plaintiff regarding benefits. The stock drop cases addressed whether or not ERISA requires an affirmative duty to disclose. The Enron court in particular found that such a duty might exist if there are "special circumstances" with a potentially "extreme impact" on the "plan as a whole." The next wave of ERISA litigation also hinges on this affirmative duty to disclose and has been focused on disclosure of plan fees and expenses. This duty-to-disclose issue continues to be litigated and to develop, and ERISA fiduciaries might be wise to overdisclose rather than underdisclose information that may be relevant to plan participants.

The Department of Labor has issued new rules, expected to go into effect in July of 2012, that will expand the disclosure responsibilities of ERISA plan providers, particularly in the area of fee disclosures. Under the amended disclosure rules, "[r]etirement plan providers are required to disclose fee and service information to plan sponsors, in order to help them fulfill their fiduciary duties."[33]

The DOL summarized the new rule as requiring "that certain service providers to employee pension benefit plans disclose information to assist plan fiduciaries in assessing the reasonableness of contracts or arrangements, including the reasonableness of the service providers' compensation and potential conflicts of interest that may affect the service providers' performance. These disclosure requirements are established as part of a statutory exemption from ERISA's prohibited transaction provisions. This regulation will affect employee pension benefit plan sponsors and fiduciaries and certain service providers to such plans."[34]

The Supreme Court recently determined that ERISA fiduciaries must consider the conflict of interest that may arise from the dual role of paying out plans and determining eligibility for benefits.[35] In *Metropolitan Life Insurance Company v. Glenn* (2008):

> . . . an employee was diagnosed with a severe heart condition. MetLife, the insurance company administering the plan on behalf of the employer, determined that she qualified for short term benefits. MetLife also suggested that the employee apply for federal Social Security disability benefits (an offset to benefits under the employer's long term disability plan), for which she subsequently applied and qualified. The employee then applied for benefits under the employer's LTD plan. MetLife denied her claim for the extended benefit because it found that she was "capable of performing full time sedentary work." The employee appealed her claim, but the appeal was also denied. The employee subsequently brought suit in federal district court under section 502 of ERISA, seeking judicial review of MetLife's denial of benefits.[36]

In upholding the employee's claim, the Court found that although the structural conflict of interest within the fiduciary's role is permissible, it must be weighed when considering discretionary abuse in denial of benefits. Emphasizing that this consideration must be made on the basis of the particular facts in each case, the *Glenn* ruling enlarges the scope of discovery in denial of benefits cases and shifts the burden of proof to the fiduciary to show that discretionary power was not abused. Recent lower court decisions have contested the degree of discovery required by *Glenn*, however, and produced varying interpretations of the conflict of interest consideration it requires.[37]

Eligibility and Vesting Rules

vesting
Becoming legally entitled to receive a benefit that cannot be forfeited if employment is terminated.

ERISA and the tax code require that all employees age 21 or over who have completed one year of employment must be covered by their employer's pension plan. **Vesting** means acquiring rights that cannot be taken away. ERISA and the tax code provide that an employee's right to her or his pension benefit becomes 100 percent nonforfeitable after three years of employment or gradually nonforfeitable over six years (20 percent per year, beginning in the second year). In either case, the employee's right is vested, but the employee may not obtain the money or use it until retirement. Once an employee's rights in the plan are vested, the employee cannot lose the pension benefits, even if she or he switches employers. Regardless of vesting schedules with regard to pension benefits for contributions by employers on behalf of employees, employees are *always* 100 percent vested in their *own* contributions, though there are variable tax penalties for early withdrawal.

Funding Requirements for Defined Benefit Plans

To ensure that adequate funds are available under defined benefit plans to pay employees on their retirement, ERISA establishes minimum standards on how those plans should be funded throughout the years. Such standards require that employers fund the costs associated with accruals of benefits based on service in each year and amortize any prior service or actuarial gains or losses on investment over a set period of years.

In addition, employers with defined benefit plans must purchase insurance from the Pension Benefit Guarantee Corporation (PBGC) to cover potential losses of benefits if the plan is terminated without sufficient funds to pay all promised benefits. The PBGC was established by ERISA and is similar to the FDIC in that it acts to insure pensions to a certain guaranteed limit in the event that the plan and the employer are unable to pay all promised benefits. The pensions of retired workers generally are insured for the full amount owed, while the pensions of vested but still employed workers are covered only to the extent that their vested interests have accrued at the time the plan terminates, but only to a level guaranteed by the PBGC. Accordingly, workers can lose promised and accrued benefits. This result is what happened to workers at

Exhibit 16.9 *Employee Benefit Plans Overview*

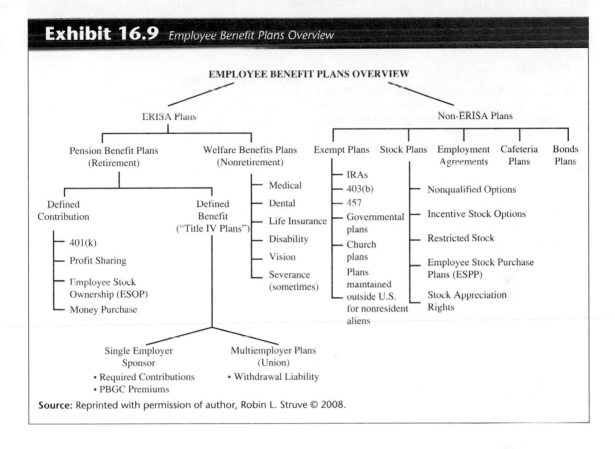

EMPLOYEE BENEFIT PLANS OVERVIEW

ERISA Plans

Non-ERISA Plans

Pension Benefit Plans (Retirement)

Welfare Benefits Plans (Nonretirement)

Exempt Plans   Stock Plans   Employment Agreements   Cafeteria Plans   Bonds Plans

Defined Contribution

Defined Benefit ("Title IV Plans")

- Medical
- Dental
- Life Insurance
- Disability
- Vision
- Severance (sometimes)

- IRAs
- 403(b)
- 457
- Governmental plans
- Church plans
- Plans maintained outside U.S. for nonresident aliens

- Nonqualified Options
- Incentive Stock Options
- Restricted Stock
- Employee Stock Purchase Plans (ESPP)
- Stock Appreciation Rights

- 401(k)
- Profit Sharing
- Employee Stock Ownership (ESOP)
- Money Purchase

Single Employer Sponsor
- Required Contributions
- PBGC Premiums

Multiemployer Plans (Union)
- Withdrawal Liability

Source: Reprinted with permission of author, Robin L. Struve © 2008.

United Airlines, for instance, when their pension plans were terminated in its bankruptcy proceedings.

When a firm considers modifying a retirement plan for its employees, it must be wary since the employees may have been making decisions in reliance on the original benefit plan. Even if a proposed plan offers greater benefits than those originally included, an employer has a fiduciary duty to notify all employees of the changes that might take effect once the employer gives the proposal "serious consideration." Consider the perspective of someone who is about to retire but who might have greater benefits if she simply waits a month or two until a new plan is implemented. She would prefer to know about the possibility, wouldn't she?

Where a plan is being given serious consideration, managers must truthfully and forthrightly offer the information to all employees. If notice of the possible changes are not given to employees, the firm should make eligibility for plan participation retroactive to the date of serious consideration. (See Exhibit 16.9, "Employee Benefit Plans Overview," for an overview of benefit plans, and Exhibit 16.10, "ERISA," for ERISA provisions.)

REPORTING AND DISCLOSURE

Participants

- *Summary Plan Descriptions (SPD)*—Within 90 days after an employee becomes a participant in the plan, or 120 days after the plan becomes subject to ERISA. Updated SPD must be provided every 5 years if amendments are made to the plan or 10 years if no amendments are made. Note: The Pension Welfare Benefits Administration has become the Employee Benefits Security Administration.
- *Summary of Material Modifications*—210 days after the end of the plan year in which the modification or change was adopted.
- *Summary Annual Reports*—Within nine months after the close of the plan year. Model notice available.
- *Notice to Participants of Underfunded Plans*—Defined benefit plans that are less than 90% funded two months after the deadline for filing Form 5500 for such plan. Model notice available.
- *Notice of Right to Diversify Investments*—Public companies that provide for investment in employer stock under a defined contribution plan must provide notice of the participant's right to diversify investments out of employer stock.
- *COBRA Notices.*
- *Blackout Period Notices*—30-day advance notice, with limited exceptions.
- Plan documents upon request.

IRS/DOL
- Form 5500.

PBGC
- Premiums—defined benefit plans only.

Penalties
- Daily penalties for failure to file required reports or provide required disclosure.
- Penalties for failure to provide required participant disclosure—generally $110/day per participant.
- DOL/IRS penalties range from $25 per day to $110 per day for delinquencies.
- Criminal penalties can apply.
- DOL delinquent filer program available with reduced set penalties.

FIDUCIARY DUTIES

- Plan assets held exclusively for the purposes of providing benefits to participants and beneficiaries.
- Prudent person rule.
- Investment diversification.
- Must abide by plan document.
- Participant-directed accounts.
- Plan assets must be invested as soon as possible, but no later than 15 business days after the end of the month in which payroll withholding occurs.
- Prohibited Transactions:
  —Loans.
  —Sales/purchases.
  —Providing services.
  —Using plan assets for own account.
- Breach of fiduciary duty is a personal liability. Make sure to have indemnification!

GENERAL WELFARE PLAN ISSUES

- *Severance Plans*—ERISA plans if they have an "administrative scheme." If not, then no.
- *Cafeteria Plans*—Not ERISA plans but still subject to IRS Form 5500 reporting (waived at this time). Cafeteria plan contributions not subject to FICA.
- *Disability*—When is an employee no longer "employed" once on disability? ADA concerns.

GENERAL PENSION PLAN ISSUES

- *401(k) Plans*—Non-discrimination/plan operation issues. Investments in employer stock. Fees regarding administration and investment management.
- *Cash Balance Plans*—Age discrimination and funding issues.
- *Defined Benefit Pension Plans*—Funding and cost of administration issues.

Source: By Robin L. Struve, "What Everyone Should Know About ERISA." © 2008. Reprinted with permission of the author.

ERISA Litigation

The collapse of Enron was the impetus behind many legal and regulatory reforms in the area of corporate governance. It also contributed to substantial litigation involving complex ERISA issues regarding fiduciary liability. Although, ultimately, the Enron ERISA litigation settled out of court, the few judicial decisions and the briefs that DOL filed in the Enron case influenced many cases claiming breach of fiduciary duty when the value of employer stock in retirement plans declined suddenly.[38] The outcomes of these "stock drop" cases differ, with some being decided during the pleading stage, before the case goes to the jury, and most of them settling out of court. However, such cases provide insight into who is or is not a fiduciary, as well as whether such fiduciaries have an affirmative duty to disclose information that may be relevant to a participant regarding his or her benefits. Generally, these cases find that a fiduciary will be *anyone who has functional discretionary control over the plan.* In addition, these cases generally hold that fiduciaries have a duty to be truthful, under the *Varity* standard discussed earlier, but may not always have an affirmative duty to disclose all financial details of the company merely due to the ability of participants to invest in company stock.[39]

The plaintiffs in the cases found in the notes all alleged that the fiduciaries of the plans breached their fiduciary duties under ERISA in one of the following ways:

- Allowing the plan to continue to acquire and hold employer stock after the defendants knew or should have known it was an imprudent investment;

- Failing to disclose to plan participants facts that would have enabled them to make an informed judgment regarding their continued acquisition and holding of employer stock; and/or

- Affirmatively inducing participants to continue to invest in employer stock after the defendants knew or should have known it was an imprudent investment.

Some of the more interesting claims in the stock drop cases surround the issue of who are the fiduciaries of the plan. Most of these plans gave fiduciary responsibility either to the company or to an administrative committee made up of individual employees appointed by the company.

ERISA declares that a person is a plan fiduciary "to the extent that" he or she exercises discretionary authority over plan management or plan administration, regardless of whether or not the person is a named fiduciary. Until Enron and its progeny, courts tended to interpret this functional definition of a fiduciary narrowly, and held that individuals acting in the scope of their employment were not personally liable for actions of the corporation. For example, the Third Circuit in *Confer v. Custom Engineering Co.*[40] held that, "when an ERISA plan names a corporation as a fiduciary, the officers who exercise discretion on behalf of the corporation are not fiduciaries within the meaning of [ERISA] unless it can be shown that these officers have individual discretionary roles as to plan administration." But other courts such as the Fifth Circuit in *Musmeci v. Giant Super Markets, Inc.,*[41] have adopted an expanded interpretation of the functional approach to determining fiduciary status, where the court held officers and employees performing fiduciary acts on behalf of a corporation that is a fiduciary will be fiduciaries themselves.

This broad functional approach is the position taken by the Department of Labor and by the Enron court when it wrote, "[i]n view of the broad language [and] the functional and flexible definition of 'fiduciary' . . . this Court agrees with those courts which reject a per se rule of non-liability for corporate officers acting on behalf of the corporation and instead make a functional, fact-specific inquiry to assess 'the extent of responsibility and control exercised by the individual with respect to the Plan' to determine if a corporate employee . . . has exercised sufficient discretionary authority and control to be deemed an ERISA fiduciary and thus personally liable for a fiduciary breach."[42] Most of the stock drop cases followed a similar approach.

The financial crisis that hit the U.S. in the 2000s caused pension plan losses that have been estimated at $2 trillion.[43] Most of those losses were the result of drops in the value of stocks held by pension plans. Not surprisingly perhaps, ERISA-based lawsuits to recover pension plan losses have skyrocketed.[44] Paving the way to more lawsuits was a 2008 decision by the U.S. Supreme Court, *LaRue v. DeWolff, Boberg & Associations,*[45] in which the Court ruled that individuals can sue the plan trustee under ERISA for individual losses to their retirement plans. ERISA §502(a)(2) allows recovery against the trustee for "losses to the plan." The question for the Court was whether "losses to the plan" meant that the suit against the trustee must be filed by the plan itself or if one person could bring suit for his or her individual losses. Provided that the plan is a defined contribution plan, such as a 401(k) plan, which has individual accounts, individuals are allowed to file suit under ERISA to recover damages resulting from the trustee's breach of his or her fiduciary duty. In the *LaRue* case, the individual contended that his retirement account lost $150,000 because the trustee failed to carry out his investment orders.

In response to the financial crisis in 2008, the Bush administration passed the Worker, Retiree, and Employer Recovery Act, which amended several features of ERISA and the PPA.[46] The new law clarifies that employers "are required to allow non-spouse rollovers and provide direct rollover notices as a condition of plan qualification."[47] Previously, pension providers were permitted, but not required, to allow nonspouses who are designated to receive participant death benefits to "roll over" the funds into an inherited IRA. Another provision permits "smoothing" in the calculation of the value of a pension plan's assets, protecting ERISA plans from market volatility by averaging value over a two-year period. Other measures ease the transition to PPA funding rules by lowering the required funding threshold for plans that fail to meet expected annual earnings.

Consolidated Omnibus Budget Reconciliation Act of 1985 (COBRA)

The problem of an employee losing workplace health care coverage when the employee stopped working or switched jobs was addressed by the Consolidated Omnibus Budget Reconciliation Act of 1985 (COBRA) and was codified in ERISA and the tax code.[48] COBRA applies to group health plans provided by employers with 20 or more employees on a typical working day in the previous calendar year. COBRA gives participants and beneficiaries the right to maintain, at their own expense, coverage under their health plan that would be lost due to a change in circumstance such as termination of employment or divorce. However, many states have similar laws governing smaller employers. A small employer should not assume that it does not have continuation requirements if it is otherwise not covered by COBRA.

If a worker's employment terminates or she or he loses benefit coverage due to a reduction in hours, COBRA requires that employers extend employee health insurance coverage for up to 18 months and may charge up to 102 percent of the rates originally charged while the individual was still working for the employer. While the coverage is paid for by the employee, COBRA provides guaranteed coverage for an employee who leaves employment for a relatively short time where that person may have difficulty obtaining coverage. COBRA also requires employers to extend coverage to dependents who would otherwise lose coverage due to divorce or ceasing to be a dependent. General notice informing the covered individuals must be given informing them of their rights under COBRA and describing the law.

The Health Insurance Portability and Accountability Act (HIPAA)

The Health Insurance Portability and Accountability Act (HIPAA) is a federal law that amended ERISA in 1996 to promote standardization and efficiency in the health care industry.[49] HIPAA accomplishes several goals including protecting individuals from discrimination based on their health status because it restricts exclusion from coverage due to preexisting medical conditions (employers are prohibited from denying coverage or charging more for coverage based on an individual's past or present poor health); it created a uniform system for processing, retaining, and securing health care information by encouraging the use of electronic technology, mandating standardization of health-related transactions, and promoting security precautions to maintain the privacy of health information; and perhaps, most importantly, it protects the privacy of individuals with respect to their health care data, and the sharing of such data. Other HIPAA protections relate to the portability of medical coverage by individuals who experience a job loss or job change. When such an event occurs, HIPAA may increase the ability to obtain or maintain health coverage for oneself or one's dependents if the election is made within a certain time frame.

HHS delegated responsibility for enforcing HIPAA's privacy rules to the HHS Office for Civil Rights (OCR). HIPAA does not provide a private right of action for individuals to sue covered entities for alleged violations. However, covered entities may be subject to private lawsuits borne under tort or other legal theories. For example, individual state laws may offer relief that can be invoked by private plaintiffs. Further, some situations may be governed by ERISA, which would allow participants and beneficiaries to sue for enforcement of the applicable plan document.

HIPAA violations are subject to civil and criminal sanctions enforced by the Department of Justice. For instance, HHS may impose civil monetary penalties on a covered entity of $100 per failure to comply with HIPAA's privacy rules. A person who knowingly obtains or discloses individually identifiable health information in violation of HIPAA faces a fine of $50,000 and up to one year of imprisonment. The criminal penalties increase to $100,000 and up to $250,000 and up to 10 years of imprisonment if the wrongful conduct involves the intent to sell, transfer, or use individually identifiable health information for commercial advantage, personal gain, or malicious harm.

HIPAA does not preempt all state privacy laws. Furthermore, there are no provisions in HIPAA that exempt an employer from complying with other federal laws such as ERISA, ADA, and FMLA. In jurisdictions where the state privacy laws are more stringent than HIPAA, those laws or the relevant portions thereof are preserved and should be applied instead of HIPAA.[50] Therefore, a state privacy law that provides more privacy protections or greater individual rights than provided by the federal HIPAA privacy rules will generally govern the situation. Employers should initially determine whether and to what extent they are required to follow state law (including local statutes and regulations) instead of the requirements of HIPAA. The HHS Web site, http://www.hhs.gov, contains numerous links and technical assistance on HIPAA-related topics.

HIPAA Privacy Rules

HIPAA's privacy rules specifically address the permitted and prohibited use(s) and disclosure(s) of health information by organizations subject to them.[51] A covered entity is generally permitted (but not required) to use and disclose protected health information, *without* an individual's authorization, for the following purposes or situations: to the individual for "treatment," "payment," and "health care operations" as defined in the rule; to certain governmental authorities if abuse, neglect, or domestic violence is at issue; for many law enforcement activities pursuant to court orders and/or subpoenas; to funeral directors, coroners, or medical examiners to identify a deceased person or to determine the cause of death; and to the U.S. Department of Health and Human Services (HHS) when it is undertaking a compliance investigation, review, or enforcement action.

Generally, covered entities may use or disclose protected health information only if the use or disclosure is permitted or required by these privacy rules.[52] In very general terms, a group health plan may use protected health information internally or disclose it externally only under the limited circumstances and for the specific purposes articulated in the privacy rules. Otherwise, group health plans may use or disclose protected health information only with the specific permission of the individual who is the subject of the protected health information. Such permission is manifested in the form of a signed, valid authorization form. No doubt, you have signed at least one such form in the past couple of years if you have visited a doctor. Such forms must be written in plain language and they must include a number of elements, including the following:[53]

- A description of the protected health information to be used and disclosed.
- The person(s) authorized to make the use or disclosure.
- The person(s) to whom the covered entity may make the disclosure.
- An expiration date or event.
- The purpose for which the information may be used or disclosed.
- A notice of the individual's right to revoke the authorization.

In some circumstances, it may be necessary to include additional information for the authorization to be valid. There are special rules, for instance, that apply to psychotherapy notes and the use of health information for marketing purposes. The validity of an authorization also may be subject to various state laws and may be further varied depending on the subject of the health information that is being used or disclosed. Additional privacy requirements may be imposed by state law in jurisdictions where the state law provides greater protections for health information.

These privacy rules attempt to strike a balance between permitting important uses of information and protecting the privacy of people who seek medical treatment. The rule is supposedly flexible and comprehensive enough to cover the variety of uses and disclosures that need to be addressed while still promoting high-quality health care.

HIPAA applies to any entity that is a health care provider that conducts certain transactions in electronic form, a health care clearinghouse, or a health plan. Entities that fall within one or more of these categories are referred to as *covered entities.* Many varied organizations (in addition to hospitals) *may* be considered a covered entity due to the activities they conduct. For instance, a university might be considered a covered entity if it has a student health center or a mental health center that provides health care. A grocery store may be considered a covered entity if it has a group health plan managed by the benefits office for its employees.

General Obligations of Covered Entities

In general, HIPAA requires covered entities to notify patients of their privacy rights and to explain how their personal health information can be used or disclosed by the organization or its business associates. To this end, they must prepare and distribute a Notice of Privacy Practices to their patients or employees depending on the activities that they regularly conduct.

Covered entities are required to adopt and implement privacy policies and procedures. These policies should be widely publicized and distributed to all individuals within the organization. Individuals who work closely with health information or who are responsible for securing this information should receive detailed training on the organization's established policies and procedures.

All covered entities should make an effort to prevent unauthorized viewing or access to (electronic and paper) health records in their care. To this end, administrative, physical, and technical safeguards should be implemented. Specific protective steps may include the establishment of regular and ongoing training sessions for new and current employees who handle health information; documentation of office procedures for managing health information; creation of firewalls between departments to shield those departments that maintain health information from, for example, individuals who make human resources decisions; addition of locks to file cabinets that house medical information; and use of passwords and timed screen savers on all computers of individuals whose jobs require them to regularly come into contact with health information.

Organizations also must designate a privacy officer who has responsibility for ensuring that the above steps are adopted and followed, and that complaints regarding privacy violations are addressed through the organization's established procedures. The privacy officer should use a monitoring plan to randomly check on the effectiveness of the organization's privacy practices. (See Exhibit 16.11, "Sample Monitoring Plan.")

Enforcement of ERISA

Employers have the right to reduce or modify employee benefits (unless prohibited by contractual obligations), as long as similarly situated plan participants are treated alike. For instance, the employer may not reduce benefits for one full-time employee without similarly reducing the benefits for all similar employees. In order to prevail on a claim of a violation of section 510 of the act, in the case of discharge, the employee must prove that the employer terminated her or his employment with the "specific intent" to interfere with her or his benefit rights.

In *Owens v. Storehouse, Inc.,*[54] the court was asked to consider the employer's (Storehouse) choice to limit coverage for specific types of claims, a choice that could adversely impact certain employees. Specifically, the employer's insurance company notified Storehouse that it intended to cancel the firm's policy because of the high incidence of AIDS in the retail industry generally, and among Storehouse's employees specifically (five employees had AIDS at the time). Eventually, Storehouse convinced the company to continue the contract, but there was now a $75,000 deductible for AIDS-related claims, while other coverage began at $25,000. As it looked for another insurer, Storehouse considered placing a $25,000 lifetime cap on all AIDS-related claims. Owens, an employee, sued, claiming that this modification lowering the cap violated ERISA. The court held that there is no "vested" interest in the type of coverage an employer provides, even once someone begins to take advantage of that coverage, as long as the employer reserves the right to change or terminate its terms. As there was no specific intent to violate ERISA (i.e., denial of coverage in retaliation for exercising an ERISA right), the employer prevailed. (Note: This type of arrangement would now be prohibited by the ADA as it would be discriminatory against someone with a disability.)

Exhibit 16.11 *Sample Monitoring Plan*

Specific Risk (1)	Operating Control (2)	Monitoring Control (3)	Evidence of Control	Oversight Control (4)	Evidence of Oversight Control
Complaint of inappropriate use/disclosure of their PHI.	HIPAA policy forbids this action by personnel.	Violations of HIPAA policy are subject to disciplinary action.	Policy that supports disciplinary action for violation of HIPAA policy.	Complaint procedure, as outlined in university HIPAA policy.	Periodic check by component areas of complaints logged by privacy office.
New employees in component areas are not trained on HIPAA protocol.	Policy officials within each component area should train new employees in their respective areas.	Written training procedures developed by departments that handle PHI.	Training attendance forms signed by training participants once training is completed.	Training attendance forms are returned to privacy officer once training has been completed.	Training attendance forms are filed in privacy office.
Notice of privacy practices is not distributed in accordance with HIPAA.	Component areas set up procedures that govern the designated times and manner notice is to be distributed.	Random (annual), periodic auditing/monitoring by privacy office of organization's privacy practices.	Schedule of random/periodic monitoring.	Complaint procedure, as outlined in university HIPAA policy.	Periodic check by complaints logged by privacy office.
"Business associates" are not bound by agreement with the organization before they access PHI.	Component areas identify vendors and any others who may have access to PHI and provide this information to privacy officer.	Privacy officer contacts vendor and memorializes terms of agreement.	Business associate agreements.	Business associate agreements are cataloged in organization's database.	Random audits of database.
PHI is not protected by administrative, physical, and technical safeguards.	Component areas set up procedures that determine the minimum necessary disclosures to make pursuant to valid requests; in addition, component areas have to identify physical safeguards to protect PHI locks on file cabinets, passwords on computers.	Review departmental procedures and establish random, periodic auditing/monitoring by privacy officer.	Schedule of random/periodic monitoring	Complaint procedure, as outlined in HIPAA policy.	Periodic check by component areas of complaints logged by privacy office.

Management Tips

- Ensure that all employees are correctly classified so that the appropriate FLSA provisions are applied.
- Be sure to include all appropriate time in wages, such as donning and doffing time.
- Know that the Obama administration is tightening up enforcement of wage laws, so make sure the laws are handled appropriately.
- Check the status of employees carefully before granting or denying FMLA leave.
- Be aware that the Obama administration has clarified coverage of sick child laws to gays and lesbians caring for children of the relationship.
- Note that the Bush administration extended FMLA laws to better cover members of the military and their families being cared for during deployment or after returning with an injury.
- Make sure that all of your communications about your benefit plans are clear and written in a way that a reasonable person would understand. If you make any changes, those need to be communicated in writing to all affected employees.
- Under the Pension Protection Act (PPA) of 2006, you may have an additional communication requirement if you are a public company. If you allow for investment of employee contributions into your stock fund, you will need to notify employees of their right to diversify into other stock investments outside of your fund. There are other requirements along these lines, as well; so public companies need to be especially careful and diligent with respect to notification to employees.
- Individuals acting as officers and employees who are performing fiduciary acts on behalf of a corporation that is a fiduciary should be aware of the potential for a broad-scale adoption of an expanding definition of fiduciary that is tending to include them.

In *Central Laborers' Pension Fund v. Heinz,* provided for your review, the Supreme Court evaluated a similar claim with regard to the amendment of a pension plan that expanded the definition of disqualifying employment and resulted in a suspension of early retirement benefits to some participants, in possible violation of ERISA's prohibition against reducing an accrued right or benefit under a pension plan (the "anti-cutback" rule), an issue not addressed in *Owens* because those benefits were welfare benefits not protected by ERISA's accrual rule.

It should be noted that some ERISA claims also may be asserted under the Age Discrimination in Employment Act (ADEA). For instance, since benefits are more likely to become vested as a worker gains seniority and as seniority may be more likely with advancing age, employers attempting to avoid paying benefits may be more likely to terminate older workers, giving rise to a claim under both ERISA and the ADEA.

Chapter Summary

We have covered a lot of ground in this chapter.

- Employers must be aware that employees have certain rights due to them under various statutes, including the right to a minimum wage and to be paid time and a half for hours worked over 40.

- Children below a certain age may not be employed except as specified by law, and there are only certain hours they can work and certain jobs they can do.

- By law, employees who have worked for an employer for at least 12 months are entitled to take up to 12 weeks' unpaid leave for illness or to care for their children, parents, or a returning war veteran, without fear that their job will be taken from them or that their benefits or seniority will suffer.

- In addition, employees have a right to a safe workplace. Employers have a general duty to provide a safe workplace for their employees, in addition to any specific workplace safety regulations that have been developed by OSHA. OSHA inspectors have the authority to conduct unannounced inspections of a workplace, either without a warrant if the employer agrees or with a warrant if the employer insists upon one. Employers may be fined for violations of the safety regulations.

- While employers are not required to provide workplace benefits and retirement plans for their employees, if they choose to do so, they must carefully follow the applicable laws, including allowing employees to have interim coverage if they leave the job and protecting any medical information the employer may have for the employee. In providing benefits, the employer is under a duty to disclose relevant facts to employees, including contemplated changes, and to safeguard the employees' contributions from unethical or illegal interference.

- An awareness of these workplace rules is a must for an employer who wishes to avoid federal and state liability for violations.

Chapter-End Questions

1. No employer intends to harm its employees. How would you define the term *willful* that would give rise to penalties of up to $70,000?

2. The range of dangerous conditions in which employees have been forced to work has been well documented, at least since Upton Sinclair's *The Jungle*. But, what if the danger is the condition of the workplace building itself? Do the OSH Act protections extend to dangers created by, for example, a decrepit building? [*Cascades Boxboard Group*, osha.gov/pls/oshaweb/owadisp.show_doucment?p_table=NEWS_RELEASES&p_id=17393, Jan. 30, 2009.]

3. A police officer is eligible for two hours of additional leave bonus if he does not take more than 40 hours of sick leave during a year. If he loses the bonus as a result of taking FMLA leave, have his rights been violated because he has not been restored to an equivalent position before he left? Does it matter how he chooses to take his FMLA leave (i.e., as sick leave versus some other type of leave)? [*Chubb v. City of Omaha*, No. 05-1172, Eighth Circuit, Sept. 27, 2005.]

4. Allbright finds that Benito, Juana, and Lao Tsu, three of his employees, were the cause of the discovery of FLSA violations. As a result, he terminates them. Do the employees have any recourse? Explain.

5. Sasha is employed as the Winstons' babysitter when they must occasionally stay over in town because of their jobs. Sasha is becoming increasingly discontented with her wages, which are below minimum wage. What relief does the FLSA provide for Sasha?

6. A Christmas tree grower used seasonal help to assist in harvesting Christmas trees and did not pay them overtime wages since the growers deemed the employees as engaged in agriculture, which is exempted from the overtime provisions. The DOL argued that the planting, fertilizing, and all other tasks relevant to growing the trees were performed by others who were agricultural workers exempted from the overtime provisions. However, they argued, since the seasonal employees only harvested the trees, they were not engaged in agriculture, but rather in forestry and lumbering, which requires the payment of overtime wages. Which view prevails? [*DOL v. N.C. Tree Growers Association, Inc.,* 377 F.3d 345 (4th Cir. 2004).]

7. In a construction project, a company built an 18-foot-by-20-foot trench that had to be lined with a special fabric. When the workers had trouble stretching the fabric over the trench, an employee volunteered to go into the trench and fix the problem. His supervisor stopped him, saying it was too dangerous because the walls of the trench had not been properly supported. After several additional failed attempts to stretch the fabric, the supervisor relented and told the employee to go into the trench. Within five minutes, he was seriously injured when the trench collapsed. Does the supervisor's initial statement constitute an intentional act of injury by the employer, thus removing the case from the limits set by the workers' compensation statutes? Is it relevant to a jury's decision if OSHA issues a citation for a willful violation in this case before it goes to trial? [*Van Dunk v. Reckson Associates Realty Corp.,* Superior Court of NJ, Appellate Div., No. A-3548-08T2, August 30, 2010.]

8. An employee worked as a drill and machine operator at a furniture manufacturer. Employees were subject to dismissal when they accumulated seven points against them for violations based on conduct. For example, an excused absence was one point, while an unexcused absence was two points. The drill operator had five points; so, when she developed a urinary tract infection, she felt forced to work through the pain. Her doctor ultimately determined that she needed surgery to repair the urinary tract infection, so she asked for leave under the FMLA, for which the employer confirmed she was eligible.

   Meanwhile, two other relevant events occurred. First, she was arrested and spent two days in jail for writing bad checks, both days of which constituted unexcused absences. Second, she left work early one day, believing that she had been terminated, to see her union rep and was dismissed, not for accumulating too many points but for walking off the job. She was also denied her right to the FMLA because she was five days short of working for the employer for one year, as the FMLA requires. Is the employee entitled to FMLA leave? Has the employer fired her for absences attributable to a serious health condition, which is prohibited under the FMLA? Do the two days spent in jail constitute an unexcused absence, thus allowing the employer to fire her? Was she retaliated against for going to see her union rep, in violation of the FMLA? [*Gurley v. Ameriwood Industries, Inc.,* No. 4:01 CV 355 DDN, E.D. Mo., 2002.]

9. Jared requested FMLA time off from his job to care for his partner, Samuel, who was suffering from a particularly acute case of adult mumps. Is the leave likely to be granted?

10. Nine months after coming to work for Gaggle, Inc, Sarah was diagnosed with breast cancer. The prognosis was not good. Sarah underwent surgery and a chemotherapy regimen that physically depleted her. When Sarah's sick leave was used up, Sarah asked her employer for 12 weeks of FMLA leave. Will Sarah be granted the FMLA leave for her health?

End Notes

1. The federal regulations of the Wage and Hour Division can be found at 29 C.F.R. chapter V, http://www.dol.gov/esa/whd/flsa/index.htm.

2. http://www.dol.gov/whd/statistics/2008FiscalYear.htm.

3. Toni Randolph, "Wal-mart to Pay $54.25 M to Settle Minnesota Lawsuit," MPRNews, 12/9/2008, http://minnesota.publicradio.org/display/web/2008/12/09/wall_mart_suit/.

4. "The Labor Department—which has set new records for aggressive Wage and Hour enforcement—now has strong new standards in place to better protect workers' pay," http://www.dol.gov/claws/overtime.htm; Cynthia Stamer, "The DOL's announcement of the recovery of more than $1.5 million in back pay under these two settlements in less than a week highlights the rising risks U.S. employers run if their overtime, wage and hour, worker classification or recordkeeping practices don't comply with the Fair Labor Standards Act or other federal wage and hour laws." 1/24/2011, http://cynthiastamer.com/get_docID2a.asp?fileID=7PB1gVYd7l1hpbBzI5MEOVY8u.

5. Steve Greenhouse, "Growth of Unpaid Internships May Be Illegal, Official Says," *The New York Times*, 4/2/2010, http://nytimes.com/2010/04/03/business/03intern.html.

6. Ibid.

7. 593 F.3d 449 (5th Cir. 2010).

8. For a list of state minimum wage laws regarding tipping, see, the Wage and Hour Division of the Department of Labor's information at http://www.dol.gov/whd/state/tipped.htm.

9. 160 F.3d 294 (6th Cir. 1998).

10. *Chou v. Starbucks,* No. GIC 836925 (Cal. Super. Ct. Mar. 19, 2008).

11. www.courtinfo, ca.gov/opinions/archive/D053491.pdf.

12. "U.S. Department of Labor recovers more than $1M in overtime wages for employees of U.S. Army contractor in Southern California: Back wages paid to 864 employees working at Ft. Irwin," 1/13/2011, http://www.dol.gov/whd/media/press/whdpressVB3. asp?pressdoc=Western/20110113.xml.

13. www.dol.gov/esa/whd/fmla/ndaa_fmla.htm.

14. "U.S. Department of Labor clarifies FMLA definition of son and daughter: Interpretation is a win for all families no matter what they look like," news release, U.S. Department of Labor, 6/22/2010, http://www.dol.gov/opa/media/press/WHD/WHD20100877.htm.

15. http://oversight.house.gov/story.asp?ID=1878.

16. Society for Human Resource Management, "FMLA and Its Impact on Organizations," July 2007, http://www.shrm.org/Publications/HRNews/Pages/CMS_022292.aspx.

17. "U.S. Department of Labor final rule will expand FMLA for military families and clarify rules for workers and employers," Department of Labor news release, 11/17/2008, http://www.dol.gov/opa/media/press/esa/archive/esa20081703.htm.

18. 278 F.3d 847 (8th Cir. 2002).

19. No. 09-1775 (7th cir. 2/14/11).

20. No. 09-CV-4055 (W. D. Ark 1/27/2011).

21. Occupational Safety and Health Administration, "OSHA Enforcement: Vital to a Safe and Healthy Workforce," 2007, http://www.osha.gov/dep/enforcement/ enforcement_results_06.html.

22. *Solis v. Summit Contractors, Inc.*, No. 07-2191, Feb. 26, 2009, Eighth Circuit.

23. http://www.osha.gov/recordkeeping/new-osha300form1-1-04.pdf.

24. U.S. Dept. of Labor, "U.S. Department of Labor's OSHA proposes $2.78 million fine against Cintas Corp.," OSHA press release (Aug. 16, 2007), http://www.osha.gov/pls/oshaweb/owadisp.show_document?p_table-NEWS_RELEASE&p_id-14397.

25. OSHA, "U.S. Dept. of Labor, Cintas Settle Pending Federal OSHA Cases," OSHA trade news release (Dec. 18, 2008), http://www.osha.gov/pls/oshaweb/owadisp.show_document?p_table=NEWS_RELEASES&p_id=17213; U.S. House of Representatives, Committee on Education and Labor, "Woolsey, Hare Assail Cintas Settlement," press release (Dec. 19, 2008), http://www.house.gov/apps/list/speech/edlabor_dem/1219Cintas.html.

26. Tom Parsons, "Tyson Foods Fined," Softcom.com/Associated Press, April 9, 2004.

27. 445 U.S. 1 (1980).

28. 528 F.2d 564 (5th Cir. 1976).

29. See Maureen Milford, "UC Takes Charge of Enron Suit," *National Law Journal*, March 7, 2002.

30. *Moench v. Robertson*, 62 F.3d 553 (3d Cir. 1995).

31. Stephen Rosenberg, "The Ninth Circuit Adopts Moench and Why It Matters," Boston ERISA & Insurance Litigation Blog (October 8, 2010), http://www.bostonerisalaw.com/archives/401k-plans-the-ninth-circuit-adopts-moench-and-why-it-matters.html (accessed 2/26/11).

32. *Quan v. Computer Sciences Corp.*, 623 F. 3rd 870 (9th Cir. Sept. 30, 2010); Yolanda Montgomery, "Third Time's the Charm: The Ninth Circuit Finally Adopts *Moench* Presumption of Prudence," *The ERISA Litigation Newsletter* (November 2010), http://www.proskauer.com/news/detail.aspx?news=5783.

33. Danielle Andrus, "To Aid with Compliance of DOL's ERISA Rules, Principal Releases White Paper," AdvisorOne (January 11, 2011), http://www.advisorone.com/article/aid-compliance-dols-erisa-rules-principal-releases-white-paper.

34. Department of Labor, 29 CFR Part 2550, Reasonable Contract or Arrangement under Section 408(b)(2)—Fee Disclosure; Interim Final Rule.

35. 128 S.Ct. 2343 (2008).

36. W. Mark Smith & Jasper B. Smith, "United States: Supreme Court Addresses Conflicts of Interest in ERISA Benefit Claims," Sutherland Asbill & Brennan LLP, August 13, 2008 (originally published, July 1, 2008), mondaq.com.

37. See *Murphy v. Deloitte & Touche Group Ins. Plan*, 619 F.3d 1151 (10th Cir. 2010); *Crosby v. La. Health Serv. & Indem. Co.*, Case No. 10-30043, 2010 WL 5356498 (5th Cir. Dec. 29, 2010). See also, Jeannine Jacobson, "Will the 10th Circuit's Advice Rein in ERISA Conflict Discovery?," Sedgwick, Detert, Moran & Arnold LLP, *Healthcare Law Newsletter*, January 31, 2001, sdma.com.

38. See *In re WorldCom Inc. ERISA Litig.*, 263 F. Supp. 2d 745 (S.D. N.Y. 2003); *In re Polaroid ERISA Litig.*, 362 F. Supp. 2d 461 (S.D.N.Y 2005); *In re McKesson HBOC,*

Inc. ERISA Litig., 291 F. Supp. 2d 812 (N.D. Cal. 2005); *In re Goodyear Tire & Rubber Co. ERISA Litig.,* 438 F. Supp. 2d 783 (N.D. Ohio 2006); *DiFelice v. US Airways,* 436 F. Supp. 2d 756 (E.D. Va. 2006); *In re Electronic Data Systems Corp. "ERISA" Litig.,* 305 F. Supp. 2d 658 (E.D. Tex. 2004); *In re Sears Roebuck & Co. ERISA Litig.,* No. 02 C 8324, 2004 U.S. Dist. LEXIS 3241 (N.D. Ill. Mar. 3, 2004); *In re Tyco Int'l Ltd., Multidistrict Litig.,* 2004 U.S. Dist. LEXIS 24272 (D.N.H. Dec. 2, 2004).

39. See *Kelley v. Household International, Inc.,* 312 F. Supp. 2d 1165 (N.D. Ill. 2004), and *Hill v. Bellsouth Corp.,* 313 F. Supp. 2d 1361 (N.D. Ga 2004).

40. 952 F.2d 34 (3d Cir. 1991).

41. 332 F.3d 339, 350–52 (5th Cir. 2003).

42. *Title v. Enron Corp.,* 2003 WL 22245394 at 85 (S.D. Tex. September 30, 2003).

43. Mike Caggeso, "Retirement Blues: Financial Crisis Pulls Billions from Pension Plans, Crimping Consumers' Dreams and Corporate Profits," *Money Morning,* January 29, 2009, moneymorning.com/2009/01/29/pension-plans.

44. See, for example, Sean F. Driscoll, "More Retirement Plan Lawsuits Filed as Stock Market Slumps, *Rockford Register Star,* Dec. 11, 2010, www.rrstar.com/businessrockford/x1757258400/More-pension-fund-lawsuits-filed-as-stock-market-falls.

45. 128 S.Ct. 1020 (2008).

46. Worker, Retiree, and Employer Recovery Act of 2008. H.R. 7327 (December 23, 2008).

47. Keith McCurdy, "Worker, Retiree and Employer Recovery Act Changes Required Minimum Distributions," *Employee Benefits Legal Blog,* December 22, 2008, employeebenefits.foxrothschild.com.

48. Consolidated Omnibus Budget Reconciliation Act of 1985, Pub. Law No. 99-272 (April 7, 1986).

49. Health Insurance Portability and Accountability Act of 1996, Pub. Law No. 104-191 (August 21, 1996).

50. For instance, Illinois has more stringent requirements regarding use and disclosure of genetic health information. See 410 Ill. Comp. Stat. 513/15 et seq.—the Genetic Information Privacy Act—regarding the use and disclosure of mental health information. See also 740 Ill. Comp. Stat. 110/1 et seq., the Mental Health and Developmental Disabilities Confidentiality Act.

51. Though certain information may be released pursuant to permitted uses and disclosures, the amount of released information should be limited to the "minimum necessary" that is needed to accomplish the intended purpose of the use, disclosure, or request, as defined in the rules.

52. See 45 C.F.R. § 164.502(a).

53. See 45 C.F.R. § 164.508.

54. 984 F.2d 394 (11th Cir. 1993).

Cases

Case 1

Reich v. Circle C Investments, Inc. *998 F.2d 324 (5th Cir. 1993)*

The court analyzes whether topless nightclub dancers who received no compensation except tips from customers are employees subject to FLSA or "business women renting space, stages, music, dressing rooms and lights from the club," not subject to the law. The court determined that they were, in fact, employees for FLSA purposes.

Reavley, J.

***

The secretary of labor alleges that a topless nightclub has improperly compensated its dancers, waitresses, disc jockeys, bartenders, doormen, and "housemothers" and has failed to keep accurate records of the hours worked by its employees. The district court determined that the topless dancers and other workers are "employees" under the FLSA and that the club willfully violated its minimum wage, overtime and record-keeping provisions.

The dancers receive no compensation from the club. Their compensation is derived solely from the tips they receive from customers for performing on stage and performing private "table dances" and "couch dances." At the end of each night, the dancers must pay the club a $20 "tip-out," regardless of how much they make in tips. The club characterizes this tip-out as stage rental and argues that the dancers are really tenants. According to the club, the dancers are neither employees nor independent contractors, but are business women renting space, stages, music, dressing rooms, and lights from the club.

To determine employee status under the FLSA, we focus on whether the alleged employee, as a matter of economic reality, is economically dependent upon the business to which she renders her services, or in business for herself. To make this determination, we must analyze five factors.

The first factor is the degree of control exercised by the alleged employer. The district court found that the club exercises a great deal of control over the dancers. They are required to comply with weekly work schedules, which the club compiles with input from the dancers. The club fines the dancers for absences or tardiness. It instructs the dancers to charge at least $10 for table dances and $20 for couch dances. The dancers supply their own costumes, but the costumes must meet standards set by the club. The dancers can express a preference for a certain type of music, but they do not have the

final say in the matter. The club has many other rules concerning the dancers' behavior; for example, no flat heels, no more than 15 minutes at one time in the dressing room, only one dancer in the restroom at a time, and all dancers must be "on the floor" at opening time. The club enforces these rules by fining infringers.

The club attempts to de-emphasize its control by arguing that most of the rules are directed at maintaining decorum or keeping the club itself legal. The club explained that it publishes the minimum charge for table and couch dances at the request of the dancers to prevent dancers from undercutting each others' prices. Finally, it stresses the fact that it does not control the dancers' routines. We believe, however, that the record fully supports the district court's findings of significant control.

The second factor is the extent of relative investments of the worker and alleged employer. The district court found that a dancer's investment is limited to her costumes and a padlock. The amount spent on costumes varies from dancer to dancer and can be significant. The club contends that we should also consider as an investment each dancer's nightly tip-out, which it characterizes as rent. The district court rejected this argument, and so do we. It is the economic realities that control our determination of employee status.

Third, we must look at the degree to which the workers' opportunity for profit and loss is determined by the alleged employer. Once customers arrive at the club, a dancer's initiative, hustle and costume significantly contribute to the amount of her tips. But the club has a significant role in drawing customers. Given its control over determinants of customer volume, the club exercises a high degree of control over a dancer's opportunity for "profit." Dancers are far more closely akin to wage earners toiling for a living than to independent entrepreneurs seeking a return on their risky capital investments.

The fourth factor is the skill and initiative required in performing the job. Many of the dancers did not have any prior experience with topless dancing before coming to work at the club. They do not need long training or highly developed skills to dance at the club. A dancer's initiative is essentially limited to decisions involving costumes and dance routines. This does not exhibit the skill or initiative indicative of persons in business for themselves.

Finally, we must analyze the permanency of the relationship. The district court found that most dancers have short-term relationships with the club. Although not determinative, the impermanent relationship between the dancers and the club indicates non-employee status.

Despite the lack of permanency, on balance, the five factors favor a determination of employee status. A dancer has no specialized skills and her only real investment is in her costumes. The club exercises significant control over a dancer's behavior and the opportunity for profit. The transient nature of the workforce is not enough here to remove the dancers from the protections of the FLSA. AFFIRMED.

Case Questions

1. Does any of the case surprise you? Explain.

2. If you were the club owner and did not want the dancers to be employees, after receiving this decision, how would you change things?

3. Do you think the dancers should have been considered employees? Why or why not?

Case 2

Mullins v. City of New York *626 F.3d 47 (2nd Cir. 2010)*

A group of police officers sued their police department for violations of the FLSA, specifically for failing to pay them for overtime. In the course of that lawsuit, the police department took depositions of some of the police officers. Following those depositions, the police department ordered its Internal Affairs Bureau to become involved in the lawsuit, both by collecting various documents and by attending future depositions. The officers claimed that IAB's involvement constituted retaliation, which is prohibited by the FLSA, and they sought a preliminary injunction stopping all such intimidation. The trial court granted the injunction and the police department appealed to the Second Circuit.

Pooler, J.

***

Plaintiff-Appellees are approximately 4300 current and former New York City police sergeants who filed suit against the City of New York (the "City") and the New York City Police Department ("NYPD") on April 19, 2004, claiming systematic violations of their overtime rights under the Fair Labor Standards Act of 1938 ("FLSA"). Because of the sheer volume of plaintiffs, the parties agreed in May of 2005 to limit depositions to "test plaintiffs"—individuals from seventeen job categories, who would be organized into three groups.

The record reflects that, at some point in January 2006, NYPD's outside counsel, Seyfarth Shaw LLP, met with Charles Campisi, Chief of the "Internal Affairs Bureau" ("IAB"), as well as other high level IAB officials and NYPD lawyers regarding the "topic of deposition

testimony." On January 19, 2006, Seyfarth Shaw sent transcripts from depositions of the first group of test plaintiffs to Appellants. The next day, the NYPD ordered lieutenants from IAB to collect command logs, memo books, activity reports, overtime slips, and requests for leave reports from all of the test plaintiffs as well as individuals who worked with them. Some of the IAB document collectors were plaintiffs in this lawsuit—they were promoted to lieutenants after the action was filed. The pool of plaintiffs from whom documents were collected included both those who had been deposed and those who had not.

Counsel for the test plaintiffs immediately objected to the use of IAB to collect documents on the ground that certain plaintiffs understood IAB's involvement to mean they were under investigation. Sergeant Paul Capotosto, Citywide Secretary of the Sergeants Benevolent Association, described the document collection process as a "raid." During his testimony at the preliminary injunction hearing, Sergeant Capotosto chronicled at least a dozen phone calls he received from worried plaintiffs, who expressed concern to him that the NYPD was retaliating against them for their participation in the lawsuit. Among these callers was IAB Lieutenant Ed Heim, a plaintiff in this action, who described being "forced" to collect documents from other plaintiffs and communicated his apprehension to Sergeant Capotosto about the NYPD's approach. Another sergeant referred to IAB's actions as "goon tactics."

Testimony at the preliminary injunction hearing about the unusual nature of the process used to collect documents confirmed that plaintiffs' concerns were not unfounded. Sergeant Anthony Lisi of the Emergency Services Unit of the NYPD testified that document collection is typically conducted by Administrative Lieutenants or Integrity Control Officers assigned to a particular command. In addition, Sergeant Brian Coughlan, Sergeant Supervisor of Detectives in the Bomb Squad, testified that IAB is involved in most cases only when an officer is being arrested or removed from his post.

In March 2006, shortly after the document collection, IAB sent an Integrity Control Officer to attend the deposition of Sergeant Edward Scott. As of his deposition date, Sergeant Scott, who was a plaintiff in the lawsuit against the City and NYPD, had given no testimony in connection with the action. Sergeant Scott, who testified by affidavit at the preliminary injunction hearing, explained that Integrity Control Officers do not normally attend depositions, and he was, therefore, "surprised and concerned" by the officer's presence. He also testified that he found the officer's presence to be "intimidating." When Sergeant Scott's retirement was administratively deferred pending resolution of an unspecified "disciplinary matter" some months later, it came to light that he was under investigation for testimony he had given during his deposition. Sergeant Scott stated that, at the time, "I believed that if I withdrew from this FLSA lawsuit, the City would close its investigation into my deposition testimony."

FLSA provides that it is "unlawful for any person . . . to discharge or in any other manner discriminate against any employee because such employee has filed any complaint or instituted or caused to be instituted any proceeding under [FLSA]." 29 U.S.C. § 215(a)(3). FLSA retaliation claims are subject to the three-step burden-shifting framework established by *McDonnell Douglas Corp. v. Green,* 411 U.S. 792 (1973). Thus, a plaintiff alleging retaliation under FLSA must first establish a *prima facie* case of retaliation by showing (1) participation in protected activity known to the defendant, like the filing of a FLSA lawsuit; (2) an employment action disadvantaging the plaintiff; and (3) a causal connection between the protected activity and the adverse employment action. An employment action disadvantages an employee if "it well might have 'dissuaded a reasonable worker from making or supporting [similar] charge[s]. . . .'" Although the application of pre-existing disciplinary policies to a plaintiff "without more, does not constitute adverse employment action," a causal connection between an adverse action and a plaintiff's protected activity may be established "through evidence of retaliatory animus directed against a plaintiff by the defendant," or "by showing that the protected activity was closely followed in time by the adverse action."

Regarding the causal connection between the NYPD's actions and Appellees' participation in this lawsuit, we think the link is self-evident, and the district court did not err in concluding as much—IAB investigated the veracity of testimony given by the sergeants as part of the lawsuit. Moreover, the sequence, timing and nature of events only reinforces the connection. The day after the NYPD received transcripts from the depositions of certain test plaintiffs, IAB was dispatched to collect documents from the first group of plaintiffs. As testimony indicated, this was unusual in and of itself, because such documents are typically collected by Administrative Lieutenants or other officers in the individual precincts—not IAB. For the foregoing reasons, we AFFIRM the order of the district court.

Case Questions

1. Do you agree with the court that IAB's involvement constituted retaliation? Why or why not?

2. To what extent did the police department culture play a role in this decision?

3. What steps could the police department have taken to prevent these actions from constituting retaliation?

Varity Corp. v. Howe *516 U.S. 489 (1996)*

Case 3

At the time employer Varity Corporation transferred its money-losing divisions in its subsidiary Massey-Ferguson, Inc., to Massey Combines, a separate firm (it called the transfer "Project Sunshine"), it held a meeting to persuade its employees of these failing divisions to change benefit plans. Varity conveyed the impression that the employees' benefits would remain secure when they transferred. In fact, Massey Combines was insolvent from the day it was created, and by the end of its receivership, the employees who had transferred lost all of their nonpension benefits. The employees sued under ERISA, claiming that Varity breached its fiduciary duty in leading them to withdraw from their old plan and to forfeit their benefits. The district court held for the employees, and the court of appeals affirmed.

Breyer, J.

***

. . . The second question—whether Varity's deception violated ERISA-imposed fiduciary obligations—calls for a brief, affirmative answer. ERISA requires a "fiduciary" to "discharge his duties with respect to a plan solely in the interest of the participants and beneficiaries." To participate knowingly and significantly in deceiving a plan's beneficiaries in order to save the employer money at the beneficiaries' expense, is not to act "solely in the interest of the participants and beneficiaries." As other courts have held, "[l]ying is inconsistent with the duty of loyalty owed by all fiduciaries and codified in section 404(a)(1) of ERISA."

Because the breach of this duty is sufficient to uphold the decision below, we need not reach the question of whether ERISA fiduciaries have any fiduciary duty to disclose truthful information on their own initiative, or in response to employee inquiries.

We recognize, as mentioned above, that we are to apply common-law trust standards "bearing in mind the special nature and purpose of employee benefit plans." But we can find no adequate basis here, in the statute or otherwise, for any special interpretation that might insulate Varity, acting as a fiduciary, from the legal consequences of the kind of conduct (intentional misrepresentation) that often creates liability even among strangers.

We are aware, as Varity suggests, of one possible reason for a departure from ordinary trust law principles. In arguing about ERISA's remedies for breaches of fiduciary obligation, Varity says that Congress intended ERISA's fiduciary standards to protect only the financial integrity of the plan, not the individual beneficiaries. This intent, says Varity, is shown by the fact that Congress did not provide remedies for individuals harmed by such breaches; rather, Congress limited relief to remedies that would benefit only the plan itself. This argument fails, however, because, in our view, Congress did provide remedies for individual beneficiaries harmed by breaches of fiduciary duty.

Case Questions

1. What should Varity have done in order to avoid liability under ERISA?

2. How can an employee ensure that she or he knows all of the facts relevant to a question such as the one present in this case?

3. Why do you think Varity handled this in the way that it did?

Central Laborers' Pension Fund v. Heinz
541 U.S. 739 (2004)

Retirees who had been receiving early retirement benefits from a multiemployer pension fund sued the fund under ERISA's anti-cutback rule after their plan was amended to expand which types of postretirement employment triggered suspension of such benefits. Heinz understood that, if he were to work as "a union or non-union construction worker" ("disqualifying employment'), his pension would be suspended during that time. However, he also understood that his benefits would not be suspended if he chose to work in a supervisory capacity. Heinz therefore took a job in central Illinois in 1996, after retiring, as a construction supervisor, and the plan continued to pay out his monthly benefit.

In 1998, the plan's definition of disqualifying employment was expanded by amendment to include any job "in any capacity in the construction industry (either as a union or non-union construction worker)." The plan took the amended definition to cover supervisory work and warned Heinz that if he continued on as a supervisor, his monthly pension payments would be suspended. Heinz kept working, and the plan stopped paying.

Heinz sued to recover the suspended benefits on the ground that applying the amended definition of disqualifying employment so as to suspend payment of his accrued benefits violated ERISA's anti-cutback rule. The District Court granted judgment for the plan, only to be reversed by a divided panel of the Seventh Circuit, which held that imposing new conditions on rights to benefits already accrued was a violation of the anti-cutback rule. The Supreme Court granted certiorari in order to resolve the resulting Circuit Court split and affirms the Seventh Circuit in favor of the retirees.

Souter, J.

***

With few exceptions, the "anti-cutback" rule of the Employee Retirement Income Security Act of 1974 (ERISA) prohibits any amendment of a pension plan that would reduce a participant's "accrued benefit." The question is whether the rule prohibits an amendment expanding the categories of postretirement employment that triggers suspension of payment of early retirement benefits already accrued. We hold such an amendment prohibited.

II.

A.

There is no doubt about the centrality of ERISA's object of protecting employees' justified expectations of receiving the benefits their employers promise them. "Nothing in ERISA requires employers to establish employee benefits plans. Nor does ERISA mandate what kind of benefits employers must provide if they choose to have such a plan. ERISA does, however, seek to ensure that employees will not be left empty-handed once employers have guaranteed them certain benefits. . . . [W]hen

Congress enacted ERISA, it wanted to . . . mak[e] sure that if a worker has been promised a defined pension benefit upon retirement—and if he has fulfilled whatever conditions are required to obtain a vested benefit—he actually will receive it."

ERISA's anti-cutback rule is crucial to this object, and (with two exceptions of no concern here) provides that "[t]he accrued benefit of a participant under a plan may not be decreased by an amendment of the plan. . . ." After some initial question about whether the provision addressed early retirement benefits, a 1984 amendment made it clear that it does. Now § 204(g) provides that "a plan amendment which has the effect of . . . eliminating or reducing an early retirement benefit . . . with respect to benefits attributable to service before the amendment shall be treated as reducing accrued benefits."

Hence the question here: did the 1998 amendment to the Plan have the effect of "eliminating or reducing an early retirement benefit" that was earned by service before the amendment was passed? The statute, admittedly, is not as helpful as it might be in answering this question; it does not explicitly define "early retirement benefit," and it rather circularly defines "accrued benefit" as "the individual's accrued benefit determined under the plan. . . ." Still, it certainly looks as though a benefit has suffered under the amendment here, for we agree with the Seventh Circuit that, as a matter of common sense, "[a] participant's benefits cannot be understood without reference to the conditions imposed on receiving those benefits, and an amendment placing materially greater restrictions on the receipt of the benefit 'reduces' the benefit just as surely as a decrease in the size of the monthly benefit payment." Heinz worked and accrued retirement benefits under a plan with terms allowing him to supplement retirement income by certain employment, and he was being reasonable if he relied on those terms in planning his retirement. The 1998 amendment undercut any such reliance, paying retirement income only if he accepted a substantial curtailment of his opportunity to do the kind of work he knew. We simply do not see how, in any practical sense, this change of terms could not be viewed as shrinking the value of Heinz's pension rights and reducing his promised benefits.

B.

The Plan's responses are technical ones, beginning with the suggestion that the "benefit" that may not be devalued is actually nothing more than a "defined periodic benefit the plan is legally obliged to pay," so that § 204(g) applies only to amendments directly altering the nominal dollar amount of a retiree's monthly pension payment. A retiree's benefit of $100 a month, say, is not reduced by a post-accrual plan amendment that suspends payments, so long as nothing affects the figure of $100 defining what he would be paid, if paid at all. Under the Plan's reading, § 204(g) would have nothing to say about an amendment that resulted even in a permanent suspension of payments. But for us to give the anti-cutback rule a reading that constricted would take textual *force majeure*, and certainly something closer to irresistible than the provision quoted in the Plan's observation that accrued benefits are ordinarily "expressed in the form of an annual benefit commencing at normal retirement age."

The Plan also contends that, because § 204(g) only prohibits amendments that "eliminat[e] or reduc[e] an early retirement benefit," the anti-cutback rule must not apply to mere suspensions of an early retirement benefit. This argument seems to rest on a distinction between "eliminat[e] or reduc[e]" on the one hand, and "suspend" on the other, but it just misses the point. No one denies that some conditions enforceable by suspending benefit payments are permissible under ERISA: conditions set before a benefit accrues can survive the anti-cutback rule, even though their sanction is a suspension of benefits. Because such conditions are elements of the benefit itself and are considered in valuing it at the moment it accrues, a later suspension of benefit payments according to the Plan's terms does not eliminate the benefit or reduce its value. The real question is whether a new condition may be imposed after a benefit has accrued; may the right to receive certain money on a certain date be limited by a new condition narrowing that right? In a given case, the new condition may or may not be invoked to justify an actual suspension of benefits, but at the moment the new condition is imposed, the accrued benefit becomes less valuable, irrespective of any actual suspension.

***

This is not to say that § 203(a)(3)(B) does not authorize some amendments. Plans are free to add new suspension provisions under § 203(a)(3)(B), so long as the new provisions apply only to the benefits that will be associated with future employment. The point is that this section regulates the contents of the bargain that can be struck between employer and employees as part of the complete benefits package for future employment.

The judgment of the Seventh Circuit is AFFIRMED.

Justice Breyer, with whom the Chief Justice, Justice O'Connor, and Justice Ginsburg join, CONCURRING.

Case Questions

1. Notwithstanding the law as applied, do you believe an employer should be able to change the terms of pension plan qualifications once individuals have begun to avail themselves of the benefits? Can you think of *any* circumstances where you might be persuaded that the employer should be able to modify the plan in this regard?

2. The Court does not seem to be persuaded at all by the plan's arguments, though the district court found in its favor. Are you persuaded by *any* of the plan's arguments?

Glossary

A

ADA and Rehabilitation Act protection   As long as an individual with a disability is otherwise qualified for a position, with or without reasonable accommodation, the employer may not make an adverse employment decision solely on the basis of the disability.

adverse employment action   Any action or omission that takes away a benefit, opportunity, or privilege of employment from an employee.

affinity orientation   Whom one is attracted to for personal and intimate relationships.

affirmative action   Intentional inclusion of women and minorities in the workplace based on a finding of their previous exclusion.

affirmative action plan   A government contractor's plan containing placement goals for inclusion of women and minorities in the workplace and timetables for accomplishing the goals.

Age Discrimination in Employment Act   Prohibits discrimination in employment on the basis of age; applies to individuals who are at least 40 years old. Individuals who are not yet 40 years old are not protected by the act and *may* be discriminated against on the basis of their age.

agency shop clause   Requires nonunion members to pay union dues without having to be subject to the union rules.

AIDS   Acquired immune deficiency syndrome, a syndrome in which the individual's immune system ceases to function properly and during which the individual is susceptible, in most cases fatally, to opportunistic diseases. AIDS is not transmitted through casual contact; to transmit the disease, there must be an exchange of fluids. The disease may be transmitted through sexual contact, during which there is an exchange of bodily fluids; needle sharing; or an exchange of blood.

Americans with Disabilities Act   Extends Rehabilitation Act protection to employees in the private sector, with few modifications.

antifemale animus   Negative feelings about women and/or their ability to perform jobs or functions, usually manifested by negative language and actions.

antiretaliation provisions   Provisions making it illegal to treat an employee adversely because the employee pursued his or her rights under Title VII.

arbitration   The selection of a neutral or third party to consider a dispute and to deliver a binding or nonbinding decision.

assumption of risk   A defense to a negligence action based on the argument that the injured party voluntarily exposed herself or himself to a known danger created by the other party's negligence.

at-will employment   An employment relationship where there is no contractual obligation to remain in the relationship; either party may terminate the relationship at any time, for any reason, as long as the reason is not prohibited by law, such as for discriminatory purposes.

availability   Minorities and women in a geographic area who are qualified for a particular position.

B

back pay   Money awarded for time an employee was not working (usually due to termination) because of illegal discrimination.

bargaining unit   The group of employees in a workplace that have the legal right to bargain with the employer.

BFOQ   Bona fide occupational qualification, discussed more thoroughly in Chapter 2's discussion of the *prima facie* case of disparate treatment.

bi-gender affinity orientation   Someone attracted to both genders.

bona fide occupational qualification (BFOQ) Permissible discrimination if legally necessary for an employer's particular business.

business agent   The representative of a union, usually a craft union.

business necessity   Defense to a disparate impact case based on the employer's need for the policy as a legitimate requirement for the job.

C

claimant or charging party The person who brings an action alleging violation of Title VII.

closed shop Employer hires only union members.

collective bargaining Negotiations and agreements between management and labor about wages, hours, and other terms and conditions of employment.

collective bargaining agreement Negotiated contract between labor and management.

common law Law made and applied by judges, based on precedent (prior case law).

common-law agency test A test used to determine employee status; the employer must merely have the right or ability to control the work for a worker to be classified as an employee.

community of interests Factors employees have in common for bargaining purposes.

comparable worth A Title VII action for pay discrimination based on gender, in which jobs held mostly by women are compared with comparable jobs held mostly by men in regard to pay to determine if there is gender discrimination.

compelled self-publication Occurs when an ex-employee is forced to repeat the reason for her or his termination and thereby makes a claim for defamation.

compensatory damages Money damages given to a party to compensate for direct losses due to an injury suffered.

conciliation Attempting to reach agreement on a claim through discussion, without resort to litigation.

constructive discharge Occurs when the employee is given no reasonable alternative but to end the employment relationship; considered an *involuntary* act on the part of the employee.

continual-training requirement OSHA requires that the employer provide safety training to all new employees and to all employees who have been transferred into new positions.

contributory negligence A defense to a negligence action based on the injured party's failure to exercise reasonable care for her or his own safety.

corporate management compliance evaluation Evaluations of mid- and senior-level employee advancement for artificial barriers to advancement of women and minorities.

covenant of good faith and fair dealing Implied contractual obligation to act in good faith in the fulfillment of each party's contractual duties.

craft unions Unions composed of skilled craftworkers not situated at any one workplace.

D

debar Prohibit a federal contractor from further participation in government contracts.

defamation An intentional tort involving the publication of false statements about another.

defendant One against whom a case is brought.

defined benefit Retirement plan where the benefit payable to a participant is defined up front by a formula, the funding of which is determined actuarially.

defined contribution Retirement plan where the benefits payable to a participant are based on the amount of contributions and earnings on such contributions.

de novo **review** Complete new look at an administrative case by the reviewing court.

disability A physical or mental impairment that substantially limits one or more of the major life activities of an individual; a record of such impairment; or being regarded as having such an impairment.

disparate treatment Treating similarly situated employee differently because of prohibited Title VII factors.

disparate/adverse impact Effect of facially neutral policy is deleterious for a Title VII group.

duty to reasonably accommodate The employer's Title VII duty to try to find a way to avoid conflict between workplace policies and an employee's religious practices or beliefs.

E

economic realities test A test to determine whether a worker qualifies as an employee. Courts use this test to determine whether a worker is economically dependent on the business or is in business for himself or herself. To apply the test, courts look to the degree of control exerted by the alleged employer over the worker, the worker's opportunity for profit or loss, the worker's investment in the business, the permanence of the working relationship, the degree of skill required by the worker, and the extent to which the work is an integral part of the alleged employer's business.

EEO investigator   Employee of the EEOC who reviews Title VII complaints for merit.

eligibility testing   Tests an employer administers to ensure that the potential employee is capable and qualified to perform the requirements of the position.

emergency temporary standards   Standards are imposed by OSHA without immediately going through the typical process where an employee is exposed to grave danger from exposure to substances and the standards are necessary to protect employees from the danger.

employee benefit plan (or plan)   A contractual obligation either through a plan, fund, or arrangement by which an employer or an employee organization such as a labor union agrees to provide retirement benefits or welfare benefits to employees and their dependents and beneficiaries.

equitable relief   Relief that is not in the form of money damages, such as injunctions, reinstatement, and promotion. Equitable relief is based on concepts of justice and fairness.

essential functions of a position   Those tasks that are fundamental, not marginal or unnecessary, to the fulfillment of the position's objectives. The employer may not take an adverse employment action against a disabled employee based on the disability where the individual can perform the essential functions of the position.

exhaustion of administrative remedies   Going through the EEOC administrative procedure before being permitted to seek judicial review of an agency decision.

F

face validity   A test that looks well suited to its purpose.

facially neutral policy   Workplace policy applies equally to all appropriate employees.

fellow servant rule   An employer's defense to liability for an employee's injury where the injury occurred on the job and was caused by the negligence of another employee.

fetal protection policies   Policies an employer institutes to protect the fetus or the reproductive capacity of employees.

fiduciary   Someone who has discretionary authority over the investment or management of plan assets of others.

forum selection clause   A clause in a contract that identifies the state law that will apply to any disputes that arise under the contract.

four-fifths rule   Presumption of discrimination where the selection rate (for any employment decision) of the protected group is less than 80 percent of the selection rate of the nonminority group. Often arises in questions concerning testing or other selection tools or screening devices. If presumption is shown, the device must then be shown to serve a legitimate business necessity.

free riders   Bargaining unit employees who do not pay union dues but whom the union is still obligated to represent.

front pay   Equitable remedy of money awarded to a claimant when reinstatement is not possible or feasible.

fundamental right   A right that is guaranteed by the Constitution, whether stated or not.

G

gender identity statutes   Laws providing protection for transgenders.

"gender-plus" discrimination   Employment discrimination based on gender and some other factor such as marital status or children.

gender/sexual reassignment surgery   The surgery required to change a person's gender due to gender dysphoria, the condition of one's physical gender not matching the emotional/psychological gender.

gender stereotypes   The assumption that most or all members of a particular gender must act a certain way.

general duty clause   A provision of the act requiring that employers furnish to each employee employment and a place of employment free from recognized hazards that cause or are likely to cause death or serious physical harm to the employee.

genetic testing   Investigation and evaluation of an individual's biological predispositions based on the presence of a specific disease-associated gene on the individual's chromosomes.

greater hazard defense   An employer may use the greater hazard defense to an OSHA violation where the hazards of compliance are greater than the hazards of noncompliance, where alternative means of protection are unavailable, and where a variance was not available.

Guidelines on Discrimination Because of Religion or National Origin Federal guidelines that apply only to federal contractors or agencies and that impose on these employers an affirmative duty to prevent discrimination.

H

HIV Human immunodeficiency virus, the virus that causes AIDS.

hostile environment sexual harassment Sexual harassment in which the harasser creates an abusive, offensive, or intimidating environment for the harassee.

hostile work environment A work environment in which harassment of an employee exists to such an extent that a reasonable employee would dread or fear going to work.

I

impairment "Any physiological disorder or condition . . . affecting one or more of the following body systems: neurological; musculoskeletal; special sense organs; respiratory, including speech organs; cardiovascular; reproductive; digestive; genitourinary; hemic and lymphatic; skin, and endocrine; or any mental or psychological disorder" that substantially limits one of life's major activities. [From the EEOC regulations.]

implied contract A contract that is not expressed, but, instead, is created by other words or conduct of the parties involved.

independent contractor Generally, a person who contracts with a principal to perform a task according to her or his own methods, and who is not under the principal's control regarding the physical details of the work.

industrial union Union composed of all employees across an industry, regardless of the type of job held.

inevitable disclosure Theory under which a court may prohibit a former employee from working for an employer's competitor if the employer can show that it is inevitable that the former employee will disclose a trade secret by virtue of her or his position.

injunction A court order requiring individuals or groups of persons to refrain from performing certain acts that the court has determined will do irreparable harm.

IRS 20-factor analysis List of 20 factors to which the IRS looks to determine whether someone is an employee or an independent contractor. The IRS compiled this list from the results of judgments of the courts relating to this issue.

J

job analysis Information regarding the nature of the work associated with a job and the knowledge, skills, and abilities required to perform that work.

job group analysis Combines job titles with similar content, wage rates, and opportunities.

judicial affirmative action Affirmative action ordered by a court as a remedy for discrimination found by the court to have occurred, rather than affirmative action arising from Executive Order 11246.

judicial review Court review of an agency's decision.

L

liquidated damages Liquidated damages limit awards to a predetermined amount. As used in the ADEA, liquidated damages are equal to the unpaid wage and are available in cases involving "willful violations" of the statute.

lockout Management does not allow employees to come to work.

M

major life activities "[F]unctions such as caring for one's self, performing manual tasks, walking, seeing, hearing, speaking, breathing, learning and working." [From the EEOC regulations.]

make-whole relief Attempts to put a claimant in position he or she would have been in had there been no discrimination.

management security clause Parties agree that management has the right to run the business and make appropriate business decisions as long as applicable laws are complied with.

mandatory arbitration agreement Agreement an employee signs as a condition of employment, requiring that workplace disputes be arbitrated rather than litigated.

mandatory retirement Employee must retire upon reaching a specified age. Deemed illegal by the 1986 amendments to the ADEA, with few exceptions.

mandatory subject of bargaining Wages, hours, and other conditions of employment, which, by law, must be negotiated between labor and management.

midterm negotiations Collective bargaining negotiations during the term of the contract rather than at its expiration.

minimum wages   The least amount a covered employee must be paid in hourly wages.

N

national origin   Individual's, or her or his ancestor's, place of origin (as opposed to citizenship), or physical, cultural, or linguistic characteristics of an origin group.

national origin discrimination protection   It is unlawful for an employer to limit, segregate, or classify employees in any way on the basis of national origin that would deprive them of the privileges, benefits, or opportunities of employment.

negligence   The failure to do something in such a way or manner as a reasonable person would have done the same thing; or doing something that a reasonable person would not do. Failing to raise one's standard of care to the level of care that a reasonable person would use in a given situation.

negligence   The omission to do something a reasonable person would do, when guided by those considerations that ordinarily regulate human affairs, or something that a prudent and reasonable person would not do.

negligence   Failing to do something in such a way or manner that a reasonable person would have done; doing something that a reasonable person would not do; or failing to raise one's standard of care to the level of care that a reasonable person would use in a given situation, any of which results in damage to another person or person's property.

negligent hiring   Employment of a person who causes harm that could have been prevented if the employer had conducted a reasonable and responsible background check on the employee. The standard against which the decision is measured is when the employer knew or should have known that the worker was not fit for the job.

no-fault   Liability for injury imposed regardless of fault.

no reasonable cause   EEOC finding that evidence indicates no reasonable basis to believe Title VII was violated.

non-compete agreement (or covenant not to compete)   An agreement signed by the employee agreeing not to disclose the employer's confidential information or enter into competition with the employer for a specified period of time and/or within a specified region.

no-strike, no-lockout clause   Labor and management agree that labor will not strike and management will not stage a lockout.

O

organizational profile   Staffing patterns showing organizational units, their relationship to each other, and gender, race, and ethnic composition.

P

performance appraisal   A periodic assessment of an employee's performance, usually completed by her or his immediate supervisor and reviewed, at times, by others in the company.

permissive subjects of bargaining   Nonmandatory subjects that can be negotiated between labor and management.

picketing   The carrying of signs, which tell of an unfair labor practice or strike, by union members in front of the employer's business.

placement goal   Percentage of women and/or minorities to be hired to correct underrepresentation, based on availability in the geographic area.

plaintiff   One who brings a civil action in court.

polygraph   A lie-detecting device that measures biological reactions in individuals when questioned.

preemployment testing   Testing that takes place before hiring, or sometimes after hiring but before employment, in connection with such qualities as integrity, honesty, drug and alcohol use, HIV, or other characteristics.

prima facie **case**   Presenting evidence that fits each requirement of a cause of action.

private sector   That segment of the workforce represented by private companies (companies that are not owned or managed by the government or one of its agencies).

public policy   A legal concept intended to ensure that no individual lawfully do that which has a tendency to be injurious to the public or against the public good. Public policy is undermined by anything that harms a sense of individual rights.

public sector   That segment of the workforce represented by governmental employers and governmental agency employers. In some situations, this term may include federal contractors.

punitive damages   Money over and above compensatory damages, imposed by a court to punish a defendant for willful acts and to act as a deterrent.

Q

qualification standards   The EEOC regulations define qualification standards as "the personal and professional attributes, including the skill, experience, education, physical, medical, safety and other requirements established   as requirements which an individual must meet in order to be eligible for the position held or desired."

qualified for the position   Able to meet the employer's legitimate job requirements.

quid pro quo sexual harassment   Sexual harassment in which the harasser requests sexual activity from the harassee in exchange for workplace benefits.

R

reasonable accommodation   An accommodation to the individual's disability that does not place an undue burden or hardship (courts use the language interchangeably) on the employer. The reasonableness of the accommodation may be determined by looking to the size of the employer, the cost to the employer, the type of employer, and the impact of the accommodation on the employer's operations. It is important to understand that each case will be determined by looking to the *particular* job responsibilities as they are impacted by the employee's or applicant's *particular* disability. Courts have referred to this inquiry as one that is "fact intensive and case specific."

reasonable cause   EEOC finding that Title VII was violated.

reasonable factor other than age (RFOA)   May include any requirement that does not have an adverse impact on older workers, as well as those factors that do adversely affect this protected class but are shown to be job-related. For example, if an employee is not performing satisfactorily and is terminated, her failure to meet reasonable performance standards would constitute a reasonable factor other than age.

reasonable person standard   Viewing the harassing activity from the perspective of a reasonable person in society at large (generally tends to be the male view).

reasonable victim standard   Viewing the harassing activity from the perspective of a reasonable person experiencing the harassing activity including gender-specific sociological, cultural, and other factors.

recklessness   Conscious disregard for safety; conscious failure to use due care.

record keeping and reporting requirements   Title VII requires that certain documents must be maintained and periodically reported to the EEOC.

respondent or responding party   Person alleged to have violated Title VII, usually the employer.

retirement or pension plan   A plan that provides for compensation at retirement or deferral of income to periods beyond termination of employment.

retroactive seniority   Seniority that dates back to the time the claimant was treated illegally.

reverse discrimination   Claim brought by a majority member who feels adversely affected by the use of an employer's affirmative action plan.

right-to-sue letter   Letter given by the EEOC to claimants, notifying them of the EEOC's no-cause finding and informing them of their right to pursue their claim in court.

right-to-work laws   Permits employees to choose not to become a part of the union.

S

screening device   Factor used to weed out applicants from the pool of candidates.

search   A physical invasion of a person's space, belongings, or body.

secondary boycott   Union pressure on management by getting others who do business with management to cease.

Section 503 of the Rehabilitation Act   Prohibits discrimination against otherwise-qualified individuals with disabilities by any program or activity receiving federal assistance. Requires affirmative action on the part of federal contractors and agencies to recruit, hire, and train disabled workers.

706 agency   State agency that handles EEOC claims under a work-sharing agreement with the EEOC.

severe and/or pervasive activity   Harassing activity that is more than an occasional act or is so serious that it is the basis for liability.

shop steward   Union member chosen as an intermediary between union members and employers.

social media   User-created content, including text, video, audio, and other multimedia, published or otherwise communicated in an environment that enables scalable interactivity and dialogue, such as a blog, wiki, or other similar site.

substantially limited   "[U]nable to perform a major life activity that the average person in the general population can perform; or significantly restricted as to the condition, manner, or duration under which an individual can perform a major life activity." [From the EEOC regulations.]

T

tort   A private (civil) wrong against a person or her or his property.

transgender   Someone whose physical gender does not match his or her emotional/psychological gender; may or may not undergo gender reassignment surgery.

U

under color of state law   Government employee is illegally discriminating against another during performance of his or her duties.

underrepresentation or underutilization   Significantly fewer minorities or women in the workplace than relevant statistics indicate are available or their qualifications indicate they should be working at better jobs.

undue hardship   A burden imposed on an employer, by accommodating an employee's religious conflict, that would be too onerous for the employer to bear.

union shop   Union and management agree that employees must be members of the union.

union shop clause   Provision in a collective bargaining agreement allowing a union shop.

V

validation   Evidence that shows a test evaluates what it says it evaluates.

valuing diversity   Learning to accept and appreciate those who are different from the majority and value their contributions to the workplace.

vesting   Becoming legally entitled to receive a benefit where the benefit cannot be forfeited if employment is terminated.

vicarious liability   The imposition of liability on one party for the wrongs of another. Liability may extend from an employee to the employer on this basis if the employee is acting within the scope of her or his employment at the time the liability arose.

W

waiver   The intentional relinquishment of a known right.

wildcat strike   A strike not sanctioned by the union.

Y

yellow dog contract   Agreement employers require employees to sign stating they do not belong to a union and will not join one; now illegal.

Subject Index

A

Aaron Rentals, 388
Accent
  discrimination, 269
  national origin and, 305
  speech characteristics and, 305
Acceptable attire, 471
Accessibility accommodations, 582
Accommodation, 304. *see also* failure to
    accommodate
  expenses, 581
  refusal to consider, 514–515
Accounting scandals, 772
Ace of Spades (Matthews), 286
Achtenberg, Roberta, 441
ADA Amendments Act (ADAAA)
  alcoholism as disability under, 606
  disability definition changes under,
    575, 576
  impairment under, 571
  major life activity definition, 574
  "mitigating" measure rules, 576
  otherwise qualified person
    under, 577
  purpose and applicability, 566–567
Adaptive skill areas, 593
Adcock case, 35
Added points, 226
Adverse effect, 228
Adverse employment action, 307, 319,
    525, 528, 577
Adverse employment effect, 297
Advertising/advertisements, 351
  age discrimination in, 526–527
  for applicants, 226
  neutral solicitation, 144–145
  promoting from within, 144
  venue recruiting, 144
  walk-in applicants, 144
  word-of-mouth recruiting, 142–143
Affinity orientation, 405
  as basis for adverse employment
    decisions, 449
  definition, 433
  examples of, 433, 435–436
  gay student recruitment, 449
  issues, 348
  terminology of, 424–435
Affinity orientation discrimination,
    432–475
  AT&T, 443, 444
  affinity orientation as a basis for
    adverse employment
    decisions, 448–450

employers with policies on, 438
employment benefits, 454–460
gay employees, 443
gender identity discrimination,
    452–454
heterosexual realities, 440
lesbians in political positions, 441
management considerations, 460–462
management tips, 462
out of the closet, 433–448
same-gender sexual harassment,
    450–452
state laws on, 437
statutory basis, 433
terminology, 434–435
summary, 463
Affirmation, 46
Affirmative action, 199–241, 564
  affirmative action and veterans, 237
  applicability to, 209
  defined, 201
  design and unstable history of,
    201–221
  in employment, 220
  under Executive Order 11246,
    221–229
  judicial affirmative action, 230–231
  management tips, 242
  misconceptions about, 207
  negative attitudes about, 212
  obligations from, 221
  productivity impact study, 213
  race-conscious, 248
  reverse discrimination, 233–236
  statutory basis, 200–201
  statutory basis for, 200
  unfairness claims, 215
  use of for remedies, 214
  valuing diversity, 232, 237–241
  voluntary affirmative action,
    231–233
  summary, 243
Affirmative action, described, 210–221
  employment research findings,
    212–213
  life under Jim Crow, 211
  Mississippi Sovereignty
    Commission, 217–218
  U.S. House of Representatives
    resolution apologizing for
    slavery, 216–217
Affirmative action, design and unstable
    history of
  1980s media statements regarding
    affirmative action, 203–204

about, 201–202
affirmative action described, 210–221
affirmative action realities, 207
affirmative action's
    misunderstandings based on
    race, 202, 205, 207
clearing the air, 207–210
voting under Jim Crow, 203–204
Affirmative action plans, 222, 251
African Americans
  actresses, 286
  beatings, 204
  black Miss America, 285
  colonial settlement, 272
  de jure segregation of, 216
  at Democratic national convention,
    203, 204
  discrimination against, 181
  life governed by racial mistreatment,
    273–274
  post Civil War relationships, 98
  racial history, 272
  Title VII of the Civil Rights Act
    impact on, 202
  voting rights, 205
Age discrimination, 516–559
  age as BFOQ, 553
  Age Discrimination in Employment
    Act (ADEA), 518, 520–539
  age limits on hiring, 553
  age stereotypes, 517–520
  complaints, 520
  distinctions among benefit plans, 544
  employee retirement income security
    act, 543–544
  goal of statutes, 535
  management considerations,
    544–545, 547
  management tips, 546
  as motivating factor, 527
  older workers and age
    discrimination, 519
  proof in case, 529
  remedies, 543
  statutory basis, 518
  use of statistical evidence, 542–543
  waivers under the older workers'
    benefit protection act of
    1990, 539–542
  summary, 547–548
Age Discrimination in Employment Act
    of 1967 (ADEA)
  age discrimination measure of
    proof, 525
  BFOQ under, 528

Case Index